Microsoft® Exchange Server 2003 Resource Kit

Kay Unkroth, Elizabeth Molony, Pav Cherny, Brian Reid, Fergus Strachan, and Bill English with the Microsoft Exchange Server Team

PUBLISHED BY
Microsoft Press
A Division of Microsoft Corporation
One Microsoft Way
Redmond, Washington 98052-6399

Library of Congress Control Number 205920807

Printed and bound in the United States of America.

2 3 4 5 6 7 8 9   QWT   9 8 7 6 5

Distributed in Canada by H.B. Fenn and Company Ltd.

A CIP catalogue record for this book is available from the British Library.

Microsoft Press books are available through booksellers and distributors worldwide. For further information about international editions, contact your local Microsoft Corporation office or contact Microsoft Press International directly at fax (425) 936-7329. Visit our Web site at www.microsoft.com/learning/. Send comments to *rkinput@microsoft.com.*

Acquisitions Editors: Martin DelRe, Hilary Long, and Megan Camp
Project Editor: Maureen Williams Zimmerman
Technical Reviewer: Wadeware

mediaService Corporation
Project Manager: Kay Unkroth
Copy Editors: Camilla Paynter and Barbara Fandrich
Desktop Publisher: Gerhard Alfes
Proofreader: Fran Tooke
Indexers: Camilla Paynter, Nikolaus Loesken and Pav Cherny

Body Part No. X10-87090

Contents

What do you think of this book? We want to hear from you!	Microsoft is interested in hearing your feedback about this publication so we can continually improve our books and learning resources for you. To participate in a brief online survey, please visit: *www.microsoft.com/learning/booksurvey/*

Foreword

When Exchange 5.5 was being designed in the mid 1990s, e-mail was being deployed in most enterprises. As we were designing Exchange 2003, many customers were telling us that e-mail had become more important than their telephones. What an amazing change in just five years! Our goal with Exchange 2003 was to meet these new customer expectations with a release that would be easy to deploy and would lower our customers' costs, secure their environment, and increase their information-worker productivity. This book is the key to unlocking these benefits for your organization.

When it came to cost reduction, we focused our efforts on two areas: disaster recovery and site consolidation. We recognized the pain involved in a server restore and responded with recovery storage group and volume snapshot support. We recognized the complexity in managing servers distributed across multiple geographic locations—and introduced tools to enable these "sites" to be consolidated back to central, more easily managed locations. We doubled down on the development of our Microsoft Operations Manager (MOM) management pack, encoding thousands of event patterns and knowledge of how to respond.

During development of Exchange 2003, we devoted a large effort to making this release the most secure communications infrastructure a customer can deploy. We re-reviewed all of our code for modern best practices, changed all of our default settings to be secure, and added support for Kerberos between client and server—and server to server. For secure e-mail itself, we added support for SMIME to Outlook Web Access and Pocket Outlook. Last but not least, the travesty of spam was overwhelming our mailboxes. We responded with the Intelligent Message Filter, support for domain block subscriptions, and recipient filtering.

Certainly, one of the biggest achievements of Exchange 2003 was our partnership with the Outlook team to deliver an integrated productivity experience across the PC, Web browser, and mobile devices. Outlook 2003 introduces cached Exchange mode, with a newly tuned client-server protocol that maintains information worker productivity regardless of network latencies. Outlook 2003 also introduced terrific usability features such as the reading pane, smart folders, and quick flags. Outlook Web Access matched each of these, to deliver a consistent roaming experience for Outlook users. Personally, now that I'm addicted to these new features, I could never go back.

As you deploy Exchange 2003, I hope you will find that we've met your expectations for your e-mail and scheduling infrastructure. It would be great to hear from you within our Exchange communities at *http://www.microsoft.com/exchange*. Your feedback will be listened to carefully as we plan the future releases of Microsoft Exchange Server.

Terry Myerson
General Manager of Exchange, Microsoft Corporation

Acknowledgments

This book would not have been possible without the support of the Microsoft Exchange Server team and other Microsoft teams. We owe special thanks to Derek Murman and the Microsoft Identity Integration Server (MIIS) team. Many other individuals contributed to this book, in particular Brendon Bennett and Susan Bradley of the Microsoft Exchange Server team. The Exchange Server expert technical reviewers and contributing writers who contributed to this book are listed here.

Technical Reviewers

Alex Uelsberg
Bill Ashcraft
Chris Vandenberg
Eric Ashby
Jian Yan
Mike Lee
Nagendra Sitharamaiah MCSE, CISSP
Nino Bilic
Rafael Reyes
Sean O'Brien
Steven Halsey

Ayla Kol
Chris Frediani
Doug Blanchard
Evan Dodds
Jon Hoerlein
Mohammad Nadeem
Nick Rosenfeld
Paul Ford
Ross Smith IV
Simon Attwell
Teresa Appelgate

Contributing Writers

Christopher Budd, CISSP, CISM
Joey Masterson
Jon Hoerlein
Kweku Ako-Adjei
Susan Hill
Teresa Appelgate
Michele Martin
Nagendra Sitharamaiah, MCSE, CISSP

Jens Trier Rasmussen
John Speare
Jyoti Kulkarni
Ryan Wike
Tammy Treit
Thom Randolph
Patricia Anderson

Introduction

Welcome to the *Microsoft Exchange Server 2003 Resource Kit*. This book is designed to provide a comprehensive reference to Microsoft Exchange Server 2003, including helpful scripts, setup instructions, and procedures to assist in the design, implementation, administration, and troubleshooting of an Exchange organization.

The "About This Resource Kit" section below provides an overview of the parts and chapters in this book. For styles used in this book, see the "Document Conventions" section. The *Exchange Server 2003 Resource Kit* includes a companion CD filled with procedures, sample scripts and programs, and instructions to help understand the topics covered in this book.

About This Resource Kit

This book is organized into four parts. The parts cover vital aspects of using Exchange Server 2003, including designing an Exchange organization, using Exchange, optimizing Exchange features for your environment, and troubleshooting problems in an Exchange organization.

Part I: Designing Your Exchange Server 2003 Organization

The first part of the *Exchange Server 2003 Resource Kit* deals with the preliminary steps and considerations when setting up Exchange Server 2003. This section provides a product overview and introduction. It includes advanced design and configuration topics, such as consolidations and migrations, and information for setting up a hosted Exchange environment. Specifically, the following chapters are included:

- Chapter 1, "Exchange Server 2003 Product Overview," gives details about Exchange Server 2003 components, requirements, and capabilities. To aid in understanding, test scenarios and a test environment setup are included on the companion CD.

- Chapter 2, "Exchange Server 2003 Design Basics," covers the elements and components of an Exchange organization that can be configured to structure mailbox management, server administration, and message routing. Logical placements for optimal administration and performance as well as physical topology considerations are discussed.

- Chapter 3, "Exchange Server 2003 in Enterprise Environments," builds on design considerations when deploying an Exchange organization and deals with design elements to consider when deploying Exchange Server 2003 in an enterprise environment. Such an environment might include departments, business units, or other complex structures with the need for specialized and segregated messaging systems.

- Chapter 4, "Upgrading to Exchange Server 2003," provides strategies and tools for upgrading to Exchange Server 2003 from previous versions.

- Chapter 5, "Migrating to Exchange Server 2003," provides strategies and tools for migrating to an Exchange organization. Migration differs from upgrading in that in an upgrade scenario, there is an existing Exchange organization and resources are added and removed. In a migration scenario, resources are moved between separate messaging systems or organizations.

- Chapter 6, "Server and Site Consolidation Strategies," explains how to consolidate servers, sites, and Exchange organizations. Consolidation involves a movement of resources within an organization for more centralized control and less overhead. Consolidation can also involve the combination of separate systems and organizations into a single entity.

- Chapter 7, "Hosting Exchange Server 2003," explains how to host Microsoft Exchange Server 2003 in an environment based on Microsoft Solution for Windows-based Hosting.

Part II: Managing Your Exchange Server 2003 Organization

The second part of the *Exchange Server 2003 Resource Kit* focuses on operations and administration tasks typically encountered in Exchange organizations. This section discusses how to manage directory information, Internet-related services, Exchange Store resources, and how to secure Exchange Servers. Specifically, the following chapters are included:

- Chapter 8, "Operating an Exchange Server 2003 Organization," explains the typical tasks performed in an Exchange organization. The tasks are split into daily, weekly, monthly, and as-needed tasks. This chapter is intended as a reference of the processes required for operating and maintaining Exchange servers.

- Chapter 9, "Managing Directory Information," focuses on how directory information is managed in a Microsoft Exchange Server 2003 organization. It explains the types of recipient objects, where the recipient objects live in Microsoft Active Directory, recipient object attributes, and how object attributes are replicated between global catalog servers. This chapter also covers communication between Active Directory and Exchange.

- Chapter 10, "Configuring Exchange Store Resources," covers the architecture of Microsoft Exchange Server 2003 storage and the administrative requirements for effectively managing that storage. It explains the types of technologies involved in Exchange Server storage and how storage is configured on an Exchange

Server, including requirements for creating multiple storage groups and stores on a server.

- Chapter 11, "Connecting to the Internet," discusses the flow of e-mail messages via the Simple Mail Transfer Protocol (SMTP) to and from an Exchange organization.

- Chapter 12, "Maintaining IIS Virtual Servers," further explains how to add, remove, and configure Internet Information Services (IIS) virtual servers. The chapter includes topics and discussion on implementing and configuring security and RPC over HTTP.

- Chapter 13, "Implementing Exchange 2003 Security," covers how to secure an Exchange organization. The chapter examines the various parts of an Exchange organization that can be secured, such as server/client communication, Active Directory, gateways, messaging connectors, and routing groups. The chapter also examines possible ways to secure parts of an Exchange organization.

Part III: Optimizing Your Exchange Server 2003 Organization

The third part of the *Exchange Server 2003 Resource Kit* concentrates on tuning, optimizing, and getting the most out of Exchange Server 2003. Included in the section are overviews and detailed information about monitoring, using Exchange Management Pack, and how to use Exchange in a clustered environment. Specifically, the following chapters are included:

- Chapter 14, "Streamlining Message Routing," addresses the message routing and transport concepts and the connectors for Exchange Server 2003.

- Chapter 15, "Managing Clustered Exchange 2003," explains how to cluster multiple servers running Microsoft Exchange Server 2003 according to their specific roles in an Exchange organization.

- Chapter 16, "Standard Monitoring Tools," provides an overview of monitoring tools, such as System Monitor, Exchange System Manager, Network Monitor, and other tools to help monitor an Exchange organization.

- Chapter 17, "Exchange Management Pack," covers how to set up and configure Exchange Management Pack for Microsoft Operations Manager. The chapter includes potential areas to monitor with Exchange Management Pack and how to troubleshoot Exchange Management Pack.

- Chapter 18, "Tuning Exchange Server Performance," explains how to fine-tune an Exchange server for optimal performance.

Part IV: Troubleshooting Exchange Server 2003

The fourth part of the Exchange Server 2003 Resource Kit focuses on troubleshooting Exchange Server 2003. This part includes disaster recovery considerations and strategies, and general troubleshooting guidelines. Specifically, the following chapters are included:

- Chapter 19, "Exchange Server 2003 Troubleshooting Strategies," addresses general procedures for diagnosing Exchange Server 2003 problems, and it explains how to use Microsoft troubleshooting and debugging tools to gather information about the health and configuration of a server running Exchange Server 2003.

- Chapter 20, "Troubleshooting Active Directory Communication," examines the communication between Active Directory and Exchange, potential trouble spots, and how to troubleshoot them.

- Chapter 21, "Disaster Recovery Planning for Exchange Server 2003," discusses how to develop a disaster recovery plan for Exchange Server 2003. The chapter focuses on how to design your Exchange organization with failures and disasters in mind, the data that you must protect to ensure that Exchange can be recovered, different types of backup strategies, and the tools that an administrator needs to address any recovery issues that might arise.

- Chapter 22, "Implementing a Backup Solution," concentrates on the processes required to back up Exchange Server and the Windows operating system.

- Chapter 23, "Restoring Exchange Server 2003," explains how to recover from failures in an Exchange environment. It covers what you need to know from the rebuilding of individual servers and cluster nodes to the restoration and recovery of Exchange database data and individual configuration components.

Document Conventions

In this book, you will find special sections offset with icons that point out items of interest, provide tips, or warn of possible damaging consequences. These reader alerts should provide additional help with understanding and using Exchange Server 2003. This book also includes style conventions used when dealing with scripts and working with the command line.

Readeraid Conventions

Readeraids are used throughout this guide to notify you of essential as well as supplementary information. The following table explains the meaning of each readeraid:

Readeraids	Meaning
	Tip Alerts you to supplementary information that is essential to the completion of the task at hand.
	Note Alerts you to supplementary information.
	Important Alerts you to supplementary information that is essential to the completion of a task.
	Caution Alerts you to possible data loss, breaches of security, or other serious problems.
	Warning Alerts you to a potentially serious problem, and points out that failure to take or avoid a specific action might result in harm to you, the hardware, or the software.

Style Conventions

The following style conventions are used in documenting scripting and command-line tasks throughout the book.

Element	Meaning
Bold font	Characters that you type exactly as shown, including commands and parameters. User interface elements are also bold.
Italic font	Variables for which you supply a specific value. For example, *File.ext* can refer to any valid file name.
`Monospace font`	Code samples.

Resource Kit Companion CD

The companion CD includes a variety of informational aids that may be used throughout the book. For example, the CD includes instructions for setting up various test environments, as well as step-by-step procedures and instructions for configuring features, installing components, and performing modifications necessary to examine particular Exchange topics covered in the Exchange 2003 Resource Kit. The companion CD also includes helpful scripts and configuration files to automate processes and provide examples of Exchange features. Additionally, the CD includes e-Books for Microsoft Encyclopedia of Networking, Encyclopedia of Security, and Microsoft Windows 2000 Scripting Guide as well as links to Exchange Server tools and the Exchange SDK Development Tools and Documentation.

The companion material is organized by chapter. Located within the Aids_and_Tools folder are folders organized by chapter. Within each chapter's root folder, you can find documents that contain installation instructions and step-by-step procedures. Each document outlines prerequisites to accomplish the outlined procedures successfully. Some procedures depend on procedures in other documents. In this case, the prerequisites section will list the relevant documents. If a procedure requires you to run an admin script or install other tools, the prerequisites section will inform you where to find these tools. For example, you can generally find admin scripts in the \Scripts subfolder under each chapter's root folder.

In complex scenarios, documents with installation instructions and step-by-step procedures are organized in subfolders, so that you can selectively pick the topics that interest you and leave others aside. In Chapters 5 and 7, documents are furthermore assigned a sequence number so that you can quickly see which documents to work with first. These chapters feature massive sample scenarios that might require more than 20 computers. To build such complex test environments, we recommend that you use virtual server technology, such as Microsoft Virtual PC, instead of physical computers. Microsoft does not support Exchange Server 2003 on virtual servers, but this is primarily an issue for production environments.

The scripts, tools, installation instructions, step-by-step procedures, and other materials that you can find on the companion CD are for test installations only. If you use these components or perform the procedures in a production environment, you can cause serious problems. These problems may require you to reinstall your entire Windows Server, Active Directory, and Exchange Server environment. Do not apply the instructions, procedures, scripts, tools, and other components to a production environment without thorough testing on a reference system.

Using the Companion CD

When using the procedures and scripts on the companion CD with virtual servers, you will need to use a computer that can handle multiple virtual servers. Your test computer should have the following:

- An Intel Pentium or compatible 1 GHz processor computer with at least 2 GB of RAM. Because virtual servers use the RAM installed on the test computer, the amount of RAM installed determines how many virtual servers you can run at the same time.

- A hard disk with 200 GB or more of free space. A typical virtual server requires at least 2 GB of disk space.

To view the files on the companion CD, the following is required:

- An Intel Pentium or compatible 300 MHz computer with at least 128 MB of RAM and a CD-ROM drive.

■ Microsoft Word 2000 or later or Microsoft Word Viewer for viewing the setup procedures and steps.

Resource Kit Support Policy

Microsoft does not support the software supplied in the *Exchange Server 2003 Resource Kit*. Microsoft does not guarantee the performance of the tools or scripting examples, response times for answering questions, or bug fixes for the tools or scripts. However, Microsoft Press provides a way for customers who purchase the *Exchange Server 2003 Resource Kit* to report any problems with the software and receive feedback for such issues. To report any issues or problems, send e-mail to RKInput@microsoft.com. This e-mail address is only for issues related to the *Exchange Server 2003 Resource Kit*. For issues related to the Windows operating system, please refer to the support information included with the product.

Microsoft Press also provides corrections for books and companion CDs through the World Wide Web at *http://www.microsoft.com/learning/support*. To connect directly to the Microsoft Press Knowledge Base and enter a query regarding a question or issue that you may have, go to *http://microsoft.com/mspress/support/search.asp*.

Part I

Designing Your Exchange Server 2003 Organization

In this part:

Chapter 1

Exchange Server 2003 Product Overview

About This Chapter

This chapter discusses the most important features of Microsoft Exchange Server 2003 and available licensing options that you should be aware of when planning a deployment of Exchange 2003 in your company. To keep the explanations practical, this chapter outlines a basic test system, so that you can evaluate Exchange 2003 without impact on a production environment. The worksheets that you can find on the companion CD in the \Companion Material\Chapter01 folder contain step-by-step instructions to install a test environment.

It is assumed that you are already familiar with Microsoft Windows server technology and the administration of user accounts and other resources in a Windows domain, but you can also start without any knowledge of Windows Server 2003 or the concepts of Active Directory directory service if you follow the step-by-step instructions in the worksheets closely. Keep in mind, however, that familiarity with Windows 2003 and Active Directory is imperative for Exchange administrators. If you are unfamiliar with Windows Server 2003 or Active Directory, you must familiarize yourself with these technologies prior to deploying Exchange 2003 in a production environment. For more information about Windows Server 2003, see Windows Server 2003 Technology Centers at *http://www.microsoft.com/windowsserver2003/technologies.*

What You Need to Know

Microsoft Exchange Server 2003 is a leading messaging and collaboration platform that builds on proven database, directory, and connectivity technologies, brings advances in reliability, performance, and security, and enhances the functionality of the products in the Microsoft Office System. There are many features that you can use to support local, remote, and mobile information workers better than with any previous version of Exchange Server. Interesting are the features in Exchange 2003 that an organization can use to protect its users from spam and malicious e-mail messages. Exchange 2003 also includes advanced administrative tools, such as Exchange Management Pack for Microsoft Operations Manager (MOM), which you can use to streamline daily operations in a complex Exchange organization.

Microsoft Exchange Server 2003 Service Pack 1 (SP1) is the first major update for Exchange 2003. The Exchange development team provides service pack releases on a regular basis to fix known issues, apply design changes, and implement new features. For example, Exchange 2003 SP1 comes with improved deployment tools, such as a Mailbox Move Wizard that supports moving mailboxes across sites and administrative groups in mixed-mode organizations that contain Exchange servers running Microsoft Exchange Server 5.5, Microsoft Exchange 2000 Server and Exchange Server 2003. Other important improvements are buried deep in the architecture of Exchange 2003. For example, the database engine of Exchange 2003 SP1 Ese.dll contains error checking and correcting (ECC) code that uses 64-bit checksums, so that the Extensible Storage Engine (ESE) can fix single-bit database corruption issues automatically to avoid a database recovery from backup. All database versions of Exchange prior to Exchange 2003 SP1 have only 32-bit checksums. If you consider that approximately 40 percent of all database corruption issues in Exchange 5.5 and Exchange 2000 that are handled by Microsoft Product Support Services are caused by single-bit errors, you can understand the significance of this feature. Error correction code in Exchange 2003 SP1 is one compelling reason for companies to upgrade all Exchange servers that hold mailboxes or public folders to Exchange 2003 and update to Exchange 2003 SP1.

Beginning with Exchange 2003, Microsoft provides most of the tools that traditionally shipped on the Exchange product CD in the form of Web releases. Web releases provide a framework for Microsoft to keep the tools updated after the standard release cycle, and also to introduce new tools as they become available. For example, a Domain Rename Fixup (XDR-Fixup) tool was added to the tools collection with Exchange 2003 SP1. You can use the XDR-Fixup tool to fix Exchange configuration information in Active Directory after renaming a Windows 2003 domain using Rendom.exe. Because it is not possible to update material that ships on CDs or DVDs, the tools are no longer available on the product CD. They are also not included on the companion CD of the Exchange Server 2003 Resource Kit. You can download the tools at *http://www.microsoft.com/exchange/downloads/2003.asp*.

Installing a Basic Test Environment for Exchange Server 2003

The most basic environment for testing product features available in Exchange 2003 consists of a single server and a workstation, as illustrated in Figure 1-1. For detailed step-by-step instructions about how to install a test environment, see the document Preparing a basic test environment.doc, which you can find in the \Companion Material\Chapter01 folder on the companion CD.

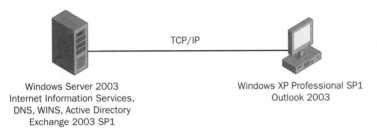

TCP/IP

Windows Server 2003
Internet Information Services,
DNS, WINS, Active Directory
Exchange 2003 SP1

Windows XP Professional SP1
Outlook 2003

Figure 1-1   A basic test environment for Exchange 2003

> **Note**   This chapter outlines test environments without regard to specific requirements or planning considerations. It is very important to keep the test systems strictly separate from a production environment, including Active Directory domain controllers and DNS servers. To minimize the risk of conflicts with production systems, you must install a separate Active Directory forest, and you should use non-routed IP addresses to isolate the test servers from production servers. Ideally, the test systems are physically not connected to the production network.

The test server runs the following software:

- **Windows Server 2003**   The full feature set of Exchange 2003 is only available when you install Exchange Server 2003 on a server running Windows Server 2003. Features such as remote procedure call (RPC) over Secure Hypertext Transfer Protocol (HTTPS), front-end and back-end IP Security (IPSec) encryption, and database snapshots based on the Volume Shadow Copy service are not available when installing Exchange 2003 on a Windows 2000 server. You can download a Windows Server 2003 Evaluation Kit from *http://www.microsoft.com/windowsserver2003/evaluation/trial/evalkit.mspx*.

- **Active Directory directory service**   The test server must run Active Directory to establish the directory that Exchange 2003 uses to maintain recipient information and all configuration information about the Exchange organization.

An Exchange 2003 organization is a collection of Exchange servers and other resources, such as recipient objects, that are in the same Active Directory forest. A single Exchange organization cannot span multiple forests.

■ **Domain Name Service (DNS)**   Active Directory requires DNS. Running DNS servers on domain controllers enables you to integrate DNS zones with Active Directory. An advantage of Active Directory-integrated zones is that zone information is stored in Active Directory and replicated between domain controllers as part of Active Directory replication.

■ **Windows Internet Naming Service (WINS)**   WINS is, strictly speaking, not a requirement in a test environment with only one network segment, where Network Basic Input/Output System (NetBIOS) name resolution can rely on broadcasts. Nevertheless, you should install WINS, because NetBIOS name resolution requires WINS in a production environment with multiple segments, where network nodes block broadcasts. Running Exchange 2003 without WINS represents an unsupported configuration. Your test system should be based on a supported configuration.

■ **Internet Information Services (IIS) 6.0**   The server must run IIS 6.0, because the Simple Mail Transfer Protocol (SMTP) service that Exchange 2003 uses to implement the message transport subsystem is an IIS component. Internet clients, such as Microsoft Office Outlook Web Access, Microsoft Office Outlook Mobile Access, or Post Office Protocol version 3 (POP3) and Internet Mail Access Protocol version 4 (IMAP4) clients, also communicate with Exchange 2003 through protocol virtual servers that are integrated with IIS 6.0. You can read more about the features of messaging clients in an Exchange organization later in this chapter.

■ **Exchange Server 2003 Enterprise Edition**   Exchange Server 2003 is available in two editions: Standard Edition and Enterprise Edition. The Enterprise Edition provides the full feature set of Exchange 2003, such as support for multiple databases for each server without size restrictions and Windows Clustering support. The Standard Edition does not support Windows cluster configurations, and supports only one mailbox database and one public folder database in a single storage group. In the Standard Edition, the messaging databases are limited to 16 gigabytes (GB). A trial version of Exchange Server 2003 Enterprise Edition is available at *http://www.microsoft.com/exchange/evaluation/trial/2003.asp*. Remember to update Exchange 2003 with Service Pack 1.

The workstation runs Microsoft Windows XP Professional with Service Pack 1 or later and Microsoft Office Outlook 2003. You can connect the computers through a crossover cable, but it is more advantageous to use a network switch with five or more ports. Using a network switch, you can extend the test environment with additional servers or workstations. The network protocol must be Transmission Control Protocol/Internet Protocol (TCP/IP). Exchange 2003 relies on TCP/IP because it uses

SMTP as the native message transfer protocol and relies on Active Directory for directory services. SMTP and Active Directory are based on TCP/IP.

Implementing a Separate Domain Controller

When installing a test environment for Exchange 2003, you must decide whether to install Exchange 2003 on a domain controller. Exchange experts are discussing the benefits of this configuration since the first versions of Exchange. There is no straightforward answer to this question, but in a test environment, installing Exchange 2003 directly on the domain controller running Active Directory works under almost all circumstances. Remember, however, that you must not change the role of the server after Exchange 2003 is installed. For example, demoting a domain controller running Exchange 2003 to a member server leads to an unsupported server configuration. Promotion of a member server running Exchange 2003 to a domain controller is also not supported. For more information about whether to install Exchange 2003 on a domain controller, see Chapter 2, "Exchange Server 2003 Design Basics."

Although you can install Exchange 2003 directly on a domain controller, this chapter recommends implementing a separate server for Active Directory. You can then use Microsoft Network Monitor (Netmon.exe) to capture the network traffic between the Exchange server and Active Directory to analyze how Exchange 2003 interacts with Active Directory. Figure 1-2 shows the test environment with a separate domain controller. In a production environment, you install additional domain controllers to provide redundancies for fault tolerance. However, fault tolerance is seldom a requirement for a test environment. A single domain controller configured as a global catalog server is usually sufficient for an Exchange 2003 test installation.

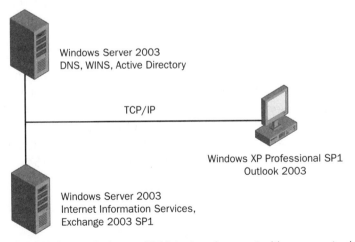

Figure 1-2 An Exchange 2003 test environment with a separate domain controller

The Client Workstation

The primary messaging client for Exchange 2003 is Microsoft Outlook. You might be tempted to install Outlook 2003 directly on the test server to eliminate the requirement for an extra workstation, but you should not do so, because this results in an unsupported configuration. Microsoft does not support installing MAPI clients, such as Outlook, on an Exchange server. Exchange server components, such as Exchange Development Kit (EDK)-based connectors and Exchange System Manager, use MAPI, but the MAPI subsystem that is installed with Exchange 2003 differs from the MAPI subsystem that is included with Outlook. Exchange 2003 installs a copy of the Mapi32.dll file in the Winnt\System32 folder. In Outlook 2000 and later, the MAPI subsystem moves to the Program Files\Common Files\System\Mapi\1033\NT folder. Typically, Outlook installs a "stub" version of MAPI in the Winnt\System32 folder, which routes MAPI calls to the Outlook implementation. The MAPI subsystem of Outlook, however, is not optimized for Exchange server operation, and server components that require specific features from the Exchange MAPI implementation might fail to operate reliably with the Outlook MAPI version.

Suppose that you want to install Outlook on a server running Exchange 2003 SP1. When Exchange 2003 is running, the Mapi32.dll file is loaded. Installing Outlook 2000 or later on the server in this situation leads to an error, because the stub DLL cannot replace a loaded Mapi32.dll. Exchange 2003 continues to use the MAPI subsystem that is optimized for Exchange 2003. On the other hand, stopping the Exchange services and installing Outlook enables the Outlook Setup program to replace the MAPI DLL, and if you restart Exchange 2003, the server then uses an incorrect DLL that is not the latest version. The Exchange 2003 SP1 version of Mapi32.dll is then replaced with an older MAPI subsystem, possibly a version as old as Outlook 2000, which is an undesirable server configuration.

> **Note**   If you must install Outlook and Exchange 2003 on the same computer, for example, because a non-Microsoft solution, such as a MAPI-based backup program, requires Outlook components, read Microsoft Knowledge Base article 266418, "XCCC: Microsoft Does Not Recommend Installing Exchange 2000 Server and Outlook 2000 or Later on the Same Computer" (*http://support.microsoft.com/default.aspx?scid=kb;en-us;266418*).

The Management Workstation

You can use Exchange System Manager directly on the test server or remotely using Windows 2003 Remote Desktop, but installing a dedicated management workstation has the advantage that you can use Network Monitor to capture the network traffic between the management workstation and Exchange server and analyze how

Exchange System Manager interacts with Exchange 2003 and Active Directory. Remember that in Exchange 2003, all Lightweight Directory Access Protocol (LDAP) communication between Exchange System Manager and Active Directory is signed and cannot be read directly, but you can see how Exchange System Manager establishes connections to Active Directory, and you can see Distributed Authoring and Versioning (DAV) communications when managing public folders, and RPC interaction when interacting with the Exchange store through MAPI. We recommend that you use a separate workstation for Exchange System Manager, because it is not supported to install Outlook together with Exchange System Manager on a workstation. Exchange System Manager is designed to work with the Mapi32.dll file that is included with Exchange 2003. Figure 1.3 shows the error message that Exchange System Manager displays if an incorrect version of Mapi32.dll is detected.

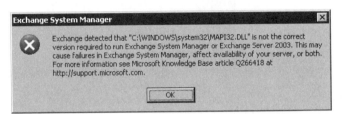

Figure 1-3   Running Exchange System Manager with an incorrect MAPI32.dll

Table 1-1 lists the advantages and disadvantages of using Exchange System Manager directly on the server versus on a management workstation.

Table 1-1   Exchange 2003 administration scenarios

Management scenario	Advantages	Disadvantages
Logging directly on to the server (Console session)	■ No extra setup required. ■ No extra hardware required.	■ Increased risk. Administrators can inadvertently delete files or introduce viruses.
Using Remote Desktop or Terminal Server	■ No extra setup required. ■ Can manage from outside of the data center. ■ Administrators can perform most tasks without leaving their desks.	■ Increased risk. Administrators can inadvertently delete files or introduce viruses. ■ Number of remote connections is limited to the number of Terminal Server licenses purchased.
Using a dedicated management station	■ Can place management station in convenient location. ■ Can analyze the Exchange System Manager communication using Network Monitor.	■ Extra setup required. ■ Extra hardware required.

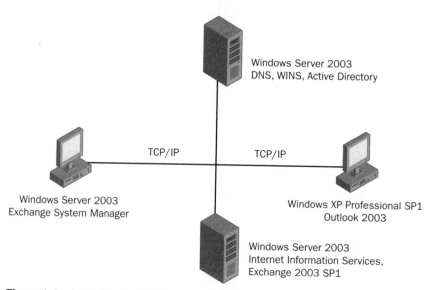

Figure 1-4   An Exchange 2003 test environment with a separate management workstation

As you notice in Figure 1-4, Exchange System Manager is installed on a workstation running Windows Server 2003. This is not a strict requirement for Exchange System Manager. Exchange System Manager runs on Windows XP Professional with Service Pack 1 or higher. The Windows 2003 workstation configuration is necessary because Network Monitor is not included with Windows XP. Windows XP includes only a command-line tool called Network Monitor Capture Utility (Netcap.exe) that is installed when you install the Windows XP Support tools. The graphical Network Monitor tool is only provided with Windows Server products and Microsoft Systems Management Server (SMS). For more information about using Network Monitor, see Microsoft Knowledge Base article 148942, "How to Capture Network Traffic with Network Monitor" *(http://support.microsoft.com/default.aspx?scid=kb;EN-US;148942).*

Exchange Server 2003 Hardware Requirements

The hardware requirements for an Exchange 2003 test server to check out basic product features are moderate. Any workstation-type x86-based personal computer should be able to run Windows 2003 and Exchange 2003. Multiple processors and additional RAM up to four gigabytes (GB) can enhance the administrator and user experience. However, remember that Exchange 2003 does not run on 64-bit processors and cannot use more than four GB of RAM. These limitations apply to all 32-bit Windows programs unless they use physical address extension (PAE) to address RAM above four GB. For example, Microsoft SQL Server 2000 uses PAE, but Exchange 2003 does not.

Exchange 2003 requires the following minimum hardware configuration:

- **Intel Pentium or compatible processor running at 133 megahertz (MHz) or faster**   Although Exchange 2003 can run on a computer with a 133 MHz processor, we recommend that in your test environment you use at a minimum an x86-compatible processor with a speed of 500 MHz or faster.

- **128 megabyte (MB) RAM (recommended minimum is 256 MB)**   An amount of 128 MB might be sufficient, but causes Exchange 2003 to run slowly. You might want to provide at least 256 MB on a test server. For even better response times, consider 512 MB of RAM or more.

- **500 MB disk space for the Exchange 2003 executable files**   We recommend that you install the executable files of Exchange 2003 on a disk drive that has at least 500 MB of free space to have sufficient room for the binary files and database files, as well as for support tools and documentation that you might want to download from the Exchange 2003 downloads site at *http://www.microsoft.com/exchange/downloads/2003.asp* and install on the test server in addition to Exchange 2003.

- **200 MB available on the system drive**   Windows Server 2003 requires several hundred megabytes of free disk space on the system drive. Consider 200 MB of free space the absolute minimum. If possible, keep one GB of disk space available for the operating system.

- **A 100 megabit per second (Mbit/s) network card**   As a messaging system, Exchange 2003 requires a functioning TCP/IP network. It is sufficient to use a 100 Mbit/s network card in a test computer. Production systems, however, will benefit from multiple gigabit per second (Gbit/s) network cards.

Note   The minimum hardware specification is rarely suitable for a production server running Exchange Server 2003. The design of a production server involves many variables and requires a thorough analysis of requirements, as explained in Chapter 2, "Exchange Server 2003 Design Basics," and in Chapter 18, "Tuning Exchange Server Performance."

File System Requirements

In addition to the minimum hardware specification, you might want to consider providing a separate disk drive for Exchange 2003 database files. Figure 1-5 shows a possible hardware configuration for a basic Exchange 2003 test server.

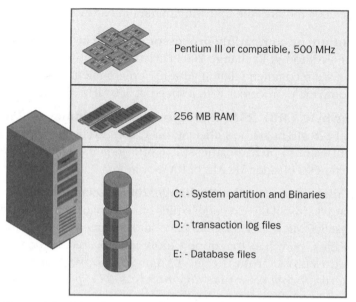

Figure 1-5   A hardware configuration for an Exchange 2003 test server

We recommend that you assign the hard disks of your test server as follows:

- **Drive C: for the system partition and for Exchange binaries**   Install the operating system and Exchange 2003 on the system partition. The operating system files consist of the Windows folder, which contains executables for Windows programs, services, and also Active Directory partitions, if the computer is a domain controller. We recommend that you use the default C:\Windows for the directory of the operating system when installing Windows Server 2003 and the default C:\Program Files\Exchsrvr when installing Exchange Server 2003.

- **Drive D: for Exchange transaction log files**   After Installing the Exchange 2003 program files on drive C, you should move the Exchange transaction log files to a separate physical drive to increase the performance of the Exchange store. For more information about how to configure Exchange databases, see Chapter 10, "Configuring Exchange Store Resources."

- **Drive E: for Exchange database files**   Following the installation of Exchange 2003, it is a good idea to start Exchange System Manager and move the database files to a dedicated drive to separate them from the transaction log files. For detailed step-by-step instructions about how to accomplish this task, see the document Preparing a basic test environment.doc, which you can find in the \Companion Material\Chapter01 folder on the companion CD.

Note If your test server has multiple disks or redundant arrays of independent disks (RAID), map these disks directly to drives C, D, and E. If your test server has only one hard disk, you can partition the single disk into three volumes to simulate a system with three independent drives. This is sufficient for a test server, but in a production system, it is strongly recommended that you place the database files on a separate physical disk subsystem for fault tolerance and increased performance, as discussed in Chapter 10, "Configuring Exchange Store Resources." Format all partitions with the NTFS file system.

Operating System Requirements

Exchange Server 2003 supports the following operating systems:

- Windows 2000 Server, Standard, Advanced, or Datacenter Editions, with Service Pack 3 or higher

- Windows Server 2003, Standard, Enterprise, or Datacenter Editions

As mentioned earlier in this chapter, the full feature set of Exchange 2003 is available only when installing Exchange 2003 on Windows 2003.

Active Directory Requirements

Before installing Exchange Server 2003, you must deploy Active Directory. Ensure that the Active Directory configuration meets the following requirements:

- **The computer network supports TCP/IP**   Active Directory uses LDAP and requires TCP/IP for network communication. You should use static IP addresses for both the server running Exchange 2003 and the domain controller. The workstation running Windows XP Professional SP1 and Outlook 2003, as well as the management workstation running Exchange System Manager, can be configured using Dynamic Host Configuration Protocol (DHCP), but in a test environment it is also sufficient to assign these workstations static IP addresses if DHCP is not available. We recommend that you use IP addresses from a private address range, such as 192.168.1.0/24.

- **Domain Name Service (DNS) is available in the Windows network**   You can install a DNS server when you promote your test computer to a domain controller. For the purposes of the test environment, it is sufficient to configure a root DNS server. It is not required to integrate this DNS server into an existing DNS infrastructure.

- **The domain controller is configured as a global catalog** This is the default configuration for the first domain controller installed in a new Active Directory forest.

> **Note**   Exchange 2003 is supported in native Windows 2000, mixed Windows 2000, and Windows 2003, and native Windows 2003 Active Directory environments. While Windows 2000 Server Service Pack 2 domain controllers can be present, the domain controllers and global catalog servers that Exchange 2003 uses must run Windows 2000 Service Pack 3 or later. It is assumed that you are running Exchange 2003 in a native Windows 2003 Active Directory test environment.

Internet Information Services Requirements

Exchange 2003 requires a number of IIS services and components to be installed prior to running the Setup program of Exchange 2003. You will not be able to install Exchange 2003 if these services and components are not present on the server.
Ensure that the following IIS services and components are installed:

- **Simple Mail Transfer Protocol (SMTP) Service**   Exchange 2003 extends this service with additional components so that this service can perform message routing and delivery functions in the Exchange 2003 organization.

- **Network News Transfer Protocol (NNTP) Service**   Exchange uses and extends the NNTP service to participate in USENET discussions and provide access to Exchange public folders for newsreader clients through NNTP.

- **World Wide Web Publishing Service**   Exchange relies on the Web service to support Internet-based clients, such as Outlook Web Access and Outlook Mobile Access.

- **.NET Framework**   The .NET Framework is a Windows component for building and running Windows applications and Web services. For example, Outlook Mobile Access, a component of Exchange 2003 that enables mobile users to communicate with Exchange 2003, is based on the .NET Framework.

- **ASP.NET**   ASP.NET integrates with .NET Framework to provide a unified programming environment for developing Web applications, such as Web services. Outlook Mobile Access is based on ASP.NET. It should be noted, however, that Outlook Web Access is not based on the .NET Framework or ASP.NET.

> **Note** On Windows 2000, the Setup program of Exchange 2003 installs .NET Framework and ASP.NET automatically if they are not already present. On Windows 2003, you must install ASP.NET manually prior to running the Exchange 2003 Setup program.

Permission Requirements

To install Exchange 2003 successfully, administrative permissions are required on the test server, as well as in the Active Directory environment. In a test environment with only one domain, you can use the Administrator account to install Exchange 2003 However, if you want to test Exchange security, you might want to use a separate account. The Administrator account has full control over the domain, including the permissions of an enterprise administrator, schema administrator, domain administrator, and local administrator.

> **Note** If you want to install Exchange 2003 on a member server, ensure that you are logging on with a domain account. Local accounts are available only on the local server and will not have the required permissions to access Active Directory on a domain controller.

To install Exchange 2003, you must have the permissions of the following accounts:

- **Schema administrator** You must be a schema administrator in the test environment because the Setup program of Exchange 2003 extends the Active Directory schema during the installation of the first server. For subsequent installations, permissions of a schema administrator are not required.

  A schema administrator can also run the Exchange 2003 Setup program with the /ForestPrep parameter to prepare the Active Directory environment for you prior to installing the first Exchange 2003 server, in which case, you do not need to be a schema administrator when you install the server. See Table 1-2 for a list of permissions required to run Setup in ForestPrep mode.

- **Domain administrator** You must be a domain administrator because the Setup program of Exchange 2003 creates group objects for Exchange servers called Exchange Domain Servers and Exchange Enterprise Servers in Active Directory. This process can succeed only if you have domain administrator permissions. A domain administrator can also prepare the domain in which you want to install Exchange 2003 for you by running the Exchange 2003 Setup program with the /DomainPrep parameter. See Table 1-2 for a list of permissions required to run Setup in DomainPrep mode.

- **Local administrator**   The Setup program of Exchange 2003 places numerous files in the \Program Files\Exchsrvr directory on the test server's local hard disk, extends the SMTP service with additional components, and configures registry settings for the various services included in Exchange 2003. You must be a local administrator on the server on which you install Exchange 2003 to accomplish these tasks successfully.

> **Note**   If a schema administrator has prepared the Active Directory forest for you, you must install the first Exchange 2003 server with the account that the schema administrator specified during the ForestPrep operation. If the schema administrator specified a group instead of an individual account during ForestPrep, your account must be a member of that group, or you must be working with an account that is a member of the Enterprise Administrators group or the Domain Administrators group in the root domain of your forest. These accounts have the permissions of an Exchange Full Administrator at the Exchange organization level. If you want to install Exchange 2003 on an additional server in the organization, you must be an Exchange Full Administrator at the organization level or at the level of the administrative group to which you want to add the server.

Table 1-2 lists the permissions that you need to run Setup in ForestPrep or DomainPrep mode.

Table 1-2   Permissions required for ForestPrep and DomainPrep

ForestPrep	DomainPrep
- Schema administrator	- Domain administrator
- Enterprise administrator	- Local administrator
- Domain administrator	
- Local administrator	

Outlook 2003 Requirements

A messaging system is not very useful without a messaging client, and a good choice for Exchange 2003 is Outlook 2003. As discussed, you should install Outlook 2003 in your test environment on a separate computer to avoid an unsupported server configuration. If you cannot install a separate computer in your test environment to run Outlook, consider installing Outlook directly on a domain controller (if the domain controller is not running Exchange 2003) or use Outlook Web Access instead of Outlook 2003 as the messaging client.

Office Outlook 2003 has the following system requirements:

- Intel Pentium 233 MHz or higher processor. Pentium III or higher recommended.

- 128 MB of RAM or more.

- 150 MB of available hard disk space. The optional installation file cache will require an additional 200 MB of hard disk space.

- Microsoft Windows 2000 with Service Pack 3 (SP3) or later, or Windows XP or later.

- Super VGA or higher-resolution monitor.

Note Outlook 2003 integrates tightly with the other applications in the Microsoft Office suite, such as Microsoft Office Word 2003. If you want to evaluate the full spectrum of Outlook 2003 functionality, install Microsoft Office 2003 on your test workstation. For example, you can then use Word 2003 as the e-mail editor in Outlook 2003, which has the advantage that you can use Word features, such as the Word spelling checker, when you compose e-mail messages.

Exchange System Manager Requirements

The installation of Exchange System Manager on a management workstation is more involved than the installation of Outlook 2003 on a client workstation. This is because Exchange System Manager is installed using the Exchange 2003 Setup program, and this Setup program expects to find certain components on the computer, such as the SMTP service and Active Directory Users and Computers, which it extends to make them Exchange 2003-aware. Furthermore, to manage Exchange 2003, the management workstation must be joined to the same forest as your Exchange servers. You cannot manage Exchange servers in a different forest, but client workstations running Outlook can be in a workgroup or a foreign forest with or without trust relationships.

Exchange System Manager has the following software requirements:

- **Microsoft Windows XP Professional SP1 or later or Windows Server 2003** The management workstation must be a member of a domain in the forest of Exchange 2003.

- **Windows Administrative Tools Pack** Installing this tools pack installs Active Directory Users and Computers and other tools on the management workstation that enable you to remotely manage servers running Windows 2003.

To install Windows Server 2003 Administration Tools:

a. Open the \i386 folder on the Windows Server 2003 product CD.

b. Double-click Adminpak.msi.

c. Click Next, and then click Finish.

■ **SMTP service**   The Exchange 2003 Setup program must install SMTP service components that enable Exchange System Manager to communicate with an SMTP service running on an Exchange 2003 server. This communication is required, for example, when enumerating messages currently awaiting delivery in message queues. It is required to have the SMTP server to run the Setup program successfully, but it is not required to run the SMTP service on the management workstation. Following the installation of Exchange System Management Tools, you can stop the SMTP service and configure the service for manual startup using the Service tool.

Note   You might also want to install the Windows 2003 support tools by double-clicking Suptools.msi from the \Support\Tools folder on the Windows Server 2003 product CD. Among other things, the Windows 2003 support tools include the Active Directory Schema snap-in that you can use to view and edit the Active Directory schema and the ADSI Edit tool, which is a low-level Active Directory tool that you can use to view and modify directory objects and attributes.

For detailed step-by-step instructions about how to install Exchange System Manager on a management workstation, see the document Preparing a basic test environment.doc, which you can find in the \Companion Material\Chapter01 folder on the companion CD.

Key Features of Exchange Server 2003

Having accomplished the deployment of an Exchange 2003 test environment, you can take a first look at the features that Exchange 2003 provides. Most of these features you configure using Exchange System Manager.

Features in Exchange System Manager

Exchange System Manager is the main administrative interface to configure settings for Exchange 2003 server resources. You can find this tool on the server or the management workstation in the Microsoft Exchange program group. By default, Exchange System Manager provides the following top-level containers:

- **Global Settings**   Includes features to configure system-wide settings. These settings apply to all servers and recipients in an Exchange organization. Global settings are also available for Exchange ActiveSync and Outlook Mobile Access. Global settings determine:

    - **Internet Message Formats**   Specify how Exchange 2003 converts MAPI messages to Multipurpose Internet Mail Extensions (MIME) messages, and how Exchange 2003 handles automatic responses destined for an SMTP domain. For an example of how to configure Internet message formats for an SMTP domain, see the document Configuring Internet message formats.doc, which you can find in the \Companion Material\Chapter01 folder on the companion CD.

    - **Message Delivery**   Specifies how Exchange 2003 handles messages for recipients in the Exchange organization. For example, you can specify message size limits and a maximum number of recipients for each message, as well as sender, recipient, and connection filters to block spam and other unsolicited e-mail messages. For an example of how to configure message delivery options, see the document Configuring message delivery options.doc, which you can find in the \Companion Material\Chapter01 folder on the companion CD.

    - **Mobile Services**   Specify which Exchange ActiveSync and Outlook Mobile Access features are enabled and can be used to define mobile carriers for each SMTP domain. For an example of how to configure mobile service options, see the document Configuring mobile services.doc, which you can find in the \Companion Material\Chapter01 folder on the companion CD.

- **Recipients**   Includes features to manage objects and settings for recipients in your organization. You can manage address lists, offline address lists, recipient update services, recipient policies, mailbox management settings, details templates, and address templates. For an example of how to configure a recipient policy, see the document Configuring recipient policies.doc, which you can find in the \Companion Material\Chapter01 folder on the companion CD.

- **Servers**   Holds server-specific configuration objects, such as queues, mailbox stores, public folder stores, and protocols information. For an example of how to configure Exchange store resources, see the document Configuring messaging databases.doc, which you can find in the \Companion Material\Chapter01 folder on the companion CD.

- **Connectors**   Holds configuration objects for connectors to non-Exchange messaging systems, such as Connector for Lotus Notes, Connector for Novell GroupWise, and Calendar Connector. Connectors to non-Exchange messaging systems are discussed in Chapter 5, "Migrating to Exchange Server 2003."

- **Tools**   Contains tools that help you to monitor your Exchange organization, track messages, and recover mailboxes. For an example of how to verify the current state of an Exchange server, see the document Verifying server status.doc, which you can find in the \Companion Material\Chapter01 folder on the companion CD.

- **Folders**   Displays public folder hierarchies. A public folder stores messages or information that can be shared with all designated users in your organization. Public folders can contain different types of information, from simple messages to multimedia clips and custom forms.

In an Exchange organization with only one server, Exchange System Manager by default does not display administrative groups or routing groups. You can display these containers when you right-click on the organization object, such as Tailspin Toys (Exchange), select Properties, and then select the check boxes Display routing groups and Display administrative groups on the General tab. The Servers, Folders, and Connectors containers are then moved under the administrative group container to which they belong. You must restart Exchange System Manager to fully activate the changes.

Mailbox-Enabling and Mail-Enabling Recipients

If you are familiar with the Exchange Administrator program of Exchange Server 5.5, you might notice one significant difference in Exchange System Manager: Exchange System Manager is not the tool to create mailboxes. In an Exchange 2003 organization, mailboxes are managed primarily using Active Directory Users and Computers because mailbox settings are stored in the attributes of user accounts. There is no separate mailbox object in Active Directory. Chapter 9, "Managing Directory Information," explains in detail how to manage recipient settings.

For step-by-step instructions about how to mailbox-enable or mail-enable user accounts, see the document Mailbox-enabling and mail-enabling recipients.doc, which you can find in the \Companion Material\Chapter01 folder on the companion CD.

Microsoft Management Console Integration

All graphical administration tools included in Exchange 2003 are based on Microsoft Management Console (MMC). MMC is an extensible host environment for management applications provided in the form of snap-ins. Collections of snap-ins can be saved in .msc files to create administrative tools. For example, Exchange System Manager is a tool that consists of snap-ins saved in a pre-configured MMC file named Exchange System Manager.msc.

Snap-ins are Component Object Model (COM) objects implemented in COM in-process server DLLs. A COM in-process server DLL can expose one or more COM objects that run within the process of a client application that uses these objects. In contrast to a stand-alone application that runs as a separate process in Windows, snap-ins run in the MMC process (MMC.exe). For example, most of the snap-ins that comprise Exchange System Manager are implemented in Exadmin.dll, which you can find in the \Program Files\Exchsrvr\bin directory.

The Active Directory Users and Computers tool that you can use to manage user accounts and mailboxes also consists of various snap-ins provided by Dsadmin.dll. This tool is saved in a pre-configured MMC file named Dsa.msc, which resides in the \Windows\System32 directory. Exchange 2003 includes another MMC file named Users and Computers.msc that also loads the Active Directory Users and Computers snap-ins. The Users and Computers.msc file is in the \Program Files\Exchsrvr\bin directory. Dsa.msc and Users and Computers.msc look the same, because both .msc files load the same snap-ins. You should note, however, that the Active Directory Users and Computers snap-in and the Active Directory Users and Computers tools are not the same. The snap-in is a COM component. The tools are .msc files that include the snap-in.

Note   Microsoft Knowledge Base articles often use inexact terminology by referring to .msc files as snap-ins. For example, you do not start a snap-in when you click Start, point to All Programs, point to Microsoft Exchange, and then click System Manager. You actually start MMC.exe and load the Exchange System Manager.msc file, which in turn loads all the snap-ins.

Examining Snap-In Registrations

Each snap-in is assigned a globally unique identifier (GUID) that identifies the snap-in as a unique COM class object within an in-process server dynamic-link library (DLL). These identifiers, known as class identifiers (CLSIDs), must be registered for each object in the HKEY_CLASSES_ROOT\CLSID registry key. For example, {1B600AEA-10BA-11d2-9F28-00C04FA37610} is the CLSID of the *SystemMgr Class*. The *SystemMgr Class* can be found in an in-process server DLL named Exadmin.dll, which is located in the \Program Files\Exchsrvr\bin directory. The entries under the CLSID registry key define, among other things, the threading model for the COM classes, the ProgID, and the version number of the COM class.

To locate the CLSIDs of the various Exchange System Manager snap-ins, perform these steps on your management workstation:

1.   Start Registry Editor by typing Regedit.exe at a command prompt.

Warning   Using Registry Editor incorrectly can cause serious problems that may require you to reinstall your operating system. Microsoft cannot guarantee that problems resulting from the incorrect use of Registry Editor can be solved. Use Registry Editor at your own risk.

2. Right-click the HKEY_CLASSES_ROOT hive and select the Find command.

3. In the Find dialog box, under Find what, type Exadmin.dll, and then click Find Next.

4. Regedit.exe will jump to the first registration entry for the Exchange Queue Viewer snap-in. You can determine the ProgID of the snap-in in the ProgID registry key.

5. Press the F3 key to search through the remainder of the HKEY_CLASSES_ROOT hive. Repeat this step to iterate through all snap-in entries that point to Exadmin.dll.

To define COM components as MMC snap-ins, the CLSIDs must also be registered under the HKEY_LOCAL_MACHINE\Software\Microsoft\MMC\SnapIns key. For example, if you search for a CLSID key of {1B600AEA-10BA-11d2-9F28-00C04FA37610} under the SnapIns key (that is, the CLSID of the SystemMgr Class), you find that this entry belongs to the Exchange System snap-in, which is the core snap-in of Exchange System Manager. Table 1-3 lists the entries for snap-ins under the SnapIns key.

Table 1-3   Registry parameters for MMC snap-ins

Parent Key	Parameter	Type	Comments
{CLSID}	NameString	REG_SZ	The NameString value specifies the display name of the snap-in, as it appears in the MMC user interface when adding a snap-in to a console. For example, Namestring=Exchange System defines the display name for the Exchange System snap-in.
{CLSID}	About	REG_SZ	The About value contains the CLSID of the object that is used to provide an icon, a description, and the About dialog box for the snap-in. For example, About= {1B600AEB-10BA-11d2-9F28-00C04FA37610} points to a specific CLSID. If you look up this CLSID under HKEY_CLASSES_ROOT\CLSID, you find that this is the CLSID for the *AboutSystemMgr Class*, which also resides in Exadmin.dll.

Table 1-3   Registry parameters for MMC snap-ins (Continued)

Parent Key	Parameter	Type	Comments
{CLSID}	NameString-Indirect	REG_SZ	The NameStringIndirect value provides a resource DLL name and string identifier, as an indirect means to retrieve the name of the snap-in. For example,
			NameStringIndirect=@C:\\Program Files\\Exchsrvr\\bin\\exadmin.dll,-12577 specifies the name of the Exchange System snap-in, as found in Exadmin.dll. If NameStringIndirect does not exist, or if its value data does not lead to a successful string load, MMC then uses the NameString value as the name string.
{CLSID}\ StandAlone	N/A	N/A	An existing StandAlone key indicates that the snap-in is a stand-alone snap-in. You can add stand-alone snap-ins to an MMC console in the Add/Remove Snap-in dialog box. You can also add stand-alone snap-ins to subnodes of other snap-ins, using the stand-alone snap-in in much the same way as an extension snap-in.
			The StandAlone key is missing for extension snap-ins. Therefore, the snap-in cannot be added to an MMC console without first adding a stand-alone snap-in that provides the nodes that the extension snap-in is designed to extend. For example, the Exchange Information Store extension snap-in extends the System Manager snap-in. Therefore, you can add only this extension snap-in when you add the System Manager snap-in to your MMC console. Extension snap-ins are listed as available extensions for a stand-alone snap-in in the Add/Remove Snap-in dialog box on the Extensions tab.

Table 1-3   Registry parameters for MMC snap-ins (Continued)

Parent Key	Parameter	Type	Comments
{CLSID}\ NodeTypes	{CLSID}	N/A	Nodes refer to the configuration objects in the MMC console tree. For example, in Exchange System Manager, the individual server objects in the Servers container under an administrative group are a specific node type. Node types are registered in the NodeTypes key. The NodeTypes key contains subkeys that are the GUIDs of the node types. MMC uses these GUIDs to enumerate the node types of the snap-in and then uses that list of node types to obtain the extension snap-ins for those node types. The set of extension snap-ins is then displayed as available extensions for the snap-in in the Extensions tab of the Add/Remove Snap-in dialog box.
KEY_LOCAL_-MACHINE\Soft-ware\Microsoft\ MMC\NodeTypes	{CLSID}	N/A	All extensible node types have their own subkey (that is, the GUID of the node type) registered under the ..\MMC\Node-Types key. Each GUID key contains an Extensions subkey and the Extensions key contains additional subkeys that represent the actual types of extensions that this node type can have. Each extension-type subkey contains values that represent the CLSIDs of the snap-ins that extend that node type. For example, the Exchange POP3 Container Object (GUID {F54E0C6b-11FF-11d2-9F28-00C04FA37610}) is an extensible node type of the Exchange Protocols snap-in. Likewise, the key ..\Node-Types\{F54E0C6b-11FF-11d2-9F28-00C04FA37610} has an Extensions subkey that lists the CLSID of the Exchange POP3 extension snap-in in the ContextMenu and NameSpace subkeys. This indicates that the Exchange POP3 extension snap-in extends the namespace and the context menu in Exchange System Manager for the Exchange POP3 container object. The namespace is the hierarchy of all objects that can be managed through an MMC console.

Creating Custom MMC Tools

One of the key features of MMC snap-ins is that they can be used to create custom MMC consoles. For example, you can include the Exchange Message Tracking Center snap-in in a separate MMC tool and provide this tool to administrators that are only responsible for message tracking. MMC extensibility can also be used to create tools that provide more functionality than standard tools. For example, you can include both the Exchange System snap-in and the Active Directory Users and Computers snap-in in a custom MMC tool that is reminiscent of an Exchange 5.5 Administrator program. Exchange 5.5 administrators planning to migrate to Exchange 2003 might find this useful.

Figure 1-6 shows a custom MMC tool that combines the Exchange System snap-in and the Active Directory Users and Computers snap-in. For step-by-step instructions about how to create this tool, see the document Exchange System Administrator.doc, which you can find in the \Companion Material\Chapter 01 folder on the companion CD.

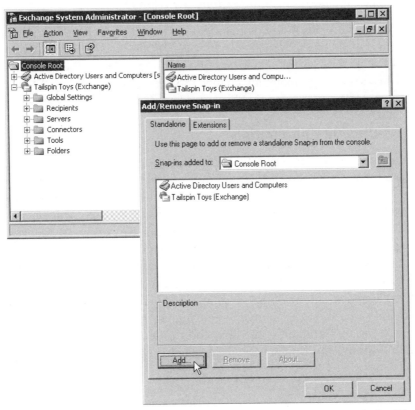

Figure 1-6   A custom MMC tool combining the Exchange System and Active Directory Users and Computers snap-ins

MMC consoles can run in one of two modes, author mode or user mode. You use author mode to create new consoles or modify existing consoles. You use user mode to work with existing consoles for system administration. You can specify the console mode when you open the Console menu and click Options.

There are three levels of user mode:

■ **User mode - full access**   When running a console in this mode, the user can use all available functionality of the snap-ins, but the user cannot add or remove snap-ins or save changes to the console.

■ **User mode - limited access, multiple window**   When running a console in this mode, the user cannot add or remove snap-ins or save changes to the console, nor can they close any windows that were open when the console author last saved the console.

■ **User mode - limited access, single window**   Running a console in this mode, the user cannot add or remove snap-ins or save changes to the console, and additional subwindows cannot be opened.

You can use the MMC command line switch /a to open a saved console in author mode and make changes to saved consoles. When saved consoles are opened using the /a switch, they are opened in author mode, regardless of their default mode. However, this does not permanently change the default mode setting. When you omit the /a switch, MMC opens console files according to their default mode settings.

Active Directory Integration

When you use Network Monitor to capture the network traffic generated on your management workstation while starting Exchange System Manager, you can see that a substantial number of data packets are exchanged with a domain controller running Active Directory. This is because Exchange Server 2003 uses Active Directory to store most of its configuration data, including settings for servers, server resources, and messaging connectors. Exchange System Manager must somehow access this information so that you can manage the Exchange organization. Exchange System Manager uses Active Directory Service Interfaces (ADSI) to communicate with Active Directory, and ADSI in turn relies on the LDAP protocol. For example, the first datagram after starting Exchange System Manager is usually an LDAP UDP SearchRequest to locate a domain controller, and the second datagram is usually an LDAP SearchResponse of a domain controller (Figure 1-7).

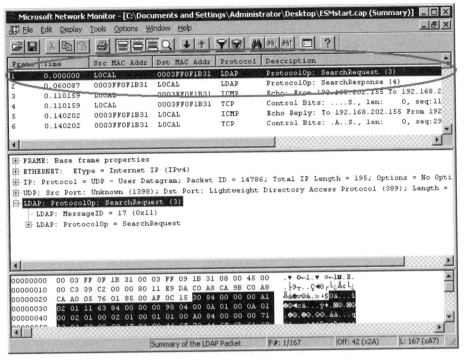

Figure 1-7   LDAP SearchRequest and SearchResponse datagrams

Subsequently, ADSI performs several suitability tests to determine if the domain controller is functioning properly before actually binding to it, but this is beyond the scope of the current discussion. The important point is that most of the Exchange 2003 configuration information is in Active Directory, specifically in the configuration naming context (NC).

The following three Active Directory naming contexts contain Exchange-related data:

- **Domain NC**   Exchange recipient and system objects are stored in the domain NC in Active Directory. The domain NC is replicated to every domain controller in a given domain. A partial replica of the domain NC is replicated to the global catalog.

- **Configuration NC**   Exchange configuration objects, such as administrative groups, global settings, recipient policies, system policies, and server information are stored in the configuration NC. The configuration NC is replicated to all domain controllers in the forest.

- **Schema NC**   Exchange schema modifications (for example, classes and attributes) are stored in the schema NC. The schema NC is replicated to all domain controllers in the forest.

> **Note**   Not all configuration information is stored in Active Directory. Exchange also uses the local registry, the IIS metabase, and in special situations, configuration files.

NCs are root container objects, also called partitions, in Active Directory, which you can display using ADSI Edit. Figure 1-8 shows ADSI Edit, the three naming contexts, and the Exchange configuration information in the configuration NC. For step-by-step instructions about how to configure the ADSI Edit tool to display the Active Directory NCs, see the document ADSI Edit and Active Directory NCs.doc, which you can find in the \Companion Material\Chapter 01 folder on the companion CD.

> **Warning**   If you use the ADSI Edit snap-in and you incorrectly modify the attributes of Active Directory objects, you can cause serious problems. These problems may require you to reinstall Windows 2003, Exchange 2003, or the entire Active Directory forest. Microsoft cannot guarantee that problems that occur if you incorrectly modify Active Directory object attributes can be solved. Use ADSI Edit at your own risk.

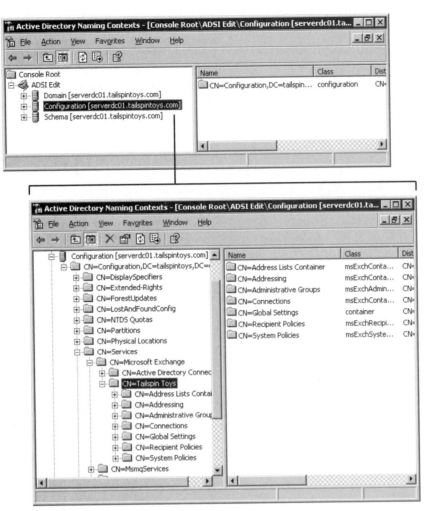

Figure 1-8   An Exchange organization in the configuration naming context

Active Directory integration has the following consequences for Exchange 2003:

- **Active Directory forest limitation**   Because Active Directory does not replicate naming context information to domain controllers in other forests, an
Exchange organization cannot span multiple forests. A single forest also cannot
host more than a single Exchange organization. Theoretically, it might be possible for a single configuration NC to hold more than one Exchange organization
container. However, several dependencies exist that prevent this form of
deployment. Among other things, the Setup program of Exchange Server 2003
does not give you a choice to create a second organization if an organization
object already exists in the configuration NC of Active Directory.

- **Combined user account and mailbox administration**   Windows administration and Exchange administration are closely linked, and this is an advantage because resources such as user accounts and their messaging-related properties can be administered from a single perspective, usually through Active Directory Users and Computers. There is a one-to-one relationship between user accounts and mailboxes. This is noticeably different from Exchange 5.5, where a particular Windows NT user can have multiple mailboxes. In Exchange 2003, a particular user might have multiple mailboxes, but you must create a separate user account for each mailbox and then configure access permissions to grant the actual user access to all the mailbox-user accounts. This different way of dealing with multiple mailboxes for a single user in Exchange 2000 and Exchange 2003 might confuse Exchange 5.5 administrators at first. The best way to deal with this issue is to create several mailboxes for a particular user in a test environment to familiarize yourself with how this process works. For an example, see the document Creating Multiple Mailboxes for the Administrator account.doc, which you can find in the \Companion Material\Chapter 01 folder on the companion CD.

- **Group Policies and System Policies**   Windows Server 2003 and Exchange Server 2003 provide policies that administrators can use to apply settings to a collection of Active Directory objects, including users, computers, and Exchange objects, such as servers and mailbox stores. The group policy structure of Windows 2003, is a powerful and extensible platform that provides standard settings for directory objects and also allows additional policies to be written and applied for particular environments. For example, auto-enrollment of X.509 certificates that enable users to sign and encrypt e-mail messages can be performed through the use of Group Policy.

  Exchange 2003 includes two other kinds of policies: recipient policies and system policies. Recipient policies are policies that are applied to mailbox-enabled or mail-enabled recipient objects to generate e-mail addresses. System policies are policies that are applied to a collection of servers, mailbox stores, or public stores to reduce administrative overhead in larger environments with multiple servers, mailbox stores, or public stores through a single configuration object. For an example of how to configure a system policy in Exchange 2003 to apply mailbox quotas to all users in a mailbox store, see the document Configuring a mailbox store policy.doc, which you can find on the companion CD in the \Companion Material\Chapter 01 folder.

- **Dynamic (Query-based) Distribution Groups**   Exchange 2003 supports query-based distribution groups that perform the same function as normal distribution groups in Active Directory, except that their membership is determined dynamically when the groups are used to transfer messages. Membership of a query-based distribution group is determined using an LDAP query against mailbox-enabled or mail-enabled objects in Active Directory, for example to "All existing user accounts" or "All full-time employees" in a company. This method provides for lower administrative overhead, because the lists do not require manual maintenance, but it results in more processing overhead on the server for distribution list expansion, depending on the number of members. Query-based distribution groups are supported only in native-mode Exchange organizations that contain only servers running Exchange 2000 SP3 or higher and Exchange 2003.

> **Note**   When you deploy query-based distribution lists in a multi-site environment, it is important to understand group nesting and the role of the expansion server to minimize processing and network traffic costs. For more information about configuring distribution groups, see Chapter 9, "Managing Directory Information."

■ **Command-line tools and programmable administrative interfaces**   The fact that Exchange 2003 uses Active Directory to store recipient information and most of its configuration data means that you can use Active Directory command-line tools and application programming interfaces (APIs) to manage an Exchange 2003 organization. Using command-line tools, such as Ldifde.exe and Csvde.exe, you can perform bulk export and import operations that are beyond the capabilities of the graphical administrative tools. Ldifde.exe and Csvde.exe have the same command-line parameters, yet Csvde.exe provides only limited functionality in the sense that you cannot perform update operations on existing directory objects. For detailed information about Ldifde.exe, see Microsoft Knowledge Base article 237677, "Using LDIFDE to Import and Export Directory Objects to Active Directory" *(http://go.microsoft.com/fwlink/ ?linkid=3052&kbid=237677)*.

   With basic Microsoft Visual Basic Scripting Edition (VBScript) programming skills, it is also possible to create custom scripts that implement specific management features. The most important APIs that an advanced Exchange administrator should be familiar with are Active Directory Service Interfaces (ADSI) and Collaboration Data Objects for Exchange Management (CDOEXM). The \Companion Material\Chapter 01\Scripts folder on the companion CD contains a sample script called SetMailboxQuotas.wsf that you can use to apply individual mailbox quotas to all mailbox-enabled user accounts in a specified organizational unit. You can use the Scheduled Task Wizard of Windows 2003 to configure this script to run automatically based on a scheduled event, for example, you can run this script every day at midnight. You can automatically enforce mailbox size limits for all Exchange users in the restricted organizational unit without affecting users in other organizational units and without changing the default quotas for the mailbox stores. You only need to create or move the restricted user accounts into the monitored organizational unit, and the size limits are applied automatically when the SetMailboxQuotas script runs. For details about the advantages of managing an Exchange organization using custom admin scripts, see Chapter 8, "Automating Exchange Configuration Tasks."

The following code example illustrates how to perform an Exchange management task programmatically. SetMailboxQuotas.wsf uses this code in a slightly modified form to support command-line parameters. Keep in mind that the code below is not a complete .wsf script. For more information how to use this code in a script, try out SetMailboxQuotas.wsf and read the document SetMailboxQuotas.doc, which you can find in the \Companion Material\Chapter 01\Scripts folder.

```
Procedure SetMbxLimits
'
'    Sets Mailbox limits for an Exchange user
Sub SetMbxLimits(oUser)
    'Set the quotas in KB
    oUser.EnableStoreDefaults = False
    oUser.StoreQuota = 1000
    oUser.OverQuotaLimit = 2000
    oUser.HardLimit = 3000

    'Save the settings
    oUser.SetInfo
End Sub
```

■ **Single-seat administration**   The configuration NC is replicated to all domain controllers in the forest, which means that each domain controller has a complete replica of the Exchange organization. Any changes to a configuration object are replicated. Thus, you do not need to connect to a particular domain controller to perform management tasks. In fact, the default setting for Exchange System Manager is Any Writable Domain Controller (Figure 1-9).

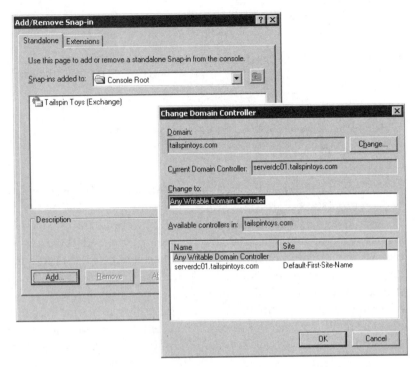

Figure 1-9   Connecting to any domain controller to perform Exchange management tasks

Exchange 2003 administration does not depend directly on the physical network structure, so a company can implement a centralized administration model for Exchange Server 2003 even across multiple geographical locations. For example, regardless of a server's physical location, an Exchange administrator at the organization level, such as a member of the Enterprise Administrators group, can run the following LDIFDE command to export the distinguished name, version information, and server name of all the Exchange servers in an Exchange organization that are not running Exchange 2003 SP1 (the example uses a domain controller named SERVERDC01 in the domain tailspintoys.com): ldifde -f c:\serverlist.txt -s SERVERDC01 -d "CN=Microsoft Exchange,CN=Services,CN=Configuration,DC=tailspintoys,DC=com" -p subtree -r "(&(objectClass=msExchExchangeServer)(!serialNumber=Version 6.5*Service Pack 1*))" -l "serialNumber, name." The resulting serverlist.txt file will list all the servers that you might want to update to Exchange 2003 SP1 in the various locations of your company. You can replace ldifde with csvde to export the information into a comma-separated values (.csv) file that you can then process further using Microsoft Excel.

The following is an LDIFDE sample output for a server running Exchange 2000 Service Pack 3:

```
dn: CN=SERVER02,CN=Servers,CN=First Administrative Group,CN=Administrative
Groups,CN=Tailspin Toys,CN=Microsoft Exchange,CN=Services,CN=Configuration,DC=tail-
spintoys,DC=com

changetype: add

serialNumber: Version 6.0 (Build 6249.4: Service Pack 3)

name: SERVER02
```

Version 6.0 stands for Exchange 2000. Servers running Exchange 2003 have a version number of 6.5.

Exchange System Manager communicates both with Active Directory and with services running on the Exchange server being managed. For example, Exchange System Manager communicates with the SMTP service to obtain dynamic information about message queues and with the Remote Registry service to configure settings stored in the registry. This communication requires support for remote procedure calls (RPCs). Thus, Exchange 2003 administration is not entirely independent of the physical network structure. In order to access the configuration information that is in Active Directory, a domain controller must be available through LDAP.

Additional Administrative Tools

Exchange 2003 includes a variety of administrative tools that you can use to accomplish specific tasks. Some of these tools, such as Message Tracking Center and Mailbox Recovery Center, are directly integrated with Exchange System Manager. You can find these tools under the Tools node. Other tools are provided as stand-alone applications on the Exchange 2003 product CD, such as Exchange Server Deployment Tools that can help you to install Exchange 2003 on the first server or additional servers in an Exchange organization and to perform post-installation tasks. Further tools are available in form of Web releases. You can download these tools in one package at *http://www.microsoft.com/downloads/details.aspx?FamilyId=E0F616C6-8FA4-4768-A3ED-CC09AEF7B60A&displaylang=en*.

The following administrative tools are available for Exchange 2003:

- **Exchange Server Deployment Tools**   You can find these tools in the \Support\Exdeploy folder on the Exchange 2003 product CD. You can start these tools by clicking on the Exchange Deployment Tools link in the Welcome to Exchange Server 2003 Setup screen that is displayed automatically when you insert the product CD into the CD-ROM drive on your computer, but you can also start the deployment tools directly by double-clicking on Exdeploy.hta. The latest version of the Exchange Server Deployment Tools is included in the Web release package.

The Exchange Server Deployment Tools include tools and documentation that lead you through the entire installation process. You can run specific tools and utilities to verify that your server, Active Directory, and the computer network are ready for the Exchange 2003 installation. When upgrading from Exchange 5.5, the Exchange Deployment Tools also help to ensure that Exchange 5.5 is properly integrated with Active Directory prior to running Exchange 2003 Setup.

Note To ensure that all of the required tools and services are installed and running properly, we recommend that you run Exchange 2003 Setup through the Exchange Server Deployment Tools.

- **Active Directory Connector**   You can find this tool in the \ADC\i386 folder on the Exchange 2003 product CD. An updated version is available with Exchange 2003 SP1. Active Directory Connector is an important tool when upgrading from Exchange 5.5 to Exchange 2003. Upgrading requires integrating Exchange 5.5 with Active Directory, which is accomplished using Active Directory Connector (ADC). Active Directory Connector populates and synchronizes Active Directory with Exchange 5.5 directory, including mailbox, custom recipient, distribution list, and public folder information. For more information about using ADC, see Chapter 4, "Upgrading to Exchange Server 2003."

- **Active Directory Account Cleanup Wizard**   You can find this tool in the Start menu under All Programs\Microsoft Exchange\Deployment. The executable file is Adclean.exe, which is in the \Program Files\Exchsrvr\bin directory. You can use this tool to merge duplicate Active Directory user accounts and contact objects into a single user account. Duplicated accounts might be generated when you migrate Exchange 5.5 users from a Windows NT environment to Active Directory and Exchange 2003. Chapter 4, "Upgrading to Exchange Server 2003," discusses how to bring Exchange 5.5 users to Exchange 2003.

- **Exchange Migration Wizard**   You can find this tool in the Start menu under All Programs\Microsoft Exchange\Deployment. The executable file is Mailmig.exe, which is in the \Program Files\Exchsrvr\bin directory. This tool automates the migration of mailboxes and server-based data to Exchange 2003. Exchange Migration Wizard extracts folders, messages, and address books from the source messaging system and converts the data to Exchange format before importing the data into Active Directory and the selected target Exchange store. You can migrate data from Exchange servers and non-Exchange messaging systems, such as Lotus Notes and Novell GroupWise. For a detailed discussion of the Exchange Migration Wizard, see Chapter 5, "Migrating to Exchange Server 2003."

- **Message Tracking Center**   You can find this tool in Exchange System Manager under the Tools node, but the Message Tracking Center is also available as a stand-alone MMC snap-in. You can use this tool to analyze the transfer paths that messages take across your organization. Among other things, you can locate messages that have failed to arrive in your users' mailboxes, such as messages that are stuck in a connector's message queue. You can also track system messages, such as public folder replication messages that Exchange stores exchange with each other to keep public folder instances on separate servers synchronized. By default, message tracking is not enabled.

- **Exchange Queue Viewer**   You can find this tool in Exchange System Manager in the form of a Queues node under each individual Exchange server object. You can use the Exchange Queue Viewer tool to maintain and administer message queues and to identify and isolate mail flow issues. Exchange 2003 maintains message queues for all virtual servers, the Exchange Message Transfer Agent (MTA), and all installed messaging connectors.

- **Mailbox Recovery Center**   You can find this tool in Exchange System Manager under the Tools node. You can use this tool to reconnect deleted or orphaned mailboxes to user accounts. By default, Exchange 2003 holds deleted mailboxes in the Exchange store for 30 days. Within this time frame, you can reconnect those mailboxes to their original user accounts using Mailbox Recovery Center. An orphaned mailbox is a mailbox for which the corresponding user account is deleted. For example, when you delete a mailbox-enabled user account in Active Directory Users and Computers, you leave behind an orphaned mailbox in the Exchange store that by default is purged after thirty days. Using Mailbox Recovery Center, you can match the orphaned mailbox to a different user account or export information from the mailbox into an LDAP data format (LDF) file and create a new user account for the mailbox with Ldfide.exe. Mailbox recovery is discussed in detail in Chapter 23, "Restoring Exchange Server 2003."

- **Recover Mailbox Data Wizard**   You can find this tool in Exchange System Manager when you restore a mailbox store from a backup into a recovery storage group. A recovery storage group is an additional storage group that you can create in Exchange Server 2003 for recovery operations on mailboxes. The recovery storage group differs from ordinary storage groups in that it does not interact with the organization by way of standard protocols, system and mailbox policies, maintenance procedures, or by connecting mailboxes to Active Directory accounts using Mailbox Recovery Center. Recovery storage groups are accessible only through MAPI.

Recovery Storage Groups can be used in the following scenarios:

- Recovering deleted items purged from a user's mailbox.

- Repairing or recovering an alternative copy of a database from backup, usually with the intention of merging data back into the production database.

- Recovering a database on a server other than the original server.

You can start the Recover Mailbox Data Wizard in Exchange 2003 SP1 when you right-click a mailbox in a restored mailbox store and select the Exchange Tasks command. The wizard enables you to merge or copy data from a restored mailbox into the actual mailbox. Data can be merged from the recovery storage group into a storage group on the same server or on a different server in the same administrative group. For more information about recovering an Exchange 2003 server, see Chapter 23, "Restoring Exchange Server 2003."

> **Note** To use Recover Mailbox Data Wizard, you must work with Exchange System Manager in Exchange 2003 SP1, and you must have at least one server running Exchange 2003 or later to host the recovery storage group.

- **Exchange Mailbox Merge Wizard**   You can find this tool in the Web release tools for Exchange 2003. You can use this tool to extract data from mailboxes on an Exchange server and merge this data into mailboxes on another Exchange server. The Exchange Mailbox Merge Wizard copies data from the source server into personal folder (.pst) files and then merges the data in the .pst files into mailboxes on the destination server. The Exchange Mailbox Merge Wizard can copy user items, as well as folder rules and permissions. You can filter the data to be merged based on subject, sender, date, and other message properties. Chapter 23, "Restoring Exchange Server 2003," discusses the Exchange Mailbox Merge Wizard.

- **Exchange Management Pack for MOM**   You can find this tool together with a Management Pack Configuration Wizard in the Web release tools for Exchange 2003. This is a component for Microsoft Operations Manager (MOM) that administrators can use to manage multiple Exchange 2003 servers from a single console or Web page. Exchange Management Pack monitors the performance, availability, and security of Exchange 2003 servers, alerting administrators to events that have a direct impact on the server and helping to proactively protect Exchange from critical problems before they occur. It is noteworthy that Exchange Management Pack can monitor all types of Exchange installations, including back-end, front-end, clustered, and stand-alone servers.

Some of the activities the Management Pack performs are:

- *Monitors access to various services,* such as the Active Directory service, the Microsoft Exchange Information Store service, Extensible Storage Engine (ESE), Outlook Web Access, and Internet protocols such as SMTP, POP3, and IMAP.

- *Monitors Exchange services* that should be running on the server.

- *Monitors critical data* such as server queue lengths and disk space.

- *Monitors Exchange performance counters* and sends alerts in situations that indicate possible service problems, including possible denial-of-service attacks.

- *Detects, alerts, and responds to critical events* in order to correct and possibly prevent some Exchange problems, such as service outages.

   The Exchange Management Pack also provides sophisticated reporting features that enable administrators and managers to produce tailored information about the health of their Exchange servers, including resource usage, client connection response times and errors, as well as server up-time information for service level reporting. To use Exchange 2003 Management Pack, you must deploy a MOM environment, as explained in Chapter 17, "Exchange Server 2003 Management Pack."

- **Additional tools in the Web release**   The Web release tools for Exchange 2003 include maintenance and troubleshooting tools that you can use on a server running Exchange 2003. Some tools, such as the Notes application analyzer, might be useful only in specific situations, while others are more generally useful. For example, you can use the Loadsim and Jetstress tools to simulate a large number of users and activities on a test server to find out how much hardware your production servers need in order to provide messaging services at desired response times. Table 1-4 lists the additional tools that you can find in the Web release.

Table 1-4   Maintenance and troubleshooting tools in the Web release for Exchange 2003

Tool	Description
Add Root Certificate Tool	Enables you to add a root certificate to a Pocket PC device running Pocket PC 2002 so that you can use secure sockets layer (SSL) when synchronizing or accessing a server. Pocket PC 2003 devices do not require a separate tool to install certificates.
Auto Accept Agent	Automatically accepts meeting requests and replaces auto accept scripts written for Exchange 5.5 and Exchange 2000. The Auto Accept Agent is an event sink based on the Exchange store events.

Table 1-4   Maintenance and troubleshooting tools in the Web release for Exchange 2003 (Continued)

Tool	Description
ArchiveSink Tool	Enables message archiving and logs all message and recipient details of an e-mail message as it passes through the SMTP transport subsystem of Exchange 2003.
Up-to-Date Notifications Troubleshooting Tool	Displays a Web page that shows a list of portable devices configured for a user, the delivery methods and device addresses, and when the device expires. You can use this tool to send a test e-mail message to the specified devices.
Authoritative Restore Tool	Enables you to force a restored Exchange directory database to replicate to other servers after restoring from a backup. Exchange Server 2003 maintains an Exchange directory database in mixed mode when the Site Replication Service (SRS) is running. You can read more about the Site Replication Service in Chapter 4, "Upgrading to Exchange Server 2003."
Badmail Deletion and Archival Script	Enables you to schedule the automatic deletion or archiving of files in the Badmail directory of specified SMTP virtual servers on an Exchange 2003 server. This script ensures that the size of the Badmail directory does not exceed the specified size limit.
Up-to-Date Notifications Binding Cleanup Tool	Enables you to clean up orphaned event bindings associated with up-to-date notifications of Exchange ActiveSync.
Importer for Lotus cc:Mail Archives	Imports Lotus cc:Mail archive files to folders in a mailbox store, or to one or more personal folder (.pst) files.
Application Analyzer for Lotus Notes	Compiles raw data about Lotus Notes applications. You can also use this tool to view an executive summary report. Application Analyzer for Lotus Notes supports Lotus Notes up to and including release 6.
Disable Certificate Verification Tool	Enables users with Windows mobile devices to connect to Exchange servers using SSL without verifying the root certificate authority against the certificate trust list on the device.
DNS Resolver Tool	Simulates the internal code path of the SMTP service and prints diagnostic messages that indicate how DNS name resolution is proceeding. DNS Resolver works only on Exchange 2003 running on Windows 2003.

Table 1-4   Maintenance and troubleshooting tools in the Web release for Exchange 2003 (Continued)

Tool	Description
Envelope Journaling Tool	Enables you to augment the standard journaling feature of Exchange 2003 and capture more message data, such as blind carbon-copy (Bcc) information that does not appear by default in journaled messages.
Error Code Lookup Tool	Enables you to determine error values from decimal and hexadecimal error codes in the Windows operating systems.
Address Rewrite Tool	Rewrites return e-mail addresses on outgoing messages sent from an external messaging system to Exchange 2003 and destined for external or Internet addresses.
Inter-Organization Replication Tool	Replicates free/busy information and public folder content between Exchange organizations to support calendar and public folder features between separate Exchange organizations.
SMTP Internet Protocol Restriction and Accept/Deny List Configuration Tool	Provides a programmatic interface to connection and relay control for SMTP virtual servers on Exchange 2003. Connection filtering enables you to configure IP addresses for which you want to accept or deny connections to limit the computers that can connect to a virtual server or that can relay e-mail messages outside of the Exchange organization. The SMTP Internet Protocol Restriction and Accept/Deny List Configuration tool includes a Visual Basic script and a COM object called ExIPSec to provide a programmatic interface to the following: ■ SMTP Virtual Server Connection Control settings and Relay Control settings available on an individual SMTP virtual server's properties. ■ The global accept and deny lists configured in Connection Filtering in Global Settings.
Exchange Profile Update Tool	Modifies the default Outlook profile so that users can successfully log on to their mailboxes after you move mailboxes across Exchange organizations or administrative groups.
GUIDGen Tool	Generates GUIDs that you can use as unique identifiers in configuration files and registry keys.

Table 1-4   Maintenance and troubleshooting tools in the Web release for Exchange 2003 (Continued)

Tool	Description
Jetstress Tool	Enables you to verify the performance and stability of the disk subsystem. Jetstress does this by simulating Exchange disk input/output (I/O) load. Specifically, Jetstress simulates the Exchange database and log file loads produced by a specified number of users. You can use System Monitor, Event Viewer, and the Performance tool with Jetstress to verify that your disk subsystem meets or exceeds the established performance criteria.
LegacyDN Tool	Enables you to change the names of Exchange organizations and administrative groups in a test environment.

> **Note**   Do not use the LegacyDN tool to make changes in a production system. Doing so renders all Exchange databases inoperable. Use this tool in a test environment only. For example, it might be required to use this tool on a non-production server to restore messaging databases from a different server. You can read more about disaster recovery strategies in Chapter 23, "Restoring Exchange Server 2003."

Tool	Description
Load Simulator 2003 (Loadsim)	Simulates the delivery of multiple MAPI client messaging requests to an Exchange server, thereby causing a mail load. Load Simulator is a benchmarking and capacity-planning tool that tests the effect of an isolated client MAPI load on a server. Note that it does not account for usage from other protocols and activities, such as content indexing.
Information Store Viewer Tool	Enables you to work with the low-level contents (raw data) of Exchange store databases using the MAPI interface. The Information Store Viewer is also named MDBVu32.
Exchange Server Stress and Performance 2003 Tool	Enables you to stress test Exchange 2003. This tool includes multiple modules and can simulate a large number of Internet client sessions while accessing one or more Exchange servers concurrently. You can use this tool to test several workload scenarios. This tool is also referred to as Medusa.

Table 1-4   Maintenance and troubleshooting tools in the Web release for Exchange 2003 (Continued)

Tool	Description
MTA Check Tool	Analyzes and corrects problems in the Exchange MTA. Run MTA Check if you suspect corruption in the MTA database or if you see errors written to the Event Log.
Web based Admin Tool for Outlook Web Access (OWA)	Enables you to manage manually configured settings for Outlook Web Access.
WinRoute Tool	Enables you to determine the link state routing information that is known to the routing group master. WinRoute presents the link state information in a human-readable format.
Exchange Domain Rename Fixup Tool	Fixes Exchange attributes after you rename a Windows 2003 domain that contains Exchange 2003 servers using Rendom.exe.

Supported Messaging Clients

Exchange 2003 supports a wide variety of messaging clients, including Microsoft Outlook, Outlook Web Access, Internet-based clients, such as Netscape Communicator, Eudora Mail, or Microsoft Outlook Express, as well as mobile clients.

Microsoft Office Outlook 2003

Users experience the features of Exchange 2003 through a client interface. The client that best uses all available Exchange 2003 features is Outlook 2003. Outlook combines e-mail, calendar, contacts, and task management, as well as workgroup capabilities, and integrates with other Microsoft Office applications. Outlook is a personal information manager, rather than a simple messaging client. For information about the individual features of Outlook 2003, see Outlook online Help and the Outlook product documentation at *http://office.microsoft.com/assistance/topcategory.aspx?TopLevelCat=CH790018071033&CTT=98&Origin=CH790018071033*.

For an Exchange system architect, perhaps the most interesting aspects of Outlook 2003 are the performance and security enhancements and other improvements designed to improve the messaging experience that Outlook 2003 provides compared to earlier versions. The most important features of Outlook 2003 that Exchange architects should be familiar with are:

- **RPC compression and buffer packing**   When using Outlook 2003 to access a mailbox on a server running Exchange 2003, content is compressed on the Exchange server before it is sent to the Outlook 2003 client. In addition, the data is packaged in large and optimized buffer packets, thereby reducing the number of requests that must be transferred over the network between the Outlook client and the server running Exchange 2003. Both MAPI compression and buffer packing significantly lower the network bandwidth requirements for client/server communication and enable users to access an Exchange server with acceptable response times even over slow connections.

■ **Cached Exchange Mode**   This feature enables Outlook 2003 to download all items from the server-based mailbox and to keep them synchronized in a cache on the local workstation. After a full copy of the mailbox is downloaded, the client performs most e-mail related tasks from the local computer. Communication with the server is required only during folder synchronization, when downloading new items to the workstation or uploading added or changed items to the server, or when sending messages. For step-by-step instructions about how to configure and test this feature see the document, Cached Exchange Mode.doc, which you can find in the \Companion Material\Chapter 01 folder on the companion CD.

Cached Exchange Mode is especially interesting for Exchange architects because it not only reduces the bandwidth consumption in the computer network, but also improves the remote or branch office user's experience with Outlook. Access to items stored in the local cache is always fast, no matter how slow or unreliable the network connection, and access to the items in the local cache does not depend on server availability. Because the client always works with a local copy of the data, users do not need to restart Outlook to an offline profile when network interruptions occur or when the server is shut down temporarily for maintenance reasons. However, several operations are still performed on the server, such as the generation of out-of-office messages and the processing of Inbox rules.

In Cached Exchange Mode, users can choose from the following download options:

■ **Download full items**   This is the best option when using Cached Exchange Mode over fast and reliable network connections. The client downloads all items to the client immediately.

■ **Download headers first, then full items**   With this option, the client performs a header download first so that the user can see the list of new items quickly. Following the header download, the client performs a full download to bring all data to the client. Users who want to see all new items in their Inbox as quickly as possible might want to choose this option.

■ **Download headers only**   This is the best option over slow and unreliable network links, such as dial-up connections. The client downloads only the message headers so that the user can see the size of the e-mail and attachments in the Inbox and other folders and can decide which items to download. The client downloads a message when the user opens the message in Outlook.

Note   We recommend that you enable Cached Exchange Mode over local area network (LAN) as well as wide area network (WAN) connections.

- **Improved Outlook synchronization performance**   The Outlook 2003 performance in Cached Exchange Mode is further improved by reducing the number of change notifications between the client and the server. The server informs the client about the number and size of messages to be downloaded, and when items are marked as read or unread, or flagged or slightly modified in other ways, only the header that lists the change is sent back to the server. When full items are downloaded, the server sends only the native format of messages to the client. MAPI compression ensures efficient data communication.

  It should be noted that the synchronization in Outlook 2003 is incremental. That is, if a synchronization cycle is interrupted unexpectedly, the synchronization process resumes where the interruption occurred, instead of starting the entire synchronization process again. Items marked as bad or conflicting are moved to the Sync Items folder, which allows the synchronization to continue.

- **Web beacon blocking**   Web beacons are a common tool that spam e-mail senders use to verify that an e-mail account exists. These beacons are based on a simple mechanism. When the e-mail client downloads Web content in an HTML message, the IP address of the client can be logged at the Web server. To prevent this, Outlook 2003 does not download external elements automatically when viewing HTML-formatted messages. A placeholder that enables you to download the content manually replaces all external content.

- **Junk mail filtering**   Outlook 2003 features SmartScreen technology. The junk mail filter uses safe and blocked sender and recipient lists that are determined by the user's preference. Messages from senders listed in a safe sender list are always considered acceptable, even if other characteristics, such as specific phrases in the message content would identify them as junk e-mail. Messages from senders listed in a blocked sender list, on the other hand, are always considered junk e-mail. To add a sender of junk e-mail to the blocked sender list, right-click on the received junk e-mail message, point to Junk E-Mail, and then select Add Sender to Blocked Senders List. By default, Outlook 2003 moves messages that are identified as junk e-mail to the Junk E-Mail folder. For step-by-step instructions about how to configure junk mail filters, see the document Configuring junk mail filters.doc, which you can find in the \Companion Material\Chapter 01 folder on the companion CD.

- **AutoArchiving**   This feature creates a personal folder store called Archive Folders, which mirrors the folder structure of the mailbox. The Archive Folders store is saved in a .pst file on the user's workstation. You can then specify on a per-folder basis whether to perform message archiving automatically. Outlook determines which messages to archive based on the last modified date and time information (Figure 1-10).

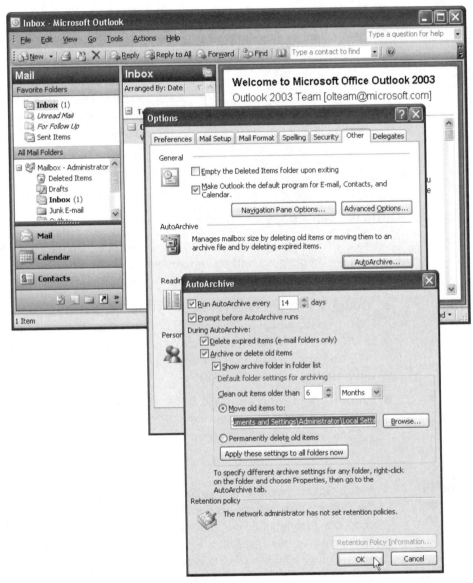

Figure 1-10   Enabling autoarchiving for an entire mailbox

Archiving is a process in which Outlook 2003 moves messages from the mailbox to the Archive Folders store. Archived messages no longer exist on the server. This helps to keep individual mailbox sizes within the limits of mailbox quotas specified for each mailbox store or individual user. For step-by-step instructions about how to configure autoarchiving, see the document Configuring autoarchiving.doc, which you can find in the \Companion Material\Chapter 01 folder on the companion CD.

- **Outlook performance monitoring**   Outlook 2003 collects latency and performance information and sends it to Exchange Server 2003 so that organizations can identify performance bottlenecks relating to poor bandwidth conditions or poor connectivity. The performance data is stored on the Exchange server in performance counters, as well as reported in the event log. Organizations can use tools, such as the Performance console, Microsoft Exchange 2003 Management Pack for Microsoft Operations Manager (MOM), or non-Microsoft tools, to monitor response times on a continuous basis and to create performance reports over any given period of time. Analyzing the performance data centrally on the server can help organizations to identify when local or remote Outlook clients are experiencing connectivity issues.

Outlook Web Access

Outlook Web Access (OWA) is one of the components in Exchange Server 2003 that has been updated significantly compared to Exchange 2000. In Exchange 2003, there are two distinct versions of Outlook Web Access:

- **Outlook Web Access Premium**   This is the full-featured version of Outlook Web Access, which has a similar appearance and functionality to the Outlook 2003 client. Outlook Web Access Premium is designed for Internet Explorer (IE) 5.01 and above, although features such as encrypted e-mail and data compression support require IE6.0 SP1.

- **Outlook Web Access Basic**   This version of Outlook Web Access provides only a subset of the features of the premium client. The basic version is designed for browsers earlier than Internet Explorer 5.01 and non-Microsoft browsers.

> **Note**   Outlook Web Access supports a logon page with the ability to select the Outlook Web Access version to use, along with improved security when connecting from public computers. For step-by-step instructions about how to enable this page, see the document Enabling the OWA logon page.doc, which you can find in the \Companion Material\Chapter 01 folder on the companion CD.

The following key enhancements are available in the Premium version of Outlook Web Access:

- **Functionality enhancements**   One of the key user interface enhancements in Outlook Web Access is drag-and-drop functionality, which makes it easy to move messages and folders within Internet Explorer. Context sensitive menus, or shortcut menus, are displayed when a user right-clicks on a message, folder, or other object, from which relevant commands can be selected. Users can also assign various colored flags to messages in order to sort or prioritize them.

  The most important functionality enhancements in Outlook Web Access include:

  - **Server-side-rules**   Outlook Web Access provides support for server-side rules to process messages automatically when they arrive in a user's Inbox. Rules created in Outlook Web Access provide fewer processing options than those created in Outlook 2003, and Outlook-created forms with complex processing appear grayed out in Outlook Web Access. However, support for server-side rules represents a significant enhancement in Outlook Web Access functionality. For a demonstration of how to configure Inbox rules, see the document Configuring server-side rules.doc, which you can find in the \Companion Material\Chapter 01 folder on the companion CD.

  - **Tasks functionality**   Outlook Web Access now provides access to the Tasks folder, allowing users to create single and recurring tasks, add attachments, set reminders, and mark tasks as complete. Assigning tasks to other users is still a feature only in Outlook 2003.

  - **Keyboard shortcuts**   Outlook Web Access now supports a number of keyboard shortcuts to more closely match the keyboard shortcut behavior in Outlook 2003. For example, Ctrl+N creates a new item depending on which folder you presently have open. From the Inbox folder, Ctrl+N will create a new message item, Ctrl+N from within the Calendar folder will create a new calendar item, and so forth. Another important shortcut is Ctrl+K, which resolves recipients in a new message. When using recipient validation in this way, Outlook Web Access suggests recipients and contacts from the Global Address List and from your personal Contacts, which is another useful feature.

Note   For a comprehensive list of keyboard shortcuts see the document Keyboard Shortcuts in OWA.doc, which you can find on the companion CD in the \Companion Material\Chapter 01 folder.

- **Security**   As part of Microsoft's trustworthy computing initiative, Exchange 2003 technology has been enhanced to provide more security. The following are some of the ways in which this is achieved in Outlook Web Access:

  - **Cookie-based authentication**   When you enable forms-based authentication in Outlook Web Access, user credentials are stored in a cookie, which is cleared either at logout or after a period of inactivity. Depending on whether the user selects Public or shared computer or Private computer, the cookie times out by default after 15 minutes or 24 hours, respectively. These values can be changed in the Exchange server's local registry.

> **Note**   When the logon page is not used, the logoff process is also more secure. Users do not have to close the browser to clear the credentials cache. This happens when the user clicks the Log Off button in Outlook Web Access.

  - **Secure MIME (S/MIME)**   Support for S/MIME gives Outlook Web Access users the ability to sign and encrypt e-mail messages. E-mail signatures are a means of verifying originator information in received messages. E-mail signatures can also be used to verify that a message was not tampered with during transmission. Message encryption, on the other hand, is a method to prevent disclosure of information to unintended users, such as an eavesdropper. Only a user with the correct encryption key is able to decrypt the message and read the information. For more details about S/MIME support in Outlook Web Access, see Chapter 13, "Implementing Exchange 2003 Security."

  - **Web beacon blocking**   Similar to Outlook 2003, Outlook Web Access does not download external elements automatically. All external content is replaced by a placeholder that enables you to download the content manually. Figure 1-11 shows an HTML-formatted message with blocked external content.

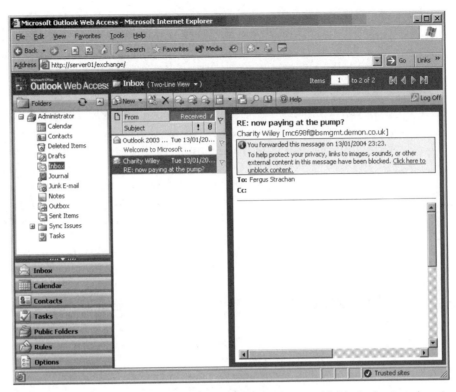

Figure 1-11 A message displayed in Outlook Web Access with blocked external content

Outlook Mobile Access

Outlook Mobile Access is a new component in Exchange Server 2003 that replaces Microsoft Mobile Information Server. Outlook Mobile Access provides access to Exchange 2003 through a number of protocols, such as HTML, CHTML, or XHTML, to allow users of mobile devices to access their e-mail, Contacts, Calendar, and Tasks folders.

Outlook Mobile Access provides access through the following protocols:

- **Hypertext Markup Language (HTML)** The standard markup language for the Internet. Devices such as Microsoft Pocket PC 2002, Microsoft Pocket PC Phone Edition devices, Microsoft Smartphones, and standard PC Internet browsers use HTML.

- **Compact HTML (CHTML)** CHTML is a scaled-down version of the HTML protocol, designed specifically for mobile devices such as Personal Digital Assistants and mobile phones. CHTML retains HTML features such as hyperlinks, formatted text, frames, and GIF images but excludes features such as JPG image support, style sheets, and backgrounds. CHTML uses four buttons for navigation rather than two-dimensional cursor movement.

- **Extensible Hypertext Markup Language (XHTML)**   As an application of XML used to describe Web pages, XHTML enables programmers to define a schema to present data in a particular way. XHTML is a standard not only for mobile devices, but also for web pages that are viewed by using Internet Explorer, Opera, Netscape, or other browsers.

Even without a mobile device, you can view Outlook Mobile Access output by using Internet Explorer on your client workstation, which can be a good idea when working over a particularly slow network connection. Open Internet Explorer and type in http://SERVER01/OMA. The interface is uncomplicated and well-suited for mobile devices. It should be noted, however, that Outlook Mobile Access is not enabled by default. To enable this feature, see the document Enabling and testing OMA.doc, which you can find in the \Companion Material\Chapter 01 folder on the companion CD.

Figure 1-12 shows how to access Outlook Mobile Access through Internet Explorer.

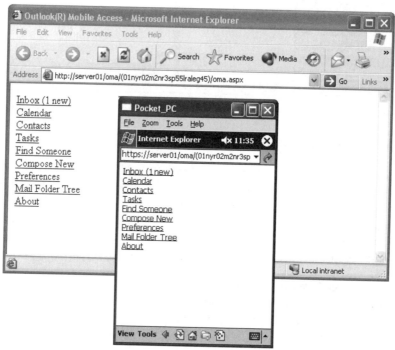

Figure 1-12   Outlook Mobile Access in Internet Explorer on a PC and on a Pocket PC

Exchange ActiveSync

Exchange ActiveSync is a new server-side feature that enables Windows Mobile-based devices to store and synchronize Exchange content with a high level of security and without the need for a PC, a device cradle, and synchronization software. Exchange ActiveSync retrieves native Exchange data, including attachments that are not available through Outlook Mobile Access, and the mobile device's Pocket Outlook renders this data locally. ActiveSync supports a synchronization of the Inbox, Calendar, and Contact folders. Figure 1-13 shows synchronized calendar and contact items on a Pocket PC.

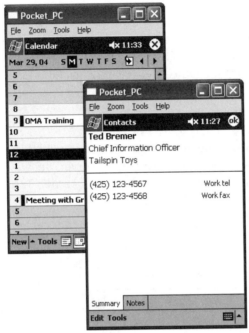

Figure 1-13 Synchronized appointments and contacts on a Pocket PC

Synchronization using Exchange ActiveSync is enabled by default, and provides synchronization by a number of methods:

- **User-initiated synchronization** Provides the ability for mobile device users to synchronize their devices manually with the Exchange server. This method gives the user the most flexibility.

- **Up-to-date notification** Sends a notification to the mobile device when a new message is received, instructing it to synchronize with the server. Using this method, along with over-the-air synchronization (that is, synchronization over a wireless carrier) enables users to keep up to date when they are out of the office. When the mobile device receives notification from the Exchange server, it initiates synchronization with Exchange over the wireless network. Figure 1-14 illustrates this process. If using a corporate wireless carrier, this carrier object must be created in Exchange System Manager under Mobile Services. This method standardizes the delivery of notification messages and makes operation and troubleshooting more manageable.

> **Note** The notification process uses an algorithm that includes intelligent batching of notification messages so that, for example, users receiving five e-mails in the space of a minute do not receive five notification messages within that minute.

- **Delivery to User-Specified SMTP Addresses** Enables users to use any mobile carrier to carry the notification message from the Exchange server. On receipt of this notification message, the device will contact the Exchange server and initiate the synchronization procedure.

> **Note** When using this option, the administrator is not required to configure the corporate wireless carrier on the Exchange server, because each device will be configured individually using each user's carrier. The device address is configured on the mobile device itself.

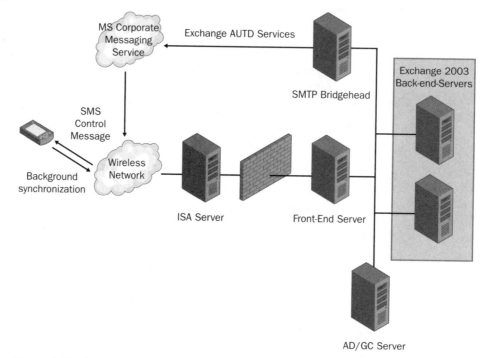

Figure 1-14   The ActiveSync Auto-Up-To-Date process

Exchange 2003 Security Features

Exchange 2003 takes full advantage of the security features of Windows 2003 for controlling access to Exchange resources. Windows 2003 provides authentication services for Exchange 2003 and discretionary access control lists (DACLs) determine which person is allowed to access which resource, with what level of permissions. For example, user account administrators are typically allowed to write user account objects in an organizational unit, which usually also makes them mailbox administrators. Besides the DACL, resources might also have a security access control list (SACL), which determines what security-related events are written to the security event log if auditing is enabled in the operating system.

Exchange 2003 can also benefit from advanced security features, such as a public key infrastructure based on Windows 2003 Certificate Services, to issue X.509 certificates. In addition, you can deploy a patch management infrastructure based on the Windows Update service to distribute security patches and other critical updates automatically to all Exchange servers in the organization. To review current environment and make recommendations on patches for Exchange 2003, use Microsoft Baseline Security Analyzer for Exchange.

The following are important security features in Exchange 2003 that you can use to protect your Exchange organization:

- **Secure/Multipurpose Internet Mail Extensions (S/MIME)** Exchange Server 2003 uses the Certificate Services of Windows Server 2003 to enable digital signatures and message encryption. Users can obtain X.509 certificates, manually or automatically through auto-enrollment, from a Windows Server 2003 Certificate Authority. X.509 certificates are required to sign and encrypt e-mails. One advantage of using the underlying Windows security infrastructure is that X.509 certificates can also be used in other applications, such as encrypting parts of the file system with the Encrypting File System. Exchange Server 2003 also provides an S/MIME ActiveX control that can be downloaded from the Exchange server in order to enable e-mail signing and encryption in Outlook Web Access. This control requires Internet Explorer 6 with Service Pack 1 or later. Chapter 14, "Implementing Exchange 2003 Security," discusses how to integrate Exchange 2003 with a public key infrastructure based on Windows 2003 Certificate Services.

- **Anti-spam features** Exchange 2003 administrators can maintain a list of IP addresses to accept or deny certain sources of e-mail messages. For instance, known spam e-mail senders can be placed on a deny list, while partners and customers can be placed on an accept list. In addition to blocking incoming messages through a deny list, Exchange Server 2003 also can be configured to examine each incoming message and compare the sender's e-mail address (not the IP address) against a list of blocked e-mail addresses. If there is a match, Exchange can be configured to either drop the incoming message or to archive it. As mentioned earlier in this chapter, you can use the SMTP Internet Protocol

Restriction and Accept/Deny List Configuration Tool to programmatically set IP restrictions on SMTP virtual servers.

Exchange 2003 also supports inbound recipient filtering to block incoming messages destined for non-valid recipients or restricted internal addresses. When inbound recipient filtering is enabled, Exchange Server simply rejects messages for nonexistent or blocked recipients during the SMTP session, rather than sending a non-delivery report (NDR) back to the sender. Suppressing NDRs is a good idea, because spam typically originates from spoofed addresses or addresses of innocent Internet users.

Exchange Server 2003 can also forward the IP address of each incoming message to one or more anti-spam service providers. Anti-spam service providers are sources on the Internet that maintain lists of known spam e-mail senders. The Realtime Blackhole List (RBL) service provider indicates a status code for each incoming message to Exchange 2003 to determine whether an incoming message should be accepted or rejected and returned to the sender with the appropriate error code.

> **Note**   For an example of how to configure Exchange 2003 to use an RBL service provider, see the document Integrating an RBL SP.doc, which you can find in the \Companion Material\Chapter 01 folder on the companion CD.

You can also integrate a non-Microsoft anti-spam product with Exchange Server 2003 to scan each incoming SMTP message. The anti-spam product attaches a numeric score, or Spam Confidence Level (SCL), to the message, indicating the degree of probability that the message is spam. Based on a threshold set by an administrator, the message will be forwarded to either the recipient's Inbox or to a Junk E-mail folder.

- **Virus Scanning**   Exchange 2003 supports the Virus Scanning API (VSAPI) version 2.5, which is Microsoft's answer to e-mail borne viruses. VSAPI enables software vendors to develop antivirus solutions that scan Internet messages during message transfer before they actually reach a mailbox store. VSAPI 2.5 also makes it possible to prevent infected e-mail from leaving an organization by scanning outgoing mail. If a message is infected, the antivirus solution can automatically send a warning message back to the sender that a virus was detected and the e-mail was deleted.

  Exchange 2003 SP1 now also supports the scanning of message attachments in Transport Neutral Encapsulation Format (TNEF) and opaque signed (that is, digitally signed and encrypted) messages. Exchange 2003 transfer messages in TNEF format to other Exchange servers in the same routing group and between routing groups if a routing group connector or SMTP connector is used. Opaque messages, on the other hand, appear to be one long binary, previously unscannable MIME attachment. You should deploy a VSAPI-based antivirus solution on all your Exchange 2003 servers.

- **Client Attachment Blocking**   Outlook and Outlook Web Access enable administrators to prevent users from viewing, sending, and receiving e-mail attachments with certain file extensions, such as executable files. Attachment blocking is a new feature in Outlook Web Access, with the following characteristics:

  - **Prevent access to attachments of certain file types**   By default, all new Exchange 2003 installations block attachments of potentially dangerous file and MIME types, such as .exe files and scripts. A warning message in the InfoBar informs the user that the attachment has been blocked.

  - **Prevent sending of attachments**   By default, Outlook Web Access will not allow users to send attachments that may contain viruses. Files with corresponding file extensions are not allowed to be uploaded into Outlook Web Access.

- **RPC over HTTPS**   RPC over HTTPS enables MAPI clients such as Outlook 2003 to connect to an Exchange server over the Internet without requiring a virtual private network (VPN) connection. By encapsulating remote procedure calls (RPCs) into HTTP traffic that is encrypted using Secure Sockets Layer (SSL), users can use the same network and firewall infrastructure for Outlook 2003 that also provides them with access to Outlook Web Access over the Internet. RPC over HTTPS uses the same network ports and encryption methods. Exchange servers involved must be running on Windows Server 2003, and the servers that deal with client requests (Exchange front-end server or Internet Security and Acceleration server) must be running Windows Server 2003 with the RPC over HHTP Proxy component configured. Additionally, the client computer must be running Windows XP with Service Pack 1 or later with the "Windows XP Patch: RPC Updates Needed for Exchange Server 2003."

Note   You must enable SSL encryption to support RPC over HTTP securely.

Figure 1-15 shows the recommended configuration for an RPC over HTTPS deployment. An alternative configuration is to have a front-end Exchange server as the proxy server in the perimeter network; although this is disadvantageous because it requires opening the internal firewall for RPC-based MAPI communication.

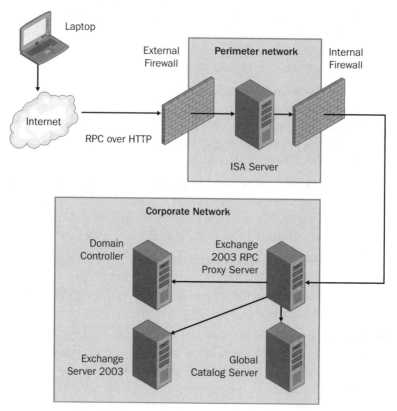

Figure 1-15   A recommended RPC over HTTPS configuration

The connection between the Outlook client and the Exchange 2003 RPC Proxy server is purely an HTTPS connection. The RPCs are encapsulated in HTTP packets and sent through the HTTPS pipe to the RPC Proxy server. This server unwraps the RPC requests and forwards them to the servers specified in the RPC request, such as a global catalog server or the user's mailbox server.

With Exchange 2003 SP1, you can use Exchange System Manager to configure the RPC over HTTPS environment. Each server object provides an RPC-HTTP tab that you can use to specify if the server is a RPC-HTTPS front-end server, RPC-HTTPS back-end server, or not part of an RPC-HTTP topology (Figure 1-16). Chapter 12, "Maintaining IIS Virtual Servers," explains in detail how to configure RPC over HTTPS using Exchange 2003 SP1.

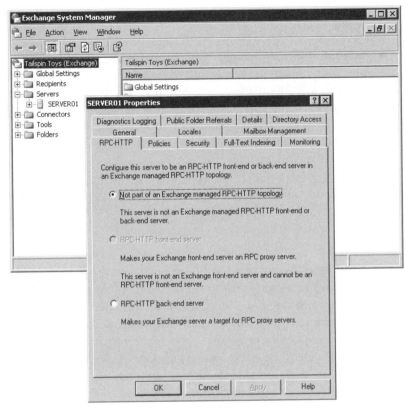

Figure 1-16   The RPC-HTTP tab of an Exchange 2003 server

■ **Information Rights Management**   Outlook 2003 works in conjunction with Windows Server 2003 to provide rights management capabilities that enable individuals and companies to protect corporate information. E-mails and documents stored in Exchange can be configured to allow or not allow view, read-only, copy, print, save, forward, and time-based permissions. To enable Information Rights Management, you must deploy Windows Rights Management Services (RMS) within your Windows 2003 environment. For more information about Information Rights Management, see the article "Information Rights Management in Microsoft Office 2003," available at *http://www.microsoft.com/technet/prodtechnol/office/office2003/operate/of03irm.mspx.*

Performance Improvements

One of the key design goals of Exchange Server 2003 is to increase performance, scalability, and reliability over previous Exchange versions. This is important if you want to reduce the cost of IT operations by consolidating server locations and servers. Consolidation strategies are discussed in detail in Chapter 6, "Server and Site Consolidation Strategies."

IT managers and decision makers should consider the following when planning to consolidate servers:

■ **Virtual memory usage and monitoring**   Exchange server automatically tunes server memory usage and manages the allocation of virtual memory. Servers with more than 1 GB of RAM, however, require some manual optimization. Exchange 2003 is efficient in the way it reuses blocks of virtual memory, reducing fragmentation of memory and improving server efficiency.

Exchange 2003 provides performance counters for virtual memory that can be used to proactively monitor Exchange servers, either using Performance Monitor (Perfmon.exe) or Microsoft Operations Manager with the Exchange Management Pack. Important monitors include VM Largest Block Size, VM Total 16MB Free Blocks, VM Total Free Blocks, and VM Total Large Free Block Bytes. For information about how to optimize memory usage, see Chapter 18, "Tuning Exchange Server Performance."

■ **Windows Cluster service**   Server clusters offer a high-availability solution for Windows server applications, such as Exchange 2003, by providing service failover from one node in the cluster to another node. In contrast to the single-server approach, in which a problem on the server can bring down the services it is running, clusters fail over from non-operating nodes to operating nodes in order to restore services with minimum downtime. Clustered server arrangements can play a major role in server consolidation by bringing all mailboxes together into a single, highly available, and centrally maintainable system. Simplified hardware and software maintenance is another reason organizations deploy Windows clusters. You can move the virtual servers around to alternate nodes and then perform hardware or software upgrades on the now passive node. An upgrade of hardware or software in this way is also called a rolling upgrade.

Exchange Server 2003 offers the following flexibility when implementing server clusters on Windows Server 2003:

   ■ **8-node clusters**   Exchange Server 2003 Enterprise Edition provides active-passive clustering of up to eight nodes. Figure 1-17 shows an eight-node cluster with one passive node, sometimes also called a hot-spare. In a cluster with more than two nodes, you must leave at least one node without a virtual server so that this passive node can take over a virtual server from a failing node without performance impact. Exchange 2003 SP1 enforces an active/passive configuration in clusters with more than two nodes by blocking multiple Exchange virtual servers on a single cluster node. It is important to note that Microsoft does not support active/active configurations in cluster configurations with more than two nodes.

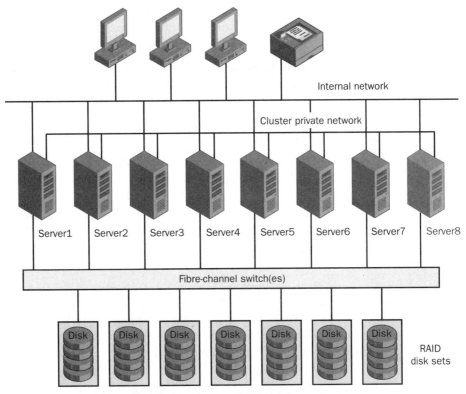

Internal network

Cluster private network

Server1 Server2 Server3 Server4 Server5 Server6 Server7 Server8

Fibre-channel switch(es)

Disk Disk Disk Disk Disk Disk Disk

RAID
disk sets

Figure 1-17 An eight-node Windows Server 2003 cluster system

■ **Support for volume mount points** Volume mount points are directories that point to specified disk volumes. Using this feature, you can present multiple drives as a single volume. Volume mount points are supported in Exchange clusters. Volume mount points bypass the limitation imposed by assigning drive letters to persistently mapped volumes.

■ **Failover performance** The developers flattened the service hierarchy in Exchange 2003 so that the Exchange services are quicker to start on a node during a failover process. Protocol services are no longer dependent on the Microsoft Exchange Information Store service and are now dependent only on the System Attendant. Failover detection time is also reduced on Windows Server 2003 servers, so downtime for both planned and unplanned failovers is reduced.

■ **Security** Security of Exchange clusters has been improved to offer the same features as in single server arrangements. Internet Protocol Security (IPSec) support for front-end and back-end servers enables the encryption of data between front-end and clustered back-end servers. This configuration is supported when Exchange Server 2003 is running on Windows Server 2003 on both front- and back-end servers. Permissions on cluster servers have also been changed and are less restrictive. For example, the cluster service account no longer needs to have the Exchange Full Administrator role at the organization or administrative group level.

■ **Performance Improvements**   Exchange Server 2003 provides a number of performance improvements that lessen the client load on the server and thus enable a higher mailbox to server ratio. This can assist in the consolidation of Exchange servers in larger environments.

Performance improvements include:

■ **Client performance improvements**   Microsoft Office Outlook 2003 and Office Outlook Web Access 2003 are key elements in server consolidation scenarios. Outlook 2003 should be used in Cached Exchange Mode so that users can work with a local mailbox copy for normal operations, synchronizing changes and periodically updating from the Exchange server. This decreases the amount of data sent to and from the server and virtually increases response times on the local machine. When using Outlook 2003 with an Exchange Server 2003 server, data between client and server is also compressed in order to reduce the amount of traffic on the network.

Outlook Web Access performance improvements are support for data compression when using Internet Explorer 6 or later and on-demand download of scripts and files, rather than downloading all content at logon time. This helps to improve the users' experience with Outlook Web Access. The level of compression is specified on the Exchange Server 2003 server. Exchange 2003 can compress static pages (low compression) or static and dynamic pages (high compression). To enable this function, users' mailboxes must reside on Exchange Server 2003 servers, the Exchange servers must be running on Windows Server 2003, and client computers must be running Windows 2000 or later.

■ **Server performance improvements**   Performance improvements are also noticeable in several internal Exchange components. For example, Exchange 2003 uses improved caching algorithms in its DSAccess component so that directory lookups can be completed more efficiently, resulting in a 60 percent reduction of Active Directory queries in comparison to Exchange 2000 Server. Virtual memory management also has been improved, to address memory fragmentation that can occur on large server installations. The Exchange 2003 Technical Reference contains more information about the internal components of Exchange 2003.

When deploying Exchange 2003 in an environment with multiple routing groups, Exchange replicates link state information among all servers in the organization to inform all servers about the availability of message paths. The propagation of link state information among servers has also been optimized to reduce network traffic. You can read more about the routing group design in Chapter 2, "Exchange Server 2003 Design Basics."

Server and Client Licensing

Microsoft has introduced new licensing options with Windows Server 2003 and Exchange Server 2003. Microsoft Exchange client access licenses (CALs) can now be purchased on a per-user or per-device basis.

Traditionally, Microsoft has used the client licensing and server licensing models, where licenses are required for each installation of the server software and also for each device connecting to the server via the network. The latter is called a per-device CAL, and is necessary for each device, whether it is a PC, Pocket PC, Smartphone or other mobile device. Each Exchange 2003 CAL also includes Microsoft Office Outlook 2003 and permits access from Outlook Web Access, Outlook Mobile Access, Exchange ActiveSync, or any standard Internet messaging client.

You can choose from the following licensing models:

- **The Per-Device CAL** The Exchange 2003 per-device CAL is required for each device that will access the server and entitles access rights to an unlimited number of users sharing the device. An example of such a device is a kiosk computer running Outlook Web Access that is shared by several employees (for example, users who work in shifts).

- **The User CAL** Because of recent changes in the way companies conduct business, specifically the way that employees access distributed information from multiple devices and locations, the per-device CAL model is no longer appropriate for users who access their mailboxes from a home PC, notebook computer, Pocket PC, and office PC. Under previous licensing arrangements, the company would be obliged to pay for four licenses for this user. In a world where people demand access to their data from multiple clients, this represents a shortcoming in the licensing model for many companies.

  The User CAL introduces an alternative method of licensing clients for access to server systems. The User CAL, an equivalently priced license to the Device CAL, licenses a single person as opposed to a device. This means that a company can purchase licenses for each user, and those users can access their server data freely from any device they choose.

> **Note** Although it is possible to have a mixed environment with Device CALs and User CALs together, it is not recommended, because it can lead to an unnecessarily complex licensing arrangement.

- **The External Connector license** The other change in recent licensing for Exchange Server 2003 is the introduction of the External Connector (EC) license. This license is an alternative to User or Device CALs for providing access to your server data to people who are not employees of your company (for example, partners or customers). For small numbers of people requiring external access, companies can still buy individual CALs.

Companies enrolled in the Software Assurance (SA) program can convert existing Device CALs to User CALs, or vice versa, upon renewal of the SA program. If the CALs are not associated with SA, the choice is permanent.

Best Practices

It is a good idea to evaluate Exchange Server 2003 in a test environment before digging deeper into product details. Evaluation versions of Windows Server 2003 and Exchange Server 2003 are available for download. The Windows 2003 Evaluation Kit is available at *http://www.microsoft.com/windowsserver2003/evaluation/trial/eval-kit.mspx*, and the Exchange 2003 Evaluation Kit is available at *http://www.microsoft.com/exchange/evaluation/trial/2003.asp*. A separate workstation is required to run Outlook 2003, because it is not supported to install this MAPI client directly on the server.

Having installed a test environment, you might want to create some test users using Active Directory Users and Computers so that you can send messages back and forth using Outlook. To configure server settings, such as recipient policies and mailbox quotas, you typically use Exchange System Manager. The graphical user interface (GUI) tools make the configuration of an Exchange server intuitive, but for advanced configuration tasks, command-line tools and custom scripts can also be used. Exchange 2003 provides administrators with many possible options to manage an Exchange organization. For details about how to manage an Exchange organization, see the Microsoft Exchange online guides, available for download at *http://www.microsoft.com/exchange/library*.

Chapter 2

Exchange Server 2003 Design Basics

About This Chapter

This chapter discusses the basic design elements of Microsoft Exchange Server 2003 and explains how to use these elements to structure mailbox management, server administration, and message routing in an Exchange organization. Because Exchange 2003 relies heavily on the Active Directory directory service, this chapter also covers important Active Directory features that influence the Exchange 2003 design. Further important topics concern what server types to deploy in the Exchange organization. For more information about planning, designs, and deployment, see the books "Planning an Exchange Server 2003 Messaging System" *(http://go.microsoft.com/fwlink/?LinkId=21766)* and "Exchange Server 2003 Deployment Guide" *(http://go.microsoft.com/fwlink/?LinkId=21768)*.

It is assumed that you are familiar with Microsoft Windows server technology and the logical and physical design elements of Active Directory. Whether you are designing a new Exchange organization or upgrading an existing organization to Exchange 2003, you must review the existing Windows and Active Directory infrastructure to ensure that the deployment of Exchange 2003 does not lead to an overload of networking services, such as Domain Name System (DNS) and Active Directory. For detailed information about how to design or restructure a

Windows 2003 Active Directory environment, see the book "Designing and Deploying Directory and Security Services" in the Windows Server 2003 Deployment Kit, available for download at *http://www.microsoft.com/downloads/details.aspx?FamilyID=6CDE6EE7-5DF1-4394-92ED-2147C3A9EBBE&displaylang=en*.

What You Need to Know

An Exchange organization is a collection of servers, messaging clients, and other resources (such as connector objects and recipient objects) that share the same directory information. Active Directory provides this shared directory service for Exchange 2003. There is a one-to-one relationship between Exchange 2003 and Active Directory. A single Active Directory forest cannot have more than one Exchange organization, and a single Exchange organization cannot span multiple forests.

An Exchange 2003 organization can operate in native mode or in mixed mode. Native mode offers full Exchange 2003 (and Exchange 2000) functionality, but mixed mode offers interoperability with Exchange 5.5. When you install Exchange 2003, your Exchange organization is in mixed mode by default. This default setting ensures interoperability with Exchange 5.5.

Similar to Active Directory, the design of an Exchange organization is divided into logical and physical structures. In Active Directory, the logical design consists of the forest, domains within the forest, and organizational units within the domains. In Exchange 2003, the logical design is based on a flat arrangement of administrative groups. The physical structure of Active Directory, on the other hand, relies on the concept of sites and replication links. In Exchange 2003, the physical design is represented by routing groups and messaging connectors.

An administrative group in Exchange 2003 is a collection of Exchange-related directory objects that are grouped together for the purpose of permissions management. An administrative group can contain policies, routing groups, public folder hierarchies, and configuration objects for server-based resources. The content of an administrative group depends on the choices that you make when you design an Exchange organization.

A routing group in Exchange 2003 is a collection of Exchange servers that are grouped together for the purpose of message routing. Routing groups can also be used to structure public folder access. Within a routing group, all servers communicate directly with each other over direct TCP/IP connections using SMTP. Messages sent between any two servers within a routing group are transferred directly from the source server to the destination server. Between routing groups, however, a routing group connector must be used to transfer messages.

By default, an Exchange server assumes many different functions in an Exchange organization, but you can also configure dedicated servers to distribute the tasks among a number of servers. In large organizations, configuring dedicated servers can lessen the workload on each particular server, and it enables you to design the hardware configuration more precisely for each server. An Exchange server can have one (or in some cases more than one) of the following roles in an Exchange organization:

- **Front-end server**   A server that receives requests from Internet-based clients and relays them to the appropriate back-end server. Front-end servers do not store any user mailboxes. Companies that want to provide Internet users with a single access point to mailboxes regardless of the actual mailbox location often deploy front-end servers. You can read more about front-end server arrangements in Chapter 7, "Hosting Exchange Server 2003."

- **Back-end server**   A server that stores user mailboxes, public folders, or both. Front-end servers connect to back-end servers when relaying requests from clients. The design of back-end servers for a very large number of users is discussed in Chapter 6, "Server and Site Consolidation Strategies."

- **Bridgehead server**   A server that transfers messages across routing group boundaries by means of a messaging connector. All messages to destinations outside the local routing group must use a messaging connector. You define the local and remote bridgehead servers in the connector configuration. The configuration of bridgehead servers for load balancing and fault tolerance is discussed in Chapter 14, "Understanding and Configuring Message Routing and Transport."

- **Mailbox server**   A server that hosts user mailboxes in one or multiple mailbox stores. On a dedicated mailbox server, all public folder stores have been removed. By configuring dedicated mailbox servers you can eliminate public folder replication traffic on servers that host mailbox resources. For more information about how to configure mailbox servers, see Chapter 10, "Configuring Exchange Store Resources."

> **Note**   Dedicated mailbox servers are typical configurations in an active/active server cluster, where only one Exchange virtual server can host the MAPI-based public folder store. Non-clustered Exchange servers are usually configured as both mailbox servers and public folder servers to keep the public folder hierarchy available to all clients with mailboxes on the server. You can read more about the configuration of server clusters for Exchange 2003 in Chapter 15 "Managing Clustered Exchange 2003 Servers."

- **Public folder server**   A server that hosts public folders in one or multiple public folder stores. Microsoft recommends deploying a dedicated public folder server for routing groups that contain more than three servers to simplify public folder management. For more information about how to configure public folder servers, see Chapter 10, "Configuring Exchange Store Resources."

As discussed in Chapter 1, "Exchange Server 2003 Product Overview," Exchange 2003 supports a wide variety of messaging clients, including Microsoft Office Outlook, Microsoft Office Outlook Web Access, and Internet-based clients, such as Netscape Communicator, Eudora Mail, or Microsoft Outlook Express, as well as mobile clients. Which clients you deploy influences the design of the Exchange 2003 organization. For example, MAPI-based clients, such as Outlook require direct remote procedure call (RPC) connectivity to domain controllers, mailbox servers, and public folder servers, and cannot benefit from front-end server arrangements (unless your front-end servers are running Windows 2003 so that you can configure an RPC proxy on these servers to support RPC over Secure Hypertext Transfer Protocol (HTTPS), which enables Outlook users to communicate through RPCs encapsulated in HTTP traffic over the Internet).

Planning an Exchange 2003 Organization

The individual steps to implement an Exchange organization will differ depending on whether you are deploying a new Exchange 2003 organization, upgrading an existing Exchange organization, or migrating from a non-Exchange messaging system. However, before you choose an appropriate deployment path to implement a target design, you must define the target design itself. The ultimate goal of the Exchange 2003 design is the definition of an Exchange organization according to the requirements of your company.

An Exchange organization can contain up to 1,000 Exchange servers, 1,000 administrative groups, 1,000 routing groups, and 100 domains. We recommend, however, that you keep the number of administrative groups and routing groups at a much lower limit to reduce the complexity of the Exchange organization. Optimally, an Exchange organization should have no more than 150 routing groups. Small and medium Exchange organizations typically have less than 10 routing groups.

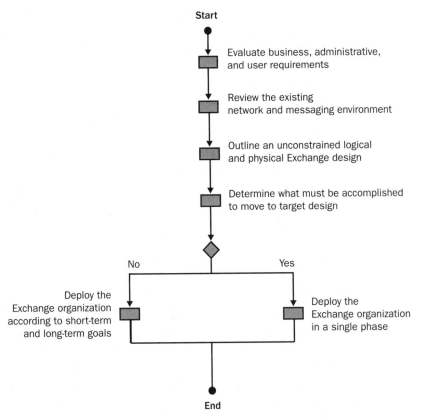

Figure 2-1   General steps to planning and deploying Exchange 2003

As indicated in Figure 2-1, planning an Exchange 2003 deployment typically includes the following steps:

1. **Evaluating business, administrative, and user requirements**   Business requirements that you need to identify before you can begin to plan an Exchange organization include Service Level Agreements (SLAs) and budget constraints. SLAs determine what storage, clustering, and backup and recovery technologies you must use to achieve the required level of availability and recoverability in the Exchange organization, including message delivery time, percentage of server uptime, amount of storage per user, and amount of time to recover an Exchange database. The budget determines the extent to which you must work within the existing network infrastructure, hardware, and software, or whether it is feasible to deploy entirely new server systems and client software.

Furthermore, your company's administrative requirements have a significant impact on the logical design of the Exchange organization because these requirements determine whether you can implement a centralized management model, or if you must use a distributed model or a combination of the two. Strict administrative requirements might even force you to implement separate Active Directory forests and multiple Exchange 2003 organizations. For more information about the administrative design of an Exchange 2003 organization, see "Structuring the Administrative Topology of an Exchange Organization" later in this chapter.

Some of the user requirements that influence how you arrange servers in your Exchange organization include remote, Web, and mobile access requirements. Companies whose offices are geographically dispersed might require a virtual private network (VPN) or RPC over HTTPS to connect the offices to the data center. Users might also require the ability to access their mailboxes from mobile devices, for example, from a Microsoft Pocket PC 2003 device. For more information about how to address the needs of users in an Exchange 2003 organization, see "Structuring the Physical Topology of an Exchange Organization" later in this chapter.

2. **Reviewing the environment in which you plan to deploy the Exchange organization**   To determine an existing environment's readiness for Exchange 2003, you should document and review the current physical and logical network design. The physical design includes local area network (LAN) segments, wide area network (WAN) links, and the hubs, switches, routers, firewalls, Internet access points, and remote access servers in the network topology. Your documentation should provide detailed information about existing servers and workstations that could potentially run Exchange 2003 or Outlook. This includes hardware standards, including manufacturers, type and number of CPUs, the amount of random access memory (RAM) and whether it can be expanded, available hard disk space, the type of network card(s), and any special hardware that is not on the Hardware Compatibility List (HCL). You should also document the operating systems, communications protocols, and the backup and recovery software installed on each server.

From a logical standpoint, Exchange 2003 depends primarily on the IP routing topology, DNS, and Active Directory. Your computer network must support TCP/IP in all locations so Exchange 2003 servers can communicate with each other. Name resolution mechanisms, namely DNS and Windows Internet Naming Service (WINS), must also work reliably, because any problems that prevent your systems from locating each other implicitly prevent your servers and clients from communicating with each other and your messaging system from functioning. Exchange 2003 typically places a significant load on Active Directory, so your Active Directory design must also be sound. You should document and review all these network components. In addition, you should document naming conventions for servers, workstations, and user accounts, as well as any existing messaging systems that you want to connect or migrate to Exchange 2003. You can find a worksheet entitled Documenting a Network Infrastructure.doc on the companion CD in the \Companion Material\Chapter 02\DocTemplates folder. This worksheet provides basic guidelines on how to document a network and Active Directory environment. Chapter 4, "Upgrading to Exchange Server 2003," and Chapter 5, "Migrating to Exchange Server 2003," explain how to deal with existing messaging systems in an Exchange 2003 deployment.

3. **Outlining an unconstrained logical and physical design of the Exchange organization** According to the information that you determine in the previous steps, you should create an unconstrained view of the future Exchange organization as it best meets the messaging requirements of your company, as explained later in this chapter. It is not necessary to take any budget constraints or existing messaging systems into consideration at this point. Budget constraints will later determine to what extent the Exchange organization can be deployed, and existing messaging systems might influence how the Exchange organization must be implemented, but these specifics should not restrict you when you define the ultimate strategic goal of the deployment. The ultimate goal is usually an Exchange 2003 organization running in native mode for all users in the company.

4. **Performing a gap analysis between what is and what should be** With the design of an ideal Exchange 2003 organization in mind, you can perform a gap analysis by comparing the existing environment with the desired future environment to determine what changes you must introduce to your existing environment, including network infrastructure, hardware, and software upgrades. The gap analysis reveals overall budget requirements for new server systems, server and client upgrades, and so forth. The gap analysis can also help to identify potential points of network failures that you must eliminate prior to deploying Exchange 2003, as well as options for reducing the network's complexity.

5. **Constraining the design of the Exchange organization** It is not uncommon that substantial changes must be applied to a network infrastructure to prepare it for an Exchange 2003 deployment. For example, you must deploy Active Directory before you can deploy Exchange 2003, which might represent a substantial challenge if your Exchange organization is still on Microsoft Windows NT Server 4.0 and Microsoft Exchange Server 5.5. For more information about upgrading your organization to Exchange Server 2003, see Chapter 4, "Upgrading to Exchange Server 2003." If you must introduce complex changes

or if the project budget does not allow you to implement the ideal Exchange 2003 design to its full extent in a single step, you can implement the Exchange 2003 organization in stages. It is advantageous to define short-term and long-term goals for staged deployment projects. After each deployment step, you might want to perform a new gap analysis to measure progress and to outline remaining tasks according to the current stage of the deployment.

> **Note**   We recommend that you verify the design of the future Exchange organization in test environments and pilot deployments before deploying Exchange 2003 in a product environment. If you must deploy Exchange 2003 in stages, you should separately test each interim design before you deploy it. Virtualization technology, such as Microsoft Virtual PC 2004 and Microsoft Virtual Server 2005, is very useful if you want to deploy a large number of test servers.

Structuring the Administrative Topology of an Exchange Organization

At this point, we assume that you have gathered all of the business and administrative requirements for your Exchange organization, and that you have documented the existing network and Active Directory infrastructure. You can use the worksheet Documenting a Network Infrastructure.doc in the \Companion Material\Chapter 02\DocTemplates folder on the companion CD as a guideline to get the groundwork done, or you can use methodologies unique to your company to gather the required information.

One crucial piece of information concerns how much autonomy the departments and divisions in your company need to manage their resources and whether each group needs to isolate their resources from other groups. Autonomy involves independent but not exclusive control over resources. Administrators can manage their resources autonomously even if other administrators with equal or greater authority, such as enterprise administrators, can take control over resources if necessary. Security isolation, on the other hand, means that a group of administrators has exclusive control over the resources and that there are no other administrators with equal or greater authority.

It is important to understand that in a single Active Directory forest and Exchange organization, there is no security isolation because the forest owner and enterprise administrators can always obtain full access to all resources. If divisions in your company must operate independently from the rest of the organization or if security and legal requirements demand that divisions operate in isolated environments, you must implement multiple Active Directory forests, which complicates the Exchange 2003 design. As mentioned in the beginning of this chapter, a single Exchange organization cannot span multiple forests. For more information about designing Exchange 2003 organizations for companies with isolation requirements, see Chapter 3, "Exchange Server 2003 in Enterprise Environments."

> **Note**   Creating a design to achieve non-isolated autonomy is generally less expensive than creating a design to achieve isolation.

Administrative Boundaries in an Exchange 2003 Organization

There are three types of administrative boundaries that you must be aware of when you design the administrative topology of an Exchange organization:

- **Enterprise management**   This involves control over all services provided by Active Directory and Exchange 2003.

- **Server management**   This involves control over all or part of the Exchange servers and their resources in an Exchange organization.

- **Recipient management**   This involves control over all or part of the recipient objects stored in Active Directory.

Translated into the administrative topology of an Exchange organization, this means that enterprise administrators have full control over the entire Exchange organization, and that recipient or server administrators do not have the ability to prevent enterprise administrators from taking control of recipient objects or server resources. You can verify this in Active Directory Sites and Services or in Exchange System Manager if you enable the Security tab for organization and administrative group objects using the following registry parameter.

> **Warning**   Using Registry Editor incorrectly can cause serious problems that may require you to reinstall your operating system. Microsoft cannot guarantee that problems resulting from the incorrect use of Registry Editor can be solved. Use Registry Editor at your own risk.

Location	HKEY_CURRENT_USER\Software\Microsoft\Exchange\ExAdmin
Name	ShowSecurityPage
Type	REG_DWORD
Value Data	0x1
Description	Enables the Security tab for all configuration objects in Exchange System Manager. If the value is 0x0 or not present, the Security tab is displayed only on the following objects:

- Address lists
- Global address lists
- Mailbox and public folder databases
- Top level public folder hierarchies

Because you are modifying a key within HKEY_CURRENT_USER, the change only affects the user who is logged on to the computer on which you are working.

> **Note** Use caution when changing permissions on Exchange objects. If you incorrectly assign deny permissions, you may render objects unmanageable in Exchange System Manager.

To verify the effective security settings in Active Directory Sites and Services, you must enable the Show Services Node option on the View menu. If you then expand the Services node, display the properties of the Exchange organization object, and click the Security tab, you can see that the Enterprise Admins group has full control over the Exchange organization (Figure 2-2). The Domain Admins group from the root domain of the Active Directory forest also has far-reaching control over the entire Exchange organization. The permissions are inherited from the root container in the configuration naming context.

> **Note** Active Directory Sites and Services and Exchange System Manager do not display the root container in the configuration naming context, but you can use ADSI Edit to examine the security settings for this directory object. See the document ADSI Edit and Active Directory NCs.doc for instructions how to use ADSI Edit. You can find this file in the \Companion Material\Chapter 01 folder on the companion CD.

It is possible to block inheritance or deny Enterprise Admins and Domain Admins permissions at the Exchange organization level, but this is not a recommended configuration, and it does not prevent an enterprise administrator from seizing ownership of the Exchange organization object and then re-granting access permissions. If it is unacceptable that an enterprise administrator has full control over a particular region or group of Exchange resources; you must implement a separate Active Directory forest and Exchange organization for that group to enforce a strict security boundary. The procedures outlined in the document Autonomy of an Exchange organization.doc demonstrate how an enterprise administrator can gain access to a resource despite denied permissions. You can find this file on the companion CD in the \Companion Material\Chapter 02 folder.

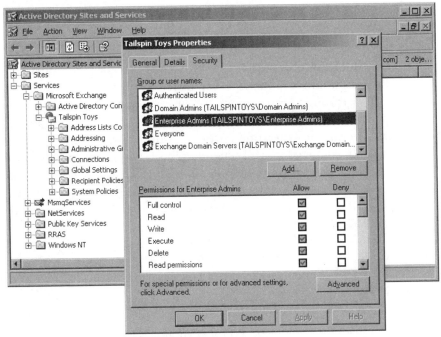

Figure 2-2   Full control permissions for Enterprise Admins

> **Note**   In the list of accounts with far-reaching permissions over the Exchange organization, you can also find an Exchange Domain Servers group from each domain in your Active Directory forest that grants the Exchange servers in each domain access to the Exchange configuration information in Active Directory. Do not modify these permission settings, because Exchange 2003 servers cannot function without access to the Exchange configuration information in Active Directory.

Structuring Server and Resource Management

Although enterprise administrators have full control over an entire forest, explicit Exchange server administrators should have control only over those resources in the Exchange organization that they are actually responsible for. As illustrated in Figure 2-3, you can delegate Exchange administrator permissions at the following two levels:

- **Organization level** Exchange administrators with permissions at the organizational level can manage global settings in addition to the resources in all administrative groups of the Exchange organization. In Exchange 2003, centralized administration is enforced for Internet message format definitions, message delivery settings, mobile services, recipient policies, and address book settings. These resources are available across the entire organization and do not belong to a specific server.

- **Administrative group level** Exchange administrators with permissions at the administrative group level can manage only those resources that exist in the particular administrative group for which administrative permissions have been granted. It is important to understand, however, that an Exchange administrator with permissions for one particular administrative group is also implicitly granted read access to all other administrative groups in the organization. All Exchange administrators require at least read access at the organization level (otherwise they cannot navigate to the administrative group that they are supposed to manage). Read permissions at the organization level are then inherited by all administrative groups.

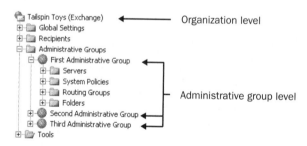

Figure 2-3   Administrative boundaries in an Exchange organization

To delegate administrative permissions at the organization or administrative group level, use the Exchange Administration Delegation Wizard, which you can start in Exchange System Manager by right-clicking the organization object or target administrative group and then selecting Delegate Control. Table 2-1 lists the roles that you can assign an Exchange administrator. For step-by-step instructions that demonstrate how to grant Exchange administrators specific roles at the organization and administrative group level, you can use the worksheet Delegating administrative permissions in an Exchange organization.doc, which you can find in the \Companion Material\Chapter 02 folder on the companion CD.

Table 2-1   Administrative Roles in Exchange Server 2003

Role	Description
Exchange View Only	Grants permissions to list and read the properties of all objects in the Exchange organization or administrative group. If the administrator needs to manage recipient objects and mailboxes, but does not need to manage server resources, assign this role.
Exchange Administrator	Grants all permissions except for the ability to take ownership of configuration objects or change permissions. If the administrator needs to add objects or modify object properties, but does not need to manage permission settings on objects, assign this role.
	To fully manage an Exchange server, the administrator must also be a member of the server's local Administrators group.
Exchange Full Administrator	Grants all permissions to all objects in the Exchange organization or administrative group including the ability take ownership of configuration objects and to change permissions. Assign this role only to administrators who are installing Exchange servers or who are required to delegate permissions to configuration objects.
	Installing Exchange 2003 requires Exchange Full Administrator permissions. The first server in any domain requires the administrator to have Exchange Full Administrative permissions at the organization level. Additional servers in the same domain can be installed with accounts that have Exchange Full Administrator permissions at the administrative group level.

Note   We recommend assigning permissions to security groups rather than to individual user accounts.

Centralized Versus Decentralized Administration

By deciding whether you grant administrative permissions at the organization or administrative group level, you are essentially determining whether you want to implement a centralized or decentralized administration model for the Exchange organization. The administrative model of Exchange 2003 is fairly independent of the physical infrastructure, so you can centralize administration even if your company consists of several branch offices, and you can decentralize administration even if all servers are deployed in a central location. Keep in mind, however, that Exchange System Manager requires RPC connectivity to the Exchange servers being managed. Thus, the administration model is not entirely free of physical constraints if you cannot implement a virtual private network (VPN) to support RPCs or use another solution for remote administration. A decentralized server infrastructure might limit the ability of a central Information Technology (IT) department to manage server resources across an Exchange organization.

Figure 2-4 provides guidelines for centralizing or decentralizing Exchange administration based on physical constraints. Creating multiple administrative groups because of network connectivity issues is similar to the site model in Exchange Server 5.5 and earlier versions. Keep in mind, however, that organizational reasons might still require you to implement a decentralized administrative model even if network connectivity supports a centralized model.

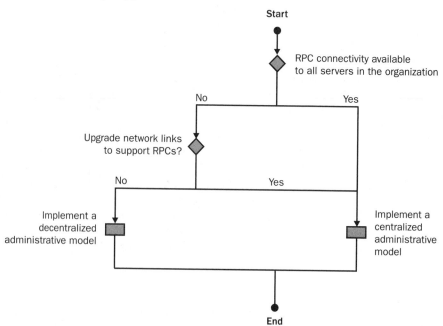

Figure 2-4   Centralizing or decentralizing Exchange administration

The centralized administrative model, typically characterized by a single administrative group, is better suited for Exchange Server 2003 than is a decentralized model. Arguably, you can place all servers in the default administrative group regardless of RPC connectivity, but this does not lead to a clearly structured administrative model. An administrative group should not contain unmanageable servers. If you want to place all servers in a single administrative group for centralized administration, consider consolidating all servers in a data center or upgrading the network links to all locations with Exchange servers to support RPCs so all administrators can manage all server resources to their full extent.

Figure 2-5 shows two Exchange administrators in different locations that are unable to manage Exchange stores and other server resources even though both have been granted full administrative permissions at the organization or administrative group level. Installing SERVER02 in a second administrative group can lead to a better administrative structure.

> **Note**   Microsoft does not support managing an Exchange organization using Exchange System Manager over network connections that do not support RPCs. Without an RPC connection to the server being managed, you can only control configuration settings that are stored in Active Directory, but you cannot manage storage groups, mailbox stores, public folder stores, or message queues, which means, in essence, that you cannot manage the server.

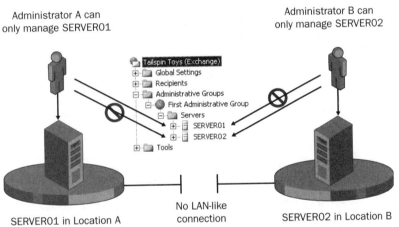

Administrator A can only manage SERVER01

Administrator B can only manage SERVER02

SERVER01 in Location A

No LAN-like connection

SERVER02 in Location B

Figure 2-5   A single administrative group for two locations without a LAN-like network connection

> **Note**   In Exchange 2003, you cannot move Exchange servers between administrative groups. You must create the server's target administrative group prior to installing the server, and, you must then specify the target administrative group during setup. Exchange Full Administrator permissions are required to install Exchange 2003.

Centralizing a Decentralized Administrative Model

As shown in Figure 2-6, servers are not the only type of resources organized in administrative groups. Administrative groups are also the parent containers of public folder hierarchies (grouped together under the Folders container), routing groups, and system policies. In a decentralized environment, you might have to implement separate administrative groups for these resources, so administrators from different administrative groups can manage these resources centrally. Figure 2-6 illustrates how this works based on an example with two administrators each separately responsible for an individual administrative group and both jointly managing folder hierarchies, routing groups, and system policies in a third administrative group. It is also possible to grant an administrator permissions for only the third administrative group, if this administrator is not supposed to manage server resources in individual administrative groups.

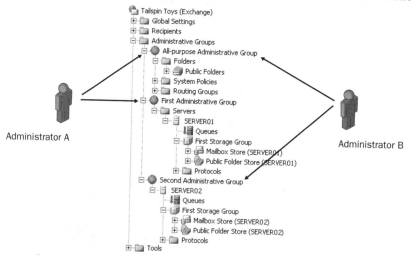

Figure 2-6   Centralizing resource management in a decentralized Exchange organization

Independent of server placement in administrative groups, you can delegate the following tasks to administrators in an Exchange organization:

- **Routing Group Management**   In an Exchange 2003 organization running in native mode, the routing topology is independent of the administrative model. Thus, you can create a dedicated administrative group for all routing groups and then grant all those administrators access to this administrative group who are supposed to manage the messaging routing topology in the Exchange organization. You can read more about routing groups under "Structuring the Physical Topology of an Exchange Organization" later in this chapter.

    This administrative model is only available if you have no Exchange 5.5 servers in the organization and are running in native mode. In an Exchange 2003 organization running in mixed mode, routing groups can only contain servers from the local administrative group to maintain an infrastructure similar to the site concept of Exchange Server 5.5. For more information about interoperability with Exchange Server 5.5, see Chapter 04, "Upgrading to Exchange Server 2003."

■ **System Policies Management**   As mentioned in Chapter 1, "Exchange Server 2003 Product Overview," Exchange Server 2003 supports system policies that you can use to apply settings to a collection of Exchange server resources. Using policies you can define global settings for message tracking, mailbox stores, and public folder stores, and you can apply these policies to all or a number of your Exchange servers to specify common settings in a uniform way. Implementing a dedicated administrative group for system policies enables you to achieve a certain level of centralized server and Exchange store management even in a distributed administration model.

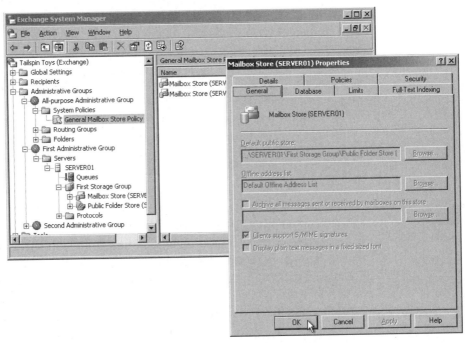

Figure 2-7 Enforcing resource settings through system policies

Figure 2-7 illustrates that an administrator cannot change settings on a resource if that resource is assigned a system policy. To change the settings, the configuration must be changed using the system policy object, or you remove the resource from the system policy, in which case the resource can be managed individually. Only Exchange administrators for the "system policy" administrative group are able to configure policy settings. However, Exchange administrators from local administrative groups can always remove their server resources from a central system policy even if they only have list and read permissions on the "system policy" administrative group. For information about how to work with a dedicated "system policy" administrative group, see the document Centralizing system policies.doc, which you can find in the in the \Companion Material\Chapter 02 folder on the companion CD.

- **Public Folder Hierarchy Management**   Public folder hierarchies, also called public folder trees, are created and managed using Exchange System Manager. By default, only the MAPI-based public folder hierarchy exists in an Exchange organization (alternative hierarchies must be created manually). Among other things, you can use this hierarchy object to manage top-level folder permissions, configure replication settings for public folders, and administer system public folders that are not visible in Outlook. You can read more about public folder management under "Structuring Public Folder Management" later in this section.

    Note that each public folder hierarchy corresponds to a single configuration object in Active Directory, although it is possible to associate multiple public folder stores with a particular hierarchy and replicate public folder instances between Exchange servers. For example, by placing the MAPI-based public folder hierarchy in a separate administrative group, you can decide which administrators are allowed to configure public folders at the highest level. To manage public folder hierarchies, however, administrators must be able to connect to a public folder server over a connection that supports Hypertext Transfer Protocol (HTTP) and Distributed Authoring and Versioning (DAV). Exchange 2003 automatically replicates any changes on a public folder to all other Exchange servers that hold a public folder store associated with the hierarchy.

Note   Administrators always have the ability to create system policies in the local administrative group and then assign these policies to servers, mailbox stores, or public folder stores. You can use the script SystemPolicy-Check.wsf, located in the \Companion Material\Chapter 02\Scripts folder on the companion CD to list all system policies in an Exchange organization with their assigned resources. You can also list all those resources that have not been assigned to a system policy.

Note   Administrators can create and manage additional public folder trees in their own administrative groups. If your public folder administrators have only administrative permissions for the "public folder" administrative group, they will not be able to manage these additional hierarchies. To move an object to a new administrative group, you must have at least Exchange Administrator permissions on both the source and the target administrative group.

Structuring Public Folder Management

If you are planning to use Exchange 2003 primarily for messaging and Microsoft Windows SharePoint Services for workgroup solutions, a sophisticated public folder management model might not be required. If you plan to use public folders, however, you must decide how Exchange administrators and regular users should perform public folder management tasks. To create and maintain public folder resources, a user does not necessarily have to be an Exchange administrator.

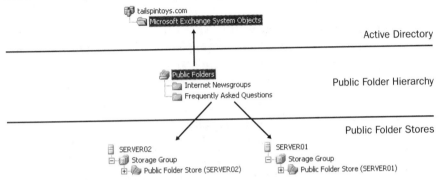

Figure 2-8   Public folder architecture

As indicated in Figure 2-8, a public folder resource can consist of several individual components that influence how public folders are managed, as follows:

- **Active Directory**   Public folders can be mail-enabled so that your users can send messages to them, even though by default they are hidden from the address book. For example, you can mail-enable a public folder and add it to a distribution group, in this way creating a message archive for all group-related messages. It is also possible to make public folders visible in the address book by clearing the **Hide from Exchange address book** check box on the **Exchange Advanced** tab in the public folder properties. Users must have permissions to create items in a public folder if they want to send messages to it. You can read more about the configuration of public folders in Chapter 10, "Configuring Exchange Store Resources."

    When you e-mail enable a public folder, you create a recipient object for the folder in the Microsoft Exchange System Objects container in Active Directory. You can view this container in Active Directory Users and Computers if you enable the **Advanced features** option on the **View** menu. When you use Exchange Administration Delegation Wizard to delegate administrative permissions to an Exchange administrator for an administrative group in which the public folder hierarchy resides, the wizard grants the administrator read and write access to the Microsoft Exchange System Objects container. You can also customize the permission settings for this container by using Active Directory Users and Computers to determine specifically which Exchange administrators are able to manage e-mail-related public folder settings. You can also specify directory rights on a per-public folder basis on the Permissions tab in the public folder properties in Exchange System Manager.

■ **Public folder hierarchy**   The public folder hierarchy defines the tree of public folders in a public folder store. Top-level folders can contain subfolders, and those can contain other subfolders. The hierarchy also holds folder-specific configuration settings, such as client permissions. Exchange 2003 supports two types of hierarchies:

   ■ **MAPI-based hierarchy**   This is the public folder tree that users of MAPI-based clients, such as Outlook, and users of Outlook Web Access or Internet Mail Access Protocol version 4 (IMAP4)-based clients can use to share information. There can only be one MAPI-based hierarchy in an Exchange 2003 organization.

   ■ **General purpose hierarchy**   These are additional public folder trees that you can create for Web-based workflow and workgroup solutions. General purpose hierarchies are not available in Outlook, and are therefore not suitable for discussion forums and other instant workgroup solutions that rely on Outlook features, such as Outlook task or calendar items.

   Exchange administrators use public folder hierarchies primarily to manage permissions (Table 2-2). As mentioned earlier in this chapter, you can place public folder hierarchies in a dedicated administrative group. All administrators with permissions on that administrative group implicitly have full administrative permissions over the hierarchy and can create and manage public folder instances. For step-by-step instructions about how to grant specific users the right to create and manage top-level folders in the MAPI-based hierarchy, you can use the worksheet Managing top-level folder permissions.doc, which you can find in the \Companion Material\Chapter 02 folder on the companion CD.

Table 2-2   Important Permissions for Public Folder Hierarchies

Permission	Description
Create Public Folder	Specifies who can create a public folder in this hierarchy.
Create Top-Level Public Folder	Specifies who can create top-level folders, which represent the first level in the tree structure.
Mail-Enable Public Folder	Specifies who can mail-enable a public folder in this hierarchy.
Modify Public Folder Admin ACL	Specifies who can change administrative permissions.

- **Public folder stores** A particular public folder hierarchy can be associated with multiple public folder stores (Figure 2-8) to replicate the hierarchy, and possibly public folder contents, between multiple servers. Note that an administrator does not require full permissions on a public folder hierarchy to associate the hierarchy with a public folder store in the local administrative group. Exchange View Only Administrator permissions are sufficient for the administrative group in which the hierarchy object resides. Administration Delegation Wizards implicitly grants Exchange administrators these permissions on all administrative groups in an Exchange organization. For step-by-step instructions about how to associate a hierarchy with a public folder store and create public folder replicas without administrative control over the hierarchy, see the document Managing top-level folder permissions.doc, which you can find in the \Companion Material\Chapter 02 folder on the companion CD.

  Exchange administrators use public folder store objects in Exchange System Manager primarily to manage replication settings and public folder size and age limits. You can also apply these settings within a system policy for multiple public folder stores. With Exchange Administrator permissions on a public folder store, you can add or remove public folder instances on the server. Public folder replication will ensure that all public folder instances in a hierarchy are synchronized. Administrative permissions at the public folder store level are determined by the administrative group in which the Exchange server resides. You can read more about the configuration of public folder stores and public folder replication in Chapter 10, "Configuring Exchange Store Resources."

- **Public folder instance** The actual public folders within a public folder hierarchy can be managed using Outlook or Exchange System Manager. Creating folders in Exchange System Manager has the advantage that you can specifically select the public folder servers on which to place the public folder. When you create public folders in Outlook, these settings are inherited from the parent folder. Outlook users cannot control folder location or replication settings. Table 2-3 lists different key features that you can manage for public folders in Outlook and Exchange System Manager.

Table 2-3   Public Folder Management Features Available in Outlook and Exchange System Manager

Outlook	Exchange System Manager
■ Specify default and custom views for public folders and configure public folder rules. You also have the option to create moderated public folders.	■ Manage e-mail addresses for mail-enabled public folders.
■ Manage electronic forms associated with public folders and define a standard form to be used when posting new items.	■ Specify a simple display name and determine whether to show or hide mail-enabled public folders in the address book.
■ Specify a Web page, such as a digital dashboard, to be displayed when the user selects the public folder.	■ Specify delegate permissions and forwarding addresses for a public folder.
■ Specify client permissions for public folders.	■ Determine whether read/unread information should be maintained for this folder.
■ Synchronize public folder contents with offline copies.	■ Specify storage and age limits and deleted item retention times.
	■ Configure client permissions, directory rights, and administrative rights on the public folder.
	■ Specify which servers contain replicas and set times at which this public folder is replicated.
	■ Configure system public folders that are not visible in Outlook.

The creator of a public folder becomes automatically the owner of the public folder with full control over the configuration settings, but you can also explicitly specify public folder owners in the client permissions. This enables you to create top-level folders for the departments and divisions in your company and then delegate the folder ownership to a folder administrator in each business unit. The folder administrators can then create subfolders underneath their individual top-level folders according to the specific needs of their teams. Subfolders inherit the parent folder's configuration settings.

Over-Designing the Administration Model of Exchange 2003

If you enable the **Security** tab for all objects in Exchange System Manager by using the ShowSecurityPage registry parameter discussed earlier in this chapter, you can examine the inherited and directly assigned permission settings on all directory objects in the Exchange organization. You can also change the permission assignments to control what accounts have access to what resources. For example, you can deny a particular organization administrator access to an administrative group, or to a particular server in an administrative group, or to a particular Exchange store on a server. You can also grant an administrator access to a public folder hierarchy but not to a public folder store, or grant an administrator full access to the Microsoft Exchange

System Objects container in the domain naming context but no access to public folder hierarchy objects in the configuration naming context. However, we do not recommended designing the administrative model of Exchange 2003 on that basis.

The problem with using the Security tab for direct permission assignments is that it is very easy to overlook important access rights and very difficult to determine what access rights to assign and maintain for a number of administrators with varying responsibilities. For example, if you use Exchange Administration Delegation Wizard to assign an account the Exchange Administrator role for an administrative group that contains the MAPI-based public folder hierarchy, you actually grant this account read and write access permissions at various levels in the domain and configuration naming context. To illustrate this fact, Figure 2-9 shows the security settings for the Microsoft Exchange container in ADSI Edit. Ted Bremer has been assigned read permissions for this container because he is an Exchange Administrator for an administrative group. The Microsoft Exchange container is not exposed in Exchange System Manager, but nevertheless, Exchange Administration Delegation Wizard configures its security settings when you delegate Exchange administrator roles.

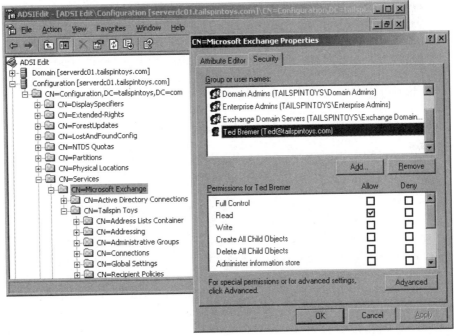

Figure 2-9 Permission settings for an Exchange administrator one level above the Exchange organization object

> **Note**   It is not a good idea to design the administrative model for
> Exchange 2003 based on individual permission assignments or denials. If
> your departments require strict security boundaries, consider placing
> resources in separate forests and creating multiple Exchange organizations.
> Within a single Exchange organization, however, strive for administrative
> simplicity. Organize the server resources in administrative groups and use
> Exchange Administration Delegation Wizard to delegate administrative per-
> missions at the organization and administrative group level. Use dedicated
> security groups instead of individual administrator accounts to assign
> Exchange administrator roles.

Structuring Recipient Management

In Exchange Server 2003, server resources are managed using directory objects that
reside in the configuration naming context of Active Directory. Recipient objects, on
the other hand, are directory objects that reside in the domain naming context. Thus,
recipient management is entirely separated from server management in
Exchange 2003. This is fundamentally different from Exchange Server 5.5. You can
read more about the integration of Exchange Server 5.5 with Exchange Server 2003 in
Chapter 04, "Upgrading to Exchange Server 2003."

Recipient Objects and Mailboxes

Recipient objects in Exchange 2003 are mailbox-enabled user accounts and mail-
enabled contacts, user accounts, or groups. You can also mail-enable public folders,
as discussed earlier in this chapter. This creates public folder recipient objects in the
domain naming context. It is important to understand that Exchange-specific recipient settings are maintained in standard Windows 2003 domain objects.
Exchange 2003 extends the Active Directory schema when running Setup in Forest-
Prep mode (launched automatically when you install the first Exchange server in a
forest) so contacts, user accounts, and groups can have Exchange-specific attributes.

Figure 2-10 illustrates the relationship between mailbox-enabled recipients and
their mailboxes. The important point is that the recipient object is not the mailbox
itself. The recipient is an object in the domain naming context, and the mailbox is a
container for messages and other items in the Exchange store. This is more obvious
for mail-enabled recipients, which do not have any resources in an Exchange store.
Mail-enabled recipients refer to recipients outside the local Exchange organization.
On the other hand, attributes of mailbox-enabled recipient objects (such as the msExchMailboxGuid attribute) establish the association between the recipients and their
mailboxes within the local Exchange organization.

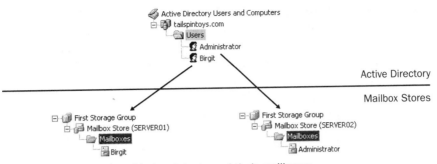

Figure 2-10   Mailbox-enabled recipients and their mailboxes

   The relationship between mailbox-enabled recipients and their mailboxes is important because mailbox resources in an Exchange store are managed primarily through settings applied to their recipient objects. Thus, permissions granted at the level of domains and organizational units determine who can manage the recipient objects and their associated mailboxes. Translated into the administrative model of Exchange 2003, this means that a mailbox administrator does not require any permissions on mailbox stores or other resources in the Exchange organization. In fact, an Exchange server does not even have to be available for an administrator to create a new mailbox on that server. For a step-by-step demonstration of this, see the document Managing mailboxes without Exchange store access.doc, which you can find in the \Companion Material\Chapter 02 folder on the companion CD.

> **Note**   We recommend granting mailbox administrators the Exchange View Only Administrator role at the organization or administrative group level.

Globalized Recipient Management

In an Active Directory forest with Exchange 2003, recipient management is always global and cannot be restricted to an administrative group. In other words, account operators with full permissions on organizational units can place mailboxes on any mailbox store in an Exchange organization. Microsoft often states that at a minimum Exchange View Only Administrator permissions are required on the administrative group where the Exchange server with the target mailbox store resides, but this is slightly misleading because it suggests that you cannot create the mailbox without view only permissions. However, Exchange View Only Administrator permissions are required only if you want to mailbox-enable a user account or move a mailbox in Active Directory Users and Computers by using Exchange Task Wizard. Exchange Task Wizard requires read access to the target administrative group so it can enumerate available mailbox stores and read the attributes, such as the mailbox store's distinguished name, from the target mailbox store object in the configuration naming context. The wizard then writes this information into the attributes of the recipient object to establish the association between the recipient object and its mailbox. The Exchange store creates the actual mailbox later when the user logs on to the mailbox for the first time or when other users send the newly created recipient messages.

If you know the distinguished name of the target mailbox store and the legacyExchangeDN information of the target Exchange server, you can mailbox-enable a user account by using ADSI without having read access to the Exchange organization. The following code demonstrates this by creating a new mailbox-enabled user account in a domain called tailspintoys.com and then setting Exchange-related attributes to indicate that the user has a mailbox in SERVER01's default mailbox store, called Mailbox Store (SERVER01):

```
'--- Create a new user object in the Users Container ----
Set ou = GetObject("LDAP://CN=Users,DC=tailspintoys,DC=com")
Set usr = ou.Create("user", "CN=Birgit")
'--- Mandatory Attributes ----
usr.Put "samAccountName", "Birgit"
usr.SetInfo

'---- Optional Attributes, you can optionally skip these ----
usr.Put "sn", "Seidl"
usr.Put "givenName", "Birgit"
usr.Put "userPrincipalName", "Birgit@tailspintoys.com"
usr.SetInfo

'---- Reset the user's password and enable the account ----

usr.SetPassword "1qw$t9x"
usr.AccountDisabled = False
usr.SetInfo

'---- Mailbox-enable the user account ----
usr.Put "mailNickname", "Birgit"
usr.Put "homeMDB", "CN=Mailbox Store (SERVER01),CN=First Storage Group," _
        & "CN=InformationStore,CN=SERVER01,CN=Servers," _
        & "CN=First Administrative Group,CN=Administrative Groups," _
        & "CN=Tailspin Toys,CN=Microsoft Exchange,CN=Services," _
        & "CN=Configuration,DC=tailspintoys,DC=com"
usr.Put "msExchHomeServerName", "/o=Tailspin Toys/" _
        & "ou=First Administrative Group/cn=Configuration/" _
        & "cn=Servers/cn=SERVER01"
usr.SetInfo
```

If the homeMDB and msExchHomeServerName attributes are specified correctly, the user account will be mailbox-enabled, and the recipient update service will then stamp the newly created recipient with the remaining directory information, such as e-mail addresses generated according to recipient policies. You can read more about the management of recipient objects in Chapter 9, "Managing Directory Information."

Note   An account operator can determine the required homeMDB and msExchHomeServerName information from existing recipient objects in the domain. For example, you can use the following command to export this information from all existing mailbox-enabled user accounts: ldifde -f <output file> -s <domain controller> -d "<distinguished name of target OU>" -r (homeMDB=*) -l "homeMDB,msExchHomeServerName" (such as ldifde -f output.txt -s serverdc01.tailspintoys.com -d "CN=Users,DC=tailspintoys,DC=com" -r (homeMDB=*) -l "homeMDB, msExchHomeServerName"). Read access to the Exchange organization is not a requirement.

Delegating Mailbox Management at the Administrative Group Level

If you are planning to use standard tools, such as Exchange Task Wizard, for mailbox management, you must grant account operators read access to the Exchange organization. In a large organization, you might want to restrict the list of servers and mailbox stores available to an account operator in Exchange Task Wizard by delegating the Exchange View Only Administrator role at the administrative group level to that person. Granting this role at the administrative group level gives the account operator read access specifically to the Exchange organization object and the selected administrative group. Other administrative groups do not inherit the read permissions on the Exchange organization object, so the account operator cannot enumerate mailbox stores from other administrative groups.

Note   Delegating the Exchange View Only Administrator role at the administrative group level allows you to narrow down the mailbox store choices an account operator has in Exchange Task Wizard, but it does not affect the operator's ability to create, manage, and delete mailboxes on any store in the organization.

Delegating Recipient Management at the Domain Level

The above explanations make clear that mailbox management is primarily an account operator task in Exchange 2003 and as such, it is structured using the logical design of Active Directory. Within a forest, you can use the following Active Directory elements to structure recipient management

- **Domains**   Windows domains enable you to partition recipient objects for optimized directory replication. Domain controllers replicate the domain naming context only within the domain. Domain controllers in other domains do not have access to the local domain's user account and recipient information. For Exchange 2003 to provide a consistent global address book in a multi-domain environment, partial domain information must be replicated to global catalog servers. You can read more about global catalog server dependencies later in this chapter.

> **Note**   In an Active Directory forest, a domain should not be used as a security boundary, because it is not possible for domain administrators to prevent enterprise administrators from other domains from accessing user account information in a domain.

- **Organizational units**   You can use organizational units to group user account and other objects in a hierarchical structure for administrative purposes. In a process similar to that for an administrative group in an Exchange organization, you can delegate administrative permissions for organizational units to individual administrators using the Delegation of Control Wizard in Active Directory Users and Computers.

In general, Active Directory domains are used to control the replication of user account information, and organizational units are used to delegate administration. Control over an organizational unit is determined by the access control lists (ACLs) on that organizational unit. In multi-domain environments, you must define the hierarchy of organizational units for each domain separately.

Splitting User Account and Recipient Management

Companies upgrading from Exchange Server 5.5 to Exchange 2003 might want to split user account and recipient management to preserve the existing administrative model. In Exchange Server 5.5, recipient and server management are combined based on the concept of sites. User account management, on the other hand, is based on the concept of Windows NT domains. Accordingly, companies running an Exchange 5.5 organization often have dedicated Exchange administrators and dedicated Windows account operators.

This paradigm shifts in Exchange 2000 and Exchange 2003. With the merger of Exchange directory and Windows NT domain database into an overall directory service called Active Directory, user accounts and recipients are no longer separate objects. The information is combined into mailbox-enabled and mail-enabled Windows accounts, thus combining user account management with mailbox management. Splitting user account and recipient information again means granting account operators and mailbox managers full control over different sets of properties on the same directory objects. For example, by denying an account operator permissions for the homeMDB and msExchHomeServerName attributes, you can prevent this administrator from creating mailboxes for user accounts in the selected organizational unit.

If you want to split user account and recipient management, you must delegate property-specific permissions to your administrators by using Delegation of Control Wizard. You must create a custom task instead of selecting a common administrative task in the wizard to grant property-specific permissions, yet the configuration at this level is very burdensome. You have to make your choices from approximately 200 properties, and some properties, such as displayName and mailNickname, you might have to delegate to all administrators. Separating the user account administration from recipient management complicates the administrative infrastructure tremendously and is therefore best avoided if possible.

Note   In Exchange 2003, we recommend combining user account and recipient management. If you must split these responsibilities, consider implementing a resource forest for Exchange 2003 to establish a strict security boundary that separates user accounts from mailbox accounts. Resource forest deployments are discussed in Chapter 03, "Exchange Server 2003 in Enterprise Environments."

Structuring the Physical Topology of an Exchange Organization

In a computer network with permanent and reliable TCP/IP connections, Exchange Server 2003 can operate with a single routing group. However, by structuring the routing topology of an Exchange organization along the physical topology of the computer network, you can optimize bandwidth consumption, increase performance, and increase reliability of messaging services. The physical characteristics of the computer network, including distributed networking services, such as DNS and Active Directory, are important design factors that influence how you arrange servers, message transfer paths, and messaging clients. However, SLAs might also influence the design. It is assumed that you have gathered the required information in a previous step.

The physical design of an Exchange organization consists of the following elements:

- **Active Directory site topology**   The Active Directory site topology describes where in the computer network domain controllers and global catalogs are located and what mechanisms these servers use to replicate directory information. Because Exchange 2003 depends on Active Directory, and because the Active Directory design greatly influences the reliability and performance of Exchange 2003, the physical topology of Active Directory must be considered an important Exchange design element. Exchange 2003 has a significant impact on Active Directory and introduces requirements not present in an Active Directory forest without Exchange 2003. You must review the Active Directory design to ensure that it is ready for Exchange Server 2003.

■ **Message routing topology**   The message routing topology describes how Exchange transfers messages from one server to another within the Exchange organization and to external messaging systems. By default, all servers are in the same routing group and message transfer is direct. By implementing a more sophisticated routing topology, you can optimize WAN link usage.

■ **Server infrastructure**   The server infrastructure describes where in the computer network Exchange servers should be deployed and what roles these servers should assume in the Exchange organization. The server infrastructure depends on the number of users in the Exchange organization, the geographical profile of the environment, and whether or not you must connect Exchange to non-Exchange messaging systems.

■ **Client access topology**   The client access topology describes the network connections that messaging clients use to access mailboxes and public folders. Client access might be direct over a local or remote network connection, or indirect using front-end servers. For remote connections, the client access topology should also outline the remote access infrastructure and firewall arrangements, so internal resources are appropriately protected from unauthorized users.

Active Directory Site Topology

The site topology of Active Directory, defined through sites, subnets, site links, and site link bridges, determines the efficiency of Active Directory queries and replication traffic. Many components of Exchange 2003 act as Active Directory clients performing Active Directory queries to look up both configuration and recipient information. Efficient directory replication ensures that configuration changes are made available to all Exchange servers in the organization in a timely manner.

The site topology elements of Active Directory have the following purposes:

■ **Subnets**   A subnet is a segment of a TCP/IP network that is connected to a router and identified by a range of IP addresses. Computers within a subnet communicate with each other directly. Computers in different subnets must communicate with each other indirectly by means of the router device. Subnet objects in Active Directory identify the segments in the network by means of their IP address ranges.

■ **Sites**   A site is a collection of subnets that are connected to each other through reliable and fast network connections. Within a site, domain controllers replicate directory information when changes occur, without the overhead of data compression, to replicate the data with minimum delays. Between sites, the data is compressed to minimize transfer costs over WAN links. Each domain controller in a forest is associated with a site according to its subnet (identified by its IP address). When replication occurs between sites, a single domain controller in the source site communicates the directory changes at a scheduled time to a domain controller in the target site. The receiving domain controller then communicates the directory changes to all other domain controllers in the local site.

Active Directory sites also define client affinities. Domain controllers can inform Active Directory clients about the nearest domain controller in the network and Active Directory clients can then establish a connection to the nearest domain controller to avoid communications over slow network links. To ensure that every site has a preferred domain controller, domain controllers advertise themselves through a site-specific service (SRV) resource record in DNS. If no domain controllers exist in a site, a domain controller from the closest site with the lowest cost site link relative to other connected sites advertises itself as the nearest domain controller. This ensures that all Active Directory clients can communicate with Active Directory as efficiently as possible.

Note   Sites are not related to domains. A site can host domain controllers from more than one domain, and a domain can also span multiple sites.

- **Site links**   A site link establishes an inter-site connection for Active Directory replication across site boundaries. You must manually connect sites with each other by using site links so domain controllers in one site can replicate directory changes to domain controllers in the other sites.

- **Site link bridges**   A site link bridge represents a set of site links, in which all the sites can communicate by using a common network communication mechanism. Site link bridges enable domain controllers that are not directly connected by means of a communication link to replicate with each other.

Domain Controller and Global Catalog Servers

To ensure that Exchange 2003 can operate fast and reliably, you must ensure that domain controllers and global catalog servers are available to each Exchange server in the organization over fast and reliable network connections. Ordinary domain controller communication takes place over TCP port 389 for Lightweight Directory Access Protocol (LDAP) connections and over TCP port 636 for LDAP connections over Secure Sockets Layer (SSL). Global catalog servers also listen on TCP port 3268 for global catalog-specific requests and on port 3269 for global catalog-specific requests over SSL.

Exchange 2003 servers communicate with domain controllers and global catalog servers for the following reasons:

- **Global catalog servers**   Without global catalogs, account and recipient information is only replicated between domain controllers in the local domain, but not with domain controllers in other domains. Thus, in a forest with multiple domains, individual domain controllers do not have all recipient objects. To provide a complete global address book, however, all recipients must be present in the directory. This is where global catalog servers come into play. Domain controllers replicate domain information between domain controllers in the local domain and partial domain information to a global catalog server independent of their domain. The global catalog replication includes only those account properties that are marked for global catalog replication to reduce the replication overhead. Global catalog servers contain a complete replica of all objects in the domain and a partial replica of all objects in the forest.

> **Note**   In a single-domain forest, there is no global catalog replication overhead because the domain is the forest root domain and contains all of the user, contact, and group accounts in the forest. Because all domain controllers have a full replica of the domain, they can all be configured as global catalog servers without increasing replication traffic.

Note that Exchange 2003 and MAPI-based clients direct almost all recipient-related Active Directory queries to global catalogs, such as those for client logons and resolving recipient information. Therefore, high-speed access to a global catalog server is key to an optimal Exchange and Outlook performance. In addition, you must ensure that the hardware of global catalog servers can cope with the increased workload that Exchange 2003 and MAPI-based clients place on Active Directory. For information about designing global catalog server hardware, see the book "Designing and Deploying Directory and Security Services" in the Windows Server 2003 Deployment Kit *(http://www.microsoft.com/ downloads/details.aspx?FamilyID=6CDE6EE7-5DF1-4394-92ED- 2147C3A9EBBE&displaylang=en)*.

- **Domain controllers**   Exchange 2003 also directs requests to domain controllers that are not operating as global catalog servers, for example, to obtain configuration information and to write configuration information. The domain controller that Exchange 2003 uses to write directory information is called the configuration domain controller. If domain controllers exist in the local site that are not configured as global catalog servers, then Exchange 2003 prefers one of these domain controllers as the configuration domain controller. Global catalog servers are the second choice, and domain controllers in other sites are the last choice, if no domain controller or global catalog server is available in the local site.

Note In a single-domain forest, there is no need for extra domain controllers, because all global catalog servers are also domain controllers that Exchange 2003 can use to read and write directory information.

Active Directory Load Balancing and Fault Tolerance

By default, only the first domain controller in a forest is a global catalog server, which is usually not a sufficient configuration for Exchange 2003. For example, the test environment discussed in Chapter 1, "Exchange Server 2003 Product Overview," has a severe weakness in that the entire environment relies on a single domain controller for all directory services configured as a global catalog server. If this server is down for any reason, Outlook clients cannot connect to Exchange 2003, because MAPI-based clients cannot log on to mailboxes without communicating with a global catalog server. Likewise, Exchange 2003 services cannot perform their functions.

Figure 2-11 shows critical errors that Exchange 2003 writes to the server's application event log if the Exchange server cannot access a domain controller or global catalog server. For a demonstration of the effects that Active Directory unavailability has on an Exchange 2003 organization, see the document Shutting down the one and only GC in a test environment.doc, which you can find in the \Companion Material\Chapter 02 folder on the companion CD.

To increase the resilience of an Exchange 2003 organization, you must deploy a minimum of two domain controllers and configure both as global catalog servers. Figure 2-12 illustrates an enhanced test environment with two global catalog servers. If SERVERDC01 is unavailable for any reason, Exchange 2003 can continue to communicate with Active Directory through SERVERDC02. For step-by-step instructions about how to add a second global catalog to a forest, see the document Adding a second GC to a test environment.doc, which you can find in the \Companion Material\Chapter 02 folder on the companion CD.

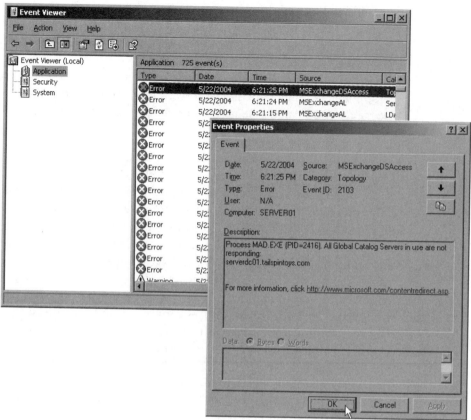

Figure 2-11   Critical errors resulting from Active Directory unavailability

Note   You should also configure all domain controllers in a forest with Exchange 2003 as DNS servers with Active Directory-integrated zones to provide fault tolerance for the DNS infrastructure. The document Adding a second GC to a test environment.doc outlines how to install a DNS server on an additional domain controller.

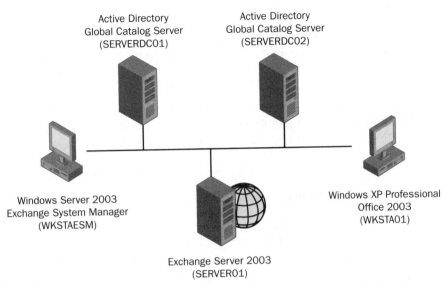

Figure 2-12   An Exchange 2003 test environment with two global catalog servers

Unless you are planning to deploy a single Exchange 2003 server directly on a domain controller, we recommend to have at least two global catalog servers in the computer network for load balancing and fault tolerance. In fact, we recommend that you have two global catalog servers in each site that contains Exchange servers. In a large site, you might want to deploy even more global catalog servers. Exchange 2003 can use a maximum of 10 global catalog servers to balance the load on a round-robin basis to avoid overloading a single global catalog server with directory queries. On the other hand, if there are no global catalog servers in the local site, or if none of the global catalog servers in the local site are available or considered operational, then Exchange servers use a maximum of 200 global catalog servers that are in other sites with lowest costs.

Exchange 2003 can load-balance configuration queries between up to 10 domain controllers in the local site as well. If there are no domain controllers in the local site, or if none of the domain controllers are available or considered operational, then Exchange 2003 uses up to 200 domain controllers that are in other sites with the lowest costs. However, while Exchange 2003 can read from multiple domain controllers concurrently, write operations are only directed to a single domain controller. This avoids conflicts when applying configuration changes to Active Directory. If the configuration domain controller becomes unavailable for any reason, then Exchange 2003 selects another domain controller as its configuration domain controller.

> **Note**   Unless you have installed Exchange 2003 on a domain controller or have hard-coded domain controllers and global catalog servers in the registry, Exchange 2003 re-evaluates and re-generates its list of global catalog servers and domain controllers every 15 minutes using a topology discovery process and suitability tests. For more information about how Exchange 2003 uses domain controllers and global catalog servers, see Chapter 9, "Managing Directory Information."

Message Routing Topology

The test environment depicted in Figure 2-12 does not require you to design a message routing topology, because the Exchange server does not need to route messages to deliver them from local senders to local recipients. Message routing is only required if you must use messaging connectors to transfer messages, but the Exchange server is able to send and receive messages without a messaging connector. If a connection to the Internet exists and if you integrate your internal DNS system with the public Internet DNS, the Exchange server can also send and receive messages to and from the Internet without a messaging connector.

When a user sends a message to an Internet recipient, the Exchange server performs a DNS lookup to find a mail exchanger (MX) host for the destination Simple Mail Transfer Protocol (SMTP) domain. When it discovers a target SMTP host, the server determines the IP address of that host, establishes an SMTP connection to that host, and then transfers the message across. To receive inbound messages, you also must register your Exchange server as an MX host in the Internet DNS. Remote SMTP hosts can then determine the IP address of your server, establish an inbound SMTP connection, and send your users e-mail messages. To protect your computer network, you must plan and deploy a firewall system, but you do not have to plan a topology for message routing or deploy any messaging connectors in an Exchange organization with just one server. For detailed information about connecting Exchange 2003 to the Internet, see the Exchange Server 2003 Transport and Routing Guide available at *http://www.microsoft.com/exchange/library.*

You likewise do not need to design a sophisticated routing topology if you deploy additional servers in the same location. By default, only a single routing group called First Routing Group exists in an Exchange organization, and all servers are added to this routing group during setup. Within a routing group, all servers communicate directly with each other, and if all servers are also able to communicate with hosts on the Internet, no configuration of messaging connectors is necessary to streamline message transfer. Figure 2-13 shows a test environment with multiple servers that do not require a sophisticated routing topology.

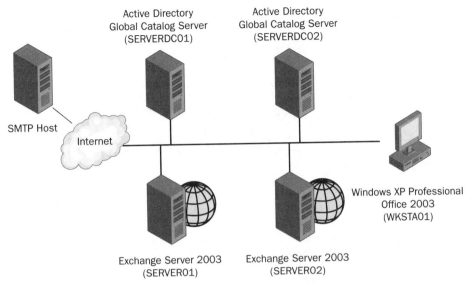

Figure 2-13   Two Exchange servers communicating directly over the Internet

Note   You should strive to design the routing topology of your Exchange 2003 organization with the least number of routing groups possible.

Defining a Smart Host for Internet Messaging

It is not a good idea to connect mailbox servers directly to the Internet, because this configuration exposes important messaging servers and data to viruses, worms, and other attacks from the Internet. It is better to implement a smart host for message transfer to and from the Internet that does not contain any mailboxes or data. This smart host might not even run Exchange 2003. The SMTP service of Windows 2003 can be configured to operate as a smart host, but you can also use a UNIX- or Linux-based Sendmail host. Figure 2-14 illustrates this configuration in a test environment.

Message transfer through a smart host has the advantage that you can perform virus scanning and junk e-mail blocking directly on this host before the messages actually reach the Exchange organization. It is also possible to isolate the smart host from the internal computer network by means of a perimeter network, separated from the Internet and from the internal network through firewalls (Figure 2-14). For information about how to secure an Exchange organization, see Chapter 13, "Implementing Exchange 2003 Security."

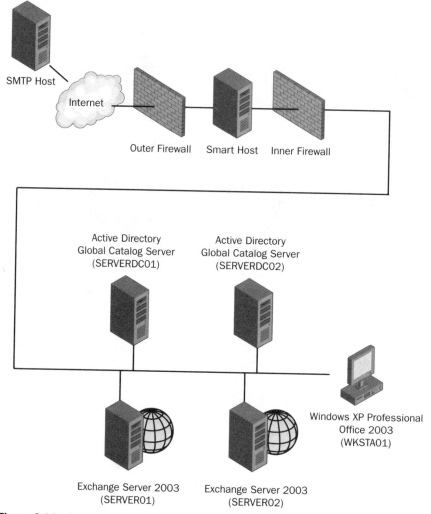

Figure 2-14   Sending and receiving Internet messages through a smart host

Internal Exchange servers only need to be able to communicate with the smart host over TCP port 25 for SMTP. All direct communication between the Internet and the internal Exchange servers can and should be blocked. For load balancing and fault tolerance, you can implement multiple smart hosts and cluster them using a network load balancing solution. The smart host is the only system that you must register in an MX record in the public DNS on the Internet. Internal Exchange servers do not have to be registered in the public DNS and are completely hidden from the Internet.

You have two options to force Exchange 2003 servers to forward all outbound messages to a smart host:

- **Virtual server forwarding**   Small organizations with only a single server running Exchange Server 2003 can send outbound messages directly to destinations in the Internet, or use a smart host at their Internet service provider (ISP). You can specify the smart host in the advanced delivery settings of your Exchange SMTP virtual server (Exchange System Manager, in the SMTP virtual server's properties, on the **Delivery** tab, click **Advanced**). In an organization with a single Exchange server, an explicit SMTP connector configuration is not required, unless your ISP has specific requirements, such as remote-triggered message transfer using the ETRN command.

- **SMTP Connector**   Configuring an explicit SMTP connector to the Internet is the recommended approach for organizations with multiple Exchange servers. As soon as you configure an SMTP connector in an Exchange organization with a general address space of SMTP:* for all messages to the Internet, all Exchange servers in the organization will stop sending messages directly and start routing SMTP messages over this connector. It is possible to specify single or multiple Exchange servers as local bridgehead servers for the SMTP connector. For information about how to use an SMTP connector to concentrate message traffic to the Internet, see the document Implementing a smart host in a test environment.doc, which you can find in the \Companion Material\Chapter 02 folder on the companion CD.

Defining a Central Smart Host in a Dispersed Environment

Although it might sound surprising, separate routing groups are also not required in an Exchange organization with regional offices as long as each regional office has only a single Exchange mailbox server. Implementing separate routing groups in this situation has no advantage. Routing groups are supposed to group multiple servers together for the purpose of message routing. If only a single Exchange server exists in each location, there is no need to "group" each server using a separate routing group. Placing each server in a separate routing group does not improve WAN link usage.

Figure 2-15 illustrates an environment with mailbox servers in separate locations, but all placed in the default routing group.

Exchange 2003 can accomplish the message transfer successfully and efficiently if all servers are configured as local bridgeheads for the SMTP connector to the smart host. All outbound SMTP message transfer is then direct, but you can also implement a central bridgehead if you prefer a more indirect routing path. For inbound messages, the smart host can deliver the messages to any server based on MX records in DNS. The Exchange servers will forward messages to each other if the recipients are on other servers. This is no different from Exchange users on different servers sending each other messages.

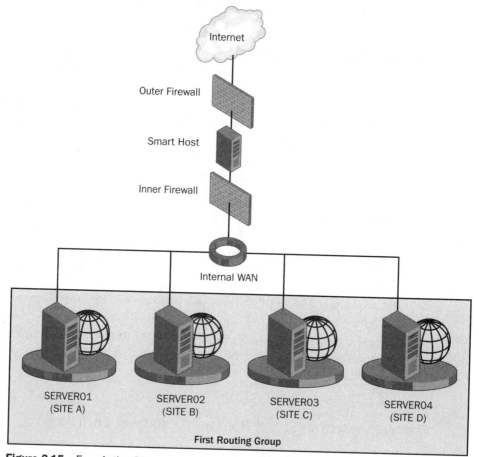

Figure 2-15   Four Active Directory sites, but one Exchange routing group

Figure 2-15 is a perfect example of how Active Directory sites do not necessarily match the routing group topology. The internal WAN may not support RPCs, for example, thus forcing you to implement separate Active Directory sites for directory replication over SMTP. However, Exchange 2003 servers do not have RPC dependencies, because these servers always communicate with each other over SMTP. Remember, however, that Exchange 2003 servers must also be able to establish a TCP/IP connection to the routing group master over TCP port 691. The routing group master is a special role that a single Exchange 2003 server assumes in each routing group. For information about how to configure an Exchange server as a routing group master, see the document Changing the routing group master in a test environment.doc, which you can find in the \Companion Material\Chapter 02 folder on the companion CD.

Note In Exchange 2003, server-to-server communication works well over any type of TCP/IP connection. Therefore, a routing group does not necessarily define regions on a computer network with high network bandwidth. Routing groups can span a slow network connection, if the connection is permanent and reliable.

Implementing Multiple Routing Groups

There are a number of reasons that you might be forced to implement separate routing groups in an Exchange organization, including:

- **WAN communication generates costs** All Exchange servers in a routing group periodically poll the routing group master, which is especially important if communication over WAN connections generates costs. To minimize costs, you might want to schedule oversize message transfer for off-peak hours, for example, or control the server-to-server communication in other ways that require implementing multiple routing groups.

- **WAN uses dial-up connections** Exchange 2003 does not support dial-up connections directly. Instead, Exchange uses dial-up connections by means of Routing and Remote Access Service (RRAS). Hence, if you want to connect to a remote location over an on-demand dial-up connection, you need to install and configure your modem or Integrated Services Digital Network (ISDN) card on a server that will act as a demand-dial network router. In this configuration, Exchange 2003 is not aware that a dial-up connection exists. The server polls the routing group master in the routing group as if it were using a LAN connection. To avoid unnecessary connection establishment due to polling, place the servers on either side of the dial-up connection in separate routing groups.

- **No connections over TCP ports 25 and 691** If your network locations are connected with each other over a WAN that does not support TCP/IP, such as an X.25 packet switching network, you must implement a separate routing group for each location. To connect the individual routing groups over the X.25, you must use X.400 connectors.

Note X.400 connectors are available only in Exchange Server 2003 Enterprise Edition.

- **Unstable connections over TCP ports 25 and 691**   If you have some servers in your computer network that are connected by a slower or unstable WAN link, it is best to group these servers in a separate routing group. One server with unreliable network connectivity in a single routing group can generate link state traffic to trigger updates to the message routing tables on all other servers. Because all other servers need to be notified if this server or a routing group connector on this server becomes unavailable, the routing group master (the server that is responsible for communicating information about the routing topology to servers within a routing group) must propagate changes in this server's status to all the servers in the routing group. For more information about link state traffic and updates to the message routing table, see Chapter 14, "Streamlining Message Routing."

- **Imposing administrative restrictions on message transfer**   Messaging connectors enable you to configure delivery restrictions and content restrictions. Using delivery restrictions, you can specify users who are allowed to send messages across a connector and users who are rejected. Content restrictions enable you to define what priority (low, normal, or high) and what message types (system and non-system messages) you want to support. You can also define a message size limit for a routing group connector, which might be a good idea over slow network links.

  Be aware that enabling delivery restrictions on messaging connectors is extremely process-intensive and can affect server performance. For each message that is sent through this connector, distribution groups must be expanded to their individual recipients to enforce the restriction. This expansion is costly in terms of performance. Therefore, we recommend that you use delivery restrictions on a connector only in cases in which distribution groups are small or you are certain that the performance impact is acceptable to your users.

  An alternative that avoids the performance impact is using routing groups to restrict messaging connectors to a subset of users in the Exchange organization. This is achieved by designating a routing group scope for the connector. In Figure 2-16, for example, you can restrict the scope of the SMTP connector to the first routing group to prevent users in the second routing group from using this Internet connection. This might make sense if the second routing group has its own Internet connection and you want the users in each routing group to use only their local Internet access points.

- **Exchange organization with multiple administrative groups running in mixed mode**   In mixed mode, routing groups can only contain servers from the local administrative group for backward compatibility with Exchange Server 5.5. Hence, if you have servers in multiple administrative groups and you have Exchange 5.5 in the organization, you must implement at least one separate routing group for each administrative group.

■ **Separate locations with multiple mailbox servers** Exchange servers in the same routing group always transfer messages directly to the target server. If a user sends a message to recipients on multiple of servers, this means that the source server must send the message multiple times. In a process called bifurcation, Exchange 2003 creates a separate message copy for each destination, places the relevant subset of recipients on each message copy, and transfers each message copy individually to its target server. By grouping the target servers together by means of a separate routing group, you can eliminate redundant message traffic over slow or expensive WAN connections.

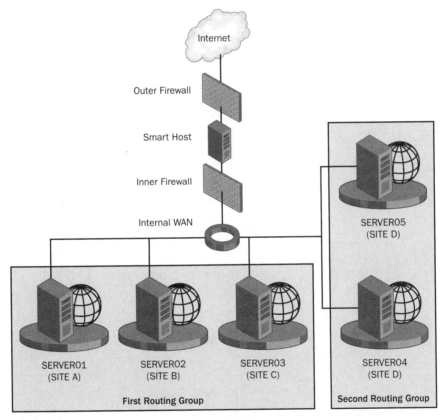

Figure 2-16 An Exchange organization with two routing groups

Figure 2-16 shows the environment of Figure 2-15 with a second Exchange mailbox server in site D. To avoid redundant message traffic over the internal WAN connection, a second routing group is used to group the servers in site D (SERVER04 and SERVER05) together to create a single node for the purpose of message routing. All other servers remain in the first routing group. For step-by-step instructions about how to create a separate routing group and place Exchange servers in that routing group, see the document Creating a routing group topology in a test environment.doc, which you can find in the \Companion Material\Chapter 02 folder on the companion CD.

If a user in the first routing group now sends a message to recipients on SERVER04 and SERVER05, the message is first transferred as a single instance over the WAN to the second routing group using a routing group connector. The Exchange 2003 source server transfers the message only once instead of twice, and WAN bandwidth is preserved. The receiving bridgehead server in the second routing group then bifurcates the message, delivers one copy to the recipients on the local server, and transfers the other message copy to the second server in the routing group. For example, if SERVER04 is used as the bridgehead, then SERVER04 forwards the message to SERVER05 for the subset of all those recipients that have their mailboxes on SERVER05, as illustrated in Figure 2-17.

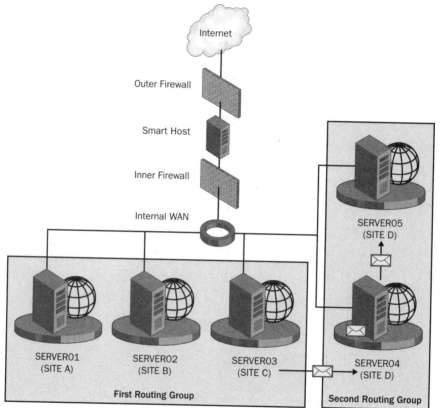

Figure 2-17 Preserving WAN bandwidth by concentrating message traffic through bridgehead servers

Defining Routing Group Boundaries

As a general guideline, you should define additional routing groups only when necessary. The fewer routing groups you have, the less complex and more manageable the Exchange organization is. You can use the flowchart shown in Figure 2-18 to determine appropriate routing group boundaries.

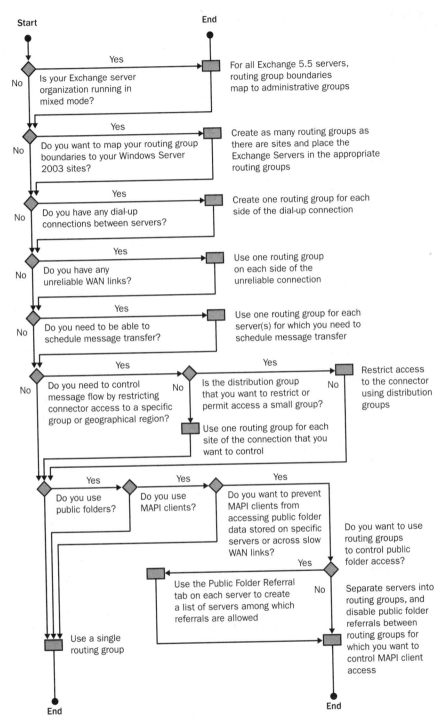

Figure 2-18 Determining routing group boundaries

Routing Group Connectors

Message transfer does not take place between routing groups without an explicit configuration of a routing group connector. Note that routing group connectors are one-way routes for outgoing messages, which means that messages travel outbound to the connected routing group. For two routing groups to communicate, a routing group connector must exist in each routing group to send messages outbound to the other routing group.

The following Exchange connectors can be used to establish message transfer paths between routing groups:

- **Routing Group Connector**   A Routing Group Connector provides a one-way connection path in which messages are routed from servers in one routing group to servers in another routing group. Routing Group Connectors use SMTP to communicate with servers in connected routing groups. Routing Group Connectors provide the best connection between routing groups.

- **SMTP connector**   An SMTP connector can be used to connect routing groups, but this is not recommended. SMTP connectors are designed for external message delivery. SMTP connectors define specific paths for e-mail messages that are destined for the Internet or an external destination, such as a non-Exchange messaging system.

- **X.400 connectors**   Although you can use X.400 connectors to connect routing groups, X.400 connectors are designed to connect Exchange servers with other X.400 systems or to servers running Exchange Server 5.5 outside an Exchange organization. An Exchange 2003 server can then send messages over this connector using the X.400 protocol.

Note   The Routing Group Connector (note the capitalization) is a specific type of connector that can only be used to connect routing groups with each other. Other connectors that can connect routing groups are the SMTP connector and X.400 connector. However, these connectors can also be used to connect an Exchange organization to an external messaging system through SMTP or X.400. To avoid confusion, the Resource Kit uses the "Routing Group Connector" to refer to the specific connector that can only be used between routing groups and "Routing Group Connector" to refer to all types of connectors that can be used to connect routing groups.

Load Balancing and Fault Tolerance through Multiple Bridgehead Servers

Load balancing between routing groups can be achieved using one Routing Group Connector with multiple bridgehead servers or using multiple routing group connectors with individual bridgehead servers. The recommended approach is to use one Routing Group Connector with multiple bridgehead servers. For example, in Figure 2-17, SERVER04 and SERVER05 can be specified as remote bridgehead servers for a Routing Group Connector in the first routing group. If SERVER04 is down for some reason, the bridgehead in the first routing group can still transfer the message to the second routing group using SERVER05 and all users on SERVER05 will receive the message. When SERVER04 is restarted, SERVER05 will then transfer the message to SERVER04 if the message contained recipients on that server.

Figure 2-19 shows a Routing Group Connector with two remote bridgehead servers. Exchange 2003 can in this case randomly select the bridgehead server that should be used for each particular message, thereby load balancing the message transfer across all bridgehead servers. It is best to specify multiple source and destination bridgeheads for a single routing group connector between two routing groups. This practice improves load balancing and fault tolerance.

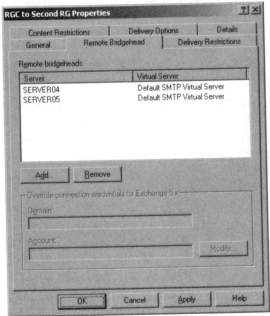

Figure 2-19   Multiple remote bridgeheads for a Routing Group Connector

When you create a routing group connector, you have the option of either keeping all the servers as bridgehead servers for that connector, or specifying that only a selected set of servers act as bridgehead servers for that connector. Table 2-4 compares the advantages of each approach.

Table 2-4   Selecting the Number of Bridgehead Servers in a Routing Group

Number of bridgehead servers	Advantages
All servers in a routing group	■ Provides more efficient message flow, because all of the servers in the routing group can directly deliver messages to other routing groups.
	■ Capitalizes on configurations where all of the servers in a routing group have the same network connectivity to the servers in other routing groups.
	■ Direct point-to-point connectivity can provide load balancing.
Only a select few servers in a routing group	■ Makes troubleshooting message flow easier because there are limited points of contact between routing groups.
	■ Distributes messaging if you anticipate heavy message flow between routing groups.
	■ Allows you to specify server roles of bridgehead servers and mailbox servers in large environments where you do not want mailbox servers handling the traffic sent through a bridgehead server.
	■ Makes mail flow more reliable and efficient in those configurations where some servers have better network connectivity than others.

True load balancing is not achieved when configuring multiple connectors to the same routing group, each with a single source and destination bridgehead server. Exchange 2003 calculates the routing path only one time, selects on available connector, caches this information, and then routes all messages of the same type over the same connector. The second connector is used only if the first connector fails. However, a second server might select the second connector and in this way balance the load to some degree.

Exchange 2003 also cannot distinguish between local and remote routing group connectors. This can lead to a situation in which a server transfers the messages for the connected routing group to another source bridgehead server, even if the local server is also a source bridgehead that could transfer the message. This could lead to inefficient message transfer, and so it is not a good idea to use multiple connector instances between routing groups for load balancing. You can only achieve true load balancing with a Routing Group Connector that uses multiple source and remote bridgeheads.

Note Only the Routing Group Connector supports multiple source and remote bridgeheads. X.400 connectors and SMTP connectors can only connect a single source bridgehead to a single remote bridgehead.

Designing Routing Group Topologies

After you identify the server locations that you want to represent through individual routing groups, you can approach the task of designing the message routing topology of your Exchange organization. Designing a routing group topology is a two-step process:

1. *Outlining the routing group topology* You should design the routing group topology along the physical links of your computer network. Figure 2-20 illustrates how a questionable message routing topology can lead to increased network traffic and waste of bandwidth. In the example, Headquarters was chosen as a central message routing hub, although the physical network topology included separate network segments with multiple routers in a chain-like arrangement between the regional offices and the headquarters. As a result, messages sent from Regional Office A to Regional Office B unnecessarily flow back and forth through the network segments between Regional Office B and Headquarters. This is clearly not a desirable message routing topology. To solve this problem, Regional Office A should connect to Regional Office B in addition to Headquarters.

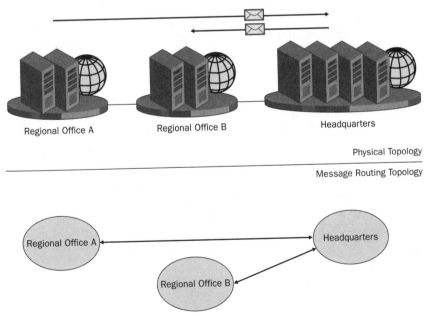

Figure 2-20 An inefficient message routing topology

2.   *Connecting the routing groups*   Subsequently, you must determine the appropriate type of routing group connector to use between any two routing groups in the topology. It is not required to standardize on a single connector type in your Exchange organization, but we recommend using Routing Group Connector wherever possible for its support of multiple source and remote bridgehead servers. X.400 connector and SMTP connector are secondary choices.

Hierarchical Versus Meshed Routing Group Topologies

The challenge in designing a routing group topology is to determine how to connect the routing groups together for optimal message transfer. There are several message routing topologies that you can choose from, including:

- **Chain**   A routing group chain is a message routing topology in which routing groups are connected with each other in a linear fashion. For example, the inefficient message routing topology depicted in Figure 2-20 features a routing group chain: Regional Office A - Headquarters - Regional Office B. It is important to understand that routing group chains do not scale well to a large number of routing groups. Consider this chain: RG A - RG B - RG C - RG D - RG E. It could not be any more indirect and slow to get a message from A to E.

- **Full mesh**   A much better choice than a routing group chain is to connect all routing groups directly with each other. For example, by introducing a routing group connector between Regional Office A and Regional Office B you can resolve the inefficient message transfer issue discussed above. However, the full mesh also does not scale well to a large number of routing groups. For example, in an Exchange organization with just six routing groups (RG A through RG F), you would have to configure 35 connectors. Keep in mind that you must configure routing group connectors in each routing group separately.

- **Hub–spoke**   In a hub–spoke topology, a central routing group assumes the role of a message switch. This central routing group is called the hub. Smaller branch office locations then connect to this hub only. There are no direct connections between the branch offices. The routing group connections between the hub and the branch offices represent the spokes in this topology. For example, in Figure 2-20, adding a third regional office to Headquarters would result in a hub–spoke arrangement in which Headquarters is the hub. Typically, all servers in the central hub are grouped together in a single routing group where all servers have reliable network connectivity.

The most significant advantage of the hub–spoke architecture is its scalability. You must configure only a minimum number of routing group connectors to gain total control over the message transfer. All messages to recipients in other routing groups traverse through the hub because alternate paths between any two routing groups do not exist. Routing groups that have only a single inbound routing group connector and a single outbound routing group connector in exact opposite direction are often called leaf-node routing groups. If no alternate path exists for a connector that connects to or from a leaf-node routing group, Exchange 2003 considers the connector state as always available. Exchange 2003 no longer changes the connector state to unavailable if the connector is down but no alternate path exists. Instead, Exchange queues mail for delivery and sends it when the connector becomes available again. This change enhances performance because it reduces the propagation of link state changes, which is particularly relevant in a distributed messaging environment with a large number of routing groups. No link state traffic is generated, and the network is not affected.

The most significant disadvantage of this hierarchical routing topology is, however, that this architecture may not reflect the network infrastructure very well. For example, Regional Office A and Regional Office B would again communicate inefficiently with each other. There is also the disadvantage that Exchange 2003 cannot perform message rerouting in case a connector is down, because alternate paths between any two routing groups do not exist. Furthermore, if the hub routing group is unavailable, all message transfer between routing groups stops. For this reason, it is vital to deploy multiple bridgeheads in the hub routing group.

- **Hybrid** If your Exchange organization is too complex to configure routing group connectors between all routing groups, but you want to avoid inefficient message transfer in a hub-spoke arrangement, you can create routing topology of fully meshed sub-backbones in a global hub-spoke arrangement. This allows you to route messages optimally, according to the WAN topology of your network. Large companies often use X.400 to establish a global messaging backbone that connects fully meshed local messaging system together, but you can also use SMTP. Figure 2-21 shows a hybrid routing group design.

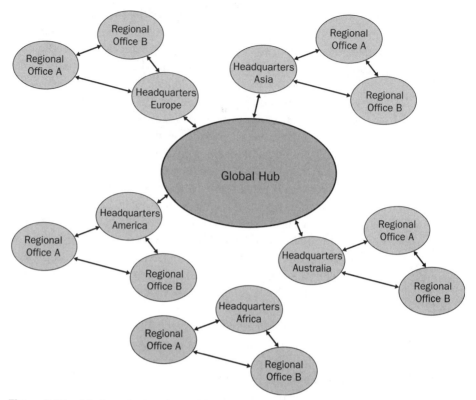

Figure 2-21   A hub-spoke topology of fully meshed sub-backbones

Connecting Routing Groups

After you determine the desired routing group topology, you can connect the routing groups through appropriate connectors. You should consider the following questions:

- **To which routing group does this connector deliver messages?**   This information is critical. Identifying the routing group to which the connector delivers messages establishes the relationship between the sending and receiving routing groups and the rest of your topology. You need to know how the sending and receiving routing groups fit into your topology so you can determine a cost for the associated connector.

- **What cost should this connector have?**   Cost is the variable that Exchange uses to determine the most efficient messaging route. Exchange considers the lowest cost route the most efficient. Exchange uses a more expensive route only if a server or connector is unavailable on the route with the lowest cost. You should assign the lowest costs to the routes with the highest available network bandwidth.

- **Which servers in the routing group can act as bridgehead servers?** Only designated bridgehead servers can send messages across the connector to the connected routing group. The default and preferred setting is to have the servers in the local routing group send mail using this connector. Use this default option when all servers in the routing group can connect directly over the network to the remote bridgehead server and share the same messaging load. Connecting directly to the remote bridgehead server provides more efficient message flow. However, you may have better direct network connectivity between specific servers in the local routing group and the designated remote bridgehead server. In this case, you should specify the servers that have the better direct network connectivity as the bridgehead servers.

- **What are the remote bridgehead servers to which this connector can send messages?** The remote bridgehead servers are the servers in the connected routing group that receive all messages destined for this routing group. The remote bridgehead servers also receive link state information from the bridgehead servers for the connector.

Server Infrastructure

Within each routing group, you must decide what types of servers to deploy. By default, every Exchange 2003 server is a mailbox and a public folder server, and as mentioned, you can also use all servers in a routing group as bridgehead servers. With so many responsibilities, however, the servers might not be able to achieve top performance. As the number of users per server increases, splitting the roles across several servers becomes an interesting alternative. Designing a server infrastructure using dedicated server configurations gives you the ability to dedicate the server hardware to specific tasks, and it allows you to structure the administration according to individual server roles. For instance, you could install all bridgehead servers in a separate administrative group and delegate full control permissions to routing administrators only.

Dedicated Mailbox Servers

The mailbox server is at the core of an Exchange 2003 organization, so you should design the server hardware generously to prepare for future growth. You might want to consider additional processors with two gigabytes (GB) or more of memory and a reliable storage subsystem based on a redundant array of independent disks (RAID) that has a capacity of at least two or three times the estimated size of your messaging databases. You might also want to cluster mailbox servers using Windows Clustering service. For more information about configuring mailbox servers for a large number of users, see Chapter 6, "Server and Site Consolidation Strategies."

The following factors influence your Exchange server hardware design:

- **Connected users versus total users**   When you design server hardware, estimate how many users will connect to the server concurrently. Performance requirements might be lower if not all users connect at the same time, for example, if users work in shifts. However, the server background activity increases as the number of mailboxes increases, even when users are not logged on to the system. For example, database defragmentation activity increases on a server storing thousands of mailboxes. Always consider background activities when you design server hardware.

- **Location and use of message stores**   Exchange users can store their messages in server-based mailboxes or in personal folders (.pst files) on their local client computers or on a network drive. Users can reduce a server's storage and processing workload by setting their default delivery locations for messages to their personal folders. For example, when a user opens or saves an item in a personal folder, the Microsoft Exchange Information Store service on the server is not involved. However, when you decide whether to use personal folders in this way, consider the fact that storing all messages in personal folder stores on local client computers makes it impossible to back up messages centrally.

> **Note**   To require users to store messages in .pst files on their client computers, configure mailbox quotas for the mailbox stores. If a mailbox exceeds its size limits, the user must reduce the amount of data by downloading messages to the .pst file or deleting them. Otherwise, the user cannot continue to receive and send e-mail messages.

- **User habits and messaging clients**   When you design server hardware, consider the number of messages users send and receive per day. Also consider the types of clients that they use. Outlook 2003 and Outlook Web Access 2003 place different workloads on a server. If your users primarily use Outlook Web Access 2003, assume additional processing requirements for Internet Information Services (IIS).

Table 2-5 lists general processor and memory configuration recommendations for mailbox servers.

Table 2-5   Processor and Memory Configurations for Mailbox Servers

Number of Users	CPUs	Memory
Fewer than 500	1 – 2	512 MB – 1 GB
500 – 1,000	2 – 4	1 GB – 2 GB
1,000 – 2,500	4 – 8	2 GB – 4 GB
2,500 or more	4 – 8	4 GB

The figures in Table 2-5 are recommendations for an optimal configuration, but it is also possible to support a greater number of users and at the same time use less hardware. To make the best use of server hardware, you can configure dedicated mailbox servers. A dedicated mailbox server is a server where all public folder stores are removed and only mailbox stores exist. However, when configuring dedicated mailbox servers, keep in mind that at least one public folder store must exist in the organization that is associated with the MAPI-based public folder hierarchy. It is not possible to remove the public folder stores from all Exchange servers in the organization.

To determine the number of mailboxes you can place on a server, use the following capacity planning tools:

■ **Capacity Planning and Topology Calculator**   The Capacity Planning and Topology Calculator helps you determine the size of the servers that you need for your Exchange 2000 or Exchange 2003 topology. The Capacity Planning and Topology Calculator can be found at *http://go.microsoft.com/fwlink/ ?LinkId=1716.*

■ **Microsoft Exchange Server Load Simulation Tool (LoadSim.exe)**   With Microsoft Exchange LoadSim, you can simulate the load of MAPI clients against Exchange. You simulate the load by running LoadSim tests on client computers. These tests send messaging requests to the Exchange server, causing a load on the server. For more information about the LoadSim tool or to download Load-Sim, see the "Load Simulator" section of Microsoft Exchange 2000 Server Resource Kit *(http://go.microsoft.com/fwlink/?LinkId=1710).*

■ **Exchange Stress and Performance (ESP) tool**   The Exchange Stress and Performance tool (ESP) is a highly scalable stress and performance tool for Exchange. It simulates large numbers of client sessions by concurrently accessing one or more protocol services. Scripts control the actions that each simulated user takes. The scripts contain the logic for communicating with the server. Test modules, dynamic link libraries (DLLs), then run these scripts. Test modules connect to a server through Internet protocols, call to application programming interfaces (APIs), or through interfaces like OLE DB. For more information about the ESP tool or to download ESP, see the Microsoft Exchange 2003 Tools and Updates website *(http://go.microsoft.com/fwlink/?LinkId=21316).*

- **Jetstress (Jetstress.exe)**   Exchange 2003 is a disk-intensive application that requires a fast, reliable disk subsystem to function correctly. Jetstress is a tool in Exchange to help administrators verify the performance and stability of the disk subsystem prior to putting their Exchange server into production. The Jetstress tool can be found at *http://www.microsoft.com/downloads/details.aspx?FamilyId=94B9810B-670E-433A-B5EF-B47054595E9C&displaylang=en.*

> **Warning**   Because some of these tools create accounts that have insecure passwords, these tools are intended for use in test environments, not in production environments.

Dedicated Public Folder Servers

The public folder design is an important aspect of every Exchange organization, even if you do not plan to use public folders for discussion boards or workgroup applications, because the public folder store also contains important system folders, such as the Schedule+ free/busy folder and offline address book folder. In general, we recommend deploying a dedicated public folder server for administrative groups that contain more than three mailbox servers. The public folder server, in turn, does not have to host any mailboxes, but it does require a mailbox store, because internal message queues are maintained in the mailbox store. You can then configure the mailbox servers to use the dedicated public folders server as the default public folder store. For step-by-step instructions about how to separate mailbox and public folder server tasks, see the document Configuring a dedicated public folder server in a test environment.doc, which you can find in the \Companion Material\Chapter 02 folder on the companion CD.

In an environment with multiple locations, you have the following options for public folder placement:

- **Public folder server in remote locations**   Public folder replication allows you to address network topology issues. If a direct connection to a remote public folder server is not possible, you can place public folder replicas on local Exchange servers so each location has a replica of public folders from other locations. Replicas are useful for distributing the user load on servers, distributing public folders across geographical areas, and backing up public folder data. All replicas of a public folder are equal, so there is no master replica.

   Table 2-6 lists the advantages and disadvantages of placing public folder instances on public folder servers in each routing group.

Table 2-6   Advantages and Disadvantages of Replicated Public Folders

Advantages	Disadvantages
The public folder is available in all locations for local access.	New items posted in a public folder instance are not immediately available in all other locations due to public folder replication latency.
Client access over WAN connections is eliminated.	Public folder replication latency increases the chance of conflicts due to concurrent changes to existing items in multiple public folder instances.
Fault tolerance between multiple servers is available.	Public folder replication must be configured manually, but new subfolders inherit the settings of their parent folders.
Load balancing between multiple servers is possible.	Public folder replication relies on e-mail messages and increases message traffic.
Public folder replication can be scheduled.	

■ **Public folder server in data center**   You can also store all public folders on a public folder server in the data center or hub so you maintain a single source of data. Within the routing group of the central public folder server, users can work with the public folders directly. Between routing groups, however, public folder referrals determine whether access to public folder servers in other routing groups is allowed. By default, public folder referrals are enabled across connectors connecting routing groups. However, network traffic increases when users access a public folder in a remote routing group. If your routing groups are connected by slow network links, or if your network might not be able to handle the additional traffic, you should disable public folder referrals and replicate the public folders to a public folder server in each routing group.

Table 2-7 lists the advantages and disadvantages of placing public folder instances on central public folder server in a data center routing group.

Table 2-7   Advantages and Disadvantages of Non-replicated Public Folders

Advantages	Disadvantages
Public folder maintenance is centralized because only one public store is affected.	Bottlenecks in public folder access are possible if the public folder server is overtaxed.
No additional disk space on further servers is required.	Public folders are not available during server maintenance or unplanned downtime.
There is no overhead or latency due to public folder replication.	Underlying network topology determines quality of public folder access.

Be aware that potentially all users in an organization may access a central public folder server. For this reason, you should design public folder servers generously. If you decide to consolidate public folder servers in a data center, you must configure public folder referrals so users in other routing groups can gain access. You have the following two options to configure public folder referrals on an Exchange server (Figure 2-22):

■ *Use Routing Groups* If you choose to use routing groups for public folder referrals, the routing group connector determines whether access to the central public folder server is allowed. Every routing group connector provides a Do Not Allow Public Folder Referrals setting, which, if enabled, denies public folder access across the routing group boundary. The cost value of the connector establishes the public folder affinity. If multiple routing groups exist, the lowest cost determines the preferred routing group in which to look for the folder contents. Keep in mind that public folder referrals are transitive. If access is allowed between routing group A and routing group B, and between routing groups B and C, then it is implicitly allowed between groups A and C.

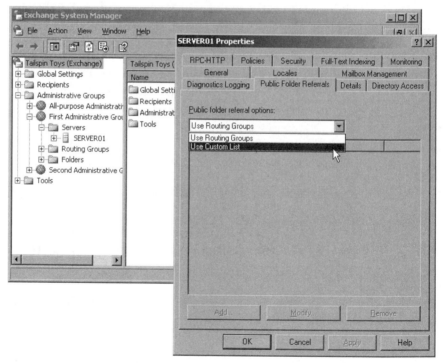

Figure 2-22   Public folder referral options

■ *Use Custom List* If you choose to use a custom list for public folder referrals, you can use the Public Folder Referrals tab in the server's properties dialog box to specify the central public folder directly. If you have replicated the public folders between multiple public folder servers, you can specify each server with a cost value to establish a preferred public folder server. You can also assign all public folder servers the same cost value for load balancing.

Note   Access to public folders is subject to the latency inherent in your network connections. If the locations are connected by low-bandwidth, high-latency network connections, public folder access does not benefit from cached Exchange mode the way that mailbox access does. Unlike mailbox data, public folder data is not cached locally on the client computer (unless you add a public folder to your offline "Favorites," which are kept synchronized with the server's data). Therefore, requests for public folder data are directed over the remote connection to an Exchange server in the data center.

Dedicated Bridgehead Servers

It is not unusual to deploy dedicated bridgehead servers in routing groups to offload the workload for message transfer to other routing groups from mailbox and public folder servers. Besides routing group connectors, bridgeheads might also host connectors to non-Exchange messaging systems. It is important to note that bridgeheads require at least one mailbox store because the message queues of many connectors reside in the Exchange store. Many message queues are located in hidden system mailboxes.

If you intend to build large routing groups with a significant number of users who communicate heavily with users in other routing groups and external messaging systems, bear in mind that there is a high risk of overwhelming a single bridgehead server. Growing message queues and delays in message transfer are indicators of this problem. The workload on bridgeheads can be very high. Message routing requires the bridgehead server to frequently retrieve routing information from Active Directory. Messages addressed to recipients in different routing groups must be bifurcated into separate copies, and message transfer to non-Exchange messaging systems requires conversion of recipient information and message formats. If the sum of these activities represents a substantial workload, configure multiple bridgehead servers to run the connectors. Very large organizations often opt to run no more than one connector per bridgehead.

Special Purpose Servers

Besides mailbox, public folder, and connector servers, an Exchange organization also contains servers with very specialized purposes. This includes the following server roles:

- **Routing group masters**   Coordinate the update of message routing tables on all servers in the routing group. For more information about the role of a routing group master in a routing group, see Chapter 14, "Understanding and Configuring Message Routing and Transport."

- **Site replication servers**   Run the site replication service (SRS) in a mixed mode organization to replicate configuration information with Exchange 5.5. For information about how to integrate Exchange 2003 with Exchange 5.5, see Chapter 4, "Upgrading to Exchange Server 2003."

- **Recipient update servers**   Run the recipient update service in each domain of your forest to stamp new Exchange users with e-mail addresses as defined in a recipient policy. For details about the recipient update service, see Chapter 9, "Managing Directory Information,"

- **Offline address book servers**   Stores the offline address lists that Outlook users can download to have address information available when working in offline mode. You should choose an appropriate server to generate and update offline address lists. For increased server performance, select a server that is not busy performing other tasks. If you use cached Exchange mode, you should consider the impact on the server when users download offline address lists. This impact could be significant. Not only do first-time users download offline address lists, but users on a daily basis download these lists. You may want to consider setting up one or two public folder servers to handle offline address books. The offline address book folder is a hidden system folder stored in the public folder store. For step-by-step instructions about how to configure replication settings for the offline address book folder, see the document Replicating offline address lists between multiple servers.doc, which you can find in the \Companion Material\Chapter 02 folder on the companion CD.

- **Free/busy folder servers**   Stores the Schedule+ free/busy folders of your administrative groups. The Schedule+ free/busy folder is a hidden system folder in the public folder store that contains information that Exchange users can use to view the availability of others when scheduling meetings. Access to free/busy information is therefore an important design consideration. For step-by-step instructions about how to configure replication settings for Schedule+ free/busy folders, see the document Replicating free/busy information between multiple servers.doc, which you can find in the \Companion Material\Chapter 02 folder on the companion CD.

Each administrative group has one free/busy folder. If your administrative model calls for multiple administrative groups, you can place replicas of free/busy folders from any or all of the other administrative groups on a free/busy folder server in each routing group. Replication occurs just as it does for regular public folders. Because each administrative group has one free/busy folder and an administrative group can span multiple routing groups, you might need to add a folder replica in each routing group. Replicating all free/busy folders to a public folder server in each routing group ensures that free/busy information is always available locally. If you decide not to replicate a Schedule+ free/busy folder to a public folder server in the local routing group, be sure to verify the public folder referrals configuration. Remember that if users must access free/busy folder data over WAN connections, they might experience a delay in receiving other users' free/busy information when scheduling meetings.

- **Front-end servers**   Proxy incoming connections of Internet-based clients to back-end servers where the mailboxes reside. You can read more about front-end server configurations in Chapter 07, "Hosting Exchange Server 2003."

Remote Access Topology

If you are planning to provide remote and mobile users with access to mailboxes and public folders over Internet or dial-up connections, you must design a client access topology that outlines how firewalls and remote access servers are arranged to support remote connections in a secure way. For detailed information about how to use the Internet to best support remote and mobile users, see Chapter 11, "Connecting to the Internet."

You have the following options to provide remote and mobile users with access to an Exchange organization:

- **Virtual private network (VPN) connections**   VPNs are a good solution for remote users who request full connectivity to the internal network. VPNs leverage TCP/IP-based networks, such as the Internet, to connect remote clients and offices through an encrypted channel, known as a tunnel or VPN connection. When the data enters the VPN connection, the IP data packets are placed in Point-to-Point Protocol (PPP) or Layer 2 Tunneling Protocol (L2TP) frames, which in turn are encapsulated into IP datagrams before they are sent over the network. When the data leaves the VPN connection on the receiving side, it is decrypted. Clients and servers are not aware that tunneling took place.

- **RPC over HTTP**   RPC over HTTPS connections are a good solution for remote users who want to use Outlook over the Internet, but who do not need to access any other services in the internal network. Configuring Exchange to use RPC over HTTP involves deploying an RPC proxy server. The RPC proxy server then handles all RPC over HTTP requests on behalf of the client and proxies the request to the appropriate back-end resource. Additionally, back-end resources, including the global catalog server and the back-end Exchange servers, must be specially configured to communicate with the RPC proxy server. RPC over HTTPS is covered in Chapter 11, "Connecting to the Internet."

- **Front-end servers** Front-end servers are useful in Exchange organizations with multiple mailbox servers that want to provide a single namespace to users of Internet-based messaging clients. Without a front-end server, each user must know the name of the server that stores his or her mailbox. This need to know the server name complicates administration and compromises flexibility, because every time your organization grows or changes and you move some or all mailboxes to another server, you must inform the users. With a single namespace, users can use the same URL or POP and IMAP client configuration, even if you add or remove servers or move mailboxes from server to server. In addition, creating a single namespace ensures that Outlook Web Access, POP, or IMAP access remains scalable as your organization grows. You can read more about front-end server configurations in Chapter 7, "Hosting Exchange Server 2003."

- **Terminal server** Over slow or unreliable network connections, you might want to consider using Remote Desktop to connect to a server running Terminal Services in the internal network. The server runs the actual client applications directly in the internal network, so users using Remote Desktop can work as if they were sitting directly in front of an office workstation. Using Remote Desktop over unreliable connections has the advantage that connectivity problems do not affect the client applications running on the server. If the terminal server connection drops for any reasons, Outlook keeps running on the server. When the user reconnects, the user can continue working at the point where the work was interrupted.

Best Practices

When planning the placement of Exchange servers and the administration of directories and servers, it is usually recommended that you start with a centralized model and add servers, routing groups, and administrative groups only when necessary. With the features available in Exchange 2003, Windows Server 2003, and Outlook 2003, businesses may be encouraged to adopt more centralized messaging systems than were possible in the past. In addition, with the proliferation of higher speed and higher bandwidth connections, companies composed of geographically dispersed offices can consider centralizing their hardware and administration so they can reduce the number of servers required in remote locations.

Keep the following recommendations in mind when designing your Exchange organization:

- **Centralize the hardware that serves remote offices**   Your might want to consolidate your sites and administrative groups to reduce operational costs. Exchange 2003 has a number of features that facilitate this task. In addition, cached Exchange mode in Outlook 2003 can help you reduce the number of servers located in remote locations that are connected with high latency.

- **Reduce the number of servers**   You might decide to reduce the number of servers needed by investing in high-end servers, including high performance processors and servers with multiple processors. Reducing the number of servers can help to reduce operational costs.

- **Centralize server administration**   Your might want to combine and centralize server administration to reduce operational costs.

- **Minimize the number of routing groups**   You might want to keep the number of routing groups in your organization at a minimum to reduce the overhead associated with creating and maintaining routing group connectors.

Chapter 3

Exchange Server 2003 in Enterprise Environments

About This Chapter

This chapter discusses design elements that you must consider when planning a deployment of Microsoft Exchange Server 2003 in a complex enterprise environment. In the context of this chapter, a complex enterprise environment is an environment with departments, divisions, or other business units that operate independently from each other and the rest of the company. For example, in a financial institution, an off-shore location might have a legal requirement to operate in an isolated environment so it can maintain the confidentiality of private client financial records. Research departments in the private business sector, government organizations, and military divisions that work with highly classified data, are also seldom integrated with non-confidential entities. These environments are considered complex because they require a deployment of multiple Active Directory forests. This chapter explains how to deploy Exchange Server 2003 in these situations so the messaging environment appears to be unified, although participants are isolated.

This chapter assumes that you are familiar with Microsoft Windows server technology and the basic logical and physical design elements of an Exchange 2003 organization, as discussed in Chapter 2, "Exchange Server 2003 Design Basics."

> **More Info**   For more information about planning, designs, and deployment, see the books "Planning an Exchange Server 2003 Messaging System" (*http://go.microsoft.com/fwlink/?LinkId=21766*) and "Exchange Server 2003 Deployment Guide" (*http://go.microsoft.com/fwlink/?LinkId=21768*).

What You Need to Know

Simplicity is the key to a well-designed Exchange 2003 organization. In your design, you should strive for a streamlined administrative topology, a straightforward routing topology with a minimum number of routing groups, and a server infrastructure that is able to cope with the workload imposed by messaging clients. A well-designed Exchange 2003 organization can help reduce administrative overhead and total cost of ownership while providing fast message transfer and optimal client/server response times. Within a complex enterprise environment, however, these objectives are not always easy to achieve.

A number of factors can complicate the design of an Exchange 2003 organization, including:

- **Isolation**   Business units that require data and service isolation for legal or other reasons or that have separate directory schema requirements might have to keep their resources in separate Active Directory forests.

- **Windows NT environments**   Business units that are still in a Microsoft Windows NT Server 4.0 domain might not want to move to Microsoft Windows Server 2003 and Active Directory directory service.

- **Mergers and acquisitions**   Business units that already have deployed Active Directory and Exchange independently from each other might not want to merge their environments into a unified Active Directory forest and Exchange organization.

To adequately address these issues, you must design an environment that includes multiple Active Directory forests. A single Exchange 2003 organization cannot span multiple Active Directory forests, but this does not mean that you cannot deploy Exchange 2003.

You can deploy Exchange 2003 in an environment with multiple forests in one of the following ways:

- **Dedicated resource forest**   A dedicated resource forest is an Active Directory forest dedicated to running Exchange and hosting mailboxes, while the user accounts associated with the mailboxes are in separate forests without

Exchange 2003. The resource forest is a good option for companies with business units that require strict security boundaries for user accounts and data, but that can share a centrally managed Exchange organization. A resource forest deployment is also a good option for companies with business units that are still on Windows NT domains, as illustrated in Figure 3-1.

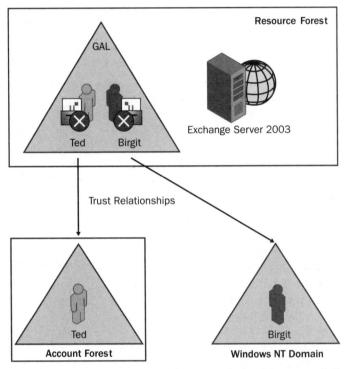

Figure 3-1   A resource forest with trust relationships to an Active Directory forest and a Windows NT domain

The resource forest concept is similar to that of a Microsoft Exchange Server 5.5 organization. In an Exchange Server 5.5 organization, a single directory (that is, the Exchange directory) holds all recipients and configuration information, and the user accounts are located in separate Windows domains. In Exchange 2003, the resource forest resembles what used to be the Exchange directory maintaining recipient and configuration information. The user account forests and Windows NT domains, on the other hand, host the user account databases. Similar to Exchange Server 5.5, in which you must establish an explicit association between a Windows account and a mailbox by means of a primary Windows NT account, Exchange 2003 requires that you establish an association between the user accounts and their mailbox accounts. Options for establishing this association are explained in the section "Provisioning Exchange 2003 Resources in a Resource Forest" later in this chapter. Trust relationships must exist for users from external domains to access resources in the resource forest.

Table 3-1 lists the advantages and disadvantages of a resource forest deployment.

Table 3-1   Advantages and Disadvantages of a Resource Forest Deployment

Advantages	Disadvantages
Provides a strict security boundary between Active Directory forests.	Because Exchange resources and user accounts are maintained separately, the resource forest model does not leverage the benefits of integrating Exchange and Active Directory administration.
Because all Exchange resources are in a single forest, a single global address list (GAL) contains all users across the entire environment.	Creating, changing, or deleting user accounts in Active Directory forests or Windows NT domains is not automatically reflected in Exchange.
Well-suited for an environment with Windows NT domains or where user account and mailbox administration must be separated.	If you cannot place all Exchange servers in a single location, you must deploy duplicate domain controllers and global catalog servers in all sites where Exchange will run, which can increase total cost of ownership.

On the Resource Kit CD   You can find a document named Preparing a Resource Forest Test Environment.doc with step-by-step instructions for installing a resource forest on the companion CD in the folder \Companion Material\Chapter 03\Resource Forest.

■ **Non-dedicated resource forest**   Companies that cannot afford to deploy separate domain controllers and global catalog servers for a dedicated resource forest can host Exchange 2003 in one of their existing forests. The forest hosting Exchange is then considered a non-dedicated resource forest. Investment requirements might be lower in comparison to the dedicated resource forest model, but user account management is somewhat more complicated, because different types of mailbox accounts must be created in the non-dedicated resource forest for local users and users from other forests or Windows NT domains. For local Exchange users, you must create enabled mailbox-enabled user accounts. For Exchange users in other forests, you typically create disabled mailbox-enabled user accounts, which are then associated with the actual enabled user accounts in these other forests. Figure 3-2 illustrates this difference.

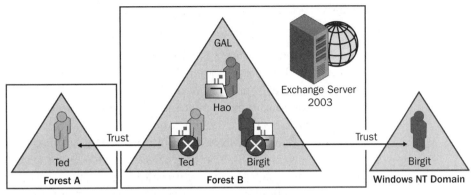

Figure 3-2   An Exchange 2003 deployment in one production forest of a multiple forest environment

Table 3-2 lists the advantages and disadvantages of deploying Exchange 2003 in a non-dedicated resource forest.

Table 3-2   Advantages and Disadvantages of Deploying Exchange 2003 in One Production Forest

Advantages	Disadvantages
Leverages an existing Active Directory structure.	It is not possible to implement a common user account and mailbox administration model across all forests. For example, user accounts in the Exchange forest are mailbox-enabled, but user accounts in other forests must be configured as associated external accounts.
Because the Exchange organization uses existing domain controllers and global catalog servers, total cost of ownership does not increase as much as in a dedicated resource forest scenario.	Creating, changing, or deleting user accounts in Active Directory forests is only partially reflected in Exchange. In general, administration is clumsy.
Provides strict security boundaries between forests.	Because a subset of Exchange resources is maintained separately from external user accounts, the forest administrators must determine how to share or divide responsibilities for managing NT user accounts, Active Directory and Exchange objects.

■ **Multiple forests all running Exchange**   If the business units in your company require rigid security isolation and cannot share a centrally managed Exchange organization, you must deploy an individual Exchange organization in each individual Active Directory forest. Mergers and acquisitions might also lead to a situation in which multiple Exchange organizations must coexist for a time. Such organizations might still be running Exchange Server 5.5 in a

Windows NT domain, or Exchange 2000 or Exchange 2003 in Active Directory forests.

As shown in Figure 3-3, individual Exchange organizations are, by default, not integrated with each other. There is no explicitly defined message transfer path, and there is no common global address list. To make the individual Exchange organizations appear integrated with each other, you must establish messaging connectors explicitly, and you should synchronize directories using tools, such as Active Directory Connector (ADC) or Microsoft Identity Integration Server 2003 (MIIS). You might also want to synchronize calendar information, so users across all organizations can check each other's free/busy information when booking meetings. For more information about how to accomplish these tasks, see the section "Integrating Exchange Organizations in Multiple Forest Environments" later in this chapter.

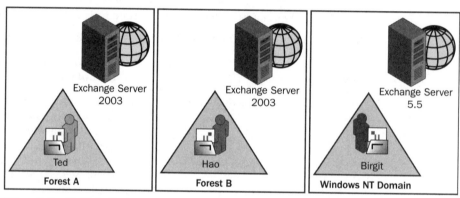

Figure 3-3   Multiple Exchange organizations in a single environment

Table 3-3 lists the advantages and disadvantages of deploying Exchange 2003 in multiple forests.

Table 3-3   Advantages and Disadvantages of Deploying Multiple Exchange 2003 Organizations

Advantages	Disadvantages
Because Exchange resources are maintained only for user accounts in the local forest, there is no need to share or divide responsibilities for managing Active Directory and Exchange objects with other business units.	Messaging features, such as delegate mailbox access, are not supported between users in different Exchange organizations.

Table 3-3   Advantages and Disadvantages of Deploying Multiple Exchange 2003 Organizations (Continued)

Advantages	Disadvantages
Strict data isolation and security boundaries are enforced.	If a group from another forest is represented as a contact, you cannot view the group's members. Group membership is not expanded until mail is sent to the source forest. This is not an issue for groups with hidden membership information, however.
Administrators from other forests are unable to seize control over the resources in the local forest.	Although you can synchronize free/busy information across forests and use it to schedule meetings, you cannot use the Open Other User's Folder feature in Microsoft Office Outlook to view the calendar details for a user in another forest.
Companies do not have to abandon their existing Exchange organizations after a business merger or acquisition.	A front-end server cannot proxy requests to a back-end server in a different forest. This limitation applies whether you are using a front-end server for Outlook Web Access or Outlook Mobile Access.

Deploying Exchange 2003 in Multiple Forest Environments

Deploying Exchange 2003 in a multiple forest environment requires you to choose from two mutually exclusive options: splitting the messaging environment into multiple Exchange organizations or keeping everything in a global organization. In general, it is better to deploy a global Exchange organization rather than multiple individual organizations because of lower administrative overhead. A company that must maintain multiple Exchange organizations typically requires more Exchange administrators per Exchange users and must deploy and maintain several synchronization tools that are not needed in a single Exchange organization.

Figure 3-4 provides guidelines to determine the right form of deployment for your company.

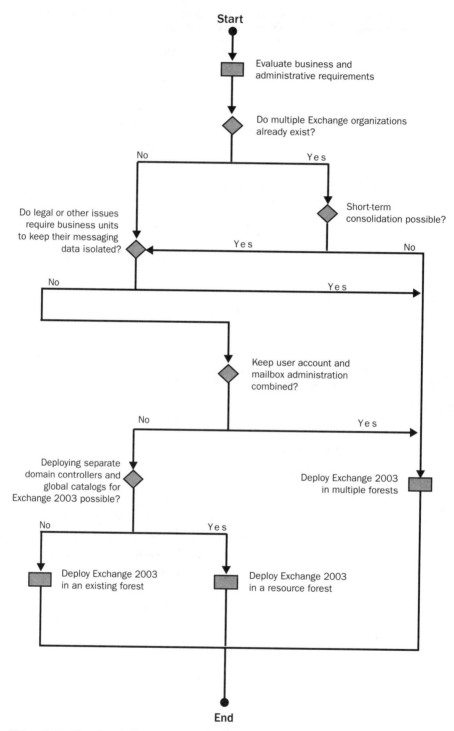

Figure 3-4   Planning an Exchange 2003 deployment in a multiple forest environment

The result of the planning is either a resource forest (dedicated or non-dedicated) or a multi-forest design with the following dependencies:

- **Resource forest deployment** Because user account administration and mailbox administration are performed in different forests, administrators must coordinate their activities with each other. You must set up a provisioning process so that when an administrator creates, changes, or deletes a user account in an account forest, a mailbox account is also created, changed, or deleted in the resource forest. You can automate the account provisioning process using custom scripts or commercial tools, such as Microsoft Identity Integration Server (MIIS).

- **Multi-forest deployment** Companies that plan to deploy Exchange 2003 in separate forests face a number of challenges from the interoperability limitations between Exchange organizations. To maximize the level of interoperability between Exchange organizations, you must:

  - **Synchronize directories** You must find a way to synchronize the global address lists in the various Exchange organizations with each other so all users have consistent address books. A variety of tools is available to perform this synchronization, including Microsoft tools such as Identity Integration Server and non-Microsoft tools, such as SimpleSync from CPS Systems, Novell Nsure Identity Manager (formerly called DirXML), or HP LDAP Directory Synchronizer. The tool that you choose depends on the functionality that you need and what systems you want to synchronize. Identity Integration Server 2003, for example, supports a wide variety of directories and comes with a preconfigured global address list synchronization agent.

  - **Integrate routing topologies** You must find a way to share the same Simple Mail Transfer Protocol (SMTP) domain space between your Exchange organizations, if your company wishes to hide the complexity of the internal messaging environment from external business partners and Internet users. The ultimate goal here is to provide all users with an SMTP address from the same public SMTP domain, such as @tailspintoys.com, regardless of the Exchange organization in which the mailboxes actually reside.

  - **Replicate free/busy information** You must find a way to replicate free/busy information between your Exchange organizations, if the business units in your company work closely together and collaborate in meetings. Free/busy information facilitates the planning of meetings, because meeting organizers can determine when all attendees are available. To replicate free/busy information between organizations, you can use the Inter-Organization Replication tool that you can download from *http://www.microsoft.com/downloads/details.aspx?FamilyId=E7A951D7-1559-4F8F-B400-488B0C52430E&displaylang=en*.

- **Synchronize public folder content**   You must find a way to replicate public folders between multiple Exchange organizations, if the business units in your company want to share discussion forums or other public folder-based workgroup solutions. The Inter-Organization Replication tool, which you can use to replicate free/busy information, can also be used to synchronize public folder content. However, the Inter-Organization Replication tool has several limitations. For example, access control lists are not synchronized, which can lead to a disclosure of potentially confidential information. Hence, we recommend that you look for alternatives before using the Inter-Organization Replication tool. Microsoft Windows SharePoint Services (WSS) is an interesting technology that you can use to implement workgroup solutions and discussion forums for users in different forests. To download Windows SharePoint Services and for detailed product information, see *Windows SharePoint Services* in the *Microsoft Windows Server 2003 Technology Centers*, at *http://www.microsoft.com/windowsserver2003/technologies/sharepoint/default.mspx.*

Provisioning Exchange 2003 Resources in a Resource Forest

In the resource forest deployment scenario, you must decide what type of mailbox accounts you want to create in the resource forest for the actual users in their account forests. In Exchange 2003, mailbox accounts are mailbox-enabled user accounts, but you must decide whether to create enabled or disabled mailbox-enabled user accounts. Your choice influences how you establish the association between the mailbox accounts and the user accounts. We recommend that you use disabled mailbox accounts, because they have the advantage that users cannot use a disabled mailbox account to log on to the resource forest directly.

> **Note**   In this chapter, the term mailbox account refers to a mailbox-enabled user account in a resource forest. The mailbox account might be enabled or disabled.

You can associate mailbox accounts and user accounts with each other in the following ways:

- **No account association**   You can decide not to associate user accounts with mailbox accounts to reduce administrative overhead. For each user, just create an enabled mailbox account, and then ask the user to use the mailbox account credentials directly in Outlook 2003 to log on to the resource forest. The disadvantage of this approach is that the user must perform a separate logon and must work with two different accounts and passwords (the mailbox account and the user account), but this is not much different from using a non-Microsoft messaging system that is not integrated with the Windows security subsystem.

■ **Configure delegate access**   To eliminate the need for a separate logon account, you can associate a user account with a mailbox account by granting the user account delegate access permissions for the mailbox account. This simplifies the user environment because the user does not have to work directly with an additional mailbox account. When you establish an outgoing external trust relationship from the resource forest to the account forest, you can grant the user delegate access to the mailbox account.

To provide delegate access to a mailbox, you must grant the user account the following permissions:

■ **Full Mailbox Access**   In the properties of the mailbox account, switch to the Exchange Advanced tab, and click Mailbox Rights to grant this access permission. Users with full mailbox access can open a mailbox and all mailbox folders, such as Inbox and Calendar, by using a messaging client such as Outlook.

■ **Send As**   In the properties of the mailbox account, switch to the Security tab, and grant the user account this access permission. Users with Send As permissions in addition to full mailbox access can send messages on behalf of the mailbox account.

On the Resource Kit CD   For an example of how to configure delegate mailbox access, see the document Creating Multiple Mailboxes for the Administrator account.doc in the \Companion Material\Chapter 01 folder on the companion CD.

You should not disable the mailbox accounts in the resource forest at this stage, although the document Creating Multiple Mailboxes for the Administrator account.doc suggests disabling the accounts. Disabling mailbox-enabled accounts works in the example included in Chapter 1 because the administrator account used to access additional mailboxes is also a mailbox-enabled user account itself. In a resource forest scenario, however, the actual user accounts are typically not mailbox-enabled, because they exist in forests without Exchange 2003. Accordingly, the Exchange store cannot determine an active Exchange user and delegate access to a disabled mailbox account fails. In this event, the Exchange store writes the following information into the application event log:

```
Event Type: Warning
Event Source: MSExchangeIS
Event Category: General
Event ID: 9548
Description: Disabled user /o=Tailspin Toys/ou=First Administrative Group/
cn=Recipients/cn=Ted does not have a master account SID. Please use
Active Directory MMC to set an active account as this user's master account.
```

- **Associated external account** For delegate access to a disabled mailbox account in a resource forest to work, you must specify an associated external account for the mailbox. This associated external account is also called the master account or mailbox owner. Together, the disabled but mailbox-enabled mailbox account and the enabled but mailbox-disabled external account form an entity that Exchange 2003 considers enabled and mailbox-enabled (Figure 3-5). Because both accounts together are considered a unit, you cannot have more than a single master account per mailbox, and you cannot assign multiple mailboxes to a single master account. Furthermore, the mailbox account and associated external accounts must not belong to the same forest.

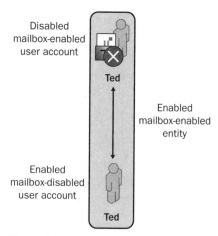

Disabled
mailbox-enabled
user account

Ted

Enabled
mailbox-enabled
entity

Enabled
mailbox-disabled
user account

Ted

Figure 3-5 Associating an enabled user account with a disabled mailbox account

To specify a master account for a mailbox, you must grant the account the Associated External Account mailbox right in the properties of the mailbox account (on the Exchange Advanced tab, click the Mailbox Rights button). You must also grant the external account Full Mailbox Access permissions so the user can open the mailbox folders, and also Send As permissions so the user can send messages on behalf of the mailbox account. If you want the user to be able to modify personal information in the address book directly, you must also grant the master account the permissions Read Personal Information and Write Personal Information on the Security tab of the mailbox account.

In summary, to grant an account all required and optional rights, you must grant:

- Associated External Account mailbox right

- Send As permission

- Read Personal Information permission

- Write Personal Information permission

> **On the Resource Kit CD**   For an example of how to configure an associated external account for a disabled mailbox account, see the document Creating disabled mailbox accounts in a resource forest.doc in the \Companion Material\Chapter 03\Resource Forest folder on the companion CD.

In Active Directory Users and Computers, Exchange Task Wizard can facilitate associating a mailbox account with a mailbox owner. If you create a mailbox for an existing disabled user account, Exchange Task Wizard automatically displays a Create Mailbox dialog box that allows you to specify an associated external account (Figure 3-6). Exchange Task Wizard grants the selected account the mailbox right Associated External Account, Full Mailbox Access, and Send As. If you select the Grant Read and Write Personal Information privileges to the selected account checkbox in addition, Exchange Task Wizard also grants the Read Personal Information and Write Personal Information rights.

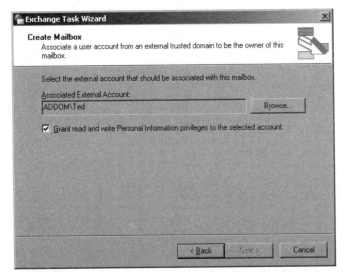

Figure 3-6   Specifying a mailbox owner by using Exchange Task Wizard

You should note, however, that Exchange Task Wizard does not display the Create Mailbox page when creating a disabled user account and mailbox-enabling it at the same time. In this situation, you must configure the security settings manually, as outlined in the document Creating disabled mailbox accounts in a resource forest.doc, or you can start Exchange Task Wizard after the user account has been created by right-clicking on the user account and selecting Exchange Tasks. In Exchange Task Wizard, you can then select the option Associate with an External Account on the Available Tasks page. Another option for associating mailbox accounts and external user accounts is using an automated provisioning system, as discussed later in this section.

Account Associations through SIDHistory

Product documentation (such as the book "Planning an Exchange Server 2003 Messaging System") sometimes suggests that account associations can also be established using the SIDHistory attribute. While it is technically correct that you can use SIDHistory information for this purpose, you should refrain from doing so, for the following reasons:

- **SIDHistory requires enabled mailbox-accounts**   You must create enabled mailbox accounts if you want to provide external users with access to their mailboxes based on SIDHistory, because the Exchange store checks objectSID and SIDHistory only for enabled user accounts that rely on their own security context to be granted permissions in Exchange store access control lists (ACLs). Disabled mailbox-enabled accounts, however, have their msExchUserAccountControl attribute set to a value of 2 instead of 0, which causes the Exchange store to check the msExchMasterAccountSid attribute instead of objectSID and SIDHistory. Exchange 2003 does not evaluate SIDHistory when using the msExchMasterAccountSid, and so the Exchange store denies access to a mailbox with a disabled user account.

- **SID filtering must be disabled on external trust relationships**   To support SIDHistory across forest boundaries, you must disable security identifier (SID) filtering for outgoing trusts in the resource forest using the following command: netdom trust <resource domain> /domain:<account domain> /Quarantine:No. Disabling SID filtering, however, weakens security significantly because users in the trusted forests can then misuse the SIDHistory attribute to gain unauthorized access to mailboxes.

On the Resource Kit CD   To see a demonstration of how an administrator in an account forest can grant a user unauthorized access to another user's mailbox if SID filtering is disabled, see the document Gaining unauthorized access to a mailbox in a resource forest.doc, which you can find in the \Companion Material\Chapter 03\Resource Forest folder on the companion CD.

Note SID filtering, enabled by default for all external trust relationships, prevents mailbox access based on SIDHistory. We do not recommend disabling SID filtering. We strongly recommend that you leave SID filtering enabled.

- **Error-prone configuration** Setting the SIDHistory attribute to the correct value and maintaining this configuration for a large number of users is a tedious task. While you can use advanced tools, such as Active Directory Migration Tool (ADMT), to copy user accounts from a source domain into a target domain and preserve the source account's SID in the target account's SIDHistory attribute, such tools seldom make sense in a resource forest scenario where users continue to use their source accounts. You can use ADMT to copy the accounts to the resource domain, but the SIDHistory is written into the mailbox accounts, where it is not needed. The users continue to work with their source accounts, which still do not have a SIDHistory. You must use a low-level tool, such as sidhist.vbs (included in the Windows 2003 support tools), to copy the SIDs in the opposite direction from the mailbox accounts into the SIDHistory attributes of the user accounts.

On the Resource Kit CD For instructions about how to use sidhist.vbs, see the document Gaining unauthorized access to a mailbox in a resource forest.doc, which you can find in the \Companion Material\Chapter 03 \Resource Forest folder on the companion CD.

- **No support for Windows NT domains** The SIDHistory attribute was first introduced with Microsoft Windows 2000 Server to facilitate migrations from Windows NT domains to Active Directory. Windows NT user accounts, however, do not support the SIDHistory attribute, and so you cannot use the sidhist.vbs script or any other tool to write a mailbox account SID back into a Windows NT user account. Thus, it is not possible to support Windows NT users in a resource forest based on SIDs.

Tip To establish associations between mailbox accounts and user accounts use explicit permission assignments instead of SIDHistory information.

Account Provisioning Using Custom Scripts

If you follow the recommended approach for establishing associations between mailbox accounts and user accounts, you are essentially performing a security operation (that is, granting Associated External Account, Full Mailbox Access, and Send As permissions to an external user account). Setting permissions is quickly accomplished in Active Directory Users and Computers if the number of mailboxes is small and user accounts in the account forests do not change often. However, if you have to deal with a large number of users in possibly multiple account forests and Windows NT domains, manually creating mailbox accounts and then configuring mailbox and Send As permissions can be a burdensome task. To reduce administrative overhead, you might want to automate this task by means of custom scripts using Active Directory Service Interface (ADSI) and Collaboration Data Objects for Exchange Management (CDOEXM).

To programmatically create a disabled mailbox account for an existing external user account and associate it with the external account, you must:

- **Read attributes from the external user account**   The mailbox account should identify the actual user participating in the Exchange organization and so it makes sense to copy user information, such as user name and account name from the source account into the target account. The following lines of code read the full name and the account name of a Windows user in either a trusted Windows NT domain or in a trusted Active Directory forest. The code uses a WinNT path, which works for both Windows NT domains and Active Directory forests:

```
'--- Get the source user object ----
Set oSRCUser = GetObject("WinNT://ADDOM/Ted")
sFullName = oSRCUser.FullName
sName    = oSRCUser.Name
```

- **Create a disabled user account in the resource forest**   The following lines of code use the full name and the account name of the Windows user to create a mailbox account in the Users container of the resource domain.

```
'--- Create a new user object in the Users Container ----
Set oOU    = GetObject("LDAP://CN=Users,DC=resdom,DC=msn")
Set oMBXUser = oOU.Create("user", "CN=" & sName)

'--- User Attributes ----
oMBXUser.FullName = sFullName
oMBXUser.Put "samAccountName", sName
oMBXUser.userAccountControl = 546
oMBXUser.SetInfo
```

Particularly interesting is the userAccountControl attribute. A value of 546 stands for a disabled user account that does not require a password (ACCOUNT-DISABLE + PASSWD_NOTREQD + NORMAL_ACCOUNT). Table 3-4 lists possible flags that you can combine in an AND operation to create the desired userAccountControl value. Write mode is not enabled.

Table 3-4   Flags for the userAccountControl Attribute

Property flag	Value in hexadecimal	Value in decimal
SCRIPT	0x0001	1
ACCOUNTDISABLE	0x0002	2
HOMEDIR_REQUIRED	0x0008	8
LOCKOUT	0x0010	16
PASSWD_NOTREQD	0x0020	32
PASSWD_CANT_CHANGE	0x0040	64
ENCRYPTED_TEXT_PWD_ALLOWED	0x0080	128
TEMP_DUPLICATE_ACCOUNT	0x0100	256
NORMAL_ACCOUNT	0x0200	512
INTERDOMAIN_TRUST_ACCOUNT	0x0800	2048
WORKSTATION_TRUST_ACCOUNT	0x1000	4096
SERVER_TRUST_ACCOUNT	0x2000	8192
DONT_EXPIRE_PASSWORD	0x10000	65536
MNS_LOGON_ACCOUNT	0x20000	131072
SMARTCARD_REQUIRED	0x40000	262144
TRUSTED_FOR_DELEGATION	0x80000	524288
NOT_DELEGATED	0x100000	1048576
USE_DES_KEY_ONLY	0x200000	2097152
DONT_REQ_PREAUTH	0x400000	4194304
PASSWORD_EXPIRED	0x800000	8388608
TRUSTED_TO_AUTH_FOR_DELEGATION	0x1000000	16777216

■ **Mailbox-enable the target account**   Now that you have created the user account, you must mailbox-enable it. This step does not differ between enabled or disabled user accounts. The following lines of code place the mailbox on a server called SERVER01 in an Exchange organization called Tailspin Toys:

```
'---- Mailbox-enable the user account ----
oMBXUser.Put "mailNickname", sName
oMBXUser.Put "msExchHomeServerName", "/o=Tailspin Toys/" _
    & "ou=First Administrative Group/cn=Configuration/" _
    & "cn=Servers/cn=SERVER01"
oMBXUser.Put "homeMDB", "CN=Mailbox Store (SERVER01)," _
    & "CN=First Storage Group,CN=InformationStore," _
    & "CN=SERVER01,CN=Servers," _
    & "CN=First Administrative Group," _
    & "CN=Administrative Groups,CN=Tailspin Toys," _
    & "CN=Microsoft Exchange,CN=Services," _
    & "CN=Configuration,DC=resdom,DC=msn"
oMBXUser.SetInfo
```

The mailNickname must be unique in your Exchange organization, msExchHomeServerName must point to an existing Exchange server, and homeMDB must point to an existing mailbox store on that server. Further information is not required to mailbox-enable a user account. ADSI and CDOEXM stamp the user account with additional Exchange attributes, such as homeMTA, legacyExchangeDN, and msExchMailboxGUID. You do not have to specify this information manually. ADSI and CDOEXM also initialize the msExchMailboxSecurityDescriptor attribute to grant the mailbox-enabled user account access to the mailbox resource in the Exchange store. Figure 3-7 shows the resulting default msExchMailboxSecurityDescriptor in the graphical user interface of Active Directory Users and Computers.

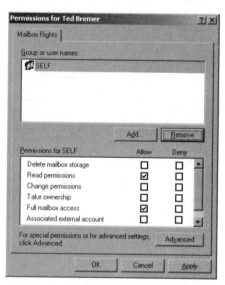

Figure 3-7   Default mailbox permissions

Once the user account is mailbox-enabled, the recipient update service of Exchange 2003 adds further Exchange-related attributes to the account, such as proxyAddresses, textEncodedORAddress, msExchALObjectVersion, msExchPoliciesIncluded, and msExchUserAccountControl. The msExchUserAccountControl attribute is most important for the resource forest scenario. The recipient update service sets this attribute to a value of 2 for disabled mailbox-enabled user accounts to inform the Exchange store that it should check the msExchMasterAccountSid attribute instead of the objectSid attribute to determine the mailbox owner. Note, however, that at this point the msExchMasterAccountSid attribute does not exist, because an associated external account has not been specified.

■ **Set the msExchMasterAccountSID attribute to the SID of the external Windows NT or Active Directory user account**   You can query the source Active Directory forest through ADSI for the objectSid attribute of the desired external user account and write this SID into the msExchMasterAccountSid attribute of the mailbox account. For Windows NT users, the attribute is called SID. You also must grant the external user account the mailbox permissions Associated External Account and Full Mailbox Access. In fact, if you set these permissions correctly, CDOEXM sets the msExchMasterAccountSid attribute automatically for you, thus saving you the effort of querying the source Active Directory forest explicitly. The following code explicitly sets the msExch-MasterAccountSid attribute of a mailbox account to the objectSID of an external user account, but this code is not needed in your script:

```
sSID = oSRCUser.Get("objectSID")

oMBXUser.Put "msExchMasterAccountSID", sSID
oMBXUser.SetInfo
```

■ **Modify the mailbox security descriptor to add an access control entry (ACE) with the trustee set to the external user account and with Associated External Account and Full Mailbox Access permissions**   The following lines of code add a user account (here, ADDOM\Ted) as the associated external account to the mailbox account created in the previous steps. Note the use of the MailboxRights method, which returns the currently effective mailbox permissions in the form of a security descriptor. The code then adds a new ACE to this security descriptor to grant the user the permissions of an associated external account.

You should not access the msExchMailboxSecurityDescriptor attribute directly to obtain the mailbox security descriptor, as in oMBXUser.Get("msExch-MailboxSecurityDescriptor"). Exchange 2003 applies the msExchMailboxSecurity-Descriptor attribute only once, when initializing the mailbox security descriptor at the time the Exchange store creates the actual mailbox. As explained in Chapter 2, this happens when the user accesses the mailbox the first time or when another user sends an e-mail message to the mailbox. After the mailbox is created in the Exchange store, the mailbox security descriptor is maintained in the Exchange store and the msExchMailboxSecurityDescriptor attribute is merely used as a shadow copy. Changes to the msExchMailboxSecurityDescriptor attribute in Active Directory have no effect for existing mailboxes. To access the mailbox security descriptor, always use the MailboxRights method.

```
CONST ADS_ACETYPE_ACCESS_ALLOWED = 0
CONST ADS_ACEFLAG_INHERIT_ACE = &h2
CONST RIGHT_DS_MAILBOX_OWNER = &h1
CONST RIGHT_DS_PRIMARY_OWNER = &h4
CONST ADS_RIGHT_DELETE = &h10000

' Get the Mailbox security descriptor (SD) and
' extract the Discretionary Access Control List (DACL)
Set oSecurityDescriptor = oMBXUser.MailboxRights
Set dacl = oSecurityDescriptor.DiscretionaryAcl
```

```
' Create and set an Access Control Entry (ACE)
' to make ADDOM\Ted an associated external account
' with full mailbox access
Set Ace1 = CreateObject("AccessControlEntry")
Ace1.AccessMask = ADS_RIGHT_DELETE _
        + RIGHT_DS_PRIMARY_OWNER _
        + RIGHT_DS_MAILBOX_OWNER
Ace1.AceType  = ADS_ACETYPE_ACCESS_ALLOWED
Ace1.AceFlags = ADS_ACEFLAG_INHERIT_ACE
Ace1.Flags    = 0
Ace1.Trustee  = "ADDOM\Ted"

'Add the new ACE to the DACL
dacl.AddAce Ace1

' Add the modified DACL to the security descriptor
oSecurityDescriptor.DiscretionaryAcl = dacl

' Save new security descriptor in the mailbox account
' and commit the changes
oMBXUser.MailboxRights = Array(oSecurityDescriptor)
oMBXUser.SetInfo
```

- **Modify the Active Directory security descriptor**   The final step is to grant the associated external account Send As permissions. However, these permissions are not maintained in the mailbox security descriptor. They are maintained in the Active Directory security descriptor of the mailbox account instead. Accordingly, you must add an ACE for the Send As permissions and set the trustee to the external user account to the Active Directory security descriptor. In addition, you might want to add a second ACE to grant the associated external account default read and list permissions.

    The following code sample demonstrates how to add a user account (here ADDOM\Ted) as a trustee to the list of accounts with permissions for the mailbox account. The code grants Ted Send As permissions and default read and list permissions:

```
CONST ADS_ACETYPE_ACCESS_ALLOWED = 0
CONST ADS_ACETYPE_ACCESS_ALLOWED_OBJECT = 5
CONST ADS_FLAG_OBJECT_TYPE_PRESENT = &h1
CONST ADS_ACEFLAG_INHERIT_ACE = &h2
CONST ADS_RIGHT_ACTRL_DS_LIST = &h4
CONST ADS_RIGHT_DS_READ_PROP = &h10
CONST ADS_RIGHT_DS_CONTROL_ACCESS = &h100
CONST ADS_RIGHT_READ_CONTROL = &h20000

' Get the Active Directory security descriptor (SD) and
' extract the Discretionary Access Control List (DACL)
Set oSecurityDescriptor = oMBXUser.Get("ntSecurityDescriptor")
Set dacl = oSecurityDescriptor.DiscretionaryAcl

'Create an ACE for the Send As right
Set Ace1 = CreateObject("AccessControlEntry")
```

```
Ace1.AccessMask = ADS_RIGHT_DS_CONTROL_ACCESS
Ace1.AceType   = ADS_ACETYPE_ACCESS_ALLOWED_OBJECT
Ace1.AceFlags  = 0
Ace1.Flags     = ADS_FLAG_OBJECT_TYPE_PRESENT
Ace1.ObjectType = "{AB721A54-1E2F-11D0-9819-00AA0040529B}"
Ace1.Trustee   = "ADDOM\Ted"

'Create an ACE for default read and list permissions
Set Ace2 = CreateObject("AccessControlEntry")
Ace2.AccessMask = ADS_RIGHT_READ_CONTROL _
        + ADS_RIGHT_DS_READ_PROP _
        + ADS_RIGHT_ACTRL_DS_LIST
Ace2.AceType   = ADS_ACETYPE_ACCESS_ALLOWED
Ace2.AceFlags  = ADS_ACEFLAG_INHERIT_ACE
Ace2.Flags     = 0
Ace2.Trustee   = "ADDOM\Ted"

'Add the ACEs to the DACL
dacl.AddAce Ace1
dacl.AddAce Ace2

' Add the modified DACL to the security descriptor.
oSecurityDescriptor.DiscretionaryAcl = dacl

' Save new security descriptor in the mailbox account
' and commit the changes
oMBXUser.Put "ntSecurityDescriptor", oSecurityDescriptor
oMBXUser.SetInfo
```

On the Resource Kit CD   You can find a complete example of how to create a mailbox account for an existing external user account on the companion CD in the \Companion Material\Chapter 03\Scripts folder on the companion CD. The script is called CreateMBXandSetExternalAccount.wsf.

Note   For more information about programming access control settings using ADSI, see the topic "Controlling Access to Active Directory Objects" in the Microsoft Platform Software Development Kit (SDK), available at *http:// msdn.microsoft.com/library/en-us/ad/ad/ controlling_access_to_active_directory_objects.asp*.

Account Provisioning Using MIIS 2003

As demonstrated, creating mailbox accounts and associating them with external user accounts can be accomplished through ADSI code. However, you must also ensure that the resource forest and account forests or Windows NT domains stay synchronized. When an administrator in an account forest deletes a user account, you must also delete the corresponding mailbox account in the resource forest. If the account operator renames a user account, you might also want to rename the mailbox account in the resource forest to reflect the changes in the global address list, and so forth. However, developing a full-featured custom provisioning solution based on ADSI to accomplish these tasks is a major undertaking. You might find that the costs for developing such a solution outweigh the costs of commercially available software.

Note   Whether you are developing a custom directory synchronization solution or use commercially available software, you must carefully design the directory synchronization topology to avoid account mismatching, duplication, or even accidental account deletion. It is imperative to test your directory synchronization solution on a reference system physically separated from the production environment.

MIIS 2003 is a good example of a commercial solution that you can use to implement a professional provisioning system. MIIS ships with management agents that allow you to integrate many different types of directories, including Microsoft Windows NT, Active Directory, Novell NDS and eDirectory, SunONE/iPlanet Directory, X.500 systems, and other metadirectory products, as well as e-mail systems such as Lotus Notes/Domino and Microsoft Exchange 5.5. If you only need to integrate Active Directory forests, you can use Identity Integration Feature Pack for Microsoft Windows Server Active Directory instead of the full-featured MIIS. Identity Integration Feature Pack for Microsoft Windows Server Active Directory is available as a no-cost Web download to customers who have already licensed Windows Server 2003, Enterprise Edition (*http://www.microsoft.com/downloads/details.aspx?FamilyID=d9143610-c04d-41c4-b7ea-6f56819769d5&DisplayLang=en*).

Note   Identity Integration Server and Identity Integration Feature Pack for Microsoft Windows Server Active Directory require Microsoft SQL Server 2000 with Service Pack 3 (SP3) as the data store, installed on a server running Microsoft Windows Server 2003 Enterprise Edition. Microsoft Identity Integration Server 2003 Enterprise Edition requires SQL Server 2000 Enterprise Edition. Identity Integration Feature Pack can run with SQL Server 2000 Standard Edition or Enterprise Edition.

Identity Integration Server 2003 in a Resource Forest Environment

Figure 3-8 illustrates how Identity Integration Server can be deployed in a resource forest environment. The computer running Identity Integration Server does not have to be a member of an Active Directory forest or Windows NT domain, but it might be a good idea to install MIIS on a server that is a member of the resource forest so Exchange administrators can have full control over the provisioning system. The advantage of this deployment is that you do not need to deploy any additional software in the account forests or Windows NT domains.

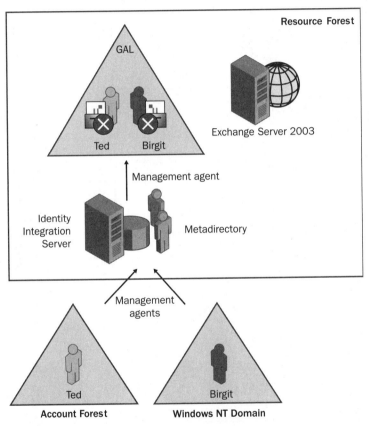

Figure 3-8   MIIS in a resource forest environment

Identity Integration Server Architecture

At the core of Microsoft Identity Integration Server (MIIS) is an SQL Server database named MicrosoftIdentityIntegrationServer that represents the central repository for consolidated identity information from multiple connected data sources. Because this database collects information from multiple directories, it is also called the metadirectory. In a resource forest environment, the data sources are Active Directory forests and Windows NT domains that contain the user accounts and mailbox accounts that you want to associate with each other. Data sources are connected to the metadirectory by management agents. Each management agent is responsible for importing data from a particular data source into the metadirectory. A management agent can also export data out of the metadirectory to keep the connected data source synchronized. In a resource forest environment, there is at least one importing management agent for each account forest and Windows NT domain, and one exporting management agent for the resource forest, as indicated in Figure 3-8.

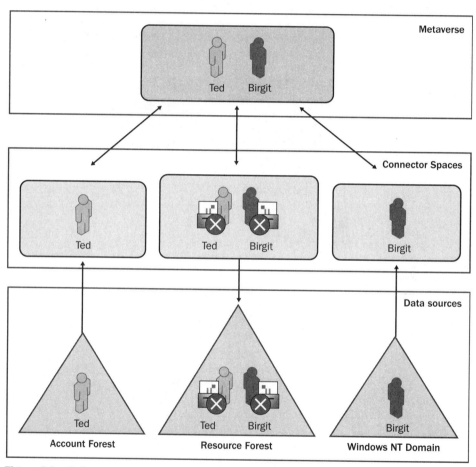

Figure 3-9   Data sources, connector spaces, and metaverse

It is very important to understand that the MIIS metadirectory is separated into two logical namespaces: the metaverse and the connector space. As shown in Figure 3-9, there is only one metaverse, which contains the integrated identity information from multiple connected data sources. For each management agent connecting a data source to MIIS, however, there is a separate connector space.

MIIS connector spaces and metaverse have the following purposes:

- **Connector space**   MIIS uses the connector space as a staging area for directory information that management agents import from or export into connected data sources. Each individual connector space is essentially a mirror of its connected data source. The management agent synchronizes all objects of a given type (such as user or group) between a connected data source and its connector space without applying any filters or rules.

  The management agent always synchronizes key attributes that allow a reliable association between the source object and the corresponding object in the connector space, such as the objectGUID and distinguished name for an Active Directory user account. You must specify additional attributes in the management agent configuration explicitly. For example, for a user account in an Active Directory forest, you can specify to synchronize common name (cn), surname (sn), givenName, displayName, sAMAccountName, objectSID, and so forth. A Windows NT user account, on the other hand, has fewer attributes to offer. You can configure a Windows NT 4.0 management agent to synchronize full_name, sAMAccountName, comment, and SID.

On the Resource Kit CD   For an example of how to configure Active Directory and Windows NT 4.0 management agents, see the document Adding MIIS to the Resource Forest Test Environment.doc, which you can find in the \Chapter 03\Resource Forest folder on the companion CD.

Figure 3-10 illustrates the relationship between an Active Directory user account and its corresponding entry in the connector space.

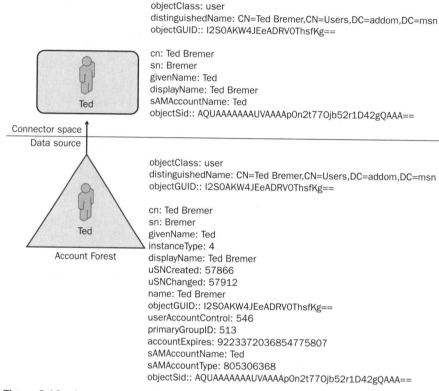

objectClass: user
distinguishedName: CN=Ted Bremer,CN=Users,DC=addom,DC=msn
objectGUID:: I2SOAKW4JEeADRVOThsfKg==

cn: Ted Bremer
sn: Bremer
givenName: Ted
displayName: Ted Bremer
sAMAccountName: Ted
objectSid:: AQUAAAAAAAUVAAAApOn2t77Ojb52r1D42gQAAA==

Connector space
Data source

objectClass: user
distinguishedName: CN=Ted Bremer,CN=Users,DC=addom,DC=msn
objectGUID:: I2SOAKW4JEeADRVOThsfKg==

cn: Ted Bremer
sn: Bremer
givenName: Ted
instanceType: 4
displayName: Ted Bremer
uSNCreated: 57866
uSNChanged: 57912
name: Ted Bremer
objectGUID:: I2SOAKW4JEeADRVOThsfKg==
userAccountControl: 546
primaryGroupID: 513
accountExpires: 9223372036854775807
sAMAccountName: Ted
sAMAccountType: 805306368
objectSid:: AQUAAAAAAAUVAAAApOn2t77Ojb52r1D42gQAAA==

Figure 3-10   A user account in data source and connector space

- **Metaverse**   The metaverse is the ultimate MIIS repository where all identity information about a specific entity, such as a person or a group, is synthesized into a single entry. A globally unique identifier (GUID) establishes the association between the metaverse entry and the connector space entry. You can also use join criteria to merge accounts from different data sources. For example, a user can have a separate account in two forests in an account forest and in a resource forest, which correspond to separate entries in two connector spaces, but in the metaverse, these two entries are merged into a single object. This is how MIIS accomplishes account synchronization. When you change the attributes of the user account in the account forest, and you run a management agent to import the changes into a connector space, the changes eventually flow from the connector space into the associated object in the metaverse, and the metaverse then sends those changes to the connector spaces of other connected data sources that the affected metaverse object is associated with, such as the management agent exporting the information to the resource forest.

Figure 3-11 illustrates the relationship between a metaverse object and a connector space object. Note that the attributes in the metaverse and connector space are not necessarily the same. In the example, cn, sn, givenName, and objectSID attributes are mapped directly to corresponding attributes in the metaverse. The sAMAccountname attribute, however, is mapped to the uid attribute, because by default, the person object in the metaverse has no sAMAccountname attribute. The ou and homeMDB attributes, again, do not exist in the connector space. These attributes are assigned constant values that you can specify directly in the management agent configuration. The displayName attribute is customized using a rules extension to add a tag that indicates the account forest of the user. The distinguished name and objectGUID attributes are not mapped into the metaverse at all, because this information is relevant only to the connected data source and does not need to be propagated to other data sources. Within the management agent, you must configure attribute mappings and rules that govern how attributes flow into and out of the metaverse.

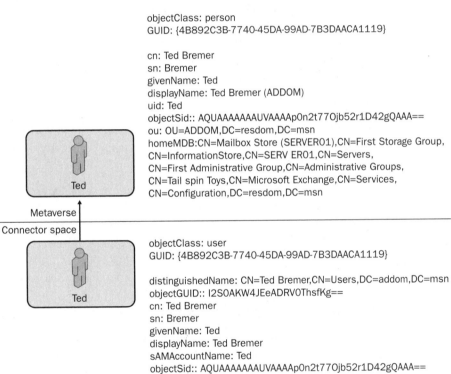

Figure 3-11   Attribute flow into the metaverse

Connector and Disconnector Objects

The terms connector object and disconnector object both refer to entries in the connector space. A connector object is a connector space entry that is linked to an object in the metaverse. Figure 3-11 shows a connector object. On the other hand, a disconnector object is a connector space entry that is not linked to an object in the metaverse.

As mentioned earlier, a management agent imports all objects of a given type from the connected data source into the connector space. At this point, all these objects are disconnectors. To make these entries connector objects, you must specify within the configuration of the management agent how the information should be passed on to the metaverse. You have two configuration options:

- **Project**   When projecting a connector space object into the metaverse, you are creating a new metaverse object for each connector space object. MIIS links each new metaverse object to its corresponding connector space object by means of a GUID. In a resource forest environment, you typically project user accounts and groups from the account forests into the metaverse.

- **Join**   Based on join clauses that you can define in the management agent, you can establish an association between a connector space object and an existing metaverse object. The management agent then applies the information from the connector space object to the existing metaverse object. If no metaverse object exists, the connector space object remains a disconnector object. Joining objects is useful if you want to consolidate user information from different directories. For example, a user might have a user account in Active Directory, a record in a human resources database, and telephone numbers in the telephone system. MIIS enables you to join this information into a single metaverse object, but joining information from multiple directories is usually outside the scope of a resource forest scenario.

In the management agent configuration, you can also apply filters that determine which objects you want to propagate into the metaverse and which you do not want to propagate. Objects that are not propagated remain disconnector objects excluded from provisioning and synchronization. For example, you can specify not to propagate the Administrator account and other system accounts from an account forest to avoid provisioning mailbox accounts for them.

Configuring Management Agents in a Resource Forest Environment

Creating and configuring a management agent to connect a data source to MIIS is a straightforward process. Identity Manager includes a wizard that guides you through all of the important steps. To configure management agents, you must be logged on as a member of the MIISAdmins security group.

To configure a management agent complete the following steps:

1. **Defining general properties**   In the first step, you must select the type of management agent that you want to create, specify a name for the agent, and optionally add an administrative description. For Active Directory forests, create an Active Directory management agent. For Windows NT domains, select a Windows NT 4.0 management agent instead.

In the general properties, you can also choose to run the management agent in a separate process. By default, the management agent runs in the same process space as the Identity Integration Server service. This improves overall performance and consumes less memory space, but if a management agent does not operate reliably, it might cause the Identity Integration Server service to fail. Management agents included in MIIS can be considered reliable, so you can leave these management agents running in the process of the Identity Integration Server service.

2. **Connecting to the data source**   Next, you must specify the data source that you want to synchronize with MIIS in form of a fully qualified forest name or Windows NT domain name. You must also provide a user name with administrator rights and password and a logon domain name. The management agent uses this information to log on to the connected data source to read or write to the directory.

3. **Selecting directory partitions**   For Active Directory management agents, you must select the directory partitions you want to include in the synchronization process. To synchronize user accounts, you must include the domain partition. You can also specify a preferred domain controller and alternate user credentials to read and write the domain partition, but this is not necessary if the account you specified in the previous step has administrative rights for the forest or domain. More important is the Containers button at the bottom of the wizard page, which you can use to select individual organizational units and containers to include. By default, all containers and organizational units are selected, but if account operators use only specific organizational units to maintain user accounts, you can narrow the scope of the management agent to these containers. For example, you can exclude all but the Users container if the administrators in the account forests have not created a more sophisticated organizational unit structure. Windows NT domains do not support directory partitions, so this configuration step is not available for Windows NT 4.0 management agents.

4. **Selecting object types**   Next, you must determine what object types to include in the synchronization. If you want to provision mailbox accounts for your users, you must include user objects. Optionally, you can also decide to include groups. Account operators can then maintain their own distribution groups and synchronize them with distribution lists in the Exchange organization. For Active Directory management agents, you will notice that container and domainDNS checkboxes are by default also selected. You should leave these object types included, because without container information MIIS is not able to construct distinguished names for account objects.

5. **Selecting attributes to synchronize**   On the next wizard page, you must specify the source attributes that you want to import into the metadirectory or export into Active Directory. Selecting all attributes is a practicable strategy, but you can

optimize data transfer and database space consumption by selecting only the attributes of interest, such as common name (cn), surname (sn), givenName, displayName, sAMAccountName, and objectSID for Active Directory management agents and full_name, sAMAccountName, and SID for Windows NT 4.0 management agents. If you want to fully synchronize user account information, however, select all available attributes. If you include groups into the provisioning system, remember to include the member attribute so group membership information is propagated.

6. **Configuring connector filters**   In the next step, you should specify filters for user and group objects respectively, to exclude from the provisioning process all the accounts to which you do not want to assign a mailbox account or e-mail address. For example, you might want to exclude the Administrator account, service accounts, and the Guest account. For groups, you can define synchronization criteria so not all Windows groups from the account forests end up as distribution lists in the Exchange 2003 organization. For example, you can specify a filter in the form of "cn does not start with Exchange" to filter out all groups except those that have a group name that starts with Exchange.

7. **Configuring join and projection rules**   In a resource forest scenario, all importing management agents should be configured to project source objects into the metaverse. Group objects are projected as group objects, and user objects are projected as person objects. You must configure a separate projection rule for each object type. For the management agent exporting information to the resource forest, a projection rule does not need to be defined, because the flow of information is one-way from the metaverse to the resource forest. You must create connector space objects for metaverse objects using a metaverse extension DLL.

8. **Configuring attribute flow**   Perhaps the most complex configuration step is the attribute mapping between connector spaces and the metaverse. The following tables list attributes that you can map directly from Active Directory objects to metaverse objects. Mapping as many attributes from the source account forests as possible enables you to provide complete organizational information for each Exchange user in the Exchange global address list.

Table 3-5   Typical User-to-Person Import Attribute Flow Mappings

Connector Space User Object Attribute	Metaverse Person Object Attribute	Mapping Type
CN	CN	Direct
TelephoneNumber	TelephoneNumber	Direct
displayName	displayName	Direct
SN	SN	Direct
C	C	Direct

Table 3-5   Typical User-to-Person Import Attribute Flow Mappings (Continued)

Connector Space User Object Attribute	Metaverse Person Object Attribute	Mapping Type
Company	Company	Direct
Department	Department	Direct
Division	Division	Direct
employeeID	employeeID	Direct
employeeType	employeeType	Direct
givenName	givenName	Direct
Manager	Manager	Direct
O	O	Direct
Title	Title	Direct
UserCertificate	UserCertificate	Direct
UserSMIMECertificate	UserSMIMECertificate	Direct
streetAddress	streetAddress	Direct
St	St	Direct
postalCode	postalCode	Direct
Co	Co	Direct
physicalDeliveryOfficeName	physicalDeliveryOfficeName	Direct
otherTelephone	otherTelephone	Direct
homePhone	homePhone	Direct
otherHomePhone	otherHomePhone	Direct
facsimileTelephoneNumber	facsimileTelephoneNumber	Direct
Mobile	Mobile	Direct
telephoneAssistant	telephoneAssistant	Direct
Pager	Pager	Direct
Info	Info	Direct
L	L	Direct
Initials	Initials	Direct

Table 3-6   Typical Group-to-Group Import Attribute Flow Mappings

Connector Space Group Object Attribute	Metaverse Group Object Attribute	Mapping Type
CN	CN	Direct
displayName	DisplayName	Direct
Member	Member	Direct
GroupType	GroupType	Direct

Direct attribute mappings are quickly configured in Identity Manager. However, complex attribute flow might require you to program rules extensions using Microsoft Visual Studio. NET 2003. For details about how to configure attribute mappings in a resource forest scenario, see the section "Attribute Flow between Connector Space and Metaverse" later in this chapter.

> **On the Resource Kit CD**   You can find more information in the document Adding MIIS to the Resource Forest Test Environment.doc, which you can find in the \Chapter 03\Resource Forest folder on the companion CD.

9. **Specifying deprovisioning actions**   Next, you must decide how to deal with user accounts and group objects that are deleted in the connected data sources. For importing management agents, it is sufficient to accept the default setting **Make them disconnectors**. For the exporting management agent, you should select the option **Stage a delete** on the option for the next export run, so the management agent deletes the affected user account from the resource forest when the external user account is deleted from the account forest. Alternatively, you can select the option **Determine with a rules extension**, if you want to implement advanced logic for deprovisioning user accounts.

10. **Adding a rules extension**   Finally, you must specify the. dll file that contains your program code to handle custom filtering, attribute mappings, or deprovisioning. The DLL must reside in the \Program Files\Microsoft Identity Integration Server\Extensions folder.

Attribute Flow between Connector Spaces and the Metaverse

Configuring the flow of attributes into and out of the metaverse requires an understanding of the information that you must eventually pass to the resource forest in order to create a mailbox account that is associated with an external user account. Some attributes you can pass directly from the source user account to the target mailbox account. Other attributes you might have to modify, and additional attributes you must add to the connector objects in MIIS yourself. For example, the source user accounts do not have any Exchange-specific attributes because Exchange is not deployed in the account forests, so you must add these attributes, such as homeMDB and mailNickname, to the connector object explicitly before exporting the objects to the resource forest. As outlined in the section "Account Provisioning using Custom Scripts" earlier in this chapter, you must also specify ACEs in the msExchMailboxSecurityDescriptor and nTSecurityDescriptor attributes to grant the associated external accounts the required access rights. By mapping the objectSid attribute of the source user account to the msExchMasterAccountSid attribute of the mailbox account, you can designate the source accounts as the associated external accounts. Figure 3-12 shows an example of how selected attributes must flow through the metadirectory to create a mailbox account in the resource forest for a user account from an account forest.

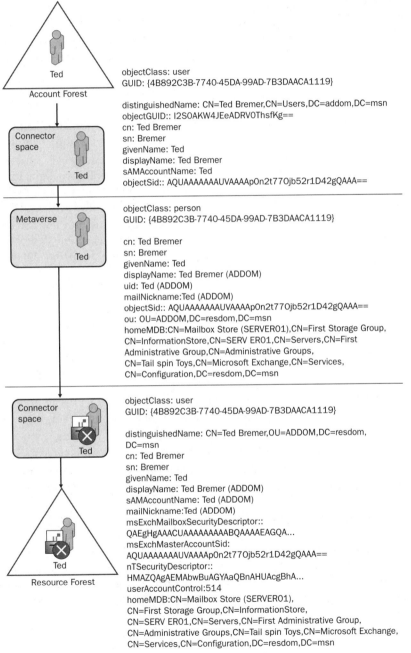

objectClass: user
GUID: {4B892C3B-7740-45DA-99AD-7B3DAACA1119}

distinguishedName: CN=Ted Bremer,CN=Users,DC=addom,DC=msn
objectGUID:: I2S0AKW4JEeADRV0ThsfKg==
cn: Ted Bremer
sn: Bremer
givenName: Ted
displayName: Ted Bremer
sAMAccountName: Ted
objectSid:: AQUAAAAAAUVAAAAp0n2t77Ojb52r1D42gQAAA==

objectClass: person
GUID: {4B892C3B-7740-45DA-99AD-7B3DAACA1119}

cn: Ted Bremer
sn: Bremer
givenName: Ted
displayName: Ted Bremer (ADDOM)
uid: Ted (ADDOM)
mailNickname:Ted (ADDOM)
objectSid:: AQUAAAAAAUVAAAAp0n2t77Ojb52r1D42gQAAA==
ou: OU=ADDOM,DC=resdom,DC=msn
homeMDB:CN=Mailbox Store (SERVER01),CN=First Storage Group,
CN=InformationStore,CN=SERV ER01,CN=Servers,CN=First
Administrative Group,CN=Administrative Groups,
CN=Tail spin Toys,CN=Microsoft Exchange,CN=Services,
CN=Configuration,DC=resdom,DC=msn

objectClass: user
GUID: {4B892C3B-7740-45DA-99AD-7B3DAACA1119}

distinguishedName: CN=Ted Bremer,OU=ADDOM,DC=resdom,
DC=msn
cn: Ted Bremer
sn: Bremer
givenName: Ted
displayName: Ted Bremer (ADDOM)
sAMAccountName: Ted (ADDOM)
mailNickname:Ted (ADDOM)
msExchMailboxSecurityDescriptor::
QAEgHgAAACUAAAAAAAABQAAAAEAGQA...
msExchMasterAccountSid:
AQUAAAAAAUVAAAAp0n2t77Ojb52r1D42gQAAA==
nTSecurityDescriptor::
HMAZQAgAEMAbwBuAGYAaQBnAHUAcgBhA...
userAccountControl:514
homeMDB:CN=Mailbox Store (SERVER01),
CN=First Storage Group,CN=InformationStore,
CN=SERV ER01,CN=Servers,CN=First Administrative Group,
CN=Administrative Groups,CN=Tail spin Toys,CN=Microsoft Exchange,
CN=Services,CN=Configuration,DC=resdom,DC=msn

Figure 3-12 Attribute mappings to provision mailbox accounts in a resource forest

As indicated in Figure 3-12, the management agent modifies and adds information when importing attributes into the metaverse. Table 3-7 lists these attributes.

Table 3-7   Modified Attributes Propagated to the Metaverse

Connector Space Group Object Attribute	Metaverse Group Object Attribute	Mapping Type
displayName	displayName	Rules extension to append name of management agent.
sAMAccountName	Uid	Rules extension to append name of management agent and to ensure uniqueness.
sAMAccountName	mailNickname	Rules extension to append name of management agent and to ensure uniqueness.
---	Ou	Set to a constant value that specifies the target organizational unit for the mailbox account in the resource forest, such as OU=ADDOM,DC=RESDOM,DC=msn.
---	homeMDB	Set to a constant value that specifies the distinguished name of the target mailbox store in the Exchange organization, such as Mailbox Store (SERVER01),CN=First Storage Group,CN=InformationStore,CN=SERVER01,CN=Servers,CN=First Administrative Group,CN=Administrative Groups,CN=Tail spin Toys,CN=Microsoft Exchange,CN=Services,CN=Configuration,DC=resdom, DC=msn.

Changing the display name to indicate the source forest is optional. A direct mapping also works. Changing the sAMAccountName, however, might be required because this value must be unique in the target forest. Because you are importing accounts from different forests, it is possible that two accounts have the same sAMAccountName, which would lead to a provisioning error in the resource forest. The mailNickname must also be unique.

Attribute Flow Based on Rules Extensions

Checking attributes for uniqueness or adding information to an attribute dynamically requires you to program a rules extension. Rules extensions are implemented in .NET components that inherit from the IMASynchronization interface. You must program these extensions using Visual Basic .NET 2003 or Visual C# .NET 2003.

The following lines of code show how to append the name of a management agent to the displayName attribute when projecting the connector space object to the metaverse. Provided you name the management agent according to the connected account forest, the metaverse object's displayName attribute indicates the location of the user in the resource forest environment.

```
Public Sub MapAttributesForImport( _
    ByVal FlowRuleName As String, _
    ByVal csentry As CSEntry, _
    ByVal mventry As MVEntry) _
    Implements IMASynchronization.MapAttributesForImport

  Dim thisMA As ManagementAgent = csentry.MA
  Dim sDisplayName As String

  Select Case FlowRuleName.ToString.ToLower
    Case "displaynamemapping"
        sDisplayName = csentry("displayName").Value
             + " (" + thisMA.Name.ToString + ")"
        mventry("displayName").Value = sDisplayName
    Case Else
       Throw New EntryPointNotImplementedException
  End Select
End Sub
```

To use this code, you must configure a rules extension for the displayName-to-displayName attribute mapping under Configure Attribute Flow in the importing management agent, and you must add the rules extension DLL to the management agent under Configure Extensions. It is important to name the flow rule "DisplayNameMapping" (Figure 3-13), so the code can identify the rule and perform the correct action. The code obtains the displayName value from the connector space entry, adds to it the name of the management agent enclosed in brackets, and then assigns the resulting value to the displayName attribute of the metaverse entry.

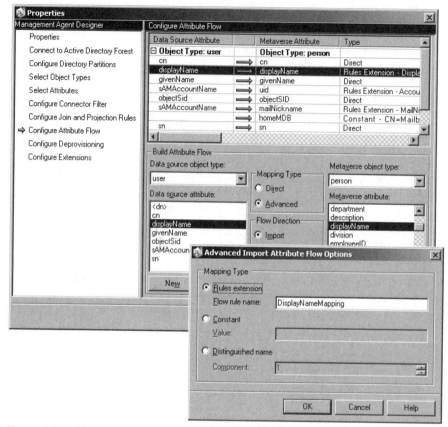

Figure 3-13   Mapping attributes by using a rules extension

Similarly, you can map the sAMAccountName attribute of the connector space object to the uid and mailNickname attributes of the metaverse object, with the added requirement that you must ensure the uniqueness of the values. You can use the following code to check any attribute (specified in the sAttribName parameter) for uniqueness. The code attempts to find another object with the same value in the metaverse, and if it does, it assigns the value a counter, which the code increases until a unique attribute value is generated or the code exceeds the maximum limit specified in RETRY_NUM_LIMIT.

```
Private Const RETRY_NUM_LIMIT = 1000

Private Function GetUniqueValue(ByVal sAttribName As String, _
            ByVal sValue As String, _
            ByVal sMAName As String, _
            ByVal mventry As MVEntry) As String
  Dim findResultList() As MVEntry
  Dim mvEntryFound As MVEntry
  Dim sUniqueValue As String = sValue + " (" + sMAName + ")"
  Dim iSuffix As Integer
```

```
' Create a unique naming attribute by adding a number to
' the existing mailNickname value.
For iSuffix = 1 To RETRY_NUM_LIMIT
   ' Check if the passed mailNickname value exists
   ' in the metaverse by using
   ' the Utils.FindMVEntries method.
   findResultList = Utils.FindMVEntries(sAttribName, sUniqueValue, 1)
   Select Case findResultList.Length
      Case 0
         ' The value does not exist in the metaverse,
         ' so it is unique.
         Exit For
      Case 1
         ' The value does exist in the metaverse,
         ' but it might be our own mventry,
         ' in which case it is still unique.
         mvEntryFound = findResultList(0)
         If mvEntryFound Is mventry Then
            Exit For
         Else
            ' Okay, it is not our mventry,
            ' so the current value is not unique.
            ' Loop again to make it unique.
            sUniqueValue = sValue + _
                  " (" + sMAName + iSuffix.ToString + ")"
         End If
      Case Else
         ' More than one item found,
         ' so the current value is not unique.
         sUniqueValue = sValue + _
               " (" + sMAName + iSuffix.ToString + ")"
   End Select
   Next
GetUniqueValue = sUniqueValue
End Function
```

You now must only extend the Select statement in the MapAttributesForImport method of your rules extension DLL, as shown in the following code, and configure advanced attribute flow rules named AccountNameMapping and MailNicknameMapping for the sAMAccountName-to-uid mapping and the sAMAccountName-to-mailNickname mapping.

```
Public Sub MapAttributesForImport( _
   ByVal FlowRuleName As String, _
   ByVal csentry As CSEntry, _
   ByVal mventry As MVEntry) _
   Implements IMASynchronization.MapAttributesForImport

   Dim thisMA As ManagementAgent = csentry.MA
   Dim sDisplayName As String

   Select Case FlowRuleName.ToString.ToLower
      Case "accountnamemapping"
```

```
                       ' Set the value for the uid attribute
                       ' to the source account's sAMAccountName attribute,
                       ' but ensure it is a unique value.
                       mventry("uid").Value = GetUniqueValue("uid", _
                               csentry("sAMAccountName").Value, _
                               thisMA.Name.ToString, mventry)
                 Case "mailnicknamemapping"
                       ' Set the value for the mailNickname attribute
                       ' to the source account's sAMAccountName attribute,
                       ' but ensure it is a unique value.
                       mventry("mailNickname").Value = GetUniqueValue( _
                               "mailNickname", _
                               csentry("sAMAccountName").Value, _
                               thisMA.Name.ToString, mventry)
                 Case "displaynamemapping"
                       sDisplayName = csentry("displayName").Value
                       sDisplayName = sDisplayName + " (" + _
                               thisMA.Name.ToString + ")"
                       mventry("displayName").Value = sDisplayName
                 Case Else
                   Throw New EntryPointNotImplementedException
                 End Select
          End Sub
```

Implementing a Metaverse Provisioning Extension

Having accomplished the configuration of attribute flow from the source accounts to the metaverse, you must now configure the attribute flow from the metaverse to the connector space that eventually will be exported to the resource forest. Before attributes can flow, however, you must create the connector space objects programmatically using a metaverse rules extension that implements the IMVSynchronization interface. You cannot create the connector space objects by importing them from the connected data source because the objects do not yet exist in the resource forest. You can program metaverse extensions using Visual Basic .NET 2003 or Visual C# .NET 2003.

To create a metaverse extension DLL, open the Tools menu in Identity Manager and click Configure Extensions. You can then select the Enable metaverse rules extension checkbox and the Provisioning rules extension checkbox (Figure 3-14). By clicking on Create Rules Extension Project, you can conveniently set up a Visual Studio project skeleton for your metaverse extension.

On the Resource Kit CD   You can find a sample metaverse rules extension project in the \Chapter 03\MIIS\MVExtensionfolder on the companion CD.

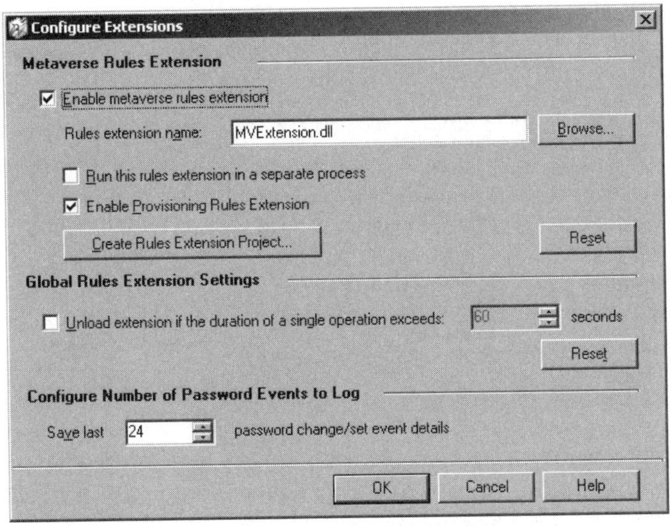

Figure 3-14   Enabling a provisioning rules extension

The most important method that you need to work with in the code is the Provision method. MIIS passes the metaverse entry that is currently being synchronized to this method. Depending on the situation, you must provision a connector space object for the metaverse object, change the distinguished name of the object, or deprovision the connector space object. The following code shows how to accomplish these tasks:

```
Public Sub Provision(ByVal mventry As MVEntry) _
        Implements IMVSynchronization.Provision
  Dim resMA As ConnectedMA = mventry.ConnectedMAs("RESDOM")
  Dim csentry As CSEntry
  Dim dn As ReferenceValue

  Select Case resMA.Connectors.Count
    Case 0
      ' The object does not exist in the connector space yet
      ' so create a new connector object
      Select Case mventry.ObjectType
        Case "person"
          ' It is a user account, create a mailbox for it.
          csentry = CreateResourceMailbox(mventry, resMA)
        Case "group"
          ' It is a group account, create an e-mail address
          csentry = CreateResourceMailAddress(mventry, resMA)
        Case Else
          Exit Sub
      End Select
    Case 1
      ' The object exists in the resource connector space.
      csentry = resMA.Connectors.ByIndex(0)
      If mventry.ConnectedMAs.Count.Equals(1) Then
        ' If the object only exists in the resource connector,
```

```
            ' but in no other connector space,
            ' then deprovision (delete) the object.
            csentry.Deprovision()
        Else
            ' The object's cn might have been changed.
            ' Update the distinguished name.
            dn = resMA.EscapeDNComponent("CN=" + _
                    mventry("cn").Value _
                    ).Concat(mventry("ou").Value.ToString)
            csentry.DN = dn
        End If
    Case Else
        Throw New UnexpectedDataException(PROV_ERR_MULTI_CONN + _
                    resMA.Connectors.Count.ToString)
    End Select
End Sub
```

The code first determines the exporting management agent (here named RES-DOM) and then checks the number of connector objects linked to the current metaverse entry in that agent's connector space. If the value is 0, no exported connector object exists yet, so you must create (provision) a new connector object that the management agent will eventually export to the resource forest. When provisioning a new connector object, you must check the type of metaverse object that is currently being synchronized. For users mapped to the metaverse object type person, you must create a mailbox-enabled account in the resource forest. For groups, you must create a mail-enabled distribution list. The functions CreateResourceMailbox and CreateResourceMailAddress accomplish these tasks, as explained later in this section. For any other types, you do not need to perform any provisioning actions.

If the resMA.Connectors.Count value is 1, then an exported connector object already exists in the exporting management agent's connector space. You now need to find out whether it is safe to delete (deprovision) the existing connector object, or whether you must rename the connector object (that is, change its distinguished name). The number of management agents that the current metaverse entry is associated with reveals the answer to this question.

- **mventry.ConnectedMAs.Count is 1** There is no importing management agent remaining. The exporting management agent is the only management agent associated with the metaverse entry, which means that the source account was removed, and it is safe to deprovision the existing connector object.

- **mventry.ConnectedMAs.Count is greater than 1** There still is an importing management agent, which implies that the source object still exists. You must not deprovision this object. Instead, you must determine whether you have to rename the object. This is accomplished by updating the distinguished name of the target account in the resource forest. The code above re-creates the target distinguished name by combining the cn attribute with the ou attribute of the metaverse entry. The ou attribute is a constant value. The common name of the user account, however, changes when an administrator renames the user account in the account forest. By recreating the distinguished name and reassigning the new distinguished name to the connector space object, you cause the exporting management agent to rename the target account during the next export cycle. On the other hand, if the source account was not renamed (that is, the common name has not changed), then the re-created distinguished name is the same as before. Reassigning the same distinguished name to the connector space object has no effect during the next export process.

Creating Mailbox-Enabled Accounts in the Resource Forest

If you determine that the metaverse object being synchronized is a person object that is not yet linked to an exported connector object, you must provision a new connector object. Furthermore, you must set the attributes of the new connector object to values that cause the creation of a mailbox account in the resource forest with an associated external account that is granted the correct mailbox and Active Directory rights. This sounds more complicated than it is. You can use the ExchangeUtils.CreateMailbox method that MIIS provides to accomplish these tasks in a single step.

The ExchangeUtils.CreateMailbox method requires the following parameters:

- **ResourceMA**   The exporting management agent for which to create the connector space object.

- **dn**   The distinguished name of the target account in the resource forest. The code constructs the target distinguished name based on the common name of the metaverse object and its ou attribute value.

- **nickName**   The mailNickname, which was set to a unique value during the import into the metaverse.

- **mailboxMDB**   The homeMDB, which was set to the distinguished name of the target mailbox store during the import into the metaverse.

- **sid**   The objectSID, which was mapped directly into the metaverse object from the source account.

The following code shows how to use the ExchangeUtils.CreateMailbox method:

```
Private Function CreateResourceMailbox(ByVal mventry As MVEntry, _
            ByRef ResourceMA As ConnectedMA) _
            As CSEntry
  Dim cnForObject As String = mventry("cn").Value.ToString()
  Dim nickName, mailboxMDB As String
  Dim dn As ReferenceValue
  Dim sid As Byte()

  ' Construct the distinguished name and obtain other information
  dn = ResourceMA.EscapeDNComponent("CN=" + _
          cnForObject).Concat(mventry("ou").Value.ToString)
```

```
nickName = mventry("mailNickname").Value
mailboxMDB = mventry("homeMDB").Value
sid = mventry("objectSID").BinaryValue

CreateResourceMailbox = ExchangeUtils.CreateMailbox(ResourceMA, _
                        dn, _
                        nickName, _
                        mailboxMDB, _
                        sid)
End Function
```

> **Note** For more information about the ExchangeUtils.CreateMailbox method, see the Microsoft Identity Integration Server 2003 Developer Reference in the Microsoft Platform SDK (*http://msdn.microsoft.com/library/ en-us/mmsdev/mms/portal.asp*).

Creating Distribution Lists in the Resource Forest

Creating distribution lists for Windows groups from account forests is also a straightforward task if you use the ExchangeUtils.CreateDistributionlist method that MIIS provides. The ExchangeUtils.CreateDistributionlist method requires the following parameters:

- **ResourceMA**   The exporting management agent for which to create the connector space object.

- **dn**   The distinguished name of the target group account in the resource forest. The code constructs the target distinguished name based on the common name of the metaverse object and its ou attribute value.

- **nickName**   The mailNickname, which was set to a unique value during the import into the metaverse.

The following code shows how to use the ExchangeUtils.CreateDistributionlist method:

```
Private Function CreateResourceMailAddress(ByVal mventry As MVEntry, _
                     ByRef ResourceMA As ConnectedMA) _
                     As CSEntry
  Dim cnForObject As String = mventry("cn").Value.ToString()
  Dim dn As ReferenceValue
  Dim nickName As String

  ' Construct the distinguished name
  dn = ResourceMA.EscapeDNComponent("CN=" + _
           cnForObject).Concat(mventry("ou").Value.ToString)
  nickName = mventry("mailNickname").Value
```

```
CreateResourceMailAddress = ExchangeUtils.CreateDistributionlist( _
                            ResourceMA, _
                            dn, _
                            nickName)
End Function
```

> **Note** For more information about the ExchangeUtils.CreateDistributionlist method, see the Microsoft Identity Integration Server 2003 Developer Reference in the Microsoft Platform SDK (*http://msdn.microsoft.com/library/ en-us/mmsdev/mms/portal.asp*).

Configuring Outbound Attribute Flow

Now that a connector object exists and is linked to the metaverse object, MIIS can synchronize further attributes. Because you already prepared the attributes during the import into the metaverse, exporting the attributes from the metaverse into the connector space object can be accomplished through direct mappings. Figure 3-15 shows an example. Note that the flow direction is set to Export to apply the information from the metaverse object to the connector space object being exported. Note also that the common name is not mapped. The distinguished name of the exported connector object contains and defines the common name of the target mailbox account.

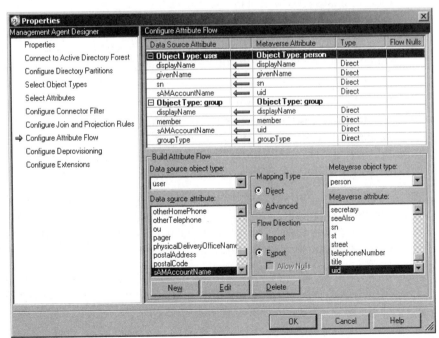

Figure 3-15 Exporting attributes from the metaverse through direct attribute mappings

Running Management Agents

Management agents do not run automatically. For each management agent, you must configure run profiles, which specify the actions that the agent is supposed to perform. A particular run profile can include multiple actions, but it is also possible to configure multiple run profiles for a particular management agent. At least one run profile with at least one action is required to run a management agent.

On the Resource Kit CD   For step-by-step instructions about how to configure run profiles for management agents, see the document Adding MIIS to the Resource Forest Test Environment.doc, which you can find in the \Chapter 03\Resource Forest folder on the companion CD.

You can configure run profiles to perform the following actions:

- **Delta Import (Stage Only)**   Select this action to import into the connector space only the objects that have changed in the connected data source since the last import run. Information is not propagated to the metaverse.

- **Full Import (Stage Only)**   Select this action to import all objects and attributes from the connected data source to the connector space. Information is not propagated to the metaverse.

- **Delta Import and Delta Synchronization**   Select this action to import into the connector space only the objects that have changed in the connected data source since the last import run, and then apply synchronization rules to those objects that have changed in the connector space to synchronize these objects with the metaverse.

- **Full Import and Delta Synchronization**   Select this action to import all objects and attributes from the connected data source to the connector space, and then apply synchronization rules to the objects that have changed in the connector space to synchronize those objects with the metaverse.

- **Full Import and Full Synchronization**   Select this action to import all objects and attributes from the connected data source to the connector space, and then apply synchronization rules to all objects in the connector space to synchronize those objects with the metaverse.

- **Delta Synchronization**   Select this action to apply synchronization rules to the objects staged in the connector space that have changed to synchronize those objects with the metaverse.

- **Full Synchronization**   Select this action to apply synchronization rules to all objects staged in the connector space to synchronize those objects with the metaverse.

- **Export**   Select this action to export from a connector space to a connected data source the objects and attributes that have been created, changed, or deleted since the last export run. An export is always a delta synchronization.

Sequence of Synchronization Steps

Although it might seem surprising, the very first action that you should perform is a Full Import (Stage Only) run of the exporting management agent that connects the resource forest to MIIS. This import is required because the exporting management agent must discover what target containers and organizational units exist in the resource forest. If the target organizational unit does not exist in the resource forest, MIIS will report an error when attempting to assign a connector space object a distinguished name that points to the non-existent organizational unit. For example, you must create an organizational unit called ADDOM in the resource forest (resdom.msn) so you can place the mailbox account for Ted Bremer into this organizational unit by assigning the corresponding connector space object the distinguished name CN=Ted Bremer,OU=ADDOM,DC=resdom,DC=msn. The Full Import (Stage Only) run ensures that the exporting management agent has the required information about the ADDOM organizational unit. Note that you must include the target containers and organizational units in the management configuration on the Selecting directory partitions page.

Having accomplished the initial full import, you can perform an import and synchronization for each importing management agent. During the synchronization, the provisioning code will stage connector objects in the export connector space. It is usually sufficient to run delta imports and delta synchronizations, but if you suspect the directory information to be out of sync, you can run a full import and full synchronization.

When you have all the objects that you want in the export connector space, you can perform an export run of the management agent that connects MIIS to the resource forest. New mailbox-enabled accounts are then created in the target organizational units. Existing mailbox accounts are renamed, and deprovisioned mailbox accounts are deleted. It is important to keep the export connector space synchronized with the resource forest, so you should perform a Delta Import (Stage Only) run after the export to update the connector space.

Automating Management Agents

You can run synchronization profiles for each management agent manually using Identity Manager, but you can also automate the processing using a custom script. This is a good idea, especially if you have a large number of account forests and Windows NT domains. You can use the Scheduled Tasks tool in Windows 2003 to automatically run a custom script that triggers management agent runs at non-peak usage hours, when network traffic is low.

The following code demonstrates how to control a management agent called RESDOM on an MIIS server called SERVER02 programmatically using Windows Management Interface (WMI) Provider for Microsoft Identity Integration Server 2003.

```
set oWMILocator = CreateObject("WbemScripting.SWbemLocator")
set oWMIService = oWMILocator.ConnectServer("SERVER02", _
            "root/MicrosoftIdentityIntegrationServer")
Set oManagementAgent = oWMIService.Get( _
            "MIIS_ManagementAgent.Name='RESDOM'")
runResult = oManagementAgent.Execute("Export")
```

On the Resource Kit CD   For a complete script that uses the WMI provider for MIIS, see the document runMAProfile.wsf, which you can find in the \Companion Material\Chapter 03\Scripts folder on the companion CD. In addition, the document Adding MIIS to the Resource Forest Test Environment.doc on the companion CD outlines a batch file that uses this script to run a complete synchronization cycle over all management agents in the test environment.

Integrating Exchange Organizations in Multiple Forest Environments

You can also use Identity Integration Server or Identity Integration Feature Pack for Microsoft Windows Server Active Directory to integrate Exchange organizations in multiple forest environments with each other. Specifically, you can use the Active Directory global address list (GAL) management agent that is included in both products to synchronize recipient information between Active Directory forests that contain Exchange 2000 Server or Exchange Server 2003 organizations (Figure 3-16).

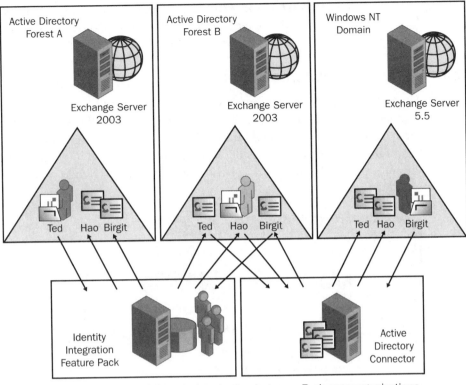

Figure 3-16 Global address list synchronization between Exchange organizations

As indicated in Figure 3-16, Identity Integration Server-based GAL synchronization does not include Exchange Server 5.5. Although MIIS comes with management agents for Exchange Server 5.5, these management agents include no "out of the box" GAL synchronization logic. You therefore must implement GAL synchronization manually, similar to provisioning mailbox accounts in a resource forest, but with the added complexity that all management agents must perform both import and export operations. It is not a trivial task to coordinate various different importing and exporting Active Directory and Exchange 5.5 management agents and to create correct connector space objects for each connected Active Directory forest and Exchange 5.5 directory. Instead of using Identity Integration Server for GAL synchronization between Exchange Server 2003 and Exchange Server 5.5, you might want to use a more readily available and cost effective solution.

We recommend that you use the following tools for GAL synchronization:

- **GAL synchronization with Exchange 2000 Server or Exchange Server 2003 organizations** Use Identity Integration Feature Pack for Microsoft Windows Server Active Directory and configure Active Directory GAL management agents.

- **GAL synchronization with Exchange Server 5.5 organizations** Use Active Directory Connector (ADC), included in Exchange Server 2003 Service Pack 1, and configure inter-organizational connection agreements.

Global Address List Synchronization

The GAL contains all recipients within the organization, including all mailbox-enabled users, mail-enabled users, groups, and contacts. If not all recipients are in the same organization, users might find it difficult to locate each other. Figure 3-17 shows the address books of the users depicted in Figure 3-16 without aggregation of recipient information through GAL synchronization. The Exchange organizations appear isolated.

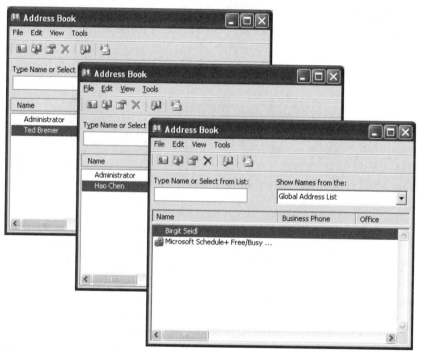

Figure 3-17   Address lists from a multiple forest test environment without GAL synchronization

To solve this problem, you must create recipients in each organization that represent the external users. Table 3-8 lists the directory objects that you can use to import address information from other Exchange organizations into a global address list.

Table 3-8   Recipient Objects for External Users in Exchange Address Lists

Exchange Version	Recipient Object	Comments
Exchange Server 5.5	Custom recipient	A custom recipient is a recipient in Exchange 5.5 that has no mailbox in the local organization. Instead, the custom recipient is associated with an external e-mail address to facilitate messaging between the local organization and the external user.
Exchange 2000 Server or Exchange Server 2003	Mail-enabled user account	A mail-enabled user account is an Active Directory account that represents a user in the local Active Directory forest who does not have a mailbox in the Exchange organization. For example, a user of a non-Exchange messaging system in the local environment might work with an Active Directory account in the local forest. It is possible to mail-enable the user account to include the e-mail address of the non-Exchange user in the Exchange global address list.
	Mail-enabled contact	An Active Directory account that represents a recipient outside the local Active Directory forest. A contact is a non-security principal, meaning the account cannot be used to log on to the domain. You typically use mail-enabled contacts to represent external recipients, such as users, distribution groups, or custom recipients that exist in an external messaging system. This recipient object is similar to a custom recipient in Exchange Server 5.5. Note that you should create mail-enabled contacts for recipients from other Exchange organizations, because these recipients are not in the local Active Directory forest.

Active Directory Synchronization

Global address list synchronization is available for native mode Exchange 2003 organizations and Exchange 2003 organizations in mixed mode running any combination of Exchange 5.5, Exchange 2000, and Exchange 2003. The main consideration is that the recipient information must be available in Active Directory so you can use the Active Directory global address list (GAL) management agent.

Deploying Identity Integration Feature Pack

In an environment with multiple Exchange 2003 organizations, you can synchronize all forests using a single server running Identity Integration Feature Pack or Identity Integration Server. Figure 3-16 depicted a configuration with a single MIIS server. This arrangement is also called a hub-spoke topology, because a single server running MIIS acts as a hub to consolidate all recipient information and propagates this information to each connected forest. The GAL management agents form the spokes in this topology. A separate management agent is required for each forest participating in the synchronization. Each GAL management agent imports recipients from the connected forest into the metadirectory and can then be used to export recipient information in the form of mail-enabled contacts to a specified target organizational unit in the connected forest. You must use different source and target containers or organizational units for imported and exported recipient information.

On the Resource Kit CD For step-by-step instructions about how to deploy a hub-spoke GAL synchronization topology, see the document Adding MIIS to the Multiple Forest Test Environment.doc, which you can find in the \Companion Material\Chapter 03\Multiple Forests folder on the companion CD.

You must configure at least one Active Directory GAL management agent per forest, but you can also use separate GAL management agents for imports and exports. Furthermore, you can use multiple servers running MIIS in a meshed topology. Deploying a hub-spoke synchronization topology is recommended, because a single server running MIIS is easier to maintain than multiple servers, but security considerations might require you to install a separate MIIS server in each forest. If business units in your company are reluctant to provide you with accounts that have administrative permissions in target domains and organizational units (a requirement for exporting directory information into a connected forest by using a GAL management agent), you can provide each business unit with an individual MIIS server to export directory information into each forest. Figure 3-18 illustrates this topology.

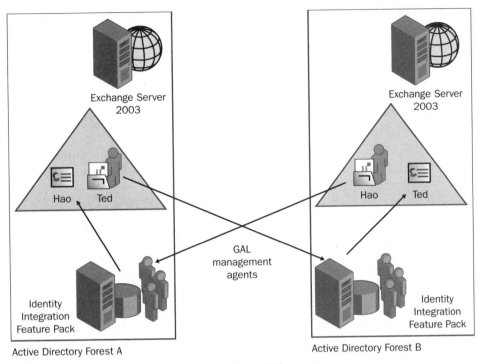

Figure 3-18   GAL synchronization using multiple MIIS servers

Note   To ensure that management agents can export contacts to target forests, the server running Identity Integration Feature Pack or Identity Integration Server 2003 must be able to connect to a domain controller in each of the participating forests through LDAP. Management agents can manage multiple domains, but they must access domain controllers instead of global catalog servers, because global catalog servers do not provide write access to domain information. Furthermore, Identity Integration Feature Pack and Identity Integration Server 2003 require permissions on the entire directory partition to use the dirsync control API provided by Active Directory. The Identity Integration Server service account must be granted replicate directory changes permissions on the appropriate partition, which grants MIIS read access on all objects in the partition.

Single-Master Replication

GAL synchronization does not support a multi-master replication model. In other words, a single recipient cannot have multiple authoritative recipient objects. If you must use separate management agents on the same or separate MIIS servers to import and export directory information for a connected forest, you must carefully design the GAL synchronization topology to avoid conflicts. Among other things, you must ensure that exported directory information does not flow back to the originating forest. For example, in Figure 3-18, the organizational unit that you specify in Forest A as a target container for contact objects from Forest B must not be used as a source container to import recipient information from Forest A into Forest B.

This is important because when you import exported recipient information, MIIS might merge the information in the metaverse with the original user information based on the join rules preconfigured for the GAL synchronization agents. If the directory information was changed during the export (for example, a display name was appended with further information) or if an administrator in Forest A changed any information on the contact object manually, this information might flow back into Forest B, causing a change of attribute values on the original user object. Even worse, if the administrator in Forest A deleted the contact, the user in Forest B might find his or her user account deleted after the next synchronization cycle.

You should avoid configurations in which organizational units that are designated as target containers in one management agent serve as source containers in other management agents. Such configurations run the risk of creating circular topologies. An exception to this rule is chain topologies, in which recipient objects from Forest A are exported into an organizational unit in Forest B, and then this organizational unit is used as a source container in a management agent exporting recipient information into Forest C. This configuration works, as long as you do not re-import the Forest A recipients through any synchronization path back into Forest A.

> **Note**   Active Directory GAL synchronization agents are best deployed in a hub-spoke topology because of the reduced risk of creating a situation in which multiple recipient objects are authoritative for a particular recipient or creating synchronization loops.

Synchronizing Distribution Groups

By default, Active Directory GAL management agents create mail-enabled contact objects in target organizational units to represent users, groups, or contacts from an external messaging system. Mail-enabled contacts are a perfect choice for external users and contacts, but have the following limitations when representing external distribution groups:

- Contact objects do not reveal group memberships in the address book.

- Message transfer might be inefficient if a group contains recipient objects from multiple forests. For example, if an administrator creates a distribution group in

Forest B and adds recipients from Forest A and Forest B to that group, and if that group is then synchronized as a contact into Forest A, messages from Forest A that are addressed to this group contact will first travel to Forest B, where the group is expanded to route the message to each member, and will then be transferred back into Forest A for all Forest A group members.

■ Users cannot send encrypted messages to a distribution group in another forest, because the client cannot expand the group membership to determine the X.509 certificate and public encryption key for each individual user.

Inefficient message transfer is the main reason that you might want to exclude group objects from GAL synchronization in the management agent configuration. Doing so, however, means that administrators must create and maintain distribution groups in each forest individually. Another option is to reprogram the GALSync.dll file, which implements the provisioning logic. The source code is installed with Identity Integration Server and can be found in the \Program Files\Microsoft Identity Integration Server\SourceCode\GalSync folder.

You must use Visual Studio .NET 2003 to program GALSync.dll. If you open the GALMV.vb file, you can find a method called AddOrRenameConnector in which the ExchangeUtils.CreateMailEnabledContact method is called to provision contact objects for all types of MVEntry objects. You must check the MVEntry property named ObjectType to see if you are provisioning a group object, and then call the ExchangeUtils.CreateDistributionlist method instead of ExchangeUtils.CreateMailEnabledContact for groups. The source code, discussed earlier in this chapter, demonstrates the use of mventry.ObjectType and the ExchangeUtils.CreateDistributionlist method.

However, before changing the provisioning logic, consider the following disadvantages of synchronizing groups as groups instead of as contacts:

■ **Possible lost messages**   GAL synchronization cannot guarantee that all group members are synchronized. For example, a group might contain the Administrator account, but if you decided to filter out this account, it is not replicated to external forests. In the target forest, the group is now missing a member, and if a user in that forest sends a message to the group, the Administrator account does not get the message.

■ **Increased synchronization traffic**   Changes to group memberships must be replicated to all external forests.

■ **Messages reach non-members**   If changes to group membership are replicated infrequently, recipients who have been removed from distribution groups might, for a period of time, continue to receive e-mail messages from external users addressed to those groups. This can potentially lead to disclosure of confidential information.

- **Inconsistent group membership**   Administrators in target forests might add members to distribution groups imported from other forests. You must not re-import directory information into the source forest, so any changes to group memberships applied in other forests will not be reflected on the original group. When users in Forest A now send a message to the distribution group, they might reach a different set of recipients than the users in Forest B.

- **Possible disclosure of hidden memberships**   If you synchronize groups as groups, Identity Information Server replicates membership information to the external forests that might be hidden in the original forest. You can implement code to hide the group membership information from the Exchange address books, but you cannot hide the group membership information from administrators in the external forests. External administrators can use Active Directory Users and Computers to analyze the membership information of potentially security sensitive groups.

- **Expansion servers in the original forest cannot be used**   Distribution groups with specific expansion servers will not be expanded on those servers when users in other forests send messages to the distribution group. Exchange 2003 can only use expansion serves in the local Exchange 2003 organization.

- **No support for query-based distribution groups**   The query-based distribution group is a type of group, first introduced in Exchange 2003, that uses a real-time LDAP query to the global address list to generate group membership information dynamically rather than using a static list of group members as in a conventional distribution group. For example, you can use the following LDAP filter to include all Exchange users in a query-based distribution group: (&(objectClass=user)(homeMDB=*)(!msExchHideFromAddressLists=TRUE)). Yet, if you reprogram GALSync.dll to synchronize this query-based distribution group as a group to another forest, then the LDAP query is performed against a different global address list. Messages addressed to this query-based distribution group will then reach an entirely different set of recipients in each forest.

Synchronizing Additional Exchange Recipient Objects

The Active Directory GAL management agent included in Identity Feature Pack and Microsoft Identity Integration Server 2003 supports synchronizing users, conventional distribution groups, and contacts, but an Exchange 2003 organization can have more than these three standard types of recipients. Additional objects that you can mailbox-enable or mail-enable in an Exchange 2003 organization include:

- **InetOrgPerson accounts**   The inetOrgPerson class is defined in RFC 2798 and is generally used in directories other than Active Directory to define user accounts. A company that uses directory applications requiring inetOrgPerson objects or that has other directory compatibility requirements can create ine-tOrgPerson objects in Active Directory instead of creating ordinary user accounts. In Windows 2003, the inetOrgPerson class is derived from and fully compatible with the user class.

- **Query-based distribution groups**   A company can use query-based distribution groups to lower administrative cost and effort associated with maintaining group memberships. You do not have to add members to groups on an ongoing basis. You only need to populate the user attributes systematically in Active Directory Users and Computers, and whenever the query-based distribution group is used, the users are automatically included in the resultant query.

- **Public folders**   You can mail-enable public folders in Exchange System Manager so you can use them as recipients in e-mail messages. In fact, public folders in the MAPI-based tree are automatically mail-enabled, although they are hidden from the address book by default. You can make public folders visible in the address book by deselecting the Hide From Address Book check box on the Exchange Advanced tab, which the Exchange System Manager displays in the public folder properties.

As soon as you display a public folder in the client's address book, users can select the folder as a message recipient. It is also possible to add a public folder to a distribution group, which allows you to keep track of discussions in teams, workgroups, and so forth. This frees team members from having to maintain personal discussion folders for distribution lists. Users must have permissions to create items in a public folder if they want to send messages to it. Otherwise, a non-delivery report informs the sender about the missing permissions. By default, everyone has permissions to create items in a public folder.

To synchronize inetOrgPerson accounts, query-based distribution groups, and public folders, you must adjust the Active Directory GAL management agent configuration. You must include the object types inetOrgPerson, msExchDynamicDistributionList, and publicFolder, and you must configure join and projection rules to propagate the recipient information to the metaverse.

On the Resource Kit CD   For step-by-step instructions about how to support inetOrgPerson, msExchDynamicDistributionList and publicFolder objects, see the documents Synchronizing inetOrgPerson Recipients in the Multiple Forest Test Environment.doc, Synchronizing Dynamic Distribution Groups in the Multiple Forest Test Environment.doc, and Synchronizing Public Folder Recipients in the Multiple Forest Test Environment.doc, which you can find in the \Companion Material\Chapter 03\Multiple Forests folder on the companion CD.

As shown in Figure 3-19, user and inetOrgPerson objects can be mapped to person objects in the metaverse. Group and msExchDynamicDistributionList objects are mapped to group objects, and publicFolder objects are also treated as groups because these objects have similar recipient information and can be used to reach multiple users.

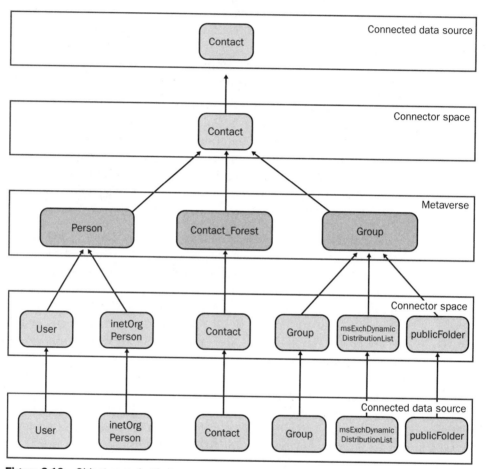

Figure 3-19   Object mapping between source and target directories

The advantage of mapping inetOrgPerson, msExchDynamicDistributionList, and publicFolder objects to existing object types in the metaverse (instead of creating new object types) is that you can use existing join and projection rules and GAL synchronization logic to provision contacts in the connected target forest. You can use existing rules for connector filters, as well as existing rules extensions that handle import and export attribute flow. The default GALSync.dll file included in Identity Feature Pack and Identity Integration Server 2003, however, is not aware of inetOrgPerson, msExchDynamicDistributionList, and publicFolder objects.

On the Resource Kit CD You must replace the default GALSync.dll file in the \Program Files\Microsoft Identity Integration Server\Extensions folder with an extended GALSync.dll version, available in the \Companion Material\Chapter 03\MIIS folder on the companion CD.

Table 3-9 compares both GALSync.dll versions.

Table 3-9   Synchronizing Exchange Recipient Objects Through GALSync.dll

Recipient Object	GALSync.dll available in Identity Feature Pack and Identity Integration Server 2003	GALSync.dll available in \Companion Material\Chapter 03 \MIIS folder on the companion CD
User	Yes	Yes
Group	Yes	Yes
Contact	Yes	Yes
InetOrgPerson	No	Yes
Query-based distribution group	No	Yes
Public Folder	No	Yes

Modifying Attribute Flow

In the default configuration, Active Directory GAL management agents use a very straightforward attribute mapping, which is sufficient for most attributes.

On the Resource Kit CD The document Synchronizing inetOrgPerson Recipients in the Multiple Forest Test Environment.doc, which you can find in the \Companion Material\Chapter 03\Multiple Forests folder on the companion CD contains a table that details the attribute mapping for user (inetOrgPerson) accounts, for example.

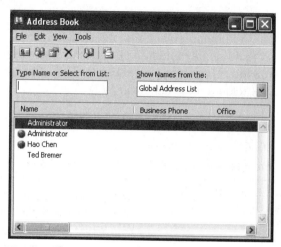

Figure 3-20   A synchronized address book without display name customization

However, a direct mapping of attributes might not always be an optimal choice. As shown in Figure 3-20, different organizations can have recipients with similar display names, but similar looking address book entries make it difficult for users to select the correct recipient. This becomes an increasingly more serious problem the more Exchange organizations you synchronize, as users might accidentally send confidential messages to the wrong recipients. To mitigate this risk, you should include information in the display name that allows the users to identify each recipient more specifically. For example, you might want to include the name of the Exchange organization in each external user's display name.

The GALSync.dll file that you can find in \Companion Material\Chapter 03\MIIS folder on the companion CD includes code for an attribute flow rule called DisplayNameMapping that extracts the name of the Exchange organization from the recipient's legacyExchangeDN attribute and then appends this information enclosed in brackets to the display name when importing the recipient into the metaverse. If you replaced the original GALSync.dll file in the \Program Files\Microsoft Identity Integration Server\Extensions folder with the extended GALSync.dll version, you can change the display name mapping in your GAL management agents to use this attribute flow rule.

On the Resource Kit CD   For detailed step-by-step instructions about how to configure the attribute mapping, see the document Changing the DisplayName Attribute Flow.doc, which you can find in the \Companion Material\Chapter 03\Multiple Forests folder on the companion CD.

Figure 3-21 shows the resulting address book information.

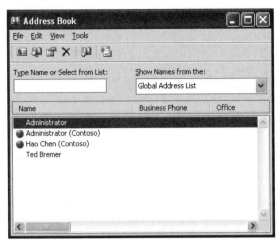

Figure 3-21   A synchronized address book with display name customization

   The following code example, taken from GALMA.vb, shows the DisplayNameMapping logic. Before appending the display name with the organization name extracted from the legacyExchangeDN attribute, the code checks to confirm whether the legacyExchangeDN attribute exists, and whether the display name may be appended. Otherwise, the display name is mapped directly without additional information.

```
Private Sub IAFDisplayName( _
          ByVal csentry As CSEntry, _
          ByRef mventry As MVEntry)

  Dim sDisplayName As String = csentry(DISPLAY_NAME).Value

  If csentry(LEGACY_EXCHANGE_DN).IsPresent _
        AndAlso AppendOK(sDisplayName) Then
    mventry(DISPLAY_NAME).Value = sDisplayName + " (" _
    + GetExchangeOrgName(csentry(LEGACY_EXCHANGE_DN).Value.ToString) _
          + ")"
  Else
    mventry(DISPLAY_NAME).Value = sDisplayName
  End If
End Sub

Private Function GetExchangeOrgName(ByVal sLegacyExchangeDN As String) _
                          As String
  'legacyExchangeDN format: /o=Organization/ou=/cn=/cn=
  Dim i As Integer
  Dim sName As String

  i = InStr(4, sLegacyExchangeDN, "/")
  If i > 4 Then
    sName = Mid(sLegacyExchangeDN, 4, i - 4)
  Else
    ' Organization name not extractable, use a default value
```

```
      sName = "Extern"
   End If
      GetExchangeOrgName = sName
End Function

Private Function AppendOK(ByVal sValue As String) As Boolean
   Dim x, y As Integer

   ' By default, append
   AppendOK = True

   x = InStr(1, sValue, "(")
   y = InStr(1, sValue, ")")

   If y > x Then
      ' There is a "(...)", so it is not okay to append
      AppendOK = False
   End If
End Function
```

The AppendOK method determines if a display name can be appended based on the criteria that an opening and closing parenthesis must not exist yet. If an opening and closing bracket already exists, then the display name already has additional information. A recipient object might already have a modified display name, for example, in a topology in which separate GAL management agents synchronize recipient information. Consider a chain topology between Forest A and Forest B, and Forest B and Forest C. Recipients replicated into Forest B will already have a modified display name, which must not be appended again during the next replication cycle.

Note If the naming conventions for recipient objects in your organization rely on parenthesis in the display name, you must modify GALMA.vb to use different criteria for checking that a display name can be appended. Another option is to change the naming conventions.

Exchange Server 5.5 Directory Synchronization

GAL synchronization does not work for pure Exchange 5.5 organizations because these organizations do not maintain recipient information in Active Directory. However, you can integrate Exchange 5.5 and Active Directory by using Active Directory Connector (ADC). In doing so, you have two options. You can deploy multiple servers each synchronizing a single forest with Exchange 5.5, or you can deploy a single server running Active Directory Connector in a hub-spoke topology, as shown in Figure 3-22.

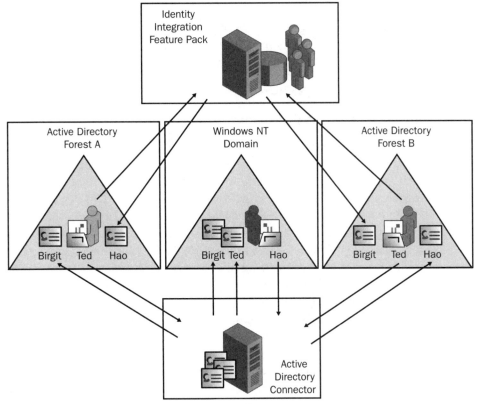

Figure 3-22 Synchronizing multiple Exchange 2003 organizations with an Exchange 5.5 organization

A significant disadvantage of synchronizing each forest individually with Exchange 5.5, as shown in Figure 3-22, is increased administrative overhead. You must maintain separate connection agreements for each forest. Coordinating the Active Directory Connector topology with a GAL synchronization topology and avoiding synchronization loops is also a complex task that becomes increasingly more difficult with the number of Exchange organizations, Active Directory Connector installations, and connection agreements. Perhaps a better approach is to deploy Active Directory Connector only between one forest and the Exchange 5.5 organization and then use the GAL synchronization infrastructure to replicate the recipient information to all remaining forests. Active Directory Connector replicates Exchange 5.5 recipients as mail-enabled contacts to Active Directory. You can then use MIIS or Identity Feature Pack to synchronize these Active Directory contacts across all forests. In the forest connected to Exchange 5.5, Active Directory Connector also replicates the Exchange 2003 recipients as custom recipients into the Exchange 5.5 directory. Figure 3-16 earlier in this chapter illustrates this topology.

> **Note** To integrate Exchange 5.5 with Exchange 2003, use the Exchange 2003 version of Active Directory Connector. You must have at least one server in each Exchange site running Exchange 5.5 SP3.

Inter-Organizational Connection Agreements

The way in which you integrate Exchange 5.5 with Active Directory depends on whether you plan to upgrade the Exchange 5.5 organization eventually to Exchange 2003. If you are planning to upgrade to Exchange 2003, you should first upgrade the Windows NT domain to Active Directory. Next, deploy recipient connection agreements to replicate Active Directory with Exchange 5.5 directory information, and then add an Exchange 2003 server to the organization. Having accomplished these steps, you can use MIIS or Identity Feature Pack to synchronize recipient information across forests. For more information about upgrading from Exchange 5.5 to Exchange 2003, see Chapter 4, "Upgrading to Exchange Server 2003."

On the other hand, if you are not planning to upgrade, you must configure inter-organizational connection agreements between the Exchange 5.5 organization and an Exchange 2003 organization in an Active Directory forest. Inter-organizational connection agreements create mail-enabled contact objects in Active Directory or custom recipients in the Exchange 5.5 directory. The synchronization is always one-way, so you must configure two connection agreements that point in opposite directions to enable full synchronization. The logic of the one-way connection agreement assumes that the source object is authoritative and the target object is not. There is no coordination between inter-organizational connection agreements pointing in opposite directions, so it is important not to use the target container of the first connection agreement as the source container of the second connection agreement. You also must coordinate source and target containers with GAL management agents. The synchronization topology determines what containers you must specify in an inter-organizational connection agreement (Table 3-10).

Table 3-10   Source and Target Containers for Inter-organizational Connection Agreements

Topology	To Active Directory	To Exchange 5.5 Directory
Hub-spoke or chain topology	Specify a common organizational unit for Active Directory Connector and GAL management agent, as follows: Active Directory Connector uses the organizational unit as the target for Exchange 5.5 recipient information. GAL management agent uses the organizational unit as a source container to replicate contacts to other forests.	Specify a common recipient container. Active Directory Connector will replicate all recipients that are possibly from multiple source containers in Active Directory into a single recipient container.
Mesh topology	Specify separate organizational units for Active Directory Connector and GAL management agent. Because additional inter-organizational connection agreements will replicate Exchange 5.5 recipients into each forest individually, you must exclude the ADC target container from GAL synchronization.	Specify a common or separate recipient container for each forest. Do not include recipient containers for Exchange 2003 users as source containers in inter-organizational connection agreements, because this recipient information is separately replicated between forests using GAL management agents.

On the Resource Kit CD   For an example of how to configure inter-organizational connection agreements and GAL management agents to synchronize Exchange 5.5 and Exchange 2003 recipient information across a multiple forest environment, see the document Adding ADC to the GAL Synchronization Topology.doc, which you can find in the \Companion Material\Chapter 03\Multiple Forests folder on the companion CD.

Extending Inter-organizational Connection Agreements

Inter-organizational connection agreements replicate only standard recipient objects, such as users, distribution lists, and contacts, between Exchange 5.5 and Exchange 2003 organizations, but as listed in Table 3-11, an Exchange 2003 organization can have more recipient objects.

Table 3-11 Standard Recipient Mapping in Inter-organizational Connection Agreements

Exchange 5.5 Recipient	Exchange 2003 Recipient
Mailbox	User
Custom recipient	Contact
Distribution list	Group
Not mapped	Query-based distribution group
Not mapped	inetOrgPerson
Not mapped	publicFolder

You can extend standard recipient connection agreements to synchronize mail-enabled query-based distribution groups and inetOrgPerson objects as custom recipients from Active Directory to Exchange 5.5. This is an advanced customization task that you cannot perform using the Active Directory Connector snap-in. You must use a low-level tool, such as ldp.exe or ADSI Edit (AdsiEdit.msc), or program a solution based on ADSI.

On the Resource Kit CD The script ManageICA.wsf, which you can find in the \Companion Material\Chapter 03\Scripts folder on the companion CD, demonstrates how to customize the configuration of connection agreements through ADSI.

Note It is important that you thoroughly test and document any advanced customizations to ensure good supportability. You must carefully test the behavior of any changes described in the following steps, including LDAP search filters and schema mapping rules. Microsoft cannot support issues that arise as a result of modification in any of these areas. If you have made any of these customizations and subsequently call Microsoft Product Support Services about problems with inter-organizational connection agreements, let Product Support Services know about the changes that you have made.

To extend an inter-organizational connection agreement to replicate query-based distribution groups and inetOrgPerson objects as contacts into an Exchange 5.5 organization, accomplish the following steps:

1. **Change the LDAP search filter rule**   Inter-organizational connection agreements have an attribute called msExchServer1SearchFilter that contains an LDAP search filter that specifies the object classes to be included in the replication from Active Directory to Exchange 5.5. The replication from Exchange 5.5 to Active Directory, on the other hand, is governed by an LDAP search filter specified through the msExchServer2SearchFilter attribute. The '1' in msExchServer1SearchFilter stands for Active Directory, and a '2' represents the Exchange 5.5 directory.

    For example, if you configured an inter-organizational connection agreement to replicate users, groups, and contacts from Active Directory to Exchange 5.5, then the msExchServer1SearchFilter will look as follows: `(|(objectclass=user)(objectclass=contact)(objectclass=group))`. The vertical bar at the beginning of the string indicates this is an OR filter. The syntax of LDAP search filters is defined in RFC 2254.

    If you want to include query-based distribution groups and inetOrgPerson objects in addition, you must modify the msExchServer1SearchFilter. You can use ADSI Edit for this purpose. Display the properties of the desired connection agreement under CN=Active Directory Connections,CN=Microsoft Exchange,CN=Services in the configuration naming context. Select the msExchServer1SearchFilter attribute, and then type in the following LDAP search string: `(|(object-`
`class=user)(objectclass=contact)(objectclass=group)(objectclass=msExchDynam-`
`icDistributionList)(objectclass=inetOrgPerson))`.

> **Warning**   If you use the ADSI Edit snap-in or a custom ADSI tool, and you incorrectly modify the attributes of Active Directory objects, you can cause serious problems. These problems may require you to reinstall Windows 2003, Exchange 2003, or both. Microsoft cannot guarantee that problems that occur if you incorrectly modify Active Directory object attributes can be solved. Use ADSI Edit at your own risk.

2. **Change the attribute mapping table**   After you include msExchDynamicDistributionList and inetOrgPerson objects in the msExchServer1SearchFilter, you must customize the rules for matching attributes between Active Directory and Exchange 5.5. Matching rules are defined in an ADC Policy object so they can be applied to multiple connection agreements. Each connection agreement's msExchCASchemaPolicy attribute points to the ADC Policy object being used. By default, only one ADC Policy object, named Default ADC Policy, exists. You can find this object under CN=Active Directory Connections,CN=Microsoft Exchange,CN=Services in the configuration naming context.

The ADC Policy object has two attributes:

- **msExchServer1SchemaMap**   Represents   attribute   mappings   from Active Directory to Microsoft Exchange Server 5.5.

- **msExchServer2SchemaMap**   Represents attribute mapping from Exchange Server 5.5 to Active Directory.

Active Directory Connector validates object class matches by searching through the attribute maps to see if at least one rule is specified for each object class. If a rule is specified, the mapping is considered a valid match. If no rules are specified, the mapping is not valid. Because by default no rules exist for msExchDynamicDistributionList and inetOrgPerson objects, you must modify the msExchServer1SchemaMap to include at least one rule for each of these object classes.

Each line in the attribute mapping files has the following syntax:

```
comment#src-class#tgt-class#src-attr#tgt-attr#prefix#dn-syntax#flags#
```

The first field in the attribute mapping syntax is a comment that you can set to any value. The second field represents the source object class. For msExchDynamicDistributionList objects, you must specify msExchDynamicDistributionList$top, and for inetOrgPerson objects you must specify inetOrgPerson$user$organizationalperson$person$top as the object class. The third field is the target object class. Because inter-organizational connection agreements create custom recipients in the Exchange 5.5 directory, you must always specify the object class remote-address$person$top. In the fourth and fifth field, you can then specify source and target attributes. Table 3-12 summarizes the individual fields in the attribute mapping syntax.

> **Note**   When ADC determines which rule to use to map an attribute, the first choice is a rule that is complete with object class. If ADC finds such a rule, it uses that rule. If ADC does not find such a rule, the next choice is a generic rule (without an object class).

Table 3-12   Attribute Mapping Syntax

Field	Description
comment	Field is ignored and can contain anything
src-class	The source object class (optional)
tgt-class	The target object class (optional)
src-attr	The source attribute name
tgt-attr	The target attribute name
Prefix	SMTP$ or X400$ (special case for proxy address fields)

Table 3-12   Attribute Mapping Syntax (Continued)

Field	Description
dn-syntax	A distinguished name-linked attribute
Flags	A set of special flags that have the following meaning:

- **0x0001**   Maps a multivalued attribute to a single-valued attribute.
- **0x0002**   Lazy distinguished name conversion. Causes Active Directory Connector to postpone the resolution of the attribute, so that resolution of the attribute is the last operation that Active Directory Connector performs before it replicates the entry. This improves performance, because all linked distinguished names are resolved at the end of the process with fewer searches to the directory service.
- **0x0004**   Maps a single-valued attribute to a multivalued attribute.
- **0x0008**   Links a multivalued attribute to a single-valued attribute.
- **0x0010**   Disables replication. The disable replication flag has the same effect as removing the line from the file. The Active Directory Connector Management snap-in sets or resets this attribute every time that you clear or select this attribute to be replicated.
- **0x0020**   The source attribute is an ADC internal attribute.
- **0x0040**   The target attribute is an ADC internal attribute.
- **0x0100**   Hides the attribute in the Active Directory Connector Management snap-in, so the attribute cannot be disabled or enabled.
- **0x0200**   Merges the attribute into the target instead of replacing it.
- **0x0400**   Distinguished name attribute that can only be resolved if Exchange 2000 Server is installed.
- **0x0800**   Allows mapping of strings to distinguished names and distinguished names to strings.

To combine flags, add the value of the flags and use the hexadecimal number that results (without "0x"). To best use these flags, observe how they are used in the Remote.map and Local.map files.

While you can use ldp.exe or ADSI Edit to edit the msExchServer1SchemaMap attribute, you might find that it is very difficult to add the attribute mappings this way. You have the following alternatives to apply custom attribute mappings:

- **Change the mappings prior to installing Active Directory Connector** The Active Directory Connector Setup program uses two files called Remote.map and Local.map to import attribute mappings into the Default ADC Policy object. The Remote.map file contains the values for the msExchServer1SchemaMap attribute, and the Local.map file contains the values for the msExchServer2SchemaMap attribute. These files are located on the Exchange Server 2003 Service Pack 1 CD in the \ADC\i386 folder. If you want to edit these files prior to installing Active Directory Connector, copy the \ADC folder to a temporary folder on a hard disk, remove the read-only flag, and then make the necessary changes to the Remote.map file. You can also replace the Remote.map file with the Remote.map file that you can find in the \Companion Material\Chapter 03\ADC folder on the companion CD. This file contains all necessary msExchDynamicDistributionList and inetOrgPerson mappings. To apply the changes, install Active Directory Connector from the temporary folder.

If you want to update an existing Active Directory Connector installation, you must keep in mind that the Setup program does not replace existing attributes in the Default ADC Policy object. You must delete the msExchServer1-SchemaMap attribute before you run the Active Directory Connector Setup program from the temporary folder.

On the Resource Kit CD   For step-by-step instructions about how to update an existing installation, see the document Extending the capabilities of inter-org connection agreements manually.doc, which you can find in the \Companion Material\Chapter 03\ADC folder on the companion CD.

- **Import the mappings from a customized Remote.map file using an ADSI script**   You can also update an existing Active Directory Connector installation by loading a customized Remote.map file directly into the msExchServer1SchemaMap attribute through ADSI.

On the Resource Kit CD   For a demonstration of the use of a custom script for this purpose, see the document Extending the capabilities of inter-org connection agreements through scripting.doc, which you can also find in the \Companion Material\Chapter 03\ADC folder on the companion CD.

The following code example shows how to accomplish this task:

On the Resource Kit CD   For a complete solution, see the document ManageICA.wsf, which you can find in the \Companion Material\Chapter 03 \Scripts folder on the companion CD.

```
adcPolicyDN = "CN=Default ADC Policy," _
      & "CN=Active Directory Connections," _
      & "CN=Microsoft Exchange," _
      & "CN=Services,CN=Configuration," _
      & "DC=ADDOM-A,DC=msn"

Set oADCPol = GetObject("LDAP://" & adcPolicyDN)
Set oFileSys = CreateObject("Scripting.FileSystemObject")
Set oFile = oFileSys.OpenTextFile("c:\Remote.map", 1, False, -1)
strContents = oFile.ReadAll()

' Write the information into the ADC policy.
oADCPol.Put "msExchServer1SchemaMap", strContents
oADCPol.SetInfo
```

> **Note**   Changing any of the attribute mappings can have adverse effects and can possibly cause data corruption in the Exchange 5.5 directory or Active Directory. You should carefully consider and test changes prior to deployment. If you install service packs, you must reapply the custom mapping, using the new map files that were introduced with the new service pack.

Limitations of Inter-organizational Connection Agreements

Unfortunately, it is not possible to replicate public folder recipient objects across organization boundaries because Active Directory Connector uses a separate type of connection agreement, the public folder connection agreement, to replicate public folder information. Public folder connection agreements cannot be used between Exchange organizations. If you must provide users in other organizations with recipient objects that represent public folders, consider creating distribution groups with the same display names as the public folders. You can then add each public folder as a member to the group with the same name (display the properties of the public folder in Exchange System Manager, and click the Member Of tab). To avoid duplicate recipient entries in the local address book, you can hide the public folder by selecting the Hide from Exchange address book checkbox on the Exchange Advanced tab. The configuration is similar in Exchange 5.5.

Another limitation of Active Directory Connector is that you cannot apply advanced rules extensions to the attribute flow. Using the Active Directory Connector snap-in, you can control to some extent which attributes to synchronize from one directory to another, and you can customize attribute mappings, but you cannot append further information. For example, you cannot customize the display names during synchronization to append an organization name. You can specify a prefix in the display name mapping entry in the msExchServer1SchemaMap and msExchServer2SchemaMap attributes, but it is not possible to specify a suffix. The following line demonstrates how to customize the display name mapping by specifying a prefix that indicates the version of the user's Exchange organization.

- **msExchServer1SchemaMap**   remote###displayName#cn#(Exchange 2003)
  ##0#

- **msExchServer2SchemaMap**   remote###cn#displayName#(Exchange 5.5)
  ##0#

However, adding information at the beginning of a user name might not comply with the naming conventions in your organization. You have the following alternatives:

- **Include the information in the source objects**   For example, if you specify the home Exchange organization of the user directly in the display name, Active Directory Connector will replicate the information correctly to Active Directory.

- **Modify the contacts in Active Directory before synchronizing the recipients with other forests**   Using a custom ADSI script you can add the missing information to the recipient objects after they have been replicated to Active Directory.

On the Resource Kit CD   For an example of how to append an organization name to the display name of all contact objects in an organizational unit, see the script AddOrgInfoToContacts.wsf, which you can find in the \Companion Material\Chapter 03\Scripts folder on the companion CD. If you run this script as a scheduled task, you can ensure that the display names of external recipients adhere to your naming conventions.

Note   During a full synchronization, Active Directory Connector overwrites any changes you apply directly to contact objects replicated from an Exchange 5.5 organization. You should run the script to adjust recipient information each time you run an inter-organizational connection agreement.

Configuring Message Routing Between Forests

After setting up GAL synchronization, you must ensure that mail flows properly between organizations and the Internet. For basic mail flow, the only requirement is that a route can be resolved to each adjoining forest. Trusts between the forests are not required.

Mail flow is determined by the network connectivity between forests and the way in which SMTP proxy addresses are configured. From an Exchange perspective, the ideal configuration is to have direct network connectivity between the forests with no firewalls. (If there are firewalls between the forests, you must ensure that the firewalls do not block the server communication.)

> **Note**   No link state information or routing topology information is shared between forests.

You must also set up SMTP connectors between the forests. Furthermore, we recommend that you enable authentication across the forests. Enabling authentication has the following benefits:

- User name resolution (*ResolveP2* registry key) between forests is automatic, which means that a user's e-mail address resolves to the user's name that is stored in Active Directory.

- Additional scheduling and mail features, such as mail forwarding, are available.

To prevent the forging of identities (spoofing), Exchange 2003 requires authentication to resolve a sender's name to its display name in the GAL. In a multiple forest environment, we recommend that you configure authentication so users who send mail from one forest to another are resolved to their display names in the GAL, rather than to their SMTP addresses. To enable cross-forest SMTP authentication, you must create connectors in each forest that uses an authenticated account from another forest.

> **On the Resource Kit CD**   For step-by-step instructions to configure SMTP connectors and enable cross-forest SMTP authentication, see the document Configuring SMTP Connectors in the Multiple Forest Test Environment.doc, which you can find in the \Companion Material\Chapter 03 \Multiple Forests folder on the companion CD.

Configuring Extended Mail Features

You may have several Exchange organizations but only a single namespace that represents your company on the Internet (for example, tailspintoys.com). In this case, to retain individual forest namespaces but still route mail properly to the individual forests, you must distinguish the forests from one another. In addition, to enable or disable mail features such as out-of-office responses, automatic replies, and delivery reports, you might have to configure global settings.

Configuring a Shared SMTP Namespace

When GAL Synchronization creates contacts from mail recipients in a source forest, it uses SMTP addresses to create a targetAddress attribute for each contact. Therefore, when users in a forest send mail to a contact, the mail is delivered to the contact's targetAddress, even if the user manually entered the primary reply address. To determine which targetAddress GAL Synchronization should assign to a contact, it compares the recipient's proxyAddresses property to the SMTP address for which the Exchange organization is responsible. Each organization must have a unique SMTP domain namespace so contacts receive a unique targetAddress. If your forests do not have unique namespaces, you can add a unique SMTP address to the appropriate recipient policies for each Exchange organization that contains users to be replicated across forests. After you do this, messages sent to a contact are routed directly to the source forest, where the target address resolves to the actual mailbox, and the message is delivered.

You can also route contacts on a forest-by-forest basis. When setting up management agents for GAL synchronization, you can select whether mail sent to contacts that were imported into a forest should route back through the source forest. If you have a connector to a foreign messaging system, mail that is intended for a contact is routed to the source forest (the forest that manages the connector) by default. However, the forest administrator can change this routing configuration.

As an example of SMTP routing in a multiple forest environment, consider two forests that each have a default recipient policy with an SMTP proxy address of tailspintoys.com. To set up unique namespaces, you would do the following in each Exchange organization:

- **In Organization 1**   Add an SMTP proxy address of Org1.tailspintoys.com to the default recipient policy.

- **In Organization 2**   Add an SMTP proxy address of Org2.tailspintoys.com to the default recipient policy.

In both cases, when adding the proxy address, you select the This organization is responsible for all mail delivery to this address check box. Also, you leave the tailspintoys.com proxy as the primary address so, when a user sends mail, their reply address is user@tailspintoys.com (rather than user@Org1.tailspintoys.com or user@Org2.tailspintoys.com).

Another example illustrates mail flow in a hub-spoke topology. In this example, multiple Exchange organizations are present, but all users can be addressed in a single domain space (for example, @tailspintoys.com). In this case, all external mail addressed to @tailspintoys.com flows into a central hub organization called OrgA. OrgA is configured with secondary SMTP proxy addresses that represent each spoke organization. One of these addresses is @OrgB.tailspintoys.com. When mail addressed to UserB@tailspintoys.com arrives at OrgA, the mail resolves to the contact, and the mail is redirected to OrgB. When the message leaves OrgA, the To line is changed to the targetAddress attribute to allow for routing, but the Reply To address remains UserB@tailspintoys.com.

> **On the Resource Kit CD**   For more information, see the document Deploying a Central Hub Organization in the Multiple Forest Test Environment.doc, which you can find in the \Companion Material\Chapter 03\Multiple Forests folder on the companion CD.

If you want to use an SMTP relay server to route all mail from the Internet to the correct forest, we recommend that you create SMTP connectors on the SMTP relay server to all of the other forests so mail routes directly to each forest. This configuration allows you to add SMTP servers as needed for load balancing. You can also add SMTP connectors to route all outbound Internet mail through the new forest.

Configuring Global Settings

To enable or disable mail features such as out-of-office responses, automatic replies, and delivery reports, you must configure Internet message formats for the appropriate domains. Three methods for configuring Internet message formats are:

- Configure the Default domain (*) so all domains have the same settings.

- Add a separate Internet message format domain for each SMTP namespace (for example @OrgA.tailspintoys.com), and then configure each domain differently.

- Add an Internet message format domain that represents domains with a common suffix (for example @*.tailspintoys.com) and then configure each entry differently.

Internet message formats are located in Exchange System Manager under Global Settings.

Sharing Free/Busy and Public Folder Data

In companies that have multiple Exchange organizations, a common requirement is the ability to coordinate meetings, appointments, and contact information with users in different Exchange organizations. Therefore, to replicate these free/busy system folders between forests, you can use the Inter-Organization Replication tool. If your company uses public folders, you can also use the Inter-Organization Replication tool to share public folder data across Exchange organizations.

> **Note**   You can find a link called *Inter-Organization Replication (English only)* to download the Inter-Organization Replication tool on the Exchange Server 2003 Downloads website (*http://go.microsoft.com/fwlink/ ?LinkId=21316*) under the section Interoperability and Coexistence.

The Inter-Organization Replication tool consists of two programs: the Exchange Server Replication Configuration tool (Exscfg.exe) and the Exchange Server Replication service (Exssrv.exe). Exscfg.exe creates a configuration file that Exssrv.exe uses to continuously update information from one server to another. The server that sends updates is the publisher, and the server that receives updates is the subscriber. All replication takes place over MAPI sessions that are established between servers in the organizations.

The Inter-Organization Replication tool publishes free/busy data for mailbox-enabled user objects and contact objects to other organizations, if equivalent contact objects exist in the target organization (as created by GAL Synchronization). The contacts are matched by their SMTP addresses. (When setting up the Inter-Organization Replication tool, use the Publish custom recipient free/busy data option.) You can then replicate all or a portion of the free/busy data from one organization to another. However, free/busy data replicates only in one direction. Therefore, to update free/busy data in both directions, you must configure two sessions.

> **On the Resource Kit CD**   For an example of how to configure the Inter-Organization Replication tool to synchronize free/busy information, see the document Deploying the Inter-Organization Replication tool in the Multiple Forest Test Environment.doc, which you can find in the \Companion Material\Chapter 03\Multiple Forests folder on the companion CD.

You cannot use the Inter-Organization Replication tool to modify address books or directories. Address book changes are not propagated to other organizations. These changes must be made independently.

Similarly to how you replicate free/busy data, you can replicate all or a portion of public folder data from one organization to another. However, unlike free/busy data, public folder data can be replicated from publisher to subscriber or bi-directionally, resulting in fewer sessions. In addition, a single instance of the Inter-Organization Replication tool can support up to fifteen sessions. This means that a public folder server can subscribe to multiple publisher servers. You can specify individual folders or both folders and subfolders. Furthermore, you can configure the replication frequency, message and folder replication logs, and the amount of processing power you want dedicated to the replication process.

Note The Inter-Organization Replication tool does not replicate permissions for public folders. When a public folder is replicated to another forest, the administrator for that forest must set permissions on the public folders.

Whether you should configure the Inter-Organization Replication tool in a mesh configuration or in a hub-spoke configuration depends largely on the number of organizations in your environment. A mesh configuration is feasible for up to four organizations. However, if you have more than four organizations, it might be easier to manage the Inter-Organization Replication tool in a hub-spoke configuration.

Note A ring topology is not recommended for inter-organizational replication. Because there is potential for high replication latency along the ring, a user could update information in a forest that has not yet received the replication update. As a result, the most recent update is overwritten by the replicated update. Another problem with a ring topology is that if one connection breaks, the loop is broken.

More Info For more information about the Inter-Organization Replication tool, see the following Microsoft Knowledge Base articles:

238573, "XADM: Installing, Configuring, and Using the InterOrg Replication Utility"
(*http://go.microsoft.com/fwlink/?linkid=3052&kbid=238573*)

238642, "XADM: Troubleshooting the InterOrg Replication Utility"
(*http://go.microsoft.com/fwlink/?linkid=3052&kbid=238642*)

Best Practices

Deploying Exchange Server 2003 in a multiple forest environment requires that you carefully design the inter-forest topology to control costs and administrative overhead. In general, deploying a resource forest and concentrating Exchange resources in a central location is advantageous. You can then implement an automated provisioning solution so users in their account forests and Windows NT domains can collaborate.

If you must work with multiple Exchange organizations, consider using Identity Integration Feature Pack and Active Directory GAL management agents to synchronize recipient information. With relatively moderate effort, you can extend the GAL synchronization logic. If you must integrate Exchange 5.5 organizations as well, consider using Active Directory Connector and inter-organizational connection agreements. Although Active Directory Connector is not designed for cross-forest synchronization, it is a good solution to synchronize one forest with the Exchange 5.5 directory. If you find that the Active Directory Connector functionality does not cover your needs, consider using Identity Integration Server 2003 and a custom solution based on Active Directory GAL and Exchange 5.5 management agents. However, you might find that the costs for implementing such a solution are only justified in long term coexistence scenarios. In fact, a more cost-effective solution might actually be a migrating to Exchange 2003, because you can then use Identity Integration Feature Pack to perform GAL synchronization. Integration Feature Pack is available as a no-cost Web download to customers who have already licensed Windows Server 2003 Enterprise Edition.

It is also good practice to implement a central hub for Internet message traffic to hide the complexity of the internal messaging environment from external business partners and Internet users. You can then provide all users with an SMTP address from the same public SMTP domain, such as @tailspintoys.com, regardless of the Exchange organization in which the mailboxes actually reside. You can also perform virus scans and spam filtering in the hub organization centrally. We recommend that you deploy direct SMTP connectors between your Exchange organizations so you can enable cross-forest SMTP authentication. This enables Exchange 2003 to resolve users who send mail from one forest to another to their display names in the global address list, rather than to their SMTP addresses.

In addition, a deployment with multiple Exchange organizations is inferior to deploying a resource forest because there are interoperability limitations. For example, delegate access does not work across organization boundaries. Certain interoperability issues, however, you can address using the Inter-Organization Replication tool. For example, you can use the Inter-Organization Replication tool to replicate free-busy information between organizations, and you can replicate public folders. Detailed configuration information for the Inter-Organization Replication tool is provided when you download the tool.

Chapter 4

Upgrading to Exchange Server 2003

About This Chapter

This chapter explains how to upgrade from Microsoft Exchange Server 5.5 or Microsoft Exchange 2000 Server to Microsoft Exchange Server 2003, using a variety of strategies and upgrade tools. Upgrading is a process that entails deploying Exchange Server 2003 in an existing organization, and then moving mailboxes, public folders, and other resources, such as messaging connectors, over to Exchange 2003. This is in contrast to migrating to Exchange 2003, where you deploy an Exchange 2003 organization separate from existing organizations, and then move resources across organizational boundaries, which is explained in Chapter 6, "Server and Site Consolidation Strategies."

What You Need to Know

It is assumed that you are familiar with Microsoft Windows server technology, Active Directory directory service, and the basic design elements of an Exchange 2003 organization. For more information about how to upgrade from Windows NT Server 4.0 and Windows 2000 domains to Windows 2003, see the book *Designing and Deploying Directory and Security Services* that you can find in the Windows Server 2003 Deployment Kit (*http://www.microsoft.com/windowsserver2003/techinfo/reskit/deploykit.mspx*). For more information about designing an Exchange 2003 organization, see Chapter 2, "Exchange Server 2003 Design Basics" as well as the Exchange online book *Planning an Exchange Server 2003 Messaging System* (*http://go.microsoft.com/fwlink/?linkid=21766*).

Exchange Server 2003 Upgrade Dependencies

To deploy Exchange 2003, you must have a stable Domain Name Service (DNS) and Active Directory environment. Thus, if you are running Exchange Server 5.5 in a Windows NT domain environment, you must first deploy DNS and Active Directory. To support Exchange 2003, domain controllers must run Windows 2000 Server Service Pack 3 (SP3) or Windows Server 2003.

You might want to migrate your existing Windows domain environment to Active Directory prior to rolling out Exchange Server 2003, but you do not necessarily have to complete the Active Directory deployment before you can upgrade to Exchange 2003. For example, in a multi-domain environment, you can deploy Exchange 2003 in an Active Directory domain, but still have Exchange 5.5 users with Windows NT user accounts in other domains. For all Exchange 5.5 users with Windows NT accounts, Active Directory Connector will create a placeholder account in Active Directory, so that Exchange 2003 users have a complete global address list (GAL). You can use the placeholder accounts to manage mailboxes, even if the actual Windows user accounts reside in a Windows NT domain. This includes moving mailboxes from an Exchange 5.5 server to an Exchange 2003 server, adding or removing e-mail addresses, and so forth. However, it should be noted that you should not use the placeholder accounts to manage user account settings. Use the Windows NT accounts instead. For example, you can disable a user's Windows NT account to prevent this user from logging on and accessing his or her mailbox or you can reactivate a locked-out Windows NT account, but you should not enable any placeholder accounts because these are not the actual user accounts. When you merge or upgrade Windows NT domains to Active Directory later on, make sure the Windows user accounts are separate from the placeholder accounts. You can then run Active Directory Cleanup Wizard to merge the mailbox information from the placeholder accounts into the Windows user accounts.

Note   Exchange 2003 does not support directly upgrading a server running Exchange Server 5.5. You must install Exchange 2003 on a separate computer.

Upgrading from Exchange Server 5.5 to Exchange 2003 includes the following steps:

1. You must have at least one Active Directory domain so that you can deploy Exchange 2003. Either upgrade an existing Windows NT domain or set up a new domain.

2. Prepare the Exchange Server 5.5 directory for synchronization with Active Directory. This includes running the Exchange 5.5 directory service consistency adjuster to remove outdated account information from access control lists (ACLs), and it also includes identifying user and resource mailboxes as explained later in this chapter.

3. Deploy Active Directory Connector (ADC) and configure connection agreements to populate Active Directory with Exchange recipient information and keep both directories synchronized. You can use Exchange Server Deployment Tools included with Exchange Server 2003 to accomplish this task. Exchange Server Deployment Tools guide you through the recommended steps and include diagnostic tools and setup links to help you successfully install Active Directory Connector and Exchange 2003. In complex topologies, however, you must configure ADC connection agreements individually instead of using Exchange Server Deployment Tools.

4. Having synchronized Exchange 5.5 directory information with Active Directory, you can deploy Exchange Server 2003 in the organization. Update each server installation to the latest Exchange Server 2003 Service Pack right away. If you are running Exchange 2003 in a server cluster, be sure to read Microsoft Knowledge Base article 867624, "How to install Exchange Server 2003 Service Pack 1 in a clustered Exchange environment" (*http://support.microsoft.com/?id=867624*).

Note   To support interoperability between Exchange 5.5 and Exchange 2003, each Exchange 5.5 site must contain at least one server running Exchange 5.5 SP3.

5. As soon as Exchange 5.5 and Exchange 2003 coexist in the same organization, you can move mailboxes and public folders to Exchange 2003. There must be an account in Active Directory to hold the mailbox settings in order to have a mailbox on Exchange 2003. This can be a regular mailbox-enabled Windows account, an enabled placeholder account representing a mailbox with a Windows NT account, or a disabled placeholder account with a Windows NT account that has been granted the permission of an associated external account, as explained in Chapter 3, "Exchange Server 2003 in Enterprise Environments."

6. You must also migrate existing messaging connectors to Exchange Server 2003. If you are using connectors that are not included in Exchange 2003, such as Connector for Lotus cc:Mail or non-Microsoft connectors, you must devise a plan to replace these components with alternative solutions. For example, messaging connectivity to Lotus cc:Mail may be established using SMTP and non-Microsoft vendors may provide updated connector components for Exchange Server 2003. On the other hand, if an alternative solution is not available, you must leave an Exchange 5.5 bridgehead server in place to run legacy connector components in a mixed-mode Exchange 2003 organization.

7. Once all resources are moved to servers running Exchange Server 2003, you can decommission the legacy Exchange servers. Decommissioning Exchange 5.5 entails analyzing what specific services each Exchange 5.5 server provides in the organization and how these services are provided through Exchange 2003. Some connectivity components that are available in Exchange 5.5 are not included in Exchange 2003, such as Connector for Microsoft Mail for PC Networks. If you find that you require such components, you must leave at least one Exchange 5.5 server running for these components in the organization.

More Info   For more information about how to remove the last Exchange 5.5 server from an administrative group, see Microsoft Knowledge Base article 822450, "How to remove the last Exchange Server 5.5 computer from an Exchange Server 2003 administrative group" (*http://support.microsoft.com/default.aspx?scid=kb;en-us;822450*).

8. Having eliminated all Exchange 5.5 servers from the Exchange organization, you can switch the organization into native mode using Exchange System Manager to unlock the full potential of Exchange 2003. You cannot switch back to mixed mode.

The steps to upgrade from Exchange 2000 to Exchange 2003 are different from the steps for an Exchange 5.5 upgrade because you can assume that Windows NT domains are already integrated with Active Directory. Even if Exchange 5.5 and Exchange 2000 coexist in the same organization, you can assume that Active Directory is already implemented, and Active Directory Connector is running to keep Exchange 5.5 directory and Active Directory synchronized. However, to support Exchange Server 2003, you must upgrade all Active Directory Connector instances to the ADC version provided with Exchange Server 2003. We recommend that you update to the version included in the latest Exchange Server 2003 Service Pack.

Deploying Active Directory Connector is not necessary if you are planning to upgrade an Exchange 2000 organization that is operating in native mode because there is no Exchange 5.5 directory. In general, you have two options to upgrade a server running Exchange 2000: upgrade directly or deploy Exchange 2003 on new server hardware. The latter approach has the advantage that you can replace outdated server hardware during the upgrade project.

> **Note**   If you have deployed Exchange 2000 Server in a front-end/back-end topology, upgrade the front-end servers before upgrading any back-end servers.

Deploying Active Directory in an Exchange 5.5 Environment

An important question that influences how you deploy Active Directory in your environment is whether you want to restructure your domain topology or not. In Windows NT 4.0, domains are often deployed in a master and resource domain topology to structure account and resource management. In Active Directory, you can use organizational units for this purpose, so it is recommended to consolidate all existing domains into a single-domain Active Directory forest unless security requirements or other business reasons prevent you from consolidating. The advantages of single-domain forests for Exchange 2003 are discussed in Chapter 2, "Exchange Server 2003 Design Basics."

You have the following options to deploy Active Directory in a Windows NT environment:

- **Perform an in-place upgrade**   This is an efficient, time-saving approach, although Microsoft recommends installing new domains instead of performing an in-place upgrade. At a minimum, you must upgrade the primary domain controller (PDC) in a Windows NT domain to perform an in-place upgrade. During the in-place upgrade, all domain accounts are converted to Active Directory accounts. The original security identifiers (SIDs) of the user accounts are preserved, which greatly simplifies system integration because it avoids the creation of duplicate user objects.

> **On the Resource Kit CD**   The document Performing a full Windows NT in-place upgrade.doc in the \Companion Material\Chapter 04\Full In-Place Windows Upgrade folder on the companion CD outlines how to perform an in-place Windows NT upgrade.

Active Directory supports mixed domains containing computers running Windows NT Server 4.0, Windows 2000 Server, and Windows Server 2003. If you decide to perform an in-place upgrade of a Windows NT domain, you must upgrade the PDC first, followed by backup domain controllers (BDCs), and then member servers. Another option is to remove the BDCs from the domain and to install Windows Server 2003 domain controllers from scratch. Keep also in mind that you cannot upgrade servers that run software not compatible with Windows 2003, such as Exchange Server 5.5. For example, if you have installed Exchange Server 5.5 on the PDC, you cannot upgrade the domain to Windows 2003 because you must upgrade the PDC before any other server.

You have the following options to deal with domain controllers running Exchange 5.5:

1. **Promote a BDC that is not running Exchange Server 5.5 to a PDC and then upgrade this server to Windows Server 2003.**   You must operate the domain in mixed mode if you cannot decommission the former PDC (now a BDC) running Exchange 5.5.

> **On the Resource Kit CD**   The document Performing a partial Windows NT in-place upgrade.doc in the \Companion Material\Chapter 04\Partial In-Place Windows Upgrade folder on the companion CD explains how to accomplish this task.

Figure 4-1 illustrates a mixed Active Directory domain with Exchange 5.5 running on a member server and on a BDC. The PDC has been upgraded to a Windows 2003 domain controller.

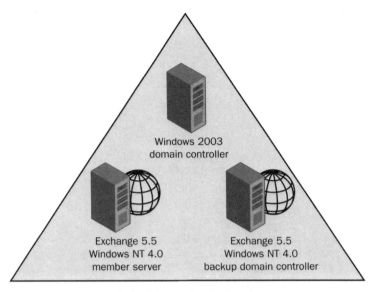

Active Directory in mixed mode

Figure 4-1   A mixed Active Directory domain with Exchange 5.5

2. **Move all resources from the Exchange server (PDC) to another Exchange server in the site.**   If you uninstall Exchange 5.5 on the PDC, you can upgrade the PDC directly. It is a good idea to eliminate all Exchange servers that are running on domain controllers, so that you can upgrade all Windows NT domain controllers to Windows 2003.

> **On the Resource Kit CD**   The document Performing a full Windows NT in-place upgrade.doc in the \Companion Material\Chapter 04\Full In-Place Windows Upgrade folder on the companion CD about explains how to remove Exchange 5.5 from a domain controller and how to upgrade the domain controller to Windows 2003.

Figure 4-2 illustrates an Active Directory domain with Exchange 5.5 running on a member server. Exchange 5.5 was uninstalled from the domain controller, and both PDC and BDC have been upgraded to Windows 2003. In this configuration, you can enable the Windows Server 2003 domain functional level because there are no legacy domain controllers left. The relevance of domain functional levels for Exchange 5.5 upgrades is explained later in this chapter.

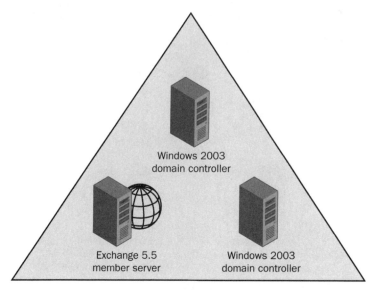

Active Directory domain

Figure 4-2   An Active Directory domain with Exchange 5.5 on a member server

Note   Before moving Exchange 5.5 resources to another Exchange 5.5 server, you should verify that the target Exchange 5.5 server can handle the additional workload. If you cannot move the resources to another Exchange 5.5 server, consider promoting a BDC that is not running Exchange 5.5 to a primary domain controller (PDC).

3. **Upgrade the PDC to Windows 2000 Server.** It is supported to run Exchange Server 5.5 on Windows 2000 domain controllers. By upgrading the PDC to Windows 2000, you can implement an Active Directory environment for Exchange Server 2003. This option might be a good choice for companies that are not planning to deploy Windows 2003. Do not forget to update the domain controller to at least Windows 2000 Server SP3.

   Figure 4-3 illustrates a Windows 2000 Active Directory domain with Exchange 5.5 running on a Windows 2000 domain controller and a Windows NT member server.

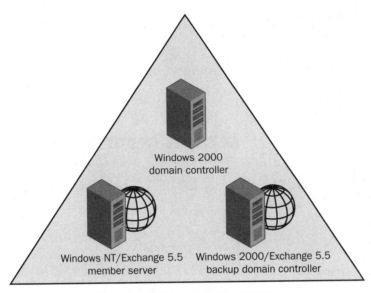

Figure 4-3   A Windows 2000 Active Directory domain with Exchange 5.5

Active Directory Connector performs directory synchronization based on Lightweight Directory Access Protocol (LDAP). Remember this when upgrading a PDC or BDC running Exchange Server 5.5 to a Windows 2000 Server. The Exchange 5.5 directory supports LDAP and so does Active Directory, but both expect incoming LDAP connections on TCP port 389, by default. Port 389 is the well-known TCP port for LDAP. On a Windows 2000 domain controller, Active Directory locks TCP port 389 for its own use. When the Exchange 5.5 directory service starts, it cannot access the same port and cannot communicate via LDAP until you change the LDAP port for the Exchange directory to a port other than 389, such as TCP port 379. We recommend changing the LDAP port for the Exchange directory service prior to upgrading to Windows 2000 and Active Directory.

Figure 4-4 shows the dialog box to change the LDAP port for all Exchange servers in an Exchange 5.5 site.

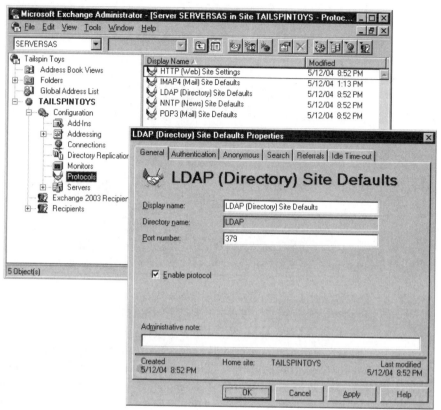

Figure 4-4   Changing the LDAP port for the Exchange 5.5 directory

■ **Deploy a new Active Directory domain**   If you are planning to restructure the domain topology, or if you cannot upgrade your Windows NT domains for any reason, you can deploy a new Active Directory domain. You can then use Active Directory Connector to create separate accounts for your users in Active Directory and synchronize these accounts with mailbox information from the Exchange 5.5 directory. You can also use the Active Directory Migration Tool to migrate user accounts and then use Active Directory Connector to keep these accounts synchronized. However, when upgrading Windows NT domains later on, you may end up with duplicated user accounts because Windows NT accounts are converted to Active Directory accounts but they are not automatically merged with other existing accounts. You must merge duplicated user accounts into a single account using Active Directory Cleanup Wizard.

On the Resource Kit CD   The document Deploying SERVERDC01 in a separate Active Directory domain.doc in the \Companion Material\Chapter 04\New Active Directory Domain folder on the companion CD outlines how to deploy a new Active Directory domain for an upgrade to Exchange 2003.

Figure 4-5 illustrates a Windows 2003 Active Directory domain and a Windows NT domain with Exchange 5.5. A two-way trust relationship has been established between both domains, and Active Directory Connector is used to propagate recipient objects to Active Directory.

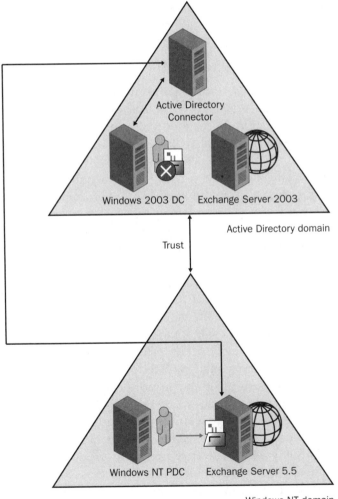

Figure 4-5   Active Directory and a Windows NT domain with Exchange 5.5

> **Note**   The strategy you choose to upgrade your domains from Windows NT 4.0 to Active Directory depends on the business needs of your organization. Most organizations prefer migrating user accounts using Active Directory Migration Tool instead of creating new user accounts using Active Directory Connector. A detailed discussion of user account migration strategies is beyond the scope of this chapter. For details, see the topic "Upgrading Windows NT 4.0 Domains to Windows Server 2003 Active Directory" in the book *Designing and Deploying Directory and Security Services* of the Microsoft Windows Server 2003 Deployment Kit. (*http:// www.microsoft.com/resources/documentation/WindowsServ/2003/all/ deployguide/en-us/Default.asp?url=/resources/documentation/Win- dowsServ/2003/all/deployguide/en-us/DSSBE_UPNT_OVERVIEW.asp*).

Universal Security Group Requirements

We highly recommend that you enable the Windows 2000 native or Windows Server 2003 domain functional level in at least one Active Directory domain to facilitate public folder migration and Windows NT user account migration. You can enable these functional levels only in a domain that does not contain any domain controllers running Windows NT 4.0. If you cannot upgrade all existing domain controllers in your domain to Active Directory, consider implementing a separate Active Directory domain. You can then activate the Windows Server 2003 domain functional level in this domain.

One reason for this requirement involves support for universal security groups. Exchange 5.5 uses distribution lists to set permissions on public folders. When you integrate Exchange 5.5 with Active Directory, Active Directory Connector creates universal distribution groups for Exchange 5.5 distribution lists. However, you cannot use universal distribution groups to specify public folder permissions in Exchange 2003. To support public folder migration, the Microsoft Exchange 2003 Information Store service will attempt to convert any distribution groups present in the access control list of a public folder to universal security groups. This conversion will fail in a mixed domain containing Windows NT 4.0 domain controllers because universal security groups are only supported in native mode domains (that is, domains operating at the Windows 2000 native or Windows Server 2003 domain functional level). Public folders with distribution lists in their Exchange 5.5 access control lists will not show correct security settings in Exchange 2003. If the distribution lists are not successfully converted to security groups in Active Directory, default permissions are applied, which could mean that access to the public folder is denied.

Hence, if you cannot upgrade a Windows NT domain completely, you should consider deploying a separate Active Directory domain, enable the Windows 2000 native or Windows Server 2003 domain functional level for it, and then let Active Directory Connector create all distribution groups in this domain. You can create a separate recipient connection agreement for distribution list synchronization. If you use ADC Tools, select the native domain as the default domain. This will create recipient connection agreements that manage the synchronization of the distribution groups to the native domain.

> **On the Resource Kit CD**   For instructions about how to configure an Active Directory domain for distribution groups, see the document Adding a Domain for Distribution Groups to the In-Place Upgrade Test Environment.doc in the \Companion Material\Chapter 04\Partial In-Place Windows Upgrade folder on the companion CD.

> **Note**   Exchange Server 2003 attempts to convert only those universal distribution groups that have been specified in Exchange 5.5 public folder permissions.

Integrating Exchange Server 5.5 with Active Directory

By upgrading Windows NT domains, you move user account management to Active Directory. Mailbox management, however, is still performed in the Exchange directory. To consolidate user account and mailbox information, you must deploy Active Directory Connector and synchronize Exchange directory and Active Directory through connection agreements. As soon as user account and mailbox information is present in Active Directory, you can use Active Directory tools, such as Active Directory Users and Computers, to perform both user account and mailbox management. However, we recommend that you use the Exchange 5.5 Administrator program to manage Exchange 5.5 mailboxes and Active Directory Users and Computers to manage Exchange 2003 mailboxes.

> **Note** To upgrade from Exchange Server 5.5 to Exchange Server 2003, you must synchronize Exchange 5.5 directory with Active Directory and you must synchronize Active Directory with Exchange 5.5 directory. In other words, you must enable bidirectional directory synchronization using two-way connection agreements or one-way connection agreements that are pointing in opposite directions.

Exchange Server Deployment Tools

Before installing Active Directory Connector and configuring connection agreements, you must verify that at least one Exchange server in each site of your organization is running Exchange Server 5.5 with SP3 or later. You should also check your Active Directory environment and fix any inconsistencies before installing Active Directory Connector. This is best accomplished using Exchange Server Deployment Tools. See the document Adding ADC to the Test Environment.doc in the \Companion Material\Chapter 04\Full In-Place Windows Upgrade folder for an example of how to use Exchange Server Deployment Tools.

You should accomplish the following checks to prepare for a deployment of Active Directory Connector:

- **Check operating system requirements.** You should ensure that Windows 2000 Server SP3 or later, Windows 2000 Advanced Server SP3 or later, or Windows Server 2003 is installed on the server running Active Directory Connector.

- **Check Internet Information Services (IIS) requirements.** If you are planning to install Exchange Server 2003 on the server running Active Directory Connector, you must verify that the Network News Transfer Protocol (NNTP), Simple Mail Transfer Protocol (SMTP), and World Wide Web services are installed and enabled on the server. If you are running Windows Server 2003, verify that ASP.NET is installed.

> **Note** IIS is not required on a server running Active Directory Connector. IIS is only required if you are planning to deploy Exchange Server 2003 on the server in a subsequent step.

- **Check the Exchange 5.5 directory.**   You should run the DSScopeScan tool included in Exchange Server Deployment Tools to create a report about the existing Exchange 5.5 organization. The DSScopeScan tool writes all information into an ExDeploy.log to indicate whether the tool ran successfully and includes any errors or warnings. You must specify the path to the ExDeploy.log file in the DSScopeScan tool parameters.

  DSScopeScan runs the following tools:

  - **DSConfigSum**   Reports the total number of Exchange 5.5 sites and the total number of servers in each site.

  - **DSObjectSum**   Reports the total number of public folders, system folders, distribution lists, distribution lists with hidden membership, and contact objects in the Exchange 5.5 directory.

  - **UserCount**   Reports the total number of users in each Exchange 5.5 site and the total number of users in the Exchange 5.5 directory.

  - **VerCheck**   Reports the server name and Exchange version for each server for each server in the Exchange organization. It is highly recommended that you verify that at least one server at each site is running Exchange 5.5 with SP3 before you install Active Directory Connector.

Note   To run the DSScopeScan tool successfully, you need at a minimum the permissions of a View Only Admin. in the Exchange 5.5 sites and configuration containers.

- **Check domain controller health and network connectivity.**   You should check your DNS and Active Directory environment and fix any inconsistencies before installing the ADC. This is accomplished quickly using the Domain Controller Diagnostics tool (DCDiag) and the Network Connectivity Tester tool (NetDiag). Both tools are included in the Windows Support Tools, which you can find on the Windows 2003 product CD in the \Support\Tools folder. Make sure you install the support tools on the ADC server in a folder in the system search path. You can then simply type **dcdiag** and **netdiag** at the command prompt to launch a test.

Note   Be sure that you have local administrator permissions on the server you are planning to run these tools. It is a good idea to verify network connectivity to domain controllers on all servers running Active Directory Connector or Exchange Server 2003.

Deploying Active Directory Connector

Before you install Active Directory Connector by running Setup.exe from the \ADC\i386\ folder on the Exchange Server 2003 product CD, you should prepare the Active Directory environment for a later deployment of Exchange Server 2003. This is accomplished by using ForestPrep and DomainPrep.

Using Exchange Server Deployment Tools, you can perform the installation of Active Directory Connector through the following steps:

1. Run the Exchange 2003 Setup program with the /ForestPrep option to extend the Active Directory schema with Exchange-specific classes and attributes. ForestPrep also creates the container object for the Exchange 2003 organization in the configuration naming context of Active Directory. Because ForestPrep extends the schema, you must run ForestPrep in the Active Directory domain where the schema master resides. Setup will inform you if you are running ForestPrep in an incorrect domain. It is a good idea to run ForestPrep directly on the schema master. To run ForestPrep, you must be a member of the Enterprise Admins group and the Schema Admins group. During ForestPrep, you will designate an account that will have Exchange Full Administrator permissions to the organization object. By default, the Exchange Setup program suggests the account you are currently using to run /Forestprep, but you should change this account information according to the specific requirements of your company.

Note   In Exchange 2003, the schema files that ship with Active Directory Connector are identical to the core Exchange Server 2003 schema files. Therefore, you only need to update the schema once.

2. Run the Exchange 2003 Setup program with the /DomainPrep option to create the groups and permissions within the domain necessary for Exchange servers to read and modify user attributes in Active Directory. DomainPrep creates two new domain groups known as Exchange Domain Servers (a Windows global security group) and Exchange Enterprise Servers (a Windows domain local security group). DomainPrep also creates the Public Folder proxy container in

the current Active Directory domain named Microsoft Exchange System Objects in the Active Directory domain. Active Directory Connector public folder connection agreements will create recipient objects for public folders in this container. To run DomainPrep, you must be a member of the Domain Admins group. You must run DomainPrep once in each domain that contains an Exchange 2003 server and in any domain that hosts Exchange users, as well as in the root domain of the forest.

3. Run the OrgPrepCheck tool to validate Active Directory schema extensions, domains, and security descriptors before installing Active Directory Connector. The OrgPrepCheck tool runs the following tests:

    ■ **OrgCheck**   The OrgCheck tool validates the schema extensions created by ForestPrep, verifies that the proper domain groups exist and are populated, ensures that the correct security descriptors are assigned, confirms that the Exchange configuration container exists in Active Directory, and checks connectivity to a global catalog server. A global catalog server must be available in a domain in which DomainPrep has been run. You should check that a global catalog server is available in the same site as the ADC server or a site directly adjacent to the ADC server's site.

    ■ **PolCheck**   The PolCheck tool checks that all domain controllers in the local domain have the Manage auditing and security logs permission for the Exchange Enterprise Servers group. The PolCheck tool reports any domain controllers that do not have this permission.

4. To run the ADC Setup, deploy the Active Directory Connector version that ships with Exchange Server 2003 or the one that ships with Exchange Server 2003 SP1. The Setup.exe is located on the Exchange Server 2003 product CD in the \ADC\i386 directory. We recommend that you install ADC directly on a domain controller, preferably a global catalog server. Keep in mind, however, that the hardware must be able to handle the extra workload. To distribute the workload, you can deploy ADC on multiple domain controllers and split the connection agreements across the Active Directory Connector instances. However, this complicates the ADC deployment and is only necessary in complex or very large environments. If the network connection to the nearest global catalog server is fast and reliable, you can also install ADC on a member server. To install ADC, your account must be a member of the Domain Admins and Enterprise Admins groups, and have the permissions of a local administrator.

> **Note**   You should update all Active Directory Connector installations by installing the ADC version included with Exchange Server 2003 SP1 by running Setup.exe and choosing the Reinstall option. If you have not deployed Active Directory Connector yet, you can directly install the SP1 version. The slipstreamed Setup.exe does not need an existing Exchange 2003 version.

Active Directory Connector consists of the following two separate components, which should both be installed on the ADC server:

5. Microsoft Active Directory Connector service is the Windows 2000 service that performs the actual directory synchronization. The account being used to run the ADC service must be a member of the local Administrators group.

6. The Active Directory Connector Manager snap-in is the management tool that configures directory synchronization based on connection agreements. Connection agreements are explained later in this section.

ADC Connection Agreements

To synchronize Exchange 5.5 directory and Active Directory, you must configure ADC connection agreements. You can accomplish this task using the Active Directory Connector Manager snap-in. Among other things, you must specify the servers that Active Directory Connector will to connect to, the directory object types to synchronize, the synchronization direction, and a synchronization schedule. You also must specify credentials to access Active Directory and the Exchange 5.5 directory. Remember that connection agreements must read information from the source directories and write information to the target directories. Keep also in mind that for an upgrade from Exchange 5.5 to Exchange 2003, you must use the Active Directory Connector version included in the latest Exchange Server 2003 Service Pack.

Active Directory Connector supports the following types of connection agreements:

■ **Recipient connection agreement**   Synchronizes Exchange 5.5 mailbox objects, distribution lists, and custom recipients with Active Directory user accounts, mail-enabled groups, and contacts.

> **Note** In addition to user accounts, groups, and contacts, Exchange Server 2003 in native mode also supports inetOrgPerson objects and query-based distribution groups. However, Active Directory Connector does not synchronize inetOrgPerson objects or query-based distribution groups because these object types are not available in a mixed-mode organization.

- **Public folder connection agreement** Synchronizes directory objects that represent mail-enabled public folders between Exchange 5.5 and Active Directory. In Exchange 5.5, all public folders are mail-enabled by default. In Exchange 2003, you can mailbox-enable or mailbox-disable public folders. Public folders that have a corresponding recipient object in Active Directory are mail-enabled.

- **Configuration connection agreement** Synchronizes recipient policies and Exchange configuration information. You cannot create configuration connection agreements manually. The Exchange 2003 Setup program automatically creates a configuration connection agreement when you install the first Exchange 2003 server in an Exchange 5.5 site. By synchronizing configuration information between directories, Exchange Server 2003 servers and Exchange 5.5 servers share a common configuration and can coexist. Each server is aware of other servers, sites, routing, and connectors of the other. It is for this reason that the ADC must be installed before the first Exchange Server 2003 server can be joined to an Exchange 5.5 organization.

Configuring Directory Synchronization

To help you successfully configure recipient and public folder connection agreements, the Active Directory Connector Manager snap-in includes an ADC Tools node that provides access to relevant wizards and configuration utilities. You should use ADC Tools to prepare the Exchange 5.5 directory for directory synchronization.

You can perform the following steps to check the Exchange 5.5 directory:

1. Specify the target Exchange 5.5 server that ADC Tools should contact to gather and write Exchange 5.5 directory information. If the server you specify uses an LDAP port other than the default port of 389, such as port 379, you must also specify the custom port number, so that Active Directory Connector can successfully establish an LDAP connection.

2. Collect directory data about the recipient objects in the Exchange 5.5 directory to verify that Exchange 5.5 is ready for directory synchronization. Specifically, you must examine the Exchange 5.5 directory for user accounts that are associated with multiple mailboxes. For example, if you follow the steps outlined in

the document Installing Exchange Server 5.5.doc in the \Companion Material\Chapter 04 folder on the companion CD, you have assigned the Administrator account two mailboxes named Administrator and Postmaster. This configuration represents an issue because in Active Directory, every mailbox-enabled user has exactly one mailbox and every mailbox corresponds to exactly one user object, so the Administrator account cannot have two mailboxes in Active Directory.

3. Run Resource Mailbox Wizard prior to configuring connection agreements if you have users with multiple mailboxes in Exchange 5.5, or you might synchronize the wrong Exchange 5.5 mailbox information with Active Directory user accounts. Active Directory Connector synchronizes the first mailbox with a user object, where the SID of the primary Microsoft Windows NT account matches the SID of the user account in Active Directory. For any additional mailboxes, Active Directory Connector either creates an enabled or disabled user account depending on the connection agreement configuration.

   To match the appropriate primary mailbox to its Active Directory account, you must mark all remaining mailboxes as resource mailboxes so that they are not accidentally matched to the Active Directory account. For example, the Postmaster mailbox mentioned above might be a resource mailbox for the Administrator account. Identifying a mailbox as a resource mailbox can be achieved by setting the custom attribute 10 of the resource mailbox to a value of "NTDS-NoMatch." You can make these changes manually, semi-automatically using a comma-separated value (.csv) import file in the Exchange Administrator program, or fully automated using Resource Mailbox Wizard. Resource Mailbox Wizard provides a convenient user interface to select primary and resource mailboxes, which the wizard stamps accordingly with the NTDSNoMatch value. Resource Mailbox Wizard checks the Exchange 5.5 directory for mailboxes with the same primary Windows NT account, determines whether the mailbox alias matches the Windows account name, and, if it does not, suggests configuring the mailbox as a resource mailbox by applying the NTDSNoMatch value. You can adjust the configuration in the wizard's Select Primary and Resource Mailboxes screen before applying the changes.

> **On the Resource Kit CD**   The document Adding ADC to the Test Environment.doc in the \Companion Material\Chapter 04\Full In-Place Windows Upgrade folder on the companion CD provides an example of how to run Resource Mailbox Wizard.

Synchronizing Resource Mailboxes

Figure 4-6 illustrates the process of synchronizing resource mailboxes with Active Directory. When Active Directory Connector finds the NTDSNoMatch value in custom attribute 10, it does not match the mailbox to any existing user accounts. Instead, Active Directory Connector creates a separate user account for the resource mailbox.

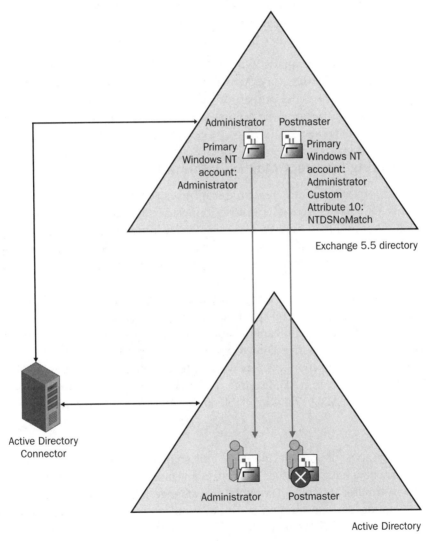

Figure 4-6   Synchronizing a resource mailbox with Active Directory

When synchronizing resource mailboxes, Active Directory Connector performs the following steps:

1. Creates a new user account for the resource mailbox in Active Directory, and grants the original user account Full Mailbox access so the original account can open the resource mailbox.

2. Grants the original account the Send As right so the original account can send messages on behalf of the resource account.

3. Grants the original account the permissions Read Personal Information and Write Personal Information so the original account can modify personal information of the resource account in the address book.

4. Changes the primary Windows NT account for the resource mailbox in the Exchange 5.5 directory. Active Directory Connector specifies the newly created user account as the primary Windows NT account. Access to the resource mailbox works because the original account has the required access permissions in Active Directory.

Correcting Incorrect Mailbox Information

It is important to identify resource mailboxes prior to configuring connection agreements. Otherwise, Active Directory Connector might match the wrong accounts with each other and may overwrite existing directory information. For example, if Active Directory Connector matches the Postmaster mailbox with the Administrator account, you will notice that the display name of the Administrator account changes to Postmaster.

If Active Directory Connector has synchronized a user object with the wrong mailbox information, you must clean up both Exchange 5.5 directory and Active Directory. However, you cannot simply delete the existing user accounts from Active Directory because Active Directory Connector would then delete the corresponding mailboxes from Exchange 5.5 as well. Instead, you must use a low-level tool, such as ADSI Edit or a custom ADSI script, to reset Active Directory Connector–specific directory attributes. ADSI Edit is available in the support tools of Windows Server 2003.

Warning If you use the ADSI Edit snap-in, a custom ADSI script, or the Exchange Administrator program in raw mode and you incorrectly modify the attributes of Active Directory or Exchange 5.5 directory objects, you can cause serious problems. These problems may require you to reinstall Exchange 5.5, Windows 2003, or Exchange 2003. Microsoft cannot guarantee that problems that occur if you incorrectly modify Active Directory or Exchange 5.5 directory object attributes can be solved. Use ADSI Edit, custom ADSI scripts, and Exchange Administrator in raw mode at your own risk.

User Accounts in Windows NT Domains

If Active Directory Connector cannot match user accounts, for example, because the accounts are in Windows NT domains and no corresponding object exists in Active Directory or because Custom Attribute 10 is set to NTDSNoMatch, Active Directory Connector must create new Active Directory accounts. When creating new accounts, Active Directory Connector grants the original Windows NT account Full Mailbox Access permissions. The new account is placed in the OU identified as the default destination for new objects in the configuration of your recipient connection agreement. If you configured the recipient connection agreement to create disabled mailbox-enabled user accounts for Exchange 5.5 mailboxes, Active Directory Connector also grants the original Windows NT account the Associated External Account permission, so the original Windows NT user can still access the mailbox even it is moved to Exchange 2003 later on.

> **More Info**   For more information about the purpose of Associated External Account configurations, see Chapter 3, "Exchange Server 2003 in Enterprise Environments."

On the other hand, if you decided to create enabled mailbox-enabled user accounts for Exchange 5.5 mailboxes in a user account migration scenario, you must keep in mind that Active Directory Connector cannot migrate passwords; therefore, creating enabled user accounts fails by default in Windows 2003. Enabled user accounts with no passwords do not meet the default Windows 2003 security requirements for complex passwords. In this case, Active Directory Connector will report errors with an event identifier of 8270 in the application event log. The following listing shows a shortened example:

```
Event Type:Error
Event Source:MSADC
Event Category:LDAP Operations
Event ID:8270
Description:
LDAP returned the error [35] Unwilling To Perform when importing the transaction
dn: cn=Ted Bremer,ou=Recipients,
OU=Exchange 5.5 Recipients,DC=ad,DC=tailspintoys,DC=com
changetype: Add
...
```

To avoid this issue, you must configure Group Policy settings for the domain that you have specified as the destination for new objects in the configuration of your recipient connection agreement. Specifically, you must configure the password policy in the Default Domain Policy to allow empty passwords.

> **Note**   You should not create mail-enabled user accounts for Exchange 5.5 users in the local Exchange organization. This is an unsupported feature that is present only for inter-organizational connection agreements.

ADC Attributes Mapping

Active Directory Connector maps most mailbox attributes to appropriate user account attributes. For example, the Hide-From-Address-Book attribute in Exchange 5.5 is mapped to the msExchHideFromAddressLists attribute in Active Directory to ensure that hidden objects remain hidden from address books across the entire environment. If required, you can exclude specific attributes from directory synchronization when you right-click the root object named Active Directory Connector Management in Active Directory Connector Manager, and then select Properties. You can customize the Exchange-to-Active Directory and Active Directory-to-Exchange attribute flow on the From Exchange and From Windows tabs. Using these tabs, you can also customize how Active Directory Connector matches mailboxes to Active Directory accounts.

> **Note**   If you customize object matching rules, you cannot use ADC Tools to configure connection agreements. Microsoft does not recommend changing object matching rules or attributes mappings. Microsoft only supports Active Directory Connector with the default matching rules and attribute mappings.

Customizing Attributes Mapping

It might be required to customize the mapping of attributes in Active Directory Connector if you use Exchange 5.5 custom attributes to include special recipient information in the address book, such as the license plate number of employee vehicles. The schema of the Exchange 5.5 directory is not flexible enough to support customization. To address this issue, Exchange Server 5.5 supports 15 custom attributes, which you can rename in the Exchange Administrator program (DS Site Configuration object, Custom Attributes tab). For example, you might have given Custom Attribute 1 the label Car License to identify the information contained in this field as license plate numbers.

Tip Microsoft does not support Active Directory Connector installations with customized attribute mappings. When troubleshooting Active Directory Connector, verify that the problem also occurs with default mappings before contacting Microsoft Product Support Services.

Exchange Server 2003 supports Exchange 5.5 custom attributes via 15 extension attributes, and Active Directory Connector synchronizes these attributes accordingly. By design, you cannot rename the extension attributes because extension attributes exist for backward compatibility reasons only, so you cannot give Extension Attribute 1 the label Car License, for example. If you find that the extension attributes do not meet your requirements for custom information, you can use other attributes or modify the Active Directory schema to implement your own attributes. Active Directory provides a flexible database schema. It should be noted, however, that modifying the Active Directory schema to implement custom attributes causes a complete rebuild of all global catalogs. In a complex Active Directory forest with multiple domains, this can lead to excessive replication traffic, so plan your custom attributes carefully. Remember that you cannot remove custom attributes once the schema is extended. You can only deactivate attributes once they are implemented.

To continue the license plate example, user accounts in Active Directory have a carLicense attribute that you can use for the purpose of specifying license plate information. The carLicense attribute is a standard attribute. You do not have to extend the schema in order to use it, but you must change the Active Directory Connector attribute mapping to synchronize Custom Attribute 1 with carLicense instead of Extension Attribute 1. To synchronize the information correctly, you must change the Active Directory Connector attribute mapping rules.

Attribute mapping rules have the following characteristics that apply to all connection agreements:

- Active Directory-to-Exchange matching rules are stored in the msExchServer1-SchemaMap attribute of the Default ADC Policy object.

- Exchange-to-Active Directory matching rules are stored in the msExchServer2-SchemaMap attribute of the Default ADC Policy object.

- The Default ADC Policy object resides in the configuration naming context under Configuration\Services\Microsoft Exchange\Active Directory Connector. You can use ADSI Edit to examine the attributes.

As explained in Chapter 3, "Exchange Server 2003 in Enterprise Environments," you can modify these attribute mapping rules using ADSI Edit, but this is a very burdensome undertaking because of the large number of mapping rules stored in these single-valued fields. It is more convenient to customize the mapping rules in a text file and then use a custom ADSI script to import the information into msExchServer1-SchemaMap and msExchServer2SchemaMap.

On the Resource Kit CD   You can use the ImportCustomMappings.wsf script in the \Companion Material\Chapter 04\Scripts folder on the companion CD for this purpose. Also see the document Customize ADC Attribute Mapping Example.doc in the \Companion Material\Chapter 04\CarLicense folder on the companion CD for step-by-step instructions on how to implement a Custom Attribute 1 to carLicense attribute mapping.

Designing a Connection Agreement Topology

Having prepared the Exchange 5.5 directory, object matching rules, and attribute mapping rules, you can configure connection agreements and start synchronizing user and mailbox information. In a single-domain Active Directory forest, you can use the Connection Agreement Wizard included with ADC Tools for this purpose. This wizard enables you to configure required public folder connection agreements and recipient connection agreements based on your Exchange 5.5 directory and Active Directory configuration. Depending on the number of users, it can take several hours to fully synchronize Exchange Directory with Active Directory.

In a more complex domain environment, it may be necessary to configure connection agreements manually. For example, if you have deployed a separate native-mode Active Directory domain for distribution lists, you might want to synchronize recipient object types selectively. The Connection Agreement Wizard can suggest a configuration if you specify the native-mode domain as the default target, but if you want to synchronize user accounts with a different domain, the default configuration might not be sufficient. In this situation, you must create separate connection agreements with different destinations: one recipient connection agreement to synchronize user accounts and contacts with a mixed-mode domain, and another recipient connection agreement to synchronize distribution lists with the native-mode domain. Figure 4-7 illustrates this topology.

Note   It is recommended that you use ADC Tools or Exchange Deployment Tool (Exdeploy.exe) to verify the replication of your connection agreements.

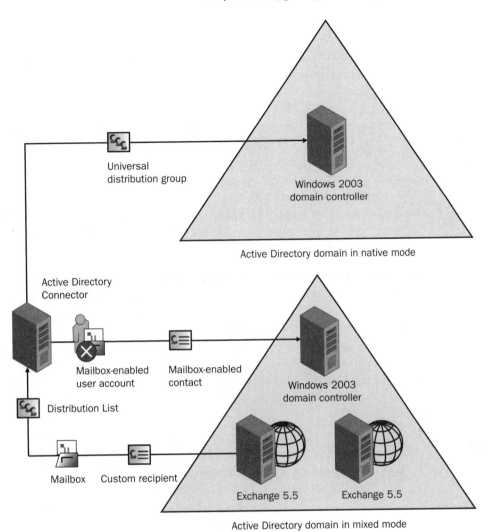

Figure 4-7 A separate destination for distribution lists

Multiple-Site and Multiple-Domain Topologies

Exchange 5.5 organizations with multiple sites and Active Directory forests with multiple domains complicate the connection agreement design. Within an Exchange 5.5 organization with multiple sites, Exchange servers fully replicate directory information to each other, but directory objects from remote sites are read-only. If you want to write information into the Exchange 5.5 directory, you must configure an explicit connection agreement to a server in each site. Similarly, in Active Directory, domain controllers do not contain information about user accounts from other domains. Only global catalog servers hold a partial replicate of each domain naming context in the forest, but this replica is likewise read-only. Therefore, if you want to write information into Active Directory, you must configure separate connection agreements for each domain as well.

Having multiple connection agreements write information into a directory, however, bears the risk of creating duplicate recipient objects. For example, assume you have an Active Directory forest with two domains. What happens if you create a new mailbox in Exchange 5.5? You may end up with duplicated user accounts in Active Directory—one in each domain. To prevent this, Active Directory Connector supports the concept of primary and secondary connection agreements, which you can specify on the Advanced tab in the connection agreement's properties. A primary connection agreement synchronizes existing directory objects and creates new objects for those that could not be matched to an existing object. A secondary connection agreement, on the other hand, synchronizes existing objects but does not create new objects.

In complex topologies, you should deploy primary and secondary connection agreements as follows:

- **Single Active Directory domain with multiple Exchange sites**   In general, there should only be one primary connection agreement per domain to an Exchange organization. Applied to an Active Directory domain with a multi-site Exchange organization this means that you should configure one primary connection agreement to the nearest site, and secondary connection agreements to all other Exchange sites. All connection agreements can then write changes back into Exchange 5.5 recipient objects, but new recipients created in Active Directory are created only in the Exchange site of the primary connection agreement.

Note   To configure a secondary connection agreement to Exchange 5.5, clear the This is a primary Connection Agreement for the connected Exchange Organization check box on the Advanced tab.

- **Single Exchange site with multiple Active Directory domains**   Similarly, there should only be one primary connection agreement from an Exchange organization to an Active Directory forest. You might want to choose an Active Directory domain in native mode for the primary connection agreement, so that you do not have to configure a separate connection agreement for distribution lists. To all remaining Active Directory domains, configure secondary connection agreements.

Note   To configure a secondary connection agreement to Exchange 5.5, clear the This is a primary Connection Agreement for the connected Windows Domain check box on the Advanced tab.

■ **Multiple Active Directory domains with multiple Exchange sites**   The configuration of connection agreements can be very complex in environments with multiple Exchange sites and multiple domains. To prevent accidental creation of duplicated accounts, it is recommended that you first configure all connection agreements as secondary two-way agreements. Two-way connection agreements help reducing the overall number of required connection agreements. You must synchronize the directories in both directions to support Exchange Server 2003.

Having deployed secondary two-way agreements between domains and sites, you can configure an additional primary one-way connection agreement to synchronize Exchange 5.5 recipient information to Active Directory. In general, one primary connection agreement is sufficient for the entire Active Directory forest. This requires you to identify a domain where accounts should be created. This domain should operate in native mode. Make sure you include all Exchange recipient containers in the connection agreement. On the From Exchange tab, simply select the organization object under Exchange Recipients Containers. You also must specify an appropriate OU under Default Destination. Active Directory Connector then automatically creates sublevel OUs in this location for all recipient containers. This may not represent an ideal OU structure, but in the Active Directory Users and Computers console, you can easily move newly created objects to other OUs. As mentioned earlier, Active Directory Connector retains the relationship between directory objects based on object matching rules, which work independent of the object locations.

To support seamless coexistence, you also must configure primary connection agreements from Active Directory to the Exchange 5.5 directory. This requires you to identify one connection agreement per domain and enable its This is a primary Connection Agreement for the connected Exchange Organization check box. Make sure that only one connection agreement per domain is able to create new objects and that the default destination points to the desired recipient container in Exchange 5.5.

> **Note** In multi-domain environments, you should deploy Active Directory Connector on a global catalog server to ensure that all requested objects are included in the directory synchronization.

Adding Exchange 2003 To an Exchange 5.5 Organization

Following the synchronization of Exchange Server 5.5 with Active Directory, Exchange 2003 can be installed in the organization. For backward compatibility, Exchange 2003 includes an Exchange 5.5 directory service, named Site Replication Service (SRS), that enables Exchange 2003 to participate seamlessly in an Exchange 5.5 site. Exchange 2003 servers appear in the Exchange Administrator program just as any other server running Exchange. Similarly, Exchange System Manager displays all servers running Exchange 5.5 alongside Exchange 2003 server objects. However, remember not to mix administrative tools. You must use the Exchange Administrator program to manage Exchange 5.5 servers and Exchange System Manager to manage Exchange 2003 servers. Exchange System Manager displays Exchange 5.5 servers as read-only to prevent you from configuring these servers, but Exchange Administrator does not include such precautions.

Exchange Server 2003 in Mixed Mode

Exchange Server 2003 can operate either in mixed mode for backward compatibility or in native mode for full functionality. The default is mixed mode to ensure you can integrate the system with Exchange 5.5. As long as Exchange 5.5 servers exist in your organization, switching the Exchange organization to native mode is not possible.

Table 4-2 summarizes the features available in native mode and mixed mode.

Table 4-2 Native Mode vs. Mixed Mode Features

Feature	Available in mixed Exchange 5.5, Exchange 2000, and Exchange 2003 organization?	Available in pure Exchange 2003 organization that is in native mode?
Move system folders and public folders across routing groups	No, may prevent e-mail delivery to the public folder	Yes
Move mailboxes between servers in the same administrative group	Yes	Yes

Table 4-2   Native Mode vs. Mixed Mode Features (Continued)

Feature	Available in mixed Exchange 5.5, Exchange 2000, and Exchange 2003 organization?	Available in pure Exchange 2003 organization that is in native mode?
Move mailboxes between servers in different administrative groups	Yes, with Exchange 2003 SP1	Yes
Create an administrative group that spans multiple routing groups	No	Yes
Use query-based distribution groups	No	Yes
InetOrgPerson object can be mail-enabled or mailbox-enabled	No	Yes

Exchange 2003 Installation

You must add the first Exchange 2003 server in your organization to an existing site. Subsequently, you can create additional administrative groups in Exchange System Manager and install Exchange 2003 in these groups. An important requirement to remember when installing the first Exchange 2003 server in an existing Exchange 5.5 site, is that all servers in an Exchange 5.5 site must use the same service account for server-to-server communication based on remote procedure calls (RPCs). You must ensure that the site services account is in Active Directory so that servers running Exchange Server 2003 can participate in this communication. This can be accomplished by upgrading the PDC of the site services account domain or by moving the site service account to an Active Directory domain.

 On the Resource Kit CD   The document Changing the Exchange 5.5 Site Services Account.doc in the \Companion Material\Chapter 04\New Active Directory Domain folder on the companion CD explains how to move the site services account.

To add Exchange Server 2003 to an existing Exchange organization, you must:

- Use an account that is a member of the local Administrators group on the server that you are installing and a Permissions Admin in the Exchange site.

- Know the password of the site services account.

> **Note**   Having installed Exchange Server 2003, you can verify the site services account in Exchange System Manager, on the General tab, in the properties of the administrative group that corresponds to the Exchange site to which you added the Exchange 2003 server.

Resource Consolidation

An upgrade to Exchange 2003 is a good opportunity to consolidate server resources on fewer but more powerful computers. Exchange 2003 includes a number of improvements over Exchange Server 5.5 and Exchange 2000 Server, including support for Volume Shadow Copy service, improved virtual memory management, and improved caching algorithms so that directory lookups can be completed more efficiently. If you intend to consolidate messaging resources, keep in mind that certain mixed-mode restrictions may limit your flexibility when resources are in different Exchange sites.

You have the following options to consolidate Exchange 5.5 resources from different Exchange sites onto fewer Exchange 2003 servers:

- **Postpone consolidation until all servers run Exchange Server 2003** You can then switch the organization to native mode and move the mailboxes across administrative group boundaries. A disadvantage of this approach is that you must initially deploy a larger number of Exchange 2003 servers and administrative groups than in a consolidated Exchange 2003 organization.

- **Move Exchange 5.5 servers to the same site using the Move Server Wizard** It might be possible to move Exchange 5.5 into a consolidated site prior to installing Exchange 2003 Active Directory Connector. Move Server Wizard is available in SP3 of Exchange Server 5.5 and later. However, once Exchange 2003 Active Directory Connector is installed, the mixed-mode organization exists in Active Directory, and you should no longer use Move Server Wizard to move servers between sites in the same organization.

> **Note**   If you move Exchange 5.5 servers between sites, give the Exchange directory time to replicate the changes to all servers in the organization before you install Exchange Server 2003.

■ **Consolidate sites using Exchange Server 2003 SP1 Deployment Tools**   It might not be possible to wait with resource consolidation until the Exchange organization is in native mode, and it is likewise not an easy task to use Exchange 5.5 Move Server Wizard. The good news is that Exchange Server 2003 SP1 supports mailbox moves across administrative groups in mixed mode. Chapter 6, "Server and Site Consolidation Strategies," covers mixed-mode consolidation in more detail.

Exchange 5.5 Directory Replication

Active Directory Connector replicates Exchange 5.5 and Active Directory information, but Active Directory does not store directory information in Exchange 5.5 format. To achieve seamless coexistence, Exchange 2003 and Exchange 5.5 must also fully replicate their directory information with each other through the Exchange 5.5 directory replication protocol based on RPCs. This is accomplished using Site Replication Service. The SRS contains much of the executable code of the former directory service, which ensures full compatibility. The Exchange 2003 Setup program activates SRS on the first Exchange 2003 server in a site. On all other Exchange 2003 servers, this service is deactivated by default.

SRS maintains a separate database named SRS.edb to hold Exchange Server 5.5 directory information. This database is not the Active Directory database. SRS.edb resides on the file system in the \Program Files\Exchsrvr\SRSData directory. To synchronize SRS with Active Directory, you must use Active Directory Connector, as illustrated in Figure 4-8. The Exchange 2003 Setup program automatically creates a configuration connection agreement so that Active Directory Connector can synchronize the SRS database with Active Directory. Active Directory will then propagate the configuration information to all domain controllers in the forest. In the other direction, SRS will replicate directory changes with Exchange 5.5 servers in the local site. The configuration connection agreement object is read-only in Active Directory Connector Manager.

Note   You should place the Exchange 2003 server running SRS close to the server running the Active Directory Connector configuration connection agreement.

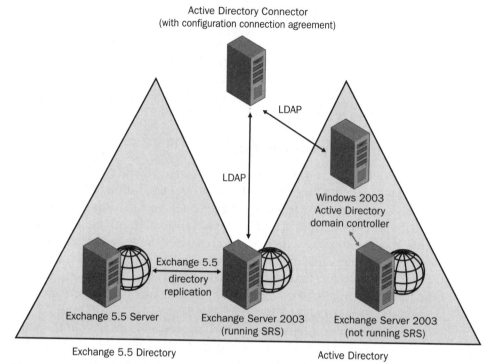

Figure 4-8   Directory replication between SRS, Active Directory, and Exchange directory

SRS has the following characteristics:

- The name service provider interface (NSPI) in the SRS is disabled to prevent MAPI-based clients, such as Outlook, from connecting to SRS and retrieving directory information from this service.

- The SRS replicates directory information only with Exchange 5.5 directories, it does not directly replicate directory information with Active Directory.

- To synchronize configuration information, Active Directory Connector communicates with SRS through LDAP. SRS uses TCP port 379 to avoid port conflicts with Active Directory.

- SRS is not supported in a Windows cluster configuration. Therefore, the first Exchange 2003 server in an Exchange 5.5 site cannot be a clustered server.

- SRS only exists in mixed mode. Exchange 2003 removes all SRS instances as soon as you switch the organization into native mode.

Note When installing or enabling SRS, existing Exchange 5.5 administrators in the local site inherit the permissions to manage the SRS environment because the SRS permissions are a copy of the permissions from the Exchange 5.5 directory. Administrators who are granted permissions to the Exchange 2003 organization in Active Directory at a later time will not receive any permission in the SRS database. These administrators will therefore not be able to manage SRS unless you grant them permissions explicitly using the Exchange Administrator program. Connect to the Exchange 2003 server and grant the desired user accounts the appropriate rights at the organization, site, and configuration levels. You need the rights of a Permissions Admin to accomplish this step.

Exchange 5.5 and Exchange 2003 Interoperability

Replication of configuration information between Exchange Server 5.5, SRS, and Active Directory is the basis for seamless system integration. Exchange 5.5 servers are then able to locate and use resources on Exchange 2003 servers, and vice versa. However, several interoperability issues exist due to differences in system architectures. For instance, Exchange Server 2003 uses LSI from a link state table (LST) to make routing decisions, whereas Exchange Server 5.5 relies on a Gateway Address Routing Table (GWART). Moreover, Exchange Server 5.5 maintains security information in the Information Store to grant or deny users access to the resources, whereas Exchange Server 2003 uses primarily Active Directory for access control.

Note As long as your bridgehead servers run Exchange Server 5.5, message routing decisions are based on GWART. Only Exchange 2000 and Exchange 2003 servers are able to make smart routing decisions based on an LST. If possible, you should migrate messaging connectors to bridgehead servers running Exchange Server 2003. In other words, you should migrate your bridgehead servers to Exchange 2003 early on.

Message Routing between Exchange 5.5 and Exchange 2003

For backward compatibility, Exchange Server 2003 generates a GWART and replicates it through SRS to Exchange 5.5 servers, so all users in the organization can use messaging connectors running on Exchange 2003, such as an SMTP Connector linking the messaging organization to the Internet. Exchange Server 2003 also receives routing information from Exchange 5.5 through SRS, which Exchange 2003 incorporates into the LST. Thus, Exchange 2003 users can use connectors running on Exchange 5.5, such as connectors not available in Exchange 2003, including Connector for Microsoft Mail for PC Networks, Connector for Lotus cc:Mail, Connector for Professional Office System (PROFS), Connector for System Network Architecture Distribution Services (SNADS), or any Exchange 5.5–specific third-party gateway.

Figure 4-9 illustrates a mixed-mode Exchange organization. An Exchange 2003 SMTP Connector has replaced the Exchange 5.5 Internet Mail Service (IMS), but a Connector for PROFS remains running on an Exchange 5.5 bridgehead server so that all users can communicate with PROFS.

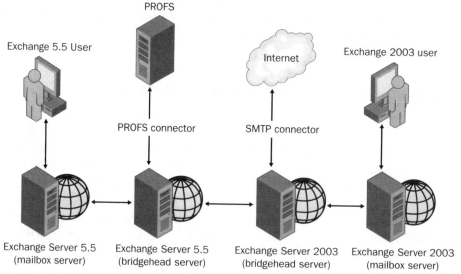

Figure 4-9   Connector coexistence in mixed mode

Exchange 5.5 and Exchange 2003 users can send messages via any connector regardless of the Exchange Server version. However, some connectors may be restricted in scope, which may present an interoperability issue. Exchange Server 2003 supports connector scopes at the organization and routing group levels, but Exchange 5.5 supports an additional scope at the server-location level for which no counterpart exists in Exchange 2003. Message routing may be inefficient as long as connectors with a server-location scope are used in an Exchange 5.5 site. Table 4-3 lists the differences in connector scopes between Exchange 5.5 and Exchange 2003.

Table 4-3   Connector Scope Differences

Scope in Exchange 5.5	Scope in Exchange 2003	Comments
Organization	Organization	Connectors with an organization-wide scope are available everywhere in the organization.
Site	Routing group	Site-level connectors are restricted to the local Exchange 5.5 site and Exchange 2003 routing group in which they exist.
Server location	Not applicable	Locally scoped connectors do not have a counterpart in Exchange 2003. Connectors with a server-location scope are available to all Exchange 2003 users in the routing group, which by default refers to the entire site. Perhaps the best way to address this issue is to create an additional routing group in the administrative group that corresponds to the Exchange 5.5 server location.
		It should be noted that, in mixed mode, you cannot place servers from different administrative groups in the same routing group. However, you can create multiple routing groups in a single administrative group.

Exchange-to-Exchange Message Transfer

During the phase of coexistence, it is vital for all Exchange servers running any version to communicate with each other based on the mechanisms supported by Exchange Server 5.5. Message transfer between Exchange 2003 servers, however, is not affected by the presence of Exchange 5.5 servers in the organization and always relies on SMTP, the native communication mechanisms of Exchange 2003.

There are two different scenarios in which an Exchange 2003 server might have to communicate with an Exchange 5.5 server:

- **Communication within sites**   Exchange 5.5 message transfer agents (MTAs) do not use a messaging connector for e-mail transfer within a site. Within an Exchange 5.5 site, MTA communication is always direct and based on RPCs. If Exchange Server 2003 is deployed in an existing Exchange 5.5 site, messages are exchanged with Exchange 5.5 through RPCs using the Microsoft Exchange MTA Stacks service. It is important that you keep the Microsoft Exchange MTA Stacks service running on every Exchange 2003 server.

- **Communication between sites** Between sites, Exchange 5.5 and Exchange 2003 servers communicate by means of a messaging connector. In Exchange 5.5, sites are usually connected using Site Connector and Site Connector communication takes place using RPCs. In Exchange 2003, routing groups are the equivalent of Exchange 5.5 sites for the purposes of message routing. Exchange 2003 routing groups are usually connected using Routing Group Connector. Between Exchange 2003 servers, Routing Group Connector uses SMTP.

  You can also use Site Connector to connect an Exchange 5.5 site to an Exchange 2003 routing group, and you can use Routing Group Connector to connect an Exchange 2003 routing group to an Exchange 5.5 site. Exchange 2003 can communicate with a Site Connector instance configured on an Exchange 5.5 server over RPCs. If you configure a Routing Group Connector instance to connect to an Exchange 5.5 server in a remote site, Routing Group Connector also automatically switches to RPCs, instead of SMTP, for backward compatibility with Exchange 5.5.

Note   You can also use SMTP or X.400 between sites and routing groups. For SMTP connectivity, you must deploy Internet Mail Service in Exchange 5.5 and an SMTP connector in Exchange 2003. For X.400 connectivity, use X.400 connectors at both sides. It is recommended, however, to use Site Connector and Routing Group Connector for their support of load balancing and fault tolerance.

Outlook Web Access Interoperability

Both Exchange Server 5.5 and Exchange Server 2003 support Outlook Web Access, but the technologies are very different. The Exchange Server 5.5 version of Outlook Web Access relies on Collaboration Data Objects (CDO) version 1.2.1, whereas the version of Exchange 2003 uses the OLE DB interface of the Exchange store. Because the OLE DB interface is not available in Exchange 5.5, you cannot access resources, such as mailboxes or public folders, that reside on an Exchange 5.5 server using the Exchange 2003 version of Outlook Web Access. Outlook Web Access 5.5, on the other hand, is able to communicate with Exchange 5.5 and higher versions because all Exchange versions support CDO 1.2.1. The only exception is alternate public folder hierarchies on an Exchange 2003 server. These hierarchies are unavailable to OWA 5.5 because CDO 1.2.1 is based on MAPI.

If your users require Outlook Web Access in a mixed-mode organization, you should use the Exchange Server 5.5 version. To support Exchange 2003 Outlook Web Access, you must move the mailboxes and all public folder resources to an Exchange 2003 server. Table 4-4 lists typical Outlook Web Access interoperability issues.

Table 4-4   Outlook Web Access Interoperability

Feature	Exchange Server 5.5	Exchange Server 2003
Mailbox on Exchange 2003	Yes	Yes
Mailbox on Exchange 5.5	Yes	No
MAPI-based public folders on Exchange 2003	Yes	Yes
MAPI-based public folders on Exchange 5.5	Yes	No
Alternate public folders on Exchange 2003	No	Yes

Offline Address Book Interoperability

There are also significant differences in the implementation of offline address books, which users can download to their Outlook clients to compose messages while disconnected from the server. Exchange Server 5.5 generates site-specific offline address books in ANSI format from recipient information in the Exchange Directory. Exchange Server 2003, on the other hand, generates organization-specific offline address books from Active Directory objects. There is no upgrade or synchronization of offline address books between Exchange Server 5.5 and Exchange 2003.

Users with mailboxes on an Exchange 5.5 server can only download offline address books that an Exchange 5.5 server generated. Thus, as long as Exchange 5.5 servers exist in the site/administrative group, offline address books cannot reside on an Exchange 2003 server. You should move the offline address books to the Exchange 5.5 server in the site that you are planning to decommission last. To do so, open the Exchange Administrator program, display the properties of the DS Site Configuration object from the Configuration container of your site, click the Offline Address Book tab, and then specify the other Exchange server in the Offline Address Book Server list box.

Public Folder Interoperability

In a mixed-mode organization, you can place public folders on Exchange 5.5, Exchange 2003, or both, and all users should be able to access these folders whether their mailboxes reside on Exchange 5.5 or Exchange 2003. To provide all users with the same level of access to all public folders, you must synchronize the complete set of public folder information.

In Exchange Server 5.5, public folders are always mail-enabled, meaning they have associated directory objects, although these are hidden from the address book by default. The legacy Exchange Administrator program, for instance, expects to find a directory object for every public folder in the organization. Exchange Server 2003, operating in mixed mode, likewise mail-enables public folders by default for backward compatibility.

If you create a public folder on an Exchange 5.5 server, the associated public folder recipient object exists in the Exchange 5.5 directory. In Exchange 5.5, these objects are in the Recipients container. If you create a public folder on an Exchange 2003 server, the recipient object exists in Active Directory instead, specifically in the Microsoft Exchange System Objects container, which you can display in Active Directory Users and Computers if you enable the Advanced Features setting on the View menu. To synchronize public folder recipient objects between Exchange 5.5 directory and Active Directory, you must configure a public folder connection agreement. When you create a public folder connection agreement, Active Directory Connector will automatically select the Microsoft Exchange System Objects container and Exchange 5.5 Recipients container. You cannot change these settings. Public folder connection agreements are always two-way connection agreements, and they are always primary for the connected Exchange organization. You must create a separate public folder connection agreement for each Exchange site, but only one connection agreement should be configured as a primary connection agreement for each connected Active Directory domain.

> **Note**   Public folder connection agreements synchronize public folder directory objects, but not the actual public folder hierarchy or the public folder contents.

Public Folder Coexistence

In the Exchange store, public folders consist of two separate entities: a public folder hierarchy and the public folder contents. Hierarchy and contents are replicated differently across the organization. The hierarchy information (that is, the list of public folders) is replicated to all servers that hold a public folder database associated with the hierarchy. The content, on the other hand, is replicated only to those servers specified in the folder configuration.

For example, the MAPI-based hierarchy is associated with a public folder store on every Exchange server by default. The Exchange store therefore replicates the MAPI-based hierarchy to all servers in the organization (unless you remove the public folder store from an Exchange server, which excludes this server from hierarchy replication). The contents, in contrast, might reside only on one server or might be replicated to a subset of servers, but it is seldom that all servers in an Exchange organization hold a replica of a particular public folder. If a user wants to access a public folder instance and the public folder does not reside on the user's home server where the mailbox is located, the Exchange server returns a referral list to the client to redirect the client to a location that has the folder contents available. The client connects to the server where the public folder is hosted and displays the items. This redirect is transparent to the user.

As illustrated in Figure 4-10, an Exchange 2003 user might be redirected transparently to an Exchange 5.5 public folder server. The public folder contents appear as if they were hosted on the user's home server.

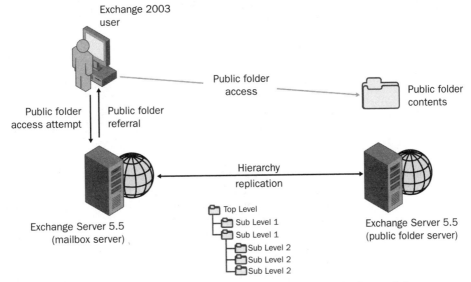

Figure 4-10   Public folder referral between Exchange 2003 and Exchange 5.5

Public Folder Interoperability Issues

To access public folder contents, clients may connect to an Exchange 5.5 server or an Exchange 2003 server, but the systems manage access to public folder resources differently. Table 4-5 lists the most important differences that affect public folder access.

Table 4-5   Public Folder Access Issues

Issue	Exchange Server 5.5	Exchange Server 2003	Comments
Public folder permissions	Exchange Server 5.5 controls access to public folder. resources based on distinguished names of Exchange directory objects. Security information is stored in separate database tables in the public folder database.	Exchange Server 2003 uses Active Directory access control lists (ACLs) to control access to public folders. ACLs are properties of the public folders in the hierarchy. No extra database tables are maintained.	Exchange Server 2003 must incorporate the Exchange 5.5 public folder permissions into Active Directory ACLs. If this process is not accomplished or fails, the folder will not be visible to Exchange 2003 users. It should be noted that, in Exchange Server 2003, the Exchange store maintains public folder ACLs in the messaging databases, but the accounts granted or denied permissions in these ACLs are Active Directory accounts.
Public folder affinities	Exchange Server 5.5 stores affinities at the site level in a separate table (that is, the affinity table) of the Exchange directory database. Public folder affinities are not transitive.	Exchange Server 2003 can use the routing table or server-specific settings to calculate public folder affinities. Public folder affinities are transitive.	Public folder affinities are not upgraded. You must reconfigure them manually after upgrading to Exchange Server 2003. You can read more about the design of routing group topologies and public folder access strategies in Chapter 2, "Exchange Server 2003 Design Basics."

To give users access to a public folder, the public folder hierarchy must be available and the contents must reside on a server that can be reached according to public folder affinities. The public folder affinity defines a cost value or preference level for public folder instances in a remote location. The public folder hierarchy is always replicated as long as RPC communication and e-mail transfer work. However, Exchange 2003 users might not be able to see all Exchange Server 5.5 public folders if Exchange 2003 cannot upgrade public folder permissions.

> **Note** Exchange System Manager provides access to all public folders in the hierarchy, even if public folders are not displayed in messaging clients.

Folder permissions are replicated as part of the hierarchy, but Exchange 2003 does not use Exchange 5.5 access control lists to grant or deny access to public folders. Exchange Server 2003 must convert Exchange 5.5 ACLs into Active Directory ACLs to provide Exchange 2003 users with access to the contents. This conversion can fail for the following reasons:

- Accounts specified in public folder permissions have been deleted from the Exchange 5.5 directory.

- Accounts specified in public folder permissions do not exist in Active Directory.

- Accounts specified in public folder permissions exist in Active Directory, but have no msExchMailboxSecurityDescriptor or msExchMasterAccountSID attribute.

- Distribution lists specified in public folder permissions have been synchronized with universal distribution groups, but the automatic conversion into universal security groups failed (possibly because the domain does not operate in native mode, as explained earlier in this chapter).

If the conversion of a folder's ACL fails, Exchange 2003 writes an error to the server's application event log and the folder remains invisible to Exchange 2003 users. It is advisable to examine the event log after the installation of Exchange Server 2003 and correct the client permissions in Exchange System Manager to ensure that the security information is upgraded successfully.

> **On the Resource Kit CD** For step-by-step instructions about how to examine and troubleshoot conversion failures, see the document Public folder ACLs in Exchange 2003.doc in the \Companion Material\Chapter 04\Public Folder Upgrades folder on the companion CD.

Avoiding ACL Conversion Issues

To avoid issues relating to failed folder ACL conversions, we recommend that you run the ADCConfigCheck tool included in Microsoft Exchange Deployment Tools. ADCConfigCheck verifies the Exchange 5.5 directory configuration to ensure that Exchange 5.5 directory objects are properly replicated to Active Directory. ADCConfigCheck accomplishes this by searching Active Directory using the Exchange 5.5 object's ADCglobalNames attribute. ADCConfigCheck lists any Exchange 5.5 configuration objects that are missing from Active Directory. It is highly recommended that you run this tool after Exchange Server 2003 Setup. To run ADCConfigCheck, your account must have Domain Administrator permissions and Exchange 5.5 Administrator permissions.

You should also follow these steps to upgrade public folders to Exchange Server 2003:

1. Use the Exchange Administrator program to display the client permissions for existing public folders and document them carefully.

2. Use the Exchange Administrator program to check the Information Store/Directory consistency on the Exchange 5.5 server. Enable the option to remove unknown user accounts from public folders. Removing unknown accounts helps to prevent permission-related upgrade problems.

> **Note**   You should not run the DS/IS consistency adjuster after joining a server to a site unless directory replication within the site has completed.

Follow these steps:

  a. In the Exchange Server 5.5 Administrator program, click on your Exchange 5.5 Server computer that contains the public folder database.

  b. On the File menu, click Properties, and then click the Advanced tab.

  c. Click Consistency Adjustment.

  d. Select the Remove unknown user accounts from public folder permissions and the Remove unknown user accounts from mailbox permissions check boxes, and then click All Inconsistencies.

  e. Clear all other check boxes, and then click OK.

6. Install Exchange Server 2003 and configure public folder connection agreements to create public folder objects in Active Directory that correspond to the public folder objects in the Exchange 5.5 directory.

7. Use Exchange System Manager to verify that the Exchange 2003 server has a complete list of all public folders in its MAPI-based hierarchy. Hierarchy replication is an automatic process.

8. Use Event Viewer to check that the folder permissions were mapped correctly to Active Directory ACLs during the upgrade process. Specifically, check the application event log to find any errors with the event ID 9551.

> **On the Resource Kit CD**   For an example of this event, see the document Public folder ACLs in Exchange 2003.doc on the companion CD.

9. Use Exchange System Manager to check the public folder ACLs. Display the properties of a public folder in the MAPI-based hierarchy, click the Permissions tab, press the CTRL key, and then click Client Permissions. This displays the Exchange 2003 ACLs in Windows format. If only the Anonymous Logon account is listed, you must correct the configuration. Close the dialog box and click Client Permissions again, this time without pressing the CTRL key. This displays the Client Permissions dialog box, which provides a consistent user interface with the Exchange Administrator program and Outlook. Verify that your users have the correct access permissions.

10. Use Exchange System Manager to examine the directory rights and also check the administrative rights for users and groups who administer the public folders.

Solving ACL Conversion Issues

The recommended approach to prevent ACL conversion issues is to run the DS/IS consistency adjuster against the Exchange 5.5 store before migration. However, if you have already migrated all of your accounts or are in the process of migrating your accounts to Exchange 2003, you may not be able to move mailboxes back to Exchange Server 5.5 just to run the DS/IS consistency adjuster one more time.

You have the following options to deal with ACL conversion issues:

■ **Fix ACLs manually**   You can use Exchange System Manager to adjust the client permissions. If you remove the problematic accounts, Exchange 2003 can convert the ACLs the next time the public folder is accessed.

■ **Ignore problematic distribution lists and other critical accounts specifically**   If the content in the public folder is not confidential or sensitive, you can configure a REG_SZ registry parameter named DNDeadList on the Exchange 2003 server at the following location: `HKEY_LOCAL_MACHINE\System\CurrentControlSet\Services\MSExchangeIS\ParametersSystem`, which you must set to a text file that contains the distinguished names that Exchange 2003 should ignore during the conversion process.

On the Resource Kit CD   For an example of how to configure a Deadlist.txt file see the document Fixing ACL conversions using DNDeadList.doc in the \Companion Material\Chapter 04\Public Folder Upgrades folder on the companion CD.

- **Ignore all problematic user accounts**   If the content in the public folder is not confidential or sensitive, you can decide to ignore all user accounts that are not represented in Active Directory in the ACLs of mailboxes and public folders. User accounts that are not represented in Active Directory can lead to a range of access problems, including delays in public folder access and ACL conversion issues. To ignore these accounts, configure a REG_DWORD registry parameter named Ignore zombie users on the Exchange 2003 server at HKEY_LOCAL_MACHINE\System\CurrentControlSet\Services\MSExchangeIS\Parameters-System.

On the Resource Kit CD   For details, see the document Fixing ACL conversions by ignoring zombie users.doc in the \Companion Material\Chapter 04\Public Folder Upgrades folder on the companion CD.

Note   These workarounds are supported for situations where the migration has occurred and the server cannot be restored to a pre-migration state, so performing the DS/IS consistency check is not a possibility. However, these workarounds can also be a replacement for running the DS/IS consistency adjuster in the first place.

Moving Public Folders and Mailboxes to Exchange 2003

Security-related issues may also arise after the deployment of Exchange Server 2003 when users create new public folders on an Exchange 5.5 server. For this reason, it is a good idea to relocate all public folders to an Exchange 2003 server early in the migration process. Having moved all public folders to Exchange 2003, Exchange 2003 maintains all public folder ACLs, which gives all Exchange 2003 users access to the resources. Exchange 2003 also calculates public folder permissions in legacy format and replicates this information as part of the public folder hierarchy to Exchange 5.5 servers, so that Exchange 5.5 users can work with the public folders as well.

> **Note** As mentioned earlier, offline address books should remain on an Exchange 5.5 server as long as there are Exchange 5.5 users in the organization. Exchange maintains offline address books in system folders, which are hidden public folders. You should move these folders to Exchange 2003 when you have finished moving your user's mailboxes.

Moving Public Folders

It is not a trivial task to move a public folder between servers, although it might seem simple at the first glance. In Exchange 5.5, public folders have a home server for the purposes of message delivery; however, in Exchange 2003 they do not because message routing in Exchange 2003 can direct the messages to any public folder instance. To ensure that messages can be delivered, you should move public folders to an Exchange 2003 server in the same routing group as the original public folder home server.

Moving public folders relies on public folder replication. The principle is straightforward. You replicate a public folder to an Exchange 2003 server, and when replication is complete, you remove the original replica from the Exchange 5.5 server (see Figure 4-11). However, it is difficult to identify when public folder replication is complete. For example, Microsoft Knowledge Base Article 327191 "XADM: How to Verify Public Folder Content After You Migrate from Exchange Server to Exchange 2000" suggests you should use Outlook or the M: drive (disabled on Exchange 2003 servers by default) to count the number of items in the original and replicated public folder instances, but this strategy does not work well if you are dealing with a large number of public folders. Perhaps a better approach is to use the old Exchange 5.5 Public Folder Replication Verification Tool (Replver.exe) in the Microsoft Exchange Server Resource Kit for Microsoft Exchange Server 5.5, which is part of the Microsoft BackOffice Resource Kit, Part Two. Using Replver.exe, you can verify public folder replication and compare public folders on servers in multiple sites to determine if public folder contents have been successfully replicated. Replver.exe compares items in public folders and the MAPI properties of the items and the folders.

If you do not have the Public Folder Replication Verification Tool at hand, you can also use Exchange System Manager to view the replication status of each public folder. Keep in mind, however, that this information is not reliable. For example, a public folder replica on an Exchange 2003 server might show a replication status of In Sync even after an Exchange 5.5 user has changed the contents on a Exchange 5.5 server. Fortunately, items are not lost even if you remove a public folder instance from an Exchange 5.5 server before the last changes were replicated. The old replica remains on the Exchange 5.5 server until the replication has taken place and the contents are entirely transferred to the new replica.

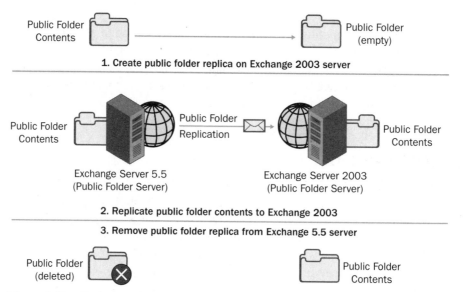

Figure 4-11   Moving a public folder to Exchange 2003

Public folder replication is not a super-fast process because it is based on e-mail messages. If you remove an original replica too early, you might end up with an empty folder on the Exchange 2003 server. This effect disappears as the Exchange servers complete the replication, yet depending on the replication schedule and the importance of the folder, this could cause confusion in the interim. It is also advisable not to uninstall the Exchange 5.5 public folder server immediately after you move the public folders. Outlook clients cache the names of public folder servers in the MAPI profile and if a server has been removed, the client may hang when attempting to access a public folder on that server. To avoid this problem, wait until all Outlook users have accessed the folders on the new server. Depending on the situation, this may take a week or longer.

You can use the following tools to move public folders:

- **Exchange System Manager**   To move a public folder using Exchange System Manager, display the properties of the folder, click the Replication tab, add the Exchange 2003 server to the list of servers that hold a replica, wait until contents are replicated, and then remove the replica from Exchange 5.5 servers using the Replication tab. To assign configuration changes to all folders in a tree, you can propagate replication settings from parent folders to child folders.

- **Microsoft Exchange Public Folder Migration tool**   To move a public folder using the Public Folder Migration (pfMigrate) tool, you must run the pfMigrate.wsf script located on the Exchange Server 2003 product CD in the \Support Tools\i386 folder. pfMigrate enables you to create replicas of your public folders on the new Exchange 2003 server. You can also use the pfMigrate tool to remove replicas from an Exchange 5.5 server. The Exchange 5.5 server and the Exchange 2003 server must reside in the same routing group. pfMigrate does not enable you to create replicas of your system folders and public folders across routing groups. In mixed mode, moving folders across routing groups could prevent e-mail delivery to public folders. Once the PFMigrate tool has run, you should wait until the Public Folders have replicated to the Exchange 2003 server prior to removing the public folders from the Exchange 5.5 server.

On the Resource Kit CD   For an example of how to use the pfMigrate tool for public folder migration, see the document Moving public folders to Exchange 2003.doc in the \Companion Material\Chapter 04\Public Folder Upgrades folder on the companion CD.

To use the pfMigrate.wsf script, you must log on to the Exchange 2003 server with an account that has the following privileges:

- Exchange Administrator privileges in Exchange Server 2003
- Exchange Administrator privileges in the Exchange 5.5 site
- Administrator permissions on the public folders you want to move

> **Note** The default scripting host is WScript, which provides output via dialog boxes. The pfMigrate tool, however, is designed to run with CScript instead. You might want to change the default scripting host to CScript, so pfMigrate can provide output into a command window throughout the processing. To use CScript as the default scripting host, use the following command: **CSCRIPT //H:CScript.**

Moving Mailboxes

All versions of Exchange support a move mailbox feature that enables you to relocate single or multiple mailboxes to a different home server in the same organization. The move mailbox feature moves the entire mailbox, including hidden objects such as inbox rules and folder views, without data conversion or data loss. To the user, a mailbox move is usually transparent because the old Exchange server automatically redirects the messaging client the next time the user attempts to access the mailbox. If users are online while you move their mailboxes, they will be disconnected, but they can immediately reconnect (close and restart Outlook) as soon as the mailboxes are on the Exchange 2003 server. Hence, it is a good idea to schedule mailbox upgrades when few users are accessing their mailboxes, such as on a weekend. You do not need to move all mailboxes at once. In fact, moving mailboxes gradually will minimize the impact of unanticipated problems, such as corrupted messages causing a mailbox move to fail. You can move mailboxes individually or in small groups, and you can move resources from different Exchange servers to the same Exchange 2003 server.

> **Note** After you have successfully moved mailboxes from Exchange 5.5 to Exchange Server 2003, perform a full online backup of the new Exchange Server 2003 database. Otherwise, if a disaster strikes before you back up the system, you have to restore the old messaging databases on the Exchange 5.5 server, adjust the Directory/Information Store consistency, and then repeat the entire upgrade process.

Preparing a Mailbox Move

It is vital that you perform several preparation steps before actually moving mailboxes to ensure that mailboxes can be moved successfully. For example, you should remove old items from your Exchange 5.5 users' mailboxes using the Clear Mailbox feature in the Exchange Administrator program. Figure 4-12 illustrates the user interface. You might also remind your users to empty their Deleted Items folders to avoid moving obsolete data to Exchange 2003. The less data you have to move to Exchange 2003, the quicker the mailbox move process and the less likely the chances of issues related to problematic messages in your users' mailboxes.

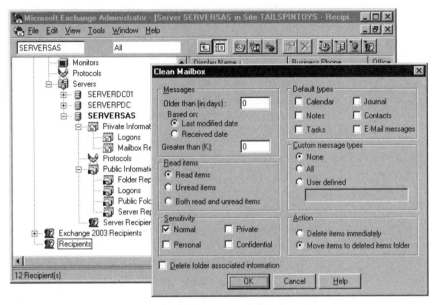

Figure 4-12   Cleaning mailboxes in Exchange 5.5

The following are typical problems that prevent a successful mailbox move to Exchange 2003:

- **Insufficient access rights for the migration account**   To move mailboxes from a server running Exchange 5.5 to a mailbox store on an Exchange 2003 server, you must be logged on to the server with an account that has Exchange Administrator privileges in both the Exchange Server 2003 organization and the Exchange 5.5 site. You must also be a member of the Account Operators group or the Domain Admins group with Change Property rights on the Windows accounts so you can write user attributes in Active Directory.

- **Source mailboxes are corrupted**   Corrupted items in source mailboxes can cause the move mailbox processes to fail. It is recommended that you check the source mailboxes using the Private Folder DS/IS Check tool (PrivFoldCheck) that is included in Exchange 2003 Deployment Tools. PrivFoldCheck relies on the Exchange 5.5 DS/IS consistency adjuster to synchronize Exchange 5.5 directory and information store. Inconsistencies between the directory and the information store can occur when there is an entry for a mailbox in the directory database without a corresponding entry in the information store, or vice versa.

To run PrivFoldCheck, your account must have Exchange 5.5 Administrator permissions with rights to view objects in the Exchange directory.

PrivFoldCheck runs the DS/IS consistency adjuster with the following options:

- **Synchronize with the directory and create new directory entries for mailboxes that do not have a corresponding directory entry.** If a mailbox exists in the Exchange 5.5 mailbox store, but not in the directory, PrivFoldCheck creates a recipient object in the directory.

- **Remove unknown user accounts.** PrivFoldCheck removes access control entries from mailboxes and folders within mailboxes if the user accounts no longer exist in the Exchange 5.5 directory. Removing these accounts avoids ACL conversion issues, as discussed earlier.

- **User accounts are corrupted or have incorrect settings in Active Directory** Users can end up with incorrect settings in Active Directory; for example, if you enable user accounts that Active Directory Connector created as disabled user accounts for resource mailboxes, or if you deployed Exchange 2003 in a separate Active Directory domain and used Active Directory Connector to create disabled user accounts for Exchange 5.5 users. An enabled user account with the msExchMasterAccountSID attribute set represents an invalid configuration, which can cause problems with delegate access and public folder permissions when the Exchange store attempts to convert the SID to a legacyExchangeDN. Only disabled users should have the msExchMasterAccountSID attribute set.

A user account can also be considered corrupted or in a critical state if the account is mailbox-enabled but contains no homeMDB, homeMTA, or msExchHomeServer attribute for any reason, or if it is both mail enabled and mailbox enabled. To check Active Directory for any issues prior to moving mailboxes, you should run the RecipientDSInteg tool included in Exchange 2003 Deployment Tools. RecipientDSInteg runs checks on each recipient object in Active Directory to see if user, group, contact, and public folder attributes are in a consistent state. You must be a Domain Administrator with permissions to view objects in Active Directory to run this tool successfully. If you discover any account inconsistencies, you can use LDAP Data Interchange Format Directory Exchange (LDIFDE) to correct the settings.

On the Resource Kit CD   For an example with step-by-step instructions on how to use LDIFDE for account cleanup purposes, see the document Correcting invalid Active Directory Attribute Settings.doc in the \Companion Material\Chapter 04\New Active Directory Domain folder on the companion CD.

Performing a Mailbox Move

Having checked and prepared Exchange 5.5 directory and Active Directory, you can perform the mailbox move using Exchange Task Wizard. This wizard is available in Active Directory Users and Computers as well as in Exchange System Manager. In fact, Exchange 2003 Deployment Tools recommends using Exchange System Manager for mailbox moves. In Exchange System Manager, expand Administrative Groups, and then expand the administrative group/site of the source Exchange 5.5 server. Expand Servers, expand the Exchange 5.5 server object, such as SERVERSAS, expand the storage group, such as First Storage Group, and mailbox store, such as Private Information Store (SERVERSAS), and then click Mailboxes. Select the mailboxes you want to move, and then on the Action menu, click Exchange Tasks.

For the purposes of migrating mailboxes, you might want to use Active Directory Users and Computers instead of Exchange System Manager. The wizard is the same, but the problem with Exchange System Manager is that the Mailboxes container might not list all mailboxes, so you might leave mailboxes behind in your migration. As explained in Chapter 3, "Exchange Server 2003 in Enterprise Environments," mailboxes only exist in the Exchange store when a user accesses a mailbox for the first time or when other users send messages to the mailbox. In other words, if an administrator created a mailbox in Exchange 5.5 and the user has not logged on to the mailbox yet, the mailbox is not in the Exchange store and thus not listed in the Mailboxes container of the mailbox store.

The document Moving mailboxes to Exchange 2003 using Exchange Tasks Wizard.doc in the \Companion Material\Chapter 04\Mailbox Upgrades folder on the companion CD demonstrates how to work with Exchange Tasks Wizard from within Active Directory Users and Computers. It demonstrates how to use a saved LDAP query to find all users with mailboxes on an Exchange 5.5 server and how to move these users at once using Exchange Tasks Wizard.

Another option is to use Collaboration Data Objects for Exchange Management (CDOEXM) to move mailboxes programmatically. The script MoveAllMailboxes.wsf in the \Companion Material\Chapter 04\Scripts folder on the companion CD uses CDOEXM. The script queries Active Directory for all users with a mailbox on an Exchange 5.5 server, and then moves these mailboxes to a specified mailbox store.

The code to move mailboxes is very straightforward, as illustrated in the following modified listing:

```
' Get the user account in Active Directory
Set oUser = GetObject("LDAP://CN=Administrator,CN=Users," _
                     DC=ad,DC=tailspintoys,DC=com ")
' Move the mailbox to a mailbox store on an Exchange 2003 server
sMbxStorePath = "CN=Mailbox Store (SERVER01)," _
            & "CN=First Storage Group,CN=InformationStore," _
            & "CN=SERVERDC01,CN=Servers,CN=TAILSPINTOYS," _
            & "CN=Administrative Groups,CN=Tailspin Toys," _
            & "CN=Microsoft Exchange,CN=Services,CN=Configuration," _
            & "DC=ad,DC=tailspintoys,DC=com"
objUser.MoveMailbox sMbxStorePath
```

The distinguished name of the mailbox store might seem complex, but you can use the ListMailboxStores.wsf script in the \Companion Material\Chapter 04\Scripts folder on the companion CD to determine the distinguished names of all mailbox stores configured on an Exchange 2003 server.

> **On the Resource Kit CD**   For details about how to use MoveAllMail-boxes.wsf and ListMailboxStores.wsf, see the document Moving mailboxes to Exchange 2003 using a custom script.doc in the \Companion Material\Chapter 04\Mailbox Upgrades folder on the companion CD.

Mailbox Move Details

The actual steps to move a mailbox are the same whether you are moving mailboxes using Exchange Tasks Wizard or CDOEXM. Whichever tool you use, a mailbox move is a copy process. Thus, if a mailbox move fails for any reasons, for example, if a corrupted message causes trouble, the user can continue working with the mailbox on the Exchange 5.5 server until you locate and eliminate the source of the problem.

When moving a mailbox, Exchange 2003 accomplishes the following steps:

1. The administrative tool connects to the Exchange stores on the source and target servers. If any of these connection attempts fails, the move operation fails, and the mailbox remains on the source system.

2. As soon as the connections are established, the administrative tool copies the mailbox data from the source to the target mailbox store. If this copy process fails, any data already copied is deleted and the mailbox remains on the source system. The complete set of private folders and messages is still available in the source mailbox.

3. When the copy process is completed, the recipients in the Exchange 5.5 directory and Active Directory are updated to reflect the new home server. If this process fails for any of the directories, the system rolls back the changes and the mailbox remains on the source system. The original mailbox is still available on the source server.

4. When the copy process and directory updates complete successfully, the mailbox has been moved to the target server successfully. The administrative tool now deletes the old mailbox from the source mailbox store. The mailbox is now on the target system and contains the complete list of private folders and messages. If the deletion of the mailbox fails, it will be removed from the original mailbox store database during the next maintenance cycle because the mailbox's home server attribute now points to the new server.

Migrating Windows NT Accounts after Mailbox Migration

You must take extra care of mailbox-enabled user accounts if you deployed a new Active Directory domain for Exchange 2003 and created, enabled or disabled user accounts in this domain for Windows NT users. You can move the mailboxes to Exchange 2003 and users can access these mailboxes using the original Windows NT accounts because Active Directory Connector grants the original accounts full mailbox access, but if users attempt to log on to mailboxes using Active Directory accounts (for example, if you want to decommission the old Windows NT domain), access to the mailboxes is denied even if you enabled the user accounts and cleared the msExchMasterAccountSID attribute. This is one of the most important reasons why you should migrate your Windows NT environment to Active Directory before moving mailboxes.

On the Resource Kit CD   The document Correcting invalid Active Directory Attribute Settings.doc in the \Companion Material\Chapter 04\New Active Directory Domain folder on the companion CD explains how to deal with incorrect attribute settings.

Exchange 2003 prevents these Active Directory users from accessing their associated mailboxes because Active Directory Connector does not grant Active Directory user accounts created for Windows NT users mailbox access permissions. Active Directory Connector grants access permissions only to the original Windows NT accounts. Figure 4-13 illustrates the difference. The Administrator account to the left only permits the Windows NT user TAILSPINTOYS\Administrator access to the mailbox. The Administrator account to the right permits the Active Directory Administrator account (through the special account named NTAUTHORITY\SELF) full mailbox access. Another difference is noticeable for the Associated External Account permission. Active Directory Connector sets this permission when the user's logon account is not migrated to Active Directory and is still in a Windows NT 4.0 domain. The account to the right does not have this permission set because NTAUTHORITY\SELF is not an external account.

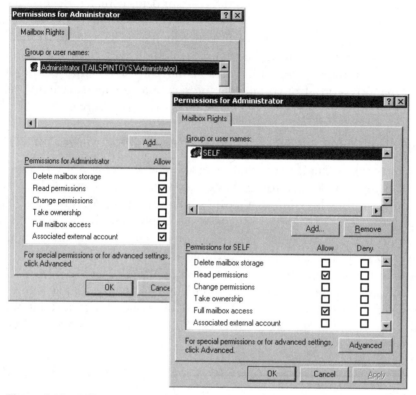

Figure 4-13   Differences in access permissions for mailbox-enabled user accounts

If you want Windows NT users to use enabled user accounts created through Active Directory Connector in Active Directory, you must correct the security settings as follows:

1. Grant the NTAUTHORITY\SELF account Full Mailbox Access permissions as well as the rights Read, Receive As, Send As, and optionally, Read Personal Information and Write Personal Information rights.

2. Remove the original Windows NT account from the lists of accounts with mailbox rights and Active Directory rights.

You might also have to reset user account names because Active Directory Connector assigns disabled user accounts a random logon name, such as ADC_NKOHFBCWZGCMJCNZ. These random logon names are difficult to handle.

Your users might want to work with their original logon names. For example, you can obtain the original logon name from the associated external account and then reassign this account name to the user account's samAccountName attribute. You can also set the user's userPrincipalName attribute using the original account name. Finally, as a more cosmetic change, you might change the description attribute of your user accounts. For disabled accounts, Active Directory Connector sets this attribute to "Disabled Windows user account," which does not reflect reality if you enable the accounts.

The following code snippet illustrates how to determine and remove an associated external account from an Active Directory account. Note that the code writes the original account name into a string variable named sTrustee. This variable is used in a later step to assign the Active Directory user account the original account name.

```
sUserADsPath = "LDAP://CN=Ted Bremer,OU=Recipients," _
               " "OU=Exchange 5.5 Recipients,DC=ad,DC=tailspintoys,DC=com"


'--- Get the user object ----
Set oUser = GetObject(sUserADsPath)
'--- Get the mailbox security descriptor ----
Set oSecurityDescriptor = oUser.MailboxRights
' Get the DACL from the security descriptor.
Set dacl = oSecurityDescriptor.DiscretionaryAcl

' Loop through the DACL and find the ACE of the
' associated external account, which has the AceFlags
' set to ADS_RIGHT_ACTRL_DS_LIST = &H4
For Each ace In dacl
        sTrustee = ""
        If (ace.AccessMask AND ADS_RIGHT_ACTRL_DS_LIST) = _
                                     ADS_RIGHT_ACTRL_DS_LIST Then
            ' Remember the account name
            sTrustee = ace.Trustee
            ' Remove the ACE to get rid of the external account
            dacl.RemoveAce ace
            ' Exit the loop, we have found what we are looking for
            Exit For
        End If
Next
' Reorder the DACL for the security descriptor.
Set dacl = ReorderACL(dacl, True)
' Add the modified DACL to the security descriptor.
oSecurityDescriptor.DiscretionaryAcl = dacl
' Save new security descriptor onto the user.
oUser.MailboxRights = Array(oSecurityDescriptor)
' Commit changes from the property cache to the Exchange store.
oUser.SetInfo

' Now, clean Active Directory security settings
Set oSecurityDescriptor = oUser.Get("ntSecurityDescriptor")
Set dacl = oSecurityDescriptor.DiscretionaryAcl
For Each ace In dacl
    ' Remove the ACE if it specifies the original Windows NT account
```

```
        If UCase(ace.Trustee) = UCase(sTrustee) Then
            dacl.RemoveAce ace
        End If
Next


' Reorder the DACL for the Security Descriptor.
Set dacl = ReorderACL(dacl, True)
' Add the modified DACL to the security descriptor.
oSecurityDescriptor.DiscretionaryAcl = dacl
oUser.Put "ntSecurityDescriptor", oSecurityDescriptor
oUser.SetInfo


' Now, clean up the user account's samAccountName and other attributes
' The user account name has the form DOMAIN\Account.
' Get rid of the 'DOMAIN\' portion
i = Instr(1, sTrustee, "\")
If i > 0 Then
    samName = Mid(sTrustee, i+1)
    oUser.Put "samAccountName", samName
    oUser.Put "userPrincipalName", samName & "tailspintoys.com"
    oUser.Description = "Activated and cleaned"
    oUser.SetInfo
End If

Set oUser = Nothing
```

Having cleaned the user account object, you can grant the NTAUTHOR-ITY\SELF trustee the required access permissions, similar to the procedures discussed in Chapter 3, "Exchange Server 2003 in Enterprise Environments." For a fully functional custom script that performs all the steps of resetting ACEs and user account attributes, see the script named ResetAccountPermissions.wsf in the \Companion Material\Chapter 04\Scripts folder on the companion CD.

> **On the Resource Kit CD**   The document Resetting External Account Permissions.doc in the \Companion Material\Chapter 04\New Active Directory Domain folder on the companion CD explains with step-by-step instructions about how to use the ResetAccountPermissions.wsf script in a test environment.

You can also use the ResetAccountPermissions.wsf script to enable user accounts if they are currently disabled. Keep in mind that Windows 2003 security policies prevent you from enabling user accounts without passwords, by default. Because Active Directory Connector does not migrate passwords, you must set the user passwords to a default value and force the users to change their passwords when they first log on to Active Directory. The following code snippet demonstrates how to accomplish these tasks. ResetAccountPermissions.wsf uses a similar approach.

```
' Reset the password to 1qw$t9x
sPassword = "1qw$t9x"
oUser.SetPassword sPassword
' Mark the account so that the user must
' change the password at first logon
oUser.Put "pwdLastSet", CLng(0)
' Enable the account
oUser.AccountDisabled = False
' Commit the changes
oUser.SetInfo
```

Moving System Folders

Having migrated all public folders and mailboxes to Exchange 2003, you can move system folders, such as OFFLINE ADDRESS BOOK, EFORMS REGISTRY and SCHED-ULE+FREE BUSY. You can use Exchange System Manager for this purpose if you expand the Folders node, right-click Public Folders, and then select View System Folders. The configuration steps and replication procedures are the same for public folders and system folders.

On the Resource Kit CD   You can also use the pfMigrate tool to move system folders if you specify the /SF command line switch, as demonstrated in the document Moving system folders to Exchange 2003.doc in the \Companion Material\Chapter 04\Public Folder Upgrades folder on the companion CD.

Decommissioning Exchange 5.5 and Enabling Native Mode

When moving public folders and mailboxes to Exchange Server 2003, do not decommission your Exchange 5.5 servers as soon as all resources are moved. You should leave the legacy servers in place for some time so that the servers can redirect clients to the new mailbox locations. If you remove the old mailbox server before a client is redirected, the client cannot reconnect automatically and you must reconfigure the MAPI profile on the client manually. You can avoid this unnecessary trouble if you wait with server removals until all users have reconnected to their mailboxes. Exchange System Manager displays the time of the last logon for each mailbox in the Logons container that you can find under each mailbox store.

> **Note**   Outlook users who access additional mailboxes will have to reconfigure their MAPI profiles to access these mailboxes at their new locations. For step-by-step instructions to include additional mailboxes in an Outlook profile, see the document Creating Multiple Mailboxes for the Administrator account.doc that you can find in the \Companion Material\Chapter 01 folder on the companion CD.

The same is true for public folders. When moving public folders to Exchange 2003, you can remove the old replica in the Exchange System Manager without waiting for the contents to replicate. The old replica remains on the original Exchange server until the contents are replicated, but if you remove the old Exchange server too quickly, users might end up with an empty folder in Exchange 2003. You should wait until all Outlook users have accessed public folders on the new server before proceeding with the server removal, so that Outlook can cache the names of public folder servers in the MAPI profile.

Decommissioning Exchange Server 5.5

In general, you should not uninstall any servers unless you are absolutely sure they are no longer required in the mixed-mode organization. Before decommissioning any servers, shut them down for an extended period of time (such as a week or more). Should users complain about access problems, restart the old server, correct the configuration, finish the directory and public folder replication, then shut down the server again for an extended period of time.

It is safe to remove Exchange servers under the following conditions. If there are multiple resources on one server, more than one criterion may apply:

- **Directory replication bridgehead server**   If you replaced a replication bridgehead server with a server running Exchange 2003,as soon as the desired Exchange 2003 server running SRS is displayed in the directory replication connector configuration on all remote replication bridgeheads, the old Exchange server is no longer considered a directory replication server and can be removed safely.

- **Mailbox server**   Ensure that all mailboxes are moved successfully to an Exchange 2003 server, and then wait until all users have reconnected to their mailboxes.

- **Messaging bridgehead server**   Configure messaging connectors on Exchange 2003, and then set the cost value for the connectors on the Exchange 5.5 bridgehead to 100. Connectors with a cost value of 100 are excluded from message routing, although they are still available and can empty their message queues. You can use the message-tracking center in Exchange System Manager, diagnostics logging, and SMTP protocol logs to verify that the Exchange 2003 connectors are transferring the messages. When the Exchange 5.5 bridgehead server has emptied its message queues, and when no further messages are routed to Exchange 5.5 connectors, you can decommission the Exchange 5.5 bridgehead server. Keep in mind that you cannot remove bridgeheads that run connectors unsupported in Exchange 2003 Server. These servers must remain in the organization until they are no longer needed.

- **Offline address book server**   By default, the first server in the Exchange site assumes the role of the offline address book server holding the offline address books for all MAPI-based clients. As long as Exchange 5.5 users exist in the site, the offline address book must reside on an Exchange 5.5 server. It is possible to move the offline address books to any Exchange 5.5 server in the site.

- **Public folder server**   Ensure that public folder hierarchy and contents are replicated completely before you decommission Exchange 5.5 public folder servers. Do not forget to replicate the system folders, such as the SCHEDULE+ FREE BUSY folder to Exchange 2003. Verify that the public folders show a status of In Sync in Exchange System Manager or use another tool, such as Replver.exe, to verify public folder replication. When you remove replicas from Exchange 5.5 public folder servers, make sure that users still have access to the public folders on the new server.

- **Routing recalculation server**   The routing recalculation server updates the GWART in the Exchange site. Directory replication will then propagate the new GWART to all other Exchange servers. A routing recalculation server is required as long as there is an Exchange 5.5 server in the site. You can assign this task to any Exchange 5.5 server. Launch the Exchange Administrator program, display the properties of the Site Addressing object, after choosing the Configuration container of the site, and then change the server in the General tab, under Routing Recalculation Server.

To decommission an Exchange 5.5 server, start the Exchange Server 5.5 Setup program directly on the server you want to remove, and select the Remove All option. After that, log on to an existing Exchange 5.5 server, start the Exchange Administrator program, and delete the old server reference from the Exchange 5.5 directory. You can also use the Exchange Administrator program that ships with Exchange Server 2003. The Exchange 5.5 directory replicates the configuration changes to the SRS where the configuration connection agreement propagates the changes to Active Directory.

Switching to Native Mode

You should switch the Exchange organization into native mode as soon as all Exchange 5.5 servers are decommissioned to eliminate mixed-mode limitations. In Exchange System Manager, display the properties of the organization object, and then on the General tab, click the Change Mode button. However, you might notice that you cannot click this button even if the last Exchange 5.5 server has been uninstalled. In this case, the Exchange directory still requires manual cleanup.

The last Exchange 5.5 server must be deleted from the SRS database manually because no other Exchange directory service exists in the site to accomplish this via directory replication. You must use the Exchange Administrator program and specify the Exchange 2003 server that runs the SRS as the server to connect to. You can then remove the remaining Exchange 5.5 server reference. Active Directory Connector will propagate the changes to Active Directory, and once the last Exchange 5.5 server is removed from Active Directory, you can remove SRS and switch the organization into native mode. You must remove the existing Active Directory Connector connection agreements manually. Follow these steps to remove Exchange SRS:

1. From the Active Directory Connector Tool MMC snap-in, navigate to your recipient connection agreements. To remove any recipient connection agreements that exist in your Exchange organization, right-click the connection agreement, and then click Delete. You should also remove any public folder connection agreements.

2. Either from another Exchange 5.5 server, or directly from the Exchange 2003 server that is running SRS, open the Exchange 5.5 Administrator program. This is typically the first Exchange 2003 server installed in an Exchange 5.5 site. Click File, click Connect to Server, and then type the name of the Exchange 2003 server running SRS.

3. In the Exchange 5.5 Administrator program, expand the local site name (displayed in bold), expand Configuration, click Directory Replication Connectors, and then delete any directory replication connectors that exist.

> **Important**   Do not delete the ADNAutoDRC connector listed under Directory Replication Connectors.

4. Allow time for the changes that you made in Exchange Administrator to replicate to Active Directory through configuration connection agreements (Config CAs).

5. In Exchange System Manager, ensure that no Exchange 5.5 computers are displayed in any administrative groups.

6. In Exchange System Manager, expand Tools, and click Site Replication Services. From the details pane right-click each SRS, and then click Delete. When you do so, the SRS and corresponding Config CA for that SRS are deleted.

7. After all instances of SRS are deleted, uninstall the ADC service.

After you complete these steps, you can convert the Exchange organization to native mode.

> **Note**   Switching to native mode irreversibly disables interoperability with Exchange 5.5. Do not switch to native mode if Exchange Server 5.5 may be needed in the foreseeable future; for instance, to run messaging connectors not supported in Exchange Server 2003.

Upgrading from Exchange 2000 Server

In general, you choose between two upgrade strategies to go from Exchange 2000 Server to Exchange Server 2003. You can either install Exchange Server 2003 directly on a server running Exchange 2000 Server, thus performing an in-place upgrade, or add a new Exchange 2003 server to the organization, and then move mailboxes and other resources to Exchange 2003, which corresponds to a move-mailbox upgrade.

> **Note**   To upgrade an Exchange 2000 server, you must use an account that has Exchange Full Administrator permissions at the organization or administrative group level and is a local administrator on the computer.

Operating System Dependencies

If you are operating an Exchange 2000 organization in mixed or native mode, you already have deployed Active Directory. However, you should keep in mind that Exchange 2000 is designed to operate with Windows 2000, while Exchange 2003 is designed to run on Windows 2000 SP3 (or later) or Windows Server 2003. Hence, you should upgrade Exchange 2000 to Exchange 2003 first, and then upgrade operating systems and Active Directory.

The following features of Exchange Server 2003 are not available in a Windows 2000 environment:

- **Eight–node clustering** Only four-node clustering is supported on Windows 2000 Datacenter Server.

- **Support for volume mount points**   You cannot overcome the 24-drive letter limitation on a server.

- **Volume Shadow Copy service**   You cannot use a database backup solution that uses Volume Shadow Copy service to back up Exchange 2003 messaging databases.

- **Internet Protocol Security (IPSec) support for front-end and back-end communication**   You cannot encrypt the data communication between Exchange 2003 servers in a front-end and back-end topology.

- **Internet Information Services (IIS) 6.0**   IIS 6.0 provides new security and dedicated application mode functionality, but IIS 6.0 is only available on Windows 2003.

- **HTTP access from Outlook 2003**   You cannot use RPC over HTTP to provide MAPI-based clients with connectivity to Exchange 2003 Servers.

Note   Domain controllers and global catalog servers must be running Windows 2000 SP3 or later or Windows Server 2003 to support Exchange Server 2003.

Installing Exchange Server 2003

You should perform the following steps when upgrading Exchange 2000 to Exchange 2003. Most of these steps are standard for any Exchange 2003 installation; however, you should ensure that your existing environment, including DNS and Active Directory, is ready for Exchange 2003. If you have deployed front-end and back-end servers in your Exchange 2000 organization, you must upgrade your front-end servers before you upgrade your back-end servers.

Perform these steps to install Exchange 2003 (you can use Exchange 2003 Deployment Tools as a guideline):

1. **Verify that your organization meets the Exchange 2003 requirements**
   Exchange 2003 requires a reliable DNS environment and Windows 2000 Server SP3 or Windows Server 2003 Active Directory.

2. **Run the DCDiag and NetDiag tools**   We recommend that you install the Windows 2003 Support Tools, and then run DCDiag and NetDiag to ensure that your computer network is ready for a deployment of Exchange 2003.

3. **Run ForestPrep**   The schema extensions supplied with Exchange 2003 are a superset of those supplied with Exchange 2000. Hence, Exchange 2003 extends

the Active Directory schema. To run ForestPrep, you must be a member of the Enterprise Admins and the Schema Admins groups.

> **Note**   You must run in the domain where the schema master resides in your Active Directory forest.

4. **Run DomainPrep**   Even if you previously ran Exchange 2000 DomainPrep, you must run Exchange 2003 DomainPrep to perform Setup pre-installation checks in each domain. Running DomainPrep does not require any Exchange permissions. Only Domain Administrator permissions are required in the local domain. However, you should run DomainPrep in the root domain of your Active Directory forest, in all domains that will contain Exchange 2003 servers, in all domains that will contain Exchange recipient objects, and in all domains that contain global catalog servers that Exchange directory access components may potentially use.

5. **Run Exchange Setup**   Before you begin the Exchange 2003 installation, you should back up your Exchange 2000 servers and databases, Active Directory, and ensure that the databases can be mounted on backup servers. The Exchange Server 2003 Setup program must be able to contact a domain controller running Windows 2000 SP3 or later or Windows Server 2003 within the local Active Directory site.

> **Note**   In Exchange, the default size limit for sending and receiving messages is 10,240 KB. This default size limit applies to new installations and to upgrades from Exchange 2000 for which no size limit was set. If you specify a size limit other than the default, the existing setting is preserved. If you want the size limit to be unlimited, you can manually change the setting to **No limit**.
>
> Additionally, the maximum item size limit for public folder stores is set to 10,240 KB. As with the default message size limit, this setting applies to new installations and to upgrades for which no size limit was set. Existing size limits are preserved during an upgrade.

Performing a Move-Mailbox Upgrade

Although it is possible to install Exchange 2003 directly over Exchange 2000, you might want to consider the option of upgrading to Exchange 2003 using a move-mailbox strategy. This approach has the advantage that you can modernize the server infrastructure and consolidate resources from different Exchange 2000 servers onto a single Exchange 2003 server. Server and site consolidation is discussed in Chapter 6, "Server and Site Consolidation Strategies."

The tools and procedures to move mailboxes from Exchange 2000 to Exchange 2003 are the same tools that you would use when upgrading from Exchange 5.5. Specifically, Exchange Tasks Wizard or custom ADSI scripts can facilitate this task, as discussed earlier in this chapter. You can schedule mailbox moves for low-peak hours, such as over a weekend. An advantage of the move-mailbox upgrade is that you can keep server downtime at a minimum. If you move mailboxes over a weekend, for example, users may not be affected. Another advantage is that you do not have to clean up Exchange 2000–specific performance parameters, which you might have to correct if you perform an in-place upgrade, as discussed later in this chapter.

Performing an In-Place Upgrade

The in-place upgrade is only supported over Exchange 2000 Server SP3 or later. When you launch the Exchange 2003 Setup program directly on a server running Exchange 2000 Server SP3, the previous version is detected automatically, and Setup switches into upgrade mode, not allowing you to add additional components or change the existing configuration in any way. To make any changes, you must start Setup again after you accomplish the upgrade. It is important to note that if you are upgrading an Exchange 2000 server to Exchange 2003, you must remove the following items first because they are not supported in Exchange 2003:

- **Microsoft Mobile Information Server Exchange Event Source.**   This component is replaced by Outlook Mobile Access in Exchange 2003.

- **Instant Messaging Server, Microsoft Exchange 2000 Chat Service, Microsoft Exchange 2000 Conferencing Server, Key Management Service, Microsoft Exchange Connector for Lotus cc:Mail, and Microsoft Exchange MS Mail Connector.**   If you want to retain these services in your organization, you should not install Exchange 2003 on the servers running these components; you can retain an Exchange 2000 server to run such components. Another option is to use alternative technologies to replace these services, such as Microsoft Office Live Communications Server.

- **Third-party components and services.**   You should also check third-party components that you have installed on your Exchange 2000 servers to ensure that they are supported with Exchange 2003. Examples include backup systems, antivirus applications, and Exchange Development Kit (EDK)–based connectors (such as a fax connector).

When upgrading to Exchange 2003, the current state of the Post Office Protocol version 3 (POP3), Internet Message Access Protocol version 4 (IMAP4), and NNTP services is preserved. Furthermore, if you are upgrading to Exchange 2003 on a server running Windows 2000, Exchange Setup installs and enables the Microsoft .NET Framework and ASP.NET components automatically, which are prerequisites for Exchange 2003.

> **Note**   Unless it is necessary that you run a particular service, you should disable it. For example, if you do not use POP3, IMAP4, or NNTP, you should disable these services on all of your Exchange 2003 servers after you install Exchange 2003.

Upgrading International Versions of Exchange

When upgrading from Exchange 2000 to Exchange 2003, you must upgrade to the same language version of Exchange 2003. For example, you cannot use Exchange Setup to upgrade a German version of Exchange 2000 to a French version of Exchange 2003.

> **Important**   You can use Exchange Setup to upgrade an English version of Exchange 2000 to the Chinese Simplified, Chinese Traditional, or Korean versions of Exchange 2003. The Novell GroupWise connector, however, is not supported on any of these language versions. Therefore, if this connector is installed on your English version of Exchange 2000, you must remove it before you can upgrade to Exchange 2003.

Removing Exchange 2000 Tuning Parameters

Many Exchange 2000 tuning parameters (for example, those parameters listed in the *Microsoft Exchange 2000 Internals: Quick Tuning Guide* (*http://go.microsoft.com/ fwlink/?linkid=1712*), are no longer applicable in Exchange 2003; in fact, some of these parameters cause problems. If you previously tuned your Exchange 2000 servers by adding any of the settings listed in this section, you must manually remove them on your servers running Exchange 2003. The tools you use to remove those settings are Registry Editor, Internet Information Services Manager, and ADSI Edit. For information about how to use Registry Editor, Internet Information Services Manager, and ADSI Edit, see Windows Server Help.

> **Warning**   Incorrectly editing the registry can cause serious problems that may require you to reinstall your operating system. Problems resulting from editing the registry incorrectly may not be able to be resolved. Before editing the registry, back up any valuable data.

Initial Memory Percentage

The Initial Memory Percentage registry key no longer works with Exchange 2003. Therefore, use Registry Editor to delete the following registry parameter when Exchange 2003 is installed.

Location:	`HKEY_LOCAL_MACHINE\SYSTEM\CurrentControlSet\Services\MSExchangeIS\ParametersSystem`
Parameter:	`Initial Memory Percentage (REG_DWORD)`

Extensible Storage System Heaps

The optimum number of heaps is now automatically calculated with Exchange 2003. Therefore, use Registry Editor to delete the following registry parameter when Exchange 2003 is installed.

Location:	`HKEY_LOCAL_MACHINE\SOFTWARE\Microsoft\ESE98\Global\OS\Memory`
Parameter:	`MPHeap parallelism (REG_SZ)`

DSAccess Memory Cache Tuning

If you previously tuned the user cache in DSAccess, you can now remove your manual tuning. Exchange 2000 had a default user cache of 25 MB, whereas Exchange 2003 defaults to 140 MB. Therefore, use Registry Editor to remove the following registry parameter when Exchange 2003 is installed.

Location:	`HKEY_LOCAL_MACHINE\SYSTEM\CurrentControlSet\Services\MSExchangeDSAccess\Instance0`
Parameter:	`MaxMemoryUser (REG_DWORD)`

Cluster Performance Tuning

If you previously added the following registry parameters, use Registry Editor to remove them when Exchange 2003 is installed.

Location	`HKEY_LOCAL_MACHINE\SYSTEM\CurrentControlSet\` `Services\SMTPSVC\Queuing`
Parameter:	`MaxPercentPoolThreads (REG_DWORD)`

Location:	`HKEY_LOCAL_MACHINE\SYSTEM\CurrentControlSet\` `Services\SMTPSVC\Queuing`
Parameter:	`AdditionalPoolThreadsPerProc (REG_DWORD)`

Outlook Web Access Content Expiration

You should not disable content expiry for the \Exchweb virtual directory. The default expiration setting of **1 day** should be used in all scenarios. You can view and modify this setting in Internet Information Services Manager.

Log Buffers

If you previously tuned the msExchESEParamLogBuffers parameter manually [for example, to 9000 (an Exchange 2000 SP2 recommendation), or 500 (an Exchange 2000 SP3 recommendation)], clear the manual tuning. Exchange 2003 uses a default value of 500. Previously, Exchange 2000 used a default value of 84.

To return this setting to the default setting of <Not Set>, open the following parameter in ADSI Edit, and then click Clear.

Location:	`CN=Configuration/CN=Services/CN=Microsoft Exchange/`
	`CN=<`*`Exchange Organization Name`*`>/CN=Administrative Groups/`
	`CN=<`*`Administrative Group Name`*`>/CN=Servers/CN=<`*`Server`*
	`Name``>/CN=Information Store>/CN=<`*`Storage Group Name`*`>`

Parameter:	`msExchESEParamLogBuffers`

Max Open Tables

If you tuned the msExchESEParamMaxOpenTables parameter manually, you should clear the manual tuning. When the value of the parameter is cleared, Exchange 2003 automatically calculates the correct value for you; for example, on an eight-processor server, a value of 27600 is used.

To return this setting to the default setting of <Not Set>, open the following parameter in ADSI Edit, and then click Clear.

Location:	`CN=Configuration/CN=Services/CN=Microsoft Exchange/`
	`CN=<`*`Exchange Organization Name`*`>/CN=Administrative Groups/`
	`CN=<`*`Administrative Group Name`*`>/CN=Servers/CN=<`*`Server`*
	`Name``>/CN=Information Store>/CN=<`*`Storage Group Name`*`>`

Parameter:	`msExchESEParamMaxOpenTables`

Best Practices

An upgrade from an earlier version of Exchange is a complex task that is best approached with careful planning and preparations. For example, the way you upgrade Windows NT domains to Active Directory can simplify or complicate the Exchange migration. It is best to update the Windows NT domains directly and enable the Windows Server 2003 domain functional level. That way, Active Directory Connector can synchronize existing user accounts with Exchange 5.5 mailbox information, saving you the extra effort of cleaning up and resetting user accounts using low-level tools or custom ADSI scripts.

Careful preparation of the upgrade project should include verifying that the DNS and Active Directory environment is ready for Exchange Server 2003, and that the Exchange 5.5 organization is in a consistent state. It is highly recommended that you use the tools from the Exchange 2003 Deployment Tools suite and work through the checklists provided with Exchange 2003 Deployment Tools to make sure all tests are performed and completed successfully. Better to measure twice and cut once! It is easier to fix inconsistencies and configuration issues before integrating Exchange 5.5 with Active Directory than afterward. For example, you cannot simply delete objects in Active Directory because it results in deleted mailboxes in Exchange 5.5.

Chapter 5

Migrating to Exchange Server 2003

About This Chapter

This chapter describes how to connect and migrate non-Exchange messaging systems to Microsoft Exchange Server 2003. It explains connectivity components available in Exchange Server 2003, discusses their advantages and disadvantages, and explains fundamental interoperability options and migration strategies that you should take into consideration when planning a migration to Exchange 2003. This chapter also explains how to move user data from one system to another using a variety of tools, such as Microsoft Office Outlook and Microsoft Exchange Migration Wizard.

It is assumed that you are familiar with Microsoft Windows server technology, Active Directory directory service, and the basic design elements of an Exchange 2003 organization. For more information about designing an Exchange 2003 organization, see Chapter 2 "Exchange Server 2003 Design Basics" as well as the Exchange online guide "Planning an Exchange Server 2003 Messaging System" at *http://go.microsoft.com/fwlink/?linkid=21766*.

> **More Info**   For detailed information about the architecture of connector components and troubleshooting connectivity issues, directory synchronization, and Exchange Migration Wizard, see the "Exchange Server 2003 Interoperability and Migration Guide" at *http://www.microsoft.com/technet/ prodtechnol/exchange/2003/library/interopmig.mspx*.

What You Need to Know

An Exchange 2003 messaging migration includes planning and design steps as in any Exchange 2003 deployment. In addition, you must connect the new Exchange 2003 organization to the legacy messaging system so that non-migrated and migrated users can communicate with each other during the migration phase. Seamless interoperability also includes directory synchronization, so all users have complete address lists. It possibly also includes calendar integration, so non-migrated and migrated users can check each other's free/busy information when planning appointments and meetings. Interoperability between the systems is not necessary, however, if you can move all of your users to Exchange 2003 at once.

Exchange 2003 messaging migration typically entails:

- **Planning and designing the future Exchange 2003 organization**   Standardizing an entire messaging infrastructure on Exchange 2003 can help lower administrative overhead and total cost of ownership (TCO) in comparison to running multiple messaging systems. It is therefore a good idea to plan a future messaging infrastructure that relies exclusively on Exchange 2003 and does not have to coexist with non-Exchange messaging systems. However, there are circumstances that might force you to keep a non-Exchange messaging system in place. For example, you might have implemented complex workgroup applications based on a non-Exchange messaging system that are difficult to replace with comparable Windows- or Exchange-based solutions. If you cannot replace a non-Exchange messaging system quickly, you must take long-term interoperability into consideration in your Exchange 2003 design. For details about planning and designing an Exchange 2003 organization, see Chapter 2 "Exchange Server 2003 Design Basics."

- **Assessing the existing messaging system**   It is important to assess and document the existing messaging environment so that you can identify interoperability and migration opportunities. You must know where legacy post offices or servers are located and how many there are. You must also know the number of users on each post office or server, and you must identify potential gateway or bridgehead servers that you can use for message transfer and directory synchronization. Table 5-1 lists important information that you should gather about the existing messaging environment.

Table 5-1   Important Characteristics of a Messaging System

Item	Comments
Post offices or servers that host mailboxes	Document the following information: ■ The number of post offices or servers that host mailboxes, and their names and locations. ■ The number of mailboxes on each post office or server. ■ The installed messaging systems. ■ The names of administrators. ■ Any special configuration settings (such as post office passwords and database versions). ■ The administrative tools that are used to manage the systems and their versions.
Post offices or servers that host workgroup and workflow applications	Document the following information: ■ The number of post offices or servers that host workgroup applications, and their names and locations. ■ The installed messaging systems. ■ The purposes of these workgroup applications, such as discussion forums, document libraries, as so on. ■ The number of users who access these workgroup applications. ■ The names of administrators. ■ Any special configuration settings, such as post office passwords and database versions. ■ The names of the administrators and developers who are responsible for those workgroup applications.
Messaging backbone infrastructure	Document the following information: ■ The WAN and LAN topology, central transfer routes, and their communication protocols. ■ The names and locations of bridgehead servers and connections to other messaging systems and the Internet. ■ The names of the administrators who are in charge of the messaging backbone.

Table 5-1   Important Characteristics of a Messaging System (Continued)

Item	Comments
Directory synchronization topology	Document the following information: ■ The messaging systems and directories that participate in directory synchronization. ■ The post offices or servers that have specific roles in the directory synchronization topology and their names and locations. ■ The number of recipients included in the global address list and specific conventions for the global address list structure. ■ The interval at which directory synchronization is performed. ■ The mapping of standard and custom directory attributes between the messaging systems. ■ The administrators who are responsible for the directory synchronization configuration and maintenance.
Backup and restore procedures	Document the following information: ■ The backup schedule and backup validation policies for the individual messaging systems in your environment. ■ The storage location of backup media and product CDs. ■ Step-by-step procedures to back up and recover the messaging systems.
Messaging clients	Document the following information: ■ The types of messaging clients that are currently in use and their versions. ■ The configuration standards for messaging clients, including hardware, client software, and other messaging or groupware applications. ■ The methods messaging clients use to access mailboxes and workgroup applications, such as local versus remote access. ■ The messaging habits of your users, such as the number of messages in mailboxes and current storage requirements, and the number of messages that are generated by the users in each location on a typical business day. ■ The locations where users store their messaging data, such as server vs. workstation. ■ The security technologies, if any, that are used to encrypt messages. ■ The main contacts for end-user support.

- **Developing an interoperability and migration strategy**   Based on your assessment of the existing messaging infrastructure, you can decide how to move to Exchange Server 2003. You have the following general options:

- **Single-phase migration**   In a single-phase migration you move all your users at once. The key advantage of this approach is that there is no need for interoperability, but only small organizations with one or two messaging servers might be able to accomplish a migration in a single step.

- **Multiphase migration**   Medium and large organizations typically move to Exchange 2003 in multiple phases so that they can control the pace of the migration and react to issues that can arise during the migration. Because non-migrated users must be able to communicate with migrated users, you must connect Exchange 2003 to the non-Exchange messaging system and perform directory synchronization to provide seamless interoperability, as explained later in this chapter.

- **Long-term coexistence**   Long-term coexistence is essentially a multiphase migration without an end point. As mentioned earlier, long-term coexistence can be a requirement if you must deal with complex workgroup applications, such as a Lotus Notes business application, that you cannot replace with an adequate alternative solution in the short-term.

    Table 5-2 lists advantages and disadvantages of these migration strategies. For more information about planning a migration to Exchange 2003, see "Exchange Server 2003 Interoperability and Migration Guide" at *http://www.microsoft.com/technet/prodtechnol/exchange/2003/library/interop-mig.mspx*.

Table 5-2   Advantages and Disadvantages of Migration Strategies

Strategy	Advantages	Disadvantages
Single-phase migration	<ul><li>Yields quick results because all users are migrated at once.</li><li>No need for messaging connectivity between the existing messaging system and Exchange 2003.</li><li>Preserving existing e-mail addresses is straightforward, because the Exchange 2003 organization replaces the existing messaging system.</li></ul>	<ul><li>It is difficult to stage server and client deployments. You must establish the entire Exchange organization before you migrate users.</li><li>It is not possible to control the pace of the migration. You cannot migrate divisions or departments individually, for example.</li><li>The migration of large numbers of users or large amounts of data results in unacceptable downtime.</li></ul>

Table 5-2   Advantages and Disadvantages of Migration Strategies (Continued)

Strategy	Advantages	Disadvantages
Multiphase migration	■ It is possible to complete the migration in incremental and manageable steps. ■ Migration risks are minimized. If one particular operation in the multiphase migration is not successful, a limited number of users are affected; those users can continue to work with their old mailboxes until the problem is solved. ■ It is possible to minimize the system downtime for messaging users. If you choose to perform the migration during non-business hours, you might be able to nearly eliminate downtime for users. ■ It is possible to synchronize the reconfiguration of the messaging client and end-user training with the migration of mailboxes. ■ You can stage server and client deployments according to your migration phases. It is not necessary to establish the entire Exchange organization before you migrate users.	■ Compared to single-phase migrations, multiphase migrations are more time consuming and therefore more expensive. ■ The legacy messaging system and the Exchange 2003 organization must interoperate as seamlessly as possible. You must deploy a messaging connector and configure directory synchronization between the systems. ■ The computer network experiences an increased amount of data traffic, which results from the need to communicate with users on the legacy messaging system, as well as from directory synchronization and calendar interoperability. ■ Preserving existing e-mail addresses is difficult, because message transfer processes use address information to distinguish the legacy system from the Exchange organization. ■ You must maintain both the legacy messaging system and Exchange 2003 for a period of time.

Table 5-2   Advantages and Disadvantages of Migration Strategies (Continued)

Strategy	Advantages	Disadvantages
Long-term coexistence	■ It is possible to preserve investments in existing technologies. However, it is important to evaluate and test your legacy application's ability to support users with mailboxes in the Exchange 2003 organization. ■ Autonomous sites can use diverse messaging systems that communicate with each other over a corporate messaging backbone or central message switch.	■ The legacy messaging system and the Exchange 2003 organization must interoperate as seamlessly as possible. You must deploy a messaging connector and configure directory synchronization between the systems. ■ The computer network experiences an increased amount of data traffic, which results from the need to communicate with users on the legacy messaging system, as well as from directory synchronization and calendar interoperability. ■ Preserving existing e-mail addresses is difficult, because message transfer processes use address information to distinguish the legacy system from the Exchange organization. ■ Users must work with multiple clients, for example, Outlook to participate in the Exchange 2003 organization and another client (such as Lotus Notes or a Web-based interface) to work with the legacy business application (such as a Lotus Notes solution). ■ TCO is high because administrators must maintain multiple messaging systems, and users must use multiple clients, which is support-intensive.

- **Deploying the new Exchange 2003 organization**   Having decided how to migrate to Exchange 2003, you can design and deploy the new organization in whole or in part. Small companies that plan to migrate in a single step will have to deploy the Exchange 2003 organization in whole so that they can migrate all users at once. Deploying the entire organization prior to migration is usually not an issue if the organization consists of one ore two Exchange 2003 servers. On the other hand, if you are planning to deploy an Exchange 2003 organization with a large number of servers or with multiple geographic sites, it is a good idea to migrate in multiple phases, because then you do not have to wait until Exchange 2003 is fully deployed before you can start migrating users. The Exchange 2003 organization can evolve as the migration project progresses.

- **Connecting Exchange 2003 to the legacy messaging infrastructure**   This step is not a requirement in a single phase migration because the non-Exchange messaging system is replaced at once. In a multiphase migration, however, you should implement connectivity components for message transfer, directory synchronization, and free/busy synchronization. Table 5-3 lists typical connectivity requirements in a multiphase migration.

Table 5-3   Typical Connectivity Requirements

Requirement	Comments
Message transfer	When you connect Exchange 2003 to an existing messaging infrastructure, you must accomplish the following tasks:
	■ Deploy messaging connectors that enable migrated and non-migrated users to send each other messages.
	■ Preserve external message paths so that migrated and non-migrated users can continue to communicate with external users, such as Internet users.
	■ Verify and optimize the message-routing topology to avoid performance bottlenecks, such as implement multiple bridgehead servers between the legacy messaging system and Exchange 2003.

Table 5-3   Typical Connectivity Requirements (Continued)

Requirement	Comments
Directory synchronization	You have the following options to provide accurate directory information in both the legacy messaging system and Exchange 2003 so that users can select migrated and non-migrated recipients from their global address lists:

- Perform automated directory synchronization through Exchange connectors. Exchange Development Kit (EDK)-based connectors, such as Connector for Lotus Notes and Connector for Novell GroupWise, include directory synchronization features that you can use to synchronize the non-Exchange directory with Active Directory.

- Perform automated directory synchronization through Microsoft Identity Integration Server (MIIS) or an equivalent third-party solution. MIIS is a comprehensive solution, but the costs justify its use only in long-term coexistence scenarios or in environments that already use MIIS for other purposes, such as for synchronizing identity information between Active Directory accounts and a human resources database.

- Perform automated directory synchronization using custom applications based on Microsoft Visual Basic, Scripting Edition (Visual Basic script), ADSI and CDOEXM. For example, you can create a script that synchronizes directory information and run this script automatically using the Task Scheduler service. This approach is flexible but requires programming skills.

- Perform semi-automated directory synchronization using import and export files in conjunction with low-level tools. For example, you can use Ldifde.exe to extract Active Directory information into Lightweight Directory Access Protocol (LDAP) Data Interchange Format (LDIF) files or import LDIF files into Active Directory.

- Perform manual directory synchronization using the standard administrative tools of your messaging systems. For example, you can use Active Directory Users and Computers to create mail-enabled recipients for non-migrated users in Active Directory. This strategy works well if you are migrating a small number of users.

Table 5-3   Typical Connectivity Requirements (Continued)

Requirement	Comments
Free/busy synchronization	If the non-Exchange messaging system includes calendar features, you have the following options to provide migrated and non-migrated users with access to each other's free/busy information:

- Use Exchange 2003 Calendar Connector to synchronize free/busy information between the non-Exchange messaging system and Exchange 2003. Calendar Connector relies on Connector for Lotus Notes and Connector for GroupWise.
- Publish free/busy information in a shared location by using Microsoft Office Outlook Internet Free/Busy (IFB) publishing. Outlook can publish free/busy information using the Microsoft Office Internet Free/Busy service or at a location in the internal network. For more information about the Office IFB service, go to the "Exchange Server 2003 Interoperability and Migration Guide" at *http://go.microsoft.com/fwlink/?LinkId=25927.*
- Implement a custom solution based on Collaboration Data Objects for Exchange (CDOEX) that displays the free/busy status of Exchange 2003 users in an ASP.NET page. The non-Exchange messaging system should also include application programming interfaces (APIs) that enable you to implement a custom solution for displaying free/busy information.

- **Deploying Outlook or Microsoft Office Outlook Web Access**   Users who are familiar with Outlook, such as those who already use Outlook for Internet messaging, will find a migration to Exchange 2003 very straightforward. However, novice users might face a steep learning curve because Outlook offers a comprehensive set of personal information management (PIM) features. You can alleviate this situation by providing appropriate user training and by deploying Outlook on all workstations early on in the migration project. This approach can greatly facilitate the migration. If you deploy Outlook on all desktops before migration and use an appropriate MAPI transport driver to connect to the non-Exchange messaging system (see Table 5-4), users can familiarize themselves with the new messaging client. You can also advise your users to download all messages in Outlook to their client computers. It is then not necessary to move server-based user data to Exchange 2003. After migration, you need only to reconfigure Outlook profiles to connect to Exchange 2003.

Note   If your users are unfamiliar with Outlook, it is reasonable to assume that the helpdesk call volume will increase during the first six months after the migration to Outlook and Exchange 2003 is complete. It is a good idea to dedicate one or more well-trained helpdesk specialists specifically to Outlook-related questions.

Table 5-4   MAPI Transport Drivers for Non-Exchange Messaging Systems

Messaging system	MAPI transport driver
Lotus Notes	You can use Microsoft Outlook 2002 Connector for IBM Lotus Domino to help your users become familiar with Outlook while they continue to work in the Domino environment. Through this connector, your users can use Outlook to access e-mail messages, calendar, address book, and To Do (task) items on Lotus Domino R5. The Outlook Connector is available for download from *http://go.microsoft.com/fwlink/ ?LinkId=25930*. Alternately, you can use Lotus iNotes Access 6 for Microsoft Outlook if this connector is already deployed.
Novell GroupWise	You can use Novell GroupWise 5.5 Plug-in for Outlook. However, note that if you want to run the GroupWise client and Outlook on the same computer, they must use different MAPI profiles. Both clients rely on MAPI, but cannot share the same profile.
POP3- or IMAP4-based messaging systems	You can use the POP3 or IMAP4 transport driver. Outlook works with a personal folder (.pst) file to download all messages from the host, and users can use Outlook to manage their personal information on their workstations.
Proprietary messaging systems	Check with your vendor to see if an appropriate MAPI transport driver is available for your messaging system. For example, you can use the Microsoft Mail transport driver, available in the Outlook, to work with a mailbox on a Microsoft Mail post office. If a direct MAPI transport driver is not available, consider using POP3 or IMAP4 for mailbox access. Most modern messaging systems support POP3 and IMAP4.

- **Moving user data and porting business solutions** You have several options to migrate user data to Exchange 2003. As mentioned, you can deploy Outlook in the legacy messaging system, and ask all users to download important messages to .pst files on their local workstation prior to migration. That way, you might be able to eliminate all server-based user data prior to migration. Another option is to upload all messages from local non-Outlook clients to the post office or server. You can then move the data on behalf of the users to Exchange 2003 using Exchange Migration Wizard. The Exchange Migration Wizard as a key migration tool is covered later in this chapter. A third option is to skip moving existing data and start with a fresh and empty Exchange 2003 organization, but this is seldom a good choice for companies that rely on e-mail in their daily business operations.

  Migrating data to Exchange 2003 also entails porting existing workgroup and workflow applications. This can be a complex task, especially if such business solutions use technologies not directly supported in Exchange 2003, such as LotusScript or external data sources. You should evaluate your business solutions to decide whether you want to migrate them or not. For those that you must migrate, consider using Windows SharePoint Services instead of Exchange APIs. Windows SharePoint Services provides advanced features for information sharing and document collaboration without dependencies on Exchange public folders.

> **Note**   Migrating workgroup and workflow applications to Exchange 2003 is beyond the scope of this chapter. For information about Windows Share-Point Services and Exchange APIs, such as Windows Management Instrumentation (WMI), Collaboration Data Objects for Exchange 2000 Server (CDOEX), or Microsoft ActiveX Data Objects (ADO), see the Microsoft Platform SDK (*http://msdn.microsoft.com/platformsdk*).

- **Decommissioning the non-Exchange system** As soon as you have migrated messaging connectors, users, workgroup applications, and possibly other services that the non-Exchange messaging system provided, you can uninstall the non-Exchange messaging system. This can be a straightforward undertaking if no further post offices or servers remain in the legacy environment. However, if you migrate to Exchange 2003 in multiple phases—post office-by-post office or server-by-server—decommissioning a particular post office or server must include a thorough dependencies check. For example, a particular non-Exchange server might be a messaging bridgehead to the Internet. If you decommission this server without first moving the bridgehead role to another server, you will break the message transfer path. Another server might be responsible for directory synchronization, and yet other servers might be required for other services, such as free/busy updates or workgroup applications. You should check the documentation about your legacy messaging system to see if it is safe to decommission a particular post office or server. Some messaging systems also include tools that you can use to check for dependencies. For example, you can run the IBM Lotus Decommission Server Analysis tool before decommissioning a Lotus Domino server.

Tip   A good strategy is to shut down the non-Exchange post office or server without actually decommissioning it for a period of time, such as a month, to see if any dependencies are noticeable. If this is the case, you can quickly restart the non-Exchange post office or server, and then transfer the responsibilities to another system.

Implementing Messaging Connectivity

Exchange 2003 includes several connector components that you can use to implement connectivity to a non-Exchange messaging system, as listed in Table 5-5. It should be noted, however, that Exchange 2003 includes fewer messaging connectors than previous versions of Exchange Server. For example, Connector for Microsoft Mail for PC Networks (MS Mail) and Connector for Lotus cc:Mail, included in Microsoft Exchange 2000 Server, are not included in Exchange 2003. Microsoft removed these connector components because MS Mail and Lotus cc:Mail are no longer supported by Microsoft or Lotus Corporation. If you want to use these connectors, you can deploy Exchange 2000 in your organization. Third-party vendors also provide messaging connectors that you can use to connect Exchange 2003 to a non-Exchange system. Novell GroupWise Gateway for Microsoft Exchange is an example of such a product.

Table 5-5   Exchange 2003 Connectors to Non-Exchange Messaging Systems

Connector	Comments
Connector for Lotus Notes	Connects an Exchange 2003 organization to a Lotus Domino messaging system. This direct connector also supports directory synchronization and calendar integration between Domino and Exchange.
Connector for Novell GroupWise	Connects an Exchange 2003 organization to a Novell GroupWise messaging system. This direct connector also supports directory synchronization and calendar integration between GroupWise and Exchange.

Table 5-5   Exchange 2003 Connectors to Non-Exchange Messaging Systems

Connector	Comments
SMTP connector	Connects an Exchange 2003 organization to one or multiple Simple Mail Transfer Protocol (SMTP)-based messaging systems This general messaging connector does not support directory synchronization or calendar integration.
X.400 connector	Connects an Exchange 2003 organization to an X.400-based messaging system, such as DEC All-In-One. This general messaging connector does not support directory synchronization or calendar integration.

Choosing a Messaging Connector

In general, you should choose direct messaging connectors over general messaging connectors because direct connectors can handle advanced message types, such as meeting requests. Furthermore, direct messaging connectors, included in Exchange Server 2003, support directory synchronization. This functionality is not available "out of the box" when choosing a general messaging connector, such as an SMTP connector. If you choose the SMTP connector for messaging connectivity, for example, you must implement custom solutions for directory synchronization and calendar integration. Nevertheless, all modern messaging systems support SMTP. An advantage of the SMTP connector is that you do not need to deploy and maintain additional third-party client components on your bridgehead servers.

> **Note**   The X.400 connector has the same benefits and limitations as the SMTP connector, but its configuration is complicated. If you are not specifically connecting to an X.400 messaging system, choose SMTP over X.400. This chapter focuses on SMTP connectivity.

Limitations of Direct Messaging Connectors

Direct messaging connectors follow the paradigm that connectivity between two messaging systems is best implemented in a direct way. However, direct connectivity also has limitations. For example, direct messaging connectors are difficult to maintain and do not scale. To overcome these limitations, companies typically connect messaging systems together using a messaging backbone based on a common standard. SMTP is the most widely accepted standard for messaging connectivity.

Figure 5-1 shows the general architecture of a direct Exchange messaging connector. It is important to note that the connector uses proprietary interfaces to communicate with both messaging systems. For example, direct connectors based on the

Exchange Development Kit (EDK) use MAPI to access their message queues in the Exchange store. On the side of the non-Exchange messaging system, the direct connector uses a proprietary third-party API. For example, Connector for Lotus Notes uses Lotus Notes Client API to communicate with a Lotus Domino server, and Connector for Novell GroupWise uses Novell GroupWise API Gateway to interact with GroupWise.

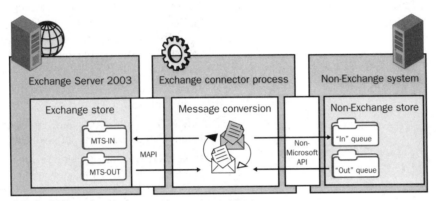

Figure 5-1   Direct messaging connector architecture

Note   You can find detailed information about the architecture of Exchange messaging connectors in the "Microsoft Exchange Server 2003 Technical Reference Guide," available at *http://www.microsoft.com/technet/prodtech-nol/exchange/2003/library/techrefgde.mspx.*

Using proprietary interfaces in a messaging connector has the following disadvantages:

- **Limited scalability**   Due to the use of proprietary APIs, you cannot run multiple instances of the same connector type on a single Exchange server, and a particular connector cannot connect to more than one non-Exchange system (that is, a Lotus Domino server or Novell GroupWise API Gateway, for instance). If you want to provide redundant message transfer paths, you must deploy multiple bridgehead servers and install an individual connector instance on each bridgehead.

- **Increased administrative overhead and costs**   To provide the required non-Microsoft APIs, you must install non-Microsoft software on the bridgehead server. This increases administrative overhead because you must configure and maintain these components. This also increases costs because you must obtain separate software licenses for the non-Microsoft components. Table 5-6 lists the non-Microsoft software required to run the messaging connectors included in Exchange Server 2003.

Table 5-6   Additional Software Required for Direct Messaging Connectors

Messaging connector	Additional components and versions
Connector for Lotus Notes	Lotus Notes client release 4, 5, or 6
Connector for Novell GroupWise	Novell GroupWise API Gateway version 4.1 with Novell GroupWise Patch 2 for API
	Novell NetWare client 4 when connecting to Novell GroupWise API Gateway on a NetWare server over TCP/IP
Calendar Connector	Lotus Notes client release 4, 5, or 6, when connecting to Lotus Domino
	Novell GroupWise API Gateway version 4.1 with Patch 2, when connecting to Novell GroupWise
	Novell NetWare client 4 when connecting to Novell GroupWise API Gateway on a NetWare server over TCP/IP

- **No support for Internet-based message formats**   When a direct messaging connector obtains a message, it expects the message to be in the native format of the source system. The connector must know how to handle the source format in order to perform the required conversion into a format supported by the target system. However, the message might not be in a known format if you use either Exchange or the non-Exchange messaging system as the central gateway to the Internet. In this situation, you route Internet messages over the direct messaging connector. The messages might arrive at the messaging connector with HTML formatting structures that the messaging connector cannot convert. As a result, HTML-formatted messages will not be delivered. You must use SMTP to deliver HTML-formatted messages.

> **More Info**   For more information regarding the lack of support for Internet-based message formats, see Microsoft Knowledge Base article 303986, "XFOR: Exchange Notes Connector Does Not Send HTML" (*http://support.microsoft.com/default.aspx?scid=kb;EN-US;303986*).

- **Complicated troubleshooting**   Troubleshooting interoperability issues between components from different software vendors can be a complicated and time-consuming task. If you are experiencing trouble with a messaging connector, you might have to contact Microsoft and the third-party software vendor, and the non-Microsoft vendor might choose to "solve" the issue by referring you back to Microsoft even if the problem is actually related to the non-Microsoft components. However, it is impossible for Microsoft to support or fix non-Microsoft components. As a result, it can take a very long time before a solution to an issue becomes available. For example, you might experience stability issues when using Connector for Lotus Notes with Lotus Notes R6.5.1 running on Windows Server 2003. Until IBM Lotus decides to fix these issues, you must revert back to an earlier version of the client API, such as Lotus Notes R6.

- **No support for multiple messaging systems per gateway connector** A particular type of gateway connector can connect Exchange 2003 only to a particular type of non-Exchange messaging system, such as Lotus Domino or Novell GroupWise, but not both. If you are planning to migrate a variety of messaging systems to Exchange 2003, you must deploy and maintain a variety of messaging connectors and non-Microsoft components. Furthermore, a direct messaging connector might not be available for all of your systems. For example, Connector for Novell GroupWise is not supported in the Chinese Simplified, the Chinese Traditional, or the Korean versions of Exchange 2003. In this situation, you must use a general messaging connector, such as an SMTP connector, to implement connectivity.

Implementing Connectivity Using Connector for Lotus Notes

If you are planning to migrate from Lotus Notes and Lotus Domino to Exchange 2003 in multiple phases and find that the limitations of a direct messaging connector do not represent an issue in your environment, you should deploy Connector for Lotus Notes because of its support for special message type conversions, directory synchronization, and calendar integration. Table 5-7 shows how Connector for Lotus Notes converts different message types between Exchange 2003 and Lotus Domino.

Table 5-7   Message Conversion Between Lotus Domino and Exchange 2003

Exchange 2003 feature	Lotus Domino feature	Lotus Domino to Exchange 2003	Exchange 2003 to Lotus Domino
E-mail messages	Messages	Yes	Yes
E-mail delivered receipt	E-mail delivered receipt	Yes	Yes
E-mail read receipt	E-mail read receipt	Yes	Yes
Non-delivery report	Non-delivery report	Yes	Yes
Importance	Importance	Yes	Yes
Voting buttons	No feature	No	No
Embedded OLE object	Embedded OLE object	Yes	Yes
Embedded file attachment	Embedded file attachment	Yes	Yes

Table 5-7 Message Conversion Between Lotus Domino and Exchange 2003

Exchange 2003 feature	Lotus Domino feature	Lotus Domino to Exchange 2003	Exchange 2003 to Lotus Domino
Message expiry date	Message expiry date	No	No
No feature	Reply by	No	No
Web URL	Web URL	Yes	Yes
No feature	URL hotspot	No	No
Meeting requests	Appointments	Yes	Yes
Meeting accepted	Meeting accepted	Yes	Yes
Meeting declined	Meeting declined	Yes	Yes
Meeting tentatively accepted	Meeting accepted	Appears as accepted	Appears as accepted
Meeting request read	Meeting request read	Yes	Yes
Meeting request delivery	Meeting request delivery	Yes	Yes
Meeting updates	Meeting updates	Appear as new meeting requests containing the word "Updated" in the subject line	Appear as new meeting requests containing the word "Updated" in the subject line
Meeting cancellation	Meeting cancellation	Yes	Yes
Task requests	Tasks	Task requests appear as e-mail messages or tasks	Appear as e-mail messages
All day meeting requests	No feature	No	Appear as meetings with midnight as the start and end time
No feature	Phone messages	Appear as e-mail messages	No
Other messages	Other messages	Default to e-mail messages	Default to e-mail messages

Note Connector for Lotus Notes does not support signed or encrypted messages.

Installing and Configuring Connector for Lotus Notes

You must complete the following steps to install and configure Connector for Lotus Notes (for step-by-step instructions, see the document 01_Installing Connector for Lotus Notes.doc in the \Companion Material\Chapter 05\Connector for Lotus Notes folder on the companion CD):

- **Ensure that prerequisites are met**   Before you install Connector for Lotus Notes on a new Exchange 2003 server, you must ensure that the Exchange 2003 server has network connectivity to the Lotus Domino server and can resolve the name of the Lotus Domino server. All access to Lotus Domino from Exchange 2003 is accomplished through standard Lotus Domino APIs. To use Lotus Domino APIs, the Lotus Notes client software (release 4.6 or later) must be installed on the Exchange 2003 server running Connector for Lotus Notes. The Lotus Domino server must run Lotus Domino 4.6 or later.

> **Note**   When you are deciding which version of the client to install, consider the information in Microsoft Knowledge Base article 316035, "XFOR: Lotus Notes Client Versions That Are Tested with the Exchange Notes Connector" (*http://go.microsoft.com/fwlink/?linkid=3052&kbid=316035*).

In addition, remember not to use Lotus Domino as the SMTP mail gateway to and from the Internet for your Exchange organization. If a Lotus Domino server is configured as the inbound SMTP mail gateway, the addresses for SMTP messages sent to Exchange users from the Internet will be corrupted. This is because all messages sent to Exchange through Connector for Lotus Notes are appended with the Lotus Domino domain name. To avoid this problem, configure Exchange, not Lotus Domino, as the inbound SMTP mail gateway for messages inbound from the Internet.

> **More Info**   For more information about the SMTP address issue, see Microsoft Knowledge Base article 255160, "XFOR: SMTP Messages from Lotus Notes SMTPMTA to Exchange 2000 Append @NotesDomain to the Sender's Address" (*http://go.microsoft.com/fwlink/?linkid=3052&kbid=255160*).

- **Prepare the Lotus Domino environment**   Before configuring Connector for Lotus Notes, the following tasks must be performed on the Lotus Domino server:

- **Use Lotus Domino Administrator to register a connector identifier**   To transfer messages between Lotus Domino and Exchange 2003 and synchronize directories, Connector for Lotus Notes must have its own Lotus Domino user identifier (ID). If you decide not to specify a password for this user ID, you cannot store the ID information in the Lotus Domino directory. Instead, create an ID file, and use this file later to configure Lotus Notes on the Exchange server that runs Connector for Lotus Notes. Remember the location of the user ID file because you must copy it later to the Exchange 2003 server and Connector for Lotus Notes.

Note   If your security policies require you to create a password for the connector user ID, create an ID file and specify the password in the connector configuration.

- **Create the Lotus Domino databases for routing mail to Exchange**   Lotus Domino requires two mailbox databases to route messages to Exchange 2003: a connector mailbox and a mailbox for badmail. Badmail refers to e-mail messages that cannot be delivered to your Exchange organization. The connector mailbox stores mail being routed from Lotus Domino to Exchange. Later, you create the foreign domain document to register the Exchange organization as an external foreign domain in the Lotus Domino Directory and configure Connector for Lotus Notes. At that time you also specify the name of the connector mailbox. All mail routed from Lotus Domino to Exchange 2003 is then sent to the connector mailbox, from which it is retrieved by Connector for Lotus Notes. The mailbox for badmail stores any mail that failed to transfer to Exchange 2003.

Note   If the user ID for Connector for Lotus Notes has Lotus Domino permissions to create new databases (configured in Lotus Domino Administrator on the Security tab of the Lotus Domino server Server document), these two databases are created automatically when you configure Connector for Lotus Notes. By default, Lotus Domino gives this permission to everyone, but most Lotus Domino administrators restrict this permission to privileged users. We recommend that you create these databases manually.

- **Prevent the new user ID from being synchronized to Active Directory**   You might not want the new Lotus Domino user ID for Connector for Lotus Notes to appear in the Exchange address list after you synchronize with Lotus Domino because this connector does not represent a user in your environment. To prevent propagation of this user ID, use Lotus Domino Administrator to hide the new user ID from Exchange users or downstream Lotus Domino domains.

- **Grant Depositor access to the server mailbox**   This is the level of access required by Connector for Lotus Notes. You must ensure that the user ID that you created for Connector for Lotus Notes has Depositor access to the server mailbox. Connector for Lotus Notes uses the server mailbox (mail.box, by default) to deposit mail from Exchange 2003 that is bound for Lotus Domino mailboxes. In most Lotus Domino environments, new user IDs are automatically granted Depositor access.

- **Grant Editor access to the Lotus Domino directory**   To update the Lotus Domino directory, Connector for Lotus Notes requires Editor level access to the directory of the Lotus Domino target server. In addition, ensure that the Delete documents permission is granted to Connector for Lotus Notes.

- **Grant Reader access to other Lotus Domino databases**   Lotus Domino allows users to create links between documents. These links are named DocLinks. Connector for Lotus Notes converts these links to one of three formats: OLE document link, Rich Text Format (RTF) attachment, or URL shortcut.

> **Note**   Database links and view links are not supported. Exchange users receive an error message if database or view links are sent to them from Lotus Domino users.

If you choose to convert links to RTF attachments, Connector for Lotus Notes requires Reader access to the document associated with the link. Otherwise, it cannot generate and send the linked file as an RTF attachment. Therefore, the Lotus Domino user ID in Connector for Lotus Notes must be given Reader access in the access control list (ACL) to every database that might be linked or that contains a document to which a Lotus Domino user might link. One option is to update the ACL on each database in Lotus Domino Administrator. Alternately, you can add the user ID for Connector for Lotus Notes to a group in the Lotus Domino directory that has Reader access to the necessary databases.

■ **Identify Exchange as a foreign domain**   For messages to be routed correctly from Lotus Domino to Exchange 2003, the Exchange organization must be identified to Lotus Domino as a foreign domain in Lotus Domino Administrator.

> **Note**   Incorrect settings in the foreign domain document can prevent Lotus Domino from routing messages to the connector's mailbox database (exchange.box).

■ **Install Exchange 2003 with Connector for Lotus Notes**   After you configure your Lotus Domino environment, you install Exchange 2003 on a dedicated bridgehead server. As part of this setup, you install Connector for Lotus Notes. To install Exchange 2003 on the server, you must have Exchange Administrator permissions in the administrative group in which the Connector for Lotus Notes target routing group exists. You must also be a member of the Administrators group on the server on which you install Exchange 2003.

■ **Prepare the Exchange 2003 environment**   After you install Exchange 2003 with Connector for Lotus Notes, you must install and configure Lotus Notes Client and enable Lotus Domino proxy addresses on the same server, as follows:

■ **Install and configure Notes Client**   Before you install the Lotus Notes client on the Exchange 2003 connector server, make sure that you have a Lotus Notes Client access license for the connector. After the installation, copy the user ID file that you created earlier to the directory of your Lotus Notes client (for example, e:\lotus\notes, where e is the drive letter with Lotus Notes client installed). After you copy the file, configure the Lotus Notes client for the user ID that you created for Connector for Lotus Notes so that Connector for Lotus Notes can use it to connect to the Lotus Domino server.

> **Note**   It is important to include the Lotus Notes directory in the system search path on the connector server. Do not simply copy the nnotes.dll file from the Lotus Notes directory to \%windir%\System32. Also, to avoid connector problems, do not select another user ID on the connector server that uses the Switch ID command in Lotus Notes.

- **Enable Lotus Domino Proxy Addresses** Lotus Notes users see Exchange users as recipients in another Lotus Domino domain, as identified by the foreign domain created for the connector. By default, the Lotus Notes e-mail address format that is used for Exchange 2003 users is based on the user's display name and the name of the Exchange organization. Because Exchange organization names sometimes contain characters that are not valid for an e-mail address type, you can modify the address generation rule in a recipient policy. The Recipient Update Service automatically generates the NOTES addresses for each mailbox and mail-enabled account. The address rule uses a set of symbols to determine how Exchange recipients appear in the Lotus Domino organization.

The resulting addresses must be unique within the address space. If the rule does not create a distinctive address, the Lotus Domino e-mail address generator modifies the address to ensure that it is unique.

The following is the default format for Lotus Notes addresses that are assigned to Exchange users:

&d/organization@domain name

The *&d* part of this address signifies the Lotus Notes display name (typically the full name) of the user, *organization* is the name of the user's Exchange organization, and *domain name* is the Lotus Domino foreign domain name that represents the Exchange organization. This is the name that you specified when you configured the connector's foreign domain document in Lotus Domino Administrator. You can use the placeholders listed in Table 5-8 to customize the NOTES address generation.

Table 5-8   Proxy Address Configuration Symbols

Information	Placeholder
The user's alias	&M or &m
The user's initials	&I or &i
The user's display name	&D or &d
The first name of the user	&G or &g
The last name of the user	&S or &s
An ampersand (&)	&&

For example, if you set the address format to &d@Exchange, a user whose display name is Pilar Ackerman receives the following Lotus Notes address:

Pilar Ackerman@Exchange.

> **Caution**   After directory synchronization, the connector creates secondary proxy addresses for Lotus Domino recipients. These addresses, which do not display bold formatting on the E-Mail Addresses tab, are used as unique identifiers for Lotus Domino recipients. Do not delete these secondary proxy addresses. You should delete only the addresses that you create manually.

1. **Configure Connector for Lotus Notes**   Connector for Lotus Notes is configured using Exchange System Manager. You can find the corresponding configuration object in the routing group where you installed the connector. Among other things, you must specify the location of the Notes.ini file and the name of the connector mailbox that you configured earlier on your Lotus Domino server; for example, exchange.box. Also specify the name of the server mailbox on the Lotus Domino bridgehead server to which Connector for Lotus Notes connects (the default is mail.box).

    You might want to adjust the polling interval that Connector for Lotus Notes uses to check for new messages delivered to Exchange, and specify how to convert Lotus Notes DocLinks. Another important configuration parameter is the address space that you must specify for the connector so that Exchange 2003 can route messages to Lotus Notes. Use wildcards (*) where appropriate, to allow all users to connect to Lotus Domino using Connector for Lotus Notes.

2. **Test e-mail connectivity**   To ensure that the message routing works, send test messages from Lotus Notes to Exchange 2003 and from Exchange 2003 to Lotus Notes. Use your NOTES proxy address to specify an Exchange recipient in Lotus Notes; for example, Administrator/First Administrative Group/Tailspin-toys@Exchange. To find your proxy address, start Active Directory Users and Computers, and display the E-Mail Addresses tab for your user account.

Deploying Multiple Connector for Lotus Notes Instances

If you want to use multiple connector instances to connect an Exchange 2003 organization to a Lotus Domino environment, you must distribute the users in your Exchange organization across multiple Lotus Domino foreign domains. You can configure multiple recipient policies to generate NOTES addresses according to different formats. For example, you might assign Ted Bremer the address Ted Bremer/Tailspin-toys@Exchange1, and the administrator might have the address Administrator/Tail-spintoys@Exchange2.

The environment illustrated in Figure 5-2 corresponds to an Exchange 2003 organization with two foreign domains defined in the Lotus Domino directory. You must point these foreign domains to separate mailbox databases of different connectors in Lotus Domino Administrator. In this way, multiple connector instances can share the message traffic to Exchange 2003.

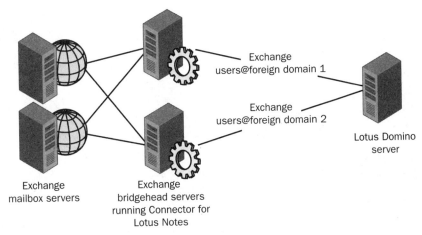

Figure 5-2   Multiple Connector for Lotus Notes instances

Note   When you implement multiple connector instances, carefully design the directory synchronization topology to avoid duplicating address information. Directory synchronization configuration is covered later in this chapter.

Specifying Routable Lotus Domino Domains

Just as an Exchange 2003 organization can have multiple administrative groups, a Lotus Domino environment can have multiple domains. These domains can transfer messages indirectly to the Exchange 2003 organization through another domain in which the connector's Lotus Domino server resides. Connector for Lotus Notes can allow all users in all domains to communicate with each Exchange user, but additional configuration is required to support message transfer in the opposite direction. You must identify downstream domains in the Advanced tab of the connector object in Exchange System Manager. Click the Add button under Routable Domains, and type the domain names in the Add Routable Domains dialog box. You can identify Lotus Domino domains that are referenced in connection, foreign domain, and non-adjacent domain documents. Exclude the foreign domains created for Exchange 2003. In addition, you must assign correct address space information to the Connector for Lotus Notes to allow for proper message routing.

Figure 5-3 illustrates a configuration in which Exchange users can communicate with Domino users in multiple domains over a single Connector for Lotus Notes instance.

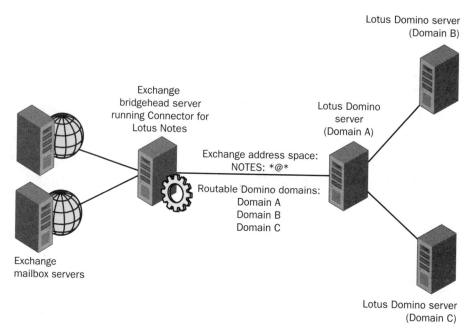

Figure 5-3 A single Connector for Lotus Notes instance to multiple Lotus Domino domains

Implementing Connectivity Based on Connector for Novell GroupWise

You can deploy Connector for Novell GroupWise if you are planning to migrate from Novell GroupWise to a language version of Exchange 2003 that supports this connector. Similar to Connector for Lotus Notes, Connector for Novell GroupWise supports special message type conversions, directory synchronization, and calendar integration.

> **Note** Microsoft does not officially support Connector for Novell GroupWise when connecting to Novell GroupWise 6.0 or later. However, because the underlying technologies remain the same as in previous versions of GroupWise, Microsoft Product Support Services offers commercially reasonable effort support.

Table 5-9 shows how Connector for Novell GroupWise converts different message types between Exchange 2003 and Novell GroupWise.

Table 5-9   Message Conversion Between Novell GroupWise and Exchange 2003

Exchange 2003 feature	GroupWise feature	GroupWise to Exchange 2003	Exchange 2003 to GroupWise
E-mail messages	Messages	Yes	Yes
E-mail read receipt	E-mail read receipt	Yes	Yes
Non-delivery report	Non-delivery report	Yes	Yes
Importance	Importance	Yes	Yes (low priority does not have a representation in GroupWise)
Sensitivity	Sensitivity	Yes	Yes
Meeting requests	Appointments	Yes	Yes
Meeting accepted	Meeting accepted	Yes	Yes
Meeting declined	Meeting declined	Yes	Yes
Meeting tentatively accepted	Meeting accepted	Appear as "Accepted"	Appear as "Accepted"
Meeting request read	Meeting request read	Yes	Yes
Meeting request delivery	Meeting request delivery	Yes	Yes
Meeting updates	Meeting updates	Appear as new meeting requests containing the word "Updated" in the subject line	Appear as new meeting requests containing the word "Updated" in the subject line
Meeting reminder times	Meeting reminder times	No	No
Meeting cancellation	Meeting cancellation	No	Yes
Task requests	Tasks	Task requests appear as e-mail messages	Tasks appear as e-mail messages
All day meeting requests	Meeting requests	Yes	Appear as meeting requests, however if the meeting extends over multiple days, it is placed as a single instance on the first day with the date range in the message field
N/A	Phone messages	Appear as e-mail messages	N/A
Other messages	Other messages	Default to e-mail messages	Default to e-mail messages

> **Note**   Connector for Novell GroupWise does not support signed or encrypted messages.

Installing and Configuring Connector for Novell GroupWise

You must complete the following steps to install and configure Connector for Novell GroupWise (for step-by-step instructions, see the document 01_Installing Connector for Novell GroupWise.doc in the \Companion Material\Chapter 05\Connector for Novell GroupWise folder on the companion CD):

- **Ensure that prerequisites are met**   Before you install Connector for Novell GroupWise on a new Exchange 2003 server, you must ensure that the Exchange 2003 server has Novell NetWare connectivity and can resolve the name of the Novell NetWare server running the API Gateway. All access to Novell GroupWise from Exchange 2003 is gained through the API Gateway using keyword-based text files. To communicate with Novell NetWare, either Gateway and Client Services or Novell NetWare Client for Windows must be installed on the Exchange 2003 server and Connector for Novell GroupWise. The server must be running Novell NetWare 3.x or later and Novell GroupWise 4.1 or later.

> **Note**   If your Novell NetWare environment is based on TCP/IP, use Novell NetWare Client for Windows to integrate the Exchange 2003 server into your Novell NetWare environment. Novell NetWare 4.8 is the preferred Novell Directory Services (NDS) client. If you want to use Gateway and Client Services instead, remember that this system configuration requires the NWLink (IPX/SPX) protocol between the Exchange 2003 server and the Novell API Gateway server. You must configure IPX routing in your TCP/IP-based Novell NetWare network to support Gateway and Client Services.

- **Prepare NDS and Novell GroupWise**   To support Connector for Novell GroupWise, you must deploy a dedicated API Gateway and configure a foreign GroupWise domain for your Exchange 2003 organization in the Novell NetWare Administrator program. You must work with Novell NetWare Administrator on a workstation where the GroupWise administration files have been installed. You must complete the following steps to prepare NDS and Novell GroupWise for interoperability with Exchange 2003:

- **Install the Novell GroupWise API Gateway on a Novell NetWare server**   You should use the NLM version of the API Gateway for Connector for Novell GroupWise. For installation, copy the corresponding gateway files to a directory on your NetWare server. Before you start the actual installation, it is a good idea to create a gateway directory in the \Wpgate subdirectory of your GroupWise domain (for example, \API41). On the System Console, run NWConfig to install the API Gateway in the NetWare Configuration program.

> **Note** We recommend that you install Patch 2 for the GroupWise 4.1 API Gateway for NLM on the Novell NetWare server that is running the API Gateway. This patch is available from Novell in the form of a self-extracting file named GW41API2.exe, at *http://support.novell.com*.

- **Configure the API Gateway in the Novell GroupWise domain**   After you have installed the GroupWise API Gateway files, you must start the Novell NetWare Administrator program and create a gateway object in the Novell GroupWise domain. You must create a GroupWise Gateway in the GroupWise domain object. Remember to enable directory synchronization for this object.

- **Create a foreign domain document for the Exchange organization in the Novell GroupWise domain, and link it to the API Gateway**   To complete the configuration, create an external foreign domain for your Exchange organization. Configure the link table of the GroupWise domain to connect the external foreign domain to your GroupWise domain through the API Gateway or Novell GroupWise cannot route messages to Exchange users.

- **Configure security for the API Gateway directory**   We recommend that you restrict access to the API Gateway directory, because the gateway is able to perform management functions similar to a Novell NetWare Administrator. Table 5-10 lists the most important API Gateway directories.

- **Table 5-10   Important API Gateway Directories**

Directory	Comments
API_IN	Receives incoming message header files from non-GroupWise systems.
API_OUT	Holds outgoing message header files to non-GroupWise systems
ATT_IN	Receives incoming message bodies and attachments from non-GroupWise systems.
ATT_OUT	Holds outgoing message bodies and attachments to non-GroupWise systems.

Table 5-10   Important API Gateway Directories (Continued)

Directory	Comments
WPCSIN	The Novell GroupWise Message Transfer Agent (GWMTA) inbound queue where incoming messages are placed after they are processed through the API Gateway.
WPCSOUT	The GWMTA outbound queue where outgoing messages are located before they are converted into keyword-based text files and placed into API_OUT and ATT_OUT through the API Gateway.

To identify Connector for Novell GroupWise and grant it permissions to read and write messages in the API input and output directories, a dedicated Novell NetWare account is required. You must create this account using Novell NetWare Administrator, and then use Exchange System Manager to configure the connector (on the General tab) to use this account for API Gateway access.

Note   The connector's NetWare account must be a member of a special group named NTGATEWAY, which you need to create using Novell NetWare Administrator. The connector's NetWare account requires permissions to create, read, write, and delete files in the API Gateway directories.

- **Install Exchange 2003 with Connector for Novell GroupWise**   After you configure your Novell GroupWise environment, you can install Exchange 2003 on a dedicated connector server. As part of this setup, you install Connector for Novell GroupWise. You must have Exchange Administrator permissions in the administrative group where the connector's target routing group exists to install Exchange 2003 on the server, and you must be a member of the local Administrators group on the server on which you install Exchange 2003.

- **Prepare the Exchange 2003 environment**   Next, you must enable Novell GroupWise proxy addresses on the server running Exchange 2003 with Connector for Novell GroupWise installed on it. By default, Novell GroupWise users see Exchange users as recipients in an external foreign domain named Exchange. The post office name corresponds to the administrative group name. The Recipient Update Service automatically generates the proxy addresses for each mailbox- and mail-enabled account in the Exchange organization using a proxy address generator. The GroupWise proxy address generator is GWXPX-GEN.DLL, which resides in the Program Files\Exchsrvr\Address\Gwise\i386 directory.

It is possible to customize GWISE proxy addresses through recipient policies in Exchange System Manager. Make sure that GWISE address is enabled, and then customize the address generation rule. For example, you might want to shorten or change the reference to the post office name, which by default refers to the administrative group, but you cannot remove the post office name portion of the address. GroupWise addresses must conform to the GroupWise naming convention of domain.post office.user alias. Do not change the domain name portion until you have created a corresponding external foreign domain in GroupWise.

You can use the placeholders listed in Table 5-8 earlier in this chapter to customize GWISE address generation. For example, you can set the address format to **Exchange.First Administrative Group.&d**. A user whose display name is Pilar Ackerman receives a Novell GroupWise address of Exchange.First Administrative Group.Pilar Ackerman.

Caution   After directory synchronization occurs, the connector creates secondary proxy addresses for Novell GroupWise recipients. These addresses, which do not display bold formatting on the user's E-Mail Addresses tab, are used as unique identifiers for Novell GroupWise recipients. Do not delete these secondary proxy addresses. In general, you should delete only the addresses that you create manually.

1. **Configure Connector for Novell GroupWise**   Connector for Novell GroupWise is configured using Exchange System Manager. You can find the corresponding configuration object in the routing group where you installed the connector. Among other things, you must specify the Universal Naming Convention (UNC) path to the root directory of the connector's API Gateway, identify the connector account (which must be a member of the NTGATEWAY group, as mentioned earlier), and define message routing information for the connector. Alternately, you can configure delivery restrictions to specify users and groups that are permitted or denied message transfer through Connector to Novell GroupWise.

2. **Test e-mail connectivity**   To ensure that the message routing works, send test messages from Novell GroupWise to Exchange 2003 and from Exchange 2003 to GroupWise. Use your GWISE proxy address to specify an Exchange recipient in Novell GroupWise; for example, Exchange.First Administrative Group.Administrator. To find your proxy address, start the Active Directory Users and Computers MMC snap-in and display the E-Mail Addresses tab for

your user account. After the message is received in Microsoft Outlook, reply to it and verify that the reply is received in Novell GroupWise.

Implementing Multiple Connector for Novell GroupWise Instances

You can configure multiple recipient policies to generate GWISE addresses according to different formats. For example, you might assign Birgit Seidl the address Exchange1.First Administrative Group.Birgit Seidl, while the Administrator might have the address Exchange2.First Administrative Group.Administrator. This corresponds to an Exchange organization with two external foreign domains in Novell GroupWise. You must create an external foreign domain in Novell GroupWise for Exchange1 and one for Exchange2 using Novell NetWare Administrator. To distribute the workload across multiple gateway instances, either point to the same API Gateway or to separate gateways, possibly in different GroupWise domains. In this way, multiple connector instances can share the message traffic to Exchange 2003. To distribute outbound message traffic to GroupWise domains across multiple Connectors for Novell GroupWise, assign detailed GWISE address spaces to each connector.

Figure 5-4 shows a configuration with two Connector for Novell GroupWise instances.

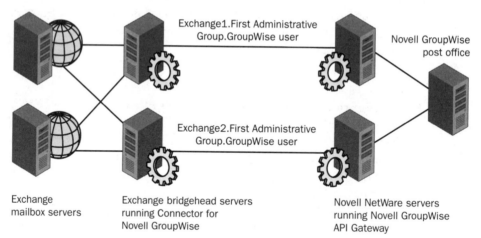

Exchange1.First Administrative
Group.GroupWise user

Novell GroupWise
post office

Exchange2.First Administrative
Group.GroupWise user

Exchange
mailbox servers

Exchange bridgehead servers
running Connector for
Novell GroupWise

Novell NetWare servers
running Novell GroupWise
API Gateway

Figure 5-4   Multiple connector instances between Exchange 2003 and Novell GroupWise

Note   When you are implementing multiple connector instances, carefully design the directory synchronization topology to avoid duplicating addresses.

Specifying Routable Novell GroupWise Domains

Just as an Exchange 2003 organization can have multiple administrative groups, a Novell GroupWise environment can have multiple domains. These domains can transfer messages indirectly to the Exchange 2003 organization through another domain in which the connector's API Gateway is installed.

As illustrated in Figure 5-5, a single Connector for Novell GroupWise instance can allow all users in all GroupWise domains to communicate with each Exchange user. Correct address space information must be assigned to the Connector for Novell GroupWise to allow for proper message routing. For example, assign an address space of GWISE:* to the connector to route messages to all GroupWise users through your connector instance. Additional configuration might be required in the Novell GroupWise environment. You must ensure that the routing configuration of the connector's GroupWise domain meets your GroupWise routing requirements. The GroupWise MTA must be able to route inbound messages that are received from the API gateway to their GroupWise destinations.

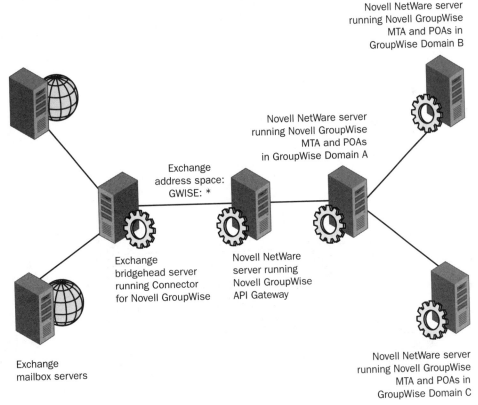

Figure 5-5   A single Connector for Novell GroupWise instance for multiple Novell GroupWise domains

Implementing Connectivity Based on SMTP Connectors

In comparison to direct messaging connectors, SMTP-based connectivity is relatively straightforward to implement. In fact, Exchange 2003 can communicate with other messaging systems over SMTP even without the explicit configuration of an SMTP connector because the internal transport subsystem of Exchange 2003 is based on SMTP. You need only make sure that required mail exchanger (MX) records exist in Domain Name System (DNS) and that the hosts can establish TCP/IP connections over TCP port 25. Nevertheless, SMTP connectivity to internal messaging systems is best implemented through explicit SMTP connectors, so you can deploy dedicated bridgehead servers in a large Exchange organization and establish well-defined transfer paths between Exchange 2003 and non-Exchange messaging systems. As soon as you configure an SMTP connector to another messaging system, all servers in the Exchange organization will route their messages to this destination over the SMTP connector. For more information about message routing in Exchange 2003, see *Exchange Server 2003 Transport and Routing Guide*, available at *http://www.microsoft.com/technet/prodtechnol/exchange/2003/library/extransrout.mspx*.

Figure 5-6 illustrates a deployment of a single bridgehead server. For fault tolerance and load balancing, you can define multiple bridgehead servers in the SMTP connector configuration.

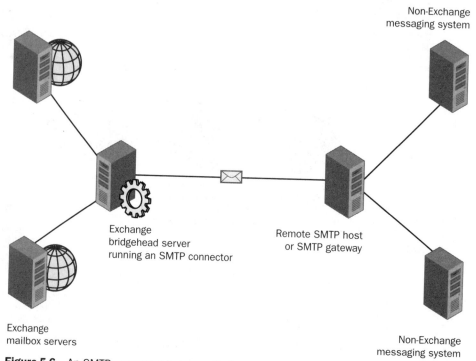

Figure 5-6   An SMTP connector between Exchange 2003 and a non-Exchange messaging system

E-Mail Addresses and Internal Message Routing

SMTP-based systems use Internet domain names to perform message routing, which implies that you must assign the Exchange 2003 organization a different Internet domain name than the non-Exchange messaging system. For example, if non-Exchange users have an e-mail address of *<user>*@tailspintoys.com, then Exchange users must have a different domain name portion in their e-mail addresses, such as *<user>*@exchange.tailspintoys.com. Otherwise, SMTP hosts are not able to distinguish the Exchange from the non-Exchange messaging system.

The requirement for different domain names represents an issue that you must address to avoid disruption in the delivery of e-mail messages during a migration. Disruption can occur because your users' e-mail addresses will change when you move them to Exchange 2003. For example, Ted Bremer's e-mail address might change from Ted@tailspintoys.com to Ted@exchange.tailspintoys.com. When users continue to send messages to Ted@tailspintoys.com these messages are routed to the non-Exchange messaging system where Ted's mailbox does not exist anymore. The sender will receive a non-delivery notification stating that Ted could not be reached.

To avoid this problem, you must configure the non-Exchange messaging system so that it forwards messages to migrated users to the Exchange organization. One way to accomplish this is to configure forwarding rules that automatically redirect all incoming messages to the new SMTP addresses. However, forwarding rules are difficult to maintain and there is a risk of creating message loops with forwarding rules. A better approach is to create a recipient object in the non-Exchange directory for each migrated Exchange 2003 user. These recipient objects in the non-Exchange directory can be associated with the original and the new SMTP address. If the non-Exchange system receives a message addressed to the original SMTP address, it can replace the original with the new SMTP address that points to a recipient in the Exchange 2003 organization. Having replaced the SMTP address, the non-Exchange messaging system can redirect the message to Exchange 2003 without having to use forwarding rules.

If your non-Exchange messaging system is not capable of redirecting messages, you can use Exchange 2003 for this purpose, but you need to flip the domain names. For example, you can assign the Exchange 2003 organization the Internet domain name tailspintoys.com after you change the domain name of the non-Exchange messaging system to legacy.tailspintoys.com. In other words, you must assign all non-Exchange users new SMTP addresses that will revert back to the original addresses as you move the users to Exchange 2003. To ensure message delivery in the meantime, you must configure mail-enabled recipient objects in Active Directory that point to the users in the non-Exchange messaging system. Exchange will perform the address translation and message redirection as required. For example, a message sent to Ted@tailspintoys.com will reach the Exchange organization first. If Ted now has a mail-enabled recipient object in Active Directory that points to the address of Ted@legacy.tailspintoys.com, Exchange replaces the addresses and routes the message to its non-Exchange destination.

E-Mail Addresses and External Message Routing

Changing e-mail addresses are also an issue for communication with external users, such as customers and business partners. With the strategies discussed above, you can ensure that messages from external users sent to Ted@tailspintoys.com are delivered, but when Ted himself sends messages to external users, those messages will show his changed e-mail address, such as Ted@exchange.tailspintoys.com or Ted@legacy.tailspintoys.com. This is usually not desirable. Ideally, Ted's address remains Ted@tailspintoys.com in all outbound messages prior to and after the migration.

You have the following options to preserve the existing e-mail addresses:

■ **Use a central smart host as the SMTP gateway to the Internet**   This straightforward approach is often used by companies that want to hide the complexities of their internal messaging infrastructures. A central smart host has a global alias list, mapping internal to external addresses. In outbound messages, the smart host specifies the user's external address in the sender information. In inbound messages, the smart host replaces the external address with the internal address in the recipient information before routing the message further to Exchange 2003 or the non-Exchange messaging system. A disadvantage of this approach is that you must maintain a separate alias list in addition to Exchange and non-Exchange address lists.

Figure 5-7 shows an arrangement of messaging systems with a central smart host performing the address mapping between internal and external e-mail addresses.

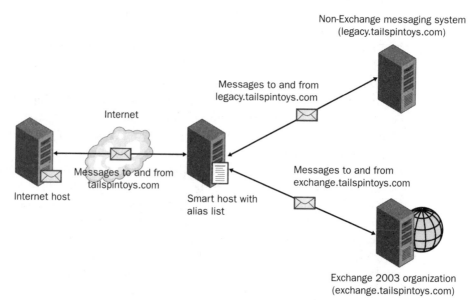

Figure 5-7   A smart host as the SMTP gateway to the Internet

■ **Use the non-Exchange messaging system as the SMTP gateway to the Internet** If the existing messaging system is connected directly to the Internet and capable of replacing sender information in outbound messages, you can use the non-Exchange system for inbound and outbound Internet e-mail. For example, if Ted is sending messages as Ted@exchange.tailspintoys.com and you route these messages through the non-Exchange messaging system, the non-Exchange messaging system must replace Ted@exchange.tailspintoys.com with Ted@tailspintoys.com before routing the outbound message to the Internet. A disadvantage of this approach is that all Internet communication depends on the system from which you are migrating.

Figure 5-8 shows an arrangement with a non-Exchange messaging system performing the address mapping between internal and external e-mail addresses for Exchange users. For this arrangement to work, the non-Exchange messaging system must be able to process all inbound and outbound Internet messages.

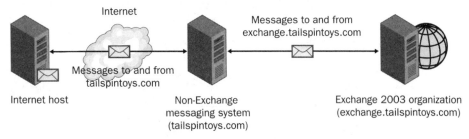

Figure 5-8   A non-Exchange messaging system as the SMTP gateway to the Internet

■ **Use Exchange 2003 as the SMTP gateway to the Internet** It is preferable to use Exchange 2003 for all inbound and outbound SMTP messages. This approach requires you to assign the Exchange organization the original domain name and change the domain name in the non-Exchange messaging system, as discussed earlier. To change the e-mail addresses of non-Exchange users in the sender information of outbound messages, however, you must enable Address Rewrite on your Exchange 2003 bridgehead servers. Address Rewrite is a feature that replaces SMTP addresses in messages that are received through SMTP from a non-Exchange system and are destined to the Internet with the sender's primary SMTP address. To use Address Rewrite successfully, you must have a mail-enabled recipient object in Active Directory for each user in the non-Exchange system, and you must specify for each sender the primary SMTP address that you want to use as the reply address in outgoing messages.

On the Resource Kit CD   The document 01_Using Exchange 2003 as the SMTP gateway to the Internet.doc in the \Companion Material\Chapter 05\SMTP Connector folder on the companion CD illustrates how to use the Address Rewrite feature.

More Info   For more information about Address Rewrite (Exarcfg.exe), also consult the Readme file that accompanies the tool. You can download tool and documentation from *http://go.microsoft.com/fwlink/?LinkId=25932*.

Figure 5-9 shows an arrangement with an Exchange 2003 bridgehead server performing the address mapping between internal and external e-mail addresses for non-Exchange users. In this arrangement, you must install the Address Rewrite tool on the bridgehead server.

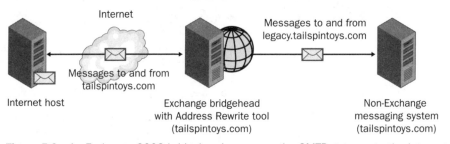

Figure 5-9   An Exchange 2003 bridgehead server as the SMTP gateway to the Internet

Resolving E-Mail Addresses on Anonymous Connections

If possible, you should configure your internal SMTP hosts to use authentication when establishing connections to an Exchange 2003 bridgehead server. Exchange 2003 can then resolve address information for external users in e-mail messages to their recipient objects in Active Directory, as illustrated in Figure 5-10. However, not all SMTP hosts are able to perform authentication. For example, you cannot configure Lotus Domino R6.5.1 for authentication over outbound SMTP connections. To address this shortcoming, you must enable address resolution over anonymous connections in Exchange System Manager. The document 01_Using Exchange 2003 as the SMTP gateway to the Internet.doc on the companion CD illustrates how to do this.

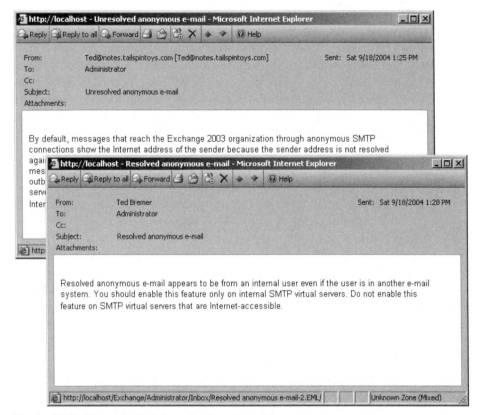

Figure 5-10   Unresolved and resolved sender addresses

It must be noted, however, that you should not enable address resolution over anonymous connections on Internet-accessible SMTP virtual servers. Otherwise, attackers from the Internet can submit messages with a falsified return address, and Exchange will resolve these spoofed addresses, making it difficult for Exchange users to differentiate between authentic messages and spoofed messages. To minimize this possibility, you should use different Exchange bridgehead servers for Internet and internal communication, or create a second SMTP virtual server with a custom port number for internal message transfer. You can then restrict access to the SMTP virtual server to the IP addresses of your Exchange and non-Exchange messaging servers.

Encapsulating Message Properties

SMTP, as a "simple" message transfer protocol, describes a plain-text message as a sequence of 7-bit ASCII characters. To support formatted text or attachments, the original content must be encoded using UUENCODE or Multipurpose Internet Mail Extensions (MIME) and inserted into the body as a 7-bit ASCII character stream. Modern messaging systems also support e-mail messages formatted in HTML. For example, Outlook users can configure their clients to compose messages in HTML format by default.

If your users choose to use Microsoft Word as their e-mail editor, they can use the full HTML editing set available with Word when composing e-mail messages. The recipient's client must also support HTML mail to display the content with correct formatting. However, some administrators prefer to block HTML-formatted messages because HTML mail can include scripts that contain malicious code, such as worm viruses.

Another option is to send messages in Exchange RTF—provided that the recipient works with a client that supports Exchange RTF, such as Outlook or Outlook Express. Users can decide individually whether to send messages in RTF, but you can also enable this feature in Exchange System Manager for an SMTP domain if you know that all users in that domain work with an Exchange RTF-aware client. Exchange 2003 encapsulates RTF messages in Transport Neutral Encapsulation Format (TNEF) to preserve all message properties even if the messages are routed over non-Exchange messaging systems. However, clients that do not understand TNEF will display a plain-text or HTML-formatted message with an additional attachment named winmail.dat. The winmail.dat file contains the message and all attachments, but recipients will not be able to access the contents, unless they are using a specialized decoder such as Biblet Computer Services WMDecode (*http://www.biblet.freeserve.co.uk/*). You should not send Exchange RTF to SMTP domains if you are not sure that the recipients work with an Exchange RTF-aware client.

On the Resource Kit CD The document 02_Using Exchange RTF between Exchange and IMAP4 users.doc in the \Companion Material\Chapter 05\SMTP Connector folder on the companion CD illustrates how to configure Exchange 2003 to send messages in RTF to an Internet domain with IMAP4-based Outlook users.

Configuring SMTP Connectivity

You must complete the following steps to configure an SMTP connector to a non-Exchange messaging system:

- **Ensure that prerequisites are met** Before you configure an SMTP connector on a bridgehead server running Exchange 2003, you must ensure that the Exchange 2003 server can resolve the name of the remote SMTP host to an IP address and can open a TCP/IP connection to TCP port 25, which is the standard port for SMTP. It might be necessary to verify the internal DNS configuration so that the Exchange bridgehead server and the remote SMTP host can locate each other. An alternative is to specify the remote SMTP host in the SMTP connector configuration directly, and provide similar configuration settings in the remote messaging system, so messages can be transferred in both directions without DNS lookups.

■ **Prepare the non-Exchange messaging environment**   To support proper message routing between Exchange 2003 and the non-Exchange messaging system, you might have to change the SMTP domain name in the non-Exchange messaging system, as mentioned earlier. Depending on the option you choose to preserve existing e-mail addresses, you might also have to deploy a central smart host and configure an alias file or install an Exchange 2003 bridgehead server with Address Rewrite.

■ **Prepare the Exchange 2003 environment**   If the Exchange 2003 organization already exists, you might have to change the SMTP domain name of your Exchange users as well. You do this by changing the default recipient policy in Exchange System Manager. Recipient policy objects reside in the Recipient Policies container under the Recipients node. Display the properties for the Default Policy object, switch to the E-Mail Addresses (Policy) tab, and then change the SMTP address reference. For example, specify **@exchange.tailspintoys.com** instead of @tailspintoys.com. Remember that you must implement a solution to preserve the existing e-mail addresses of your users so that e-mail communication with external users, such as customers and business partners, is not disrupted. Do not change the domain name until you have decided how to resolve this issue.

■ **Configure the SMTP connector and Internet message formats**   The SMTP connector is installed and configured using Exchange System Manager. At a minimum, you must specify whether the SMTP connector should use DNS to determine the remote SMTP host through MX records, or provide the host name or IP address of the remote SMTP host directly on the General tab. You also must specify the local bridgehead servers that will use this connector instance to transfer messages. It is possible to specify multiple bridgehead servers. You must also define an address space for the connector on the Address Space tab to identify the SMTP domain to which this connector instance connects (for example, legacy.tailspintoys.com).

On the Resource Kit CD   For an example showing how to configure an SMTP connector, see the document 01_Using Exchange 2003 as the SMTP gateway to the Internet.doc in the \Companion Material\Chapter 05\SMTP Connector folder on the companion CD.

■ **Test e-mail connectivity**   To ensure that message routing works, send test messages from the non-Exchange messaging system to Exchange 2003, and then reply to these messages to ensure that message transfer also works in the opposite direction. You should also send test messages to an Internet recipient, such as a Hotmail address, to verify that external e-mail addresses are preserved correctly for migrated and non-migrated users.

> **Note**   Always test newly configured Exchange connectors in both direc-
> tions.

Synchronizing Recipient Information

Having implemented messaging connectivity based on a direct or general Exchange connector, you are ready to approach the second task in establishing seamless interoperability—directory synchronization. You must perform directory synchronization to provide both Exchange and non-Exchange users with consistent global address lists. Directory synchronization is also an important tool to ensure delivery of Internet messages. As discussed earlier, if you use Exchange 2003 as the central SMTP gateway to the Internet, you must create a mail-enabled recipient object for each non-Exchange user in Active Directory so that Exchange 2003 can route incoming messages to these users.

> **Note**   It is important to synchronize directories after each migration step because recipient information changes during the migration. If you omit this step, messages might be delivered to wrong locations.

You have several options to synchronize Exchange and non-Exchange address information. For example, you can use the directory synchronization features of a direct messaging connector. Another option is to use a separate product for directory integration, such as Microsoft Identity Integration Server (MIIS) or a non-Microsoft tool. A business solutions developer can also create a custom directory synchronization solution based on Active Directory Service Interfaces (ADSI) and Collaboration Data Objects for Exchange Management (CDOEXM). You can also perform manual directory synchronization or bulk export and import operations using low-level Active Directory tools, such as Ldifde.exe and Csvde.exe. Ldifde.exe works with LDAP Data Interchange Format (LDIF) files. Csvde.exe uses comma-separated value (.csv) files.

Synchronizing Directories Using Direct Messaging Connectors

Direct messaging connectors support automatic directory synchronization. For example, you can use Connector for Lotus Notes to synchronize Active Directory and Domino directories. The same principle applies to Connector for Novell GroupWise. If you are using Exchange 2000 on a bridgehead server, you can also use Exchange Connector for Microsoft Mail and Connector for Lotus cc:Mail to perform automatic directory synchronization with Microsoft Mail or Lotus cc:Mail.

When you use these connectors, you can configure a number of settings, including:

- **Attributes to be synchronized**   If you do not want all of the attributes for each user to be synchronized to the other messaging system, you can exclude attributes from the directory synchronization.

- **Directory objects to be synchronized**   For example, you might choose to synchronize the directory information for all mailbox-enabled user accounts but not synchronize contacts or mail-enabled groups.

- **Organizational units in Active Directory**   Based on the organizational units that you select, you can specify which recipient objects are synchronized with the legacy messaging system. You can also specify a target organizational unit for all recipient objects that point to legacy mailboxes.

- **Types of recipient objects to be created**   You can create disabled Windows user accounts, enabled Windows user accounts, or contacts in Active Directory.

- **Whether to replicate groups or distribution lists**   When you configure the connector to replicate distribution lists from the non-Exchange messaging system, a mail-enabled contact object is created in Active Directory for that distribution list. When Exchange users send messages to that contact, the messages are sent to the e-mail address that is specified on the contact, and the message is delivered to the other messaging system, where the list is expanded, and the e-mail messages are distributed to all of the recipients in the list.

On the Resource Kit CD   For step-by-step instructions detailing how to configure directory synchronization with Lotus Notes or Novell GroupWise, see the documents 02_Configuring Directory Synchronization with Lotus Notes.doc and 02_Configuring Directory Synchronization with Novell GroupWise.doc in the \Companion Material\Chapter 05\Connector for Lotus Notes and \Companion Material\Chapter 05\Connector for Novell GroupWise folders on the companion CD.

Customizing Directory Synchronization

Connector for Lotus Notes and Connector for Novell GroupWise use a common directory synchronization agent that relies on schema definition files and mapping rule files that determine the attributes included in the directory synchronization processes. You can edit the schema definition files and mapping rule files in Notepad to customize the attribute mappings from one directory to the other directory. Table 5-11 lists the schema definition files and mapping rule files that you can edit to customize directory synchronization. In addition, there are also control files, such as EXTERNAL.TBL, GWPCTA.TBL, and MEXPCTA.TBL, which you should not edit manually.

> **Note** Remember to stop the connector services before you edit these files to ensure that the directory synchronization is not active. If you edit schema definition and mapping rule files using Notepad or another text editor, ensure that you save backup copies of the original files. In addition, do not use the Tab key when making changes. You must use the Space key to enter white-space characters.

Table 5-11 Schema Definition Files and Mapping Rule Files

File	Location	Purpose
AMAP.TBL	\Program Files\Exchrvr\Conndata\Dxamex	Defines the Exchange mailbox attributes to be synchronized.
AMAP.TBL	\Program Files\Exchrvr\Conndata\Dxanotes	Defines the Lotus Notes attributes to be synchronized.
GWAMAP.TBL	\Program Files\Exchrvr\Conndata\Dxagwise	Defines the GroupWise schema attributes to be synchronized.
MEXAMAP.TBL	\Program Files\Exchrvr\Conndata\Dxagwise	Defines the Exchange schema attributes to be synchronized.
MAPMEX.TBL	\Program Files\Exchrvr\Conndata\Dxanotes	Determines the attribute mapping from Exchange 2003 to Lotus Notes.
MAPMEX.TBL	\Program Files\Exchsrvr\Conndata\Dxagwise	Determines the attribute mapping from Exchange 2003 to Novell GroupWise.
MAPNOTES.TBL	\Program Files\Exchrvr\Conndata\Dxamex	Determines the attribute mapping from Lotus Notes to Exchange 2003.
MAPGWISE.TBL	\Program Files\Exchrvr\Conndata\Dxagwise	Determines the attribute mapping from Novell GroupWise to Exchange 2003.

Most attributes are mapped in a straightforward way. For example, if you check out \Program Files\Exchrvr\Conndata\Dxanotes\MAPMEX.TBL, you can find out that when a Domino directory is synchronized with Active Directory, the Exchange 2003 attribute *Company* is assigned the value of the Lotus Domino directory attribute *Company*. However, there are also more complicated constructs, such as `LastName = ISEQUAL( LastName, "", FullName, LastName )`, which states that the DXA should map *LastName* to *LastName* unless *LastName* is empty (""), in which case the directory synchronization agent should map *FullName* to *LastName*. Table 5-12 lists the functions that you can use to customize attribute mappings.

Table 5-12   Attribute Mapping Functions

Function	Comments
AND()	Returns the concatenation of two non-null strings, or the null string if either of the two strings specified is null.
CFGPARM()	Returns a value from the connector's .ini file.
ISEQUAL()	Returns a configurable value, depending on whether or not two expressions are equal.
LEFT()	Returns the left n characters of an expression, padded on the right if necessary.
LOWER()	Converts a field to lower-case characters.
NAMEF()	Returns a person's first name or initial from a pre-formatted string.
NAMEL()	Returns a person's last name or initial from a pre-formatted string.
NAMEM()	Returns a person's middle name or initial from a pre-formatted string.
POS()	Determines the position of a particular string within an attribute.
PROPER()	Converts a name field to proper-name format.
REPLACE()	Replaces selected characters with substitute characters.
RIGHT()	Returns the right n characters of an expression, padded on the left if necessary.
SUBSTR()	Returns a specified sub-string of a string, padded with extra characters if necessary.
STRIP()	Locates the left-most or right-most occurrence of one string in another and removes characters.
TRIM()	Returns a field with leading and/or trailing blanks removed.
UPPER()	Converts a field to upper-case characters.
WORD()	Returns a specified number of words from a string.
X500()	Extracts an attribute from an X.500-style hierarchical address.

> **More Info** For detailed information about customizing the directory synchronization, see Microsoft Knowledge Base article 180517, "XFOR: Customizing Directory Synchronization Between Exchange and Notes" (*http://go.microsoft.com/fwlink/?linkid=3052&kbid=180517*).

Synchronizing SMTP Addresses Instead of NOTES or GWISE Addresses

Although it is relatively difficult to customize schema definition and attribute mapping files in Notepad, you can achieve astonishing configurations through customized directory synchronization. For example, you can tweak Connector for Lotus Notes and Connector for Novell GroupWise to synchronize SMTP addresses instead of NOTES or GWISE addresses. In this way, you can use an SMTP connector for all message transfer, which is a good idea if you want to support HTML mail between the messaging systems, for example. Figure 5-11 illustrates this configuration.

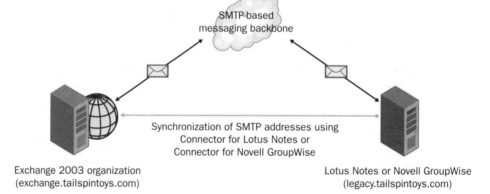

Figure 5-11 SMTP address synchronization with Lotus Notes or Novell GroupWise

Customizing Directory Synchronization with Lotus Notes

To synchronize SMTP address information between Exchange 2003 and Lotus Notes, you must accomplish the following steps:

1. **Edit the schema definition file for Lotus Notes attributes (Dxanotes\ Amap.tbl)** You must edit this file to include the Lotus Notes attributes *InternetAddress*, *MailAddress*, and *MailSystem* into directory synchronization. These attributes correspond to the Internet address, Forwarding address, and Mail system fields in a Domino Person document.

2. **Edit the schema definition file for Active Directory attributes (Dxamex\ Amap.tbl)** You must edit this file to include the primary SMTP proxy address of Exchange recipients into directory synchronization. In schema definition files, the primary SMTP proxy address is referred to as ProxyAddresses(SMTP:).

3. **Edit the attribute mapping from Exchange 2003 to Lotus Notes (Dxanotes\Mapmex.tbl)**   You must edit this file to specify how the SMTP proxy address of an Exchange recipient should be mapped to the relevant fields in a Domino Person document. Specifically, you must assign the *MailSystem* attribute a numeric value of **5** to set the Mail system field for Exchange recipients in the Domino directory to Other Internet Mail, and you must assign the *MailAddress* attribute the primary SMTP proxy address of the Exchange recipient.

4. **Edit the attribute mapping from Lotus Notes to Exchange 2003 (Dxamex\Mapnotes.tbl)**   You must edit this file to change the *targetAddress* attribute for mail-enabled recipient objects that you create in Active Directory for Lotus Notes users. Instead of a NOTES address, you must specify an SMTP address. For example, you can map the Active Directory *targetAddress* attribute to the Domino *MailAddr* attribute. However, not all Notes users might have a forwarding address, in which case, you might want to map the Notes user's *InternetAddress* to the *targetAddress* attribute. If the *InternetAddress* attribute is empty as well, you should construct a valid SMTP address based on the Notes user's full name and Domino domain information. Using the functions listed in Table 5-12 you can check *InternetAddress* and *MailAddress* for their values and generate the required SMTP address accordingly.

> **On the Resource Kit CD**   The document 03_Configuring SMTP Directory Synchronization with Lotus Notes.doc in the \Companion Material\Chapter 05\SMTP Connector\Notes Connector SMTP DirSync folder on the companion CD provides step-by-step instructions to synchronize SMTP address information between Exchange 2003 and Lotus Notes. This document shows how to use the functions *ISEQUAL()*, *Replace()*, and *Strip()* to generate valid *targetAddress* information.

Customizing Directory Synchronization with Novell GroupWise

To synchronize SMTP address information between Exchange 2003 and Novell GroupWise, you must accomplish the following steps:

1. **Create an external foreign domain for the Exchange organization**   By default, Connector for Novell GroupWise requires you to configure an external foreign domain for Exchange, and then link this domain to Novell GroupWise API Gateway. However, if you want to use Novell GroupWise Internet Agent instead of GroupWise API Gateway for message transfer, you must define an Internet domain name in the properties of the external foreign domain. Defining the Internet domain name causes Novell GroupWise to route all messages to this domain through the GroupWise Internet Agent.

Unfortunately, however, you cannot include the actual SMTP address information directly into directory synchronization with Novell GroupWise because GroupWise API Gateway requires address information to be in Group-Wise format. To tackle this issue, you can define a preferred address format for the external foreign domain in GroupWise so that you know exactly how GroupWise generates the SMTP addresses for Exchange users. For example, you can set the preferred address format for the external foreign domain in Group-Wise to *UserID@Internet domain name*. The *UserID* corresponds to the user part in the GroupWise address, such as Pilar in Exchange.First Administrative Group.Pilar. If the *Internet domain name* of the external foreign domain is set to tailspintoys.com, GroupWise will assume an Internet address of Pilar@tail-spintoys.com. To ensure that your Exchange users have GWISE and an SMTP addresses with matching user identifiers, you should also configure matching address generation rules in a recipient policy in Exchange System Manager. Make sure you use the same placeholders. For example, the rules `GWISE: Exchange.First Administrative Group.&m` and `SMTP: %m@tailspintoys.com` result in GWISE and SMTP addresses with matching user identifiers.

On the Resource Kit CD   The document 03_Configuring SMTP Directory Synchronization with Novell GroupWise.doc in the \Companion Material\Chapter 05\SMTP Connector\GroupWise Connector SMTP DirSync folder on the companion CD demonstrates how to configure a recipient policy for matching user identifiers in GWISE and SMTP addresses.

2. **Edit the attribute mapping from Novell GroupWise to Exchange 2003 (Dxagwise\Mapgwise.tbl)**   The fact that GroupWise API Gateway cannot handle SMTP address information implies that there are no additional attributes to include into directory synchronization with Novell GroupWise. However, you must edit the Mapgwise.tbl file to change the *targetAddress* for mail-enabled recipient objects that you create in Active Directory for GroupWise users. Instead of a GWISE address, you must specify an SMTP address. For example, you can map the *UserID* (referenced through the *Object* attribute) to the *targetAddress* and append the *Internet domain name*, such as **@gwise.tailspintoys.com** (see the document 03_Configuring SMTP Directory Synchronization with Novell GroupWise.doc on the companion CD).

Synchronizing Directories Using LDAP

Most modern messaging systems include directory services that support LDAP, which is a simplified version of the X.500 Directory Access Protocol (DAP). For example,

Exchange 2003 relies on Active Directory and Active Directory supports LDAP. The current version of LDAP is defined in Request for Comments (RFC) 2251, RFC 3377, and others. As a widely accepted Internet standard, LDAP is an ideal choice for directory synchronization between Exchange 2003 and non-Exchange messaging systems. A key advantage of an LDAP-based directory synchronization solution is that you do not need to use proprietary APIs, such as Lotus Notes Client API or GroupWise API Gateway.

MIIS is a good example of a directory-integration system that includes numerous management agents connecting to LDAP-based directory servers such as Sun ONE (formerly known as Netscape/iPlanet) and Novell eDirectory. There is also an LDAP Interchange Format (LDIF) management agent that you can use to integrate almost any LDAP system capable of importing and exporting LDIF files. However, MIIS is more than a simple directory synchronization tool. It is a full-featured identity integration system, and the costs to implement this system warrant its use only in situations in which directories coexist for an extended period of time or permanently. MIIS is discussed in Chapter 3 "Exchange Server 2003 in Enterprise Environments."

If you are planning to entirely replace an existing messaging system with Exchange 2003 in the next six to twelve months, you might want to use an alternative solution, such as CPS Systems SimpleSync version 4, Imanami Directory Transformation Manager, or HP LDAP Directory Synchronizer.

We have randomly selected CPS Systems SimpleSync as an example to synchronize directories using LDAP. SimpleSync normally uses LDAP to connect to a source directory and to write directory information into the destination directory. In the SimpleSync configuration, you specify source and destination directory, user account information to log on to these directories, and LDAP filters to select the directory objects to synchronize. Unlike MIIS, SimpleSync does not include an intermediary repository for directory information or a metaverse.

In SimpleSync, a particular connection synchronizes information only in one direction. To implement bidirectional directory synchronization, you must configure two SimpleSync connections reversing the source and destination directory. Remember, however, that you must exclude those recipient objects from synchronization that the opposite connection creates to avoid returning recipient objects back to their original directory. If you want to synchronize more than two directories, you can configure multiple SimpleSync connections. For example, you can use Active Directory to consolidate information from all LDAP directories, and then synchronize these directories in a hub-spoke arrangement.

Figure 5-12 illustrates a hub-spoke topology in an environment with Active Directory, Lotus Domino, Novell GroupWise, and Alt-N MDaemon. It should be noted that you must write-enable the LDAP interface in Lotus Domino to support synchronization from Active Directory to Domino. Novell GroupWise, on the other hand, does not provide an LDAP interface, but you can synchronize Active Directory with Novell NDS or Novell eDirectory. If you deploy Novell eDirectory, you can configure an association between GroupWise and eDirectory in Novell ConsoleOne so that e-mail addresses and other information match between the directories. If you do not install Novell eDirectory, you must manually update the mail attributes of your users in NDS. Other LDAP directories, such as Alt-N MDaemon/LDaemon, might not support recipient objects for users in other messaging systems. In this situation, the only possible direction is unidirectional to Active Directory. For example, MDaemon users do not have a server-based address list that includes non-MDaemon users, but these users can configure an LDAP address book that connects to Active Directory to access the complete set of recipient information,

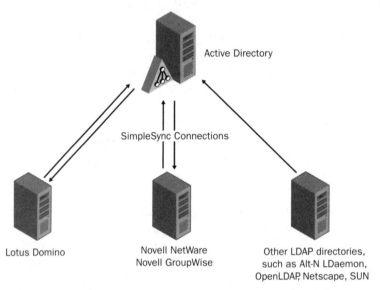

Figure 5-12   Synchronizing multiple directories through SimpleSync

On the Resource Kit CD   For step-by-step instructions to establish the configuration shown in Figure 5-12, see the worksheets in the \Companion Material\Chapter 05\SMTP Connector\SimpleSync folder on the companion CD.

Synchronizing Directories Using a Custom Solution

If budget constraints or other reasons prevent you from using a commercially available directory synchronization solution, you must synchronize directory information manually through Ldifde.exe and other tools or implement a custom solution based on ADSI and CDOEX. At a minimum, you should create recipient objects for all non-Exchange users in Active Directory so that you can use an Exchange 2003 bridgehead server as the SMTP gateway to the Internet, as discussed earlier. You should also implement a solution to synchronize the non-Exchange directory, if the non-Exchange system provides appropriate import and export capabilities or programming interfaces. For details about how to import directory information, contact the vendor of your non-Exchange messaging system. An alternative is to provide non-Exchange users with access to Active Directory so that these users can access complete address lists through an LDAP address book, as discussed for MDaemon users above.

Extracting Source Directory Information

The first step in performing manual directory synchronization is to obtain the source information that you want to transfer into Active Directory. One way to obtain directory information is to use directory export features included in the administrative tools of the non-Exchange messaging system. Another way is to use an LDAP-based tool, such as Exchange Migration Wizard, to extract the information, provided the non-Exchange system supports LDAP.

If you are planning to use Exchange Migration Wizard, you must remember that the Exchange Migration Wizard expects user accounts to have an object class of inetOrgPerson. If your LDAP directory uses another object class, the migration wizard cannot identify the user accounts unless you edit a file named mlmigad.ini, located in the \Program Files\Exchsrvr\Bin directory, and specify the object class of the user account in the ADSI_*ObjectClass* line. For example, Active Directory uses an object class of organizationalPerson for user accounts. Table 5-13 lists all settings that you can specify in an mlmigad.ini file.

Table 5-13   Mlmigad.ini Configuration Parameters

Parameter	Default value	Required	Description
ADSI_ObjectClass	inetOrgPerson	yes	Used to determine which objects are mail users.
ADSI_UserID	uid	yes	When extracting LDAP information for a subsequent migration of IMAP4 mailboxes, this parameter is used by the IMAP extractor to log on to the IMAP mailbox. This is a required attribute.
ADSI_MailServer	mailhost	yes	When extracting LDAP information for a subsequent migration of IMAP4 mailboxes, this parameter is used by the IMAP extractor to log on to the IMAP mailbox. This is a required attribute.

Table 5-13 Mlmigad.ini Configuration Parameters (Continued)

Parameter	Default value	Required	Description
ADSI_EmailAddress	mail	yes	When extracting LDAP information for a subsequent migration of IMAP4 mailboxes, this parameter is used as a secondary proxy address in Exchange.
			Mail sent to this address is routed to the Exchange mailbox. This is a required attribute.
ADSI_FullName	not specified	no	Used to create a display name in Exchange. If this is left blank, the display name is created from other attributes, such as the e-mail address. This is an optional attribute.
ADSI_FirstName	givenname	no	The user's first name. This is an optional attribute.
ADSI_LastName	sn	no	The user's last name. This is an optional attribute.
ADSI_Initials	initials	no	The user's middle initial(s). This is an optional attribute.
ADSI_NickName	uid	no	The user's short name, also used for the Exchange alias. This is an optional attribute.
ADSI_Title	title	no	The user's title. This is an optional attribute.
ADSI_Company	not specified	no	The user's company name. This is an optional attribute.
ADSI_Department	ou	no	The user's department name. This is an optional attribute.
ADSI_Office	roomnumber	no	The location of this user's office. This is an optional attribute.

Table 5-13   Mlmigad.ini Configuration Parameters (Continued)

Parameter	Default value	Required	Description
ADSI_PostalAddress	*postaladdress*	no	The user's postal address. This is an optional attribute.
ADSI_City	*l*	no	The user's city. This is an optional attribute.
ADSI_StateOrProvince	*st*	no	The user's state or province. This is an optional attribute.
ADSI_PostalCode	*postalcode*	no	The user's postal code. This is an optional attribute.
ADSI_Country	*not specified*	no	The user's country. This is an optional attribute.
ADSI_TelephoneNumber	*telephonenumber*	no	The user's business telephone number. This is an optional attribute.
ADSI_TelephoneNumber2	*not specified*	No	The user's second business telephone number. This is an optional attribute.
ADSI_TelephoneHome	*homephone*	no	The user's home telephone number. This is an optional attribute.
ADSI_TelephoneHome2	*not specified*	no	The user's second home telephone number. This is an optional attribute.
ADSI_TelephoneMobile	*mobile*	no	The user's mobile telephone number. This is an optional attribute.
ADSI_TelephonePager	*pager*	no	The telephone number of the user's pager. This is an optional attribute.
ADSI_TelephoneFax	*facsimiletelephonenumber*	no	The telephone number of the user's fax machine. This is an optional attribute.
ADSI_AssistantName	*secretary*	no	The name of the user's assistant. This is an optional attribute.
ADSI_AssistantPhone	*not specified*	no	The telephone number of the user's assistant. This is an optional attribute.

Table 5-13 Mlmigad.ini Configuration Parameters (Continued)

Parameter	Default value	Required	Description
ADSI_AlternateAddress	*mailalternateaddress*	no	Used as an additional SMTP address for the user in Exchange. This is an optional attribute.
ADSI_Comment	*description*	no	The comment for this user. This is an optional attribute.

On the Resource Kit CD You can find several customized mlmigad.ini files in the \Companion Material\Chapter 05\Mlmigad Examples folder on the companion CD. You can use these files to extract directory information from various sources, such as Active Directory, Lotus Domino, and Novell Group-Wise. For step-by-step instructions to use Exchange Migration Wizard to extract LDAP directory information, also see the documents in the \Companion Material\Chapter 05\SMTP Connector\Exchange Migration Wizard Sync folder on the companion CD.

Preparing and Importing Data into Active Directory

Exchange Migration Wizard extracts directory information into a primary migration file named Directory.pri. This is a comma-separated value (csv) text file that you cannot import directly into Active Directory without further processing. The tool that you use to import directory information into Active Directory determines how you must structure the data. If you want to use LDIFDE.exe, for example, you must convert the csv format into LDIF. LDIF is defined in RFC 2849.

The following LDIF listing shows how to create a mail-enabled contact object in Active Directory using LDIFDE.exe:

```
dn: cn=Pilar Ackerman,CN=USERS,DC=TAILSPINTOYS,DC=COM
changetype: add
objectClass: contact
cn: Pilar Ackerman
targetAddress: SMTP:Pilar@tailspintoys.com
mail: SMTP:Pilar@tailspintoys.com
displayName: Pilar Ackerman
givenName: Pilar
sn: Ackerman
proxyAddresses: SMTP:Pilar@tailspintoys.com
mailNickname: Pilar
```

On the Resource Kit CD   The document 06_Converting PRI into LDIF files and importing contacts into Active Directory.doc in the \Companion Material\Chapter 05\SMTP Connector\Exchange Migration Wizard Sync folder on the companion CD demonstrates how to convert Directory.pri files into LDIF files and how to use LDIFDE.exe to import recipient objects for non-Exchange users into Active Directory.

Maintaining Recipient Objects with LDIFDE

After directory information is imported into Active Directory, you must also ensure that directory information is kept up-to-date in both directories. For example, if you change or delete a user in the non-Exchange system, the corresponding recipient object must also be updated or deleted in Active Directory. Changing or deleting an existing recipient object requires that you find the existing object in Active Directory, and then perform the update.

The following LDIF listing shows how to update an existing mail-enabled contact object in Active Directory with new e-mail address information:

```
dn: cn=Pilar Ackerman,CN=USERS,DC=TAILSPINTOYS,DC=COM
changetype: modify
replace: targetAddress
targetAddress: SMTP:Pilar@nonExchange.tailspintoys.com
-
replace: mail
mail: SMTP:Pilar@nonExchange.tailspintoys.com
-
replace: proxyAddresses
proxyAddresses: SMTP:Pilar@nonExchange.tailspintoys.com
-
replace: proxyAddresses
proxyAddresses: smtp:pilar@tailspintoys.com
-
```

If you want to delete this mail-enabled contact object from Active Directory instead, use the following lines:

```
dn: cn=Pilar Ackerman,CN=USERS,DC=TAILSPINTOYS,DC=COM
changetype: delete
```

Identifying Required Import Operations

To identify the import operation for a particular recipient, such as creating, updating, or deleting the recipient object in Active Directory, you must keep track of those recipient objects that you have already imported during a previous synchronization cycle. The easiest way to do this is to preserve the old .pri file. By comparing the old with the current .pri file, you can determine the required import operation according to the following criteria:

- **Objects that exist in the current .pri file but not the previous .pri file**
These are recipients that have been added to the non-Exchange directory since the last import into Active Directory. You must create the recipient objects in Active Directory. For non-Exchange users, you can create the following types of user accounts in Active Directory:

    - **Disabled Windows user accounts**   Create disabled Windows user accounts if your non-Exchange users are not in your Active Directory environment yet, but will be after migration to Exchange 2003.

    - **Enabled Windows user accounts**   Create enabled Windows accounts for non-Exchange users who work in your Active Directory environment prior to migration.

    - **Windows contacts**   Create Windows contacts for non-Exchange users who are not in your Active Directory environment. The Exchange Migration Wizard can convert these contact objects to user accounts during the migration process.

- **Identical objects that exist in both .pri files**   These are recipients that have been previously imported into Active Directory and that have not been changed since that import. No action is necessary.

- **Objects that exist in both .pri files but are not identical**   These are recipients that have been previously imported into Active Directory and that have been changed in the non-Exchange directory since that import. You must update the recipient objects in Active Directory.

> **Note**   The custom solution discussed in this section performs a unidirectional import operation. It is assumed that you do not change imported recipient objects in Active Directory. The non-Exchange messaging system is still considered the authoritative system for these recipient objects.

- **Objects that exist in the previous but not in the current .pri file**   These are recipients that have been deleted in the non-Exchange directory since the last import into Active Directory. You must delete the recipient objects in Active Directory.

On the Resource Kit CD   The script PRI2LDIF.wsf in the \Companion Material\Chapter 05\Scripts folder on the companion CD uses this logic to convert .pri files to LDIF files. The script creates LDIF files to import recipients as mail-enabled contacts. The document 06_Converting PRI into LDIF files and importing contacts into Active Directory.doc in the \Companion Material\Chapter 05\SMTP Connector\Exchange Migration Wizard Sync folder on the companion CD shows how to use this script.

If you have not preserved the old .pri file, you must search Active Directory to find all those recipients that have been imported in a previous synchronization cycle. You can use the e-mail address of the recipient object to locate its counterpart in Active Directory because the primary e-mail address of the Active Directory object is the SMTP address of the recipient in the non-Exchange messaging system. However, you must account for situations in which e-mail addresses do not match. The user's original e-mail address might have changed (for example, a user is given a new SMTP address in the non-Exchange messaging system). In this situation, matching e-mail addresses does not work, and you must use additional attributes to find the matching recipient object. You can use the common name, display name, or alias of the user in the non-Exchange system or any other attribute that allows you to establish a reliable association between the source and target recipient objects.

However, finding a target object in Active Directory is complicated when the source object has been deleted from the non-Exchange messaging system. The deleted source object no longer exists, so it cannot be used as a reference to locate a corresponding counterpart in Active Directory. If you do not know specifically which objects were deleted, you must compare the complete address list from the non-Exchange messaging system with the complete list of corresponding recipient objects in Active Directory to determine which objects you must delete from Active Directory. You might be able to use the SMTP domain name of the non-Exchange messaging system to associate the recipient objects that you create in Active Directory with their non-Exchange messaging system. Another option is to use an organizational unit exclusively for the recipient objects that belong to a specific legacy messaging system. You can then compare the objects in that organizational unit to the list of recipients in the non-Exchange system. A third, and perhaps the most reliable way to compare address lists, is to write specific information about the home messaging system into an attribute of the recipient objects in Active Directory. You can then use this attribute as the basis for an LDAP query. You can either use an extension attribute or the attribute named *importedFrom* to register your specific synchronization information. For example, the PRI2LDIF.wsf script sets the *importedFrom* attribute to a value of PRI2LDIF. You can then use the following command to export all recipient objects that you created using PRI2LDIF.wsf and LDIFDE.exe into an LDIF file named pri2ldif.ldf: **ldifde -f pri2ldif.ldf -r "(importedFrom=PRI2LDIF)"**.

Implementing Calendar Interoperability

Messaging clients, such as Outlook, Lotus Notes, and Novell GroupWise, include a calendaring component that users can use to schedule appointments and plan meetings. A meeting is an appointment with multiple attendees. When an organizer invites other users to a meeting, a meeting request message is generated and sent to the invitees so that the invitees can accept or decline the invitation. Connector for Lotus Notes and Connector for Novell GroupWise can convert meeting request messages. Modern messaging clients, such as Outlook, Outlook Web Access, and Lotus Notes, also support the iCalendar standard so that meeting requests can be transferred over SMTP and the Internet. The iCalendar standard is defined in RFC 2445.

Figure 5-13 shows a meeting invitation that an Exchange user has sent to a Lotus Notes user over SMTP. Collaboration is seamless because both clients adhere to the iCalendar standard.

Figure 5-13   Inviting a Lotus Notes user to a meeting

Note   Non-Exchange messaging clients that do not support the iCalendar standard, such as Novell GroupWise, will display a plain-text version of the meeting request. Non-Exchange users must then book the meeting manually. Alternately, these users can use Outlook with an appropriate transport driver for calendaring.

To facilitate the planning of meetings, you must ensure that users can see when other users are available without having to open the other user's calendar. In Exchange, the availability information is stored in the form of free/busy items in a system folder (a hidden public folder) named SCHEDULE+ FREE BUSY. Each Exchange user has an individual free/busy item. You can display the free/busy items in Outlook Web Access if you access the SCHEDULE+ FREE BUSY folder in the non-IPM public folder subtree (that is, http://*<Exchange server name>*/public/non_ipm_subtree/ SCHEDULE+ FREE BUSY). A subfolder exists for each administrative group in the Exchange organization.

Outlook and Outlook Web Access write your free/busy items in the background when you create appointments, and these clients also read free/busy items for all specified attendees in a meeting request if you click on the Availability tab. Free/busy information does not enable you to see the details of a particular user's appointments, but you can determine available time slots so that you can pick a time for the meeting that likely suits all attendees. To provide free/busy information from non-Exchange users, you must create a free/busy item for each non-Exchange user in the SCHEDULE+ FREE BUSY folder.

Synchronizing Free/Busy Information Using Calendar Connector

Exchange 2003 includes Microsoft Exchange Calendar Connector for the purpose of synchronizing free/busy information with Lotus Notes and Novell GroupWise. Although the specific components vary between Lotus Notes and Novell GroupWise, the process that is used to synchronize free/busy information is similar for both messaging systems.

Note   Calendar Connector requires Connector for Lotus Notes or Connector for Novell GroupWise to be installed on the same server or on another Exchange server in the same administrative group.

The following describes the process that occurs when an Exchange 2003 user queries the free/busy information for a user on either Lotus Notes or Novell GroupWise:

1. Calendar Connector monitors the SCHEDULE+ FREE BUSY folder on the server on which Calendar Connector is installed. When an Exchange user queries another user's free/busy information, Calendar Connector intercepts the request.

2. If the free/busy information was updated for the requested user within a pre-configured period of time, Calendar Connector returns the information to the user who is requesting it. Otherwise, Calendar Connector requests updated free/busy information from the server that is running Lotus Notes or Novell GroupWise. The request uses programmable interfaces specific to the non-Exchange messaging system. If Calendar Connector does not receive a response in time, it returns the information currently stored in the SCHEDULE+ FREE BUSY public folder.

3. Through the programmable interfaces, Calendar Connector activates the scheduling component on the non-Exchange messaging system to locate the calendar information for local users. The scheduling component returns the free/busy information to the appropriate programmable interface.

4. Calendar Connector receives the free/busy information and translates it into Exchange format. Calendar Connector then adds the free/busy information to the user's free/busy item in the SCHEDULE+ FREE BUSY folder and sends the updated information to the Exchange 2003 user who requested it.

The following is a description of the process that occurs when a user on the non-Exchange messaging system queries the calendar information for an Exchange 2003 user:

1. When a non-Exchange user queries an Exchange user's free/busy information, the request is sent to the non-Exchange calendaring component.

2. The non-Exchange calendaring component detects that the requested information is located on a remote server or post office, and forwards the request to that system.

3. Because the remote server or post office is actually an Exchange 2003 server, Calendar Connector intercepts the request for calendar information.

4. Calendar Connector processes the request, checks the SCHEDULE+ FREE BUSY public folder for the requested free/busy information, and returns the response to the non-Exchange messaging system.

5. The information is translated into the appropriate format and provided to the user who requested the information.

On the Resource Kit CD   For step-by-step instructions to install Calendar Connector to synchronize free/busy information with Lotus Notes, see the document 03_Installing and Configuring Calendar Connector.doc in the \Companion Material\Chapter 05\Connector for Lotus Notes folder on the companion CD. For step-by-step instructions to install Calendar Connector to synchronize free/busy information with Novell GroupWise, see the document 03_Installing and Configuring Calendar Connector in a Novell Group-Wise Environment.doc in the \Companion Material\Chapter 05\Connector for Novell GroupWise folder on the companion CD.

More Info   For detailed information about the architecture and limitations of Calendar Connector, see the "Exchange Server 2003 Interoperability and Migration Guide" (*http://www.microsoft.com/technet/prodtechnol/ exchange/2003/library/interopmig.mspx*).

Supported Calendar Synchronization Implementations

Exchange supports the following implementation scenarios:

- A single Calendar Connector with a single connection to a Lotus Domino domain or Novell GroupWise organization

- A single Calendar Connector, in a single routing group, with separate connections to each Lotus Domino domain or Novell GroupWise organization

- Multiple administrative groups, each with its own Calendar Connector, connected to the same Lotus Domino domain or Novell GroupWise organization

- A single Calendar Connector that queries users on an upstream domain

  Exchange does not support the following implementation scenarios:

- Multiple Calendar Connectors within a single administrative group connected to the same Lotus Domino domain or Novell GroupWise organization

- Free/busy switching or querying from one coexistence partner to another using Exchange as a backbone

- Lotus Domino or Novell GroupWise as a backbone between two Exchange systems

Synchronizing Free/Busy Information Using iCalendar Interoperability

Calendar Connector is not available for non-Exchange messaging systems other than Lotus Notes or Novell GroupWise when connected to the Exchange 2003 organization through Connector for Lotus Notes or Connector for Novell GroupWise. In other words, if you are migrating from another system, such as an Internet-based messaging host, you cannot synchronize free/busy information using components included in Exchange 2003. However, you can work around this limitation by using the free/busy publishing feature of Microsoft Office Outlook 2003. Outlook users can use this feature to publish free/busy information in a shared location in the internal network so that other users, who otherwise would not have access to the information, can retrieve it. You can use a Web server on the intranet, an internal File Transfer Protocol (FTP) server, or a file server to provide the shared repository. The only difference among these options is the Uniform Resource Locator (URL) that you must specify in your Outlook configuration for the location where free/busy information should be published. You can use any valid URL format, such as: *http://*, *file://*, or *ftp://*.

> **On the Resource Kit CD**   Novell GroupWise and Lotus Notes users can participate in free/busy publishing if they use Outlook in an IMAP4 or POP3 configuration to access their GroupWise or Domino server. For more information, see the documents 06_Configuring Outlook for POP3 access to Lotus Domino.doc and 07_Configuring Outlook for POP3 access to Novell GroupWise.doc in the \Companion Material\Chapter 05\FreeBusy Integration folder on the companion CD.

Figure 5-14 illustrates how POP3 and IMAP4 users connecting to different messaging systems can share their free/busy information in Outlook.

Publishing free/busy information works well if all users work with Outlook in an Internet mail configuration. Other messaging clients might also support publishing free/busy information, because this feature is based on the iCalendar standard and VFREEBUSY components as defined in RFC 2446. VFREEBUSY is an emerging standard for requesting, publishing, and replying free/busy information. However, Microsoft does not support publishing free/busy information if you use Outlook with the MAPI transport service for Exchange. If you enable free/busy publishing in an Exchange configuration, Outlook will continue to use the SCHEDULE+ FREE BUSY system folder for all Exchange recipients that are in the server-based address lists and will not check a shared free/busy location on another server. Exchange recipients include all Exchange users and also all non-Exchange recipients that you synchronized with Active Directory.

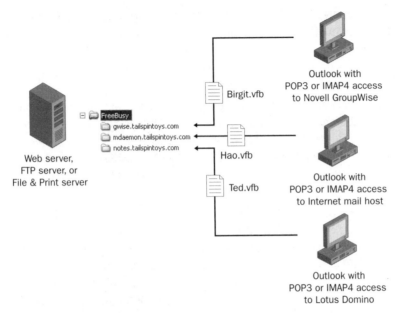

Figure 5-14   Free/busy publishing with Outlook

Note   Microsoft supports the free/busy publishing feature only when Outlook is configured for the Internet Mail Only mode.

Importing Free/Busy Information into Exchange 2003

To provide non-Exchange free/busy information to Exchange users working with Outlook in an Exchange configuration or with Outlook Web Access, you must import the VFREEBUSY information from the shared repository into the SCHEDULE+ FREE BUSY system folder. This requires you to create an individual free/busy item for each non-Exchange recipient. Because the location and subject of a free/busy item corresponds to the recipient's legacyExchangeDN, you must ensure that a recipient object exists for each non-Exchange recipient in Active Directory. Otherwise, Exchange users cannot locate the free/busy item.

To give an example, assume that the Lotus Notes user Ted Bremer has a mail-enabled contact object in Active Directory with a legacyExchangeDN of /o=Tailspin Toys/ou=First Administrative Group/cn=Recipients/cn=tbremer. Provided that SERVER01 hosts the SCHEDULE+ FREE BUSY folder, this legacyExchangeDN translates into the following URL for Ted's free/busy item: *http://SERVER01/public/NON_IPM_SUBTREE/ SCHEDULE+ FREE BUSY/EX:_xF8FF_o=TAILSPIN TOYS_xF8FF_ou=FIRST ADMINIS-TRATIVE GROUP/USER-_xF8FF_cn=RECIPIENTS_xF8FF_cn=TBREMER.EML.* The string "_xF8FF_" is the URI-encoded form of a forward slash ("/") when it is not used as a path separator. In this URL, organization and administrative group name are part of the folder name that contains the free/busy item, and recipient container and user name are part of the free/busy item's subject.

> **Note**   You can display all free/busy items of an administrative group in Outlook Web Access if you specify the folder URL without the USER part, such as: *http://SERVER01/public/NON_IPM_SUBTREE/SCHEDULE+ FREE BUSY/ EX:_xF8FF_o=TAILSPIN TOYS_XF8FF_OU=FIRST ADMINISTRATIVE GROUP/*.

Although you can open free/busy items directly in Outlook Web Access, it is not possible to read or write free/busy information because this information is not stored in VFREEBUSY format in the message body. Exchange free/busy items contain extended MAPI properties that store free/busy data in binary form, and these properties are not exposed in Outlook Web Access. To import free/busy information from .vfb files, you must use a tool that is aware of the Exchange free/busy MAPI properties, such as the VFREEBUSY Import service in the \Companion Material\Chapter 05\FreeBusy Integration\vFreeBusy Service folder on the companion CD.

> **On the Resource Kit CD**   For step-by-step instructions to setup and configure the VFREEBUSY Import service, see the documents in the \Companion Material\Chapter 05\FreeBusy Integration folder on the companion CD.

Providing Free/Busy Information to Non-Exchange Users

Importing free/busy information into Exchange provides Exchange users with the desired information, but non-Exchange users still have no way to check the availability of Exchange users when planning meetings. One way to address this issue is to develop a custom tool that exports free/busy information of Exchange users into .vfb files. This is not a very complex task because Exchange readily provides this information formatted in XML. You have only to process the information and place it into appropriate .vfb files in the FreeBusy share. For example, the following URL returns free/busy times for Administrator and Pilar in the month of October 2004: *http://server01/public/ ?Cmd=freebusy&start=2004-10-01T00:00:00Z&end=2004-11-01T00:00:00Z&interval=60&u=SMTP:Administrator@tailspintoys.com&u=Pilar@tailspintoys.com.*

Perhaps a better solution is to implement an ASP.NET application that directly returns the free/busy information in a format that Outlook is able to understand—VFREEBUSY. Because you have imported free/busy information for non-Exchange users into Exchange, users can use this ASP.NET application as a central search location for Exchange and non-Exchange VFREEBUSY items. Among other things, this frees you from having to grant non-Exchange users Read permissions to the FreeBusy share. Having Read and Write permissions enables users to misuse the FreeBusy share as a temporary file repository. Removing the Read permission prevents this misuse. Outlook does not require Read permissions to publish free/busy information.

Figure 5-15 illustrates a configuration in which non-Exchange users publish free/busy times using a Web, FTP, or file server. The VFREEBUSY Import service imports this information immediately into Exchange. Non-Exchange users can then use an ASP.NET solution that directly reads Exchange free/busy items and returns VFREEBUSY items to obtain free/busy information for Exchange and non-Exchange users. Exchange users can query Exchange free/busy items directly, as usual.

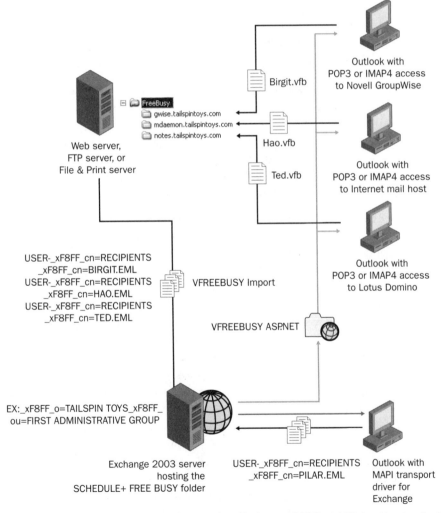

Figure 5-15   Free/busy integration based on Exchange 2003 and iCalendar standard

> **On the Resource Kit CD**   You can find a completed ASP.NET application that provides access to free/busy information on an Exchange server in VFREEBUSY format in the \Companion Material\Chapter 05\FreeBusy Integration\VFREEBUSY ASP.NET folder on the companion CD. See also the documents in the parent folder for installation and configuration instructions.

Implementing the iCalendar Interoperability Solution

You must complete the following steps to share free/busy information using Outlook, VFREEBUSY Import service, and VFREEBUSY ASP.NET application. For the purposes of this section, it is assumed that all non-Exchange and Exchange users work with Outlook 2003. For step-by-step instructions, see the documents in the \Companion Material\Chapter 05\FreeBusy Integration folder on the companion CD.

Complete the following steps to install the VFREEBUSY system:

1. **Create the FreeBusy share on a Web, FTP, or File server**   You can use the InitFbFolders tool in the \Companion Material\Chapter 05\FreeBusy Integration\InitFbFolders folder on the companion CD to initialize the folder structure as required by the VFREEBUSY Import service. The InitFbFolders tool queries Active Directory to determine the Internet domain names of any recipient objects in your global address lists. This tool creates a corresponding subfolder for each Internet domain in the FreeBusy share.

2. **Deploy VFREEBUSY Import service and VFREEBUSY ASP.NET application**   To install VFREEBUSY Import service and VFREEBUSY ASP.NET application use the Setup programs that come with these tools. It is not required to install these applications directly on an Exchange server or the server that hosts the FreeBusy share. The VFREEBUSY Import service uses a .NET FileSystemWatcher object to monitor the FreeBusy share on a file server. The FileSystemWatcher works locally and over the network. When a user publishes a .vfb file, the FileSystemWatcher object informs the VFREEBUSY Import service about this event. The VFREEBUSY Import service then parses the .vfb file, extracts the free/busy information, and imports it into the user's free/busy item in Exchange—provided that the user has a mail-enabled recipient object in Active Directory.

   The VFREEBUSY Import service and VFREEBUSY ASP.NET application communicate with Exchange 2003 through XML requests. However, these applications must send their XML requests directly to an Exchange server that has the free/busy item available locally. To check whether an Exchange server contains a replica of the free/busy system folder for the target administrative group, in Exchange System Manager, open the Folders container, right-click Public Folders, and then select View System Folders. Free/busy folders reside in the SCHEDULE+ FREE BUSY container. Display the properties of the system folder for your local administrative group, and switch to the Replication tab. Ensure that the public store of the Exchange server that you use with the VFREEBUSY Import service is listed in the list of stores.

> **Note**   You can specify an Exchange server that hosts the SCHEDULE+ FREE BUSY folder in the configuration of VFREEBUSY Import service and VFREEBUSY ASP.NET application.

3. **Configure Outlook to publish free/busy information**   To publish free/busy information, you must enable the option to publish and search for free/busy information at an internal location. You can find corresponding configuration options in Outlook by clicking Tools, clicking Options, clicking Calendar Options on the Preferences tab, and then clicking Free/Busy Options. Type the fully qualified path to the server in the text box that becomes available when you select the Publish At My Location option. You can specify the location in HTTP, FTP, or FILE URL format. If you are using an FTP server with Anonymous Login disabled, you must specify the user and password information in the FTP URL as follows:

ftp://User:Password@ftp.domain.com/<SMTP domain>/<SMTP alias>.vfb

User is the user name of the account and Password is the password associated with the account. SMTP domain corresponds to the user's SMTP domain name, and SMTP alias refers to the user's e-mail address within the SMTP domain. Because the name portion of an e-mail address is guaranteed to be unique within an SMTP domain, this way of organizing .vfb files prevents naming conflicts. Free/busy files typically have an extension of .vfb. If you want to use a different file name extension, you must adjust the -MSK parameter in the configuration of the VFREEBUSY Import service.

More Info   The VFREEBUSY Import service determines a user's SMTP address by combining the name of the .vfb file with the name of the parent folder. For example, if Ted Bremer has an e-mail address of Ted@notes.tail-spintoys.com, then Ted must publish his free/busy information using the location \notes.tailspintoys.com\Ted.vfb. If Ted specifies a different parent folder or file name, the VFREEBUSY Import service will not update Ted's free/busy item in Exchange. The VFREEBUSY Import service will update free/busy items only if the ORGANIZER address in the .vfb file matches the SMTP address generated by combining parent folder and file name (unless you set Extension Attribute 7 for a mail-enabled recipient in Active Directory to a value of "Allow Unknown Overwrite").

4. **Set the global free/busy search path in Outlook**   If all of your users have their free/busy information in Exchange 2003, you can set the search path for this information globally to the VFREEBUSY ASP.NET application. The VFREEBUSY ASP.NET application expects to find the SMTP address of a recipient that you want to look up in a QueryString parameter named *a*. You can specify the required information using the *%NAME%* and *%SERVER%* substitutions in the Search locations text box in the Free/Busy Options dialog box. For example, you can specify the URL *http://SERVER01/FREEBUSY/?a=%NAME%@%SERVER%*.

Tip   You can also set the search path specifically for each SMTP recipient, which is useful if the location of free/busy information varies by recipient. First, create a contact object for the recipient in your Contacts folder. You can then specify the path to that recipient's free/busy information in the Address text box in the Internet Free-Busy section on the Details tab.

Migrating Mailboxes to Exchange 2003

Having integrated Exchange and non-Exchange messaging systems in a seamless way, you are ready to move mailboxes and migrate users. One of the key migration tools that enables you to move mailboxes and data is Exchange Migration Wizard. This tool is installed together with Exchange System Manager on your Exchange 2003 server. Exchange Migration Wizard extracts user data from various messaging systems, and it converts folders, messages, and address books, where applicable. You can use Exchange Migration Wizard to connect to the non-Exchange messaging system, extract the user data into temporary migration files, and then connect to the target Exchange 2003 server to place the data into the corresponding mailboxes. The wizard can even create the mailboxes automatically for you during this process. You can complete the entire process in one step, or in two steps if you want to modify the migration files.

> **Note**   As a tool dedicated to extracting and importing data, the Exchange Migration Wizard is not designed to analyze security settings. Consequently, the wizard does not preserve delegate permissions to other mailboxes, Inbox rules, or other special configuration settings that are applied to individual mailboxes. Your users must apply their specific Inbox rules, views, access permissions, and so on to their new mailboxes in the Exchange 2003 organization.

Available Source Extractors

Source extractors connect to source mail systems and extract the data to save in a set of migration files. The Exchange Migration Wizard can use a variety of source extractors for several messaging systems, including Microsoft Mail for PC Networks, Lotus cc:Mail, Lotus Notes/Domino, Novell GroupWise, and IMAP4 hosts, as well as LDAP-conforming directories. You choose the source extractor that you want on the Migration Wizard page that appears when you click Next in the Welcome page of the wizard. Some source extractors might require additional software to be fully functional, such as the Lotus cc:Mail Export.exe tool, a Lotus Notes client, or a Novell GroupWise client installed on the local computer.

The following source extractors are available:

- **Lotus Notes and Lotus Domino**   The Exchange Migration Wizard supports Lotus Notes and Lotus Domino release 4.6 and 5.x, and with Microsoft Exchange Server 2003 Service Pack 1. Exchange Migration Wizard also supports Lotus Domino release 6 or later. For complete procedures with step-by-step instructions for migrating Lotus Notes and Domino users to Exchange 2003 using the Exchange Migration Wizard, see the document 04_Migrating from Lotus Domino to Exchange 2003.doc in the \Companion Material\Chapter 05\Connector for Lotus Notes folder on the companion CD.

- **Novell GroupWise**   Exchange Migration Wizard supports Novell GroupWise version 4.1 and later. However, Microsoft does not officially support interoperability with or migration from Novell GroupWise 6 or later because Novell does not provide Novell GroupWise API Gateway for versions higher than 4.1. Instead, Novell provides patches for Novell GroupWise API Gateway so that it works with higher Novell GroupWise versions as well. Microsoft cannot guarantee that Novell GroupWise API Gateway works reliably with GroupWise 6 or higher, but Microsoft Product Support Services (PSS) will offer "commercially reasonable effort" support. For complete procedures with step-by-step instructions for migrating Novell GroupWise users to Exchange 2003 using the Exchange Migration Wizard, see the document 04_Migrating from Novell GroupWise to Exchange Server 2003.doc in the \Companion Material\Chapter 05\Connector for Novell GroupWise folder on the companion CD.

- **Internet mail systems that support IMAP4**   The Exchange Migration Wizard supports IMAP4. For messaging connectivity, deploy an SMTP connector between Exchange 2003 and the Internet mail system. For complete procedures with step-by-step instructions for migrating Internet mail users to Exchange 2003 using the Exchange Migration Wizard, see the document 04_Migrating from an Internet Messaging System to Exchange 2003.doc in the \Companion Material\Chapter 05\SMTP Connector folder on the companion CD.

- **Microsoft Mail for PC Networks**   The Exchange Migration Wizard supports Microsoft Mail for PC Networks. However, a direct messaging connector is not available in Exchange Server 2003. You can use Microsoft Exchange Connector for Microsoft Mail if you are running an earlier version of Exchange in your organization, such as Microsoft Exchange 2000 Server. Connector for Microsoft Mail supports automated directory synchronization.

    For Exchange Server 2003 messaging connectivity, consider deploying a Microsoft Mail gateway to SMTP or a Microsoft Mail gateway to X.400. You can use the Exchange Migration Wizard to create a user list; however, the migration wizard will export Microsoft Mail for PC Networks address information, which you must replace with SMTP addresses before you import the recipients into Active Directory.

- **Microsoft Mail for AppleTalk Networks**   The Exchange Migration Wizard does not directly support Microsoft Mail for AppleTalk Networks or StarNine Technologies' Quarterdeck Mail. You must use the Microsoft Mail for AppleTalk source extractor to copy the data from Microsoft Mail for AppleTalk version 3.0 or later to migration files. You can then import these migration files to Exchange 2003 using the Exchange Migration Wizard.

- **Lotus cc:Mail**   The Exchange Migration Wizard supports the Lotus cc:Mail DB6 and DB8 formats. However, a direct messaging connector is not available in Exchange Server 2003. You can use Microsoft Exchange Connector for Lotus cc:Mail if you are running an earlier version of Exchange Server in your organization, such as Microsoft Exchange 2000 Server. Connector for Lotus cc:Mail supports automated directory synchronization.

    For Exchange 2003 messaging connectivity, consider using the built-in SMTP feature available in Lotus cc:Mail. You can use the Exchange Migration

Wizard to create a user list; however, the migration wizard will export Lotus cc:Mail address information, which you must replace with SMTP addresses before you import the recipients into Active Directory. Alternately, you can use the Import and Export tools that are included with Lotus cc:Mail for directory import and export operations.

- **IBM PROFS, IBM OfficeVision/VM, Fischer TAO, and other PROFS-based systems**   The Exchange Migration Wizard does not directly support host-based messaging systems, such as IBM PROFS. You must use the PROFS and OfficeVision/VM source extractor to copy the data from PROFS to migration files. You can then import these migration files to Exchange 2003 using the Exchange Migration Wizard. For messaging connectivity, consider using a host-based SMTP solution, such as TBS Software OfficePath/SMTP-Send (OP/SS), or an X.400 gateway. Alternately, you can use Microsoft Exchange Connector for IBM OfficeVision/VM, if you still have a server running the Enterprise edition of Microsoft Exchange Server 5.5 in your organization.

- **Verimation MEMO**   The Exchange Migration Wizard does not directly support Verimation MEMO. You must use the MEMO source extractor to copy the original MEMO documents to migration files. You can then import these migration files to Exchange 2003 using the Exchange Migration Wizard. For messaging connectivity, consider using a host-based SMTP solution, such as MEMO Integrator and MEMO SMTP Connector or MEMO/X400. Alternately, you can use Microsoft Exchange Connector for SNADS, if you still have a server that runs the Enterprise edition of Exchange Server 5.5 in your organization.

- **Digital All-In-1**   The Exchange Migration Wizard does not directly support Digital All-In-1. You must use the All-In-1 source extractor to copy the original documents to migration files. You can then import these migration files to Exchange 2003 using the Exchange Migration Wizard. For messaging connectivity based on SMTP or X.400, consider using Digital MAILbus 400.

Note   For detailed information about how to migrate from non-Exchange messaging systems using protocols other than IMAP4, consult the Exchange Migration Wizard documentation and the documentation for the source extractor that you want to use. To obtain a stand-alone source extractor for your legacy messaging system, contact Microsoft Product Support Services. For information about Product Support Services, including how to contact them, go to *http://support.microsoft.com.*

Migration Files

Exchange Migration Wizard uses its internal migration file importer component to inject messages, calendar information, and collaboration data into the selected Exchange store and recipient information into Active Directory. Although there are many different types of source extractors, there is only one migration file importer.

Migration files are .csv files and can be opened in a text editor or using Microsoft Excel. The Directory.pri file discussed earlier in this chapter in the context of directory synchronization is an example of such a migration file. You can edit the migration files before using Exchange Migration Wizard to import them into Active Directory and Exchange 2003. In this way, you can change mailbox aliases or generate first name and last name fields based on display names. You can also add additional information, such as telephone numbers, department names, and so on. Furthermore, you can delete all messages sent before a certain date.

The Exchange Migration Wizard migration file importer requires the following three types of files to accomplish a migration:

- **Packing list file**   This is used to identify the primary and secondary migration files, as required by the Exchange Migration Wizard to determine all primary and secondary files involved in the migration.

- **Primary files**   These include directory information as well as message headers and pointers to secondary files. There is one primary file, named directory.pri, containing the directory information for all users and their attributes, such as display name, alias, and e-mail addresses. There is also one primary file for each user that contains corresponding message header information, such as To, From, Cc, Subject, Date, and Time, and pointers to secondary files. Primary files for users are named in numbered sequence; for example, 00000001.pri, 00000002.pri, 00000003.pri, and so on.

- **Secondary files**   These contain raw data, such as message bodies, attachments, and so on.

> **Warning**   Do not edit secondary migration files. Changes to secondary files invalidate all offsets and pointers in the corresponding primary file. Editing primary migration files can also lead to incorrect data. Save a copy of the original migration files, and test your changes carefully before applying them in the production environment.

The Exchange Migration Wizard does not change or delete messages from the source mailboxes. The source mailboxes remain intact and continue to receive mail after you perform a migration. There is no option to delete old mailboxes automatically. You must reconfigure the message routing and decommission the legacy system.

Preparing for a User Migration

Perform the following steps to prepare the existing environment for a migration to Exchange 2003:

1. **Prepare a migration server**   We recommend that you configure a dedicated migration server to run the Exchange Migration Wizard. This computer must be able to communicate with the legacy messaging system, Active Directory, and Exchange 2003. Installing Exchange System Manager through the Exchange 2003 Setup program installs Exchange Migration Wizard on your migration server.

> **Note**   We recommend that you install multiple migration servers to distribute the workload. For example, you can use five migration servers to migrate 100 users and balance the load so that each migration server handles 20 users. Powerful hardware is not required for your migration servers.

2. **Prepare the user mailboxes**   It is a good idea to run any available mailbox maintenance tools on the non-Exchange messaging system that you want to migrate to eliminate inconsistencies in the messaging data. If you discover problems with individual mailboxes, you might need to run the maintenance tools more than once to repair the messaging data.

   In addition to running maintenance tools, you might want to perform the following tasks:

   - Delete mailboxes in the legacy messaging system for users that no longer exist in the environment.

   - Instruct users to delete old messages and calendar data to reduce the amount of data that must be migrated. Users should also flush their deleted items folders or wastebaskets.

   - Check the file system on which the messaging data resides to repair any problems on data volumes.

   - Ensure that the time on all servers across the network is consistent.

   - Delete old mail from all mail queues.

> **Note** You must be an Exchange Full Administrator in the target administrative group and an account administrator in the target Active Directory domain or organizational unit to import mail data and directory information.

Performing a Lotus Domino Migration to Exchange 2003

The following guidelines are recommended for most migrations from Lotus Domino to Exchange 2003, and consist of extracting data from the Lotus Domino server and immediately importing it into Exchange 2003.

> **On the Resource Kit CD** The following section is a conceptual discussion of configuration steps. For complete procedures with step-by-step instructions for migrating Lotus Domino/Notes users to Exchange 2003 using the Exchange Migration Wizard, see the document 04_Migrating from Lotus Domino to Exchange 2003.doc in the \Companion Material\Chapter 05\Connector for Lotus Notes folder on the companion CD.

A Lotus Domino to Exchange 2003 migration consists of the following steps:

1. **Grant access to users' mailboxes** To migrate data from Lotus Domino to Exchange 2003, the Exchange Migration Wizard requires access to the mailbox for each user who is migrated. By default, only the owner of the mailbox has access. Everyone else, including Lotus Domino administrators, is denied access. There are two ways for the user ID used by the Exchange Migration Wizard to gain access to users' mailboxes:

   - **Have users grant access to their mailboxes using Lotus Notes** The most direct way to gain access to a user's mailbox is for the user to grant it. Using their Lotus Notes clients, all users should grant access to the user ID used by Connector for Lotus Notes. Each user who migrates to Exchange should first perform the following procedure. In Lotus Notes, on the menu bar, click File, point to Database, and then click Access Control.

   - **Create a link from the local database to the Lotus Domino database** The second way to gain access to a user's mailbox is to establish a link to the Lotus Domino database from the local database, and then update the ACL on the user's mailbox through the link in Lotus Domino Administrator. For security reasons, you should delete the folder link after you update the ACLs on the users' mailboxes.

2. **Migrate data from Lotus Domino to Exchange 2003**   The next step in performing a migration from Lotus Domino to Exchange 2003 is to migrate the users and mailboxes from the Lotus Domino server to the Exchange 2003 server. You do this by running the Exchange Migration Wizard on an Exchange 2003 server with Lotus Notes installed (for example, the server you configured to run Connector for Lotus Notes). Before you start, ensure that the installation path for the Lotus Notes client on the Exchange 2003 server is in the system path. The Exchange Migration Wizard stops responding if the Lotus Notes installation path is not in the Windows system path.

Note   Stop the Connector for Lotus Notes service during migration to prevent directory synchronization from deleting Lotus Domino mailboxes before you verify that migration is successful. If a migration attempt ends unsuccessfully, delete any mailboxes and recipient objects created during the migration attempt from Active Directory. Restart the Connector for Lotus Notes, and perform a manual directory synchronization.

The Exchange Migration Wizard creates a mailbox-enabled Active Directory account for each user being migrated. All new user accounts are placed in the target organizational unit that you select on the Container For New Windows Accounts page. If accounts already exist in Active Directory, for example, because you created disabled Windows accounts for all Lotus Notes users through directory synchronization beforehand, you must verify that the accounts are matched correctly. You can associate the correct account using the Find Existing Account option on the Windows Account Creation And Association page. You can also create a new account, using the Create New Account option. For new accounts, the Exchange Migration Wizard can generate a random strong password, which is stored in the Accounts.Password file in the \Program Files\Exchsrvr\Bin directory on the Exchange 2003 server.

After migration is complete, review the application log for information about the migration progress. Look for event log messages, the source of which is MSExchangeMig. It might be helpful to configure and apply a filter in Event Viewer to list only those event log messages from the Exchange Migration Wizard.

3. **Migrate calendar information**   The Exchange Migration Wizard migrates calendar information by generating a SCHEDULE+ FREE BUSY public folder import file for each user. This file contains the user's schedule information. Users receive this file as an attachment to a new message in their Inboxes. Your users must manually import their schedule data.

Performing a Novell GroupWise Migration to Exchange 2003

The following guidelines are recommended for most migrations from Novell Group-Wise to Exchange 2003 and consist of extracting data from a Novell GroupWise post office and immediately importing it into Exchange 2003. We recommend that you configure a dedicated migration server rather than performing the migration through the connector server.

On the Resource Kit CD   The following section is a conceptual discussion of configuration steps. For step-by-step instructions for migrating Novell GroupWise users to Exchange 2003 using the Exchange Migration Wizard, see the document 04_Migrating from Novell GroupWise to Exchange Server 2003.doc in the \Companion Material\Chapter 05\Connector for Novell GroupWise folder on the companion CD.

Performing a Novell GroupWise to Exchange 2003 migration consists of the following steps:

1. **Set up a migration server for Novell GroupWise and Exchange 2003**   The computer that you use to run the Exchange Migration Wizard is generally referred to as a migration server. The migration server must be able to communicate with Novell GroupWise and Exchange 2003. To install the Exchange Migration Wizard on the migration server, run the Exchange 2003 Setup program and select the option to install Exchange System Manager. For best results with the Exchange Migration Wizard, use the following software versions on the migration server:

2. **GroupWise 5.2.5**   This recommendation pertains only to the migration server. GroupWise users can use the latest GroupWise client.

3. **Novell NetWare 4.8**   This recommendation pertains only to the migration server. Users can use the latest NDS client.

Note   We recommend that you install multiple migration servers to distribute the workload. For example, you can use five migration servers to migrate 100 users and balance the load so that each migration server handles 20 users. Powerful hardware is not required for your migration servers. You can use a workstation-type computer (a single-processor computer with 128 MB of RAM or more).

4. **Prepare the users' Novell GroupWise mailboxes** To migrate data from Novell GroupWise to Exchange 2003, the Exchange Migration Wizard requires access to the mailbox for each user who is migrated. By default, only the owner of the mailbox has access. Novell GroupWise users must grant proxy access to the GroupWise account that you are using to perform the migration. It is also a good idea to run the Novell GroupWise Check (GWCheck) tool on the Group-Wise accounts that you want to migrate to ensure that database inconsistencies are eliminated. The GWCheck tool is available from Novell. If you discover GroupWise database problems, you might have to run the GWCheck tool several times to repair a user's messaging database.

   If the GWCheck tool is unable to clear existing corruption, you might be able to solve the problem by creating a new Novell GroupWise post office in another location and moving the mailboxes that have problems into the new post office. This typically clears any corruption that is not resolved by the GWCheck tool. You can then migrate the users from the new post office to Exchange 2003 or move the users back to the old post office before migration.

   In addition to running the GWCheck tool, you might want to perform the following Novell GroupWise tasks:

   - Delete users that no longer exist from Novell GroupWise.

   - Run the Novell VREPAIR tool, available from Novell, to repair any problems on traditional Novell NetWare volumes.

   - Run the Novell Timesync tool, available from Novell, at the server console to ensure that the time on all servers across the network is consistent.

   - Clean all mail queues of old mail.

5. **Migrate data from Novell GroupWise to Exchange 2003** The next step in performing migration from Novell GroupWise to Exchange 2003 is to migrate the users and mailboxes from Novell GroupWise to the Exchange 2003 server. You do this by running the Exchange Migration Wizard on an Exchange 2003 server with Novell NetWare client and Novell GroupWise client installed (for example, the server that you configured to run Connector for Novell Group-Wise). The Exchange Migration Wizard uses the Novell GroupWise client API to access GroupWise mailboxes.

> **Note**   Stop the Connector for Novell GroupWise service during migration to prevent directory synchronization from propagating migrated Novell GroupWise accounts as Exchange 2003 mailboxes before you verify that your migration is successful. If a migration attempt ends unsuccessfully, delete any mailboxes and recipient objects created during the migration attempt from Active Directory. Restart Connector for Novell GroupWise and perform a manual directory synchronization to bring both messaging systems back in sync.

The Exchange Migration Wizard creates a mailbox-enabled Active Directory account for each user being migrated. All new user accounts are placed in the target organizational unit that you select on the Container For New Windows Accounts page. If accounts already exist in Active Directory, for example, because you created disabled Windows accounts for all Novell GroupWise users through directory synchronization beforehand, you must verify that the accounts are matched correctly. You can associate the correct account using the Find Existing Account option on the Windows Account Creation And Association page. You can also choose to create a new account using the Create New Account option. For new accounts, the Exchange Migration Wizard can generate a random strong password, which is stored in the Accounts.Password file in the \Program Files\Exchsrvr\Bin directory on the Exchange 2003 server.

After migration is complete, review the Application Log for information about the migration progress. Look for event log messages with the source MSExchangeMig. It might be helpful to configure and apply a filter in Event Viewer to list only those event log messages from the Exchange Migration Wizard.

6. **Migrate calendar information**   The Exchange Migration Wizard migrates calendar information by generating a SCHEDULE+ FREE BUSY public folder import file for each user. This file contains the user's schedule information. Users receive this file as an attachment to a new message in their Inboxes. Your users must manually import their schedule data.

Performing an Internet Mail Migration to Exchange 2003

The following guidelines are recommended for most migrations from Internet mail messaging systems to Exchange 2003 and consist of extracting data from the Internet mail host through IMAP4 and immediately importing it into Exchange 2003. You can migrate users from any messaging system that supports IMAP4, including Lotus Domino and Novell GroupWise. We recommend that you configure a dedicated migration server.

On the Resource Kit CD   The following section is a conceptual discussion of configuration steps. For step-by-step instructions for migrating Internet mail users to Exchange 2003 using the Exchange Migration Wizard, see the document 04_Migrating from an Internet Messaging System to Exchange 2003.doc in the \Companion Material\Chapter 05\SMTP Connector folder on the companion CD.

You must complete the following steps to perform an Internet mail to Exchange 2003 migration:

1. **Prepare an IMAP4 migration file for the Exchange Migration Wizard**   To migrate data from an Internet mail system to Exchange 2003, the Exchange Migration Wizard requires access to the mailbox of each user who is migrated. By default, only the owner of the mailbox has access, so you must specify each individual user name and password. You can provide this information during the migration process in a .csv file that contains information about the mailboxes being migrated, their SMTP addresses, as well as the user accounts and passwords to log on to each individual mailbox. The IMAP4 server where the mailbox resides can be specified through a fully qualified host name or IP address.

   Table 5-14 lists the possible fields for the IMAP4 user list file.

Table 5-14   IMAP4 User List Fields

Field	Description
IMAP_Mailbox	Internet Message Access Protocol version 4 (IMAP4) mailbox account name.
SMTP_Address	Exchange destination mailbox SMTP address. Optionally, you can provide the alias of the Exchange destination mailbox. If you do not add the destination mailbox alias, the Exchange Migration Wizard migrates the mail to the mailbox with the SMTP address that you specify.
IMAP_Server	The IMAP4 server name.
Ex_Mailbox	Exchange mailbox alias. If each user does not already have a mailbox in Exchange, the wizard creates one using the IMAP4 mailbox name and the SMTP address that you specify. This is an optional field.
IMAP_Port	IMAP port. You can specify an alternate TCP/IP port for the Exchange Migration Wizard to use to bind to the IMAP server. The default IMAP port is 143. If you do not add the optional IMAP port field to the user list file, the wizard will try to connect through port 143. This is an optional field.

Table 5-14   IMAP4 User List Fields (Continued)

Field	Description
IMAP_SSL	You can specify whether to encrypt the transmission of each user's mailbox contents using Secure Sockets Layer (SSL). By default, if the IMAP_SSL field is not in the user list file, information is not transmitted using SSL. This is an optional field that can have the following values: **Y, Yes, T, or True** The Exchange Migration Wizard uses SSL when transmitting the contents of that mailbox. **N, No, F, or False** The Exchange Migration Wizard does not use SSL.

Note   If you receive errors during an IMAP4 migration, check the user list file to verify that you have specified the correct IMAP4 server name and port number.

The following is an example of a .csv file for an IMAP4 migration:

```
IMAP_Mailbox,SMTP_Address,IMAP_Password,IMAP_Server
Ted,Ted@notes.tailspintoys.com,1qw$t9x,192.168.202.122
Hao,Hao@mdaemon.tailspintoys.com,1qw$t9x,192.168.202.123
Birgit,Birgit@gwise.tailspintoys.com,1qw$t9x,192.168.202.160
```

If you create this file, remember to include the header line, and remember that each line must have exactly four pieces of information, separated from each other by a comma. If, however, your Internet mail system also supports LDAP, you can perform an LDAP directory migration as a first step to automatically create a .csv file named Imapusr.csv, which Exchange Migration Wizard places in the migration files directory. After you edit this file to verify the account and server information, you are ready to approach the actual IMAP4 migration.

Note   When migrating from Internet mail systems to Exchange 2003, we recommend that you first create a user list file, named **Imapusr.csv**, using the Internet Directory component of the Exchange Migration Wizard.

2. **Migrate server-based data to Exchange 2003**   The next step in performing a migration from an Internet mail system to Exchange 2003 is to migrate the users and mailboxes from the Internet host to the server running Exchange 2003. You do this by running the Exchange Migration Wizard.

Table 5-15 lists the data elements that the Exchange Migration Wizard preserves during migration.

Table 5-15   Data Elements That Are Preserved in IMAP4 Migrations

Item	In Exchange
IMAP4-compliant mail messages	MAPI or HTML messages (for Microsoft Office Outlook Web Access).
Attachments	Attachments.
Calendar information	Plain text message.
Encrypted messages	Encrypted messages. Users must move their private keys and certificates to Outlook to be able to use Outlook to read migrated encrypted mail. Alternately, users can reconfigure the IMAP client that contains their certificates and keys so that they can read the encrypted mail from their Exchange mailboxes.

The Exchange Migration Wizard creates a mailbox-enabled Active Directory account for each user who is being migrated. All new user accounts are placed in the target organizational unit that you specify on the Container For New Windows Accounts page. If accounts already exist in Active Directory, for example because you created disabled Windows accounts for all Internet mail users through a semi-automated directory synchronization process beforehand, you must verify that the accounts are matched correctly. You can associate the accounts using the Find Existing Account option on the Windows Account Creation And Association page. You can also choose to create a new account using the Create New Account option. For new accounts, the Exchange Migration Wizard can generate a random strong password, which is stored in the Accounts.Password file in the \Program Files\Exchsrvr\Bin directory on the server running Exchange 2003.

After migration is complete, review the application log for information about the migration progress. Look for event log messages for which the source is MSExchangeMig. You might find it helpful to configure and apply a filter in Event Viewer to list only those event log messages from the Exchange Migration Wizard. If a migration attempt ends unsuccessfully, you can delete any mailboxes and recipient objects that were created during the migration attempt from Active Directory. Perform a manual directory synchronization to bring both messaging systems back in sync.

3. **Migrate local messaging data**   The Exchange Migration Wizard migrates only data stored on the IMAP4 server. Internet messaging clients, however, often store messaging data and calendar information locally. Data stored in local archives on client computers is not migrated. To migrate local data and calendar information, users must use Outlook to import the data after Exchange mailboxes have been created using the Exchange Migration Wizard. Outlook can

import local messaging data from Eudora Pro and Outlook Express. Outlook Express also provides a mail importer component for Netscape Communicator and Netscape Mail.

IMAP4 users can also place message items back into their server-based mailboxes prior to migration. However, this can greatly increase the amount of data that must be migrated if large amounts of e-mail data are stored on the users' workstations. You must ensure that your Internet mail system and Exchange 2003 server have sufficient disk space to store the data. If you are concerned that migrating local data will impede your migration process, you might want to consider migrating local data only for executives and employees with specific permission.

Note   After migration is complete, your users can create local personal folder store (.pst) files to store the e-mail data that was previously stored in local folders on the client computer.

4. **Migrate personal address books**   The Exchange Migration Wizard cannot migrate personal address books from Internet mail users. Users must migrate their personal address books after they connect to Exchange 2003 using Outlook. Outlook detects and silently imports information from supported messaging clients, such as Netscape Messenger 4.0 and Outlook Express. For unsupported clients, you might be able to use an address book converted in Outlook Express before you import the data into Outlook. Outlook Express supports a number of address book formats, including LDIF, Netscape Address Book, Netscape Communicate Address Book, and .csv files. If an address book converter is not available, you might be able to export personal address books from the old messaging client into text-based files that can be converted into .csv files using a macro in Microsoft Excel, for example. The main task is to reorder the fields to match the layout required by Outlook. Outlook is able to import Contact objects from a .csv file.

To determine the order of fields in a .csv file for Outlook, create a sample contact object in Outlook, and then export this contact into a .csv file using the Import and Export command on the File menu in Outlook 2003. Choose Export To A File, and then select Comma Separated Values (Windows). Select the Contacts folder where you created the sample contact, and complete the export procedure. Open the resulting .csv file in Excel. You should find the list of fields in the first row. The following is a list of all header fields that Outlook recognizes:

```
"Title","First Name","Middle Name","Last Name",
"Suffix","Company","Department","Job Title","Business Street",
```

```
"Business Street 2","Business Street 3","Business City",
"Business State","Business Postal Code","Business Country",
"Home Street","Home Street 2","Home Street 3","Home City","Home State","Home
Postal Code","Home Country","Other Street",
"Other Street 2","Other Street 3","Other City","Other State",
"Other Postal Code","Other Country","Assistant's Phone",
"Business Fax","Business Phone","Business Phone 2","Callback",
"Car Phone","Company Main Phone","Home Fax","Home Phone",
"Home Phone 2","ISDN","Mobile Phone","Other Fax","Other Phone",
"Pager","Primary Phone","Radio Phone","TTY/TDD Phone","Telex",
"Account","Anniversary","Assistant's Name","Billing Information",
"Birthday","Business Address PO Box","Categories","Children",
"Directory Server","E-mail Address","E-mail Type","E-mail Display Name",
"E-mail 2 Address","E-mail 2 Type","E-mail 2 Display Name",
"E-mail 3 Address","E-mail 3 Type","E-mail 3 Display Name","Gender","Government
ID Number","Hobby","Home Address PO Box",
"Initials","Internet Free Busy","Keywords","Language","Location",
"Manager's Name","Mileage","Notes","Office Location",
"Organizational ID Number","Other Address PO Box","Priority",
"Private","Profession","Referred By","Sensitivity","Spouse","User 1",
"User 2","User 3","User 4","Web Page"
```

> **Note** Users can recreate personal contacts, as well as personal distribution lists, in a Contacts folder in Outlook.

Best Practices

It is important to assess the existing messaging environment before migrating users and data so that you can identify interoperability and migration opportunities. At a minimum, you must decide whether to migrate in a single step or in multiple stages to Exchange Server 2003. Companies with a large number of users will find that it is best to migrate in multiple stages to control the pace of the migration and mitigate migration risks. There are also factors that might force you to coexistence long-term between messaging systems, for example, if you cannot migrate complex workgroup applications.

Migrating in multiple stages or long-term coexistence requires you to integrate the existing non-Exchange messaging system with the future Exchange 2003 organization in a way that enables non-migrated and migrated users to communicate with each other seamlessly. Seamless interoperability requires you to establish message transfer paths, directory synchronization, and calendar integration. The technologies and tools you choose to achieve seamless interoperability depend on the messaging system you are migrating from and your project budget.

If you are migrating from Lotus Notes and Lotus Domino or Novell GroupWise to Exchange 2003, you can use Connector for Lotus Notes or Connector for Novell GroupWise and Calendar Connector for seamless interoperability. If you use these components to provide connectivity, synchronize directories, and keep free/busy information updated, non-Exchange and Exchange users can communicate with each other as if they exist in the same messaging system. Users can send each other messages and meeting requests, can find each other in server-based address lists, and can check each other's free/busy information when planning meetings. However, Connector for Lotus Notes, Connector for Novell GroupWise, and Calendar Connector also have disadvantages. For example, these components depend on proprietary APIs, which limits their scope of use and increases the difficulty to implement and maintain these components.

An interoperability alternative to direct connector components is connectivity components based on widely accepted Internet standards, such as SMTP, LDAP, and iCalendar. Using SMTP, you can connect to any kind of modern non-Exchange messaging system. Implementing SMTP connectivity is a straightforward undertaking. Through LDAP, you can synchronize any modern directory with Active Directory to create mail-enabled recipient objects for non-Exchange users, and you can keep these objects updated. Both Microsoft and non-Microsoft tools are available to implement LDAP-based directory synchronization. Based on the iCalendar standard, Internet mail users can also share their free/busy information with each other in Outlook. It is possible to integrate an Exchange organization into the free/busy publishing system.

Having established seamless interoperability, you can move mailboxes and data to Exchange 2003. We recommend that you use Exchange Migration Wizard for this purpose. Exchange Migration Wizard supports a long list of messaging systems. Using a common messaging standard, such as IMAP4, you can also migrate mailboxes and data from messaging systems where a direct source extractor is not available. It is a good idea to prepare the non-Exchange messaging system prior to using Exchange Migration Wizard. For example, you should delete any outdated message items from the server and perform database maintenance to eliminate any corrupted items. You should also devise a solution to migrate data that users keep locally on their workstations.

During and after the migration, it is important to provide users with training and support. This is especially critical if your users have not worked with Outlook in the non-Exchange messaging system. It is a good idea to deploy Outlook as soon as possible so that users can familiarize themselves with their new messaging clients, and it is also a good idea to provide a specifically trained helpdesk specialist to deal with Outlook-related issues that might arise as users start using Outlook for messaging and personal information management.

Chapter 6

Server and Site Consolidation Strategies

About This Chapter

This chapter explains how to consolidate servers, sites, and Exchange organizations. Consolidation involves a movement of resources within an organization for more centralized control and less overhead. Consolidation can also involve the combination of separate systems and organizations into a single entity.

Understanding Consolidation Strategies

When consolidating sites, servers, Exchange organizations, and Exchange components, two types of consolidations to keep in mind are consolidations within an Exchange organization and consolidations of separate Exchange organizations. Each scenario is discussed in the following sections.

Consolidating Within an Exchange Organization

An Exchange organization can greatly benefit from consolidation. The goal of consolidation is to centralize operations and reduce the total cost of ownership (TCO) of the messaging infrastructure. Consolidation can take place on both a centralized administrative model, in which resources are managed from a single location, or a distributed administrative model, in which separate locations retain administrative control. Consolidation can provide benefits to an existing Exchange organization, as follows:

- **Lower expenses** Reducing the number of servers or sites reduces the expenses of procuring, managing, and maintaining the servers and sites.

- **Better use of existing resources** If an organization has a centralized data center with staff and centralized administration, consolidating servers and sites leverages the existing infrastructure and reduces overall cost. Centralized data centers often have very high service level agreements (SLAs) to ensure availability and performance. Combining resources into a centralized model leverages this advantage of a centralized data center.

- **Lower overhead** Consolidating servers and sites has the potential to decrease network traffic over low-bandwidth links. Exchange transfers mail, resolves recipients against Active Directory, routes incoming and outgoing mail, and performs other tasks that require network connectivity. If there is a high-bandwidth connection, such as one available in a centralized data center, the overhead is lower than with connections to remote sites that have low-bandwidth connections such as ISDN or frame relay.

Considerations

When you assess the existing messaging infrastructure or Exchange organization, it is important to consider the following:

- **Topology and environment** For an overview of the existing infrastructure, you should create a graphical schematic that includes routing and administrative groups, and defines geographic regions and sites.

- **Servers and functions** The domain controllers, global catalog servers, back-end and front-end servers, or servers that perform other functions, such as connecting messaging systems, should be documented. One way to do this is to assemble a list of computers and their roles along with the graphical schema of network topology.

- **Network connectivity** Bandwidth, link latencies, and reliability are important to consider, especially in remote sites. During migration, large amounts of data might need to be sent. It is best to schedule some tasks during off-peak hours for minimal disruption for users. You should also ensure that the new hardware can handle the consolidation. To do this, gather data about the load on existing servers and check it against the new hardware.

Figure 6-1 illustrates a recommended approach to identifying consolidation opportunities.

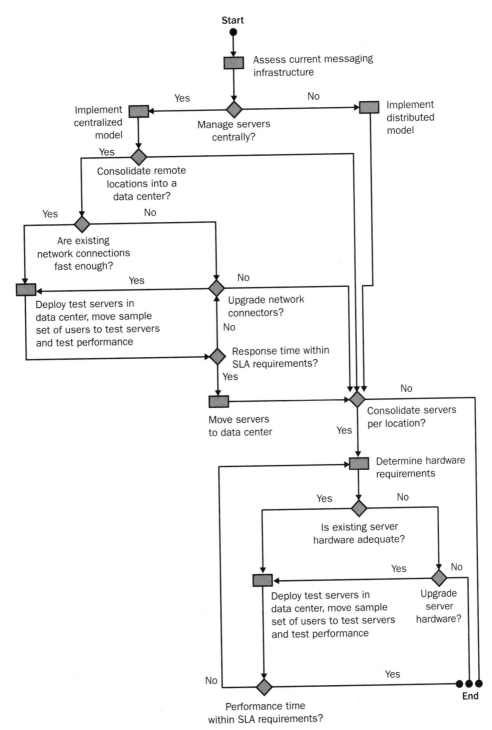

Figure 6-1   Determining server consolidation opportunities

In choosing an approach for consolidating, consider the following questions:

1. **Is it possible to implement a central administration model?**   You can implement a centralized administration model to reduce costs and overhead. Depending on the company needs and structure, a centralized administration might be the best solution. For example, if all business is done in one location, and if no business units have unique needs for separate messaging systems or for separate forests and segregated environments, then a centralized model can be used. This approach fosters easier server consolidation by having resources in one location. If you cannot implement a completely centralized administration, consider implementing a hybrid model in which a different Information Technology (IT) department is responsible for each individual geographical region in the organization. Each department is then centrally responsible for all those remote locations that belong to its assigned region. It might then be possible to consolidate servers into regional data centers.

2. **Is it possible to consolidate remote locations into a data center?**   Remote locations that fall under the same administrative authority are good candidates for site consolidation if sufficient network bandwidth is available to support client/server communication with acceptable response times. Outlook 2003 in Exchange cached mode can work over slow or unreliable network connections. However, you should conduct performance tests and pilot projects to determine whether the existing bandwidth is sufficient. An organization might have to upgrade network connections that cannot accommodate the workload or refrain from eliminating mailbox servers in regional offices.

3. **Is it possible to consolidate servers within each location?**   To identify servers that can be consolidated within a data center or geographical location, you must analyze the various tasks that the existing servers currently manage. Some server types are more eligible for an actual physical consolidation than others. For example, some servers might be responsible only for storing mailboxes (mailbox servers), while others might serve only the purpose of message transfer (bridgehead servers). You should consolidate mailbox servers, but it is not necessarily a good idea to consolidate bridgehead servers or Web servers onto mailbox servers in large organizations. Bridgehead servers and Web servers, due to their need for high network bandwidth, are more suited for server farms that are based on load-balancing technologies, such as Microsoft Application Center 2000.

4. **Is it necessary to replace the existing server hardware in order to manage the expected workload?**   After you identify the servers that can be consolidated, calculate the final number of users that each of these servers must support. Based on these figures, estimate each server's approximate workload to determine its hardware requirements.

Consider whether the existing server hardware can accommodate future demands. Reusing existing hardware might help to reduce costs.

> **Warning**   Do not upgrade existing Pentium Pro or Pentium II multi-processor computers to Windows Server 2003 and Exchange 2003. Intel discovered that an upgrade to Windows Server 2003 on servers that have two or more Pentium Pro or Pentium II processors might cause instability, data corruption, or other unpredictable results. Upgrading these platforms will force Windows Server 2003 into single-processor mode, which is a supported configuration. However, a single processor that is operating at 200 MHz is not a good choice for server consolidation.

When you consolidate onto fewer servers, consider replacing existing server hardware and storage technology. Table 6-1 lists basic processor and memory configuration recommendations for mailbox servers.

Table 6-1   Processor and Memory Configurations for Mailbox Servers

Number of users	CPUs	Memory
Fewer than 500	1 – 2	512 MB – 1 GB
500 – 1,000	2 – 4	1 GB – 2 GB
1,000 – 2,500	4 – 8	2 GB – 4 GB
2,500 or more	4 – 8	4 GB

5. **Is the server hardware correctly designed according to SLAs?**   You can use Exchange 2003 stress and performance tools on a test server to verify whether its hardware is designed to accommodate the number of mailboxes you want to place on the server. For example, you can use Load Simulator (LoadSim) (LoadSim.exe) to test how an Exchange 2003 server responds to a large number of Outlook 2003 clients. Another useful tool is JetStress (JetStress.exe), which you can use to simulate disk input/output (I/O) load to verify the performance and stability of your disk subsystem. You can download these tools from the "Exchange Server 2003 Tools" website (*http://go.microsoft.com/fwlink/ ?LinkId=23490*). To determine how many mailboxes Exchange 2003 servers of a given class can support, you might also want to read the performance benchmark studies at the "Performance and Scalability for Exchange Server 2003" website (*http://go.microsoft.com/fwlink/?LinkId=23430*). Another source of information on this topic is "Troubleshooting Exchange Server 2003 Performance" (*http://go.microsoft.com/fwlink/?LinkId=23454*).

Server Design Considerations

When designing Exchange servers to be used in a consolidation environment, consider the following factors:

- **Connected users versus total users**   Server use varies with the time of day. The beginning of the day might be a time of heavy use, as users log on to retrieve messages. Consider aspects like these when determining server specifications. For example, out of 3,000 users, the maximum number with concurrent connections might be 500. This scenario requirement might have lower requirements than a scenario in which 1000 users routinely connect out of 1500 users. Keep in mind that the server background activity increases as the number of mailboxes increases, even when users have not logged on to the system. For example, database defragmentation activity increases on a server storing thousands of mailboxes. Always consider background activities when you design server hardware.

- **Location and use of message stores**   Exchange users can store their messages in server-based mailboxes or in personal folders (.pst files) on their local client computers or on a network drive. Users can reduce a server's storage and processing workload by setting their default delivery locations for messages to their personal folders. For example, when a user opens or saves an item in a personal folder, the Microsoft Exchange Information Store service on the server is not involved. However, when you decide whether to use personal folders in this way, consider the fact that storing all messages in personal folder stores on local client computers makes it impossible to back up messages centrally.

- **User habits and messaging clients**   When you design server hardware, consider the number of messages users send and receive each day. Also consider the types of clients that they use. Outlook 2003 and Outlook Web Access 2003 place different workloads on a server. If your users primarily use Outlook Web Access 2003, assume additional processing requirements for Internet Information Services (IIS).

- **Public folder usage and replication**   Public folders can have a significant impact on server performance, depending on folder size, frequency of access, number of different views for each folder, number of replicas, replication schedule, and frequency of content changes. Place large public folder repositories on a dedicated Exchange server that does not store any user mailboxes. Exchange servers that store public folders are sometimes called public servers.

- **Connectors and gateways**   Connectors and gateways are messaging components that can substantially increase a server's workload. Message transfer involves server-to-server communication and might require message conversion. As mentioned previously, do not configure connectors or gateways on large mailbox servers. An organization can benefit from servers that are dedicated to message transfer. Another option is to migrate all messaging systems to Exchange 2003, thereby eliminating the need for messaging gateways.

Consolidating Servers

Server consolidation is the process of using fewer servers to accomplish the same task as before. Server consolidation involves having more mailboxes on back-end servers, and possibly reducing front-end and bridgehead servers. You might want to consolidate servers to reduce overhead or if the existing loads on a server do not justify having a dedicated server for the particular environment.

Organizations that deploy Exchange 2003 can achieve these objectives by using the following general strategies:

- **Consolidate multiple small servers on fewer large servers**   You can use Exchange 2003 to accommodate more users on each server than by using any previous version of Exchange, while maintaining usable backup windows. Exchange 2003 runs on Windows Server 2003 clusters with up to eight nodes. Backup agents can use the new Volume Shadow Copy service available in Windows Server 2003 to reduce the time required for Exchange 2003 backup operations. Exchange 2003 also features a Recovery Storage Group and a Mailbox Recovery Center. You can use the Recovery Storage Group to restore individual mailboxes from a database backup quickly and conveniently. The Mailbox Recovery Center, on the other hand, provides bulk reconnection of mailboxes to the appropriate users in Active Directory, which supports disaster recovery scenarios.

- **Physically move servers from multiple geographic locations to one central location**   This approach is often referred to as site consolidation and entails placing all servers in a data center. Outlook 2003 enables site consolidation in an Exchange 2003 organization. With over-the-wire MAPI compression and client-side caching in Cached Exchange Mode, Outlook 2003 is more resilient under unstable network conditions and requires less network bandwidth than any previous version of Outlook. Site consolidation helps to lower administrative overhead and makes it easier for information workers to access messaging resources when they work remotely.

- **Automate the maintenance of multiple servers using a reduced number of management interfaces**   This approach is sometimes referred to as virtual consolidation, which means managing multiple servers as one virtual server system. Individual servers may reside in a data center or in different geographic locations. Integration with Active Directory and new administration tools, such as Exchange 2003 Management Pack for Microsoft Operations Manager, are key catalysts for virtual consolidation in Exchange 2003 organizations. For example, Exchange Management Pack enables organizations to monitor the performance, availability, and security of all Exchange servers in the organization from a single Microsoft Operations Manager console or Web page.

Consolidating Sites

Site consolidation refers to the aggregation and removal of remote sites in favor of a more centralized administrative model. Figure 6-2 shows a comparison between server consolidation and site consolidation.

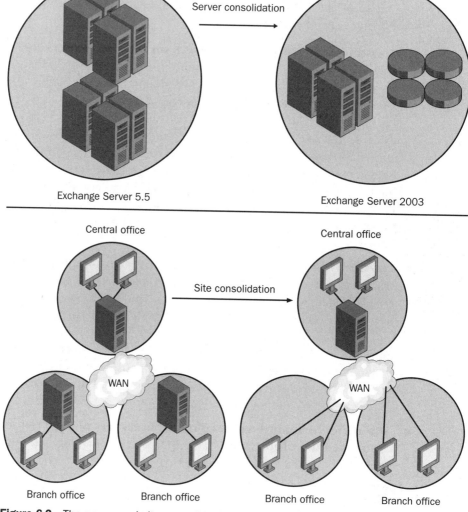

Figure 6-2   The server and site consolidation

When consolidating sites, you should consider the following factors, in addition to the general consolidation factors mentioned previously:

- **User details**   The users of the remote site should be considered. Consider the number of users, the methods used to access mail (MAPI, POP3, IMAP4, and so on), and the message load during typical use. You should create a profile of the users, mailboxes, public folders, distribution lists, and other components to help in site consolidation or to determine whether or not to consolidate sites.

- **Site details**   The biggest consideration with site details is the available bandwidth for messaging and typical bandwidth used for messaging. Messaging communication can be within the remote site, or there might be heavy traffic between sites.

Consolidation Tools

After obtaining a clear understanding of site and user details, you can use site consolidation tools bundled with Exchange Server 2003 Service Pack 1 (SP1) to consolidate sites. You can download the tools at *http://www.microsoft.com/downloads/ details.aspx?FamilyId=271E51FD-FE7D-42AD-B621-45F974ED34C0&display-lang=en*.

To facilitate site consolidation, you can do the following:

- **Use Outlook 2003 with offline address book**   Outlook 2003 includes Cached Exchange Mode functionality. Cached mode decreases traffic between the Outlook client and the Exchange server by using a local copy of the mailbox. To use Cached Exchange Mode, Outlook users need an offline address book (OAB), which is stored on a public folder server. Outlook uses the OAB in a number of cases. For example, Outlook downloads the OAB when a user accesses a mailbox for the first time after a mailbox move, or when there are changes to the Exchange topology.

- **Use Exchange 2003 SP1 Active Directory Connector**   The SP1 Active Directory Connector (ADC) enables you to update distribution lists and user objects in a site consolidation so that Active Directory replication reflects the changes.

- **Consolidate supporting servers and functions**   When consolidating messaging systems, sites, and servers, you can also consolidate domains. It is possible to rename domains in Exchange 2003 SP1. Renaming domains is accomplished by the Exchange Domain Rename Fixup tool (XDR-Fixup). To rename a domain, you need to use the released version of Rendom included with SP1, and the XDR-Fixup tool. XDR-Fixup is a part of the Web Release tools for Exchange 2003. You can download the Domain Rename Fixup tool at *http:// www.microsoft.com/exchange/downloads/2003/default.mspx*.

> **Note** When consolidating Exchange 5.5 sites, there is a known bug with the IS consistency checker. You must apply a hotfix to resolve the problem. To do a cross-site move in an Exchange mixed-mode environment, you must first install the hotfix. This update addresses known problems with the Microsoft Exchange Server 5.5 information store. You must install the update on all Exchange Server 5.5 computers that are in the Exchange organization and that have public folder stores configured. For more information, see *http://go.microsoft.com/fwlink/?linkid=3052&kbid=836489*.

When consolidating sites, you can use the following tools:

- **Move Mailbox Wizard** With the Move Mailbox Wizard, you can move mailboxes from one administrative group to another. The Move Mailbox Wizard in Exchange 2003 SP1 includes the functionality to map an Exchange 5.5 site to an administrative and a routing group in Exchange 2003 SP1. This tool is included in SP1.

- **Exchange Profile Update tool** With the Exchange Profile Update tool, users can update their Outlook profiles after mailboxes are moved across administrative groups.

> **Note** You can download Exchange Profile Update at *http://www.microsoft.com/downloads/details.aspx?FamilyId=56F45AC3-448F-4CCC-9BD5-B6B52C13B29C&displaylang=en*.

- **Public Folder Migration tool** With the Public Folder Migration tool, you can move public folders from one server to another. The tool includes the option to move public folders across administrative groups.

- **Object Rehome tool** With the Object Rehome tool, you can move contacts and distribution lists from one server to another. This tool is especially helpful in consolidating Exchange 5.5 sites because you can use the tool to update the LegacyDN value for distribution lists and recipients so that messages are delivered to the correct mailbox after consolidation.

Site Consolidation Practices and Issues

Assuming you have an existing central site running Exchange Server 2003 SP1 with SP1 Active Directory Connector that is used to consolidate remote sites, you should be aware of practices and issues with user moves, moves across administrative groups, public folder moves, and object rehoming.

Active Directory Connector Behavior

ADC fosters the replication of Active Directory data during site consolidation. However, you should be aware of ADC behaviors to help consolidate sites.

During site consolidation, when an object such as a mailbox, contact, distribution list, or public folder, is rehomed to another site, ADC removes the previous distinguished name from links, such as distribution lists, and adds the new distinguished name to the link. For example, with public folders' objects in a distribution list, ADC does the following:

1. Removes the old public folder object from the distribution list.

2. Updates DN link information.

3. Leaves a stub public folder until distribution list membership is replicated.

4. Removes the stub public folder through the PFMigrate process.

The PFmigrate process assigns a `X500:ADCDeleteWhenUnlinked` proxy value to indicate that the object should be deleted when the object no longer belongs to a distribution list.

To enable faster replication when moving mailboxes from a remote site to a central site, you can select Replicate Now in the ADC interface. If there is a delay in replication, and if an Exchange 5.5 user on a remote site sends e-mail messages to users who have been moved to the new site, the messages cannot be delivered until replication completes.

Public Folder Moves

When moving public folders, you should be aware of the following issues:

- **Temporary inaccessibility**   If not all content is replicated, or if the replica list isn't updated and users are directed to the old location, public folders may be inaccessible.

- **Inbox rules**   Rules that move messages to and from public folders that are based on folder ID (FID) will not work after public folders have been moved across administrative groups. You may receive a message such as "Unable to find Destination Folder."

If you have any client or server side inbox rules that are based on a user and the user's Exchange *LegacyExchangeDN*, the rules will be broken when you move cross-administrative groups because the *LegacyExchangeDN* of a user changes. However, inbox rules do not break if the user resides on an Exchange Server 2003 SP1 or later-based server. Inbox rules work in Exchange Server 2003 SP1 after a cross-administrative group move because changes to the mailbox store allow rules to work even when the *LegacyExchangeDN* of a user changes. Instead of relying on the *LegacyExchangeDN* attribute, the additional X500 proxy-address added during the cross-administrative group move can be used during rule processing on Exchange 2003 SP1 servers. If the user is not homed on Exchange Server 2003 SP1, the inbox rules based on a cross-administrative, group-moved person must be recreated.

- **Moved public folders in the global address list**   Public folders that are moved across administrative groups may disappear from the global address list (GAL) in Exchange Server 5.5. This behavior may occur if the original Exchange Server 5.5 object in the old site is hidden before the new Exchange Server 5.5 object is replicated to the new site from Active Directory. Cross-administrative moved public folders are not affected in Active Directory, the Exchange 2000 Server GAL, or Exchange Server 2003 GAL.

- **Journaling**   Journaling will not work if a public folder that is used for Exchange Server 5.5 or Exchange 2000 Server Journaling is moved across administrative groups. This issue occurs because the *LegacyExchangeDN* attribute is changed.

- **Organizational forms**   Organizational forms are not moved cross-site by the PFMigrate script. Organizational forms are part of the system folders, and administrators must manually update the public folder replica list for this and other system folders.

- **Third-party programs based on public folders**   Third-party programs that are based on a public folder and the *LegacyExchangeDN* of that public folder may not work after a public folder is moved cross-site.

- **Proxy addresses**   Public folders will retain their original proxy addresses from their old sites. Additionally, public folders will not gain new proxy addresses from being moved across administrative groups, even if the recipient policy is based on administrative group membership. The Recipient Update Service (RUS) will not stamp updated proxies if the public folder already has proxies of that type. To receive a new proxy address for a recipient policy that would now apply to the user, based on the new administrative group membership, click Apply Now on the recipient policy, and then rebuild the RUS. It is best to do this during non-peak hours to minimize performance impact. Although proxy addresses are not updated, mail flow will not be affected. However, if your system is performing some very specific restriction checking, you may experience an issue if the addresses are not updated.

■ **Running the Directory Service/Information Store consistency adjuster rehome option** After a cross-site move of a public folder, it is best that you do not run the Directory Service/Information Store (DS/IS) consistency adjuster until all directory replication has completed. You must wait until public folder cross-site moves are complete before running the DS/IS consistency adjuster. If you run the DS/IS consistency adjuster shortly after cross-site moves of public folders, it may rehome your public folders to a site other than the target site specified by PFMigrate. This behavior may occur under the following conditions:

  ■ You run PFMigrate to add public folder replicas for all public folders in a site to a target server in a new site.

  ■ You run PFMigrate to delete all public folder replicas from all servers in the source site.

  ■ An administrator runs the DS/IS consistency adjuster before homed attributes have replicated back from Active Directory to the Exchange Server 5.5 directory.

  However, after Active Directory replicates with Exchange Server 5.5, there is no risk in running the DS/IS consistency adjuster.

■ **Free/busy information and resource mailboxes** Free and busy information must be republished after a cross-site mailbox move. For user mailboxes, this will occur 15 minutes after the user uses Outlook to log on to the Exchange server and the user performs a calendar action. For example, if the user approves, removes, or creates a meeting request, the calendar free and busy information is republished 15 minutes later. The owner of a resource mailbox, for example, a meeting room, must open the mailbox and perform a calendar action to republish the free and busy information. This behavior occurs because there will not be a free/busy message for the user's new *LegacyExchangeDN* attribute in the target site, but Outlook will not publish an update until a calendar change is made, and the Outlook local free/busy cache is dirtied. This behavior also occurs if you run through the GUIDGen process to reset site system folders. Alternately, the UpdateFB tool can be used to automate this Free/Busy republishing process. For more information about the UpdateFB tool, see *http://support.microsoft.com/default.aspx?scid=kb;EN-US;294282.*

■ **X500 Addresses** Although rare, the X500 addresses may be overwritten when contacts are moved across sites. A contact is created in an organization by inter-organizational connection agreement to represent mailboxes in another organization. If the contact is cross-site moved, the original directory name of the contact from the source site is stamped onto the cross-site moved contact in the form of an X500 address. However, if the mailbox that the contact represents is changed, the change is replicated back to the cross-site moved contact object, and the ADC will overwrite the X500 address. To work around this issue, use one or more of the following suggestions:

■ Reconfigure the ADC to a new site, and run the tool, losing all X500 addresses.

■ Export the *LegacyExchangeDNs* from Exchange Server 5.5 before the cross-site move, and then import the *LegacyExchangeDNs* as X500 addresses on the Exchange Server 5.5 mailboxes.

■ Switch to Exchange Native Mode and do not move the contacts.

Using a Resource Forest in Consolidation

When consolidating servers and sites, there may be some cases where using a resource forest is the optimal solution. For example, using a resource forest might make sense when dealing with a company merger using different messaging systems, there might be a Windows NT environment that must be retained, or strict boundaries must exist for managing Exchange resources and Active Directory resources.

You can use a resource forest in a similar way to using a central site in site consolidation. User accounts can be maintained in one forest, while Exchange servers, mailboxes, public folders, and other Exchange components and features can be maintained in the Exchange forest.

Note   A resource forest scenario is not limited to one Exchange forest and one user forest. You can run multiple user forests and use a common GAL for address resolution and mail transport. For more details about resource forests, as well as site consolidation, see the "Planning an Exchange Server 2003 Messaging System" whitepaper at *http://www.microsoft.com/ downloads/details.aspx?FamilyID=9FC3260F-787C-4567-BB71- 908B8F2B980D&displaylang=en.*

Figure 6-3 shows a resource forest scenario.

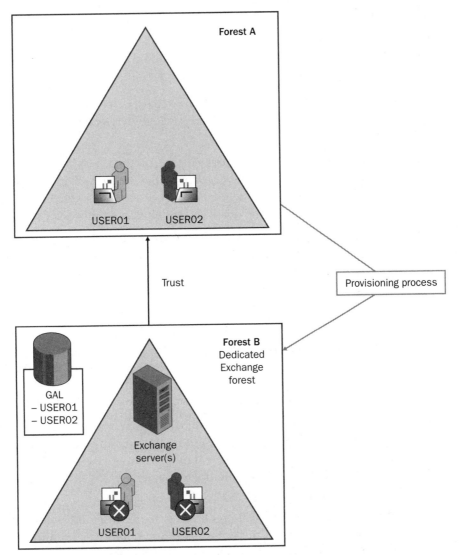

Figure 6-3   Resource forest

For a resource forest to function, a user in the account forest is associated with a disabled user with a mailbox on the Exchange forest. Trusts enable communication, and provisioning between forests helps to create new accounts with proper permissions and rights.

Issues in Using a Resource Forest

When using a resource forest, you should be aware of specific concerns and configuration steps that must be taken in order for mail transport to work effectively for Exchange users. You should be aware of the following:

- **Trusts**   As briefly mentioned, trusts must exist between forests. The trusts must be configured with at least one-way privilege between the Exchange and user account forests.

- **User moves**   When administering user accounts, it is important to keep in mind the logical attributes associated with the accounts. For example, although the user might be a part of the overall organization, he or she might belong to a specific forest. Knowing the details helps when providing user support.

- **Name resolution, synchronization, and replication**   In an Exchange 5.5 upgrade scenario, when the Exchange 5.5 directory replication connectors are disconnected, no information is replicated to other forests. This can be resolved by using a synchronization tool such as Microsoft Identity Integration Server (MIIS).

- **Mailbox moves and Outlook**   When users are moved across forests, their Outlook profiles must be updated to include the back-end server on which the mailbox now resides. Use the Exchange Profile Update tool (Exprofre.exe) to update Outlook profiles. If a user runs the Cached Exchange Mode feature in Outlook, check the new profile to ensure that the profile uses accurate .ost files.

- **Feature preservation**   Both rules and mailbox access control lists (ACLs) are not preserved during a cross-forest move. Also, published certificates are not migrated. You must transfer Key Management Service certificates before a migration because certificates are not recovered.

- **Permissions and access**   Users from different forests cannot access each other's mailboxes. Users in different forests are represented as contacts and contacts cannot have access permissions. When mailboxes are moved, the delegated permissions are not preserved. Similarly, groups are also contacts, and you cannot see the group's members by expanding the details.

- **Free/busy**   Free/busy data can be synchronized across forests, but users in different forests cannot view each other's calendar details.

- **Front-end servers**   Front-end servers can only proxy to a back-end server in the same forest.

- **SMTP Namespace**   In case there are several Exchange organizations that use one namespace and separate forest namespaces, Exchange uses GAL Synchronization and SMTP addresses to create the *TargetAddress* property to determine a contact's address. Each contact must have a unique *TargetAddress* property.

To accomplish a single shared namespace across multiple forests, you can do the following:

- Use SMTP routing to specify a recipient policy with a proxy address of the single namespace. For example, with name.tailspintoys.com and second-name.tailspintoys.com, each organization can specify the other organization's proxy address in the recipient policy and select the This Organization Is Responsible For All Mail Delivery To This Address check box.

- Use a central server to process mail for all Exchange organizations. In this setup, using the two organizations from the previous example, a central hub contains proxy addresses to name.tailspintoys.com and second-name.tailspintoys.com and directs mail to the proper destination.

In a shared namespace and a resource forest, when users are moved, mail delivery is possible by the *LegacyExchangeDN* property. GAL Synchronization creates a secondary X.500 proxy address for the user who was moved so that old messages can be properly routed to the user's new mailbox, based on the *legacyExchangeDN* property. For example, UserA sends mail to UserB, who is in the same organization. Later, UserA is moved to a different organization. The mail originally sent by UserA still specifies UserA's *legacyExchangeDN* property. GAL Synchronization creates a contact for UserA in the old organization and assigns an X.500 address with the old *legacyExchangeDN* property. This allows UserB to reply to the old mail, which, in turn, is properly routed to the *TargetAddress* property for UserA.

Site Consolidation in International Environments

When you consolidate users from different sites, maybe regional sites, on to the same Microsoft Exchange 2003 server, the users might have different nationalities. You will therefore be in a situation where you need to support different languages used by these users.

The areas that need to be addressed when supporting multiple languages are as follows:

- **Sorting of the online address book**   Users in different languages might sort address book entries differently. For example, the Scandinavian sort order differs from the English sort order because Scandinavian languages use characters not found in the English alphabet.

- **Sorting of the offline address book**   Microsoft Outlook can download an offline version of the server-based address information to the workstation. The sort order should be the same in online and offline mode.

- **Address and detail templates**   Microsoft Outlook uses address and detail templates to display the address book information. These templates need to be presented in the appropriate languages.

- **Organizational forms**   Microsoft Outlook can use forms to display information in a specific way. These forms can be stored based on their language, and the appropriate form should be presented to the clients.

- **Locales**   Users of different languages need to have currency, date, and time displayed according to the appropriate languages.

- **Outlook Web Access Help**   Users of Outlook Web Access need to be able to have the online help available in their local languages.

Regional and Language Settings

Before discussing issues that revolve around sort orders, address and detail templates, and so forth, we need to clarify where clients store the language settings.

When we talk about language it has two implementations:

- **The language of the application used to access Exchange**   For the Microsoft Outlook application it is the locale ID of the Outlook profile that specifies the language used, and it will typically correspond to the language version of Emsmdb32.dll. Emsmdb32.dll is a core component of the Exchange provider for the MAPI subsystem. By default, this file resides in the \Program Files\Common Files\System\MSMAPI\1033 directory.

    For the Outlook Web Access application, it is the language specified in the Accept-Language of the HTTP header. This will typically correspond to the Languages setting in Internet Explorer. To access the Languages setting in Internet Explorer, click Tools, click Internet Options, and select Languages.

- **The Regional and Language setting of the Windows client**   The Regional and Language setting of the Windows client is stored in the registry in the following key.

Location	HKEY_CURRENT_USER\Control Panel\International\
Key	Locale
Type	REG_SZ
Value	Locale ID or code page
Description	The value of the locale key is the locale ID or code page. For more information see the Microsoft Knowledge Base article 221435, "List of supported locale identifiers in Word 2000" (*http://support.microsoft.com/default.aspx?scid=http://support.microsoft.com:80/support/kb/articles/q221/4/35.asp&NoWebContent=1*).

Sorting the Online Address Book

This area focuses on the issue of ensuring that the information in the Microsoft Outlook Personal Address Book is sorted and formatted accordingly to the rules of the language used, for example that names starting with the Danish characters Æ, Ø and Å are placed correctly accordingly to the Danish alphabet in the Outlook address book.

Starting with Microsoft Exchange 2000, the Outlook address book is serviced by the global catalog component of Active Directory. It is the global catalog server that sorts and formats the information presented to the Outlook address book.

When the Microsoft Outlook client needs to present the Outlook address book, the Exchange address book provider requests the information from a global catalog server based on the locale of the current user as defined in the locale registry key explained in the previous section. If the global catalog server supports the requested language, Active Directory returns the requested information sorted and formatted according to the requested language. If the global catalog server does not support the requested language, Active Directory will return the information sorted appropriately for English (U.S.). The locale ID for English (U.S.) is 0x00000409.

You must make sure that the appropriate Windows language files are installed on the global catalog servers. To verify that the appropriate Windows language files are installed:

1. Open the Control Panel.

2. Double-click Regional And Language Options.

3. Click the Languages tab.

4. Click the language family you need under "Supplemental language support."

Take the following steps to verify that the required locales and code pages are loaded on a global catalog server:

1. Start Registry Editor (Regedit.exe).

2. Click to expand the following subkey in the registry:

   `HKEY_LOCAL_MACHINE\Software\Microsoft\Ntds\Language`

3. Check to see if the appropriate values are listed.

As an example, the following registry keys must be added to support English (U.S.), Swedish, and French. You must restart the global catalog server to have the settings take effect.

Location	`HKEY_LOCAL_MACHINE\SOFTWARE\Microsoft\NTDS\Language`

Values	`"Language 0000041d"=dword:0000041d`
	`"Language 0000040c"=dword:0000040c`
	`"Language 00000409"=dword:00000409`

Description	Adding additional languages to the global catalog server generates a new index per language. The amount of data replicated between global catalog servers is not impacted by these additional indexes because the indexes are generated locally. However, the size of the Active Directory database (ntds.dit) will increase.

Figure 6-4 shows how the different components interact when an online Outlook client accesses the address book.

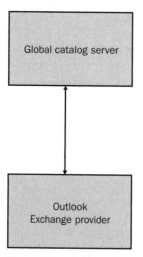

Figure 6-4   Online address book access

To ensure correct sort order for all the Microsoft Outlook users, you must load the appropriate locales and Windows code pages on all the global catalog servers used by the users. Microsoft Exchange 2003 is able to use up to 10 global catalog servers and will refer Microsoft Outlook clients to any of them. It is therefore important that you load the appropriate locales and Windows code pages on all global catalog servers referable by your Microsoft Exchange 2003 servers.

Also be aware that Microsoft Outlook 2000 or later will store the global catalog server it is using in the profile and it will continue to use that global catalog server as long as it responds. There is therefore a possibility that some Microsoft Outlook clients of site consolidated users still will use local global catalog servers. Therefore, they must also have the appropriate locales and Windows code pages loaded.

The Offline Address Book

To enable users to browse the address book while not being connected, Microsoft Outlook supports the OAB. The OAB is generated by a designated Microsoft Exchange 2003 server running as the offline address list server. It is generated by the OABGen component of the Microsoft Exchange System Attendant (MAD.EXE). The default OAB information is stored in subfolders of the system public folder `OFFLINE ADDRESS BOOK\/o=Organization/cn=addrlists/cn=oabs/cn=Default Offline Address`. It is possible to have more than one OAB.

Each OAB system public folder contains two subfolders, "OAB Version 2" and "OAB Version 3a." The actual OAB content is stored as a number of items with attached files. The items can contain a full OAB or the changes that have been made since the last change or full OAB was generated.

Previous versions of Microsoft Outlook and Microsoft Exchange only supported the OAB in the American National Standards Institute (ANSI) character encoding standard. The ANSI OAB is stored in the "OAB Version 2" system public folder. Microsoft Outlook 2003 and Microsoft Exchange 2003 now also support the OAB in the Unicode character encoding standard. The Unicode OAB is stored in the "OAB Version 3a" system public folder. For more information, see Table 6-2.

Table 6-2   Attachments Found on Items in the Offline Address Book System Public Folders

ANSI OAB version 2	Unicode OAB version 3a	Description
Browse2.oab	browse2_o.oab	This main file for the offline address book contains pointers to the data in the other .oab files.
Details2.oab	details2_u.oab	The details address book information.
Rdndex2.oab	rdndex2_u.oab	Distinguished name index.
Anrdex.oab	anrdex2_u.oab	Ambiguous name resolution index.
Lng*xxx*.oab	Lng*xxx*.oab	Localized templates for display and addressing data, where *xxx* is the locale ID in hex.
mac*xxx*.oab	mac*xxx*.oab	Macintosh templates for display and addressing data, where *xxx* is the locale ID in hex.
changes.oab	Changes.oab	The changes made since last time the offline address book was generated.

With Microsoft Exchange 2003, Exchange System Manager can view the contents of public folders, including system public folders. To view system public folders:

1. Open Exchange System Manager.

2. Expand the organization object, Folders, and then Public Folders.

3. Right-click Public Folders, and then select View System Folders.

4. Expand Offline Address Book.

5. Expand the distinguished name of the offline address book. For example, the default offline address book will be: /o=*Organization*/cn=addrlists/cn=oabs/cn=Default Offline Address List.

6. Click the "OAB Version 2" folder or the "OAB Version 3a" folder.

7. In the right window, click the Content tab.

8. Enter the credentials for a mailbox in order to view the folders. (All accounts should have access to view the OAB messages.) Then, the items can be seen.

In both Microsoft Exchange 2000 and 2003 versions, Outlook Web Access can be used to view the system public folders by taking the following steps:

1. Go to *http://<ExchangeServer>/public/NON_IPM_SUBTREE/*. For example, on the Exchange server itself, go to *http://localhost/public/NON_IPM_SUBTREE/*.

2. Then, go to Offline Address Book.

The offline address book Exchange provider component of Microsoft Outlook downloads the offline address book from a replica of the appropriate system public folder and creates the offline address book on the PC. The offline address book is comprised of the following files stored in the directory \Documents and Settings\\<*Windows alias*>\Local Settings\Application Data\Microsoft\Outlook\. For more information, see Table 6-3.

Table 6-3 Offline Address Book Files on the PC

ANSI file	Unicode file	Description
Browse.oab	ubrowse.oab	The main file for the offline address book, it contains pointers to the data in the other .oab files.
Details.oab	udetails.oab	The details address book information.
Rdndex.oab	urdndex.oab	Distinguished name index.
pdndex.oab	updndex.oab	Table of parent domain names.
Anrdex.oab	uanrdex.oab	Ambiguous name resolution index.
tmplts.oab	utmplts.oab	Templates

Apart from the offline address book, Microsoft Outlook also provides the ability to view some or all of your mailbox or public folders available when you are not connected to the Microsoft Exchange 2003 server. The folders are stored in the offline folder file, also referred to as the OST file.

Previous versions of Microsoft Outlook support the offline folder in the ANSI character encoding standard. Microsoft Outlook 2003 now supports having the offline folder in the Unicode character encoding standard. The offline folder can now also be larger than 2 GB in size.

An existing offline folder in ANSI mode will not automatically be converted to Unicode mode when you upgrade to Microsoft Outlook 2003. You must delete the existing offline folder and re-create it to use Unicode mode. This is important to note, since you will not be able to have a Unicode offline address book unless you have a Unicode mode offline folder.

Sorting the Offline Address Book

Having specified the required settings on all relevant global catalog servers in your environment, users with different language settings can enjoy working with correctly sorted address book information in their messaging clients when working online. However, users might find that Microsoft Outlook falls back to an incorrect sort order when working in offline mode. This is because Microsoft Outlook 2003 working offline in cached mode or previous versions of Microsoft Outlook in offline mode do not communicate with global catalog servers, but use the offline address book.

The key difference between the online and offline scenario is which component is requesting the information from the global catalog server and which language it is requesting it in. This is shown in Figure 6-5.

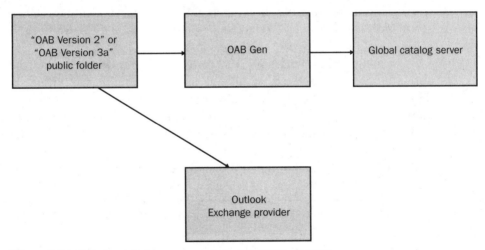

Figure 6-5   Global catalog server component request diagram

In the offline scenario it is OABGen that requests the information, and it will request it in the language defined as the default server locale. The default server locale is stored in the registry in the following key:

Registry key	`HKEY_USERS\.Default\Control Panel\International\Locale`
Description	The locale ID in hex and stored as a string; for example, `00000409` for English (U.S.)

The offline address book sort order will default to English (U.S.), if the global catalog server used by OABGen does not support the requested language. It is important to understand how OABGen determines which global catalog server it talks to. The global catalog server is given to OABGen by the Microsoft Exchange System Attendant. The System Attendant does not use DsAccess to get a global catalog server, rather it uses the Windows 32 API *DsGetDCName*. The same API is used to get a global catalog server for other tasks performed by the System Attendant including Move Mailbox. Its specific usage of *DsGetDCName* means that it will return any global catalog server in the Windows 2000 site of the Microsoft Exchange Server. So, to ensure that the offline address book is generated in the appropriate language, it is important to configure support for the language on all global catalog servers in the Windows 2000 Site of the Microsoft Exchange Server generating the offline address book.

To understand which global catalog server OABGen is using, you can increase Diagnostic Logging for MSExchangeSA->OAL Generator and the event 9117 will be generated in the application event log. The event 9117 will contain the name of the global catalog server used by OABGen.

Microsoft Exchange 2003 only requests and generates the offline address book for one language. It is possible to change the default server language to another language than English (U.S.) to have the offline address book generated to support the sorting and formatting of that language. If a user is not using the language on the server, the user is presented with the language that is on the server for formatting and sorting options.

To mitigate this limitation when using the offline address book, inform the users about the problem, and explain that all users are listed in the offline address book, they are just not placed alphabetically correctly in the list. If the users type the display name in the To, Cc, or Bcc and use the Check Name functionality of Microsoft Outlook, the display names will be resolved to the correct entry in the offline address book.

It is possible to determine the language of the OAB on the Microsoft Outlook client by examining the registry keys as follows:

Registry key	`HKEY_CURRENT_USER\Software\Microsoft\Exchange\Exchange Provider\OAB Sort LocaleU`
Description	The locale ID for the Unicode OAB in hex and stored as binary; for example, `09 04 00 00` for English (U.S.)

Registry key	`HKEY_CURRENT_USER\Software\Microsoft\Exchange\Exchange Provider\OAB Sort Locale`
Description	The locale ID for the ANSI OAB in hex and stored as binary; for example, `09 04 00 00` for English (U.S.)

Organizational Forms Library

The Microsoft Exchange Organizational Forms Library exists by language. The library to use is determined by the Microsoft Outlook client language version.

In order to create a language-specific Organizational Forms Library, use the Exchange System Manager as follows:

1. Open Exchange System Manager.

2. Expand the Organization container, Folders, and then Public Folders.

3. Right-click Public Folders, and then select View System Folders.

4. Expand EFORMS REGISTRY.

5. Right-click EFORMS REGISTRY and select to Create A New Organizational Forms Library using the appropriate language.

After you have created the Organizational Forms Library, remember to add the required forms to it, either by using third-party installation and setup programs or by publishing the forms from within an appropriate localized version of Microsoft Outlook.

Address and Detail Templates

Microsoft Outlook uses templates to display the address book information, such as details on mailboxes, public folders, custom recipients and distribution lists, send options, and search dialogue.

In order to support different Microsoft Outlook client languages, the appropriate Address and Detail template needs to be loaded on the Exchange server. This will be done by Exchange Setup during installation.

It is possible to check which Address and Detail templates have been loaded by taking the following steps in Exchange System Manager:

1. Open Exchange System Manager.

2. Expand the Recipients and then access Address Templates.

3. Expand the Recipients and then access Details Templates.

Locales

In order to provide correct display of currency, date, and time settings for different Microsoft Outlook client languages, the appropriate locales should be installed on the Microsoft Exchange 2003 server.

To add or remove locales, perform the following steps in the Exchange System Manager:

1. Open Exchange System Manager, and go to the server in question.

2. Right-click and select Properties.

3. Select the Locales tab.

4. Add the appropriate languages.

Outlook Web Access Help

In order to provide the appropriate localized Outlook Web Access help, you need to install the help files. They are found on the Microsoft Exchange 2003 product CD in the directory setup\i386\exchange\exchweb. Select the appropriate languages and install them.

Known Symptoms if the Correct Languages Are Not Loaded on the Global Catalog Server

If the global catalog server being accessed by the Exchange address book provider does not support the requested language, the following symptoms can be seen:

- **Check Name Against The Global Address List fails**   The user is not able to check his/her alias against the global address list and is therefore prevented from creating an Outlook profile.

- **Distribution list membership is not shown**   When the user selects to view the membership of a distribution list, the membership list is empty.

Best Practices

In site and server consolidation, planning and verification are the primary tasks in implementing a consolidation strategy. Site and server considerations have already been discussed, and include taking an inventory of the existing configuration, listing used resources, anticipating load and growth, evaluating network availability and use, and planning for business needs.

There are other best practices you should remember when consolidating servers and sites. They are as follows:

- **Conflicts**   Planning consolidations includes planning for conflicts. Ask what naming conflicts are possible in the namespace and in Active Directory. Contacts must have unique *TargetAddress* properties, so evaluate consolidations and plan for possible conflicts to ensure that users can send and receive mail. Check for known issues, such as certificate transference and distribution list moves. Also, check for connectivity issues. The OAB takes a long time to download with many users running cached mode. Ensure that enough bandwidth is available for the tasks.

- **Synchronization**   GAL synchronization is vital for resource forests and scenarios with multiple forests. Ensure that InterOrg replication takes place to have a combined GAL. As an additional option, you can use the LDAP directory synchronization utility to help integrate Exchange organizations.

- **Migration**   Use tools such as the Migration Wizard and ADC to help move and rehome objects.

This chapter lists best practices and suggestions for site and server consolidation. By preplanning and preserving user profiles and Exchange features, sites and servers can be consolidated systematically to benefit both centralized and distributed network administration models.

Chapter 7

Hosting Exchange Server 2003

About This Chapter

This chapter explains how to host Microsoft Exchange Server 2003 in an environment based on Microsoft Solution for Windows-based Hosting. After providing a brief introduction to core Windows-based Hosting technologies, the chapter discusses the deployment of an Exchange 2003 organization to provide hosted messaging services, including full Microsoft Office Outlook 2003 support. This chapter further explains how to share an Exchange organization between consumer and business customers, how to implement a centralized management system and a reseller model, and how to automate routine administrative tasks, such as creating resellers, business organizations, user accounts, and vanity Simple Mail Transfer Protocol (SMTP) domains.

On the companion CD, you can find a \Companion Material\Chapter 07 folder with worksheets that detail how to deploy a basic hosted Exchange 2003 test environment. Deploying this test environment enables you to follow the explanations in this chapter with practical steps. For information about deploying and configuring a full-featured production environment, see the Windows-based Hosting documentation or contact Microsoft. Microsoft Consulting Services and Microsoft Certified Partners can assist you with designing, deploying, and operating a Windows-based Hosting solution for Exchange 2003. To obtain Microsoft Solution for Windows-based Hosting, go to the Microsoft website for service providers at *http://www.microsoft.com/servicepro-viders.* You must register as an ASP.NET service provider to download the software.

What You Need to Know

Microsoft Solution for Windows-based Hosting relies on a centralized hosting infrastructure based on Microsoft Windows Server 2003 and Active Directory directory service. This infrastructure enables you to host websites and e-commerce solutions based on Internet Information Services (IIS) and Microsoft SQL Server 2000, messaging services based on Exchange 2003, and collaboration solutions based on Microsoft Windows SharePoint Services. Microsoft recommends deploying a unified Active Directory environment for all hosted application services so that you can centralize management and reduce costs and efforts required to manage the hosting infrastructure.

Figure 7-1 shows an example of a Windows-based Hosting design, developed and tested by Microsoft Consulting Services. The hosting infrastructure relies on the following key elements defined in the Windows-based Hosting design:

- **Internet router** The Internet router, also known as a border router, represents the initial access point connecting the hosting infrastructure to the Internet. The Internet router also serves as a first line of defense against attacks by limiting the traffic allowed into the perimeter network. You should block all traffic that appears to be spoofed (that is, inbound traffic from the Internet that is structured to appear as if it originated in the hosting infrastructure or perimeter network). You should also block all traffic that is not relevant to the hosted sites. Internet Control Message Protocol (ICMP) should be blocked, for example, because attackers can exploit ICMP redirects and other types of ICMP messages. It should be noted, however, that blocking all ICMP messages prevents Internet users from pinging your hosts. If you want to support Ping, you must allow ICMP echo-requests and ICMP echo-replies.

    Traffic that you might want to allow also includes File Transfer Protocol (FTP), Hypertext Transfer Protocol (HTTP), SMTP, Domain Name System (DNS), Internet Message Access Protocol version 4rev1 (IMAP4), and POP3 (Post Office Protocol version 3, with or without Secure Sockets Layer (SSL).

More Info The Windows-based Hosting documentation that you can find on the Microsoft Solution for Windows-based Hosting CD in the Documentation folder provides details on how to configure protocol filters.

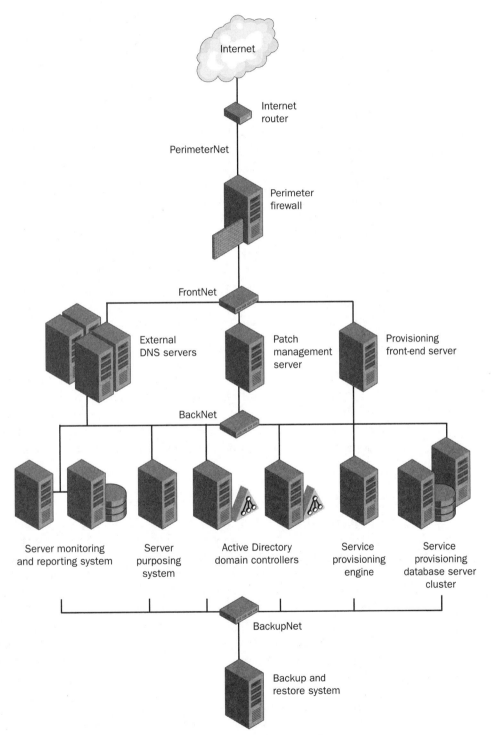

Figure 7-1   A Windows-based Hosting infrastructure example

> **Note**   Do not forget to protect the administrator accounts of your Internet routers through very strong passwords.

- **Perimeter firewall**   The perimeter firewall is the preliminary access point connecting the hosting infrastructure to the perimeter network, also known as the demilitarized zone (DMZ). Interfaces connected to the perimeter network, such as the Internet-facing network card of the perimeter firewall, use public IP addresses, and must therefore be considered vulnerable to attacks despite basic protection through the Internet router. The perimeter firewall (or an arrangement of firewalls) separates and protects the hosting infrastructure from the perimeter network. To provide the required level of security, the perimeter firewall should perform network address translation (NAT), packet and port filtering, Secure SSL termination, stateful inspection of data traffic, and, optionally, content load balancing. For more information about configuring firewall systems to connect an Exchange 2003 organization to the Internet in a secure way, see Chapter 11, "Connecting to the Internet."

> **Note**   If you already have a network with outer and inner firewalls separating Internet, perimeter network, and internal networks, you can use the existing infrastructure in your Windows-based Hosting environment. You might have to adjust the network configuration, but it is not required to deploy a completely separate firewall infrastructure for Windows-based Hosting.

- **External DNS**   At the core of the Internet-accessible part of the hosting infrastructure, named the FrontNet, are the external DNS servers. External DNS servers provide host name resolution services so that FrontNet hosts can establish outbound connections to Internet hosts and Internet hosts can establish inbound connections to published FrontNet systems. For example, you must register the SMTP hosts of your hosted SMTP domains in mail exchanger (MX) records in the external DNS so that Internet users can send your users messages. On the other hand, Internal servers in the BackNet, such as Active Directory domain controllers, should not be registered in the external DNS because these systems are not Internet accessible.

At a minimum, you require two external DNS servers for redundancy, configured as a primary server and a secondary server. You must integrate these DNS servers with Internet DNS so that name queries on the Internet can be directed to your DNS servers. Your external DNS servers must also be able to resolve names on the Internet (usually by forwarding queries to a root name server) so that your SMTP servers can establish outbound connections to Internet SMTP hosts.

On the Resource Kit CD   For step-by-step instructions illustrating the config-uration of external DNS Servers, see the document Installing and configuring external DNS servers.doc in the \Companion Material\Chapter 07\Hosting Infrastructure\Deploying external DNS folder on the companion CD.

The hosting infrastructure depicted in Figure 7-1 features four instead of two external DNS servers in a split-DNS configuration. The split-DNS design protects effi-ciently against DNS attacks. For example, DNS spoofing is a common attack in which a DNS cache is filled with incorrect entries (cache poisoning) to redirect SMTP hosts to wrong destinations so that an attacker can intercept e-mail messages. DNS spoofing can also be used to redirect Web access to the wrong hosts in order to capture pass-words, for example. Cache poisoning is possible if a DNS server is configured to per-form both host name resolution services and advertising services. The split-DNS configuration prevents this form of attack by delegating these services to different DNS servers. Resolving DNS servers listen only for queries originating from the Front-Net. Advertising DNS servers, on the other hand, listen only for queries originating from the Internet.

Note   The FrontNet uses private IP addresses that the perimeter firewall translates into public IP addresses. Thus, servers connected to the Front-Net can access the Internet and are accessible from the Internet through publishing rules configured on the perimeter firewall.

On the Resource Kit CD   The document Installing and configuring external DNS servers.doc that you can find in the \Companion Material\Chapter 07 folder on the companion CD illustrates how to implement a split-DNS config-uration based on a primary resolving server, a cache-only resolving server, and two advertising DNS servers.

■ **Patch management system**   The Windows-based Hosting design relies on Microsoft Systems Management Server (SMS) and Software Update Service (SUS) for patch management and software distribution, enabling service providers to stay aware of critical updates, hotfixes, and patches to known vulnerabilities. Within the hosting infrastructure, SMS uses standard Microsoft security tools, such as Microsoft Baseline Security Analyzer (MBSA), to determine missing security updates and to identify any configuration options that leave Windows servers open to potential security threats. SMS also provides a method for testing updates on a reference system for compatibility and for distributing updates to production servers.

Deploying a patch management and software distribution system based on SMS is beyond the scope of this chapter. For more information about deploying SMS in the hosting infrastructure, see the Windows-based Hosting documentation. For further details regarding patch management through SMS, also see the technical guide, "Patch Management Using Microsoft Systems Management Server 2003," available at *http://www.microsoft.com/technet/itsolutions/techguide/msm/swdist/pmsms/2003/pmsms031.mspx.*

- **Active Directory and internal DNS**   At the core of the internal hosting infrastructure, named the BackNet, is Active Directory with two domain controllers. Both domain controllers are configured as global catalog servers to provide full redundancy. These domain controllers provide centrally managed authentication services in the hosting infrastructure, enforce security policies, and also host the internal name resolution services, DNS and WINS. It is important to note that both FrontNet and BackNet systems use the internal DNS servers. You must configure the internal DNS servers to forward any DNS queries for Internet hosts to the external DNS servers so that these name queries can be resolved.

Note   To increase security and to separate user traffic from internal server-to-server communication, the internal hosting infrastructure is physically isolated from the Internet-accessible part. BackNet servers, such as domain controllers, do not need to communicate with systems on the Internet. However, BackNet servers and FrontNet servers must be able to communicate with each other. If there is a firewall between the FrontNet and BackNet, you must ensure that the firewall does not block the FrontNet-to-BackNet communication.

In the hosting infrastructure, Active Directory provides the foundation for centralized management of servers, administrators, resellers, and users. A single Active Directory forest with a single domain is shared by the service provider and all subscribers. Within this shared domain, Windows-based Hosting uses separate hierarchies of organizational units (OUs) for the internal infrastructure

(Servers organizational unit tree) and each subscriber (Hosting organizational unit tree), as illustrated in Figure 7-2. The document 03_Configuring organizational units and group policies.doc in the \Companion Material\ Chapter 07\Hosting Infrastructure\Deploying Active Directory folder on the companion CD outlines how to configure the organizational units in the Servers organizational unit hierarchy and how to apply group policies. The organizational unit structure in the Hosting hierarchy, on the other hand, is discussed later in this chapter. The Microsoft Provisioning System (MPS) uses the Hosting organizational unit hierarchy.

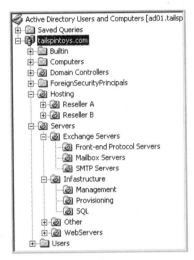

Figure 7-2 Active Directory organizational units for Windows-based Hosting

- **Provisioning system** To support the provisioning of hosted services, Windows-based Hosting relies on MPS. MPS components run on several servers deployed in FrontNet and BackNet. Subscribers can access the provisioning front-end server to request services, which the front-end server passes to the provisioning engine to activate the requested services. The provisioning engine performs the actual provisioning tasks against Active Directory, Exchange Server, and SQL Server. The provisioning engine is a transaction-oriented COM+ service that uses MPS providers to communicate with the actual server systems, such as Exchange Server 2003. You can find detailed information about the architecture of MPS in the Windows-based Hosting documentation. The section "Provisioning Hosted Exchange Services" later in this chapter explains how to use MPS in a hosted Exchange 2003 environment.

  In the hosting infrastructure, MPS enables you to:

  - Create user accounts, groups, and organizational units in Active Directory

  - Provision mailbox-enabled user accounts in an Exchange organization

  - Provision messaging services, such as Microsoft Office Outlook Web Access

- Create vanity SMTP domains

- Create databases with service plans for customers

- Configure Microsoft Windows registry and file system settings

- Provision installation packages and custom scripts

- Track billable events (such as mailbox created or deleted)

    MPS uses SQL Server to store its databases, including the Configuration database, Transaction log, Audit and Recovery Service, and Audit log, as well as databases that enable you to implement predefined customer service plans and track provisioning events for billing purposes. Because the data store is an important component of MPS, Windows-based Hosting recommends deploying SQL Server for MPS in a two-node cluster in active/passive configuration.

On the Resource Kit CD   For step-by-step instructions about how to deploy MPS in a test environment, see the worksheets in the \Companion Material\Chapter 07\Hosting Infrastructure\Provisioning System folder on the companion CD.

Note   You must install the provisioning engine on a computer running Windows 2000 Server. MPS 1.0 is not supported on Windows Server 2003. The next version of MPS will support Windows Server 2003.

- **Monitoring and reporting system**   Proactive monitoring, alerting, reporting, and trend analysis are key tasks in maintaining a reliable hosting infrastructure. Windows-based Hosting relies on Microsoft Operations Manager (MOM) to accomplish these tasks. MOM uses management packs to provide intelligent operations management. Management packs are available for a wide variety of server applications. For example, if you want to monitor an Exchange 2003 organization you can use the Exchange 2003 Management Pack for MOM 2000 SP1. You can read more about the Exchange 2003 Management Pack in Chapter 17, "Exchange Server 2003 Management Pack."

    Windows-based Hosting includes specialized management packs that enable service providers to monitor core and application services in the hosting infrastructure. Windows-based Hosting also includes HTTP and remote procedure call (RPC) Pinger tools and a Performance Warehouse Database (PWDB). Pinger tools enable MOM to verify that specific services are available. The PWDB database is a repository for data extracted from the MOM database for long-term storage and for generating performance reports based on the extracted data. MOM keeps track of all system information in a SQL Server database named OnePoint. For performance and scalability, Windows-based Hosting uses a dedicated server running SQL Server 2000 to host the OnePoint and PWDB databases.

On the Resource Kit CD   For details regarding the Windows-based Hosting management packs, Pinger tools, and PWDB, see the Windows-based Hosting documentation. For step-by-step instructions about how to deploy MOM and the MOM tools included in Windows-based Hosting, also see the documents in the \Companion Material\Chapter 07\Hosting Infrastructure\Monitoring and Reporting folder on the companion CD.

- **Server purposing system**   The server purposing system is an optional component in the hosting infrastructure. This system is based on Automated Deployment Services (ADS). ADS includes imaging tools and a scripting engine that you can use to automate Windows server deployments. It is important to note that server hardware must be Pre-Boot eXecution Environment (PXE)-compliant so that you can deploy the operating system automatically. Service providers running a large number of servers can use ADS to lower deployment costs. In a test environment, however, it is sufficient to install servers manually.

  ADS requires Windows Server 2003 Enterprise Edition. It is available for download at *http://www.microsoft.com/downloads/details.aspx?FamilyID=b7a 79e10-46ae-4576-ab30-b7f26affc60f&displaylang=en*. For detailed technical information, see also the Automated Deployment Services section in Microsoft Technology Centers (*http://www.microsoft.com/windowsserver2003/technologies/management/ads/default.mspx*). For information about how to implement and run a server purposing system based on ADS in a hosting infrastructure, see the Windows-based Hosting documentation.

- **Backup and restore system**   Data centers typically deploy automated tape libraries for centralized backup and data archiving. For performance reasons, we recommend deploying a separate physical network segment for backup and recovery operations to eliminate this traffic from FrontNet and BackNet. If you have deployed a server purposing solution, you can also use the backup segment to deploy new server systems over this network. In a Windows-based Hosting test environment, a backup and recovery solution is an optional component. In a production environment, however, a backup and recovery solution is imperative. See Chapters 21, 22, and 23 for detailed information about backing up and restoring Exchange 2003 servers.

Deploying Exchange 2003 in a Hosting Infrastructure

Having deployed the basic hosting infrastructure, you can implement Exchange 2003 to provide hosted messaging services to subscribers. According to the FrontNet/Back-Net architecture of the hosting environment, you should deploy Exchange 2003 in an arrangement of front-end and back-end servers.

An Exchange front-end server is a computer located in the FrontNet that receives incoming client connections and redirects them to an appropriate back-end server, located in the BackNet. It is important to understand that an Exchange front-end server does not store any user data. The Exchange back-end server hosts the mailboxes and public folders. This server is not directly Internet accessible, which increases security. Exchange 2003 supports front-end and back-end configurations for Internet protocols, such as IMAP4, POP3, and HTTP. You can also support MAPI-based clients, such as Outlook, if you configure your front-end servers as RPC over HTTP proxies, as explained later in this chapter.

Figure 7-3 illustrates a basic Exchange front-end and back-end configuration within a Windows-based Hosting infrastructure.

Note   Windows-based Hosting recommends deploying Exchange front-end servers in a network segment that directly connects the front-end servers to back-end servers, Active Directory domain controllers, and global catalog servers. It is not strictly necessary to deploy a firewall between front-end and back-end servers. In other words, you do not have to deploy front-end servers in the perimeter network. For a detailed discussion of front-end and back-end topologies and their advantages and disadvantages, see the technical guide Exchange Server 2003 and Exchange 2000 Server Front-End and Back-End Topology, available at *http://www.microsoft.com/technet/ prodtechnol/exchange/2003/library/febetop.mspx.*

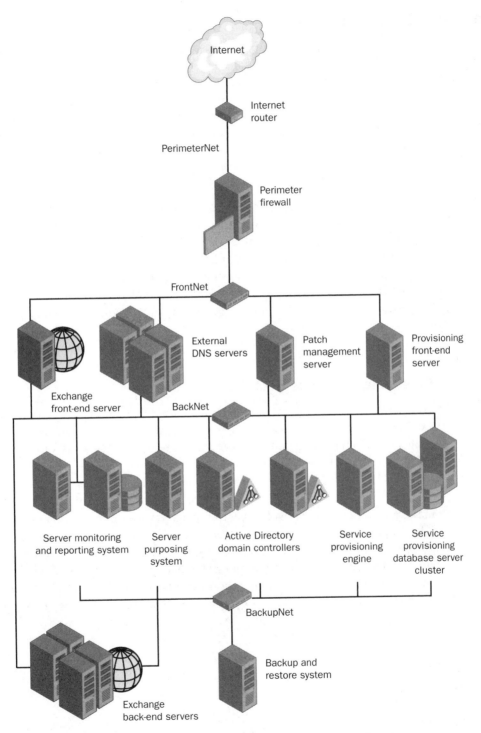

Figure 7-3 A hosting infrastructure with Exchange front-end and back-end servers

Deploying Back-End Servers

Exchange back-end servers are dedicated to storing mailboxes and public folders and as such should be designed with a reliable, high-performance storage subsystem. As discussed in Chapter 6, "Server and Site Consolidation Strategies," Exchange Server 2003 Enterprise Edition includes several features, such as improved memory management, unlimited Exchange store with multiple storage groups and databases, and support for server clusters with up to eight nodes, that enable you to place more mailboxes on an Exchange server than with any earlier version.

Note   The Exchange back-end server design is driven by the number of mailboxes and also by user traffic loads and usage patterns. To ensure that the hosting environment achieves the desired performance, test your server design on a reference system before deploying production servers. For details about designing server hardware, see the "Exchange Server 2003 Performance and Scalability Guide" that you can download at *http:// www.microsoft.com/technet/prodtechnol/exchange/2003/library/perfscal- guide.mspx.*

Clustering Exchange Back-End Servers

To guarantee a very high availability of hosted Exchange services, you should deploy Exchange back-end servers in an active/passive cluster configuration. Active cluster nodes run Exchange virtual servers to provide users with access to mailboxes and public folders, while passive cluster nodes stand by to take over should an active node fail. In this way, active/passive server clusters based on the Windows Cluster Service allow you to keep system downtime at a minimum (and availability at a maximum). It is also relatively easy to replace hardware in a server cluster or to add additional nodes if the number of users increases. The Windows-based Hosting documentation recommends deploying five-node active/passive Exchange 2003 clusters, but you can vary the number of active and passive nodes according to your specific availability requirements. You can find more information about clustering Exchange back-end servers in Chapter 15, "Managing Clustered Exchange 2003 Servers."

> **Note** You should not run SQL Server for MPS or MOM on the same cluster as Exchange back-end servers. We strongly recommend deploying SQL Server and Exchange Server 2003 in separate server clusters. If you deploy these platforms in the same server cluster, a single node might have to run both Exchange 2003 and SQL Server at the same time, which can lead to performance issues and system failures due to insufficient processing resources.

Storage Technologies for Exchange Back-End Servers

Exchange 2003 store supports three key storage technologies for the messaging databases. Depending on the budget and the number of mailboxes you want to host, you can choose among the following technologies:

- **Storage Area Networks (SANs)** Windows-based Hosting documentation recommends using a SAN for the Exchange store because SANs add an extra layer of reliability, provide smart backup and restore features, and support sophisticated storage management. For example, you can increase the storage capacity in a SAN without impacting system availability. However, SANs can be more expensive than alternate solutions, and can confront the administrator with complex configuration challenges.

- **Network-attached storage** If you are planning to provide a hosted Exchange solution with a low or medium storage capacity, you should evaluate Microsoft Windows Storage Server 2003 Feature Pack. Windows Storage Server 2003 Feature Pack allows you to place the Exchange store on a network-attached storage device running Windows Storage Server 2003. At present, Windows Storage Server 2003 Feature Pack is the only supported network-attached storage solution for Exchange Server 2003.

- **Locally attached disks** If you do not have Windows Storage Server 2003 or a comparable Exchange-aware network-attached storage solution, you can also deploy Exchange back-end servers on two-node clusters with locally attached cluster disks or on non-clustered servers, although this configuration must be considered a low-end solution because non-clustered servers do not achieve the same degree of availability as clustered systems and so would not be a typical solution for a hosted environment.

> **Note**   The document 01_Installing Exchange Front-End and Back-End Servers.doc in the \Companion Material\Chapter 07\Exchange Infrastructure folder on the companion CD shows how to deploy a non-clustered Exchange back-end server in a hosting infrastructure. This is sufficient for the test environment in this chapter, but you can also replace the non-clustered system with a server cluster to come closer to a production system. In a production environment, you should deploy a server cluster. Check out the document Deploying an eight-node (5+3) Exchange 2003 Cluster.doc in the \Companion Material\Chapter 15\Server Clustering\ActivePassive folder.

Deploying Front-End Servers

Exchange front-end servers do not require a high-performance storage subsystem because these servers do not host mailboxes or public folders. Front-end servers are primarily responsible for network communication and should therefore be equipped with fast processors, 512 MB of RAM or more, and high-performance network interfaces (1 GB per second) to best handle the communication between messaging clients and back-end servers.

Depending on the number of users, a dual-processor system can be advantageous, but it is also possible to achieve excellent response times with single-processor server configurations if you deploy multiple front-end servers in a load-balancing cluster. Load balancing also eliminates single points of failures and in this way increases front-end server availability. Another important advantage of a front-end server cluster is that you can provide a single point of access to all messaging resources regardless of the number of front-end servers installed. For example, you can use Windows Network Load Balancing, available in Windows Server 2003, to include up to 32 Exchange front-end servers in a single load-balancing cluster. Internet users can then access their mailboxes and public folders through the IP address of the load-balancing cluster. They do not need to access a particular front-end server because any server in the load-balancing cluster can forward the request to the appropriate back-end server. Load balancing is discussed in more detail in Chapter 15, "Managing Clustered Exchange 2003 Servers."

> **On the Resource Kit CD**   For an example of how to configure Exchange front-end servers in a Windows Network Load Balancing (NLB) cluster, see the document Configuring Network Load Balancing for Front-End Servers.doc in the \Companion Material\Chapter 15\Network Load Balancing folder on the companion CD.

Note A general recommendation is to deploy one Exchange front-end server for every four Exchange back-end servers and cluster the servers using NLB. To test front-end server performance, you can use the Exchange Server Stress and Performance 2003 (English only) tool, available for download at *http://www.microsoft.com/downloads/details.aspx?FamilyId=773AE7FD-860F-4755-B04D-1972E38FA4DB&displaylang=en*.

Enabling Exchange Front-End Server Components

By default, every Exchange 2003 server is an Exchange back-end server until you activate the This Is A Front-End Server Check Box on the General tab in the server properties in Exchange System Manager. To apply the changes, you must restart IIS and Exchange services, which you can most conveniently accomplish by rebooting the entire server, but you can also restart the services individually using the Services tool. When the services restart, Exchange 2003 loads the following components to proxy HTTP-, IMAP4-, and POP3-based communication:

- **Exprox.dll** Front-end servers proxy HTTP traffic to back-end servers when users work with Office Outlook Web Access or Outlook Mobile Access, or synchronize mobile devices using Exchange ActiveSync.

- **IMAP4fe.dll** Users of IMAP4-based messaging clients can access mailboxes and public folders through a front-end server. The front-end server loads IMAP4fe.dll instead of IMAP4be.dll on a back-end server to activate the proxy component.

- **POP3fe.dll** Front-end servers load POP3fe.dll instead of POP3be.dll to proxy requests of POP3-based messaging clients to Exchange back-end servers.

Because these front-end server components proxy the client communication, it is possible to separate the back-end server physically from the Internet-accessible part of the hosting infrastructure. In the hosting infrastructure, Exchange front-end servers are dual-homed (that is, equipped with two network cards). One network card is connected to the FrontNet for communication with Internet users and the second network card is connected to the BackNet for communication with back-end servers. This arrangement achieves a high level of security because Internet users cannot access back-end servers directly. Figure 7-4 illustrates this configuration.

> **On the Resource Kit CD**   For step-by-step instructions on how to configure a front-end server, see the document 02_Configuring Exchange Front-End Servers.doc in the \Companion Material\Chapter 07\Exchange Infrastructure folder on the companion CD.

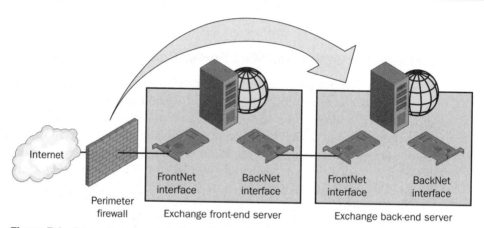

Figure 7-4   Protecting user data from direct Internet access

An Exchange front-end server always contacts a back-end server over the default port that corresponds to the client access protocol. If the back-end server's protocol virtual server is listening at a custom port number, communication cannot take place. Exchange front-end servers listen on the default non-SSL and SSL ports, and Exchange back-end servers must listen on the non-SSL port. Table 7.1 lists the default TCP ports for Internet access protocols.

Table 7-1   Default TCP Ports for Internet Access Protocols

Access protocols	Front-end server	Back-end server
HTTP	TCP port 80 (without SSL) and TCP port 443 (with SSL)	TCP port 80
IMAP4	TCP port 143 (without SSL) and TCP port 993 (with SSL)	TCP port 143
POP3	TCP port 110 (without SSL) and TCP port 995 (with SSL)	TCP port 110

Note   IIS virtual servers that differentiate themselves from other virtual servers only by port numbers are not supported in a front-end and back-end configuration. IIS virtual servers on back-end servers must differentiate themselves by IP addresses or host headers.

HTTP-Based Access To Mailboxes Through Front-End Servers

By default, every Exchange 2003 server has two HTTP virtual directories that Outlook Web Access users can use to access resources: Exchange and Public. Furthermore, there is an OMA virtual directory for access to Outlook Mobile Access, and a virtual directory named Microsoft-Server-ActiveSync that Exchange uses to synchronize mobile devices. To access a mailbox, Outlook Web Access users can use the URL *http://<FQDN of front-end server>/Exchange*. Outlook Mobile Access users can use *http://<FQDN of front-end server>/OMA*.

When a user accesses an HTTP virtual directory on a front-end server, the front-end server prompts the user for account information (that is, user name and password), authenticates the user, and as soon as the user is authenticated, the user's Windows account is known and the front-end server can query Active Directory for the user's home server and mailbox store information. In Active Directory, every mailbox-enabled user object has an msExchHomeServerName attribute that points to the server and a homeMDB attribute that points to the Exchange store of the mailbox.

Note   When accessing a mailbox through a front-end server, the user does not need to know where the mailbox actually resides. The user only needs to access a front-end server, and the front-end server will determine the actual mailbox location dynamically.

The back-end server requires user authentication before access is granted, but the front-end server supplies this information automatically. The user is not prompted a second time. However, authentication on front-end servers requires RPC-based communication between front-end servers and Active Directory domain controllers, which will not work if a firewall is located between the FrontNet and the BackNet blocking RPC traffic. If you cannot have RPC traffic passing this inner firewall, you must disable authentication on the front-end servers and enable anonymous access to the HTTP virtual directories. This is known as pass-through authentication because the front-end server passes authentication requests and responses between the client and the back-end server without performing authentication itself. The back-end server challenges the user for his or her credentials. However, it is important to note that with pass-through authentication, access to mailboxes using a generic URL (that is, *http://<FQDN of front-end server>/Exchange*) does not work anymore because the front-end server cannot determine which back-end server to contact. To access a mailbox without authentication on a front-end server, you must specify the mailbox directly in the URL, such as *http://www.tailspintoys.com/Exchange/user-id,* where user-d is the user's alias. The front-end server can then extract the mailbox name from the URL and perform a directory lookup to find the corresponding mailbox-enabled user account in Active Directory.

Note   In a hosting infrastructure, it is a good idea to let the front-end server authenticate users. You can use forms-based authentication, enabled directly on the front-end servers. Using forms-based authentication, users can access Exchange resources through a generic URL, and can then specify explicit account information to access the desired mailbox.

On the Resource Kit CD   The document Enabling the OWA logon page.doc in the \Companion Material\Chapter 01 folder on the companion CD illustrates how to enable forms-based authentication.

HTTP-Based Access To Public Folders Through Front-End Servers

Outlook Web Access users have the ability to access public folders to participate in discussion groups or access Web-based workflow applications. Access to the MAPI-based public folder hierarchy is possible through the Public virtual directory. For alternate public folder hierarchies, no virtual directory exists by default. If you want to provide users with access to alternate public folder hierarchies, you must create the HTTP virtual directories manually in Exchange System Manager. Remember that you must configure all virtual servers and virtual HTTP directories on the Exchange front-end and back-end servers identically so that front-end servers can properly proxy client connections. For example, if Internet users are supposed to access an alternate public folder hierarchy through a virtual-directory-named alternate, then you should create and configure that HTTP virtual directory on all Exchange front-end servers and all Exchange back-end servers that host the alternate public folder hierarchy. You can read more about the configuration of protocol virtual servers in Chapter 12, "Maintaining IIS Virtual Servers."

Access to MAPI-based public folders differs depending on whether the front-end server performs authentication or not, as follows:

- **Front-end server performs authentication**   For authenticated users, the front-end server can determine the default public store that is associated with the user's mailbox store through Active Directory. You can verify the default public folder store of a mailbox store database in Exchange System Manager (in the properties of the mailbox store on the General tab). The front-end server proxies the client connection to the back-end server that holds the default public folder store to give the user access to the same set of folders that the user would access using Outlook. However, the presence of the MAPI-based public folder hierarchy on a back-end server does not necessarily mean that the server also has the public folder content available. The content may exist on another Exchange server. In this case, the contacted back-end server returns a referral list to the front-end server with the Exchange servers that have the content. The front-end server picks one server from this list and redirects the client connection. If the front-end server cannot contact the selected back-end server over HTTP for any reason, the back-end server is marked as offline and the front-end server chooses another Exchange server. The front-end server marks an unavailable back-end server as offline for a period of 10 minutes to minimize further communication attempts to the offline server.

- **Front-end server does not perform authentication**   If the front-end server cannot authenticate the user, it cannot determine the default public folder store. The user is anonymous until a back-end server performs the authentication. In this scenario, the front-end server queries Active Directory to obtain a list of Exchange servers that host the MAPI-based public folder hierarchy. The front-end server then randomly selects and contacts one of these servers to balance the workload. If the contacted public folder server does not have the contents, the back-end server returns a referral list to the front-end server, as explained earlier. If the front-end server cannot contact the selected back-end server over HTTP for any reason, the back-end server is marked as offline and the front-end server chooses another Exchange server. The front-end server marks an unavailable back-end server as offline for a period of 10 minutes to minimize further communication attempts to the offline server.

Note   Alternate hierarchies are not associated with any mailbox stores. Thus, there is no default public server for an alternative hierarchy. Access to an alternate public folder always works exactly as for unauthenticated access to MAPI-based public folders.

POP3 and IMAP4-Based Access Through Front-End Servers

Access to mailboxes based on POP3 or IMAP4 via front-end servers is straightforward. The user specifies a front-end server and mailbox account in the client configuration, and, when the user starts the client, the account information is passed to the front-end server. Based on this information, the front-end server determines the appropriate back-end server to which to proxy the client communication. The back-end server receives the client request via the front-end server, performs user authentication, determines whether the user is allowed to access the mailbox, and, if this is the case, sends the mailbox data back to the front-end server, which in turn delivers the information to the client.

IMAP4 clients are also able to access public folders. If the public folder does not reside on the user's home server, the client is redirected. To accomplish this, the user's home server returns an IMAP referral to the client, which the front-end server intercepts. The front-end server handles the referral process and redirects the client connection to the appropriate public folder server right away. To the IMAP4 client it appears as if all public folders reside on the front-end server and the user has access to the entire public folder hierarchy. Public folder access only applies to IMAP4 clients, because POP3 clients are unable to access public folders.

> **Note**   POP3 and IMAP4 clients use SMTP to send messages. Your users can specify the front-end server or a bridgehead server as the host for outgoing messages, but the SMTP virtual server is not part of the front-end and back-end configuration.

In Exchange 2003, IMAP4 and POP3 services are not enabled by default. If you want to support IMAP4 and POP3, you must enable these services on the front-end servers as well as on the back-end servers, as shown in the document 02_Configuring Exchange Front-End Servers.doc in the \Companion Material\Chapter 07\Exchange Infrastructure folder on the companion CD. For detailed information Internet-based client access, see also "Exchange Server 2003 Client Access Guide," available at *http://www.microsoft.com/technet/prodtechnol/exchange/2003/library/cliaccgde.mspx*

RPC over HTTP Access Through Front-End Servers

Microsoft Windows XP with Service Pack 1 or later and Microsoft Windows Server 2003 operating systems support RPC communication over HTTP with SSL (HTTPS) connections, and Microsoft Office Outlook 2003 can use RPC over HTTP when communicating with Exchange Server 2003. Because RPC communication is tunneled through HTTPS, service providers do not need to deploy a separate infrastructure based on virtual private network (VPN) technology to provide full Outlook support to their subscribers. With RPC over HTTP, Outlook 2003 client requests are handled similarly to HTTP requests from Outlook Web Access. The difference is that the e-mail client is Outlook 2003.

Figure 7-5 illustrates how an Internet client running Office Outlook 2003 can access a mailbox and public folders on an Exchange back-end server through an arrangement of firewalls and an Exchange front-end server. It is important to understand that no special components are required on the firewalls. Firewalls see RPC over HTTP traffic as regular HTTP traffic encrypted using SSL (TCP port 443) directed at the /rpc virtual directory of an Exchange front-end server. The Exchange front-end server, configured as an RPC over HTTP proxy, then forwards the communication to the back-end server.

On the Resource Kit CD   The document 03_Configuring RPC Over HTTP for Outlook 2003.doc in the \Companion Material\Chapter 07\Exchange Infrastructure folder on the companion CD shows with step-by-step explanations on how to configure an Exchange front-end server as an RPC over HTTP proxy.

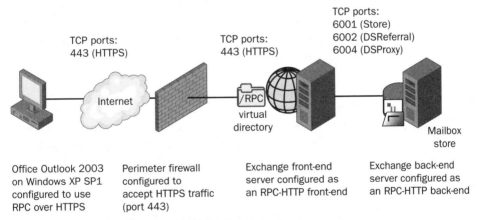

Figure 7-5   RPC over HTTP in a hosting infrastructure

Note   For a discussion of alternative configurations, such as placing a firewall between front-end and back-end servers or using RCP over HTTP without front-end servers, see the technical guide "Exchange Server 2003 RPC over HTTP Deployment Scenarios," available at *http://go.microsoft.com/ fwlink/?linkid=24823*.

Recommended Software for RPC over HTTP

To use RPC over HTTP, you should use the software listed in Table 7.2. The use of Exchange Server 2003 Service Pack 1 (SP1) and Windows XP Service Pack 2 (SP2) is strongly recommended because these service packs include several RPC over HTTP improvements, including:

- **Exchange 2003 SP1** The Microsoft Exchange System Attendant service is redesigned to discover Exchange servers configured as RPC-HTTP back-end servers through Active Directory. Exchange System Manager provides a new user interface to configure these settings. This eliminates the need to configure the Windows registry manually to enable RPC over HTTP. System Attendant updates the front-end server configuration to register all available RPC-HTTP back-end servers automatically. Exchange 2003 SP1 also eliminates the need for the front-end server to communicate with an Active Directory global catalog server through RPC over HTTP. With Exchange 2003 SP1, the front-end server passes all RPC over HTTP communication to the back-end server. On the back-end server, the DSProxy component of System Attendant proxies the communication to Active Directory.

- **Windows XP SP2** It is important to install Windows XP SP2 on all workstations that are configured to use RPC over HTTP. Windows XP SP2 includes several RPC over HTTP fixes. For example, logons using user principal names (UPNs) only work with Windows XP SP2 (or later). The advantages of UPNs in a hosted environment are explained later in this chapter in the section Provisioning Hosted Exchange Services.

> **Note** If you want to use Outlook and RPC over HTTP on a computer running Windows XP SP1 or Windows Server 2003, you must install the Windows XP Patch: RPC Updates Needed for Exchange Server 2003 (*http://go.microsoft.com/fwlink/?LinkId=16687*).

Table 7-2 Recommended Configurations for RPC over HTTP

Client	RPC-HTTP front-end	RPC-HTTP back-end	Global catalog
■ Windows XP SP2	■ Windows Server 2003	■ Windows Server 2003	■ Windows Server 2003
■ Office Outlook 2003 SP1	■ Exchange Server 2003 SP1 or later	■ Exchange Server 2003 SP1 or later	

Deploying RPC over HTTP

The configuration of RPC over HTTP is a straightforward undertaking if you have deployed front-end servers running Exchange 2003 SP1, as detailed in the document 03_Configuring RPC Over HTTP for Outlook 2003.doc that you can find in the \Companion Material\Chapter 07\Exchange Infrastructure folder on the companion CD.

To deploy RPC over HTTP, you must perform the following three steps:

1. Install the Windows RPC over HTTP networking component on the Exchange front-end servers.

2. Configure the Exchange front-end servers as RPC-HTTP front-end servers.

3. Configure the Exchange back-end servers as RPC-HTTP back-end servers.

When you install the Windows RPC over HTTP networking component, you automatically create the /RPC virtual directory in IIS. Office Outlook 2003 will connect to this virtual directory over HTTPS, so it is required to enable SSL for it. It is also important to enable the correct client authentication method in the properties of the /RPC virtual directory. Windows-based Hosting recommends enabling Basic authentication over SSL because Basic authentication is firewall-independent and can be used regardless of the client's domain membership. In a hosting environment, the clients typically do not belong to the internal Active Directory domain.

> **Note** When you identify an Exchange front-end server as an RPC-HTTP front-end server in Exchange System Manager SP1, Exchange System Manager configures the required settings for the /RPC virtual directory.

Deploying the RPC over HTTP Client Configuration Website

To use RPC over HTTP in Office Outlook 2003, users must specify Exchange proxy settings in their client configurations through the following steps:

1. In Outlook, on the Tools menu, click E-Mail Accounts, select View Or Change Existing E-Mail Accounts.

2. Click Next, select the Microsoft Exchange e-mail account, and then click Change.

3. Click More Settings, and then click the Connection tab.

4. Under Exchange Over The Internet, select Connect To My Exchange Mailbox Using HTTP.

5. Click Exchange Proxy Settings, and then specify the proxy server under Use This Url To Connect To My Proxy Server For Exchange. You should also select the check boxes On Fast Networks, Connect Using HTTP First, Then Connect Using

TCP/IP and On Slow Networks, Connect Using HTTP First, Then Connect Using TCP/IP.

6. It is also important that you enable SSL communication with Basic authentication, which is required when using RPC over HTTP.

To facilitate the configuration of an Outlook profile, you can deploy the RPC over HTTP Client Configuration website included in Microsoft Solution for Windows-based Hosting. The RPC over HTTP Client Configuration website automates the deployment of Office Outlook 2003. From this website, the user can download an Outlook profile file and script to configure Office Outlook 2003 on the local computer without having to perform the configuration steps manually.

> **On the Resource Kit CD**   The document 09_Deploying the RPC over HTTP Client Configuration Web Site.doc in the \Companion Material\Chapter 07\Exchange Provisioning folder on the companion CD explains how to deploy the HTTP Client Configuration website, and the document 04_Configuring Outlook 2003 for RPC over HTTP.doc in the \Companion Material\Chapter 07\Sample Scenarios\BizzOrg folder on the companion CD illustrates how to use this website to configure Office Outlook 2003.

Securing Exchange Front-End Servers

As Exchange front-end servers reside in an Internet-accessible location, you must take extra steps to secure these servers and keep them secure. Among other things, you should deactivate unnecessary services, such as the Microsoft Exchange MTA Stacks service, and apply all relevant security patches.

> **Note**   Make sure you configure all of your Exchange front-end servers identically, and carefully test the configuration settings on a reference system.

Use the following steps as a guideline to secure your Exchange front-end servers:

1. Enable and enforce SSL for all Exchange virtual servers so that all communication between the clients and the front-end servers is encrypted. This is important because HTTP, IMAP4, and POP3 are clear-text protocols transmitting user data, such as e-mail messages, in non-encrypted form. Even more important, front-end servers can only perform Basic authentication, which is likewise based on clear-text communication. To protect the account information and passwords of your users, you must enable and enforce SSL.

Note You should enable SSL only on front-end servers. You cannot enable SSL-based encryption between front-end servers and back-end servers. If you must encrypt the front-end and back-end communication, you can use IPSec.

2. Dismount and delete the public folder stores in Exchange System Manager. If you intend to use dedicated bridgehead servers for SMTP-based message transfer, you can also dismount and delete the mailbox stores. However, if you are planning to use the front-end server as bridgehead, you cannot delete the mailbox store. The SMTP service requires access to a mailbox store, for example, when generating non-delivery reports.

On the Resource Kit CD For step-by-step instructions, see the document 02_Configuring Exchange Front-End Servers.doc in the \Companion Material\Chapter 07\Exchange Infrastructure folder on the companion CD.

3. Stop and disable all unnecessary services on the Exchange front-end server. Table 7.3 lists the required Exchange services for each Internet access protocol. You should stop and disable all other Exchange services. However, one exception to this rule is the Microsoft Exchange System Attendant service. Although not required for several protocols, certain tasks are only accomplished if System Attendant is running. For example, System Attendant maintains the DSAccess cache mentioned earlier and runs the metabase update service that transfers relevant configuration changes from Active Directory into the IIS metabase so that the changes can take effect. System Attendant is also responsible for updating the configuration of the RCP-HTTP front-end server if you add further RCP-HTTP back-end servers. Another exception is the Windows License Logging Service. This service must be running on all Exchange front-end servers because IIS does not allow more than ten simultaneous SSL connections unless this service is running.

Table 7-3   Exchange Services Required for Client Access

Client access method	Services required
HTTP (Outlook Web Access, Outlook Mobile Access, Exchange Active Sync)	World Wide Web Publishing Service (W3SVC)
POP3	Microsoft Exchange POP3 (POP3Svc)

Table 7-3   Exchange Services Required for Client Access (Continued)

Client access method	Services required
IMAP4	Microsoft Exchange IMAP4 (IMAP4Svc)
SMTP	Simple Mail Transfer Protocol (SMTPSVC)
	Microsoft Exchange System Attendant (MSExchangeSA)
	Microsoft Exchange Information Store (MSExchangeIS)
	Microsoft Exchange Routing Service (RESVC)

4. Run the Urlscan tool that you can download at *http://www.microsoft.com/down-loads/details.aspx?displaylang=en&familyid=23d18937-dd7e-4613-9928-7f94ef1c902a.* The document 02_Configuring Exchange Front-End Servers.doc on the companion CD demonstrates how to run this tool on an Exchange 2003 front-end server.

> **More Info**   For further information, see Microsoft Knowledge Base article 823175, "Fine-tuning and known issues when you use the Urlscan utility in an Exchange 2003 environment" (*http://support.microsoft.com/ ?kbID=823175*).

5. If you are providing hosted IMAP4 and POP3 services, you can change the IMAP4 and POP3 banners to avoid disclosing system and version information to Internet users. The document 02_Configuring Exchange Front-End Servers.doc on the companion CD shows how to edit the IIS 6.0 metabase to change these banners.

6. Include the front-end servers into your patch management and software distribution system to ensure the servers are updated and have the required security patches installed.

Optimizing Directory Access on Front-End Servers

Exchange front-end servers query Active Directory through the Directory Service Access (DSAccess) component of the Microsoft Exchange System Attendant service. The advantage of querying Active Directory through DSAccess is that DSAccess can dynamically determine the global catalog server to query and can store the results of directory queries temporarily in a cache. The default time period is 10 minutes and the default cache size is 4 MB. DSAccess can measurably reduce the number of queries sent to Active Directory, especially on busy Exchange front-end servers.

The longer you hold information in the DSAccess cache, the more you reduce the network traffic and workload on global catalog servers, but this also increases the chance of the front-end server using outdated directory information. However, increasing the size of the DSAccess cache can help you achieve a high performance on front-end servers. To adjust the expiration interval and size of the DSAccess cache, you must configure registry parameters. It is also possible to disable the DSAccess cache entirely, which may be useful in troubleshooting situations.

> **Warning** Incorrectly editing the registry can cause serious problems that may require you to reinstall your operating system. Problems resulting from editing the registry incorrectly may not be able to be resolved. Before editing the registry, back up any valuable data. Remember to carefully test any configuration changes in your computer lab.

Location	HKEY_LOCAL_MACHINE\System\CurrentControlSet\Services\MSExchangeDSAccess
Name	CachingEnabled
Type	REG_DWORD
Value Data	0x2
Description	To deactivate the DSAccess cache, create the CachingEnabled value and set it to **0x2**. Deleting this value or setting it to **0x1** enables the DSAccess cache again.

To specify an expiration interval or memory size limit, create a new key and call it *Instance0*. The settings under the *Instance0* key influence how DSAccess handles information from the configuration naming context.

Location	HKEY_LOCAL_MACHINE\System\CurrentControlSet\Services\MSExchangeDSAccess\Instance0
Name	CacheTTL
Type	REG_DWORD
Value Data	0x258
Description	Specifies the expiration time for data in the DSAccess cache in seconds (such as **0x258** for ten minutes).

Location	HKEY_LOCAL_MACHINE\System\CurrentControlSet\Services\MSExchangeDSAccess\Instance0
Name	MaxMemory or MaxEntries
Type	REG_DWORD

Value Data	`0x0`
Description	Specifies the expiration time for data in the DSAccess cache in seconds (such as **0x258** for 10 minutes). MaxMemory and specifies the size in kilobytes (such as **0x1000** for 4 MB). Alternately, you may create a REG_DWORD value named MaxEntries and specify the maximum number of entries allowed in the DSAccess cache, but MaxMemory usually gives you more control over the cache size. A MaxEntries value of 0x0 stands for an unlimited number of entries in the DSAccess cache. It should be noted that the minimum memory size limit of the DSAccess cache is 2 MB. *MaxMemory* values of less than 2 MB are ignored.

Offloading SSL from Front-End Servers

You can further increase the performance of your Exchange front-end servers by off-loading SSL to a dedicated device, such as an SSL accelerator card. Installing an SSL accelerator card is a good option for service providers with a small number of front-end servers. For service providers with a large number of front-end servers, on the other hand, an external accelerator device might be a more cost-effective solution. For example, you can use an advanced firewall system, such as Microsoft ISA Server 2004, in front of your Exchange front-end servers to terminate SSL at the perimeter firewall.

SSL Offloading and Outlook Web Access

When using SSL to access mailboxes and public folders in Outlook Web Access, Outlook Web Access must generate the URL for each item using the HTTPS instead of the HTTP protocol identifier. For example, each message in a user's inbox must have a URL that starts with *https://* if SSL is used. In a front-end and back-end configuration, the front-end server informs the back-end server that SSL is used by passing the HTTP header "Front-End-Https: on" in all requests to the back-end server. The back-end server can then generate the URLs in the correct format. However, if SSL is terminated at an external device, the front-end server does not know that an HTTP request was made using SSL, and therefore doesn't pass the "Front-End-Https: on" header to the back-end server.

To solve this issue, you must configure the external accelerator device to pass the HTTP header "Front-End-Https: on" to the front-end server. The front-end server then passes this header unchanged to the back-end server. If you are using an external accelerator device that does not support adding a custom header, you can install an Internet Server Application Programming Interface (ISAPI) extension DLL named ExFeHttpsOnFilter.dll on the front-end server. This ISAPI DLL will add the required header. You must contact Microsoft Product Support Services to obtain ExFeHttpsOnFilter.dll.

More Info   For information about how to configure ExFeHttpsOnFilter.dll, see Microsoft Knowledge Base article 327800, "A new option that allows Exchange and OWA to always use SSL (HTTPS)" (*http://go.microsoft.com/ fwlink/?linkid=3052&kbid=327800*).

Microsoft ISA Server is a good example of a firewall system that supports adding custom headers, which spares you the installation of ExFeHttpsOnFilter.dll on all front-end servers. You can configure ISA Server to generate the "Front-End-Https: on" header by configuring a REG_DWORD parameter named AddFrontEndHttpsHeader in the registry.

More Info   For information about the configuration of ISA Server 2000 for "Front-End-Https: on" support, see Microsoft Knowledge Base article 307347, "Secure OWA Publishing Behind ISA Server May Require Custom HTTP Header" (http://go.microsoft.com/fwlink/?LinkID=3052&kbID= 307347).

Warning   Incorrectly editing the registry can cause serious problems that may require you to reinstall your operating system. Problems resulting from editing the registry incorrectly may not be able to be resolved. Before editing the registry, back up any valuable data.

To enable SSL offloading on a server running ISA Server 2000:

1. Start Registry Editor (regedit32.exe) and open the following registry key: HKEY_LOCAL_MACHINE\SYSTEM\CurrentControlSet\Services\W3Proxy\Parameters.

2. Open the Edit menu, point to New, and then click DWORD Value.

3. Type the name of the new value **AddFrontEndHttpsHeader** and press ENTER.

4. Double-click AddFrontEndHttpsHeader.

5. In the Edit DWORD Value dialog box, type the value **1**.

6. Click OK.

> **Note**   You must restart the World Wide Web Publishing Service to make these changes effective.

SSL Offloading and Forms-Based Authentication

The "Front-End-Https: on" header enables Outlook Web Access to format URLs correctly, but it does not allow you to use forms-based authentication. Forms-based authentication requires SSL. If you offload SSL from the front-end server, you must enable forms-based authentication over non-SSL connections by configuring a REG_DWORD parameter named *SSLOffloaded.*

> **Warning**   Incorrectly editing the registry can cause serious problems that may require you to reinstall your operating system. Problems resulting from editing the registry incorrectly may not be able to be resolved. Before editing the registry, back up any valuable data.

To enable forms-based authentication with SSL offloading:

1. Start Registry Editor (regedit32.exe) and open the following registry key: HKEY_LOCAL_MACHINE\SYSTEM\CurrentControlSet\Services\MSExchangeWeb\OWA.
2. Open the Edit menu, point to New, and then click DWORD Value.
3. Type the name of the new value **SSLOffloaded** and press ENTER.
4. Double-click SSLOffloaded.
5. In the Edit DWORD Value dialog box, type the value **1**.
6. Click OK.

> **Note**   You must restart the World Wide Web Publishing Service to make these changes effective.

SSL Offloading and RPC over HTTP

SSL offloading also represents an issue for Exchange front-end servers configured as RPC over HTTP proxies. In this case, you must configure RPC over HTTP for non-encrypted connections by setting a *REG_DWORD* registry parameter named

AllowAnonymous. Keep in mind, however, that the data now arrives unencrypted at the front-end server. If you must protect the client/server communication between the SSL-offloading device and the front-end server through encryption, you can use IPSec.

> **Warning** Incorrectly editing the registry can cause serious problems that may require you to reinstall your operating system. Problems resulting from editing the registry incorrectly may not be able to be resolved. Before editing the registry, back up any valuable data.

To configure an RPC proxy server for non-SSL connections:

1. On the RPC proxy server, start Registry Editor (regedit).

2. In the console tree, locate the following registry key: HKEY_LOCAL_MACHINE\ Software\Microsoft\Rpc\RpcProxy

3. Create a DWORD Value with the name AllowAnonymous.

4. Double-click the AllowAnonymous value and in the Value data field, enter **1**.

5. On the RPC virtual directory security settings in IIS, under Authentication methods, verify that the check box next to Enable anonymous access is cleared.

> **Note** You must restart the World Wide Web Publishing Service to make these changes effective.

Deploying SMTP Bridgehead Servers

In an Exchange organization with a large number of Internet users, it is advantageous to separate bridgeheads from front-end servers so that message processing and transfer does not impact the front-end server performance. A front-end server that is busy processing a large number of messages will respond slowly to client requests. For this reason, Windows-based Hosting recommends installing dedicated Exchange bridgehead servers. While you can use a non-Exchange system (such as the Windows SMTP service without Exchange extensions) to implement SMTP smart hosts, Exchange bridgehead servers can simplify system configuration and maintenance. For example, it is straightforward to configure an SMTP connector to the Internet on an Exchange front-end server. Exchange back-end servers will automatically forward all outbound messages to the SMTP connector.

On the Resource Kit CD   For step-by-step instructions about how to deploy an SMTP connector on a bridgehead server, see the document 03_Configuring SMTP Bridgehead Servers.doc in the \Companion Material\Chapter 07\Exchange Infrastructure folder on the companion CD.

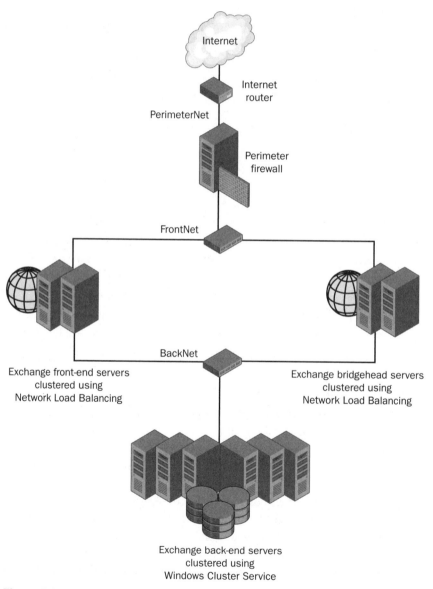

Figure 7-6   Separate front-end servers and bridgehead servers, load-balanced in a hosting infrastructure

Figure 7-6 shows a hosting infrastructure with dedicated front-end servers and bridgehead servers. It is a good idea to deploy two or more bridgehead servers for redundancy. You can cluster multiple bridgeheads using network load balancing or register multiple MX hosts in DNS. Network load balancing is generally the better option because it enables you to specify exactly how to balance the workload and it hides the details of the hosting infrastructure from the Internet.

Intelligent Message Filter on Bridgehead Servers

Exchange bridgehead servers are also an ideal location to perform connection, recipient, and sender filtering, as well as antivirus checks to reduce spam and drop malicious messages. For example, you can configure your bridgehead servers to use a block list provider for connection filtering, as demonstrated in the document Integrating an RBL SP.doc in the \Companion Material\Chapter 01 folder on the companion CD.

In addition, you can install Microsoft Exchange Intelligent Message Filter on your bridgehead servers. Intelligent Message Filter evaluates the textual content of incoming messages from anonymous sources, such as Internet hosts connecting to your Exchange bridgehead servers through SMTP. Intelligent Message Filter assigns each message a rating based on the probability that the message is spam. This rating is persisted with the message when the front-end server sends the message to an Exchange back-end server. You can download Intelligent Message Filter at *http:// www.microsoft.com/downloads/details.aspx?FamilyID=c1b08f7b-8caf-4147-b074-8c9c8f277071&displaylang=en.*

On the Resource Kit CD   The document 04_Configuring SMTP Bridgehead Servers.doc in the \Companion Material\Chapter 07\Exchange Infrastructure folder on the companion CD shows how to install and configure Exchange Intelligent Message Filter.

With Intelligent Message Filter installed, Exchange 2003 performs the following steps for message filtering:

1. During an inbound SMTP session, Exchange applies connection filtering using the following criteria:

   a. Connection filtering checks the global accept list. If an IP address is on the global accept list, no other connection, recipient, or sender filtering is applied, and the message is accepted.

   b. Connection filtering checks the global deny list. If the IP address of the sending server is found on the global deny list, the message is automatically rejected and no other filters are applied.

c. Connection filtering checks the real-time block lists of any providers that you have configured. If the sending server's IP address is found on a block list, the message is rejected and no other filters are applied.

4. After connection filtering is applied, Exchange checks the sender address (the P1 information specified in the SMTP conversion by the MAIL FROM command) against the list of senders you configured in sender filtering. If a match is found, Exchange rejects the message and no other filters are applied.

5. Exchange checks the recipient against the recipient list that you have configured in recipient filtering. If the intended recipient matches an e-mail address that you filter, Exchange rejects the message and no other filters are applied.

6. After recipient filtering is applied, Exchange checks the resolved sender address (the P2 data) against the list of senders you configured in sender filtering. If the sender matches an address on the sender list, Exchange filters the message based on the options you configured and no other filters are applied.

7. If a message is not filtered by connection, recipient, or sender filtering, Intelligent Message Filter is applied. If Intelligent Message Filter assigns the message an SCL rating that is higher than the threshold that you have specified for blocking UCE on gateway servers (in the Message Delivery Properties on the Intelligent Message Filter tab in Exchange System Manager), Intelligent Message Filter takes the action that you selected on the same tab under When Blocking Messages (such as, Archiving, Deleting, Rejecting, or No Action).

Note   As a service provider, you might want to set the Intelligent Message Filter action to No Action so that all UCE is passed to the Junk Mail folders of your users.

8. If Intelligent Message Filter assigns the message an SCL rating that is lower than or equal to your gateway threshold, the message is accepted and the Exchange front-end server forwards the message to the back-end server that hosts the user's mailbox store.

9. The receiving Exchange store compares the message's SCL rating with the store threshold you configured in the Message Delivery Properties on the Intelligent Message Filter tab. If the user is using Outlook 2003 or Exchange 2003 Outlook Web Access and has configured blocked and safe senders lists, one of two things happens:

- If the message rating is lower than or equal to the store threshold, the Exchange store checks the user's blocked senders list configured in Outlook or Outlook Web Access, and either one of the following will happen:

If the sender of the message is not on a blocked senders list configured in Outlook or Outlook Web Access, or if a blocked senders list is not available or defined, the message is delivered to the recipient's Inbox.

If the sender appears on the blocked senders list configured in Outlook or Outlook Web Access, the message is delivered to the user's Junk E-mail folder.

- If the message rating is higher than the store threshold, the mailbox store checks the user's safe senders list configured in Outlook or Outlook Web Access, and one of two things happens:

If the sender appears on the safe senders list, the message is delivered to the recipients Inbox.

If the sender does not appear on the safe senders list or if a safe senders list is not available or defined, the message is delivered to the recipient's Junk E-mail folder. However, if your users have versions of Outlook earlier than Outlook 2003, the mailbox store thresholds have no effect and messages filtered in step 7 are instead delivered to the users' Inboxes. However, if your clients can access e-mail using Outlook Web Access 2003, the store thresholds are applied as described in step 7.

Note By default, Intelligent Message Filter does not process messages of authenticated users, such as IMAP4 users that authenticate to send messages through your bridgehead servers. The document Configuring SMTP Bridgehead Servers.doc outlines how to configure Intelligent Message Filter to process messages of authenticated users as well.

For more information about Intelligent Message Filter, see Chapter 11, "Connecting to the Internet" and also the "Microsoft Exchange Intelligent Message Filter Deployment Guide," available at *http://www.microsoft.com/downloads/details.aspx?FamilyID=b1218d8c-e8b3-48fb-9208-6f75707870c2&displaylang=en*.

Securing Exchange Bridgehead Servers

In general, the same security rules apply to Exchange bridgehead servers and Exchange front-end servers. You should remove the public folder store and disable all unnecessary services. However, you must not dismount or remove the mailbox store. The SMTP-based transport subsystem of Exchange 2003 requires a mailbox store to function properly. For example, the mailbox store is required so that the SMTP-based transport subsystem can generate non-delivery reports successfully.

To secure an Exchange bridgehead server, follow these steps:

1. Dismount and delete the public folder stores that exist on the bridgehead server in Exchange System Manager.

2. Stop and disable all unnecessary services on the Exchange front-end server. Exchange bridgehead servers require only the following Exchange services:

    ■ Simple Mail Transfer Protocol (SMTPSVC)

    ■ Microsoft Exchange System Attendant (MSExchangeSA)

    ■ Microsoft Exchange Information Store (MSExchangeIS)

    ■ Microsoft Exchange Routing Service (RESVC)

3. Change the SMTP banner that the SMTP service sends as a greeting to hosts that establish an SMTP connection in order to avoid disclosing system and version information.

> **On the Resource Kit CD**   You can use the script SMTPBanner.wsf in the \Companion Material\Chapter 07\Scripts folder on the companion CD to change the SMTP banner.

4. Disable authentication to protect your bridgehead servers from possible dictionary attacks. In a dictionary attack, a malicious user runs through a list of words and typical password strings, performing a logon attempt for each, in order to guess another user's password. However, you cannot disable authenticated access on an SMTP virtual server if IMAP4 or POP3 users specify the SMTP virtual server as the outgoing mail host in their client configurations. By default, only authenticated users are permitted to relay messages through an Exchange SMTP virtual server. If authentication is disabled, POP3 and IMAP4 users cannot send messages to external SMTP domains.

5. Include the Exchange bridgehead servers into your patch management and software distribution system to ensure the servers are updated and have the required security patches installed.

Provisioning Hosted Exchange Services

As a service provider, you have two general options to provide hosted Exchange services to subscribers. You can implement a separate Exchange organization for each subscriber or share a single Exchange organization. Implementing separate Exchange organizations is a good idea if you have subscribers with a large number of users. Small- and medium-sized customers, on the other hand, are best hosted in a shared Exchange organization to maximize the ROI into the hosting infrastructure. For example, it is more cost-efficient to host business organizations with less than 50 users in a shared organization than each in a separate organization with dedicated Active Directory domain controllers and Exchange front-end servers and back-end servers. Windows-based Hosting achieves cost efficiency by sharing an Exchange organization.

Sharing an Exchange Organization

To share an Exchange organization, you must structure the messaging system in a way that users from different business organizations work with different sets of resources. For example, if you split the server-based address lists so that users of a particular business organization can see only users from their own business organization in the address book, the Exchange organization will appear as if it belonged exclusively to these users. The address book will give these users no indication that other business organizations are hosted in the same Exchange organization as well. However, server-based address lists are not the only type of resource that you must take into consideration.

To provide a distinct environment to each subscriber in a shared Exchange organization, you must divide the following resources:

- **Active Directory domain** You must split user account management in Active Directory by means of organizational units so that administrators from each business organization can manage their user accounts but not the user accounts of other business organizations, and you must use UPN suffixes in user logon names so that users can log on to their mailboxes without having to know the shared domain name. Table 7.4 lists advantages of UPNs in hosted environments.

> **Note** You can support authentication based on UPNs on IIS virtual directories if you enable Basic authentication and set the default domain to a backslash "\." Outlook 2003 running on Windows XP also supports the use of UPNs. Because Outlook Web Access can handle Basic authentication using any valid UPN, you do not need to provide an individual virtual directory for each hosted Exchange organization.

Table 7-4   Advantages of UPNs in Hosted Environments

Advantage	Comments
Hide shared domain name	Users can log on using their e-mail addresses, such as Ted@Fabrikam.com. E-mail addresses are generally easier to handle than Windows NT-style logon names, which include the domain name as in TAILSPINTOYS\Ted. Furthermore, the e-mail address can be business organization-specific while the domain name refers to the shared Active Directory domain, which is the same for all hosted organizations.
Provide a unique namespace	UPNs can be used to provide a unique namespace for each hosted organization. The logon names do not need to be unique as long as the UPNs are distinctive and used for logon and user identification. For example, you can create two special Guest accounts and name them Guest@FourthCoffee.com and Guest@Fabrikam.com.
Reveal company information in log files	Security-related events, written to the server's event log, allow you to identify the user and his or her company from the user logon name.

- **Internet domain**   You should register a separate Internet domain for each business organization to provide all users with SMTP addresses that reflect their individual organizations. You can then register your Exchange front-end servers in the external DNS as hosts of each Internet domain so that the users of a business organization can access messaging resources through an individual address. For example, a company named Fabrikam, Inc. might want to provide its users with a host name of mail.fabrikam.com to access the Exchange organization, while a company named Fourth Coffee might want to use a host name of mail.fourthcoffee.com.

Note   Internet domains, which you register for the purpose of providing your subscribers with individual URLs and e-mail addresses, are often known as vanity domains. Windows-based Hosting supports vanity domains for business organizations and individual consumers.

- **IIS virtual servers**   When you enable SSL directly on Exchange front-end servers, you must configure individual virtual servers for each business organization so that you can use organization-specific SSL certificates. For example, you cannot point both *https://mail.fabrikam.com* and *https://mail.fourthcoffee.com* to the same HTTP virtual server because a particular SSL certificate cannot be issued to more than one host name. If the certificate is issued to mail.fabrikam.com then users accessing Outlook Web Access through *https:// mail.fourthcoffee.com* will receive a security warning that the host name specified in the URL does not match the name registered in the SSL certificate. Configuring multiple virtual servers on a front-end server for SSL requires you to assign the front-end server multiple IP addresses because Exchange front-end servers only support SSL communication over default ports, such as TCP port 443 for HTTPS, as mentioned earlier in this chapter, and the IP address/TCP port combination must be unique for each virtual server.

Note If you are planning to host a large number of Internet domains, you should consider offloading SSL encryption from front-end servers so that you can use a single virtual server for all domains. The more virtual servers and virtual directories you create in Exchange System Manager, the more information System Attendant must replicate from Active Directory into the local IIS metabase.

If you are offloading SSL through an external SSL accelerator or perimeter firewall, you must associate the correct SSL certificates on this device. Figure 7-7 shows an example where SSL connections are terminated on a perimeter firewall. This configuration has the advantage that you do not need to configure additional virtual servers on Exchange servers. The default virtual servers can handle non-SSL communication for all Internet domains hosted in the Exchange organization.

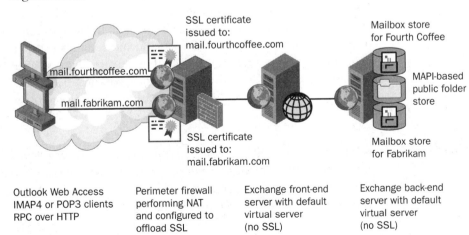

Figure 7-7 Offloading SSL for multiple Internet domains

■ **Exchange store**   As shown in Figure 7-7, you might also want to configure separate mailbox stores for each business organization. This allows you to delegate permissions selectively to the appropriate administrators responsible for mailbox management in each business organization. Splitting the Exchange store also facilitates the configuration of offline address books. You should configure a separate offline address book for each business organization so that users do not download address information from other companies.

> **Note**   Exchange Server 2003 supports four storage groups plus one recovery storage group per server, and each storage group can hold up to five mailbox stores. This implies that if you want to provide each hosted Exchange organization with an individual mailbox store, you cannot host more than 20 organizations per server. Hosted Exchange 2003 bypasses this limitation by configuring offline address book settings on a per recipient basis. With Hosted Exchange 2003, hosted organizations can share a single mailbox store, so you can host more than 20 organizations per server if it is not required to provide each hosted Exchange organization with an individual mailbox store.

If you want to provide subscribers with access to public folders, you must also split the public folder store. However, there is only one MAPI-based public folder hierarchy per Exchange organization, so all business organizations work with the same public folder hierarchy and can access all public folders, by default. To provide each business organization with a different set of MAPI-based public folders, you must assign each organization a dedicated top-level folder and set access permissions on it so that the top-level folder is only visible and accessible to the users of that organization. Underneath the top-level folder, users of a business organization can then create their organization-specific public folders for discussion forums and other workgroup applications. It is possible to configure multiple top-level public folders for a single business organization.

> **Note**   Keep the right to create top-level folders in the MAPI-based hierarchy restricted to the system administrators of the data center so that subscribers cannot create additional top-level folders, which, by default, would be visible to all users in the shared Exchange organization.

- **Address lists** As mentioned earlier, you must split the server-based address lists, such as the global address list (GAL), to deliver the impression that only the users from a particular business organization belong to the same Exchange organization. Among other things, you must delete the address list definitions in Exchange System Manager under All Address Lists in the Recipients container because these definitions include recipient objects regardless of the business organization they belong to. However, you should not delete the default GAL definition that you can find under All Global Address Lists. System components, such as the SMTP service, need access to a complete address list. Instead, you should change the access permissions on the GAL definition object so that users from business organizations cannot read the default GAL, as outlined in the document 06_Configuring Exchange Server Default Address Lists.doc in the \Companion Material\Chapter 07\Exchange Infrastructure folder on the companion CD.

Provisioning Services Through MPS

Microsoft Provisioning System (MPS) is a key component in Windows-based Hosting because it enables you to automate the tasks that you must accomplish to share an Exchange organization between multiple business organizations. MPS does not only automate series of complex configuration steps, it also tracks provisioning activities in an audit database and provides a platform for delegating provisioning tasks to resellers and customers.

Figure 7-8 shows the architecture of MPS based on a configuration with separate servers. It is also possible to install all components on a single server, but a single server cannot support the FrontNet/BackNet design discussed in this chapter.

> **On the Resource Kit CD** The documents in the \Companion Material\Chapter 07\Exchange Provisioning folder on the companion CD outline how to deploy MPS with separate servers running front-end components, provisioning engine, and databases.

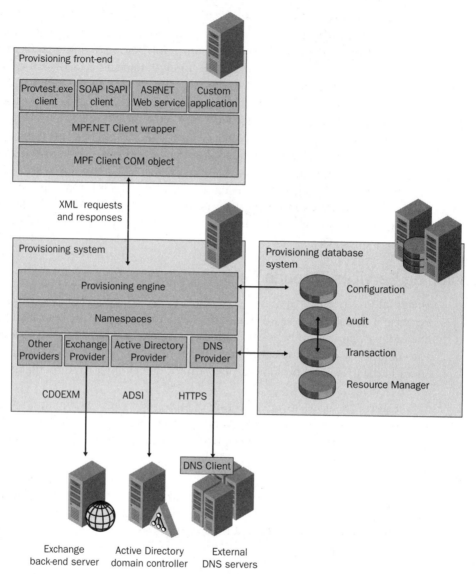

Figure 7-8 MPS architecture with separate front-end server, provisioning engine, and database cluster

MPS handles provisioning tasks as follows:

1. A user with administrative permissions (such as a data center administrator, a reseller, or a consumer) connects to the provisioning front-end server and requests a provisioning action, such as the creation of a new vanity domain. MPS for Windows-based Hosting includes an ASP.NET Web service that accepts configuration requests in the form of XML documents and a sample Exchange provisioning website based on this Web service to create provisioning requests,

but you can also develop your own management applications. Windows-based Hosting includes API documentation and a developer toolkit.

Note   The document Deploying the Hosted Exchange Sample Web Service Client.doc in the \Companion Material\Chapter 07\Sample Scenarios folder on the companion CD illustrates how to install the sample Web Service Client that is included with Windows-based Hosting. The Web Service Client demonstrates how to perform Exchange provisioning tasks through the Web service and .ASPX pages.

2. The Web service (or custom application) passes the provisioning request in the form of an XMP document to MPF .NET Client Wrapper, and MPF .NET Client Wrapper passes the request to the MPF Client COM object. The MPF .NET Client Wrapper and MPF Client object both reside on the same computer as the calling .NET application.

3. The MPF Client forwards the request unchanged to the provisioning engine.

4. Although every provisioning request maps to a single procedure, that procedure can include calls to lower-level procedures as well. For example, it is possible that a high-level provisioning procedure chains together calls to other procedures to involve multiple providers. Accordingly, the provisioning engine must parse the XML request and query the configuration database to expand the request into individual actions that the engine must perform to carry out the provisioning task.

Note   In MPS, namespaces are used to group procedures together. Each namespace is registered in the configuration database. You can view the namespaces and procedures that they contain in MPS Provisioning Manager under the Namespaces node. For example, you can find many of the provisioning procedures important for a hosted Exchange environment in the Hosted Exchange namespaces, such as *CreateMailbox*, *CreateSMTPDomain*, and *CreatePublicFolder*.

5. Based on the actions identified in the expanded request, the provisioning engine calls the relevant providers. A provider is a set of COM objects that contain the code for making API calls to external applications, such as Exchange 2003 or Active Directory. For example, MPS uses Collaboration Data Objects for Exchange Management (CDOEXM) to perform Exchange 2003 functions, and ADSI to perform management actions against Active Directory.

6. The providers carry out the requests and return the results to the provisioning engine. The providers also write transaction data to the transaction database so that MPS can rollback the transactions if a subsequent provider call in the current transaction fails. The transaction data is moved from the transaction log to the audit database for historical reference.

7. The provisioning engine returns the results to the MPF client in XML format.

8. The MPF client returns the results to the client wrapper, which in turn provides them to the calling application.

Provisioning a Reseller Organization

In Windows-based Hosting, a reseller is an entity that leases infrastructure capacity from the service provider and sells it to its customers. A particular reseller can have multiple customers for which the reseller can perform management tasks, such as creating a business organization. A particular business organization can have only one reseller, although a particular reseller can have multiple customers. This relationship between resellers and customers maps to a hierarchical structure of organizational units in Active Directory. At the top is a single organizational unit, named Hosting for example, and underneath it are all reseller organizational units that contain sublevel organizational units for customers. Placing all resellers and customers into the same tree facilitates the delegation of administrative permissions on reseller and customer organizational units. Permissions granted on higher-level organizational units are inherited by lower-level organizational units, and so an administrator of a reseller is also an administrator for all the reseller's customers.

Figure 7-9 shows a sample organizational unit hierarchy with two resellers and their customers. ConsolidatedMessenger and TailspinToys are the reseller organizational units. Fourth Coffee, Litware, Inc., Contoso, Ltd., and Northwind Traders are the customer organizational units.

Figure 7-9 A sample hierarchy of reseller and customer organizational units

Creating a Reseller Organizational Unit

To create a reseller organizational unit through MPS, you must call the *CreateReseller-rOrganization* procedure from the Hosted Exchange namespace. The following XML document shows how to create a reseller named ConsolidatedMessenger. The most important parameters that you must pass to the *CreateResellerOrganization* procedure are the LDAP path of the parent organizational unit in which MPS is supposed to create the new reseller organizational unit, the name of the reseller organization, and the preferred domain controller that MPS should connect to.

```
<?xml version="1.0" encoding="utf-8" ?>
<request xmlns:xsl="http://www.w3.org/1999/XSL/Transform">
  <procedure xmlns:xsl='http://www.w3.org/1999/XSL/Transform'>
    <execute namespace="Hosted Exchange"
                 procedure="CreateResellerOrganization" impersonate="1">
      <executeData>
        <container>LDAP://OU=Hosting,DC=TailspinToys,DC=Com</container>
        <name>ConsolidatedMessenger</name>
        <description>Hosted E-mail account reseller</description>
        <preferredDomainController>
            ad01.tailspintoys.com
        </preferredDomainController>
      </executeData>
      <after source="executeData" destination="data" mode="merge"/>
    </execute>
  </procedure>
</request>
```

The *CreateResellerOrganization* procedure is explained in detail in the Windows-based Hosting documentation.

> **On the Resource Kit CD**   The document 05_Creating a Reseller OU and Admin User.doc in the \Companion Material\Chapter 07\Exchange Provisioning folder on the companion CD demonstrates how to use the MPS provisioning test tool (Provtest.exe) to pass this XML document to the provisioning engine.

You can also use the Hosted Exchange 2003 Sample Web Site to create resellers conveniently through a Web page (CreateResellerOrg.aspx). CreateResellerOrg.aspx renders the XML data based on the information that you submit in an HTML form and passes the XML document to the provisioning engine through the MPS Web service.

Structuring Service Administration

Besides creating a reseller organizational unit and registering the reseller organization in the configuration database of MPS, the *CreateResellerOrganization* procedure also creates a number of security groups in Active Directory. Most important are the following two groups:

- **Admins@<reseller>**   This security group is for service provider administrators. If you create a service administrator account for a reseller, you add this account as a member to this group.

- **CSRAdmins@<reseller>**   This security group is for customer service representatives (CSRs) of the reseller. MPS differentiates between service administrators and CSRs. For example, you can restrict the set of MPS procedures available to CSRs so that CSRs can manage user accounts but cannot create or delete business organizations.

Note If you enable Advanced Features on the View menu in Active Directory Users and Computers, you will also notice a hidden _Private container in each hosting organizational unit. The _Private container holds various security groups and sub-level container objects that MPS requires for internal operations. For example, the AllUsers@<organization> group is used to grant user accounts Read and List Contents permissions on their organizational units. The sub-level container objects enable MPS to determine the organization type of an organizational unit, such as hosting, reseller, or customer.

To provide a reseller with an administrative account, you must create a user account and add it to the Admins@<reseller> or CSRAdmins@<reseller> group. You can use the *CreateBusinessUser* procedure from the Hosted Exchange namespace for this purpose, as shown in the following listing:

```
<?xml version="1.0" encoding="utf-8" ?>
<request xmlns:xsl="http://www.w3.org/1999/XSL/Transform">
  <procedure xmlns:xsl='http://www.w3.org/1999/XSL/Transform'>
    <execute namespace="Hosted Exchange"
                     procedure="CreateBusinessUser" impersonate="1">
      <executeData>
        <preferredDomainController>
          ad01.tailspintoys.com
        </preferredDomainController>
        <container>
      LDAP://OU=ConsolidatedMessenger,OU=Hosting,DC=Tailspintoys,DC=Com
        </container>
        <policy>Reseller</policy>
```

```
  <userPrincipalName>
    Admin@ConsolidatedMessenger
  </userPrincipalName>
  <displayName>ConsolidatedMessenger Administrator</displayName>
  <givenName>Admin</givenName>
  <middleName>Admin</middleName>
  <sn>Admin</sn>
  <initials>AD</initials>
  <newPassword do-not-log="1">1qw$t9x</newPassword>
  <description>Consolidated Messenger Administrator</description>
  <isAdmin>1</isAdmin>
  <properties>
  </properties>
  </executeData>
  <after source="executeData" destination="data" mode="merge"/>
  </execute>
 </procedure>
</request>
```

The LDAP path specified in the <container> tag enables MPS to associate the user account with the reseller organizational unit. MPS creates the user account with the specified account information and password, and then adds this account to the Admins@ConsolidatedMessenger group because the <isAdmin> tag is set to a value of 1. Membership in the Admins@ConsolidatedMessenger group grants the account the permissions of a system administrator in the reseller organizational unit hierarchy of ConsolidatedMessenger. Also noteworthy is the <userPrincipalName> tag. As mentioned earlier in this chapter, UPNs are a means to provide users with accounts that reflect their individual organizations. For example, the administrator of Consolidated-Messenger can now log on with the account name Admin@ConsolidatedMessenger and does not have to know or specify the shared domain name (which is TAILSPIN-TOYS in the test environment of this chapter).

On the Resource Kit CD For step-by-step instructions on how to create administrator accounts for a reseller, see the document 05_Creating a Reseller OU and Admin User.doc on the companion CD.

Note MPS does not create a mailbox for the administrator account specified in the XML document listed above because the reseller organization is not Exchange-enabled and a service plan was not specified.

Provisioning Business and Consumer Organizations

Business organizations and consumer organizations are entities that lease infrastructure resources from a reseller organization or directly from the service provider. In Active Directory, business and consumer organizations are represented by organizational units that typically reside within reseller organizational units, as indicated previously in Figure 7-9. However, unlike reseller organizations, business and consumer organizations are Exchange-enabled, meaning they consume resources in the Exchange organization.

Managing Exchange Resources

To prevent overuse of resources, MPS includes a resource manager component that controls how much space a business or consumer organization can consume in the Exchange store. Resource manager accomplishes this task by subtracting provisioned resources from a pool of available resources. You must add resources available in the shared Exchange organization to this pool before you can provision your first business or consumer organization.

> **On the Resource Kit CD**   The document 03_Installing Hosted Exchange 2003 Sample Service Plans.doc in the \Companion Material\ Chapter 07\Exchange Provisioning folder on the companion CD contains a sample XML listing and demonstrates how to add resources available in the shared Exchange organization to MPS resource manager through the *AddExchangeResources* procedure from the Exchange Resource Manager Ex namespace

Table 7.5 lists the types of resources that you must initialize for Exchange resource management.

Table 7-5   Exchange Resources Managed by MPS Resource Manager

Resources	Properties	Comments
ConsumerMailStore	■ serverName ■ mailStoreName ■ megabytes ■ warningPC ■ defaultMaxFillPC	Identifies a mailbox store that MPS can use for consumer mailboxes. The *megabytes* property defines the size of the disk storage available for the database.
		The *defaultMaxFillPC* property defines the maximum percentage of allocation for the resource and *warningPC* defines the percentage of resource allocation before MPS issues warnings about available resources. To add storage space to a consumer mail store, you can use the *ReAllocateConsumerMailStore* procedure from the Exchange Resource Manager Ex namespace.
		It is important to note that the mailbox store name must be unique in the Exchange organization. Windows-based Hosting recommends a naming scheme of "Mailbox Store N (ServerName)" where N is an integer that is unique on the server.
FrontEndServer	■ serverName	Defines Exchange front-end server that is available in the shared organization. You can use the *QueryAllFrontEndServers* procedure from the Exchange Resource Manager Ex namespace to obtain a listing of all front-end servers that have been added to MPS.
MailStore	■ serverName ■ mailStoreName ■ megabytes ■ shared	Identifies a mailbox store that MPS can use for mailboxes of business customers. The *megabytes* property defines the overall storage space available for mailboxes. The *shared* property indicates whether the Exchange store may be shared by multiple business organizations. A value of 1 indicates that the Exchange store may be shared; otherwise MPS will allocate the mailbox store to a single business organization.
		It is important to note that the mailbox store name must be unique in the Exchange organization. Windows-based Hosting recommends a naming scheme of "Mailbox Store N (ServerName)" where N is an integer that is unique on the server.

Table 7-5   Exchange Resources Managed by MPS Resource Manager (Continued)

Resources	Properties	Comments
PublicStore	■ serverName ■ publicStoreName ■ megabytes	Identifies a public folder store that MPS can use for public folders of business customers. The *megabytes* property defines the overall storage space available for public folders.

MPS resource manager keeps track of available resources as follows:

■ MPS receives a provisioning request for a business organization, business user, or consumer specifying the total amount of space required.

■ MPS resource manager checks the pool of available resources to determine those resources that have sufficient space available for the provisioning request. For example, if you provision a business user, MPS resource manager will determine all MailStore resources that can hold the mailbox.

■ If multiple resources of a given type are available, MPS resource manager selects the resource with the least free space available to maintain a tight packing of resources.

■ MPS resource manager decrements the estimate of space available within that resource by the total amount of space required for this provisioning request.

Note   MPS resource manager does not monitor the actual resource consumption. For example, users might not use all of their allocated mailbox capacities and so the actual store size may be considerably less than what is allocated in MPS resource manager.

Provisioning a Business Organization

Having identified the overall set of resources available in the shared Exchange organization, you can begin provisioning business organizations.

On the Resource Kit CD   You can use the *CreateBusinessOrganization* procedure from the Hosted Exchange namespace or the sample Exchange Web service client, as demonstrated in the document 01_Creating a Business Organization and Business User.doc in the \Companion Material\Chapter 07\Sample Scenarios\BizzOrg folder on the companion CD.

The following XML document creates a business organization named Fourth Coffee:

```
<request xmlns:xsl="http://www.w3.org/1999/XSL/Transform">
  <procedure xmlns:xsl='http://www.w3.org/1999/XSL/Transform'>
    <execute  namespace="Hosted Exchange"
             procedure="CreateBusinessOrganization" impersonate="1">
      <executeData>
        <container>
         LDAP://OU=ConsolidatedMessenger,OU=Hosting,DC=Tailspintoys,DC=Com
        </container>
        <name>FourthCoffee</name>
        <mailStore>
          <megabytes>1000</megabytes>
          <shared>1</shared>
        </mailStore>
        <publicStore>
          <megabytes>1000</megabytes>
        </publicStore>
        <SMTPDomain>FourthCoffee.com</SMTPDomain>
        <preferredDomainController>
          ad01.Tailspintoys.com
        </preferredDomainController>
          <availablePlans>
            <planName>BaseMail</planName>
            <planName>GoldMail</planName>
            <planName>PlatinumMail</planName>
          </availablePlans>
      </executeData>
      <after source="executeData" destination="data" mode="merge"/>
    </execute>
  </procedure>
</request>
```

The *CreateBusinessOrganization* procedure performs the following steps to create the business organization:

1. Creates the business organization in Active Directory.

2. MPS creates an organizational unit and security groups for service administrators and customer service representatives in Active Directory, similar to those resources created for a reseller organization.

3. Track the creation of a new business organization in the MPS databases.

4. MPS adds a new record for the business organization to the customer plan database and logs a created event.

5. Exchange-enable the business organization.

6. MPS calls the *ExchangeEnableOrganization* procedure from the Hosted Exchange namespace to enable the business organization for Exchange mailboxes and public folders. This procedure allocates the amount of space specified for the mailbox store and the public folder store for the organization, and it creates the organization's primary SMTP domain. By default, MPS creates a recipient policy for the SMTP domain in the shared Exchange organization.

> **Note**   Business organizations are limited to one mailbox store, and there are no procedures for moving organizations and user mailboxes to another store.

7. Create an association between service plans and the organization in the customer plan database. In this optional step, MPS can restrict the business organization to a specified set of service plans. For example, it is possible to specify that a business organization can only use basic mail features as defined in the BaseMail sample service plan. You can read more about service plans later in this chapter.

Provisioning a Consumer Organization

Provisioning a consumer organization does not differ from provisioning a business organization. Using the *CreateBusinessOrganization* procedure, you must specify how much mailbox storage the consumer organization can allocate an SMTP domain. A consumer organization typically does not need a public folder store, but you should specify which service plans MPS should make available to consumers.

> **On the Resource Kit CD**   For an example of how to create a consumer organization, see the document 06_Creating the Consumer OU and Admin User.doc in the \Companion Material\Chapter 07\Exchange Provisioning folder on the companion CD.

> **Note** The difference between a business organization and a consumer organization results from using different methods to create users. Business users have mailboxes in a MailStore resource and consumer users have mailboxes in ConsumerMailStore resources. MailStore and ConsumerMail-Store are specifically designed to isolate mail stores intended for use by business organizations and those intended for use by consumer e-mail accounts.

Provisioning Mailboxes and Public Folders

The Hosted Exchange namespace provides the following three procedures to create mailboxes and public folders in a shared Exchange organization:

- **CreateConsumerUser** Using this procedure, you can create a consumer user with attributes based on a specified service plan. Among other things, you must specify a valid LDAP path of the organizational unit where the new user will be created, the UPN of the user, the sAMAccountName, and a preferred domain controller. Optionally, you can also specify a password for the new user account. The service plan that you specify in the *planName* property determines the set of e-mail features available to the consumer user. You can also use *CreateConsumerUser.aspx* in the Hosted Exchange Sample Web Client to sign-up consumer users over a Web page.

> **On the Resource Kit CD** For an example of how to use the *CreateConsumerUser* procedure in an XML document, see the CreateConsumerUser.xml file in the \Companion Material\Chapter 07\Scripts folder on the companion CD.

> **Note** By default, consumer users do not have access to a server-based address list or public folders. Furthermore, the *CreateConsumerUser* procedure does not add the consumer user as a member to the AllUsers@<ConsumerOrg> security group. MPS uses this group to grant users List Object access to their organization OU. To give consumer users proper access, you must add the Domain Users group to the organizational unit of the consumer organization and give it List Object permissions (see 06_Creating the Consumer OU and Admin User.doc on the companion CD).

- ***CreateBusinessUser*** Using this procedure, you can create a user in a business organization. This is not much different from creating an administrator for an organization, as discussed earlier in this chapter for a reseller organization. The difference is that you must specify a service plan in the *planName* property to mailbox-enable the user, and you do not need to set the *isAdmin* property if you do not want to grant the user administrative permissions. You can also use *CreateBusinessUser.aspx* in the Hosted Exchange Sample Web Client to create business users in a Web page.

On the Resource Kit CD For an example of how to use the *CreateBusinessUser* procedure in an XML document, see the CreateBusinessUser.xml file in the \Companion Material\Chapter 07\Scripts folder on the companion CD.

Note MPS resource manager subtracts space from the business organization's mailbox store as you create business users. If all space is used up, no more users can be provisioned for that organization. In this case, it may become necessary to increase the space an organization has on a mail store by using the *ReAllocateOrganizationMailNoMove* procedure.

- ***CreateFolder*** Using this procedure, you can create public folders in the MAPI-based public folder hierarchy and configure access control lists. Among other things, you must specify the organization for which you want to create the public folder so that MPS resource manager can subtract the space from that organization's resource pool. The megabytes tag specifies the maximum size of the public folder. MPS also uses this value to configure the folder's Prohibit post at setting. The *folderPath* property, on the other hand, specifies the location of the public folder in the MAPI-based public folder hierarchy. If you want to create a top-level folder for a business organization, you should specify a forward slash "/." Business users can then create sub-level folders in Outlook.

    If you want to create a top-level folder, you must set permissions on the folder so that only users from the business organization are able to see and work with the public folder. This is accomplished using the Permissions tag. Each permission entry must specify a MAPI role (owner, publishing editor, author, editor, publishing author, non-editing author, contributor, or none) and the LDAP path to a user account or security group to which you want to assign this role.

On the Resource Kit CD   The CreatePublicFolder.xml file in the \Companion Material\Chapter 07\Scripts folder on the companion CD demonstrates how to create a top-level public folder and set permissions on it.

Using Exchange Mailbox Service Plans

As mentioned earlier, to mailbox-enable a user account, you must specify a service plan in the *CreateConsumerUser* or *CreateBusinessUser* procedure. A service plan is a collection of attributes that describe the features that you want to enable for a user. When provisioning a new business organization, the provisioning process includes selecting which service plans are available to users within that organization. When a plan is then assigned to a user, MPS enables the specified features. The provisioning system for Hosted Exchange 2003 includes a Service Plan database and several sample service plans. You can also create your own custom service plans through the *CreatePlanFeatureTypes* and *CreateMailboxPlan* from the Hosted Exchange namespace. However, creating a custom service plan is optional and not required for a successful deployment. For more information, see the section "Creating a Custom Exchange Mailbox Service Plan" in the Windows-based Hosting documentation.

Table 7.6 lists the sample service plans that ship with the provisioning system for Hosted Exchange 2003.

On the Resource Kit CD   The document 03_Installing Hosted Exchange 2003 Sample Service Plans.doc in the \Companion Material\Chapter 07\Exchange Provisioning folder on the companion CD provides step-by-step installation instructions.

Table 7-6   Hosted Exchange 2003 Sample Service Plans

Service plan	Features	Comments
BaseMail	■ 10 megabytes mailbox space ■ POP3 and IMAP4 ■ Basic Outlook Web Access features	MPS set the storage limits for BaseMail users as follows: ■ **Issue warning at (KB):** 9000 ■ **Prohibit send at (KB):** 10000 ■ **Prohibit send and receive at (KB):** 50000 MPS configures the storage quotas so that Exchange issues warnings at 90 percent of the quota limit, prevents the user from sending e-mail when the quota limit is reached, and, additionally, prohibits message reception at five times the quota limit. Furthermore, MPS enables only the basic features of Outlook Web Access by setting the msExchMailboxFolderSet directory attribute for that user to a bitmask value of 0x00018205, which corresponds to a combination of the following features: ■ **Messaging** 0x00000001 ■ **Contacts** 0x00000004 ■ **Rich client** 0x00000200 ■ **Themes** 0x00008000 ■ **Junk e-mail** 0x00010000 To learn more about Outlook Web Access segmentation, see Microsoft Knowledge Base article 833340, "How to modify the appearance and the functionality of Outlook Web Access by using the segmentation feature in Exchange 2003" (*http://support.microsoft.com/ ?id=833340*).

Table 7-6   Hosted Exchange 2003 Sample Service Plans (Continued)

Service plan	Features	Comments
GoldMail	■ 20 megabytes mailbox space ■ POP3 and IMAP4 ■ Enhanced Outlook Web Access features	MPS set the storage limits for GoldMail users as follows: ■ **Issue warning at (KB):** 18000 ■ **Prohibit send at (KB):** 20000 ■ **Prohibit send and receive at (KB):** 100000

MPS enables enhanced features of Outlook Web Access by setting the *msExchMailbox-FolderSet* directory attribute for that user to a bitmask value of 0x0001A70F, which corresponds to a combination of the following features:

- **Messaging** 0x00000001
- **Calendar** 0x00000002
- **Contacts** 0x00000004
- **Tasks** 0x00000008
- **New mail notification** 0x00000100
- **Rich client** 0x00000200
- **Spelling checker** 0x00000400
- **Signature** 0x00002000
- **Themes** 0x00008000
- **Junk e-mail** 0x00010000

MPS set the storage limits as for GoldMail users and enables the full set of Outlook Web Access features by setting the *msExchMailboxFolder-Set* directory attribute for that user to a bitmask value of 0x0001FFFF, which corresponds to a combination of the following features:

- **Messaging** 0x00000001
- **Calendar** 0x00000002
- **Contacts** 0x00000004
- **Tasks** 0x00000008
- **Journal** 0x00000010
- **Sticky notes** 0x00000020
- **Public folders** 0x00000040
- **Reminders** 0x00000080
- **New mail notification** 0x00000100
- **Rich client** 0x00000200
- **Spelling checker** 0x00000400
- **S/MIME** 0x00000800
- **Search folders** 0x00001000
- **Signature** 0x00002000
- **Rules** 0x00004000
- **Themes** 0x00008000
- **Junk e-mail** 0x00010000

Table 7-6   Hosted Exchange 2003 Sample Service Plans (Continued)

Service plan	Features	Comments
■ 20 megabytes mailbox space ■ POP3 and IMAP4 ■ Full Outlook Web Access features ■ RPC over HTTP for Outlook client support enabled	■ PlatinumMail	■ MPS set the storage limits and Outlook Web Access features as for PlatinumMail users and enables support for MAPI-based clients by setting the showInAddressLists attribute in the service plan definition. If MPS finds the *<showInAddressLists>* attribute in the service plan definition, it checks if the organization already has address list definitions for the user's business organization. If no address lists exist, MPS creates them so that the user account can be assigned correct information in the *showInAddressBook* attribute. MAPI-based clients must find the user account in a server-based address list; otherwise the user will not be able to log on to the mailbox.

Splitting the Server-Based Address Book

Address book functionality differs between Outlook Web Access and MAPI-based clients such as Office Outlook 2003. While Outlook Web Access users must query Active Directory explicitly based on display name, alias, or other account information to locate other users in the organization, Outlook 2003 can conveniently pick recipients from the global address list. Figure 7-10 shows the different user interfaces.

To restrict Outlook Web Access address book searches so that users can only search for recipients in their own business organization (that is, their own organizational unit in Active Directory), MPS sets the msExchQueryBaseDN attribute for the user to the distinguished name of the business organization's organizational unit. However, the msExchQueryBaseDN attribute does not apply to the Office Outlook 2003 address book. Exchange 2003 determines the recipient information displayed in the Office Outlook 2003 address book based on server-based address list definitions.

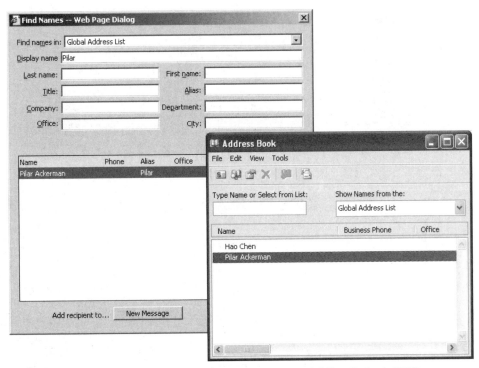

Figure 7-10   The address book in Outlook Web Access and Office Outlook 2003

Managing Server-Based Address Lists

As mentioned earlier, MPS creates address list definitions for a business organization if you provision the first business user with full Outlook support (that is, with the <showInAddressLists> attribute set in the service plan). You can verify the existence of address list definitions in Exchange System Manager under the All Address Lists and All Global Address Lists containers. Figure 7-11 shows an example of address list definitions for two separate business organizations.

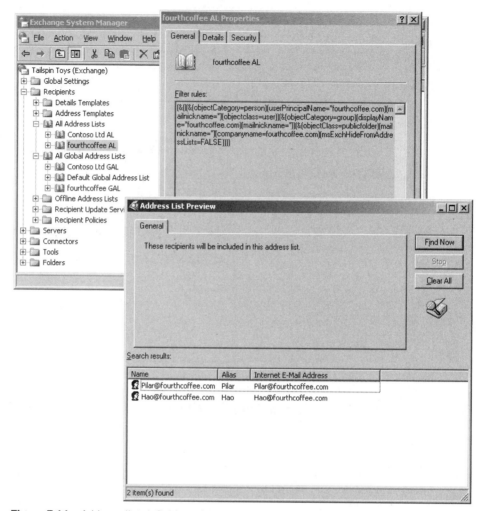

Figure 7-11   Address list definitions for separate business organizations

When you display the properties of an address list object, you can examine the filter rule that MPS has specified to include only those users that belong to a particular business organization. For example, the following rule only applies to recipient objects that have a UPN suffix or company name of FourthCoffee.com or that have a display name ending with fourthcoffee.com (if it is a mail-enabled group):

```
(&(|(&(objectCategory=person)(userPrincipalName=*fourthcoffee.com)(mailnickname=*)(o
bjectclass=user))(&(objectCategory=group)(displayName=*fourthcoffee.com)(mailnicknam
e=*))(&(objectClass=publicfolder)(mailnickname=*)(companyname=fourthcof-
fee.com)(msExchHideFromAddressLists=FALSE))))
```

You can see the results of the LDAP filter if you click the Preview button on the General tab (see Figure 7-11). MPS grants the Admins@<customer> and AllUsers@<customer> groups Read access to their address list objects so that Outlook 2003 displays correct information in the address book.

> **Note** By default, Exchange 2003 supports a maximum of 1,000 global address list definitions, which can be an issue for a service provider that wants to host more than 1,000 business organizations with Outlook 2003 users in a shared Exchange organization. Windows-based Hosting includes a tool named makeGalLinked.exe that you can use to remove this limit by changing the Global-Address-List definition in the Active Directory schema. For more information, see the section "Configuring the Active Directory Schema update for Global Address Lists" in the Windows-based Hosting documentation.

Provisioning Offline Address Books

The offline address book (OAB) is a client-based replica of the server-based address lists. It is created on the server and downloaded to the user's local computer to provide recipient information when no connection to the server exists and the client operates in offline mode. On the server, the OAB items reside in a hidden public folder; on the client, the offline address information is in files with an .oab extension. To avoid the download of full address information, MPS creates a customized, partial OAB for each business organization. A separate offline address list (OAL) object defines the properties for each OAB. You can find the OAL objects in Exchange System Manager in the Offline Address Lists container.

Assigning an Offline Address Book To a User

By default, a user is permitted to download only the OAB that is associated with the mailbox store that holds the user's mailbox. This mechanism works well as long as you provide each business organization with a separate mailbox store. However, this configuration does not scale because it does not permit you to share mailbox stores between smaller companies with Outlook 2003 users. To enable sharing of mailbox stores without disclosing address information through OABs, MPS configures the msExchUseOAB attribute of each business user directly. The msExchUseOAB attribute contains the distinguished name of the OAL object in Active Directory, such as `CN=fourthcoffee OAL,CN=Offline Address Lists,CN=Address Lists Container,CN=Tailspin Toys,CN=Microsoft Exchange,CN=Services,CN=Configuration,DC=tailspintoys,DC=com`.

> **More Info**   For more information about the msExchUseOAB attribute, see Microsoft Knowledge Base article 280435, "How to create an offline address list that contains a filtered copy of the global address list" (*http:// support.microsoft.com/default.aspx?scid=kb;EN-US;280435*).

Updating Offline Address Books

By default, Microsoft Exchange System Attendant service uses an internal Offline Address Book Generator component implemented in OABGEN.dll to build the offline address books on a scheduled basis. OABGEN.dll retrieves address information from Active Directory and creates the OAB items in the appropriate offline address book folders. OAB folders are hidden system folders that you can display in Exchange System Manager when you view the system folders in the MAPI-based public folder hierarchy (see Figure 7-12).

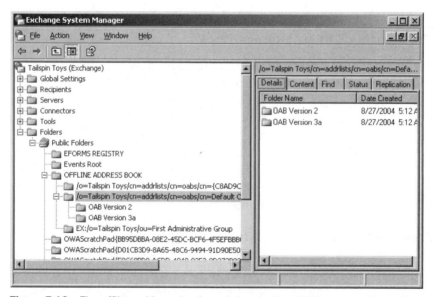

Figure 7-12   The offline address book container in the MAPI-based public folder store

Unfortunately, System Attendant cannot generate more than 1,000 OABs. To bypass this limitation, MPS disables the automatic generation of offline address books by setting the OAB Update Interval to Never Run. To update OABs, you must use the Hosted Exchange OAB Update tool (HeOabUpdate.exe) included with Windows-based Hosting. HeOabUpdate.exe enables you overcome the OAB scalability issue by placing OABs across dedicated OAB servers.

On the Resource Kit CD   The document 08_Installing the OAB Update Application.doc in the \Companion Material\Chapter 07\Exchange Provisioning folder on the companion CD explains how to deploy the Hosted Exchange OAB Update tool.

Note   Each particular Exchange 2003 OAB server can hold a maximum of 1,000 OABs. To track available OAB servers and their available capacity, Windows-based Hosting includes the namespace Exchange Offline Address Book (OAB) Resource Manager. The Exchange OAB Resource Manager keeps track of all OABs that have been allocated and enforces the 1,000 OAB per server limit.

Provisioning SMTP Domains

To successfully create a business organization using the *CreateBusinessOrganization* procedure, you must specify an *smtpDomain* property in the XML document and set it to the business organization's primary SMTP domain name, for example, FourthCoffee.com. Accordingly, MPS registers the *smtpDomain* information in the plan database and sets it as the primary domain for the business organization. In the default configuration, MPS also creates a recipient policy to inform Exchange 2003 that it is responsible for mail delivery to recipients in this domain.

In Exchange 2003, a recipient can have multiple SMTP addresses. Correspondingly, you can assign a business organization multiple SMTP domains through the *CreateSMTPDomain* procedure from the Hosted Exchange namespace. Using this procedure, you can add the following types of SMTP domains to the plan database:

- **PrimaryDomain**   This is the default SMTP Domain for a business organization. When you create a user in a business organization using the *CreateBusinessUser* procedure, MPS assigns the user a primary SMTP address based on the user's UPN prefix and the organization's SMTP Domain; for example, Hao@FourthCoffee.com. Exchange 2003 uses the primary SMTP address in all outbound messages to the Internet.

- **SecondaryDomain**   This is an additional SMTP domain that Exchange accepts as an inbound domain for a business organization. For example, the users in the business organization of FourthCoffee.com might also want to receive messages addressed to an SMTP domain of FourthCoffee.net. Keep in mind that you must register a mail exchanger for the secondary domain in the public DNS so that users can receive messages from the Internet. Provisioning DNS zones is explained later in this chapter.

> **On the Resource Kit CD**   The document 01_Creating a Business Organization and Business User.doc in the \Companion Material\Chapter 07\Sample Scenarios\BizzOrg folder on the companion CD contains a section that demonstrates how to add a secondary SMTP domain to a business organization.

- **VanityDomain**   This is a domain for an individual consumer user. You can use the *CreateConsumerVanityDomain* procedure from the Hosted Exchange namespace to add an SMTP domain name to a consumer user as the primary domain. As always, you must register a mail exchanger for the vanity domain in the public DNS so that the user can receive messages from the Internet.

> **On the Resource Kit CD**   The document 06_Creating a Vanity Domain for a User.doc in the \Companion Material\Chapter 07\Sample Scenarios\Reseller folder on the companion CD outlines how to add a vanity domain to a consumer.

SMTP Address Information and Recipient Update Service

In a non-shared Exchange 2003 organization, recipient update service (RUS), an internal component of the Microsoft Exchange System Attendant service, generates the e-mail addresses for mailbox-enabled and mail-enabled recipient objects. RUS is also responsible for keeping server-based address list information up-to-date. Whenever changes occur in a recipient policy or address list definition, RUS updates the recipient attributes in Active Directory. RUS runs on a schedule that you can configure in the properties of the RUS configuration object in Exchange System Manager.

Unfortunately, running recipient updates on a scheduled basis is not suitable for hosted environments because it causes latencies between the creation of a user account, the generation of e-mail addresses, and the update of address lists. A user must wait with the first logon to a mailbox until RUS has updated the user account. This can take five minutes or more depending on the RUS configuration. To prevent delays and provide users with immediate access to their mailboxes, MPS bypasses the recipient update service and assigns all relevant attributes and address information to newly created user accounts as part of the automated provisioning process. This includes the proxyAddresses attribute that holds the e-mail addresses of a user as well as the showInAddressBook attribute that specifies the address lists in which the recipient is included. MPS also sets the user account's mail attribute to the primary e-mail address and the msExchUserAccountControl attribute to a value of 0 to indicate that the account is an enabled user account in the local domain.

> **Note** The Hosted Exchange 2003 Companion Installer only disables the Recipient Update Service that is responsible for updating recipient objects in the domain naming context by setting its Update Interval to **Never run**. However, Hosted Exchange 2003 does not disable the Enterprise RUS that is responsible for processing Exchange system objects in the configuration naming context. The Enterprise RUS should not be disabled, and you should not delete the default recipient policy because the Enterprise RUS requires access to this policy.

Bypassing Recipient Policies

Windows-based Hosting maintains recipient policies primarily for the purpose of identifying inbound SMTP domains that the local Exchange organization is responsible for. If you are hosting a large number of business organizations and support secondary and vanity domains in addition, you can quickly reach the 1,000 configuration objects limit with recipient policies. To address this issue, Windows-based Hosting includes an SMTP domain event sink that enables the SMTP transport subsystem in Exchange 2003 to identify SMTP domains as inbound based on a text file named Domains.dat instead of recipient policies.

> **On the Resource Kit CD** For step-by-step instructions to install the SMTP domain event sink, see the document 10_Installing and Configuring the SMTP Domain Event Sink.doc in the \Companion Material\Chapter 07\ Exchange Provisioning folder on the companion CD.

The SMTP domain event sink solution consists of two key components: a dynamic-link library (DLL) named smtpdomx.dll that you must install on all your SMTP bridgehead servers and an SMTP data file generator DTS package that you must install on the MPS database system. The DTS package generates an updated Domains.dat file on a scheduled basis, which you must then copy to your SMTP bridgeheads. Smtpdomx.dll is the actual SMTP domain event sink that uses the Domains.dat file. Figure 7-13 illustrates the architecture of the SMTP Domain Event Sink solution.

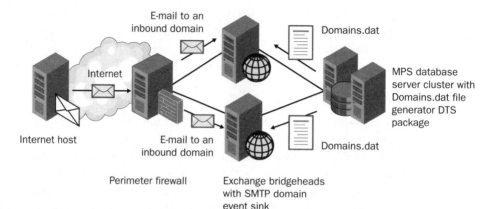

Figure 7-13   Distributing the Domains.dat file to identify inbound SMTP domains

Supporting Vanity Domains for ActiveSync Users

Exchange ActiveSync will not work for users who use a non-Exchange default SMTP address. To support users who have their primary SMTP address set to a vanity domain, you must configure the following ActiveSync registry parameter.

> **Warning**   Incorrectly editing the registry can cause serious problems that may require you to reinstall your operating system. Problems resulting from editing the registry incorrectly may not be able to be resolved. Before editing the registry, back up any valuable data.

To set up the registry for ActiveSync users who do not use the default SMTP address:

1. Start Registry Editor (regedit32.exe) and open the following registry key: HKEY_LOCAL_MACHINE\SYSTEM\CurrentControlSet\Services\MasSync\Parameters.

2. Open the Edit menu, point to New, and then click String Value.

3. Type the name of the new value **SMTPProxy** and press Enter.

4. Double-click SMTPProxy.

5. In the Edit String Value dialog box, type the default SMTP address for the shared Exchange organization, such as **tailspintoys.com**.

6. Click OK.

> **Note**   You must repeat these steps on all front-end servers running Active-Sync.

Configuring External DNS for Hosted SMTP Domains

To integrate hosted SMTP domains with the Internet, you must create DNS zones and configure resource records. A DNS zone for a primary SMTP domain should include the following resource records:

- **Name server (NS)**   NS records should point to the advertising DNS servers in your hosting infrastructure.

- **Host records (A)**   A records should point to the Web hosts and RPC over HTTP proxies that users employ to access messaging resources.

- **Mail exchanger (MX)**   MX records should point to the Exchange bridgehead servers in your hosting infrastructure.

Secondary and vanity domains do not need to include A records for Web hosts or RPC over HTTP proxies, but should include NS records and MX records so that Internet hosts can locate your Exchange bridgehead servers to transfer messages addressed to the secondary or vanity domain.

Maintaining DNS Zones Through the Provisioning System

Small- and medium-sized service providers might find it sufficient to maintain external DNS zones manually. With an increasing number of hosted SMTP domains, however, you can lower maintenance efforts by automating DNS configuration tasks through MPS. MPS includes a DNS provider and a DNS provider client that handle zone configurations as part of the automated provisioning process.

Figure 7-14 illustrates the architecture of the DNS provider. The DNS provider component resides on the provisioning engine and communicates with the DNS provider client component through .NET Remoting and a virtual directory named /DnsProvider. You must run Windows Server 2003 and ASP.NET on your external DNS servers as required by .NET Remoting. The DNS provider client performs the actual DNS configuration tasks on the local server through the DNS Windows Management Instrumentation (WMI) provider.

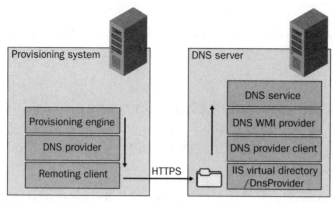

Figure 7-14 DNS provider architecture

To perform DNS configuration, the DNS provider must be authenticated with administrative permissions on the DNS server. This is accomplished in IIS using Basic authentication when the remoting client accesses the /DnsProvider virtual directory. Because Basic authentication relies on passwords in clear-text format, you must install an SSL certificate on the IIS so that the DNS provider communication can take place over HTTPS. It is important that the provisioning system trusts the SSL certificate and that the SSL certificate is issued to the fully qualified domain name of the DNS server. You can check the validity of the SSL certificate by accessing the /DnsProvider virtual directory in Internet Explorer. If Internet Explorer displays a security warning, you must correct the configuration.

Alternately, you can also configure the remoting client to use HTTP instead of HTTPS. This might be appropriate on a test system, but in a product environment, you should protect your administrative accounts using SSL.

On the Resource Kit CD The document 01_Installing the DNS Provider Client.doc in the \Companion Material\Chapter 07\DNS Provider folder on the companion CD shows how to enable DNS provider communication over HTTP. However, you should not enable HTTP without SSL in a test environment if you want to stay close to the production system.

Provisioning DNS Zones and Resource Records

To create a DNS zone through the provisioning system, you use the *CreateDNSZone* procedure from the DNS Provider namespace. In this procedure, you must identify the DNS server on which you want to create the new zone, provide account information to log on to the DNS server with administrative privileges, and specify the name of the new zone and the zone type. The following XML document creates a new primary DNS zone for Contoso.com on DNS01:

```xml
<?xml version="1.0" encoding="utf-8" ?>
<request xmlns:xsl="http://www.w3.org/1999/XSL/Transform">
  <procedure xmlns:xsl='http://www.w3.org/1999/XSL/Transform'>
    <execute  namespace="DNS Provider" procedure="CreateDNSZone">
      <executeData>
        <serverIdentifier>DNS01</serverIdentifier>
        <userName>WORKGROUP\Administrator</userName>
        <password>1qw$t9x</password>
        <zoneName>Contoso.com</zoneName>
        <debugLevel logging="high" check-only="on"/>
        <zoneType>Primary</zoneType>
      </executeData>
      <after source="executeData" destination="data" mode="merge"/>
    </execute>
  </procedure>
</request>
```

Having created the DNS zone, you can add resource records. For example, the following XML document adds a host (record) for an Exchange front-end server to the DNS zone.

```xml
<?xml version="1.0" encoding="utf-8" ?>
<request xmlns:xsl="http://www.w3.org/1999/XSL/Transform">
  <procedure xmlns:xsl='http://www.w3.org/1999/XSL/Transform'>
    <execute  namespace="DNS Provider" procedure="CreateResourceRecord">
      <executeData>
        <serverIdentifier>DNS01</serverIdentifier>
        <userName>WORKGROUP\Administrator</userName>
        <password>1qw$t9x</password>
        <zoneName>contoso.com</zoneName>
        <rrType>MicrosoftDNS_AType</rrType>
        <debugLevel logging="high" check-only="on"/>
        <properties>
          <property name="ContainerName">contoso.com</property>
          <property name="DnsServerName">dns01</property>
          <property name="IPAddress">192.168.202.131</property>
          <property name="OwnerName">webmail.contoso.com</property>
        </properties>
      </executeData>
      <after source="executeData" destination="data" mode="merge"/>
    </execute>
  </procedure>
</request>
```

MX records require different information than A records. To map an SMTP domain to an SMTP host, you must specify the host name of the mail exchanger and a preference level. A DNS zone can contain multiple MX records and the preference level which mail exchanger Internet hosts choose to transfer messages. The following XML document shows how to add an MX to a DNS zone.

```xml
<?xml version="1.0" encoding="utf-8" ?>
<request xmlns:xsl="http://www.w3.org/1999/XSL/Transform">
  <procedure xmlns:xsl='http://www.w3.org/1999/XSL/Transform'>
    <execute  namespace="DNS Provider" procedure="CreateResourceRecord">
      <executeData>
        <serverIdentifier>DNS01</serverIdentifier>
        <userName>WORKGROUP\Administrator</userName>
        <password>1qw$t9x</password>
        <zoneName>contoso.com</zoneName>
        <rrType>MicrosoftDNS_MXType</rrType>
        <debugLevel logging="high" check-only="on"/>
        <properties>
          <property name="ContainerName">contoso.com</property>
          <property name="DnsServerName">dns01</property>
          <property name="MailExchange">
            smtp.consolidatedmessenger.com
          </property>
          <property name="OwnerName">contoso.com</property>
          <property name="Preference">10</property>
        </properties>
      </executeData>
      <after source="executeData" destination="data" mode="merge"/>
    </execute>
  </procedure>
</request>
```

On the Resource Kit CD   For further XML samples that demonstrate how to query for DNS zone information and resource records, see the XML documents in the \Companion Material\Chapter 07\DNS Provider folder on the companion CD.

Monitoring Hosted Exchange Services

Microsoft Provisioning System keeps track of configuration information for business organizations and users, and MPS resource manager helps prevent overuse of resources, but MPS does not track the actual use of resources or the state of the systems in the hosting infrastructure. Windows-based Hosting relies on Microsoft Operations Manager (MOM) for monitoring and reporting.

Windows-based Hosting includes the following tools and components to monitor hosted Exchange organizations and create system reports:

■ **Monitoring components**   Monitoring components include the Hosted Exchange 2003 Monitoring Management Pack, the Exchange 2003 Management Pack, and additional monitoring applications such as the RPC Pinger tool. You can use the RPC Pinger tool to verify RPC over HTTP connectivity. The management packs include MOM processing rules to monitor the health, availability, and performance of servers in an Exchange 2003 organization. The rules in the Hosted Exchange 2003 Monitoring Management Pack are optimized to meet typical service provider needs. The Exchange 2003 Management Pack monitors general Exchange system parameters. The features of the Exchange 2003 Management Pack are covered in detail in Chapter 17, "Exchange Server 2003 Management Pack."

■ **Reporting components** Reporting components include the Hosted Exchange 2003 Reporting Management Pack and data collection applications, such as CollectWmiLogonInformation.exe and ExchangeWmiDataInsert.exe. The Hosted Exchange 2003 Reporting Management Pack has reporting rules that use the data collection applications. For example, the reporting rule named Execute CollectWmiLogonInformation in the MOM processing rule group User Count – Exchange runs CollectWmiLogonInformation.exe to determine which users have logged on and accessed a mailbox in the previous 24 hours as well as the current mailbox size for each user. CollectWmiLogonInformation.exe writes the information into XML files and raises a completion event which causes MOM to run ExchangeWmiDataInsert.exe. ExchangeWmiDataInsert.exe extracts the data from the XML files and updates the reporting database.

■ **Performance warehouse database (PWDB) and sample Web charting application** The performance warehouse database and sample Web charting application demonstrate how you can pull statistical data from the MOM database and generate reports about the overall performance of the Hosted Exchange 2003 environment. The Windows-based Hosting solution also includes a PWDB Import Customer Data DTS package that you can use to import provisioning information from the provisioning database into the performance warehouse database. This information is required to generate reports based on service plan types and customer information. The sample Web charting application uses the performance warehouse database to create performance charts based on date range, servers, aggregation types, and performance counters.

On the Resource Kit CD   The worksheets in the \Companion Material\Chapter 07\Monitoring and Reporting folder on the companion CD explain with step-by-step instructions how to deploy the monitoring and reporting components in a hosting infrastructure and how to use performance warehouse database and sample Web charting application.

Best Practices

If you are planning to provide hosted services based on Windows Server technologies, you should register with Microsoft as an ASP.NET service provider at *http://www.microsoft.com/serviceproviders*. You can then download the Microsoft Solution for Windows-based Hosting software package, which includes detailed documentation and tools to deploy a Windows-based Hosting infrastructure. It is a good idea to start with a test environment, such as the one outlined in the worksheets in the \Companion Material\Chapter 07 folder on the companion CD.

A Windows-based Hosting infrastructure is best deployed in a FrontNet/BackNet topology with all user data in the BackNet where it is not directly Internet accessible. The FrontNet should be protected through an arrangement of Internet and perimeter firewalls, but it is not necessary to deploy a firewall system between FrontNet and BackNet. Front-end servers deployed in the FrontNet can communicate directly with back-end servers through a separate physical network segment. The primary task of a front-end server is to proxy communication for authenticated users to the appropriate back-end servers. For example, you can configure Exchange servers as front-end servers for POP3 and IMAP4 clients and for HTTP-based Outlook Web Access and mobile clients. To support MAPI-based clients, you must configure your Exchange front-end servers also as RPC over HTTP proxies. It is a good idea to deploy Exchange 2003 SP1 because enhancements available in this service pack simplify the RPC over HTTP configuration.

To achieve the highest possible level of availability and fault tolerance, it is recommended that you cluster your Exchange servers. Exchange front-end servers are best included into a load-balancing cluster. Windows Network Load Balancing, for example, can include up to 32 front-end servers. Exchange back-end servers, on the other hand, are best clustered using the Windows Cluster service. You should use an active/passive cluster configuration in a cluster with up to eight nodes.

Having deployed the Exchange 2003 infrastructure, you can create business organizations and users to provide hosted messaging services. This is a complex task that is best automated to reduce the operational costs and increase efficiency. Windows-based Hosting relies on Microsoft Provisioning System and is a very flexible tool to automate administrative tasks for DNS, Active Directory, Exchange 2003 and other systems such as IIS. MPS is based on XML and includes a Web service that you can use to develop custom Web-based management applications. A sample Hosted Exchange Web service client is included in Windows-based Hosting. This sample client demonstrates how resellers and business organizations can manage their own accounts and resources. Consumer users might also be provided with a custom Web-based solution so that they can create and manage their own accounts. For example, a consumer might want to change personal information or create a vanity domain for his or her mailbox.

To further increase the efficiency of your hosting operations, you should deploy MOM and install Exchange 2003 Management Pack. You should also install Hosted Exchange 2003 Monitoring Management Pack and Hosted Exchange 2003 Reporting Management Pack so that you can monitor important services in your shared Exchange organization and create performance reports and charts. You should also include all of your servers into a patch management system to ensure the latest security patches are applied in a timely manner.

Before you deploy a full-featured production environment, contact Microsoft Consulting Services or Microsoft Certified Partners for assistance with designing, deploying, and operating a Windows-based Hosting solution for Exchange 2003.

Part II

Managing Your Exchange Server 2003 Organization

Chapter 8

Operating an Exchange Server 2003 Organization

About This Chapter

This chapter discusses monitoring from both theoretical and practical perspectives. On the theoretical level, the chapter explains how Microsoft Operations Framework (MOF) is a guide for structuring operations tasks. On the practical level, the chapter discusses best practices and necessary processes for daily, weekly, and monthly activities.

This chapter is organized to guide you through the steps to create or improve an operations plan. A test environment illustrates concepts and ideas. Specifically, this chapter covers the following:

- **Microsoft Operations Framework overview**   Read this section to understand the processes and methodologies of the Microsoft Operations Framework (MOF), which is a suggested approach to operating an IT environment.

- **Best practices**   This section includes suggestions for implementing and designing an operations plan. It follows the MOF model and applies it specifically to an Exchange organization.

- **Daily, weekly, and monthly processes**   Operations tasks, including monitoring, administration, and troubleshooting are separated into daily, weekly, and monthly activities in this section. This section discusses what to do to maintain a healthy Exchange organization.

- **Tools and technologies**   For automation, convenience, and flexibility, you can use additional tools and technologies to operate an Exchange organization. This section covers some of them.

Understanding Microsoft Operations Framework

Operating an Exchange organization requires a sound understanding of best practices that contribute to effective monitoring, such as Microsoft Operations Framework (MOF). MOF is discussed in this chapter, as are practical tasks to perform when monitoring an Exchange organization.

Microsoft Operations Framework Overview

Microsoft Operations Framework (MOF) combines models, best practices, and ideas into a comprehensive body of knowledge to help guide system operations. MOF includes methods to reach and maintain system availability, performance, and reliability.

MOF includes four key components:

- **MOF Process Model for operations**   The MOF Process Model is a model for instituting and operating an IT environment. It includes a cycle of processes to help achieve an available and reliable environment.

- **MOF Team Model for operations**   The MOF Team Model complements the MOF Process Model by providing best practices and guidance on how to arrange operations and processes for optimal performance and availability.

- **MOF Risk Management Discipline for operations**   Managing risk is a necessary part of managing and operating an Exchange organization. The MOF Risk Management Discipline provides a structured approach to risk management.

- **Service Management Functions**   Service Management Functions (SMFs) provide roles and tasks for people and teams responsible for monitoring components and an overall computing environment.

The following sections describe the four MOF components and how they relate to operating an Exchange organization.

The MOF Process Model

Historically, as technological administration and technology in general became more standardized, IT management best practices were documented by the Office of Government Commerce (OGC) in the United Kingdom. This practical advice and guidance is held in the IT Infrastructure Library (ITIL). MOF builds upon ITIL best practices and adapts them for use with Microsoft technologies, including Exchange Server 2003.

MOF is intended to be a part of the overall IT lifecycle. The IT lifecycle includes other components, such as Microsoft Solutions Framework (MSF) and contains a model for running an IT environment. Specifically, MOF and MSF combined provide guidance as four steps to solve IT problems or modify existing solutions. The steps are as follows, and are shown in Figure 8-1:

- **Use MSF and MOF to plan the solution**   This includes research into existing configurations and requirements, and performing needs analysis to create the solution.

- **Use MSF to build the solution**   Building the solution requires a step beyond planning. In the building stage, you create the features and components of the solution.

- **Use MOF and MSF to deploy the solution**   Implement a smooth deployment into the production environment using strong release management processes and automation.

- **Use MOF to operate the new IT environment**   Use the MOF operations models (discussed in this section) for operations and management of the Exchange organization.

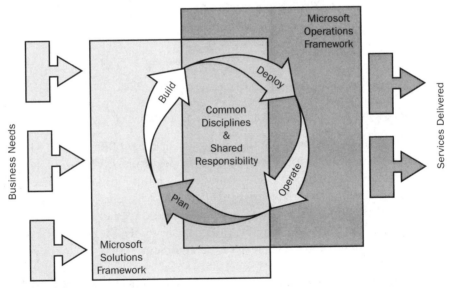

Figure 8-1   IT lifecycle

The four-step approach to managing an IT organization enables change at multiple levels. For example, a new business unit might require a network separate from the main organization, but it must be able to share resources. Using MOF, you can recognize the problem and follow suggested processes to plan, deploy, manage, and improve the solution. The need for a new business unit arises in the normal course of company expansion. New problems might also arise, which require that you generate solutions using MOF.

This chapter focuses specifically on operations tasks on a daily, weekly, monthly, and as-needed basis. The MOF process model specifically applies to these operations tasks and organizes them as part of an operations cycle. Figure 8-2 shows how MOF describes this cycle in a four-quadrant model.

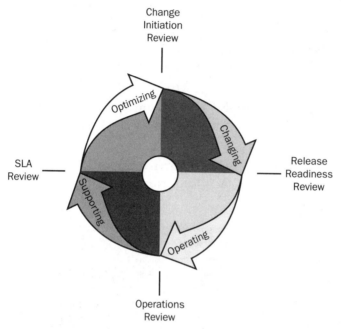

Figure 8-2   The Microsoft Operations Framework cycle

Although MOF is a continuous cycle, it most often begins when a proposed change is introduced for deployment and operations. Before the release is approved and the processes in the cycle continue, a change initiation, or release readiness review determines if the release is ready for deployment. If the decision is supportive of the proposed change, it is deployed and introduced to a production environment. Along the way, Service Management Functions (SMFs) help to guide through the definite processes of the cycle. Service Management Functions are covered in the next section.

After a successful deployment, the solution must be managed and operated. The Operating quadrant includes processes and SMFs to deal with this. The Operating stage involves tasks such as monitoring, administration, and systems management. In the tasks of the Operating quadrant, there is an Operations Review. The goal of an Operations Review is to provide the procedures and tools to make supporting the system as simple and efficient as possible.

With any solution, problems might arise. The Supporting quadrant includes processes and SMFs to deal with supporting users and resolving operational problems. Typical tasks in this quadrant include identifying incidents and cases, troubleshooting and analyzing cases, assigning them for resolution, and finally resolving problems. The Supporting tasks are typically handled by a support team or a helpdesk. In the Supporting quadrant, there is a service level agreement (SLA) review. The SLA review is a measurement of how effectively the system is performing. Issues arising from the SLA review might highlight areas where improvements are necessary.

The final quadrant in the MOF process model is the Optimization quadrant. During the optimization stage, costs, effectiveness, and future needs are assessed. The current solution is reviewed for effectiveness and to determine whether it meets current and future needs. Also, costs are considered to decide if a better solution exists. In this stage, there are proposals for change, which are built and suggested for implementation for the Changing quadrant. In this way, the process begins anew.

At the end of each phase, there is a review point. In the case of a large IT department, this is likely to be a review meeting between the various people or teams involved, such as release management, operations, and security. In a small company, the review points might only constitute useful points at which to stop and check that you are ready to proceed.

Table 8-1 summarizes the mission of service and the operations management reviews for each of the four quadrants.

Table 8-1   Mission of Service and Operations Management Review for Each Quadrant

Quadrant	Mission of Service	Operations Management Review	Evaluation Criteria
Changing	Introduce new service solutions, technologies, systems, applications, hardware, and processes. Performed prior to new release.	Release Readiness	■ The release (the changes) ■ The release package (all of the tools, processes, and documentation) ■ The target (production) environment and infrastructure ■ Rollout and rollback plans ■ The risk management plan ■ Training plans ■ Support plans ■ Contingency plans

Table 8-1   Mission of Service and Operations Management Review for Each Quadrant (Continued)

Quadrant	Mission of Service	Operations Management Review	Evaluation Criteria
Operating	Execute day-to-day tasks effectively and efficiently. Performed periodically.	Operations	■ IT staff performance ■ Operational efficiency ■ Personnel skills and competencies ■ Operations level agreements
Supporting	Resolve incidents, problems, and inquiries quickly. Performed periodically.	Service Level Agreement	■ SLA-defined targets and metrics ■ Customer satisfaction ■ Costs
Optimizing	Drive changes to optimize cost, performance, capacity, and availability in the delivery of IT services. Performed at change identification.	Change Initiation	■ Cost/benefit evaluation of proposed changes ■ Impact to other systems and existing infrastructure

Service Management Functions

Each MOF quadrant includes specific tasks and processes to be used at various stages of the operations cycle. For example, performing weekly status meetings to review main trouble tickets is best done in the optimization part of the cycle, while new server deployment to meet demand is part of routine operations. Although these processes can be used in more than one quadrant, they tend to concentrate around a specific area. SMFs are especially useful from a project management perspective. A manager must delegate tasks and define roles and processes for a team to ensure that the organization functions and all necessary tasks are completed.

MOF includes 20 SMFs. Each one can be attributed to a specific quadrant, as shown in Figure 8-3.

As the tasks in the MOF cycle progress, the various roles and processes complement each other to ensure a smooth transition from idea creation to deployment, operations, and optimization. The quadrants and their related SMFs are discussed in the next section.

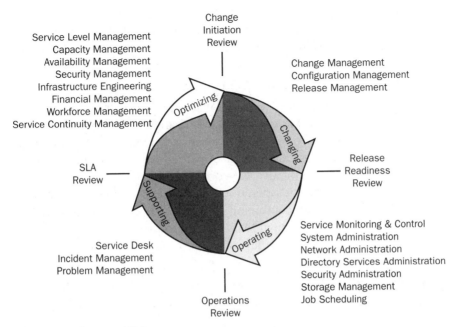

Service Level Management
Capacity Management
Availability Management
Security Management
Infrastructure Engineering
Financial Management
Workforce Management
Service Continuity Management

Change
Initiation
Review

Change Management
Configuration Management
Release Management

Optimizing

Changing

SLA
Review

Release
Readiness
Review

Supporting

Operating

Service Desk
Incident Management
Problem Management

Service Monitoring & Control
System Administration
Network Administration
Directory Services Administration
Security Administration
Storage Management
Job Scheduling

Operations
Review

Figure 8-3   SMFs in MOF

Changing Quadrant

In the Changing quadrant, an idea is brought for implementation to solve a problem, increase existing performance, or address a change in anticipation of growth. The processes in this quadrant seek to maintain the existing environment and not interfere with existing operations, while introducing new changes and smoothly deploying a solutions plan.

Three SMFs are included in the Changing quadrant, as follows:

- **Change management**   The goals of change management are to first identify the systems that will be affected by the proposed change, and second, to identify ways to ease the change. For example, if an upgrade is proposed from Exchange 2000 Server to Exchange Server 2003, the adverse effect might be downtime or mailbox unavailability. As part of the change management SMF, the risk is mitigated or eliminated. In this case, if downtime is necessary, users and others impacted by the change are notified as part of the change management process.

- **Configuration management**   The primary goal during the configuration management process is to identify various components of the existing organization and IT environment, and determine how the components are interrelated. For example, in an upgrade scenario, the components might include front-end servers, back-end servers, Active Directory global catalog servers, and so on. In the configuration management process, these components are identified and documented to facilitate understanding the present state of the organization. Configuration management is especially useful during complex changes that involve multiple configuration items, because changes made before deployment that alter configuration details must be recorded.

- **Release management**   The focuses of the release management SMF are to facilitate the introduction of software and hardware releases into managed IT environments and to ensure that all changes are deployed successfully. Typically, this includes the production environment, as well as the managed preproduction environments. Release management coordinates and manages all releases and is typically the coordination point between the development release team and the operations groups responsible for deploying the release into production. In combining MSF and MOF in an end-to-end IT lifecycle, this is the key point at which MSF-developed projects and solutions integrate fully with the MOF deployment process into a release product.

Operating Quadrant

The processes in the operating quadrant seek to perform the necessary tasks to operate an IT environment. The typical activities are administrative in nature and involve monitoring, managing, and maintaining the IT environment to meet SLA levels. The tasks in this quadrant also include creating and maintaining defined procedures for operations tasks.

Seven SMFs are included in the Operating quadrant, as follows:

- **System administration**   The system administration SMF processes ensure that the various systems in the IT environment operate properly. The system administration processes encompass a variety of tasks. For example, in an Exchange environment, system administration can refer to maintaining the messaging system, services, databases, underlying hardware, and operating system.

- **Security administration**   Security administration involves ensuring that a safe and secure IT environment exists. A primary goal of the Security Administration SMF is to make data available to the proper people, inaccessible to others, and accurate when retrieved. Typically, the tasks for this SMF include security audits, log analysis, and intrusion detection.

- **Directory services administration**   Directory services allow users and applications to find network resources such as users, servers, applications, tools, services, and other information. The directory services administration SMF deals with the day-to-day operations, maintenance, and support of the enterprise directory. The goal of directory services administration is to ensure that information is accessible through the network using a simple and organized process by any authorized requester. Directory services administration addresses directory-enabled applications, metadirectories, user, group, and resource creation, management, and deletion, and daily support activities such as monitoring, maintaining, and troubleshooting the enterprise directory.

- **Network administration** The goal of the processes in the network administration SMF is both to prevent potential disruptions in network operations and to monitor, manage, and maintain all networks and their components. Typical network administration tasks include managing routers, hubs, firewalls, and switches. Network administration covers LANs, WANs, virtual private networks (VPNs), and support activities, such as troubleshooting and maintenance.

- **Service monitoring and control** The service monitoring and control SMF is composed of two parts: service monitoring and service control. In the monitoring component of the process, server loads, response times and latencies, status, and availability are monitored. In the control component, solutions are generated to respond to problems detected during service monitoring.

- **Storage management** The storage management SMF deals with data storage and media. This involves storage software and hardware, recordkeeping, and defined storage procedures. In an Exchange organization, for example, the task of ensuring that enough hard disk space is available for mailboxes on back-end servers is handled by the processes in the storage management SMF.

- **Job scheduling** Job scheduling seeks to maximize efficiency of all running processes, loads, and jobs and to meet organizational requirements and SLAs. Job scheduling entails defining the following:

  - **Job schedules** The workloads are organized by time periods (daily, weekly, monthly, annually) and jobs are scheduled for execution according to business needs, length of job, storage requirements, and associated dependencies.

  - **Scheduling procedures** Schedules are set up and maintained, conflicts and problems pertaining to scheduling are managed, and special needs (for example, as-needed jobs) are accommodated.

  - **Batch processing** Jobs are executed according to the work schedule, run priority, and job dependencies.

Supporting Quadrant

The SMFs within the Supporting quadrant are designed to meet user needs for help and support. However, the processes involved for supporting are not confined only to a helpdesk. In the supporting quadrant, service levels are met both by anticipating problems and planning for failures and by responding to user problems and needs. A key aspect of processes in the Supporting quadrant is that they monitor the overall state of services and availability against a defined threshold. That is, they are not responsible for overall monitoring, but rather for monitoring within specified criteria customized to the environment.

Three SMFs are included in the Supporting quadrant:

- **Service desk**   The service desk SMF is a main function of the Supporting quadrant. It acts as hub between users and IT providers. Users use the helpdesk to inquire about features, report problems, and for general support. The service desk is a single point of contact between the users and the provider of IT services. As part of service desk operations, daily support tasks, such as problem resolution and investigation, as well as optimization tasks that more proactively support users, are included.

- **Incident management**   Incident management is the process of managing and controlling faults and disruptions in the use or implementation of IT services, including applications, networking, hardware, and user-reported service requests.

  The following list summarizes the principle activities within the Incident Management SMF:

  - **Incident communication**   Communicating to the enterprise the existence of and current status of service-disrupting incidents.

  - **Incident control**   Ensuring that incidents are resolved as quickly as possible with minimal impact.

  - **Incident origin determination**   Determining the component or components that are causing the disruption.

  - **Incident recording**   Ensuring that incidents are recorded as quickly as possible into the appropriate databases and support tools.

  - **Incident alerting**   Communicating to all involved in the incident in order to ensure immediate action toward resolution.

  - **Incident diagnosis**   Accurately determining the nature and cause of the incident.

  - **Incident classification**   Recording the incident and accurately allocating the correct resources for resolution.

  - **Incident investigation**   Researching to determine whether the incident is unique or has been experienced before.

  - **Incident support**   Providing support throughout the entire life cycle of the incident in order to resolve the incident as quickly as possible and with the least impact to business processes.

  - **Incident resolution**   Resolving the incident as quickly as possible through the effective use of all appropriate tools, processes, and resources available.

  - **Incident recovery**   Returning the affected environment to stability after the incident is resolved.

■ **Incident closure**   Effecting proper closure of the incident, ensuring that all pertinent data surrounding the life cycle of the incident is properly discovered and recorded.

■ **Incident information management**   Properly recording and categorizing incident-related information for future use by all levels and organizations within the enterprise.

■ **Problem management**   The problem management SMF seeks to proactively identify and document problems in the IT environment. This is done by creating workarounds, or requesting that changes be made to a component. Through the processes in the problem management SMF, problems are investigated, solved, resolved, and closed.

Optimizing Quadrant

The goals of the Optimizing quadrant are first, to identify processes, components, and performance across the IT organization and second, to discover ways to improve and optimize performance and availability.

The Optimizing quadrant includes eight SMFs:

■ **Service level management**   Service level management entails discovering needs and expectations for service levels and evaluating how service levels are being met. For example, the service level for a remote office in an Exchange organization might require connectivity only at specified time of day. In this case, it makes sense to have a service level that meets only that requirement, as opposed to striving for constant 99.999 percent uptime, which is sometimes needed for large organizations.

Within the service level management SMF, identifying and meeting service levels require planning and budgeting. If resources are unavailable to ensure that service levels are met, then it is futile to attempt to meet them. Setting standard procedures for identifying and meeting service levels is also a part of the processes in this SMF.

■ **Financial management**   The processes and activities in the financial management SMF seek to ensure cost-efficient solutions and the continued functioning of the IT organization within available funds. Planning for financial needs might include budgeting, cash flow forecasting, cost-benefit analysis, expense tracking, customer billing, and so on. The tasks in the financial management SMF are not a substitute for a company's accounting systems; however, they apply accounting principles to the IT environment. For example, a needs analysis done in an Exchange organization might show that a solution of a Lotus Notes messaging system across a newly acquired company did not meet messaging needs. A migration to Exchange 2003 was proposed. The processes in the financial management SMF take the proposal, evaluate costs of retiring the old system and costs of planning, deployment, support, and so on, and evaluate benefits, needed budgets, breakeven points, and so on. This results in financially viable solutions that meet needs while minimizing costs.

- **Capacity management**   Capacity management processes seek to plan and manage the capacity of resources to meet service levels and user needs. Meeting service levels is necessary at both a large and small scale. For example, in planning for disk space for Exchange stores, a task in the capacity management SMF might be to check current use and track growth over the last year, then implement an upgrade plan for projected needs. Capacity management is also concerned with current operations and performance both on an overall IT systems scale and at the component level.

  To manage system capacities, it is important to keep records of processes and calculations used at either initial or ongoing capacity evaluation. This is important because as business needs change, so must capacities. Suppose a past operating system upgrade required three technicians working full time for 80 hours to complete an upgrade of 50 computers. Using these numbers, it is possible to approximate resources and capacities needed to implement a plan, or to anticipate future needs.

- **Availability management**   Availability management is concerned with timely delivery of a needed service. For example, when a user wants to retrieve mail, the back-end mail server must be operational, functional, and able to transmit data across the network to the user. In other words, availability is concerned with uptime. Optimal uptime can be achieved by using redundant systems, failover technologies, clustering, and other tools. However, improving uptime also requires proactively monitoring and managing the IT organization and correcting problems and potential problems before they are apparent to the user. If a service is unavailable, but users do not need to access the service, it is still considered available. Therefore, proactive systems management must be a part of organizational monitoring and optimization.

- **Continuity management**   Continuity management deals with disaster and recovery planning. Its focus is on minimizing the disruption of mission-critical systems. An IT disaster is defined as a loss of service for protracted periods, which requires that work be moved to an alternative system in a non-routine way. Continuity management also provides guidance on safeguarding the existing systems by the development and introduction of proactive measures and reactive countermeasures. IT service continuity management also considers which activities need to be performed in the event of service outages that are not classified as disasters.

- **Workforce management**   The goal of the processes in the workforce management SMF is to have a highly skilled and able workforce. This is accomplished by setting, developing, and practicing recruiting, hiring, development, training, and knowledge transfer processes. This SMF concerns human resources, how to motivate the workforce and ensure that it is working to meet IT needs.

- **Security management** The goal of the security management SMF is to define and communicate the organization's security plans, policies, guidelines, and relevant regulations, as defined by the associated external industry or government agencies. Security management strives to ensure that effective information security measures are taken at the strategic, tactical, and operational levels. It also has overall management responsibility for ensuring that these measures are followed, as well as for reporting to management on security activities. Security management has important ties with other processes. Some security management activities are carried out by other SMFs, under the supervision of security management.

- **Infrastructure engineering** The infrastructure engineering SMF includes processes that act as connectors between various other teams and SMFs. Infrastructure engineering acts as a creative director, who identifies design and strategy and verifies that it is executed and measured. These processes seek to manage and coordinate the overall existing IT environment by evaluating risks, finances, capacities, availability, business needs, and so on.

The MOF Team Model

The Service Management Functions and MOF models are somewhat abstract. They provide guidance on the IT cycle, its integration with MSF, and typical tasks and goals within each quadrant. In a real-world scenario, these tasks often overlap and are performed by the same team or person. MOF recognizes this and includes the idea of role clusters within its framework. The MOF Team Model is composed of seven role clusters that can be adopted by teams or individuals to complete the processes explained in the SMFs.

The role clusters are as follows:

- **Release** The release team manages the roll-out of changes into the production environment, is responsible for configuration management, maintains licensing information, and forms a liaison between development and operations groups.

- **Service** The service team ensures that customer needs are addressed and met. This is done by evaluating needs, drafting and managing SLAs, and managing customer relationships.

- **Infrastructure** The infrastructure team performs the planning and management of the IT infrastructure, including capacity forecasting, management of standard builds and system images, and monitoring system availability and connectivity.

- **Support** The support team represents the user helpdesk's liaison with users. This team manages compliance with SLAs, provides incident and problem resolution and maintains a knowledge base of common resolutions. This team is also responsible for providing customer feedback to design teams.

- **Operations**   The operations team manages user accounts and mailboxes, monitors performance and availability of systems, manages connectivity with external systems, monitors queues and logs, and maintains firewalls.

- **Partner**   The partner team is responsible for the liaison with suppliers and partners, such as Internet Service Providers. This team manages contractual Service Level Agreements (SLAs) with third parties, performs commercial evaluation of alternative suppliers, manages procurement, and makes purchasing decisions.

- **Security**   The security team is responsible for detecting virus attacks, intrusion attempts, and denial-of-service and other attacks. This team must monitor the use of IT resources and compliance with standards, and perform audit tracking and reporting. This team is often also responsible for managing Public Key Infrastructure (PKI) technologies required for message signing and encryption, as well as for conducting external testing, including mail relay testing and penetration testing.

Figure 8-4 shows how these role clusters combine within MOF.

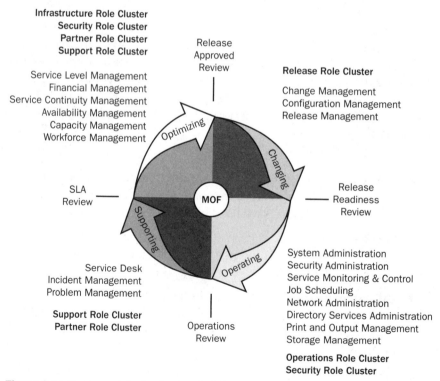

Figure 8-4   Team model role clusters in MOF

The MOF Team Model is based on the concept that an operations team must achieve a number of key quality goals, or missions of service, to be successful. These goals direct the team and help define the Team Model within MOF. The seven role clusters identified in the MOF Team Model each have a distinct set of objectives. Their quality goals are:

- Controlled release and change management, and accurate inventory tracking of all IT services and systems (Release Role Cluster).

- Efficient management of physical environments and infrastructure tools (Infrastructure Role Cluster).

- Quality customer support and a service culture (Support Role Cluster).

- Predictable, repeatable, and automated day-to-day system management (Operations Role Cluster).

- Protected corporate assets, controlled authorization to systems and information, and proactive planning for emergency response (Security Role Cluster).

- Efficient and cost-effective, mutually beneficial relationships with service and supply partners (Partner Role Cluster).

- Delivery of a portfolio of business-aligned IT services (Service Role Cluster).

MOF Risk Management Discipline

Risk management is vital to an IT organization, because it enables the organization to proactively anticipate an uncertain future. By assessing risk at a global level, in each process, and with each person, risks can be identified and mitigated. The MOF risk management discipline is composed of six steps:

1. **Identifying risks in operations**   The first step in managing risk is identifying it. Identification requires expressing the risk in a statement with the root cause and the effect on parties involved. Often, this step requires brainstorming and communication between various units to define causes and effect of existing and potential risk. This step helps risk management to identify probabilities and indicators of risk events to develop solutions and answers.

2. **Analyzing and prioritizing risks**   The second step of risk management is to formulate the information from the first step and use it in making decisions. In the second step, risk probability, impact, and exposure are identified for each risk. Doing this helps to put the risks in a hierarchy and allocate resources to deal with the most urgent risks.

3. **Planning and scheduling risk actions**   The third step of managing risk is planning and scheduling action items. First, this step helps to set a course of action by creating responses to risks, ordering the importance of actions within each risk, and creating an overall action response plan for the risks. Second, this

step involves scheduling. Scheduling integrates the tasks required to implement the risk action plans into daily operations by assigning them to individuals or roles and by actively tracking their status.

4. **Tracking and reporting risk**   The fourth step is tracking and reporting risk. In the process of IT operations, risks change in kind, severity, and detail. Recording these changes helps to deal with risk. Specifically, you should note three things in the process of risk tracking: whether the risk materializes; whether conditions, probabilities, or impacts change; and whether the mitigation plan progress changes.

   Risk reporting should operate at two levels, the internal level and the external level. For IT operations (internal), regular risk status reports should consider four possible risk management situations for each risk:

   - **Resolution**   A risk is resolved, completing the risk action plan.

   - **Consistency**   Risk actions are consistent with the risk management plan, in which case the risk plan actions continue as planned.

   - **Variance**   Some risk actions are at variance with the risk management plan, in which case corrective measures must be defined and implemented.

   - **Changeability**   The situation has changed significantly with respect to one or more risks. This usually involves reanalyzing the risks or re-planning an activity.

5. **Controlling risk**   The fifth step is controlling risk. This step assumes that the risk has materialized and must be managed. In this step, the plans previously developed to deal with risk are put into action. Successes and failures in execution, measurements, and benchmarks are recorded and incorporated into a contingency plan status and outcome report, so that that information becomes part of the operations risk knowledge base.

6. **Learning from risk**   The sixth step is learning from risk. This step focuses on three key objectives:

   - Providing quality assurance on the current risk management activities so that the IT operations group can gain regular feedback.

   - Capturing knowledge and best practices, especially those pertaining to risk identification and successful mitigation strategies. This contributes to the risk knowledge base.

   - Improving the risk management process by capturing feedback from the organization.

Daily, Weekly, and Monthly Processes

One of the most important factors in determining the success or failure of the management of your Exchange organization is planning a monitoring strategy. This section discusses daily, weekly, and monthly monitoring tasks. Monitoring can be systematized into a routine set of tasks that involve checking the status of services and systems, responding to problems, and preparing for future problems by mitigating risk and developing a response plan.

Planning a monitoring strategy is sometimes done spontaneously by assigning tasks and expecting the end result to be satisfactory. However, this is not the optimal approach. By using Microsoft Operations Framework (MOF) and Microsoft Solutions Framework (MSF) together with roles and SMFs, it is possible to plan a comprehensive monitoring approach, implement it, and optimize the strategy. This should be the starting point of monitoring an Exchange organization.

Exchange monitoring and operations management is best done proactively. Early detection and handling of problems before they escalate prevents the disruption of service levels and ensures that no major outages occur. Proactive monitoring is accomplished by regularly checking known and potential weak points. Established procedures for daily, weekly, and monthly tasks define what you must do to monitor an Exchange organization.

Daily Operations Tasks

In daily operations tasks, it is important to be thorough in checking the various components of the Exchange organization. These components include software, hardware, physical environment, human resources, and so on. It is helpful to develop a checklist and record data for typical resource usage for capacity planning. In daily operations tasks, you should focus on the following:

- **Performing physical environment checks**   Inspecting the physical environment for security problems or physical problems is the first step in daily tasks.

- **Maintaining backups**   Rotating backup media and performing backups helps in case of a disaster.

- **Checking disk use**   Ensuring that enough disk space is available for your organization's needs is an important daily task.

- **Checking CPU and memory use**   Resources might use too much CPU time or memory. Knowing when resources are overextended is an important part of capacity planning and monitoring.

- **Checking system response times**   Checking response times can help alert you to any existing or future problems.

- **Checking message paths**   Knowing message paths can help you track points of failure and respond appropriately.

- **Checking logs**   Event logs can alert you to recurrent problems and pinpoint causes and points of failure. Security issues usually happen over time, as an intruder attempts to exploit vulnerability. Checking through logs helps uncover problems before they escalate.

- **Virus Scanning**   Monitoring for viruses is important, because e-mail is the most common way that viruses enter an organization, and a functioning messaging system is important in today's world.

Performing Physical Environment Checks

Before checking for performance, availability, and functionality of your Exchange organization and its components, you should check the physical environment to ensure that it functions according to your expectation. For example, the temperature might need to be lowered, or a network cable might need to be replaced. Specifically, you should check for the following:

- **Physical security measures**   Physical security protection such as locks, dongles, doors, and restricted-access rooms must be secure. Check for unauthorized and forced entries and signs of equipment damage.

- **Temperature and humidity**   High temperature and humidity can cause hardware components to overheat. Check temperature and humidity to ensure the environmental systems, such as heating and air conditioning, function correctly.

- **Devices and components**   The Exchange organization relies on a functioning physical network and hardware. Check to ensure that routers, switches, hubs, physical cables, and connectors are operational.

Maintaining Backups

There are two steps that you should perform to maintain backups:

- **Checking backup logs**   Check backup logs for any problems. For example, a backup might not have completed, or the media might not have enough space. In this step, verify that backups complete successfully.

- **Rotating backup media**   After you verify that backups are complete, label the media and store it in the archive. Old archives can be put away for permanent storage and the latest backup can be made available nearby in case of failure.

Checking Disk Use

Disks are a critical component of your exchange organization. Without adequate free disk space, the operating system and Exchange databases cannot function. You should monitor three categories of disks, as follows:

- **System partition disks**   The disk that contains the operating system files and page file is vital to an Exchange server. You can check free disk space by checking the drive in Windows Explorer, or by checking the \logicalDisk % Free Space counter in System Monitor.

- **Transaction log disks**   Check disks with transaction logs, because they are vital to message integrity.

- **Database volume disks**   Check disks with the database volume for errors and available free space. You can use event logs to check for disk-related data.

Using System Monitor with Disks

You can monitor disk performance with System Monitor. System Monitor includes two main objects for monitoring disks, Physical Disk and Logical Disk. Each is discussed next.

- **Physical Disk object**   The two counters to monitor for the Physical Disk object are % Disk Time, and Current Disk Queue Length. % Disk Time indicates the percentage of time the disk is reading and writing. A value greater than 50 might indicate excessive use. The Current Disk Queue Length counter measures the number of I/O requests waiting for the disk drive. A value greater than two might indicate a potential bottleneck.

- **Logical Disk object**   In the Logical Disk object, monitor the Average Disk/sec read and Average disk/sec write counters. If these values are very high, the disk cannot keep up with requests for data reads and writes. This might cause poor performance for users with Outlook.

Checking CPU and Memory Use

CPU and memory are two resources that affect performance. Monitoring typical and peak use can help prevent problems and address needs for growth. For example, constant overuse of CPU resources by a non-Exchange component might decrease system response times and create unavailability for users. The following sections describe some ways to check for CPU and memory use.

Check Performance Monitor Counters

Many Performance Monitor counters exist to monitor CPU and memory use. When checking the counters and instances, use a worksheet to record the measured values to help with later performance analysis. You can use System Monitor in combination with Server Monitors in Exchange System Manager to create notifications for CPU and memory use that exceeds a threshold.

CPU Counters

There are two important counters for the Processor object in Performance Monitor:

- **Interrupts/sec**   Interrupts/sec is the average rate, in incidents per second, at which the processor received and serviced hardware interrupts. This value is an indirect indicator of the activity of devices that generate interrupts, such as the system clock, the mouse, disk drivers, data communication lines, network interface cards, and other peripheral devices. These devices normally interrupt the processor when they have completed a task or require attention.

- **%Processor Time**   % Processor Time is the percentage of elapsed time that the processor spends to execute a non-idle thread. It is calculated by measuring the duration of time for which the idle thread is active in the sample interval, and subtracting that time from interval duration. Each processor has an idle thread that consumes cycles when no other threads are ready to run. This counter is the primary indicator of processor activity and displays the average percentage of busy time observed during the sample interval. It is calculated by monitoring the time for which the service is inactive, and subtracting that value from 100 percent.

Memory Counters

Three distinct objects can be used to monitor memory: Memory, Paging File, and Process. When checking these objects and counters, it is important to check them against a baseline number. A baseline number reflects the typical usage within the Exchange organization when server load is neither abnormally low nor abnormally high. The individual counters and methods for ensuring memory availability are as follows:

- Counters for the Memory object are:
  - **Committed Bytes**   Committed Bytes is the amount of committed virtual memory, in bytes. Committed memory is the physical memory that has space reserved on the disk paging file(s). One or more paging files can exist on each physical drive. This counter displays the last observed value only; it is not an average.

- **Pages/sec**   Pages/sec is the rate at which pages are read from or written to disk to resolve hard page faults. This counter is a primary indicator of the kinds of faults that cause system-wide delays.

- **Page Reads/sec**   Page Reads/sec is the number of reads from the page file per second. This number should be below 100. If the value is high over a period of time, then consider increasing total system memory.

- **Page Writes/sec**   Page Writes/sec is the number of writes to the page file per second. This number should not exceed 100. If the value is high over time, then consider increasing total system memory.

- **% Committed Bytes In Use**   % Committed Bytes In Use refers to the committed memory, which is the physical memory in use for which space has been reserved in the paging file in case it needs to be written to disk. The commit limit is determined by the size of the paging file.

- **Available Mbytes**   Available Mbytes is the amount of physical memory, in megabytes, immediately available for allocation to a process or for system use.

- Counters for the Paging File object are:

  - **% Usage**   The % Usage represents the amount of the page file instance in use. This counter should be below 70 percent.

- Counters for the Process object are:

  - **Page Faults/sec**   Page Faults/sec is the rate at which page faults by the threads executing in this process occur. A page fault occurs when a thread refers to a virtual memory page that is not in its working set in main memory. This might cause the page to not be fetched from disk if it is on the standby list and hence is already in main memory, or if it is in use by another process with which the page is shared. Monitor this counter for excessive faults compared with an established baseline recorded under normal operating conditions.

Check System Response Times

In your daily monitoring tasks, it is important to assume the role of a user to check how Exchange performs in real life. Events and counters are useful, but can be limited in how much they can relate about the user experience. When using Exchange, it is important to note availability and system response times. If resources are overextended, the messaging system may slow down significantly enough to impact users. For example, consider e-mail messages that are delayed by six hours and that outline important details between vendors and a company unit. Specifically, you should check for MAPI performance and SMTP performance.

SMTP Transport Engine Performance

The SMTP transport engine involves complex and various interactions with Exchange services. The numerous queues, event sinks, and processes make it a vital component, the failure or performance degradation of which is disastrous to an organization. To check the SMTP transport engine, you can send a test e-mail message to see if it is processed correctly. The Message Tracking Center in Exchange System Manager is helpful for monitoring SMTP performance.

MAPI Client Performance

Outlook 2003 is the MAPI client used to access full Exchange collaboration features. In a deployment that includes Outlook clients, you should monitor performance and availability. You can do this in three ways: by using Performance Monitor, by using Event Viewer, and by performing test logons and operations to the Exchange server.

Using System Monitor

The MSExchangeIS Transport driver and MSExchangeIS objects include counters to monitor MAPI performance is. These counters are as follows:

- **Client Moved List** When messages that are submitted for routing and delivery are delayed or congested, the Client Moved List counter tracks and measures how many messages are moved to Transport Temporary Tables. This value might vary at times from normal operations. A growing number of messages moved to Transport Temporary Tables indicates sluggish performance.

- **Client Submit List** Messages sent to outboxes in a MAPI client are processed and put into appropriate queues. When the messages are not processed, you should check to ensure that messages are routed and delivered, and that related services such as SMTP and IIS are running. Monitor the Client Submit List counter for excess growth. This value should not constantly grow over time, and is generally very small or zero.

- **MSExchangeIS\RPC Requests** Indicates the number of MAPI Remote Procedure Call (RPC) requests presently being serviced by the Microsoft Exchange Information Store service. The Microsoft Exchange Information Store service can service only 100 RPC requests (the default maximum value, unless configured otherwise) simultaneously before rejecting client requests. This number should be below 30 at all times.

- **MSExchangeIS\RPC Averaged Latency** Indicates the RPC latency in milliseconds (ms), averaged for the past 1024 packets. It should be below 50 ms at all times.

Using Event Viewer

When a MAPI client logon fails, the event is recorded in the Application event log. Specifically, the System Attendant (MSExchangeSA event source) records event 1022 when the Exchange store logon fails. When the client cannot log on to the Exchange store, there might be a problem with store availability.

Note   For more information about related events, see Microsoft Knowledge Base articles Q262456, Q288598, Q316709, and Q327352.

Performing Test Logons and Operations

Perhaps the most direct method to verify MAPI client availability and performance is to use a MAPI client to log on to the Exchange server and verify that messages are delivered.

To test MAPI client availability through synthetic logons:

1. Create test accounts on each Exchange server and one test account outside of the Exchange organization.

2. Send a test message from each account to all test account recipients.

3. Log on to each test account mailbox with a MAPI client to verify that the messages were delivered to their recipients.

Checking Message Paths

Sending test messages is an excellent method of checking for performance and availability of the overall Exchange System. The goal of successful Exchange operations is to create a secure environment that can deliver messages. To check for message delivery, consider the user experience and check actual performance.

Sending Test Messages

To test for and ensure that messages are queued and delivered to recipients you can send test messages. Sending test messages is a practical way to check for proper SMTP transport functionality.

Using Link Monitors

You can check link status in the Status container. It is listed as available or unavailable. To troubleshoot and monitor links, you can do the following:

■ Configure an e-mail or script notification to alert you when a link becomes unavailable.

■ Use Queue Viewer for the specific protocol that you are troubleshooting.

Using Message Tracking Center

You can use the Message Tracking Center to check for each instance of when a message is sent to a queue by a component of SMTP transport. You can use Message Tracking Center to track messages that have problems in routing or delivery. To effectively check and ensure SMTP transport health, you can perform the following steps:

1. Select an Exchange server by choosing it from within the Message Tracking Center interface. Click Server, type the name of the desired server, and click OK.

2. Find the test messages sent to all other Exchange servers.

3. Open each test message and check that it was delivered successfully. An example of a message that was not delivered is shown in Figure 8-5.

4. Repeat the above steps for each Exchange server in the organization.

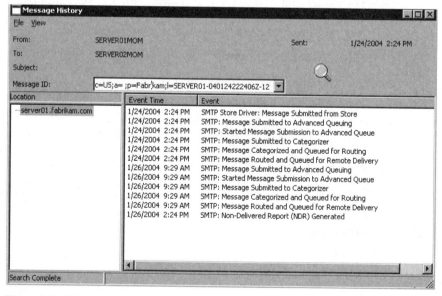

Figure 8-5   Message tracking history

Checking Queues with Exchange System Manager

To complement the ability to track messages, Exchange System Manager includes an interface to monitor queues, as shown in Figure 8-6.

You can use the Queues interface in several ways when you monitor your Exchange organization:

■ **Checking in conjunction with the Message Tracking Center**   You can check the queue related to a transport failure that was found through the Message Tracking Center. When you know the specific instance of what caused a message to not reach its recipient, you can design an appropriate response to maintain system health.

■ **Checking based on state and number of messages**   You can check the state of all queues by looking at the State column. Queues in the ready state and queues that are delivering messages properly usually have few messages queued for transfer. When a queue retries to send a message, this might indicate that a service is not running. The most significant indicator that you should monitor is queue growth. If the number of messages is increasing, and if the queue is in a retry state, this might indicate that the queue cannot deliver messages.

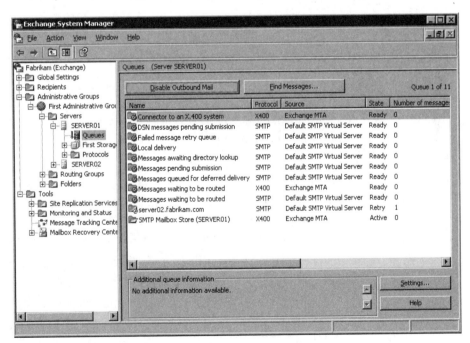

Figure 8-6   Queues interface

Checking Logs

The System and Application event logs, as well as service-specific event logs, such as Exchange and IIS, are useful monitoring resources. Typically, the logs contain a large number of event entries, as well as errors and warnings. These errors and warnings can be filtered and examined to determine the root causes and resolve the problems. When checking logs, perform the following tasks:

- **Searching For Errors and Warnings and Check Overall System Health** A quick method to diagnose problems is to filter errors and warnings in the logs. You can check for every error and warning or check for specific components, such as transport-related errors.

- **Checking Security Logs**   Security problems often have identifying events in logs. Check IIS, Exchange, and firewall logs for events that indicate unauthorized access, repeated unsuccessful logins, modified log times and data, and other suspicious activity. You can filter data to see the type of log entry that you want.

Virus Scanning

The performance of your Exchange organization depends not only on hardware and software availability, but also on proper configuration and preventive measures. Handling viruses and worms before they become a widespread problem is a vital aspect of your daily operations tasks.

Viruses and worms have the capacity to slow server performance to a crawl by introducing excess network traffic. You should regularly scan computers and update virus definitions on all client and server computers in your organization. Some of the different kinds of scanning solutions available are as follows:

- **File-level scanners**   File-level scanners can be used on client computers and servers. File-level scanners can be on-demand scanners, which scan at a scheduled interval or when desired, or memory-resident scanners, which check accessed files in memory and on the computer disk at all times. File-level scanners must be configured not to scan key Exchange files and directories such as:

  - Exchange databases and log files across all storage groups. By default, these are located in the Exchsrvr\Mdbdata folder.

  - Exchange MTA files in the Exchsrvr\Mtadata folder.

  - Additional log files, such as the Exchsrvr\server_name.log directory.

  - The Exchsrvr\Mailroot virtual server folder.

  - The working folder that is used to store streaming .tmp files that are used for message conversion. By default, this folder is Exchsrvr\Mdbdata.

- The temporary folder that is used in conjunction with offline maintenance utilities such as Eeseutil.exe. By default, this folder is the location from which the .exe file is run.

- Site Replication Service (SRS) files in the Exchsrvr\Srsdata folder.

- Microsoft Internet Information Services (IIS) system files in the %System-Root%\System32\Inetsrv folder.

- **MAPI scanners** These scanners perform a MAPI logon to each mailbox and then scan it for known viruses.

- **Virus scanning API scanners** Virus Scanning Application Programming Interface, or AVAPI, enables antivirus scanning of Exchange messages. In the scanning process, the scan is initiated when a client tries to open a message. Then, a comparison is made to ensure that the message body and attachment were scanned by the current virus signature file. If the current virus signature file has not scanned the content, the corresponding message component is submitted to the antivirus vendor product for scanning before that message component is released to the client. The client can be using a conventional MAPI client or an Internet Protocol (IP)-based client such as Post Office Protocol version 3 (POP3), Microsoft Outlook Web Access (OWA), and Internet Message Access Protocol, Version 4rev1 (IMAP4).

- **ESE-based scanners** ESE-based scanners use an interface between the information store and the Extensible Storage Engine (ESE). When you use this type of software, you run the risk of database damage and data loss if there are errors in the implementation of the software.

Regardless of your scanning solution, you must ensure that the following is done:

1. Implement a daily method to manually update virus definitions on all computers, both server and client, in the organization or set up automatic updates.

2. Create an action plan for when a virus is detected. For example, on a client computer, you can isolate the infected computer and disinfect it, educate users on steps to take when they become infected, and update software with any necessary patches to prevent further vulnerability.

3. Ensure that your solution has the capability to scan message attachments for viruses. New viruses and worms that can do extensive damage by causing heavy network traffic can spread through e-mail messages. Additionally, when new viruses that propagate through e-mail attachments appear, educate users on proper steps to take.

> **Note** For an overview of scanning solutions, their features, advantages and disadvantages, see Microsoft Knowledge Base Article 823166, Overview of Exchange 2003 and antivirus software (*http://support.microsoft.com/?id=823166*).

Best Practices in Virus Defense

To ensure optimal virus defense, you must not only educate users, update virus definitions, scan for viruses, and plan for responding to viruses, but you must also perform preventive and maintenance tasks such as the following:

- Quarantine files that you suspect are infected. Then, check files to see if they are critical and necessary components. If they are necessary and if the files cannot be disinfected, you must replace the files from a backup or other source.

- Check the quarantine and empty unneeded content. Files placed in quarantine that can be safely deleted should be deleted. The quarantine is a depository for administrative inspection, and should not be overloaded with files. Also, clean files should not be in quarantine.

- For added security and protection, you can set up filtering rules to filter messages in addition to using virus-scanning software.

Weekly Operations Tasks

The daily operations tasks in an Exchange organization focus on what you must do to maintain system health and availability. Weekly operations tasks provide an overview of the larger picture and enable for feedback, planning, and review. There are two tasks that should be done on a weekly basis, status meetings, and status reports.

Conducting a Status Meeting

A status meeting is the weekly opportunity to discuss the status of an IT environment. Status meetings provide time to evaluate past problems and responses, discuss current solutions, and plan for the future. Although the format and style of status meetings vary among organizations, they should include at least the following:

- Server and network status for the overall organization and segments
- SLA reviews
- Incident report reviews
- Risk analysis and evaluation
- Capacity, availability, and performance reviews

Creating Status Reports

Status reports are vital when monitoring an Exchange organization because they provide an overview of past events and create data for comparison. Reports can be used in capacity planning, in SLA reviews, for ease of determining performance, and other reasons. You can create reports by using recorded data with basic tools such as Excel or with an in-house solution. Alternatively, Microsoft Operations Manager with Exchange Management Pack includes reporting capability.

> **Note**   For more information on Exchange Management Pack, see Chapter 17, "Exchange Server 2003 Management Pack."

In addition to status reports, you should create incident reports. Incident reports can be part of the trouble ticket system used to resolve problems, or they can be generated independently whenever an incident occurs. Using incident reports helps to evaluate common and recurring problems to understand bottlenecks and weak areas.

Monthly Operations Tasks

Monthly tasks continue the overview and analysis processes from the weekly tasks, as well as performing operations tasks that are not required on a daily basis. Monthly tasks provide an excellent opportunity to do high-level planning and the tasks and processes in the Optimizing quadrant of MOF. The following sections discuss some necessary monthly tasks.

Performing Patch Management

Software development cycles typically include revisions to released programs, updates, and service packs. Often, the updates include fixes for detected security flaws or enhancements to the product. Updates can be created for various components of the software for an Exchange organization. For example, an update might be to a Windows component, such as Internet Explorer through Windows Update, or it might be a service pack, such as SP1 for Exchange Server 2003.

A best practices procedure for updates is to create a list of all software installed on servers and workstations, and systematically update all computers when an update is released. The update process can be automated by using group policies and scripts in Windows Server 2003.

> **Note**   To facilitate updates and help recognize potential security misconfigurations, you can use Microsoft Baseline Security Analyzer. For more information, see the Microsoft Baseline Security Analyzer website at *http:// www.microsoft.com/technet/security/tools/mbsahome.mspx*

It is also a good idea to maintain a test environment for deploying major updates and service packs before going live in a production environment.

> **Note**   If you are running Exchange Management Pack, you can specify the updates that you want each monitored computer to have. When a computer does not have a specified update, an alert is generated informing you of the condition.

Disaster Recovery Fire Drill

A monthly operations task that requires department-wide cooperation is the disaster recovery fire drill. In this exercise, a disaster is simulated and subsequently overcome. This helps to ensure that procedures are in place to recover from a major failure with minimal downtime. A recovery fire drill consists of two major components:

- **System recovery toolkit**   The recovery toolkit includes clear instructions for what to do in case of an emergency. A regular fire drill has clear plans for where each section of a building exists in case of a fire. Similarly, a disaster recovery toolkit should include what to do in case of individual component failure, such as database corruption, or a more widespread failure, such as a network outage or server failure. Check the toolkit and update the knowledge during monthly recovery fire drills.

- **Test recoveries**   Simulating fire drills puts a plan to the test. It can help uncover any contingencies with no plan, familiarize administrators with recovery procedures, and anticipate changes and failures in the organization. Test recoveries are an excellent risk-mitigation strategy.

Scheduling System Changes

With software and hardware updates, temporary system unavailability can occur. Updates sometimes require verification and configuration to ensure that services are working as expected. Informing users about changes and scheduling them during off-peak hours helps to maintain good availability.

When planning for change, consider performance issues and capacity issues. For example, memory and CPU performance might be low, while at the same time there is an anticipated addition of another business unit because of organizational growth. The increased users might require a dedicated server, and the current CPU might require an upgrade. Scheduling these tasks simultaneously or scheduling a planned outage and informing users are helpful in scheduling system changes.

More Info   For more information on how to monitor the server and establish performance baselines, as well as understand current capacities and limitations, see "Troubleshooting Exchange Server 2003 Performance" at *www.microsoft.com/exchange/library*.

Ad Hoc Tasks

The Exchange tasks suggested in this section are intended as a guide for developing a monitoring plan. They are necessary and encompass the majority of operations scenarios typically encountered. However, sometimes an unexpected situation or emergency arises because of an unforeseen risk. Follow best practices in accordance with MOF discussed earlier in this chapter to resolve these problems.

Tools and Technologies

The basic set of tools for administering Exchange servers and users includes the Windows Server 2003 administrative tool pack and the Exchange Server 2003 exchange system management tools. This section will give an outline of some of the tools that are available for managing the operations of an Exchange Server 2003 organization.

These management tasks and tools can be broadly divided into six categories:

1. **Active Directory and permissions management**   Exchange Server 2003 is tightly integrated with Active Directory. User attributes pertaining to Exchange server (e-mail address, ability to connect using POP3, mailbox server, and so on) are stored as user attributes in Active Directory. Therefore, one of the most important tools for managing Exchange users is Active Directory Users and Computers.

2. **Patch management and software updates**   Messaging systems can be especially vulnerable to malicious attacks, because the vast majority of messaging systems are connected to the Internet and must be capable of accepting unsolicited connections from unknown systems. It is vital to apply all security updates to servers exposed to public networks as soon as they are available. To check that your servers are up to date and report back on missing service packs and

hotfixes for the operating system and applications, you can use Microsoft Baseline Security Analyzer (MBSA). Microsoft Baseline Security Analyzer should be used to perform audits on systems. MBSA is free to download from Microsoft at *www.microsoft.com/security.*

> **Note** MBSA checks for security updates on Exchange Server 5.5 and above. It does not check the way in which Exchange is configured.

Software Update Services is a tool for automatically deploying security updates and other crucial updates. It is especially useful for updating workstations, but can also be used to update servers. Software Update Services automatically downloads each update over the internet as it is released by Microsoft. It provides the ability for you test a new update before deploying it automatically. Using Active Directory, you can control which computers receive updates and how the updates are applied. Workstations can be configured to download and install updates, rebooting as necessary without any manual intervention. Servers are usually configured to only download updates, waiting for an administrator to manually install the updates and reboot the server at a convenient time.

3. **Microsoft Operations Manager** In medium to large enterprises or in organizations where high availability is important, consider using an automated tool to track the performance and availability of servers and for capacity management. These tools can be configured to report on long-term trends, such as a gradual drop in response to MAPI clients as the number of clients increases. They can also be used to alert support staff in the event of a failure or rapid degradation of service.

> **Note** Microsoft Operations Manager is a package for monitoring and alerting, managing event logs, reporting, and trend analysis. It is used to monitor servers and will automatically log and analyze events and statistics from many computers.

4. **Systems Management Server** Systems Management Server is a tool that allows you to automate configuration management tasks by gathering information on hardware and software assets, storing this data in an SQL Server database and allowing custom queries and reports to be generated. In addition to performing the reporting duties of configuration management, Systems Management Server can also deploy software, service packs and hotfixes. System

Management Server can be configured to automatically discover devices on a network and to deploy agents to each server or workstation. Each agent gathers configuration data from the device and passes the information back to the central database. It can therefore be used to automate many of the regular changes discussed earlier in this chapter.

Windows Server 2003 software deployment services can be used to deploy software to computers or users across an organization or in a specific department or business unit.. Systems Management Server can be much more flexible and can, for example, deploy software only to clients within a specific department that are running Windows XP and that have at least 2 gigabytes (GB) of free disk space and at least 256 megabytes (MB) of RAM.

5. **Exchange 2003 tools**   Standard tools for managing an Exchange 2003 organization include Exchange System Manager and Exchange Migration Wizard. The use of Exchange System Manager in performing standard tasks is covered in more detail in later chapters. Exchange Migration Wizard is a tool for migrating user mailboxes from legacy messaging systems, such as Exchange 5.5, Microsoft Mail for PC Networks, or Lotus cc:Mail, to Exchange Server 2003.

6. **Automation tools and scripts**   Many administrative tasks related to Active Directory can be automated by using scripts. Windows Scripting Host is the host application that allows scripts to be run and that is installed by default on Windows Server 2003 and Windows XP Professional. Of the various scripting languages, VBScript (a derivative of the Visual Basic language) is the most commonly used for administrative tasks, where speed of writing is more important than the elegance and efficiency of the code.

Note   There are many examples of useful scripts to be found on the Web, and these can be customized to suit your particular need. A good starting point with plenty of useful examples can be found at *http://www.microsoft.com/technet/community/scriptcenter/default.mspx.*

Best Practices

Operating an Exchange Server 2003 organization requires close attention to the details and components that Exchange uses to operate. To effectively operate, you should understand and systematize the tasks that you should perform on a daily, weekly, and monthly basis. A good way to systematize the processes is to use the Microsoft Operations Framework. With MOF, you can evaluate the current operations and monitoring approach, identify areas that can be improved, and design and execute a solution.

When planning for operations and operating an Exchange organization, it is important to have a baseline that can be used in the future to plan growth, to compare usage, and to evaluate performance. An operations plan must additionally deal with disasters and emergencies. Fire drills, recovery plans, and failover systems help complete an operations plan and create good performance and availability.

Chapter 9

Managing Directory Information

About This Chapter

This chapter discusses how directory information is managed in a Microsoft Exchange Server 2003 organization. It explains the types of recipient objects, where the recipient objects live in Microsoft Active Directory, recipient object attributes, and how object attributes are replicated between global catalog servers. The chapter explains how communication occurs between Exchange and Active Directory and how address lists are maintained and displayed. Lastly, the chapter discusses managing recipient objects.

Prior to Exchange 2000 Server, Exchange used its own database to hold messaging system and directory information, including mailbox, custom recipient, distribution list, and public folder directory objects. Although mailbox objects were linked to the Microsoft Windows NT security database through the primary Windows NT account, no other link between the operating system and messaging directory existed. Beginning with Exchange 2000 Server, all that changed. The directory service was removed from Exchange Server, and now Active Directory, a core component of the Windows Server operating system, stores all Exchange objects.

Exchange stores its configuration information in Active Directory and relies on information in Active Directory to generate the global address list (GAL), which is the list that contains all mail-enabled and mailbox-enabled objects in Active Directory.

This chapter assumes that you are familiar with Microsoft Windows server technology and Active Directory directory service. To familiarize yourself with Windows Server 2003 or Active Directory, see Windows Server 2003 technology centers at *http://www.microsoft.com/windowsserver2003/technologies*. For additional information about Exchange Server 2003 directory information, also see Chapter 20, "Troubleshooting Active Directory Communication."

Recipient Objects in Active Directory

Active Directory user and group account information is used for Exchange recipients. An Exchange recipient is an object in Active Directory that Exchange can deliver messages to, such as a user or group.

In an Exchange 2003 environment, Active Directory users and groups marked with Exchange-specific attributes indicate whether they are mail-disabled, mail-enabled or mailbox-enabled. Exchange 2003 makes the following distinction between a mail-enabled object and a mailbox-enabled object:

- A mail-enabled object is an Active Directory object with at least one defined e-mail address.

- A mailbox-enabled object is an Active Directory object that has an Exchange mailbox associated with it. The Exchange mailbox takes up storage space on one of the Exchange servers.

Types of Recipient Objects

Not all Active Directory objects can be Exchange recipient objects. Recipient objects are categorized into four different types: user, contact, group, and public folder. User, contact, and group recipients are managed through Active Directory Users And Computers. Public folders are created using Microsoft Office Outlook, Outlook Web Access, or Exchange System Manager, and they are managed through Exchange System Manager.

User Recipients

User recipients are security principals in Active Directory. A security principal is a directory object that is assigned a security ID (SID), which can be used to access domain resources (that is, an object that can log on). There are two types of user recipients—mailbox-enabled users and mail-enabled users.

- A mailbox-enabled user has an account in Active Directory, an Exchange mailbox, and an e-mail address. This user can send and receive e-mail messages by using the Exchange infrastructure in the organization. For example, a corporate employee is likely to be a mailbox-enabled user.

■ A mail-enabled user has an account in Active Directory and an external e-mail address associated with it but no Exchange mailbox. A mail-enabled user is listed in the GAL. This enables other users to easily locate and send e-mail to a mail-enabled user even though he or she does not have a mailbox in the Exchange organization and cannot send or receive e-mail by using the Exchange infrastructure in the organization. For example, you may create a mail-enabled user for onsite contract employees who require access to the network but who want to continue receiving their e-mail through an external system, such as their Internet service provider (ISP).

Note Exchange 2003 includes the InetOrgPerson recipient object, which functions like a user object and can be mail-enabled or mailbox-enabled. The InetOrgPerson recipient object, although similar to the Windows user object, has extended attributes to improve compatibility with non-Microsoft Lightweight Directory Access Protocol (LDAP) and X.500 directory services that use InetOrgPerson objects. The InetOrgPerson is used to facilitate migrations from other directory services to Active Directory. InetOrgPerson is used only in a native Exchange Server 2003 topology, in which all computers in the Exchange organization are running Exchange Server 2003. You can create InetOrgPerson objects only if you are running a Microsoft Windows Server 2003 domain controller.

When a user recipient is disabled, Exchange does not provide access to it by standard e-mail protocols. From an e-mail perspective, the server does not recognize the address unless the recipient is enabled.

Contact Recipients

Contacts that are configured with e-mail addresses are known as mail-enabled contacts. A mail-enabled contact is neither a security principal in Active Directory nor has an Exchange mailbox in the associated Exchange organization. Mail-enabled contacts are visible in the GAL but cannot send or receive e-mail by using the Exchange infrastructure. An internal user can address an e-mail message to a contact simply by selecting the contact from the appropriate address list. For example, you might create a mail-enabled contact for a customer who does not need to access your network but whose e-mail address you would like to include in Exchange address lists.

Group Recipients

Groups are collections of users, groups, and contacts. Groups that are configured with e-mail addresses are known as mail-enabled groups. They are similar to distribution lists in Exchange Server 5.5. You can mail-enable any type of Active Directory group, although we recommend that you only mail-enable universal groups in multi-domain organizations. After a group is mail-enabled, it has an e-mail address and appears in address lists. All members of the group who have e-mail addresses correctly defined in Active Directory are able to receive messages that are sent to the group's e-mail address.

More Info   Query-based distribution groups are mail-enabled distribution groups that have their membership determined by an LDAP query. For more information about query-based distribution groups, see the section "Working with Mail-Enabled Groups" later in this chapter.

Public Folder Recipients

All public folders are not mail-enabled by default. As with other recipient objects, public folders can be mail-enabled as necessary. After a public folder is mail-enabled, it has an e-mail address and appears in address lists. By mail-enabling a public folder, users can easily send an e-mail message to a public folder by selecting the public folder name from the appropriate address list instead of posting to the folder directly.

Table 9-1 summarizes the characteristics of each recipient object type.

Table 9-1   Recipient Object Types

Recipient object type	Security principal	E-mail address	Mailbox location
Mailbox-enabled user	Yes	Mailbox in Exchange mailbox store or forwarding address.	Exchange mailbox store.
Mail-enabled user	Yes	Mailbox on external e-mail system.	External e-mail system.
Mail-enabled contact	No	Mailbox on external e-mail system.	External e-mail system.
Mail-enabled distribution group	No	Group address where mail is routed to group members.	None. The group serves as a distribution list.
Mail-enabled security group	Yes	Group address where mail is routed to group members.	None. The group serves as a distribution list.
Mail-enabled public folder	No	Public folder in Exchange public folder store.	Public folder in Exchange public folder store.

Working with Mail-Enabled Groups

In Exchange 2003, an Active Directory group is similar to an Exchange Server 5.5 distribution list. Active Directory contains two types of groups, and each group type has a scope attribute. The scope of a group determines who can be a member of the group, and where you can use that group in the network. The domain functional level limits the choice of group type and group scope.

Group Types

There are two types of groups—security groups and distribution groups. Both types of groups can be mail-enabled.

- **Security groups**   Security groups in Windows are used for security-related purposes, such as granting permissions to gain access to public folders and other resources. You can mail-enable security groups and use them to send e-mail messages to multiple users. Sending an e-mail message to a group sends the message to all mail-enabled and mailbox-enabled members of the group.

- **Distribution groups**   Distribution groups are used only for sending e-mail messages to groups of users. You cannot grant permissions to distribution groups.

Table 9-2 compares the advantages and disadvantage of each group type.

Table 9-2   Group Type Comparison

Group type	Advantage	Disadvantage
Security groups	They can be mail-enabled by assigning a Simple Mail Transfer Protocol (SMTP) address, allowing the group to act as a distribution list equivalent. They can be used for assigning permissions to public folders in Exchange 2003. They can be useful if you want to also assign network permissions to the group members. They can lower the number of groups and the amount of maintenance required for Active Directory and the messaging system because they can act as pseudo-distribution groups.	Users might gain unauthorized access to network resources if they are accidentally placed in the wrong group.
Distribution groups	They can be used for bulk mailing. They can be used as universal groups, even in a mixed-mode domain.	Permissions cannot be assigned to network resources. Permissions cannot be assigned to public folders in Exchange 2003.

Group Scopes

Before you mail-enable Active Directory groups, you must have a clear understanding of the effects of group scope on the messaging capability of these groups. There are three scopes for groups—domain local, global, and universal.

- **Domain local group**   The membership of this group is not published to the global catalog. This means that Exchange users cannot view the full membership of a mail-enabled domain local group when their user accounts are located in domains other than the domain in which the group exists.

  We recommend that you use domain local groups under the following conditions:

  - Limiting replication overhead is a priority for your company.

  - Most mail is sent from the local domain to recipients in the local domain.

  - You want to control access to public folders but do not want to switch your Windows domain to a functional level of Windows 2000 native or Windows Server 2003 so that you can use a universal group.

- **Global group**   The membership of this group is not published to the global catalog. This means that Exchange users cannot view the full membership of a mail-enabled global group when their user accounts are located in domains other than the domain in which the group exists.

  Global groups are recommended for similar reasons as domain local groups but we recommend that you use global groups instead under the following conditions:

  - You want to assign access permissions to resources that are located in the same domain in which you create the global group.

  - You want to organize users who share the same job tasks and network access requirements.

- **Universal group**   The membership of this group is published to the global catalog and replicated to all global catalog servers in a forest. This means that Exchange users in any domain can view full membership of mail-enabled universal groups. If you have multiple domains in your environment, we recommend that you only mail-enable universal groups and not domain local or global groups. Universal security groups are needed for granting permissions to public folders.

  Another point to consider is the impact on network and server performance when deploying universal groups. Universal group membership is listed in the global catalog, so any membership change causes replication traffic. Although Active Directory supports property-level replication, the membership for a group is held in a multi-valued property on the group object. Therefore, if the group is large, a significant amount of replication traffic can be generated. To mitigate this risk, place user objects in other universal groups and then nest these groups under an umbrella universal group. When the membership changes for a user in the group, the large universal group object is not changed and no replication traffic is created. Universal group membership is enumerated when a user logs on, which can also affect performance when large numbers of universal groups are used.

When you implement universal groups, Microsoft Outlook users can still view full memberships of both the umbrella group and its subgroups. You can use global groups instead of universal groups. However, global groups do not have their membership listed in the global catalog, and this can impact the ability of an Outlook client to view membership at the recipient level.

If you want to use a universal security group, you must create that group in a Windows domain that has a domain functional level of Windows 2000 native or Windows Server 2003.

We recommend that you use universal groups under the following conditions:

- You want to nest global groups or domain local groups or both.

- Active Directory has multiple domains.

- You want to use access control lists (ACLs) on a public folder that will be used across multiple domains.

- Most mail is sent from a remote domain.

Expansion Servers

An expansion server is a server that is used to resolve or expand the membership of a mail-enabled group whenever a message is sent to that group. We recommend that you use universal groups in multi-domain organizations. However, if you must use domain local or global groups, use an expansion server. Because of the limited scopes of a domain local group or a global group, Exchange users in one domain are not able to view the membership of groups that are defined in another domain. Exchange is unable to deliver messages sent by users in one domain to groups defined in another domain. To resolve group membership, you must use an expansion server when mail-enabling domain local groups or global groups in environments that have multiple domains. The expansion server that you choose must exist in the same domain as the mail-enabled group. Expansion servers are identified on a group-by-group basis.

Query-Based Distribution Groups

A query-based distribution group is a new type of distribution group introduced in Exchange 2003. It provides essentially the same functionality as a standard distribution group. However, instead of specifying static user memberships, a query-based distribution group enables you to use an LDAP query to specify membership in the distribution group (for example, all employees in an accounting department or all employees in a particular office building).

Advantages of Query-Based Distribution Groups

By using query-based distribution groups, you can considerably lower the administrative overhead in maintaining certain distribution groups, especially those that have memberships that change frequently. Administrators do not have to add members to their group on an ongoing basis. For example, suppose an employee joins the company in the marketing department in the Spokane office. Usually, if you use static groups, the administrator has to manually go in and add this new account to at least three groups: All Employees, All Employees in the Spokane office, and All Marketing Personnel. For large organizations, adding and removing static memberships is an ongoing, tedious task. If, instead, you set up query-based distribution groups once, all you need to do is populate the user attributes systematically in Active Directory Users And Computers, and whenever the query-based distribution group is used, the user will automatically be included in the resultant query.

Disadvantages of Query-Based Distribution Groups

Query-based distribution groups require higher performance cost in terms of server resources, such as high CPU utilization and an increased working set, because each message to the query-based distribution group causes a corresponding LDAP query to be run against the Active Directory directory service to determine its membership. In addition, a query-based distribution group can be created only in an organization that is running Exchange 2003 and a domain that has been raised to the Windows Server 2003 functional level.

Message Delivery Process

When a message is submitted to a query-based distribution group, Exchange treats the message slightly differently than messages that are destined for other recipients. When a message is sent to a query-based distribution group:

1. A message is submitted through the Exchange store driver or through SMTP to the submission queue.

2. The categorizer, a transport component that is responsible for address resolution, determines that the recipient is a query-based distribution group.

3. The categorizer sends the LDAP query request to a global catalog server.

4. The global catalog server runs the query, and then it returns the set of addresses that match the query.

5. After receiving the complete set of addresses that match the query, the categorizer generates a recipient list that contains all the users. The categorizer must have the complete set of recipients before it can submit the message to routing.

If an error occurs during the expansion of the query-based distribution group to its individual recipients, the categorizer must start the process over.

6. After the categorizer sends the complete and expanded list of recipients to routing, the standard message delivery process continues, and the message is delivered to the users' mailboxes.

The process is slightly different if you use a dedicated expansion server, a single server that is responsible only for expanding distribution groups, for query-based distribution groups. In this case, instead of sending a query to the global catalog server for expansion, the message is first routed to the dedicated expansion server. After the message arrives at the expansion server, the expansion occurs. The delivery follows the same process that is described above.

Query-Based Distribution Group Guidelines

The following list describes the guidelines on using query-based distribution groups:

- They are mail-enabled by default and cannot be disabled.

- They can have restrictions set to limit who can send to the query-based distribution group.

- They can be configured to expand on a dedicated server.

- They can be nested, but we recommend that you use a universal distribution group to group together multiple query-based distribution groups.

- They cannot be security principals.

- They cannot be used in an Exchange mixed-mode environment that includes Exchange Server 5.5 or earlier.

- They cannot use an external directory service for LDAP queries. You must replicate the external objects to Active Directory.

- Filters must use attributes that are in the global catalog; use of the Preview option is strongly recommended to view the filter results.

- Index the attributes that are used in the query. Indexing greatly improves the performance of the query and reduces the time that it takes to expand the distribution group and to deliver the message to the intended recipients.

More Info For additional information about indexing attributes, view the Microsoft Knowledge Base article 313992, "How to Add an Attribute to the Global Catalog in Windows 2000" (*http://support.microsoft.com/ default.aspx?scid=kb;en-us;313992*).

■ You must use an Exchange 2003 version of Exchange System Manager and of Active Directory Users And Computers to create a query-based distribution group.

Improving Performance Using Windows 2000 Global Catalog Servers

To configure an Exchange 2000 Service Pack 3 (SP3) server for improved reliability in organizations where query-based distribution groups are expanded with Windows 2000 global catalog servers, follow these steps:

1. Start the Registry Editor.

2. Expand the following registry key:

   `HKEY_LOCAL_MACHINE\SYSTEM\CurrentControlSet\Services\SMTPSVC\Parameters`

3. Right-click Parameters, select New, and then click DWORD Value.

4. Type **DynamicDLPageSize**, and then press Enter.

5. Right-click DynamicDLPageSize, and then click Modify.

6. In Edit DWORD Value, under Base, click Decimal.

7. Under Value Data, type **31**, and then click OK.

Query-based distribution groups will not work reliably if you are running any version of Exchange earlier than Exchange 2000 SP3 in your environment.

Working with Query Types

With query-based distribution groups, you can have AND and OR type operations on the query-based distribution groups. This means that if you can create a query using two attribute values, the query would include results that meet both of the specified conditions. For example, if you create a query that includes users on Mailbox Store 1, and then users located in Seattle, the results would include only users who are on Mailbox Store 1 and who are located in Seattle.

If you want to create a query-based distribution group based on an OR operator, you can create multiple query-based distribution groups and combine them in a single distribution group. For example, to include all users who are on Mailbox Store 1 or who are located in Seattle, you would need to create a query-based distribution group for users in Seattle, and a second distribution group for users residing on Mailbox Store 1. Then you could create a standard distribution group and include these two queries within that group.

Viewing Membership

You cannot view the membership of a query-based distribution group in the GAL because it is dynamically generated each time mail is sent. However, you can see the dynamic list if you right-click the distribution group, click Properties, and then click the Preview tab (Figure 9-1).

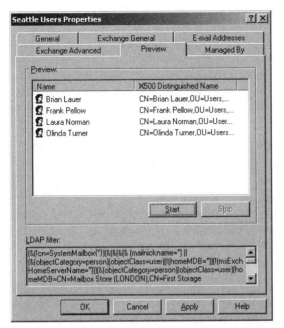

Figure 9-1   Query-based distribution group Preview tab

Be aware that two areas will affect the results you see when you use the Preview tab when you are creating a query-based distribution group. The first is the security context of the user who is logged in. When the query-based distribution group forms its membership, it uses the security context of the Exchange Server account. For this reason, the results that are displayed in the Preview tab may vary from the actual results when the query is run, if the security privileges of the current user and Exchange Server account are different.

The second is whether or not the attributes you are using in your query are replicated to the global catalog servers. When you use the Preview tab, the query executes against the available attributes on the global catalog server. You can see whether the result is what you're expecting or if the query result or preview is empty, and adjust the query if required.

More Info   For additional information about troubleshooting query-based distribution groups, view the Microsoft Knowledge Base article 822897, "How to Troubleshoot Query-Based Distribution Groups" (*http://support.microsoft.com/default.aspx?scid=kb;en-us;822897*).

Exchange 2003 and Active Directory

Exchange 2003 uses a single Active Directory forest to store all Exchange system information. Each Exchange object is represented in the Active Directory global catalog and, as a result, is replicated throughout the forest when the global catalog changes. The Active Directory forest is the boundary of the Exchange organization. It is not possible to have more than one Exchange organization running within the same Active Directory forest.

Companies that choose to deploy multiple Active Directory forests might deploy Exchange in more than one forest. When more than one Exchange organization exists, an inter-organizational GAL synchronization strategy is required to provide users with a single GAL. Provisioning software, such as running Identity Integration Feature Pack or Identity Integration Server can be used to provide a single GAL. For more information on deploying Exchange 2003 in multiple Active Directory forests, see Chapter 3, "Exchange Server 2003 in Enterprise Environments."

The Exchange requires more classes and attributes than Active Directory provides. Object classes describe the possible directory objects that can be created. Attributes are the characteristic of an object; for example, a network printer is an object and its attributes include its location, whether it can print in color, and its print job capacity. Each object class is a collection of attributes.

When Exchange Server Setup is run with the ForestPrep option, the Active Directory schema is extended to accommodate the Exchange containers and properties. New classes are added and existing classes are extended with new attributes. Extending the schema enables Active Directory to accommodate all of the classes and attributes that are specific to Exchange 2003. Exchange 2003 attributes have names that start with ms-Exch; for example, ms-Exch-OAB-Default. The schema is extended by using LDAP Data Interchange Format (LDIF) files. You can examine which attributes have been added to Active Directory by viewing the LDIF files on the Exchange 2003 compact disc.

Domain Information and Global Catalogs

Domain controllers and global catalog servers are critical for an Exchange organization. They enable users in various locations to log on and for global address list information and Exchange objects to be replicated throughout the Active Directory forest.

Domain Controllers

The core unit of the logical structure in Active Directory is the domain. A domain is a collection of computer, user, and group objects, defined by an administrator, that share a common directory database, security policies, and security relationships with other domains. Each domain has a unique name within the Active Directory forest and provides access to the centralized user accounts and group accounts maintained by the domain administrator.

Domains are also units of replication. In each domain, computers named domain controllers contain a writable copy of the Active Directory data for that domain. All of the domain controllers in each domain can receive changes to information in Active Directory, and they can replicate these changes to all of the other domain controllers in that domain.

Domain controllers contain an Active Directory directory service structure within the context of their domains; in addition, the Active Directory structure contains a configuration, schema, and domain naming context. They also provide the authentication services that are necessary for clients to log on and access services in Exchange.

Global Catalog

The global catalog is a repository of information that contains a subset of the attributes of all objects in Active Directory. The global catalog contains a complete replica of all objects in the domain and a partial replica of all objects in the forest. The global catalog is the component of Active Directory that Exchange queries to create the global address list, and Exchange clients query to obtain information about recipients located in the global address list. By default, the attributes that are stored in the global catalog are those that are most frequently used in queries, such as a user's first name, last name, and logon name. The global catalog contains the information that is necessary to determine the location of any object in the directory.

A global catalog server is a Windows Server domain controller that stores a writable copy of the domain naming context for its domain and the forest-wide configuration and schema naming contexts. The Active Directory domain naming context contains all of the objects (such as users, groups, contacts, and computers) in the directory for the domain. The global catalog also contains a partial set of the attributes for every object from every domain in the forest. Domain data in each domain is replicated to every domain controller in that domain, but not beyond that domain.

A global catalog server is a domain controller that stores copies of all queries and processes the queries to the global catalog. Both Exchange and Outlook need a local global catalog server. The global catalog server is critical for Exchange Server services, including log on, group membership, store services, and access to the GAL.

The global catalog makes the directory structure within a forest transparent to users who perform a search. For example, if you search for all of the printers in a forest, a global catalog server processes the query in the global catalog, and then returns the results. Without a global catalog server, this query would require a search of every domain in the forest.

Exchange balances requests among available global catalog servers. Each time an address book search occurs and each time a message is routed, Exchange uses the closest global catalog server.

Global Catalog Servers

All domain controllers are accessed through TCP port 389. The entire object can be seen on port 389 of the domain controller for the domain that contains the object. In addition to port 389 exposed by domain controllers, a global catalog server also exposes TCP port 3268. Even though an object is available on ports 389 and 3286, only a partial set of attributes is visible on 3286. MAPI properties appear only on global catalogs. Outlook users within a forest can see directory details for users in other domains because MAPI properties replicate to the global catalog.

Accessing Active Directory Data

Exchange services require access to Active Directory, as do Exchange clients, such as Outlook. Exchange management tools, such as Exchange System Manager, also require access to Active Directory. The process that each of these items uses to access Active Directory varies and is discussed in greater detail in the sections that follow.

- All Exchange 2003 services that require Active Directory access, either for reading configuration information or for writing new entries to the directory, use the Directory Service Access Application Programming Interface (DSAccess API), also referred to as DSAccess.

- Exchange clients perform address book searches using Active Directory. Depending on the Exchange client, the client may require a referral to access information in Active Directory using the client referral process, DSProxy.

- Exchange System Manager does not use DSAccess but instead uses a separate process to discover domain controllers.

Exchange 2003 Access to Active Directory

DSAccess is an internal process in Exchange 2003 that is used for accessing and storing directory information. Exchange 2003 queries Active Directory for both user and configuration information. The most important part of DSAccess is the shared cache, which caches search results between different services in Exchange 2003.

DSAccess can be configured to either statically or dynamically detect directory service servers that may exist in the topology where the Exchange Server computer resides.

Note   Any configuration changes to DSAccess apply to a single Exchange Server computer.

Global Catalog and Domain Controller Access   DSAccess partitions the set of available directory service servers into the following three (possibly overlapping) categories: global catalog servers, domain controllers, and the configuration domain controller.

During initialization, DSAccess dynamically detects available directory service servers within the domain, unless you manually configure static entries. There are two kinds of detection algorithms.

DSAccess generates a list of available global catalog servers and domain controllers, which it periodically updates as directory service state changes are detected. This list can be shared out to other directory consumers that do not necessarily use DSAccess as their gateway for accessing the directory service (for example, Categorizer, DSProxy, and the System Attendant service).

For access to a domain controller, DSAccess first queries domain controllers within the same site and domain as the server running Exchange. If no such domain controller is available, DSAccess queries domain controllers outside the site but still within the same domain. If more than one domain controller is available, DSAccess selects one by using the round-robin method. If the desired information is not stored on one of the domain controllers, DSAccess makes a Domain Name System (DNS) query for the nearest global catalog server, and then requests the information again.

DSAccess uses DNS to provide a list of all of the domain controllers in the local domain and the local Active Directory site. DSAccess saves up to ten domain controller names in its cache; it load balances the usage of these domain controllers in a round-robin fashion.

For access to the global catalog, DSAccess first queries the Windows Server site to which the server running Exchange 2003 belongs. If all global catalog servers in that site are unavailable, DSAccess queries other sites.

Global catalog server detection is different from traditional service detection. To detect global catalog servers, DSAccess uses the LDAP connection to the domain controller that DSAccess is currently bound to. On the domain controller, DSAccess reads the Options attribute of the Microsoft Windows NT Directory Service Settings object for each directory service server, if any, in the site that contains the server running Exchange 2003. DSAccess detects which of the listed domain controllers are also global catalog servers. The global catalog servers are added to the DSAccess profile, and load balancing takes place.

If DSAccess does not find any global catalog servers in the local domain and site, a remote global catalog server is selected. Using a global catalog server in a remote site is not an optimal solution, however, because the global catalog servers in other Active Directory sites may be located across slow links and may not be load balanced.

DSAccess performs a full network redetection whenever the Kerberos version 5 authentication protocol ticket times out (there is a default period of ten hours) or a configuration change is made, such as the addition of a new domain controller or global catalog server.

Defining Domain Controllers and Servers DSAccess contacts an Active Directory server by making a DNS query. You can require a server running Exchange 2003 to always use the same Active Directory server through the Directory Access page (Figure 9-2) on the properties of the server object or by changing the registry settings.

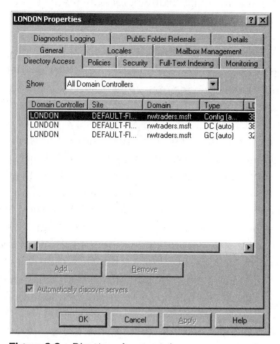

Figure 9-2 Directory Access tab

DSAccess can be statically configured to channel directory service loads for user-context searches to a specified set of directory service servers. This is accomplished in the registry. Upon initialization, DSAccess first reads the registry to determine if any domain controllers or global catalog servers have been statically configured. If any domain controllers or global catalog servers are statically configured, then no dynamic domain controller detection is performed. Conversely, if no static configurations are made to the registry, DSAccess dynamically detects those directory service servers in the topology.

More Info For additional information about manually configuring domain controller and global catalog servers for use by DSAccess using the registry, view the Microsoft Knowledge Base article 250570, "Directory Service Server Detection and DSAccess Usage" (*http://support.microsoft.com/ default.aspx?scid=kb;en-us;250570*).

When DSAccess has been statically configured, DSAccess will never fall back and use any other domain controller or global catalog server that might otherwise be dynamically detected. As a result, if all the statically configured domain controllers or global catalog servers are down, then no DSAccess operations will succeed.

If you manually configure global catalog servers, but do not specify domain controllers, DSAccess dynamically detects and uses any available domain controller. Similarly, if you manually configure domain controllers but do not specify any global catalog servers, DSAccess dynamically detects and uses any available global catalog servers. Multiple domain controllers and global catalog servers can be specified for load balancing, but only one Configuration-Context Domain Controller can be configured.

The configuration domain controllers that will be used for configuration-context searches can be dynamically detected, detected when the Exchange System Attendant starts, or by statically configuring the server using the registry.

In Exchange 2003, the Microsoft Exchange System Attendant will choose the Configuration Domain Controller only on the first service start, which occurs during setup or upgrade. In all cases, the choice by the System Attendant is ignored if the configuration domain controller is statically configured in the registry. Static configuration domain controller configuration is taken by DSAccess as a suggestion. This means that if the configuration domain controller is statically configured, DSAccess prefers this domain controller for configuration-context requests. If this domain controller becomes unavailable, an alternative domain controller is chosen from the list of available domain controllers. In this event, DSAccess fails over the configuration domain controller by choosing an available User domain controller, behaving as if the configuration domain controller registry keys were not set.

Client Access to Active Directory

Exchange clients also access information in Active Directory. The client requests range from resolving user names when addressing e-mail messages, to showing objects from the global address list. Depending on the client software, how Active Directory is accessed may change.

The DSProxy service runs within the Exchange System Attendant (mad.exe) rather than as its own service. DSProxy provides compatibility for earlier versions of MAPI-based clients, such as Outlook, that are connected to an Exchange 2003 server. These clients assume that the storage and directory services are on the same server, as they were in Exchange 5.5. DSProxy enables Outlook clients to access the data within a global catalog, and isolates the clients from global catalog failure, because the DSProxy service always finds the nearest global catalog server by using DSAccess service.

Exchange Client, Outlook 97, and Outlook 98   Earlier versions of Microsoft Outlook (Exchange Client, Outlook 97, and Outlook 98) make Messaging Application Programming Interface directory service (MAPI DS) requests to a server running Exchange 2003, rather than to a domain controller. To make Exchange 2003 backward compatible with the existing MAPI client base, a server running Exchange 2003 will proxy any MAPI DS requests to a local global catalog server on the network. The DSProxy process on the Exchange server accomplishes this by forwarding the client request. It does not change the request into LDAP. Active Directory supports a number of protocols, including LDAP and MAPI directory service, so an Outlook directory request is valid, even when made directly to a global catalog server.

The following steps are the communication process for a one-recipient name lookup:

1. The MAPI client sends one network packet to the Exchange 2003 server. The packet contains the search name in plain text.

2. The Exchange 2003 server sends the request to a local global catalog server.

3. The local global catalog server returns the result to the Exchange 2003 server.

4. The Exchange 2003 server returns the result to the MAPI client.

5. The MAPI client returns an acknowledgement to the Exchange 2003 server.

6. The Exchange 2003 server sends the acknowledgement to the local global catalog server.

The directory search produces about six frames on the network. Even when multiple names are searched for in the directory, the name fragments go into a one-request packet.

If the user browses the GAL, the same process takes place. A few extra frames are produced on the network as the user scrolls through the address list, thus causing the client to retrieve more information.

Outlook 98 SP2, Outlook 2000 and Later   For more recent versions of Microsoft Outlook (Outlook 98 SP2, Outlook 2000 and later), the client can directly access Active Directory. The first time the client connects to a server running Exchange 2003, the client will look for the Directory Service on the server. If Outlook is connected to Exchange 2003, Exchange 2003 will initiate the DSProxy process for the very first session. After the client has contacted the DSProxy service, a referral will be passed back to the client, informing it that all future directory requests should be sent directly to the global catalog server.

Non-MAPI Clients   Non-MAPI clients, such as Post Office Protocol version 3 (POP3) and Internet Message Access Protocol version 4 (IMAP4) clients, retrieve directory information, such as addresses, by using the LDAP. During setup, a POP3 or IMAP4 user specifies which directory service they want to use by machine name or by TCP/IP address, and then contacts the specified service through the standard LDAP port 389.

A server running either Windows Server Active Directory or Exchange 2003 can accept these LDAP requests. If the client computer is configured with the name or address of a server running Exchange 2003, and if this server is installed as a member server, then that server running Exchange 2003 uses DSProxy to proxy the LDAP requests.

Exchange also proxies request for directory information for Outlook Web Access clients.

Exchange System Manager Access to Active Directory

Exchange System Manager does not use DSAccess to discover the domain controller (domain controller or global catalog server) that it will communicate with. Exchange System Manager uses Active Directory Service Interfaces (ADSI) to perform a server-less binding to the directory. Typically, this does not create any problems. Occasionally, the domain controller referred to your server by DSAccess is different than the domain controller that Exchange System Manager is bound to. This can happen when the computer used to run Exchange System Manager and the Exchange Server are in different Windows sites. If this happens, there may be a delay when settings are modified due to replication not having occurred yet.

To configure Exchange System Manager to communicate with a specific domain controller, you can create a custom Microsoft Management Console (MMC). When you create a custom MMC for the Exchange System snap-in, you are presented with a dialog box to select a domain controller.

1. Click Start, select Run, type **mmc**, and then press Enter.

2. In the Console1 window, on the File menu, select Add/Remove Snap-in. The Add/Remove Snap-in dialog box is displayed.

3. On the Standalone tab, click Add.

4. In the Add Standalone Snap-in dialog box, in the Available Standalone Snap-ins list, select Exchange System, and then click Add.

5. In the Change Domain Controller dialog box, in the Available Controllers list, select the domain controller that you want to connect to, and then click OK.

6. In the Add Standalone Snap-in dialog box, click Close.

7. In the Add/Remove Snap-in dialog box, click OK.

Attributes Included in Global Catalog Replication

The Windows 2003 schema contains a large number of object attributes that administrators can use. The attributes typically required by Windows 2003 are enabled by default when the first domain controller is installed; a number of these attributes are used by both Active Directory and the global catalog. These attributes have the Index This Attribute In The Active Directory and Replicate This Attribute To The Global Catalog options selected in their properties. Figure 9-3 is an example of an attribute, mailNickname, configured to appear in both Active Directory and the global catalog.

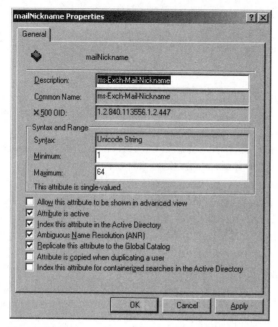

Figure 9-3   Properties of the mailNickname attribute

When you install Exchange 2003, the Active Directory schema is extended with new attributes that all start with ms-Exch-; for example, ms-Exch-OAB-Default. Existing Active Directory attributes are modified, some of which affect what Outlook users see in the global address list. The global catalog stores only a partial set of attributes for these objects, which includes any attribute in the schema having its isMemberof-PartialAttributeSet property set to TRUE.

More Info   For additional information about default attributes in Active Directory and global catalog, view the Microsoft Knowledge Base article 257203, "Common Default Attributes Set for Active Directory and Global Catalog" (*http://support.microsoft.com/default.aspx?scid=kb;en-us;257203*).

For additional information about modifying the schema, view the Microsoft Knowledge Base article 216060, "Registry Modification Required to Allow Writing to Schema" (*http://support.microsoft.com/default.aspx?scid=kb;en-us;216060*).

Table 9-3 lists the common attributes and LDAP names for an Active Directory, mailbox-enabled, user object. The table illustrates how these attributes differ between standard installations of Active Directory and Active Directory when it is enabled for

Exchange 2003. The "In global catalog" columns indicate whether the attribute is tagged by default for global catalog server replication.

Table 9-3   Attributes in Active Directory Before and After Exchange 2003 Installation

Attribute	LDAP name	In index before	In global catalog before	In index after	In global catalog after
First name	GivenName	Yes	No	Yes	Yes
Initials	Initials	No	No	No	Yes
Last name	Sn	Yes	No	Yes	Yes
Display name	DisplayName	Yes	No	Yes	Yes
Alias	MailNickname	N/A	N/A	Yes	Yes
Mailing address	StreetAddress	No	No	No	Yes
City	L	Yes	No	Yes	Yes
State	St	No	No	No	Yes
ZIP code	PostalCode	No	No	No	Yes
Country or region	C	No	No	No	Yes
Job title	Title	No	No	No	Yes
Company	Company	No	No	No	Yes
Department	Department	No	No	No	Yes
Office	PhysicalDelivery-OfficeName	Yes	No	Yes	Yes
Telephone	TelephoneNumber	No	No	No	Yes
Fax	FacsimileTelephone				
Number	No	No	No	Yes	
Home telephone	HomePhone	No	No	No	Yes
Manager	Manager	No	Yes	No	Yes
SMTP Address	Mail	Yes	No	Yes	Yes
Custom attributes (all)	ExtensionAttribute-xx	N/A	N/A	No	Yes

Selecting Attributes to Replicate to the Global Catalog

With earlier versions of Exchange and Outlook, users rely on the directory data that is populated to the Exchange directory. For example, users can look up each other's telephone numbers through this mechanism.

With Exchange Server 4.0 and Exchange Server 5.0, any directory data present in one Exchange server has to be replicated to every other Exchange server within a company. To reduce network traffic, Exchange Server 5.5 implements selectable-field replication, which prevents certain attributes (but not objects) from replicating between Exchange sites. Many companies do not take advantage of this new feature because users frequently rely on the directory information.

Active Directory has a similar feature, in which selected attributes can be tagged for replication to the global catalog server. A difference between this feature in Active Directory and earlier versions of Exchange is that, by default, not all attributes are tagged for replication. Exchange administrators control attributes tagged for replication through the Active Directory schema console.

By default, the global catalog does not replicate all attributes that were included in previous versions of Exchange, although additional attributes can be configured to replicate and display in the global catalog. For example, the attributes for first name, last name, and SMTP address are tagged for global catalog replication by default. However, the attribute for mailing address is not.

If you need to display a non-default attribute in the global address list, you must modify it for replication to the global catalog. During messaging evaluation, examine all attributes to determine if modifications are required. Modifying the replicated attributes triggers replication to the global catalog. It is important to plan and ensure that business processes are not affected when this happens.

You can change both the number of attributes selected and which specific attributes are used by using the Active Directory Schema snap-in in MMC. In most cases, there is no need to modify any of these attributes. To make the Active Directory Schema snap-in available, you must first register the Active Directory Schema DLL as follows: Click Start, select Run, type **Regsvr32 schmmgmt.dll**, and then press Enter.

To change which attributes replicate to the global catalog, right-click the attribute in the Active Directory Schema MMC snap-in, choose Properties, and then select or clear the Replicate This Attribute To The Global Catalog check box, as shown in Figure 9-4.

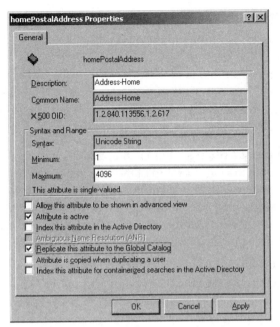

Figure 9-4 Properties in the Active Directory Schema snap-in of homePostalAddress attribute

Making Schema Changes

The Active Directory schema can grow to accommodate a company's changing needs. Keep in mind that Active Directory schema modifications affect the company's infrastructure and replication mechanisms. For example, if you deploy Active Directory and then decide to tag another attribute for global catalog replication, you can make the change easily in the Active Directory Schema Manager snap-in. However, this causes all global catalogs to set their Update Sequence Numbers to zero. As a result, all objects (not just the changed property) in Active Directory must replicate to each global catalog again, consuming significant network bandwidth.

In addition, if you install an application (such as Exchange) that tags attributes for replication in the global catalog, it will have the same impact on Active Directory. Plan your schema to minimize replication time for an Exchange installation.

Managing Recipient Policies

Recipient policies are designed to replace the function of site addressing in Exchange Server 5.5, with a little more flexibility. Site addressing in Exchange 5.5 applied proxy addressing rules to all users in a site, whereas recipient policies in Exchange 2003 give more flexibility on how you group the users to whom the addressing rules apply.

Types of Recipient Policies

Exchange 2003 features two kinds of recipient policies: one is for e-mail addresses and the other affects mailboxes. E-mail address policies generate e-mail addresses for your users, contacts, and groups, while mailbox policies restrict the age and size of messages stored in users' mailboxes. Both kinds of recipient policies can be created, modified, and prioritized through Exchange System Manager, and both can be applied to all users or only a select few.

- **E-Mail Address Recipient Policies**   For each e-mail address recipient policy you create, you can define the membership of the recipient policy and select the address types for policy members. E-mail addresses are used to define the valid formats for addressing inbound e-mail to the Exchange system. E-mail addresses identify recipients to the gateways and connectors that connect Exchange with other messaging systems, such as Lotus Notes and Novell GroupWise.

- **Mailbox Recipient Policies**   For each mailbox recipient policy you create, you can define the membership of the recipient policy and choose to move or delete messages from some or all folders in the mailboxes of all policy members. Exchange Mailbox Manager regularly scans and processes user mailboxes in order to enforce corporate e-mail retention policies and conserve disk space on the local Exchange server.

Adjusting Default Recipient Policy Settings

When Exchange 2003 is installed, a recipient policy is created with a default SMTP recipient address and a default X.400 recipient address. Depending on the size and complexity of your Exchange organization, you may want to modify the default recipient policy or create additional recipient policies. For example, a large company might want to create a recipient policy for each department, or a company with an international presence might want to create a recipient policy for each branch office.

E-mail address recipient policies create the appropriate e-mail addresses for users in your Exchange organization. You cannot modify the membership of the default recipient policy, but you can modify the address types on the default recipient policy. For each new recipient policy you create, you can define the membership of the recipient policy and select the address types for policy members.

In addition to the default policy, you can create multiple recipient policies and assign priorities to each one of the policies. The default policy has the lowest priority and is always processed first so that higher priority policies can override it as necessary. The policy with the highest priority is processed last.

Adding Recipient Policies

Depending on the purpose of the recipient policy, you can use either the E-mail Address (Policy) tab or the Mailbox Manager Settings (Policy) tab to configure a recipient policy. Use the E-mail Address (Policy) tab to configure e-mail addresses for Active Directory recipients. Use the Mailbox Manager Settings (Policy) tab to configure mailbox management settings for Active Directory recipients.

Query and Search Criteria

When you create a recipient policy, you must define the search criteria that determine the recipients to which the policy is applied. This search criteria is known as filter rules. You define the search criteria by using the Find Exchange Recipients Advanced tab to build an LDAP query.

This query filters Active Directory to identify only the set of recipients for which the search criteria is true. For example, assume that your company has the following needs:

- Your company has offices in Europe and the United States.

- All users are part of the default recipient policy. The default recipient policy defines the primary SMTP address as alias@nwtraders.msft.

- Users in Europe must have a secondary SMTP address of alias@contoso.msft defined for them.

To apply a secondary SMTP address to only users in Europe, you must create another recipient policy with a higher priority than the default policy. As part of this policy, you will configure a query that searches Active Directory for users whose office location is Europe, as shown in Figure 9-5. This causes the policy to be applied only to users based in Europe.

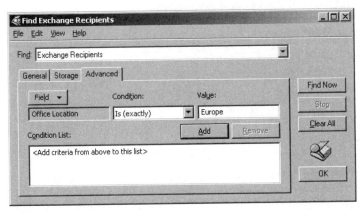

Figure 9-5   Recipient policy filter rules

E-Mail Address Settings

You use the E-Mail Addresses (Policy) tab to define primary and secondary e-mail addresses, which are used by external users to send messages to users in your Exchange organization. If you create multiple e-mail addresses of the same type in a recipient policy, the first one created is the primary e-mail address for that address type. The primary address appears in the From field of messages that users send outside of your Exchange organization. Each subsequent e-mail address defined in the policy is a secondary address for that address type.

The default address types are listed here:

- Custom Address

- X.400 Address

- Microsoft Mail Address

- SMTP Address

- cc:Mail Address

- Lotus Notes Address

- Novell GroupWise Address

By default, the SMTP address uses the alias of the recipient to define the left side of the SMTP address. You can override this default by using variables. For example, say that the default SMTP address for users is alias@domainname. To generate the SMTP address firstname.lastname@domainname, you can create a new recipient policy that specifies the SMTP address value as follows:

%g.%s@<*domainname*>

Use the variables in Table 9-4 to define e-mail address values in your recipient policy.

Table 9-4   Variables to Define E-Mail Addresses

Variable	Value
%g	Given name (first name)
%i	Middle initial
%s	Surname (last name)
%d	Display name
%m	Exchange alias
%xs	Uses first x letters of surname so that if x=2, the first two letters are used
%xg	Uses first x letters of given name so that if x=2, the first two letters are used

Although recipient policies can add additional e-mail addresses to user accounts, removing these addresses from the policy will not remove them from the user accounts. You must either remove them manually or by using a script.

Recipient Update Service is the service that builds and maintains address lists. You can force a recipient policy to be applied immediately by right-clicking the recipient policy that you want to be applied and then click Apply This Policy Now. Recipient Update Service is covered in detail in the next section of this chapter.

Mailbox Manager Settings

You use the Mailbox Manager Settings (Policy) tab to define the action that the Mailbox Manager will take when processing mailboxes and folders that contain messages that exceed policy limits. Mailbox Manager actions include generating reports on mailboxes containing messages that exceed policy limits, moving messages that exceed policy limits to the Deleted Items folder or the System Cleanup folder, and deleting messages exceeding policy limits immediately. You can use the settings on this tab to define whether Exchange will send e-mail messages to users after their mailboxes have been processed. You can also exclude specific message classes from deletion.

More Info   For additional information on configuring recipient policies in Exchange, view the Microsoft Knowledge Base article 249299, "How to Configure Recipient Policies in Exchange" (*http://support.microsoft.com/ default.aspx?scid=kb;en-us;249299*).

Recipient Update Service

Recipient Update Service is a service that builds and maintains address lists. It runs as a thread of the System Attendant service. Recipient Update Service polls Active Directory for updated recipient information on a predetermined schedule, which is once a minute by default. If there are new recipients, new address lists, or changes to the existing address lists, Recipient Update Service updates the address lists. This ensures that you always have accurate address list memberships that reflect all modifications you have made.

If you create a mailbox for a user, the Recipient Update Service is responsible for the automatic generation of the user's SMTP address and any other proxy addresses that you have defined for your recipients. However, in the Active Directory Users and Computers tool, the proxy addresses are not displayed immediately because a short latency period occurs before the Recipient Update Service produces the new e-mail addresses. This latency occurs even if you have configured the Recipient Update Service to run continuously.

Recipient Update Service also updates the e-mail addresses of recipients based on the settings of recipient policies. By default, two Recipient Update Service objects are created.

- **Recipient Update Service (Enterprise Configuration)**   This object updates the e-mail addresses of the objects that are in the configuration partition (or configuration naming context) of Active Directory, such as the Exchange store object, the message transfer agent (MTA) object, and the System Attendant object. There is only one instance of this Recipient Update Service in the organization.

- **Recipient Update Service (installation Active Directory domain)**   This object is created for each Active Directory domain that contains mailbox-enabled users. It updates e-mail addresses for recipient objects in Active Directory, and it updates address lists based on changes in recipient objects in that domain.

> **Tip**   Recipient policies that modify e-mail addresses are applied to all recipients based on the filter rules set on the policy. If there are any recipients that match the filter rules that you do not want the e-mail address changes applied to, you must clear the Automatically Update E-Mail Addresses Based On Recipient Policy check box on the E-mail Addresses tab of the recipient object before you apply the recipient policy.

Each instance of the domain Recipient Update Service associates one Exchange 2003 computer (where the Recipient Update Service runs) with one Windows 2000 or Windows Server 2003 domain controller (where the Active Directory objects are updated). Only one Recipient Update Service can be associated with any Active Directory domain controller.

Recipient Updates in Multiple Domain Environments

Each domain where mail-enabled objects will exist requires a Recipient Update Service, and some domains may require several instances of the Recipient Update Service. This may require you to create additional instances of the Recipient Update Service.

You can have multiple instances of the Recipient Update Service on an Exchange 2003 computer, but each domain controller in a domain can only participate in one Recipient Update Service. If you want multiple Recipient Update Service instances for a domain, that domain must have multiple domain controllers.

The Exchange 2003 computer and the Windows domain controller that are associated with a particular Recipient Update Service are displayed in the details pane of Exchange System Manager. Click the Recipient Update Services container in the console tree to display this information in table form.

When you are creating a Recipient Update Service, you cannot select the domain controller; you can only select the domain that you want the new Recipient

Update Service to be associated with. After you have finished creating the Recipient Update Service, you can edit the properties of the Recipient Update Service and select the domain controller that you want.

Manually Updating the Recipient Update Service

You can manually update an address list instead of waiting for scheduled updates to occur. The manual updating process incorporates the changes that you have made to address list memberships since the last scheduled update. You can force an address list to be updated by running Recipient Update Service.

To run Recipient Update Service, you can perform an update operation or a rebuild operation as follows:

- **Update operation** If you perform an update operation, proxy e-mail addresses are generated immediately for all new users. This operation forces address book membership to be recalculated for recently altered Exchange recipients. Perform an update operation if you are running the Recipient Update Service on a schedule and you want to complete mailbox creation before the next scheduled update runs.

- **Rebuild operation** If you perform a rebuild operation, all proxy e-mail addresses are recalculated and all address list memberships are verified. Perform a rebuild operation if you make a change to organizational policy on SMTP addressing, such as changing from a .com to a .net location or if you change the DNS domain name. A rebuild operation may take several hours; we recommend that you perform this operation only during hours when the network is not busy.

More Info For additional information on working with Recipient Update Service, view the Microsoft Knowledge Base article 823153, "How to Work with the Recipient Update Service in Exchange Server 2003" (*http://support.microsoft.com/default.aspx?scid=kb;en-us;823153*), and article 253828, "How the Recipient Update Service Populates Address Lists" (*http://support.microsoft.com/default.aspx?scid=kb;en-us;253828*).

Managing Server-based Address Lists

People who use Exchange as their e-mail server typically search for other e-mail users in their company by using the GAL. This includes all the e-mail messaging recipients, including contacts with external addresses and mail-enabled groups, in the Exchange organization. The GAL is retrieved from the global catalog servers in Active Directory and used by Exchange clients to address e-mail messages or find information about recipients in the organization. When you first install Exchange, a default GAL is created automatically. The GAL is the default address list that users will use in their address book.

Starting with Exchange 2000, Exchange Server 5.5 address book views were replaced with address lists. An Exchange 5.5 address book view was a virtual container created based on field groupings. For example, to create a virtual container of all users in the Sales Team, the Exchange 5.5 administrator creates a view grouped by the field Department. In Exchange 2003, an address list is a collection of recipient objects that are returned by using an LDAP query and are based on attributes in Active Directory. Each address list can contain one or more types of recipient objects; for example, users, contacts, groups, or public folders. Exchange 2003 address lists also provide administrators with a mechanism to divide mail-enabled objects in Active Directory so that users of MAPI clients, such as Outlook, can more quickly locate the recipients to whom they want to send e-mail. Address lists are dynamic, which means that as new recipient objects are added or changed, membership of the address lists change automatically.

Exchange 2003 supports four types of address lists: default, global, offline, and custom address lists.

You can create a container that has a build rule for the address lists associated with it through the Exchange System Manager console. These rules use the LDAP search filter syntax, as defined in RFC 2254, and they are extremely flexible. For example, if you want to create an address list of all permanent employees in the Toronto Marketing department, you could create a single container named Marketing with a rule of:

```
(&(mail=*) (&(department=Marketing)(l=Toronto)(!(Extension-Attribute-3=Contractor))))
```

Default Address Lists

A default address list is an address list that is automatically created based on the values of specific attributes of Active Directory objects. Default address lists are available to Exchange users without any administrator action. Exchange 2003 includes the following five default address lists that you can use in their default state:

- Default Global Address List
- All Contacts
- All Groups
- All Users
- Public Folders

Use the default address lists if the users in your organization do not need any address list customization, such as having the lists grouped by office location or by job titles.

Address List Contents

The default address lists, configured in Exchange 2003, appear in Table 9-5.

Table 9-5   Default Exchange 2003 Address Lists

Address list name	Syntax based on RFC 2245
Default Global Address List	(& (mailnickname=*) (	(&(objectCategory=person)(objectClass=user) (!(homeMDB=*))(!(msExchHomeServerName=*))) (&(objectCategory=person)(objectClass=user)(	(homeMDB=*) (msExchHomeServerName=*))) (&(objectCategory=person)(objectClass=contact)) (objectCategory=group)(objectCategory=publicFolder) (objectCategory=msExchDynamicDistributionList)))
All Contacts	(& (mailnickname=*) (	(&(objectCategory=person)(objectClass=contact))))
All Groups	(& (mailnickname=*) (	(objectCategory=group)))
All Users	(& (mailnickname=*) (	(&(objectCategory=person)(objectClass=user) (!(homeMDB=*))(!(msExchHomeServerName=*))) (&(objectCategory=person)(objectClass=user)(	(homeMDB=*) (msExchHomeServerName=*)))))
Public Folders	(& (mailnickname=*) (	(objectCategory=publicFolder)))

Offline Address Lists

An offline address list is a collection of address lists that are available to Exchange users when they are working offline. Exchange administrators can choose which address lists are available for their users who work offline by associating the offline address list with a mailbox store. Exchange users copy the contents of a server-based address list into a set of offline address book files (files with an .oab extension) on the local client's hard disk. Users can search the content of the offline address lists, compose e-mail messages, and address the messages without being connected to the server. The next time the user is online, these messages are sent automatically.

When you first install Exchange, a default offline address list is created based on the default GAL. You can create additional offline address lists and associate them with the users' mailbox store to enable your users on that store to download smaller address lists to use when they are offline—this saves users' time when they are offline and looking for other people in their address book. For example, suppose that you work for a large company with many locations and that your GAL is very large. The users in the European Sales division tell you that when they travel, they communicate only with other users in the Europe division. You can create an offline address list that only has recipients from your Europe division in it to reduce the size of the offline address book that these users must download and search. Typically, the default GAL is used as the source for generating additional offline address lists because it is the most comprehensive address list.

Office Outlook 2003 Cached Mode

As companies adopt Outlook 2003 cached mode for their users, the offline address books become increasingly important. When Outlook 2003 users open the GAL or use name resolution, the offline address book is used instead of making requests to a global catalog server. The offline address book itself consists of a set of .oab files that are attached to a message object and stored in a special public folder, commonly known as a system folder. The size of these files will vary depending on how many mail-enabled users you have in Active Directory and how many attributes are present on each object.

The offline address book is typically generated once a day. OABGen, which is part of the Exchange System Attendant process (mad.exe), runs on one nominated Exchange server. The process first looks at the previous day's offline address book, and creates a new message object with an attached changes.oab file. This includes all the changes that were made in the past 24 hours, and is the mechanism that Outlook uses to download incremental updates. Next, OABGen will refresh the main .oab files which is a complete copy of the offline address book.

The offline address book system folder (named OAB Version 3a in Exchange 2003) has a default aging limit of 30 days. The Exchange server retains 30 days' worth of changed objects before it starts automatically removing old generations. Outlook users can download incremental offline address book updates at up to 30-day intervals. If a user downloads the offline address book and then waits 35 days, it won't be possible to download an incremental update. Outlook will automatically download the full offline address book again.

Custom Address Lists

A custom address list is an address list that you create to meet the specific needs of your Exchange organization—typically, to make it easier for people to find other e-mail users in their address books. For example, you might create a custom address list for users in the Marketing department because they want to be able to more quickly find other users in their department. You can create and nest multiple address lists, and the address lists that you create can be based on recipient categories or fields, which can be used as filters to search Active Directory.

Filter Rules

You can use address lists to group your users according to a number of different criteria to benefit your organization by making it easier to find mail recipients in Outlook. To add an address list, you must define a filter rule.

Filter rules aid in creating the LDAP query that enables you to define the type of Exchange 2003 objects that are displayed in a particular address list.

You can define the search filters for address list membership by performing one of the following tasks:

- Define filters using the Exchange recipients search category, such as users with Exchange mailbox or contacts with external e-mail addresses.

- Define filters based on mailbox storage, including mailboxes on a specific Exchange server, any Exchange server, or a particular mailbox store.

- Define filters using the user, contact, group, or public folder attributes, and then define whether the attribute must meet a specific condition and value using:

  - Starts With

  - Ends With

  - Is (Exactly)

  - Is Not

  - Present

  - Not Present

> **Tip** You can add further conditions, but remember that the logic is "AND." Therefore, all conditions must be true for a match to be displayed.

- Define filters using the custom search category beyond the standard Exchange recipient object types. Custom searches also enable you to directly enter an LDAP query. By entering an LDAP query you can create a filter rule that uses the "OR" operator as a condition. This is especially useful if you want to create a complex query.

  For example, you are the Exchange administrator for Contoso, Ltd., and you want to create an address list that contains members from the Finance or the Marketing departments of your company. You would enter the following LDAP query:

  ```
  (&(&(objectCategory=user)(|(department=Marketing)(department=Finance))))
  ```

  In this example, the objectCategory field contains the type of object to query. The objectCategory is set to user, which means that this query will search through all the user account objects. The OR operator (|) indicates that the department field may contain the value of Marketing or Finance. Figure 9-6 shows the Advanced tab in the custom search dialog box used to create this query.

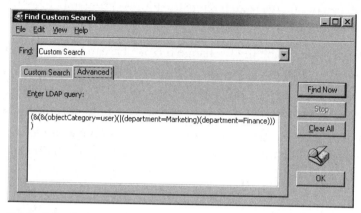

Figure 9-6   Custom search

Creating Nested Lists Under All Address Lists

An address list is a folder that contains a dynamic listing of the Exchange 2003-enabled objects in an organization. You can nest address lists; for example, you can organize the top-level lists by country, the next level by city, and the bottom level by office. When you plan address lists, you must think about the best way to group the Exchange 2003-enabled objects in your organization to make it easier for people to find the person or the distribution list to which they want to send an e-mail message.

You can create nested address lists that are located under a custom address list. However, in the subordinate address lists you must specify the conditions that you used to create the parent list and add any extra conditions to distinguish the child list from the parent list. Nested address lists do not inherit their rules from the parent address list.

To create empty address lists, do not define any filter rules. Empty address lists are useful for organizing nested address lists because the empty parent address list does not have any members. The default "All Address Lists" list is an example of an empty list.

Updating Address List Information

The Recipient Update Service populates the defined address lists by entering the list name and location to the showInAddressBook attribute on the user objects in the directory. Each mail-enabled object has this attribute, including users, contacts, groups, public folders and any other object in Active Directory that supports the showInAddressBook attribute and has a mailNickname attribute.

Every time that a user, a group, or any object is added or modified in Active Directory, the Recipient Update Service picks up that object, determines which of the available address lists it belongs to, and adds that address list to the showInAddress-Book attribute of the object.

One exception for this is if the mailbox is hidden. In that case, the msExchHide-FromAddressLists attribute is set to TRUE, so the Recipient Update Service will not stamp any address lists, and will remove any that are already present on the attribute.

The showInAddressBook attribute has two purposes. The first is to let users see the entry listed in the address list by means of MAPI clients, such as Outlook. The second purpose is to allow users to resolve a name on a MAPI client.

You can use ADSI Editor (ADSI Edit) to view these values. ADSI Edit is part of the Windows Support Tools. You installed the Windows Support Tools by running Setup in the \Support\Tools directory on the Windows Server installation CD.

Figure 9-7 shows an example of a user, Aaron Con, who is a member of the manufacturing department at Northwind Traders. Using ADSI Edit, you can display the user object's properties in the domain naming context. The showInAddressBook attribute lists the distinguished names of the Exchange address lists that Aaron's user account is a member of.

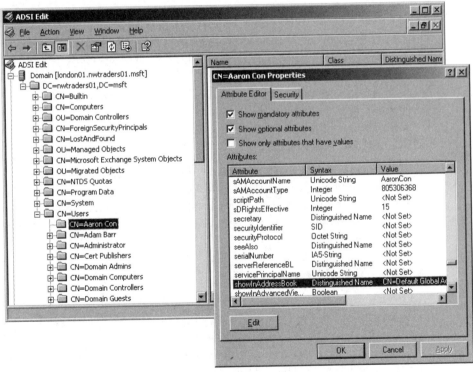

Figure 9-7 showInAddressBook attribute on the properties of a user object

For example, if Aaron's user account belonged to just the default address lists in Exchange and was not hidden from the Exchange address lists, the showInAddress-Book attribute would display the distinguished names as follows:

```
CN=All Users,CN=All Address Lists,CN=Address Lists Container,
    CN=Northwind Traders01,CN=Microsoft Exchange,CN=Services,
    CN=Configuration,DC=nwtraders01,DC=msft
CN=Default Global Address List,CN=All Global Address Lists,
    CN=Address Lists Container,CN=Northwind Traders01,
    CN=Microsoft Exchange,CN=Services,CN=Configuration,
    DC=nwtraders01,DC=msft
```

If Northwind Traders created an address list named Manufacturing, then the showInAddressBook attribute for Aaron's user account would display the distinguished names as follows:

```
CN=All Users,CN=All Address Lists,CN=Address Lists Container,
    CN=Northwind Traders01,CN=Microsoft Exchange,CN=Services,
    CN=Configuration,DC=nwtraders01,DC=msft
CN=Default Global Address List,CN=All Global Address Lists,
    CN=Address Lists Container,CN=Northwind Traders01,
    CN=Microsoft Exchange,CN=Services,
    CN=Configuration,DC=nwtraders01,DC=msft

CN=Manufacturing,CN=All Address Lists,CN=Address Lists Container,
    CN=Northwind Traders01,CN=Microsoft Exchange,CN=Services,
    CN=Configuration,DC=nwtraders01,DC=msft
```

If Aaron's user account was hidden from Exchange address lists, the showInAddressBook attribute would display <Not Set>.

Address and Detail Templates

Address and detail templates control the way information is displayed when an Exchange client, such as Outlook, addresses an e-mail message or displays the properties of a recipient object. Both templates have property pages that enable you to customize the template for two types of users: Outlook users and MS-DOS users using the Exchange Client.

Address Templates

Address templates control the appearance of the dialog boxes that appear when a user addresses a message to a recipient that is not in the global address list.

Templates make the address type available to Outlook users when they are creating one-off addresses, either directly in e-mail messages or for storage in their personal address books. The default address types are: X.400 Address, Microsoft Mail Address, Internet Address, MacMail Address, cc:Mail Address, and Other Address. They enable users to create addresses without knowing the details of address-type syntax.

The address entry template object works with a corresponding address syntax program, the proxy generation dynamic-link library (DLL) that generates proxy addresses for the address type. This program converts the data entered in the dialog box by the client into an actual proxy address string.

Customizing Address Templates

Every gateway has an associated address type that corresponds to the address format of the foreign system that the gateway serves, such as Lotus Notes or Novell Group-Wise. This address type is represented by an addrType object. If the address type for your gateway does not already exist in Active Directory, you must install the addrType object and any associated information when you install the gateway itself.

If you provide a new addrType object with your gateway, you should also provide a new address entry template object. This template displays a dialog box into which the user enters information to create an address of the type supported by the gateway.

To create an address entry template object, you first create a text file that describes the data entry fields of the address entry dialog box your template will display. Then you use the TEMPLATE.EXE utility provided by the Exchange Software Development Kit (SDK) to convert the text file into a binary file. The Exchange Server address book provider uses this binary file to create the address entry dialog box.

The text file has nine fields for each dialog box control, separated by commas. Table 9-6 describes these fields.

Table 9-6 Address Entry Template Object Fields

Field	Type	Description
1	Integer	X position of control.
2	Integer	X length of control.
3	Integer	Y position of control.
4	Integer	Y height of control.
5	Integer	Type of control. The following entries are valid: **DTCT_BUTTON** Creates a command button; **DTCT_CHECKBOX** Creates a check box; **DTCT_EDIT** Creates an edit field for user input; **DTCT_GROUPBOX** Creates a group box; **DTCT_LABEL** Creates a text label; **DTCT_LBX** Creates a list box; **DTCT_MVLISTBOX** Creates a multi-valued list box; **DTCT_PAGE** Introduces a new page in the property sheet.

Table 9-6   Address Entry Template Object Fields (Continued)

Field	Type	Description
6	Integer	Control flags. These are used only for DTCT_EDIT entries. Valid entries can be a combination of the following: ■ **0x00000001** Creates a multi-line edit control; ■ **0x00000002** Allows the edit control to be edited; ■ **0x00000004** Requires edit from the user upon OK; ■ **0x00000010** Displays an asterisk (*) when the user types a character in the edit control, for example for a password. To combine these flags, bitwise OR them, and enter the result in this field.
7	Integer	Property tag that controls are mapped to. This value will be used by the address generation code to access field information entered by the user. The following entries are valid: ■ 0x3001001E – PR_DISPLAY_NAME (display name of contact). ■ 0x6800001E – 0xFFFE001E – Custom string properties. Note that the low-order bits for the custom string property are always 001E, which indicates that the property is a string.
8	Integer	For DTCT_EDIT fields, the maximum length of input.
9	Text	Label text for control. This can be text or an asterisk.

The following example shows the content of a text file that creates a new property sheet that has a text label named Display Name, with an edit box that enabled input for up to 256 characters.

```
0, 0, 0, 0, DTCT_PAGE,0x00000000, 0x00000000, 0,New Address
12, 50, 20, 8, DTCT_LABEL,0x00000000, 0x00000000, 0,Display Name:
75, 141, 18, 12, DTCT_EDIT,0x00000006, 0x3001001E, 256,*
```

Once you have created the text file, you must save it in Unicode format. You then use the TEMPLATE.EXE utility to produces a binary file that is used as an attribute for the Address-Template object. Lastly, you use the ADDRTEMP sample application from the Exchange SDK to install the templates associated with an address type.

More Info   For more information on customizing address templates, view the Microsoft Exchange Server 2003 SDK documentation on the Microsoft Developer Network (MSDN) website (*http://msdn.microsoft.com*).

Details Templates

Details templates control the appearance of the dialog boxes that appear when a user views the recipient properties in an address list. Exchange users use these dialog boxes when they view the properties of a recipient object using Outlook. You can change the appearance of address lists by modifying details templates using Exchange System Manager.

Extension Attributes vs. Custom Attributes

When you install Exchange 2003, the Active Directory schema is extended with many new attributes, including 15 additional extension attributes that you can use to add information about your users that does not easily fit into the existing fields. The fields are accessible through Custom Attributes on the Exchange Advanced tab of a recipient's properties. The custom attribute field can be used to display information such as the employee identification (ID) number or cost center in the GAL.

You can also use custom attributes values to create custom searches, and then use these to organize recipient objects.

When planning for utilizing custom attributes, you must consider the following limitations:

- You cannot enter multiple-value strings in custom attributes. You can only enter a single string of text.

- You cannot enter a custom attribute value with more than 1024 characters. Custom attributes have a maximum length of 1024 characters; any additional characters beyond that limit are not saved.

- You cannot change the display names for the extensionAttribute*x* attribute in the user account properties, nor can you change the Custom Attribute *x* entry in the field list in the Find Users, Contacts, And Groups dialog box.

Adding Custom Attributes to Details Templates

Let's say you use extensionAttribute1 to record an employee's cost center and that you wanted to add the cost center to the details template below the existing phone entry. You can follow these steps to add Cost Center to the details templates:

1. Start Exchange System Manager.

2. Expand the Recipients container.

3. Expand the Details Templates container, and then click the language that you want.

4. In the details pane, right-click User, and then click Properties.

5. Click the Templates tab to load the schema.

6. After the schema loads, the current details template properties appear.

7. To add another field:

   a. Click Add, click Label under Choose A Control Type, and then click OK.

   b. In the Label Control dialog box, type the coordinates, the width and the height, and the name of the field in the Text box, using the following information, and then click OK.

Item	Value
X:	189
Y:	140
W:	70
H:	8
Text:	Cost &Center

   c. In the Value column, click Cost &Center, and then click Move Down.

   d. Click Add, click Edit, and then click OK.

   e. In the Edit Control dialog box, type the coordinates, and then type the width and the height of the field using the following information.

Item	Value
X:	259
Y:	140
W:	100
H:	12

   f. In the Field list, click ms-Exch-Extension-Attribute-1, and then click OK.

   g. In the Value column, click ms-Exch-Extension-Attribute-1, and then click Move Down.

8. Click Test to preview the modified template (Figure 9-8).

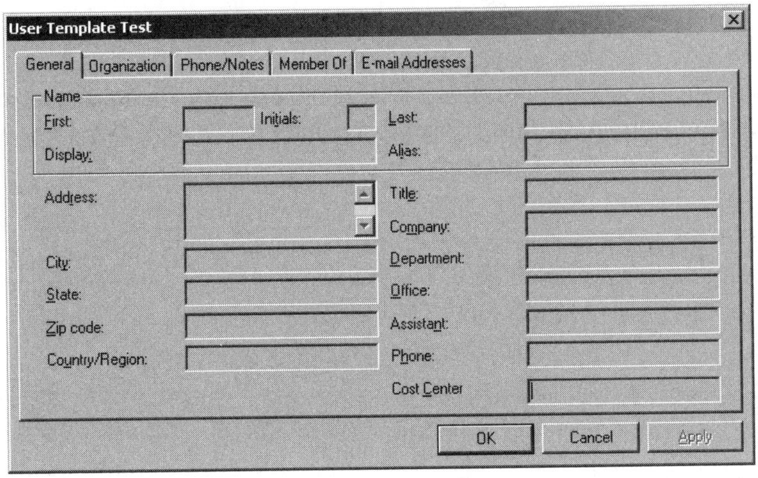

Figure 9-8   Preview of modified details template

> **More Info**   For more information about modifying details templates in Exchange 2003, view the Microsoft Knowledge Base article 313962, "How to modify Exchange 2000 or Exchange 2003 details templates" (*http://support.microsoft.com/default.aspx?scid=kb;en-us;313962*).

Customizing Display Names in Address Lists

You can customize display names to meet the specific needs of your organization. For example, if you have a large Exchange organization, you may want the names in the address list sorted by last name (surname). Exchange displays address lists based on the Full Name field in Active Directory. By default, the Full Name field contains recipient names in this order: First Initial Last (First I. Last). Although you can change the Full Name field on a recipient object, you can also change the default on the Exchange 2003 server.

You can change the way the Full Name field is generated by modifying the display specifier for a user or contact. The high-level steps for customizing display names by using the ADSI Edit MMC snap-in are as follows:

1. Browse to the following location in the ADSI Edit snap-in:

```
Configuration Container,CN=Configuration,CN=DisplaySpecifiers,CN=409
```

More Info   409 is the name of the local container for US-English. For more information about locales, see the Table of Language Identifiers page of the Microsoft website at *http://msdn.microsoft.com/library/default.asp?url=/library/en-us/intl/nls_238z.asp*.

2. Modify the createDialog property of the user-Display or contact-Display object to specify how the Full Name field is generated. For example, if you want the Full Name to be Last, First, type the following entry for the value of the create-Dialog property:

```
%<sn>, %<givenName>
```

Tip   The text added in the createDialog property is case sensitive.

In this example, sn stands for Surname, which is the LDAP field name for Last Name, and givenName (case sensitive) stands for Given Name, which is the LDAP field name for First Name.

Managing Recipient Objects

Administrators perform many tasks relative to recipient objects. Some tasks, such as assigning mailbox rights, may be performed only occasionally, and there may be no requirement to automate the task. Other tasks, such as the creation of recipient objects, may be ongoing and are good candidates for automation.

Assigning Mailbox Rights

In Exchange 2003, by default, only the mailbox owner has permission to access his or her mailbox. There are two methods in Exchange 2003 that you can use to configure a mailbox so that users other than the mailbox owner can use that mailbox to send messages.

- You can permit one or more users to send messages on behalf of a particular mailbox owner by granting "Send on Behalf" permissions.

- You can also permit one or more users to send messages as a particular mailbox owner by granting "Send As" permissions.

Granting "Send on Behalf" Permissions

If you grant a user "Send on Behalf" permissions for another user's mailbox, that user can send mail on behalf of the mailbox owner. The name in the From box of these messages appears as

From: DelegateUser on behalf of MailboxOwner

DelegateUser is the name of the user to whom you granted "Send on Behalf" permissions and *MailboxOwner* is the name of the user who owns the mailbox.

For example, if you want to grant UserB "Send on Behalf" permissions for UserA's mailbox so UserB can send messages on behalf of UserA, follow this procedure:

1. Start Active Directory Users And Computers.

2. In the console tree, click Users.

3. In the details pane, right-click the mailbox of UserA, and then click Properties.

4. Click the Exchange General tab, and then click Delivery Options.

5. Under Send On Behalf, click Add.

6. Type **UserB**, click Check Names to verify the name, and then click OK.

7. Click OK twice.

8. Close Active Directory Users And Computers.

When UserB sends a message on behalf of UserA, the From box in these messages appears as:

From: UserB on behalf of UserA

Granting "Send As" Permissions

You can grant a user "Send As" permissions for another user's mailbox, the *DelegateUser* can send mail as the *MailboxOwner*. The From box in these messages appears as follows:

From: MailboxOwner

For example, if you want to grant UserB "Send As" permissions for UserA's mailbox so UserB can send messages as UserA, follow this procedure:

1. Start Active Directory Users And Computers.

2. On the View menu, click to select Advanced Features.

3. In the console tree, click Users.

4. In the details pane, right-click the mailbox of UserA, and then click Properties.

5. Click the Security tab.

6. Click Add, and then type **UserB**.

7. Click Check Names to verify the name, and then click OK.

8. Verify that UserB is selected, and then click to select the Allow check box next to Send As and Receive As in the Permissions list.

9. Close Active Directory Users And Computers.

If you grant UserB "Send As" permissions for UserA's mailbox, UserB can send messages that appear to be sent from UserA. The From box in these messages appears as follows:

From: UserA

Occasionally, granting "Send On Behalf" or "Send As" permissions may not be sufficient for delegating e-mail administration. For example, you might have a customer satisfaction mailbox that several people in your organization must access. Consider granting these people mailbox owner permissions.

Export and Import Features

To make changes to individual recipient objects, you use Active Directory Users And Computers. However, there are times when you may need to make bulk changes to the directory. For example, if your company acquires another company, you will need to import the directory information of the acquired company into your existing directory. In this scenario, you can export the directory information of the acquired company into a bulk export file. You can then use this file to import the directory information into Active Directory.

LDIFDE and CSVDE Utilities

Exchange 2003 uses LDAP to access Active Directory. You can use the following two utilities to import data to or export data from Active Directory:

- LDAP Data Interchange Format Directory Exchange (Ldifde) uses an LDAP Data Interchange Format (LDIF) file as input to create, modify, and delete directory objects.

  You can also use Ldifde to extend the schema, export Active Directory user and group information to other applications or services, and populate Active Directory with data from other directory services.

- Comma Separated Value Directory Exchange (CSVDE) uses a Comma Separated Value (CSV) file as input to import and export data from Active Directory.

You can use these utilities to add users, contacts, and groups to Active Directory. You can also use Ldifde to create mailboxes for users or establish e-mail addresses for users, contacts, and groups.

Performing Bulk Operations Using Ldifde and CSVDE

To make changes to Active Directory by using Ldifde or CSVDE, you must prepare an input file that contains the information about the modifications to be made.

LDIF File Format

The LDIF file consists of a series of records separated by a blank line. A record consists of the attributes and values that are necessary for adding, deleting, or modifying an object in Active Directory. Attribute names in an LDIF file are not case sensitive.

For example, you want to create a mailbox-enabled user object named Suzan Fine in the Marketing organizational unit of the Nwtraders' domain. The LDIF file would look like this:

```
DN: CN=Suzan Fine,CN=Marketing,DC=nwTraders,DC=msft
changeType: add
objectClass: user
sAMAccountName: suzanf
mailNickname: suzanf
homeMDB: CN=Mailbox Store (LONDON),CN=First Storage Group,
CN=InformationStore,CN=LONDON,CN=Servers,
CN=First Administrative Group,CN=Administrative Groups,
CN=Northwind Traders,CN=Microsoft Exchange,CN=Services,
CN=Configuration,DC=nwtraders,DC=msft
UserAccountControl: 512
```

To use Ldifde, at the command prompt, type **ldifde** followed by one or more parameters. For example, if the LDIF file is named Ldif.txt, then at the command prompt, type:

ldifde –I –f ldif.txt –v

This will import the file ldif.txt in verbose mode, which displays detailed information at the command prompt during import. The default import mode does not display any detailed information at the command prompt during import.

CSV File Format

The CSV file consists of one or more lines of data, with each value separated by a comma. The first line in the CSV file is the header, which contains the names of each attribute. Any lines that follow the header must list the values for each attribute in the same order as the header line.

The following is an example of the content of a CSV file that can be used to create three user objects:

```
DN,objectClass,samAccountName,userPrincipalName,displayName,1,
department,title,description,telephoneNumber,company,
userAccountControl,Manager,Name,givenName,sn,
```

```
physicalDeliveryOfficeName,mail
"CN=Michelle Alexander,OU=Users,OU=Managed Objects,
DC=nwtraders,DC=msft",user,MichelleAlexa,MichelleAlexa@nwtraders.msft,
Michelle Alexander,London,Legal,Administrative Assistant,
Administrative Assistant,555-0013,Northwind Traders,514,
"CN=Amy Alberts,OU=Users,OU=Managed Objects,DC=nwtraders,DC=msft",
Michelle Alexander,Michelle,Alexander,Building 2,
MichelleAlexa@nwtraders.msft
"CN=Gregory Alderson,OU=Users,OU=Managed Objects,
DC=nwtraders,DC=msft",user,GregoryAlder,GregoryAlder@nwtraders.msft,
Gregory Alderson,London,Legal,Lawyer,Lawyer,555-0011,
Northwind Traders,514,"CN=Amy Alberts,OU=Users,
OU=Managed Objects,DC=nwtraders,DC=msft",Gregory Alderson,
Gregory,Alderson,Building 2,GregoryAlder@nwtraders.msft
"CN=Karen Archer,OU=Users,OU=Managed Objects,
DC=nwtraders,DC=msft",user,KarenArche,KarenArche@nwtraders.msft,
Karen Archer,London,Legal,Lawyer,Lawyer,555-0018,Northwind Traders,
514,"CN=Amy Alberts,OU=Users,OU=Managed Objects,DC=nwtraders,DC=msft",
Karen Archer,Karen,Archer,Building 2,KarenArche@nwtraders.msft
```

You can only use the CSVDE utility to add objects to Active Directory. You cannot use CSVDE to modify or delete objects. As a result, there is no changeType attribute in a CSV file used by CSVDE. All other attributes are identical to those in the Ldifde format. As with an LDIF file, attribute names in the CSV file are not case sensitive.

To use CSVDE, at the command prompt, type **csvde** followed by one or more parameters. For example, if the CSV file is named Import.csv, then at the command prompt, type:

csvde -i -f import.csv -k -j c:\logs

This command will import the file Import.csv, ignore errors during import, and log output to c:\logs\csv.log, where csv.log is the file automatically created by CSVDE.

CSVDE Export Examples

Although there are many ways of exporting information from Active Directory, one of the easiest is to use the CSVDE tool.

Table 9-7 provides examples on exporting mail-enabled user and group objects.

Table 9-7   CSVDE Export Examples

Object type	CSVDE command
Users	csvde -f c:\users.txt -r "(&(objectCategory=user)(proxyAddresses=*))"
Groups	csvde -f c:\dls.txt -r "(&(objectCategory=group)(proxyAddresses=*))"

These command examples will export all mail-enabled user and group objects. To specify which attributes to export, you can use the list option:

```
-l list - List of attributes (comma separated) to look for in an LDAP search
```

To control the scope of the LDAP search, use the SearchScope option:

```
-p SearchScope - Search Scope (Base/OneLevel/Subtree)
```

Automating Mailbox Administration

You can enhance the efficiency of mailbox administration by using scripts and available programming technologies. Being able to automate administration is particularly important if you are managing mailboxes for hundreds or thousands of users in your Exchange organization.

You can use a variety of programming technologies to access Exchange configuration settings and data. These technologies and their purposes are listed in Table 9-8.

Table 9-8   Programming Technologies to Access Exchange Data

Programming technology	Purpose
Microsoft ActiveX Data Objects (ADO)	Technology used to access data residing in an Exchange store.
Active Directory Service Interfaces (ADSI)	Method used to access information stored in Active Directory.
Collaboration Data Objects (CDO)	Server-side collaborative component that is the primary way that applications access and control Exchange information such as mailboxes and recipients.
Exchange OLE DB (ExOLEDB) provider	Method for programmers to access items in the Exchange store.
LDAP	Protocol that supports accessing the data stored in Active Directory.
Store events	Technology that enables collaboration and workflow applications to receive automatic notification when events occur in the Exchange store. You can register code that will be run when the triggering event occurs.
Web Distributed Authoring and Versioning (WebDAV)	Protocol that remote client applications can use to access items and property information in the Exchange store.
Windows Management Instrumentation (WMI)	The Microsoft implementation of Web-Based Enterprise Management (WBEM), an interface for accessing system management information, often by using a Web browser. WMI can be used with any programming language that is compatible with Component Object Model (COM).

These programming technologies make it possible to access Exchange store and Active Directory data. You can use Microsoft Visual Basic Scripting Edition (VBScript) to create scripts that automatically create and configure mailboxes.

> **More Info**   For additional information on extending Exchange functionality using programming technologies and scripts, view the Microsoft Exchange Server 2003 SDK documentation on the Microsoft Developer Network (MSDN) website at *http://msdn.microsoft.com*.

Summary of Tools for Managing Directory Information

Table 9-9 provides a quick overview of tools that you can use to manage directory information and a brief description of their use. Although no list of tools is ever all-inclusive, these are the most common tools that are used to manage directory information in an Exchange environment.

Table 9-9   Tools for Managing Directory Information

Tool	Description
Active Directory Users and Computers	Used to create new recipient objects, mail-enable or mailbox-enable existing recipient objects, assign mailbox permissions and ownership.
Exchange System Manager	Used to create and manage address lists and public folders.
Active Directory Sites and Services	Used to manage Active Directory replication.
ADSI Edit	Used to view and edit attribute values of objects in the configuration, schema, or domain naming context of Active Directory.
Active Directory Schema Manager	Used to view and edit replication properties of attributes in the Active Directory schema naming context. Used to activate or deactivate classes in the Active Directory schema naming context.
LDAP Data Interchange Format Directory Exchange (Ldifde)	Used to create, modify, and delete recipient objects in Active Directory, extend the Active Directory schema, and export Active Directory recipient information. Also used to mailbox-enable or mail-enable recipients.
Comma Separated Value Directory Exchange (CSVDE)	Used to import and export data from Active Directory.

Best Practices

■ Always use mail-enabled universal groups, particularly in multiple domain environments. Use of mail-enabled domain local and of global groups, even of nested groups, does not work in a multi-domain environment because their membership is not replicated to all global catalog servers.

■ Use security groups as the primary group type, but only mail-enable the groups when appropriate.

■ Use distribution groups for lists that include non-trusted recipients.

■ When deciding on the number of global catalog servers needed to support an Exchange deployment, consider the number of clients supported by each global catalog server. As a general rule, you should have one global catalog server processor per four Exchange server processors. For scalability and resilience, place at least two global catalog servers per Windows Server site. If a Windows Server site spans multiple domains, configure a global catalog server for each domain where Exchange servers and clients are situated.

■ When creating custom address lists, target address list search variables against fields where the variations in value are not large. For example, address lists that organize people by their office numbers may not be effective for large offices. However, address lists that organize people by location or department are more effective because people often send messages to people in their own departments.

■ Changes to the way display names are generated only apply to new recipient objects. Existing recipients are not modified and would require scripting to automate updating existing recipient objects. If you plan to change how display names are generated, you should perform the change early in your Active Directory deployment.

■ Make changes or additions to the schema only after careful consideration and planning. After you make additions, you can only disable them, you cannot delete them. Additional attributes may increase the time required for their replication.

Chapter 10

Configuring Exchange Store Resources

About This Chapter

This chapter discusses the architecture of Microsoft Exchange Server 2003 storage and the administrative requirements for effectively managing that storage. It explains the types of technologies involved in Exchange Server storage and how storage is configured on an Exchange Server, including requirements for creating multiple storage groups and stores on a server. It further explains how to manage mailbox and public folder resources.

Understanding Exchange Server 2003 Database Technologies

To effectively manage data storage in Exchange 2003, you must understand the technology that Exchange data storage is based on and where Exchange stores data. Understanding the database technologies that Exchange 2003 uses can help you to better understand how to tune your Exchange servers' performance. It is also useful in understanding and designing a backup and restore strategy for Exchange.

Extensible Storage Engine

Extensible Storage Engine (ESE) is the technology behind both the Microsoft Active Directory directory service and Exchange 2003 data storage. ESE is the database engine used by the Exchange Information Store. ESE provides an interface to the underlying database structures in Exchange. The main function of ESE in Exchange is to manage changes that are made to the Exchange database. ESE makes database changes as a series of operations that culminate in a transaction. An operation is the smallest change, such as inserting or deleting data, that can be made to the database. A transaction is the result of several operations made with the same goal, such as updating a user's mailbox. All operations that are part of a transaction must complete successfully. If an operation fails, the transaction fails, and all operations in the transaction are rolled back. When all of the operations are completed, and the change has been made in the database, the transaction is referred to as committed.

For example, moving a message from your Inbox to your Deleted Items folder is a transaction composed of a series of operations. For the transaction to be committed, the following operations must complete successfully: the message must be deleted from the Inbox folder and added to the Deleted Items folder, and the properties of both folders must be updated. If the transaction was committed without each of these operations completing successfully, this can result in inconsistencies such as having two copies of the message or having the item count for the folder not match the actual folder contents.

ESE provides stability and fault tolerance to Exchange data storage by ensuring that transactions change the database from one reliable state to another reliable state. ESE ensures that changes to the database take effect only after transactions are committed. ESE will either complete all transactions, leaving the system in a stable state, or, if it cannot complete all transactions, it will roll back whatever transactions are in progress and return the system to its previous stable state.

Exchange Stores and Storage Groups

Exchange 2003 supports multiple Exchange stores on each Exchange server. Exchange servers store data in logical databases called *stores*. Exchange Server 2003 Enterprise Edition provides database support for databases of up to 16 terabytes. Exchange Server 2003 Standard Edition databases are limited to 16 gigabyte (GB).

Exchange Stores

There are two types of Exchange stores: mailbox stores and public folder stores. Mailbox stores store data that is private to an individual and contain mailbox folders generated when a new mailbox is created. Public folder stores maintain data in public folders that can be shared.

Each Exchange store is composed of two database files:

- The rich-text database file (.edb) which contains data placed into the store by MAPI clients, such as Microsoft Office Outlook. The .edb file stores the following items:
  - All of the MAPI messages
  - Tables used by the Store.exe process to locate all messages
  - Checksums of both the .edb and .stm files
  - Pointers to the data in the .stm file
- The streaming database file (.stm), which contains native Internet formatted content, such as native Multipurpose Internet Mail Extensions (MIME). The streaming database file is used to support non-MAPI clients, such as Outlook Express.

When a MAPI client, such as Outlook, sends a message using Exchange, the message is saved directly in the rich-text database. When a MAPI client reads that message, the text comes directly from the rich-text database. When a non-MAPI client reads the same message, the content is converted into the appropriate Internet format and passed on to the client. This conversion is referred to as an on-demand, in-memory content conversion, because the data is not moved out of the .edb file into the .stm file.

When a non-MAPI client submits a message, the message data is physically stored in the streaming database. There is some automatic property promotion to the rich-text database of the message header and other data. If a MAPI client attempts to read the message, the message data in the streaming database is fully promoted to the rich-text database (attachments are left in the streaming database and converted in memory). Promotion occurs only from the streaming database to the rich-text database. There are no circumstances in which data is promoted to the streaming database. All client conversions are performed in memory to provide better performance.

If the user at the MAPI client changes the message and then saves it, the edited version is added to the rich-text database so that the message will not need to be converted the next time a MAPI client opens it. The original version of the message remains in the streaming database.

> **Note**   Mailbox moves will impact the rich-text and streaming databases. Internet protocol clients such as Post Office Protocol version 3 (POP3) and Internet Message Access Protocol version 4 (IMAP4) use the streaming database (.stm file) for reading and writing data. When you use the move mailbox function in Active Directory Users and Computers, data is moved from the .stm into the .edb file because the move mailbox function is a MAPI operation. Non-MAPI clients will experience a performance degradation, because they will be reading from the rich-text database.

The .edb and .stm files function as a pair. The streaming database contains only raw document content and must apply information from the rich-text database to format its content properly. A database signature is stored as a header in both files and is used to match the edb, .stm, and transaction logs files. The database signature is a 32-bit number in versions of Exchange prior to Exchange 2003 Service Pack 1 (SP1) and a 64-bit number in Exchange 2003 SP1, that is combined with the time the database was created. The database signature changes whenever the physical topology of the database is altered, such as when the database is defragmented or repaired.

The .edb and .stm files are organized into four-kilobyte (KB) pages. In the .edb file, the pages are organized into a balanced-tree (B-tree) structure to store data. Each page in the database file is a node in the B-tree structure. However, in the .stm file, the pages are grouped in a clustered block similar to a file system such as NTFS. These pages are stored in 64-kilobyte blocks (16 consecutive pages of four KB each) within the .stm file on the hard disk.

Checksum

The checksum (also called a message hash) is an 8-byte string (four-byte string prior to Exchange 2003 SP1) that is calculated and then added to the page. Every .edb file is made up of four-kilobyte pages and the integrity of these pages is verified through a checksum and a four- byte page number in the header of the database page. The first 82 bytes of the database page contain the header information, which contains flags for the type of page and information about what kind of data the page contains. When Exchange reads pages out of the database, the pages are compared for the correct page number and for the checksum, which is calculated to ensure that the data in the page is undamaged. If the data is damaged, ESE returns an error, the database is stopped, and an event is logged informing you of damage and actions to take (for example, completing a restore). This process ensures the optimal integrity of the database by informing you immediately if your database is damaged.

More Info   With Exchange Server 2003 SP1, a new checksum model was introduced that allows the database engine to correct single-bit database page checksum errors. This change reduces the number of checksum errors (error 1018 – Checksum Error on a Database Page) recorded in the event log that indicate that there is corruption in an Exchange database. For more information about the new checksum model in Exchange 2003 SP1, see Microsoft Knowledge Base article 867626, "New error correcting code is included in Exchange Server 2003 SP1" (*http://go.microsoft.com/fwlink/?LinkId=3052&kbid=867626*).

Database GUID

A database globally unique identifier (GUID) is assigned to the store database, and a matching GUID is stored in Active Directory. This is important, because the database will not mount if the GUIDs do not match.

Mailbox GUID

Each mailbox in the database has a GUID. The user account in Active Directory has the GUID of the mailbox that it owns, which means that although you can delete a user from Active Directory, the mailbox still exists in the database. Therefore, you can reconnect the same mailbox to a different user. If the user account is accidentally deleted, you can fix it by reconnecting the mailbox. Reconnecting the mailbox adds the mailbox GUID as a property field to the user account in Active Directory. The mailbox itself has a default retention period of 30 days.

Exchange Storage Groups

Exchange uses storage groups, which are sets of stores that share the same set of transaction log files. An Exchange storage group consists of the .edb and .stm files, the set of log files for all the databases in the storage group, and a checkpoint file (Figure 10-1).

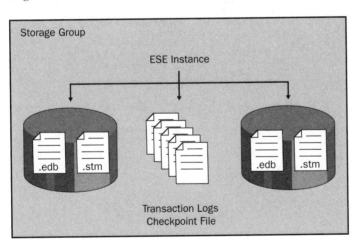

Figure 10-1   Storage Group files

Exchange uses storage groups to reduce the overhead that results from multiple sets of transaction log files. A storage group can contain up to five stores that use one set of transaction log files, and these stores can be managed as a group or independently. Exchange manages each storage group with a separate server process.

Transaction Log Files

Transaction log files record the history of server activity. These files store a sequential list of every operation that is performed on a database page in memory. Each storage group uses its own set of transaction log files. For example, if a storage group contains five stores, all transactions for all five stores are recorded in a single series of transaction log files. Exchange log files are always five megabytes (MB) in size, 5,242,880 bytes when viewed in Windows Explorer. Having a log file that is a fixed size when it is created provides better performance over having a log file that grows as transactions are written to it. If a log file does not show this exact size, this typically means that it is damaged.

When ESE makes a database modification, it copies the page into memory to make the transaction as fast as possible. However, while the transaction is being processed, it is vulnerable to system problems, such as a power failure, that can cause a loss of all uncommitted transactions from the server's memory. To protect your data during transactions, ESE uses log files to record every transaction as it progresses.

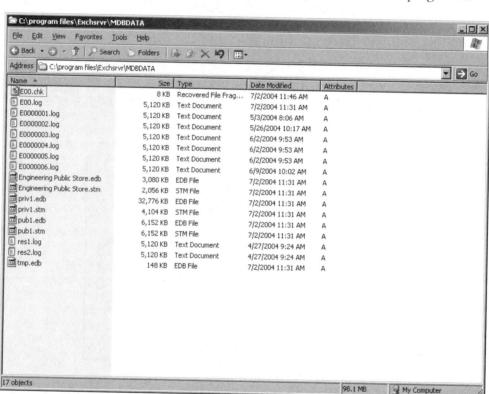

Figure 10-2 Transaction log files

When Exchange starts for the first time, it creates a five-megabyte transaction log file named E*xx*.log by default. (Where E*xx* is the log file prefix assigned to the storage group by the server, for example, the default storage group, named First Storage Group, uses the prefix E00. If you create additional storage groups, the prefix number is incremented to E01, E02, and E03.) Because Exchange logs every transaction, this log file eventually fills its five megabytes of space. ESE renames the file to

E*xx*0000*y*.log (where *y* is the generation number for the log file) and creates a new log file named E*xx*.log. When that log file is full, it will also be renamed. Figure 10-2 shows an example of a series of log files created for a storage group.

Checkpoint Files

Exchange creates a checkpoint file, named E*xx*.chk, to track the content of the log files. This checkpoint file points to the oldest log file in the storage group that has all its transactions successfully committed to the database (Figure 10-3). When all the pages that are changed by transactions in a given log file write to the database file, the checkpoint advances to the next log file in the series which contains the next unwritten entry. Separate E*xx*.chk files are maintained for each storage group.

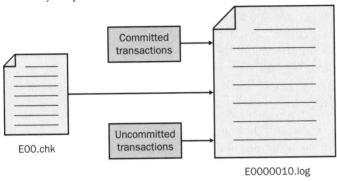

E00.chk

Committed transactions

Uncommitted transactions

E0000010.log

Figure 10-3   Checkpoint file

If a failure occurs, ESE reads the checkpoint file when Exchange starts up again. It uses the checkpoint file information to find the correct transaction log file to recover any transactions lost by the failure. ESE recovers the lost transactions by writing to the database all transactions that are newer than the checkpoint file. Uncommitted transactions are discarded. The E*xx*.chk file is not required to replay transactions. ESE determines which transactions are already written by examining the transaction log files. However, using the checkpoint saves ESE from starting at the first log file that is on the disk and checking every operation.

Reserve Log Files

For each storage group, ESE reserves two log files, res1.log and res2.log, which are stored in the log directory. Reserved log files are used as placeholders for extra disk space that can be used if the service runs out of space. They have the same size and function as normal log files.

If the server has less than five megabytes of disk space available, it cannot create a new log file. When this happens, ESE uses the reserved log files. Any operations in the server's memory are recorded in the reserved log files, starting with res2.log, and then the databases in the storage group are dismounted. When mailboxes and public folders are dismounted, they are inaccessible to users.

How Log Files Work

Log files form in the following way:

1. When the current log file fills, the E*xx*temp.log file starts.

2. The original log file name changes to the true generation number, so it has the E*xx* prefix, followed by a five-digit hexadecimal number. If the first generation file name is E01000A1.log, the next log file name is E01000A2.log.

3. The file E*xx*temp.log becomes E*xx*.log and the process repeats.

Log File Signature

Because it is possible for log files to have the same name, the ESE stamps the header in each file series with a unique signature so it can distinguish between different series of log files. Unlike database signatures that change whenever the physical topology of the database is altered, log signatures do not change after the E*xx*000001.log file is created.

Circular Logging

Circular logging is a feature that allows log files to be overwritten by new log files after the transactions in the original log file are committed to the database. Circular logging is defined at the storage group level, and it should be taken into consideration when managing stores and storage groups. Although circular logging uses transaction log techniques, it does not maintain previous transaction log files for long periods of time. Instead, Exchange maintains a few log files (typically, a set of four log files), renames older logs, and overwrites the oldest log when a new transaction log file is needed. You can enable or disable circular logging for each storage group independently using Exchange System Manager. By default, circular logging is disabled in Exchange 2003.

The main advantage of circular logging is that it reduces the use of hard disk space. You can use circular logging to reduce the buildup of transaction log files. The main disadvantage of circular logging is that if the database fails, you cannot replay transaction log files when you recover data; thus, you cannot restore data beyond the most recent backup. Another disadvantage when circular logging is enabled is that you can only perform full backups. You cannot perform backups that rely on transaction log files, such as differential or incremental backups.

Circular logging should not be used for mailbox stores. You should use circular logging only if data recovery is not important. For example, you can use it on a front-end server that does not have mailboxes or public folders and where data never needs to be recovered. Other possible scenarios are when you move large numbers of mailboxes between servers or when a storage group is dedicated to receiving information that is supplied by a Network News Transfer Protocol (NNTP) newsfeed.

How Circular Logging Works

When you enable circular logging, multiple log files might be present in the storage group folder. The presence of multiple log files in the storage group folder is normal, because the ESE typically uses four log files before reusing one of the existing four log files. For example, logs E0000010.log, E0000011.log, E0000012.log, and E0000013.log become E0000014.log, E0000011.log, E0000012.log, and E0000013.log, respectively. The circular log numbers are hexadecimal, and they increase in increments of one. If the checkpoint is still referring to the lowest numbered log file, and a new log file must be created, ESE increases the set of log files from four to five to avoid overwriting the checkpoint.

Understanding Single Instance Storage

To help control the size of mailbox stores, Exchange supports single instance message storage. When a message is sent to more than one mailbox in the same mailbox store, only one instance of the message is stored, in one mailbox. The other mailboxes contain pointers to the stored message. If the message is sent to mailboxes in a different mailbox store, the message is written one time to each mailbox store.

Exchange maintains single instance message storage on a per-store basis. When mailboxes are moved, single instance storage might not be maintained. During a move of users, Exchange checks every incoming message against its own internally assigned IDs. If Exchange determines that the incoming message is a duplicate, it merely sets up a pointer for that existing message pointing to the newly moved user. If Exchange determines that the incoming message is not a duplicate, it creates a new instance of that message. For example, suppose two mailboxes are on the same mailbox store and share a message (single instance storage for that message), and both of those mailboxes are moved to a different mailbox store. In this case, single instance storage of the message is maintained. On the other hand, if only one of the mailboxes is moved to a different mailbox store, single instance storage for that message is lost, and a copy of the message exists in both mailbox stores.

Configuring Exchange Server 2003 Storage

Each server that runs Exchange Server 5.5 or earlier is limited to a single mailbox and public folder store per server. Starting with Exchange 2000 Server, this is no longer the case. A server running Exchange Server 2003 Standard Edition can have one storage group that contains one mailbox store and one public folder store. A server running Exchange Server 2003 Enterprise Edition can have up to four storage groups, each of which can contain up to five databases (either mailbox stores or public folder stores).

The ability to have multiple stores enables a single server to support more users than with previous versions of Exchange. It also enables individual stores to be dismounted without affecting the users on the remaining stores.

Creating Additional Storage Groups and Exchange Stores

Determining when to create additional storage groups and Exchange stores will depend on many factors, including backup and restore requirements, performance requirements, and administration requirements. Use the following recommendations for determining when to create additional storage groups and additional Exchange stores.

Creating Storage Groups

When a new Exchange server is installed, the default First Storage Group is created, containing a mailbox and a public folder store. You might want to add a storage group when:

- Your company requires more than five databases on a single Exchange server. Creating additional stores is discussed later in this section.

- You want to group together databases that require the same backup schedule. (You can use the storage group as a unit for backups.)

- You want to implement circular logging to reduce log file build-up on a set of specific databases.

- You are hosting multiple companies on the same server. It is best to keep different companies in separate storage groups, because this keeps all transaction logs for each company separate from each other. Hosting companies in the same storage group results in all transactions for each company sharing the same set of transaction logs, which may cause billing or legal issues for your customers.

> **More Info**   For more information about hosting multiple companies on Exchange 2003, see Chapter 7, "Hosting Exchange Server 2003."

Creating Exchange Stores

You can use multiple mailbox stores to increase the reliability and recoverability of your Exchange organization. If your users are spread across multiple mailbox stores, the loss of a single store affects only a subset of the users instead of the whole organization. Additionally, reducing the number of users per store reduces the time that you need to recover a damaged store from a backup. Consider adding stores when:

- You want to minimize the impact of store failures and restores on users. Create multiple small mailbox stores or public folder stores instead of having one large store. Smaller stores allow for faster restore than large stores.

- You want to maximize backup efficiency. You can estimate the maximum time required to perform a backup of each store based on the speed at which your backup hardware performs in megabytes per hour. You can then constrain your stores to a maximum size limit, which enables you to back up all stores in a storage group within the time that you have allocated for backups each night.

- You want to provide priority service and fast restores to a group of users, such as your senior management. Create a dedicated mailbox store for those users. When considering this scenario, weigh the increased administrative cost against the benefits. Also consider the impact that a mailbox store failure will have if all users of a particular department or group, such as senior management, are on the same mailbox store.

- You want to maximize single instance storage. Place similar users, such as users in the same department, in the same mailbox store. Users in the same department or other groups of similar users tend to use Reply All or send large attachments to each other. If you place these similar users together, you maximize single-instance message storage, which minimizes disk space requirements.

- You want to implement full-text (content) indexing. Place information that requires full-text indexing in a separate mailbox store or public folder store, and enable full-text indexing for that store. This can minimize indexing overhead.

- You want to implement Exchange system policies. Exchange system policies enable you to apply a collection of configuration settings to one or more Exchange stores. For example, you might want to control the size of all mailboxes on a single mailbox store.

- You want to consolidate dedicated servers, such as mailbox-only, public folders-only, or NNTP-only servers, into a single server to improve manageability.

More Info   Full-text indexing and Exchange policies are covered in more detail later in this chapter.

Configuring Exchange Stores

Some Exchange store configurations are applicable to both mailbox stores and public folder stores. Some configuration settings are specific to the type of Exchange store. Your primary tool for configuring Exchange stores in Exchange 2003 is Exchange System Manager.

Configuring Settings Specific to Mailbox Stores

Three settings that are specific to mailbox stores are configuring a default public folder store to associate with the mailbox store, configuring an offline address list to associate with the mailbox store, and configuring message archiving (also known as journaling) for the mailbox store. Each of these items is configured using the General tab of the mailbox store object.

Associating Public Folder Stores

When you create a mailbox store, you must associate it with a public folder store. The public folder store can be on the local server or another server. When you associate a public folder store with the mailbox store, you are associating a public folder store that is associated with the Public Folders tree (also named the MAPI public folder tree). The public folder store associated with the mailbox store is used when the client first attempts to connect to a replica of a public folder.

You should identify a public folder store that is physically close to the server on which the mailbox store is defined. By doing so, you will minimize network traffic when clients download the public folder list from the default public folder store each time they expand the All Public Folders container.

Note   Using the default public folder store on the same server as the mailbox store might improve performance when users access public folders, and can make it easier to troubleshoot public folder access problems.

More Info   Public folders and public folder trees are covered in more detail later in this chapter.

Associating Offline Address Lists

Client applications, such as Outlook, use address lists when creating and addressing e-mail messages. By default, the address list used is the global address list (GAL), which is a list of all mail-enabled recipients (not hidden from the address list) in the Exchange organization. When users disconnect from the network, the GAL is not available to them. If Outlook users want to compose e-mail messages even when they are disconnected from their Exchange server, they must download an offline address list.

By default, there is an offline address list (Default Offline Address List) that contains all recipients in the GAL. The Default Offline Address List is associated with every mailbox store. You can create additional offline address lists and use any address list in the Exchange organization to populate them. This allows you to associate a specific offline address list with each mailbox store. For example, if you have grouped similar users together on the same mailbox store, such as users from the same department, you can create an offline address list that contains the common addresses used by that department, and associate it with the mailbox store for those users. This enables the users to download a subset of the GAL to use when they are working offline, which saves client hard disk space and download time.

More Info   For more information about address lists, see Chapter 9, "Managing Directory Information."

Enabling Message Archiving

Many companies have a legal requirement to retain all messages that are handled by a mailbox store. Archiving (also referred to as journaling) communications that are sent via e-mail is common in financial services, insurance, and healthcare industries to comply with government and industry regulations. There are three different types of journaling that you can enable in Exchange 2003.

Message-only Journaling   Message-only journaling creates a copy of all messages, and the corresponding P2 message header data to and from users on a mailbox database and sends the message copy to a specified mailbox. The P2 message header contains only the message recipient data that the sender declared to the recipients. If an external message is received from the Internet, Exchange journals the P1 message headers. The P1 message header is the address information that is used by message transfer agents (MTAs) to route mail. By default, when message-only journaling is enabled, Exchange does not account for blind carbon copy (Bcc) recipients, recipients from transport forwarding rules, or recipients from distribution group expansions.

Message-only journaling is enabled on the General tab of the mailbox store object by configuring a mailbox that will receive all journalized messages for senders on the mailbox store. We recommend that the archive mailbox be located on a dedicated, secure server rather than on a mailbox server, to provide an additional level of security for the mailbox content.

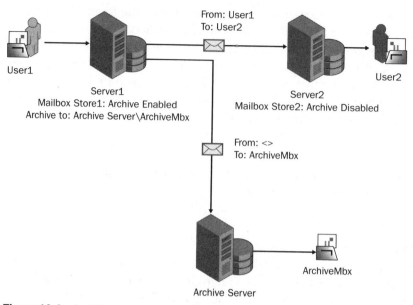

Figure 10-4 Archiving messages on a single mailbox store

Figure 10-4 illustrates an example of message-only journaling on a single mailbox store. In this example, User1 has a mailbox on Server1 in Mailbox Store1, where message archiving is enabled. User1 sends a message to User2. User2's mailbox is on Server2, in Mailbox Store2, where message archiving is not enabled. Archive Server is a mailbox server that hosts only one mailbox: ArchiveMbx. Archive Server is a dedicated archive recipient mailbox server.

Exchange performs several actions before a message leaves the sender's Exchange server:

1. Exchange sets an archiving property on the message, which identifies it as an archived message. This property travels with the message to its various destinations in the Exchange organization.

2. Exchange adds a list of archive recipient mailboxes (ArchiveMbx in the example) to the archive property.

3. Exchange looks up the recipient's address information. Exchange specifically uses the recipient's home mailbox database attribute as the destination. If archiving is enabled on Mailbox Store2, the recipient's archive mailbox and the recipient information is added to the archive property on the message.

4. When the message is sent to User2, a message is also sent to ArchiveMbx for archiving. Server2 receives the message, reads the archiving property (which specifies that the archive message has been recorded and sent), and delivers the message to User2's mailbox. When Archive Server receives the message, it creates an envelope message that specifies User1 as the sender and User2 as the

recipient, attaches the original message to the envelope message, and delivers it to ArchiveMbx's mailbox.

Bcc Journaling   Bcc journaling is message-only journaling with the added ability to capture the Bcc recipients. When Bcc journaling is enabled, Exchange captures all recipients (including Bcc recipients) that are known at the originating server. If this recipient list includes hidden distribution lists, query-based distribution lists, or distribution lists that are expanded on another server, the recipients for these lists are not be included in the journalized mail. This functionality is enabled by setting a registry key. For more information about setting this registry key, see Microsoft Knowledge Base article 810999, "XADM: Bcc Information Is Lost for Journaled Messages in Exchange 2000" (*http://go.microsoft.com/fwlink/?LinkId=3052&kbid=810999*).

Envelope Journaling   Envelope journaling differs from message-only journaling and Bcc journaling because it archives P1 message headers. This includes information about the recipients who actually received the message, including Bcc recipients and recipients from distribution groups. Envelope journaling delivers messages that are flagged to be archived by using an envelope message that contains a journal report together with the original message. The original message is delivered as an attachment. The body of the journal report contains the transport envelope data of the archived message.

Envelope journaling is enabled using the exejcfg tool available in the Exchange Server 2003 SP1 download. The exejcfg tool modifies the Exchange organization object in Active Directory, so you must run the tool from a server that has access to Active Directory. We recommend that you run the tool from a domain controller for better performance. From the directory where you installed exejcfg, type **exejcfg –e** at the command prompt to enable envelope journaling.

More Info   For more information on message archiving, see the book "Journaling with Exchange Server 2003" (*http://www.microsoft.com/technet/ prodtechnol/exchange/2003/library/journaling.mspx*).

Configuring Settings Specific to Public Folder Stores

A public folder can exist in an Exchange organization either as a single copy or as multiple copies. Multiple copies of a public folder are named replicas. The schedule at which replication updates are sent to other servers that maintain replicas of folders and the message size that contains the updates are both configured using the Replication tab of the public folder store object. Settings configured on the Replication tab can be overridden on individual public folders. Replication settings are specific to public folder stores.

Configuring Replication Interval

By default, the replication interval is every 15 minutes. You should determine a schedule for replication that is appropriate for the type of content in your public folders and the network bandwidth available between public folder servers. For example, a public folder that contains the employee handbook might not change often and might need to be replicated only once a week, whereas a public folder that contains critical customer data that users in your organization rely on to make business decisions might need to be replicated every couple of hours.

Configuring Replication Message Size Limit

The smallest unit of content replication is an individual update to a folder. Exchange uses the replication message size limit to determine how many updates can be grouped together into a single replication message. An individual update to a folder is not split up into multiple messages, but multiple updates can be combined into a single message, up to the message size define by the replication message size limit. By default, the replication message size limit is 300 KB. This means that up to 300 KB of changes are packaged into a single replication message. It does not mean that 900 KB are divided up into three separate replication messages. For example, suppose you post 40 updates of 10 KB each into a pubic folder. The store will package 30 updates into one replication message (300 KB), and another 10 updates into a second replication message (100 KB). However, if you post a single 5-MB update into a public folder, the store generates one 5-MB replication message.

> **Note**   Replication messages differ from typical e-mail messages in that Exchange treats replication messages as system messages. This means that replication messages are not bound by the typical restrictions that are applied to user e-mail messages, such as size and delivery restrictions. Because of this, if you have multiple routing groups and have defined message size limits on the connectors, for example to control bandwidth usage, you should take that into consideration when configuring your public folder stores. To prevent large replication messages, limit the maximum message size that can be posted to a public folder by configuring Maximum Item Size on the Limits tab of either the public folder store or the individual public folder.

Configuring Settings Common on Both Mailbox and Public Folder Stores

Configuration settings that control the location of the databases that make up each Exchange store, size limitations for items in the store, retention periods, and policies that are applied to the store are the same, or similar, for both mailbox and public folder stores.

Configuring Exchange Databases

Exchange database configurations are performed using the Database tab of the store object. You can identify a disk on which the rich-text and streaming database files will be located. When determining the location of your database files, you should consider performance and reliability.

■ By separating database and transaction log files, you increase your options for recovering from a disk failure. Depending on how current your backup is and whether you lose the disk drive with your database or your transaction logs, you can perform a restore and recover all or most of the information that was in store at the time of failure. For example, if you lose the hard disk containing the Exchange databases, you can replace the damaged disk and then restore the most recent database backups. After you restore the databases, Exchange automatically replays all transactions committed to the transaction log files that occurred after the backup, and brings the databases up to date.

■ By separating database and transaction log files, you can maximize performance. Data in log files is accessed sequentially; data in database files is accessed randomly. By separating database and transaction log files onto separate disk drives, you can optimize your disk I/O (input/output).

Table 10-1 shows an example of partitioning Exchange data using six separate disk drives.

Table 10-1 Exchange Hard Disk Partitioning Example

Disk	Drive configuration
Disk 1	Drive C — Windows operating system files and swap file
Disk 2	Drive D — Exchange binaries and additional server applications, such as antivirus software
Disk 3	Drive E — Transaction log files for storage group 1
Disk 4	Drive F — Database files for storage group 1
Disk 5	Drive G — Transaction log files for storage group 2
Disk 6	Drive H — Database files for storage group 2

More Info For more information about configuring storage for Exchange 2003, see Chapter 18 "Tuning Exchange Server Performance" and the book "Exchange Server 2003 High Availability Guide" (*http://www.microsoft.com/technet/prodtechnol/exchange/2003/library/highavailgde.mspx*).

Configuring Database Maintenance

Exchange store maintenance refers to a series of operations performed by the Exchange store to ensure logical consistency in the databases. These operations are performed automatically based on the schedule that is defined on the Database tab of the store object. By default, the maintenance schedule is set to run between 1:00 A.M. and 5:00 A.M. (local time).

Use the following guidelines when determining the schedule for each Exchange store:

■ Schedule maintenance to occur when most of your users are offline. This minimizes the impact of maintenance on the performance of your server.

■ When multiple storage groups are on a single server, stagger the maintenance schedule so that the online maintenance schedules do not overlap. For example, if the server has three storage groups, have storage group 1 perform maintenance from 1:00 A.M. to 2:00 A.M., storage group 2 from 2:00 A.M. to 3:00 A.M., and storage group 3 from 3:00 A.M. to 4:00 A.M.

■ Coordinate the maintenance schedule with your backup schedule. Backup does not preempt the tasks performed by the Exchange store, but initiating a backup of a database suspends the online defragmentation process until the backup is completed.

Understanding Database Maintenance   Database maintenance performs 10 tasks during the Exchange store maintenance window. These 10 tasks are performed by the store process (Store.exe). An additional task, online defragmentation, is also performed during the maintenance window and is handled by ESE. If the maintenance window ends before one of the 10 tasks is completed, the last task running is recorded and will be allowed to complete. During the next maintenance window, the Exchange store determines the last task in progress and resumes with the next task.

It is important to understand the tasks that are performed during the maintenance window to ensure that you allow the optimum amount of time for maintenance to occur. The ten tasks that are performed during Exchange store maintenance are:

1. **Purge indexes on both mailbox and public folder stores.** ESE dynamically creates indexes when information is resorted or requested in a different sort order. The Exchange store monitors these indexes by assigning them an expiry time. Information about the index is added to an internal table referred to as the Indexing Aging Table. During maintenance, the value of ptagIndexDeleteTime for each entry in the Index Aging Table is compared to the current time. If the index has expired, the index is removed. This maintenance task runs every 24 hours during the Exchange store maintenance cycle and by default, removes entries older than 40 days for Exchange 2003. The default settings are configurable through Registry Editor or through Active Directory Service Interfaces Editor (ADSI Edit).

2. **Tombstone maintenance on mailbox and public folder stores.** Each folder maintains a list of deleted messages for a folder in ptagMidsetDeleted on the folder object. When a message is deleted from a folder, an entry is made in ptagMidsetTombstones. If the folder is replicated, it gives an indication of the message delete operations that need to be synchronized. When the propagation occurs, the entries are moved from ptagMidsetTombstones and merged into ptagMidsetDeleted. If a folder is not replicated, the entry must be cleaned up through the Exchange store maintenance cycle. This maintenance task runs every 24 hours and is not configurable.

3. **Dumpster cleanup on mailbox and public folder stores.** When a message is deleted by a user a flag, ptagMsgDeleted, is set to indicate that the message was deleted. By default, client software does not display messages that have this flag set. In order to view these messages, the user must use the Recover Deleted Items (the Dumpster) feature in Outlook or Outlook Web Access. If Dumpster functionality is not enabled, deleted messages are removed from the folder during this task of the maintenance cycle. If Dumpster functionality is enabled, only messages that were deleted and exceeded the retention period are removed during this maintenance routine. This maintenance task also checks for folders that exceed the retention period and removes them as well. The interval at which the store attempts to purge unused indexes is configurable through the registry.

4. **Public folder expiry on public folder stores.** All messages in public folders are examined, and any message that exceeds the expiry time is removed. The interval at which the store removes items that exceed the retention period is configurable through the registry.

5. **Age folder tombstone on public folder stores.** When a public folder is deleted, a tombstone is put in place for replication. This enables items that are deleted to be tracked during the replication process. During this maintenance task, any deleted public folders that exceed the tombstone lifetime are removed. The default interval to keep tombstones is 180 days and is configurable through the registry.

6. **Folder conflict aging on public folder stores.** When two users edit and modify the same message in a public folder, the resulting saved messages are defined as being in conflict. Typically, message conflicts are resolved by the public folder owner. If the conflict is not resolved within the Conflict Age Limit, this maintenance task takes the appropriate action based upon the property *PR_RESOLVE_METHOD* on the folder. The interval for how long items in conflict are allowed to exist is configurable through the registry.

7. **Update server versions on public folder stores.** This maintenance task updates the version information as necessary for any public folder databases that contain a replica of the system configuration folder. No configurable settings are available.

8. **Site folder check on public folder stores.**   Every hour a public store checks to ensure no duplicate site folders exist within an Administrative Group. If duplicate site folders are found, they are removed. No configurable settings are available for this maintenance task.

9. **Cleanup deleted mailboxes on mailbox stores.**   This maintenance task looks at mailboxes that currently do not have Active Directory objects. After a default of 30 days, the mailboxes are deleted. This process runs every 24 hours, and no interval adjustments are available.

10. **Check messages table.**   This maintenance task examines the message table for a given database and then looks for messages that currently have a reference count of zero indicating no folder currently has a reference to the message. Messages encountered are deleted. This maintenance task runs every 24 hours and no interval adjustment is available.

By default, if at least one of the maintenance tasks was able to complete within the maintenance schedule, the Exchange store requests that ESE begin an online defragmentation cycle. This process will run for at least 15 minutes at the end of the maintenance window. The purpose of online defragmentation is to free pages in the database by compacting records into the fewest number of pages possible, thus reducing the amount of disk I/O. Online defragmentation does not reduce the overall file size of the database on disk. You can configure the defaults for how online defragmentation runs during the maintenance window through the registry.

Use the following registry parameters to configure the amount of time that online defragmentation will run after completing at least one of the Exchange store maintenance tasks:

Registry parameter	Description
Path	`HKEY_LOCAL_MACHINE\SYSTEM\CurrentControlSet\Services\` `MSExchangeIS\`*ServerName*`\Public-`*GUID* -or- `HKEY_LOCAL_MACHINE\SYSTEM\CurrentControlSet\Services\` `MSExchangeIS\`*ServerName*`\Private-`*GUID*
Parameter	`OLD Minimum RunTime`
Type	`REG_DWORD`
Default	15 minutes
Value	In minutes

Use the following registry parameters to configure the amount of time that online defragmentation will run beyond the maintenance window:

Registry parameter	Description
Path	HKEY_LOCAL_MACHINE\SYSTEM\CurrentControlSet\Services\ MSExchangeIS*ServerName*\Public-*GUID*
	-or-
	HKEY_LOCAL_MACHINE\SYSTEM\CurrentControlSet\Services\ MSExchangeIS*ServerName*\Private-*GUID*
Parameter	OLD Completion Time
Type	REG_DWORD
Default	3600 seconds
Value	In seconds

More Info   For more information on online maintenance, see Chapter 18, "Tuning Exchange Server Performance" and the Microsoft Exchange server team blog article "Store Background Processes Part I - IS Maintenance" (*http://blogs.msdn.com/jeremyk/archive/2004/06/12/154283.aspx*).

Configuring Storage Limits

Storage limit configurations are performed using the Limits tab of the store object. You can control how large mailboxes and public folders are allowed to grow, and how deleted items from mailboxes and public folders are retained.

Mailbox stores enable you to configure the maximum size that messages in each mailbox are allowed to occupy. When calculating the value for the Prohibit send and receive at (KB) setting, consider your backup strategy and the ability to complete a full backup within the timeframe that is allotted for backup. It is also important that you control the growth of mailboxes to accurately plan the capacity of your Exchange servers. You can configure three levels of storage limit thresholds for mailbox stores:

Option	Configuration
Issue warning at (KB)	Identifies the size to which this mailbox is allowed to grow before a warning is issued. The mailbox continues to function normally when it exceeds this limit.
Prohibit send at (KB)	Identifies the maximum size allowed on your hard disk for this mailbox before it can no longer send messages. This triggers a warning to be sent to the mailbox owner.

Option	Configuration
Prohibit send and receive at (KB)	Identifies the size allowed on your Exchange server for this mailbox before it can no longer send or receive messages. This triggers a warning to be sent to the mailbox owner. The mailbox can no longer send or receive messages.

Similarly, public folder stores allow you to configure the maximum size that items in the public folder are allowed to occupy. This size should be based on the maximum size of your public folder store. You can also configure the maximum size of an item posted to a public folder to prevent users from posting large files. For example, if most of the items that you expect to see posted are Microsoft Word documents that occupy less than 500 KB and you want to prohibit users from posting files larger than 1,000 KB, set this value to be 1,000 KB. The three storage limit thresholds that you can configure for public folder stores are:

Option	Configuration
Issue warning at (KB)	Identifies the size to which this public folder is allowed to grow before a warning is issued to the public folder's owner.
Prohibit post at (KB)	Identifies the maximum size allowed on your hard disk for this public folder before it can no longer receive message posts. This triggers a warning to be sent to the public folder's owner.
Maximum item size (KB)	Identifies the maximum size allowed for an item posted to a public folder. Posts larger than this size are not permitted.

Both mailbox and public folder stores have deleted item retention settings. When you determine how you will retain individual items, consider that Exchange does not support individual item recovery from backup media. For mailbox stores, you can also define how long a mailbox will be retained before it is deleted. Retention settings work in conjunction with the maintenance tasks that are performed by the Exchange store.

By allowing Exchange to retain deleted items, Outlook users can retrieve deleted items using Outlook's Recover Deleted Items function. By allowing Exchange to retain deleted mailboxes, mailboxes that belong to users who were deleted from Active Directory can be recovered by associating them with existing users who do not have mailboxes (this is covered later in this chapter). If you configure Exchange to maintain deleted items and deleted mailboxes, remember to accommodate for the extra data when planning your Exchange storage.

Age Limit Settings and System Folders   Age limit settings affect some system folders and also affect regular public folders. Age limit settings can have the following effects:

- **Free/Busy folder**   Outlook typically publishes three months of a user's free/busy data at a time and updates this information every time the user modifies his or her calendar. As long as the age limit is large enough (for example, 90 days), and the user modifies his or her calendar regularly, the age limit removes only information that is out of date.

- **Offline Address List folder**   Exchange rebuilds this folder regularly, based on a schedule that is set in Exchange System Manager. Ensure that the update interval is shorter than the age limit.

- **System Configuration folder**   This folder is not affected by the public folder store's age limit settings. Do not set age limits on the System Configuration folder.

- **Application Configuration folder**   This folder is not affected by the public folder store's age limit settings. Do not set age limits on the Application Configuration folder.

> **Warning**   Do not set an age limit on public folders that contain Contact or Calendar items.

Configuring Stores Using Exchange System Policies

An Exchange policy is a collection of configuration settings that is applied to one or more Exchange objects of the same type. Policies are designed to enable flexible and efficient administration of large numbers of Exchange objects. For example, you can implement a policy that controls the storage limit settings across multiple Exchange stores in your Exchange organization. When you need to change the storage limits setting on the Exchange stores, you can simply edit the policy and have the changes applied to all the Exchange stores in a single operation.

Exchange system policies are policies that control the configuration settings for Exchange server and Exchange store (mailbox store and public folder store) objects. System policies reside in the System Policies container, which is created under the Administrative Group object in Exchange System Manager. You can configure your Exchange stores using one of two types of system policies:

- **Mailbox store policies**   You can use this type of system policy to configure the properties of multiple mailbox store objects in one application. For example, you can use mailbox store policies to apply storage limits, indexing updates, maintenance intervals, mappings to public folder stores, and offline address lists on multiple mailbox stores.

- **Public store policies** You can use this type of system policy to configure the properties of multiple public folder stores in one application. For example, you can use public store policies to configure maintenance schedules, replication intervals, storage limits, and index updates on multiple public folder stores.

Using System Policies Exchange system policies are most useful in medium to large companies that have multiple servers, mailbox stores, and public folder stores. Changes to operational guidelines in these companies tend to result in significant administrative changes to the Exchange organization, thereby affecting multiple servers or stores. As a result, it becomes more efficient to create and apply a system policy than to manually configure each individual server and store.

When determining how you will use Exchange system policies, you must consider the permissions required to create and apply system policies. Creating a system policy requires that you have Exchange Administrator permissions in the administrative group container or the organization container in which a System Policies container resides. Applying a system policy to an object requires that you have Write permissions for the object to which the system policy is to be applied.

You must also consider how policies are applied. You can only apply one system policy tab to a server or store object at any given time. You should configure system policies so that each system policy controls the settings on only one tab. You can apply multiple system policies to the same object only when there is no conflict in the tabs that these system policies control. If conflicts occur, you must remove the original conflicting system policy before applying the new system policy. For example, if you have two mailbox store policies with the Limits tab configured, you can apply only one policy to a specific mailbox store. However, if you have two mailbox store policies, one with the Limits tab configured and the other with the Database tab configured, both policies can be applied to the same mailbox store.

If an option, such as the Limits tab, is controlled by a policy, the settings cannot be overridden on the Exchange store object itself (the option will be grayed out). If the option that is controlled by a policy is available on a mailbox or public folder object, the settings can be overridden for that object. For example, suppose that you configured a mailbox store policy to limit mailbox storage to 50,000 KB before a user is prohibited from sending and receiving messages. By accessing the properties of the mailbox store object, you will not be able to change the storage limit settings. You can, however use Active Directory Users and Computers to access an individual user's mailbox and clear the Use mailbox store defaults option (by using the Storage limits option on the Exchange General tab). Once the option is cleared, you can define specific storage limits for that mailbox that will override the policy settings.

Tip   Exchange system policies can also be used to quickly configure default settings for servers. Create an Exchange system policy that defines the tabs and settings that you want to use as the default values to populate your Exchange server or Exchange store object. Apply the policy to the server or Exchange store object. After the policy is applied, remove the policy from the server or Exchange store object. The settings defined by the policy will remain, but by removing the policy, you allow your local administrators the ability to modify settings as needed.

Overriding Exchange Store and Exchange System Policy Settings

You cannot override settings that are controlled through Exchange system policies by configuring the Exchange store object to which the policy was applied. You can override settings for individual mailboxes and public folders that will override the Exchange store settings regardless of whether the settings were configured on the individual store or applied to the store by using Exchange system policies. Use the following list to determine how to override settings:

- You can override the store's limits settings by using Active Directory Users and Computers to configure limits settings for individual users.

- You can override the setting for deleted item retention that is set on the mailbox store by using Active Directory Users and Computers to configure limits settings for individual users. If you choose to override the limit set on the mailbox store, you also have the choice to not permanently delete an item until the store is backed up, adding even greater recovery opportunities for that user.

- You can set limits on individual public folders that override the store settings. If you use only the store settings, the same folder might have different limits on different servers. If you use individual folder settings, the limits are the same for all replicas of the folder.

- You can set additional age limits, which affect only a specific public folder replica. These limits override limits set on the folder (using the folder's Properties dialog box), but only in the public folder store where you set them. Other replicas of the public folder (on other servers) are not affected.

More Info   For more information about configuring Exchange stores in Exchange 2003, see the book "Exchange Server 2003 Administration Guide" (*http://www.microsoft.com/technet/prodtechnol/exchange/2003/library/admingde.mspx*).

Managing Exchange Server 2003 Store Resources

Mailboxes are created using Active Directory User and Computers. Mailbox store configuration and monitoring of individual mailboxes are performed using Exchange System Manager. Public folders can be created using client software, such as Microsoft Office Outlook, or using Exchange System Manager, but the administration of public folders is performed using Exchange System Manager.

The task of managing mailboxes and public folders is performed separately from the tasks of managing storage groups and stores that contain the mailbox and public folder objects.

Managing Mailbox Resources

Mailbox management tasks include managing mailbox permissions, moving and deleting mailboxes, and managing data retention.

Understanding Mailbox Permissions

In Exchange Server 5.5, access control lists (ACLs) use MAPI permissions to control access to mailboxes. Exchange 2003 substitutes MAPI permissions for Windows Server permissions to control access to mailboxes and the messages that they contain.

- When an administrator is using Active Directory Users and Computers to manage mailbox permissions using the Mailbox Rights option on the Exchange Advanced tab, Windows-compatible permissions are displayed (Figure 10-5).

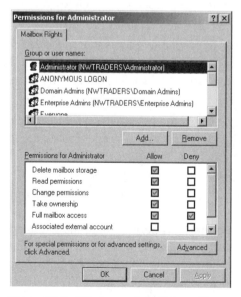

Figure 10-5   Windows-compatible mailbox permissions

■ When Outlook clients are managing permissions to their mailboxes (sharing folders or delegating access), they are using MAPI, so Exchange converts the permissions to MAPI permissions (Figure 10-6) when displaying them to the user. If the user modifies the permissions, Exchange converts them back to Windows-compatible permissions to save them.

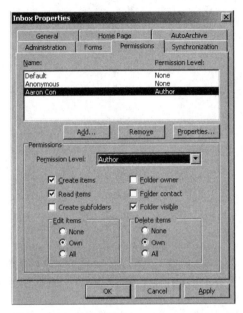

Figure 10-6   MAPI mailbox permissions

■ When Exchange 5.5 and Exchange 2003 are co-existing, permissions are replicated using the MAPI format. When the permissions replicate back to Exchange 2003 servers, Exchange 2003 converts them to the Windows-compatible format before saving them.

Exchange handles all conversions between Windows-compatible permissions and MAPI permissions automatically. However, as an administrator, you should be aware that when you use Exchange System Manager to set permissions, you might be required to work with either Windows-compatible permissions or MAPI permissions, depending on the type of object you are securing.

When you create a new mailbox, Exchange uses information from the mailbox store to create the default permissions for the new mailbox. The default folders (Inbox, Calendar, and so on) inherit permissions from the mailbox itself. Users can modify the permissions on folders in their mailbox by using Outlook.

Exchange provides a set of default levels of access that you can use when you are setting permissions on mailboxes using MAPI permissions. These levels of access are called roles. Table 10-2 summarizes MAPI roles and the permissions associated with them.

Table 10-2   MAPI Roles

Role	Permissions						
	Create Items	Read Items	Create Subfolders	Edit Items	Folder Owner	Folder Visible	Delete Items
Owner	Yes	Yes	Yes	All	Yes	Yes	All
Publishing Editor	Yes	Yes	Yes	All	No	Yes	All
Editor	Yes	Yes	No	All	No	Yes	All
Publishing Author	Yes	Yes	Yes	Own	No	Yes	Own
Author	Yes	Yes	No	Own	No	Yes	Own
Nonediting Author	Yes	Yes	No	None	No	Yes	Own
Reviewer	No	Yes	No	None	No	Yes	None
Contributor	Yes	No	No	None	No	Yes	None
None	No	No	No	None	No	Yes	None

There are times that you, as an administrator, might need access to a user's mailbox. Typically, you want to access a user's mailbox to perform troubleshooting tasks. You might also have occasion to assign one user access to another user's mailbox.

To assign access to a mailbox, you must access the mailbox in Active Directory Users and Computers, then using the Exchange Advanced tab, access Mailbox Rights. You then have the ability to select from the following access levels when you assign another user access to the mailbox:

- **Read Permissions**   The specified user can read the contents of a mailbox.

- **Change Permissions**   The user can modify or delete items in the mailbox.

- **Take Ownership**   The user is granted ownership of a mailbox.

- **Full Mailbox Access**   The specified user has the same access rights as the owner.

If you give a user the access level of Full Mailbox Access, Exchange treats that user as the mailbox owner. If you give a user an access level other than Full Mailbox Access, the original mailbox owner can use Outlook to set permissions for the other user on folders in the mailbox.

The following rights are also available, but it is typically best to let Exchange manage them:

- **Delete mailbox storage**   The mailbox from the mailbox store can be deleted. By default, only administrators have permission to do this. Users cannot delete their own mailboxes.

- **Associated external account**   This option is used when a user's Windows account resides in a different forest than the Exchange mailbox.

> **Note**   Each Exchange mailbox must be associated with an Active Directory object, such as a user, in the same forest as the mailbox. If the intended user account resides outside the forest where Exchange is, Exchange first associates the mailbox with an account in its same Active Directory forest. That account is disabled. Then, the mailbox is associated with the external account.

- **Special permissions**   Access special permissions by clicking the Advanced button on the Mailbox Rights page to work more granularly with permissions, for example, to change inheritance.

> **More Info**   For more about permissions in Exchange 2003, see the book "Working with Store Permissions in Microsoft Exchange 2000 and 2003" (*http://www.microsoft.com/technet/prodtechnol/exchange/2003/library/storperm.mspx*).

Moving Mailboxes

Using Exchange Task Wizard from either Active Directory Users and Computers or Exchange System Manager, you can move a mailbox from one mailbox store to another. You can select a single mailbox to move, or you can select multiple mailboxes. Exchange Task Wizard also enables you to schedule the mailbox move using the task scheduler, so that the move can occur at a future time, such as in the evening when users are not likely to be accessing their mailboxes. For example, you can schedule a move of a large number of mailboxes for midnight on Friday, ending automatically at 6:00 A.M. on Monday, so that the mailbox move does not impact users during regular business hours.

Before Exchange Server 2003 SP1, mixed mode Exchange organizations functioned much like Exchange 5.5 organizations in that mailbox moves were limited to moving between servers in the same administrative group. With SP1, you can move mailboxes across administrative groups in a mixed mode Exchange organization.

Deleting Mailboxes

You can use the Exchange Task Wizard to delete a mailbox. When you delete the mailbox, it is not removed from the store immediately but is marked to be deleted the next time the mailbox management process runs. The mailbox remains in the store and is viewable using Exchange System Manager for the length of time that is specified by the mailbox store settings Keep Deleted Mailboxes For (Days) and Do Not Permanently Delete Mailboxes And Items Until The Store Has Been Backed Up. The mailbox is purged automatically after the deleted mailbox retention interval has passed. Recovering the mailbox that was already purged from the Exchange store requires that you restore from your latest backup.

You can also delete a mailbox-enabled user in Active Directory Users and Computers. If you use Active Directory Users and Computers to delete a user, the mailbox information in the mailbox store is not deleted. The next time the mailbox management process runs, it marks the mailbox as unowned. Unowned mailboxes are purged automatically according to the store's Keep deleted mailboxes for (days) and Keep deleted items for (days) setting.

You can reconnect the mailbox during the mailbox retention period by associating it with a user without a mailbox. You can reconnect mailboxes by using one of two methods:

- By using the Reconnect command from the mailbox object in Exchange System Manager. This is appropriate when you want to recover a single mailbox. You will be prompted for the name of the new user for the mailbox.

- By using Mailbox Recovery Center (Figure 10-7) in Exchange System Manager. This is appropriate when you want to recover one or more mailboxes on one or more mailbox stores.

To use the Mailbox Recovery Center:

1. In Exchange System Manager, expand Tools.

2. Right-click Mailbox Recovery Center and then click Add Mailbox Store.

3. If you want to export the mailbox properties, right-click the mailbox that you want to export, and then click Export.

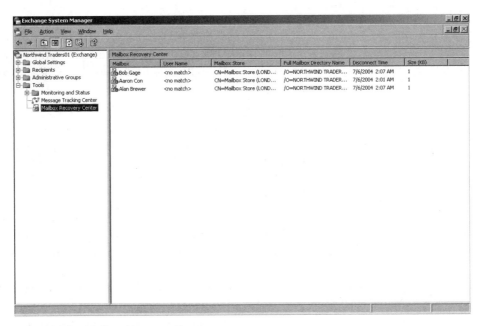

Figure 10-7   Mailbox Recovery Center

4. To allow a user to access the mailbox, perform one of following tasks to reconnect the mailbox:

   a. To associate a user with a mailbox, right-click the mailbox that you want to match to a user (or group), and then click Find Match.
   If a mailbox matches more than one user (or if no match exists), right-click the mailbox, and then click Resolve Conflicts. Follow the instructions in the Mailbox Conflict Resolution Wizard to identify a single matching user.

   b. To reconnect the mailbox, select the mailbox, right-click the selected mailbox, and then click Reconnect.

5. When you have finished reconnecting mailboxes, remove the mailbox stores from the Mailbox Recovery Center.

Managing E-Mail Retention

Similar to managing storage limits using Exchange system policies, managing recipient policies can be accomplished using e-mail retention policies.

   Recipient policies are policies that you apply to recipient objects such as users, groups, contacts, and folders. These policies can control how e-mail addresses are configured for recipient objects and also enforce e-mail retention by using the Mailbox Manager Settings to define the action that the Mailbox Manager takes when processing mailboxes and folders that contain messages that exceed policy limits. Mailbox Manager actions include generating reports on mailboxes containing messages that exceed policy limits, moving messages that exceed policy limits to the Deleted Items folder or the System Cleanup folder, and immediately deleting messages that exceed policy limits. You can use the settings to define whether Exchange will send e-mail messages to users after their mailboxes are processed. You can also exclude specific message classes from deletion.

> **More Info**   For more information about using recipient policies to manage e-mail addresses, see Chapter 9, "Managing Directory Information."

Unlike system policies, mailbox recipient policies are not necessarily linked to servers or stores. As a result, you can use recipient policies to simplify administration regardless of the number of Exchange servers, mailbox stores, and public folder stores that you have in your organization.

Use mailbox recipient policies to apply mailbox management settings to Active Directory mailbox-enabled user objects. For example, suppose that your organization defines its employee job titles in Active Directory. You want to configure Exchange to purge the Deleted Items folder of all purchasing employees when items in the Deleted Items folder are 60 days old. To do so, you create a recipient policy that queries Active Directory for users whose job title is equal to Purchasing and then configure the policy to purge deleted items that are 60 days old (Figure 10-8).

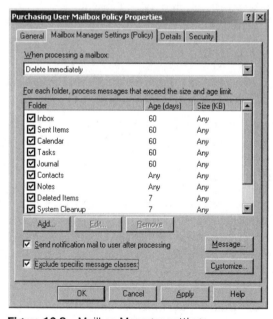

Figure 10-8   Mailbox Manager settings

Mailbox Recipient policies are created in the Recipient Policies container using Exchange System Manager. When you create a mailbox recipient policy:

1. You define the membership of the policy by defining search filters to specify the membership of the recipient policy.

2. You then select the mailbox folders that the policy will monitor, as well as the age and size limits for messages in those folders.

3. You apply the mailbox recipient policy by right-clicking the recipient policy that you want to apply and then clicking Apply this policy now.

4. You must then schedule when you want Mailbox Manager to clean mailboxes affected by the policy by using the Mailbox Management tab on each server that the policy will affect.

Recipient Update Service is responsible for managing the mailbox membership of the policy. When a new mailbox recipient policy is created, Recipient Update Service assigns a unique ID to member mailboxes. This ID associates the mailboxes to the policy, which is how Mailbox Manager knows which mailbox recipient policy to apply to a given mailbox. If the mailbox recipient policy membership is modified, the Apply this policy now command immediately associates new mailboxes to the policy without waiting for Recipient Update Service to run. The member mailboxes are not updated by Recipient Update Service until the next time that it runs, at which time the membership is updated.

> **Note**   Only one mailbox recipient policy can be applied to each user. If you have more than one mailbox recipient policy, you must ensure that policy membership does not overlap. If two mailbox recipient policies are applied to the same user, the priority of the policies determines which is used and only the higher policy is applied.

Monitoring Mailbox Resources

When a new mailbox is created, the mailbox is not immediately accessible. Although Active Directory attributes for the mailbox are configured immediately, the attributes for the mailbox in the Exchange store are not configured completely until the mailbox has been initialized, either by the owner of the mailbox accessing the mailbox for the first time or when a message is sent to the mailbox. After the mailbox is initialized, you can use Exchange System Manager to monitor mailbox statistics.

> **Tip**   You might want to send new e-mail users an introductory message automatically after their accounts are configured to ensure that the mailbox is initialized.

From the mailboxes node of the mailbox store in Exchange System Manager (Figure 10-9), you can monitor the following items by default:

■ Who last accessed a mailbox.

■ How many items are in the mailbox.

■ The last time a user logged on to a mailbox.

■ The last time a user logged off from a mailbox.

You can add additional columns to your view to be able to monitor deleted items and storage limits, as well as other columns.

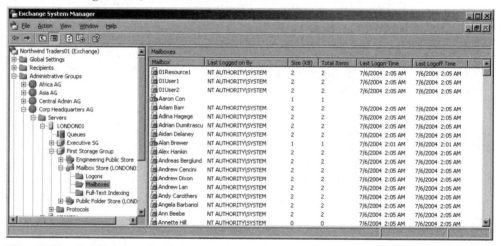

Figure 10-9   Monitoring mailboxes by using the mailboxes node

You can also use Microsoft Exchange Server 2003 Management Pack for Microsoft Operations Manager (MOM) 2000 to automate the monitoring and reporting of your mailbox statistics. The Exchange Server 2003 Management Pack contains a series of report collection rules. The rules run scripts to collect information for Exchange 2003 reports. They include the following rule groups for monitoring mailbox statistics:

■ **Mailbox Statistics Analysis**   These rules run once a night to collect information about the number of items and the size of the largest 100 mailboxes.

- **Mailboxes Per Server Analysis** This rule collects information about the number of mailboxes in each database for use by an Exchange report.

- **MAPI Logon Check and Availability Reporting**   These rules check whether the Exchange store can be accessed by doing a logon using MAPI. The resulting data is used to alert administrators of problems, as well as for a server availability report.

More Info For more information about using MOM to monitor Exchange 2003, see Chapter 17, "Exchange Server 2003 Management Pack."

Managing Public Folder Resources

Public folder management tasks include managing public folder trees, public folder permissions, and public folder replication. You create and manage public folders by using either Exchange System Manager or Outlook, but to have full control over the creation and management of public folders, you must use Exchange System Manager.

A public folder is a repository for different types of information, such as e-mail messages, text documents, and multimedia files, which can be shared with users who are in an Exchange organization, as well as with NNTP and Hypertext Transfer Protocol (HTTP) users who are outside of the Exchange organization.

The public folder structure is made up of a series of components. Public folders are contained in public folder stores. Each mail-enabled public folder has a directory entry in the Active Directory directory service. The public folder listing that is viewed by the client (for example, Outlook) is arranged in a tree structure that is called a public folder tree (also referred to as a hierarchy). Any public folder that contains subfolders is referred to as a parent folder. The public folders that are contained in a parent folder are referred to as child folders. Public folders that are created at the root of a public folder tree are referred to as top-level folders.

Public Folder Trees

There are two types of public folder trees: the default public folder tree and general-purpose public folder trees.

- The default public folder tree, also referred to as the MAPI public folder tree, is the public folder tree that is automatically created by the Setup program when you install the first Exchange server. The default public folder tree is listed in Exchange System Manager as Public Folders and it is displayed in Outlook as All Public Folders. The default public folder tree contains the list of all public folders that are within the tree. However, the default public folder tree does not contain the content of the folders themselves.

The default public folder tree is replicated to each Exchange server that contains a public folder store that is associated with that tree. As a result, users with mailboxes on different servers can easily browse the public folder hierarchy. By default, this public folder tree is replicated to every public folder server in an Exchange organization. Only one MAPI public folder tree can exist in an Exchange organization.

■   General-purpose public folder trees are the additional public folder trees that you can create. Similar to the default public folder tree, a general-purpose public folder tree is replicated to each server running Exchange 2003 that contains a public folder store associated with that tree. As a result, you can create additional public folder trees that are replicated to selected public folder servers in the Exchange organization.

    You can use a general-purpose public folder tree when you want to store custom applications. You can use separate general-purpose public folder trees to store custom collaboration applications according to the functional, business, or geographic requirements of your users. For example, you can use one tree to store a personnel department application and another tree to store a research and development application.

Accessing Different Public Folder Tree Types

Different types of clients have access to different types of public folder trees. Table 10-3 shows the supported client access for each tree.

Table 10-3   Public Folder Tree Client Access

Tree type	Support for client access
Default public folder tree	MAPI clients, such as Microsoft Office Outlook
	NNTP clients, such as Microsoft Outlook Express
	HTTP clients, such as Internet Explorer
General-purpose public folder trees	NNTP clients, such as Outlook Express
	HTTP clients, such as Internet Explorer

Because general-purpose public folder trees do not support MAPI clients, general-purpose public folder trees that you create are accessible only to your Outlook users when they use the Folder Home Page feature in Outlook. Additionally, to allow users to access a general-purpose public folder tree from a browser, you must implement an HTTP virtual server or HTTP virtual directory under the Protocols node for the server that holds the new store by using Exchange System Manager.

Note   Initially HTTP virtual servers and virtual directories are created using Exchange System Manager; however, settings such as enabling protocol logging on a virtual server are configured through Microsoft Internet Information Services (IIS) Manager.

More Info   For more information about creating virtual directories in Exchange 2003, see Chapter 12, "Maintaining IIS Virtual Servers."

Configuring Public Folder Permissions

Public folder permissions are the permissions that control the creation, management, and use of public folders and their contents. Permissions are either obtained through inheritance or are assigned by the administrator. When a MAPI public folder is created, the creator of the folder is assigned the role of Owner, Default is assigned the role of Author, and Anonymous is assigned the role of Contributor.

Public Folder Inheritance

A public folder inherits its permissions from parent objects. For example, a top-level folder inherits permissions from the administrative group and the Exchange organization. Similarly, a child folder inherits permissions from its parent folder in the public folder tree.

Child folders only inherit parent folder settings at the time at which they are created. Changes that you make to the parent folder are not automatically inherited by existing child folders. Therefore, if you want the client permission changes that you make to a parent folder to be applied to all of the existing child folders in the public folder tree, you must propagate the permissions to the child folders by choosing to propagate the folder rights from the context menu of the parent folder in the folder tree. Additionally, any changes that you make specifically to a child folder will be lost if you choose to propagate those settings from the parent folder. It is recommended that you configure permissions on parent folders before any child folders are created, so that child folders inherit the appropriated permissions.

Assigning Public Folder Permissions

As a messaging administrator, when you create a public folder, you need to assign permissions that specify the individual users or security groups that will have the rights to perform designated activities in that folder. You can assign both client access permissions and administrative rights to the folder.

There are three categories of permissions for public folders in Exchange, as shown in Table 10-4.

Table 10-4 Categories of Public Folder Permissions

Permission	Description
Client Permissions	Enables you to control the permissions of the users who are accessing the public folder. For example, you can control who has read/write permissions on a public folder.
Directory Rights	Enables you to control which users can manipulate a mail-enabled public folder object that is stored in Active Directory.
Administrative Rights	Enables you to assign specific administrative permissions to specific administrators. For example, you might want to grant only three of the 10 administrators at your company the rights to replicate certain sensitive public folders. Administrative rights are inherited by child folders from their administrative group. Administrative rights applied to a folder are not inherited by child folders by default, but can be propagated to child folders.

By default, client permissions for folders in the default public folder tree are displayed as MAPI permissions for both a MAPI client and for an administrator using Exchange System Manager. An administrator can see Windows-compatible permissions by holding down the Ctrl key and clicking on Client Permissions. Similar to mailbox permissions, MAPI client permissions are managed by using roles. A role is essentially a permissions template that grants to clients the permissions that they need to access folders and folder items.

Permissions for folders in a general-purpose public folder tree are not role-based and are displayed as Windows-compatible permissions.

Figure 10-10 shows an example MAPI permissions on a folder in the default public folder tree and Windows-compatible permissions on a folder in a general-purpose public folder tree.

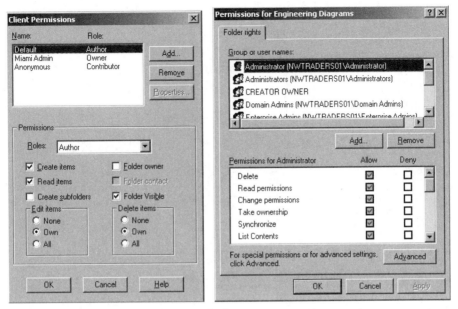

Figure 10-10 Public folder client permissions

Client permissions are applied to a user based on the following rules:

- If the user is explicitly granted permissions to the public folder, only those granted permissions are applied to the user.

- If the user is a member of a security group that has permission to the public folder, the user's permissions are the least restrictive of either the group permissions or the default permissions for the public folder.

- If the user is a member of multiple security groups that have permission to the public folder, client permissions for each of the security groups of which the user is a member are compared to determine the most restrictive. The result is then compared to the default permissions for the public folder. The least restrictive of the client permissions are applied to the user.

You can configure specific administrative rights to a folder by selecting the Administrative Rights option on the folders' Permissions tab (Figure 10-11).

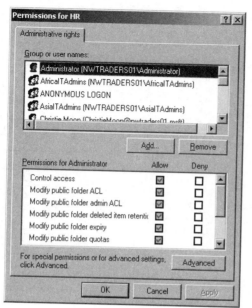

Figure 10-11   Public folder administrative rights

More Info   For more information about permissions in Exchange 2003, see the book "Working with Store Permissions in Microsoft Exchange 2000 and 2003" (*http://www.microsoft.com/technet/prodtechnol/exchange/2003/library/storperm.mspx*).

Public Folder Replication

By default, when you create a public folder, only one copy of the public folder content exists within the Exchange organization. Public folder content can exist in an Exchange organization either as a single copy or as multiple copies.

Public folder replication is process of keeping copies of public folders on other servers up to date and synchronized with each other. Public folder replication is an e-mail-based process. Replication messages are sent by using the same protocols and connectors as any other e-mail message that is sent on your network. The only difference is that that Exchange treats replication messages as system messages. This means that replication messages are not bound by the typical restrictions that are applied to user e-mail messages, such as size and delivery restrictions.

Exchange uses a multimaster replication model. A replica copied from one server to another is a separate instance of a public folder and its content. All replicas of a public folder are equal and contain exactly the same content. There is no master replica, which means that modifications to any replica are replicated to other replicas equally.

Understanding Replication Components and Replication Services

Different components of public folder replication are controlled by different services:

- The Exchange Information Store service controls the replication of public folder trees (hierarchy). Each public folder server that contains a public folder store that is associated with a given public folder tree will maintain a replica of that tree.

- The Exchange Information Store service controls the replication of the content of the public folders. Content is considered to be the message headers, message body, and any attachments. A messaging administrator controls the destination and frequency of the replication of public folder content.

- Active Directory replication (not Exchange public folder replication) controls the replication of mail-enabled public folder directory objects. Mail-enabled public folder directory objects are replicated to domain controllers and global catalog servers in the same way that user accounts are replicated.

The overall process of public folder replication within Exchange can be divided into four processes:

- **Hierarchy replication**   Hierarchy replication is the replication of the public folder tree, which contains the Folder ID (FID) for all of the folders in the tree; and the folder properties, such as MAPI public folder permissions, replica list, and age and storage limits, to all of the associated public folder stores that are in the Exchange organization. A hierarchy replication message is generated whenever the hierarchy is modified to replicate the modification to all associated public folder stores. Hierarchy modification includes: creating, deleting, or renaming a folder; modifying folder permissions or descriptions; changing the replication schedule and priority settings; adding content to or removing content from a folder; modifying replica lists; and moving the folder in the hierarchy.

  In Exchange 2003, you can push or initiate hierarchy replication between specific servers in Exchange System Manager by selecting the Send Hierarchy option from the public folder hierarchy. You can specify specific source servers to send the hierarchy to specific target servers, and you can specify the number of days of changes that are pushed between servers. This is helpful when you are troubleshooting public folder hierarchy replication issues.

Note The range of changes to replicate starts with the number of days in the past that you specify and ends at the last replication cycle. For example, you can replicate all changes made over the past two days, except for any changes made during the past 15 minutes (the default replication interval).

- **Content replication**   Content replication is the replication of the data contained in the public folder between public folder replicas. When the data contained in a replica is modified, system messages are generated to replicate the changes to other replicas that the administrator identifies.

    In Exchange 2003, you can also use Exchange System Manager to push the public folder content from one server to another using the Send Content option from the public folder. This is useful when you are troubleshooting public folder replication.

Note Manual replication (hierarchy and content) affects only changes that should already have replicated at least one time. Changes made after the last replication message was sent are not included.

- **Backfill replication**   Backfill replication refers to the process that enables public folder stores that have missed updates to become synchronized with other stores. Backfill replication occurs when a store is determined to be out of sync after it exchanges status information with other stores. You can view that replication of a specific public folder by using the Replication tab in the right pane of Exchange System Manager.

- **Content conflict resolution**   A content conflict occurs when two users edit the same item on different servers before the item is synchronized. There are two types of content conflicts: message edit conflicts and folder edit conflicts:

- **Message edit conflict**   A message edit conflict occurs when two or more users modify the content or the properties of the same message stored in a replica before the message is synchronized, and save the modifications to the same original message. A conflict resolution message is generated and sent to the folder contact, who then chooses to keep one or both messages.

- **Folder edit conflict**   A folder edit conflict occurs when two or more public folder contacts or owners change a public folder design before the folder is synchronized. When a public folder design is changed before the folder is synchronized, the last design is saved, overriding all previous changes.

Determining When to Replicate Public Folders

By replicating public folders you can provide fault tolerance and load balancing to your shared data. There are several reasons to replicate public folders in your environment:

- Public folder replication provides fault tolerance for your public folders by providing additional copies of the public folder content. A failure of a single public folder server will not prevent access to the folder content.

- Public folder replication provides load balancing to your network. With multiple replicas, public folder traffic is distributed across multiple servers.

- Public folder replication minimizes client traffic across the wide area network (WAN). You replicate public folders to servers in remote locations, so these users can access a local replica instead of having to cross the WAN to access a public folder. Accessing a local replica can significantly reduce the traffic on your network.

Depending on the nature of the public folder, you might not want to replicate a particular public folder. For example, you might have a public folder that contains time sensitive customer data that the users in your organization rely on to make business decisions. To give confidence to your users that the information that is contained in the public folder is completely up-to-date, you should consider not replicating that particular public folder, as any replication process will have some amount of replication latency. In this situation, you might need to upgrade the physical network links to ensure better access across your network.

When you consider replicating a public folder, you should also weigh network traffic against client traffic. A folder that contains constantly changing information, such as a newsgroup downloaded from an external site, is probably not a good candidate for replication. Replicating such a public folder could result in more network traffic than simply allowing users to access it across the WAN.

Figure 10-12 provides guidelines for determining when to replicate public folders.

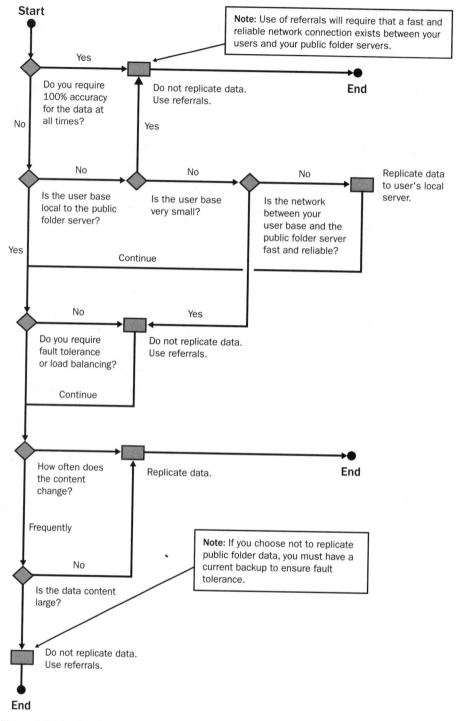

Figure 10-12   Public folder replication guidelines

Creating Public Folder Replicas

Public folders are not replicated automatically. You must use a public folder's Replication property tab (Figure 10-13) to configure which stores contain replicas of the folder and how frequently replication occurs.

■ To add or remove replicas, use the Add or Remove buttons in the Replicate content to these public stores section of the Replication tab to specify the public folder stores that will keep replicas of the folder.

■ Determine the replication schedule for the folder. By default, folders in a specific public folder store replicate according to the store's schedule. If you have several folders that must replicate more frequently or less frequently than others, you can set a specific replication schedule for those folders on the folder's Replication tab.

■ If you want replication messages from the public folder to be delivered to the target public folder store with a higher priority than other replication messages received by the target public folder store, set the replication message priority setting on the folder's Replication tab.

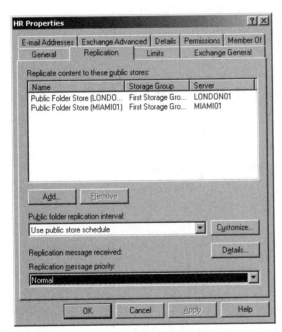

Figure 10-13   Public folder Replication tab

Client Access to Public Folders

When a client attempts to access public folder data, the client must be able to connect to a server that contains a replica of that data. Such a server can be either in the same routing group as the client or in a different routing group from the client. To maximize efficiency, the client attempts a connection to servers in the following order:

1. If the public folder is located on the user account's default public folder store, the client is directed to this store for the public folder contents. The default public folder store is defined on the General tab in the Properties dialog box of the mailbox store for the user account.

2. If the public folder server where the public folder store resides is in the same routing group as the user's default public folder server, the client is sent to this public folder server.

3. If there is not a copy of the public folder contents in the local routing group, the public folder store initiates the process of calculating the lowest-cost route to another server in the organization that has a copy of this public folder.

    For a client to be able to access a replica on a remote server in a routing group that is different from the one to which the client belongs, the connector between the routing groups must be configured to allow public folder referrals. You can enable public folder referrals by using either one of the following methods:

    - Implement and configure a connector between two routing groups. The connector is unidirectional and requires that you configure two instances for bidirectional traffic. You can configure public folder referrals for the routing group going in each direction. Public folder referrals are enabled by default.

    - Provide a public folder store with a referral list. Exchange then forces the client to choose a store only from the referral list.

> **Note**   These two methods for enabling public folder referrals are mutually exclusive. You cannot use both methods at the same time.

4. If no public folder replica exists in the local routing group, or in the routing groups that allow public folder referrals, the client will not be able to view the contents of the requested public folder.

Viewing System Folders by Using Exchange System Manager

System folders (also referred to as the NON_IPM_SUBTREE) are not accessed by users directly. Client applications such as Outlook use these folders to store information such as free/busy data, offline address lists, and organizational forms. Other system folders hold configuration information that is used by custom applications or by Exchange itself. The Public Folders tree contains extra system folders, such as the EFORMS REGISTRY folder, that do not exist in general-purpose public folder trees.

By default, Exchange System Manager displays public folders instead of system folders. You can display system folders (Figure 10-14) by right-clicking the Public Folders object, and then clicking View System Folders.

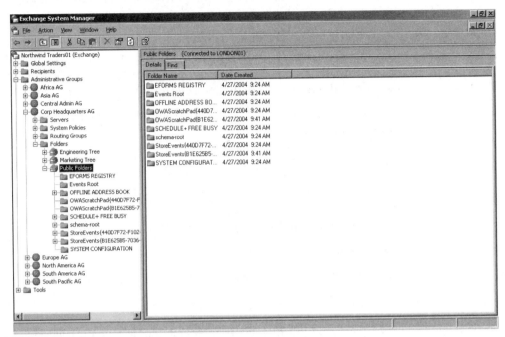

Figure 10-14   Exchange system folders

You will need to view system folders in order to replicate any of the folders to other servers.

Indexing Public Folders

Exchange 2003 supports full-text indexing (also referred to as content indexing). When you enable full-text indexing for a public folder store, users have the ability to quickly search all of the contents in the store and locate the specific piece of information that they need. You can configure full-text indexing by using Exchange System Manager.

Note   Full-text indexing can be enabled on mailbox stores also, but this is not recommended because full-text indexing is resource intensive, and mailbox data changes frequently. Therefore, keeping an up-to-date index of a given database is a very resource intensive process. Full-text indexing is better suited for public folders.

The benefits of using full-text indexing include the following:

- Individual store configuration. This feature enables you to configure each store individually. This includes the ability to determine which store to index and what the index settings, such as the update interval, should be.

- Faster searching (logarithmic search performance). The default search is similar to searching an entire book for a word. Full-text indexing is comparable to looking for a word in an index in the back of a book and then going directly to the location in the book where that word is found.

- Searching of attachments. By default, only the following types of attachments can be searched:

    - Microsoft Word (.doc)

    - Microsoft Excel (.xls)

    - Microsoft PowerPoint (.ppt)

    - Hypertext Markup Language (HTML) (.html, .htm, .asp)

    - Text files (.txt)

    - Embedded MIME Messages (.eml)

Note   Microsoft provides filters to search the attachments listed above. To search other types of attachments, third-party filters, such as the PDF filter provided by Adobe, are required.

- Search results include related words, as determined by the word-breaker for the language. For example, word-breaker considers "tester," "tested," and "tests" equivalent, but considers "testament" equivalent only to "testaments."

Tip   With full-text indexing, pattern-matching does not work. Instead, you can only search for whole words. For example, if you search for "test," you will not find "testament." Additionally, you cannot perform a search by using wildcard characters (for example, replacing a character with an asterisk).

Consider the following issues when you decide whether or not to use full-text indexing:

- The time involved in building the index and the CPU usage can be considerable.

- The amount of space that the index occupies can be considerable. The index occupies roughly 20 percent of the hard disk space of the data being indexed. For example, the index corresponding to a five-gigabyte (GB) database occupies 1 GB of disk space. The actual size of your index depends on the types of files that you store and the type of items being indexed. For example, when users post items to multiple newsgroups, the items are stored only once in the database, but they are indexed multiple times. This can cause the size of the index to exceed the size of the database.

- Incomplete search results are possible if users are searching by using an index that is currently being populated. You can avoid incomplete search results by specifying that the index cannot be used until it is finished populating. To disable searching of the index, clear the This index is currently available for searching by clients check box. Also, search results are only as accurate as the last time the index was updated.

Creating and Populating Full-Text Indexes

Before you create full-text indexes on your Exchange server, you must set the server language correctly. Full-text indexing references the server language that is specified in Control Panel when breaking words and stemming (a process that allows a search for "travel" to return "travels," "traveled," and "traveling"). Full-text indexing works best when the query language of the client computer matches the language of the files that are being indexed. The server language is sometimes used for the query language when the client computer language is unknown, so it is best for the server language to match the language of most of the documents on the server.

> **Tip**   If your environment supports multiple languages, consider partitioning Exchange data across servers based on the content language of the documents to provide better control over the time it takes to populate the index. For example, populating an index on a server containing documents written mostly in East Asian languages can take more than five times longer than for a server containing documents that are written in Western languages.

Once you have determined that your server language settings are correct, you can use Exchange System Manager to create an initial index (catalog) for each public folder (or mailbox) store that you want to index. This process will create the required file structure, which you modify when you are optimizing the index. To create the initial full-text index, right click the public folder store that you want to index, and then click Create Full-Text Index.

After you create the index, you must run a full population (also referred to as a crawl) to fill the index with data. To start a full population of the index, right-click the public folder store that you want to index, and then click Start Full Population.

> **Note**   You should ensure that full-text searches are unavailable during full population to prevent users from performing searches on incomplete indexes and receiving unexpected results. You can disable searches for the public folder store from the Full-Text Indexing tab of the public folder store object.

The initial full population can take a long time. Hardware, type and size of messages, and the content language of the documents being indexed all have an impact on the time required to fully populate the index. With a typical Exchange Server 2003 configuration, population performance typically ranges from 10 to 20 messages per second.

You can view the status of the population process by viewing the Full-Text Indexing node of the public folder store. During the initial population, the status is Crawling. You can determine if the population is complete by looking at this status or by looking in Event Viewer for Microsoft Search service messages.

Once the index has been initially populated, you can configure a schedule which will run incremental populations to update the index. It is a good idea to schedule incremental population at least one time daily (more frequently if your environment requires it). The schedule for the incremental population determines only when the population process can start. It does not put a time limit on the population process. Therefore, it is possible that an incremental population will continue to completion outside the scheduled time. You configure incremental updates by configuring the Update Interval on the Full-Text Indexing tab for a store object.

There will be times when a new full population will be required. You must fully populate the index in the following cases:

- When a word-breaker is changed. A word-breaker is used by full-text indexing to identify where individual words start and end in a particular text.
- When noise words are changed. For information about changing noise words, see "Customizing Full-Text Indexing" in the Microsoft Exchange Server 2003 SDK Documentation (*http://go.microsoft.com/fwlink/?LinkId=25925*).
- When new document format filters are added.
- When the schema file is changed.
- When the Simple Mail Transfer Protocol (SMTP) address of the store changes.
- When you perform disaster recovery.

Locating Full-Text Indexing Files

By default, all of the full-text indexing files are stored in the Exchsrvr\ *ExchangeServer_servername* directory on the drive on which you have Exchange installed. However, you can optimize the performance of full-text indexing by relocating these files to more appropriate storage locations. Table 10-5 explains the various file types, their recommended locations, and the relocation methods.

Table 10-5   Full-Text Indexing Files

File type	Description	Recommended location	How to specify the location
Catalog	The main index. There is only one catalog for each mailbox store or public folder store in Exchange.	RAID array	Use Exchange System Manager to specify its location. If the index was already created elsewhere, move it by using the Catutil tool, which is located in the Program Files\Common Files\System\MSSearch\Bin directory.
Property store	A database containing various properties of items indexed in the catalog. There is only one property store per server.	RAID array	Use the Pstoreutl tool, which is located in the Program Files\Common Files\System\MSSearch\Bin directory.
Property store logs	Log files that are associated with the property store database.	RAID array in the same location as the property store.	Use the Pstoreutl tool, which is located in the Program Files\Common Files\System\MSSearch\Bin directory.
Temporary files	Files containing temporary information that is used by the Microsoft Search service (MSSearch).	RAID array. If using a cluster, place these files on a drive that will not fail over, such as a local drive.	Use the SetTmpPath tool located in the Program Files\Common Files\System\MSSearch\Bin directory.
Gather logs	Log files containing log information for the indexing service. One set of logs exists for each index.	Leave in the default location, or move to any location that you prefer.	Assign the location in the StreamLogsDirectory registry key.

More Info   For more information about configuring and troubleshooting full-text indexing in Exchange 2003, see the book "Exchange Server 2003 Administration Guide" (*http://www.microsoft.com/technet/prodtechnol/exchange/2003/library/admingde.mspx*) and the book "Working with the Exchange Server 2003 Store" (*http://www.microsoft.com/technet/prodtechnol/exchange/2003/library/default.mspx*).

Monitoring Public Folder Resources

Public folder can be monitored using Exchange System Manager. The most common task for monitoring public folder is monitoring the replication status of a folder.

Viewing Folder Status

To view updated information about a specific public folder's replication status, use the Replication tab in the right pane of Exchange System Manager (Figure 10-15). The Replication tab lists the servers that hold content replicas of the specific public folder, the replication status of each server, the last time a replication message was received, and the average transmission time.

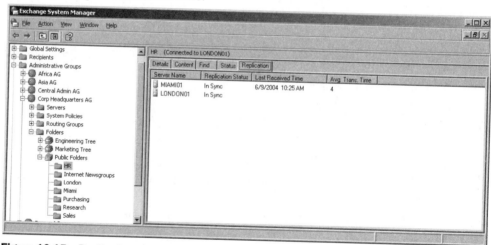

Figure 10-15   Replication status

Note   You can see the same information by clicking Details on the Replication tab of the folder's Properties dialog box.

From either the public folders node under the public folder store object in Exchange System Manager or from the Status tab (Figure 10-16) of the public folder object, you can monitor the following items:

- The size of the public folder.

- The number of items in the public folder.

- The last time the public folder was accessed.

- The last time the public folder replica was updated.

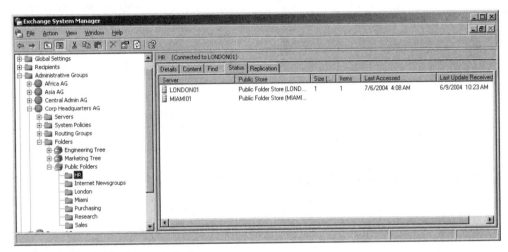

Figure 10-16   Public folder statistics

If you are using public folders node under the public folder store object to monitor public folders, you can add additional columns to your view to be able to monitor deleted items, number of contacts, and number of owners, as well as other columns.

Viewing Folder Content

You can use Exchange System Manager to view the actual content of public folders. You do this though Outlook Web Access integration with Exchange System Manager. Use the Content tab in the right pane of Exchange System Manager (Figure 10-17). You will be prompted with a logon box before you can view the content.

Automating Monitoring Tasks

You can also automate the monitoring and reporting of your public folder statistics. The Exchange Server 2003 Management Pack includes the following rule group for monitoring public folder statistics:

- **Public Folder Statistics Analysis**   These rules run once a night to collect information about the number of items and the size of the largest 100 public folders. These rules require an account named *<server>*MOM to be configured on each server to be monitored.

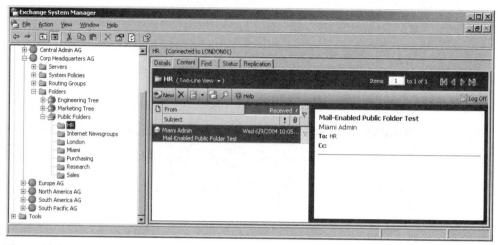

Figure 10-17   Public folder content

Configuring Dedicated Servers

Although each server running Exchange Server frequently performs several roles in a smaller organization or in a remote office, it is often preferable to dedicate servers to perform specific roles. This is especially true in medium to large companies.

Distributing functions among several different servers enables you to provide faster response time and reduced downtime. Distributing roles also helps prevent servers from becoming overloaded, and removes the dependencies between services. Dividing server roles provides additional flexibility in determining server placement, whether your Exchange organization manages its servers from a central data center or from regional offices.

When using dedicated servers, consider the following when determining how to configure the servers:

- The role of the server in the Exchange organization. For example, a mailbox server will require more hard disk space than a bridgehead server.

- The expected workload that the server will perform. For example, if your company has 50 users, less hardware or smaller servers would be required to handle the workload and meet performance requirements than if your company has 5,000 users.

- The location of servers on the network. For example, users can access their mailboxes locally, or they can access their mailboxes from a centralized data center across a WAN.

Planning Server Roles

Each role that a server running Exchange performs has design considerations that you should take into account. You need to consider each server role, not only Exchange-specific roles but also Active Directory server roles. Server roles can include:

- Mailbox servers.

- Public folder servers.

- Front-end servers control access for POP3, IMAP4, and HTTP users by separating authentication traffic from data access traffic.

- Connector and bridgehead servers for message routing.

- Domain controller and global catalog servers for authentication and directory lookup.

- Domain Name System (DNS) and Windows Internet Name Service (WINS) servers for name resolution.

When determining server roles for your Exchange organization, you must take into consideration the business requirements and goals of your messaging system. For example, a company that heavily uses public folders might want to dedicate a server to be a public folder server to localize the impact of public folder searches. A company that wants to expose a single, consistent namespace for their Internet clients might implement a front-end and back-end server topology. Another company might provide high availability by separating the domain controller role from the Exchange server, thereby allowing users to authenticate for access to network resources even if the Exchange server fails.

Dedicated Mailbox and Public Folder Servers

Depending on your business requirements and your budget, you may create dedicated mailbox and public folder servers or decide to combine this role with other server roles.

When designing mailbox and public folder servers, you need to understand:

- The impact on your budget of deploying dedicated server roles for mailboxes and public folder servers. Dedicated servers will provide a single function, thus requiring that more servers be deployed than when you deploy combined server roles. If dedicated servers are used to consolidate multiple mailbox and public folder servers into a single server, the reduction in the number of servers requires investing in high-end servers, including high-performance processors and servers with multiple processors.

- The impact on your service level agreements. Larger servers typically take longer to back up and restore. Larger servers require that you create storage groups and stores to reduce the time required to back up groups of mailboxes or public folders, which in turn will allow you to meet your service level agreements.

A dedicated mailbox server would perform no other function in the Exchange organization other than to host user mailboxes. To configure a dedicated mailbox server:

1. Associate a new public folder store with any mailbox stores that point to the public folder store that you are removing.

2. Replicate any system folders that are maintained by the local public folder store to another server.

3. If the server stores an offline address list, select a new server for the address list.

4. Replicate to another server any public folders that have their sole replicas in public folder stores on the server.

5. Once public folder replicas exist on other servers, remove the public folder store from the server.

6. Remove the public folder database files from the server's hard drive.

A dedicated public folder server would perform no other function in the Exchange organization other than to host public folders. To configure a dedicated public folder server:

1. Move any mailboxes that are on mailbox stores on the server to mailbox stores on another server.

2. Once there is no mailbox on the mailbox store, remove the mailbox store from the server.

3. Remove the mailbox database files from the server's hard drive.

Planning Server Sizing

The number of users and public folders that each server can support depends primarily on the usage profile for each user. When planning for mailbox and public folder server sizes, your primary consideration should be storage and storage capacity. The amount of storage required for mailbox and public folder servers is influenced by:

- Default storage limit on mailboxes and public folders.
- Data retention policies.
- Deleted item retention policies.
- Backup requirements.

As a general rule, use the following formula to calculate the amount of data that you can store on a single server:

(Number of mailboxes × maximum size of mailbox limit) × % of pad

The pad amount is a percentage of storage not accounted for in the mailbox size limit, such as storage for deleted items.

To accurately plan your server size, you should complete these three steps:

- Determine the usage profile.

  Usage profiles define how your users use e-mail and enable you to select server hardware based on the demand on the CPU and disk subsystem. E-mail usage can be broken down into the following categories:

  - Heavy e-mail users whose jobs depend heavily on e-mail.

  - Medium e-mail users whose jobs depend heavily on e-mail but who might also use mobile devices.

  - Light e-mail users who typically have small mailbox quotas.

  - Very light e-mail users who typically use POP3 clients and have small mailbox quotas.

- Select hardware and calculate if the hardware (CPU and disk) is adequate for the usage profile.

  Usage profiles enable you to calculate how many users a server can support based on CPU usage and disk I/O. Once you understand your usage profile, you can calculate your CPU and disk subsystem requirements. Use the System Monitor tool to monitor the Processor\% Processor Time and Physical Disk\Disk Transfers/sec counter over the peak two hours of server activity to determine the usage profile of your users.

- Validate the performance of the disk subsystem.

  Because Exchange performance is dependent on the performance of the disk subsystem that you choose, you must validate your disk subsystem capacity. Test the throughput of the hardware to ensure that it meets your requirements by using a tool such as Jetstress tool (jetstress.exe) to simulate database read/write access.

More Info For more information about sizing Exchange 2003 servers, see the book "Exchange Server 2003 Performance and Scalability Guide" (*http://www.microsoft.com/technet/prodtechnol/exchange/2003/library/ perfscalguide.mspx*).

Planning Server Location

Where to place Exchange servers depends on whether your messaging system is centralized or distributed.

Mailbox Servers

For remote locations connected by slow or unreliable network connections, you must determine how interruptions in service affect business and to what extent interruptions are acceptable. If access to updated Exchange data is critical at all times, you must place Exchange servers in your company's remote locations. If, after weighing the costs of deploying additional servers against cost savings of a more centralized model, you decide that a certain level of service interruption is acceptable, you might be able to deploy all Exchange servers in a data center. If you deploy Microsoft Office Outlook 2003 in the remote locations, by default your remote users will use cached mode and any problems with connectivity or performance across the link will be minimized.

Public Folder Servers

If your organization is comprised of multiple remote locations, you can place public folder replicas on local Exchange servers so that each location has a replica of public folders from other locations. Alternatively, you might want to consider storing all public folder information in a central server in the data center or hub so that you maintain a single, accurate source of data. This decision is based on the balance between accuracy and convenience and depends on user requirements and usage patterns.

System folders need to be considered when planning the location of public folder server.

- **Free/busy servers** Consider how users in your organization schedule meetings when you plan free/busy server placement. If it is critical that users always have access to up-to-date scheduling information, you must host free/busy folders in a centralized location. If the need for up-to-date information is not as critical as the need for fast access, you can deploy local Exchange servers to host free/busy information. Recognize, however, that delays in receiving updated free/busy information over the network might occur. You should determine what level of delay is acceptable to your business.

- **Offline address list servers** Exchange uses Active Directory to provide offline address list services. The address list files that Exchange generates are stored in a public folder. Users working offsite can connect to Exchange and download these offline address lists remotely to retrieve information about other users in the organization.

  When you generate an offline address list, address lists specified for the offline address list are converted to several sets of files and stored in a system public folder. When Exchange generates offline address book files, it attaches the files to e-mail messages and places the messages in special public folders. Outlook retrieves the messages from the folder and downloads the attached files. Exchange supports several different formats for the offline address book:

■ **OAB Version 1** If the offline address book is configured with the Exchange 4.0 and 5.0 compatibility option, Exchange generates a set of files in the offline address book version 1 format (OAB Version 1). The DOS, Windows 16 bit, and Exchange 4.0 clients use OAB Version 1 information. This information is not used with Outlook clients.

■ **OAB Version 2** For non-Unicode (ANSI) clients, Exchange generates files in the offline address book version 2 format (OAB Version 2). These files are attached to messages in the OAB Version 2 folder. All Outlook clients can use these files.

■ **OAB Version 3a** For Unicode Outlook clients, Exchange 2003 generates files in the offline address book version 3a (OAB Version 3a) format. These files are attached to messages in the OAB Version 3a folder. Outlook 2003 clients can use these files.

Table 10-6 lists the files that Exchange 2003 generates for the different offline address book formats.

Table 10-6   Table 10-6   Files Generated for Offline Address Books

ANSI OAB Version 1 (root folder)	ANSI OAB Version 2	Unicode OAB Version 3a	Description
Browse.oab	Browse2.oab	Browse2_u.oab	This file keeps the pointers to the data in the other .oab files.
Details.oab	Details2.oab	Details2_u.oab	This file contains the details records. You cannot customize the attributes included in the details records. Outlook users can specify whether to download the details file by selecting the Full Details option in Outlook.
Rndex.oab	Rndex2.oab	Rndex2_u.oab	Outlook uses this index when looking up distinguished names.
Anrdex.oab	Anrdex.oab	Anrdex2_u.oab	Outlook uses this index file to help resolve ambiguous names.

Table 10-6 **Table 10-6 Files Generated for Offline Address Books (Continued)**

ANSI OAB Version 1 (root folder)	ANSI OAB Version 2	Unicode OAB Version 3a	Description
Lng*xxx*.oab	Lng*xxx*.oab	Lng*xxx*.oab	These files contain the Display and Addressing template data for localized (language) information. In the template, *xxx* is the locale ID, which is used to identify the language. Outlook renames this to Tmplts.oab at download time.
Mac*xxx*.oab	Mac*xxx*.oab	Mac*xxx*.oab	This file contains the Display and Addressing template data for Macintosh information, where *xxx* is the code page. The client renames this to Tmplts.oab at download time. The Unicode file is created for possible future use, as Macintosh clients, including Outlook 2001, use the non-Unicode offline address book files.
Changes.oab	Changes.oab	Changes.oab	This file is also referred to as the diff (or difference) file. It contains the differences between the current offline address book and the previously generated offline address book. Outlook uses the information in this file to determine whether to download an update to its copy of the offline address book or to download a complete offline address book. This file is included as an attachment in a separate message.

More Info   If your users are using Outlook 2003 Cached Exchange Mode, you might want to consider additional replicas of the offline address list folder to distribute the load placed on the server from clients downloading the offline address list at initial logon. Or you might want to evaluate the client's Outlook 2003 download settings. If the Outlook client is running in cached mode, we recommend that you select Full Details. If the client has limited hard disk space, the user might choose to select No Details.

You must choose an appropriate server to generate and update offline address lists. The more address lists contained in an offline address list, the harder the server you choose for the offline address list must work.

More Info   For more information about configuring offline address lists and configuring Outlook 2003 cached Exchange mode clients, see the book "Working with the Exchange Server 2003 Store" (*http:// www.microsoft.com/technet/prodtechnol/exchange/2003/library/ default.mspx*).

Best Practices

- Optimize your storage by grouping users that typically communicate with each other on the same mailbox store, such as users in the same business unit. This enables Exchange to store a single copy of a message when a user in the business unit sends the same message to other members of their business unit.

- Plan and optimize you disk subsystem. Exchange performance is dependent on the performance of your disk subsystem. Use Jetstress tool (jetstress.exe) to simulate database read/write access to test the throughput of the hardware you choose before deploying it to ensure that it meets your requirements. Ensure that online defragmentation completes on databases to reduce disk I/O. Separate database and transaction log files onto separate disk drives to optimize disk I/O. Additionally, avoid sharing disk drives between Exchange and other sequential databases, such as Microsoft SQL Server.

- Understand the impact on your service level agreements when you plan disk storage. Larger servers typically take longer to back up and restore. Create multiple storage groups and stores to reduce the time required to back up groups of mailboxes or public folders.

■ Control the amount of data stored on your Exchange servers. Configure Exchange system policies to set maximum sizes for mailboxes and public folders. Define deleted items retention policies that support your company's requirements. Use mailbox recipient policies to control mailbox and public folder data retention policies.

Chapter 11

Connecting to the Internet

About This Chapter

E-mail is a great collaborative tool, but without the ability to connect with people outside of your organization it would not be as popular as it is today. In this chapter we will look at the flow of e-mail messages via the Simple Mail Transfer Protocol

(SMTP) to and from an Exchange organization. We will also consider the best security steps to take and how to reduce Internet-borne attacks against your e-mail environment through the Internet gateway.

Understanding Internet Connectivity

To successfully and securely connect your Exchange organization to the Internet requires considerable planning. For small companies with a single office and one Internet connection this is quite easy, but for large multi-office and multinational enterprises this can take considerable work to achieve.

Once a company has made the decision to host its own Exchange organization, regardless of company size, the following will need to be taken into account:

- Domain Name System (DNS) infrastructure
- Active Directory infrastructure
- Internet connectivity and firewalls
- Antivirus and anti-spam solutions
- Exchange configuration

Some companies, mostly dependant upon government laws and controls, may need to implement message archiving and logging of Internet traffic as well.

DNS Infrastructure

First and most important of all the above list of prerequisites is the configuration of your DNS zone to allow the receipt of e-mail. Without a working DNS infrastructure for your company, e-mail will not find its way to you. To consider the different ways to set up the DNS infrastructure we will take a look at two example companies. The first is the School of Fine Art. This is a small company with 30 administrative and teaching staff and up to 100 students at various times of the year. It is based in Oxford in the United Kingdom. The second example company is Woodgrove Bank. This is an investment bank with over 40,000 employees and offices around the world.

For the typical small company, once the domain name, for example fineartschool.net, has been purchased and the DNS zone configured, the correct host (A) and mail exchanger (MX) records will need to be placed in an external DNS zone. These DNS zones are either hosted by the company through whom your domain name was purchased (and each hosting company will have a different way for you to update this information), or hosted by your own DNS servers. Once you know the process for changing your external DNS records you will need to obtain the following information:

1. Purchase your preferred e-mail domain name. In the example used here it is @fineartschool.net. This domain name will form all or part of the domain

portion of your e-mail addresses. For example, the School of Fine Art could use "@*something*.fineartschool.net" or just @fineartschool.net.

2. You have to know the external IP address of your external firewall. In this example it is 207.46.130.108.

3. Find out if your Internet service provider (ISP) offers e-mail services, such as antivirus/antispam and SMTP backup (when your server is unavailable, they will store e-mail for you). SMTP backup is important if you do not have a permanent Internet connection and of benefit if you do.

For the typical large enterprise, the requirements are much the same though it is more likely that the DNS zone information is hosted and managed by the company itself with perhaps an Internet hosting company providing a backup copy, referred to as DNS secondary zone hosting. For the multinational company, the decision that impacts the DNS infrastructure the most is the e-mail extension that is used. For the example of Woodgrove Bank, they could choose @woodgrovebank.com or they could choose a country-specific model, such as @woodgrovebank.com; @woodgrovebank.co.uk; or @woodgrovebank.gg, assuming that they owned these domain names. The second choice will have a bigger impact on DNS than the first. If Woodgrove Bank chooses to go for country-specific top-level domains, such as woodgrovebank.gg for Guernsey or woodgrovebank.co.uk for the UK, with a central e-mail administrative structure (all e-mail enters the company via one Internet connection), then the configuration steps are the same as the woodgrovebank.com example we will look at in this chapter. It is just that these steps will be repeated for each top-level domain name. But if the company chooses to have e-mail managed and processed at each country, in a distributed administrative environment, then DNS will need to be configured differently for each domain because each domain will contain MX records pointing to different inbound e-mail servers.

Each Internet connection through which a company's inbound e-mail is delivered will need an IP address. Each of these IP addresses must be listed in the external DNS zone for the company as an A record, which is then associated with an MX record with a set priority. These priority values are associated with each MX record in the form of a number. The MX records with the lowest priority will be used first for sending e-mail to that domain name, with 0 being the lowest priority. When an SMTP server wants to send e-mail to a domain it will obtain the list of the MX records for the domain and attempt e-mail delivery to the server identified with the lowest priority. Those SMTP servers with higher priorities will only receive e-mail if the lower priority servers are not responding.

Before you make any DNS changes, it is easy to check your current MX records by using a command line tool named *nslookup*.

> **Warning** Be careful where you run nslookup from! In checking to see your MX records in your external DNS it is important to ensure that you do not run the command line from where you might be affected by an existing internal DNS of the same name (for example, one used for your Active Directory forest).

Figure 11-1 shows nslookup output when run internally on the School of Fine Art's network and Figure 11-2 shows the output when run from the administrator's home over her broadband connection. This is an example of a network that is not part of the School of Fine Art network.

```
C:\WINDOWS\system32\cmd.exe                                    _ □ ×
Microsoft Windows [Version 5.2.3790]
(C) Copyright 1985-2003 Microsoft Corp.

C:\Documents and Settings\Administrator>cd\

C:\>nslookup -querystring=MX fineartschool.net
Server:  fas-dc.fineartschool.net
Address:  192.168.5.240

fineartschool.net
        primary name server = fas-dc.fineartschool.net
        responsible mail addr = hostmaster.fineartschool.net
        serial  = 4
        refresh = 900 (15 mins)
        retry   = 600 (10 mins)
        expire  = 86400 (1 day)
        default TTL = 3600 (1 hour)

C:\>
```

Figure 11-1 nslookup executed on the School of Fine Art's network

```
C:\WINDOWS\system32\cmd.exe                                    _ □ ×
Microsoft Windows [Version 5.2.3790]
(C) Copyright 1985-2003 Microsoft Corp.

C:\Documents and Settings\Administrator>cd\

C:\>nslookup -querystring=MX fineartschool.net
Server:  ns1.adatum.com
Address:  131.107.2.200

fineartschool.net
        primary name server = ns1.adatum.com
        responsible mail addr = support.adatum.com
        serial  = 6673459
        refresh = 900 (15 mins)
        retry   = 600 (10 mins)
        expire  = 86400 (1 day)
        default TTL = 86400 (1 day)

C:\>_
```

Figure 11-2 nslookup executed on the Internet

Note The nslookup output in Figure 11-2 shows that the data has been obtained from the Internet provider used by the School of Fine Art, A Datum Corporation (adatum.com). This is unlike Figure 11-1, where it can be seen that the results come from the domain controller (FAS-DC) and therefore do not show the external DNS results for the domain.

The nslookup command in the above two figures shows that no MX records exist on the external or internal DNS zones. This can be seen with the querystring=MX portion of the nslookup command, and that no MX records are in the results displayed. With this in mind, the administrator adds the MX record to the external DNS zone, pointing the record to the IP address of the external firewall on the school's Internet connection. Additional MX records would be added if additional e-mail servers were available from the Internet, such as when the Internet provider offers SMTP backup services. If you have multiple publicly available SMTP servers on your network you should use load balancing rather than listing each SMTP server on a separate MX record.

The reason the external IP address of the firewall is given as the destination for the MX record is that the firewall will be configured to listen for and forward packets to the Exchange server on the local area network (LAN) when valid packets connect to the external firewall interface. If you have more than one IP address on your external interface, you would pick the IP address that listens for SMTP traffic as the IP address referenced by the MX record. You typically cannot provide the actual IP address of the Exchange server because the LAN will most likely operate with an RFC 1918 IP address range, for example 192.168.0.0/24. The firewall, as well as forwarding valid packets to the Exchange server, acts as a Network Address Translation (NAT) server to allow external clients to reach selected LAN resources.

The following tables show the options available for MX records in the external DNS zones of both the example companies in this chapter.

Table 11-1   MX Records for an E-Mail Server on the Internet

Record	Preference	Value
MX	mail.fineartschool.net	10

Table 11-2   MX Records When Using a Backup E-Mail Server

Record	Preference	Value
MX	mail.fineartschool.net	10
MX	smtp1.adatum.com	20

Table 11-3   MX Records When Using Load-balanced E-Mail Servers on the Internet

Record	Preference	Value
MX	10	smtp.woodgrovebank.com

> **Important**   The single MX record points to host (A) record for the actual IP address of the servers. When adding or updating MX records, ensure that there is a valid A record for each MX record. If using load balancing for each available SMTP server, only a single A record would be needed.

In Figure 11-3 you can see that the primary e-mail server for the School of Fine Art is mail.fineartschool.net with an IP address of 207.46.130.108 and that their ISP provides e-mail backup on smtp1.adatum.com.

```
C:\WINDOWS\system32\cmd.exe                                    _ □ ×
Microsoft Windows [Version 5.2.3790]
(C) Copyright 1985-2003 Microsoft Corp.

C:\Documents and Settings\Administrator>cd\

C:\>nslookup -querystring=MX fineartschool.net
Server:  ns1.adatum.com
Address:  131.107.2.200

fineartschool.net         MX preference = 20, mail exchanger = smtp1.adatum.com
fineartschool.net         MX preference = 10, mail exchanger = mail.fineartschool.
net
smtp1.adatum.com          internet address = 131.107.2.201
mail.fineartschool.net    internet address = 207.46.130.108

C:\>_
```

Figure 11-3   The MX records for the School of Fine Art on their external DNS server

Once the DNS infrastructure is in place, the next step is to configure a secure e-mail connection to and from the Internet.

Active Directory Infrastructure

To configure your Exchange servers to send and receive e-mail from the Internet does not require any additions to Active Directory, but steps should be taken to ensure that Active Directory is not broken or compromised by the installation of this Internet connection.

The first area, and the one of prime importance, is ensuring that your Active Directory DNS is not affected by the changes to your DNS infrastructure detailed earlier. In all the earlier discussions on DNS, it was always mentioned that the changes were to be made to the DNS server that hosts your *external* DNS records, and that this is probably hosted at an ISP. This separation of Internet DNS from LAN DNS is also known as a split DNS infrastructure.

The internal DNS infrastructure that you have does not need MX records for mail delivery because the Exchange server delivers directly to the next server in the message path using A records. As your internal DNS zone contains information pertaining to all your internal resources, it should never be the same DNS server that is used to publish your externally valid records to the Internet. In the case of some networks, the external DNS server is hosted by the company itself, but because it is still a split infrastructure it is held on a different server from the one that holds the internal records.

DNS Zone Names Internally and Externally

With an internal Active Directory forest that has a different naming structure than your external domain presence, things are easier. Internally, you might use woodgrove-bank.local and externally woodgrovebank.com. Placing these zones on their respective servers and blocking inbound DNS queries from the Internet on your firewall (but not outbound queries because you still need those) can help ensure that Active Directory and e-mail flow work. Additionally, when you have a different domain name internally from externally, the comment about ensuring that the nslookup command is not using the internal zone when it should be looking at the external zone is not an issue.

Configuration becomes a little harder when the same domain name, for example fineartschool.net, is used both internally and externally. Again, because your Active Directory information is stored on the internal DNS infrastructure, this should not be available from the Internet, but a selected subset of records would need to be available on the externally hosted DNS server. These records would be the MX records discussed earlier and their associated host (A) records. Additionally, records for any other resource that you need to publish to the Internet also need to be available on the externally hosted DNS server; for example the www host (A) record for your corporate website and the A record for your Outlook Web Access website. To keep things working for internal users, it is then common practice to add identical records to the internal DNS zone so that resources accessible from the Internet can also be reached from the LAN using the same name.

DNS Root Issues

In both of these cases, the way that the internal network is configured is very important in ensuring that mail can flow. With a separate internal DNS infrastructure, the most important fact is that the root of the DNS tree might also be internally managed. This will be the case if your internal DNS hosts the root (or ".") zone. If this is the case, then you will find that you cannot resolve external DNS records without having some servers use external DNS servers instead (or in preference to) internal ones. These selected servers would be typically the gateway servers for e-mail and Web browsing, such as the proxy server and possibly a few other selected servers. See Smart Host Message Transfer later in this chapter for more on forwarding your outbound e-mail to a server that has the ability to resolve externally valid DNS records when the internal network is not able to do this.

Once you have your MX and associated A records published externally, it is time to configure your firewall solution.

Internet Connectivity and Firewalls

For messages to travel between the Internet and your Exchange organization, you will need to allow port 25 to be open on your firewall infrastructure between the relevant servers. In the case of the Internet, this will typically be between all Internet hosts and the selected servers that initially receive e-mail from the Internet. If you receive inbound e-mail from only selected hosts then your firewall should be configured to allow inbound access from those addresses only.

There are a number of ways of configuring your network for inbound e-mail to be achieved successfully. The configuration will depend upon whether or not you use one or more of the following:

- Back-to-back firewall configuration
- Smart host servers
- Front-end servers
- Internet-based anti-spam/antivirus services

Back-to-Back Firewall Configurations

A back-to-back firewall configuration uses at least two firewalls, one firewall connecting the Internet to an isolated, at-risk area of the network known as the perimeter network or demilitarized zone (DMZ), and a second firewall connecting the perimeter network to the LAN.

This provision of two firewalls allows both to be configured differently, allowing traffic into the perimeter network from the Internet via one set of rules on the external firewall, and then from the perimeter network to the LAN via another set of rules on the internal firewall. The external firewall rules only allow access to the perimeter network and the internal firewall rules allow access only from the perimeter network. Complete pass-through rules are to be avoided unless no other option exists.

In terms of outbound traffic, the reverse rules are recommended. That is, specified servers on the LAN communicate to servers in the perimeter network via the internal firewall rules and only the servers in the perimeter network can get out to the Internet. An example of a server that would fit within the perimeter network in the role described previously would be a smart host server.

Smart Host Servers

A smart host is an e-mail server to which all Internet-bound e-mail is sent. This smart host server then does the actual DNS lookups and forwarding to the next server, rather than the DNS lookups being done by the sending Exchange server. Though smart host servers are used for outbound e-mail, it is possible to use the same server to be the inbound e-mail gateway as well. When this is the case, this server can be configured with anti-spam and antivirus solutions for e-mail. It is common for these technologies to be running on the inbound e-mail gateway server to filter out those e-mail messages found to contain viruses and unsolicited commercial e-mail (UCE), more commonly known as spam. Anti-spam and antivirus solutions are covered later in this chapter.

In terms of network and firewall configuration, if this smart host server is not an Exchange server it can be placed in the perimeter network. Given that the Exchange servers are domain members and require considerable connectivity to various domain services, it is not a recommended practice to place Exchange servers in the perimeter network.

Tip If your smart host server makes use of the features of Exchange Server, and your perimeter network is composed of numerous servers, then it would be wise to build a separate and isolated Active Directory forest within your perimeter network. Your smart host server could then be an Exchange server, which is part of this forest but completely isolated from your corporate Active Directory forest. This perimeter network forest can then additionally provide central authentication and group policy (among other things) to the perimeter servers.

A common firewall configuration using the smart host server in the perimeter network would be similar to that shown in Figure 11-4. Note that in this figure, not all the possible servers of the perimeter network are shown.

The inbound firewall rules that would be used in this example would be a rule on the external firewall allowing all Internet hosts to send data over TCP port 25 to the smart host server. A separate rule would exist on the internal firewall to only allow the smart host to send data on TCP port 25 to the internal Exchange servers that receive e-mail from the smart host. Outbound firewall rules could typically be the reverse of the above (though other options exist as well).

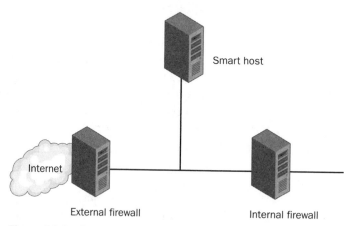

Figure 11-4   Smart host server and perimeter network configuration

Front-End Servers

Exchange servers can be configured as front-end servers to provide a common namespace for non-MAPI clients connecting to their mailboxes, SSL offloading and scalability. It is common to read in technical articles that a front-end Exchange server can be placed in the perimeter network and have communication to the back-end servers storing the mailbox. Two common misconceptions about this statement are the complexity of modern firewalls and the purpose of a perimeter network.

With modern firewall solutions such as Microsoft's Internet Security and Acceleration (ISA) Server (which start completely locked down and on which you configure which ports to open and destinations to allow) as your perimeter network boundary, you would need to open a large number of ports to all your Active Directory servers and Exchange bridgehead servers to allow the perimeter-network-based front-end Exchange servers to communicate with the LAN. This number of open ports is so great that you negate the purpose of a perimeter network by allowing all these open ports in from your perimeter network.

As mentioned previously, the perimeter network contains servers that are known to be at risk from Internet attacks and are used to protect and filter the LAN from such attacks. Therefore, the perimeter network is not the ideal place for an Exchange server that is a member of your corporate forest. It is possible to place an Exchange server in a perimeter network and to disable Remote procedure call (RPC) communication into the corporate network, leaving just the HTTP, POP3, or IMAP4 protocol that is being used across the front-end and back-end Exchange Server infrastructure. If RPC communication is disabled between the front-end server and the back-end servers, the front-end server cannot authenticate the user and it anonymously passes all inbound requests into the corporate network for authentication at the back-end server.

> **Important** Front-end servers are used to load-balance non-MAPI client requests by providing a single namespace to a user's mailbox and not as perimeter network-based servers.

Finally, the Exchange servers that must be listed in the perimeter network firewall rules are the gateway servers that receive e-mail for the Exchange organization, and the bridgehead servers that are used to send e-mail out to the Internet. All your other Exchange servers do not need to be listed in the firewall rules.

Internet-Based Anti-Spam/Antivirus Services

The typical SMTP firewall rule that you find on most external firewalls will be a rule allowing all Internet hosts to send SMTP into selected servers and for selected servers to send e-mail to all Internet hosts.

This rule will change, for example, when a company restricts the sending of e-mail to a smart host server operated by its Internet provider, or the company chooses not to communicate externally using e-mail except to a selected range of other companies, or, most commonly, the company uses the services of an Internet-based anti-spam and antivirus service provider.

These Internet-based anti-spam and antivirus service providers operate by taking all the inbound e-mail (your MX records point to their servers and not your servers), filtering it, and then passing that which is virus- and spam-free into your network. In this scenario, you will know the IP addresses used by the service provider for communicating with your e-mail servers and so can restrict your firewall to accept SMTP traffic only from these hosts. Additionally, this ensures that all received e-mail has been filtered by the Internet-based service provider.

Antivirus and Anti-Spam Solutions

The final major consideration for Internet connectivity is the antivirus and anti-spam configuration of the network. Due to the large amount of unsolicited e-mail and e-mail containing viruses, even the smallest company should have some provision for protecting itself.

If protection against these threats is not managed externally, as covered in the previous section, then the configuration of the network must ensure that all inbound and outbound e-mail goes through any e-mail server running at least antivirus software and preferably anti-spam functionality as well.

Antivirus functionality for Exchange Server is available from third-party vendors. This functionality is provided by the inclusion within Exchange Server of the APIs that these antivirus products need when checking the message flow through the Exchange server. This means that any antivirus product that checks Exchange Server data should be one that uses the provided APIs and not a MAPI or Extensible Storage Engine (ESE) antivirus scanner, as these are not recommended by Microsoft. Other antivirus products that run on the Exchange server (for example, file-scanning antivirus products) need to be correctly configured so that they do not interfere with the operation of the Exchange server.

Exchange Server 2003 antivirus products are those that make use of a technology of Exchange Server named Virus Scanning API (VSAPI). Exchange Server 2003 ships with version 2.5 of VSAPI. Antivirus products most suited to run on Exchange Server 2003 are those compatible with VSAPI 2.5, rather than those compatible with only the earlier versions of VSAPI.

The current version of VSAPI is enhanced with new capabilities, allowing antivirus vendors to develop solutions that scan e-mail messages at the entry point of the network before suspect content reaches the Exchange mailbox server. VSAPI 2.5 also makes it possible to prevent infected e-mail from leaving an organization by scanning outgoing mail. This separation of functionality allows for the SMTP routing servers in a large Exchange organization to stop viruses before they reach the mailbox server. This reduces the performance load on these back-end servers and the associated network usage in forwarding these messages to the mailbox servers.

The most problematic of the antivirus products that are installed on Exchange servers are those that do file-level scanning. When file-level scanning antivirus products are installed on the Exchange server, they must be configured to ignore any files or folders in any location used by Exchange. This includes, but is not limited to, the database and log file folders.

More Info   Microsoft Knowledge Base article 823166, "Overview of Exchange Server 2003 and antivirus software" (*http://go.microsoft.com/ fwlink/?linkid=3052&kbid=823166*) discusses the advantages, disadvantages, and troubleshooting considerations for the different types of antivirus product on an Exchange server.

A problem with Exchange Server 2000 and antivirus products was the scanning of the Installable File System (IFS) drive. The IFS drive was a view into the Microsoft Exchange Information Store service as if it were a local disk on the server. Though this functionality is not available by default in Exchange 2003, the IFS drive can be made available for compatibility with applications that have been written to use it. If it is made available, it must not be scanned by a file-level scanner. If it is scanned, potential problems include calendaring errors, failure when accessing attachments and messages, and damage to the Exchange database. Issues with mail flow can also occur.

Exclude the following from both on-demand and memory-resident file-level scanners:

- The Exchange 2003 Server IFS drive (typically M:\) if enabled.
- Exchange databases and log files. By default, these are located in the Exchsrvr\Mdbdata folder.
- Exchange MTA files in the Exchsrvr\Mtadata folder.
- Additional log files, such as the Exchsrvr\server_name.log file.
- The Exchsrvr\Mailroot virtual server folder.
- The working folder that is used to store streaming temporary files that are used for message conversion. By default, this folder is located at \Exchsrvr\MDBData, but you can configure this location.
- The temporary folder that is used in conjunction with offline maintenance utilities such as Eseutil.exe. By default, this folder is the location where the .exe file is run, but when you run the utility you can configure where you run the file from.
- Site Replication Service (SRS) files in the Exchsrvr\Srsdata folder.
- Microsoft Internet Information Service (IIS) system files in the %SystemRoot%\System32\Inetsrv folder.
- Folders that contain the Exchange.edb, .stm and .log files.

Note You may want to exclude the whole Exchsrvr folder from both on-demand and memory-resident file-level scanners.

Exchange Server 2003 contains a number of features to protect against spam. These include DNS Block List server support, global accept and deny lists, sender filtering, and inbound recipient filtering. There is also improved ability to restrict submissions to, and relaying on, SMTP virtual servers. Each of these features is covered later in this chapter. Additionally, Microsoft has made Intelligent Message Filter available for download. This is a product that integrates with Exchange Server 2003. The Intelligent Message Filter can be used to assign a rating to each message that suggests the likelihood that a message is spam, and then to take action against the message if it is.

Intelligent Message Filter

The Intelligent Message Filter is an anti-spam product that utilizes a Microsoft Research-patented, machine-learning product named SmartScreen Technology. SmartScreen Technology is the anti-spam technology currently in use in Outlook 2003, Hotmail, and MSN 8.

Intelligent Message Filter was developed to recognize the difference between e-mail that is spam versus valid e-mail. The learning process for Intelligent Message Filter involved millions of e-mail messages from Hotmail subscribers, allowing it to make a suitable assessment of the e-mail received by an Exchange 2003 server. Intelligent Message Filter is capable of not only evaluating if an e-mail is spam, but also if the e-mail is legitimate, based on over 500,000 characteristics in the e-mail. This distinction increases the likelihood that Intelligent Message Filter will not mis-categorize an e-mail.

Intelligent Message Filter is configured as part of the Exchange organization global settings and enabled on selected SMTP virtual servers. The global settings control what happens to messages that exceed a given spam confidence level (SCL) rating at the gateway SMTP virtual servers and the mailbox servers.

Note   Intelligent Message Filter does not need to be installed and enabled on all SMTP virtual servers. It is only needed on Internet SMTP gateway servers. For example, a front-end protocol server that is not an Internet bridgehead would not need to run the Intelligent Message Filter.

Each unauthenticated e-mail (assuming it is not encrypted), along with e-mail sourced from IP addresses that are specified in the Global Accept List of Exchange Server Connection Filtering are categorized and given an SCL rating. This status is associated with the message and is part of the message for its life inside the Exchange organization.

Once a message arrives at the Intelligent Message Filter server it is categorized with a rating, which is a number between -1 and 9, and then processed. An SCL rating of -1 means that the e-mail is from an authenticated source, such as someone inside your Exchange organization. Intelligent Message Filter does not filter authenticated e-mail.

More Info   More information on exposing the SCL rating inside Outlook can be found on the Exchange Team's Web blog at *http://blogs.msdn.com/ exchange/archive/2004/05/26/142607.aspx*.

The first processing occurs on the Intelligent Message Filter server, which examines the rating and compares it to a gateway threshold value set by the administrator. Messages with a rating greater than or equal to the threshold on the Intelligent Message Filter server have the gateway action taken on them. This gateway, action can be to reject, delete, archive, or ignore the e-mail. If the rating is lower than the threshold or was ignored as part of the action taken upon it at the gateway then the message is delivered to the user's mailbox server. When the gateway action is archived, the default archive directory is Exchsrvr\Mailroot\vsi *n*\UceArchive where *n* is the number of the virtual server running Intelligent Message Filter.

At the mailbox server Intelligent Message Filter processes the e-mail based on a number of criteria based on the SCL rating and any blocked or safe senders list. The message is moved into the user's Junk E-mail folder if the message rating is greater than or equal to the threshold on that mailbox server. If the client is Outlook 2003 or Outlook Web Access 2003, then the client's blocked and safe senders list comes into play. Messages from recipients that are on a client's blocked sender list will always go into the Junk E-mail folder regardless of the SCL rating on the message and messages from recipients that are on a client's safe senders list will always go into the Inbox even if the SCL rating is greater than the store threshold value.

With the functionality of Intelligent Message Filter split over both the gateway and the store, you can process spam e-mail with a high rating in a different way from that with a lower rating.

For example, Woodgrove Bank has enabled Intelligent Message Filter on their Exchange 2003 gateway server through which all their inbound Internet e-mail flows. The Gateway Blocking Configuration threshold value is set to **8** and e-mail messages with an SCL rating equal to or exceeding that are archived for further offline examination.

All messages with a threshold of below 8 are sent to the mailbox server. The second setting on the dialog box Store Junk E-Mail configuration sets the SCL threshold at which messages on the mailbox server with a rating greater than or equal to are placed in the user's Junk E-mail folder rather than in their Inbox. If this was set to **7** it would mean those messages with a rating of 7 only; as those messages with a rating of 8 and above have already been removed from the inbound message flow by being archived by the gateway server.

Intelligent Message Filter filters are the last ones to be processed on inbound e-mail from all the filtering options available within Exchange 2003. The other filters all run before Intelligent Message Filter. These include DNS Block Service Lists and Recipient Filter. This means some e-mail may be rejected before Intelligent Message Filter can process it.

When Intelligent Message Filter archives a message, it does not save the rating given with the message. The setting of the registry value `HKEY_LOCAL_MACHINE\Software\Microsoft\Exchange\ContentFilter\ArchiveSCL` (`DWORD`) to **1** will cause the X-SCL header to be added to the e-mail and this will persist with the e-mail forever. An example X-SCL header will read "X-SCL: 6 88.89%," which shows the threshold rating and the percentage likelihood that the message is spam.

In addition to the use of the registry key mentioned earlier and the Windows Performance tool to see what is happening with e-mail that Intelligent Message Filter has processed, the Event Viewer records the following event IDs:

- **7512 Informational**   Message was deleted or rejected by Intelligent Message Filter. This is only recorded if medium or higher logging is set in Exchange System Manager for the SMTP Protocol category of the MSExchangeTranport service.

- **7513 Informational**   Intelligent Message Filter was installed or the SMTP service was restarted.

- **7514 Error**   Indicates an error when starting Intelligent Message Filter.

- **7515 Error**   Indicates the Intelligent Message Filter could not process a message.

Intelligent Message Filter can be downloaded from Microsoft by setting your browser to *http://go.microsoft.com/fwlink/?LinkId=28649*. Full instructions on how to install Intelligent Message Filter can be found in the Microsoft Exchange Server 2003 Technical Documentation Library at *http://go.microsoft.com/fwlink/?LinkID=21277*.

Testing the Intelligent Message Filter

To ensure that Intelligent Message Filter is successfully installed you can use the performance counters that come with the product to show what ratings are given to all e-mail through your system. Intelligent Message Filter can be shown to be working correctly if the value of the performance counters changes with each inbound e-mail processed by the Intelligent Message Filter.

Once Intelligent Message Filter is installed and enabled on the Internet gateway SMTP virtual servers, set the threshold values to high numbers and set the gateway action to **No Action**. Messages will arrive and be processed and the performance counters for Intelligent Message Filter will record the number of messages processed and the number of messages given each SCL rating. After allowing a reasonable number of e-mail messages to be processed by Intelligent Message Filter you can examine the Intelligent Message Filter statistics in the Performance tool. You need to look at the Total Messages Assigned An SCL Rating Of # value (where # is 0 to 9). These performance counters are part of the MSExchange Intelligent Message Filter performance object. You should get a peak near 0 and another peak near 9. You can use these statistics to determine where to set your gateway and store SCL threshold ratings.

Once you have decided on the best thresholds for both the gateway and store you can, if you need to, change the gateway action. If you set the gateway action to Archive, then each message that has an SCL value greater than the gateway threshold value will be moved from the SMTP queue into the UCEArchive folder for that SMTP virtual server. This folder can be found at *<drive>*:\Program Files\Exchsrvr\Mail-root\vsi *n*\ where *n* is the number for the SMTP virtual server.

To process archived messages, open the UceArchive folder and double-click the message (.eml) file. This file will open with Outlook Express. Cancel the Internet Connection Wizard if it starts to allow you to view the e-mail. The wizard will only run the first time you start Outlook Express within a user's profile. If the message needs to be delivered to the mailbox, close the message in Outlook Express and move (not copy) the message into the Pickup folder, which can be found one level above the UceArchive folder.

> **Tip** Available to download from the Internet is a .NET tool to assist in the processing of e-mail in the UCEArchive folder. This tool, the Intelligent Message Filter Archive Manager, can be downloaded from *http://www.gotdotnet.com/community/workspaces/Workspace.aspx?id=e8728572-3a4e-425a-9b26-a3fda0d06fee.*

Exchange Configuration

The final step in connecting your Exchange system to the Internet is the configuration of the connector and additional SMTP virtual servers, although this is not necessary. That is, even without specifically configuring a connector, Exchange 2003 is able to route mail to the Internet if a valid path exists.

The default SMTP virtual server installed as part of Exchange is able to send e-mail to all domains directly. This requires that each server is able to resolve DNS lookups for remote hosts, that the firewall configuration allows that particular server to send SMTP traffic outbound, and that an IP-routed path exists from that server to the Internet.

The Internet Mail Wizard, which is available from Exchange System Manager, can be used to check if your inbound e-mail configuration is correct. For example, if your default SMTP virtual server allows anyone to send e-mail through it to any address (open relay), running the wizard will prompt you about this and allow you to change the setting.

To have more control over your Internet traffic, for example, to implement some of the configurations discussed earlier in this chapter, you can create suitable SMTP virtual servers and connectors so that e-mail flows via antivirus and anti-spam servers, via your smart hosts, and via a single-source IP address regardless of the location within your organization of the user who sent the e-mail.

For your inbound configuration, ensure that your MX records and their associated A records are valid; that your firewall allows that server to receive SMTP traffic from the Internet, that you have a recipient policy for your domain and that the

Exchange server is responsible for delivering mail to this address (this is the default setting). Once the message reaches that server it is routed as part of the internal Exchange organization connectivity, which is covered in Chapter 14.

Building this infrastructure and further configuring your secure Internet connection is covered in the remainder of this chapter.

Configuring Additional SMTP Virtual Servers

An SMTP virtual server is the configuration that Exchange Server uses to listen for and process incoming SMTP connections and to initiate outgoing SMTP connections. The virtual server is hosted within IIS 5.0 or 6.0 (depending on whether Exchange Server is running on Windows Server 2000 or Windows 2003 Server), and once Exchange Server is installed upon a server, it provides the ability to create multiple virtual servers for use within Exchange Server.

Caution   Do not confuse IIS virtual servers with Microsoft Cluster Server virtual servers. Both IIS and Cluster Server virtual servers can be used with Exchange Server, but a Cluster Server virtual server provides failover support within a Cluster Server environment, whereas IIS virtual servers provide communications and settings for the protocols used in IIS and Exchange. IIS virtual servers are used in clustered and non-clustered installations of Exchange Server.

The default virtual server created on each Exchange server is suitable for most needs, but should an organization require separation of the functionality of a virtual server (such as authentication or the application of filters) then the need to create additional virtual servers exists. Additionally, should the reason for creating a separate virtual server be based on different domain names, the administrator will need to create an SMTP connector using that virtual server as a bridgehead for the connector. For example, earlier we saw the configuration of Intelligent Message Filter. If you want to ensure that no e-mail from a partner organization is filtered, you could ensure that this organization had access to a non-filtered SMTP virtual server rather than using the default virtual server that all messages from the Internet would use.

Prerequisites to Creating Virtual Servers

Each virtual server, on the Exchange server, requires unique TCP/IP settings (the default virtual server must have different settings from another virtual server and so on). The settings that need to be unique are IP address and TCP port. Note that even though you can use a different port, SMTP travels on TCP port 25 by default, and it would be very rare for someone to choose a different port to use as this is the standard port as specified in RFC 2821. If you choose a different port, everyone who connects to you on that virtual server would need to change their configurations to communicate with you on that non-standard port. Therefore, just having a unique IP address and using TCP port 25 is the recommended best practice.

> **Important** Once you create an additional virtual server, you will not be able to run the Internet Mail Wizard unless you set the virtual server configuration back to default. You can of course manually create the connectors that the wizard would have made for you.

Creating an Additional Virtual Server

The first step in creating an additional virtual server is checking to see which virtual servers exist and noting their settings, to be sure that you choose unique settings when you create the additional virtual server. Virtual server information is available in the properties dialog box for each virtual server. The IP address can be found on the General tab and the port via the Advanced button, which is also on the General tab. Use the following steps as a guideline to create an additional virtual server:

1. Open Exchange System Manager and expand the tree until you find the Protocols node under the server you are configuring.

2. Right-click the SMTP node and choose New > SMTP Virtual Server.

3. Provide a suitable name for the virtual server.

4. Select an IP address that no other SMTP virtual server on this server is using. The All Unassigned value means all unused IP addresses. Typically, this setting is a property of the default virtual server.

Once these steps are completed, you need to wait for these changes that have been made in Active Directory to replicate to the domain controller that the target server is using. Once the configuration changes have replicated to the domain controller used by the target Exchange server, they are copied to the IIS metabase using the DS2MB process. Additionally, the file system folders that this virtual server uses are created. This will take a variable amount of time, depending on your Active Directory replication configuration. While waiting, the SMTP virtual server will display an icon with an empty white circle on it. If, before the folders are created, you open the properties of this virtual server and click OK, then an error will appear and the event log will record an error, such as *Virtual Server 2: SMTP server cannot read metabase key MailQueueDir* (the metabase is the configuration database used by the SMTP service). Once the folders are created you can open and click OK on the Properties dialog box without error. This will result in the virtual server starting, assuming it does not conflict with existing virtual servers by port and IP address. The folders are created in < *drive*>:\Program Files\Exchsrvr\Mailroot\vsi *n*\ where *n* is the next available number. If the folders are created, but the Start option is unavailable, then open the Properties dialog box and click OK. If your IP address and port settings are unique and the folders have been created, then the virtual server will start.

Virtual Server General Settings

On the Properties dialog box of the SMTP virtual server you can change the IP address, limit the number of connections, set the connection time-out, and enable logging for the virtual server.

As stated previously, the RFC for SMTP states that it listens on TCP port 25; therefore, the only recommended way to have more than one virtual server on an Exchange server is to have each virtual server on a separate IP address and have them all listening on TCP port 25. IP addressing and ports can be changed via the Advanced button on this dialog box, but if all you wish to do is change the IP address this can be set on the General property sheet in the SMTP virtual server dialog box.

Though the virtual server is set to accept an unlimited number of simultaneous connections, specific hardware and network configuration settings will enforce a true upper limit. If this upper limit is frequently reached, and performance of the server is noticeably degraded when operating at the upper limit, then the number of simultaneous connections can be set to a value suitable for your network. The maximum value for simultaneous connections is 1,999,999,999. Connection attempts in excess of the set maximum are declined with a 421 error and there will be a delay in the delivery of the messages that the connection was going to send until it can successfully connect next time. Note that changes only take effect once the settings are loaded into the metabase. This can take some time because the Exchange System Manager application changes its settings in Active Directory and the metabase is updated with these changes the next time the metabase synchronizes with Active Directory. The Exchange System Manager application does not change the metabase directly but makes its changes in Active Directory, which is replicated to the metabase with the DS2MB process. The DS2MB process is covered in Chapter 12.

The connection time-out value allows for the disconnecting of idle sessions to save resources. It is recommended that this setting is never reduced below 10 minutes because lower than 10 minutes could cause the client to be disconnected unexpectedly and possibly receive an error.

On the bottom of the general dialog box are the options to log the connections to this virtual server. One of the purposes of logging connections is for diagnostic and troubleshooting purposes and is covered in detail near the end of this chapter.

Virtual Server Advanced Settings

Once the virtual server is created, it is also possible to associate additional IP addresses and ports if you wish the virtual server to listen on more than one address/port combination but not on all unassigned ports. This is done by clicking Advanced on the General page of the virtual server properties dialog box as shown in Figure 11-5.

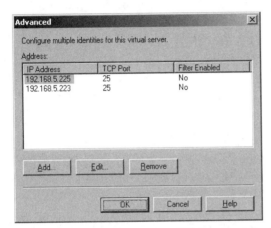

Figure 11-5 Configuring an SMTP virtual server with multiple IP addresses and ports

Additionally, enabling and disabling the global connection filters against a particular virtual server is done via the Advanced dialog box. Remember that one of the major reasons for creating an additional virtual server is to have the ability to send and receive e-mail with a different filter status than the default filter. For example, Woodgrove Bank communicates with its recently purchased subsidiary organization, Humongous Insurance, on a daily basis and needs to ensure that the global filtering that they enabled on their default SMTP virtual server does not take effect for e-mail from Humongous Insurance, which is also the name of the virtual server in the examples found here. The first step is to create a second virtual server on a dedicated IP address and keep the default setting of not having any filtering while enabling filtering on the default virtual server. Figure 11-5 shows the SMTP virtual server settings that Woodgrove Bank will use to communicate with Humongous Insurance. Note that this virtual server has no filtering enabled on it.

Virtual Server Access Settings

The Access tab in the SMTP virtual server properties dialog box controls how incoming connections to this virtual server are handled. The settings in the dialog box include Authentication and Encryption.

SMTP Virtual Server Authentication

By default, an SMTP virtual server does not require users to authenticate before using it. Anonymous access is important for all SMTP virtual servers that receive mail from the Internet because the SMTP servers that will send e-mail to your organization are not configured to provide credentials when connecting. If your Internet SMTP virtual servers require authentication, then you will fail to receive any e-mail from the Internet. The default settings in Exchange Server have all three authentication options selected, including Anonymous. If you have a single Exchange server, it is recommended to leave a virtual server capable of doing all three as it gives the greatest scope to the client's choice of authentication.

Authentication on your SMTP virtual servers is used for two types of connection. The first is to authenticate users before allowing them to send e-mail via SMTP and the second is to restrict access to a virtual server. For example, partner organizations can connect to the virtual server because they can authenticate with the right credentials.

If all the clients of your Exchange organization use Outlook configured to connect to an Exchange server to send and receive e-mail, then they never directly use SMTP and so your virtual server can be configured to allow only the relevant Exchange servers to communicate with them.

If an organization uses Exchange in a hosted environment they may choose to use POP3 or IMAP4, as the client options. Both POP3 and IMAP4 require that the user have access to an SMTP server to send e-mail. In this scenario it is very important to ensure that only valid users can connect to this hosted SMTP server because this server will need to allow relay of e-mail to all domains. If this server allows unauthenticated access and relay to all domains it becomes an open relay, and this configuration option should be avoided at all costs. To allow or deny access to the SMTP virtual server to a particular list of users, click the Users button. It is recommended that you create a Windows security group for this purpose and add only this group here. Further modifications of who is allowed or not allowed to access the virtual server can be done by simple group management. Using groups to manage permissions on the virtual server has some of the same benefits as using groups in a file system. If lots of virtual servers need the same permission, it is much easier to modify the group once than to have to modify many virtual servers each time the user list changes.

The other scenario for authentication on your SMTP virtual servers is when you have a particular range of servers that are known to be configured to connect to this virtual server and you want to keep the ability to connect limited to this range. As described previously, partner organizations make an ideal example of this type of configuration.

In the virtual server example that we have been configuring for Woodgrove Bank, we created an SMTP virtual server named *from Humongous Insurance* to listen on a different IP address from the default virtual server. This virtual server will be set to Basic authentication only. This option is set by clicking the Authentication button in the Access control area of the SMTP virtual server Access dialog box.

Integrated Windows Authentication is either Kerberos or NTLM authentication. Kerberos requires both the client and the server SMTP virtual server to be within the same forest, and if this is not the case NTLM authentication will be used. NTLM authentication does not always operate well over firewalls. In this example, Humongous Insurance is a recently purchased subsidiary of Woodgrove Bank, but not yet integrated into the woodgrovebank.com Active Directory forest. Basic authentication has no firewall or forest restrictions; however, it does send the logon password in Base64 encoding. This Base64 encoding is easy to reverse, and so Basic authentication additionally allows for the use of Transport Layer Security (TLS) encryption across the connection. TLS is a form of SSL and is used in SMTP to ensure that the normally clear-text traffic is highly encrypted. The use of TLS requires an installed SSL certificate and Basic authentication to be enabled before it to can be enabled and operate successfully, as shown in Figure 11-6. In addition to the password now being encrypted once TLS is enabled, all the message content is encrypted as well.

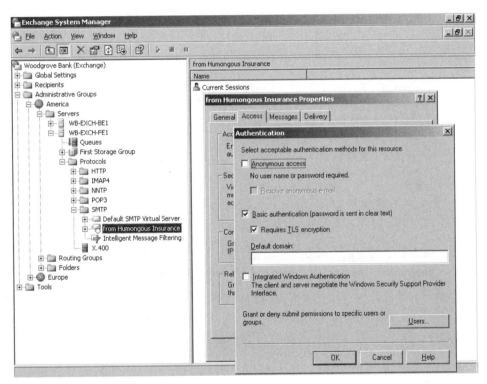

Figure 11-6   Basic authentication and TLS-enabled

SMTP Virtual Server Encryption

The ability to implement public/private key encryption on your SMTP virtual server is available from the Encryption button in the Secure communications area of the Access page of the virtual server properties dialog box.

Implementing encryption allows both SSL- and TLS-encrypted connections. If the TLS option in the Authentication properties above is enabled, but no SSL certificate is installed, the server reports the error *554 5.7.3 Unable to initialize security subsystem* when attempting to begin a TLS communication session.

Initially the Communication button on the Access property sheet is disabled because the virtual server is not configured to use a certificate to allow the encryption/decryption of messages. Full instructions on obtaining and installing certificates can be found in the next chapter. Although the next chapter discusses HTTP virtual servers, the process is the same for an SMTP virtual server.

The certificate is installed from the Certificate button, which begins the installation wizard. Once the certificate is installed, Figure 11-7 shows the result of the Communications button and the dialog box, from which a secure channel is enabled. This enables the requirement of the server to accept only connections via SSL encrypted with public/private key cryptography, and then only connections capable of providing 128-bit encryption.

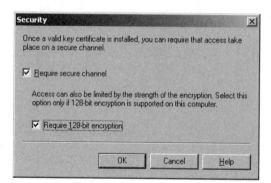

Figure 11-7   Ensuring the encryption is used for SMTP connections

Once the certificate is installed, the SMTP virtual server will be able to communicate via TLS, protecting the normally clear-text SMTP communication between selected SMTP virtual servers. The SMTP command to start a TLS session is STARTTLS as a single command followed by the EHLO command. If TLS is required and an SSL certificate is available, then attempts to communicate without TLS result in the error *530 5.7.0 Must issue a STARTTLS command* or *454 5.7.3 Client does not have permission to submit mail to this server* when anonymous access is disabled.

> **Note** The SSL options in Figure 11-7 do not need to be enabled for TLS to occur, but a certificate does need to be installed. The SSL options in this dialog box needs to be enabled if client wants SSL to protect the entire communications session from client to server, whereas TLS is used during the server-to-server communication.

The final part of the configuration involves the other SMTP virtual server in this communication and the properties of the Delivery tab and its associated SMTP connector.

Virtual Server IP Restrictions

In addition to, or instead of, the authentication and encryption settings, it is also possible to limit access to a virtual server from a particular range of computers via the Connection button in the Connection control area of the Access tab of the virtual server property dialog box. Examples for doing this might be an e-mail hosting company that provides SMTP services only to the users of its network. When a user connects over broadband or dialup, they will receive an IP address from this Internet provider. This IP address is then within the range of addresses allowed to access the SMTP virtual server.

If IP restrictions are enabled and a firewall sits between the client and the SMTP virtual server, be sure that the firewall does not change the source IP address to the firewall's internal IP address, otherwise the SMTP virtual server will not allow the connection because it appears to come from a different source.

Virtual Server Relay Settings

Relaying is the ability of an SMTP virtual server to forward e-mail messages to the correct SMTP server when the virtual server itself is not able to place them in a mailbox on that server. By default, relaying is disabled in Exchange Server 2003 by having an empty list of allowed IP addresses. Relaying is only allowed by default if you authenticate to the virtual server. Authentication is enabled on the virtual server as mentioned earlier, and so users of POP and IMAP clients who need an SMTP server can use this virtual server to relay to domains not managed by the Exchange organization.

> **Tip** If you do not have any POP or IMAP clients then you can disable the Allow Authenticated Users To Relay option to further enhance the security of your system.

If you have POP and IMAP clients you can limit the servers that can be relayed to. This will improve security. First, disable the Allow Authenticated Users To Relay option on all SMTP virtual servers on the network. Then, on the virtual servers that are used by clients to send e-mail, click the Users button and limit the authentication to a Windows security group. The members of this group are those who are allowed to relay rather than all authenticated users. A spammer obtaining or guessing a user-name and password on your network could relay with the default settings.

Open relay is the term given to an SMTP virtual server that will deliver e-mail to any address and accept connections from any client. This is a very dangerous setting to implement on your Exchange server. An Internet-connected open relay will almost certainly be found and used by someone wishing to send spam. All the spammer has to do once an open relay is found is to send the intended spam message along with a very long recipient list. The workload to ensure that the e-mail reaches every recipient now belongs to your Exchange server and not to the actual sender, who is unlikely to be using a real e-mail address and is probably untraceable. Your network suffers by being overloaded, your Exchange server suffers by being overloaded, and you are likely to be added to public lists of open relays. It is possible to configure Exchange Server to reject e-mail from known open relays, and if your server gets onto one of these lists, you will find that there are legitimate domains that you want to send e-mail to and cannot because the SMTP servers in those domains reject your Exchange server as a source of e-mail.

Virtual Server Messages Settings

A virtual server's Messages dialog box controls inbound connections (with one exception). For example, from here you could increase the maximum size of any inbound e-mail message to this virtual server and limit the number of messages that this server could send in a single session to a remote server.

Message Defaults

Size limits for SMTP can be set globally per Exchange organization on each SMTP con-nector and locally per SMTP virtual server. The Messages page of the virtual server properties dialog box is where the SMTP virtual server limits are set and are applied before the protocol processes the message. The global message size defaults to 10240 KB as the maximum receivable message size. An upgrade of an earlier version of Exchange will have its defaults increased to this value unless the previous value had been manually changed. If it was manually changed, then that value becomes the maximum message default size.

Note Individual mailboxes can have a different sending or receiving message size setting. This is enabled via the Exchange General tab, Delivery Restrictions button on the mailbox in Active Directory Users and Computers.

It is not recommended to set message size limits on the protocol as this could hinder intra-Exchange organization communication, such as public and system folder replication.

Virtual Server Incoming Message Settings

The Limit Message Size To (KB) value places an upper limit on the size of a single message accepted by the virtual server inbound, though this can hinder intra-Exchange organization communication as described previously. It does not affect the sending of messages outbound. With the original RFC for SMTP the message would have been rejected after it was sent, but to improve performance the Enhanced SMTP (ESMTP) extensions, supported by Exchange Server and most other SMTP servers, allows the sending server to communicate to the virtual server the size of the e-mail in advance of sending it. It also allows the recipient SMTP server to report the maximum message size that it will accept. This means that if the e-mail is too large it is rejected before the data is sent. This saves both the sender and recipient's bandwidth.

Tip To see the maximum message size of a foreign e-mail system, connect to port 25 on that system and enter the EHLO command. A 250-SIZE response will inform you of the maximum number of bytes that server will accept in a message. If an Exchange virtual server is configured to accept the global defaults then it will not display a value in the 250-SIZE response.

If the sending e-mail system does not understand the SIZE response then it will send the e-mail, but once it is finished it will receive the *552 4.3.1 Message size exceeds fixed maximum message size* error rather than the status 250 message for successful transmission. The ESMTP alternative to sending the entire message is the addition of the size parameter to the Mail from command. The format of this command is Mail from:<*username*> size=size_in_bytes. If the proposed size is too great then the Exchange server reports the *552 5.3.4 Message size exceeds fixed maximum message size* error before the message is sent. Note that these error messages are slightly different, based on whether the e-mail was rejected when sent (552 4.3.1) or refused in advance (552 5.3.4).

> **Note** Exchange Server is configured in kilobytes (KB), but the display that it gives to the EHLO command is shown in bytes.

The second size limitation that can be set on a virtual server is to restrict the total amount of data sent in a single connection. If a server has a number of e-mail messages queued for a domain hosted by an Exchange server, then the Limit session size to value will stop the sender server taking up too much bandwidth for extended periods by forcing the sender server to communicate in batches of data at a time. It does this by accepting each e-mail on the connection until one e-mail goes over the limit. This displays the *552 4.3.1 Session size exceeds fixed maximum session size* error and disconnects the session. The sender server will then attempt to reconnect and continue from the point when the e-mail failed. All the previously sent e-mail messages were accepted and should now have arrived at the user's mailbox.

Unlike the message size parameters, the server does not publish its session size, it just disconnects a session when it is exceeded. It is therefore important to ensure that your session limit is not less than, and preferably at least three times more than, your message size limit.

In the example SMTP virtual server that we are discussing during this section, the from Humongous Insurance virtual server could be set with a maximum message size and maximum session size greater than that which the company would typically accept from the Internet.

The third option on this dialog box is for limiting the number of messages per connection; by default this is set to 20. The fourth option limits the number of recipients in an incoming message to 64000, by default. If a message contains more than the maximum allowed number of recipients, then the sending SMTP server will need to cope with this and send the message again with the remaining recipients as a second message. A recipient of the message will see all the listed recipients even though the message connection that was used to send this particular instance of the message may not have sent the message to all the recipients. At the bottom of the Messages dialog box, the last four options affect messages that the virtual server has received successfully. The Send Copy Of Non-Delivery Report To option enables a user's mailbox to receive a copy of all e-mail messages that generated non-delivery reports (NDRs). An NDR is typically due to the misspelling of a user's e-mail address. The second most likely reason is addressing an e-mail to a common alias that does not exist, such as webmaster@ or sales@. As the Exchange organization size increases the number of NDRs is likely to increase in tandem, so leaving this option at the default is recommended. Regardless of which option is chosen, the sender (if a valid "reply to" e-mail address was provided) will receive an NDR telling them to contact the recipient directly to determine the correct e-mail address. If a user, which is typically the postmaster@ alias, receives a copy of the NDR the user can choose to forward the actual e-mail to the intended recipient. In Outlook 2003 this is achieved by clicking Send Again and addressing the e-mail correctly. The sending of the message onward to the recipient relies upon the NDR containing the original message. If the original message that the Exchange server attaches to the NDR exceeds 10 MB then it will not be attached, so the Send Again option in Outlook will not work.

The next two options on the dialog box, the BadMail and Queue folders are covered later in this chapter.

The final option on the Messages dialog box is for Forward All Mail With Unresolved Recipients To Host option. This option stops the virtual server from returning an NDR for unknown recipients and instead forwards the e-mail to another SMTP server for it to process and issue the NDRs. Care should be taken not to implement a loop in this option by setting the alternative server name to the current server name or to an alternative server name that forwards all messages back to this virtual server. This loop will result in no NDRs being sent and a significant drain on system resources on both this server and the alternative server.

The option to forward unresolved messages is typically used in organizations that have a second e-mail system holding recipients with the same domain name as the Exchange organization, but where the Exchange organization is the gateway system to and from the Internet. This is typically found in organizations that are migrating to Exchange from another e-mail platform that cannot coexist with Exchange and still have some recipients on that other platform. The unresolved recipients value can be entered as a fully qualified domain name (FQDN) or the IP address of the next hop. If an IP address is used it must be surrounded with square brackets like so: [192.168.5.10]. This is because the brackets indicate to Exchange Server that this is an IP address that can be used directly, and not a name that needs resolving.

Virtual Server Outgoing Message Setting

The third setting on the Messages dialog box controls this virtual server and its connections to other SMTP servers for the delivery of messages to them.

This setting forces multiple connections when sending, by default, more than 20 messages to a single destination server. This is a complementary setting to the maximum session size setting on the destination virtual server. If a destination virtual server has a maximum session size, the sending virtual server will not be aware of it. If that virtual server needs to send a number of e-mail messages in one session, it is more likely to exceed the session limit; therefore, this first outgoing option is to attempt to eclipse that happening by opening multiple sessions.

Virtual Server Delivery Settings

The Delivery tab contains, with one exception, settings that control this virtual server's delivery options. Care should be taken when creating a virtual server that will be used to deliver SMTP messages as delivery is often controlled by an SMTP connector. SMTP connectors have many of the same settings as a virtual server. Where the settings clash the SMTP connector takes precedence.

Outbound Delivery Options

All the options in the Outbound area of the dialog box control how often the virtual server will attempt to retry sending a message that failed when first sent. When Exchange is on a permanent network and not using dialup networking, it will attempt to deliver an e-mail as soon as it receives it by placing it in the queue and processing it when it reaches the top of the queue. This typically occurs within seconds of the e-mail arriving in the queue. Should delivery fail, retries will begin at the selected options. A virtual server that will be used to communicate with another SMTP system, such as the *from Humongous Insurance* virtual server that we have been creating in this section might require more frequent retry options than the default virtual server that is typically used to send e-mail to the Internet.

The default delivery retry times for the first three retries are at 10-minute intervals, and then every 15 minutes. After 12 hours, a delay notification will be sent to the sender. After two days, the sender will receive a #4.4.7 message saying that it was impossible to deliver the e-mail within the time limit specified.

Local Delivery Options

The two options in the Local area of the Delivery dialog box control the time outs for delivery to the mailbox and public folder stores on the server that the virtual server is running on. The major cause of items being queued for retry on local delivery will be due to a dismounted store, which could be due to a number of reasons. Topics pertaining to managing and repairing the store are covered in Chapters 22 and 23. If the store is not repaired and mounted again, the sender will receive the same error as above, stating it was impossible to deliver the e-mail within the time limit specified.

Outbound Security Delivery Options

The Outbound Security button on the Delivery options dialog box controls the type of authentication used to connect to remote SMTP hosts. Although these settings can be set here, typically they are not. A similar group of settings exist on SMTP connectors, and the use of an SMTP connector is preferred when controlling the delivery of e-mail to specific domains or servers. If an organization does not use an SMTP connector, outbound Internet e-mail will flow without further modification, but on the virtual server used for this outbound connection you would not enable any outbound security options apart from anonymous, because all Internet SMTP servers communicate anonymously.

Outbound Connections Delivery Options

The Outbound Connections button controls the virtual server's options when it connects to remote SMTP hosts.

The option Limit Number Of Connections To controls the maximum number of simultaneous outbound connections that this virtual server will make. The complementary option of Limit Number Of Connections Per Domain To controls the maximum number of simultaneous outbound connections that this virtual server will make for a single e-mail domain. The maximum number of connections defaults to 1000, and the maximum number of connections per domain defaults to 100.

If a remote server stops responding, this virtual server will disconnect after a default of 10 minutes to save connection resources, and the final option controls the port that this server will connect on. Typically, this will stay at 25, but it needs to be set to the port that the recipient SMTP server is listening for connections on.

Advanced Delivery Options

The Advanced Delivery options control mainly outbound connections and e-mail apart from the Perform Reverse DNS Lookup On Incoming Messages and Maximum Hop Count options.

The Perform Reverse DNS Lookup On Incoming Messages option adds name resolution information to an e-mail message header about the sending server. This information can then be used by spam-detecting applications or by the recipient to determine the validity of the e-mail. Exchange Server does not reject e-mail that comes from unresolved domains, unlike some anti-spam products that do attempt to reject e-mail if the reverse DNS lookup cannot be completed.

The Maximum Hop Count option, which defaults to 30 in this version of Exchange, delivers an NDR for any e-mail that has reached this virtual server after going through 30 SMTP servers before it reaches this one. As the message passes through an SMTP server, the header is appended with that SMTP server's relevant information. Each SMTP server evaluates the header and determines whether it has exceeded the maximum hop count defined. If the message has exceeded the SMTP server's maximum hop count, the message will be returned as undeliverable. Note that it does not mean 30 different SMTP servers. Consider the example where a loop between two servers has been configured. The e-mail would loop until it reached a virtual server's maximum hop count, at which point it would be deleted and an NDR issued.

The recommended setting for maximum hop count needs to allow for an e-mail to be routed through all the bridgehead servers in your organization. It also should provide for enough extra hops to allow for Internet e-mail that comes from large organizations with complex routing configurations. The value should not be too large because that could cause a looping e-mail to consume resources before being returned as an NDR.

The remaining settings in the Advanced Delivery dialog box affect outbound e-mail. The Masquerade Domain value replaces the local domain name in any Mail From lines in the e-mail message header. NDRs will be returned to the alternate domain specified, instead of the domain from which the e-mail message originated.

The Fully Qualified Domain Name option sets the name of the mail server when connected. In the initial 220 status line generated by the virtual server upon connecting to port 25, the FQDN and product/version are displayed. By default, the FQDN matches the server name but it does not need to. But it does need to resolve to an actual IP address, and the Check DNS button allows you to test this.

> **Important**   If this virtual server is accessible from the Internet, it is important that the FQDN value here is the same as the pointer (PTR) record for its Internet IP address. Some anti-spam and reverse DNS lookup systems may reject e-mail from this server as spoofed e-mail if the PTR record for the IP address does not match the FQDN.

The smart host value is covered in more detail in the section Smart Host Message Transfer later in this chapter. This setting in the SMTP virtual server causes all e-mail from this virtual server to be sent to the server specified in this field. The server specified in this field then processes the delivery of the message. If you have more than one Exchange server in your organization, you should not configure a smart host at the virtual server level or you might find that intra-organization e-mail does not work.

If the server is not using the services of a smart host and is unable to resolve Internet DNS addresses using its configured DNS servers (as these may be able to resolve only the internal DNS infrastructure), it may need DNS server addresses entered into the Configure External DNS Servers option by clicking the Configure button and entering the DNS servers to use for MX record and Reverse DNS lookup. All other requirements of DNS on this server will take the usual Windows Server method of the DNS address stored in the IP stack. Additionally, the DNS servers that Exchange Server uses need to be able to resolve TCP DNS queries and not just the standard User Datagram Protocol (UDP) DNS queries. If the DNS server rejects TCP DNS queries, which are used when looking up DNS records that are expected to return a large amount of data, then a different DNS server will be needed. This setting allows you to specify this alternate server if the DNS server used by the operating system is not able to service this type of request. The Windows 2000 and later DNS servers support queries via TCP and UDP.

Additional Virtual Server Settings

The IIS metabase is the repository of all the settings used by the SMTP service. When configuring IIS SMTP, changes can be made to the metabase using the command line or a metabase editor application. In Windows Server 2003 it is possible to edit the metabase directly using any XML editor if IIS is configured to allow you to do so.

When the IIS SMTP server has been extended by Exchange it is important to note that some of the settings are published to Active Directory by Exchange System Manager and then replicated to the IIS metabase. This replication is done by the Directory Service to Metabase Synchronization (DS2MB) process, and therefore any property controlled by this process must be modified in Exchange System Manager, or if not available in Exchange System Manager, in Active Directory using ADSI Edit. The location in Active Directory where these settings are stored is:

CN=Configuration\CN=Services\CN=Microsoft Exchange \CN=YourOrganization-Name\CN=Administrative   Groups\CN=YourAdminGroupName\CN=Servers\CN= YourServerName \CN=Protocols\CN=SMTP\CN=# where # is the virtual server instance number.

If you make a change to the IIS metabase that is also stored within Active Directory, the Active Directory setting will overwrite the metabase, assuming that the DS2MB process, which is part of the Microsoft Exchange System Attendant service, is running. Changes to the metabase are never replicated to Active Directory.

Changing the SMTP Banner

The SMTP virtual server that is published to the Internet will, upon connecting to it, display a banner indicating which e-mail server is running and what version it is. The default banner is:

220 <FQDN value> Microsoft ESMTP MAIL Service, Version: <Windows IIS SMTP Version> ready at <date> <GMT offset>

On the SMTP virtual server that is published to the Internet it is very easy to change this value to something more obscure. Note that tools exist on the Internet to fingerprint a server by sending commands to it and determining what server and version it is from the response. Changing the banner will not stop these tools from working, but blocking invalid and little-used commands such as VRFY in ISA Server can stop these tools working.

To change the SMTP server banner on a Windows Server 2003 OS (running IIS 6.0 with or without Exchange Server) open a command prompt. Change to c:\inetpub\adminscript and enter the following:

cscript adsutil.vbs set SMTPSvc/#/ConnectResponse "banner_string"

Note that # is the virtual server instance number and "*banner_string*" is the text you wish to present when connections are made to port 25. For information about completing this task on a Windows 2000 Server, see Microsoft Knowledge Base article, "How to Modify the SMTP Banner" (*http://go.microsoft.com/fwlink/ ?linkid=3052&kbid=281224*).

Working with Additional Virtual Servers

Once the virtual server has been created, it must be configured. The majority of these settings are available in Exchange System Manager, but not all of them. Occasionally, a setting needs to be changed in the metabase, which is the IIS configuration database, or in Active Directory.

To start, stop, or pause a specific SMTP virtual directory, right-click the virtual server in Exchange System Manager and choose Start, Stop, or Pause. Unavailable options, such as Pause when the server is stopped, are dimmed. If all three status options are unavailable, it is possible that the virtual server has either just been created and the folders have yet to be made or the virtual server configuration has corrupted. A paused virtual server will not accept any new connections but will continue to service existing connections until they complete and will continue to process the queue by attempting to deliver the items in the queue. The use of Pause allows a controlled shutdown of an SMTP virtual server.

Expanding the virtual server node in Exchange System Manager allows you to see the current connections and their duration. It is possible to terminate specific connections, or all connections, but note that virtual server settings, by default, will terminate a session if it is idle for 10 minutes.

Virtual servers can be renamed in the Exchange System Manager interface at any time to give them a good description for their purpose. The renaming option does not require a restart of the virtual server.

With the installation of Exchange Server 2003 SP1, one of the regular administrative tasks with a virtual server ceases to be a problem. This is the clearing out of the Badmail directory. With Exchange Server 2003 SP1, the Badmail directory is not populated with each badmail (e-mail messages contained in the BadMail folder), but rather the badmail is just discarded by the server.

Finally, the virtual server is the administrative location from which you enable filters if needed. Once the virtual server is configured and able to be used to receive e-mail, you can consider adding it to an SMTP connector to fully manage outbound e-mail.

Disabling SMTP Virtual Servers

Though it is enabled by default, not every Exchange server in the organization requires SMTP enabled on it. The SMTP services, and at least one SMTP virtual server needs to be running on all servers that host mailboxes, public folders, and all routing group bridgehead servers.

The servers that are most likely to operate without SMTP enabled are front-end servers, such as a server dedicated to processing Outlook Web Access traffic, where the front-end server is not used to route e-mail to other routing groups or the Internet. Front-end servers must not contain mailboxes, but if they are running SMTP they do need a private mail store mounted so that NDRs can be processed. If the front-end server does not take part in the delivery of e-mail around the Exchange organization, SMTP can be disabled and all information stores can be dismounted and deleted.

This dismounting of the private mailbox store stops the server from appearing in Active Directory Users and Computers when creating mailboxes. This reduces the number of servers that can be selected during mailbox enabling of an object, and ensures that users do not get their mailboxes accidentally created on a server that cannot host a mailbox.

> **Important** By setting the SMTP service to disabled, future service packs will not install, so to install the service pack, re-enable the service temporarily.

Running System Attendant on Front-End Servers

On Exchange servers that are configured as front-end servers, Exchange Server 2003 reduces the functionality of the System Attendant service by not running the DSProxy, Recipient Update Service, Offline Address Book Generation, Group Polling, Mailbox Management, and the Free/Busy service. Therefore, unlike the recommendations that exist about stopping the System Attendant service in Exchange 2000, in Exchange Server 2003 it is not necessary to do so because the System Attendant is only running that which it needs to rather than a longer list of additional, and now unneeded, processes.

Mailroot Directories for Virtual Servers

Exchange Server is a database-based application, and when the message arrives at its destination it is stored in the associated Exchange Server ESE database. While it travels across the SMTP virtual servers, the message will spend some time in folders that are on an NTFS file system. Each of these folders has a particular function, and although Exchange Server 2003 SP1 lessens the burden of checking these folders, they are needed for e-mail-flow troubleshooting.

The virtual server folders are created in *<drive>*:\Program Files\Exchsrvr\Mailroot\vsi *n*\ where *n* is the next available number.

> **Note**   A virtual server number is unavailable if the folder structure for that number exists, even though it is not used by a current virtual server.

The folders that Exchange Server creates under the \vsi *n*\ path are

- Queue
- BadMail
- Pickup
- Filter (only if using Sender Filtering with the Archive option enabled)
- UceArchive (only if Intelligent Message Filter is enabled on this virtual directory and has archived at least one message)

All these folders need to be accessible by the Exchange server and, in the cases of troubleshooting, by the Exchange Administrator, but they never need to be accessible to any users in your organization. If users were to have access to these folders and had the ability to log on locally to the Exchange server, they may be able to read confidential data in messages currently stored in these folders. To prevent this, the Exchange Server installation removes the local Users security group from the right to Log On Locally for that server. If users were to have this right, they would have permissions to the virtual server folders because these folders inherit the permissions from their parent folder, which ultimately inherits permissions from the Program Files folder. Note that this restriction does not stop the contents of e-mail messages being read as they travel across a network. SMTP does not encrypt e-mail messages by default, though options to do this do exist.

> **Important**   The virtual server folders must not be scanned by a file-level or memory-resident antivirus product because these folders queue e-mail for delivery and should not be affected by other processes. An antivirus product may cause a lock on a file in the queue, causing problems with the Exchange server's attempts to deliver that message.

The Queue Folder

The Queue folder is a store for messages that are pending delivery. When an SMTP virtual server cannot reach the next hop, the message is stored in the Queue folder. It is very important to monitor the number of messages in this folder. Performance Monitor (and any monitoring application that can read PerfMon data, such as Microsoft

Operations Manager) can have alerts set on the SMTP Server, Remote Queue Length value, and the Queue Viewer application (part of Exchange System Manager) reports on the status of messages within the queues, and thus within this folder.

For bridgehead servers that are most likely to utilize the queue, the best location for your SMTP virtual server Queue folder is to locate it on a fast RAID 0+1 (mirrored and striped) array. By default, the SMTP Queue folder is located on the same drive as the Exchsrvr folder, which is not usually the best drive choice in terms of I/O. On an Exchange server that is not a bridgehead server, it is unlikely that items will queue and is therefore unnecessary, in most cases, to move the queue.

In Exchange Server 2003, it is very easy to move the Queue folder. The current path can be found via Exchange System Manager on the Messages tab of the SMTP virtual server properties dialog box. It is changed by browsing to the new location. You do not need to move the BadMail folder when you move the queue as they can be located on different drives. In Exchange Server 2003 SP1 the BadMail folder, by default, is not populated and does not need to be moved from the default location unless it is going to be used.

> **Note** The virtual server needs to be stopped before it can be moved and manually started once it has been moved. If your queue currently contains many queued messages this may take considerable time and should only be done during virtual server creation or off-peak hours.

In Exchange 2000 Server, moving the Queue folder was achieved through ADSI Edit and Windows Explorer.

The BadMail Folder

Badmail is an e-mail message that Exchange Server cannot deliver or send an NDR for. In versions of Exchange prior to Exchange Server 2003 SP1, the maximum size for the BadMail folder was the maximum size of the partition it was installed on, and if it reached this size it would cause the SMTP service to stop.

In Exchange Server 2003 SP1, the default behavior has been changed so badmail messages are not stored. For the majority of administrators, the badmail messages are never examined and are occasionally deleted en masse, so not storing them in the first place results in proactive management of this folder for the administrator.

To change the default settings in SP1-based Exchange servers, you can make changes in the registry. The registry key is `HKEY_LOCAL_MACHINE\System\CurrentControlSet\Services\SMTPSVC\Queuing` and the two values are `MaxBadMailFolderSize` (DWORD) and `BadMailSyncPeriod`.

`MaxBadMailFolderSize` is the maximum number in kilobytes that each BadMail folder will grow to. This is a global setting for the server; that is, you cannot have different values for different badmail folders. Once the value is reached, the server will stop saving badmail messages to that folder until the folder is emptied again. A badmail folder that reaches its limit stops the future recording of badmail. It does not delete the oldest messages to keep within the limits of the registry key. Badmail messages that had been stored prior to SP1 installation remain in the folder until they are removed manually, as they are not deleted by the SP1 installation. Using a value of 0xffffffff (hex) for the `MaxBadMailFolderSize` registry key will give you the same functionality as in pre-Exchange Server 2003 SP1, which is badmail limited by available disk space. When the `MaxBadMailFolderSize` registry key is not set, or it is set to the value 0, it means no badmail is written.

Exchange Server administrators who need to process and check the BadMail folder can set the `MaxBadMailFolderSize` registry key to a sensible limit to ensure that badmail messages never fill the disk and also allow for the processing of badmail. For example, companies that send publications by e-mail may find that the BadMail folder prior to SP1 is a good source of invalid e-mail addresses. This folder can be processed with a script to remove these addresses from the publication recipient database.

Further assistance for the processing of badmail is available in the Badmail Deletion and Archiving script from Microsoft. This tool is available from the Downloads for Exchange Server 2003 website at *http://www.microsoft.com/exchange/downloads/*. This tool is installed by copying the script to a folder of choice and scheduling it to run at times of low activity. The script loops through each BadMail folder and processes the individual files that it finds in the folder. Typically, processing is the deletion of the badmail, but archiving the badmail is one of the options in the script.

To improve the performance of the script, as it uses Windows Scripting Host, ensure that the schedule is often enough so that there are not too many badmail messages to process. If you have a lot of badmail to process, such as before you run the script for the first time, we recommend that you delete the contents of the folder from the command line with **del *.*** as this will use less resources than the script.

The badmail script will also run against Exchange Server 2000 servers and Exchange Server 2003 pre-SP1 servers that do not have support for the `MaxBadMailFolderSize` registry key.

The second registry key is `BadMailSyncPeriod`. This value (in minutes) determines how frequently Exchange looks to see if the BadMail folder has been deleted. For performance reasons the server caches the size of the BadMail folder and if the contents of the folder have been deleted the system will not notice until this interval has passed. This value is used only when a `MaxBadMailFolderSize` value is specified. The `BadMailSyncPeriod` default value, if not specified in the registry, is every 12 hours. If the BadMail folder is being populated and it reaches the value of `MaxBadMailFolderSize`, then no more badmail will be saved until Exchange Server knows that the size of the BadMail folder has reduced below `MaxBadMailFolderSize`. The Exchange server only checks the size of the BadMail folder every `BadMailSyncPeriod` interval.

The Pickup Folder

The functionality of the Pickup folder was added to the IIS SMTP virtual server primarily as a way of creating e-mail by scripts. Technologies such as Collaboration Data Objects (CDO) supersede the functionality of the Pickup folder, but its functions can still be used and can assist in troubleshooting your server. Normal delivery and processing of SMTP e-mail within the Exchange server do not use the Pickup folder, but with its previously described functions it has a number of uses.

For scripting, the Pickup folder is used as a starting point for the processing and delivery of any RFC 2822 formatted e-mail placed inside the folder. As long as the message is properly formatted it will be delivered. This functionality is available in the SMTP server that comes as part of IIS, so it is also present with the Exchange SMTP server that is based upon the IIS SMTP server. Scripts can be easily written to create a file conforming to the RFC 2822 standard and saved to the Pickup folder. Once the file is saved and the handle to the file released, then the e-mail is processed.

Another use of the Pickup folder is to use it as a troubleshooting tool. If e-mail is not flowing correctly, you can check if the problem is with the SMTP virtual server rather than other parts of Exchange by creating the following file and copying it into the Pickup folder.

The structure of the RFC 2822 formatted text file is:

```
X-Sender: sender@yourdomain.com
X-Receiver: recipient@yourdomain.com
Subject: Pickup Folder Test E-mail

This is the body of a pickup folder test e-mail
```

You need to make sure that a blank line exists between the subject and the body. If correctly structured, the e-mail is delivered to the recipient on the To line. The SMTP service attempts to create the RFC-2821 (SMTP) Mail From and Rcpt To information from the pickup message. The preferred source for this information is through the X-Sender and X-Receiver headers. If this source is not found, attempts are made to figure it out from the information in the message. If the header contains both the Sender and From fields, then the Sender field takes precedence over the From field.

> **Tip**   Do not move the file into the Pickup folder because as soon as a file appears in this folder it is processed and disappears. If you move the file in, you will lose your original and have to recreate it. If you copy the file in, you can easily and repeatedly test when necessary, using the same source file.

If e-mail can be delivered from the Pickup folder but not from a client, such as Outlook, then the steps that need to be taken to fix the problem do not have to include the SMTP virtual servers, firewalls, or IP routing.

The Filter Folder

The Filter folder is created when Sender Filtering with archiving is enabled in Exchange System Manager. Sender filters are enabled from the Message Delivery Properties dialog box in Global Settings. Once a filter is enabled, remember to enable the relevant SMTP virtual servers in your organization to use these filters. (Figure 11-39 later in this chapter shows this warning.)

For example, Figure 11-8 shows the setup needed to archive e-mail from a particular source, without notifying them that it was being filtered if, for example, litigation was ongoing with that company.

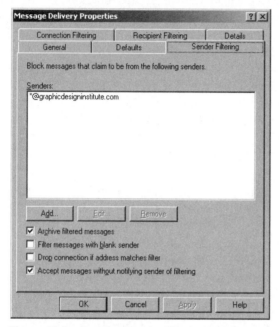

Figure 11-8   Enabling Sender Filtering with the archive option enabled

Once a message arrives that meets the filter criteria it is stored as a .tmp file in the Filter folder. This file can be opened and read by Notepad or Outlook Express. To open the file in Outlook Express, rename the file to have the .eml extension instead of the .tmp extension.

> **Tip**   Once archiving is enabled, the Filter folder could fill the disk and cause a denial of service. Plan a regular maintenance schedule for this folder.

The UceArchive Folder

This folder exists if the Intelligent Message Filter is installed and enabled on the SMTP virtual server and is configured to archive spam messages. This folder is first created when an incoming message is archived because it is greater than or equal to the Gateway Blocking Configuration threshold value for Intelligent Message Filter. If archiving has never been enabled or no message has been archived, then this folder will not exist.

The UceArchive folder can be relocated by adding the `ArchiveDir` (`STRING`) registry value. This value is created inside the `HKEY_LOCAL_MACHINE\Software\Microsoft\ Exchange\ContentFilter` registry location. The value of `ArchiveDir` is the full path to the new folder for the archive on the local server.

Controlling Incoming Connections

It is important for an Exchange Server administrator to know how SMTP works so it is possible to configure Exchange and test the changes.

SMTP is a protocol that issues readable commands and responses. It is therefore very easy to assume either the role of a sending SMTP server using Telnet or using tools such as WinsockTool (which can be downloaded from *http://isatools.org/*) to become an SMTP client or server. But before you can do this, SMTP commands need to be understood.

Exchange Server and SMTP Message Transfer Support

All Internet e-mail travels via SMTP. SMTP has been around a number of years and is now the de facto standard for e-mail communication, replacing a number of options only a few years ago. When someone gives you an Internet e-mail address, it is always an SMTP e-mail address. SMTP e-mail addresses can be identified by the @ character in the address, which separates the user's mailbox name from the domain name.

Exchange Server 2000 and Exchange Server 2003 support both the original SMTP standards, published in RFC 2821 and RFC 2822, and the ESMTP standard, published in RFC 1869, in addition to a number of other additions to SMTP published in numerous other RFCs.

How SMTP Communication Occurs

When an Exchange server communicates with another SMTP server (either another Exchange server or another SMTP server product) it will do so, by default, over TCP port 25. Communication occurs when the sending server opens a TCP session to the destination server on port 25 and waits for the destination server to respond with a message indicating that it is ready. The sending server typically finds the destination server by DNS lookup for the MX record and the destination server (if ready) will always answer with a 220 response. The 220 response may include other information but this is not used by the sender server to determine the capabilities of the destination server. For example, a server running Exchange Server 2003 SP1 will respond as follows:

```
220 <server_name> Microsoft ESMTP MAIL Service,
Version: <Windows IIS SMTP Version> ready at <date> <time> <GMT_offset>
```

The communication between Exchange Server 2003 (SMTP1) at Woodgrove Bank and an older server that supports only SMTP (SMTP2) at A. Datum Corporation (adatum.com) will be as follows:

1. SMTP1 initiates a TCP connection to SMTP2 on port 25. SMTP2 responds with "220 smtp2.adatum.com SMTP Server." The connection is now open and ready as the destination server reported 220 as the first characters in the response. The remaining characters typically list the company and the e-mail server product/ version they are using.

2. SMTP1 sends the EHLO command (extended hello greeting) followed by its full Internet name. This might look like *ehlo smtp1.woodgrovebank.com*. The destination server will respond with 500, indicating that the EHLO command is not accepted as it is an older SMTP server that does not support the ESMTP extensions. The Exchange server SMTP1 will then retry with *helo smtp1.woodgrovebank.com*. A 250 response indicates that all is okay to proceed further.

3. SMTP1 identifies the sender of the message using the *mail from: <mailbox@woodgrovebank.com>* command. Again, a successful response is identified by SMTP2 returning a 250 response.

4. Next SMTP1 identifies the recipients of the e-mail. This is in the form *rcpt to: <mailbox@adatum.com>*. Unlike the sender, which can only be specified once, multiple recipients are e-mailed by repeating the rcpt to: command with a user per line. Again, 250 is the response that signifies all is working well.

5. Once all the recipients have been listed, it is time to send the e-mail data. This is sent as 7-bit American Standard Code for Information Interchange (ASCII) text with typically no more than 1000 characters per line. The e-mail data is sent by SMTP1 sending the *data* command on a line on its own and SMTP2 responding with 354, indicating that it is ready to receive the message. Often this 354 response contains instructions on how to indicate that the data of the e-mail is finished. Like the 220 response at the start of the session, this extra text is not acted upon by the server but can be useful when testing connections to e-mail servers, and it tells the administrator what to do next.

6. When SMTP1 has finished sending the e-mail data, it indicates this to SMTP2 by sending a special sequence of characters. This sequence is Carriage Return, Line Feed, Full Stop, Carriage Return, Line Feed. This is often written as **<CRLF>.<CRLF>**. In Windows Telnet this can be entered by typing **[ENTER].[ENTER]**

7. If that is the end of the e-mail flow between SMTP1 and SMTP2, SMTP1 closes the SMTP session with the quit command. SMTP2 responds with 221 and then SMTP2 closes the connection. If SMTP1 has other e-mail to send, it issues the RSET command and starts with a new Mail from command. This whole message flow is summarized in Figure 11-9.

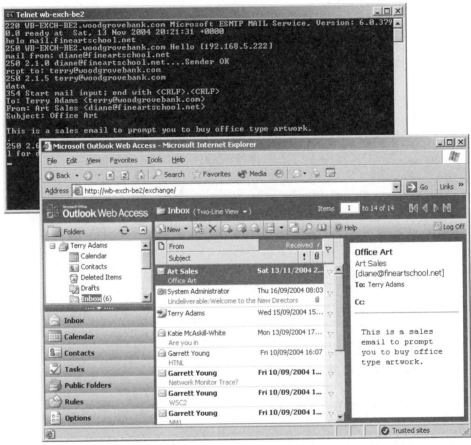

Figure 11-9 SMTP communication shown on the command line and the resulting e-mail

The transfer of SMTP follows this process typically in clear text over TCP port 25. In addition to the commands above, Table 11-4 lists the majority of SMTP commands and Table 11-5 the SMTP response codes.

Table 11-4 The Main SMTP Commands

Command	Function
HELO	Initiates SMTP between the hosts. It is also used to identify the sending SMTP server by way of the server's FQDN.
HELP	Displays the supported commands on the destination server.

Table 11-4   The Main SMTP Commands (Continued)

Command	Function
MAIL FROM:	The sender of the e-mail. Always followed by the sender's e-mail address in the form of mailbox@example.com.
RCPT TO:	Each recipient of the e-mail in the form of mailbox@example.com.
VRFY	Used to verify that the recipient exists before sending the message. This command is not typically used and is often disabled as it could provide a way for spammers to obtain valid e-mail addresses. This command does not work in Exchange 2000 or 2003 even though it is listed as a valid command. If the VRFY command is sent to an Exchange server, the response will always be 252 2.1.5 Cannot VRFY user, but will take message for <user@domain>.
DATA	Notifies the recipient server that the e-mail data is about to come.
RSET	Resets the current session. All the commands previously entered that did not result in a completed e-mail are now considered void apart from the HELO command.
TURN	Used to collect e-mail that is held on a backup e-mail server once the primary server is online. TURN is typically not used anymore because of a security flaw in the way it works. An issued TURN command will send all the queued e-mail along the current session without validating that the current session is from the primary server.
NOOP	Does not do anything but will get back a 250 response indicating that all is okay (if that is so).
QUIT	Quits the session and causes the TCP connection to be terminated.

The response codes listed in Table 11-5 are listed in four categories based on the initial digit of the response code. Responses starting 2xx mean command accepted, those that start 3xx are for general flow control, 4xx for failure in transmission, and 5xx for errors in the SMTP commands.

Table 11-5   SMTP Response Codes

Response code	Description
211	System status response.
214	Help message (this information is only useful to a human user).
220	Service ready response.
221	Service closing transmission channel.
250	Requested action okay and completed.
251	User not local. Will forward the mail onward.
354	Start mail input; end with <CRLF>.<CRLF>.
450	Requested mail action not taken because the mailbox is unavailable (e.g., mailbox busy).

Table 11-5   SMTP Response Codes (Continued)

Response code	Description
451	Requested action aborted due to local error in processing the command.
452	Requested action not taken due to insufficient system storage.
500	Syntax error, command unrecognized. This may include errors such as command line too long or spelled incorrectly.
550	Requested action not taken. For example, refusing to relay an e-mail.
554	Transaction failed.

How ESMTP Communication Occurs

ESMTP from RFC 1869 also uses TCP port 25 to communicate; however, it allows for the addition of other commands to improve the message flow between the servers. The communication between two SMTP servers, where the sending SMTP server supports ESMTP, will be as follows:

1. SMTP1 initiates a TCP connection to SMTP2 on port 25. SMTP2 responds with "220 smtp2.adatum.com ESMTP Server." Like SMTP, a 220 response means all ready and though in this example the responding server says it is an ESMTP server in the 220 line, this is not used by the sending server to determine this fact. A sending server will only know that a server supports ESMTP by a valid response to the EHLO command.

2. SMTP1 sends the EHLO command followed by its full Internet name. This might look like *ehlo smtp1.woodgrovebank.com*. The destination server will respond with 250 indicating that the EHLO command is accepted and all is okay to proceed further. In addition to this single 250 response, numerous other 250 responses precede it, each indicating an enhanced function of the server.

3. SMTP1 now uses whatever ESMTP commands it knows the destination server supports, in addition to any SMTP commands it needs to use. If the destination server does not support ESMTP it would return a 500 response. The sending server would then issue the HELO command and continue as described previously for an SMTP session.

Some of the more useful ESMTP commands are:

- **SIZE**   This tells the sending server what the maximum accepted size of e-mail will be. In SMTP, the destination server would report an error if the size is exceeded once the entire message has been transferred, but in ESMTP the sender can know in advance the maximum e-mail size without sending any data and thus save bandwidth. The size value is given in bytes.

- **CHUNKING**   SMTP in RFC 2821 defines that the DATA command initiates the message transfer and <CRLF>.<CRLF> to finish. From the point of view of the server, this means that it does not know when the data is going to finish and has to inspect each byte to see if it is the termination code. This is a very slow way of sending a data chunk, so RFC 1830 allows for the size of the message to be stated before the message is sent. In ESMTP this is done by replacing the data command with the BDAT command. The BDAT command contains the size of the message, and when the destination server has received that number of bytes it assumes that the message is finished. An Exchange 2003 server will advertise that it supports chunking via the EHLO command and will use chunking when sending e-mail to a server that also supports it.

- **PIPELINING**   SMTP requires that for each command issued, a response is given. This too is a slow way to transfer messages when the connections between servers are now much more reliable and the servers are much better at being standards-based than when the original RFC was published. This performance bottleneck is overcome by pipelining, as written in RFC 2197. This streams multiple commands from server to server without waiting for an acknowledgement between each command.

- **ETRN**   Small companies and small branch offices may require e-mail but not at the expense of a permanent connection to the Internet. Rather than have the users at these locations rely on ISP-offered e-mail servers, these companies can provide their own servers with their own backup and service-level agreements, and connect to the ISP or head office, on a schedule, collecting all the e-mail that is waiting for them. This is also an improvement on each user having a modem (or sharing a modem) to get his or her own e-mail from the ISP. At a given schedule, the server connects to the ETRN server and collects all the e-mail that has been held for it. This is implemented by listing the MX record for the ISP's SMTP server with a lower preference than the MX record for the actual destination. Because the destination server is not always connected, the majority of e-mail goes to the ISP server as that is always connected to the Internet. When the primary server comes online, it issues an ETRN command to have its stored e-mail dequeued from the ISP server. The initial implementation of ETRN is known as TURN, but TURN will send the e-mail to anyone who asks for it, based on the value given in the HELO command. Later implementations of TURN protect against this and require authentication (sometimes known as ATRN). ETRN servers open a separate connection to the primary server upon request and push the waiting e-mail messages. Should the ETRN command not be issued by a valid server, the opening of the connection to the primary server will fail (as it is still offline) and e-mail will remain stored until the primary server is online. ATRN sends the e-mail over the current connection so the authentication requirement means that only authorized servers can connect and retrieve e-mail, assuming that the username and password is not compromised.

- **TLS** The STARTTLS command for ESMTP allows the entire message communication to be encrypted with public/private key encryption. TLS is based upon SSL, but unlike SSL commonly found on websites, the port number remains the same so encrypted communications between two TLS supported servers can occur over the same open firewall ports as non-encrypted SMTP. Publicly available SMTP servers must not require the use of TLS sessions, but can offer them if the remote server wants to use them. Additionally, public MX-listed SMTP servers should never use a digital certificate from a private Certificate Authority. This will stop some Internet SMTP servers from sending messages to your SMTP server as they will try to do TLS, fail because they do not trust the certificate issuer, and then abort the session, issuing an NDR as per the STARTTLS RFC.

- **ENHANCEDSTATUSCODES** When supported, this means that this server will return additional status codes in every error message. The default SMTP error codes are described in Table 11-5 whereas ENHANCEDSTATUSCODES mean that an error might look like *550 5.7.1 <error text>*, where 5.7.1 is the enhanced status code. This ESMTP extension is described in RFC 2034.

- **8bitmime** When e-mail is transferred between two SMTP servers, it is sent in a 7-bit format. Subsequent to the initial RFCs for SMTP, the common data format of messages has changed from ASCII text to messages with attachments, HTML bodies, and character ranges not supported by ASCII. These newer uses of e-mail are typically not in 7-bit format but 8bitmime. Preventing the message body from being encoded in 7 bit and then decoded at the destination reduces overhead. When two Exchange 2003 servers communicate they will always send the message body in 8bitmime format if it is already 8bitmime format and avoid the CPU cycles associated with the conversion. 8bitmime transport can be found in RFC 1652.

- **X-LINK2STATE** This is used between Exchange 2000 and later Exchange servers to exchange link state information.

- **XEXCH50** This is used to transfer Exchange-specific information about a message between Exchange servers.

Figure 11-10 shows a Telnet session to an Exchange 2003 server and the response to the EHLO command. The response shows the ESMTP commands that are supported by this server.

```
Telnet wb-exch-be1                                                    _ □ X
220 WB-EXCH-BE1.woodgrovebank.com Microsoft ESMTP MAIL Service, Version: 6.0.379
0.0 ready at  Fri, 30 Jul 2004 19:20:08 +0100
ehlo mail.fineartschool.net
250-WB-EXCH-BE1.woodgrovebank.com Hello [192.168.5.240]
250-TURN
250-SIZE
250-ETRN
250-PIPELINING
250-DSN
250-ENHANCEDSTATUSCODES
250-8bitmime
250-BINARYMIME
250-CHUNKING
250-VRFY
250-X-EXPS GSSAPI NTLM LOGIN
250-X-EXPS=LOGIN
250-AUTH GSSAPI NTLM LOGIN
250-AUTH=LOGIN
250-X-LINK2STATE
250-XEXCH50
250 OK
```

Figure 11-10   ESMTP commands available in Exchange 2003 Server

Earlier it was stated that commands such as VRFY and TURN are known to present security issues. These commands can be blocked using ISA Server as your firewall; however, Exchange Server still advertises that your network can accept them.

More Info   For more information about how to disable commands on your Internet-connected Exchange server, see Microsoft Knowledge Base article 257569, "How to turn off ESMTP verbs in Exchange 2000 Server and in Exchange Server 2003" (*http://go.microsoft.com/fwlink/?linkid=3052& kbid=257569*).

Testing SMTP and ESMTP Connections Across Firewalls

Using the SMTP and ESTMP commands above, it is possible to test the communication path between the Internet and your Exchange server (or vice versa) using the command line. The command to type is **telnet smtp-server-fqdn 25** from your Exchange 2003 server, or if testing inbound e-mail connectivity, type **telnet exchange-fqdn 25** from a valid machine on the Internet using the correct FQDN in each case. Once the destination server responds with 220 you can start to enter EHLO or HELO commands to send a simple e-mail. Two words of caution though: the Telnet client does not allow corrections to typographical mistakes that you make, so type carefully and remember to use RSET if you need to start again, and a second caution is to use your own e-mail address in testing and not someone else's. You will want to see if the connection works by being able to read the e-mail. If you get it wrong, the NDR will come to you and not to someone else.

> **Tip** As the Windows Telnet client does not allow editing of the command before it is sent, another option is to use a free testing tool available from *http://isatools.org/winsocktool.msi* that allows you to edit your commands before sending them.

Securing Incoming Message Traffic

Once the correct configuration has been made to your default virtual server and to any additional virtual servers that you need, you can begin to securely connect these virtual servers to those sending e-mail to them. At the beginning of this chapter, we looked at the prerequisites for receiving Internet e-mail; these being the DNS configuration and a brief look at network configuration including smart hosts and front-end servers. In this section, we will look at securing your network so that only what you allow to enter will do so.

Firewalls

To protect any network it is important to install a firewall (or more than one firewall in a series) that is capable of protecting the network from all known types of attack. A few years ago the recommendation was to install a packet filtering firewall. Later on, stateful firewalls became popular. Today, it is vital that an application layer firewall is also installed.

A packet filter firewall operates up to layer 4 of the OSI network model. For the TCP/IP protocol this means that a packet filter firewall can block or allow a range of ports but cannot ensure that the data within the packet is valid for that port. Additionally, packet filtering firewalls tend to be static in their rules. You must open all the ports that could ever be used so they are typically configured to block a selection of low-numbered ports because all the ports above 1023 can be used by client communications. A company running its own Exchange server behind a packet filtering firewall would need to have TCP port 25 continually open.

Stateful firewalls were an improvement on static packet filtering firewalls because they allow the dynamic opening of a client port for outbound traffic (from the protected network to the Internet) and the return of data from that outbound connection back in again, for a limited period of time. Therefore, all ports inbound and outbound can be closed, and protocols used by clients are dynamically opened when needed. Inbound connections (Internet to the protected network) not associated with a previous outbound dynamically opened port will be blocked; therefore, a company needing to accept inbound SMTP connections must have TCP port 25 always open just like the static packet filter.

In addition to the firewall types described previously, firewalls could restrict access to the open port based upon the source of the packet, but these are typically of no benefit to the Exchange Server administrator because you typically need to be able to accept e-mail from any address on the Internet.

An application layer firewall, such as Microsoft ISA Server 2000 or 2004, is now a vital part of a network's defenses. In addition to the stateful packet filtering and restricted source IP address functionality of the previous generation of firewalls, an application layer firewall can inspect packets at OSI layer 7 (the application layer) to ensure that they meet the requirements of the network. Application layer firewalls are slower than static packet filters because they do more work on the packet, but it does not mean the end of the simple packet filtering firewall. A packet filter firewall, usually a hardware implementation, is fast, so it is a good first line of defense in filtering out all that is not needed, allowing the processing of the application layer firewall to be dedicated to the data that is going to be allowed into the network. On networks with low traffic flow, or where speed is not of the essence, one firewall able to filter at all layers is sufficient.

Application-layer firewalls must be able to change with the threats that exist on the Internet, so a product such as Microsoft ISA Server, which comes with some default filters and can have additional application layer filters installed on it, is ideal for protecting your network. ISA Server 2000 with Feature Pack 1 installed (and later) comes with two application filters and a protocol definition that can help the Exchange Server administrator. The application filters are the SMTP Filter (and optional message screener) and the URLScan HTTP filter. The new protocol definition is the Exchange RPC Server protocol. This is in addition to a built-in feature of the product where traffic to selected Web servers can be blocked if the URL requested is not allowed. Therefore, you can allow access from the Internet to your Exchange servers on your protected network for just the URLs that Outlook Web Access uses.

Protecting Your Exchange Server Network with ISA Server

An ISA Server acting as a firewall has at least two network interfaces, one interface connected to the internal network and one to the external network. Firewalls can be used in a series, and so an external network might be further protected by another firewall, where the external network of one firewall is the internal network of another. This middle network is known as a perimeter network or DMZ and the firewall configuration is referred to as a back-to-back firewall design. Depending upon the size and security needs of your company, a perimeter network can be used to hold servers that are available to the Internet that should be kept separate from the internal LAN.

Protecting Inbound SMTP E-Mail

Configuring an ISA Server to make a service that is running on a server on the internal network available to the external network is known as publishing. Publishing requires that the port used on the internal server is free to be used on the external interface of the ISA Server also. Therefore, the first step in allowing inbound SMTP traffic through an ISA Server is to publish the internal SMTP virtual server on the external interface of the ISA Server. Running the command *netstat –an | find ":25"* on the ISA Server first will show if this will be possible. If some other service, such as a locally installed SMTP server, is listening on TCP port 25 of the ISA Server, the publishing of the internal SMTP server will not work. The previous command will return nothing if there is no service listening on port 25. The result of this command is shown in Figure 11-11, with port 25 free in the top left command prompt and an example of port 25 in use in the bottom right command prompt.

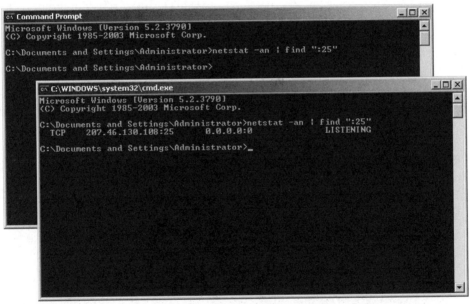

Figure 11-11   Netstat command showing that TCP port 25 is free, or not free, to use

An internal server is capable of being published on the external interface of the ISA Server as long as it can route packets to the Internet through the ISA Server. This is known as SecureNAT and is typically configured by setting the default gateway of the server to be published to the IP address of the internal network card on the ISA Server (or to a router on the server's subnet that has a default route to the Internet that goes via this internal IP address of the ISA Server). Installation of the ISA Server Firewall Client is another way to achieve this without the routing requirements of SecureNAT.

Once the routing configuration of the server is correct, it is time to configure the rules to allow inbound SMTP. It is not always the case that the server that receives e-mail from the Internet is the same server that will send them to the Internet. We will look at this scenario later when examining outbound SMTP.

The server that will have TCP port 25 published on the external interface of the ISA Server will be the server that is designated to receive e-mail from the Internet. If an organization has more than one receiving server and each needs to be published on a single ISA Server, then you will need multiple Internet IP addresses on the ISA Server, and then publish each server on a different IP address but on TCP port 25. You would not be able to publish two servers, both for TCP port 25, on the same external IP address of the ISA Server.

Publishing an internal Exchange server in ISA Server can be easily achieved by running the Mail Server Security Wizard in ISA Server 2000, shown in part in Figure 11-12 or by creating a Mail Server Publishing Rule in ISA Server 2004. These rules will publish an internal server for SMTP, and if needed, the ports for other protocols such as POP3 and IMAP4. ISA Server 2000 can also configure outbound SMTP if that option is chosen during the wizard. ISA Server 2004 requires creating an Access Rule for outbound traffic.

Manually completing Server Publishing in ISA Server for SMTP involves creating a new server publishing rule and choosing the SMTP server that will first receive Internet e-mail (the gateway server) and the external IP address on the ISA Server that will listen for connections from the Internet for that server. The Mail Server Security Wizard achieves this and other tasks based on what options are selected in it.

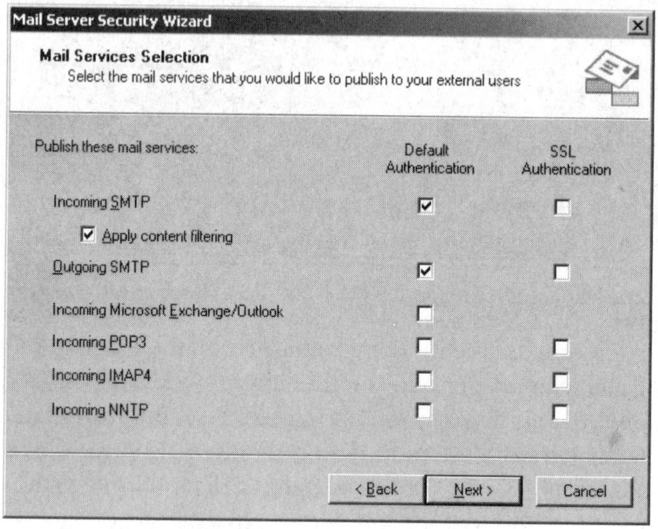

Figure 11-12   Starting the ISA Server 2000 Mail Server Security Wizard

Once the wizard is complete, you can receive Internet e-mail. The configuration is not yet complete, however, so once you have tested that you can connect to the Exchange server from the Internet you should disable the SMTP Server publishing rule (found in Server Publishing in the ISA Server 2000 management program) until the configuration is fully completed. In ISA Server 2004 the publishing rule is found on the Firewall Policy node of the management program.

Once the SMTP publishing rule is in place, the ISA Server SMTP Filter can be configured. In ISA Server 2000, if the option to Apply Content Filtering (Figure 11-12) was selected during the Mail Server Security Wizard, this application filter will already be enabled. In ISA Server 2000 the filter is found under the Extensions, Applications node of the ISA management program. ISA Server 2004 automatically enables the SMTP Filter on an SMTP Server publishing rule, and the filter can be found under the Configuration, Add-ins node of the ISA Server 2004 management program.

The SMTP Filter operates by the examination of both the properties of the SMTP connection and the content of the e-mail. For the parts of the filter that examine the content of the e-mail, the Message Screener component needs to be installed on an IIS SMTP server. Without the installation of the Message Screener, the SMTP Filter can only be used to stop the use of invalid SMTP commands. The Message Screener component is suitably replaced and improved upon by Connection Filters in Exchange Server 2003, but the command blocking component is still very useful on an ISA Server that protects an Exchange organization.

The SMTP Commands option of the SMTP Filter Properties dialog box (shown in Figure 11-13) allows you to disable and limit the use of SMTP commands. If an SMTP client then issues one of these commands, or if it issues a valid command that exceeds the allowed length of the command, the client will be disconnected. For example, it might be found that a buffer overflow exists in an SMTP server product when the EHLO command is sent with more than 1000 characters on the command line. ISA Server will protect this SMTP server even before the flaw is known because it limits the EHLO command to a maximum of 71 characters in length. ISA Server ignores commands not listed in the filter and protects all SMTP server products regardless of what commands they support.

More Info For more information about deploying application filtering with ISA Server, see Chapter 2 of the book *Introducing the ISA Server 2000 Application Layer Filtering Kit* (*http://isaserver.org/articles/spamalfkit.html*).

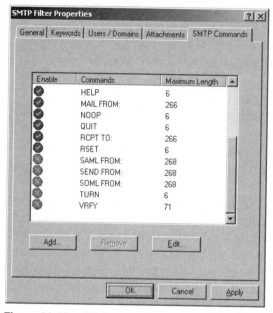

Figure 11-13   ISA Server SMTP extension with some disabled SMTP commands

Protecting Outbound SMTP E-Mail

To allow outbound SMTP connections from an Exchange server you need to create a rule to allow TCP port 25 connections from the servers that will send e-mail to the Internet. The end point of the connection will either be all Internet IP addresses, if using DNS for delivery, or a specific SMTP server if using a smart host for delivery.

Both versions of Microsoft ISA Server have a protocol object configured for TCP port 25 outbound. This protocol is named SMTP and should not be confused with the SMTP Server protocol which is the same port, but inbound. The other components of the rule are the source and destination. ISA Server 2000 outbound rules, named Protocol Rules, also require Site and Content Rule(s) to control destination. Therefore, if your ISA Server allows Web browsing to all Internet addresses, it cannot also limit outbound SMTP connections to the specific address of your smart host because the "all Internet addresses Site and Content Rule" works for both the HTTP and SMTP Protocol Rules. In ISA Server 2004 each Access Rule (a combination of the ISA Server 2000 Protocol Rule and Site and Content Rule) can allow different protocols to connect to various destinations.

Configuring your network for outbound e-mail delivery is more complex than inbound, mainly because different network designs require specific configurations. The different configurations that we will examine in this book are:

- Limiting TCP port 25 outbound

- Using a dedicated routing group for outbound e-mail

- Smart host in perimeter network

- Using the same inbound and outbound SMTP servers

- Using different inbound and outbound SMTP servers

- Providing SMTP services to customers

Limiting TCP Port 25 Outbound

A best practice for firewall design is to ensure that only the gateway SMTP servers can send e-mail to the Internet. Do not just open TCP port 25 on your firewalls for global outbound access, but limit the firewall rule to those Exchange servers that are hosting the SMTP connectors that deliver mail to Internet-located address spaces. Figure 11-14 shows a firewall rule named "SMTP Out" in ISA Server 2004 that allows a selected list of servers, Exchange Gateway Servers, to reach the Internet (External). The second rule allowing DNS Lookups is needed so the internal DNS servers can look up and resolve MX and A records on the Internet. This rule, though, only allows these requests to come from the DNS servers on the LAN. No other Internet traffic is allowed in this example, and for Internet e-mail, apart from having some method of downloading the operating system and application hotfixes, service packs, and antivirus updates, that is all you need to allow.

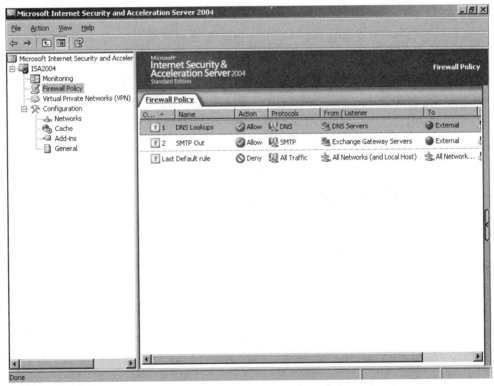

Figure 11-14   ISA Server 2004 allowing SMTP outbound to a select set of computers

From the viewpoint of SMTP servers on the Internet, the server on your network that connects to them will be the default IP address on the external interface of the external ISA Server. The Exchange Server administrator will need to know this default IP address as it will be important for some of the anti-spam technologies now beginning to come online.

Using a Dedicated Routing Group for Outbound E-Mail

In large networks, it is recommended that the gateway servers that are the last Exchange servers before the Internet should be servers dedicated to this role. This means that they do not host mailboxes nor are they front-end protocol servers for client access. The main benefit that this brings is that these servers are solely dedicated to the processing of outbound e-mail. This will include doing DNS lookups, initiating and maintaining connections to the Internet. It could also include spam filtering and virus removal. Additionally, these servers can be installed in IP load-balanced clusters to ensure outbound mail delivery even when one server needs to be restarted for maintenance.

Smart Host in Perimeter Network

The smart host is used to proxy outbound e-mail from your Exchange organization to the Internet. The smart host is an SMTP server, either on your network or on your ISP's network. Its main use is when the internal Exchange servers cannot resolve Internet DNS lookups but the smart host can. Additionally, a smart host has a use within a perimeter network of a back-to-back firewall configuration.

The smart host is located within the perimeter network and the internal firewall allows SMTP traffic to flow between the internal Exchange servers and the smart host. The external firewall has the same rule configured, except that it allows traffic to flow between the smart host and the Internet. These two rules are shown in Figure 11-15 and Figure 11-16.

It is important to note that the smart host is not a member of the internal Active Directory forest, and therefore not an Exchange server that is part of the internal Active Directory forest. This can be seen as there are no rules listed on the firewall allowing the smart host operating system to communicate with the internal network. The perimeter network is not a location for Exchange servers as they require considerable connectivity to each member of the Exchange organization and the Active Directory servers such as global catalog servers. Placing domain members in a perimeter network requires opening a considerable number of ports to internal resources and therefore reducing the effectiveness of the perimeter.

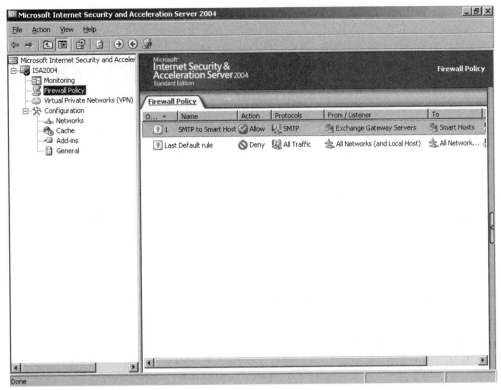

Figure 11-15   Firewall rules on the internal ISA Server 2004 in a back-to-back configuration

The message flow out of the organization means that no Internet SMTP connections are established from Exchange servers (only from the smart host), thus adding a layer of protection to the internal servers by routing all SMTP traffic via the smart host. All Internet SMTP servers that are sent messages from this organization are connected to by the smart host. Should this connection allow the smart host to be compromised, the internal network infrastructure will be unaffected, but outbound e-mail from the smart host should be considered suspect.

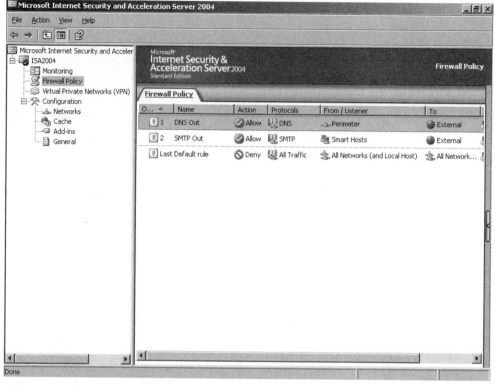

Figure 11-16   Firewall rules on the external ISA Server 2004 in a back-to-back configuration

Using the Same Inbound and Outbound SMTP Servers

If a firewall is protecting a single SMTP gateway server, it is important to ensure that inbound SMTP cannot become outbound. That is, that this server is not an open relay. Inbound e-mail must be restricted to a given list of domains and outbound e-mail should only be accepted from specific IP addresses. These specific IP addresses will be the Exchange servers that use this SMTP server as a smart host or those that authenticate.

The ISA Server 2004 rules for a single gateway for both inbound and outbound SMTP can be seen in Figure 11-17.

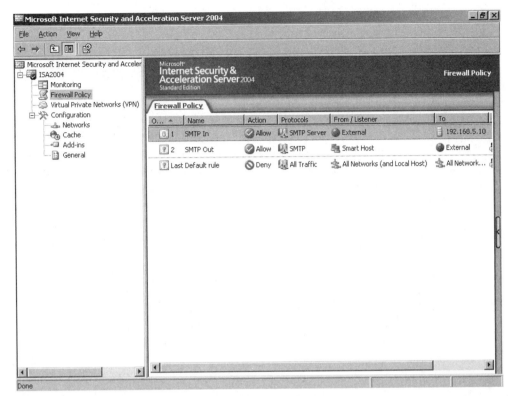

Figure 11-17   Single SMTP gateway firewall rules

In the above firewall rules, the SMTP Server protocol is TCP port 25 inbound and the SMTP protocol is TCP port 25 outbound. The SMTP In rule allows access to the IP address of the single SMTP server, whereas the SMTP Out rule allows access from that same server. Inbound (or server publishing) rules go to IP addresses, outbound (or access) rules can come from specific clients. The list of specific clients is named a Computer Set (Client Address Set in ISA Server 2000), and "Smart Host" is the Computer Set containing the single SMTP server at 192.168.5.10.

Using Different Inbound and Outbound SMTP Servers

In organizations with different paths for inbound and outbound e-mail, a change in the firewall rules is needed. The rules that need to be configured will allow inbound SMTP access from the Internet to the Exchange Server gateway. This server, if properly configured and not enabled as an open relay, will only accept e-mail destined for the address spaces listed in recipient policies.

The outbound SMTP server, or smart host, will need to be able to send mail to all locations on the Internet and so the firewall protecting this server would be configured to allow TCP port 25 outbound from this server only. As this server is stopped from inbound SMTP by the firewall, it could be configured as an open relay or, preferably, an open relay to connections from specific IP addresses. This server would then be able to relay for the Exchange organization but not for other SMTP clients on the network or Internet.

The change required to the firewall rules shown in Figure 11-17 is to ensure that the correct IP address(es) are listed in the "Smart Host" Computer Set.

Providing SMTP Services to Customers

In the open relay topic, we discussed how important it is to ensure that your inbound SMTP server does not perform open relay. This means that your network accepts and routes only the e-mail destined for your internal organization. On the other hand, outbound SMTP needs to be able to relay (send) mail to any location on the Internet.

In an environment where all SMTP clients authenticate to send e-mail, typically e-mail services provided by an ISP, relay can be easily accomplished because the outbound SMTP server can be configured to allow relay to those clients who authenticate only. This is the default behavior in Exchange Server. To ensure that the relay is available to authenticated users, on the SMTP virtual server used by your POP3/IMAP4 clients, check the option to Allow All Computers Which Successfully Authenticate To Relay, Regardless Of The List Above in the Relay Restrictions dialog box of the SMTP virtual server. The IP address list in this dialog box does not need to be populated in this example. In MAPI client environments it is recommended that you uncheck the above option to allow authenticated clients to relay as they will not need to.

> **Note**   These relay options do not need to be set for clients that connect via MAPI, HTTP, and RPC to an Exchange organization. These clients do not connect to an SMTP server to send e-mail directly, as the sending via SMTP is done by the Exchange server.

If the client cannot authenticate to send e-mail, upgrade the client to software that can. Failing that, add the client's IP addresses to the allowed list in the Relay Restrictions dialog box or restrict access to the open relay to clients of the ISP's network.

For ISPs that provide SMTP server access regardless of network, Authentication is the only option to avoid configuring an open relay, as any firewall used to protect their outbound SMTP server needs to be configured to allow access to it from any host on the Internet.

Controlling Message Relay

Message relay is the ability of an SMTP virtual server to send e-mail to domains that it does not service locally. In the case of Exchange Server, you would relay e-mail to domains that are not listed in Recipient Policies. The major factor in controlling this is to ensure that only those that are allowed to use the relay option can do so.

The default setting in Exchange Server is that relay is not allowed unless the sender authenticates first. This is an okay position to be in because an Exchange server will authenticate when communicating with other Exchange servers in the same organization. This means that messages sent from one Exchange server to another Exchange server get routed correctly because the system has authenticated. Care therefore needs to be taken whenever changes are made to the relay options on a virtual server to ensure that it is not opened for all to use without authentication.

Open Relay

Open relay is the term given to an SMTP server that will accept unauthenticated connection requests from anyone and deliver those e-mail messages to any domain, local or remote. For spammers, finding an open relay allows them to send huge amounts of e-mail that can only be traced back to your network and not to them.

SMTP servers that are known to be open relays are therefore a source of a large amount of the spam on the Internet. Closing your network to e-mail from those sources via the use of a block list service can reduce your spam intake dramatically. You might additionally reject authorized e-mail from this domain but sometimes that is an operational decision to take, in order to reduce the load on your network for a minimum amount of work and cost. If your SMTP configuration is such that you are an open relay, it is possible that you will be added to the databases maintained by these previously mentioned block list providers. This means that networks that subscribe to these block list providers will not receive e-mail that your network sends them.

> **Tip** Microsoft Knowledge Base article 304897, "SMTP relay behavior in Windows 2000, Windows XP, and Exchange Server" (*http://go.microsoft.com/ fwlink/?linkid=3052&kbid=304897*) describes how to test if an SMTP server is an open relay.

Viruses such as SoBig and Bugbear enable a simple SMTP engine on the infected computer and use that SMTP engine to send spam. A suitable firewall configuration within an organization would be to limit outbound SMTP to those servers that are authorized to send Internet SMTP and not to all clients, and secondly, to reject e-mail from computers with dynamic IP addresses. This blocking of dynamically assigned IP addresses reduces your exposure to computers infected with a spam-sending virus. A number of block list service providers provide the dynamic IP ranges of dial-up and broadband connections, allowing you to block e-mail from these sources because a dial-up or broadband user should use its ISP-provided SMTP server as a smart host and not its own directly. MessageLabs, a network-based spam filtering organization published data in October 2004 (see *http://www.messagelabs.co.uk/emailthreats/intelligence/reports/monthlies/october04/*) showing that around 70 percent of the spam MessageLabs intercepts on a daily basis has been sent via machines compromised by viruses.

Applying Message Filters

Exchange 2003 provides a number of filters within the product and is capable of having a number of other products integrate with it to help protect your e-mail.

Most of the filters are used to block e-mail from arriving at the Exchange Server gateway, or to archive it and forward it to the recipient. This means that the filters can be used to reduce the amount of spam that your network and users receive. Exchange Server 2003 introduces more filters than the previous version and the most notable addition is that of block lists. In addition to these block lists, e-mail can be filtered based on the sender or recipient e-mail address and the sending IP address.

Once filters are configured at the Global Settings level, they need to be enabled on the SMTP virtual server that will listen for and possibly reject e-mail that matches the filter.

Block Lists Services

Block Lists (also incorrectly known as Realtime Blackhole List, or RBL, which is a trademark of MAPS, one block list provider) are databases operated by service providers, typically free of charge, that maintain a DNS server that lists those IP addresses known to be associated with spam. Enabling block list lookups in Exchange Server 2003 tells your server to perform a DNS lookup to the block list provider for every incoming SMTP connection, to see if a record for the connecting IP address exists. If the connecting IP address is known to be associated as a sender (or potential sender) of spam, a response code starting with the figure 127.0.0 should be returned, though this will depend upon the accuracy of the data in the block list database. Your Exchange server then determines if the connection will be disconnected because of the response returned and therefore the e-mail rejected. If a Host Not Found response is returned from the query, your Exchange server will accept the e-mail, unless it is filtered out because it is listed via a different block list provider, or because it is covered by one of the other filters in Exchange.

Each block list can provide a number of return codes for a given IP address, and the codes will all have different meanings. Exchange Server can be configured to reject an SMTP connection that returns any 127.0.0.x response or with some investigation you can determine the codes used by your block list provider and select those you want to reject connections on. Most block lists will return the response 127.0.0.2 for open relay with other codes starting at 127.0.0 for other spam candidates. There is no standard among block list providers, so it is important to check with your chosen provider to learn which responses indicate why that IP address is listed in the database.

Block List Service Providers

A search of the Internet will return a variety of block list providers that provide a full range of service and competency. A list is maintained at *http://www.declude.com/Articles.asp?ID=97* of hundreds of block list providers, along with what is known about their performance and status. For example, this list will tell if a block list can be tested against using the IP address 127.0.0.2 and if it is free to use.

Potential Senders

Some block lists will include IP addresses that are not associated with the sending of spam but could potentially be. These are the dial-up user and dynamic IP lists and they contain the IP addresses belonging to users who obtain a dynamic IP address when they connect to the Internet. These users may not be sending spam, but when they do connect to the Internet to send e-mail, they typically use the SMTP relay provided by their ISP. The reason a dynamic IP block list is useful is that up to 70 percent of spam now comes from virus-infected PCs. For example, the SoBig virus can turn an infected PC into an SMTP engine generating spam whenever it is connected to the Internet.

One block list provider that lists dynamic IP ranges (rather than spammers directly) is SORBS. SORBS provides their list (*http://www.sorbs.net/*) for companies to block e-mail that comes directly from a dynamic IP address without going via their ISP's e-mail server. A dynamic IP address in the SORBS database will return the response 127.0.0.10.

How Block Lists Work

Block lists operate on the same principles as DNS and take requests in the form of a DNS query and respond with a DNS answer. Therefore, for your Exchange server to be able to query block lists it needs to be able to resolve DNS records on the Internet.

When Exchange Server receives an SMTP connection the block list is queried after the first RCPT TO: command. If the connection IP address is found to be on any one of the block lists that the Exchange server is using, the connection is closed with the error *550 5.7.1 w.x.y.z has been blocked by <connection filter rule name>* where w.x.y.z is the blocked IP address. Exchange Server also allows custom errors to be created, for example the error *E-mail rejected by %1 because your IP address (%0) is listed on their block list database. Visit %2 for more information* would replace %0 with the blocked IP address, %1 with the rule display name and %2 with the URL of the block list. Your custom error will be prefixed with 550 5.7.1 by the Exchange server to report an SMTP command error to the sending SMTP server.

Testing Block Lists

If a block list should stop responding or slow down in its rate of responses, it will have an impact on your ability to deliver inbound e-mail to your mailboxes. Therefore, it is important to be able to test a block list. We recommend that you do not use a block list that cannot be tested.

All block lists that can be tested should respond to a query regarding the IP address 127.0.0.2 (not to be confused with the return code of the same format). To test a block list you need to run the nslookup command and to create the correct ip4r structure for the IP address you are testing against. An ip4r record is the IP address to be tested in reverse byte format followed by the block list DNS zone. For example, if adatum.com provided a block list at the zone bl.adatum.com, and you wanted to test the 127.0.0.2 address against it, you would issue the following command:

nslookup 2.0.0.127.bl.adatum.com

The block list should return a standard DNS response containing the reason code for the block, which is typically 127.0.0.2, but it could be something else. A command prompt viewing a test against the Open Relay Database (ORDB) block list is shown in Figure 11-18.

Once you have your return code, you may be able to issue an nslookup command querying the TXT record of the domain you just found. The TXT record should give the reason why that IP address is on the block list. The inclusion of a TXT record is optional, based on the block list provider's policies.

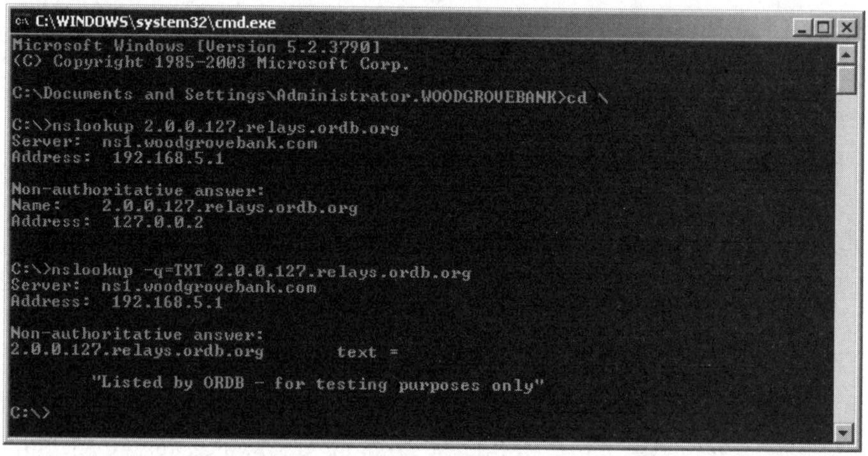

Figure 11-18   A query and TXT return from ORDB for the test IP address 127.0.0.2

In addition to being able to query the database from the command line, most block lists provide a website for you to issue a query from and some offer the ability to test to see if your e-mail system is an open relay. For example, the SORBS dynamic IP database mentioned earlier can be tested against your own home dial-up or broadband IP address.

> **Warning** If you use a system such as ORDB to test if your Exchange Server gateway is an open relay and it is found to be so, then they will add you to their list of open relays!

If you regularly need to communicate with an organization that is in your block list provider's database, it is possible to list the recipients in your organization who will be exceptions to the information returned by the block list. This can be configured via the Exceptions button on the Connection Filtering dialog box. When e-mail arrives for these listed recipients, it will always be delivered.

Configuring Exchange Server to Use Block Lists

To configure Exchange Server to use the services of a block list provider you will need to have the domain name of the provider's database. In the following examples we will use bl.adatum.com, the block list of our fictitious ISP.

1. Expand Global Settings in Exchange System Manager and right-click Message Delivery and then Properties.

2. Click the Connection Filtering tab and, to create a connection filter, click Add.

3. Enter the required values. These are a name for the connection filter, the DNS suffix of the block list zone (**bl.adatum.com** in this example) and a custom error message if needed. For an example, see Figure 11-19.

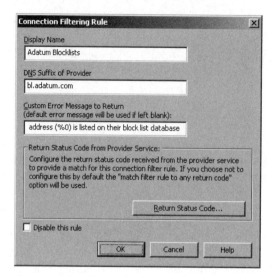

Figure 11-19   Connection Filtering Rule

4. If you want to reject SMTP connections only if they meet certain response codes from the block list provider, click Return Status Code. The Return Status Code options are:

- **Match Filter Rule To Any Return Code**   This, the default, means any return code apart from Host Not Found will result in the connection being dropped.

- **Match Filter Rule To The Following Mask**   Some block list providers record different codes for the different reasons that the IP address is in their database but return one collective code when the IP address is queried rather than each individual code. For example, a block list provider could have the code 127.0.0.1 for open relay, 127.0.0.2 for dynamic IP address and 127.0.0.4 for known virus/worm source. If the response was 127.0.0.3, the IP address is both open relay and dynamic IP address (which is .1 + .2); similarly, the response 127.0.0.6 (which is .4 + .2) would mean dynamic IP address and known virus/worm source. If you want to block a single particular combination of responses, enter the combined response code (which is known as the mask) in this field.

- **Match Filter Rule To Any Of The Following Responses**   This will disconnect the session if the IP address has any one of the given return codes listed.

5. Click OK to close all dialog boxes, confirming the notice about needing to enable the filters on the required SMTP virtual servers. Figure 11-20 shows the filters enabled on an SMTP virtual server.

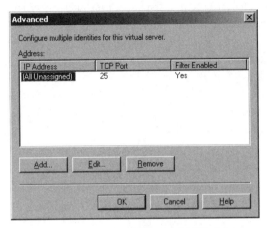

Figure 11-20   Ensuring that the SMTP virtual server uses the filters

6. As can be seen in Figure 11-21, the rejection of the e-mail due to the block list comes after the Rcpt to command is issued. Each filter in Exchange Server will cause rejections of messages at different times in the SMTP session. Figure 11-26 shows each stage of the SMTP delivery and where particular filters take effect.

Figure 11-21   The block list in action

Sender Filtering

The second filter that is configured globally for an Exchange organization is Sender Filtering. This is a list of sender e-mail addresses that are rejected by any SMTP virtual server that has the Apply Sender Filter option enabled on it. If an SMTP virtual server does not enable this filter option, the global settings do not have any effect on e-mail received on that SMTP virtual server. These sender e-mail addresses can either be entire domains in the form of "*@woodgrovebank.com" or specific e-mail addresses. Figure 11-22 shows the global settings for Sender Filtering with a specific e-mail addressed blocked from sending e-mail inbound.

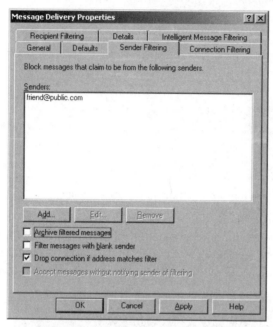

Figure 11-22   Sender Filtering global settings

The default option for Sender Filtering is to drop the connection when the sender is specified in the MAIL FROM SMTP command (known as the P1 address) or in the FROM header of the message (known as the P2 address). The first of these is shown in Figure 11-23. An alternative to blocking the e-mail, Sender Filtering allows the e-mail to be accepted by the system and for the sender not to be notified that it has been filtered. For this option to be enabled, the Drop Connection If Address Matches Filter option needs to be unchecked and the Accept Messages Without Notifying Sender Of Filtering needs to be checked. This option is useful if archiving of the filter message is also enabled. Archived messages are stored in the Filter folder.

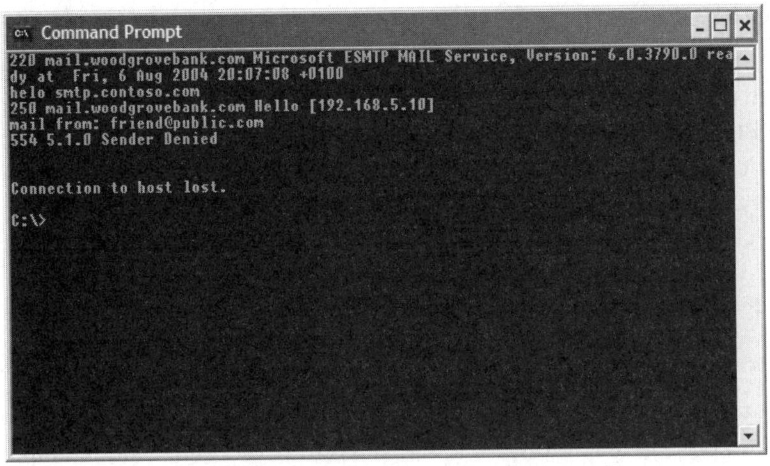

```
Command Prompt                                              _ □ x
220 mail.woodgrovebank.com Microsoft ESMTP MAIL Service, Version: 6.0.3790.0 rea
dy at  Fri, 6 Aug 2004 20:07:08 +0100
helo smtp.contoso.com
250 mail.woodgrovebank.com Hello [192.168.5.10]
mail from: friend@public.com
554 5.1.0 Sender Denied


Connection to host lost.

C:\>
```

Figure 11-23   Sender Filtering response to a blocked e-mail address

A common use of Sender Filtering is to stop e-mail messages coming into your network that claim to be from senders belonging to your organization. For example, it would be possible for Woodgrove Bank to filter out any sender claiming to have an address ending @woodgrovebank.com when the e-mail comes from the Internet. They can successfully filter this address because they know that all true senders with this address use Woodgrove Bank's e-mail system and not an external system, and so messages from these senders should not be arriving from the Internet.

Important   If your organization has users who send e-mail from outside the network, for example, via a POP3 enabled mobile telephone, then you cannot enable this option to block your own address inbound as these users may need to configure their portable devices to send e-mail from their corporate address but not via the corporate e-mail system.

As with all filters, in addition to the global settings described here, the filter needs to be enabled on the SMTP virtual server that will process e-mail from these potential sources.

Recipient Filtering

The third type of Exchange Server filtering is to block inbound e-mail to selected recipients. For example, it is common for companies to have a distribution list that covers all the employees of the company. If the e-mail address of this distribution list is included in Recipient Filtering, then it is impossible to send e-mail through the virtual servers with filtering enabled to these addresses.

Recipient Filtering can also be enabled to globally reject e-mail to recipients that are not listed in Active Directory. This is a quick way to reject e-mail messages to invalid recipients as they arrive at the Exchange organization. If the Exchange organization recipient policy does not list a particular domain name, then this filter option will not filter against this domain name using this option.

If an e-mail address is filtered because it is not listed in Active Directory, then the e-mail messages to that address are rejected during the SMTP connection with the *550 5.7.1 Requested action not taken: mailbox not available* SMTP response.

> **Important**   Globally blocking e-mail messages to recipients that are not in Active Directory can allow the discovery of valid e-mail addresses within the organization as the SMTP response for a valid address is different from an invalid address.

Restricting Sending to an External E-Mail Address

Although this is not a filter in Exchange Server 2003 by the strict definition of the word, it is possible to stop e-mail messages from being sent to specific external e-mail addresses by creating a contact in Active Directory and mail enabling the contact for the address that is to be blocked. Once the Recipient Update Service runs and the contact is mailbox-enabled, it will have an Exchange General tab on its properties dialog box in Active Directory Users and Computers. On the Exchange General tab you can configure which user accounts are allowed to send to the contact and which ones are not. If you want to block all users from sending to that address, limit the contact so that it can only be e-mailed from itself, as shown in Figure 11-24. If you want to restrict the list of users who can send e-mail to this address, then add just those users to the allowed list.

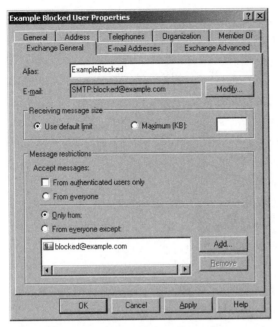

Figure 11-24   Limiting sending of e-mail to an external address

Once this limited permission contact is in place, e-mail messages to this contact from unauthorized accounts will result in the account receiving a message saying *You do not have permission to send to this recipient. For assistance, contact your system administrator.*

Restricting Receiving to an E-Mail Address

In addition to Recipient Filtering as a way to stop e-mail being sent to addresses through a virtual server, it is possible to stop the receipt of e-mail from unauthenticated connections as an alternate way of stopping e-mail coming to mailboxes from the Internet. To set this option, which is done per mailbox, check the From Authenticated Users Only option on the Exchange General tab of the mail recipient's property dialog box. This is shown in Figure 11-25.

The main difference between this option and Recipient Filtering is that this option replies with an NDR once the e-mail has been accepted from the non-authenticated source. Recipient Filtering disconnects the SMTP connection before the e-mail is sent.

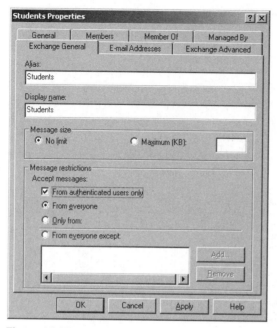

Figure 11-25   Restricting e-mail to authenticated senders only

Filtering Global Settings

There will be times when you need to ensure that e-mail that comes from a particular IP address range is accepted regardless of whether or not that IP address is listed for blocking under other filters. Exchange Server 2003 provides a global accept and deny list for IP address or range of IP addresses. The global Accept and Deny options can be found on the Connection Filtering tab of the Message Delivery Properties dialog box.

If an IP address is listed globally as denied, the connection is aborted after the Mail from command is issued and before any block lists or filtering lists are processed. If an IP address is listed in the Accept list, then it will be accepted even if the IP address is listed elsewhere (in the block list provider's database, for example).

It is important not to overlook the options available to the Exchange Server 2003 administrator provided by Connection, Sender, and Recipient filtering. Though you may have a very good antivirus and anti-spam package installed on your network, you can increase the efficiency of these systems by first filtering out all e-mail that cannot possibly be valid for your organization, using these built-in Exchange Server 2003 filters.

Figure 11-26 shows a flow chart of all the previously described filtering processes and where they take effect within an SMTP session.

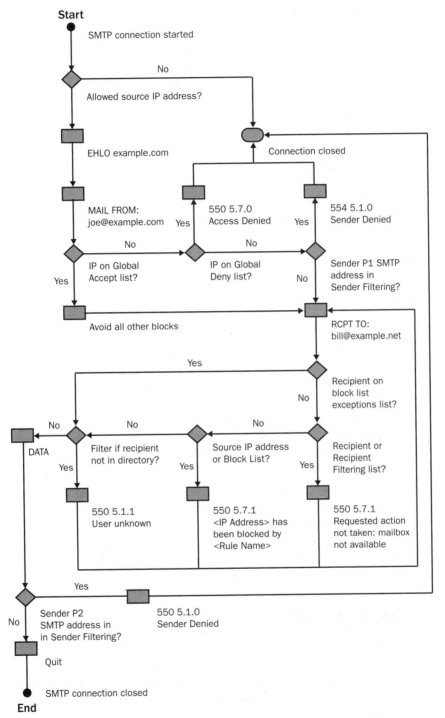

Figure 11-26 Overview flowchart of the SMTP connection process and filtering

Reverse DNS Lookups

In the Advanced Delivery options of an SMTP virtual server, you can set an option to Perform Reverse DNS Lookup On Incoming Messages. When set, the e-mail header will record if the connecting IP address and server name match. This can be used as a method of determining the validity of the e-mail against its source server.

If you select this option, the virtual server will try to check that the sender SMTP server's IP address matches the domain given by the sender server in the HELO or EHLO commands. If the reverse DNS lookup is successful, the received header will be unchanged. If the reverse DNS lookup fails, the RDNS Failed value will appear in the e-mail header. The word unverified in the header means that reverse DNS could not be completed. An example of two received headers, one for a spoofed e-mail and the second for a real e-mail, follows. In this example, the IP address listed belongs to mail.adatum.com:

1. Received: from mail.fineartschool.net ([192.168.5.10] RDNS failed) by *<server-name>*...

2. Received: from mail.adatum.com ([192.168.5.10]) by *<servername>*...

It can be seen from the two examples above, that the connection that claims to come from mail.fineartschool.net cannot be so, as the IP address the e-mail came from belongs to a different domain name. To check your reverse DNS lookup value enter **nslookup** *<SMTP_External_IP_address>* in the command line. The name returned should be the same as the FQDN value also found on the Advanced Delivery options dialog box of an Internet-connected SMTP virtual server.

Performance can be affected on the virtual server because this feature verifies all incoming messages by performing a reverse DNS lookup for each of them. This will increase network traffic to and from the Internet and add additional processing to the Exchange server.

The Reverse DNS entry for a remote host would need to be valid for this to be of much use and historically it cannot be guaranteed to be so. Proposed changes in the way SMTP operates are likely to further reduce the usefulness of this setting in the near future. More information about Microsoft's proposals for fighting spam can be found at *http://www.microsoft.com/spam/*.

Direct Message Transfer

The delivery of e-mail from the mailbox server to the Internet recipient initially follows a routing path based on the Routing Group structure of the Exchange organization. The last point for the message within the Exchange organization is the server hosting the SMTP connector for the address space that the message is going to be delivered to.

At this point, this SMTP connector hosting server has one of two options on delivery. It can either be delivered directly to the SMTP server on the Internet for that address using DNS lookups to determine that server's IP address, or to forward the message to a smart host server for onward delivery.

The default configuration for an SMTP connector is to deliver e-mail based on DNS lookups. If the connector is created as part of the Internet Mail Wizard then you will be asked which choice to make regarding smart host or direct delivery.

To accomplish direct delivery to the Internet, the server hosting the connector must be able to perform lookups from DNS zones on the Internet. By default, Exchange Server will use the Windows DNS configuration provided in the TCP/IP stack. This DNS server may be an internal server, but that does not mean that it cannot resolve Internet addresses. If you are unsure, type the following command on the Exchange server that you are configuring: **nslookup –q=MX** *domain_name* where domain_name is some Internet domain name, such as microsoft.com.

If you have Internet DNS lookups you should get back a list of the MX and A records indicating the e-mail servers for your selected domain. If you are unable to get a response, and your Internet connection is operational, you might have a network structure where external DNS records can only be found from the edge of network devices, such as proxy servers. If this is the case, you will need to configure Exchange Server with the IP addresses of DNS servers that are able to resolve records on the Internet and allow your firewall to pass these requests from your Exchange servers to these DNS servers. These DNS servers must also be able to resolve DNS requests over the TCP protocol. By default, DNS uses UDP on port 53, but responses larger than the maximum UDP packet size need to use TCP (also on port 53). Therefore, SMTP uses TCP to query its DNS servers.

Note   RFC 883 prescribes that DNS servers should be able to accept both TCP virtual circuits and UDP.

To test if your DNS server is capable of accepting TCP queries, and the Windows 2000 Server and Windows Server 2003 DNS Servers are capable of this functionality, enter **set vc** during nslookup in command line mode:

```
server <IP address of server to test>
set vc
set type=mx
domain_name
```

The response from the TCP nslookup command should be the MX and A records of the domain.

Depending upon your DNS responses, you can either leave your DNS configuration with the Windows default or override it for the SMTP virtual server in the Advanced Delivery dialog box, by clicking the Configure button.

Regardless of the DNS lookup option chosen, Windows 2000 Server and Windows Server 2003 caches DNS responses to improve performance. If an invalid DNS record is returned to the server, it will be used to attempt delivery, which will fail. To clear the DNS cache on the Exchange server enter **ipconfig /flushdns** at the command line.

Microsoft ISA Server also contains a DNS cache that operates regardless of the other caches on the network. If the Exchange server is a firewall client of the ISA Server (only necessary if direct routes to the Internet are not provided), the ISA Server will cache all DNS lookups that it passes through it. ISA Server does not cache responses for SecureNAT (routed) clients. The side effect of this cache is that the response will be cached for six hours regardless of the actual TTL on the DNS record, and it cannot be cleared without restarting the ISA Server firewall service. A registry key can be used to reduce the time of this cache on ISA Server 2000. The key location is

HKEY_LOCAL_MACHINE\SOFTWARE\Microsoft\Fpc\Arrays\{ArrayGUID}\ArrayPolicy\Proxy-WSP, a value named msFPCDnsCacheTtl (DWORD) and data for the time in seconds that the cache should retain DNS responses for. The default of 21600 (decimal) is six hours. A value of 0 stops the firewall service caching DNS responses. You will need to restart the firewall service for this registry key to take effect.

Once your DNS lookup architecture is operational, the Exchange server hosting the SMTP connector for the Internet is able to deliver e-mail.

Smart Host Message Transfer

With a smart host, instead of the message being delivered directly to the destination as a result of DNS MX record lookups, the message is passed straight to the smart host. The DNS MX record lookup is then performed by the smart host (unless it too passes the message to another smart host).

A smart host server is an SMTP server and it must be able to perform DNS MX and A record lookups as described previously or pass the message on to the next smart host. It is important to not create a looping situation when configuring smart host servers.

Though the smart host is an SMTP server it does not need to be an Exchange server or even part of your organization at all, as it could be hosted at your ISP. Microsoft IIS 5.0 and IIS 6.0 both contain an SMTP server (which must be installed before it can be used) that can provide smart host functionality, along with many third-party anti-spam and antivirus SMTP gateway products. The IIS SMTP server has an option that allows DNS lookups, and if the DNS lookup fails, it will forward the message on to another smart host. This configuration is shown in Figure 11-27.

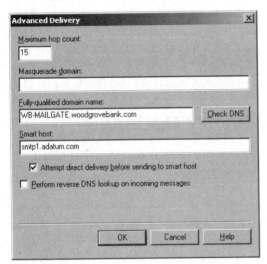

Figure 11-27   Deliver with DNS or smart host in IIS 6.0

To configure your Exchange organization to use a smart host, you either enter the smart host name or IP address on every SMTP virtual server in the organization, or enter the same details into the SMTP connector that delivers e-mail to the correct destination. The Internet Mail Wizard provides an option to configure a smart host for the Internet during the wizard. If the smart host is specified by an IP address, the address must be listed in square brackets, such as [192.168.5.1].

The two main uses of a smart host server are to provide an SMTP server in a perimeter network and to use for the direct delivery to other messaging systems.

Smart Hosts and Perimeter Networks

The smart host server becomes the last point of contact between the internal Exchange organization on the internal network and the delivery of the e-mail to the remote domain. The internal network Exchange servers no longer need to connect directly to the destination SMTP servers on the Internet and that reduces the likelihood of the internal network Exchange servers being compromised by connecting to a suspect SMTP server.

In addition to the e-mail traffic being routed via an SMTP server in the DMZ, thus protecting the internal network servers from direct Internet communication, it is often found that the antivirus and anti-spam programs additionally allow the editing of the SMTP headers in each Internet-bound e-mail, thus removing any references to internal servers that will be found in an e-mail's headers. This will help a company restrict the knowledge that a hacker could use to obtain information on the internal network.

Smart Hosts and Other Messaging Systems

When an Exchange organization needs to deliver e-mail to an alternative messaging system within the current organization, or to a specific address space to enable message delivery with specific settings such as encryption, the SMTP connector that is used can deliver the e-mail straight to the other system by entering the name or IP address into the smart host field on the SMTP connector. As before, if the remote system is identified by an IP address, the value needs to be inside square brackets.

Configuring Message Delivery Options

Once you have your configuration in place for the receipt of delivered e-mail, you can move to the easier configuration of setting your server up to deliver e-mail. By default, every Exchange server is capable of sending SMTP messages that are not stored within the Exchange organization, but just because Exchange Server can do this does not mean it is best to leave each Exchange server to the default configuration.

To improve and further control message delivery will involve configuring your Exchange organization to send e-mail via a defined path that is supported by your messaging, network, firewall, and Internet infrastructures.

The messaging configuration needs to take two factors into account. The first is if your Exchange organization is the sole location for e-mail messages to your domain, or whether it needs to forward unresolved recipients to a different messaging system within your organization. The second factor is if you have specific routes for selected domains, for example, if you need to ensure that e-mail sent to a partner organization is encrypted during its transmission.

The network configuration for outbound e-mail will depend upon whether an Exchange server can perform Internet DNS lookups or if the outbound e-mail needs to be forwarded to a server that can. Additional network configuration will control which Exchange servers can send to the Internet by restricting Internet access to specific Exchange servers, rather than allowing the entire network to have SMTP outbound. This will have an impact on the configuration of your firewall rules.

Your firewall infrastructure will have a major impact on the outbound flow of e-mail. How your LAN is connected to the Internet and the properties of the firewall rules that control traffic between the LAN and the Internet will determine the servers that can connect and send outbound e-mail.

Finally, your Internet infrastructure will control whether you are always connected to the Internet or not, and if not your Exchange servers will need to be configured to dial up to connect to the Internet on a schedule to deliver e-mail.

Once you know how each of the above four infrastructure components will affect e-mail flow, you can begin to configure your Exchange organization.

Internet Mail Wizard

The Internet Mail Wizard in Exchange System Manager is the easiest way to configure how e-mail leaves your Exchange organization for the Internet. The Internet Mail Wizard will only run if the server you select during the wizard has not had any SMTP connectors created on it. The wizard will also fail if the selected server is a cluster member (Windows Clustering or Network Load Balancing clusters), is running Exchange 5.5, or if the server is connected to multiple networks and can route between them. If you are running the wizard to receive e-mail, you cannot have additional SMTP virtual servers already created on the selected server.

The Internet Mail Wizard makes the configuration of the SMTP connector and virtual server easy, but you could configure all of it manually if you are in a position, such as in the above examples, where you cannot run the wizard.

The Internet Mail Wizard is started from Exchange System Manager by right-clicking the top node of the tree, which is your organization name.

The process for running the Internet Mail Wizard is straightforward. On the Server Selection screen you choose the server that you wish to use to send e-mail or receive e-mail. The option for sending and receiving comes on the Internet E-Mail Functions page. This follows the step when the wizard checks that it is capable of configuring the server.

The wizard will display a list of virtual servers on the selected server for you to choose which will be used for the delivery of Internet e-mail. Typically, the default virtual server is suitable for the task. Once a virtual server has been selected, you are asked a series of questions about delivery using DNS and the domains to which you want to deliver e-mail. The DNS questions cover part of the network infrastructure issues discussed previously. If your DNS infrastructure for your Exchange servers is not able to do Internet-based DNS zone lookups and you have a working Internet connection (because if your Internet connection was down or misconfigured for DNS then these lookups would also fail), then you will need to provide alternate DNS servers for Exchange Server to use when sending e-mail or enter the name or IP address of an SMTP smart host server that can do Internet DNS lookups.

The final question for the Internet Mail Wizard concerns the domains that you will use the SMTP connector it is creating to send e-mail to. If the wizard is being used for its default purpose of sending e-mail to the Internet, then you will select the default option of Allow Delivery To All E-Mail Domains.

When the wizard is finished it will have created an SMTP connector named Internet Mail SMTP Connector (SERVER_NAME). This can be found under the Connector's node of Exchange System Manager. The Connector's node is either a top-level node or, if showing Routing Groups, can be found under Routing Groups, Routing Group Name.

SMTP Connector Delivery Options

Once the Internet Mail Wizard is finished you can open the created SMTP connector and change options if need be. If you cannot use the Internet Mail Wizard, then you can create a connector that will do the same as the wizard. The following are options for the SMTP connector that matter for Internet e-mail delivery:

- **Smart Host or Direct Delivery**   On the General tab of the SMTP connector you can set or change the option for the use of a smart host or direct DNS delivery. The option to provide specific DNS servers for direct delivery that are not the same as the DNS servers listed in the TCP/IP properties of Windows is part of the SMTP virtual server shown on this dialog box.

    The Local Bridgeheads option on this dialog box sets the SMTP virtual server that is used for the sending of e-mail from this connector. Additional virtual servers in the routing group can be added for fault tolerance, but care should be taken to ensure that each virtual server has the same settings, or e-mail flow may not be as expected.

    The use of an SMTP connector with multiple bridgehead servers allows for load balancing, performance, and redundancy, but it is important to note that this is not the case for multiple SMTP connectors, each with a single bridgehead server for the same address space. When the Exchange organization has a choice of SMTP connectors to use for an address space it will select an SMTP connector based on the GUID of the sending server. This selection algorithm may not evenly distribute message flow across all the available SMTP connectors. Therefore, for load balancing use a single connector per address space with multiple bridgehead servers.

- **Whom to Deliver To and the Cost of Delivery**   The SMTP connector uses Address Space to control which SMTP domains the connector will deliver to. Figure 11-28 shows the dialog box for the SMTP connector that allows you to set the Address Space and Cost options.

    When delivering e-mail, the Exchange server determines the SMTP connector to use based on the address space value of each connector. It will use the SMTP connector that is configured for the closest address space to the domain that it is delivering to. For example, if a connector exists for woodgrovebank.com and another for * (which means all domains not managed internally by recipient policies), then an e-mail to garrett@woodgrovebank.com would use the first connector and not the second. If two connectors exist for the same address space, the connector with the lowest cost will be used unless that connector is out of service.

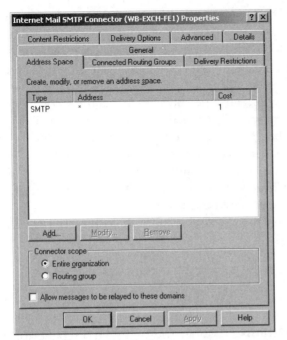

Figure 11-28   The Address Space options

An additional use of the Cost option allows you to create multiple SMTP connectors for the same address space and with higher costs than the other SMTP connectors for that address space. This configuration results in higher-cost connectors acting as backups to the primary lowest-cost connector. This means that if the server with the lowest cost is offline, or if that connector routes to a smart host that is offline, the next highest cost SMTP connector for that address space will be used. This second connector might be configured to use a backup smart host on a different Internet connection, thus avoiding whatever problem is causing the lowest cost connector to fail.

It is important to ensure that your firewall rules match your address space rules. If a server contains an SMTP connector for a particular address space, and the destination of that address is outside your firewalls, then you will need to ensure that your firewalls allow this server to send SMTP traffic outbound over TCP 25. This use of SMTP connectors restricts Internet-bound SMTP e-mail to those servers that hold the connector, allowing the firewall administrator much more precise firewall rules. Without connectors, all Exchange servers in the Exchange organization can send outbound e-mail and thus require many more open ports on the firewall.

■ **Delivery Restrictions and Non-Delivery Reports**   This property page of the SMTP connector dialog box allows control over which Active Directory users and groups can send e-mail through this connector.

The users and groups listed here will be blocked from sending e-mail through this connector if an additional registry key is enabled on the connector's bridgehead server. Because there is a performance penalty on the SMTP connector bridgehead server upon processing this restriction list, a registry key setting is required to ensure that this dialog box is not used without proper advance planning. The performance penalty is such that the recommendation is that this option should be used only when the restriction list is small or the impact is considered acceptable. The registry key that needs setting is `HKEY_LOCAL_MACHINE/System/CurrentControlSet/Services/Resvc/Parameters/` and a new value named `CheckConnectorRestrictions (DWORD)` with its data set to **1**. Once the registry key is set on the bridgehead server the Microsoft Exchange Routing Engine service and the SMTP services need to be restarted.

An additional registry key exists for the control of Delivery Status Notifications such as NDRs. A restricted SMTP connector may reject the sending of Delivery Status Notifications and so at the same registry location as above, the value `IgnoreRestrictionforNullDSN (DWORD) = 1` needs to be set to allow a restricted SMTP connector to ignore the restriction when sending Delivery Status Notifications.

- **Content Restrictions**   Another use of an SMTP connector is to restrict the types of e-mail that are allowed to go out to the Internet, such as messages with a particular priority (low, normal, or high) or type (system or non-system). Additionally, an SMTP connector can limit the size of e-mail that it can send, with this value taking priority over the similar value in the SMTP virtual server. Note that there is a potential impact to intra-Exchange organization communications with the use of message size limits on an SMTP virtual server, and though the SMTP connector overrides these settings they should be set only on the SMTP connector.

- **Delivery Options**   On networks that are not always connected to the Internet, the delivery options property sheet controls when this SMTP connector is able to send e-mail. If you have a dial-on-demand connection, or a connection that is only connected at specific times, you can configure the SMTP connector to queue outbound e-mail on a time schedule that matches your connected time or times of low expense.

For example, if the connection is less expensive to use between 6 P.M. and 6 A.M. each weekday, you could set a custom schedule to ensure that Exchange Server only sent e-mail between those hours. A second SMTP connector using the content restrictions mentioned previously could be used to ensure that high priority e-mail messages were sent immediately. Another use of the delivery options is to control when larger e-mail messages are sent, and keep them to times that have low bandwidth costs.

Note   SMTP queues that use SMTP connectors with a schedule attached to them appear in the Queue list in Exchange System Manager with a clock icon.

The queue mail for remote triggered delivery is an option that would be set on the SMTP backup mail server, which holds e-mail for a client because that client is not always connected to the Internet. This is the type of option that would be enabled at an ISP for its dial-up clients, like those in the above example, who have their own e-mail servers but do not have permanent connections to the Internet. The triggering for the delivery of remotely stored e-mail using TURN requires at least one Active Directory account to be created so that the remote client can log on to this server and issue the TURN command to force the delivery of e-mail from this SMTP server to the primary SMTP server that is now online utilizing the existing TCP/IP connection. ETRN, a more advanced method of TURN, does not use authentication as it ensures delivery to the correct SMTP server by using MX records instead.

■ **Advanced Options**   The majority of the advanced options are used by networks that are not permanently connected to the Internet, though as more and more companies are continually connected, these options can be used to protect against times of connection outage. SMTP servers that are disconnected for significant periods of time will make use of ETRN/TURN all the time, but for those organizations with a permanent connection that has failed, an ETRN/TURN SMTP backup service at an ISP will ensure e-mail does not get returned undelivered.

When the SMTP connector connects to the Internet and sends a message, the system can be configured to issue the ETRN/TURN command set to collect messages that are waiting at the SMTP backup server. If the backup server is not the one to which the e-mail messages are being sent (for example, sending e-mail messages to their destination server and not a smart host), a different ETRN/TURN server can be specified. Other options for the Exchange Server administrator include the ability to issue ETRN/TURN commands on a schedule, which domains to issue ETRN commands for, or whether to send a TURN command if your ISP does not support ETRN (TURN in Exchange Server requires authentication). Figure 11-29 shows a connector configured to issue the ETRN command every two hours and to collect stored mail from the ISP.

The only remaining Advanced options for the SMTP connector are the Authentication and Encryption options that the receiving SMTP virtual server requires. For an SMTP connector that sends e-mail to the Internet, anonymous authentication needs to be enabled, but if the connector uses TURN, or the server hosting that domain requires authentication or encryption, the correct options need to be set by clicking the Outbound Security button..

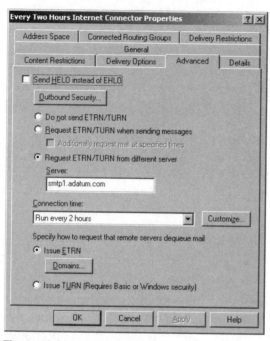

Figure 11-29   ETRN configuration on the client Exchange server

Virtual Server vs. SMTP Connector

Some SMTP connector options are the same as those on the SMTP virtual server. When an option is set on both the virtual server and the connector, the connector options always take precedence. When configuring outbound e-mail, you should know which options are available in the SMTP connector that will override the SMTP virtual server and be sure that they are set in the SMTP connector.

For example, in the Advanced Delivery tab of the SMTP virtual server you can set Authentication and Encryption options when connecting to remote SMTP servers, but you cannot choose on the virtual server which domains that virtual server will be used to send e-mail to. The SMTP connector has the Address Space option to control which domains it can send e-mail to, and it also has, again in Advanced options, the Authentication and Encryption settings. Therefore, when an SMTP connector exists for a particular address space, the Authentication and Encryption options (and others as well) will come from the SMTP connector and not the virtual server.

Forwarding Messages with Unresolved Recipients

If mail arrives at an Exchange organization and the e-mail address that it is to be delivered to cannot be found within the directory, the default behavior of Exchange Server is to issue an NDR to the sender.

This, however, will cause problems if you have two or more independent e-mail systems within an organization, all of which use the same e-mail domain.

To accommodate organizations with this configuration, it is possible for Exchange to forward mail destined for unresolved recipients onto an SMTP server that is part of another e-mail system. It then becomes the responsibility of that e-mail system to deliver any NDRs or forward mail for unresolved recipients in the second system to a third system and so on. The final messaging system in the chain needs to send NDRs for e-mail that it cannot deliver.

> **Important**   It is vital to ensure the correct processing order for this option. If the other e-mail system within an organization does not have this functionality, and therefore cannot pass unresolved recipients to the Exchange organization, the Exchange organization must be the first messaging system for inbound e-mail.

There are two ways to configure this forwarding. One is easy to configure but not very flexible, and the second is much more flexible, but harder to configure.

The first option, sharing all SMTP address spaces, is ideal in small environments, but if you require the creation of contacts in Active Directory for users on the forwarded system you cannot use this option. That is, if your Exchange server is authoritative for @humongousinsurance.com and you have a second e-mail system that also uses @humongousinsurance.com e-mail addresses, you cannot create a mail-enabled contact in Active Directory for user@humongousinsurance.com when this user is located on the forwarded system.

The second option involves sharing selected SMTP address spaces, and while allowing the creation of contacts in the domain, it involves much more configuration to make it work.

Configuring Message Forwarding

Before enabling either of the unresolved forwarding options, you need to make sure that your Exchange organization does not implement Recipient Filtering for users that are not in the directory. This option may stop the e-mail being accepted by an Exchange SMTP virtual server so it could never be forwarded on.

Option 1: Sharing All SMTP Addresses

This option is enabled on all SMTP virtual servers in the organization. On the Messaging tab of the SMTP virtual server, enter the FQDN of the SMTP server that will receive forwarded e-mail into the Forward All E-Mail With Unresolved Recipients To Host field.

If an IP address is to be used for the server, the IP address must be surrounded in square brackets. This is to stop Exchange Server from attempting to resolve the IP address as if it were a name.

If mail-enabled contacts exist in Active Directory for users in the messaging systems that unresolved recipients are being forwarded to, then this sharing of all SMTP address spaces configuration will result in a bounced e-mail. The e-mail error reads:

A configuration error in the e-mail system caused the message to bounce between two servers or to be forwarded between two recipients. Contact your administrator. <Server FQDN #5.4.6>

Option 2: Sharing Selected SMTP Addresses

The steps for sharing selected SMTP addresses involves ensuring that the selected address space does not require the Exchange organization to be responsible for its delivery. Prior to Exchange Server 2003 SP1 each namespace required a dedicated HTTP virtual server for Outlook Web Access to work for users of that namespace. Because this is not the case if you are running SP1 or later, some of the instructions required are not necessary for Outlook Web Access to work, but are needed to ensure the correct reply-to address is stamped on all outgoing e-mail.

> **Tip**   Full instructions for this procedure can be found in the Microsoft Knowledge Base article 321721, "Sharing SMTP Address Spaces in Exchange 2000 Server and Exchange Server 2003" (*http:// go.microsoft.com/fwlink/?linkid=3052&kbid=321721*).

The first step is to create an internal only address space that the Exchange organization is responsible for delivering. This ensures that Outlook Web Access remains operational in pre-SP1 installations, and because of this common choices for the address space are @owa.woodgrovebank.com or @exchange.woodgrovebank.com. This SMTP address space needs to be set in Recipient Policies on the default policy. It has to have the Exchange organization responsible for its delivery and it needs to be the primary SMTP address. This can be seen in Figure 11-30 and Figure 11-31.

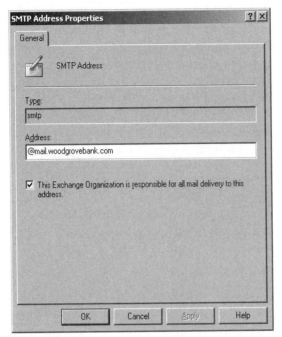

Figure 11-30   Adding a second SMTP address space and making the Exchange organization responsible for delivery to this address space

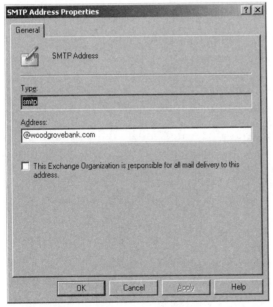

Figure 11-31   Removing the Exchange organization from delivery responsibility for the shared SMTP address space

Once the new address space is created and the shared address space modified, the new address space needs to become the default SMTP address. This is shown in Figure 11-32. This will cause the reply-to address of every mailbox-enabled object to change, so if the address space that is being shared is the primary address space for the organization, as it is in this example, then a second recipient policy needs to be created that has the shared address space set up as the primary reply-to address. This second recipient policy needs to cover all relevant users and have a higher priority than the recipient policy created/modified in the previous step. This is shown in Figure 11-33.

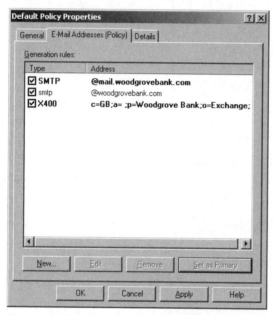

Figure 11-32   Setting the new address space as the default SMTP reply-to address

Once these recipient policies are created and modified, you can force an update of the Recipient Update Service to ensure that all mailbox e-mail addresses update correctly, though this occurs every 60 seconds by default.

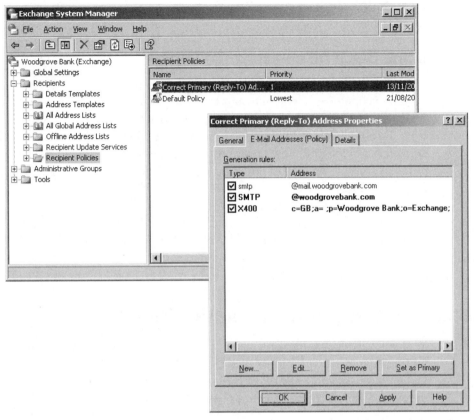

Figure 11-33   A higher recipient policy showing the corrected default SMTP reply-to address

> **Important**   For sharing some address spaces for forwarding messages, it is important not to have the configuration in place for sharing all address spaces. Therefore, be sure that the option to Forward All E-Mail With Unresolved Recipients To Host on the SMTP virtual server Message tab is blank.

The final step is in the creation of an SMTP connector to forward the unresolved messages to the next messaging system. This forwarding should be done by the use of a smart host and not DNS. Additionally, this SMTP connector requires that its address space matches the shared SMTP domain without the @. In our example, this connector would be woodgrovebank.com with a cost of 1. Finally, configuration is required on the SMTP connector to ensure that e-mail for this address space can be relayed by the server hosting the connector without that server rejecting these messages as an open relay.

These changes will operate once the Exchange server updates its configuration from Active Directory.

Implementing Catch-All on Exchange Server

Using forwarding of unresolved recipients is one way to implement a catch-all option within Exchange Server. Catch all is the ability to receive to a single mailbox all the e-mail addresses that are not associated with existing recipients.

The behavior of Exchange Server with forwarding unresolved recipients is to send the e-mail unchanged to another SMTP system. If that SMTP system is an Exchange virtual server, additional programming can be implemented on the virtual server to rewrite the recipient address to the mailbox of the user who is going to receive all these e-mail messages.

Instructions on how to program the event sink that will do the rewriting of the recipient address can be found in Microsoft Knowledge Base article 315631, "Forward Mail with Unresolved Recipients to a Single Mailbox" (*http://go.microsoft.com/fwlink/ ?linkid=3052&kbid=315631*).

Managing Outgoing Message Traffic

Setting up Exchange Server to deliver e-mail is only the start of the administration of your Exchange organization. Once e-mail is flowing, you will need to be able to manage the process and ensure that it remains operational. In Exchange System Manager the main tool for this is the Queue Viewer.

The Queue Viewer

The Queue Viewer has changed in Exchange Server 2003 and is now in an easier to manage format than Exchange Server 2000, primarily because the queues can be seen from one location within the Exchange System Manager rather than having to open each virtual server and viewing the queue on a virtual server by virtual server basis. The Queue Viewer (Figure 11-34) is located underneath each server entry in Exchange System Manager. The queues to the Internet and to other Exchange Server and messaging systems are named after the SMTP connector for that destination.

From the Queue Viewer it is possible to find messages, view information about messages, freeze and unfreeze queues, and quickly stop the delivery of outbound e-mail in the case of a virus infection. In addition to these administrative tasks, it is possible to change the refresh rate of the queues from the Settings button, or manually refresh the queues by clicking on Queues and pressing F5.

During queue administration the process that you should go through to ensure that everything is working okay is to see if a queue contains a large number of messages in the Number of Messages column. What constitutes a large number of messages will be different for different organizations. A large number that is an indication of a problem will be when it is high relative to what that queue normally runs at, though if all is working well with your system and the systems that you send e-mail to, the queue size will be at or close to zero.

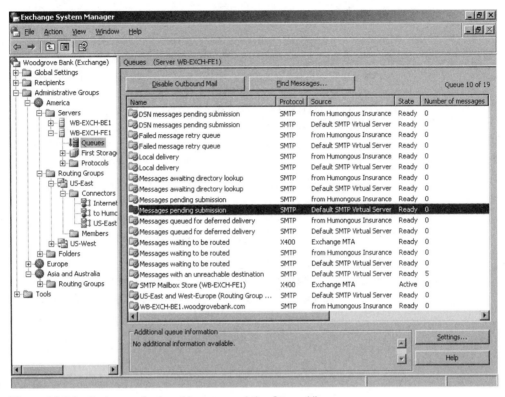

Figure 11-34 Exchange System Manager and the Queue Viewer

To check for problems in the queue, select the queue that you wish to investigate and the additional queue information at the bottom of the Queue tool will let you know the last error. If the remote system that you are connecting to is not working, and you have a queue item per remote domain because you are using DNS to send e-mail, then you will get errors such as *The connection was dropped by the remote host* or *The remote server did not respond to a connection attempt.*

If your SMTP connector uses a smart host, then you will get only one queue regardless of the number of domains that e-mail is being sent to. Queue investigation needs to move to the smart host if problems in delivery occur.

Queue Types

The following is a list of the Exchange Server 2003 queues in the order that outbound mail flows through them. The list also describes what the queue is for and how to troubleshoot the queue.

- **Messages pending submission** Once a message has been accepted by the SMTP service it will appear in this queue. Items in this queue have not been processed and this is the first queue an outbound e-mail will appear in. Performance issues with a server can cause items to remain in this queue for longer than expected. These are most likely to be performance issues with custom code (event sinks) on the SMTP service for antivirus and disclaimer placement. Occasional peaks in CPU activity on a server can also cause items to wait in this queue until CPU resources are available.

- **Messages awaiting directory lookup** While messages have their distribution lists expanded and their recipients checked against Active Directory, they will sit in this queue. This is the second queue for an outbound SMTP message. Performance issues with global catalog servers are the most likely reason for delays to items in this queue.

- **Messages waiting to be routed** This queue will exist for all SMTP connectors and the X400 delivery built into the Exchange MTA. Messages will sit in this queue while their next destination server is calculated. Once the next server is known, items will move into the queue for that server. Delays on this queue are typically due to routing problems and the first point of examination should be unnecessary delivery restrictions on the connector. The SMTP version of this queue is the third queue that Internet-bound messages will travel through on this server.

- **Domain name queues** A queue will exist for each domain name to which the server is attempting delivery if no SMTP connector exists for that address space. The domain name queue will remain in the user interface for a short while after the connection is finished. Troubleshooting this queue involves seeing if the queue state is "retry." If it is, then the Additional queue information area of Exchange System Manager will show what the problem is. If the problem is with the remote SMTP Server, and other remote delivery queues are operating fine, then the problem is most likely that the other server is unreachable. If each of the remote delivery queues is not operational you should check your DNS configuration, firewall configuration, and Internet access.

- **SMTP connector-named queues** Each connector will have a queue for either e-mail delivery to the smart host or e-mail delivery to a particular domain. An SMTP connector-based queue name will be the name of the SMTP connector, followed by the domain name and finished with "(SMTP Connector)." The queue will remain in the user interface for a short while after the connection is finished. Troubleshooting this queue is similar to the previous queue as this is a remote delivery queue also.

The remaining queues are used depending upon the destination or type of message and therefore are listed alphabetically because an outbound message may never flow through them. The X400 queue and queues for other connectors such as fax integration with Exchange are not listed here.

- **Delivery status notification message pending submission**   This queue was hidden in Exchange Server 2000. A delivery status notification is delivered from this queue into the correct queue for their destination. Delivery status notifications are primarily NDRs. Items will build up in this queue if the Information Store service is unavailable or not operational, or if a private mailbox store is offline, or if there is a problem with the Imail Exchange store component. Imail is the component that performs message conversion. Troubleshooting this queue consists mainly of looking in the Windows application event log for further details.

- **Failed message retry queue**   This queue was first visible in Exchange Server 2003. The queue contains messages that for some reason, such as DNS lookup or SMTP errors, mean that it could not be delivered to its correct queue and is awaiting a retry. Retries occur every 60 minutes. Occasionally, this queue may contain corrupt messages. If corrupt, you should notice that not all the message properties will be visible in the viewed e-mail. The time of the next retry and the oldest message in the queue can be viewed from the Queue Viewer.

- **Local delivery**   This queue contains messages destined for mailboxes stored on the current Exchange server. A delay in delivery from this queue can mean that the mailbox store is offline or corrupt, that the disk containing the folder used for the queue processing is slow, or that a looping message condition exists.

- **Messages queued for deferred delivery**   This queue was hidden in Exchange Server 2000. This queue holds messages that are awaiting a later delivery. E-mail messages could collect in this queue if they are destined for a mailbox that is corrupt, or has just been moved, or is not yet created. Also, old versions of Outlook will place items in this queue if the item has been marked for deferred delivery. Later versions of Outlook keep items for deferred delivery in the Information Store. Deferred delivery items kept in the Information Store are still visible in the Outbox in Outlook and can be manipulated by the client. If a deferred delivery e-mail disappears from the Outbox and appears in this queue, it has been sent from an old version of Outlook and cannot be stopped once it has been sent by the user, but in Exchange Server 2003 the administrator could delete the message on behalf of the user.

- **Messages with an unreachable destination** This queue is only visible if a message has ever reached this position in the recent past or if the queue contains messages. The main reason for items being in this queue is because Exchange cannot determine a route or connector to the final destination. Messages may also be moved to this queue if they remain in a queue that is in retry state for a period of time. Troubleshooting this queue is best achieved with a Microsoft download tool named WinRoute. This can be downloaded from *http:/ /www.microsoft.com/exchange/downloads/*. WinRoute shows the state of Exchange routing between routing groups in an Exchange organization. For additional information about the WinRoute tool, view the Microsoft Knowledge Base article 281382, "How to Use the WinRoute Tool" (*http://go.microsoft.com/ fwlink/?linkid=3052&kbid=281382*). If an SMTP connector or an SMTP virtual server is misconfigured so that the sender SMTP server cannot communicate with the recipient SMTP server then, once you have fixed the reason for those messages entering this queue, restart the sender SMTP virtual server used by the SMTP connector.

- **PendingRerouteQ** If a temporary link outage occurs, items are held in this queue until the outage is fixed.

Freezing and Unfreezing Queues

Pausing a queue will stop it from sending any messages to the next queue on this server or destination server. A queue can be frozen and unfrozen from the Queue Viewer in Exchange System Manager.

Managing E-Mail in a Queue

In Exchange Server 2000, before a queue would show you its contents the queue needed to be enumerated. This is no longer the case with the Exchange Server 2003 administration tools and these tools will work against an Exchange 2000 server to improve its queue management. To view messages in a queue, double-click the queue and click Find Now. To fine tune your queue management it is possible to filter the list of e-mail messages by looking for a particular sender or recipient and to change the number of returned results from the default of 100 to 500, 1000, or 10000.

Once a message has been located, it is possible to freeze (or unfreeze) individual messages and to delete a message from the queue.

When a message is deleted, you have the option to delete a message with or without sending an NDR. NDRs from messages that are deleted in the queue by an administrator contain the following error message:

This message was rejected due to the current administrative policy by the destination server. Please retry at a later time. If that fails, contact your system administrator. <Server FQDN #4.3.2>

Stopping All Outbound E-Mail

In the event of an outbreak of a virus that is able to send many hundreds and thousands of messages through the Exchange server, it is possible to halt outbound e-mail without shutting down parts of the network or firewall infrastructure until the virus is removed and the outbreak controlled.

To quickly stop all outbound messages from being delivered through a server, click the Disable Outbound Mail button in the Queue Viewer. This will disable all the queues that deliver e-mail to external sources, including routing group connectors, domain names, and SMTP connectors. During this time, assuming that your Internet connection is not overloaded with other symptoms of the virus, inbound e-mail will still arrive at a user's mailbox.

Optimizing Outbound Connections

The Exchange Server administrator has considerably more control over the configuration of outbound SMTP connections than inbound connections; however, there are more settings that control what the SMTP virtual server will accept. The majority of settings for outbound SMTP will be found on the SMTP virtual server properties dialog box on the Delivery tab, along with all the inbound properties as well.

Each property is described in detail in the section of creating additional virtual servers earlier in this chapter, but here we will concentrate on improving the performance of the virtual server for outbound traffic.

Performance can be improved by the use of the following settings:

- Global and individual message size limits

- SMTP connector content restrictions

- Outbound connections

- Smart hosts

Global and Individual Message Size Limits

Before a message is delivered to the Internet it is processed by the Exchange server and placed into a queue for delivery. The processing storage space on the disk that the queue uses and the network traffic required to deliver a message all increase as the message size increases.

Restrictions on the maximum message size that your Exchange organization clients can send can therefore help to improve disk, CPU, and network performance. As with all performance adjustments, do not enable these settings without first having a baseline of current performance activity. After implementing the limitation (or removing it), check again to see if performance, disk, and network capacity has been adversely affected.

Global Settings in Exchange System Manager controls the sending and receiving message size and the maximum number of recipients that an outbound e-mail can be addressed to. The maximum message size that can be sent is, by default, 10240 KB. The successful sending of a message close to this limit will depend upon the recipient system also, and although 10 MB is considered the default for most corporate systems, some systems, particularly those run by ISPs will have a lower maximum.

For selected individual mailboxes, an individual Sending Message Size can be set. This is enabled via the Exchange General tab, Delivery Restrictions button on the selected mailbox in Active Directory Users and Computers. E-mail messages that exceed the maximum outbound size will be returned to the sender stating:

This message is larger than the current system limit or the recipient's mailbox is full. Create a shorter message body or remove attachments and try sending it again. <Server FQDN #5.2.3>

The default value for the maximum number of recipients that an Exchange organization user can send a message to is 5000. This is the total number of recipients after any internal distribution list has been expanded. For our example company, Woodgrove Bank, the default of 5000 would stop the sending of e-mail to the all@woodgrovebank.com e-mail address, as that contains all 40,000 members of staff. If a message exceeds the allowed number of recipients then it is returned to the sender stating:

The e-mail system limits the number of recipients that can be addressed in a single message. Send the message multiple times to fewer recipients. <Server FQDN #5.5.3>

Message size is also dependant upon the format of the message. An HTML message format will take more storage to queue and require a larger amount of network traffic to deliver than the same message in plain text. The default in Exchange Server 2003 (unless upgraded from an Exchange Server 2000) is to send an e-mail as both HTML and plain text to the Internet. This option creates messages larger than either HTML only or plain text only. The encoding options can be found in Exchange System Manager, Global Settings, Internet Message Formats, Default (or, if listed, the domain to which you want to change the setting).

One encoding option is MIME. This allows for the message to be stored in the e-mail body in a number of different formats. A MIME-aware client will select and display the most richly formatted version of the message that it can find. If a client does not support MIME, it will display the entire message including all the MIME headers. Though MIME supports the storage of different message formats within the same message, global options in Exchange System Manager can control whether or not a message to the Internet will do this. The second encoding option is UUEncode (original meaning: Unix to Unix Encoding). Nearly every e-mail client is able to support UUEncode because it was one of the first encoding methods for the delivery of attachments in e-mail. A UUEncoded message will always be plain text when sent to the Internet.

If a client does not understand UUEncode (and that will be very rare), then the message will be unreadable.

It is important to choose a message format that will result in the widest readability, and MIME provides this. Even if the client does not understand MIME, the message of the e-mail will be readable, though attachments would not be. The final consideration with MIME is that the Exchange organization default is to send all messages in their HTML and plain text format, increasing the network traffic required for delivery. In networks with restricted bandwidth, the global restrictions requiring the use of plain text e-mail for Internet message delivery should be considered.

SMTP Connector Content Restrictions

In addition to limits being set globally for sending messages as discussed previously, a limit can be placed on the SMTP connector. This limit will take effect if it is smaller than the global limit. Setting the limit on the connector allows the limit to be different for different domains.

In the example used previously, Woodgrove Bank sending e-mail to their partner organization Humongous Insurance, the default global limit of 10 MB might be too low, so both Woodgrove Bank and Humongous Insurance could increase their global default for sending e-mail and set a useful limit on the SMTP connector that delivers e-mail to the Internet (the connector doing the * address space).

Outbound Connections

The SMTP virtual server controls the number of connections that it can make simultaneously. By default this is 1000, with a time out of 10 minutes if a remote SMTP server stops responding. The maximum number of connections that a virtual server can maintain is dependant upon the network capacity both on the LAN and the Internet and the number of inbound connections that same virtual server is supporting. To improve performance, this number can be changed. As with all performance work, a baseline is required beforehand to ensure that the change does not result in the system being in a worse position than before the change was made.

If server performance is the issue, then an easy performance change that can be made is to ensure that inbound e-mail does not use the same server as outbound e-mail. This is especially the case when the inbound e-mail server is running anti-spam and antivirus software.

The connection time-out of 10 minutes is sufficient in most networks and should only be increased if delivery problems due to intermittent network problems are happening. It should never need to be decreased because a properly operational SMTP session will quit and close the session when message transfer is complete. A 10-minute time out does not mean that the SMTP virtual server has to complete the entire communication within that time; it means that it will close the connection if nothing happens for the time period specified. The Queue Viewer in Exchange System Manager will display *The Semaphore Timeout Period Has Expired* upon this state occurring, and if this appears often you should increase the time out value.

Connection limiting per domain really assists the domain that you are connecting to and not your environment. The default of 100 connections to each remote domain means that a single domain will never be subject to the maximum number of connections that your network can make, and should some virus outbreak occur that tries to cause a denial of service using SMTP against another domain, your network will still have available connections to send e-mail to every other domain that you need to.

The SMTP virtual server settings control the maximum number of messages per connection. This defaults to 20, and Exchange Server will open additional connections if it needs to deliver more than 20 messages to the same domain or smart host server. This will improve performance as a queue with 21 messages in it will transmit 20 on one session and the next 20 on a second session rather than queuing all the messages to go in a series during in one session.

Smart Hosts

The use of a smart host will reduce the amount of DNS traffic generated by the Exchange Server gateway, moving this traffic to the smart host server, but because the e-mail goes through an additional server before leaving a network, an additional point exists where a delay could be introduced. Having said that, smart hosts can be used to virus-check all outbound e-mail, removing the need to check outbound e-mail on the Exchange Server gateway and thus freeing up CPU cycles for other processes.

In addition to a reduction in DNS traffic, having a smart host to channel all your e-mail through allows you to dedicate servers to the role of making Internet connections rather than allowing each Exchange server to connect to the Internet destination directly. This means that the smart host can be tuned for networking, rather than any of the other roles needed by an Exchange server, and any firewall protecting the internal network can be configured to allow outbound SMTP traffic from the smart host only.

Automatic Replies To the Internet

The Exchange organization has a number of global properties that control whether or not e-mail can be sent on a user's behalf automatically to the Internet. These settings are configured on a per-domain basis, with one default policy created that covers all domains that are not specifically listed. Each of the policies can be found in Exchange System Manager, Global Settings, Internet Message Formats, and then double-clicking the domain name (or Default) in the results pane on the right of Exchange System Manager. When you create a new domain policy, it will differ from the default policy in that it enables all of the following six options. The Exchange Server 2003 default policy only enables the last three in this list.

Exchange Server 2000 and Exchange Server 2003 have these policies as global settings, whereas in Exchange Server 5.5 they were set on the connector that delivered the e-mail. The location of this configuration has changed because the setting is based on the recipient and not the sender as it was when set per connector.

Allow Out of Office Responses

This option allows the sending of out-of-office (OOF) responses outside the Exchange organization. By default, OOF messages are not sent outside the Exchange organization. Within an Exchange organization an OOF message will always be sent if the client has set that option in Outlook.

It is becoming common practice to leave this option disabled and to create a policy for those domains that need to know this information. With the default option disabled you do not confirm an e-mail address to spammers whose e-mail arrives while a user is out, nor do you give away information to anyone on the location of your employees.

Additionally, in Exchange Server 2003 OOF messages will not be sent when the recipient receives an e-mail because it was addressed to a distribution list. They will only send OOFs if the recipient is listed in the To or Cc lines of the e-mail. This is a change in functionality from earlier versions of Exchange Server. It avoids sending an OOF message to, potentially, many mailboxes and provides an associated slight performance improvement in the product. By default, Exchange Server 2003 will send an OOF to a distribution list if the recipient is listed on the Bcc field of the e-mail. This can be disabled by the instructions in Microsoft Knowledge Base article 825370, "Out-of-Office messages are sent to distribution lists that are in the BCC field" (*http://go.microsoft.com/fwlink/?linkid=3052&kbid=825370*).

Allow Automatic Replies

If a mailbox or public folder has a rule associated with it that will automatically generate a reply to the sender, for example to confirm the acceptance of a resume to the jobs@woodgrovebank.com public folder, then the Allow Automatic Replies option needs to be enabled for the reply to leave the Exchange organization. Auto-replies within the Exchange organization happen automatically. This option is not enabled by default in Exchange Server 2003.

As with the sending of OOF messages to the Internet, there are security ramifications to consider. In addition to indicating the availability of a valid e-mail address to a spammer, consideration needs to be given to the possibility of implementing message loops. Each e-mail that arrives at the mailbox or public folder that implements the auto-reply rule sends an e-mail to the sender. But what if the sender has also implemented auto-reply? This kicks off a message back to the first e-mail address, which auto-replies, and so on. Each message is a new message, and so options such as Maximum Hop Count do not come into effect and the messages are never blocked or returned as NDRs.

Allow Automatic Forward

The option Allow Automatic Forward is not enabled in Exchange Server 2003, by default. Selecting this option will allow client rules that forward incoming mail to their mailbox to be delivered to an address outside the Exchange organization.

This example is commonly requested when users need to access their e-mail when away from the company and so have their e-mail forwarded to a Web e-mail provider such as Hotmail. Implementing Outlook Web Access or Outlook Mobile Access on your Internet connection avoids this requirement because the users should be able to reach their e-mail from any Web browser or supported mobile phone. By preventing users from automatically forwarding e-mail messages to the Internet, you stop the potential for sending confidential material outside of the company without notice.

As with auto-replies, users could implement a message loop that would cause performance problems to your network and Exchange organization. For example, an auto-forward to an ISP could cause a response saying that the mailbox is full, which would then automatically be forwarded to the ISP, and so on.

Allow Delivery Reports

As in Exchange Server 2000, the Allow Delivery Reports option is enabled in Exchange Server 2003. Deselecting this option will stop external senders receiving an automatic delivery receipt when they request it. Client programs such as Outlook 2003 will respond to an e-mail requesting a read receipt based on how the client is configured. Clients do not follow the Allow Delivery Reports option in Exchange System Manager.

Disabling this option will stop all responses to client requests for delivery receipts, which may lead users to think e-mail has not been delivered, but the disabling of the option stops automatic confirmation of a valid e-mail address to a spammer.

Allow Non-Delivery Reports

If an e-mail cannot be delivered, the Exchange server will respond with an NDR. This NDR will give the reason for the failure of delivery. Numerous reasons exist, some being immediate (user does not exist) and some being delayed (e-mail delayed for so long it became undeliverable). Disabling the Allow Non-Delivery Reports option will stop all of these NDRs from being sent outside the Exchange organization.

Preserve Senders Display Name on Message

When a user sends an e-mail outside of the Exchange organization, the e-mail is headed with both the display name and e-mail address. Clearing the Preserve Senders Display Name On Message option removes the display name before sending the e-mail externally.

Communicating with Other Exchange Organizations over the Internet

Because Exchange Server communicates using SMTP there is, on one level, nothing special about communicating with other Exchange organization over the Internet. You just send the e-mail as you would to any domain on the Internet.

On another level, though, you can set options such as authentication and message format that can be understood by the other Exchange organization. Therefore, in this section we will look at four available options when sending e-mail between two Exchange organizations:

- Using Exchange Rich Text Format (RTF) e-mail

- Authenticating e-mail between domains

- SMTP encryption between organizations

- Sending Free/Busy information between organizations.

Sending Exchange Rich Text Format Information

Rich Text Format (RTF) as used in Exchange is a form of Microsoft Word's RTF file format that is suitable for sending as e-mail. It is compressed so it results in a smaller e-mail than the same e-mail in HTML. It is not the same as an RTF document and cannot be opened by Word if it arrives as an attachment to an e-mail. RTF is a Microsoft proprietary format and is understood by Exchange Client and numerous versions of Microsoft Outlook. It is not understood by most other mail clients.

If a user chooses to send an e-mail as RTF, the e-mail is generated as both a plain text version of the contents and the RTF version of the contents. The RTF version of the contents is attached to the e-mail as a file named winmail.dat. If the receiving e-mail client can understand Exchange RTF then the attachment is not displayed as such, but its contents become the richly formatted contents of the e-mail. A mail client that does not support Exchange RTF will see the plain text e-mail and the winmail.dat attachment. They will need decoding software installed if they want to read the attachment.

Therefore, when sending e-mail to the Internet you need to ensure that Exchange RTF is either disabled or used only when sending to organizations and recipients that can understand it.

To enable RTF support in an Exchange organization go to the Advanced tab of the Internet Message Formats dialog box for the domain in question (or for default). This is the same dialog box discussed previously for out-of-office responses. The default setting on Exchange is to allow the user to decide what format to send the e-mail as. Group Policy in Active Directory can control what the default format for all new messages in Outlook will be. A reply to an e-mail will keep the same format as the original e-mail.

A user has control of the default format for individual users. This format setting can be set by double-clicking the e-mail address in the To or Cc field or by saving the e-mail address as a contact and setting it for the contact.

At the Exchange organization, the user's individual choice can be removed by choosing to Always Use or Never Use the format. Always Use should only be set on specific domains and Never Use on the default setting for Internet Message Formats.

Activating Exchange Rich-Text Information per Internet Domain

To create a global setting that forces the use of Exchange Rich Text to a particular domain you do the following:

1. In Exchange System Manager, open Global Settings and select Internet Message Formats. If the domain that you wish to set this setting for is listed, double-click the domain (see Figure 11-35), otherwise right-click Internet Message Formats and choose New to create the domain.

> **Note**   To ensure that subdomains are included, the domain name must include wildcards. For example, the domain humongousinsurance.com will control e-mail formats for user jo@humongousinsurance.com but not user jo@exchange.humongousinsurance.com. To control the format for all humongousinsurance.com domains you would need to create a policy for the *.humongousinsurance.com domain.

2. On the Advanced tab of the dialog box, choose Always Use in the Exchange Rich Text Format area.

3. On the Message Format tab select MIME with body as plain text or UUEncode. You cannot choose MIME with body as HTML or body as both when choosing to always use Exchange Rich Text Format.

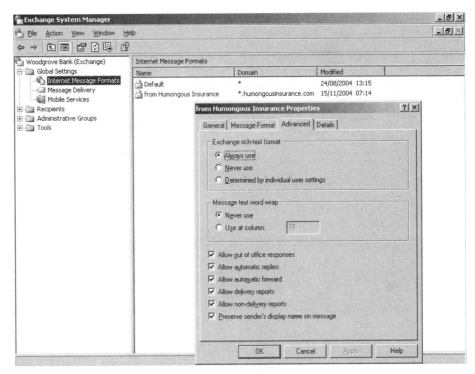

Figure 11-35   Forcing the use of Exchange Rich Text Format for a specific domain

4. Set any other specific delivery responses (on the Advanced tab) and click OK.

Authenticating E-Mail Between Domains

When e-mail is sent to a domain over an anonymous connection, Exchange Server always causes the display of both the user's display name and e-mail address in the client. Within a single Exchange organization all e-mail is authenticated (if sent using a client set to use Microsoft Exchange Server), therefore within an organization users should just see the display name and never the e-mail address. In addition, when double-clicking on the display name, the global address properties of that mail recipient will be shown. Users who are aware of this distinction can therefore tell a spoofed e-mail from an authenticated e-mail. For example, Josh Barnhill is the chief executive of Woodgrove Bank. E-mail that he sends within the organization will appear with his name only in the From header in Outlook. A spammer on the Internet can send an e-mail to any address inside Woodgrove Bank using the CEO's e-mail address as the From address. This spoof e-mail claims to come from the CEO, except the e-mail will appear differently in Outlook. Figure 11-36 shows the spoofed and real e-mail for comparison.

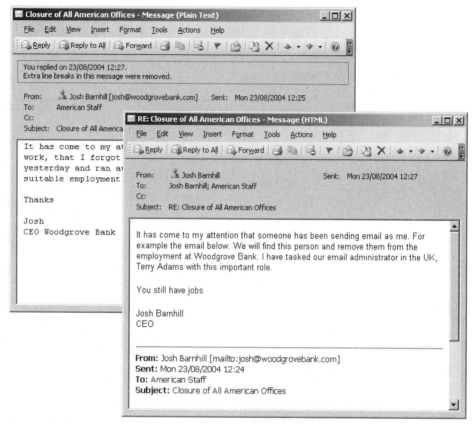

Figure 11-36   Comparing an anonymous e-mail to an authenticated e-mail

This is ideal within an organization, but when two organizations are closely connected but operate different Active Directory forests, and therefore different Exchange organizations, Exchange will not resolve an e-mail from the other forest to the global address list object because the connection is anonymous. Even if the sending user is authenticated in their forest, when the e-mail arrives at the other forest Exchange will show both the sender's display name and e-mail address. This is because the connection to the second forest was anonymous.

There are two approaches for authenticating e-mail between Exchange organizations, both of which are supported by Microsoft but one of which is not recommended.

The preferred approach is to connect the two Exchange organizations with a connector that is authenticated. The account used for the authentication must have Send As permission on the servers that host the connectors that are used for this inter-organization communication. When e-mail arrives at the second forest, because it arrives on an authenticated connection the e-mail address is resolved to the global address list object.

> **More Info**   Full steps on how to configure your Exchange organizations for authentication between organizations can be found in the "Exchange Server 2003 Deployment Guide" document available at the Microsoft Exchange Server 2003 Technical Documentation Library at *http://go.microsoft.com/fwlink/?LinkID=21277*.

The approach that is not recommended is to create an SMTP connector for the transfer of e-mail between these organizations and to configure Exchange to resolve anonymous e-mail. The option to resolve anonymous e-mail is found on the Authentication tab of the SMTP virtual server that would be used by the connector. Extended Exchange message properties (for example Intelligent Message Filter SCL ratings) are not sent on anonymous connections, so in addition to resolving anonymous e-mail these extended properties need to be propagated between organizations with the use of a registry change on both the sending and receiving Exchange servers.

SMTP Encryption Between Organizations

Exchange Server and a number of other SMTP servers support the use of TLS to encrypt SMTP sessions over port 25. TLS is an implementation of Secure Sockets Layer (SSL). When you have two Exchange organizations that need to ensure encryption of all e-mail between them, this is one option that can be enabled. The benefit of this option over the other major methods of encrypting e-mail (SMIME and PGP) is that the client does not need to be involved. All e-mail between the domains listed in the SMTP connector will be encrypted as it travels across the Internet, whereas other encryption methods that involve clients may mean that it is not always enforced. The downside to encrypting all e-mail is performance with the overhead of adding SSL to the session and the extra CPU cycles needed to encrypt and decrypt the message, though this could be offloaded to an SSL Accelerator card.

To enable TLS encryption, each bridgehead server that will receive e-mail from the other Exchange organizations will need to install a digital certificate that allows server authentication. The purchase of an SSL certificate from any public certificate authority will match this requirement, or if the organizations that are going to connect are related, partner organizations for example, then a PKI could be implemented between them to provide digital certificates for inter-organization communication. The process for obtaining and installing a digital certificate is the same for SMTP, POP3, HTTP, and IMAP4 virtual servers and so the process is described in detail in the next chapter when we look at securing HTTP virtual servers for Outlook Web Access and Outlook Mobile Access.

Once the certificate is installed on each receiving bridgehead server, the server at the sending Exchange organization needs to be configured to start a TLS session when transmitting messages to the partner domain, but not when communicating with all other domains. This is achieved with an SMTP connector, set to use the address space of the partner organization. On the Advanced tab of the SMTP connector, click Outbound Security and check TLS Encryption. A separate SMTP connector still needs to exist within the Exchange organization, without TLS enabled, going to the * address space to ensure continued delivery to Internet domain address spaces.

> **Important**   TLS security between organizations will typically only work if you have configured it to do so. And even when it is, it is still the case that most of your communications on the Internet will be in clear text.

Do not enable authentication and encryption options that are too restrictive on the receiving SMTP virtual server. This could stop connections from servers that are not configured to connect with these settings. If you are using your default virtual server you will need to ensure that TLS is not a required option, just that the certificate is installed so that the virtual server is capable of TLS. Requiring TLS will stop connections to this virtual server from other SMTP servers and clients that do not support it or expect to support it on this session.

> **Important**   Using your default virtual server means that this TLS connection from your partner organization will be subject to all the conditions of the virtual server. This will include connection filtering, time out, and message size options.
>
> See Configuring Additional SMTP Virtual Servers earlier in this chapter for the steps to create a dedicated SMTP virtual server to accept connections from, and only from, the partner SMTP virtual server.

If you are using a dedicated SMTP virtual server to receive connections from the partner organization, then you can be very restrictive with the authentication and IP address options. Though TLS does not require authentication, you can enable authentication and IP address restrictions to ensure that the only connections to the SMTP virtual server are from your partner organization. Though it is not required, changing the SMTP banner can allow you to advertise the fact that this is a restricted SMTP server.

In addition to the requirement for TLS, this same connector can be configured to authenticate to the partner domain at the same time as providing encryption. This will additionally provide resolution of a user's e-mail address to the Active Directory contact display name.

To test if everything is working, enable logging on the SMTP virtual server at the receiving organization. The default settings for the log are sufficient to generate enough data to confirm that the connection is working correctly. The following, generated by sending one e-mail, will be found in the log if all is working correctly:

```
#Fields: time c-ip cs-method cs-uri-stem sc-status
16:45:20 192.168.5.223 EHLO - 250
16:45:20 192.168.5.223 STARTTLS - 220
16:45:20 192.168.5.223 STARTTLS - 220
16:45:20 192.168.5.223 EHLO - 250
16:45:20 192.168.5.223 MAIL - 250
16:45:20 192.168.5.223 RCPT - 250
16:45:20 192.168.5.223 xexch50 - 354
16:45:20 192.168.5.223 BDAT - 250
16:45:20 192.168.5.223 QUIT - 240
```

The first two columns show the time and sending SMTP server IP address. For troubleshooting, you can see that TLS negotiation started successfully (220) and that authentication (xexch50 – 354) was also successful. A 554 error for TLS means that no certificate was installed and other 5xx errors for STARTTLS will mean invalid certificate or other error. A 504 error for the xexch50 SMTP command means failure to authenticate. This 504 error will not stop the e-mail from being sent, but the extended Exchange properties will not be included in the e-mail, resulting in an anonymous rather than authenticated session. You can also see from the above log that once a TLS session starts it negates any previously discovered information and reissues an EHLO command (for more information on TLS see RFC 3207).

> **Important**   It is vital to ensure that you do not enable the TLS Encryption option on SMTP connectors that connect to SMTP servers that do not support TLS. Doing so will cause the e-mail for these domains to remain in the queue until it times out and returns an NDR.

Once the e-mail arrives at the destination it can be checked to prove that it all worked. In the e-mail headers you should see something like:

Received: from mail.woodgrovebank.com ([192.168.5.223]) by wb-hi.humongousinsurance.com over TLS secured channel with Microsoft SMTPSVC(6.0.3790.0);

If your SMTP connector on the sending server is mismatched for the authentication and encryption options on the receiving SMTP virtual server, you will need to fix the error and wait for the Exchange organization to notice before you can continue. If, for example, your sending SMTP connector is not configured to use TLS encryption, but the receiving SMTP virtual server is, then you will get an error in the Queue Viewer tool saying *The remote SMTP service rejected AUTH negotiation.*

This error is typical of any mismatching on the Authentication and Encryption options. Fixing this error will not result in the message being sent, even if you choose to Force Connection in the Queue Viewer. Eventually, the message will move into the messages with an unreachable destination queue, as the queue state is labeled as down. You can see the state of a queue in Exchange System Manager, Tools, Monitoring And Status, Status node or with the use of WinRoute. WinRoute can be downloaded from Microsoft's Exchange Server download site (*http://www.microsoft.com/exchange/downloads/*).

Once the connector is operational in one direction, the reverse configuration can be implemented to ensure that e-mail traveling in the other direction between the organizations is also encrypted.

Replicating Free and Busy Data and Public Folder Content

Finally, in communicating with Exchange organizations across the Internet you may want to publish your calendar data. This is known as your free and busy data and is stored in a public folder that is replicated around the Exchange organization. To replicate any public folder, including the one containing free and busy data to another Exchange organization, you must use the Inter-Organization Replication Tool.

Note   To use the Inter-Organization Replication Tool to replicate free and busy data, the source and destination servers must be configured to use the same language.

You can download the Inter-Organization Replication Tool from the Downloads for Exchange 2003 website *http://go.microsoft.com/fwlink/?linkid=25097*. Full instructions on the installation of the program are contained within the download, including instructions for the configuration of firewalls to allow the transfer of RPC data over port 135.

Configuring Protocol Logging

For troubleshooting purposes, you can log the traffic that comes through the SMTP virtual server. Logging may also be required for purposes other than just troubleshooting, such as regulatory compliance and proactive security monitoring. Logging will increase the processing requirements of the virtual server, and as log files can grow very quickly they can easily consume disk space. The default location of the log files is systemdrive:\WINDOWS\System32\LogFiles\SMTPSvc*N* where *N* is the number of the virtual server (which is the same number used in the default folder path). The name of the log file is based on the logging properties of log file type and schedule and is displayed on the Logging Properties dialog box. By default, all log files' schedules change at midnight Greenwich Mean Time (GMT). If the server does not operate in a GMT time zone, you can enable Use Local Time for naming and file roll-over so that the log file change schedule operates at 00:00 hours local time. This last option only exists on Windows Server 2003, so care needs to be taken when consolidating log files from multiple servers that may be in different time zones or run different versions of Windows.

There are four log file formats, and by default the W3C Extended Log File type records by default only the following properties of the SMTP traffic in the log:

- time

- c-ip

- cs-method (the SMTP command used, i.e. MAIL or RCPT)

- cs-uri-stem (always –)

- sc-status (the status code, i.e. 250 for success).

In addition to checking the option to enable logging, when using W3C Extended Log File type, the Logging Properties Advanced dialog box can be completed. This is available by clicking the Properties button on the virtual server Properties dialog box, General tab. Take care to be very selective about the options you choose; additional values will increase the logging file size, which will speed up the filling of the disk if unmanaged. If options are selected in the Advanced dialog box, make sure to include the default options above as well. If the default options are not included, they will not be logged. Of all the available log options, most of them do not record anything as they are used primarily for website logging. The value that is not recorded by default but does contain some useful information for logging is the cs-uri-query value.

The other three log file formats all have fixed logging columns and cannot be customized. The ODBC Logging option requires a database to log to and takes up more resources than text file logging. Should the log file need to be manipulated from a database, it is recommended to enable one of the three text file logging options and import the text file to the database later for processing.

More Info   Microsoft Knowledge Base article 266686, "How to Configure an SMTP Virtual Server Part 1" (*http://go.microsoft.com/fwlink/ ?linkid=3052&kbid=266686*) shows how to configure the database for ODBC logging.

> **Note**   No log file format records the body of the e-mail

Other Log Files

Though these log files have nothing to do with protocol logging, the Internet Mail Wizard creates a log file named Exchange Internet Mail Wizard.log in the My Documents folder of the user who runs the wizard. This log file records all the steps taken during the wizard and the current settings of the SMTP virtual server, along with the results of the wizard when it completes.

If the Internet Mail Wizard is run numerous times, entries are appended to the bottom of the log file.

Best Practices

To finish this chapter we are going to look at three example networks and how these fictitious companies used the options discussed in this chapter to implement their SMTP connectivity to and from the Internet. And additionally, in the case of Woodgrove Bank and Humongous Insurance, how they connected their networks together for authenticated and encrypted e-mail.

The three best practice networks described in this chapter range from a small network operated by the School of Fine Art, a large network operated by Woodgrove Bank and the network of their subsidiary Humongous Insurance.

Small Network Example

Regardless of the size of the network that Exchange Server is operating on, a firewall and antivirus solution will be necessary, as indicated in Figure 11-37. A small company may decide that an anti-spam solution is optional if they receive a small amount of spam, but because the Microsoft's Intelligent Message Filter is a free download for Exchange Server 2003 it will be included in this network.

The School of Fine Art is a small company based in Oxford in the United Kingdom. They have 30 administration and teaching staff and up to 100 students at different times of the year. At the present time they have a Windows 2003 Active Directory forest (fineartschool.net) composed of two domain controllers, which are both global catalog servers. Both servers are located at their single site just north of the city center. They have a 100 MB Ethernet network connecting all the offices, teaching rooms, library, and the student computer room. There is one Exchange server running on their more powerful domain controller. The majority of use of the network comes from staff in their day-to-day office functions, and very occasionally when they are away from the office they may have a need to access e-mail.

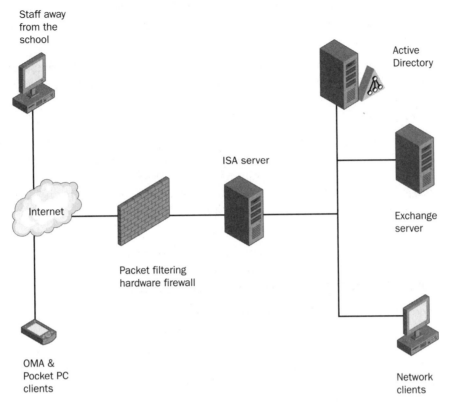

Figure 11-37   Small network high level overview

Small Network Description

Their Internet connection is a 2 MB DSL broadband connection providing an always on Internet presence with a single fixed IP address provided with the DSL connection. They have registered the fineartschool.net domain name and this is hosted by an ISP who also hosts their website, but who is not their DSL provider.

Their LAN is connected to the Internet via two firewalls. The two firewalls they operate are an ISA Server 2000 on a Windows 2003 server and their DSL modem, which provides simple stateful packet filtering firewall functionality.

Small Network DNS Settings

Before the School of Fine Art can accept any e-mail from the Internet, they need to ensure that their MX records are correct. In this network there will be one e-mail server visible to the Internet and that will be open on TCP port 25 on the IP address supplied by their DSL provider, which is 207.46.130.108. Additionally their DSL provider supplies SMTP backup services via ETRN. If the SMTP server for fineartschool.net is unavailable, then it will store and dequeue e-mail for them when they next connect. The IP address of the ETRN server is 131.107.2.200. Running `nslookup -q=MX fineartschool.net` (once the request to add the MX records has been completed by their DNS hosting company) results in:

```
fineartschool.net  MX preference = 10, mail exchanger = mail.fineartschool.net
fineartschool.net  MX preference = 20, mail exchanger = smtp1.adatum.com
mail.fineartschool.net   internet address = 207.46.130.108
smtp1.adatum.com   internet address = 131.107.2.200
```

In addition to adding their MX records they set the PTR record for the IP address the mail server uses correctly. This information needs to be set at the DSL provider, as the IP address for the external interface of the firewall belongs to them. Setting this record will assist those systems who use Reverse DNS lookups to check the validity of the SMTP server when it sends mail. Once completed, an nslookup for PTR records (`nslookup -q=PTR 207.46.130.108`) returns:

```
108.130.46.207.in-addr.arpa name = mail.fineartschool.net
```

Small Network Exchange Server Configuration

The default SMTP virtual server on the School of Fine Art Exchange server is correctly configured by default to receive inbound e-mail, with one exception. The virtual server FQDN value should be set to the Internet name of mail.fineartschool.net rather than the actual server name which it defaults to, because this is the DNS A record alias for this IP address and therefore the PTR record for Reverse DNS needs to match this name.

As the School of Fine Art have only one Exchange server, they do not need to create an SMTP connector, as all outbound e-mail can only come from one IP address, but using the Internet Mail Connection wizard to create an SMTP connector is still a recommended best practice. To ensure that the Exchange server will receive e-mail for the domain listed in the MX records (mail.fineartschool.net) the Exchange organization needs to be configured for the School of Fine Art domain name. Each user that needs to have an Internet e-mail address will need an SMTP address ending in @fineartschool.net. As this is the Active Directory domain name, this will have been completed during the Exchange Server installation. But if the external domain and the Active Directory domain do not match, the external domain name needs to be added via Recipient Policies. The name is added as a new SMTP address and the check box, which is on by default, stating that this Exchange Organization Is Responsible For All Mail Delivery To This Address needs to remain checked.

Small Network Firewall Configuration

The School of Fine Art simple stateful packet filter firewall is part of their DSL modem. Its firewall functions reach up to the TCP/UDP layer of the IP stack (layer 4 of the OSI stack). It is able to block ports or allow ports but not to examine the data in the application layer that it does allow through. Though the ISA Server that the School of Fine Art uses can do layer 4 inspection also, they decided to offload the majority of port blocking to the DSL modem firewall as this is connected directly to the Internet. The packet filter firewall allows only TCP ports 25 and 443 inbound. All other service ports (<1024) are either blocked by the packet filtering device or by their DSL provider who has additionally blocked ports 135 to 139 and 445 inbound, which they do not use on their Internet connection anyway.

The School of Fine Art's ISA Server is the next device that a packet encounters on its way into the network. The best practices for the installation of ISA Server can be found at *http://www.microsoft.com/isa/*. In this section we will look just at the configuration of this firewall for TCP port 25. The configuration for other application ports will be looked at in Chapter 13.

The external IP address is 207.46.130.108 and the internal address is 192.168.5.250. The ISA Server is also able to filter all inbound SMTP traffic to ensure that it is composed of valid SMTP commands. Should a hacker attempt to overload port 25 with non SMTP traffic in an attempt to flood the internal e-mail server or to send incorrectly structured SMTP commands in an attempt to crash the internal SMTP server then the ISA Server will terminate the connection; protecting the e-mail server.

The School of Fine Art have a single subnet network and have therefore set the default gateway on their Exchange server (at 192.168.5.241) to the internal address of the ISA Server (192.168.5.250). Once the Exchange Server gateway is routing correctly through the ISA Server the Mail Server Security Wizard can be run. Because the School of Fine Art has the same Exchange server for inbound and outbound e-mail we can use the wizard to configure both the inbound and outbound rules at the same time. The Mail Server Security Wizard will be able to select the IP address on the external interface (207.46.130.108) of the ISA Server to listen for requests on TCP port 25 and 192.168.5.241 as the address of the internal server to be published.

The School of Fine Art know that the SMTP commands VRFY and EXPN can be used by e-mail harvesting applications to determine the validity of an e-mail address for its inclusion on a list of addresses to be spammed. Also, given that most system user names match their e-mail address, it can assist a hacker in determining suitable user names for attacks into the system. Therefore, the School of Fine Art has decided to use ISA Server to disconnect any SMTP session that issues either the VRFY or EXPN command. At the same time, they are going to turn off requests that they know their e-mail server will never answer to, such as TURN to stop Internet connections using these commands. This will be achieved with the ISA Server SMTP Filter described earlier in this chapter.

For outbound SMTP connections, as the School of Fine Art have only one Exchange server (at 192.168.5.241), they will need to create a Protocol Rule (Access Rule in ISA Server 2004) to allow the Exchange server only to make SMTP connections to any address on the Internet. The remaining rules on the firewall are such that no other computer gets port 25 outbound (for example, there is not an outbound rule configured to allow all protocols to all destinations).

With the enabling of the SMTP publishing rule for inbound connections and the Protocol Rule for outbound connections in ISA Server we now have a secure barrier in front of the Exchange server. And though suspect and invalid SMTP commands are blocked by the ISA Server, one major problem exists with this network. It has no anti-virus provision. So before the School of Fine Art open their network to Internet e-mail they need to purchase and install an Exchange Server 2003 aware antivirus product.

Small Network Antivirus and Anti-Spam

The School of Fine Art have two options for protecting their messaging environment from a virus outbreak, and both options can be implemented on the same network. Both options include file-level antivirus scanners on each desktop, controlled by a central management system so that the administrator can see what the status of each desktop is at a glance. The first option is to deploy antivirus software on the ISA Server that is capable of scanning data at the application layer for TCP port 25 inbound connections and the second is to install on the Exchange server a VSAPI 2.5-compliant antivirus product. Additionally, running a file-level scanner on the desktop is sufficient because it will stop all Internet-borne inbound, virus-containing e-mail and stop the execution of viruses on the desktop. The central management of the anti-virus desktop software is important to ensure that all the desktops' antivirus signatures are up-to-date, and that policies exist to stop users from disabling their antivirus software.

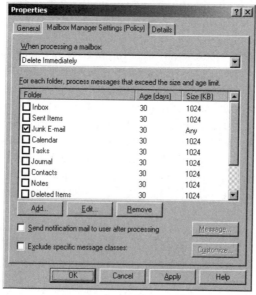

Figure 11-38   Mailbox manager policies

On the Exchange server, the School of Fine Art decide to install the Microsoft Intelligent Message Filter and for the first month after installation to just enable the filter on the SMTP virtual server. They will not change any of the global settings or archive or delete e-mail until they examine the performance logs after the first month. The one-month window allows them to see if users complain about too much spam or if relevant e-mail messages are being blocked. To further improve the management of the Exchange server, a Mailbox Manager recipient policy (Figure 11-38) is implemented to automatically delete the contents of the Junk E-mail folder every 30 days.

Another Exchange Server 2003 option that the School of Fine Art can use to reduce spam and spoofed e-mail is to implement Recipient Filtering. This will protect some of their distribution groups that have common names (for example, all@fineartschool.net) from being sent to from the Internet. Making use of the Recipient Filter requires that the default SMTP virtual server is enabled to check against the relevant filters, as shown in Figure 11-39. From now on, attempts to send unauthenticated e-mail to the selected addresses will result in the *550 5.7.1 Requested action not taken: mailbox not available* error.

Note   Recipient filter rules apply only to anonymous connections. Exchange servers and users who have logged into the network bypass these validations.

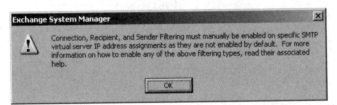

Figure 11-39   Changes to your SMTP virtual servers are required when global filters are enabled. Exchange Server warns you of this each time a filter change is made.

And finally, the School of Fine Art choose to implement Block List checking to ensure that they do not receive e-mail from SMTP servers that are configured as open relays or from IP addresses that are assigned to home user dynamic IP address systems.

Tip   More information on the configuring of these block lists can be found earlier in this chapter under "Applying Message Filters."

Large Network Example

Woodgrove Bank, shown in Figure 11-40, operates out of numerous countries and for their e-mail implementation they have two possible address namespace configurations that they could use. The first is a single address space for the entire organization (@woodgrovebank.com), and the second is one where each regional unit operates its own address space (for example @woodgrovebank.com for the United States, @woodgrovebank.co.uk for the London office and @woodgrovebank.de for the offices in Germany).

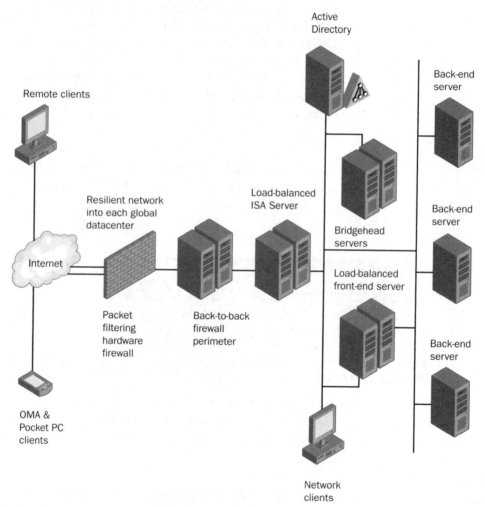

Figure 11-40 Large network high-level overview

Large Network Description

Woodgrove Bank's network spans 30 countries and they employ more than 40,000 staff. E-mail is a mission critical system and the average employee receives approximately 50 e-mail messages a day. Recently, Woodgrove Bank migrated to Exchange Server 2003 so that they could implement a consolidation of their current Exchange 5.5 server environment, and they have just finished this project. They now operate their Exchange servers out of three data centers distributed globally rather than numerous servers in each office. The mailbox server for the users of a selected office is found at their nearest data center, but for traveling users all data centers are accessible from all offices.

Each data center has a resilient 100Mb Internet connection connected to two different Level 1 Internet providers. These data centers are located in New York, London and Hong Kong. Each Internet connection is protected with a high-speed packet filter firewall with failover capability and then a load-balanced ISA Server 2000 array in a back to back perimeter network configuration.

The Internet connection at each data center provides 32 IP addresses which have been subnetted into 2 networks of 16 addresses to allow the hardware packet filters to route through to the second network those packets that are allowed further inbound. The bank hosts their own banking applications running out of the data centers and in addition to the ports open for these and other Internet applications, the packet filtering firewalls allow inbound TCP port 25 from all IP addresses.

An alternative option to accepting e-mail direct from the Internet is to have the e-mail processed by a hosted anti-spam and antivirus service provider. These service providers host the SMTP servers listed in your MX records and forward spam and virus free e-mail to the organization. In this configuration the organizations firewalls can be limited to accept e-mail only from this service provider. No e-mail would or could come direct to the organization.

Once SMTP traffic reaches the load-balanced ISA Server, it is passed into the perimeter network where Woodgrove Bank operates their anti-spam and antivirus e-mail gateway system running a 3rd party SMTP filtering product. From here e-mail passes across another firewall, delineating the perimeter network from the LAN, to the gateway Exchange servers that are in charge of receiving Internet e-mail.

Large Network DNS Settings

Each data center has the ability to receive e-mail from the Internet, but where e-mail actually gets delivered to is dependant upon the address space configuration described earlier and the DNS configuration to support that address space choice.

Woodgrove Bank's DNS settings for their MX and A records could take one of two different directions based on their choice of namespace. If Woodgrove Bank decided to opt for a single name space then they would have one MX record for each data center. If Woodgrove Bank wanted a different e-mail address name space for each office, then they would have many different zones, each with their own MX records.

For the multiple namespaces option, each DNS zone would have the highest preference MX records directed to the most suitable data center. For example, @woodgrovebank.je (in Jersey, part of the UK Channel Islands) would have the London data center as the highest preference MX record (i.e. 10) and the other data centers with lower preference MX records (i.e. 20). With this configuration e-mail is delivered to the most suitable data center for an office, and if that data center should be offline then it can be delivered to either of the other data centers.

If Woodgrove Bank decided to opt for a single namespace then they would need to decide which data center would have the highest preference for MX records. While researching the options, Woodgrove Bank found that most e-mail messages were delivered to the global data center supporting the regional offices which were open and currently doing business at any one particular time of day. Therefore the MX preference setting is altered through-out the day, and the data centre that is currently experiencing daylight appears with the lowest preference in DNS. This is achieved by a custom DNS application written in-house. The other two data centers have a lower preference and so can act as a backup in case of a data centre outage.

Without this custom application, the MX records could point to all data centers equally and e-mail would travel to a random data center before being delivered internally to the correct mailbox server. Alternatively, one data center (the largest, New York) could have a higher priority. All e-mail messages would go to that data center and from there to the users mailbox server located at the data center serving that users office.

The Woodgrove Bank MX records have a time to live (TTL) of 15 minutes, thus ensuring that no other DNS cache store the records for too long. Woodgrove Bank is using the custom DNS application to change DNS records with daylight, so the MX records at midday New York time would appear as follows:

```
woodgrovebank.com  MX preference = 10, mail exchanger =
                                 maila.woodgrovebank.com
woodgrovebank.com  MX preference = 30, mail exchanger =
                                 mailb.woodgrovebank.com
woodgrovebank.com  MX preference = 20, mail exchanger =
                                 mailc.woodgrovebank.com
mailb.woodgrovebank.com   internet address = 171.105.2.123
mailc.woodgrovebank.com   internet address = 61.107.3.26
maila.woodgrovebank.com   internet address = 204.5.43.244
```

The A records for maila point to the New York data center, mailb to London and mailc to Tokyo. The other DNS records in place would be the valid PTR records for the FQDN names of each outbound e-mail server. The outbound e-mail servers are not the same as the inbound servers, and their configuration will be covered later in this section.

Large Network Firewall Configuration

The configuration of the packet filtering and routing firewall that Woodgrove Bank use in front of their application layer firewalls is of a similar configuration to the example small network above, just that they use better and faster equipment. Additionally, this firewall operates over the dual resilient Internet connection that each data center has, ensuring that a failure of one Internet connection or firewall does not result in an inoperable data center.

Large Network Inbound Firewall Configuration

For the inbound traffic, we are only interested in the open status of TCP port 25 at this time. Only traffic on that port destined for the external load-balanced address of the ISA is accepted. Other ports are open for the bank, but they are not covered in this book.

In the same way as described in the small network example, the ISA Servers are set up to publish the internal SMTP servers. In this case, the SMTP servers that are published are those located in the perimeter network (see Figure 11-41). Once e-mail is processed by these servers, it is passed into the Exchange Server gateways on the internal network. They do this through a second layer of ISA Servers, also load-balanced. This second layer of ISA Servers allows TCP port 25 traffic, though from the perimeter network SMTP servers to the published Exchange server only. In addition, the internal ISA Servers have open only those additional ports needed to manage and obtain status reports from the perimeter network servers. These ports will vary, based on the management software in use, and it is recommended that they are changed from the default for further security. For the utmost in security, the majority of inbound network traffic has no direct connection between the Internet and the internal network.

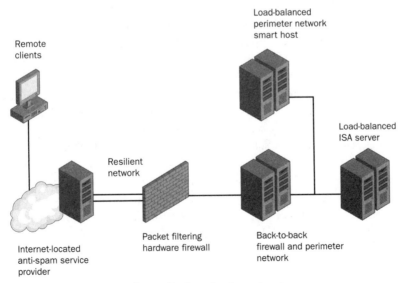

Figure 11-41   The Woodgrove Bank perimeter network

Differences do exist between the small network ISA Server 2000 configuration and this network because both the internal and external interfaces of the network cards on the ISA Server 2000 are running Network Load Balancing on a Windows Server 2003 host.

The first change is the use of the UseISAAddressInPublishing registry key. More information on this key can be found in the Microsoft Knowledge Base article 311777, "How to Enable Translating Client Source Address in Server Publishing" (*http:// go.microsoft.com/fwlink/?linkid=3052&kbid=311777*). The equivalent option in ISA Server 2004, to control the source address, is part of the server publishing properties. The second change is that the bank operates an Active Directory forest within the perimeter network, which is completely isolated from their main Active Directory. Its purpose is to provide security policies, central authorization, and Active Directory to the perimeter network. It is with this Active Directory that ISA Server 2000 Enterprise Edition can be installed. This product allows multiple servers to be configured in an array using Active Directory to centrally store their configuration. Therefore, most changes that are made to the firewall settings are replicated across all the ISA Servers in the array, ensuring that different load-balanced members do not have different configurations.

Large Network Exchange Server Configuration

The first Exchange servers the SMTP traffic reaches inside a particular data center, are those dedicated to the receipt of Internet e-mail. Each data center has four of these servers in two load-balanced groups. These servers use the default SMTP virtual server with both the FQDN corrected (mail.woodgrovebank.com) as discussed in the small network example and suitable connection filters enabled. E-mail is then routed internally within the Exchange organization to the correct mailbox server in the correct data center for its recipient. Internal routing within the Exchange organization is outside the scope of this chapter and is covered in Chapter 14. The four servers are contained within one Exchange Server routing group as two pairs of load-balanced servers. This allows incoming e-mail to be routed to one of two IP addresses on the internal network. Each of those IP addresses would be serviced by two different servers. If a server fails or needs maintenance, the IP address still operates because it is possible to reboot individual servers without loss of connectivity into the load balanced cluster; at least one server in every pair would be available at any one time.

Woodgrove Bank uses different SMTP virtual servers for the delivery of e-mail to the Internet than they use to receive e-mail from the Internet. Delivery is controlled by the creation of three SMTP connectors serving the * address space. Each of the three connectors is located in a routing group at different data centers, and configured to use an SMTP virtual server from two different Exchange servers for load balancing and fault tolerance. Figure 11-42 shows an example of one of these connectors.

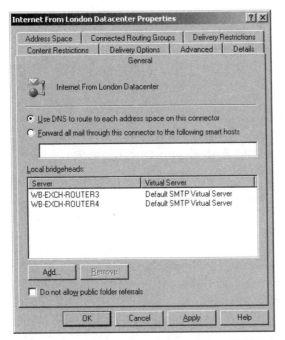

Figure 11-42   Woodgrove Bank's Internet SMTP connector general configuration

Large Network Outbound Firewall Configuration

The rules on the two ISA Server arrays that bound the perimeter network that allow SMTP outbound are similar, they just list different source addresses. The internal firewall array allows SMTP outbound from the previously described Internet SMTP connector hosting servers. These servers are listed in an ISA Server Client Address Set and SMTP outbound is limited to this set. The default route for traffic to the Internet is via both perimeter firewall arrays, so the next router that outbound SMTP traffic will go through after leaving the internal firewall array is the external firewall array. On the external firewall array, SMTP rules allow only the internal firewall array members' default IP addresses to send SMTP. Outbound SMTP appears to come from this address and not the actual source Exchange servers.

Once through the external firewall array, traffic is routed as needed to its final destination. The final destination address of the SMTP packet was discovered by an MX record lookup on the Internet SMTP connector hosting Exchange servers on the LAN. ISA Server does not change the destination address of outbound traffic.

Large Network Monitoring

Woodgrove Bank's perimeter network SMTP servers are gateway servers that filter e-mail for spam and viruses at the network edge. This filtering is done before it reaches the mailbox store servers to reduce the investment needed in transporting this extra traffic across the network. As it is vital for this system to operate successfully, these servers are monitored with Microsoft Operations Manager (MOM). Woodgrove Bank uses MOM to check the status of the antivirus service by running a MOM Service Verification script every few minutes on every perimeter network SMTP server to make sure that its status is running. If the service is found not to be running an alert is issued by MOM. For additional security, Woodgrove Bank requires additional antivirus software on every corporate standard desktop.

Large Network Antivirus and Anti-Spam Configuration

Statistics show that over 70 percent of all e-mail is spam and Woodgrove Bank remove the majority of that traffic from their network before it reaches their internal network. This measure ensures that they avoid the costly network and storage upgrades that would be needed if the spam- and virus-containing e-mail was transported to the mailbox servers and processed at the endpoint location. Note that this can result in some legitimate e-mail being blocked at the perimeter network, and IT helpdesk staff should be trained on how to find and process this e-mail should an employee query expected e-mail that is missing. In addition, you may need to fine-tune the anti-spam rules as necessary. To protect against a virus introduced on the internal network, Woodgrove Bank also install antivirus software on each Exchange server in the organization.

Partner Link Network

Humongous Insurance is a recently purchased subsidiary of Woodgrove Bank but, as shown in Figure 11-43, they have not yet linked their organizations into the same Active Directory forest; assuming they ever decide to do so. They have an immediate need for session encryption and authenticated e-mail communication between their two organizations over the Internet.

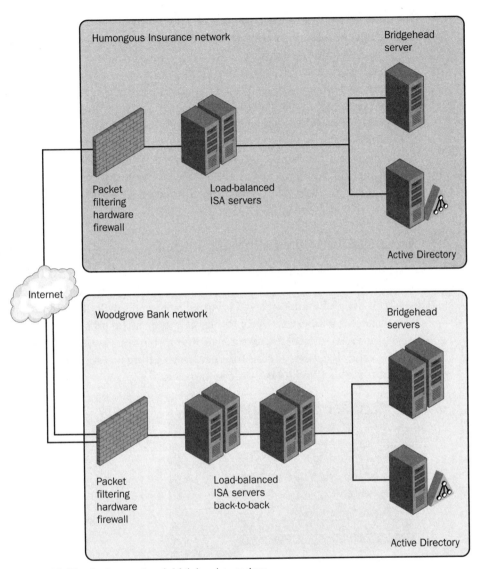

Figure 11-43   Partner network high-level overview

Partner Network Description

The Woodgrove Bank network is described above, and for the purposes of this example, Humongous Insurance have a very similar setup. Here we will describe just one side of the configuration as both sides have a similar configuration.

Partner Network DNS Settings

All e-mail to the humongousinsurance.com from Woodgrove Bank needs to go to a separate virtual server that accepts only authenticated and encrypted e-mail. Because this virtual server listens on a different IP address from the IP address identified by the existing MX records for the domain, DNS cannot be used as a delivery method in the Exchange Server SMTP connector. Therefore, the Exchange servers will use the SMTP connector smart host value to control delivery of the e-mail. Woodgrove Bank sends its Humongous Insurance destined e-mail direct to the Humongous Insurance private virtual server using the FQDN of this virtual server as the smart host. Returning e-mail flows in the opposite direction with the reverse configuration, again back to the private virtual server and not the public one identified by the domain's MX records. An IP address could not be used to identify the smart host in this example because the connection will be encrypted, and the digital certificate will identify the server by name and not IP address. The location connected to must match the certificate's CN value for the certificate to be accepted.

Partner Network Firewall Configuration

Encrypted SMTP e-mail using TLS operates over TCP port 25, so the only changes needed to the Woodgrove Bank firewalls described in the earlier section is to also server publish the additional SMTP virtual server that will accept Humongous Insurance e-mail. An ISA Server Server Publishing rule can be locked down to a specific client set, such as source address, as shown in Figure 11-44, and this configuration prevents other locations on the Internet from getting a response should they attempt to connect to this IP address/port combination.

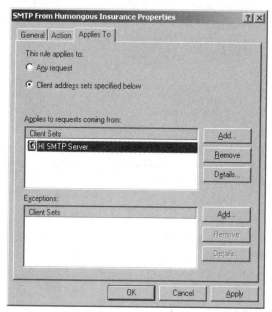

Figure 11-44 Locking down ISA Server to a specific client set address

Partner Network Exchange Server Configuration

Unlike the other two example networks, this time most of the work for configuration is on the Exchange server. At each Exchange organization a new virtual server needs to be created on the Exchange server that is designated to receive e-mail from the other company. An SMTP connector will also need to be created within the organization to ensure correct outbound delivery.

Rather than installing an entire Exchange server to receive these e-mail messages, an additional virtual server can be configured on an existing Exchange server. This virtual server will listen on port 25 like all other SMTP services, though a different port could be used. To avoid a clash with the default SMTP virtual server that is already listening on port 25 a second IP address will need to be added to the server.

Once the IP address is added and the new virtual server created, it will need to be configured as described in the "Configuring Additional Virtual Servers" section earlier in this chapter. The major changes include the removal of anonymous authentication, the requiring of TLS under Basic authentication (shown in Figure 11-45), and the removal of Windows Integrated authentication because the communicating servers are only going to use Basic authentication with TLS so the other options can be disabled. Finally, the installation of a digital certificate for server authentication will allow TLS encryption, ensuring that this certificate is trusted by both Woodgrove Bank and Humongous Insurance.

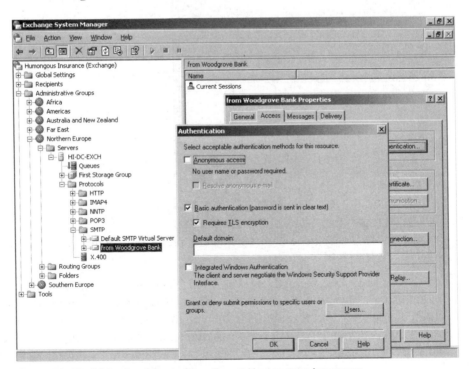

Figure 11-45 Virtual server configuration at Humongous Insurance.

Completion of the communication cannot occur until a suitable SMTP connector is installed in the other organization so that they can route e-mail addressed to the other organization over the encrypted communications channel and not over the Internet. This is covered earlier in this chapter on outbound connections. It is important not to use the same SMTP virtual server in the connector for outbound delivery as is used by the partner organization for inbound delivery; otherwise, a mail loop will be implemented. For example, Woodgrove Bank creates a new SMTP virtual server named *from Humongous Insurance*, and a new SMTP connector for the humongous-insurance.com namespace named *to Humongous Insurance*. This connector cannot use the *from Humongous Insurance* virtual server. The opposite configuration is made at Humongous Insurance. E-mail from Woodgrove Bank to any address @humongousinsurance.com will be delivered by the *to Humongous Insurance* SMTP connector, and that will be delivered to the *from Woodgrove Bank* SMTP virtual server at Humongous Insurance. One side of this connection is shown in Figure 11-46.

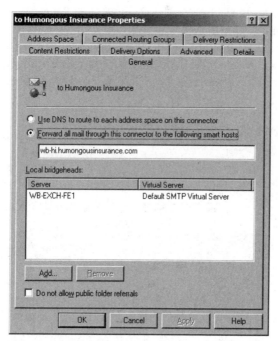

Figure 11-46   Woodgrove Bank's configuration for the sending of encrypted e-mail to Humongous Insurance

As you can see, using these best practice networks as examples, a good network administrator should have few problems in configuring a secure SMTP network for both the delivery and receipt of e-mail with the correct integration of intelligent firewalls and controlled SMTP flow, using connectors and the settings on each connector and SMTP virtual server.

Chapter 12

Maintaining IIS Virtual Servers

About This Chapter

Internet Information Services (IIS) is the set of services through which Windows Servers provide support for common Internet protocols. Exchange Server 2003 is very tightly integrated with IIS, and all its Internet communication protocols are provided through this application. Therefore, the Exchange Server administrator needs a considerable understanding of how IIS operates and how to configure and maintain IIS to ensure optimal performance and reliability of the Exchange servers.

On an Exchange server, IIS provides support for Simple Mail Transfer Protocol (SMTP), for sending e-mail between servers across the organization and Internet; Hypertext Transfer Protocol (HTTP), Post Office Protocol, version 3 (POP3), and Internet Message Access Protocol, version 4 (IMAP4), for providing client access to mailboxes; and Network News Transfer Protocol (NNTP), for access to newsgroups and public folders. Additionally, IIS provides support for the encryption of these protocols to ensure protection from network analyzers and is also the application that hosts the Microsoft Exchange Routing Engine service (RESvc). Every client that uses an IIS-supported protocol communicates with IIS on either the server hosting the client's mailbox directly or via an Exchange front-end server where its requests are proxied over the same protocol to the back-end server that holds its mailbox. The only client access method used by Exchange that is not hosted by IIS is MAPI. MAPI clients communicate directly with the Information Store on the server hosting their mailbox.

This chapter will also continue the discussion from the last chapter on how to use ISA Server to protect your Exchange servers while allowing secure access to Exchange from the Internet.

General Protocol Virtual Server Configurations

An installation of Exchange Server on a Windows 2000 Server and Windows Server 2003 requires the correct installation and configuration of IIS before you start. Though Exchange Server provides POP3 support, the POP3 service provided in Windows Server 2003 is not to be installed. Every Windows Server that is going to be an Exchange server needs IIS installed with support for HTTP, SMTP, and NNTP. POP3 and IMAP4 are provided by the Exchange Server installation, whereas the first three protocols are enhanced from their Windows Server version by the Exchange Server installation. These prerequisites for the Exchange Server installation means, that on a server with a default installation of Windows 2000 Server, the NNTP and SMTP services need to be installed, and on a default Windows Server 2003 installation IIS needs to be installed with the Web, SMTP, and NNTP services selected.

One of the easiest configuration changes that can be made by the Exchange Server administrator is enabling or disabling the different protocols on selected Exchange servers to provide distribution of services within the Exchange organization. For example, if some users require POP3 but most users connect using MAPI and HTTP, you do not need to enable POP3 on every Exchange server, just those accessed by POP3 clients. Exchange Server 2003 changes the default installation state of its protocols by having the POP3, IMAP4, and NNTP services disabled by default. In an Exchange front-end and back-end configuration, the protocols enabled on the front-end servers also need to be available on the back-end servers that hold those clients' mailboxes.

Each protocol is enabled and managed in IIS by the use of a virtual server, which is not to be confused with Microsoft Cluster Server virtual server. A virtual server is a collection of individual properties and settings for each instance of the protocol. Most Exchange Server installations will use at most one virtual server for each protocol per server, but some installations will require the creation and configuration of multiple virtual servers per Exchange server.

Administration and management of the properties of each virtual server can be done from at least one of four different places. Some properties can be changed in Exchange System Manager, others in the IIS management tools, some in Active Directory Users and Computers, and some properties can be set in the metabase. This chapter will examine each of these ways to manage the properties of the different virtual servers.

Using Exchange System Manager to Change IIS Settings

Exchange System Manager controls some of the properties of the protocol virtual servers in IIS. It does not make these changes directly; every change made in Exchange System Manager is stored in Active Directory. These changes are then applied to the IIS database (known as the metabase) at a later point in time. This means that you will need to wait for replication to complete for those changes to be enabled. Do not directly change the same setting that you have made in Exchange System Manager in IIS if you find that your recent change does not become active immediately. A change in the configuration of IIS is not recommended because the previous setting is still stored in Active Directory, and IIS will return to this previous setting the next time the Active Directory settings overwrite those held in the IIS metabase.

HTTP Virtual Servers

The HTTP virtual server is used to provide Web-based access to users' mailboxes and public folders. HTTP provides a way for users to access their mailboxes without any client software apart from a Web browser and to do that access from any location on the Internet by providing a Web mail service. For access to be from any location, correct firewall configuration needs to be implemented, and this will be discussed in detail in the "Configuring the HTTP Virtual Servers" section of this chapter.

The majority of properties that can be set on the Web server or on individual HTTP virtual servers are done in the IIS management tools. Some changes, mainly authentication and access control, must be done in Exchange System Manager, whereas other settings that can be used to affect Exchange Server users over HTTP protocols, such as implementing encryption by the installation of digital certificates and customizing error pages, need to be set in IIS Manager.

IMAP4 Virtual Servers

The IMAP4 protocol provides users with access to their mailbox, and folders within their mailbox, and is designed to run in an online network environment. IMAP4 is typically used by Internet clients and not corporate users of Exchange Server who have a MAPI client. Improvements in MAPI over IMAP include functionality like built-in support for scheduling, sharing free/busy information, and security during the connection.

The Exchange Server version of IMAP4 is IMAP4rev1, which is based on RFC 3501. IMAP4rev1 removes from the IMAP4 protocol commands that had proved to be problematic in their implementation. These problematic commands are now obsolete and are listed in RFC 2062.

IMAP4 is a common neighbor to POP3, and though they are very different protocols, they provide a similar service. IMAP is a protocol designed to operate in an online network rather than POP3, as discussed below. It does this by keeping the mail on the server, in different folders if needed, and optionally downloading first the mail headers and then the actual message to the user. This allows users to operate from multiple client computers (as their mail is centrally stored) without configuring each client to leave the e-mail on the server, and when on slow bandwidth connections to decide which messages to read and to optionally ignore larger messages and unwanted messages without downloading them. IMAP also integrates with the Multipurpose Internet Mail Extensions (MIME) message encoding standard, allowing users to download parts of a message if the client supports this functionality. For example, an IMAP client could download the text of a message but not the 5-MB video attachment that is included with the message.

IMAP4 is hosted within IIS, but fully managed from Exchange System Manager. There is no IMAP4 node in IIS Manager for additional management of the protocol, unlike HTTP.

> **Important**   IIS Manager is named Internet Information Services (IIS) Manager in Windows Server 2003 and Internet Information Services in Windows 2000 Server.

Though IMAP4 is a different protocol from POP3, the majority of the properties that can be set in Exchange System Manager are the same for both protocols.

POP3 Virtual Servers

POP3 is similar in function to IMAP4, except it is designed to operate in an offline, or occasionally connected, network. POP3 only provides access to the inbox folder of a user's mailbox and does not provide access to any other mailbox folders or public folders; therefore, it is a more basic protocol than IMAP4 in its functionality.

Like IMAP4, this protocol is typically used by Internet clients rather than corporate users of Exchange Server. The default setting of POP3 is to download the entire message to the user upon connection and to delete the message from the server unless the client requests not to delete the downloaded messages from the inbox. This means that a large message that arrived first in an inbox will download before other messages do, with no ability to delete the message on the server before downloading it. Because POP3 defaults to emptying the inbox every time it downloads messages, users can end up with messages spread across different clients if they read their e-mail from different locations. It is the responsibility of the user to ensure that its POP3 client does not delete the messages on the server so that they can be read from another client at a later time. Because POP3 clears the inbox on the server by default each time, it is a protocol preferred by Internet service providers (ISPs) because it reduces their requirement to provide storage for users' mail. ISPs that want to provide storage for users' mailboxes either provide IMAP4 or HTTP methods of accessing the mailboxes they provide.

A corporate user of Exchange Server will typically not provide POP3 support. This is because of the risk of the loss of e-mail from the server when downloaded to a client, the requirement of the management of this setting being in the hands of the user and the security issues of the protocol.

POP3 is hosted within IIS but fully managed from Exchange System Manager. There is no POP3 node in IIS Manager for additional management of the protocol, unlike HTTP.

Though POP3 is a different protocol from IMAP4, the majority of the properties that can be changed in Exchange System Manager for the protocol are the same.

NNTP Virtual Servers

NNTP is a protocol for the delivery of news and bulletin board services, both between the server and the client and between servers in a distributed NNTP environment. NNTP allows access to the public folders of an Exchange organization, but not individual mailboxes. It is typically used either by ISPs to host servers for the distribution of usenet (the public network of NNTP servers and news postings) and by corporations that need to provide bulletin board services, such as support and helpdesk services, to clients. It is more common, however, for the provision of a bulletin board as a Web application, commonly known as a forum, instead of being hosted on an NNTP news server.

The NNTP protocol is hosted within IIS, but fully managed from Exchange System Manager. There is no NNTP node in IIS Manager for additional management of the protocol once Exchange Server has been installed. On a server that does not include Exchange, NNTP can be installed because it is an optional component of IIS 5.0 and 6.0 and is managed from IIS Manager.

The major difference between the IIS and Exchange Server versions is that the IIS version stores its newsgroups and content as folders and files on either the local hard disk or a remote share, whereas the Exchange Server version of NNTP can additionally store the newsgroup articles as public folder content within an Exchange database. The second major difference between the Exchange Server and IIS versions of NNTP is that the Exchange Server version can push and pull content from news servers that provide newsgroup feeds, in order to build a replicated newsgroup network.

SMTP Virtual Servers

The final protocol managed by IIS for Exchange Server is the SMTP protocol. All of the settings and changes, and how to use SMTP for the delivery and receipt of e-mail, is covered in Chapter 11.

The SMTP protocol is hosted within IIS, but fully managed from Exchange System Manager. There is no SMTP node in IIS Manager for additional management of the protocol.

Metabase and Active Directory

The settings for each virtual server are stored in the IIS metabase. This is a database stored in the %windir%\system32\inetsrv folder. In Windows 2000 Server, this file is named metabase.bin and in Windows Server 2003 it is metabase.xml. The Windows 2000 metabase stores its data in a proprietary format and requires the use of tools such as Metabase Explorer or the use of Windows Scripting Host applications to modify it, allowing you to enable settings that cannot be changed in either IIS or Exchange System Manager. These applications and scripts also work against the XML metabase in Windows Server 2003, but additionally, the metabase in this version can be directly edited with any XML or text editor. Direct metabase editing in Windows Server 2003 needs to be enabled in IIS before the use of XML or text editors can save their changes.

Caution   Editing the metabase should not be taken lightly and comes with the same warnings that precede any editing of the registry. Changes to the metabase can make your Exchange server fail to operate and place you in a disaster recovery situation.

The metabase stores its properties in a hierarchical format. At the top of the metabase tree is the IIS_GLOBAL node, which is read only and available only when editing the XML directly (though it should not be edited). The IIS_ROOT, or "/" key follows next. Changes and additions at the IIS_ROOT key level affect all of IIS. The root node contains the (Local Machine) LM key, and under this LM key are located all the IIS services and sites on that computer. The keys below LM are organized as follows:

```
/LM/Service/Site/ROOT/Directory/File
```

Where the values above are as follows:

- Service = DS2MB, EventManager, IMAP4SVC, NNTPSVC, POP3SVC, resvc, SmtpSvc, or W3SVC. Other nodes exist, but these are the nodes that do not relate to Exchange Server.

■ Site = unique number identifier for the virtual server. Not all services have a site node. In Windows 2000 new sites gain the next available number incrementally, but in Windows Server 2003 a site number is randomly generated.
The Info key exists at the same level as Site for most services. Settings under Info affect all Sites on the server for that protocol.

■ ROOT = root virtual directory of the site. Only the W3SVC and NNTP keys have ROOT, the other Exchange Server services do not have virtual directories within the protocol.

■ Directory = a virtual or physical directory.

■ File = file name (W3SVC only).

Figure 12-1 shows the IIS Metabase Explorer application examining the properties of the Outlook Web Access Exchange virtual directory.

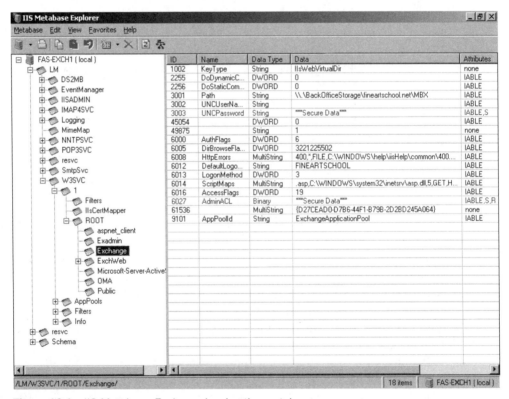

Figure 12-1 IIS Metabase Explorer showing the metabase

DS2MB Process

The Directory Service/Metabase Synchronization (DS2MB) process, which is also known as the Metabase Update process, is in charge of synchronizing the IIS settings stored in Active Directory with the metabase on the local computer. When the System Attendant service starts, it registers itself with the Config domain controller (as configured on the server properties dialog box in Exchange System Manager) so that it is notified whenever changes are made to areas of interest within the Configuration partition of Active Directory. Whenever a change is made, DS2MB is notified and it replicates the latest changes to the metabase. This should occur in less than 15 minutes within an Active Directory site as each domain controller should take, by default, no more than this length of time to replicate in the changes from any other domain controller in the same site.

Exchange System Manager always stores the changes made to IIS settings in Active Directory and never directly in the metabase. This means that running Exchange System Manager on a local management workstation will require a connection to a domain controller and not to each Exchange server that is being managed. The result of this is fast administration, but it does mean that the changes made in Exchange System Manager may not take effect on the target server for some time.

The Event Viewer can be used to see when the DS2MB process replicates changes from Active Directory to the metabase. These changes will appear from the MSExchangeMU source, but only if, in the server's properties, on the Diagnostics Logging tab, the MSExchangeMU logging level is set to minimum or greater.

The properties found in Active Directory overwrite the equivalent metabase properties whenever the System Attendant service is started or whenever the DS2MB process runs. As the client that is being used for running the administration tool may be using a different domain controller than the Exchange server that you want to see the change on, Active Directory replication will need to occur for the changes arrive at the domain controller used by the Exchange server. Once this happens, the metabase will be updated as soon as the System Attendant service is notified of the changes.

The DS2MB process is a one-way process. It will replicate changes from Active Directory to the metabase but not the other way around. A direct change to the metabase or using the IIS management tools on the Exchange server will not result in those changes populating Active Directory and being visible in Exchange System Manager. This does not mean that you cannot make changes in the IIS management tools or direct to the metabase as described above, but those properties that are changed cannot be stored in Active Directory and might be overwritten by the DS2MB process the next time it runs.

Reading and Resetting DS2MB

The DS2MB process runs in the context of the System Attendant service; therefore, if the System Attendant is not running IIS will not update with the latest changes from Active Directory.

The process is one way, from the directory service to the metabase, and stored under the DS2MB key in the metabase are values that can assist in the troubleshooting of the replication process. The `HighWaterMarks` subkey of the `DS2MB` key (`LM/DS2MB/High-WaterMarks`) in the IIS metabase contains subkeys that are the GUIDs identifying the NTDS Settings DNS alias value of the domain controllers from which changes are replicated. Inside each GUID key are three values, each identified by a number. Table 12-1 shows what these values represent:

Table 12-1   HighWaterMarks Metabase IDs

ID	Value
61472	The update sequence number (USN) of the last property change read from Active Directory. If a new change is made in Active Directory, it will get a new USN. Even though the metabase records the USN of the last change replicated, the DS2MB process does not operate like Active Directory replication does. Active Directory replication will only replicate those objects where the USN is higher than the last USN replicated.
61473	The time of the last property change.
61474	The domain controller from which the above two properties were obtained.

If Active Directory to metabase replication is not occurring, maybe because of metabase corruption, you can delete the `HighWaterMarks` subkey of the `DS2MB` key in the metabase and restart the System Attendant service. The `HighWaterMarks` key will be recreated along with a full replication of properties from Active Directory to the metabase. To manually delete the `HighWaterMarks` key, enter the following on the command line, where *drive* is the drive where Windows is installed:

cd drive:\inetpub\adminscripts

cscript adsutil.vbs delete /ds2mb/HighWaterMarks

After running the above script, you must restart the Microsoft Exchange System Attendant service and any other services that are dependant upon it. If metabase replication is still not occurring, check to ensure that your Active Directory replication is operating successfully.

> **Tip**   A manual change in the IIS metabase will only be overwritten if a change is made to the same object in Exchange System Manager. You can use the above script to reset the IIS metabase should you find that it has been edited manually and is therefore different from the configuration stored in the Active Directory HighWaterMarks subkey.

Active Directory Locations

The DS2MB process on each Exchange server reads Active Directory at the following location (where *<servername>* matches the current server name):

```
DC=<tld>,DC=<domain>,CN=Configuration,CN=Services,
CN=Microsoft Exchange,CN=<organization>,CN=Administrative Groups,
CN=<name of admin group>,CN=Servers,CN=<servername>,CN=Protocols
```

Each protocol and instance of protocol on the server can be found under this Active Directory object. Using a tool such as ADSI Edit or exporting the above container to a text file using LDIFDE, allows you to view these properties to determine if replication is working correctly. Each property that will be replicated to the metabase will be represented here, including some that are not changeable in Exchange System Manager. If the property is listed in Active Directory it can only be changed in Active Directory or Exchange System Manager. If that property is changed in the metabase it will be replaced when the DS2MB process next updates that value.

> **Important**   If changes are made using tools such as ADSI Edit, extreme care should be taken to ensure that the values entered are correct. The adding or deleting of attributes, objects, or values can cause catastrophic failure to your Active Directory, Exchange server, or Exchange organization.

Editing the Metabase

The metabase comes with the same warnings for changing it as does Active Directory above and as do changes made to the registry of a Windows computer, except that the risk of editing the metabase stops at causing failure to a single server, which in some cases could be the same as the entire Exchange organization.

To edit the metabase, either install Metabase Explorer from the IIS 6.0 Resource Kit or use the script provided on all IIS servers, named adsutil.vbs. Additionally, any XML editor can be used if the server is running IIS 6.0, though you need first to enable support for these tools.

By default, the metabase will keep 10 copies of previous metabases providing an automatic backup. Every time a change is saved to the metabase, a copy of the latest metabase is stored in the %windir%\system32\inetsrv\history folder, along with the schema in a separate XML file that exists at that point in time. A value stored on the LM key of the metabase enables the automatic backup `EnableHistory=1 (DWORD)`. The number of histories stored is set with the `MaxHistoryFiles` DWORD property also stored in the LM key of the metabase. If the `EnableHistory` property is missing, histories are enabled.

Metabase Explorer

This tool is similar in concept to the registry editor tools in Windows. In addition to being able to add, modify, and delete keys and values, it allows you to explore the metabase structure and see how it is configured.

When adding values to the metabase to enable settings not found in IIS or Exchange System Manager you need to know either the name or the ID that identifies the value that you are entering. Not all values that can be entered have names that can be selected during record creation, and if so, you need to enter the ID instead.

Command Line Tools

There are two main command line tools for editing the metabase. These are adsutil.vbs and smtpmd.exe. The first allows modifications to keys and values that already exist within the metabase and the second allows new keys and values to be created. The first tool allows creation of keys and values, but the second provides more control over that process and allows the addition of keys and values that are known only by their ID. To add a value using adsutil requires that the value has a name already defined in the metabase schema.

The adsutil.vbs command line script is installed on all servers running IIS 5.0 or IIS 6.0. The script can be found in the \inetpub\adminscripts folder and must be run from the command line. The very first time the script is run on a server it is likely that the script will default to running in Windows scripting environment (with dialog boxes) rather than via the command line. If this happens, the script will cease to run and offer to configure the server to set the command line as the default scripting environment. If this happens, the script will need to be run again. To avoid this happening while running a number of commands on a number of servers via a batch file, the script can be prefixed with CScript to force it to run in the command line scripting environment.

Example commands for adsutil.vbs are listed in Table 12-2.

Table 12-2   Example Adsutil Command Lines

Purpose	Command
To display the named values for a selected node	cscript adsutil.vbs enum w3svc\1 or cscript adsutil.vbs enum ds2mb\HighWaterMarks
To view a selected property	cscript adsutil.vbs get w3svc/1/serverbindings This shows which ports the Default Web Site is running on.
To set a property	cscript adsutil.vbs set w3svc/1/serverbindings "8080" This changes the port the Default Web Site is running on.
To delete a key	cscript adsutil.vbs delete ds2mb This deletes the DS2MB key to allow you to force Active Directory to replicate to the metabase.

The smtpmd.exe utility is not available publicly. Please contact Microsoft Product Support Services to obtain this tool. Smtpmd.exe allows more control over the creation of keys and values within the metabase than the adsutil.vbs command discussed above. For example, the following command will change the banner displayed when connecting to the default instance of the IMAP4 service:

```
smtpmd set imap4svc/1 -dtype STRING -prop 49884 -value "<banner>"
```

This property is only identified by its ID and does not have a name, therefore, it cannot be set using adsutil.vbs. Properties without names can be set using the other three tools described in this chapter, but only smtpmd.exe is scriptable via the command line. Table 12-3 shows the IDs needed to change the banner of the IMAP4 and POP3 services. Changing the SMTP banner is covered in Chapter 11.

Table 12-3   IDs for Changing Service Banner

ID	Protocol	Banner purpose
41661	POP3	Banner displayed upon connecting.
41662	POP3	Banner displayed upon disconnecting.
49884	IMAP4	Banner displayed upon connecting.
49885	IMAP4	Banner displayed upon disconnecting.

Direct Metabase Editing with XML Editors

Windows Server 2003 stores the metabase as an XML file, and therefore it can be opened with any XML editor or viewer. Editing the metabase via a text editor is considerably faster than using the IIS Manager program, especially on systems with many thousands of virtual directories, but by default the functionality of editing the metabase while IIS is running is disabled. To do direct editing requires stopping the iisadmin service. To enable direct editing of the metabase while iisadmin is running, select the Enable Direct Metabase Edit check box setting in properties of the computer in IIS

Manager (see Figure 12-2), or set the `EnableEditWhileRunning` metabase property on the `LM` key to **1**. Setting this option in IIS Manager takes effect immediately with no need to restart IIS. Changing the value in the metabase requires a restart of IIS. Regardless of which method is chosen to set this option, the `EnableHistory` metabase property described above needs to be enabled. Direct editing of the metabase cannot occur without enabling the automatic history creation.

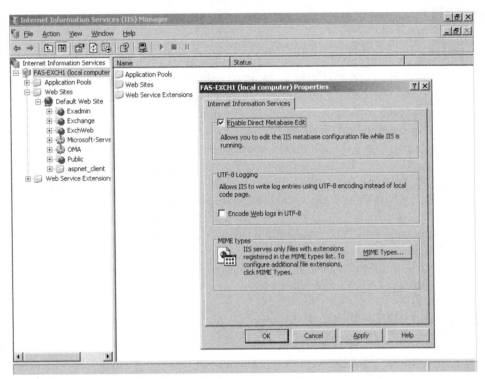

Figure 12-2   Enabling direct editing of the metabase in IIS Manager

When you are able to directly edit the metabase, the addition of keys and values is based upon typing the correct XML code in the correct place within the metabase. The following XML will set the IMAP4 server banner on both connecting and disconnecting:

```
<Custom
    Name="UnknownName_49884"
    ID="49884"
    Value="<connect_banner_string>"
    Type="STRING"
    UserType="UNKNOWN_UserType"
    Attributes="NO_ATTRIBUTES"
/>
<Custom
    Name="UnknownName_49885"
    ID="49885"
```

```
            Value="<disconnect_banner_string>"
            Type="STRING"
            UserType="UNKNOWN_UserType"
            Attributes="NO_ATTRIBUTES"
      />
```

Default HTTP, IMAP4, POP3, and NNTP Virtual Servers

Upon the installation of an Exchange server, five virtual servers are either created or expanded from their Windows installation state. Before the installation of Exchange Server the HTTP, NNTP, and SMTP protocols are installed. A virtual server for each of these protocols exists and can be modified in IIS Manager. After the installation only the HTTP virtual server remains manageable in IIS Manager but, as described above, care must be taken to ensure that the changes made in IIS Manager do not conflict with changes in Exchange System Manager because the latter will always have precedence. Once Exchange Server is installed, the management of NNTP and SMTP cannot be done from IIS Manager. Additionally, the two newly installed protocols of POP3 and IMAP4 are not visible in IIS Manager.

Each virtual server can be modified in Exchange System Manager by expanding the server node and then the protocol's node. New virtual servers can be created by right-clicking the protocol name and choosing New, and the properties, current sessions, and status of the virtual server can be viewed and changed by expanding the actual protocol node and viewing each virtual server.

The Default HTTP Virtual Server

In Exchange System Manager with the HTTP protocol node expanded (see Figure 12-3), there is a single virtual server named Exchange Virtual Server that can be seen by default. This virtual server matches the Default Web Site found in IIS Manager. Regardless of the name of the Default Web Site, an Exchange Server installation creates its default virtual server with this new name.

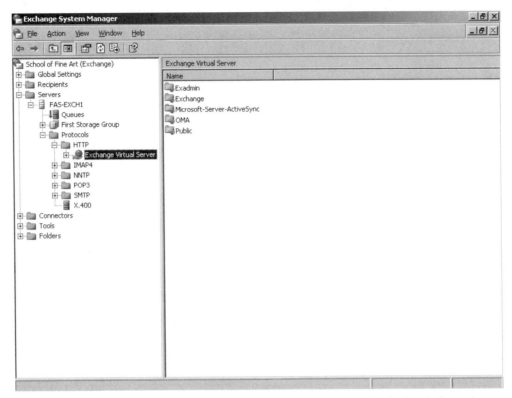

Figure 12-3   The default HTTP virtual server expanded to show the default virtual directories

The default HTTP virtual server provides a number of virtual directories that can be loosely grouped by their different Exchange Server functions. These virtual servers are Outlook Web Access (/exchange, /public, and /exchweb and /exadmin), Outlook Mobile Access (/oma), and a Web application for syncing Pocket PC and Smartphone devices directly with the server (/Microsoft-Server-ActiveSync).

Each of these virtual directories is accessible to users or devices by browsing the name of the server, followed by the virtual directory mentioned above. Any alias for this server will also work without further modification. For example, if a DNS alias for a server exists called mail, then users could browse *http://mail/exchange/* and access Outlook Web Access. This is assuming that the TCP/IP settings of the Default Web Site have not been changed. This is because the default settings of the Default Web Site listen to any connection to TCP port 80 on this server, assuming that no other additionally created HTTP virtual server is configured to listen for those settings instead.

To see what TCP/IP settings this default virtual server will answer to, you need to open IIS Manager. Because each website can listen on multiple IP addresses and ports, you will need to check for the virtual server setting in two places. The first place to check is the primary list of ports, IP addresses, and host headers. This is visible in IIS Manager if you select the Web Sites node (in Windows Server 2003) or the

Computer Name node (in Windows 2000 Server). The second check is to examine a selected website in further detail. This information can be found in the properties of a selected website, and by clicking Advanced on the Web Site tab. Both of these views can be seen in Figure 12-4.

Note   If you create additional HTTP virtual servers they need their connection settings (IP address, ports, and host header) changed in Exchange System Manager and not IIS Manager as is done for the default HTTP virtual server.

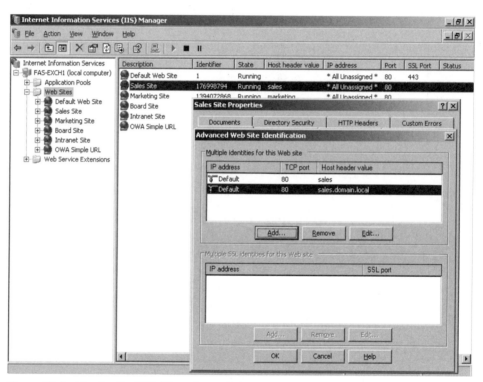

Figure 12-4   Viewing the TCP/IP settings of HTTP virtual servers

Because there is an association between the Exchange Virtual Server in Exchange System Manager and the Default Web Site in IIS Manager, some of the configuration of this site needs to be done in Exchange System Manager and some in IIS Manager. If you create additional HTTP virtual servers in IIS Manager, they cannot be used by Exchange because changes to the IIS metabase do not replicate into Active Directory, so Exchange Server does not know about these new sites. However, if you create a new HTTP virtual server in Exchange System Manager it is available for use by Exchange Server and for management in both of the administration tools, taking into account the earlier discussion about the DS2MB process.

The Default IMAP4 Virtual Server

The IMAP4 service is disabled by default in Exchange Server 2003, and so the Default IMAP4 Virtual Server is listed as not running. Before this virtual server can be started, the Microsoft Exchange IMAP4 service must be changed from disabled to manual or automatic.

The IMAP4 service is not needed in a typical corporate environment where users access their mailboxes with clients such as Outlook and Outlook Web Access. IMAP4 is often provided by ISPs that offer e-mail with a comprehensive mailbox management service. Corporations that provide IMAP4 protocol access to a user's mailbox will need to make provision to provide an SMTP server because IMAP4 has no way of sending e-mail back to the Exchange organization or Internet. Chapter 11 describes the SMTP configuration needed to support IMAP4 clients.

The Default IMAP4 Virtual Server, once enabled, listens for incoming connections on TCP port 143 on all IP addresses on the Exchange server. The IP address used by the service can be changed from the properties of the IMAP4 virtual server (Figure 12-5) with the ability to change the port available via the Advanced button on this dialog box.

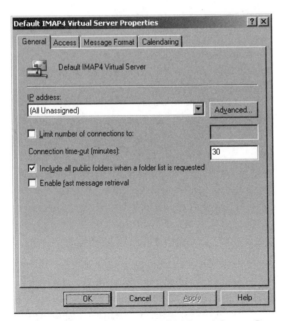

Figure 12-5 The Default IMAP4 Virtual Server Properties dialog box

If the IMAP4 service is enabled for encrypted communications from its clients using Secure Sockets Layer (SSL), the virtual server will also listen on port 993 for encrypted traffic. The use of SSL to protect the client/server communication is very important because the IMAP4 protocol sends its authentication credentials in clear text. This can be seen in Figure 12-6, which is a Microsoft Network Monitor trace of an IMAP4 client connecting to an Exchange server.

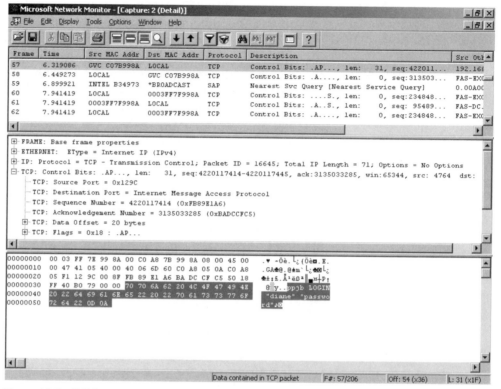

Figure 12-6   IMAP4 communication showing the authentication of a user with the password highlighted

> **Tip**   IMAP4 in Exchange Server provides NTLM as an additional authentication option. If your clients support this, then ensure that this is enabled (and not Basic Authentication) if you want to protect user names and passwords but do not mind the e-mail content being in clear text.

Exchange Server allows the creation of multiple IMAP4 virtual servers when you need to provide different sets of clients with a server supporting different functionality. For example, if most of your IMAP4 clients support the reading of e-mail in HTML format, then you can set an IMAP4 virtual server to provide the e-mail body to these clients only in this format and reduce the network traffic from that of the default installation, which provides the message body in HTML and plain text. But for those clients that do not support HTML, rather than using the defaults and providing both formats for all clients, a second virtual server configured for those users only, and for plain text only, will provide a performance improvement on the download of messages to those clients. The creation of additional virtual servers is covered later in this chapter.

Unless access to an IMAP4 virtual server is restricted via IP address or via an authenticating firewall such as ISA Server, the only way to stop users from using IMAP if the service is running is to disable the protocol on a per user basis. This is available from the Exchange Features tab of a mailbox-enabled users properties in Active Directory Users and Computers.

Tools such as ADModify.NET can be used to disable (or enable) the availability of IMAP for many users in bulk. ADModify.NET (and the previous version, ADModify) can be downloaded from the Microsoft FTP site at *ftp://ftp.microsoft.com/pss/tools/ Exchange Support Tools/ADModify/*. Also, if a user account is created by copying an existing user account that has the use of IMAP disabled, then the new user will also have IMAP disabled.

The Default POP3 Virtual Server

The POP3 service, like the IMAP4 service, is disabled by default in Exchange Server 2003. To enable the POP3 service, both the Microsoft Exchange POP3 service and the virtual server need to be started. The service should be set to automatic, unless being used temporarily for troubleshooting purposes, when manual should be sufficient.

The POP3 service is not needed in a typical corporate environment where users access their mailboxes with clients and utilities such as Outlook, Outlook Web Access, and ActiveSync. POP3 is often provided by ISPs who offer a simple e-mail service. The most common use of POP3 in a corporate environment is to allow users to download e-mail to devices such as mobile phones, but this will not allow the user full access to the mailbox, calendar, and public folders. Devices that provide POP3 access typically provide IMAP4, HTTP, and Internet access via a Wireless Application Protocol (WAP) gateway as well. Therefore, careful consideration should be given to the use of POP3 over the other three protocols. Devices such as mobile phones can access all their e-mail functionality via applications such as Outlook Mobile Access over an HTTP or WAP connection, and if running the Windows Mobile operating system they can use ActiveSync to ensure that a copy of the mailbox is on the device at all times. If ActiveSync or Outlook Mobile Access is not possible, clients should be able to access their mailboxes and public folders via IMAP4 rather than just their inboxes via POP3.

The default POP3 virtual server listens for incoming connections on, by default, all IP addresses and TCP port 110, and like IMAP does not provide a method for the delivery of e-mail back to the Exchange organization and the Internet. Therefore, when you support POP3 users, an SMTP virtual server is needed as well. Chapter 11 describes the SMTP configuration needed to support POP3 clients.

POP3 is also similar to IMAP4 in that the default authentication to the server is in clear text, and Figure 12-7 shows the user's password in clear text in Network Monitor. Exchange Server supports the use of NTLM and SSL to protect a POP3 user name and password, and when SSL is used, it further protects the entire session including passwords and message body. In addition to Exchange Server being able to support these encryption and authentication features, client support for them is also needed.

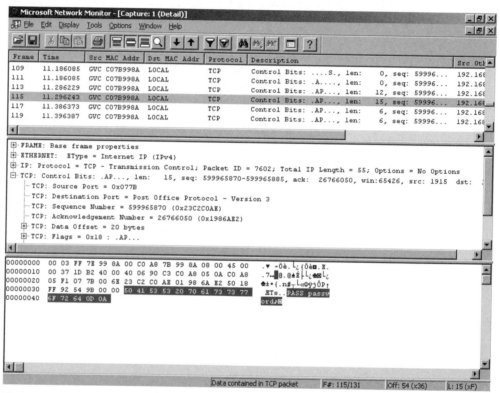

Figure 12-7 A user's password available in a POP3 session, shown by default in clear text

Useless access to a POP3 virtual server is restricted via IP address or via an authenticating firewall such as ISA Server. The only way to stop users from using POP3 if the service is running is to disable the protocol on a per-user basis. This is available from the Exchange Features tab of a mailbox-enabled users properties in Active Directory Users and Computers.

Tools such as ADModify.NET can be used to disable (or enable) the availability of POP3 for many users in bulk. ADModify.NET (and the previous version, ADModify) can be downloaded from the Microsoft FTP site at *ftp://ftp.microsoft.com/pss/tools/ Exchange Support Tools/ADModify/*. Also, if a user account is created by copying an existing user account that has the use of POP3 disabled, then the new user will also have POP3 disabled.

The Default NNTP Virtual Server

The Default NNTP Virtual Server, like the POP3 and IMAP4 virtual servers, is disabled by default in Exchange Server 2003. Enabling and starting the NNTP service will allow the virtual server to be started.

Before the NNTP virtual server can be used by clients, it needs further configuration. It provides no services upon the initial installation of the Exchange server. See Configuring NNTP Virtual Servers later in the chapter for how to configure this service.

Adding Virtual Servers

IIS and Exchange Server support the running of multiple instances of each of the protocol virtual servers available in the product. The reason for additional virtual servers is to allow for a subset of your users with different needs or domain names.

An example of different groups of users with different needs can be described by imagining a company that has a subset of IMAP4 clients who do not support the Enable Fast Message Retrieval option. Rather than disabling this feature for all users, at the impact of the increased performance and download speed penalty that this causes, a subsequent virtual server can be created with this option disabled for those clients that do not support the feature. Users then connect to the virtual server that supports their client feature set.

Prior to the installation of Service Pack 1 (SP1) for Exchange Server 2003 the major reason for the creation of multiple HTTP virtual servers was due to the way multiple SMTP-addressed spaces were handled by Outlook Web Access. Prior to SP1 each Outlook Web Access virtual directory or virtual server was tied to a single SMTP domain, and users could only use the Outlook Web Access service configured with their primary SMTP addresses. Otherwise these users could not log on. SP1 removes that limitation and allows users to log on to any Outlook Web Access virtual directory, even if it does not list their domain. This means that the major reason for multiple HTTP virtual servers is now less important, and therefore, an Exchange server running SP1 is likely to have the number of pre-SP1-created HTTP virtual servers on it reduced.

Before you can create additional virtual servers in Exchange Server, it is important to understand the restrictions that exist in any TCP/IP operating system on the running of applications that listen for connections on the TCP/IP network protocol and to understand the specifics of IIS with regard to this TCP/IP restriction.

Resolving IP Address and Port Number Conflicts

Each application that listens for incoming connections to a server needs to listen for those connections on an IP address and port that the client is aware of. If the client does not know to where to connect, it cannot connect.

The combination of the IP address and listening port is known as a socket, and is written as w.x.y.z:port. For example, the default POP3 virtual server sitting on an Exchange server with one IP address (172.16.10.5) should have socket 172.16.10.5:110. No other application on this server can bind to this socket once it is in use by Exchange Server. Conversely, if the socket is already in use by another application the POP3 virtual server cannot start on that socket.

Socket pooling is a feature of IIS that will change the default socket for IIS applications from w.x.y.z:port to 0.0.0.0:port. This is to improve the performance of a server with many virtual servers, and this is covered in detail in the next section.

Therefore, before the creation of all virtual servers, apart from those hosting HTTP (but not HTTPS), the administrator must ensure that there will not be a socket conflict with other applications or other virtual servers within Exchange Server. HTTP is different than the other protocols in that it has a property named the Host Header which allows multiple websites to run on a single socket.

> **Tip**   A list of listening and connected sockets can be seen by executing netstat –an from the command line. Windows Server 2003 can additionally show the process ID (PID) that created the socket using netstat –ano.

It is highly recommended that each Exchange Server virtual server run on its well-known port. It is commonly thought that it is a security measure to change port numbers to protect a virtual server, but it is not. All the other virtual servers except HTTP in Exchange Server identify themselves when they are connected to, so moving them to another port just adds another layer of complexity for the client. Also, an Exchange front-end and back-end scenario will not operate when non-standard ports are used.

The problem with running additional virtual servers on their well-known port is that the default virtual server instance for each protocol already runs on that port, so it is already in use. The addition of extra IP addresses is the only way to add available ports without having to use non-standard ports. Once subsequent IP addresses are added to the server, the default virtual server will use these addresses automatically until another virtual server for that protocol is created to specifically use that IP address.

It is important, therefore, when you advertise that a socket contains a virtual server with special settings, to ensure that the virtual server is created and running. If not, the default virtual server for that protocol will answer instead. The default virtual server for a protocol can, by default, answer any request for a connection because it listens on all the IP addresses where the port is not being used on the computer. If a virtual server has been created on a particular IP address, but is not currently running, then that IP address is considered as not used and is available to the virtual server listening on all unused IP addresses. The method to control whether a virtual server listens on unused IP addresses is to select All Unassigned as the IP address to listen on, as shown in Figure 12-8.

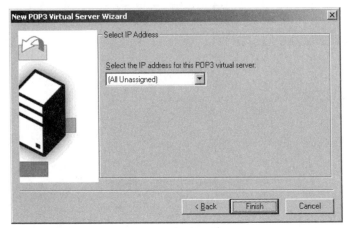

Figure 12-8   Creating a virtual server to listen on all currently unused IP addresses

Host Headers

Of all the virtual server protocols available in Exchange Server, only the HTTP protocol supports the HOST command. This command allows an incoming request to specify which website it wants to retrieve pages from because more than one website can share a socket. This allows an Exchange Server administrator to target HTTP sites, such as Outlook Web Access, to selected domain names. Different domain names connect to different websites each with different configurations, but without the use of multiple IP addresses and ports.

To configure a website to share a socket with another website, the site administrator just chooses the same IP address and port as the other site, but when doing so must provide the URL of the site as the host header. This URL, shown in Figure 12-9, is used by the browser as the value of the HOST command that will distinguish this new site from the existing sites on the server.

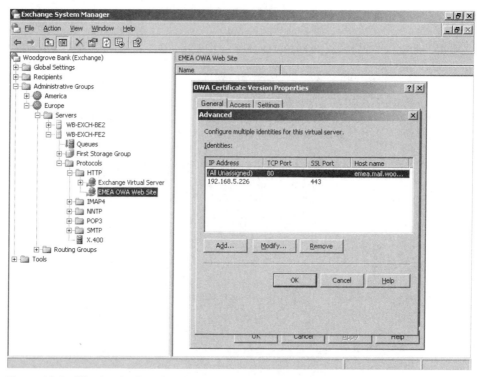

Figure 12-9 Viewing the host headers of a site in Exchange System Manager

One website on a socket can have a blank host header. The site with the blank host header will answer all requests from clients that do not send the HOST command or clients that do not support it. For global client support, at least one virtual server per socket should have a blank host header.

The host header value is only valid for the HTTP protocol, and connections that use the HTTPS protocol cannot utilize it. An HTTPS connection is encrypted using SSL, and the certificate in place on the site requires the URL to match the Common Name (CN) value of the certificate's subject field, as shown in Figure 12-10. The default HTTP virtual server socket and host header values are configured in IIS Manager, but all additional HTTP virtual servers that are created in Exchange System Manager must use Exchange System Manager to set the host header.

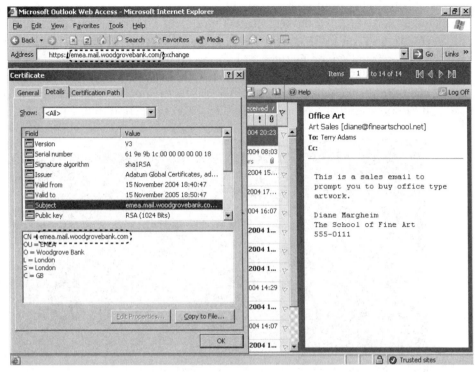

Figure 12-10 The CN value of a digital certificate must match the website URL on which the certificate is used

The use of host headers is also very important when publishing an HTTP virtual server through an application layer firewall such as Microsoft ISA Server. Application layer firewalls are able to evaluate the host header and allow or reject the site depending upon its value.

Socket Pooling

IIS 5.0 and IIS 6.0 implement a feature named Socket Pooling that collects together all of the virtual servers running on a single port and provides shared resources for them. This means two things:

1. Multiple virtual servers running on the same port can share network resources.

2. IIS runs on that port across all IP addresses on the server even if there are no virtual servers in IIS using that port.

Note With socket pooling enabled, a server can run up to three times the number of virtual servers than it can if socket pooling is disabled.

If socket pooling is enabled for a particular IIS service, the port will be listed with the IP address 0.0.0.0. For example, an IMAP4 virtual server will be listed as 0.0.0.0:143, rather than w.x.y.z:143, where w.x.y.z is each IP address used by an IMAP4 virtual server. Figure 12-11 shows an IMAP4 server listening on port 143, with socket pooling enabled, along with a single connection to that virtual server from a client. In the screenshot, the number 2596 is the process that is listening on port 143. It can be seen that a client has established a connection to that port.

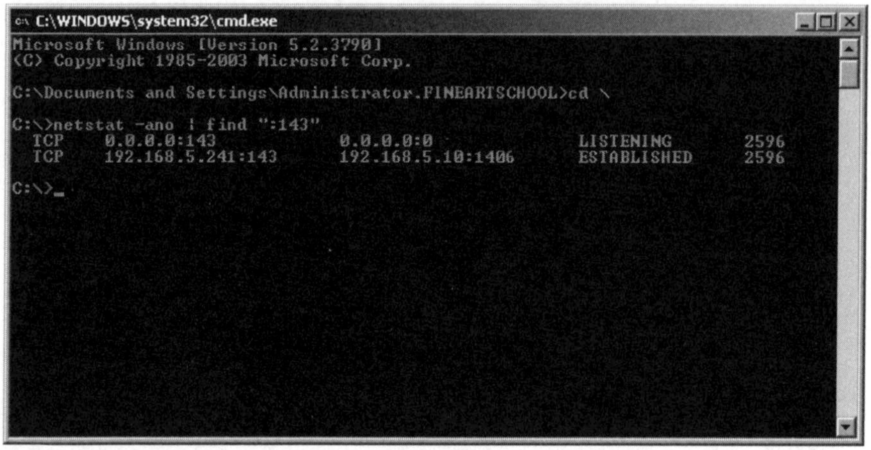

```
C:\WINDOWS\system32\cmd.exe                                             _ □ ×
Microsoft Windows [Version 5.2.3790]
(C) Copyright 1985-2003 Microsoft Corp.

C:\Documents and Settings\Administrator.FINEARTSCHOOL>cd \

C:\>netstat -ano | find ":143"
  TCP    0.0.0.0:143            0.0.0.0:0              LISTENING       2596
  TCP    192.168.5.241:143      192.168.5.10:1406      ESTABLISHED     2596

C:\>_
```

Figure 12-11   Viewing a pooled socket on an Exchange server

IIS allows a configuration change to disable socket pooling in cases where other applications need to run on the ports that IIS would use and where a service does not start because the socket is in use. Disabling socket pooling on an Exchange server is typically required in systems where an organization has a server running both Exchange and ISA Server. For ISA Server to listen for connections that IIS is already using requires the disabling of socket pooling. Disabling socket pooling in IIS 5.0 is done via the metabase, using a different command for each service. In IIS 6.0 the metabase value remains the same except when configuring HTTP virtual servers. The functionality of HTTP is operated by http.sys in Windows Server 2003 and not inet-info.exe, so it is no longer controlled by the metabase setting.

Important   We do not recommend disabling socket pooling unless the number of sites you are running is very small.

Creating Additional Virtual Servers

It is very important that additional virtual servers are created in Exchange System Manager and not IIS Manager. This is due to the nature of the DS2MB process described earlier in this chapter. If an HTTP virtual server is created in IIS Manager, it will not appear in Exchange System Manager for extending with Exchange Server functionality. Also, it is not possible to create additional SMTP and NNTP virtual servers in IIS once Exchange Server is installed. NNTP, IMAP4, and POP3 virtual servers only exist in Exchange System Manager and do not exist in IIS Manager.

Adding HTTP Virtual Servers

The steps to add an HTTP virtual server in Exchange System Manager are as follows:

1. In Exchange System Manager, locate the HTTP node under Protocols on the server that you wish to add the additional HTTP virtual server to.

2. Right-click the HTTP Protocol object and choose Properties.

3. The Properties dialog box for the new virtual server appears, as shown in Figure 12-12. Enter the name and a set of unique properties for the virtual server.

The other properties that you might want to enter are connection limits and whether this virtual server will provide mailboxes or public folders, and which domain it will provide these for. The remainder of the settings for this virtual server will be covered later in this chapter.

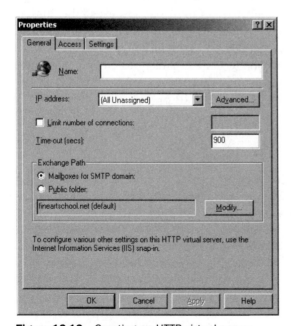

Figure 12-12   Creating an HTTP virtual server

The virtual server will start automatically (assuming that it has valid settings) once these settings have replicated to the IIS metabase on the server hosting the website. Note though that the virtual server icon in Exchange System Manager will remain partially covered in an empty white circle even though the virtual server has started, and you will need to refresh the Exchange System Manager display to see the correct running state.

> **Note**   The ExchWeb virtual directory is not visible in Exchange System Manager but is created in IIS for each HTTP virtual server automatically. The ExchWeb content is located on the server's hard disk and not the Exchange store for performance reasons, and so is not shown in Exchange System Manager.

This HTTP virtual server will get a unique identifier (ID) in IIS, starting with the number 100 and incrementing upwards. This ID is created by Exchange Server and not IIS and so does not follow the convention of either IIS 5.0 or IIS 6.0 of incrementing from 1, or random IDs, respectively. If the HTTP virtual server ID that Exchange Server creates matches an existing virtual server ID, the Exchange Server site settings will overwrite those existing in the metabase and thus overwrite that site's settings. Therefore, do not install Exchange Server on a Windows 2000 Server running IIS 5.0 with more than 99 websites, or always use a script to create the websites, using random IDs. This problem is unlikely to exist in IIS 6.0 because of the random generation of the HTTP virtual server ID by IIS, meaning that it is unlikely that an ID will have already been created that Exchange Server duplicates.

All HTTP virtual servers created in Exchange System Manager must be deleted from Exchange System Manager when they are no longer required. If not, the site will be recreated in IIS the next time the DS2MB process runs, but without most of the required values, and so will fail to start.

Adding IMAP4 and POP3 Virtual Servers

The process for creating IMAP4 and POP3 clients is the same as creating an HTTP virtual server, apart from starting the new site creation wizard from the correct location within Exchange System Manager depending upon the protocol required. The wizard for the creation of an IMAP4 virtual server is shown in steps in Figure 12-13 and Figure 12-14.

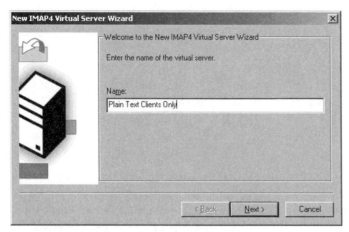

Figure 12-13   Creating a new IMAP4 virtual server by first providing a name for the virtual server

Figure 12-14   Selecting a unique IP address for a new IMAP4 virtual server

As with creating additional HTTP virtual servers, the virtual server will not start immediately upon creation because it needs to be replicated to the IIS server it will be hosted on, and this replication may take some time. If the virtual server's connection details are unique, the virtual server will start once replication completes. Exchange System Manager will need to be refreshed once the replication has occurred to see the correct status of the virtual server.

Adding NNTP Virtual Servers

Though the majority of the process for creating NNTP virtual servers is different from the POP3 and IMAP4 virtual servers, initially the same considerations of port and IP address are required.

The steps for creating an additional NNTP virtual server, once you have set your unique IP address and port (119 by default), is to choose the location where the newsgroup internal server files (its configuration files) are going to be kept on the local server hard disk, and then to choose the default location of all newsgroup content.

When newsgroups are created, their names determine their location. If a virtual directory has been created within the NNTP virtual server with that name, or part of name, then that newsgroup will be created wherever that virtual directory points to. Virtual directories can point to the local file system, a remote file share, or an Exchange public folder. If a virtual directory does not exist that matches a newsgroup name at the point of creation, the newsgroup is created in the default virtual directory.

> **Note**   The default NNTP virtual server stores its newsgroup configuration files in the drive:\inetpub\nntpfile folder, where drive is typically the same as the Windows installation drive. The default location for content on the default NNTP virtual server is the Internet Newsgroups public folder, which is created during the installation of Exchange Server.

Once an additional NNTP virtual server is created, the folder used for the configuration files should be as shown in Table 12-4.

Table 12-4   Newsgroup Internal Server Files

File/Folder name	Purpose
temp.files	Used in replicating news articles to partner feed servers.
drop	Used by Collaboration Data Objects (CDO) based applications to drop news messages on the server.
failedpickup	Contains failures from the Pickup folder below. Usually files end up here if they do not contain the headers required by the pickup folder.
pickup	Similar to the SMTP pickup folder described in Chapter 11. Text files can be composed and placed in this folder, and if they contain the correct headers they will be delivered to the correct newsgroup. Examining a .nws article file on the NNTP server will provide a idea of the headers needed.
root	A folder provided to hold newsgroup content. By default, it holds just the folders that make up the control newsgroups and a subfolder for master/subordinate newsgroup replication.
*.hsh	Three internal hash files. These should not be modified or deleted.
*.lst	Two list files used to maintain the list of the newsgroups on the server.

Adjusting Virtual Server Settings

There are many different properties that can be changed for each virtual server in Exchange System Manager or IIS Manager. Most of the settings that can be changed exclusively in IIS Manager are not covered in this book because they are general settings to any website hosted in IIS and the Microsoft IIS 6.0 Technical Reference (part of the IIS 6.0 Resource Kit) covers these in more detail. This information can be downloaded from *http://www.microsoft.com/resources/documentation/IIS/6/all/techref/ en-us/default.mspx*. The majority of the settings that can be changed in Exchange System Manager for the POP3, IMAP4, NNTP, and HTTP virtual servers will be covered in this section. All of the SMTP settings can be found in Chapter 11.

Configuring the HTTP Virtual Server

HTTP virtual servers are the only Exchange virtual server that can be changed in both Exchange System Manager and IIS Manager. As mentioned earlier, changes made in IIS Manager can be overwritten by changes made in Exchange System Manager, but this is not true for every setting. Exchange System Manager will allow changes just to the site and virtual directories of the site that Exchange Server has control over. Global server settings for HTTP and for other unrelated content can only be set in IIS Manager.

Changes made in IIS Manager at root (server) level will affect all websites, directories, and files on the Web server, including the Exchange Server virtual directories. But it is not always the case that changes at the root will override changes specifically made at the site, directory, and file levels of the Web server. If changes are going to be overwritten, you are asked to confirm this before the change can take place. Figure 12-15 shows the dialog box asking to confirm that a change made to the default document value on the entire server will change a setting on the Default Web Site and the /OMA virtual directory.

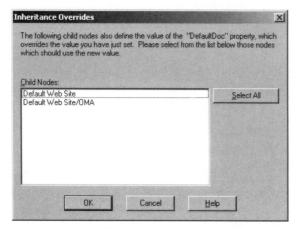

Figure 12-15   Confirming to overwrite specific IIS changes with global changes in IIS Manager

The changes made in Exchange System Manager are stored in Active Directory and replicated to the metabase upon change, so even though an administrator might select the option above to overwrite a setting on the virtual directory with a global setting, the DS2MB process can reset this within a short period of time (assuming a change has been made to Active Directory to cause this replication).

Full information on the creation of HTTP virtual servers can be found in the Microsoft Exchange Server library article "Exchange Server 2003 and Exchange 2000 Server Front-End and Back-End Topology" available at *http://go.microsoft.com/ fwlink/?LinkID=21277*.

The Default Virtual Server vs. Additional Virtual Servers

As there are two places to make HTTP virtual server administrative changes, the major issue of confusion with adjusting the settings of virtual servers is the difference in settings between the default HTTP virtual server, created when Exchange Server is installed, and any additional virtual server created in Exchange System Manager by the Exchange administrator after installation.

The HTTP virtual server created during the Exchange Server installation, known as the Exchange Virtual Server, contains five virtual directories and at the HTTP virtual server root level only the enabling of Forms Based Authentication and compression settings (Figure 12-16) can be performed from this virtual servers properties dialog box, whereas the properties dialog box for additional virtual servers allows control of more settings.

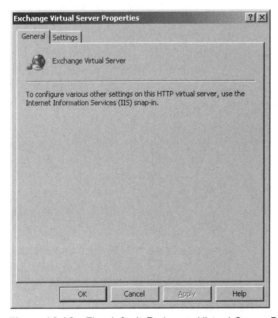

Figure 12-16   The default Exchange Virtual Server Properties dialog box

The settings, shown in Figure 12-17, can only be changed in Exchange System Manager for additional virtual servers, the equivalent settings for the default virtual server need to be changed in IIS Manager.

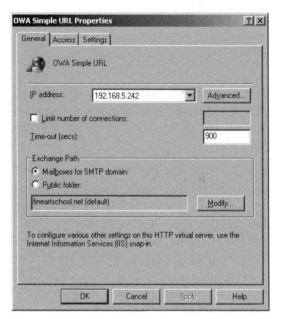

Figure 12-17   The virtual server properties dialog box for all additional HTTP virtual servers

Additional HTTP virtual servers contain a setting at the virtual server level for Exchange Path. This controls what content an HTTP virtual server shows when it is browsed to, and additional HTTP virtual servers can have mailboxes or public folders at the top of the site. This is in contrast with the default HTTP virtual server, where the mailboxes are found at /exchange by default and the public folders at /public.

Prior to SP1 for Exchange Server 2003 an HTTP virtual server was needed for each SMTP domain created in recipient policies. This led to the creation of multiple HTTP virtual servers for Exchange hosting companies with a side effect of reduced performance. SP1 for Exchange Server 2003 has removed this requirement. Prior to the service pack, it would be common for Exchange administrators to attempt performance improvements by hosting only the relevant virtual servers for a domain on the front-end servers used by those clients and on the back-end servers that hosted mailboxes for those clients. Front-end and back-end servers not used by clients of that domain did not need virtual servers created for that domain.

In Exchange Server 2003 SP1 you can use the default HTTP virtual server for all the SMTP domains that you are hosting, unless you have SSL requirements where each client has a different SSL certificate to use.

HTTP Virtual Server Authentication

The authentication settings for each HTTP virtual server need to be configured in Exchange System Manager and not IIS Manager. For more on these settings, see Authentication Methods later in this chapter.

HTTP Virtual Server Security

To change and reconfigure the security settings in an HTTP virtual server also requires the changes to be made in Exchange System Manager. See Setting Security Options later in this chapter, for more on this subject.

IIS Lockdown

When running Exchange Server on Windows 2000 Server it is very important to download and run the IIS Lockdown tool. This tool will restrict access to IIS for specified applications only, and when running the IIS Lockdown wizard the administrator will state that the server is an Exchange server and so IIS will be limited to functions needed by Exchange. For example, running this wizard on Windows 2000 Server for Exchange Server will remove the FTP service, if installed, and the /printers, /scripts, and /msadc virtual directories amongst other changes.

The IIS Lockdown Tool also installs URLScan. URLScan filters URLs, allowing only those deemed valid to actually reach the Web server. ISA Server 2004 contains the ability to scan incoming URLs, and ISA Server 2000 with Feature Pack 1 can contain a version of URLScan if installed, but it is highly recommended that URLScan run on both ISA Server and the IIS 5.0 server. Running URLScan on an ISA Server protecting IIS 6.0 is possible, but it is not necessary to run URLScan on the IIS 6.0 Web server.

> **Caution** The IIS Lockdown Tool can dramatically affect the function of your Web server and hosted sites. Before you deploy it in a production environment, always test your configuration in a secure test environment.

IIS 6.0 on Windows Server 2003 is secure by default and does not require the running of IIS Lockdown. Exchange Server installation will enable the bits of IIS needed for Outlook Web Access to operate. Features such as the /printers, /scripts, and /msadc virtual directories do not exist (unless upgraded from Windows 2000 Server, and we recommend running the IIS Lockdown Tool before the upgrade). Active Server Pages (ASP) is not needed for Outlook Web Access, so leave it disabled.

To download and install the IIS Lockdown tool and the updated subcomponent URLScan 2.5, visit *http://www.microsoft.com/technet/security/tools/locktool.mspx* and *http://www.microsoft.com/technet/security/tools/urlscan.mspx*.

HTTP Virtual Servers and Advanced Firewalls

If your Exchange server is protected by an Open Systems Interconnection (OSI) layer 7 firewall, such as ISA Server, you will need to know the virtual server URLs and virtual directories that have been created to allow them to be published.

Advanced firewalls inspect the URL and the HTTP verbs of the incoming client request and only pass that connection through to the internal server if the connection meets given criteria. In addition to the normal firewall criteria of source IP address and port, advanced firewalls can block requests to invalid URLs, virtual directories and invalid HTTP verbs. For example, the default Outlook Web Access website of Woodgrove Bank could be *http://mail.woodgrovebank.com/exchange*, but because the default website will answer to the IP address as well, the URL *http://w.x.y.z/exchange* (where w.x.y.z is the externally published IP address of the Exchange server) is a valid URL for the Outlook Web Access site. To protect against invalid requests, typically made by enumerating an indiscriminate range of IP addresses, the ISA Server can be configured to allow requests to the specific URL (mail.woodgrovebank.com) and to specified virtual directories (/exchange/*, /public/* and /exchweb/*) only. An example of the URL paths that an ISA Server 2004 installation allow is shown in Figure 12-18.

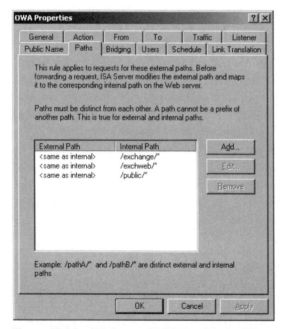

Figure 12-18   ISA Server 2004 showing the URL paths that it allows inbound following creation of a Mail Server Publishing Rule for Outlook Web Access

Attempts to access the root (/), /exadmin, and other possible virtual directories, such as /scripts that formerly existed in earlier versions of Windows, are blocked at the ISA Server firewall. Inspection of the HTTP verbs and invalid characters in the URL path are achieved with the URLScan filter which is built into ISA Server 2004 and available as an add-on in ISA Server 2000 Feature Pack 1.

> **Note** If you have an OSI Layer 7 (or advanced) firewall between your Exchange servers and Outlook Web Access clients, fully test the connection to make sure that any HTTP verb restrictions on the firewall do not stop Outlook Web Access from being 100 percent functional.

Load Balancing HTTP Virtual Servers

In an Exchange Server front-end and back-end configuration it is possible to load balance requests to users' mailboxes by passing the request via the HTTP protocol and one of a number of front-end servers. The actual mailbox is never replicated, and so protection of the back-end server using technologies such as Storage Area Networks and application or disk clusters are important but not covered in this chapter. The front-end server takes the request for the mailbox, authenticates the request, and passes it on to the correct back-end server. If a user browses to any front-end server, the request will be passed onto the correct back-end server using the HTTP protocol.

This functionality allows for a single namespace for all clients to reach their mailboxes. Rather than some clients needing to go to one back-end server, and others to a different back-end server, all clients can browse a front-end server using a single URL. To improve the reliability of the front-end server it can be clustered using Windows Network Load Balancing (NLB) or a related IP clustering technology. Front-end servers are not clustered using Microsoft Cluster Server.

When using numerous front-end servers to load balance client requests, it is important to ensure that each server has an identical HTTP virtual server configuration. This is achieved manually by the creation and modification of the HTTP virtual servers on each front-end server. Prior to Exchange Server 2003 SP1, this was considerably more work than post-SP1 because each SMTP domain would have required its own virtual server.

Configuring the IMAP4 and POP3 Virtual Servers

Although the POP3 and IMAP4 protocols are very different in their commands and functionality, within Exchange Server their administration is very similar with just three options being different between the protocols.

Similar to the SMTP virtual server discussed in Chapter 11, the IMAP4 and POP3 virtual servers can be stopped and started from Exchange System Manager by right-clicking the virtual server. Expanding the virtual server node in Exchange System Manager will show current connections and provide the ability to disconnect individual connections if necessary.

> **Note** Pausing these services will cause errors in connected clients. If the service is paused, it does not maintain existing connections.

General Settings

The General tab of the POP3 and IMAP4 protocols property dialog boxes allows the configuration of the IP address and ports used by the protocols. An example of the IMAP4 protocol dialog box can be seen in Figure 12-5 earlier in this chapter. Like the HTTP virtual server, the default protocol virtual server created by the Exchange Server installation is configured to listen to All Unassigned IP addresses, which means that it listens to all IP addresses not currently used by another POP3 or IMAP4 protocol. It is impossible to operate two virtual servers listening on the same IP address and port because the second of them will not be able to start.

The default listening ports for the two protocols are different, with the well-known port for POP3 being 110 (and 995 for POP3 over SSL) and for IMAP4 being 143 (with 993 for IMAP4 over SSL).

Like all IIS-based virtual servers, the number of connections can be limited to improve performance of the server, and the time after which an idle connection is disconnected is set to 10 minutes for POP3 and 30 minutes for IMAP4. The difference in the time out is due to the way clients use the two protocols. POP3 users connect and download, and then should disconnect immediately. IMAP4 clients remain connected after downloading messages, occasionally polling the server to see if new items have arrived.

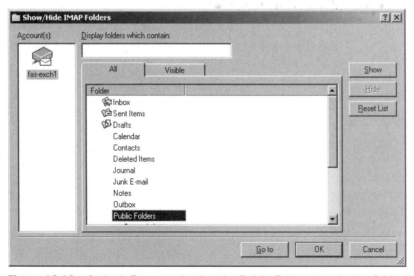

Figure 12-19 Outlook Express showing the Public Folders tree in the folder list for a client's mailbox

The Exchange Server IMAP4 virtual server provides two additional settings over the POP3 virtual server. The first of these is the inclusion of a Public Folders tree when a client requests the list of folders in a user's mailbox. Figure 12-19 shows the result of this setting in Outlook Express. The second IMAP4-only option is Enable Fast Message Retrieval. This allows Exchange Server to estimate the size of a message before the message is fully converted and delivered to the client. This improves message delivery time to the client and performance on the server because a list of message headers, including size, can be offered to the client without first rendering the entire message on the server just to calculate its exact size. Note though that not all clients support this option, and the option is not RFC compliant, so testing of this feature with your client applications is required before enabling on production systems.

Access Settings

The POP3 and IMAP4 protocols in Exchange Server support fewer authentication methods than the HTTP protocol, but how those authentication methods are implemented between the client and the server are the same and therefore covered later in this chapter.

The choice of authentication option will depend upon two factors. The first is the level of protection needed for your user names and passwords and the second is the clients in use. As with most security options there is the choice to go very secure or the choice to support a large client base. By default, the POP3 and IMAP4 protocols support both basic and NTLM authentication, and it is for the client to decide what to connect with. The problem is that because the client makes the decision on which authentication protocol to choose, the easiest to configure is often chosen. Basic authentication is often the easiest to configure because it is often the application's default authentication protocol. To increase security from basic authentication, which sends user names and passwords in clear text, usually requires stopping its use or forcing the use of SSL encryption to protect the entire connection.

Both the POP3 and IMAP4 protocols support the inclusion of Simple Authentication and Security Layer (SASL), RFC 2222. This allows the inclusion of additional authentication methods beyond those defined in the initial protocol. NTLM is included in the POP3 and IMAP4 protocols by way of this RFC. Additional methods of authentication can be enabled by the installation of suitable add-in software to Exchange Server and the correct client software or additions to existing client software.

Note   Outlook Express 5.0 and later supports NTLM by the selection of the Log On Using Secure Password Authentication (SPA) check box on the Servers tab of the Account Properties dialog box.

Messaging Settings

When a POP3 or IMAP4 client downloads a message from the Exchange server, the message may need to be converted into a suitable format for the client. This conversion is based upon how the message is stored in the Exchange store. If the message is not in the correct format for the client, the message will need to be rendered on the server into the correct format before being sent to the user. Upon arrival at the client, the format will control whether or not the message can be displayed, so the best option for compatibility is to convert messages (that need conversion) into HTML and plain text. This option however is not the best for CPU and network throughput. A message rendered into both HTML and plain text will be larger than an HTML-only message, which again will be larger than a plain text only e-mail message. The choice is a balance between performance and client compatibility. The Exchange Server default is to provide MIME encoding with the message body being presented in both HTML and plain text.

If you have a client subset that supports a different message format from other clients, an option is to create multiple virtual servers, each providing only the valid options rather than one virtual server covering all options.

Options such as BinHex for Macintosh and Exchange Rich Text Format (RTF) should only be used if all the clients connecting to this virtual server support that option because it will make the message unreadable to other clients. BinHex encoding is only readable by Macintosh clients and Exchange RTF will appear as an attachment named winmail.dat in unsupported clients. More information about winmail.dat can be found in Chapter 11.

Calendaring Settings

IMAP4 clients do not support true interactive access to the Calendar folder in a user's mailbox, and POP3 clients can only access the inbox. Therefore, when a user receives a meeting request message in the user's inbox, Exchange Server renders the e-mail to include a hyperlink to Outlook Web Access. This allows the user to view the full calendar information rather than replying with an e-mail or (if IMAP) attempting to open the Calendar folder and trying to understand the e-mail attachment that contains the calendar information.

The Calendaring settings on the POP3 and IMAP4 virtual servers control how Exchange Server renders the URL into the message. The administrator needs to configure these settings to ensure that all users get a valid hyperlink to Outlook Web Access.

Figure 12-20 shows the configuration at Woodgrove Bank to ensure that the Outlook Web Access URL will work across the Internet. The name entered into the front-end server name field is not the NetBIOS name of the front-end server, but it is the URL that ISA Server publishes that represents the front-end server cluster.

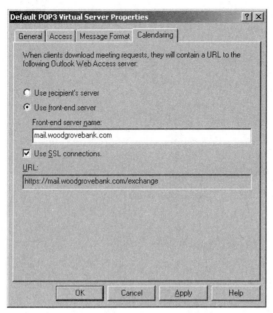

Figure 12-20   Setting the Calendaring options to provide Internet access to Outlook Web Access

An example calendar message viewed in Outlook Express can be seen in Figure 12-21.

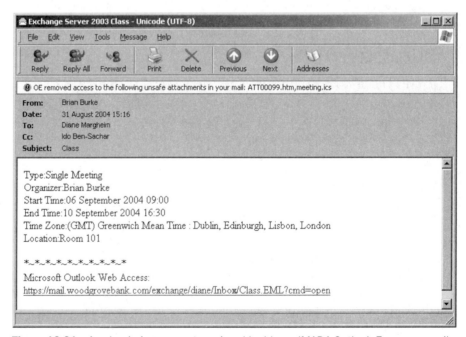

Figure 12-21   A calendaring request rendered inside an IMAP4 Outlook Express e-mail message

> **Note**   If the POP3 and IMAP4 virtual servers contain users that do not use the default Outlook Web Access website, and thus not the /exchange virtual directory, you can modify the *oWAServer* attribute of the POP3 and IMAP4 virtual server instance in Active Directory, using a tool such as ADSI Edit to generate a non-standard URL.

Configuring NNTP Virtual Servers

The NNTP service provided by Exchange Server is an extension of the same service provided in Windows servers, which is an optional installation component of IIS 5.0 or 6.0. The IIS version provides single server newsgroup support; that is, you cannot replicate other newsgroup content into the IIS NNTP server. Additionally, all content of an IIS NNTP server is stored as files and folders on a disk subsystem.

> **Important**   The IIS NNTP server is a required Windows component before Exchange Server can be installed, though once Exchange Server 2003 is installed the service is disabled.

To implement an NNTP virtual server within your Exchange organization, set the service to Automatic and then start the Default NNTP Virtual Server, and if you have created additional virtual servers, start them also. Once the Exchange Server NNTP virtual server is running, it can be configured to create newsgroups, publish existing public folders as newsgroups, configure permissions, set up replication, automatically delete news postings or articles that are out of date, and rebuild the server in the case of failure.

Newsgroup Hierarchies

The newsgroup hierarchy of a server is the layout of each newsgroup on a server in relation to all the other newsgroups. The newsgroup name determines its location within the hierarchy. An example hierarchy best describes this idea:

```
research
   archive
   current
   proposed
general-info
   sales
      local
      international
   marketing
```

This will create at least six newsgroups, two of them being research.current and general-info.sales.international. Each level of the hierarchy becomes a full stop in the newsgroup name, and names cannot have spaces in them.

Depending upon the configuration of the server the path in the above example named general-info.sales may or may not be a newsgroup. This is because some of the parts of the hierarchy can be configured to be virtual directories, but not newsgroups, whereas other parts of the hierarchy will be newsgroups within newsgroups. Virtual directories control the placement of newsgroup storage, but are not newsgroups themselves.

Therefore using the above hierarchy as an example where research is a virtual directory and archive, current and proposed are newsgroups you will get three newsgroups called research.archives, research.current, and research.proposed.

Creating Newsgroup Hierarchies

Each newsgroup on an NNTP virtual server needs to be stored somewhere. The three possible locations for storage are the local file system, a remote file share, or an Exchange Server public folder. When an NNTP virtual server is created, a default location is set for content for that virtual server, and this can be determined by viewing the path to the Default Newsgroup subtree. This setting is seen by expanding the NNTP virtual server in Exchange System Manager, and then selecting the Virtual Directories node.

Different newsgroups within the hierarchy can have different storage locations. For example, the general-info virtual directory might be stored in an Exchange public folder, whereas the research virtual directory could be kept on the local hard disk. To the client they are all part of the same hierarchy, regardless of where they are stored, but to the administrator it matters due to questions of permission, storage, and recovery.

To control where a newsgroup is stored requires creating the hierarchy before the creation of any newsgroups. If a newsgroup is created without a planned hierarchy it will be stored in the default location, but if later a hierarchy that encompasses an existing newsgroup is created, access to that newsgroup fails, and the messages are potentially lost.

The first part of the hierarchy that needs to be created is the virtual directory component. These control storage and various other settings, and if every newsgroup that is going to be created can use the default storage location and settings, then additional virtual directories do not need to be created.

Additional virtual directories that provide alternative storage locations are typically used for performance reasons or for accessibility of the news content to MAPI clients. If the news content is stored within the default public folder tree then it is accessible to MAPI clients, and if a news server is expecting lots of posts then the placement of different newsgroups within different virtual directories allows the storage requirements to be across multiple drives on the server or remote servers.

Virtual directories are created under the NNTP virtual server in Exchange System Manager and the virtual directory name must match the start of any newsgroup that will eventually be stored within the virtual directory. For example, a virtual directory named research can hold a newsgroup named research.current, but a newsgroup named sales.international could never go on the research virtual directory. Note that virtual directories are not limited to single names and a virtual directory named research.archive could be created to hold multiple newsgroups such as research.archive.2003 and research.archive.2004.

Once the virtual directory is created, its properties can be changed. For example, the research.archive virtual directory could have posting disabled on it so that it becomes read only. The other properties of a virtual directory are:

- **Directory contents**   This sets the path, either NTFS folder or Exchange Public Folder, that will store the content of the newsgroups that will be held on this virtual directory. Changing the location will remove newsgroups held on this virtual directory.

- **Secure communications**   SSL and NTFS or public folder permissions are used to set the security of the virtual directory. Note that permissions are not controlled within the NNTP virtual directory properties dialog box but, for file system stored newsgroups, via NTFS permissions, or for public folders stored newsgroups, via public folder properties within an Outlook client.

- **Access restrictions**   This stops posting to a virtual directory, making its newsgroups all read-only. You can also restrict the visibility of a newsgroup so it does not appear in a client's newsgroup listing.

- **Content control**   Content control sets the options for IIS logging and indexing. Indexing ensures that the Content Indexer service includes this virtual directory when creating an index on the server.

Creating Newsgroups

Once the virtual directories are created, the newsgroups can be created. You should not create a newsgroup before its virtual directory, otherwise the newsgroup will be stored in the default storage location for that NNTP virtual server, and if later a virtual directory is created with a name that matches the first part of any existing newsgroup, that newsgroup will become unavailable.

Newsgroups are either manually created in Exchange System Manager or via the rgroup.vbs script. Creation of a newsgroup requires that the name contains no spaces and that each part of the name is separated by a dot. If a newsgroup needs to go on a particular virtual directory, the start of the newsgroup name needs to match the virtual directory name. The wizard for creating newsgroups manually will ask for the newsgroup Description and Pretty Name values. The pretty name is just an alternate name to the default dot divided name. For example, the pretty name could be Research Archive (2003) whereas the newsgroup name would be research.archive.2003. Note that not all clients show the Pretty Name value of a newsgroup.

To create a lot of newsgroups at the same time you can use the rgroup.vbs script. This can be found in the %windir%\system32\inetsrv folder. To use this command line script requires that you have a list of the newsgroups that you want to create in the form of a text file. This file can be created by hand, or if you are going to pull content from another server you can export the newsgroup list, referred to as the active list, from that server in advance.

To export a newsgroup active list from another server, either download it from them via FTP or start Telnet from the command line and type **set logfile filename**, where filename is the name of the logfile you want to record the active list into. Then, in Telnet type **open newsserver 119** where newsserver is the fully qualified domain name (FQDN) of the NNTP server that contains the list you want. Once connected type **list active**, followed by **quit** when done. The logfile specified earlier will now contain all the newsgroups on that server in the space delineated form of group name, last posted article ID, first posted article ID and posting status (yes, no, or moderated). This file can be adjusted to create the source file needed by rgroup.vbs.

To import a manually created list of newsgroups using rgroup.vbs, a text file needs to be created or the active list downloaded and modified. The rgroup.vbs import file must start with **215 Start** on a single line, and then list each of the newsgroups you want to create on a separate line, as follows:

```
215 Start
news.public
news.private
news.current
news.archive.2003
news.archive.2004
```

Once the list is complete, it can be imported into Exchange Server by running rgroup.vbs –t l –a filename.

Moderated Newsgroups

The default configuration of a newsgroup is that anyone who has permission to post to a newsgroup will see their post a short while later (timing depends upon network configuration and replication). To ensure that posts to an NNTP server are valid for that group, posting can be moderated. This causes the post to be e-mailed to a given user, who if the post is valid will post it to the newsgroup on your behalf. Once accepted, it will appear in the newsgroup for all authorized users to see.

Before you can configure a moderated newsgroup, you need to configure the NNTP virtual server to support moderation. This involves setting the SMTP server to use and the default SMTP domain. These settings are needed because the moderator gets the posts that need moderating through e-mail.

Each moderated newsgroup will need an e-mail address configured in it so that new posts get sent to the correct moderator, and by default this e-mail address is the newsgroup-name@default.smtp.domain. If the newsgroup name contains dots, they are changed to dashes. For example, if the default domain of the newsgroup is fineartschool.net and a moderated newsgroup is research.current, then the default e-mail address used to send posts to the moderator will be research-current@fineartschool.net. If this mailbox does not exist, no message will reach the moderator, and therefore no messages will appear in the newsgroup.

The moderator will need a mail and news client that supports moderator functions. To enable Outlook Express to support a moderator, you need to set the `Moderator DWORD` registry key at `HKEY_CURRENT_USER\Identities\{GUID}\Software\Microsoft\Outlook Express\5.0\News` where {GUID} is the GUID of your Outlook Express identity (look for the User Name value of each GUID to determine which GUID you need to change) if you have more than one identity configured.

This Outlook Express identity should be configured to view the moderated newsgroups and to read the mailbox of the moderator. News posts to the group will be e-mailed to the moderator, who will drag them into the newsgroup or select Reply To Group to post those messages that are acceptable to the policies of the group.

As an alternative to moderator newsgroups, the use of the control newsgroups allows posted messages to be cancelled. This is amongst the other functions of the control groups such as the creation of newsgroups. To enable the control groups you should remove those that are not needed, for example removing all but control.cancel will only allow the deletion of messages and secure the NTFS folder (default: C:\Inetpub\nntpfile\root\control) that holds control.cancel to limit those accounts that can use the NNTP message cancel feature. Limited visibility is an option that can be used to hide the control newsgroups in NNTP clients, further limiting these folders to those who need them. Once the properties for the control newsgroups are complete, the use of control newsgroups can be enabled at the virtual server level.

Tip The server administrator can use the rcancel.vbs script to cancel messages posted by other users. The script is found in %windir%\system32\inetsrv and the command line is rcancel.vbs –m "<post_ID>" where post_ID is the ID of the post, which can be found by clicking Reply Group in the post in a NNTP client.

Warning Do not manually delete messages from the NNTP folders because they are not removed from the internal files that make up the list of current messages. The only way to delete messages (unless using a public folder) is to cancel them using the steps above.

Newsgroup Expiration Policies

For newsgroups that will contain content that will go out of date, you can use News-group Expiration Policies to delete messages after a certain period of time. News-group expiration policies do not work for newsgroups stored in Exchange public folders. Newsgroups stored in public folders should be managed the same way that all public folders are managed, that is by using system policies or the properties of the actual public folder.

Expiration policies can be set up on a date criteria, and you can have more than one policy affecting a server. If a newsgroup is affected by more than one policy, it will be acted upon by that which is invoked first.

Each policy is created to delete messages in selected newsgroups after a certain period of time in hours. The newsgroups the policy operates upon are based on the newsgroup name, and wildcards are accepted. Each policy allows you to specify more than one group and to set whether the policy will include or exclude that news-group. It is important that the Exclude entries are listed above the Include entries oth-erwise the excluded entry will be ignored. When a policy runs, it will record Event ID 418 for NNTPSVC in the system event log, recording that it ran and how many posts were deleted when it ran.

Creating Newsfeeds

A newsfeed, or feed for short, is where the Exchange Server NNTP service is able to obtain copies of news posts from other news servers both within your organization and throughout the world. These can be public or private news servers, but you typ-ically need permission to obtain a feed from a source, and to feed from a commercial source will typically require payment of subscription fees.

> **Tip**   If you need to build a replicated newsgroup structure within your orga-nization only, the easiest way is to use public folder replication.

If the content that you need to obtain is hosted externally, then you will need to agree to peer with another news provider. A news server peering agreement allows you to push and pull news articles from another news server on the Internet. News-groups are exchanged around the world by each news server peering with one or two other servers, with there being no main source server.

Once you have a server peering with an Internet news provider enabled, you can configure a master/subordinate setup to replicate the news articles around your orga-nization. The roles of peer, master, and subordinate are not directly configured within Exchange System Manager, but are the result of the feed configuration on the connect-ing server. Therefore, a server could be a peer for a set of Internet newsgroups and a master for these same newsgroups to subordinate servers on the internal network. The subordinate servers do not connect directly to the Internet peer servers, but instead pass every news article they send and receive though their master server. Table 12-5 describes each news server type by describing the feed that they implement.

Table 12-5 News Server Feed Roles

Role	Description
Master	These servers receive all new articles posted to a newsgroup (or set of newsgroups) and are in charge of distributing them to their connected subordinates and peers. A master server should not be connected to by clients. Master servers process expiry policies.
Subordinate	These servers are replication partners of master servers. They service client requests for news articles and push newly posted articles to the master server. Articles recently posted to other subordinate servers are pulled from the master for display to this subordinate's clients. Subordinates do not expire articles; they just host what the master tells them to.
Peer	Used to exchange newsgroups with the Internet.

If a company needed to operate a news server in each of three offices, all hosting the same content, they would have one peer/master server (operating both roles) and three subordinates, with the master and one of the subordinates at one office and the other subordinates at each of the remaining offices. This would mean downloading the content once into the organization rather than multiple times, with clients connecting to the subordinate servers and the peer/master replicating the content to and from the Internet.

To create a newsfeed you will need to have available the IP address or name of the other server in the feed agreement and a list of newsgroups that you wish to replicate. If you do not want to replicate all of the groups that exist on the master or peer server, create just those groups you want to replicate in advance. This is done using rgroup.vbs and importing a text file of newsgroups as described above.

To configure a master/subordinate feed relationship you first configure the subordinate server with a feed that is both inbound and/or outbound from the master server. This set of steps is then repeated on each subordinate server. Inbound news feeds are read only, in that articles posted to the subordinate server will not be replicated back to the master server. If you wish to have articles replicated both ways you need to configure an inbound and outbound feed. Each feed is configured for a set of newsgroups; for example, rec.* for all the groups starting with rec. Do not accept the default option in the wizard of * if you are unsure what newsgroups are hosted on the partner server.

Finally, once the feed has been created you will need to check the advanced settings that are not available in the wizard. These include schedules and authentication. Do not set the schedule too frequently, and provide a user name and password if the partner server does not support anonymous connections.

Once you have the subordinate-to-master feeds configured you can configure the master-to-subordinate feeds on the master server in the same way that the subordinate feeds were created. When both feeds are created, and valid newsgroups exist on both sets of servers, articles will begin to flow between the master and subordinate servers. Note that this will only happen on every scheduled interval and not immediately. For example, a schedule of 15 minutes on all feeds means that a post to a subordinate server will move to the master server within 15 minutes without being displayed on the subordinate server. Once the post is at the master server it will be pushed to all subordinate servers, including the one it came from, within 15 minutes. Therefore, it could be up to 30 minutes from the time of posting until an article appears on all the subordinate news servers.

Configuring a peer feed is similar to the master/subordinate feed described above, except this time you get to specify if the Inbound Feed is to Pull Articles From The Remote Server or to Accept A Push Feed From The Remote Server. If the remote server is an Exchange Server NNTP virtual server and the news feed is a pull feed, you need to select Allow Servers To Pull News Articles From This Server in the virtual server properties dialog box on the remote server before the feed will work.

Making Internet Newsgroups Available to Clients

With over 100,000 newsgroups available on Usenet, the most common of the Internet newsgroup systems, and other newsgroups also available, such as Microsoft's peer support servers at news.microsoft.com, it is difficult to control what users download to a network if they are granted NNTP access through a firewall.

To protect your network, and to limit downloading and uploading, it is possible to subscribe to selected newsgroups that are of relevance to your organization and to grant users access to these groups via Outlook or NNTP clients such as Outlook Express. The newsgroups of interest are downloaded to your Exchange servers via peer feeds and stored in the default public folder tree if they need to be visible to Outlook users. They are stored in any of the three storage locations of local file store, remote file store, or public folder if they need to be visible to NNTP clients.

> **Note**   Outlook is not an NNTP client and can only view newsgroups if they appear in the public folders.

With this configuration in place, the corporate firewall can be configured to allow the master Exchange server to have NNTP access to its peer server(s). If subordinate NNTP servers are needed they do not need Internet access for NNTP, just the ability to connect over port 119 to the master Exchange server. Users can now only access those newsgroups that are sanctioned by the organization, and they are protected by any antivirus product installed on the firewall or Exchange server.

News Server Configuration Tasks

In addition to the tasks of configuring virtual directories, newsgroups, expiration policies, and feeds, the Exchange administrator may also need to secure newsgroups, limit connectivity for performance, and rebuild the groups if the service will not start.

Securing a newsgroup is controlled by its storage location. If the start of a newsgroup name is the same as a virtual directory, its storage location will match that directory, with each dot in the name resulting in a subfolder. For example, if the virtual directory rec is stored on c:\news\content\rec the newsgroup rec.drinks.wine will be in the c:\news\content\rec\drinks\wine folder. Access to the rec.drinks.wine newsgroup can be restricted to those who log on to the server with permissions that match that which is allowed on the NTFS permissions set against c:\news\content\rec\drinks\wine.

If a newsgroup virtual directory uses Exchange Server public folders, each group will result in a subfolder below the parent, similar to the disk folders above, except they are stored in the Exchange public database instead. Permissions are then set using Outlook or Exchange System Manager as required.

Each Exchange Server NNTP virtual server is capable of being restricted in terms of number of concurrent sessions and for the duration of idle sessions. Exchange System Manager allows an administrator to view the current sessions and to terminate an individual session or all sessions. Additionally, the Visual Basic script rsess.vbs (in system32\inetsrv) can be used to list current sessions on a selected server and to terminate sessions by user name or IP address. Rsess.vbs is a script best run in command scripting mode and not Windows scripting mode, therefore, either set your default scripting mode using **cscript //H:cscript** or run the command explicitly in command scripting mode using **cscript rsess.vbs** from the command line.

If an NNTP virtual server will not start or starts with missing groups, it is possible to rebuild the server. This involves one of two processes:

1. The service reading the group.lst file and attempting to rebuild the configuration.

2. If that fails, rebuilding continues by reading each article and attempting to regenerate the configuration, including the .lst and .hsh files.

Rebuilding a server requires that the Network News Transport Protocol service is started, but the NNTP virtual server that is failing must be stopped. In Exchange System Manager, a stopped NNTP virtual server can be rebuilt from the All Tasks right-click menu. The two options for rebuilding match the two described processes above. The Standard Rebuild option recreates the group.lst file which holds a listing of each group. The Thorough Rebuild option recreates the entire newsgroup structure by reading each article and recreating the index files that the newsgroup uses to store the headers of every 128 messages.

Authentication Methods

Internet Information Services (IIS) provides support for a number of ways to authenticate against the server. Some of these authentication methods are Internet standards and others are proprietary Microsoft authentication methods. We will look at each in turn to see when and why they should be used.

Each virtual server protocol in Exchange Server supports a subset of these authentication methods. Table 12-6 shows which authentication methods are supported by which protocols.

Table 12-6   Protocols and Authentication Methods

Supported authentication methods	Protocol
Anonymous Access	HTTP
	NNTP
	SMTP
Forms Based Authentication/Cookie	HTTP
Basic Authentication	HTTP
	IMAP4
	POP3
	NNTP
	SMTP
Digest Authentication	HTTP
Integrated Windows Authentication (but not when server is configured as a front-end server)	HTTP
	IMAP4
	POP3
	NNTP
	SMTP
SSL Client Authentication	HTTP
	NNTP

Anonymous Authentication

Windows Servers have very limited true anonymous access. True anonymous access is where no user name and password is used to authenticate the user. In IIS, Anonymous Access is not always the same as just described. In most IIS protocols, a user name and password is stored on the server. When a user does not present any credentials during the initial connection they are logged in with these server-stored details, so it is anonymous to the user, but not to the operating system and resources. Anything that this anonymous connection needs to access has to be granted to the account that Windows uses to provide anonymous access.

Any user name and password can be stored in IIS for the use of anonymous access to an HTTP virtual server or NNTP virtual server. True anonymous access does exist for the SMTP protocol in that the server does not need to have a user account to authenticate the user on behalf of the connection. For the HTTP and NNTP virtual servers, if there is a problem with the server stored account, anonymous access will not work.

In IIS 5.0 and 6.0, the anonymous account for the HTTP virtual server is typically IUSR_*computername* where computername is replaced with the computer name during installation of IIS. If the name of the server changes, this name does not change, nor does it need to. The IUSR account, or the Internet Guest Account to describe it properly, is a member of the Guests local group, and the password is set automatically and randomly by the server. The Metabase Explorer tool allows the password to be viewed, but it should never be changed using this tool. If the Internet Guest Account is deleted then the account will be recreated upon restarting IIS using the information in the metabase. The IISAdmin Event ID 101 records the account re-creation in the Application Event Log.

IMAP4, POP3 and NNTP are used to display the contents of a user's mailbox and or public folder and so some form of authentication is required. When HTTP is used to access a user's mailbox, it too must be accompanied by a non-anonymous authentication method.

Basic Authentication

In the RFC for each virtual server protocol there is described a way to log on to the service provided. This default authentication is always referred to as basic authentication and is commonly stated as being clear text, though this is not always the case. The POP3 and IMAP4 protocols do use clear text, in that the packet on the wire is totally readable for both the user name and password. The HTTP implementation of Basic Authentication is to encode the password using the Base64 encoding method. For example, the response to an HTTP virtual server running Basic Authentication could be:

```
ZmluZWFydHNjaG9vbFxkaWFuZTpwYXNzd29yZA==
```

This Base64 string decodes to fineartschool\diane:password and will always generate that value no matter which client or server is involved. So, although a little bit of work is required to decode the string (and free decoders can be found on the Internet), it should be considered as insecure as clear text.

An Exchange Server system configured to operate in a front-end and back-end scenario supports the use of basic authentication. In Exchange Server 2000, this was the only way to configure this type of system, but Exchange Server 2003 provides support for Kerberos between the front-end and back-end servers as well as basic.

Basic authentication operates without issue over firewalls and proxy servers. The authentication information is transferred as part of the protocol connection and does not need additional ports opened on any firewall separating the connecting servers.

> **Important**   Because this type of authentication sends user names and passwords in the clear, it should really be avoided if at all possible unless an encryption technology is being used.

NTLM and Kerberos: Windows Integrated Authentication

Windows Integrated Authentication is the term used in IIS 5.0 and 6.0 to do both Kerberos, and then NTLM if Kerberos does not work. Kerberos version 5 is implemented as part of an Active Directory forest and within Exchange Server environments its main feature is that a Kerberos logon can be delegated.

Kerberos delegation is where a server that the client authenticates to can have full-network access as that client to other servers. In the Exchange Server scenario, once authentication occurs between client and server, authentication can then be passed from server to server. In Exchange Server 2000, front-end and back-end scenarios required basic authentication because Kerberos was not supported (as basic authentication can also be delegated).

Kerberos has a number of requirements before it can be used. In brief, these are Windows 2000 or later operating system and the name of the server used in the connection must be registered as a Service Principle Name (SPN). If Kerberos cannot be supported, NTLM, a Microsoft proprietary authentication method, is used instead. A Microsoft TechNet article that can be found at *http://www.microsoft.com/ windows2000/techinfo/reskit/en-us/distrib/dscd_aun_yfet.asp* covers the basics of Kerberos. The choice of which authentication protocol to use is decided by the client, with the client using the most secure that it can support.

A Service Principle Name can be registered on a Windows 2000/2003 server using SetSPN from the Windows 2000 Resource Kit. The command is **setspn -A service/new_name existing_NetBIOS_name**. For example: setspn -A HTTP/ mail.fineartschool.net fas-exch1.

The NTLM protocol is supported by Windows 95 and later. It operates by the server sending a challenge to the client. The client responds with an answer that indicates that the client knows the user name and password. The password is never sent across the wire. The server processes the same challenge that it sent to the client and the user is logged in if the server's calculation matches the client's response.

Important   Neither Kerberos or NTLM will encrypt the traffic of the connection; they just protect the user name and password.

Windows Integrated Authentication can be used in an Exchange Server 2003 front-end and back-end configuration because the Kerberos protocol is supported between the front-end and back-end servers in this release of Exchange Server.

Finally, it is worth noting that NTLM can get past a firewall, but is generally stopped by proxies, and that Kerberos can get past a proxy, but is generally stopped by firewalls. This means that if a front-end Exchange server is placed in a perimeter network (which is not recommended due to the number of ports that need to be opened in the firewall protecting the internal network), then TCP port 88 needs to be opened to support Kerberos authentication to the back-end servers. No additional ports (apart from those needed to place a front-end server in a perimeter network) are needed if the authentication between front and back-end servers uses basic authentication.

Forms Based Authentication (Cookie Authentication)

The HTTP virtual server for Outlook Web Access supports Forms Based Authentication. This method of authentication allows a custom-designed logon page to be created, and authentication is achieved by providing the client with a cookie that expires after a given amount of time.

Forms Based Authentication is only supported on Windows Server 2003 or Windows 2000 Server SP4 and later. In a front-end and back-end scenario, you can use Forms Based Authentication if your back-end servers are still running Exchange Server 2000, and though you still get the Exchange Server 2000 version of Outlook Web Access, your front-end generated logon can be forms based.

Forms Based Authentication requires an implementation of SSL. The different ways that this can be implemented are covered later in this chapter under Installing a Security Certificate on the Server.

Compression

Once Forms Based Authentication is enabled, it is possible to implement compression of the data sent to the client. This is the only authentication method that provides HTTP compression in Exchange Server without the use of the native IIS compression feature (which globally compresses all files on the server).

Note   Do not enable compression of the front-end server if the back-end servers are still running Exchange Server 2000. Unless your front-end Exchange server is running SP1, you may find that Outlook Web Access does not behave as expected when compression is enabled.

Compression reduces the size of the HTTP data by as much as 50 percent by compressing it on the fly and sending it across the wire to the client. The client then needs to uncompress it and display it. Compression support is client-driven even if the option is set on the server. On the server it is only possible to configure the level of compression used (high, low, or none), but unless the client HTTP GET request states that the client supports gzip compression (gzip compression is compatible with Exchange Server) the response will not be compressed.

Caution   We recommend that you do not enable compression in a single-server environment because compression in a single-server environment places an additional load on the server.

Compression is most effective if the time taken to download the HTTP Web page without compression is reduced by the introduction of compression. Remember that the compression/decompression steps on a slow client or server could take longer to achieve than just downloading the Web page content to the user. Compression is most effective for dial-up clients rather than clients on a LAN or faster broadband connection.

Front-End and Back-End Servers and Forms Based Authentication

When using Forms Based Authentication on the front-end server the individual virtual directories of /exchange and /public are disabled from being directly changed. Back-end Exchange Server 2003 servers require Basic Authentication or Windows Integrated Authentication enabled on them, whereas back-end Exchange Server 2000 computers require Basic Authentication.

Customizing Forms Based Authentication

The form presented during Forms Based Authentication can be changed to suit the requirements of your organization. The two easiest configuration changes that can be made is adding your own logo and removing the requirement for the user to enter the domain name during logon.

Note Microsoft cannot support changes made to the form; service packs, upgrades, and hotfixes for Exchange Server may replace your customizations with the default. Therefore, it is important to have your own backup of any modifications that you make, and to test them against any updates applied to your servers.

The owalogon.asp file at \program files\exchsrvr\exchweb\bin\auth\ redirects clients to the language-specific version of logon.asp. If a language-specific version does not exist, users are sent to the usa\logon.asp file. Customizing owalogon.asp allows you to add additional language-specific versions that do not exist. For example, a UK English version could be created by forcing the redirection of a UK English browser to the gb\ folder (which would have to be created).

The logon.asp page held in each language-specific folder can be customized in Notepad by simply changing the relevant strings at the top of the file. For example, a UK English version of the logon.asp page would need to be a copy of the USA default and then have the spelling of "unauthorized" in the L_ExpireWarning_Text value changed. Other languages would need more than this single change to be functional.

To add your own logo, copy the image to the \program files\exchsrvr\exchweb\img folder and change the references to logon_Microsoft.gif in each language specific logon.asp that you need to customize.

Because the page is HTML/ASP, additional configuration can be done to items such as more help text, disclaimers and security warnings, allowing the user name to be saved (by setting the HTML autocomplete property) and to remove the requirement for the domain name by adding it to each logon request within the page rather than getting the user to enter it. Figure 12-22 shows a customized Outlook Web Access Logon screen that is used to direct users to the front-end server nearest to their back-end server (for performance reasons) rather than the server nearest to their current location.

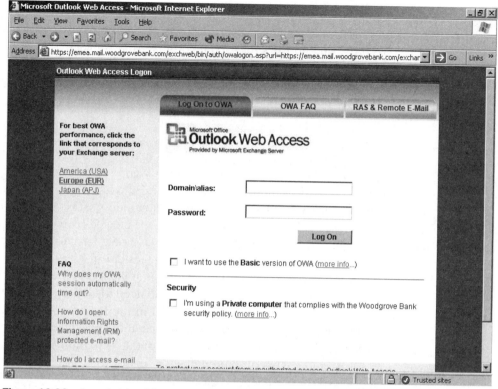

Figure 12-22   A customized Outlook Web Access Forms Based Authentication page

In addition to the customization of the logon screen, it is possible to change the cookie expiry timeouts using a registry key on each front-end Exchange server. The registry keys are TrustedClientTimeout when the Private Computer option is selected and PublicClientTimeout when the Public Or Shared Computer option is selected during log on. Both registry keys are located at HKEY_LOCAL_MACHINE\SYSTEM\CurrentControlSet\Services\MSExchangeWeb\OWA and both are of type DWORD. The value for each key is the time of expiry in minutes. Do not make the expiry time too short because a client that does not use the Outlook Web Access ActiveX control might time out while composing a long message. The premier client (that uses the Outlook Web Access ActiveX control) does not time out during message composition.

Integrating Forms Based Authentication with Other Applications

Outlook Web Access in Exchange Server 2003 allows the embedding of Outlook Web Access pages within other web-based applications. This is achieved by using specific URLs to the content that needs to be displayed. For example, a program that uses Web Parts (such as SharePoint Portal Server) shows a user's daily tasks by the use of the *http://servername/exchange/username/calendar/?cmd=contents&part=1* path. This can cause problems with Forms Based Authentication due to the issuing of the cookie. If the Web Part is from a different server than the main application, Internet Explorer's privacy settings may stop the cookie being accepted, and thus failure to log on will occur.

Web parts are seamless for the user when used with Windows Integrated Authentication because this avoids users being prompted to authenticate once for each part of the page. Therefore, in scenarios like SharePoint Portal Server, the Web Part should reference the back-end server and not a front-end server that uses Forms Based Authentication.

Digest Authentication

This authentication method was designed as a replacement for Basic authentication in HTTP. Full information on the standard can be found in RFC 2617.

To implement Digest Authentication in Windows requires a supporting browser (Internet Explorer 5 and later or Netscape 7 and later, plus others such as Mozilla and Opera), a supported Web server and configured support for the user account on Active Directory.

Digest Authentication transmits credentials across the network as an MD5 hash or message digest, where the original user name and password cannot be deciphered from the hash. Successful authentication occurs when the domain controller validating the hash sent from the client confirms that it matches the hash held on the domain controller.

For the domain controller to process the hash on a Windows 2000 domain controller, Active Directory requires that the accounts that need this authentication method be enabled to Store Password Using Reversible Encryption on the account properties in Active Directory Users and Computers. Once this setting is enabled, the user needs to change his or her password once, and after this change the password is stored both in its native Windows Active Directory form and in a reversible encryption form. A user can then authenticate to an HTTP virtual server using Digest Authentication.

Windows Server 2003-based Active Directory domains do not require the Store Password Using Reversible Encryption option to be set on accounts created once the forest scheme was updated for a Windows Server 2003 domain controller installation, but IIS 6.0 does need to be enabled to support what is now named Advanced Digest Authentication. To enable support for Advanced Digest Authentication you need to run the following command:

cscript adsutil.vbs set w3svc/UseDigestSSP 1

Note Exchange servers in a front-end and back-end scenario do not support Digest Authentication. If Digest Authentication is needed, the user must log on directly to the back-end server.

SSL Certificate Authentication

All of the previous authentication methods suffer from two potential flaws that are closely related; they require users to remember their passwords and not to disclose them to anyone.

In organizations that cannot run the risk of passwords becoming known it is possible to implement alternate authentication systems, such as SSL Certificate Authentication, which do not require the user to remember a password. The support for this mode of authentication uses digital certificates and is built into both Internet Explorer and IIS.

The digital certificate is stored either in the user's profile or on a smart card. Smart cards provide better protection than a certificate stored in the user's profile because a smart card requires two-factor authentication: to have knowledge of the PIN number and to physically have the smart card. If the digital certificate is stored in the user's profile the user can opt for Windows to prompt for a password before the certificate is used, protecting it from anyone who has been able to access the logon session.

Certificate Authentication requires an SSL session. For initial configuration you require two certificates, the first being the server authentication certificate associated with the Exchange Server virtual server that you are authenticating and the second certificate being the user's personal digital certificate, which needs to be capable of Client Authentication (see Figure 12-23).

Figure 12-23   Digital certificate capable of authenticating a client to the server

Once both the server and the user have their certificates, and the server certificate is installed by following the instructions in "Configuring SSL on a Virtual Server," found later in this chapter you will be able to allow the user to present the digital certificate as a method of authentication.

With a valid client certificate and a client application that supports certificate logon, when you attempt to connect to the server you will be prompted to select your digital certificate, unless you have only one valid certificate. If you have a single valid certificate, you will be logged on automatically unless the use of the certificate requires a password. If your certificate is installed on a smart card you will need to insert the card and enter your PIN number each time that it is inserted into the smart card reader.

Only the HTTP and NNTP services in IIS let you set SSL Certificate Authentication as a means of log on. Exchange System Manager is used to configure the NNTP virtual server and IIS Manager to configure the HTTP virtual server. The configuration of certificate authentication in IIS is done directly in IIS Manager and not Exchange System Manager, as would be expected. It is also possible to request a digital certificate as a means of logging on to a firewall such as ISA Server before that firewall forwards your request to the published server.

Implementing Client Certificates in IIS Manager

On the website that is hosting the HTTP virtual server you need to ensure that the site has a digital certificate installed and that the site can listen on the default port for SSL traffic (443).

> **Important**   The default Exchange Virtual Server has the SSL certificate and port configured in IIS Manager whereas additional HTTP virtual servers have the SSL port configured in Exchange System Manager and the certificate configured in IIS Manager.

Once the configuration for SSL is complete, in IIS Manager you enable the Require Client Certificate option, which is found in the Directory Security tab of the website you are configuring. The setting is available by clicking Edit in the Secure Communications area of the dialog box. Require Secure Channel needs to be enabled before the Require Client Certificates option can be checked. This is shown in Figure 12-24.

Figure 12-24   Enabling client certificates as a method of authentication in IIS Manager

If the client digital certificate contains an e-mail address that matches an e-mail address of a mailbox in the Exchange organization, and the digital certificate is from a trusted issuer, it will be accepted and the user will log on successfully.

Implementing Client Certificates in ISA Server

If the Outlook Web Access website is made available to the user via a Web Publishing rule in ISA Server it is possible to pre-authenticate the user when the connection reaches the firewall and to use SSL Certificate Authentication at this point. This is enabled by choosing to authenticate the Web Listener object in ISA Server 2000 or 2004.

More Info   Full instructions for the pre-authentication of user accounts for Outlook Web Access can be found in the "ISAServer.org ISA Server 2000 Exchange 2000/2003 Secure Remote E-mail Access Deployment Kit" at *http://www.tacteam.net/isaserverorg/exchangekit/2003clientcertauth/2003clientcertauth.htm*.

Authentication Precedence

When a virtual server is configured to support multiple authentication methods (in all but HTTP), the user decides which authentication method to support. For non-HTTP clients, it is common to find a setting that says which authentication method the application will support. For example, Outlook Express gives the option for the user to choose to Log On Using Secure Password Authentication, which will be any secure authentication option supported by both the client and server.

The HTTP server will send the supported authentication methods to the client upon connection, and the client browser will process them in the order received, assuming that anonymous is not an option. If anonymous authentication is enabled, the client browser will never be prompted to log on and will therefore not be presented with a list of possible ways to authenticate. If anonymous is not an option, the configured authentication methods should be sent to the client browser with the most secure first in the list. If the client does not understand the first authentication method in the list, it will downgrade to the next available method and so on, failing to authenticate if none of the server presented methods are supported by the client.

The following is an example of the headers returned by an IIS 6.0 server when requiring authentication (not all headers are shown), though it can be seen that the order of the WWW-Authenticate header is in a priority based on security with Kerberos (Negotiate) at the top of the list:

```
HTTP/1.1 401 Unauthorized
Via: 1.0 PROXY_SERVER_NAME
Content-Type: text/html
Server: Microsoft-IIS/6.0
WWW-Authenticate: Negotiate
WWW-Authenticate: NTLM
WWW-Authenticate: Basic realm="domain_name"
X-Powered-By: ASP.NET
```

Windows 2000 Server lists Digest Authentication after Basic Authentication, so to enforce Digest Authentication on a Windows 2000 Server you need to disable Basic Authentication. The order of the supported authentication methods is correct in Windows Server 2003, in that Basic is listed after Digest, which is listed after Windows Integrated.

Setting Security Options

In addition to setting the Authentication and Digital Certificate options on the HTTP virtual servers, there are a number of options that can further secure each HTTP virtual server.

Each HTTP virtual server is configured by default to support the correct configuration needed for each of the HTTP applications supported in Exchange Server. Attempts to access these applications returns HTTP/1.1 403 Forbidden if the settings are set incorrectly in Exchange System Manager. Changing the security settings in IIS Manager will result in them being overwritten when the DS2MB process next runs.

The default Access Control settings on the /exchange, /exadmin and /public virtual directories are Read, Write, Script Source Access, and Directory Browsing. If Write is disabled on /exchange or /public you cannot use Outlook Web Access to send e-mail messages, just to read them, and if Script Source Access is disabled on the same virtual directories you allow the possibility of a user executing a script on the server when it should have been downloaded for viewing.

The default Execute Permissions on the above three virtual directories is None. This is not an issue on /exadmin and /exchange, but if a workflow application is created in a public folder that relies on an ASP or Common Gateway Interface (CGI) Web-based interface, the /public virtual directory will need to have Scripts (for ASP) or Scripts and Executables (for CGI) enabled upon it to allow the application to run.

Note   The Outlook Web Access Web Administration Exchange Server download can be used to customize many of the Outlook Web Access settings described within this chapter. It can be downloaded from *http://www.microsoft.com/exchange/downloads/*.

Installing a Security Certificate on the Server

A major consideration in providing e-mail to clients, especially clients on the Internet, is the protection of the data connection from eavesdroppers. Earlier in this chapter we looked at how to protect a client's authentication to Exchange Server, but this does nothing to protect the download and upload of e-mail to Exchange Server or the protection of selected e-mail on their entire journey from the sender to the recipient.

In this section we will look at protecting the client to server communications (including the server-to-server when in a front-end and back-end topology), and in Chapter 13, "Implementing Exchange 2003 Security," we will look at how to secure an e-mail message during its entire journey, sender to recipient, which also protects it from being read if it falls into the hands of the wrong recipient.

Configuring SSL on a Virtual Server

Each of the Exchange Server virtual servers allows the transmission of the data to be encrypted using SSL. Though the configuration of SSL needs to be completed on each virtual server that wants to implement encryption, the steps are the same for each virtual server regardless of protocol.

Before you can implement any form of SSL or TLS (TLS is the version of SSL incorporated into the TCP/IP standard) you need to obtain a digital certificate for the virtual server that is able to perform Server Authentication. Different digital certificates have different purposes, and Server Authentication is the purpose assigned to a certificate that can be used to encrypt client-to-server and server-to-server communications. The certificates purpose can be found in the Enhanced Key Usage field of a digital certificate (see Figure 12-25).

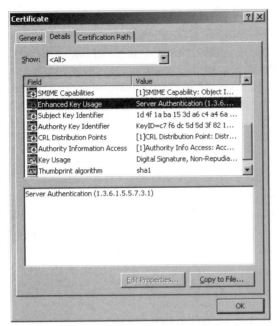

Figure 12-25   The Enhanced Key Usage field of a digital certificate

A digital certificate is easily generated by Windows, but to be a usable digital certificate it needs to be signed (or validated) by a CA. These CAs fall into one of three categories. The first of these is to validate your digital certificate with a trusted public certification authority (CA), such as Verisign or Thawte. The second is to use a private or internal organization CA, and the third is using a certificate from a test CA. Test CAs are an excellent way to prove the steps included in this book will work in your environment without the cost of purchasing a real certificate.

Tip   The majority of public certification authorities provide test certificates with a limited lifespan. To use a test CA you will need to install the CAs root certificate on all machines that will be involved in connecting to your test network.

The choice between the first and second category of CA is down to which clients/servers will use the virtual server that is being protected. If your organization has an internal CA and all the clients are configured to trust that CA (by the installation of the CAs root certificate on all the machines in the organization), and only clients on organization computers will use this virtual server, then your internal certificates will work. The moment that the virtual server will be used by computers that are from outside your organization it will require a certificate from a CA that all these parties trust.

> **More Info**   If the communication is between limited parties, a private CA that all parties trust can be installed, in order to avoid having to purchase a certificate from a public CA. Installing and configuring a Public Key Infrastructure (PKI) using Windows Server Certification Authority is covered in Chapter 13, "Implementing Exchange 2003 Security."

The steps to obtain your digital certificate will depend upon the process at the certification authority you choose to issue your Server Authentication certificate, but even before that stage you will need to generate the certificate request. The certificate request process on Exchange Server and IIS generates a file containing the public key and stores the private key on the server where the request is generated. This process of generating, storing, and processing SSL transactions is performed in Windows by the Crypto API.

> **Important**   It is important to be aware that the digital certificate is bound to the name of the server that you are protecting. A certificate is needed for each unique server name that clients and other servers will connect to.

In a network where you want to protect more than one virtual server with a digital certificate, and each virtual server is for a different protocol, then it is important to consider the placement of the secure virtual servers. If each virtual server is located on a different server, and will therefore have a different name, you will need a distinct digital certificate for each server. This could be quite costly if using a public certification authority and, regardless of cost, will introduce numerous certificates to process and manage. Therefore, consider dedicating a machine to SSL processing using the same digital certificate for all the virtual servers that need it. For example, the School of Fine Art wants to SSL-protect its Outlook Web Access installation and IMAP4 client connections. If it runs these protocols on the same Exchange server, it can purchase and manage a single digital certificate for the mail.fineartschool.net FQDN. If each protocol ran on a different server, a digital certificate would be needed for imap.fineartschool.net and owa.fineartschool.net, each of the FQDNs used for SSL.

> **Tip**   In a load-balanced environment where more than one server answers to the same name a single digital certificate is required. This certificate will be generated on one of the servers, and then copied to all the other servers once it has been validated by the certification authority.

The process of generating a digital certificate is the same regardless of which protocol it is being generated for. If you look closely at the first page of the certificate generation wizard (Figure 12-26) you will notice that the same wizard runs for each protocol regardless of which protocol was chosen as the wizard reads, "Welcome to the Web Server Certificate Wizard."

Figure 12-26   The Welcome to the Web Server Certificate Wizard

The digital certificate generation wizard is started from Exchange System Manager for all protocols apart from HTTP. For the NNTP, SMTP, POP3, and IMAP4 protocols, in the virtual server properties on the Access tab of the properties dialog box, you click the Certificate button. The screenshot, as shown in Figure 12-26, is the first page you will see. To generate a certificate request for an HTTP virtual server you need to use IIS Manager and the properties of the website that holds the Exchange virtual directories. In the properties dialog box, on the Directory Security tab, click the Server Certificate button.

The Welcome To The Web Server Certificate Wizard opens. The following is the process for completing this wizard:

■   On the Server Certificate page, choose Create A New Certificate.

- On the Delayed Or Immediate Request page, select Prepare The Request Now, But Send Later unless you are using a Enterprise CA hosted as part of your Active Directory. If you choose Send The Request Immediately To An Online Certification Authority, some of the following steps will be different from that described here.

- Enter a name for the certificate on the Name And Security Settings page. This name will be visible within the certificate. The Bit Length can remain at 1024, increasing it for more secure purposes.

- On the Organization Information page, enter the name of the Organization and Organization Unit.

- This will take you to the most important page in the wizard, the Your Site's Common Name page (as shown in Figure 12-27). The value entered here must be the same as that used by any client of the virtual server. For example, if users connect directly to this virtual server from the Internet, enter the FQDN of the server; if clients connect from internal sources only, using the NetBIOS name of the server is sufficient. If you are using SSL bridging in ISA Server (clients connect to ISA Server using HTTPS, and then the ISA Server connects to the HTTP virtual server using a new HTTPS session), choose the common name based on whether this is the certificate for the virtual server or for your ISA Server. The virtual server works best with a NetBIOS name and the ISA Server needs a certificate with the FQDN, though with a suitable host/DNS configuration the same certificate can be used on both servers.

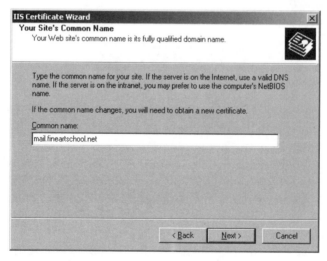

Figure 12-27   Ensuring that the common name of the certificate matches the FQDN of the virtual server that will provide SSL support

- On the Geographical Information page enter the correct details for your organization, using the full name of any state and not a shortened version (for example, Washington and not WA).

- If you are not submitting the certificate to an online CA, you will need to save the certificate request to the hard disk and upload it to the CA during the certificate signing stage. The Certificate Request File Name step provides a default name and allows you to change it.

- The final step in the creation of the certificate request file is the Request File Summary page. Here you would check that everything is correct, and then click Next.

- The Completing The Web Server Certificate Wizard reminds you of the file that you will need to submit to the CA.

Once you have the certificate request (default file name is c:\certreq.txt), you can browse to the certification authority's website. Enter the required details and upload the certificate request file. If you cannot upload the file directly and need to enter it, include all the information, such as the header and footer text, unless the CA informs you not to.

At some time following your submittal of the certificate request to the CA, you will receive the digital certificate back from the CA. This key is now digitally signed by the CA's private key, proving that they issued it, and they are happy you are who you claim to be. The process for checking your claim and the degree of trust the CA places in your claim will differ among various certification authorities. For example, the enterprise version of Microsoft Certificate Server determines trust based upon your successful logon to the CA server.

To finish the installation of the digital certificate on the Exchange server, you need to take the signed certificate given to you by the CA back to the server on which you generated the certificate request. It cannot be installed on any other machine; and if that machine has been rebuilt, or the pending request has been deleted between the request having been generated and the certificate being returned, you will have to start all over again.

Once you have the digital certificate back from the CA, return to the Certificate button on the Access tab of the virtual server properties dialog box. This time the wizard looks different and will prompt you to Process The Pending Request And Install The Certificate. This dialog box can be seen in Figure 12-28.

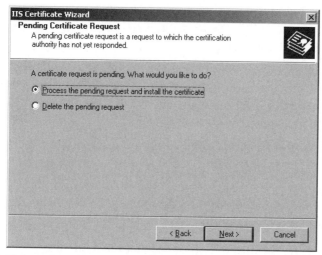

Figure 12-28   Finishing the digital certificate installation

This will involve browsing the file system for the digital certificate response file that you just received and confirming that the details in the digital certificate are correct. Once this has been done, you should delete both the certificate request file and the digital certificate returned to you from the CA because these are no longer needed. Then, it is important to do a full System State backup of the server to ensure that you have a backup of the installed digital certificate.

> **Important**   You must also install the public key (or root) certificate of the CA that signed your digital certificate on all machines that will communicate securely with this virtual server. The best CA to use is a CA whose root certificate is already trusted in Windows.

If you need the certificate on an SSL Accelerator device, you need to export the digital certificate to the other servers that need it, and on those servers import it again. If you are doing SSL offloading using ISA Server, you need to install this certificate into the computer certificate store and not the user's certificate store. This is done by creating a new Microsoft Management Console (MMC) file containing the Certificates snap-in. In ISA Server 2000, it is important that the ISA Management console is not open at this time or ISA Server will not notice the added certificate until the management program is restarted. This is not an issue with ISA Server 2004.

> **Warning** Exporting and importing the certificate requires you to set a password during exporting, and we recommend that you do not enable the option to Mark The Cert As Exportable because you should only want to be able to export the certificate from one or two servers and not all of the servers in the network that get this certificate installed on them.

Once the virtual server is configured to support SSL connections, you can set the options to stop non-encrypted connections from connecting successfully. This is covered later in this chapter in "Enforcing a Secure Communication."

Enabling SSL on Additional HTTP Virtual Servers

When you add a digital certificate to any protocol virtual server, the virtual server is able to perform secure communications immediately, though this is not the case with the additional HTTP virtual servers. If the default HTTP virtual server is already installed with a digital certificate, any additional HTTP virtual server with a certificate will not start because IIS attempts to bind port 443 to all IP addresses, only to find that this socket is taken. The System Log in Event Viewer will report:

Cannot register the URL prefix 'https://*:443/' for site '###'. The necessary network binding may already be in use. The site has been deactivated. The data field contains the error number.

To enable the additional HTTP virtual servers to listen for SSL connections, they need to be configured with two port identities using Exchange System Manager, as shown in Figure 12-29. When the additional HTTP virtual server was created, it would have needed to use a host name (what IIS calls a host header) or a unique IP address. Because SSL connections cannot use host headers, the virtual server needs to be configured to use a unique IP address for port 80 and the same IP address for port 443. The problem in this configuration comes when trying to add port 443 to the single identity already created on the virtual server.

In Exchange System Manager, you cannot set an SSL port when the standard port is already configured, so you need to add a second identity, and in this identity delete "80" from the TCP Port field. Only when the TCP Port and Host Name fields are clear does the SSL Port field become available. Ensuring the correct IP address is selected, enter port 443 into the SSL field. You cannot use ports other than 80 or 443 in a front-end and back-end configuration.

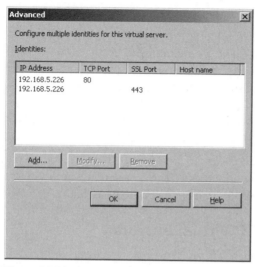

Figure 12-29   Configuring the SSL Port for additional HTTP virtual servers

Configuring SSL in a Front-End and Back-End Scenario

In a load-balanced Exchange Server front-end and back-end topology, you can choose the option to Copy Or Move The Certificate To A Remote Server Site. This option is found from the Certificate button on the virtual server's properties dialog box, Access tab.

In a front-end and back-end Exchange Server network, only the front-end servers can use SSL protection. The communication between the front-end and back-end servers is never encrypted and is always the clear-text version of the protocol. With the HTTP protocol in Exchange Server 2003, it is configured to be as secure as possible, using Integrated Windows Authentication if possible to protect the users' credentials. The POP3 and IMAP4 protocols are always clear text including the users' credentials. To protect the communication between the front-end and back-end servers you need to configure IP Security (IPSec).

The back-end Exchange servers can have SSL enabled on them for scenarios where users connect directly to them, but they need to be able to accept communications in the clear to support connections from the front-end servers.

Configuring IPSec in a Front-End/Back-End Scenario

An Exchange Server 2003 back-end server running on Windows Server 2003 will be able to use IPSec protection in communications from the front-end servers regardless of whether or not the back-end server is running with Microsoft Cluster Server. If the back-end server is running on a Windows 2000 Server platform, IPSec cannot be used to protect the connection to an Exchange Server cluster.

> **More Info** Microsoft Knowledge Base article 821839, "How to Configure IPSec on an Exchange Server 2003 Back-End Server That Is Running on a Windows Server 2003 Server Cluster" at *http://go.microsoft.com/fwlink/ ?linkid=3052&kbid=821839* discusses why IPSec does not failover in a Windows 2000 Server environment and the registry key needed to reduce the renegotiation time of IPSec in the event of unexpected failure of the cluster server when running on Windows Server 2003 clusters.

To encrypt communications between the front-end and back-end servers, you need to implement IPSec for all traffic running on port 80 (HTTP), 110 (POP3), and 143 (IMAP4). If your Exchange server is dedicated to specific protocols, you can reduce the requirements of IPSec to just those protocols. For additional information about how to configure IPSec, search for IPSec in the Windows Server 2003 Help and Support Center.

Outlook Web Access Change Password Feature

Outlook Web Access will prompt users when their passwords are due to expire, but in Exchange Server 2003, the default is not to allow password changes via Outlook Web Access, unlike earlier versions of Exchange Server. If you are running your Outlook Web Access session over a securely encrypted link, you can enable the password change functionality by setting a registry key on the Exchange server, creating a website virtual directory and implementing a change in the metabase.

The `DisablePassword` registry key (at `HKEY_LOCAL_MACHINE\SYSTEM\CurrentControlSet\Services\MSExchangeWEB`) is set to 1 by default in an Exchange Server 2003 installation. An upgrade from Exchange Server 2000 will leave the registry key value at 0. This value needs to be 0 on all back-end Exchange servers for the Change Password button to appear in the Options page of Outlook Web Access. The change does not require a restart of any service, but will be implemented for users who log on after the change has been made. Current users will not see any change until they log on again.

Once the registry key is set, a virtual directory needs to be created on each front-end Exchange server. The virtual directory must be part of the Outlook Web Access website, and if you have multiple Outlook Web Access sites, the directory will be needed under each one. The name of the directory is iisadmpwd and it must point to the %windir%\System32\Inetsrv\iisadmpwd folder. The default settings in IIS are suitable for this virtual directory (read and scripts), but the directory does not need to be a dedicated application.

Finally, if the Web server is IIS 6.0, a metabase change is needed. The w3svc/ passwordchangeflags metabase location is set by default to 6. As this metabase key is a bitmask, it means that the password change functionality of IIS is disabled (a value of 2 in the metabase key) and also that the advance notification of password expiration is disabled (a value of 4 in the metabase key). Bitmasking means that the metabase key value is the sum of all the options you want to set, and setting it to 0 implements password change over SSL connections only. A value of 1 allows password changes over non-SSL connections, but this is not recommended.

To change the metabase to allow password changes, enter **cscript adsutil.vbs set w3svc/passwordchangeflags 0** on the command line. This will set the metabase value for all websites. If you want different settings on different HTTP virtual servers, set the metabase value at **w3svc/#/passwordchangeflags** where # is the ID of the site that the change needs to be made on. A change at the site level will override a setting at the root level, leaving the value at root for all the other HTTP virtual servers on the computer.

> **Caution**   The change password functionality in Windows Server 2003 has some errors in its implementation. Please review Microsoft Knowledge Base article 833734, "You experience various problems when you use the Password Change pages in IIS 6.0" at *http://go.microsoft.com/fwlink/ ?linkid=3052&kbid=833734* before implementing it in a production environment.

Enforcing Secure Communication

Once the certificate is installed on the virtual server, you can begin to implement secure connections. With the certificate in place, you can perform both secure and clear-text communications and so the first step is to restrict selected virtual servers to secure communications only.

Before you inform clients that secure communications are available, you need to make sure that any firewall is open for the correct ports. The secure ports are not the same as the clear-text ports apart from the SMTP virtual server, where both encrypted and clear operate over TCP port 25. Table 12-7 has a list of the default secure ports for each Exchange Server virtual server protocol.

Table 12-7   Default SSL Ports

Protocol	Well-known SSL port
HTTP	443
NNTP	563
IMAP4	993
POP3	995

Viewing and Changing the SSL Port Number

In each virtual server, the port number that the protocol listens on can be found on the General tab of the properties dialog box, and then by clicking the Advanced button. As before, the default HTTP virtual server for Exchange Server needs checking in IIS Manager, but additional HTTP virtual servers are viewed in Exchange System Manager.

Adding additional secure ports or changing the default is supported apart from front-end and back-end topology where the communication between the front-end and back-end server only operates over the default non-encrypted port.

Requiring Encrypted Sessions

To force clients to only use encrypted sessions, you need to make two changes. The first is to allow just the secure ports through your firewalls, closing the default ports, and the second is to configure the virtual server to reject non-encrypted communications. The first of these stops Internet clients from using the non-encrypted ports, and the second of these enforces the same restriction on the LAN.

For the SMTP, POP3, and IMAP4 protocols this change is made on the properties dialog box of the virtual server in question using Exchange System Manager. The option to force SSL for these protocols can be found on the Access tab, and you should have the Communication button available. If the Communication button is not available, it means that this virtual server does not have a valid certificate installed. For the HTTP virtual servers, the steps are completed in IIS Manager via the Edit button in the Secure Communications area of the Directory Security tab on the properties dialog box of the website that you are making the changes on. The only way to force SSL for NNTP connections is to stop the NNTP virtual server listening on port 119.

Though each resulting dialog box looks different, the option to require SSL communications is always a check box. Once the option to enforce SSL is chosen you can further secure the connection by requiring a 128-bit session key to be used. Not all operating systems or countries support 128-bit session keys, so your client base and location will determine whether you can require 128-bit session key encryption.

Note The longer the session key the more processing that is required to manage the session, but the more secure the data will be.

SSL Offloading

SSL offloading is the use of a device between the client and the virtual server that decrypts the SSL communication into clear text before it reaches the Exchange server. This removes from the Exchange server the requirement to process the session to the virtual server over an encrypted protocol. This results in an Exchange server that is able to perform its functions faster because it does not need to do any decryption or encryption. But, this can have two side effects: the first is that part of the connection is in clear text and the second is that the Exchange server may see the connection as HTTP and so in the case of Outlook Web Access generate HTML that contains *http://* URLs and not *https://* URLs. Unless this second side effect is mitigated it will make Outlook Web Access unusable with SSL offloaders.

An SSL offloading device can be either an OSI layer 7 advanced firewall, such as Microsoft ISA Server, or an SSL Accelerator network card in the Exchange server. If the SSL Accelerator network card integrates with Windows, you will be able to select the device from the Available Providers dialog box during the digital certificate request generation. This is available by checking Select Cryptographic Service Provider (CSP) For This Certificate on the Name And Security Settings page of the wizard. Clicking Next will display the Available Providers dialog box, which is shown in Figure 12-30.

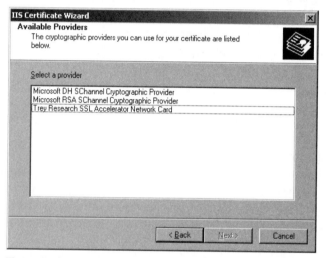

Figure 12-30   Selecting an installed SSL Accelerator card

If the SSL offloader is a separate device from the Exchange server, it works by terminating the SSL session and creating a new HTTP session to the Exchange server. This means that part of the connection is in clear text and that the Exchange server sees the connection as an HTTP connection.

The clear-text portion of the communication is always between the SSL offloader and the Exchange server, and if this is on an organization's LAN in a switched network, the possibility of interception is reduced and therefore can be an acceptable configuration. If a greater distance exists between the SSL offloader and the Exchange server, additional encryption such as IPSec should be considered.

The second problem with SSL offloading causes issues with the HTML generation of the Outlook Web Access pages because the Exchange server generates the Outlook Web Access pages based upon the connection type that it sees. If an HTTP connection terminates at the Exchange server, it will place *http://* references into the returned Web page. This will result in the client dropping back to an HTTP session. Depending upon any firewall configuration, this clear text session might be dropped, but if the firewall allows traffic inbound on TCP port 80, then the session will not be dropped but begins sending everything in clear text when the connection is initially started securely. Additionally, the use of Forms Based Authentication requires SSL. Therefore introducing an SSL offloader requires additional configuration on the Exchange server.

SSL Offloading and Outlook Web Access

Due to the way Forms Based Authentication operates, two registry keys can be used to alter its behavior. These registry keys are `AllowRetailHTTPAuth` and `SSLOffloaded`.

When using an SSL offloader and any authentication method apart from Forms Based Authentication, Exchange Server will render the Outlook Web Access pages with *http://* URLs. To generate *https://* URLs additional information must be sent to the Exchange server to indicate that the client is using an HTTPS session regardless of the session received by the Exchange server.

This happens automatically when using ISA Server 2004 to terminate the SSL session and requires the setting of the DWORD AddFrontEndHttpsHeader registry key on an ISA Server 2000. This registry key is added to `HKEY_LOCAL_MACHINE\SYS-TEM\CurrentControlSet\Services\W3Proxy\Parameters` on the ISA Server 2000 server. To complete the change, the Web proxy service needs restarting. With ISA Server 2004, or ISA Server 2000 and the registry key, the connection from the firewall to the Exchange server in HTTP includes the header Front-End-Https: On. Exchange Server receives this header and renders the pages with *https://* instead of *http://* URLs.

If you are using an SSL offloader that does not provide the above header and you can add custom HTTP headers, the addition of Front-End-Https: On solves this problem. If you cannot add custom headers, you need to install an ISAPI filter on the Exchange server to add this header for you.

More Info   More information about this filter and installation instructions can be found in the Microsoft Knowledge Base article 327800, "A new option that allows Exchange and OWA to always use SSL (HTTPS)" at *http://go.microsoft.com/fwlink/?linkid=3052&kbid=327800*.

SSL Offloading and Forms Based Authentication

Forms Based Authentication requires by default SSL to operate and the Front-End-Https: On header does not have any effect with this authentication method. To disable the use of SSL entirely when using Forms Based Authentication, the `AllowRetailHTTPAuth` registry key can be set. The `AllowRetailHTTPAuth` registry key is not present by default and should be created at `HKEY_LOCAL_MACHINE\SYSTEM\CurrentControlSet\Services\MSExchangeWeb\OWA` of type `DWORD`. To force Forms Based Authentication without SSL, set this value to **1** and restart IIS.

When an SSL offloader is used to improve SSL performance, the Exchange server running Forms Based Authentication sees the connection as HTTP and not HTTPS. This means that it will provide Basic Authentication instead of Forms Based Authentication upon connection and fall back to an HTTP session. To tell the Exchange server that the session is HTTPS when it is at the client, the `SSLOffloaded` registry key is needed. This key is type `DWORD` and needs to be created at the same location as the `AllowRetailHTTPAuth` key above. To tell the Exchange server that an SSL offloader is in use, the value of the registry key needs to be **1**.

> **Note**   In a front-end and back-end network when setting the `SSLOffloaded` registry key on the front-end server the Front-End-Https: On header is added by the front-end server on its connections to the back-end server.

The difference between `AllowRetailHTTPAuth` and `SSLOffloaded` is that the first changes all the hyperlinks in the Outlook Web Access pages to *http://* and the second, even though the connection to the Exchange server is HTTP, sets the links within Outlook Web Access to *https://*. This is because with the second option, the client is using HTTPS and if Outlook Web Access contained links stating *http://*, it would cause security errors when rendering the page on the client.

There are three different ways that Forms Based Authentication and SSL can be implemented:

- **HTTPS from the client direct to the front-end Exchange server**   This needs no additional settings on either the front-end or back-end server, but it does require the front-end server to have a digital certificate installed and answer on port 443 and not port 80.

- **HTTPS to an SSL accelerator, and then HTTP to front-end server**   The front-end Exchange servers require the `SSLOffloaded` registry key to be set to **1**. The front-end server requires no certificate installation for the support of SSL, but the certificate needs to be installed on the acceleration server.

- **HTTP used for client to front-end server**   This setting requires the `AllowRetailHTTPAuth` registry set on both the front-end and back-end Exchange servers to ensure that Outlook Web Access never contains references to *https://* URLs.

Registry Keys, SSL Offloading, and Outlook Web Access

Table 12-8 contains a summary of the success or failure of connecting to an Outlook Web Access website, depending upon the authentication option in use, the state of the `SSLOffloaded` registry key on the Exchange servers and the Front-End-Https HTTP header on any ISA Server or SSL offloader device.

Table 12-8 Outlook Web Access, SSL, ISA Server, and Authentication Summary

Auth mode	SSLOffloaded	Front-End-Https header	Result
NTLM	Not needed	0 or 1	Fail. NTLM does not work through firewalls.
Basic	Not needed	0	Fail. If the firewall allows HTTP it may appear to succeed, but it is not secure anymore. The session downgrades to HTTP and requires user to log on twice each session, once for HTTP and once for the initial HTTPS connection.
Basic	Not needed	1	Success
Forms Based Authentication	0	Not needed	Fail to do Forms Based Authentication. Basic Authentication occurs instead.
Forms Based Authentication	1	Not needed	Success

Using SSL and Windows Mobile Devices

When you are using Windows Mobile devices, such as Pocket PC 2002, 2003, and Smartphone, in a test environment with a digital certificate issued by a test or untrusted CA, you can potentially have a problem because the device does not trust the CA. To avoid the need to install the test CA public certificate on these devices, the Disable Certificate Verification tool can be downloaded from Microsoft to stop the device needing to check the validity of the certificate used during the SSL session. The session is still encrypted, it is just that the criteria of trust that is part of digital certificate environment is ignored. The Disable Certificate Verification tool can be downloaded from *http://www.microsoft.com/exchange/downloads/*.

Once your testing is finished, and you want to add a root CA certificate to your Windows Mobile devices, those based on the Pocket PC 2002 platform require the use of the Add Root Certificate tool. This tool can be downloaded from *http://www.microsoft.com/downloads/details.aspx?FamilyId=ECFDE1C7-36C9-4C13-986E-8A46790F61E4&displaylang=en*. This tool is not needed for Pocket PC 2003-based devices because they can add certificates without additional tools.

Configuring RPC over HTTP

RPC over HTTP is a new feature available to users of Outlook 2003 and Exchange Server 2003 running on a Windows Server 2003 platform. It is the ability to use Outlook over an HTTPS session across the Internet rather than needing to use Outlook Web Access. This is achieved by the encapsulation of RPC packets in HTTP packets. Outlook uses RPC to connect to an Exchange server when running on a local area network, but it is typical for firewalls to block access to TCP port 135, which would allow the use of Outlook while on the Internet. Without RPC access over the Internet, earlier versions of Outlook and Exchange Server would require a VPN session to be in place before Outlook could be used.

Outlook 2003 supports the encapsulation of its RPC packets inside HTTP packets, which can cross the Internet and pass through corporate firewalls. The Outlook clients connect to an RPC proxy server that removes the HTTP encapsulation, forwarding the RPC packets to the Exchange Server mailbox servers or to the Active Directory and global catalog servers when those services are needed.

The configuration of RPC over HTTP has been made easier upon the release of Exchange Server 2003 SP1, with the biggest change being the removal of the need to configure your global catalog servers to support this process. Additionally, in the initial release of Exchange Server, the installation of all the required components and registry key changes was a manual task. The configuration of RPC over HTTP, once SP1 has been installed, moves entirely to Exchange System Manager, removing the need for registry changes and restarts on numerous servers on your LAN. Even so, implementing this communication network should be first fully implemented on a test network and then configured on the production network at a suitable time.

The configuration instructions contained within this book will cover in brief the steps needed. Full instructions for the configuration of RPC over HTTP can be found in the article, "Exchange Server 2003 RPC over HTTP Deployment Scenarios," which is part of the Exchange library. The Exchange Server 2003 Technical Documentation Library can be reached at *http://go.microsoft.com/fwlink/?LinkID=21277*.

RPC over HTTP Installation Requirements

The following must be in place before RPC over HTTP will work:

- Global catalog servers running on Windows Server 2003.
- Exchange Server 2003 running on Windows Server 2003.
- Exchange Server 2003 SP1 on all front-end servers.
- Exchange Server 2003 on all back-end servers.
- Exchange Server 2003 SP1 on all back-end servers is optional because you can configure the back-end servers by connecting from a SP1 front-end server to complete the configuration.

- An installation of the RPC over HTTP proxy server software on each front-end server.

- Clients must use Outlook 2003 running Windows XP SP2 or SP1 and hotfix 331320 (see Microsoft Knowledge Base article 331320 for the hotfix at *http://go.microsoft.com/fwlink/?linkid=3052&kbid=331320*).

- Firewall ports configured to allow SSL traffic inbound or if using an advanced firewall such as ISA Server, to publish the /rpc/* virtual directory of each front-end server.

RPC over HTTP Deployment Scenarios

Though the recommended scenario for the deployment of RPC over HTTP is to use an advanced firewall to create your perimeter network and install the RPC Proxy software on the front-end servers, other options exist.

Front-End and Back-End Server Architecture with ISA Server on the Perimeter Network

This network design uses an ISA Server (2000 or 2004) either within the perimeter network composed of other firewalls or by using the ISA Server firewall to create the perimeter network. If the ISA Server delineates the perimeter/LAN boundary, the external firewall (perimeter/Internet boundary) needs to allow TCP port 443 inbound. This design can be seen in Figure 12-31.

The ISA Server will terminate the SSL connection, inspecting the traffic to ensure that it is composed of valid HTTP URLs and verbs and only destined for the /rpc virtual directory of the Internet published name of the RPC over HTTP service; for example, the connection must be to mail.woodgrovebank.com/rpc to be accepted. The ISA Server will then either create a second HTTPS session or initiate a clear-text session and forward the HTTP data to the RPC proxy server on the front-end servers. If ISA Server is being used to offload the SSL by creating an HTTP session to the RPC proxy server, an additional registry key will be needed on the RPC proxy server to allow HTTP sessions because the default RPC proxy configuration requires SSL.

When the data arrives at the RPC proxy server, the HTTP protocol is stripped away leaving the RPC commands, which are then sent to the relevant Exchange or Active Directory server.

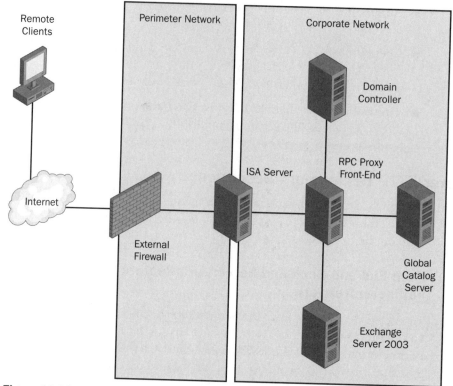

Figure 12-31   Front-end and back-end server architecture with ISA Server on the perimeter network boundary

RPC Proxy Server in Perimeter Network

This is not a recommended scenario because it requires the opening of more ports than above. The perimeter/LAN boundary firewall will need to allow TCP ports 6001, 6002, and 6004 into all the Exchange Server 2003 mailbox servers.

Single Server Environments

Although it is a supported configuration, specific settings are needed in networks where the Exchange server is the only domain controller and global catalog server. This configuration still requires firewall protection, and the use of an advanced firewall in or composing the perimeter network is recommended over a basic port filtering firewall.

Upgrading RPC over HTTP to Service Pack 1

If you have a working RPC over HTTP messaging system that was in place before the installation of Exchange Server 2003 SP1, it will remain operational after SP1 has been installed, but you might find that the RPC over HTTP dialog box in Exchange System Manager reports that your system is not configured for RPC over HTTP.

The configuration of performing the upgrade allows the further addition of RPC over HTTP systems using Exchange System Manager without needing to resort to the previously manual method of configuration. The full process for the upgrade is described in the earlier mentioned article, "Exchange Server 2003 RPC over HTTP Deployment Scenarios." The Exchange Server 2003 Technical Documentation Library can be reached at *http://go.microsoft.com/fwlink/?LinkID=21277.*

The basics of the upgrade process is that you configure each back-end server to be part of the SP1-managed RPC over HTTP environment. This will not break your existing working configuration because all it does is configure the 0x20000000 bit on the heuristics flag of the server in Active Directory and does not change the RPC over HTTP configuration in any way.

You can determine from Active Directory if a machine is a front-end- or back-end-managed RPC over HTTP server by doing an LDAP bitwise comparison of the heuristics flag against 0x20000000. Back-end servers are 0 and front-end servers are 1. The heuristics flag is an Active Directory attribute of the Exchange Server object in:

CN=server_name,CN=Servers,CN=Administrative Group Name,CN=Administrative Groups,CN=Organisation Name,CN=Microsoft Exchange,CN=Services,CN=Configuration,DC=root domain.

You will break your existing RPC over HTTP configuration if you enable the Exchange System Manager options for RPC over HTTP on the front-end servers first. The front-end servers will scan the heuristics flag of each back-end server every 15 minutes and build the correct RPC over HTTP registry key from what is discovered. If the back-end servers are not enabled for SP1 RPC over HTTP management, the registry key will disappear on each managed front-end server within 15 minutes. If you manually enter the correct values back again, it will disappear 15 minutes later.

Important   Upgrade your RPC over HTTP configuration on all the back-end servers and wait for Active Directory replication to occur. Then, and only then, upgrade the configuration on the front-end servers.

If you have many Exchange servers to configure, consider running the TopoManager script, which you can obtain from Microsoft Product Support Services. The purpose of TopoManager is to help add and remove servers to the RPC over HTTP managed topology without needing to connect to each server and configure it directly. It will scan the current RPC over HTTP configuration and update Active Directory with this information. This script can also be run to generate a report of your RPC over HTTP managed topology.

Deploying RPC over HTTP with Exchange Server 2003 SP1

The following steps will only work when all the front-end servers are installed with SP1. The back-end servers do not need to be SP1 for these steps to work, but in that case the configuration must be completed from a front-end server running SP1 connecting remotely to the back-end server.

1. Install the Windows RPC over HTTP networking component on the Exchange front-end servers. Full instructions for each of these steps can be found in the previously mentioned "Exchange Server 2003 RPC over HTTP Deployment Scenarios" article.

2. Configure the Exchange back-end server to act as a target for the Exchange front-end server configured as an RPC proxy server.

3. Configure the Exchange front-end server to act as the RPC proxy server in Exchange System Manager.

4. (Optional) Configure RPC over HTTP for SSL offloading.

5. Create an Outlook profile for your users to use with RPC over HTTP.

RPC over HTTP SP1 Installation Tips

Prior to the SP1 implementation of RPC over HTTP it was required to make a virtual directory in IIS and set numerous registry keys on both front-end Exchange servers and global catalog servers. This is now all finished with if you have a front-end and back-end environment and have installed SP1. The steps to configure RPC over HTTP are listed above and it is as simple as installing the RPC over HTTP proxy server and configuring the options in Exchange System Manager.

If you use a RPC over HTTP proxy that is not an Exchange Server 2003 front-end server, you will need to make the configuration changes manually because Exchange System Manager can only configure RPC proxy servers that have Exchange 2003 installed on them.

If the Exchange server is the server in the network that is also the domain controller and global catalog server, then a registry change will be made by Exchange System Manager to lock the global catalog ports to 6004. This change will require a restart of the server.

If the back-end Exchange servers are not global catalog servers, no changes need to be made to them, which is different from the original release of RPC over HTTP. The SP1 version of RPC over HTTP directs requests for the address book, which would normally go to a global catalog server, to the DSProxy component of the Exchange server. This avoids the need to additionally configure each global catalog server in the network. This means that if you look at the connection information in Outlook, you will not see the names of global catalog servers for the directory, just the Exchange server as a proxy for the directory.

Tip   To see the connection information in Outlook, hold down the CTRL key and right-click the Outlook icon in the notification area of the desktop. Choose Connection Status to view the Exchange Server Connection Status dialog.

Once all the changes are made, the Web Publishing Service needs to be restarted on all front-end servers, and if the back-end server is a combined Exchange Server/ global catalog server the entire server will need restarting. Once the service or server has restarted, a client can be configured and the communication to the server with RPC over HTTP can be tested. The steps to configure the correct profile settings in Outlook 2003 can be found in "Configuring Outlook 2003 to use RPC over HTTP" later in this chapter.

Deploying RPC over HTTP Manually

A number of steps are needed for the full deployment of RPC over HTTP on your network when you do not have SP1 installed or when you use an RPC over HTTP server that is not an Exchange front-end server, and some extra tips are included below.

1. Configure your RPC proxy server. This can be the Exchange front-end server, but it does not need to be when completing this task manually.

2. Configure the RPC virtual directory in Internet Information Services (IIS) on the RPC proxy server.

3. Configure the registry on the RPC proxy server.

4. (Optional) Set the NTDS port for global catalog servers acting as Exchange back-end servers.

5. (Optional) Configure RPC over HTTP for SSL offloading.

6. Create an Outlook profile for your users to use with RPC over HTTP.

RPC over HTTP Manual Installation Tips

In Step 2, if you are configuring many HTTP virtual servers on the same front-end server you will need to ensure that the /rpc virtual directory is configured correctly on each. The installation of the RPC over HTTP proxy server will only configure the /rpc virtual directory on the Default Web Site. To add the directory to other websites on which it is needed, configure the virtual directory as in Step 2 above. Then, using IIS Manager, back up the virtual directory configuration to an XML file (this is a feature of IIS 6.0 only), and create a new virtual directory on each remaining website by using this file to create each virtual directory. This saving of a virtual directory configuration to a file and creating a virtual directory from a file is achieved in IIS Manager by right-clicking the virtual directory and choosing All Tasks, Save Configuration To A File. To create a virtual directory from a file, right-click the parent virtual directory and choose New, Virtual Directory (From File).

> **Important**   In IIS 5.0 you will need to duplicate by hand the exact configuration of the /rpc folder in the Default Web Site because you cannot save the configuration of individual folders to files.

The registry key that is modified during Step 3 above needs to include the NetBIOS name of the local Exchange server twice (once for ports 6001–6002 and once for port 6004), and then repeat for these same ports for all the FQDNs that the server is identified by. For example, if the two back-end servers are wb-exch-be1 and wb-exch-be2, all in the woodgrovebank.com domain, then the registry key, set on the RPC proxy server would read:

```
wb-exch-be1:6001-6002;wb-exch-be2:6001-6002;
wb-exch-be1.woodgrovebank.com:6001-6002;
wb-exch-be2.woodgrovebank.com:6001-6002;
wb-exch-be1:6004;wb-exch-be2:6004;
wb-exch-be1.woodgrovebank.com:6004;
wb-exch-be2.woodgrovebank.com:6004
```

Step 4 is only required in networks where the back-end Exchange server is also a domain controller and global catalog server. If you have a single server network, this setting is also required. This is to fix the port that the global catalog operates on, so that it can be RPC proxied to.

For Step 5, if an ISA Server or other SSL offloader is being used, the RPC proxy setting for AllowAnonymous needs to be configured. This is not the same as the Enable Anonymous Access in IIS Manager. Additional to Step 2, if you are not using SSL offloading, you can force the need to connect to the /rpc virtual directory with SSL by configuring IIS to reject HTTP sessions. If you are doing SSL offloading you cannot set this requirement because connections to this virtual directory from the SSL offloader will be in the clear.

> **Tip**   Remember that upgrading to SP1 removes the need to do any of these steps, apart from installing the RPC proxy on the Exchange front-end server and configuring an SSL offloader if you have them.

Once all the registry keys are set, the Web Publishing Service needs to be restarted on all front-end servers. If changes have been made for Step 4, that affect the combined Exchange server/global catalog server, the entire server will need to be restarted. Once the service or server has restarted, a client can be configured and the communication to the server with RPC over HTTP can be tested.

Configuring Outlook 2003 to use RPC over HTTP

Outlook 2003 is needed to use RPC over HTTP, with some conditions. The operating system must be Windows XP running SP2 or SP1 with hotfix 331320. Once this is in place, the instructions for the configuration of RPC over HTTP can be found in the earlier referenced article.

Note that if you are not connected to the Internet network on which the Exchange servers are running when you first create your profile, Outlook will attempt to resolve your server name and mailbox name. It will fail and display the dialog box shown in Figure 12-32, followed by Figure 12-33. It is important that you click Cancel on this second box to complete the configuration of the profile. If you are connected to the LAN when creating your profile, the Exchange server name is resolved correctly and these two dialog boxes do not appear.

Figure 12-32   Failure to resolve server and user details while configuring Outlook for RPC over HTTP when disconnected from the corporate network

Figure 12-33   Click Cancel when the Check Name process fails to allow completion of the RPC over HTTP configuration when configuring Outlook offline

An Outlook profile for RPC over HTTP is similar to a standard profile for accessing the Exchange server directly on the LAN. Important points in the configuration of the profile are that the server name is the name of your mailbox server, and even though you are accessing this server across the Internet, you do not need to provide a name that can be resolved from the Internet. Remember, that in an RPC over HTTP communication, the RPC session to this mailbox server starts at the RPC proxy and is not connected to directly from the client.

The communication from the client to the RPC proxy is HTTPS and the configuration of Outlook for this server name is found in the Exchange Proxy Settings dialog box, shown in Figure 12-34. This figure shows that the server name is WB-EXCH-BE1.woodgrovebank.com, which is only resolvable internal to the Woodgrove Bank network. The Exchange Proxy Settings dialog box shows that the RPC proxy server is accessible via HTTPS only (because Basic authentication is enabled) and that the name of the RPC proxy is mail.woodgrovebank.com. The RPC proxy (or an SSL offloader device) must be configured with a digital certificate whose CN is that same name, and that digital certificate must be trusted by the client computer. If the certificate is not trusted, or if the name of the server and certificate CN do not match, then Outlook will fail to connect. There will be no error messages, it will just fail to connect.

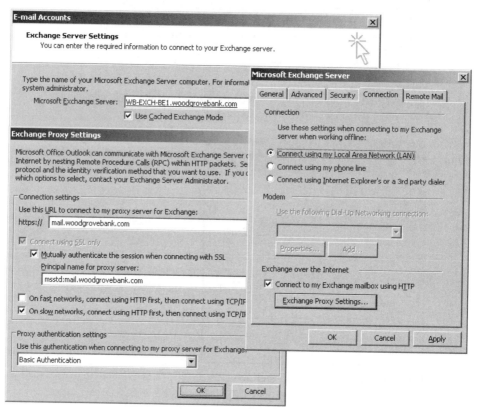

Figure 12-34   Configuring Outlook 2003 for RPC over HTTP

> **Tip**   Enabling Use Cached Exchange Mode is optional but recommended for all Outlook 2003 users because it will allow Outlook to continue to operate when contact with the Exchange server is lost or when the offline Outlook user cannot connect to the network.

To reduce the complexity of configuring profiles for users, you can configure the profiles using the Custom Installation Wizard, which is part of the Office Resource Kit. Before your initial deployment of Office 2003 consider the settings needed to implement RPC over HTTP (Figure 12-35) and include those settings into the transform file that is used to customize your Office deployment image.

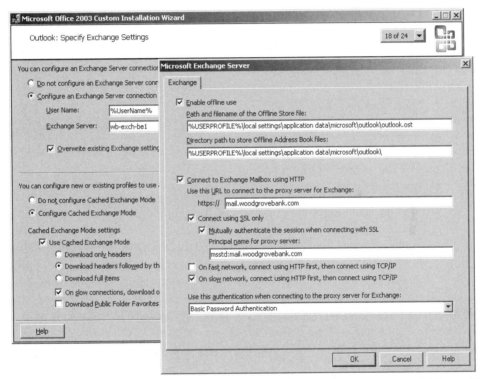

Figure 12-35   Using the Office 2003 Custom Installation Wizard to create an RPC over HTTP compatible profile

If profiles have already been deployed, because you have already deployed Office 2003, you can use the same tool to create a modified profile by clicking the Export Profile Settings button on page 20 of the Custom Installation Wizard (Figure 12-36). This results in a .prf file which can be opened on all users' machines to automatically reconfigure their existing profile.

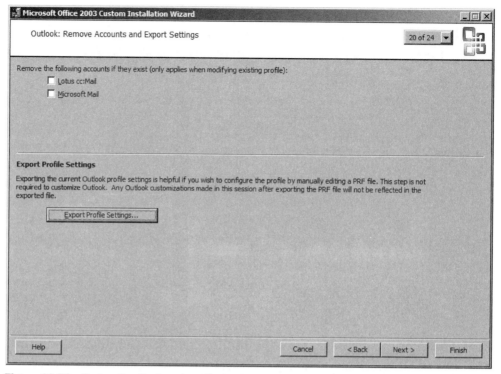

Figure 12-36   Saving the Custom Installation Wizard Outlook 2003 settings as a profile file for opening on preconfigured machines

If you are moving users' mailbox servers or administrative groups as part of the RPC over HTTP deployment, you can use the Exchange Server tool named Exchange Profile Update. This tool can be downloaded from the website *http:// www.microsoft.com/downloads/details.aspx?FamilyId=56F45AC3-448F-4CCC-9BD5-B6B52C13B29C*. It can be used to update the existing default profile and add the required RPC over HTTP settings to that profile at the same time.

Configuring ISA Server to Support RPC over HTTP

An ISA Server installation used to create your perimeter network, or installed within your perimeter network, can be used as part of your RPC over HTTP infrastructure. This section will cover the steps involved in that process. But first a word of advice: it is not wise to try to configure RPC over HTTP for the very first time through ISA Server. We recommend that you ensure that RPC over HTTP operates on the LAN first, so that the adding of the ISA Server to the infrastructure means you do not add too much complexity initially. Trying to build a RPC over HTTP infrastructure by including the ISA Server (or any other SSL offloader or firewall) right from the start can introduce numerous initial configuration issues.

Once RPC over HTTP is operational on the LAN, it is simple to add an ISA Server into the infrastructure, and the points that you need to consider for troubleshooting are now most likely to be perimeter network configuration rather than the Exchange servers or RPC over HTTP proxies.

ISA Server can be configured in the following three general ways for the support of RPC over HTTP:

- Server publishing of the RPC proxy

- SSL bridging

- SSL offloading

Server Publishing of the RPC Proxy

The RPC proxy service running on the front-end server on the LAN listens for HTTPS traffic, so it is possible to server publish this HTTPS server. Server publishing is not the default configuration for HTTP or HTTPS traffic, but rather Web Publishing is. Server publishing makes the external network interface of the ISA Server listen for, and then pass on, traffic that arrives on that interface directly to the internal server. For most server publishing rules, this is done without inspection of the data within the session. For HTTPS it means that the ISA Server firewall will block invalid ports and connection attempts, but all valid layer 4 traffic (the TCP layer) will be passed into the LAN without further inspection, and in the case of HTTPS without any decryption.

SSL Bridging

The default configuration for HTTP and HTTPS traffic is to Web publish the connection, which allows inspection of the data. This is achieved in both this and the next configuration choice. SSL bridging is where the external network interface of the ISA Server listens for HTTPS connections, as in server publishing, but instead of passing them on to the published server, the ISA Server decrypts the SSL session to get clear text and inspects the clear text to ensure that it is valid. For example, the RPC proxy server is found at the /rpc virtual directory and so the Web Publishing rule can be configured to allow access attempts only to this virtual directory. Therefore, if a hacker is attempting to gain access to the root of the Web server, and trying to mask this attempt by encrypting the data, ISA Server will prevent this by Web Publishing an HTTPS session, but could not stop it by server publishing an HTTPS session.

SSL bridging in ISA Server continues by the encryption of the traffic again, and the passing of this inspected traffic onward to the RPC proxy. This second SSL session is from the ISA Server to RPC proxy only and is not the same SSL session as the client-to-ISA Server session.

To configure ISA Server to do SSL bridging you first need to install the digital certificate onto the ISA Server that would normally go on the RPC proxy. This certificate is configured for the publicly resolvable name of the RPC over HTTP system.

> **Important** The certificate must be installed in the local computer certificate store and not the user certificate store. This is achieved by creating a custom MMC console and adding in the Certificates snap-in. You will be asked which certificates you want to view. The Computer option must be chosen and the certificate imported into the Personal store for the computer.

The RPC proxy server also needs a digital certificate, but we recommend that this is not the same certificate, to avoid name resolution issues. If the digital certificate on the RPC proxy is the same as the digital certificate on the ISA Server, the second session is made to the same FQDN that the client uses to connect to the ISA Server, but though the FQDNs need to be the same they are different servers. This means that the ISA Server needs to be able to resolve that FQDN to the internal address, whereas the client needs to resolve the same FQDN to the external address. The easiest way to do this is to add the internal server address to the HOSTS file on the ISA Server. This will stop the ISA Server trying to make the second SSL session to itself and creating a loop. Figure 12-37 shows the configuration of an ISA Server using SSL bridging for RPC over HTTP with two different certificates because this avoids the need for adjusting name resolutions on a server-by-server basis.

Once the correct digital certificates are installed on both servers, the Web publishing rule needs to be configured to pass traffic received on the SSL port onto the SSL port on the internal server. In ISA Server 2000 this is done on the Bridging tab of the Web publishing rule, and under Redirect SSL Requests As, choose SSL Requests (Establish A New Secure Channel To The Site). In ISA Server 2004 select the Bridging tab of the Web server publishing rule and select Redirect Requests To SSL Port.

The remainder of the ISA Server configuration is to ensure that the connection is made to the internal server using the same name as on the certificate installed on the internal server, and that only requests to /rpc/* can be passed through.

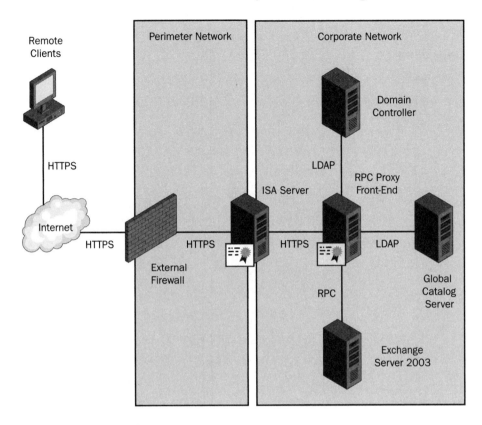

   Certificate cn=mail.woodgrovebank.com

   Certificate cn=NetBIOS *name of RPC proxy server*

Figure 12-37   An SSL bridging network design

SSL Offloading

Because the default configuration of RPC over HTTP is to require SSL, the AllowAnonymous registry key needs to be set to allow non-SSL connections.

On the ISA Server, as with SSL bridging, the digital certificate needs to be installed into the local computer certificate store, but unlike SSL bridging the internal RPC proxy does not need a digital certificate installed. Therefore, apart from the registry key on the RPC proxy, the only other configuration needed is that the ISA Server must be configured to terminate the SSL session and to connect to the internal server using an HTTP session (which optionally can be protected with IPSec). Figure 12-38 shows an example configuration of this network.

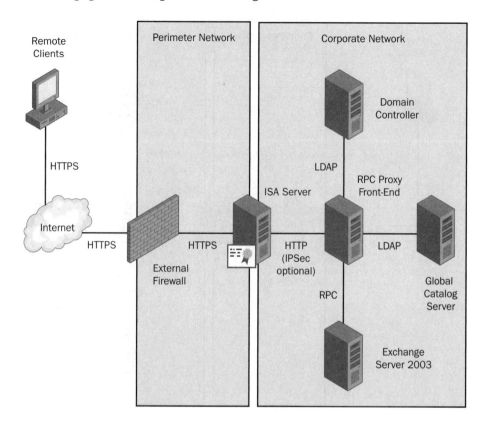

 Certificate cn=mail.woodgrovebank.com

Figure 12-38 An SSL offloading network design

General ISA Server and RPC over HTTP Settings

ISA Server 2000 with Feature Pack 1 and ISA Server 2004 both have the ability to restrict traffic to your HTTP/HTTPS servers when doing Web publishing by more than just the host header and URL. This extra restriction is known as URLScan and it blocks requests to URL's that are outside the limits set on the firewall. For ISA Server 2000 you will need to add or modify the following two sections to your URLScan.ini file on the ISA Server:

```
[AllowVerbs]
RPC_IN_DATA
RPC_OUT_DATA
[RequestLimits]
MaxAllowedContentLength=2000000000
MaxUrl=16384
MaxQueryString=4096
```

ISA Server 2004 implements the functionality of URLScan without the need to configure the .ini file. In the Web server publishing rule the above information can be added to the Filtering options on the Traffic tab of the rule.

Best Practices

When administering your Exchange organization, it is important that you try to avoid the modification of IIS metabase settings that can be set in Exchange System Manager because they could be overwritten due to the workings of the DS2MB process.

For increased security it is important that you leave disabled those virtual servers that you do not use within your organization. Not only does this improve server performance and reduce potential calls to the helpdesk, but by reducing the attack surface of your Exchange servers and network you reduce the possibility of data loss due to malicious server damage. While considering increased security, it is important to ensure that your firewall solution is capable of protecting your network. If the sum total of your firewall solution is one that can only inspect data to layer 4 of the OSI network stack (the TCP session information), and not layer 7 (the application data), then it is not good enough. At the very least you should be able to inspect inbound requests for HTTP virtual servers to ensure that the packet contains a valid request. Care though needs to be taken with the layer 7 firewall to ensure that a configuration is set that allows the HTTP features of Exchange Server 2003 to work.

If you need to provide access to your Exchange organization to remote users, you can provide Outlook Web Access, Outlook Mobile Access, IMAP4, and POP3 without additional software. A number of third-party products, such as Blackberry, exist to provide this remote view of messages. It is important to consider exactly the needs of your organization and where the users are who need remote access. Different solutions provide different advantages and disadvantages, all with their own support issues and security considerations; not to mention associated costs.

In large enterprise networks where Exchange servers are located in various corporate sites, it is important to ensure that users connect to the front-end Outlook Web Access virtual servers that are closest to their mailbox stores and not the servers closest to their present locations. Evidence shows that a user located away from his or her home office can read e-mail messages quicker by connecting to a remote front-end server that is local to the mailbox back-end server, rather than to have the front-end and back-end part of the session cover long distance. In this scenario, it is wise to customize a Forms Based Authentication page to inform users of this and provide links to the other Outlook Web Access systems available on the Internet.

Finally, if your organization is going to publish access to Outlook Web Access, Outlook Mobile Access, POP3, or IMAP4, ensure that the session is over an SSL connection to protect at least the user name and password and the content of the session too.

Chapter 13

Implementing Exchange 2003 Security

About This Chapter

Because e-mail in the twenty-first century is a mission critical business process, the servers that manage the delivery of e-mail and their associated processes need to be highly secured.

There is considerable scope for ensuring that all parts of the organization are secure. This ranges from permissions on mailboxes and public folders to limiting access to the Exchange server across a firewall from a number of different clients, and it includes controlling the type or version of client that can connect.

In this chapter we will look at how to secure your server and protect your data using the security tools of Exchange System Manager and Microsoft Active Directory directory service. Further areas of security will be examined by looking at the security protocols built into Internet Information Server (IIS) and protection using firewalling devices.

Securing Exchange Information in Active Directory

Exchange Server 2000 and 2003 use Active Directory for the storage of all the user and server information that they need to access. This is unlike Exchange Server 5.5, which came with its own directory. This means that for full administrative access on everything to do with Exchange Server, you require a high level of Active Directory permissions as well. In organizations where the responsibility for the messaging infrastructure and Active Directory are split between two or more teams of administrators, both teams will need to be aware of where their responsibilities start and end and what permissions will be needed in the two products to achieve successful administration of both systems.

Administration of an Exchange organization is basically split into these two areas, but that does not mean that Exchange administrators have no rights within Active Directory. They do, but only to selected areas, and this is only true once Active Directory has been prepared for an Exchange installation.

The very first step of an Exchange organization deployment is the loading of Active Directory with the information needed for an installation. This process is known as ForestPrep and running this part of the setup program results in two areas of Active Directory, known as directory partitions, being extended to include Exchange Server information. Directory partitions were previously known as naming contexts.

Exchange and Active Directory Partitions

The first partition that is modified by ForestPrep is the schema partition and the second is the configuration partition. Within an Active Directory forest there is only one schema partition and one configuration partition. Because the schema is one of the five operations masters in the Active Directory forest, it can be changed only via a single domain controller. The configuration partition is multi-master and can be changed on any domain controller. Changes to either the schema via the domain controller that is the schema operations master or to the configuration on any domain controller will then replicate to every other domain controller in the Active Directory forest.

Note   The configuration directory partition is located at CN=Configuration,DC=<*root_domain*>, with the Exchange Server portions of this partition at CN=Microsoft Exchange,CN=Services, CN=Configuration,DC=<*root_domain*>.

> **Note** The schema directory partition is located at `CN=Schema,CN=Configura-tion,DC=<root_domain>`.

These two partitions can be viewed in a number of different Active Directory tools, along with the other partitions that exist, such as a domain partition (where there is one for each domain in the forest). Each tool that is used to view the information in the partition will have some ability to show some of the information, for example you can use Active Directory Sites and Services to show parts of the configuration partition, but even though this tool can show the Exchange Server areas of the configuration partition, it cannot show all the information stored in Active Directory at this location.

The best tool for examining a partition is ADSI Edit. In a Windows 2000 Server this requires the installation of the Support Tools but is installed as part of a Windows Server 2003 installation and can be accessed just by running adsiedit.msc from the Run dialog box. ADSI Edit can be seen in Figure 13-1 showing the properties of an Exchange server named WB-EXCH-FE1, which is located in the America administrative group.

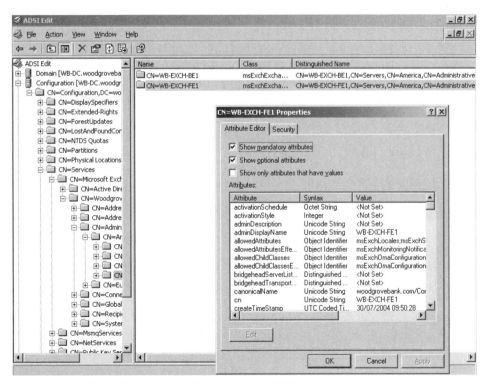

Figure 13-1 ADSI Edit running in Windows Server 2003

Initial Permissions in Active Directory

When ForestPrep is run to prepare the Active Directory forest for the installation of the Exchange organization, the setup program will ask for the user or group account that will be the main Exchange organization administrator, named the Exchange Full Administrator. Two of the steps that ForestPrep performs are to load the objects required into the Active Directory schema and configuration partitions and to set the initial permissions on the configuration partition. The execution of ForestPrep allows you to define an account that will hold the role of Exchange Full Administrator. ForestPrep will configure this account with the appropriate permissions on the organization object within the configuration partition. The Enterprise Administrator of the Active Directory forest will have full control in this area of the forest, and thus rights to the administration of the Exchange organization as well. The root Domain Admins group has a range of permissions on the configuration partition with mainly no object deletion rights. They do not get full control of the Exchange organization but can typically create objects in the configuration partition though not delete them.

All administrative users of the Exchange organization are denied the Send As and Receive As permissions. This prevents them from impersonating other users within the Exchange organization by sending e-mail messages that appear to come from them and having the ability to receive another user's e-mail messages.

ForestPrep and DomainPrep

To prepare to install the first Exchange server in an organization requires a user account with the correct security settings. An Active Directory administrator with rights to update the schema and to run ForestPrep has this level of permission. This means an account that is a member of Enterprise Admins and Schema Admins. Once the schema and configuration partitions are updated and time has been given for these changes to replicate around the forest, DomainPrep can be run. DomainPrep prepares a domain with the creation of the objects and groups needed for Exchange Server to operate in that domain. DomainPrep must be run by a domain administrator of the domain in question and can be run on any domain controller in that domain.

Once DomainPrep is complete a computer can be installed with just the Exchange admin tools. The installation of just the admin tools allows the Exchange administrative group structure to be prepared in advance of any Exchange Server installation by allowing the delegation of permissions to those who need the rights to install servers. The delegation of permissions allows additional users or groups to be granted administrative access in addition to that set during ForestPrep when only the initial Exchange Full Administrator role was configured and the default Exchange organization permissions were stored in Active Directory.

> **Note**   If you install the Exchange admin tools before installing any Exchange servers, you will see a GUID in the place of the organization name. Regardless of this, Exchange Server Delegation Wizard operates correctly. You set the organization name only when you install the first Exchange server into the Exchange organization.

Exchange Server Delegation Wizard

Exchange System Manager changes the permissions of the Exchange Server area of the configuration partition primarily by the use of Exchange Server Delegation Wizard. Exchange Server Delegation Wizard allows the easy granting of permissions within the Exchange organization for three different roles (which provide three different levels of permissions) and over two different areas of the Exchange organization. These roles are Exchange Full Administrator, Exchange Administrator and Exchange View Only Administrator. The two different areas that permissions can be applied are at the Exchange organization level or at a specific administrative group level.

The three different administrative roles provide, in brief, the following permissions. Other permissions, such as deny Send As and Receive As, are included when modify or full control permissions are granted.

- **Exchange Full Administrator**   Full control permissions to the relevant area of the configuration partition.

- **Exchange Administrator**   Modify permissions to the relevant area of the configuration partition. Apart from the ability to set most permissions within Exchange, this role is similar to Exchange Full Administrator.

- **Exchange View Only Administrator**   Read permissions to the relevant area of the configuration partition.

Exchange Server Delegation Wizard is the preferred tool for setting administrative permissions for Exchange Server in Active Directory. This is especially true when setting and removing permissions at the administrative group level. Users and groups granted permission at the administrative group level require Read access to the organization level. Exchange Server Delegation Wizard completes this task by setting the appropriate permissions at both the organization level and administrative group level automatically. This means that though Exchange Server Delegation Wizard has given you a particular level of permission at one area of the Exchange organization (your actual permissions) you may gain the same or other permissions at different levels of the organization (your effective permissions) so that your resulting permissions are not what you might expect. This is why you should use Exchange Server Delegation Wizard rather than granting the permissions manually using Active Directory tools such as ADSI Edit or by enabling the Security tab in Exchange System Manager. Using tools such as ADSI Edit or by enabling the Security tab in Exchange System Manager will result in the provision of incorrect permissions. A full list of actual permissions along with the effective permissions is shown in Table 13-1.

Table 13-1   Actual and Effective Permissions

Actual permissions	Effective permissions					
	AG: View	AG: Admin	AG: Full Admin	ORG: View	ORG: Admin	ORG: Full Admin
AG: Exchange View Only Administrator	✓*			✓		
AG: Exchange Administrator	✓	✓*		✓		
AG: Exchange Full Administrator	✓	✓*	✓*	✓		
ORG: Exchange View Only Administrator	✓			✓		
ORG: Exchange Administrator	✓	✓		✓	✓	
ORG: Exchange Full Administrator	✓	✓	✓	✓	✓	✓

* = Local administrative group only

AG = Administrative group level

ORG = Organization level

Though Exchange Server Delegation Wizard can be run at any time, use it first during the Exchange organization and administrative group preparation to delegate the building of a large Exchange Server infrastructure to multiple administrators. To run Exchange Server Delegation Wizard in Exchange System Manager you need to have Exchange Full Administrator permissions to the organization level. If you have Exchange Full Administrator permissions to an administrative group you cannot delegate permissions on that administrative group using the wizard, because as we saw in Table 13-1, you have Read permissions at the Exchange organization level. This means that though you are an Exchange Full Administrator at the administrative group level, you cannot run the wizard because it needs to set permissions at the Exchange organization level as well as administrative group level.

Using the Delegation Wizard

It is recommended that when using the delegation wizard, the permissions are granted to groups rather than users. The use of groups means that the changing of permissions in the future becomes a role for the administrator of the group rather than just those accounts that are Exchange Full Administrator.

A universal group for each of the three roles at the Exchange organization level should be created in the Active Directory forest, and then three universal groups for the roles at each administrative group level created as well. Once the groups for the Exchange Administrator and Exchange Full Administrator roles have been created they should also be granted local computer administrator permissions to the servers that are or will be Exchange servers within those administrative groups.

Important   In order to modify all server and configuration properties when you are an Exchange Full Administrator or Exchange Administrator role holder, it requires local computer Administrators group membership on the servers under your control.

Note   Unlike Exchange Server 5.5, permissions from the organization level inherit to the administrative group level and do not need to be reapplied at each administrative group.

An example of the groups that you might create to associate with the Exchange security roles when you have two administrative groups in your organization might be something like that shown in Table 13-2.

Table 13-2   Example Groups and Delegated Roles

Active Directory group name	Delegated at organization level	Delegated at Europe administrative group level	Delegated at America administrative group level
Global Exchange Full Admins	Exchange Full Administrator	Inherited from the organization level *	Inherited from the organization level *
Global Exchange Admins	Exchange Administrator	Inherited from the organization level *	Inherited from the organization level *
Global Exchange Viewers	Exchange View Only Administrator	Inherited from the organization level	Inherited from the organization level
USA Exchange Full Admins			Exchange Full Administrator *
USA Exchange Admins			Exchange Administrator *
USA Exchange View Only Admins			Exchange View Only Administrator
Europe Exchange Full Admins		Exchange Full Administrator *	

Table 13-2 Example Groups and Delegated Roles (Continued)

Active Directory group name	Delegated at organization level	Delegated at Europe administrative group level	Delegated at America administrative group level
Europe Exchange Admins		Exchange Administrator *	
Europe Exchange View Only Admins		Exchange View Only Administrator	

* These groups should also be members of the local Administrators group on each Exchange server within their associated administrative groups.

Permissions Needed to Complete Common Exchange Server Administrative Tasks

Once your groups and permissions are ready, you can start the installation of your Exchange servers. The first Exchange server in an Exchange organization or administrative group needs to be installed by someone with local computer Administrators membership and Exchange Full Administrator at the organization level. Unlike Exchange Server 2000, subsequent Exchange servers in that administrative group can be installed by anyone with local computer Administrators membership and Exchange Full Administrator at the administrative group level. If you are not a member of Domain Admins you will need to ask a domain administrator to add the computer account to the Exchange Domain Servers group in the servers' current domain.

Once Exchange Server 2003 is installed, the latest service pack can be applied. The application of a service pack to Exchange Server can be performed by an Exchange Administrator role holder for the administrative group that contains the server being upgraded.

Delegating Common Administrative Tasks

Once your Exchange Server's structure begins to take place, the creation of mail-enabled objects can be performed by any domain administrator, account operator, or another account with that delegated right within the organizational unit where the User or InetOrgPerson object is to be created. In addition to this account creation permission, you will need at least the Exchange View Only Administrator role on the administrative group containing the server where you are creating the mailbox. If an attempt is made to create a mailbox by a user with permission to create accounts but without at least Exchange View Only Administrator role membership, then the account creation wizard in Active Directory Users and Computers will not be able to get past the Create An Exchange Mailbox dialog box because the user will not be able to choose a mailbox store.

To start or stop protocol virtual servers in Exchange System Manager requires Exchange Administrator role membership of the administrative group that the computer is a member of, unless you want to start or stop the actual service in Administrative Tools. To start or stop a Windows service requires local administrator rights, which you should have because they are required when an account is an Exchange Administrator role holder.

How to Implement a Split Permission Model

A split permission model is one where the Exchange Server administration team does not have permissions on Active Directory for the modification of mailbox-enabled objects. An example of a split permission model is one where the Exchange administration team can complete mailbox management functions but not full account administration because they have only the Active Directory permissions that are needed for this role and not the Full Administrator permissions on the organizational unit that contains the object that is being modified.

Exactly what permissions are required and where they are required can be found by referencing Appendix C of the Exchange Server 2003 Technical Documentation Library book referenced at the end of this section. This book, *Working With Active Directory Permissions In Microsoft Exchange 2003,* covers the attributes that are associated with every Exchange Server property that can be changed in Active Directory Users and Computers. Using this information, you can delegate a permission model that allows the change of just those attributes needed to achieve a given role without the need to give a higher set of rights (for instance, domain admin) than those needed for the task, ultimately protecting your network from accidental or malicious damage.

Once the permission structure has been defined, you can use one of two tools to implement this change. ADSI Edit allows permissions to be changed using the dialog box that will be familiar to all Windows administrators, but to use ADSI Edit is a manual task and not suited to the implementation of a consistent permission model across multiple organizational units, domains, trees, and forests in a repeatable fashion. DSACLS, the second tool, is suited to this repetition, allowing the scripting of permissions on multiple organizational units, domains, trees, and forests. DSACLS comes with the Windows Support Tools, which can be found in the \Support\Tools folder of a Windows Server CD-ROM.

More Info   You can learn more about the permissions in an Exchange Server and Active Directory network in the Exchange Server 2003 Technical Documentation Library book, *Working With Active Directory Permissions In Microsoft Exchange 2003*. This book can be downloaded at *http:// go.microsoft.com/fwlink/?LinkID=21277.*

Securing Exchange Server Through Group Policies

With the use of group policies, both locally applied and in an Active Directory environment, it is possible to control the security of your Exchange servers. This can be achieved on a server-by-server basis with the setting of local policy files, but the recommended way to protect your network is to use Active Directory to centrally apply Group Policy, and reapply regularly. The contents of the Group Policy objects are also recommended to be based upon the Microsoft security settings, along with settings that you need and have tested within your organization.

The default security settings on a Windows Server 2003 are hardened by default, but changes may be needed due to your network environment. Microsoft recommends reviewing and implementing the recommendations found within the books *Windows Server 2003 Security Guide* and *Exchange Server 2003 Security Hardening Guide*, if your organization requires more stringent security policies. In some cases, mainly to support legacy clients, a reconfiguration of a security restriction will be needed to provide the best security for your particular Exchange organization. For example, the *Windows Server 2003 Security Guide* shows you how to stop anonymous logons to a server. If the server affected by this policy is a global catalog server, and you use Outlook 2000 and 2002 clients, this policy setting will need adjusting or the clients will have issues when they attempt to send mail to internal recipients.

More Info   For more information, the *Windows Server 2003 Security Guide* is available at *http://go.microsoft.com/fwlink/?LinkID=21638* and the *Security Hardening Guide for Exchange Server 2003* can be found in the Exchange Server 2003 Technical Documentation Library (*http://go.microsoft.com/fwlink/?LinkID=21277*).

Hardening Windows Server 2003

The first step in protecting your Exchange organization is to increase the security of the operating system. In this chapter we will introduce the Windows Server 2003 recommendations and implementations, but a similar process is available for Windows 2000 Servers. The entire process of hardening the security settings in the Windows Server 2003 operating system is covered in the *Windows Server 2003 Security Guide* mentioned previously.

More Info   The *Microsoft Windows 2000 Security Hardening Guide* can be downloaded from *http://www.microsoft.com/technet/security/prodtech/win2000/win2khg/*.

The recommended process for hardening the operating system is to use group policies. The *Windows Server 2003 Security Guide* provides a number of template security policy files that can be imported into Group Policy objects at various levels throughout your forest.

The recommended Active Directory structure for implementing the operating system security is to create an organizational unit for member servers, and within that organizational unit to create sub-organizational units for the different types of member servers. An example is shown in Figure 13-2.

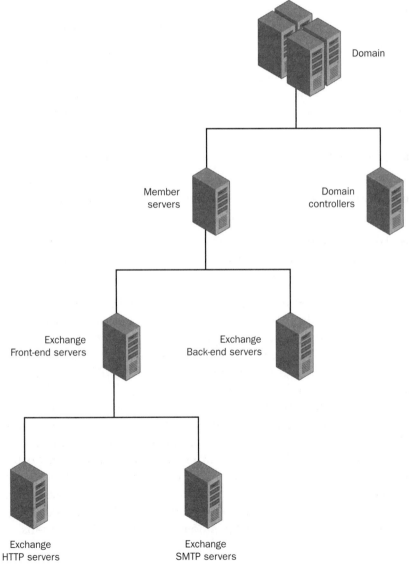

Figure 13-2   Recommended Active Directory organizational unit structure for Exchange servers

Once the correct organizational unit structure is created, you need to create Group Policy objects on all the relevant organizational units. To secure an Exchange organization this will involve creating Group Policy objects on the domain level, the domain controllers level and the member servers organizational unit.

Each Group Policy object will then be configured with the recommended security settings respective to its level within the organizational unit hierarchy. For example, the domain level object will configure settings valid for all objects in the domain, including password and security options, whereas the member servers organizational unit will be configured with settings that configure system services and other relevant settings.

If you have a network where servers operate more than one role, you will need to create an organizational unit for that combined type of server, but it is vital to ensure first that the different policies that are recommended for each of these server roles do not have conflicting settings.

The Group Policy objects are created using the templates provided with the *Windows Server 2003 Security Guide* download. The guide provides three types of templates, as follows:

- **Legacy Client**   Designed to support legacy applications and clients on your network.

- **Enterprise Client**   For use when the desire is to increase the security of Windows 2000 and later operating systems.

- **High Security**   For use when concern about security is so high that significant loss of functionality and manageability is considered an acceptable tradeoff to achieve the highest level of security.

It is common for many organizations that go through this process to apply the Legacy Client templates first and as they upgrade their infrastructure's operating systems to increase the security level by implementing the Enterprise Client templates. Some organizations further increase their security by deploying the High Security templates. An organization can stop at whatever template series provides the most suitable security for its requirements.

A Group Policy object is created as per your standard Active Directory practices. The correct security settings are applied to it by the importing of the policy template provided with the security guide. Before the Group Policy object goes live, testing needs to be performed in a lab environment that mimics or mirrors the production environment. Part of the test process is to determine the exact settings that the policy templates will apply and the effect that this will have on your network and network services. The importing of the policy template can be achieved using the Security Templates and the Security Configuration and Analysis MMC snap-ins.

Hardening Exchange Server 2003

If you implement just the hardened security settings on the operating system but not on the Exchange server, you will impact the successful operation of Exchange. Some of the impacts of the operating systems policy depend upon your client, for example the operating system policy for domain controllers is to stop most anonymous logons, and because this is applied to all your domain controllers it affects all your global catalog servers. If your Outlook clients are version 2000 or 2002, they will fail to connect to these protected global catalog servers as they attempt to connect anonymously. You must implement both the operating system and Exchange Server policies at the same time; therefore, you must test the entire security implementation in a lab environment.

> **Important**   During testing of the policies, ensure that every application you use is tested and not just the software that you know integrates with common features of Windows. It is possible that any application could be impacted by any of the many settings that could be implemented.

The *Exchange Server 2003 Security Hardening Guide*, like the Windows Security guide, provides policy templates for different Exchange Server roles (for example, front-end and back-end servers) and a template to adjust the Domain Controller templates that you will use from the Windows guide. Both the Windows guide and the Exchange guide describe in detail what each policy template does, and why it is needed to protect your environment.

The recommended approach to deploying the Exchange Server hardening templates is the same model used in hardening Windows systems: place the Exchange servers in a dedicated organizational unit within the member server's organizational unit. The two sub-organizational units that you need to create are for the front-end Exchange servers and back-end Exchange servers. Within the front-end Exchange servers organizational unit you need to create an organizational unit for each dedicated type of front-end server; for example, if you separate your HTTP servers from your IMAP servers, a policy can be applied to each type of server to ensure that the relevant security settings are applied. Figure 13-3 shows the Security Template MMC snap-in with the Exchange 2003 Backend.inf policy file open. This figure shows how this policy would change the startup values of different system services if it were deployed via a Group Policy object.

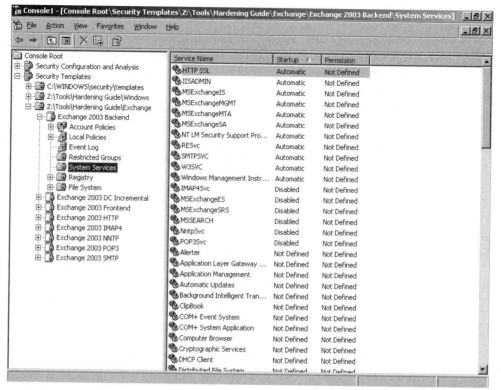

Figure 13-3 The Exchange 2003 back-end policy showing the settings it applies to system services

Protecting Your Exchange Server

The best way to protect an Exchange server is as discussed in the previous sections; using both the recommendations of the hardening guides and proper delegation of permissions on the areas of Active Directory that Exchange Server controls and uses.

In this section we will look in finer detail at some of the security considerations for Exchange Server not covered elsewhere in this chapter.

Protecting File Locations

A default installation of Exchange Server 2003 will place its folder structure in the \Program Files\Exchsrvr folder, inheriting the permissions of the \Program Files folder to most of the Exchsrvr subfolders. Information on the recommended permissions can be found in the *Exchange Server 2003 Security Hardening Guide*, but this will depend upon what services and applications you run on the server. For example, if you install the Intelligent Message Filter and delegate the task of processing archived e-mail messages to a non-administrator you will need to give that account permissions to both the UCEArchive and Pickup folders (which are subfolders of mailroot\vsi #).

If you move folders to different locations though, it becomes vital that you consider the permissions on these new folders. For example, in Exchange Server 2003 it is very easy to relocate the SMTP Queue using Exchange System Manager. This is usually done to improve the performance of the SMTP virtual server, but in doing so any template used to harden the security settings of the Exchange server would need to be modified to include this new folder, and to ensure that this new folder replicates the permissions of the original installation or the *Exchange Server 2003 Security Hardening Guide.*

The original permissions on the Exchsrvr folder are based upon the permissions granted to the parent folder that Exchange Server is installed into (\Program Files by default). If, before Exchange Server is installed, the permissions of the parent folder are changed, the majority of subfolders to Exchsrvr will gain these permission changes due to inheritance. Once Exchange Server is installed, inheritance of permissions is blocked at the Exchsrvr folder. If, after the installation of Exchange Server the Exchsrvr folders permissions are changed, these changes will affect the majority of the Exchange Server installation folder.

Of the default folders created during an Exchange Server installation, only one folder does not inherit the permissions of the parent folder: the \ExchangeServer_*servername* folder, which is used during indexing and search activities. This means that without the implementation of the security templates discussed in the *Exchange Server 2003 Security Hardening Guide*, any changes to the Exchsrvr folder permissions or the moving of any folder to a new location can result in failure of your Exchange server or a compromise of the security of the server.

The security template policies included with the *Exchange Server 2003 Security Hardening Guide* change the permissions structure of the server considerably. For example, the one folder that did not inherit permissions from Exchsrvr becomes one of only a few folders to do so because the permissions on the Exchsrvr folder are considerably tightened. Most of the folders inside Exchsrvr get specific permissions set with no inheritance from the Exchsrvr folder, reducing the risk that permission changes to Exchsrvr will propagate down the folder structure.

Important   If you make permission changes to the Exchsrvr folder after you have implemented Group Policy to control permissions, the settings in the Group Policy object will overwrite your settings within a configured period of time; 5 minutes if on a domain controller and 90 minutes with a random offset of up to 30 minutes on other servers.

Protecting Communication Ports

Exchange Server adds a number of open ports on a newly installed server, but unlike earlier versions of Exchange Server each port that is open is typically needed and only a few changes can be made to further reduce the number of open ports. If an Exchange Server 2003 installation is completed by the upgrade of an earlier version of Exchange Server, consideration should be taken to ensure that ports that were open for the process and management of the old environment are not available if not needed in the new environment.

Table 13-3 lists the ports that are open for each service.

Table 13-3   Services and Ports

Service	Inbound ports	Outbound ports	Comments
Microsoft Exchange System Attendant	TCP 135 A few TCP ports higher than 1024 which are the end-points of the 135 RPC ports. TCP 6002/6004 for RPC over HTTP	Does not initiate outbound connections.	Note that the ports greater than 1024 can change each time the service is started.
Microsoft Exchange Information Store	TCP 135 TCP 6001 (RPC over HTTP)	UDP packets to inform clients of new mail. Each MAPI client listens on a random port configured when Outlook started.	An RPC over HTTP connection does not use the outbound port listed here. Instead, the client polls the server every minute to see if new mail exists.
Microsoft Exchange MTA Stacks	TCP 135 (RPC) TCP 102 (X.400)	TCP 135 (RPC) TCP 102 (X.400)	This service needed for connections to Exchange 5.5 systems and X.400 systems only.
Simple Mail Transfer Protocol (SMTP)	TCP 25	TCP 25	Core requirement of Exchange Server 2003, and should not be stopped.
Microsoft Exchange Routing Engine	TCP 691	TCP 691	
World Wide Web Publishing Service	TCP 80 TCP 443 (SSL)	TCP 80 if front-end server to back-end servers only.	

Table 13-3 Services and Ports (Continued)

Service	Inbound ports	Outbound ports	Comments
Microsoft Exchange POP3	TCP 110 TCP 995 (SSL)	TCP 110 if front-end server to back-end servers only.	Disabled by default, but not if the Exchange server is upgraded.
Microsoft Exchange IMAP4	TCP 143 TCP 993 (SSL)	TCP 143 if front-end server to back-end servers only.	Disabled by default, but not if the Exchange server is upgraded.
Network News Transfer Protocol (NNTP)	TCP 119 TCP 563 (SSL)	TCP 119 or 563 if providing push feeds to other NNTP servers.	Disabled by default, but not if the Exchange server is upgraded.
Microsoft Exchange Site Replication Service	TCP 135 (RPC) TCP 379	TCP 135 and other RPC ports.	
Active Directory Connector	None	TCP 379 TCP 389	
Exchange Management	TCP 135 (RPC) Listens on random UDP port.		Needed for integrated management tools such as Microsoft Operations Manager that use the Windows Management Instrumentation (WMI) interfaces of the operating system.

You can determine the ports that a particular Exchange server is using at any one time from the command line. Table 13-4 lists three Windows Server 2003 command line applications that can help in determining which ports are open when Exchange Server is installed and running. Netstat running on a Windows 2000 Server does not support the "o" option and so searches on the process ID cannot be performed, therefore other tools need to be used to determine what program has which ports open. Using these tools will help you work out why a particular port is open (netstat) and which component of Exchange Server is listening on that port (rpcdump and tasklist).

Table 13-4 Applications to Assist In Determining Open Sockets

Application	Command line	Notes
Rpcdump.exe	rpcdump /v	rpcdump.exe is part of the Windows Server 2003 Resource Kit and the tools can be downloaded from Microsoft's website. This tool will report the ports used by different RPC-based Exchange services.
Netstat.exe	netstat –ano	Returns the open ports, which processes have them open, and who is connected to and from those ports.
Tasklist	tasklist /svc /fi "pid eq #"	Where # is the Process Identifier (PID) as determined using netstat. Will return the name of the application for a given PID.

Once you know the open ports and running services that you need and what is needed to connect to them, you can construct your security solution to protect the server from attack.

"Defense in depth" is a key component of protecting your network from attack by having multiple layers of defense to protect your network. It is common and vital for an organization to implement a firewall perimeter to its network, but it is a lot less common and just as vital to protect different parts of the internal network from other parts of the network. For example, in an organization that uses the Outlook client only when on the LAN, the availability of the HTTP/HTTPS protocol from the client network to the Exchange Server network is not necessary.

The concept of defense in depth is to implement a firewall and security policy to protect all your network assets and not just the interface between the internal and external networks. For example, firewalls should be used to separate one area of the network from another, the obvious example being the use of them to protect your network from the Internet, but less obvious examples include the protection of the production network from the developer and test/lab networks, ensuring that unused services/application are disabled or removed, and using Internet Protocol Security (IPSec) to limit the type of traffic accepted by a server.

As you move deeper into your network, you need to protect servers from the type of protocol rather than the protocol itself. For example, if your production network hosts your Exchange servers, you might need to allow in HTTP requests for specific URLs; but not every HTTP request that is destined for the server. You also need to limit where connections to your servers can originate or terminate. Microsoft ISA Server is an example of a product that fits the requirement of a firewall that can scan the data found in the packet, and it can also determine if the connection should be blocked by virtue of its source or destination. With its ability to inspect the data in the packet, ISA Server can allow through the firewall those packets that meet its given requirements.

Finally, you should consider local server protection. This is the level that is most often ignored. Local server protection can involve the installation of a host-based firewall on each network card on each computer but certainly should involve control of the applications and services installed on each computer to reduce how that computer can be attacked. The most basic of firewalls designed for local computer protection will block inbound connections that are not on the allowed list but will not affect outbound connections from the computer nor generate reports on activity. An example of this type of firewall is the one provided in Windows XP SP2 and Windows Server 2003 SP1. Within an already protected network these types of limited action firewalls are sufficient, especially because they can be centrally controlled by Group Policy. The use of non-Microsoft network card firewalls (also known as personal firewalls) are recommended for this part of your network's protection if your requirements exceed what the Microsoft Windows Firewall can provide.

> **Important**   A business should not be relying on this type of firewall to exclusively protect its core network but should implement defense in depth to protect its network at many points.

Within an already protected network these firewalls will assist, for example, when a virus has got in that is trying to hit all the computers on the LAN, or against someone with a grudge against the network who has physical access to it, but they should not be the only firewall that you would have between the Internet and the LAN.

In addition to the consideration of host-based firewalls, it is important to limit what can be installed on any given server, who has permissions to install software on a server to protect against viruses and to implement network encryption.

Reducing the attack profile of a server is very important, and the easiest way to do this is to ensure that you install only the minimum software required for the server to function, and that you restrict the installation of untested software or software that is vulnerable to common attacks, such as buffer overflow. For example, a feature of Windows Server 2003 is that it reduces the ability of Internet Explorer when attempting to download files from non-trusted sources. If this functionality is disabled, an administrator browsing the Web from the server console, even if just for troubleshooting purposes, could introduce code that might compromise the server.

Your antivirus policy should be implemented at numerous locations on your network including the Internet gateway (for both Web surfing and e-mail), on each server and on every client. Having an antivirus solution that does not protect from the introduction of viruses from any source leaves a potential hole in your defenses.

Protection of your network and the data carried upon it is of prime importance. Technologies such as IPSec should be considered to control the allowed inbound and outbound traffic from selected servers. Also consider the implementation of other encryption technologies such as Secure/Multipurpose Internet Mail Extensions (S/MIME) when communicating with parties outside the scope of your network.

A final level of protection is the concept of "least privilege." This ensures that users and installed service on the network must have just the correct rights to perform their tasks and no more. For example, users should not be local administrators to their workstations, and your network administrators should avoid logging on as a domain- or enterprise-level administrator unless they absolutely have to. With the principle of least privilege you restrict the ability to install or reconfigure applications or services that could profoundly impact your network.

Of all the levels of protection, the host-based firewall requires the most work and testing, followed by the implementation of least privilege. Though your external firewall should be professionally installed and secured, it is much easier to limit inbound connections to a few well-known ports and protocols than it is to protect a local server from all the connections it can receive and make. Therefore, host-based firewalls, such as the Windows Firewall, which only need configuring to allow inbound connections to selected ports or applications, are easier to configure than those that require configuring in both directions. Figure 13-4 shows the prompt that a user gets whenever an application attempts to listen for incoming connections on a firewall-protected network card.

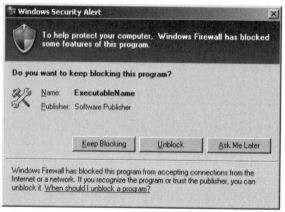

Figure 13-4   The prompt whenever a program or service on Windows attempts to listen for connections on a protected network interface

From the prompt shown, an administrator can choose whether or not the application should be allowed to listen, with the Windows Firewall default being that nothing gets in unless authorized. Selecting Unblock allows that application to operate on all its ports as if the firewall were not present.

> **Important**   If you choose to install and run an alternative network card fire-
> wall to Windows Firewall, you should disable Windows Firewall. Some net-
> work card firewall providers do this during their product's installation.
> Running two firewalls on the same network card increases the cost of
> server maintenance but does not increase server security.

Of course this needs considerable testing prior to deployment because you will not want to deploy this software on your Exchange servers and associated servers, such as domain controllers, without knowing which applications need to listen to ensure successful connectivity and which applications can be blocked from listening on the network without impact. The level of testing to ensure that host-based firewalls are protecting your network is considerable and could have a large cost associated with it. Therefore, host-based firewall protection is recommended only on specific high security networks or selected servers because the cost of implementation may outweigh the benefits of the protection gained.

Protecting the Exchange Store

The Exchange store is the collective name for the databases that store mailboxes and public folders. Each database is composed of two files, the EDB and STM along with the associated log files containing the record of the transactions that have occurred to the database files. By default, all of these files are located in \Program Files\Exch-srvr\MDBDATA but because the default location does not typically provide the best performance for Exchange Server, they will typically be moved to different locations. The best performance improvements come from the placement of the transaction log files on a different set of drives from the database files.

The protection and security of Exchange Server is ultimately about the protection and security of these files and folders. Without the databases and transaction logs you do not have a working Exchange server. Therefore, protection of this content covers a number of areas, not just the backup solution that you have in place but also to protect the information stored in these files from being compromised.

The default permissions for the database folder is that the administrator and system accounts have Full Control, that server operators get Modify along with anyone logged in through a terminal service session. User accounts get Read access by default. These permissions are all inherited from the Exchsrvr folder and can lead to compromise of the data stored in the database. If a user gains access to the server, it is possible for the user to copy the database to another location and allow offline access to the data it contains. Even though the database files are exclusively locked by the Microsoft Exchange Information Store service, some applications can read and copy the database while this service is running. If the Microsoft Exchange Information

Store service is stopped, the default permissions can allow any network user to read the contents of the database, should the user gain access to the folder on the server. The location for the storage of this folder is not shared to a user account by default and is not accessible to users by default. Note that for correct operation of Exchange Server, user accounts need Read permission to the database folder, and to stop the database from being compromised requires protection of access to the folder and server rather than the removal of the recommended permissions.

Using the security templates described earlier in this chapter, the permissions are tightened by the removal of the Terminal Services user account, and the Exchange Server 2003 setup program removes the default right for a user-level account to log on locally on a member server. Therefore, once Exchange Server is installed, users are not allowed to log on locally. Keeping with these settings, and assuming that the database folder or a parent folder is not shared, will ensure that a user cannot read the database in a low-level editing application, with the potential to read e-mail messages, because the content of the database is not encrypted.

> **More Info**   Full details of the minimum permissions that can be given to the folders containing Exchange databases and logs can be found in Appendix A of the book, Working with Store Permissions in Microsoft Exchange 2000 and 2003, which can be downloaded from the Exchange Server 2003 Technical Documentation Library at *http://go.microsoft.com/fwlink/ ?LinkID=21277.*

Therefore, because the database is not encrypted (though individual e-mail messages within the database may be), care should be taken as to where backups of the database are kept and who could restore the data from them. Further information on how to back up Exchange Server can be found in Chapter 21.

Exchange Server 2003 supports version 2.5 of the Exchange Server Virus Scanning API (VSAPI), which allows compatible antivirus products to query the contents of the Exchange store to search out viruses and remove them before they are opened by the e-mail client. The Exchange Server 2003 version of VSAPI allows the filtering out of viruses to occur on gateway servers that do not hold local mailboxes and thus remove messages containing viruses as they travel into the network and not only at the end point of the message path.

Finally, a way to protect your Exchange store and network from viruses is to stop MAPI clients that are not within a certain version range from connecting to the Exchange server. Blocking access for specific versions of Outlook allows you to ensure that those versions that do not support attachment blocking and the Object Model Guard will help to enforce a specific level of protection for your MAPI clients in your Exchange organization.

Attachment blocking stops the opening of a given list of attachments in Outlook. Attachment blocking is enabled by default in Outlook 2002 and later and can be installed in Outlook 97, 98, and 2000 by the download of an update specific to each version.

The Object Model Guard is a feature of Outlook that causes a user prompt to appear if any application attempts to send an e-mail message from the mailbox profile. The Object Model Guard is installed and enabled in Outlook 2002 and later, and can be installed in Outlook 98 or 2000 by the download of a security update specific to the version of Outlook. Outlook 97 does not support the Object Model Guard. The installation of both the attachment blocking and Object Model Guard increase the version number of Outlook so that unprotected versions are easy to identify.

To disable specific versions of MAPI clients from connecting to your Exchange organization, you need to set a registry key on each mailbox server. In Exchange Server 2000, you needed to restart the Microsoft Exchange Information Store service for this registry key to be used, but in Exchange Server 2003 the Microsoft Exchange Information Store service reads this value every 15 minutes. By setting the `Disable MAPI Clients` registry key (type `String`) to the value of the allowed version or versions of MAPI client at `HKEY_LOCAL_MACHINE\System\CurrentControlSet\Services\MSExchangeIS\ParametersSystem` you can stop those MAPI client versions that are listed in the registry key from connecting.

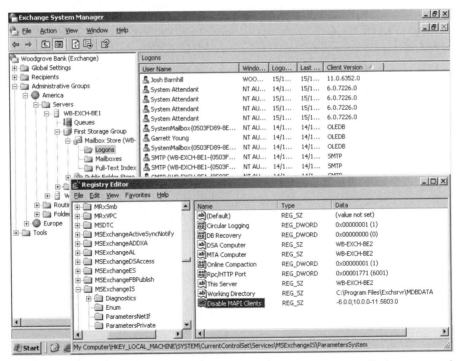

Figure 13-5   Disabling selected MAPI clients from connecting to the Exchange store based on client version number

Figure 13-5 shows the registry key value that allows only Outlook 2003 clients and later, along with Exchange System Manager (which is always 6.1.0 to 6.9999.0), to connect to the Exchange server by the setting of the registry key to **-6.0.0;10.0.0-11.5603.0**. This disables versions up to and including 6.0.0 and Outlook 2002, which is in the 10.x range.

To stop new versions of Outlook from connecting (for example, beta products or untested hotfixes), set the registry key to *x.y.z*—where *x.y.z* is one higher than the highest build of Outlook that you currently support. To disable a particular range of MAPI clients, set the registry key value to *a.b.c-x.y.z* where *a.b.c* is the lowest version of a MAPI client you will refuse connections from, and *x.y.z* is the highest version number that you will reject.

To determine the current version number of a client, log on with that client and view the Client Version column in Exchange System Manager, which can be found in the Logons node of the Exchange store containing your mailbox (also shown in Figure 13-5). A user who runs a blocked version of Outlook is prompted as shown in Figure 13-6.

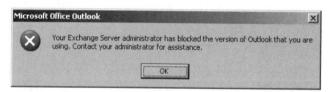

Figure 13-6   The Outlook prompt when your client is blocked from connecting to an Exchange server

To restrict all outdated versions of Outlook (Outlook 98 without the security update installed, and earlier versions), restrict all versions of Outlook with MAPI version numbers equal to or less than 5.2178.0 from connecting to Exchange. For this, the Disable MAPI Clients registry key should be set to **-5.2178.0**.

More Info   For more information, see the article, "Slowing and Stopping E-Mail Viruses in an Exchange Server 2003 Environment," available from the Exchange Server 2003 Technical Documentation Library at *http://go.microsoft.com/fwlink/?LinkID=21277*.

Protecting Public Folder Hierarchies

Exchange Server 2003, like its predecessor Exchange Server 2000, allows the use of multiple public folder trees, or hierarchies. Each public folder hierarchy that is created needs to be stored in a public folder store before it can be made available to users. Once available, users can read and write messages to the public folder hierarchy depending upon their permissions.

The default permission in Exchange Server 2003 is to deny users from having the right to create top-level public folders. This was not the case in Exchange Server 2000. If you upgrade the Active Directory schema and configuration of an Exchange Server 2000 organization with ForestPrep from the Exchange Server 2003 CD, you will set this new permission even if you have no Exchange Server 2003 servers running. This is part of Microsoft's Secure by Design philosophy.

By default, only those accounts with Exchange Full Administrator role, the local server administrator, members of, Domain Admins for the root domain, and members of Enterprise Admins can create top-level public folders. To modify this setting you need to enable the Security tab in Exchange System Manager as described in the Microsoft Knowledge Base article 264733, "XADM: How to Enable the Security Tab for the Organization Object," available at *http://go.microsoft.com/fwlink/ ?linkid=3052&kbid=264733,* and then grant the Create Top Level Public Folder permission to the user or group that needs it. By default, users get the Create Public Folder permission, but the ability to create non-top level folders depends upon the permissions they have in the folder in which they want to create a subfolder.

> **Note** The Exchange Administrator role gets the rights to change permissions on public folders even though they do not get the ability to change permissions on other parts of the Exchange organization or administrative group.

Client Permissions

Public folder permissions can be set in either Outlook or Exchange System Manager, apart from the top-level public folders, because permissions to create these are set at the administrative group level in Exchange System Manager. Permissions set in Outlook or Exchange System Manager are referred to as Client Permissions. To use Exchange System Manager to set the permissions that will affect users requires clicking the Client Permissions button, as shown in Figure 13-7.

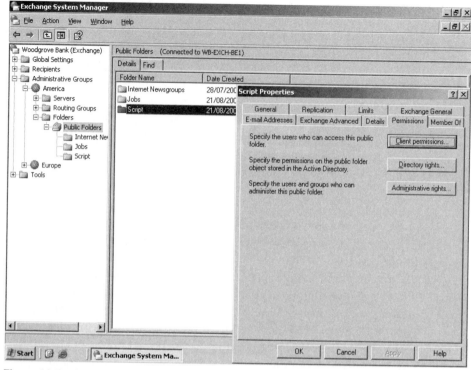

Figure 13-7   Setting public folder permissions in Exchange System Manager

The permissions set here depend upon the type of public folder that you are changing the permissions on. The default MAPI public folder tree permissions are compatible with MAPI clients and are different from the normal permissions that are set on NTFS folders and on application public folder trees, because MAPI clients operate a security model that is compliant with Exchange 5.5 Server, which is known as Exchange Canonical ACL.

The Exchange Canonical ACL requires specific settings to the layout of the access control list, which is more complex/restrictive than the list for NTFS file system permission. To that end, when you set permissions in Outlook or on the MAPI public folder tree you see a different style of permissions dialog box than you would expect in a Windows Server operating system. This dialog box is shown in Figure 13-8, whereas Figure 13-9 shows the equivalent permissions dialog box when selecting a non-MAPI public folder tree.

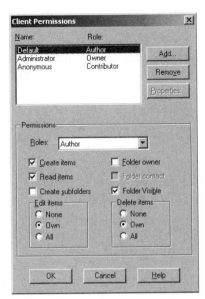

Figure 13-8   The standard MAPI permissions dialog box on public folders

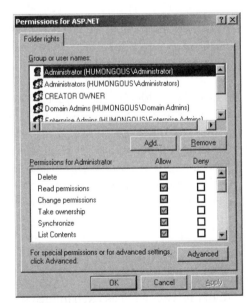

Figure 13-9   The permissions dialog box on non-MAPI public folders

It is possible to display the standard Windows permissions dialog box in Exchange System Manager when setting public folder permissions on a MAPI public folder tree by pressing the CTRL key at the same time as clicking the Client Permissions button, but this is not recommended because it can set permissions that are not in the correct order for MAPI clients to process correctly, resulting in denied access for the MAPI client.

Because public folders have two purposes, MAPI and non-MAPI, if you store NNTP content in a MAPI public folder store you need to set the permissions in Exchange System Manager or Outlook and expect the permissions to be MAPI-compliant (that is, you can give permissions to objects configured to work in Exchange Server and not all security principles). If an NNTP virtual directory is stored in the file system or in a non-MAPI public folder, the permissions will be those expected by non-MAPI users (for example, you can select user accounts that do not have mailboxes).

Directory Rights

Directory rights permissions are used to control the e-mail-related permissions of any public folder that is mail-enabled and thus has a public folder proxy object stored in the Microsoft Exchange System Objects container of the domain partition of Active Directory.

The default permission for a new object added to the Directory Rights dialog box is Full Control and includes permissions such as Send As, which allows a user to configure a public folder to send automated replies to incoming e-mail messages.

Permissions changed via the Directory Rights button give the users or groups selected permissions to the object at CN=*Public_Folder_Name*,CN=Microsoft Exchange System Objects,DC=*<domain>*,DC=*<root_domain>*, and the same permissions can be set using other Active Directory tools such as ADSI Edit and Active Directory Users and Computers.

Administrative Rights

The final permission type that can be set against a public folder (either MAPI or non-MAPI) is the right to administer that folder in tools such as Exchange System Manager or another administration tool.

Administrative changes to a public folder include setting items such as quota and replication settings.

Understanding the Dependencies of Core Exchange Services

A basic consideration when protecting the security of your Exchange server is to ensure that the server is functioning correctly and that each service that needs to run is able to. For example, be sure that it has not been disabled due to a poor understanding of what needs to run in a Windows environment to support Exchange Server. It is important to be aware of the services that can be disabled without impact, and what the minimum service requirements are for each Exchange service.

Using Table 13-5 and knowledge of your Exchange requirements, you can choose to enable or disable the services as needed. For example, if you do not have a system management tool such as Microsoft Operations Manager, you can disable the Exchange Management service. The HTTP service is required if Outlook Web Access, Outlook Mobile Access, Exchange ActiveSync, or RPC over HTTP is required, otherwise it too can be disabled. The required services of any Exchange Server installation are the Microsoft Exchange System Attendant, Microsoft Exchange Information Store, Microsoft Exchange Routing Engine, SMTP Service, and IIS Admin. This table does include the dependencies of these services, such as IIS Admin being dependant on the RPC service but not the dependencies of all services. Full service dependencies can be determined by expanding each node listed on the Dependencies tab of the service properties, as shown in Figure 13-10. The dependencies that are listed in Table 13-5 may differ on your Exchange server because of additionally installed software, hotfixes, and upgrades.

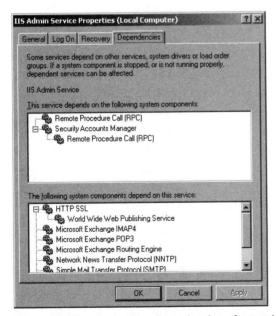

Figure 13-10 Viewing the dependencies of a service

Table 13-5   Exchange Server Dependencies

Service name	Dependencies
Event Log	No dependencies
HTTP SSL	HTTP (a driver)
IPSEC Services	IIS Admin Service
	IPSEC Driver
	Remote Procedure Call (RPC)
	TCP/IP Protocol Driver
IIS Admin Service	Remote Procedure Call (RPC)
	Security Account Manager
Microsoft Exchange Event	Microsoft Exchange Information Store
Microsoft Exchange IMAP4	IIS Admin Service
Microsoft Exchange Information Store	EXIFS (a hidden service)
	Microsoft Exchange System Attendant
Microsoft Exchange Management	Remote Procedure Call (RPC)
	Windows Management Instrumentation
Microsoft Exchange MTA Stacks	Microsoft Exchange System Attendant
Microsoft Exchange POP3	IIS Admin Service
Microsoft Exchange Routing Engine	IIS Admin Service
Microsoft Exchange Site Replication Service	No dependencies
Microsoft Exchange System Attendant	Event Log
	NT LM Security Support Provider
	Remote Procedure Call (RPC)
	Server
	Workstation
Microsoft Search	NT LM Security Support Provider
	Remote Procedure Call (RPC)
Network News Transport Protocol (NNTP)	Event Log
	IIS Admin Service
NT LM Security Support Provider	No dependencies
Remote Procedure Call (RPC)	No dependencies
Security Accounts Manager	Remote Procedure Call (RPC)
Server	No dependencies
Simple Mail Transfer Protocol (SMTP)	Event Log
	IIS Admin Service

Table 13-5   Exchange Server Dependencies (Continued)

Service name	Dependencies
Windows Management Instrumentation	Event Log
	Remote Procedure Call (RPC)
Workstation	No dependencies
World Wide Web Publishing Service	HTTP SSL
	IIS Admin Service
	Remote Procedure Call (RPC)

To ensure that all dependant services start, verify that any applied Group Policy does not inhibit any dependency. The Resultant Set of Policies or the Group Policy Management Console, can be used to determine the resulting policy when multiple Group Policies are applied on a server. If a component of Exchange Server fails to start, troubleshooting can begin by ensuring that the service or driver furthest down the chain from the failing service is working, and then making your way up the dependency chain toward the failed service. For example, if the NNTP service failed you should check, in order, the Remote Procedure Call (RPC) service, the Security Accounts Manager service, and the IIS Admin Service, along with the Event Log service.

Protecting Client/Server Communication

With Exchange Server there are a number of ways that clients can communicate with the server and through the server to the final recipient of the message. For some of these communications, a considerable amount of the information transmitted will be in plain text, and not just the message but the users' authentication credentials as well. Chapters 11 and 12 cover in detail the process behind securing the communication path when using the Internet protocols of SMTP (Chapter 11) and HTTP, POP3, IMAP4, and NNTP (Chapter 12). This section will look at the configuration of a Public Key Infrastructure (PKI) needed to support Internet-based client/server communications, the protection of the communication paths within an organization, and the protection of messages end-to-end regardless of any technologies used during parts of the connection.

Exchange and a Public Key Infrastructure

Exchange servers and clients can use two encryption technologies that are based on digital certificates. These technologies are Transport Layer Security/Secure Sockets Layer (TLS/SSL) and S/MIME. The TLS/SSL technology uses the information within a digital certificate to encrypt the communications session between either the client and the server or between two servers, but is not guaranteed to protect the entire message path. S/MIME uses digital certificates to encrypt the message body of the e-mail at the client and have it remain encrypted until read by the recipient. This means that regardless of any TLS/SSL encryption in place during the e-mail session the message will remain protected from eavesdroppers and those who attempt to change the contents of the message.

> **Note**   IPSec can also use digital certificates during any session encryption that it implements, but unlike TLS/SSL does not require a digital certificate for it to be fully implemented.

Before you can implement TLS/SSL or S/MIME, you require a digital certificate. This certificate is either a Server Authentication certificate in the case of TLS/SSL or a Secure E-mail certificate in the case of S/MIME. To have a valid digital certificate you need to have a certificate-issuing system and the ability to trust that certificate issuer. This whole collection of requirements makes, in part, your Public Key Infrastructure or PKI. An entire PKI includes more than just these pieces listed here, but this book does not go into the details of a PKI that is beyond the scope of Exchange Server.

The PKI Structure and Process

A PKI is composed of many parts. For the purposes of e-mail encryption, the main parts are the certification authority (CA) that issues certificates, the server or client that holds a digital certificate issued by that CA, and the end point of any communication. These parts are used both during the issuing of the digital certificate and the checking of the certificate during encrypted communication. These are shown in Figure 13-11. In addition to the PKI providing the means for the issuance of digital certificates, it is also used to verify the validity, authenticity, and trustworthiness of digital certificates as well as making certificates available through a directory.

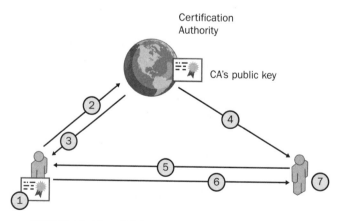

Figure 13-11   A Public Key Infrastructure for use when sending and receiving S/MIME e-mail

The process of obtaining a digital certificate for use in TLS/SSL or S/MIME, as shown in Figure 13-11, involves these elements of a PKI. In this example, a user, Anne, needs to send an e-mail message to Bob and wishes to ensure that this e-mail message can be read only by Bob:

1. Anne generates a public/private key matching pair on her computer for Secure E-mail (if this were a server we were discussing, the certificate would be for Server Authentication). The private key and public key are mathematically related. This mathematical relationship is known as a one-way function and involves very large prime numbers. The one-way function means that it is easy to compute the public key if the private key is known but it is very difficult to derive the private key if you have the public key.

2. Anne sends the public key along with information about herself to the CA. The CA then checks that Anne is who she claims to be and if satisfied with her claim will sign Anne's public key. The signing process is done by taking Anne's public key and encrypting it with the CA's private key. Anne's signed public key is her original public key and the result of the CA's encryption process. This is known as Anne's digital certificate. Recipients of Anne's digital certificate can use the information from the CA held in the key to prove that the digital certificate is from a trusted source.

3. The digital certificate is returned to Anne. Bob must go through a similar process to obtain his own unique digital certificate.

4. Bob, who needs to ensure that communications received from Anne really are from Anne, obtains a copy of the CA's public key. CAs typically make their public keys available on their websites or, for the major public CAs in the world, they are typically included in your operating system or Web browser.

5. Anne needs to encrypt the e-mail message she sends to Bob. Because it is only Bob who must be able to read this message, the original clear-text message (that is unencrypted message) must be encrypted with Bob's public key. Information encrypted with Bob's public key can only be decrypted with Bob's private key. Therefore, Anne needs to obtain Bob's public key. The easiest way to do this is for Bob to e-mail a signed message to Anne (covered later in the chapter) or for Anne to download Bob's public key from a directory service such as Active Directory.

6. Anne composes an e-mail message to Bob. The clear-text e-mail is encrypted using the information stored in Bob's public key. To prove that Anne is the sender of the message she also signs the message with her private key. Only the encrypted message is sent to Bob, the clear-text message is not sent.

7. Bob receives the e-mail and can read the message because he is able to decrypt the contents of it using his private key. Because the message was encrypted with

his public key, it can only be read by anyone with the matching, in this case, private key. Only Bob holds his private key. Bob is also sure that the message is from Anne because he is able to take the signature provided in the message and duplicate this using Anne's public key. Because Bob can complete this duplication of the signature it proves that the sender held Anne's private key while sending the e-mail message and is therefore most likely to be Anne. Bob trusts all the digital certificates used in the process because he trusts the issuing certification authority.

This entire process, which is known as digital signatures and digital encryption is covered in more detail under "Implementing Message Security" later in this chapter.

> **More Info** For more information about digital signatures and encryption, see the book *Exchange Server 2003 Message Security Guide*, which can be downloaded from the Exchange Server 2003 Technical Documentation Library at *http://go.microsoft.com/fwlink/?LinkID=21277*.

Choosing Your Certification Authority

Both Anne and Bob in Figure 13-11 use the services of the same certification authority. Anne gets her certificates signed (validated) by that CA and Bob can prove this by installing a copy of that CA's public key on this computer and checking Anne's key against this certificate. This installing of the public key is known as trusting the CA.

The CA that Anne chooses to use is based upon one major factor. Anne needs to trust that the CA will not issue certificates in her name when not requested by her. If it does, it is not trustworthy and should not be used. Bob has the same issue. If he receives an e-mail message from Anne where the question of who sent it can be determined with a public key issued by a CA he does not trust, then it might mean that although it looks as if the e-mail message was sent by Anne, it might not have been if the CA is prone to issuing digital certificates for entities (people, servers, etc.) without checking.

For secure e-mail communication that spans organizations, the best choice of CA is a commercially trusted CA. These CAs are trusted by how well they do their business and the laws and regulations they follow. You should only use the services of a CA that you trust.

For a CA to be trusted, the CA's public key needs to be installed on your computer, and only those CAs that you trust should have their public key installed on your computer. If secure e-mail communications are within an organization, between selected organizations, or between selected individuals only, the organizations or individuals in question could choose to install, and therefore trust, their own CAs.

Installing Windows Certificate Services

Windows Certificate Services is an optional component of Windows Server 2003 and Windows 2000 Server. When it is installed it can be installed in a stand-alone or enterprise configuration (Figure 13-12), where enterprise issues certificates based upon your Active Directory credentials and stand-alone issues certificates based upon whatever policy the CA administrator wants to implement.

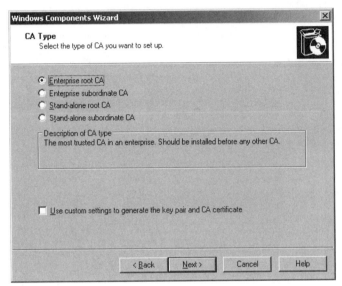

Figure 13-12   Choosing the type of installation in Windows Certificate Services

Once Windows Certificate Services is installed on a server, the server cannot be renamed or have its domain membership changed without first uninstalling Certificate Services. Also, if you plan to use the Certificate Services Web components, you should install IIS and the ASP component before installing Certificate Services. The installation steps can be found in Help or on Microsoft TechNet (*http://www.microsoft.com/technet*).

Obtaining Digital Certificates for Servers

Depending upon the type of installation of Windows Certificate Services, requests for TLS/SSL certificates can be done in two different ways. If an enterprise installation is performed, information about the existence of the CA is published to Active Directory and this allows programs such as IIS to obtain a certificate as part of the request process (Figure 13-13), rather than having to save the certificate request as a file and upload the request to the CA and wait for approval. The approval of the certificate request in an enterprise installation is all based upon the current user's logon credentials and if they have permission to request that particular type of certificate.

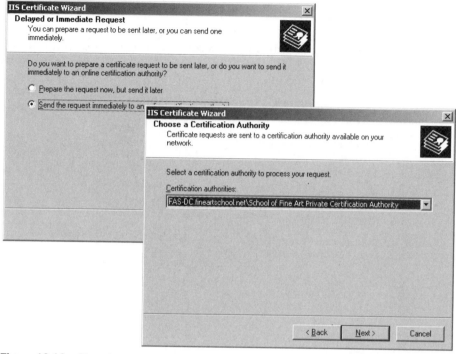

Figure 13-13 Choosing to use an online certification authority, which is a CA within your Active Directory forest installed as an enterprise CA.

If the CA is a stand-alone installation, you need to generate the request, save it as a text file, upload the request via the Certificate Services website, and wait for the CA administrator to approve your request. Once approved, you can collect the signed digital certificate, and then proceed to complete the installation of the server certificate.

> **More Info** The process for installing a digital certificate on any of the Exchange Server protocol virtual servers can be found in Chapter 12.

Obtaining Digital Certificates for Users or Servers

Once Windows Certificate Services has been installed, users can visit its website (*http://servername/certsrv/*) to request a certificate. As with the server certificate requests, if the installation is an enterprise installation, the type of certificates the users can request is based upon their Active Directory permissions. Permissions for the issuance of certificates in an enterprise installation are done via Active Directory

Sites and Services. Certificates in a stand-alone installation are issued if the CA administrator agrees that the request is within the CA's approvals policy. Microsoft TechNet includes many articles on how to customize the policy of a stand-alone certificate services installation.

It is possible for a user to request a certificate via the Certificates MMC snap-in (certmgr.msc) and for each user to automatically receive a certificate based on the Auto Enrollment settings in Group Policy as well as requesting them manually from the Certificate Services website.

Trusting a Private Certification Authority

For a user or server to complete a secure communication with another party, the end point needs to trust the CA used by the start point. In the example in Figure 13-11 earlier, Bob needed to trust the CA that Anne used to obtain her certificate.

If a user does not trust the issuer, they have no assurance that the certificate was issued by a reputable organization. Though they will get a warning (which in Windows looks like that shown in Figure 13-14) informing them of this, they can choose to ignore it. The communication is still secure from eavesdroppers, but you cannot ascertain the validity of the source because you do not trust the issuer.

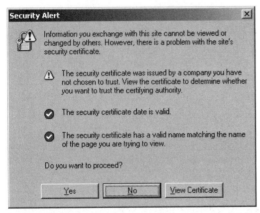

Figure 13-14   A prompt informing you that you do not trust the issuer of the digital certificate

Services or programs communicating with a TLS/SSL source cannot decide to ignore warnings such as that above, and if a digital certificate is issued by a non-trusted authority, the connection is most likely going to fail. Therefore, you need to trust any CA used by a service or program within your Exchange organization.

To trust a CA you need to install its public key into your Trusted Root Certification Authorities store (Figure 13-15 shows a warning that appears during this process). Opening the certificate from the issuer's website will begin the installation process for a user, but to install the certificate into the Trusted Root Certification Authorities for the computer or service means downloading the certificate and creating an MMC with the Certificates MMC snap-in targeted at the computer or service that needs to trust the issuer (Figure 13-16).

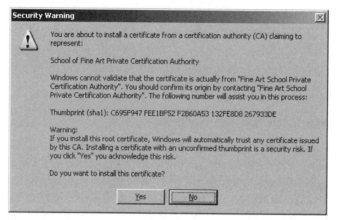

Figure 13-15   A warning when installing a root certificate that you should confirm that you are not installing an invalid certificate

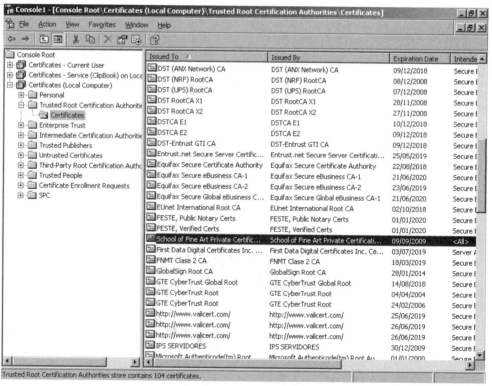

Figure 13-16   The Certificate MMC snap-in showing Trusted Root Certification Authorities for the Local Computer

Implementing Message Security

In today's interconnected world, SMTP is the protocol of choice for the delivery of e-mail. But it has security issues, with the main one being that SMTP sends e-mail messages in plaintext. This has a number of effects: a recipient has no absolute proof that the sender really was the sender, no absolute proof that the message is what that sender actually wrote, and no absolute proof that the message wasn't intercepted and read by someone else during its delivery.

The communication security options that have been discussed in this chapter and the previous chapter can help to some extent because you can encrypt the download and upload of all e-mail from the client to the server and from server-to-server, but these methods are not required, and they do nothing to protect the e-mail outside of these stages. For example, when an SMTP server uses TLS to communicate with an Exchange server, the e-mail travels across the Internet in an encrypted form and cannot be read or modified, but then it enters the queues of the SMTP virtual server on the Exchange server. If the administrator is not trustworthy or the server is not properly secured, the message and some of the headers, now in plaintext, could be modified while in the queue using several methods, including something as simple as Notepad, as can be seen in Figure 13-17.

```
NTFS_a31e764d01c4968100000001.EML - Notepad

File  Edit  Format  View  Help

Received: from mail.graphicdesigninstitute.com ([207.46.130.108]) by
mail.fineartschool.net over TLS secured channel with
Microsoft SMTPSVC(6.0.3790.0);
        Thu, 9 Sep 2004 16:28:20 +0100
Message-ID: <000a01c49681$a3ad07b0$0a05a8c0@graphicdesigninstitute.com>
From: "Shay Bashary" <shay@graphicdesigninstitute.com>
To: "Brian Burke" <brian@fineartschool.net>
Subject: How easy is SMTP to hack?
Date: Thu, 9 Sep 2004 16:28:13 +0100
MIME-Version: 1.0
Content-Type: text/plain;
        format=flowed;
        charset="iso-8859-1";
        reply-type=original
Content-Transfer-Encoding: 7bit
X-Priority: 3
X-MSMail-Priority: Normal
X-Mailer: Microsoft Outlook Express 6.00.2900.2180
X-MimeOLE: Produced By Microsoft MimeOLE V6.00.2900.2180
Return-Path: shay@graphicdesigninstitute.com
X-OriginalArrivalTime: 09 Sep 2004 15:28:20.0974 (UTC)
FILETIME=[A36920E0:01C49681]

Very easy I hear...
```

Figure 13-17   Opening an e-mail message from the SMTP virtual server Queue folder

When the modified e-mail message arrives, you cannot prove who tampered with it, if it was even noticed that the message had been altered.

> **More Info**   The *Exchange Server 2003 Message Security Guide* in the Exchange Server 2003 Technical Documentation Library (*http://go.microsoft.com/fwlink/?LinkID=21277*) covers S/MIME in much more detail than this overview. Please refer to this document and other resources on the Internet for a deeper understanding of cryptography.

To protect e-mail messages from being tampered with, you must implement end-to-end security. That is, the users must choose to encrypt their e-mail messages and the recipients need to have clients that can support the opening of those encrypted e-mail messages. This also means that both parties involved need to support the same end-to-end encryption method, and that is where S/MIME comes in. S/MIME was developed in 1995 and became one of a number of methods to provide message security, another being Pretty Good Privacy (PGP). Since then S/MIME has become standardized with two RFCs (2311 and 2312) and is now the standard for end-to-end message security for both proving the sender (digital signatures) and making the message readable only by the recipient (message encryption). S/MIME provides both digital signatures and digital encryption.

> **Note**   S/MIME version 3 is supported in Exchange Server 5.5 and later, Outlook 2000 (SR-1) and later, Outlook Express 5.01 and later, and Outlook Web Access running on an Exchange Server 2003 (depending upon the browser version and the installation of S/MIME software within that browser).

Digital Signatures

A digital signature is the most common use of S/MIME. It works by including in an e-mail a piece of information that could only be generated by someone holding unique information about the sender. This unique information comes from the sender's private key. Only the sender should hold this information and, if that is not the case, the key should be revoked to show that it is not to be trusted anymore. Revocation is a part of the PKI process not described in this book.

An e-mail client capable of providing support to add a digital signature to an e-mail message will take the body of the e-mail message and generate a mathematical hash of that information. The hash is a statistically unique output for a given input (the message body in this case), and one input will always generate the same hash output, which is extremely unlikely to be the same as the hash generated by any other input. The hash is then encrypted with the sender's private key and the encrypted hash plus the senders public key (which together is known as the digital signature), is attached to the e-mail message and sent. If the e-mail message is intercepted, though it is readable (Figure 13-18), it cannot be modified (Figure 13-19) without the recipient knowing it because digital signatures provide data integrity.

Figure 13-18   Opening a digitally signed e-mail from the SMTP virtual server Queue folder. Note the clear text portion of the e-mail

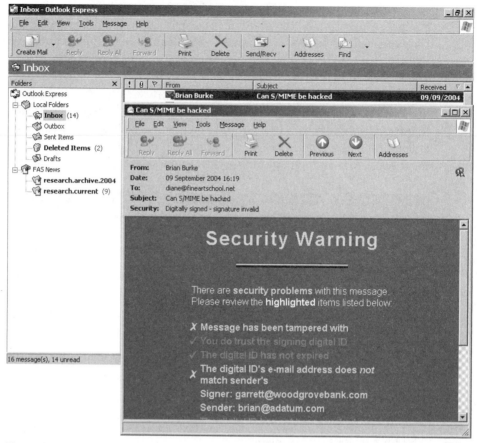

Figure 13-19   Outlook Express showing that a message has been tampered with and the sender claims to be someone other than who they are

S/MIME provides three protections for digitally signed e-mail messages. In addition to data integrity described above, and proving the sender is who they claim to be (referred to as authentication), the sender cannot claim not to have sent a message that has the sender's signature upon it. This is known as nonrepudiation, and in some areas, can make an e-mail message as legally binding as a signature on a contract.

Important   Though digital signatures provide data integrity, authentication, and nonrepudiation, they do not provide confidentiality. As can be seen in Figure 13-18, the e-mail is readable by anyone who can intercept the e-mail message.

When the e-mail message arrives at the recipient, if the e-mail client understands S/MIME encoded e-mail, the e-mail client takes the message body from the e-mail message and generates the same hash on the message body that the sender generated. The encrypted hash in the e-mail is then decrypted with the sender's public key (both contained within the digital signature), and the two hashes are compared. If they are the same, the message is valid.

If the recipient's e-mail client does not understand S/MIME e-mail, but does understand MIME encoded e-mail, the client will get the signature as an attached file named smime.p7s. This will be of no use to the client and the client will not be able to verify the digital signature. However, as long as opaque signing was not used, the client will be able to read the contents of the message because a clear-text version of the e-mail was included. Opaque signing is the translation of both the clear text and digitally signed parts of the e-mail into a single Base 64 encoded attachment. This opaque signing protects against messaging systems that can alter the e-mail during transit but means that e-mail clients that do not support S/MIME will be unable to read the e-mail.

Message Encryption

The second function of S/MIME is to encrypt the e-mail. This provides messages that are unreadable except to the recipient (known as confidentiality) and as with digital signatures, provides data integrity. However, unlike digital signatures, encryption cannot provide authentication or nonrepudiation. Authentication proves the sender and nonrepudiation guarantees that the sender sent the e-mail message.

> **Important**   Encrypted e-mail messages can additionally be signed, so a signed encrypted e-mail provides confidentiality and data integrity by the digital encryption process and authentication and nonrepudiation from the digital signature process. In practice, e-mail messages are signed and then encrypted rather than the other way around. Support for triple-wrapping also exists in Outlook Web Access. This is where the e-mail is signed, encrypted, and signed again for additional protection.

Message encryption works by the sender obtaining the intended recipient's public key and using that key to encrypt the message. Because public/private keys work as a pair, if some plaintext is encrypted with one key in the pair only, the other key in the pair can be used to decrypt the encrypted text. The sender can obtain the intended recipient's public key from a PKI directory or from a signed e-mail message sent to them by the intended recipient. By adding that user to the sender's contacts or the global address list (if that public key is needed by more than one person), the public key is available so that senders can encrypt messages to that recipient.

Note The entire message is not encrypted with the intended recipient's public key because that would introduce a considerable performance impact. Rather, a randomly generated "session" key is used to encrypt the message and the intended recipient's public key used to encrypt the session key. This session key, used for this e-mail only, does not use as complicated algorithms as public/private keys and so is a quicker process with a lower performance impact.

Once the message is encrypted, the e-mail client adds readable headers to the e-mail to allow the message to be routed through an e-mail system (Figure 13-20). Though these headers will contain the sender and recipient's names, along with e-mail addresses and the subject, these headers are included within the encrypted portion of the e-mail as well. If changed, it will have no effect on the final decryption of the e-mail message, allowing the recipient, and only the recipient, to read the message.

Figure 13-20 Intercepting an S/MIME encrypted e-mail. Notice that this e-mail contains encrypted text only

The recipient can only read the message if the recipient holds the matching private key to the public key used to encrypt the message by the sender. The recipient uses their private key to decrypt the session key that was used for the encryption of the message at the sender. The decrypted session key is then used to decrypt the message, which is faster than using public/private keys for the entire message. Table 13-6 shows which key is needed for each S/MIME process.

Table 13-6   Keys Needed During S/MIME

	Sender	Recipient
Signing	Uses own private key	Confirms with sender's public key
Encrypting	Uses recipient's public key	Decrypts with own private key

Because public/private key digital certificates have an associated date stamp on them, they should not be used after they expire, but as long as the recipient keeps a copy of all the certificates ever issued, he or she will be able to go back and read old signed e-mail messages. If you lose or delete a private key, all e-mail encrypted by the matching public key becomes unreadable.

> **Tip**   Digitally signed and encrypted e-mail messages are identified in Outlook and Outlook Express with a different icon. Digitally signed e-mail messages are shown as an envelope with a red certificate icon and encrypted e-mail messages as an envelope with blue padlock .

Configuring Clients for S/MIME

Versions of Outlook before 2000 SR-1a and before Outlook Express 5.01 do not support S/MIME. If you have these clients within your organization, they will not be able to use the functionality of digitally signed and encrypted e-mail messages.

It is possible that recipients outside of your organization could be using e-mail clients that do not support S/MIME, so you need to ensure that digitally signed e-mail messages sent to these recipients are not opaque signed because they will be unreadable. Therefore, for global readability of a digitally signed message use the Send Clear Text Signed Message When Sending Signed Messages option in Outlook 2003 (Figure 13-21) or do not use the Encode Messages Before Signing (Opaque Signing) option in Outlook Express 6 (Figure 13-22).

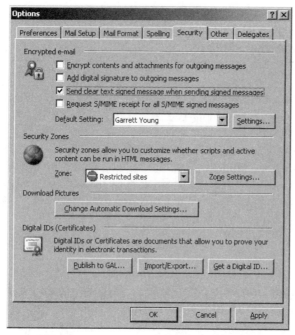

Figure 13-21   Setting Outlook 2003 to do clear text signing of e-mail messages

Figure 13-22   Setting Outlook Express 6 to not do opaque signing of e-mail messages

On supported clients, the user will need to obtain a digital certificate that contains the e-mail address that the user wants to encrypt for. For example, if a user has a digital certificate for a work e-mail address, they cannot use it to digitally sign or encrypt messages using a personal e-mail address.

Important   Support for Key Management Server, found in earlier versions of Exchange Server, does not exist in Exchange Server 2003. All certificate issuing, storage and management functions are now performed by your chosen PKI.

Support for S/MIME in Outlook Web Access has been introduced with Exchange Server 2003. For Outlook Web Access to support S/MIME the browser must be Internet Explorer 6 or later, running on Windows 2000 or later, and have Outlook Web Access S/MIME Control installed. The Outlook Web Access S/MIME Control, provides the same support for S/MIME that Outlook 2003 does, apart from not supporting secure read receipts. Without the Outlook Web Access S/MIME Control the user can read clear-text signed S/MIME messages but is not able to read encrypted messages or send digitally signed or encrypted messages.

Note   Outlook Mobile Access does not contain any S/MIME functionality. Therefore, Outlook Mobile Access users have the same S/MIME support as an Outlook Web Access user without the S/MIME control: the ability to read normal e-mail messages and clear-text digitally signed e-mail messages only.

Note   The Pocket Outlook client that runs on handheld devices that can utilize Exchange 2003 ActiveSync have the same limitations as Outlook Mobile Access users.

When using the Outlook Web Access S/MIME Control, the Exchange Server takes the part of the e-mail client. Therefore, support for the Outlook Web Access S/MIME Control must be enabled within Exchange Server 2003 before users can view encrypted messages in Outlook Web Access with the S/MIME Control installed. This support on the Exchange server requires installation of the root digital certificates of any accepted certificate issuer and the ability of the server to connect over HTTP or LDAP to retrieve revocation information.

The Outlook Web Access client and holder of the client's private key maintain all responsibility for encryption and decryption processes that use the private key. The Exchange server takes on all roles involving other users' public keys; for example, the validation, trust, and revocation of digitally signed message certificates.

On the client, the installation of the Outlook Web Access S/MIME Control can be done in two ways. The first involves the download of the control from the options page in Outlook Web Access, but this requires local administrator rights to install the software. The second is to deploy the software using Group Policy or some other software deployment process. Group Policy software deployment requires that the software to be deployed be an .msi file. The Exchange Server 2003 SP1 version, or later, of the Outlook Web Access S/MIME Control is a self-extracting .exe file that contains an .msi file. The setup package is named *setupmcl.exe* and is located in *drive:*\Program Files\Exchsrvr\Exchweb\#\Cabs (where # is the version number of each update of Outlook Web Access on the server). The latest installed release of the setupmcl.exe file will be found in the \Cabs subfolder of the highest version number folder.

Important Due to security enhancements in Windows XP SP2, it is not possible to use the original or Exchange Server SP1 S/MIME Control within Internet Explorer. An update is available for Exchange Server which does work for Windows XP SP2 users. This update can be downloaded from *http://go.microsoft.com/fwlink/?linkid=3052&kbid=883543*.

Tip To extract the .msi file (mimeclnt.msi) from *setupmcl.exe* run *setupmcl.exe –x* from the command line. You will be prompted for a location for the extracted files.

Support for Outlook Web Access S/MIME Control on the Exchange server involves the installation of the trusted root digital certificates that are used to validate users' digital certificates. These certificates must be installed in the Exchange server's Personal store or Trusted Root Certification Authorities store, and in a front-end and back-end network this needs to be done on all the back-end servers.

More Info Full information on configuring the Outlook Web Access S/MIME Control can be found in the *Exchange Server 2003 Message Security Guide*, which can be downloaded from the Exchange Server 2003 Technical Documentation Library at *http://go.microsoft.com/fwlink/?LinkID=21277*.

Securing the MAPI-based Client/Server Communication

The Outlook client uses MAPI to communicate with the Exchange server. MAPI provides for more functionality in the client/server e-mail system than the public standards of POP3 and IMAP4. It is the recommended client/server protocol for an Exchange organization. MAPI is an extensive set of functions that can be used by developers to create mail-enabled applications. It is also used to provide control over the creation of messages and the management of messages on both the client and the server. MAPI uses the RPC protocol for communication between the client and the server.

To protect the MAPI client in the client's communication to the Exchange server, you can enable the Encrypt Data Between Microsoft Office Outlook And Microsoft Exchange Server on the Security tab of the dialog box accessible from the More Settings button while configuring an Outlook profile for a Microsoft Exchange Server user. This dialog box is shown in Figure 13-23.

Note   The level of Outlook encryption is the same as that supported by Internet Explorer on the computer running Outlook with encryption enabled, therefore Windows 2000 and later can provide for 128-bit RPC encryption.

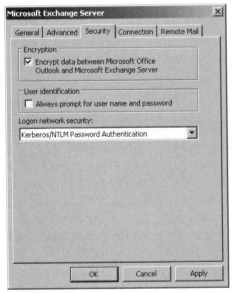

Figure 13-23   Enabling encryption of the MAPI communication between the Outlook client and the Exchange server

Because MAPI uses the RPC protocol to communicate, it works very well in a LAN environment. RPC is a synchronous protocol, requiring good and reasonably fast connectivity to ensure that the client and server can communicate within a short space of time. If the user is not on the internal network, it is possible to provide MAPI access to the Exchange server in two different ways. The first, and recommended way, is to implement RPC over HTTP as described in Chapter 12. The second is to configure an advanced firewall such as Microsoft ISA Server 2000, running Feature Pack 1 or later, to publish the RPC port of the mailbox server so that all the MAPI based RPC traffic to go between the Internet-based client and the Exchange server is intercepted by ISA Server, filtered, and if valid RPC MAPI traffic, then the traffic is allowed into the LAN.

RPC over HTTP encapsulates the RPC-based MAPI traffic inside an HTTPS session that is directed at an RPC proxy server on your LAN. The firewalls protecting your network are configured to allow HTTPS traffic to reach the RPC proxy server. At the RPC proxy server the RPC MAPI traffic is removed from the HTTPS packets and forwarded to the relevant back-end Exchange server. The RPC portion of the communication is entirely on the LAN and is capable of dealing with the synchronous issues of the RPC protocol.

Even though RPC over HTTP is the recommended method for connecting MAPI clients to Exchange Server over the Internet, it has very specific requirements that could impact its deployment in many networks. RPC over HTTP will only operate if your front-end and back-end Exchange servers are running Exchange Server 2003 on a Windows Server 2003 operating system and your client is Outlook 2003 running on Windows XP SP2 (or SP1 and a hotfix). Your global catalog servers need to run on Windows Server 2003 also. If you want to support other versions of Outlook on the Internet, you can use ISA Server to publish and protect your Exchange Server's native protocol over the Internet, remembering that a suitably reliant connection is required to support the RPC protocol.

> **Warning**   Publishing RPC involves giving your firewalls the ability to receive TCP port 135 traffic. Unfortunately, these RPC ports are the main attack destination of viruses such as Blaster and Welchia. Therefore, it is now common to find that Internet providers close access to this port over their networks. For example, you can find a page informing users of one of the United Kingdom's largest broadband ISPs of this at *http://www.ntl-world.com/tunnel.php?task=portBlocking*, including the statement that it will stop Outlook connecting to Exchange Server.

An Outlook client communicates with an Exchange server using RPC, as shown in Figure 13-24.

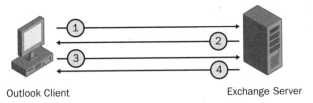

Outlook Client   Exchange Server

Figure 13-24   Outlook, Exchange Server, and RPC

The communication process is as follows:

1. The Outlook Client connects to the Exchange server on TCP port 135 (the Windows Locator Service or Endpoint Mapper port), referencing the Exchange Server components of RPC.

2. Exchange Server answers and informs the client of the randomly assigned TCP port that it should connect to.

3. The Outlook client connects to this assigned port and asks for any e-mail.

4. The Exchange server responds from this assigned port with the information required by the client.

ISA Server 2000 with Feature Pack 1 and ISA Server 2004 contain an application layer filter that is used to publish selected RPC components, which are referred to as Universal Unique Identifiers (UUIDs) and block all other RPC UUIDs. With ISA Server 2000 Feature Pack 1 installed, a protocol definition exists with the correct Exchange Server RPC UUIDs defined. It operates by accepting connections on the RPC listening port of TCP 135, after determining if the client requests a connection to Exchange Server by including in the request valid Exchange Server UUIDs. If the connection does not contain a valid UUID, the connection is dropped.

> **Tip**   The Windows Server 2003 Resource Kit includes a tool named RPC-DUMP. This tool lists all of the RPC UUIDs registered on a server at the time by entering rpcdump /i on the command line.

If the request is valid, the RPC connection is forwarded to the Exchange server, and the Exchange server answers it. The response is the port that the Outlook client can use to communicate directly with the Exchange server. This answer returns to the client via the ISA Server. The ISA Server understands this response and changes the port in the response to the port that ISA Server will open on its external interface to listen on behalf of the server. The firewall rule that ISA Server creates allows just that client to reach this port on the external interface of the ISA Server and no one else. When the client connects to this port, ISA Server forwards the request to the Exchange server. Full communication is established for just Exchange Server RPC data for that particular user on the Internet. Other users go through the same process, but other users cannot use the ports open for different users.

By blocking access to all of the RPC endpoints listed at TCP port 135, apart from those you need to publish, you disable access to your entire network apart from the services whose UUIDs are allowed through the ISA Server. The use of tools, such as RPCDUMP mentioned earlier, and viruses, such as Blaster, will not get a response from the external interface of the ISA Server because they do not request access to a specific UUID.

> **More Info**   The document "Protecting Windows RPC Traffic" at *http:// www.microsoft.com/technet/prodtechnol/isa/2000/maintain/rpcwisa.mspx* will give you more information about the ISA Server and RPC publishing. Note that this document is out-of-date with regard to its references on known exploits of RPC. It is vital that any Exchange server and ISA server are fully patched before use, in order to protect from RPC-infecting viruses, such as Blaster.

To fully configure an Outlook-to-Exchange Server RPC publishing scenario requires an IP address on the external interface of the ISA Server for each Exchange server that you need to make available. Because the protocol is MAPI, you cannot use front-end servers, so each back-end/mailbox server that will be accessed will need a unique IP address on the external interface of the ISA Server. Secondly, each internal server name for the published Exchange servers will need to be available to resolve on the Internet as well. The Internet-resolved version of the address will point to the external ISA Server IP address that is published for the matching Exchange server. To avoid this, you could create a HOSTS file entry on all remote users' computers pointing to the NetBIOS name of the server.

In Figure 13-24, once the connection is established, Exchange Server instructs the Outlook client to authenticate to Active Directory. Because Active Directory is not published over the Internet, you need to configure the Exchange server to proxy authentication requests on behalf of its clients. This is achieved by the setting of the DWORD registry value No RFR Service to 1. No RFR Service is created at HKEY_LOCAL_MACHINE\System\CurrentControlSet\Services\MSExchangeSA\Parameters, and then restarting the Microsoft Exchange System Attendant service.

Once the above is in place, you can create the firewall rule. As with all firewall rules on ISA Server, the published server must be able to route its packets via the firewall to the Internet. This is achieved by setting the Exchange server default gateway to the internal interface of the ISA server or ensuring that whatever default gateway is used on the Exchange server, it ultimately routes through the ISA server. The ISA

Server firewall rule is created in ISA Server 2000 using the Mail Server Security Wizard (Figure 13-25) and in ISA Server 2004 using the Mail Server Publishing Rule (Figure 13-26).

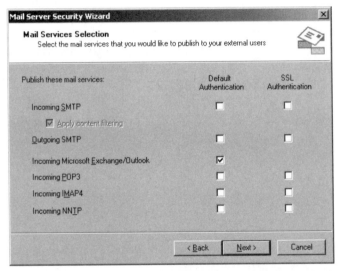

Figure 13-25   Creating the Exchange Server RPC firewall rule using the Secure Mail Server option in ISA Server 2000 Management Console

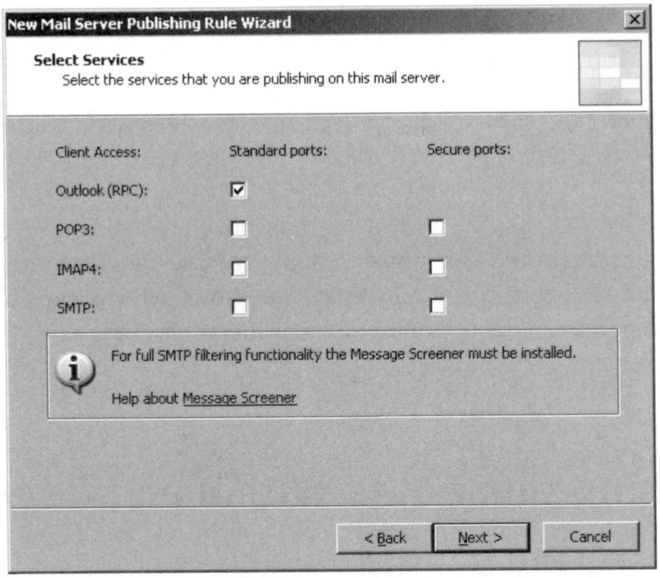

Figure 13-26   Creating an Exchange Server RPC firewall rule using the Mail Server Publishing Rule in ISA Server 2004

Finally, in Figure 13-23 you saw how to enable Outlook to encrypt the MAPI traffic between itself and the Exchange server. A registry setting in ISA Server 2000 and a firewall rule property in ISA Server 2004 allow you to enforce this option on the client and to reject the connection if it is not encrypted. In ISA Server 2000 Feature Pack 1, this is done by setting the `MinimumAuthenticationLevel` value at `HKEY_LOCAL_MACHINE\Software\Microsoft\FPC\PluginRPC` to 6 and restarting the firewall service. In ISA Server 2004, the same option is enabled by checking the Enforce Encryption option in the Configure RPC Exchange RPC Policy dialog box (Figure 13-27), which is displayed by right-clicking the firewall rule for this connection.

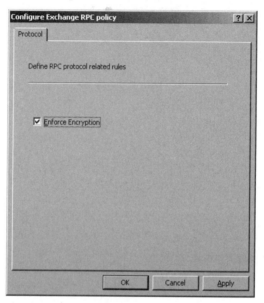

Figure 13-27   Enforcing Outlook encryption when connection is through ISA Server 2004 to Exchange Server

> **Tip**   Depending upon the version of Outlook, you may find that the client appears to have connected, and will report that it has on the status bar, but when you come to send and receive e-mail it will fail if ISA Server requires encrypted sessions and Outlook is not using them.

Protecting Transmission Paths Within and Between Routing Groups

Exchange Server 2003 uses SMTP as its primary protocol for the delivery of messages both to other Exchange servers within an organization and the Internet, though it uses the RPC or X.400 protocols (depending upon connector configuration) to deliver e-mail to Exchange 5.5 servers or earlier within the Exchange organization.

SMTP transmits its information in clear text both within your Exchange organization and to the Internet. Even though two Exchange servers will authenticate when sending messages within the organization, a network sniffer utility will be able to read the content of the e-mail to some extent. When two Exchange servers communicate, the default method of transmitting plain text e-mail messages is to use Transport Neutral Encapsulation Format (TNEF) (otherwise known as Exchange RTF). This obscures the body of a plain text e-mail from a network sniffer, but because it is not an encryption mechanism it does nothing to ensure the confidentiality of your e-mail as it travels around the Exchange organization because it is easily reversible. Additionally, if the e-mail is a HTML formatted e-mail, it is typical that the client will provide a plain text version of the e-mail as one of the MIME parts. The plain text part of the e-mail will be TNEF encoded, but the HTML portion will be readable. Therefore, it is important to consider protecting the transmission of e-mail within and between the routing groups of your Exchange organization.

Protection with IPSec

To protect your transmission paths around your Exchange organization, the easiest solution is to use IPSec. This will ensure that any communication between selected predetermined servers over selected ports will be encrypted.

By default, an Exchange organization acts as a single routing entity in that all servers running Exchange 2000 Server or later can communicate with all the other servers running Exchange 2000 Server or later without any additional routing configuration. But this makes securing your configuration difficult to do. For example, if you had eight Exchange servers located in two sites, with four servers per site and no additional configuration, your routing path would be every server direct to every other server regardless of site boundaries. Though this could be protected with IPSec, adding a new server to the organization would require changes to existing IPSec rules and would include making routing troubleshooting a complex process.

The use of routing groups and routing group connectors will help define the path that messages take and allow precise control of the use of IPSec over these paths. Figure 13-28 shows the two routing groups in the above example, but configured to allow a selected server in each routing group to communicate with the other routing group. With the assumption that the four servers in one routing group are within one office on a switched network and the same for the other office, IPSec is only needed to protect the WAN communication. If you need to protect your Exchange organization from internal attacks, you must implement IPSec on all Exchange servers in the enterprise.

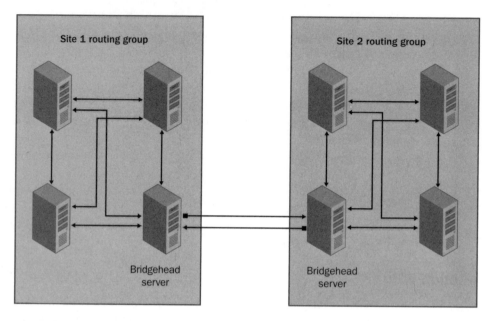

➤ = Routing group connector

Figure 13-28 Transmission paths when routing groups and bridgehead servers are configured

The disadvantage of specifying between which servers messages can flow is that failure of one of the two servers that hold the bridgehead for the routing group connector will result in queued mail on both sides. Therefore, the recommendation in scenarios that require the connector to be secured is that you have a few servers providing the connector and not just one. It is still easier and more controlled to secure message flow between known selected servers than all the servers in the default configuration.

Another advantage of IPSec for connector security is that it is transparent to Exchange Server. With the correct IPSec policy configuration you can ensure that any communication between two servers, and not just Exchange Server-related traffic, is encrypted. To save on resource usage it is best to configure your Exchange servers to use IPSec for just the ports that need protecting. In the case of routing group connectors and SMTP connectors, this is TCP port 25 and TCP port 102 for any X.400 connectors that are in place.

> **Important** X.400 connectors in an Exchange Server 2003 network are used to connect to existing Exchange Server 5.5 computers within your Exchange organization or to third-party X.400 systems. Installations of Exchange 5.5 or earlier, running on Windows 2000 or later, can use the IPSec services of the operating system. However, any installations of Exchange 5.5 running on Windows NT 4.0 will require the installation of third party IPSec software or hardware, as Windows NT 4.0 does not provide native support for IPSec.

Protection with TLS

An alternative to the use of IPSec for the protection of SMTP virtual server and SMTP connectors is the use of Transport Layer Security (TLS). Although TLS is most useful in the protection of communications between Internet-connected SMTP servers, it can be used internally. This can take more configuration than the equivalent IPSec configuration; however, it operates in places where IPSec cannot, such as to the Internet or through internal firewalls and Network Address Translation (NAT) devices that cannot support the transmission of most IPSec packets. To enable TLS on each Exchange server, each SMTP virtual server needs to be configured with a digital certificate where the subject of the certificate matches the fully qualified domain name (FQDN) of the Exchange server. This means a different certificate for each server. Once the certificates are in place, the SMTP virtual servers on each Exchange server can be configured to send and receive with TLS as a requirement. The only servers that cannot have this requirement are those that send and receive e-mail to and from the Internet. These Internet gateway servers will require two SMTP virtual servers. The first, without TLS enabled, for routing SMTP traffic to and from the Web and a second for the routing of SMTP traffic to internal SMTP virtual servers within the Exchange organization. This second virtual server would need TLS enabled.

Protecting Gateways and Messaging Connectors

In addition to the protection of the transmission paths between different Exchange servers, as discussed in the previous section, it is also important to protect the actual gateways and connectors. This protection is important because it helps to ensure the integrity of any message before and after it is delivered as e-mail is only protected by IPSec or TLS during delivery.

Protecting Exchange Connectors

The period of time that Exchange Server holds the data in the Queue folder on the disk will depend upon whatever is the next step in the delivery path. But for this period of time it is important that messages cannot be read, changed, or deleted from malicious intent. This protection involves the use of NTFS permissions to secure the Queue folders of each connector. The default Queue folder locations are found in Table 13-7.

Table 13-7   Default Queue Locations

Transport protocol	Path
SMTP	\program files\Exchsrvr\mailroot\vsi #\queue (where # is the ID of the SMTP virtual directory)
X.400	\program files\Exchsrvr\mtadata

The recommended permissions for the two folders in Table 13-7 are both the same. These are to not inherit any parent folder permissions and to set the following:

- **Local Administrators**   Full Control on this folder, subfolders, and files
- **Creator Owner**   Full Control on subfolders and files only
- **Server Operators**   Modify on this folder, subfolders, and files
- **System**   Full Control on this folder, subfolders, and files
- **Users**   Read and Execute on this folder, subfolders, and files

These permissions can be set automatically, along with all the other recommended Exchange Server backend/mailbox server folder permissions, by using the Exchange 2003 Backend.inf security template, which is part of the book *Exchange Server 2003 Security Hardening Guide*. This can be downloaded from the Exchange Server 2003 Technical Documentation Library at *http://go.microsoft.com/fwlink/ ?LinkID=21277.*

Although the Queue folder allows the Users group Read and Execute permissions, users are not allowed to log on to the Exchange server using the console. This is enforced during Exchange Server 2003 installation by the removal of the right for Domain Users to Allow Log On Locally on each individual Exchange server by modification of the local computer policy. Exchange Server 2003 does not require this right for users to log on to Outlook Web Access as was the case with earlier versions of Exchange Server.

Because the recommended permissions included users, and the default permissions are just inherited from the \Program Files folder, it is important to ensure, especially if you are not going to apply the security templates as recommended earlier, that users do not gain the right to log on locally via other means. If they gain this right there is an increased possibility of messages being tampered with while being processed through the queues.

> **Caution**   It is not possible to use file level encryption technologies such as Encrypting File System (EFS) on the Exchange Server installation folder.

Protecting Gateways

Any Exchange connector that sends its data to a network not managed by your organization should be protected in some way. This does not mean installation of firewalls for the protection of IP networks exclusively but can include telephony systems for the protection of fax and text messaging gateways.

The protection of SMTP connectors is covered in depth in Chapter 11. For guidance on the protection of other non-Internet connectors refer to the manufacturer of either the software or the network it uses.

Protecting Other Connectors

Exchange Server provides other connectors for interoperation with other e-mail systems, and software companies sell products that integrate with Exchange Server by way of a connector. The protection of these connectors is outside the scope of this book, but what you need to consider when deciding if the connector needs further security is the current level of connector security, the impact to your organization of change to the data that the connector sends, and where this change can occur in the transmission path.

Once an assessment of the potential for damage has been made, the costs of mitigating that damage can be assessed, and it can then be decided if these other connectors need additional security.

Protecting Mobile Communication Paths

Exchange Server 2003 introduces two new ways for mobile users to keep up-to-date with the contents of their mailboxes and public folders.

The first new service is Outlook Mobile Access, and the concept of this service will be familiar to users of Microsoft Mobile Information Server (MMIS). This service provides a simple view of their mailboxes to users of mobile phones. Though actually any HTTP browser can access Outlook Mobile Access, it is designed for small screen devices that connect over low or expensive bandwidth networks.

The second mobile communications feature is Exchange ActiveSync (EAS). This is used by Pocket PC devices to synchronize directly to the Exchange server via a wireless connection to the Internet rather than needing to be connected to their client PC to synchronize. If you are a current Pocket PC user, you will be aware of the Microsoft ActiveSync software. This runs on your desktop PC and enables synchronization of e-mail and other resources using a cable or infrared connection. Exchange

ActiveSync means that you do not have to be near your desktop PC, you just need some form of IP connectivity. This could include a wireless network card in your Pocket PC while you sit within range of a wireless LAN or a Bluetooth link to your mobile phone and a General Packet Radio Service (GPRS) connection via your phone provider to the Internet.

Protecting Outlook Mobile Access

By default, Outlook Mobile Access is disabled when installing Exchange Server 2003. To enable this interface to your mailbox it requires two settings in Exchange Server, a suitably secure network connection and, optionally, a setting in Active Directory Users and Computers. First, Outlook Mobile Access needs to be enabled globally for the Exchange organization. This option is available from Exchange System Manager, Global Settings, Mobile Services, and then checking the Enable Outlook Mobile Access option. The second Exchange Server option is to determine if unsupported devices will be allowed to access the application.

Outlook Mobile Access is an ASP.NET application that presents the user's mailbox in a view suitable for mobile devices, as shown in Figure 13-29.

Figure 13-29   Outlook Mobile Access viewed on the Microsoft Smartphone platform

Because each mobile device on the market can have a different range of functions with regard to its embedded browser application, the Exchange server hosting Outlook Mobile Access needs to know what mobile device is connecting and what the functionality of this device is. ASP.NET knows the functionality of a number of devices and this information can be updated through a download named device update (DU). Exchange Server 2003 installs DU2 and Exchange Server 2003 SP1 installs DU4. Each device update contains all the supported devices included in previous updates. If a device is not contained within the latest installed device update, the Exchange administrator can choose to Enable Unsupported Devices once Outlook Mobile Access is enabled, as shown in Figure 13-30.

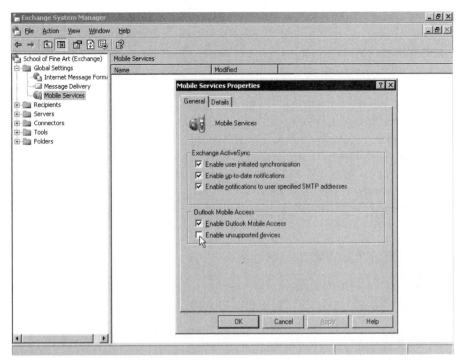

Figure 13-30   Enabling Outlook Mobile Access with the option to enable unsupported devices

> **Note**   A list of supported devices for each update, and a download of each update, is available at *http://www.asp.net/mobile/testeddevices.aspx*.

The use of an unsupported device will prompt a warning to the user when the user browses to the Outlook Mobile Access URL. In Exchange Server 2003 with SP1, the Unsupported Device Warning page has a new link displayed below the existing OK link. The new link reads OK, And Do Not Warn Me Again. When a user indicates a preference not to receive the warning page again, the user agent string of the user's current device is added to the *msExchEmbUserAcceptedDevices* property on the root folder of the user's mailbox. The property is a multi-valued string.

If a user attempts to use Outlook Mobile Access with an unsupported device and the administrator has allowed browsing with unsupported devices, Outlook Mobile Access will check the user agent against the list of user agent strings stored on the mailbox. If the user agent string matches one of the strings stored in msExchEmbUser-AcceptedDevices property, the warning page is not shown and the device will be automatically taken to the Outlook Mobile Access Browse Main Menu.

If your organization has standardized on a particular device and you find that it is not included in the supported device range, you can customize the information used by the .NET Framework by visiting the ASP.NET Device Profiling website at *http://www.asp.net/mobile/profile/default.aspx*. This provides you with a Web page to visit using your mobile device and takes you through a series of questions about the capabilities of your device. The answers to these questions are obvious when browsing through the device. For example, you will be shown a JPEG file and asked if you can see it, and if it is in color. This will answer questions on device support for graphics and color displays. Once you have finished the wizard you will be provided with a config file to add to either the web.config or the machine.config .NET Framework configuration files. To add a device for Outlook Mobile Access, you will need to modify machine.config, as web.config might be updated in future service packs and hotfixes. Once you have completed the modification to machine.config Outlook Mobile Access will be customized to the functions of that particular device, such as color, screen size, number of buttons, and so forth.

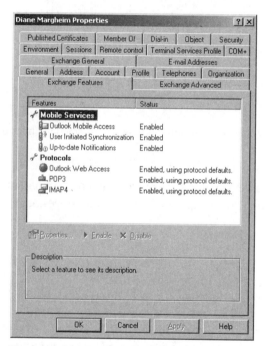

Figure 13-31   Exchange features for each user, including the ability to enable or disable Outlook Mobile Access

Once the two global settings for Outlook Mobile Access are set, the website can be configured and users enabled or disabled for access to Outlook Mobile Access. By default, all users are enabled for Outlook Mobile Access (Figure 13-31) once the global settings for Outlook Mobile Access are enabled. Tools such as ADModify.NET (which can be downloaded from the Microsoft PPS FTP site at *ftp.microsoft.com/PSS/ Tools/Exchange Support Tools/ADModify/*) can be used to bulk adjust users' settings to disable Outlook Mobile Access and many other Active Directory settings as well.

You can reach the website to access Outlook Mobile Access by browsing to the /oma HTTP virtual directory of your Exchange server. Because mobile access is almost exclusively an external-to-the-network connection, it will be typically the same FQDN as Outlook Web Access. Where Outlook Web Access is http://*fqdn*/exchange, Outlook Mobile Access will be http://*fqdn*/oma. To enable this will require adding to any advanced firewall the rules to allow the /oma/* path and, additionally, not to block the .aspx file extension.

To fully secure your Outlook Mobile Access installation you should use SSL. Unlike the decisions for Outlook Web Access, where you could use a digital certificate from either a public or private certification authority, Outlook Mobile Access requires a public certification authority. The reason for this public certificate has to do with how mobile phones connect to the Internet. Typically, the communication is over the Wireless Transport Layer Security (WTLS) protocol for the Wireless Access Protocol (WAP) session between the mobile phone and your mobile operator's WAP gateway. After this, an SSL-protected HTTP session to your Exchange server is made by your operator's WAP gateway. This means that any SSL certificate you install needs to be trusted by the mobile phone company and not by your clients' mobile phones. This almost certainly means the use of a publicly issued digital certificate, but checks should be made to ensure that your choice of public certification authority is trusted by your mobile phone company.

The /oma virtual directory is automatically created as part of the Exchange Virtual Server, even if Outlook Mobile Access is not enabled. Therefore, the /oma virtual directory can remain on the server because it serves no function if not enabled. For Outlook Mobile Access to operate the /oma and /exchange virtual directories, they need to be available on all back-end/mailbox Exchange servers and all front-end servers that will offer the service. Authentication support of Outlook Mobile Access is set to Basic authentication and cannot be changed, and thus the need for SSL is because of the unencrypted nature of basic authentication.

The only authentication option that can be changed for Outlook Mobile Access is the default domain value. It is recommended that this value be set to the most common logon domain to reduce the typing required by users on a mobile phone keypad. For example, if the Default Domain was blank, then Terry, a user at Woodgrove Bank, would need to enter **woodgrovebank\terry** to log on, whereas setting **woodgrovebank** as the Default Domain would allow him to enter just his user name (and password, of course) to authenticate. This setting of the default domain needs to be set on all the back-end Exchange servers.

When you use Outlook Mobile Access on an Exchange server that is not part of a front-end and back-end network you cannot use Outlook Mobile Access and forms-based authentication at the same time. The same is true if the /exchange virtual directory is configured to require SSL in IIS Manager or if the /exchange virtual directory does not support Kerberos authentication. The problem is that the Outlook Mobile Access application does a direct WebDAV call to the /exchange virtual directory in the

form of *http://netbios_name_of_mailbox_server/exchange/mailbox_alias.* If the /
exchange virtual directory requires SSL or if Forms Based Authentication is enabled,
the Outlook Mobile Access application cannot access the /exchange virtual directory
and so errors appear in both Event Viewer and on the mobile device. The solution is
either to connect to a front-end server or configure a new virtual directory just for the
use of Outlook Mobile Access. Instructions for this task can be found in Microsoft
Knowledge Base article 817379, "Exchange ActiveSync and Outlook Mobile Access
errors occur when SSL or forms-based authentication is required for Exchange Server
2003" at *http://go.microsoft.com/fwlink/?linkid=3052&kbid=817379.*

> **Tip**   To test Outlook Mobile Access you can use Internet Explorer. Though it
> is not a mobile phone, it will authenticate you and display your mailbox.
> Once you have confirmed that Outlook Mobile Access works in a Web
> browser, you can proceed to test it on a mobile phone.

Exchange ActiveSync

Outlook Mobile Access provides no synchronization between the user's mobile
device and Exchange Server. You need to be online and connected to your mobile
carrier to read and write messages. If you have no signal you cannot access your e-
mail. Pocket PC 2003 devices such as the Motorola MPx200 Smartphone or HP iPAQ
allow the user to have a copy of their mailbox on the device, to read and compose
messages without being connected, and then to synchronize the device to the
Exchange server as needed. This functionality is provided on Exchange Server 2003
and is known as Exchange ActiveSync (EAS). It is shown in process in Figure 13-32.

Figure 13-32   Exchange ActiveSync operating on a Microsoft Pocket PC 2003

In addition to the user choosing when to synchronize, Smartphone users can configure Up-to-date Notifications. These occur when a new message arrives in the mailbox, which causes Exchange Server to send a message to the mobile carrier, which in turn alerts the device, by way of a system notification, to start synchronizing. This means that the device is up-to-date whenever the user needs it. Up-to-date Notifications works for Windows Mobile 2003-based devices only. Devices running Windows Mobile 2002 can be configured to automatically run ActiveSync on a schedule to regularly download the latest changes to a user's mailbox because this operating system does not support Up-to-date Notifications. An example of Exchange ActiveSync network configuration is shown in Figure 13-33.

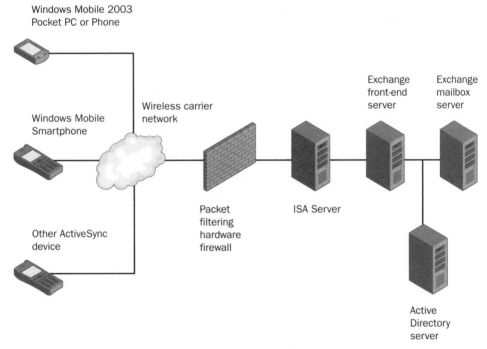

Figure 13-33   An example Exchange ActiveSync network for the support of all ActiveSync-capable devices

The default configuration of a Windows Mobile 2003 device is to synchronize on a schedule during office hours and to synchronize when e-mail arrives after hours. It is the option to synchronize e-mail when it arrives that makes use of the Up-to-date Notifications functionality.

Exchange ActiveSync is enabled by default on your Exchange Server 2003 when it is installed, and the HTTP virtual directory over which the clients connect is created in the default HTTP Exchange Virtual Server. The URL is /Microsoft-Server-ActiveSync and if you have an application filter firewall, such as Microsoft ISA Server, you will need to allow this URL to be published.

Exchange ActiveSync contains three global settings, each of which can be enabled and disabled. Figure 13-34 shows the global settings for Exchange Active-Sync. Once the global settings are correct, individual settings can be applied for each user. By default, each user is able to perform user-initiated synchronization to the Exchange server and the Exchange server can send Up-to-date Notifications to the device.

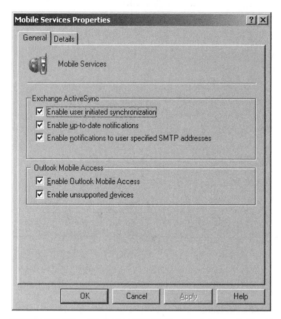

Figure 13-34   Global settings for Exchange ActiveSync

To secure your Exchange server for Exchange ActiveSync you will need to implement SSL. As with the Outlook Mobile Access security requirement of a publicly issued digital certificate to implement SSL, Exchange ActiveSync communication will need this if the device connects via a mobile carrier's gateway server. If the device connects directly to the Internet and not via a carrier gateway, you can install private certification authority certificates using the Add Root Certificate tool available from the Exchange Server downloads site (*http://www.microsoft.com/exchange/downloads*). You only need to use the Add Root Certificate tool for Windows Mobile 2002 devices; for Windows Mobile 2003 devices you can install the private certificate by browsing the certification authority website and downloading it as shown in Figure 13-35.

Figure 13-35   Installing a certification authority root certificate on a Windows Pocket PC 2003

As with Outlook Mobile Access, Exchange ActiveSync will not operate if the Exchange server that you synchronize with is a mailbox server that requires SSL on the /exchange virtual directory or implements Forms Based Authentication. Additional to these Outlook Mobile Access restrictions, Exchange ActiveSync requires the /exchange virtual directory to support Kerberos authentication. The steps to enable Exchange ActiveSync on a server that has these restrictions can be found in Microsoft Knowledge Base article 817379, "Exchange ActiveSync and Outlook Mobile Access errors occur when SSL or forms-based authentication is required for Exchange Server 2003" (*http://go.microsoft.com/fwlink/?linkid=3052&kbid=817379*).

The only communication between the Exchange organization and the mobile device that supports EAS that will not be protected by the SSL connection are the notifications for the Windows Mobile 2003 operating system. As described above, these are sent to the mobile device via the mobile carrier as an SMTP and then SMS message. The messages sent by Exchange Server 2003 contain a unique ID that informs the device that it has a reason to initiate Exchange ActiveSync, and though these messages are clear text they do not contain anything to do with the actual message(s) that they are notifying the user's mobile device about.

To allow users to configure their devices to send notifications via SMTP you should add valid carriers in Exchange System Manager. Figure 13-36 shows a Smartphone being configured to use A. Datum Mobiles. This value matches a mobile carrier configured under Global Settings, Mobile Services in Exchange System Manager.

Figure 13-36   Configuring a Windows Mobile 2003 device to use Up-to-date Notifications via an SMTP address.

The final consideration for device security is physical security. If the device is stolen or lost, the next user of the device should not be able to connect to your network just by choosing the Synchronize option. On mobile devices it is therefore very important to ensure that automatic locking of the device should occur if possible, and add the requirement of a PIN number when switching the device on.

Protecting Other Mobile Communication Paths

Other methods of communicating with the Exchange organization exist apart from Exchange ActiveSync and Outlook Mobile Access. These include both the common methods of dial-in and Virtual Private Network (VPN) connectivity to your LAN using Remote Access Services and both Outlook Web Access and RPC over HTTP.

Chapter 12 discusses the configuration of both Outlook Web Access and RPC over HTTP, and instructs that the default configuration of RPC over HTTP is to use SSL. Though SSL can be turned off for RPC over HTTP and Outlook Web Access operates without it (unless using Forms Based Authentication) the use of SSL is the way to protect these modes of communication.

Best Practices

When securing your Exchange organization it is best to ensure that you use Exchange Server Delegation Wizard to implement role-based administration rather than manually setting your own permissions in Active Directory. You should always ensure that the principle of least privilege is used. This is done to ensure that you do not give Enterprise Admin, or even Domain Admin, to your entire helpdesk.

Using the security hardening guides for both Windows and Exchange Server is vital to the protection of the operating system and e-mail platform, but only after comprehensive testing.

Never consider a firewall to be suitable if it can only block ports. With the current state of threats on the Internet and from internal users, products such as Microsoft ISA Server, which can filter data at the application layer of the network stack, are vital for the continued security of your network, but do not rely on your knowledge of a firewall to install it. Always get the advice of a firewall specialist before committing your business to Internet access.

It is a good practice when storing a secure NNTP virtual directory on a public folder not to use the MAPI default public folder. This will require security via permissions that can only be granted to mail-enabled objects and not to every security principle in your forest.

When creating your own PKI, ensure that you are able to manage it properly. If you only want a few digital certificates, it is more cost-effective to go to a public certification authority.

And a final best practice is that because S/MIME is client-driven, ensure that users who may want to send e-mail messages that will need verification or confidentiality understand the steps needed to implement this level of security. User training is always a good thing to do, and this security concept should be included for all who will need it.

Part III

Optimizing Your Exchange Server 2003 Organization

Chapter 14

Understanding and Configuring Message Routing and Transport

About This Chapter

Together, message routing and transport are responsible for message delivery internally and externally. Message routing is the way that messages flow between servers within the organization and to other servers outside of the organization. Your routing topology, based on the routing groups and connectors you define, dictates the path these messages take to reach their final destination. Transport determines the way that messages are delivered.

Simple Mail Transfer Protocol (SMTP) is the transport protocol that Exchange servers use to communicate with each other and send messages using the routing topology. SMTP is part of the Microsoft Windows Server 2003 or Microsoft Windows 2000 Server operating system. When you install Microsoft Exchange on a server running Windows Server 2003 or Windows 2000 Server, Exchange extends SMTP to support additional SMTP commands for additional functionality. Exchange extends existing event sinks in Windows Server 2003 or Windows 2000 Server, such as the Categorizer. An "event sink" is a Component Object Model (COM) component containing code that fires when an event takes place. It also adds new event sinks, such as sinks for Routing Engine and Exchange Transports, in order to provide rich functionality and features offered by Exchange Server 2003. This functionality includes the ability to communicate the link state status, available messaging routes status, and other Exchange functionality. Link state is the state of the link, whether it is UP or DOWN. Each Exchange server has a Link State Table, which holds the link state information for each link the routing topology.

In this chapter, we will focus on the message routing and transport concepts and the connectors for Exchange Server 2003.

Configuring Routing for Internal E-Mail Flow

A well-planned routing topology is essential for efficient e-mail flow within your Exchange organization if you have multiple routing groups and sites. You should carefully evaluate your existing network infrastructure before you plan your routing topology.

> **More Info**   Although this section focuses on the components of your routing topology and how they affect message flow within your organization, it does not discuss all the planning considerations and various routing topologies in detail. For more information about planning your routing topology, see the book *Planning an Exchange Server 2003 Messaging System* (*http://www.microsoft.com/technet/prodtechnol/exchange/2003/library/default.mspx*).

By default, Exchange Server 2003 places all the servers in an organization in a single routing group. That is, any Exchange server can send e-mail directly to any other Exchange server within the organization. The topology built in a single routing group environment is a full-mesh topology, and this is done automatically for you. Therefore, for those who will not have multiple routing groups, there is no planning that is involved for this part of your Exchange Server 2003 deployment.

However, in environments with varying network connectivity, you will want to create routing groups and routing group connectors in accordance with your network infrastructure. By creating routing groups and routing group connectors, servers within a routing group still send messages directly to each other, but they use the routing group connector on those servers with the best network connectivity to communicate with servers in another routing group.

Understanding Routing Groups

A routing group is a collection of servers connected by reliable network connections. Note that you define what constitutes reliable connectivity, Exchange does not do this for you. In general, by placing servers in different routing groups, you are saying that the servers between each routing group do not enjoy reliable network connectivity. You can create routing groups for other reasons, such as geographical considerations, public folder referrals, and other routing criteria, but the most common reason for creating routing groups is based on your physical topology. Within a routing group, all servers communicate and transfer messages directly to one another, as follows:

1. A user in your Exchange organization uses an e-mail client to send e-mail to another user.

2. The sender's client submits this e-mail to the SMTP virtual server on the Exchange server on which the client's mailbox resides.

3. The Exchange server looks up the recipient of the e-mail message to determine which server the recipient's mailbox resides on.

4. One of two things happens:

    a. If the recipient's mailbox is on the same Exchange server, Exchange transports the message to the recipient's mailbox by calling the Store Driver component, which delivers the message to the recipient's mailbox.

    b. If the recipient's mailbox is on another Exchange server, the first Exchange server sends the message to the recipient's home mailbox server, and it is the recipient's home mailbox server that delivers the message to the recipient's mailbox.

Although all servers communicate with each other directly within a routing group, this is not the case when a server in one routing group needs to communicate with a server in another routing group. To allow servers to communicate with servers in other routing groups, you need to create a routing group connector. Although you can use an X.400 connector or an SMTP connector to connect routing groups, the Routing Group Connector, which uses SMTP, is specifically designed for this purpose and is the preferred method of connecting routing groups.

By default, all servers within a routing group can send e-mail over the routing group connector. Servers that are capable of sending e-mail over a routing group connector are bridgehead servers. These bridgehead servers are responsible to send and receive mail through the connector on behalf of other servers in the routing group.

When creating a routing group connector, you have the option of keeping all the servers as bridgehead servers for that connector or of specifying that only a selected set of servers act as bridgehead servers for that connector. Table 14-1 compares the advantages of each approach.

Table 14-1   Number of Bridgehead Servers in a Routing Group

Number of bridgehead servers	Advantages
All servers in a routing group	Provides more efficient message flow because all the servers in the routing group can directly deliver messages to other routing groups.
	Capitalizes on those configurations where all the servers in a routing group have the same network connectivity to the servers in other routing groups.
Only a select few servers in a routing group	Makes troubleshooting message flow easier because there are limited points of contact between routing groups.
	Distributes messaging if you anticipate heavy message flow between routing groups.
	Makes e-mail flow more reliable and efficient in those configurations where some servers have more reliable network connectivity than others.
	Defines certain servers as bridgehead servers within a routing group

Figure 14-1 illustrates the basic components of routing discussed thus far, which shows message flow between servers within a routing group and between routing groups. It also illustrates a topology that uses only a single bridgehead server in each routing group.

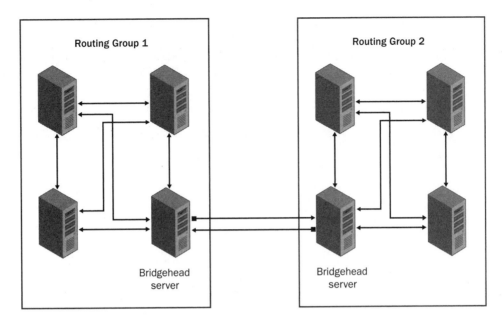

■ = Routing group connector

Figure 14-1   Communication within and between routing groups

When a topology is as simple as that shown in Figure 14-1, you do not have to consider how to best route messages between routing groups. As topologies become more complex, with large numbers of routing groups spread over varying geographical distances, message routing among groups becomes critical. You configure routing among routing groups by assigning costs to the routing group connectors used by these groups. When a user on a server in one routing group sends e-mail to a user on a server in another routing group, Exchange uses these costs (part of the link state information maintained by Exchange) to determine the most efficient route. Exchange always uses the route with the lowest cost unless a connector or server in that route is unavailable. So that every routing group knows what the various costs are for each connector and the status of those connectors, each routing group has a routing group master that updates and coordinates this information with all the other servers in a routing group.

Understanding Link State Information

Exchange Server 2003 uses link state information to determine the most effective route for delivering messages. The link state table contains information about the routing topology and whether each connector within the topology is available or unavailable. Additionally, the link state table contains costs associated with each available connector. Exchange uses this information to determine the route with the lowest cost. If a connector along the lowest cost route is unavailable, Exchange determines the best alternate route, based on cost and connector availability.

To understand how link state information and connector costs work, consider the routing topology shown in Figure 14-2, in which four routing groups exist: Seattle, Brussels, London, and Tokyo. The connectors exist between each routing group and are assigned costs based on the network speed and available bandwidth.

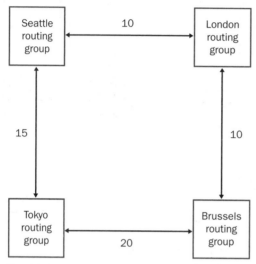

Figure 14-2   Routing group topology and costs

If all connections between the routing groups are available, a server in the Seattle routing group always sends a message to the Brussels routing group by sending the message first through the London routing group. This route has a cost of 20, the lowest cost route available. But, if the bridgehead server in London is unavailable, messages originating in Seattle and destined for Brussels travel over the higher cost route, the one that goes through the Tokyo routing group.

Understanding Routing Group Masters

When you create a routing group, the first server in that routing group is assigned the role of routing group master. The routing group master keeps track of the link state information and propagates it to the other servers within the routing group, and other servers communicate back any changes in link state. The routing group master is also responsible for propagating link state changes within its routing group to remote routing groups masters, and also propagates other routing groups' link state changes to its own routing group. For example, if a member server tries to contact another server over a connector, and this link is unavailable, the member server immediately notifies the routing group master. Likewise, when a non-master receives new link state information, it immediately transfers the link state information to the master, so that other servers can receive the information about the routing change. Link state information is always propagated ahead of other messages in the queue so that message routing efficiency is increased.

Within a routing group, the routing group master and the other Exchange servers communicate link state information over TCP/IP port 691 using SMTP; however, it is also exchanged with SMTP messages. Communication of link state information between routing groups is different. If the routing group master is not a bridgehead server for the routing group, the routing group master sends the link state information to the group's bridgehead server over TCP/IP port 691. The bridgehead server then forwards this information (over TCP/IP port 25 using SMTP) to the bridgehead servers of other routing groups.

If you do not want the first server installed in the routing group to be the routing group master (the default setting), you can change the routing group master to another server by right-clicking the server, and then selecting Set As Master.

Important   There is no automatic failover for routing group masters. If a routing group master fails, you must manually configure a new routing group master in Exchange System Manager. If a routing group master fails, the other servers in the routing group use the last known link state information until a routing group master becomes available or another routing group master is designated.

Consequences of an Unavailable Routing Group Master Server

When a server in a routing group determines that the state of a connector assigned to it has changed (gone up or down), it attempts to update link state information on the master server with the new information. If the master server is unavailable, it cannot update this information. The result is that servers in the organization continue to operate with old (possibly incorrect) information about the connectors in the routing group whose master is unavailable. Information about connectors in other routing groups continues to be updated when the connectors go up or down, and servers in the routing group with the unavailable master server continue to receive information about the state of other routing groups as e-mail is transferred. The network operates less efficiently when the master server is down, and every reasonable effort should be made to make the master server available to all servers in the routing group at all times.

> **Note**   Even if the routing group master server is down, all servers continue to operate with the current link state data.

When a Routing Master Role Is Transferred Within a Routing Group

The routing master is normally the first server installed in the routing group. In Exchange System Manager, you can determine the current routing master by clicking the routing group container, applicable routing group, Members, and right-clicking the servers. If the computer that you click is the current master, the Set As Master check box is selected.

When you change the routing master, the following behavior occurs:

1. Exchange System Manager changes the master attribute for the routing group on the domain controller it is connected to.

2. The domain controllers replicate this information to the other domain controllers.

3. The previous master domain controller is notified that a new master has been picked. The previous master sends a special Detach packet to all the non-routing masters (members) in the RG over port 691, which tells them to disconnect from the routing master and to read their directory service to find out where the new routing master is.

4. Each routing group member reads the directory service that it is connected to, to see who the routing master is. There are two possibilities:

    ■ The directory service still has the previous master listed because of replication latency. In this case, the routing group members connect to the previous master, which tells the members that it is no longer the routing master and instructs the members to read the directory service. When the domain controller's directory service receives the new master information, the members then find out where the new master is.

    ■ When the directory service contains the new master, the routing group member finds out who the new master is. If the routing group member is the routing master, then the member becomes the master and starts accepting connections. If it is not the master, the RG member connects to the new master. After the change, and before the new master finds out that it is the new master, no master is available. This period of time is defined by replication latency among the domain controllers that are used by servers in the routing group.

The link state table (LST) is a table held internally in each Exchange server that informs the server of all the possible routes to the destination along with the link information). The LST information is identified by a version number, and an era globally unique identifier (GUID). Each time a master is started, a new era for that routing group's LST begins. When you select a new master, you start a new era. There is no transfer of information between eras. The new era starts with all links marked, and then the current link states evolve.

Using Routing Groups in Native and Mixed Modes

In Exchange Server 2003, the administrative and routing functions are split into different units. Administrative groups define the logical administrative boundary for Exchange objects while the routing groups define the physical routes that messages travel over the network.

If your Exchange organization is in native mode, where all servers are running Exchange 2000 or later, this split between administrative groups and routing groups enables you to create routing groups that span administrative groups, and move servers between routing groups that exist in different administrative groups. This functionality also allows you to separate routing and administrative functions. For example, you can administer servers in two central administrative groups, placing servers from each administrative group in different routing groups, based on your network topology.

However, the functionality of routing groups in mixed mode, where some servers are running Exchange Server 2003 or Exchange 2000 while others are running Exchange 5.5, is different than in native mode. In mixed mode, you cannot have a routing group that spans multiple administrative groups nor can you move servers between routing groups that exist in different administrative groups.

This is because the routing topology in Exchange 5.5 is defined by sites, which are logical combinations of servers connected by a high-bandwidth reliable network. Sites provide the administrative, routing, and namespace boundaries in Exchange 5.5. This difference in routing topology limits the usage of routing groups when running in mixed mode. In addition, when running in mixed mode (where some servers are running Exchange 5.5), each Exchange 5.5 site will appear as a routing group to each Exchange Server 2003 server.

When you create a routing group, two containers display beneath the routing group. The first is the Connectors containers, which displays any connectors installed on the servers within the routing group. This list includes any connectors to third-party e-mail systems, such as the Lotus Notes or Novell GroupWise connector, as well as any routing group connectors, X.400 connectors, and SMTP connectors that you configure.

The second container is the Members container, which displays the servers within this routing group. By default, the routing group master is the first server added to a routing group.

Moving Servers Between Routing Groups

As discussed earlier, servers are added to the default routing group during installation. However, you can move servers between routing groups at any time. The capability to move servers between routing groups is useful if your network topology changes, and you need to combine servers with reliable connections into different routing groups. You may also need to move servers between routing groups if you are consolidating your physical sites and moving more servers into a central location.

In native mode, you can move servers between routing groups that exist in different administrative groups. In mixed mode, you can only move servers between routing groups within the same administrative group. You cannot move a server that is configured as the bridgehead server for any connectors. You must first designate a new bridgehead server, or remove the connectors before you can move the server.

Renaming a Routing Group

If necessary, you can rename a routing group after it is created. You may need to rename a routing group if you are consolidating routing groups or expanding a routing group to include more regions, and you want to change the name to reflect the new membership.

If any servers in a routing group are bridgehead servers for an X.400 connector, ensure that no messages are in the Exchange message transfer agent (MTA) queue. (Messages are submitted to this queue if they are destined for an X.400 system or an Exchange 5.5 server.) If messages are in the Exchange MTA queue when you rename a routing group, wait 114 minutes for Exchange to apply these changes, and then restart the Microsoft Exchange MTA Stacks service. You can use Queue Viewer to verify that no messages are in the Exchange MTA queue. Messages in other queues are not affected when you rename a routing group.

To rename a routing group, in Exchange System Manager, right-click the routing group, click Rename, and then type a new name for the group.

Deleting a Routing Group

Before you can delete a routing group, you must move all member servers to another routing group. After you remove the servers from the routing group, you can delete the group.

Connecting Routing Groups

When you create a routing group, you create a container that will allow you to designate a group of servers that can communicate directly with one another. As discussed earlier, for servers in different routing groups to communicate with each other, you need to connect the routing groups.

It is possible to connect routing groups with an SMTP connector or an X.400 connector. However, using these types of connectors is generally not recommended. The preferred connection method is a Routing Group Connector because this connector is designed and intended specifically for connecting routing groups. It uses SMTP to send and receive e-mail, which is more tolerant of high latency, low bandwidth environments than the X.400 connector. In addition, the SMTP connector is really used in only a limited number of situations. For most implementations, the routing group connector will be your connector of choice.

Routing group connectors are one-way routes for outgoing messages, which means messages travel outbound to the bridgehead servers in the target routing group. For two routing groups to communicate, a routing group connector must exist in each routing group to send messages outbound to the other routing group. When you create a routing group connector to a routing group, Exchange displays a message asking if you want to create a routing group connector in the remote routing group so you can send messages from the remote routing group to the routing group where you are creating the first connector. Technically speaking, you are creating two one-way connectors.

Before you create and configure a routing group connector, you should think about the following questions:

- **To which routing group does this connector deliver messages?** This information is critical. Identifying the routing group to which the connector delivers messages establishes the relationship between the sending and receiving routing groups and the rest of your topology. You need to know how the sending and receiving routing groups fit into your topology in order to intelligently assign a cost for the associated connector.

- **What cost should this connector have?** Cost is the variable Exchange uses to determine the most efficient messaging route. Exchange considers the lowest cost route the most efficient. Exchange uses routes with a higher cost only if a server or connector is unavailable on the route with the lowest cost. You should assign the lowest costs to the routes with the highest available network bandwidth.

- **Which servers in the routing group can act as bridgehead servers?** Only designated bridgehead servers can send messages across the connector to the connected routing group. The default setting is to have any of the servers in the local routing group send e-mail using this connector. Use this default option when all servers in the routing group can connect directly over the network to the remote bridgehead server. Connecting directly to the remote bridgehead server(s) provides more efficient message flow. However, you may have better direct network connectivity between specific servers in the local routing group and the designated remote bridgehead server. Should users access public folders that are not available locally using this connector?

- By default, public folder referrals are enabled across connectors connecting routing groups. However, network traffic increases when users access a public folder in a remote routing group. If your routing groups are connected by slow network connectivity or if your network may not be able to handle the additional traffic, disable public folder referrals. What are the remote bridgehead servers to which this connector can send messages?

- The remote bridgehead servers are the servers in the connected routing group that receive all messages destined for remote routing group. The remote bridgehead servers also send link state information to the source bridgehead servers for the connector.

After considering these questions, you answer the first four by setting the configurations options on the General tab in the Routing Group Connector Properties dialog box. You can answer the last question by specifying remote bridgehead servers on the Remote Bridgehead tab.

Connecting to the Internet

Exchange depends on SMTP and the Domain Name System (DNS) for Internet connectivity, as well as some other components, such as firewalls, antivirus and antispam software, and physical connections. As stated earlier, SMTP is the protocol used by Exchange to deliver e-mail internally and to the Internet. To enable Internet mail delivery in your Exchange organization, you manage the SMTP protocol by configuring SMTP virtual servers and connectors. Additionally, you must ensure that DNS is properly configured because DNS is responsible for locating mail servers outside of the organization so that SMTP can deliver e-mail to them.

After you install Exchange, you can send and receive e-mail using the default configuration of an SMTP virtual server on an Exchange server if the following conditions exist:

- You have a direct connection to the Internet.

> **Note**   Dial-up connectivity requires some additional configuration. For more information, see "Configuring SMTP in Microsoft Exchange 2000 Server" (*http://www.microsoft.com/technet/prodtechnol/exchange/2000/library/confsmtp.mspx*).

- You have DNS configured correctly to resolve Internet names and to send e-mail to your Exchange server. Specific DNS settings are discussed later in this section.

Defining SMTP Dependencies

As discussed earlier in this chapter, Exchange relies on SMTP to deliver e-mail internally and externally. This means that, for Internet mail delivery, Exchange depends on SMTP. However, before configuring Exchange for Internet mail delivery, you need to understand the components on which SMTP depends.

Internet Information Services

As mentioned earlier, the SMTP service is installed as part of the Windows Server 2003 operating system. SMTP is a component of Internet Information Services (IIS) and runs under a process called Inetinfo.exe. If you remove IIS from a server running Exchange, mail flow stops working.

The following steps assume there are no websites on this server:

1. In the Add Remove Programs, make a list of all Windows 2003 and Exchange Server 2003 service packs and hotfixes that are installed.

2. Set at least the Microsoft Exchange System Attendant service to Disabled and stop it. This will prevent Exchange from starting during subsequent restarts. Preferably, do this for all Exchange services.

3. Disable any antivirus services that are running and restart.

4. Uninstall all IIS components (from Add Remove Windows Components), this time removing metabase.bin (and all *<systemroot>*\System32\Inetsrv files).

> **Note**   The metabase.bin does not always get removed with you uninstall IIS, so you may have to delete it manually.

5. Restart.

6. Reinstall all IIS components, being *sure* to select NNTP, SMTP, and WWW Publishing services.

7. Restart.

8. Reapply whatever Windows 2003 service pack the server is running.

9. Restart.

10. (Optional) If other Windows 2003 hotfixes were installed since the service pack, install those, and restart as necessary.

11. Once the server is finished starting up, set the Exchange services back to **Automatic**, but do not start them.

12. Check the <systemroot>\system32\Inetsrv directory for its files, especially to ensure that metabase.bin was recreated.

13. Telnet to Localhost on port 25, type **ehlo**, and verify the basic SMTP verbs are there (see step 4 under "Symptoms" of Knowledge Base article 290290 "XIMS: Cannot Send Mail After Re-Installing the IIS SMTP Service" at *http://support.microsoft.com/kb/290290/EN-US/*).

14. Run the Exchange setup program from the CD and select Reinstall for the option.

15. When prompted to overwrite newer existing files during the Exchange Server 2003 reinstall, select Yes for every file. There is no "Yes to all," so you will have to select Yes multiple times.

16. Install Exchange 2000 hotfixes/service packs as per the list made in Step 1.

17. Restart.

18. Check services to make sure all are started for Exchange, as well as SMTP.

19. Telnet to Localhost on port 25, type **ehlo**, and verify the extended SMTP verbs are there (see step 4 under "Symptoms" of Knowledge Base article 290290 "XIMS: Cannot Send Mail After Re-Installing the IIS SMTP Service" at *http://support.microsoft.com/kb/290290/EN-US/*).

20. Test e-mail flow.

At this point, IIS and Exchange Server 2003 are completely installed. The Exchange Server 2003 reinstall is necessary to reregister the Exchange pieces in the IIS metabase because that is recreated when you do the reinstall of IIS. It is those missing registrations that cause the missing functionality in Exchange Server 2003 if you skipped that step.

The IIS or SMTP corruption problem is typically caused by the following:

- File level antivirus scanning on the \\<*systemroot*>\system32\inetsrv directory
- Hardware failures
- Unediting of metabase
- Ungraceful shutdown of IIS

IIS provides a framework process for Internet services such as HTTP, SMTP, and Network News Transfer Protocol (NNTP). IIS should not be confused with HTTP because several other services, such as SMTP, depend on IIS to function. After you install Exchange, the management of SMTP virtual servers moves to Exchange System Manager, even though the service itself continues to run within IIS. Because of this integration between Exchange and IIS, both the IIS component and the SMTP service that runs in IIS are required for Exchange and SMTP to function properly.

Active Directory

Exchange Server 2003 is tightly integrated with the Microsoft Active Directory directory service. Exchange stores all of its configuration information in Active Directory, including information about recipient policies, SMTP virtual server configuration, and user mailboxes. However, SMTP reads its settings from the IIS metabase. Therefore, to supply IIS with the information it needs for SMTP functionality, Exchange System Attendant, using a component called DS2MB (directory service to metabase), replicates the configuration information from Active Directory to the IIS metabase.

DNS

SMTP depends on DNS to determine the Internet Protocol (IP) address of its next internal or external destination server. Generally, internal DNS names are not published on the Internet. Therefore, SMTP must be able to contact a DNS server that can resolve external DNS names to send Internet mail, as well as a DNS server that can resolve internal DNS names for delivery within the organization.

Additionally, for your Exchange servers to receive Internet mail, your DNS server must contain a mail exchanger (MX) resource record that points to the A record with the IP address of the SMTP virtual server that is translated by your firewall into a private IP address for your Exchange server that receives Internet mail for your organization. If you are supporting multiple domains, an MX record must exist for each of these domains for DNS to accept e-mail for the domain.

Recipient Policies

Recipient policies establish the default e-mail addresses that use a specific protocol, such as SMTP, for a set of users. E-mail addresses define the valid formats for addressing inbound e-mail messages to the Exchange system. The default recipient policy sets the mail domain for which the virtual server accepts incoming e-mail messages. It specifies the default SMTP and X.400 addresses for all Exchange-based, mailbox-enabled objects. You can also create additional recipient policies if your organization receives e-mail for multiple domains, or if your default domain is used strictly for internal purposes and you use a different external mail domain.

Any SMTP domain specified in the recipient policies is replicated into the IIS metabase and set as an authoritative local domain. Setting these domains as authoritative local domains means that SMTP accepts inbound e-mail for these domains and is responsible for sending all non-delivery reports for this domain. The only time an SMTP address is not considered local is when you add the address to the recipient policy because you clear the This Exchange Organization Is Responsible For All Mail Delivery To This Address check box in the SMTP Address Properties dialog box.

Installing and correctly configuring the previous components ensures that SMTP functions properly with Exchange. With SMTP functioning properly, you can focus on configuring SMTP to meet your organization's needs.

Configuring SMTP Virtual Servers

An SMTP virtual server is defined by a unique combination of an IP address and port number. The IP address is the address on which the SMTP virtual server listens for incoming SMTP connections. The default IP address in the virtual server's properties is set to All Unassigned, which means that the SMTP virtual server listens on any of the available IP addresses. The port number is the port through which the SMTP virtual server receives communications. The default port number for inbound connections to an SMTP virtual server is port 25.

You use Exchange System Manager to control most of the SMTP settings. The property settings of the SMTP virtual server control inbound e-mail and, to a lesser degree, outbound e-mail settings.

SMTP Connectors

An SMTP connector designates an isolated route for e-mail. You can use SMTP connectors to establish a gateway for Internet mail or to connect to a specific domain, routing group or mail system. Although out-of-the-box Exchange SMTP virtual servers can send and receive e-mail just fine when provided proper DNS configuration, MX records, and Internet connectivity, there could be SMTP e-mail requirements in companies that dictate the need for one or more SMTP connectors. Please review Knowledge Base article 294736 "When to create SMTP connectors in Exchange 2000 and later" for more information.

Using an SMTP connector is recommended when you need an isolated route for e-mail destined to the Internet or specific remote domains. Additionally, more configuration options are available on an SMTP connector than on the SMTP virtual server. The following sections describe both the Internet Mail Wizard and the manual procedure for configuring Exchange to send Internet mail and include information about creating and configuring an SMTP connector to route Internet mail.

You can setup the SMTP connector using either the built-in wizard or manually. Tables 14-2 and 14-3 outline the use of the wizard for both inbound and outbound e-mail.

Table 14-2 Using Internet Mail Wizard to Configure the Sending of E-Mail

Task	Description
Select an Exchange server within your organization that will send Internet mail.	You cannot run the wizard on a server on which you have already set up SMTP connectors or created additional SMTP virtual servers. You can only use the wizard to designate Exchange 2000 or later servers.
Designate a bridgehead server or servers.	This is both the Exchange server and the SMTP virtual server on this server. The wizard creates an SMTP connector on the selected SMTP virtual server and Exchange server. The outbound bridgehead server handles all e-mail sent through this connector.

Table 14-2 Using Internet Mail Wizard to Configure the Sending of E-Mail (Continued)

Task	Description
Configure an SMTP connector to send Internet mail.	Internet Mail Wizard guides you through the process of configuring your SMTP connector.
	You can allow Internet mail delivery to all external domains, or you can restrict Internet mail delivery to specific domains.
	You can specify whether the SMTP connector sends outbound e-mail using DNS to resolve external domain names, or whether it uses a smart host that assumes responsibility for resolving external names and delivering e-mail.
Verify that your SMTP virtual server is not open for relaying.	With open relaying, external users can use your server to send unsolicited commercial e-mail, which may result in other legitimate servers blocking e-mail from your Exchange server. If your server is secured for relay, only authenticated users can send e-mail to the Internet using your server.

Table 14-3 Using Internet Mail Wizard to Configure the Receiving of E-Mail

Task	Description
Select an Exchange server within your organization that will receive Internet mail.	You cannot run the wizard on a server on which you have already set up SMTP connectors or created additional SMTP virtual servers. You can only use the wizard to designate Exchange 2000 or later servers.
Configure your SMTP server to receive Internet mail.	To receive incoming Internet e-mail messages, the server must have only one SMTP virtual server, and that virtual server must have a default IP address of All Unassigned and an assigned TCP port of 25 (dual-homed servers do not follow this requirement). If more than one SMTP virtual server exists on the Exchange server, or if the IP address or the port assignment is different than the default settings, the wizard will not continue. You can then either restore the Exchange server to its default configuration and rerun the wizard, or you can use Exchange System Manager to configure Exchange manually.
Verify that your SMTP virtual server allows anonymous access.	Other servers on the Internet expect to connect anonymously to your SMTP virtual server. Therefore, anonymous access must be permitted on your SMTP virtual server. If anonymous access is not configured, the wizard guides you through enabling anonymous access.

Table 14-3   Using Internet Mail Wizard to Configure the Receiving of E-Mail (Continued)

Task	Description
Configure your recipient policies with the SMTP domains for which you want to receive inbound e-mail.	The SMTP domains for which you want to receive Internet mail are configured in Exchange System Manager in Recipient Policies. You must have a recipient policy configured for every SMTP domain for which you want to accept Internet mail. If your default recipient policy contains the correct mail domain for your organization, use this policy.
	If you have created multiple recipient policies in Exchange System Manager, you cannot use the wizard to create additional recipient policies. In this case, to add or modify your recipient policies, you must use Exchange System Manager. To configure recipient policies manually, see "Configuring Recipient Policies" later in this chapter.
	You must configure MX records in DNS for all mail domains. If you do not have an MX record for your mail domain, DNS cannot accept messages for your domain.

Configuring a Dual-Homed Server Using the Internet Mail Wizard

When you use Internet Mail Wizard to configure Internet mail delivery on a dual-homed server (a server configured with two or more network addresses, usually with two network interface cards), the wizard performs the necessary configuration steps described in Tables 14-2 and 14-3. The wizard also creates an additional SMTP virtual server on the Exchange server. It configures Internet mail delivery in the following ways:

- To configure a server to send Internet mail, the wizard guides you through the process of assigning the intranet IP address to the default SMTP virtual server on which it creates the SMTP connector to send outbound e-mail. You assign the intranet IP address to this virtual server so that only internal users on your intranet can send outbound e-mail.

- To configure a server to receive Internet mail, the wizard guides you through the process of assigning the Internet IP address to the Internet SMTP virtual server. You assign an Internet IP address to this virtual server because external servers need to be able to connect to this SMTP virtual server to send Internet mail. Additionally, you must have an MX record on your DNS server that references this server and the IP address of the Internet SMTP virtual server.

Manually Configuring the Sending of Internet E-Mail

If your messaging environment is large or complex, you cannot use Internet Mail Wizard to configure Exchange to send Internet mail. Instead, you must manually configure Exchange to handle outbound messaging over the Internet. Configuring Exchange to send Internet mail involves the following:

- Verify that your SMTP virtual server uses the standard port for SMTP (port 25).

- Verify that your DNS server can resolve external names so that SMTP can deliver messages.

Verifying Outbound Settings on SMTP Virtual Servers

As discussed earlier, you configure most of the outbound settings that SMTP uses on the SMTP connector. However, you cannot configure the SMTP connector to control the ports and IP addresses through which Exchange sends outbound e-mail. To control these ports and IP addresses, you need to configure the SMTP virtual server. Two of the SMTP virtual server properties relate directly to configuring Exchange to send Internet mail. First, you need to ensure that the outbound port is set to port 25 (the default setting). Of the two settings related to sending Internet mail, this is the setting that you must verify. Secondly, you need to ensure that you have specified a DNS server that can resolve MX records on the Internet.

Two common methods for configuring DNS to resolve external names include configuring Exchange to point to an internal DNS server that uses forwarders to an external DNS server, and configuring Exchange to point to an external DNS server on the SMTP virtual server that is responsible for sending external e-mail.

Customizing E-Mail Delivery

One advantage of using an SMTP connector for outbound e-mail, rather than using an SMTP virtual server, is that you can specify additional configuration settings to affect how e-mail is delivered, as shown in Table 14-4. Whether you need to adjust the default values for these settings depends on how you want your SMTP connector to deliver e-mail. Unless you need the additional features provided by an SMTP connector, it is really not necessary to use the connector to send and receive Internet mail.

Table 14-4   Additional Configuration Settings for an SMTP Connector

Settings	Description
Delivery restrictions.	Restricts who can send e-mail through a connector. By default, the connector accepts e-mail from everyone. You configure these settings on the Delivery Restrictions tab of the SMTP connector's Properties dialog box.

Table 14-4   Additional Configuration Settings for an SMTP Connector (Continued)

Settings	Description
Content restrictions.	Specifies what types of messages are delivered through a connector.
	You configure these settings on the Content Restrictions tab of the SMTP connector's Properties dialog box.
Delivery options.	If you connect to an Internet service provider to retrieve your e-mail, configure a connector to run on a specified schedule, and implement advanced queuing and dequeuing features.
	You configure these settings on the Delivery Options tab of the SMTP connector's Properties dialog box.
SMTP communication.	Controls how the connector uses SMTP to communicate with other SMTP servers. Specifically, you can specify whether the connector uses SMTP or Extended Simple Mail Transfer Protocol (ESMTP) commands to initiate a conversation with another server and control the use of the ERTN and TURN commands. These commands request that another SMTP server sends the e-mail messages that it has.
	You configure these settings on the Advanced tab of the SMTP connector's Properties dialog box.
Outbound security.	Ensures that any e-mail flowing through the connector is authenticated. This setting is useful if you want to establish a more secure route for communicating with a partner company. With this setting, you can establish an authentication method and require Transport Layer Security (TLS) encryption.
	You configure these settings on the Advanced tab of the SMTP connector's Properties dialog box.

Verifying DNS Setup for Outbound E-Mail

To send Internet mail using DNS rather than forwarding mail to a smart host, the Exchange server resolves the receiving domain and IP address of the recipient's SMTP server. The server then uses SMTP over TCP port 25 to establish a conversation with the recipient's SMTP server, and deliver the e-mail. When you use DNS, the most important thing to remember is that all DNS servers that an Exchange server uses must be able to resolve external domains (also referred to as Internet domains). There are three methods that you can use to configure DNS for outbound e-mail:

- You can configure Exchange to rely on your internal DNS servers. These servers resolve external names on their own or use a forwarder to an external DNS server.

- You can have an internal DNS server be a caching server as well.

- You can configure Exchange to use a dedicated external DNS server, such as a root-DNS server on the Internet.

Manually Configuring the Receipt of Internet Mail

You can control how Exchange will receive e-mail for your users. Manually configuring Exchange to receive Internet mail involves the following:

- Create the proper recipient policies, so your Exchange server receives mail for all e-mail domains that are used by your company.

- Ensure your inbound SMTP virtual server settings are set to allow anonymous access, so other SMTP servers can connect and send mail to your SMTP virtual server.

- Verify that the correct MX records exist in DNS, so other servers on the Internet can locate your server to deliver e-mail. To verify the record is working, ping the MX record from a command prompt to ensure it correctly resolves the address record.

Configuring Inbound SMTP Virtual Server Settings

To configure your SMTP virtual server to receive Internet mail, you must ensure these default configurations exist:

- Configure the inbound port as 25 and specify the IP address. Other servers on the Internet expect to connect to your SMTP virtual server on port 25. By default, all SMTP virtual servers use this port.

- Verify that your SMTP virtual server allows anonymous access. To receive Internet mail, your SMTP virtual server must permit anonymous access. Other servers on the Internet expect to communicate anonymously with your SMTP virtual server to send Internet mail to your users.

- Verify that default relay restrictions are configured on your SMTP virtual server. By default, the SMTP virtual server allows only authenticated users to relay e-mail messages. This setting prevents unauthorized users from using your Exchange server to send e-mail messages to external domains.

Verifying DNS Setup for Inbound E-Mail

To receive Internet mail, the following DNS settings are necessary:

- Your external DNS servers or any DNS server that is authoritative for your domain must have an MX record pointing to an A record with the IP address of your mail server. The IP address must match the IP address configured on your SMTP virtual server that receives Internet mail.

- There must be external DNS resolution to your mail server's MX record

- Your Exchange server must be configured to use a DNS server that can resolve external DNS names.

To ensure that your MX records are configured correctly, you can use the NSLookup utility. You'll need to use the NSLookup utility against an internet-based DNS server, not an internal DNS server that can't resolve to the internet. To verify that your server is accessible on port 25 to other servers on the Internet, you can use Telnet.

Connecting to Exchange 5.5 Servers and Other X.400 Systems

This section focuses on using the X.400 protocol and X.400 connectors to connect to Exchange 5.5 servers or other third-party X.400 mail systems. The X.400 connector relies on the X.400 protocol and its accompanying transport stack to provide the underlying transport functionality.

Three components control the behavior of the X.400 protocol on an Exchange server, as follows:

- **X.400 protocol** An X.400 node appears under the Protocols container in Exchange System Manager on an Exchange server. Properties that are configured on the X.400 protocol determine how the protocol works on an individual server.

- **X.400 transport stacks** An X.400 transport stack contains configuration information about network software, such as TCP/IP network services, and information about hardware, such as an X.25 port adapter or dial-up connection on the computer running Exchange. Each X.400 connector requires a transport stack on which to run, and communicates using the configuration information within that stack. You can create either an X.400 TCP transport stack or an X.400 X.25 transport stack.

- **X.400 connectors** X.400 connectors provide a mechanism for connecting Exchange servers with other X.400 systems or Exchange 5.5 servers outside the Exchange organization. An Exchange Server 2003 server can then send messages using the X.400 protocol over this connector.

Important X.400 connectors are only available in Exchange Server 2003 Enterprise Edition.

Customizing the X.400 Protocol

The X.400 protocol provides the underlying functionality used by X.400 connectors and protocol stacks. The X.400 service MTA stack, located in the Protocols container under your Exchange server in Exchange System Manager, provides addressing and routing information for sending messages from one server to another. Use the X.400 Properties dialog box to configure basic settings and messaging defaults used by the X.400 protocol on your server. Any X.400 transport stacks and X.400 connectors that you create on this server inherit these settings by default, although you can override this configuration on individual connectors. The following general properties can be set on the X.400 protocol:

- The entry in the Local X.400 Name box identifies the X.400 account that Exchange uses when it connects to the remote system. This name identifies the MTA to other mail systems. By default, this name is the name of the server where the X.400 service is installed. You can change the local X.400 name by using the Modify button. You can also set a local X.400 password. Third-party systems use this password when connecting to the X.400 service.

- The Expand Remote Distribution Lists Locally option makes a remote distribution list available to users in your organization. When this option is selected and a user sends a message to a remote distribution list, the distribution list expands locally (on the server to which the user is currently connected). Exchange finds the best routing for the message, based on the location of recipients in the list. This method ensures the most efficient message handling. However, note that processing large distribution lists can affect server performance.

- The Convert Incoming Messages to Exchange Contents option changes the address and contents of incoming messages to a format compatible with MAPI clients, such as Microsoft Outlook and Exchange. Do not select this option if your users do not use a MAPI client.

- The Modify button in Message queue directory allows you to change the location of the X.400 message queue directory.

Note When you modify the location of the queue directory, you are modifying only the MTA database path and moving only the database (.dat) files. You are not moving any of the run files or the run directory. The database files are the core files that are required for starting the MTA, queue files, and message files.

Understanding X.400 Connectors

Generally, you use X.400 connectors in the following situations:

- Your environment has an existing X.25 network.
- You are connecting to an X.400 system.

> **Note** Although you can use X.400 connectors to connect routing groups within Exchange, the routing group connector is recommended.

You can create two types of connectors on Exchange Server 2003 Enterprise Edition: TCP X.400 connectors and X.25 X.400 connectors. The TCP connector enables connectivity over a TCP/IP network and the X.25 connector enables connectivity using X.25.

Creating an X.400 Protocol Stack

Before you create an X.400 connector, you must create a protocol stack on the Exchange server that will host the connector. The protocol (or transport) stack is created on individual Exchange servers and provides the underlying functionality for the connector to transport messages. The server on which you create the protocol stack processes all messages that are sent by connectors that use this stack. You create a transport stack using TCP or X.25, based on your network and the system to which you are connecting. Creating a transport stack involves the same steps for either protocol.

Creating an X.400 Connector

After you create a TCP X.400 or X.25 transport stack, you can create an X.400 connector to connect to another X.400 system. Remember that connectors send e-mail in only one direction, so the X.400 connector enables e-mail to flow from your system to the remote system or routing group. If you are connecting to a remote system, the administrator of that system must also create a connector to send e-mail to your organization.

Table 14-5 lists the configuration settings that are available for an X.400 connector. These settings are available in the Properties dialog box for an X.400 connector.

Table 14-5   Configuration Settings for an X.400 Connector

Settings	Description
Remote X.400 name.	When you configure an X.400 connector, you need to specify a valid account and password for the remote X.400 system to which you are connecting.
	You configure these settings on the General tab of the X.400 connector's Properties dialog box.

Table 14-5   Configuration Settings for an X.400 Connector (Continued)

Settings	Description
Address space.	The address space defines the e-mail addresses or domains for the e-mail messages that you want routed through a connector. You can specify the X.400 address of a third-party X.400 system or an Exchange 5.5 server to which you are connecting, so that all e-mail destined to the specified X.400 system is routed through this connector.
	You configure these settings on the Address Space tab of the X.400 connector's Properties dialog box.
Transport address information for the remote system.	You must specify transport address information for the remote X.400 system to which you are connecting.
	You configure these settings on the Stack tab of the X.400 connector's Properties dialog box.
Content restrictions.	You can specify what types of messages are delivered through a connector.
	You configure these settings on the Content Restrictions tab of the X.400 connector's Properties dialog box.
Scope.	You can select either an entire organization or a routing group for the connector's scope. For example, if you create an X.400 connector to send e-mail to an X.400 system on a server in one routing group, and an X.400 connector exists on a server in another routing group, you may choose to specify a routing group scope for these connectors so that servers in each routing group are forced to use the connector. If an X.400 connector that is set to a routing group scope becomes unavailable, messages queue in the routing group until the connector becomes available. If your user requirements permit this, you could implement the connectors with a routing group scope.
	You configure these settings on the Address Space tab of the X.400 connector's Properties dialog box.
Override options.	By default, the X.400 connector inherits the settings that are configured on the X.400 protocol.
	To override these settings, you use the Override tab of the X.400 connector's Properties dialog box.
Delivery restrictions.	You can restrict who can send e-mail through a connector. By default, e-mail is accepted from everyone.
	You configure these settings on the Delivery Restrictions tab of the X.400 connector's Properties dialog box.

Configuring Additional Options on the X.400 Connector

You can also use the General tab of the X.400 connector to configure public folder referrals and specify how messages are delivered by this connector. These additional options include the following:

- The Message Text Word-Wrap option controls whether or not text wraps at a specific column in a message.

- The Remote Clients Support MAPI option results in Exchange sending messages through the connector in Rich Text Format (RTF). Do not select this option if clients do not support MAPI because it can cause problems with message formatting on non-MAPI clients.

- The Do Not Allow Public Folder Referrals option prevents public folder referrals when you connect to another routing group. Public folder referrals enable users in a connected routing group or a remote system to access public folders through this connector.

Overriding X.400 Properties

By default, each X.400 connector inherits the settings that are configured on the X.400 protocol. You can use the Override tab on the X.400 connector to override the options that are set on the X.400 protocol. The configuration options that are available on the Override tab are as follows:

- The Name Entered In The Local X.400 Service Name box overrides the local X.400 name of the X.400 transport stack. Some X.400 systems do not support certain characters. If your local X.400 name contains characters that are not supported by the remote system to which you are connecting, use this option to connect to the remote X.400 service using a name that it can support.

- The Maximum Open Retries option sets the maximum number of times that the system tries to open a connection before it sends a non-delivery report (NDR). The default is 144.

- The Maximum Transfer Retries option sets the maximum number of times that the system tries to transfer a message across an open connection. The default is 2.

- The Open Interval (Sec) option sets the number of seconds that the system waits after a message transfer fails. The default is 600.

- The Transfer Interval (Sec) option sets the number of seconds the system waits after a message transfer fails before resending a message across an open connection. The default is 120.

To set additional override values, you use the Additional Values dialog box. To open this dialog box, click the Additional Values button on the Override tab in the X.400 connector's Properties dialog box. In the Additional Values dialog box, you can set these options:

- The options under RTS Values set the Reliable Transfers Service (RTS) values. RTS values determine message reliability parameters, such as the checkpoints to include in data and the amount of unacknowledged data that can be sent. You can use the options on an X.400 connector's Override tab to override the default X.400 service attributes, such as RTS values.

■ The options under Association Parameters determine the number and duration of connections to the remote system. Each X.400 connector uses the association parameters that are configured on the X.400 protocol, but you can configure association parameters on each individual connector to override the settings.

■ The options under Transfer Timeouts determine how long the X.400 connector waits before sending an NDR for urgent, normal, and not urgent messages. Each X.400 connector uses the transfer time out values that are configured on the X.400 MTA, but you can configure specific transfer time out values on each individual connector that override these settings.

Disabling or Removing Connectors

If necessary, you can disable or remove existing connectors in your organization. You can disable a connector that you do not want Exchange to use by setting the connection schedule to **Never**. Disabling a connector rather than deleting it allows you to retain the configuration settings if you want to enable it again in the future.

You can remove a connector that you no longer use by deleting it. You can remove a connector at any time. When you remove a connector, you are not warned of the connections you are breaking. For example, you may be breaking an established connection between two routing groups. However, you are prompted to verify that you want to remove the connector. To remove a connector, in the Exchange System Manager, right-click the connector that you want to remove, and then click Delete.

Using Queue Viewer to Manage Messages

Queue Viewer is a feature in Exchange System Manager that allows you to monitor your organization's messaging queues, as well as the messages that are contained within those queues. Queue Viewer works at a server level. In Exchange System Manager, you expand the server and then click Queues to open Queue Viewer and display the messaging queues associated with the server.

In Exchange Server 2003, Queue Viewer is enhanced to improve the monitoring of message queues. In Exchange Server 2003, you can view all the messaging queues for a specific server from the Queues node under each server. This is an improvement over Exchange 2000, where each protocol virtual server has its own Queues node, and you cannot view all queues on a server from a central location. For example, using Exchange Server 2003, you can now use Queue Viewer to view both the X.400 and SMTP queues on a server, rather than having to view each of these queues separately in each of their respective protocol nodes. Other enhancements to Queue Viewer in Exchange Server 2003 include the following:

- **Disabling outbound e-mail**   You can use a new option named Disable Outbound Mail to disable outbound e-mail from all SMTP queues.

- **Setting the refresh rate**   You can use the Settings option to set the refresh rate of Queue Viewer.

- **Finding messages**   You can use Find Messages to search for messages based on the sender, recipient, and message state. This option is similar to enumerating messages in Queue Viewer in Exchange 2000.

- **Viewing additional information**   You can click a specific queue to view additional information about that queue.

- **Viewing previously hidden queues**   Queue Viewer in Exchange Server 2003 exposes three queues that were not visible in Exchange 2000: DSN Messages Pending Submission, Failed Message Retry queue, and Messages Queued For Deferred Delivery.

The remainder of this section highlights two of these new enhancements, disabling outbound e-mail and finding messages, and also provides guidelines for how to use the SMTP and X.400 queues shown in Queue Viewer to troubleshoot message flow.

Disabling Outbound Mail

Using the Disable Outbound Mail option, you can disable outbound e-mail from all SMTP queues. For example, disabling outbound e-mail can be useful if a virus is active in your organization. If you want to prevent outbound e-mail from a particular remote queue, instead of disabling all SMTP queues, you can freeze the messages in that particular queue.

Finding Messages

You can use the Find Messages option to search for messages by specifying search criteria (such as the sender or recipient) or the message state (such as frozen). You can also specify the number of messages that you want your search to return. Using Find Messages in Exchange Server 2003 is similar to the Enumerate Messages option in Exchange 2000.

Using SMTP Queues to Troubleshoot Message Flow

During message categorization and delivery, all e-mail is sent through the SMTP queues of an SMTP virtual server. If there is a problem delivering the message at any point in the process, the message remains in the queue where the problem occurred until the problem is remedied.

Use the SMTP queues to isolate possible causes of e-mail flow issues. If a queue is in a Retry status, in Queue Viewer, select the queue and check the properties of the queue to determine the cause. For example, if the queue properties display a message similar to *An SMTP error has occurred*, you should review your server's event logs to locate any SMTP errors. If there are no events in the log, you should increase the SMTP logging level, by right-clicking the Exchange server, clicking Properties, clicking the Diagnostics Logging tab, and then selecting MSExchangeTransport. Table 14-6 lists the SMTP queues, their descriptions, and troubleshooting information for message accumulation in each queue.

Table 14-6   SMTP Queues

Queue name	Description	Causes of message accumulation
DSN messages pending submission	Contains delivery status notifications, also known as non-delivery reports (NDRs) that are ready to be delivered by Exchange. The following operations are unavailable for this queue: Delete All Messages (no NDR) and Delete All Messages (NDR).	Messages can accumulate in this queue if the store service is unavailable or not running, or if problems exist with the IMAIL Exchange store component, which is the store component that performs message conversion. Check the event log for possible errors with the store service.
Failed message retry queue	Contains messages that Exchange has failed to deliver, but that the server will attempt to send again. The following operations are unavailable for this queue: Delete All Messages (no NDR) and Delete All Messages (NDR).	Messages can accumulate in this queue if a problem exists with DNS or SMTP. Check the event log to determine whether an SMTP problem exists. Verify your DNS configuration using NSLookup or another utility. On rare occasions, a corrupted message can remain in this queue. To determine whether a message is corrupted, try to look at its properties. If some properties are not accessible, this can indicate message corruption.

Table 14-6   SMTP Queues (Continued)

Queue name	Description	Causes of message accumulation
Messages queued for deferred delivery	Contains messages queued for delivery at a later time, including messages sent by earlier versions of Outlook clients. (You can set this option in Outlook clients.) Messages sent by earlier versions of Outlook treat deferred delivery slightly differently. Previous versions of Outlook depend on the MTA for message delivery because SMTP, not the MTA, now handles message delivery. These messages remain in this queue until their scheduled delivery time. Essentially, this queue is where Advanced Queuing Engine (AQ) places messages that need some sort of administrator action; for example, if a loop is detected in SMTP. If a message is disappearing with no immediate DSN but eventually returns a 4.4.6 or 4.4.7, then it might be sitting in this queue if you cannot find it elsewhere. Other possible causes include: On Move mailbox (local delivery fails with *ecMailboxInTransit*). When the user does not yet have a mailbox created and no master account SID (local delivery fails with *ecLoginFailure*). When messages bounce between two SMTP servers. The MAPI property that uses this is PR_DEFERRED_DELIVERY_TIME. The SendQ deferred is PR_DEFERRED_SEND_TIME (used by recent versions of Outlook). If you set PR_DEFERRED_DELIVERY_TIME when you submit a message (such as using CDO to submit a MAPI message..or an older version of Outlook) it will end up in the AQ deferred delivery queue.	Possible causes of message accumulation include: Messages are sent to a user's mailbox while the mailbox is being moved. The user does not yet have a mailbox created, and no master account security identifier (SID) exists for the user. For more information, see Microsoft Knowledge Base article 316047, "XADM: Addressing Problems That Are Created When You Enable ADC-Generated Accounts" (*http://support.microsoft.com/?kbid=316047*). The message may be corrupted, or the recipient may not be valid. To determine if a message is corrupted, check its properties. If some properties are not accessible, this can indicate a corrupted message. Also check that the recipient is valid.

Table 14-6   SMTP Queues (Continued)

Queue name	Description	Causes of message accumulation
Local delivery	Contains messages that are queued on the Exchange server for local delivery to an Exchange mailbox.	Messages can accumulate in this queue if the Exchange server is not accepting messages for local delivery. Slow or sporadic message delivery can indicate a looping message or a performance problem.
		This queue is affected by the Exchange store. Increase diagnostic logging for the Exchange store as described in "Configuring Diagnostic Logging for SMTP" later in this chapter. Other possible causes include disk subsystem or Storage Area Network bottlenecks, as well as antivirus software.
Messages awaiting directory lookup	Contains messages addressed to recipients who have not yet been resolved against Active Directory. Messages are also held here while distribution lists are expanded.	Generally, messages accumulate in this queue because the advanced queuing engine is unable to categorize the message. The advanced queuing engine may not be able to access the global catalog servers and access recipient information, or the global catalog servers are unreachable or performing slowly.
		The categorizer affects this queue. Increase diagnostic logging for the categorizer as described in "Configuring Diagnostic Logging for SMTP" later in this chapter.

Table 14-6   SMTP Queues (Continued)

Queue name	Description	Causes of message accumulation
Messages waiting to be routed	Holds messages until their next-destination server is determined, and then moves them to their respective link queues.	Messages accumulate in this queue if Exchange routing problems exist. Message routing may be experiencing problems. Increase diagnostic logging for routing as described in "Configuring Diagnostic Logging for SMTP" later in this chapter.
[*Connector name| Server name| Remote domain*]	Holds messages destined for a remote delivery. The name of the queue matches the remote delivery destination, which may be a connector, a server, or a domain.	If messages accumulate in this queue, you must first identify the status of the queue. If the queue status is Retry, check the queue properties to determine the reason that it is in this state. For DNS issues, use Nslookup and Telnet to troubleshoot. If the host is unreachable, use Telnet to ensure that the remote server is responding.
Final destination currently unreachable	Contains messages for which the final destination server cannot be reached. For example, Exchange cannot determine a network path to the final destination.	Messages can accumulate in this queue if no route exists for delivery. Additionally, anytime a connector or a remote delivery queue is unavailable or in Retry for a period of time, and no alternate route exists to the connector or remote destination, new messages queue here. Messages can remain in this queue until an administrator fixes the problem or defines an alternate route. To get new messages to flow to their remote destination queue, allowing you to force a connection and get a Network Monitor (Net-Mon) trace, restart the SMTP virtual server.

Table 14-6 SMTP Queues (Continued)

Queue name	Description	Causes of message accumulation
Messages pending submission	Holds messages that have been acknowledged and accepted by the SMTP service. The processing of these messages has not begun.	Messages that are accumulating constantly may indicate a performance problem. Occasional peaks in performance can cause messages to appear in this queue intermittently.

Message accumulation in this queue can also indicate problems with a custom event sink or a third-party event sink. |

Using X.400 (MTA) Queues to Troubleshoot Message Flow

Exchange Server 2003 uses the X.400 queues to submit e-mail to and receive e-mail from Exchange 5.5 servers and to send e-mail through connectors to other mail servers. If you experience mail flow problems when you are sending e-mail to an Exchange 5.5 or earlier server, or to another mail system to which you are connecting using X.400, check the X.400 queues on the Exchange server. If you experience mail flow problems when sending e-mail to servers that are running Exchange 5.5 or earlier, you should also check the MTA queues on those servers. Table 14-7 lists the X.400 queues, their descriptions, and troubleshooting information for message accumulation in each queue.

Table 14-7 X.400 Queues

Queue name	Description	Causes of message accumulation
PendingRerouteQ	Contains messages that are waiting to be rerouted after a temporary link outage.	Messages can accumulate in this queue if a route to a connector, to a different mail system, or to an Exchange 5.5 server is unavailable.

Table 14-7   X.400 Queues (Continued)

Queue name	Description	Causes of message accumulation
Next hop MTA	Contains messages destined to one of the following: ■ Another gateway, such as a connector for Lotus Notes or Novell GroupWise. ■ An X.400 link to an Exchange 5.5 site or a destination outside of the organization. ■ An Exchange MTA over the LAN—for example, destined to an Exchange 5.5 server in a mixed-mode environment.	Messages can accumulate in this queue when Exchange Server 2003 experiences problems sending to another mail system, to an Exchange 5.5 server, or through an X.400 link. Increase diagnostic logging for the X.400 service
Messages waiting to be routed	Contains messages waiting to be routed under normal operating conditions.	Messages can accumulate in this queue when there is a problem with the network connectivity between the X.400 connector and the destination connector or server.

Configuring Diagnostic Logging for SMTP

To help you determine the cause of a transport issue, you can view events that relate to MSExchangeTransport. If you experience problems with Exchange message flow, immediately increase the logging levels relating to MSExchangeTransport. Logging levels control the amount of data that is logged in the application log. The more events that are logged, the more transport-related events that you can view in the application log. Therefore, you have a better chance of determining the cause of the message flow problem. The SMTP log file is located in the \Program Files\Exchsrvr\ *Server_name*.log folder. You can configure the logging levels in the Diagnostics Logging tab in the properties of the Exchange server in the Servers folder in the Administrative Group.

As discussed in "Using SMTP Queues to Troubleshoot Message Flow" and "Using X.400 (MTA) Queues to Troubleshoot Message Flow" earlier in this chapter, issues with specific routing and transport components can cause messages to accumulate in a queue. If you are having problems with a specific queue, increase the logging level for the component that is affecting the queue.

Enabling Debugging Level Logging

If you are experiencing mail flow issues and want to view all events, you can modify a registry key to set logging to the debugging level, which is the highest level (level 7). Remember that incorrectly editing the registry can cause serious problems that may require you to reinstall your operating system. Problems resulting from editing the registry incorrectly may not be able to be resolved. Before editing the registry, back up any valuable data.

To enable logging at the debugging level:

1. Start Registry Editor.

2. In Registry Editor, locate and click the following registry key:

   ```
   HKEY_LOCAL_MACHINE\System\CurrentControlSet\Services\
   MSExchangeTransport\Diagnostics\SMTP Protocol
   ```

3. Set the value to **7**, and then click OK.

Best Practices

There are some best practices which you should follow in your Exchange deployment. First, ensure that you are using a minimum number of routing groups and that the routing groups that you create are created because of unreliable bandwidth issues, not for other reasons. Secondly, use the default SMTP virtual server configurations for sending and receiving Internet e-mail unless you have special considerations which require you to use an SMTP connector. Thirdly, if you are new to Exchange Server 2003 and need a quick way to setup Internet e-mail, then use Internet Mail Wizard to properly configure your Exchange server. Finally, use the diagnostic logging feature in the properties of your Exchange server to log message transport events if you encounter an interruption of message flow and you need additional diagnostic assistance.

Chapter 15

Managing Clustered Exchange 2003 Servers

About This Chapter

This chapter explains how to cluster multiple servers running Microsoft Exchange Server 2003 according to their specific roles in an Exchange organization. Further important topics concern load-balancing clusters based on the Windows Network Load Balancing (NLB) feature of Microsoft Windows Server 2003, as well as server clusters based on the Microsoft Cluster Service (MSCS). Important high-availability clustering concepts, such as active/active and active/passive clustering are also explained.

A working knowledge of Microsoft Windows Server 2003 Enterprise Edition is important. This chapter assumes that you understand how to use Windows Server 2003 and Microsoft Active Directory directory service, and that you are familiar with the basic concepts of Exchange Server 2003, such as storage groups, routing and administrative groups, mailbox management, and public folders. For more information about the basic concepts of Exchange Server 2003, see Chapter 2, "Exchange Server 2003 Design Basics," as well as the Exchange online books *Planning an Exchange Server 2003 Messaging System* and *Exchange Server 2003 High Availability*

Guide, both available at http://www.microsoft.com/technet/prodtechnol/exchange/2003/library/default.mspx.

What You Need to Know

Clustered Exchange 2003 servers are typical elements of a segmented messaging environment that separates servers hosting mailboxes and public folders from servers performing message transfer and other tasks, such as communicating with Internet clients. Servers that host mailboxes and public folders are called Exchange back-end servers, and servers that handle message transfer and client communication are bridgehead servers or Exchange front-end servers. Exchange front-end servers can act as bridgeheads to offload Simple Mail Transfer Protocol (SMTP) queues, message filtering, Secure Sockets Layer (SSL) encryption, forward and reverse queries to a Domain Name System (DNS) server, and other communication-related activities from Exchange back-end servers.

According to the different roles of front-end and back-end servers in an Exchange organization, you will use different clustering technologies to increase performance and decrease downtime from hardware failures. You can cluster your bridgehead servers and Exchange front-end servers using a load-balancing solution, such as Windows Network Load Balancing. Exchange back-end servers, on the other hand, are clustered using Windows server clustering provided by the Windows 2003 Cluster service. When running on Windows Server 2003 Enterprise or Datacenter Edition, Exchange Server 2003 Enterprise Edition supports server clusters of up to eight nodes. With Windows 2000 Datacenter Server, server clusters are limited to a maximum of four nodes. The Windows Cluster service is not supported with Windows 2003 or Exchange 2003 standard editions, however.

Key benefits of load-balancing clusters and server clusters are:

- **Load-balancing clusters**   The primary benefit of using a load-balancing cluster for Exchange 2003 front-end servers is distributed workload. Exchange front-end servers, clustered using a load-balancing solution that distributes incoming TCP/IP traffic among all servers, can provide faster response times than a single Exchange front-end server. Faster response times are achieved because the servers share the workload.

- **Server clusters**   The primary benefit of using server clusters with Exchange 2003 back-end servers is failover support. If one node in the cluster fails, the failover process automatically shifts the workload of the failed server to another node in the cluster, ensuring a quick recovery of Exchange services. For example, nodes in an active/passive server cluster do not share the workload, but eliminate single points of failures. You can also trigger a failover process manually, which can help to simplify server maintenance. For example, it is straightforward to replace hardware in a server cluster. You can move an Exchange

Virtual Server to another node, then replace the node with new hardware, and then move the Exchange Virtual Server back to that node. In a server cluster, an Exchange Virtual Server is a Windows cluster group containing cluster resources, such as an IP address, a network name, and physical disks, as well as Exchange resources, such as the Exchange 2003 System Attendant.

The Windows Cluster service also permits you to add additional nodes to a cluster if processing demands increase.

A number of qualified hardware and storage vendors offer clustering products. You should only use hardware from the Windows Server Catalog for clustered Exchange 2003 back-end servers. The Windows Server Catalog lists the hardware that Microsoft has certified for Windows Server 2003. The catalog is available at *http://go.microsoft.com/fwlink/?linkid=17219*. If you want to deploy multiple servers in a Windows cluster, be sure that your hardware is listed in the catalog's "Cluster Solutions" section, and that the hardware configuration must be the same on each node.

> **Note**   Microsoft supports hardware for Windows Server 2003 clusters only if it has passed the Windows Hardware Quality Labs (WHQL) test for the Windows Server 2003 family.

Clustering Exchange 2003 Front-End Servers

An Exchange front-end server acts as a proxy for requests from Hyper Text Transmission Protocol (HTTP), Post Office Protocol 3 (POP3), and Internet Message Access Protocol 4 (IMAP4) clients. It receives a client request and directs the request to the appropriate Exchange back-end server where data resides. It is also possible to configure an Exchange front-end server as an RPC over HTTP Proxy server, so users can use full-featured Microsoft Office Outlook 2003 with RPC over HTTP to access mailboxes over Exchange front-end servers. You do not need to deploy a virtual private network (VPN) to provide connectivity for Outlook clients. Chapter 7, "Hosting Exchange Server 2003," discusses Exchange front-end servers and RPC over HTTP configurations in more detail.

Load Balancing Exchange Front-End Servers

Exchange front-end servers do not host any user data, so it is insignificant which Exchange front-end server you choose to connect to the Exchange back-end server where your mailbox is located. You can deploy multiple Exchange front-end servers and connect through any of them to your mailbox or public folder server. The Exchange front-end server that you choose determines your home server dynamically based on Active Directory information (the msExchHomeServer attribute).

> **Note**   A general recommendation is to deploy one Exchange front-end server for every four Exchange back-end servers if you wish to support Internet-based messaging clients and want to provide a central access point, and cluster the servers using Network Load Balancing. To test front-end server performance, you can use the Exchange Stress and Performance 2003 (English only) tool, available for download at *http://www.microsoft.com/downloads/details.aspx?FamilyId=773AE7FD-860F-4755-B04D-1972E38FA4DB&displaylang=en.*

Multiple Exchange front-end servers do not require the users to specify different host names if you cluster the servers by means of a load-balancing solution. Using a load-balancing solution, you can cluster two or more servers with a single IP address. To the user, it will appear as if the client is always accessing the same host. In fact, the users do not know which Exchange front-end server is actually handling their client connections. Figure 15-1 illustrates the load-balancing cluster principle. Remember, however, that you must create identical configurations on all Exchange front-end servers that are part of the load-balancing cluster. Otherwise, clients might experience different behavior, depending on the server that proxies the client connection to the Exchange back-end server. For example, if users are supposed to work with Outlook Web Access through a custom virtual directory called /mail, this virtual directory must exist on all Exchange front-end servers. If this virtual directory is missing on a front-end server, users who are directed to that front-end server will not reach Outlook Web Access.

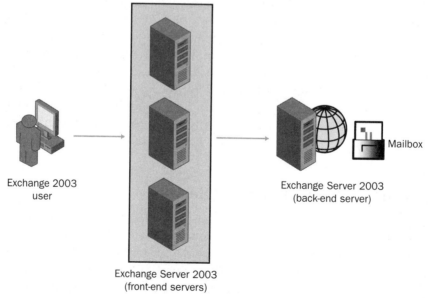

Exchange 2003 user

Exchange Server 2003 (front-end servers)

Exchange Server 2003 (back-end server)

Mailbox

Figure 15-1   Exchange front-end servers in a load-balancing environment

To cluster Exchange front-end servers, you can use one of the following technologies:

- **Domain Name Service (DNS) round robin**   This mechanism is based on the simple concept of having the same host name mapped to the IP addresses of multiple Exchange front-end servers. To distribute user connections, DNS must be configured to rotate the host records. If you use a Windows 2003 DNS for round-robin load balancing, do not forget to activate the Enable round-robin setting in the DNS snap-in; otherwise, the DNS Server service does not rotate the host records and always returns the same IP address to the client.

Note   It is not recommended to configure Exchange front-end servers as DNS servers. In an Active Directory forest, the typical configuration is to run Windows 2003 DNS on domain controllers, so you can use Active Directory-integrated zones.

Figure 15-2 shows the DNS round-robin setting for a Windows 2003 DNS server.

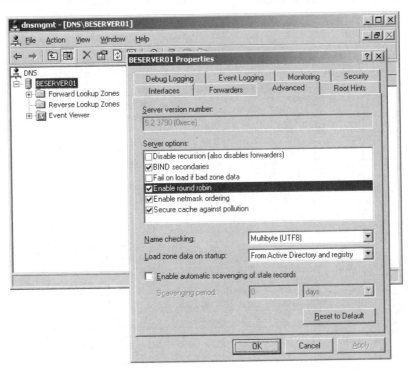

Figure 15-2   DNS round-robin setting

It should be noted, however, that DNS round robin provides only a minimum level of fault tolerance. Client requests must be repeated if a particular Exchange front-end server is not responding, which eventually should point the client to an available server. Compared to other load-balancing solutions, round robin has significant disadvantages because information about client connections or unavailable servers is not maintained.

■ **Microsoft Windows Network Load Balancing**   This load-balancing solution is available at no extra cost in Windows 2000 Advanced Server and Datacenter Server as well as all Windows Server 2003 editions. Windows Network Load Balancing is relatively easy to install and supports up to 32 Exchange front-end servers. A Windows Network Load Balancing Manager tool, included in Windows 2003, enables you to configure an entire load-balancing cluster from a single console. Figure 15-3 shows Windows Network Load Balancing Manager.

On the Resource Kit CD   For an example of how to configure Windows Network Load Balancing using Windows Network Load Balancing Manager, see the document Configuring Windows Network Load Balancing for Exchange front-end servers.doc in the \Companion Material\Chapter 15\Windows Network Load Balancing folder on the companion CD.

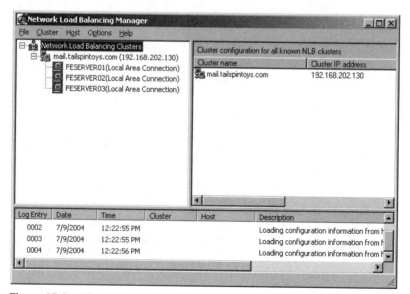

Figure 15-3   Windows Network Load Balancing Manager

An advantage of Windows Network Load Balancing is that this technology is able to automatically update its current information about the load-balancing environment when an Exchange front-end server is taken offline. Existing connections to the offline server are lost, but new client requests are redirected to one of the remaining servers. When you restart the server, the server will join the load-balancing cluster again. Windows Network Load Balancing also supports the mapping of client connections to a particular Exchange front-end server based on affinities. By default, all servers in a Windows Network Load Balancing cluster have the same affinity to distribute the workload evenly across all servers, but you can also configure affinity values for each host individually, in which case the affinity value determines the percentage of the workload that the server will handle.

- **Alternative load-balancing solutions**   If you want to increase performance or need to include more than 32 Exchange front-end servers in a load-balancing cluster, you must use an alternative load-balancing solution. In general, load-balancing solutions fall into one of two categories:

  - **Hardware load-balancing solutions**   Networking equipment, such as dedicated hardware devices like bridges or routers, might include load-balancing functionality. For example, Cisco Local Director is a network bridge that can manage and distribute the client traffic to multiple servers. Hardware load balancing might be a good choice if you want to implement a high-performance environment with a very large number of Exchange front-end servers.

  - **Software load-balancing solutions**   Software-based solutions, such as IBM eNetwork Dispatcher, can be used to load-balance network traffic. Software-based load balancing is generally slower than hardware-based load balancing, but if your network topology changes, such as when you add servers, you can reconfigure a software-based solution while you might have to wait for vendor development to address your special needs with a hardware-based solution.

When implementing a load-balancing solution, be sure to avoid single points of failures. For example, if you only have a single hardware load-balancing device (such as a router that provides load-balancing functionality), a failure to that device can render the entire load-balancing cluster unavailable even though the individual servers are still running. You might have to invest in backup systems to achieve the desired level of fault tolerance. This is not an issue with Windows Network Load Balancing because this solution runs on every server in the load-balancing cluster and does not require any extra equipment. We recommend that you implement a Windows Network Load Balancing solution for Exchange front-end servers.

Clustering Exchange 2003 Back-End Servers

In a server cluster, individual servers, called nodes, run instances of server applications, such as Exchange Server 2003. Instances of server applications running on cluster nodes are called virtual servers. For example, an Exchange server running on a cluster node is called an Exchange Virtual Server. A virtual server corresponds to a static IP address and a network name, and usually has a physical disk resource and other resources. Clients can use the network name and IP address to communicate with the virtual server without having to know the actual node that is currently running the services.

The process of transferring a virtual server from one node in a cluster to another node is called failover. The process of transferring a virtual server back to the original node when the original node is available again, is called failback. It is important to understand that the virtual server is unavailable during failover and failback procedures, but as soon as the virtual server is running on the next node, users can reconnect using the network name or IP address of the virtual server.

Failover and failback have the following characteristics:

- **Failover**   A failover can occur in two situations: Either you trigger it manually for maintenance reasons or the Cluster service initiates it automatically in case of a resource failure on the node owning the resource. Examples of cluster resources are IP address, network name, physical disks, and Exchange Server services. If a resource fails, the Cluster service first attempts a resource restart on the local node. If this does not correct the problem, the Cluster service will take the resource group offline along with its dependent resources, move it to another node, and then restart it there. Resource groups represent the virtual servers running on a server cluster. The resources within a resource group are always moved as a single unit between cluster nodes. The resources of a particular resource group are always owned by a single node.

    Because the Cluster service must decide where to move the resource group, it communicates with its counterparts on the remaining active nodes to arbitrate the ownership of the resource group. This arbitration relies on the node preference list that you can specify when creating resources in Cluster Administrator. The arbitration can also take into account other factors such as the capabilities of each node, the current load, and application-specific information. After a new node is determined for the resource group, all nodes update their cluster databases to track which node now owns the resource group. If multiple resource groups are affected, for instance because of a total node failure, the process is repeated for each resource group individually.

Note By grouping servers together in a server cluster, you can minimize system downtime caused by software or hardware failures, but you cannot provide uninterrupted services. Messaging services are interrupted when an Exchange Virtual Server fails on one node, although users might be able to reconnect almost immediately, depending on how fast the failover procedure completes. Likewise, the Windows Cluster service does not protect and does not repair Exchange stores, which remain single points of failure no matter how many nodes you add to a server cluster. For example, if a mailbox store is corrupted for any reason, causing the Exchange store to dismount this mailbox store, moving the Exchange Virtual Server from the current node to another node will not solve the issue. The Exchange store will not be able to mount the corrupted mailbox store on any of the nodes in the cluster.

- **Failback** By default, resource groups are set not to failback automatically. Groups continue to run on the alternate node after the failed node comes back online. However, if you have specified a preferred owner for a resource group, and this node comes back online, the failover manager will failback the resource group to the recovered or restarted node. The Cluster service provides protection against continuous resource failures. For example, continuous resource failures can result from repeating failback to nodes that have not been correctly recovered. The Cluster service provides protection by limiting the number of times the Cluster service attempts failback. Furthermore, you can configure specific hours of the day during which the failback of a group is prohibited, for example, at peak business hours. To configure failback and failback hours, display the properties of the desired resource group in Cluster Administrator and then click the Failback tab.

Single-Node Cluster Example

The smallest server cluster is a cluster with just one node. A single-node cluster does not help to minimize system downtime or increase availability because an Exchange Virtual Server cannot failover to another node in the cluster. However, single-node clusters are useful for test or training purposes because in a single-node cluster you can place all cluster resources on local hard disks.

On the Resource Kit CD For an example of how to install Exchange 2003 in a single-node server cluster, see the document Deploying a single-node Exchange 2003 Cluster.doc in the \Companion Material\Chapter 15\Server Clustering\Single Node folder on the companion CD.

You can also use a single-node cluster configuration for the servers in your production environment. A primary benefit of a single node cluster is that it can simplify hardware replacement processes. For example, to replace an Exchange back-end server that is part of single-node cluster, add a new Exchange back-end server as a second node in the cluster, move the Exchange Virtual Server to the second node, and then evict the outdated first node. It is by far more complicated to replace a server that is not part of an Exchange back-end cluster configuration.

Note   The above explanations apply to single-node cluster configurations as well as server clusters with multiple nodes. Hardware replacement processes are generally independent of the number of nodes in the cluster.

On the Resource Kit CD   Adding a second Node to the Server Cluster Test Environment.doc and Removing a Node from a Windows 2003 Cluster.doc that you can find in the \Companion Material\Chapter 15\Server Clustering\Single Node folder on the companion CD explain how to add a second node to a server cluster and how to remove the first node.

Figure 15-4 illustrates how to replace server hardware using a single-node cluster.

Joining a Server Cluster

When you start a server that is part of a cluster, the operating system is started as usual, mounting and configuring local, non-clustered resources. On a cluster node, the Cluster service (Clussvc.exe) is one of the server services, typically set to automatic startup. You can also start the Cluster service manually using the Services tool or the command line **net start ClusSVC**. When the Cluster service starts, the Cluster service determines the other nodes in the cluster based on the information from the local copy of the cluster registry. The Cluster service attempts to find an active cluster node called the sponsor that can authenticate the local service. The sponsor then broadcasts information about the authenticated node to other cluster nodes and sends the authenticated Cluster service updated configuration information if the authenticated node's cluster database was found outdated.

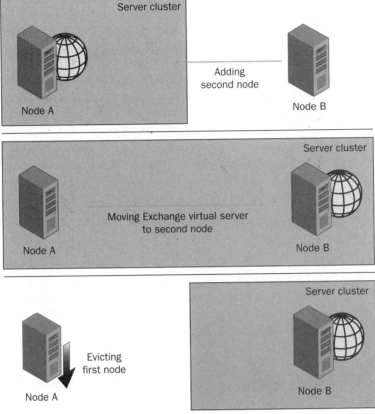

Figure 15-4 Replacing server hardware in a single-node cluster

From the point of view of other nodes in the cluster, a node may be in one of three states:

- **Offline** A node is offline when it is not an active member of the cluster.

- **Online** A node is online when it is fully active, is able to own and manage resource groups, accepts cluster database updates, and contributes votes to the quorum algorithm. The quorum algorithm determines which node can own the quorum disk. The quorum disk stores the configuration and state data of the cluster.

- **Paused** A paused node is an online node unable to take over further resource groups, such as an Exchange Virtual Server from a failed node. You can pause a node for maintenance reasons, for example.

Server Clusters and Cluster Storage

It is important to design the storage subsystem in a way that permits all nodes in the cluster to run the virtual servers. For example, if you want to move an Exchange Virtual Server from one node to another node, the Exchange Virtual Server must be able to access its mailbox stores, public folder stores, message queue directories on the file system, and possibly message tracking logs on either node. In a typical cluster configuration, you must connect all nodes to a shared Small Computer System Interface (SCSI) bus or Fiber Channel system that provides all nodes with access to the cluster disks. However, the Windows Cluster service also supports configurations in which cluster nodes do not share physical disks, such as in a geographically dispersed server cluster.

You have the following options to design the cluster storage subsystem:

- **Use local hard disks** This configuration is only appropriate for single-node clusters that you install for test or training purposes because local disks are not shared between cluster nodes. For example, if you configure an Exchange Virtual Server using a local disk resource on Node A, then Node B cannot run the Exchange Virtual Server. Attempts to move the Exchange Virtual Server to Node B will fail because the Exchange store databases, SMTP mailroot directory, message transfer agent (MTA) message queue directory, and other resources are not available on Node B. Local hard disks must be SCSI-based storage devices configured as basic disks. The Windows Cluster service does not support dynamic disks, volume sets, or Integrated Device Electronics (IDE) hard disks.

> **Caution** If you are planning to install Exchange 2003 in a single-node cluster to simplify hardware maintenance, do not use local hard disks for the Exchange Virtual Server or you will not be able to move the Exchange Virtual Server to a second node that you might want to add later on.

- **Use shared hard disks** This is the standard configuration for server clusters running Exchange Server 2003. On server clusters running Windows 2003, you can use a shared SCSI or Fiber Channel storage system. Only hardware components, especially host bus adapters and disks that are tested by Microsoft and that are on the hardware-compatibility list for server clusters, should be used for clustering. Make sure the host bus adapters and host bus adapter firmware are identical on each node. If you are using a traditional SCSI-based storage system, connect only disks and SCSI adapters to it. Do not connect tape devices, CD-ROMs, scanners, and so forth. Furthermore, ensure that the bus is terminated properly on both ends. If your cluster configuration includes unsupported hardware components or an improperly terminated shared SCSI bus, you may end up with corruption of data on shared hard disks of the cluster. Corruption of the data on your shared hard disks has a significant impact on reliability and availability of your messaging system. For server clusters with more than two nodes, we recommend that you use Fiber Channel hardware on the shared storage bus. The shared storage subsystem is best configured using redundant arrays of independent disks (RAID). You cannot use software RAID. You must use hardware RAID to protect the data.

Figure 15-5 illustrates a shared storage configuration in a two-node cluster.

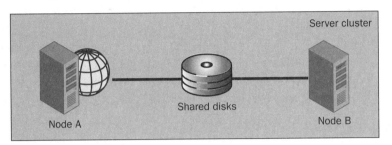

Figure 15-5   Shared disks in a server cluster

Note   The standard cluster model based on shared disks is the most appropriate cluster model for Exchange Server 2003. We recommend that you partition and format all disks on the cluster storage device before adding the first node to your server cluster. All partitions must be formatted with NTFS. For Exchange Server 2003, you should leave the partitions uncompressed.

For detailed information about how to configure the cluster disks, see *Exchange Server 2003 High Availability Guide* (*http://www.microsoft.com/ technet/prodtechnol/exchange/2003/library/highavailgde.mspx*). Also see *Designing and Deploying Server Clusters* in the book *Planning Server Deployments* of the *Microsoft Windows Server 2003 Deployment Kit* (*http:// www.microsoft.com/resources/documentation/WindowsServ/2003/all/ deployguide/en-us/Default.asp?url=/resources/documentation/WindowsServ/2003/all/deployguide/en-us/dpgsdc_overview.asp*).

■ **Implement a majority node set cluster**   In a majority node set cluster, each node maintains its own disk resources. Although you can use majority node set when the nodes of your cluster are located in close proximity, using a majority node set can be especially helpful if you choose to physically locate the nodes of the server cluster in different data centers. Configurations where cluster nodes are located in various datacenters is called a geographically dispersed cluster configuration. In such a configuration, you must ensure that the shared disks of the cluster are replicated between each datacenter. Exchange 2003 geographically dispersed cluster configurations can be complex, and the clusters must use only components supported by Microsoft. Geographically dispersed clusters should be deployed only in conjunction with vendors who provide qualified configurations. For more information about geographically dispersed clustering in Exchange 2003, see Chapter 5 of the *Exchange Server 2003 High Availability Guide*. For detailed information about geographically dispersed clusters in Windows Server 2003, see *Geographically Dispersed Clusters in Windows Server 2003* (*http://go.microsoft.com/fwlink/?linkid=28241*).

> **Note**   The hardware in a geographically dispersed cluster must be on the Microsoft Hardware Compatibility List for geographically dispersed clusters. For more information, see the Windows Server Catalog (*http://go.microsoft.com/fwlink/?LinkId=28572*).

Partitioned Data Access

Nodes that share cluster disks cannot access the disks concurrently. The Cluster service prevents concurrent access from multiple nodes to prevent data corruption. This partitioned data access model is usually sufficient for PC systems, but its disadvantage is that you cannot achieve dynamic load balancing. For instance, when you configure a resource group for an Exchange Virtual Server in a two-node cluster (as shown in Figure 15-5), only one node at a time can own this resource group and run the Exchange Virtual Server. In the event of a failure, the Windows Cluster service can move the Exchange resource group to another node in the server cluster, but it is not possible to run the same virtual server on more than one node concurrently. The node owning the resource requests exclusive access to the disk by issuing a SCSI Reserve command. No other node can then access the physical device unless an SCSI Release command is issued.

Cluster Disk Caching

In some configurations, enabling write caching on disks can help improve messaging performance. However, it is highly recommended that you do not enable this feature on cluster disks, in order to avoid losing data during failover. For example, if you enable write back cache (write through only) on an internal RAID controller, data in the cache will be lost during failover.

Alternately, it is possible to enable write cache on an external RAID controller inside the disk cabinet because the data in the cache is preserved, as the external RAID controller is not affected by a node failure. The data that was in the cache at the moment of failover is available to the node that takes ownership of the Exchange Virtual Server.

Resource Groups and Physical Disks

A resource group defines the unit of failover for a collection of cluster resources. If one resource in a resource group fails, the entire resource group is affected and the Windows Cluster service moves the resource group to an alternate node. All of the resources in the resource group are moved because a resource group can only be owned by one node at any given time. Resource groups cannot share resources. A single resource has to be a member of one and only one resource group. For example, it is not possible to include the same physical disk in two different resource groups. If Group A is owned by Node A and Group B is owned by Node B, then Node A and Node B would require access to the same physical disk, which is not possible according to the partitioned data access model.

> **Note** The resource group defines the resources of a virtual server. The difference between a resource group and a virtual server is that a resource group may not contain any resources while a virtual server is a resource group that must have a network name resource, an IP address resource, and other resources, such as a physical disk.

In a typical cluster configuration for Exchange 2003 back-end servers, you should create a minimum of three different resource groups. With these three separate resource groups in a server cluster, you need at least three physical disks in the cluster storage device. Physical disk resources in a cluster map directly to physical SCSI devices identified by an individual logical unit number (LUN), rather than to drive letters or partitions.

In a server cluster for Exchange 2003, you should configure the following resource groups:

- **Cluster Group** The default Cluster Group contains the resources for the server cluster that provide generic information and failover policies. This group is essential for cluster operation. You should not install any applications into the default Cluster Group. If a resource for an application is added to this group and the resource fails, it can cause the cluster group to fail, thus reducing the overall availability of the entire server cluster.

    A very important resource in the default Cluster Group is the quorum resource, which is typically a physical disk (although for single-node server clusters, the Local Quorum resource can also act as a quorum resource). The quorum resource provides node-independent storage for cluster configuration and state data in the form of recovery logs. The recovery logs contain details about all the changes that have been applied to the cluster database. For a detailed discussion about quorum resources, see the technical article *Quorums in Server Clusters* (*http://www.microsoft.com/technet/prodtechnol/windowsserver2003/technologies/clustering/qsvclust.mspx*).

- **Resource group for Microsoft Distributed Transaction Coordinator (MSDTC)**   The Exchange 2003 Setup program must communicate with MSDTC to register the Collaboration Data Objects (CDO) workflow event sink for the Exchange store, which is implemented in the COM+ component called Cdowfevt.dll. Therefore, MSDTC must be running in the cluster. Microsoft only supports running MSDTC on cluster nodes as a cluster resource. MSDTC running in stand-alone mode on a cluster is not a recommended or supported configuration because distributed transactions may be orphaned if a cluster failover occurs. To set up MSDTC and COM+ on a Windows Server 2003 cluster, you must create an MSDTC resource directly by using Cluster Administrator. On Windows 2000, use the COM Cluster tool (Comclust.exe) instead to configure MSDTC in clustered mode.

  An important resource that you must add to the MSDTC resource group is a shared disk resource. When you add the Distributed Transaction Coordinator resource to the resource group in the next step, MSDTC creates an MSDTC log file on the shared disk so the MSDTC transaction manager can access the MSDTC log file from any node in the cluster. MSDTC can only run on one node in the cluster at a time, but if the node running the MSDTC transaction manager fails, the Cluster service restarts the MSDTC transaction manager automatically on another node. The restarted MSDTC transaction manager reads the MSDTC log file on the shared disk to determine pending and recently completed transactions. Applications can then reconnect to MSDTC to initiate new transactions.

> **Note**   Applications running on any node in the cluster can use MSDTC. These processes simply call the MSDTC Proxy in the normal way and the MSDTC Proxy automatically forwards MSDTC calls to the MSDTC transaction manager that is controlling the entire cluster.

- **Resource group for Exchange Server 2003**   MSDTC and Exchange Server 2003 do not have to run on the same node in the cluster. To run Exchange 2003 independently of other resources, configure a dedicated resource group for Exchange 2003.

> **On the Resource Kit CD**   The document Deploying a single-node Exchange 2003 Cluster.doc in the \Companion Material\Chapter 15\Server Clustering\Single Node folder on the companion CD provides an example of how to configure a dedicated resource group for Exchange 2003.

Drive Letter Limitations

You must add at least one shared disk to the Exchange 2003 resource group for the database files and file system-based message queues. If you want to implement additional Exchange Virtual Servers in a multi-node cluster or separate Exchange database files from transaction log files, even more physical disks are required. Remember that Windows 2003 is limited to 26 drive letters. Regardless of the number of cluster nodes, the maximum number of shared disks is typically 23 because one disk must be reserved for the operating system on each node, and two additional letters are typically assigned for the floppy disk (if present) and CD (or DVD) drive. Additional drive letters might be required for network share access.

If your cluster nodes are running Windows Server 2003, Enterprise Edition or Windows Server 2003, Datacenter Edition, you can use volume mount points to avoid the 26 drive letter limitation. Another option to overcome the limitations of directly attached storage (DAS) and avoid the expenses of a storage area network (SAN) is Microsoft Windows Storage Server 2003 Feature Pack, which enables you to place the Exchange store databases and transaction logs on a system running Microsoft Windows Storage Server 2003. Remember, however, that each Exchange Virtual Server still requires at least one physical cluster disk for message queue folders, message tracking log files, and possibly database transaction log files. For detailed information about the advantages and configuration of Microsoft Windows Storage Server 2003 Feature Pack in server cluster environment, see the document *Managing Exchange Storage with the Windows Storage Server 2003 Feature Pack*, available for download at *http://www.microsoft.com/windowsserversystem/wss2003/techinfo/plandeploy/exchange_fp.mspx*.

Volume Mount Points

Volume mount points bypass the need to associate each disk volume with a drive letter, by pointing to specified disk volumes through NTFS junction points. For example, you can configure F:\Exchsrvr_SG1_Log_Files to point to one disk volume and F:\Exchsrvr_SG2_Log_Files to point to another volume.

When using volume mount points in clusters, consider the following:

- Make sure that you create unique volume mount points so they do not conflict with existing local drives on any cluster node.

- Do not create volume mount points between shared cluster disks and local disks.

- Do not create volume mount points from the cluster disk that contains the quorum disk resource. You can, however, create a volume mount point from the quorum disk resource to a clustered disk.

All physical disks that you reference using volume mount points must belong to the same resource group and must be dependent on the root disk. Specifically, the volume mount point disk will not come online unless the root disk is first online. Setting this dependency prevents time-outs and failures when starting. It is also important to note that the Exchange System Attendant resource requires a dependency on all physical disks holding Exchange data.

We recommend that you use volume mount points with Exchange 2003 clusters that have four or more nodes running Windows Server 2003, Enterprise Edition or Windows Server 2003, Datacenter Edition. You should use one root disk per storage group. You can place the logs on the root disk and place the database on the mounted drive. If there are not enough drive letters available (such as in an eight-node cluster), you can use a single root disk. However, to minimize the risk of data loss in case of disk failure, do not store data on the root disk. You need one root disk for each Exchange Virtual Server.

Handling Single Points of Failures

For a server cluster to effectively provide fault tolerance and increase availability, you must avoid a configuration in which a single component can cause the entire server cluster to fail. Table 15-1 lists potential single points of failures in a server cluster and available options to avoid them or mitigate their impact.

Table 15-1   Potential Single Points of Failures in a Server Cluster

Single Point of Failures	Comments
Power supply	You should protect all servers and the network devices, such as hubs, bridges, and routers, using uninterruptible power supply (UPS) devices to provide protection against power failures and power surges. It is also a good idea to put each cluster node on a separate power circuit.
Disks	You should configure your disks in a RAID with fault tolerance to protect against single-disk failures, such as a RAID 5 or a RAID 0+1 configuration.
SCSI controllers	A malfunctioning SCSI controller can affect the entire cluster if the component causes the cluster storage to be unavailable. It is a good idea to have a replacement controller readily available. Make sure that any spare parts exactly match the original parts. You should also maintain a backup of the RAID controller configuration.

Table 15-1   Potential Single Points of Failures in a Server Cluster (Continued)

Single Point of Failures	Comments
Network infrastructure	Consider implementing a redundant network infrastructure, including redundant hubs, bridges, and routers, as well as redundant wide area network (WAN) links, to provide secondary access to the server cluster. You should also provide redundant Active Directory domain controllers and global catalog servers in the computer network. Remember, however, that it is not supported to run Active Directory on cluster nodes that host Exchange Virtual Servers. Cluster nodes that run Exchange 2003 must be member servers in an Active Directory domain.
Network interfaces	Consider configuring the network adapters in each cluster node redundantly, in order to reduce the chance that a failure of a network interface card (NIC) will result in the failure of the entire cluster. If a cluster node has only one network adapter and this network adapter fails, communication with the remaining nodes in the cluster is interrupted. When two nodes are unable to communicate, they are said to be partitioned. When two nodes become partitioned, the Cluster service on each node might attempt to take control of the quorum resource. There is a chance that the node with the interrupted network connection will gain control of the quorum resource, in which case the entire cluster becomes unavailable.

In addition to considering using redundant network adapters for the public and private network adapters for your cluster nodes, the following list provides an introduction to each type of network, as well as related best practices when deploying your cluster communication infrastructure:

- **Public network communication**   Nodes of a server cluster use public NICs to communicate with the client computers and other server computers in the corporate network. For your NICs that connect to the public network, you should use fast and reliable network cards, such as Fast Ethernet or Fiber Distributed Data Interface (FDDI) cards.

- **Private network communication**   Nodes of a server cluster use private NICs to communicate to other nodes in the cluster. Specifically, in intervals of seconds, nodes exchange state information between each other to determine the current state of each node, which is known as a heartbeat. The private network is optional but highly recommended to implement an additional communication channel between the nodes in case the corporate network fails. For your NICs that connect to the private network, low-cost Ethernet cards are sufficient to handle the minimal cluster communication traffic between the nodes.

We recommend that you use static IP addresses for all public and private network adapters. Each network must be a unique subnet.

Windows Cluster Service Architecture

The Cluster service and its internal components rely on external components to control the cluster activities on each node. A cluster network driver, for example, monitors the status of communication path between nodes, routes messages, and detects communication failures. Another important component is the cluster disk driver, which ensures that only one node can access a shared cluster disk at a time. The cluster database is also an important component because it stores the cluster registry on each node. The cluster database is located in the %systemroot%\Cluster\CLUSDB folder. A copy of the cluster registry is also stored in the CHK*xxx*.TMP file on the quorum disk.

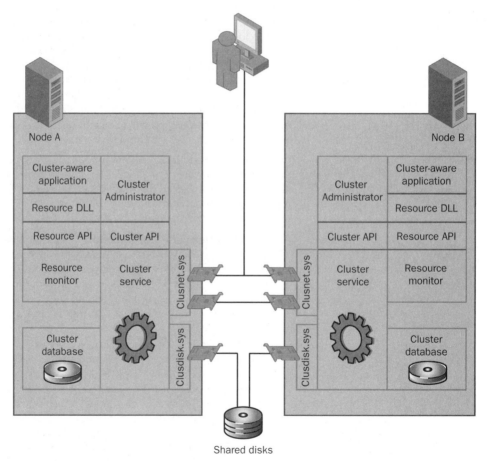

Figure 15-6 Cluster service, cluster APIs, and cluster-aware components

The health of each cluster resource is monitored by the resource monitor, which is implemented in a separate process communicating with the Cluster service via remote procedure calls (RPCs). The resource monitor provides a communication and monitoring mechanism between the Cluster service and the resources through resource DLLs. Resource DLLs are loaded into the process of the resource monitor to carry out most operations on cluster resources. Resources are any physical or logical components that the Cluster service can manage, such as disks, IP addresses, network names, Exchange services, and so forth.

Figure 15-6 illustrates the relationship between the Cluster service, its application programming interfaces (APIs), and its external components.

Internal Cluster Service Elements

Internal Cluster service elements are not illustrated in Figure 15-6 to reduce the figure's complexity. The Cluster service consists of the following internal components:

- **Node manager** The node manager maintains the list of nodes that belong to the cluster. The node manager also monitors the system state. It is this component that periodically sends heartbeat messages to the other nodes in the cluster. The heartbeat enables the node manager to recognize node faults.

- **Resource manager** The resource manager receives system information from resource monitor and node manager to manage resources and resource groups and initiate actions, such as startup, restart, and failover. To carry out a failover, the resource manager works in conjunction with the failover manager.

- **Failover manager** The failover manager provides safe and secure failover from one node in a cluster to another node. In the event of a failover, the failover manager checks all other nodes to determine the node that the resource group should be moved to. If there are any nodes in the possible owners' list for the resource that are currently not hosting a resource group, those nodes are considered a preferred target for failover.

- **Communications manager** The communications manager manages the communication among all cluster nodes through the cluster network driver.

- **Event processor** The event processor manages the node state information and controls the initialization of the Cluster service. This component transfers event notifications between Cluster service components and between the Cluster service and cluster-aware applications. For example, the event processor activates the node manager to begin the process of joining or forming a cluster.

- **Configuration database manager** The configuration database manager maintains the cluster database. The cluster database stores the cluster registry, which is separate from the local Windows Registry, although a copy of the cluster registry is kept in the Windows Registry as well. The cluster database maintains updates on members, resources, restart parameters, and other configuration information.

- **Checkpoint manager** The checkpoint manager saves the cluster configuration in a log file on the quorum disk. The quorum resource is used to communicate configuration changes to all nodes in the cluster.

- **Global update manager** The global update manager provides the update service that transfers configuration changes into the cluster database on each node.

- **Log manager** The log manager writes recovery logs to the quorum disk.

Exchange 2003 Cluster Integration

Exchange 2003 provides a cluster resource DLL called Exres.dll for communication and interaction with the Cluster service. The resource monitor component uses Exres.dll to communicate with the cluster-aware Exchange resources. Exres.dll also monitors the cluster-aware Exchange resources and notifies the Cluster service if an Exchange resource fails so the Cluster service can take action. The Cluster service is responsible for starting and stopping Exchange 2003 services through Exres.dll. Exres.dll monitors these processes and notifies the Cluster service if an operation ends unsuccessfully.

Exres.dll monitors the following Exchange resources:

- **System Attendant** The System Attendant is the fundamental resource that controls the creation and deletion of all the resources in an Exchange Virtual Server. These resources are created when you create the System Attendant resource. The resources are deleted when you delete the System Attendant in Cluster Administrator.

  To configure cluster-aware Exchange resources, Exchange 2003 extends the Cluster Administrator tool through Excluadm.dll. The Excluadm.dll file provides cluster-specific Wizards and the user interface (UI) that is associated with Exchange 2003.

- **Information Store** The Information Store resource corresponds to the Exchange store. When this resource is brought online, the Microsoft Exchange Information Store service (Store.exe) starts and begins to mount the mailbox and public folder stores. When all Exchange stores are mounted, the resource is considered to be online.

- **Protocol virtual servers** You can run protocol virtual servers, such as SMTP, HTTP, POP3, and IMAP4 virtual servers, in a server cluster. Protocol servers for SMTP and HTTP are created automatically when you add a System Attendant resource to a resource group. For POP3 and IMAP4, you must first open Services tool and enable the protocol services (POP3 service and IMAP4 service are disabled by default). You must also verify in the Protocols container in Exchange System Manager that POP3 and IMAP4 virtual servers exist. You can then add POP3 and IMAP4 resources manually to an Exchange 2003 Virtual Server using

Cluster Administrator, and bring these resources online. The configuration of protocol virtual servers is explained later in this chapter.

■ **Routing Engine**   The Routing Engine service provides topology and routing information to servers running Exchange 2003. If this service is stopped, optimal routing of messages might not be available.

■ **Message Tracking Agent (MTA)**   The MTA routes messages through X.400 and gateway connectors to non-Exchange messaging systems. In a mixed environment with servers running Exchange 5.5 in the local routing group, the MTA is also used to transfer messages between Exchange 2003 and Exchange 5.5. This occurs because Exchange 5.5 MTAs communicate with each other in the local site directly through RPCs. Exchange 2003 must rely on this communication method for backward compatibility.

   If you plan to configure multiple Exchange Virtual Servers in a cluster, remember that the MTA cannot run on more than one node in the cluster because concurrent access to the MTA message queue directory on a shared cluster disk from multiple nodes is not supported. Only one Exchange Virtual Server can contain an MTA resource in a cluster.

Exchange Virtual Servers also support full-text indexing through the MS Search service. A corresponding resource is added to an Exchange Virtual Server when you add the System Attendant resource to your resource group in Cluster Administrator. However, Exres.dll is not used to monitor the MS Search resource. The Cluster service uses an MS Search-specific resource DLL, called Gathercl.dll, to manage this resource. If you don't plan to use full-text indexing, you can delete the MS Search resource from your Exchange Virtual Server.

> **More Info**   For detailed information on how to delete the MS Search resource from an Exchange Virtual Server (and how to recreate it), see Microsoft Knowledge Base Article 830189, "Exchange Server 2003 Computer Cannot Bring the Microsoft Search Resource Online" *(http://support.microsoft.com/default.aspx?scid=kb;en-us;830189).*

Figure 15-7 illustrates the relationship between Exchange 2003 and the Cluster service.

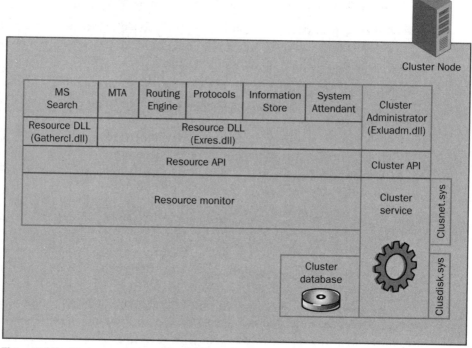

Figure 15-7   Exchange 2003 resources in a server cluster

Unsupported Exchange 2003 Components

It is important to understand that the following Exchange 2003 components do not support the Windows Cluster service:

- **Microsoft Active Directory Connector (ADC)**   Windows clustering is primarily a technology to increase the availability of mailbox servers. Active Directory Connector, on the other hand, is used to perform directory update operations, such as synchronizing an Exchange Server 5.5 directory with Active Directory directory service. Because ADC is not an important component for a mailbox server, ADC has not been implemented as a cluster-aware service. To integrate Exchange 5.5 with Active Directory, install and configure ADC on a computer that is not a node of a back-end Exchange cluster.

- **Exchange Calendar Connector**   Calendar Connector is used in conjunction with Connector for Lotus Notes or Connector for Novell GroupWise to synchronize free and busy information between Exchange and non-Exchange users. You must install and configure Calendar Connector on a bridgehead server, and that bridgehead server cannot be part of a node of a back-end Exchange cluster.

- **Exchange Connector for Lotus Notes** Similar to Calendar Connector, Connector for Lotus Notes should be installed on a dedicated (non-clustered) bridgehead server to connect an Exchange organization to a Lotus Domino/ Notes environment. You cannot install and configure Connector for Lotus Notes on a computer that is a node of an Exchange back-end cluster.

- **Exchange Connector for Novell GroupWise** Similar to Calendar Connector and Connector for Lotus Notes, Connector for Novell GroupWise is not supported on a node of an Exchange back-end cluster. You must run this connector on a dedicated bridgehead server with connectivity to the Novell GroupWise messaging environment, and that server must not be a node of an Exchange 2003 back-end cluster.

- **Microsoft Exchange Event service** The Exchange Event service supports server-side scripting agents developed for Exchange Server 5.5. This component is not critical for a mailbox server and is deactivated in Exchange 2003 by default. If you have deployed a solution that requires the Exchange Event service, you must run this component on a non-clustered Exchange server.

- **Site Replication Service (SRS)** The Site Replication Service enables seamless directory interoperability between Exchange 2003 and Exchange 5.5. The Site Replication Service communicates with the directory service of Exchange Server 5.5 through the Exchange 5.5 directory replication protocol. This component is not supported on clustered mailbox servers.

- **Network News Transfer Protocol (NNTP)** The NNTP service, a component of Internet Information Services, is required for installing Exchange 2003 in a cluster. However, after you install Exchange 2003 in a cluster, the NNTP service is not functional.

- **Intelligent Message Filter (IMF)** Intelligent Message Filter is an add-on for Exchange Server 2003 and should be installed at the bridgehead servers connecting the Exchange organization to the Internet. You should not install this component on an Exchange server cluster. As mentioned earlier in this chapter, bridgehead servers are best clustered using a Windows Network Load Balancing solution.

Load Balancing and Failover Configurations for Server Clusters

In contrast to a load-balancing cluster, server clusters do not provide load balancing in the sense that multiple nodes provide access to the same resources concurrently. A particular virtual server can only run on one node in the cluster at any given time. However, you can implement static load balancing by spreading mailboxes across multiple Exchange Virtual Servers running on separate nodes. For example, you can configure a three-node cluster with two Exchange Virtual Servers and then run each virtual server on a separate node, reserving the third node as a standby server. If one node is unavailable, the third node can run the affected Exchange Virtual Server without performance impact. The static load-balancing configuration is preserved because two separate nodes share the workload at all times. If a second node fails in this cluster configuration, however, one Exchange Virtual Server must remain offline to avoid overloading the last remaining node in the cluster. For this reason, restore the failed node as quickly as possible, so failover can occur again if another node fails.

Exchange Virtual Servers and Routing Groups

All Exchange Virtual Servers that you configure on a server cluster must belong to the same administrative group and routing group. It is not supported to move Exchange Virtual Servers to different routing groups in Exchange System Manager. Figure 15-8 shows the Cluster warning dialog box that Exchange System Manager displays if you attempt to separate Exchange Virtual Servers in different routing groups.

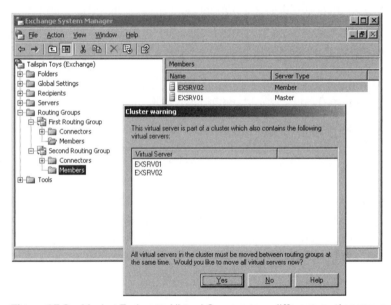

Figure 15-8   Moving Exchange Virtual Servers to a different routing group

Active/Active and Active/Passive Cluster Configurations

A server cluster with all nodes running an Exchange Virtual Server is called an active/active cluster. However, because no node is standing by to take over an Exchange Virtual Server if one node fails, active/active clustering must be considered a clustering method with limited capabilities. It is better and strongly recommended to deploy a server cluster in an active/passive configuration, in which one or multiple nodes do not run an Exchange Virtual Server in normal operation. Passive nodes stand by to run an Exchange Virtual Server if an active node fails. Passive nodes are therefore also called hot-standby servers.

Active/Active Cluster Configuration

Because of their drawbacks, Microsoft restricted active/active cluster configurations to two-node server clusters. The major drawback is that each node of the cluster runs an Exchange Virtual Server. When a failure occurs, the Exchange Virtual Server on the node that failed moves to the remaining node of the cluster, potentially overloading that node, thus leading to performance and stability issues due to the increased demand for server hardware, such as memory. This can result in memory fragmentation, which in turn can lead to issues that may even cause the overloaded node to fail, thus resulting in a situation where the entire server cluster goes down.

Active/active cluster configurations should be avoided whether you are planning to dedicate a server cluster to running only Exchange Server 2003 or want to implement a combined server cluster that runs more than one kind of server application, such as Exchange 2003 on one node and Microsoft SQL 2000 Server on another node. You must consider that in a failover situation, one node might have to run all virtual servers. For example, a node might have to run both Exchange 2003 and SQL Server. Yet, it is not advisable to run Exchange 2003 and SQL Server on the same computer because both server applications have a substantial demand for hardware resources and access memory differently. For this reason, we recommend that you configure dedicated server clusters, such as one server cluster for SQL Server and another server cluster for Exchange 2003, and that you use an active/passive configuration, as explained later in this chapter.

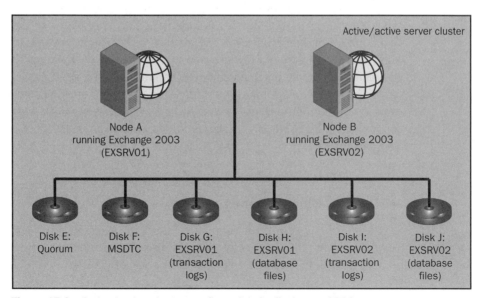

Figure 15-9   Active/active cluster configuration for Exchange 2003

Figure 15-9 illustrates a two-node server cluster running two Exchange Virtual Servers in an active/active configuration, as it may be appropriate for a small company that prioritizes hardware utilization over system availability.

On the Resource Kit CD   For step-by-step instructions to install an active/active cluster, see the document Deploying an active-active Exchange 2003 Cluster.doc in the \Companion Material\Chapter 15\Server Clustering\ActiveActive folder on the companion CD.

When designing an active/active server cluster, you must avoid overtaxing the cluster nodes in a failover situation, but there are also other factors to take into consideration. For example, a physical Exchange 2003 server cannot have more than four storage groups. If you specify that Exchange 2003 Virtual Servers in an active/active cluster have multiple storage groups, ensure that a node does not have to handle more than four storage groups. Otherwise, you might create a situation in which Exchange 2003 cannot mount databases in storage groups that exceed the limit of four, and users will not be able to connect to their mailboxes.

Note   Microsoft supports active/active clusters only with a maximum of two nodes and 1,900 MAPI clients per node because an active/active cluster can quickly create a prohibitive level of potential overload. For example, in an active/active cluster, it is imperative that you monitor on an ongoing basis the rate of virtual memory fragmentation on both nodes using Performance Monitor. You must also ensure that server processes do not consume more than 40% of CPU resources on each node. If you do not monitor the resources on an ongoing basis, you cannot ensure system availability in case of a failover. For more information about active/active cluster restrictions and load metrics, see *Exchange Server 2003 High Availability Guide* (*http://www.microsoft.com/technet/prodtechnol/exchange/2003/library/highavailgde.mspx*).

Active/Passive Cluster Configuration

Active/passive cluster configurations are strongly recommended for Exchange. Because at least one node in the cluster does not run an Exchange Virtual Server, this configuration is called active/passive or N+I Hot-Standby Server. N+I refers to having N active nodes and I passive nodes. The passive nodes take over if active nodes fail.

In a 2+1 server cluster, for example, two nodes run Exchange Virtual Servers and one node is idle. Figure 15-10 illustrates this configuration.

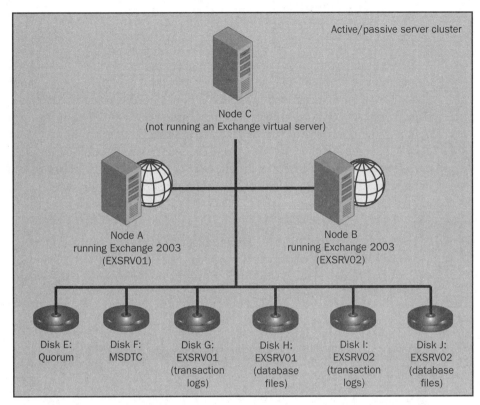

Figure 15-10   Active/passive three-node cluster configuration for Exchange 2003

> **Note**   Active/active cluster configurations are not supported on server clusters with more than two nodes running Exchange Server 2003.

Active/Passive Ratio

The more nodes you add to an active/passive server cluster, the more efficiently you can make use of hardware investments. To give an example, assume that you want to support 21,000 users with seven mailbox servers. If you would deploy server two-node active/passive clusters, you would need 14 production servers. Exactly 50 percent of the hardware is idle during normal operation. On the other hand, if you deploy an eight-node cluster (with seven active nodes and one passive node), you only need eight servers and only 12.5 percent of the hardware is idle.

Note   Clusters with more than two nodes require Windows Server 2003 Enterprise or Datacenter Edition.

With three or more nodes in a server cluster, the N+I configuration requires careful planning. A 7+1 (or 7 active/1 passive) server cluster, for example, might offer best utilization of hardware resources, but might not be able to ensure Exchange availability in a critical situation, such as when multiple nodes fail. If your service level agreements demand an extremely high level of availability, you might want to consider deploying a server cluster with more than one passive node or a geographically dispersed cluster. In any case, you might want to evaluate hardware systems from different manufacturers to meet your SLAs in the most cost efficient way.

On the Resource Kit CD   For an example of how to configure a 5+3 server cluster, see the document Deploying an eight-node (5+3) Exchange 2003 Cluster.doc in the \Companion Material\Chapter 15\Server Clustering\ActivePassive folder on the companion CD.

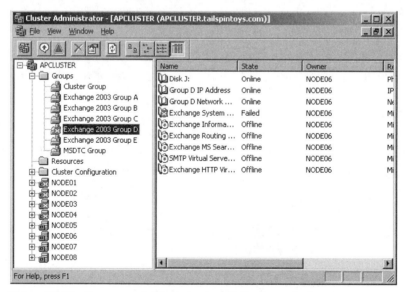

Figure 15-11   Four unavailable nodes in a 5+3 server cluster

When designing an active/passive cluster with more than two nodes, remember that Exchange 2003 prevents multiple Exchange Virtual Servers from running on a single node on clusters with more than two nodes. If you implement a server cluster with only one passive node and two node failures occur, the first Exchange Virtual Server will failover successfully, but the second will remain offline because there is no further node available that could run this Exchange Virtual Server. You can address this issue by adding multiple passive nodes. For example, in a 5+3 cluster, three nodes can fail before Exchange availability is jeopardized.

Figure 15-11 illustrates a situation where four nodes failed in a 5+3 cluster. One Exchange Virtual Server must now remain offline.

The System Attendant failed because NODE06 is already running an Exchange Virtual Server. In this situation, the Cluster service logs the following error in the application event log:

```
Event Type:Error
Event Source:MSExchangeCluster
Event ID:1022
Description:
Exchange System Attendant - (EXSERVER04): The Exchange cluster is operating
in an Active/Passive mode and cannot have more than one System Attendant
resource online on the same node.

For more information, click http://www.microsoft.com/contentredirect.asp.
Data:
```

Enforcing Failover to Passive Nodes

In a two-node active/passive server cluster, failover will always occur from the active to the passive node. In a server cluster with more than two nodes, however, Exchange Server 2003 must prevent failover from an active (failing) to an active (operational) node because the Cluster service would not be able to bring the Exchange Virtual Server online. The failover must occur to an available passive node.

To prevent failover to an active node, Exchange 2003 resource groups have a property called *AntiAffinityClassNames*, which is automatically set to a value of "*Microsoft Exchange Virtual Server*" for any group containing an Exchange Virtual Server. In the event of a failover, the failover manager in Windows 2003 uses the *AntiAffinityClassNames* to keep virtual servers apart by selecting nodes that do not own groups with the same *AntiAffinityClassNames* value. If there are any nodes that are in the possible owners' list for the resources that do not own a resource group with the same *AntiAffinityClassNames* value, those nodes are considered a preferred target for failover. This value can take higher priority over the preferred owners' list.

Tip To examine the *AntiAffinityClassNames* value of virtual servers, you can use the Cluster.exe tool with the following command: **Cluster.exe group "*<name of Exchange Virtual Server>*" /prop**. For example, to examine the *AntiAffinityClassNames* value of an Exchange Virtual Server in a resource group called *Exchange 2003 Group A*, use this command: **Cluster.exe group "Exchange 2003 Group A" /prop**. To list the names of all resource groups configured on a server cluster, use the command: **Cluster.exe group**.

Specifying Preferred Owners

Depending on the desired cluster design, you can also specify preferred owners for each Exchange resource group. This is not strictly a requirement because of the *AntiAffinityClassNames* mechanism, but might be helpful if you are running dissimilar server applications.

On the Resource Kit CD For an example of how to configure preferred owners, see the document Configuring preferred owners in an eight-node (5+3) Exchange 2003 Cluster.doc that you can find in the \Companion Material\Chapter 15\Server Clustering\ActivePassive folder on the companion CD.

The Cluster service performs a failover differently according to the preferred owner configuration, as follows:

■ **Preferred owners not specified** The Cluster service uses the subsequent node in the node list. When the Cluster service gets to the last node in the node list, it moves to the first node in the list again.

The position of a node in the node list is determined by the order in which each node joined the server cluster. You can view the order by examining the registry key \HKEY_LOCAL_MACHINE\Cluster\Nodes. For every cluster node, there is a registry key named sequentially, starting with number one. If you select one of these registry keys, you can determine the node that corresponds to the selected number based on the REG_SZ value called NodeName which lists the name of the cluster node. The first installed node is listed under the registry key 1, followed by the second node listed under the registry key named 2, and so forth.

Figure 15-12 shows the numbered registry keys under \HKEY_LOCAL_MACHINE\ Cluster\Nodes for an eight-node server cluster. The key of NODE08 is selected.

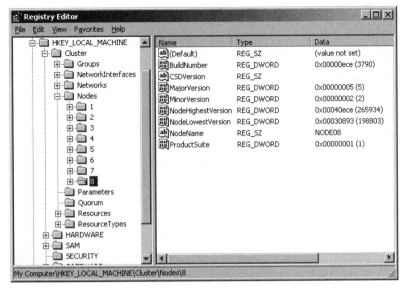

Figure 15-12   The node list of a server cluster

■ **Preferred owners specified**   If you have specified preferred owners for a resource group, the failover manager reorders the node list. Preferred owners are listed first in the list, in ascending order of their node ID, followed by the remaining nodes. Thus, failover occurs to preferred nodes first, unless no preferred owner is available, at which point the failover manager can choose any other node that is available.

Enabling Failback to Preferred Nodes

In addition to configuring preferred owners for your resource groups, you might also want to enable failback, so the Cluster service can move an Exchange Virtual Server back to its original node as soon as the node is available again. You can configure failback to happen immediately or during specified hours, such as non-business hours. For example, if you enable failback for the resource group Exchange 2003 Group D of Figure 15-11, the virtual server will failback to its original node when you restart this node. Otherwise, the virtual server remains unavailable even if all nodes are restarted. When failback is disabled, you must move Exchange 2003 Group D to an available node manually using Cluster Administrator. The document Configuring preferred owners in an eight-node (5+3) Exchange 2003 Cluster.doc, on the companion CD, demonstrates how to configure failback.

Note   It is a good idea to disable failback when maintaining a server cluster so that you can move virtual servers manually to the desired nodes.

Running Exchange 2003 in a Server Cluster

Running Exchange 2003 in a server cluster increases administrative complexity to a certain degree. For example, you must prepare your cluster nodes carefully before installing Exchange Server 2003. As soon as Exchange services and resources are added to the cluster, remember that virtual server resources are managed using Cluster Administrator. It is important *not* to start or stop clustered services using the Services tool or Exchange System Manager. For example, if you stop the SMTP service of an Exchange Virtual Server using the Services tool for any reason, the Cluster service will interpret this as a resource failure, will take the entire resource group offline, and will move it to another node in the cluster to bring it back online.

On the Resource Kit CD For step-by-step instructions on how to install Exchange 2003 in a server cluster, see the documents in the subfolders under \Companion Material\Chapter 15 on the companion CD.

Installing Exchange 2003 in a Server Cluster

To install Exchange Server 2003 in a clustered environment, the Cluster service must be installed and properly configured first. Next, you need to install Exchange Server 2003 on all nodes, one at a time, and then you should update each node to Exchange 2003 Service Pack 1. Each node must be configured exactly the same way. It is important to use the same disks and drive letters on all the nodes in the cluster. During installation, be sure to place the binary files on the local system drive of each node.

When all nodes are prepared, you can use Cluster Administrator to configure Exchange Virtual Servers. Each Exchange Virtual Server requires an IP address, a network name, and at least one disk resource. You can then add the Microsoft Exchange System Attendant resource. All remaining Exchange resources are added automatically. As soon as the configuration is complete, you can take the virtual server online.

Note You cannot install Exchange Server 2003 on a non-clustered server and then integrate this server later as a node into a server cluster. Make sure that the cluster is configured properly before installing Exchange 2003.

It is relatively straightforward to install Exchange Server 2003 on a cluster node. The Setup program detects the Cluster service automatically and installs the cluster-aware version of Exchange 2003 on the cluster node's local hard disk. The binary files are not shared between nodes. Setup installs the Exchange-specific Cluster resource DLLs and sets the Exchange services to start manually. Remember that you must use Cluster Administrator to take Exchange services online or offline.

Configuring Resource Groups and Virtual Servers

As soon as you have installed Exchange Server 2003 on all cluster nodes, you can configure resource groups for your Exchange Virtual Servers. Each virtual server requires an IP address and a network name. Your users will utilize the network name you define for the virtual server to access their mailboxes. You must not change the network name once you have created the Exchange Virtual Server, just as you must not change the Network Basic Input/Output System (NetBIOS) name of a non-clustered server once Exchange Server 2003 is installed.

Each Exchange Virtual Server also requires one or more shared disks where the mailbox and public folder databases are placed. You cannot assign a single physical disk to more than one virtual server. If you find that the number of available physical disks and drive letters limits you in your server cluster and storage group design, you can use Windows Storage Server 2003 Feature Pack to place messaging databases on a Windows Storage Server, as mentioned earlier in this chapter.

Configuring Public Stores

Public folders are repositories that allow users in an Exchange organization to share information. Apart from regular public folders that can be used to implement discussion forums, workgroup applications, or workgroup solutions, there are also system public folders that are invisible in the public folder hierarchy. Exchange stores free/busy information in such a hidden public folder, for example. Another example is the offline address book, which Exchange generates based on the recipient information available in Active Directory. Offline address books are items stored in a hidden public folder and downloaded by Outlook clients to provide address book information when working in offline mode. The new cached Exchange mode especially puts a greater strain on public folders, such as by downloading the offline address book, so providing the ability to spread the load across multiple public folder stores in a cluster allows for a better client experience.

Prior to Exchange 2003 Service Pack 1, clusters could only accommodate one public folder store associated with the MAPI-based public folder hierarchy, no matter how many nodes were present in the cluster. This limitation was due to the fact that a single Exchange store process cannot handle more than one public folder store associated with the same top-level hierarchy, and in two-node Active/Active clusters multiple virtual servers may reside on the same physical node. With Exchange 2003 Service Pack 1, now, you can configure a public folder store associated with the MAPI-based public folder hierarchy in each Exchange Virtual Server in an N+I active/passive cluster that has three or more nodes. Because Exchange 2003 prevents running multiple Exchange Virtual Servers on a single node in active/passive clustering, there is no technical reason not to allow one MAPI public folder store per Exchange Virtual Server rather than one MAPI public folder store per cluster. Because only one Exchange Virtual Server can run on a node at any time, it is not possible to run into the scenario where a single store process has to run multiple public folder stores associated with the same top-level hierarchy. The configuration of public folder stores is covered in Chapter 10, "Configuring Exchange Store Resources."

Configuring Protocol Servers

You can use Exchange System Manager to configure virtual servers for Internet access protocols such as POP3 or IMAP4. Having accomplished this step, you can use Cluster Administrator to install a corresponding resource in the Exchange Virtual Server and bring this resource online. Remember, however, that you should not use Exchange System Manager to start or stop clustered protocol servers.

To install an Internet protocol server, perform the following steps:

1. Start Exchange System Manager and verify that the desired virtual protocol server exists in the Protocols container or create the virtual protocol server.

2. Right-click the resource group of the Exchange Virtual Server, point to New, and then select Resource. Add a new resource that corresponds to the Internet protocol server that you want to create.

3. On the Possible Owners page, make sure that the nodes that can run the Exchange Virtual Server are listed in the Possible Owners list. Click Next.

4. On the Dependencies page, to the Resource Dependencies list, add the Microsoft Exchange System Attendant, and then click Next.

5. On the Virtual Server Instance page, select your virtual protocol server, and click Finish.

6. You can now bring the virtual protocol server online by right-clicking on it and selecting Bring Online.

You can read more about the configuration of Internet access protocols in Chapter 7, "Hosting Exchange Server 2003."

Exchange Clusters in Mixed-Mode Organizations

An Exchange Virtual Server cannot be the first Exchange 2003 server to join an Exchange Server 5.5 site. The first server must be a stand-alone (non-clustered) Exchange 2003 server because Site Replication Service is not supported in a cluster configuration. The first Exchange 2003 server installed in an Exchange 5.5 site runs Site Replication Service to replicate the Exchange 2003 configuration information with the Exchange 5.5 directory. For more information about Site Replication Service, see Chapter 4, "Upgrading to Exchange Server 2003."

Disaster Recovery on Clustered Servers

Exchange 2003 supports a recovery storage group to enable restores of individual mailboxes. However, in an active/active configuration (two-node cluster), you cannot create a recovery storage group on all Exchange Virtual Servers because in a failover situation, this would lead to a single Exchange server having to handle two recovery storage groups, which is not supported in Exchange 2003. This is not an issue in active/passive clusters, which allow you to create recovery storage groups on multiple virtual servers because a failover to a passive node does not lead to a situation where a single physical Exchange server has to run two recovery storage groups.

Note Databases in a recovery storage group are not mounted automatically. You must mount the databases manually, after a cluster failover or a manual restart of the Exchange store.

Remember that you cannot run Setup with the **/DisasterRecovery** option on an Exchange Virtual Server Active Directory object. This setup mode does not work on a clustered server because on a clustered server Setup only copies Exchange files. Only creating a System Attendant resource in a resource group actually creates and configures an Exchange Virtual Server.

You also cannot take a regular non-clustered Exchange computer, give it the same name as the failed Exchange Virtual Server, and then run **/DisasterRecovery** from that server. This does not work because the Active Directory object and other sub-objects that were created for the clustered Exchange Virtual Server have settings that are unique to clustered installations. These values prevent the non-clustered Exchange computer from functioning correctly.

To recover the Exchange clustered server in this situation:

1. Perform a full backup of the server in its current state, including all Exchange 2003 databases. You should also perform a full backup of Active Directory.

2. Use ADSI Edit to manually remove the server object from Active Directory.

Warning If you use the ADSI Edit snap-in or any other LDAP client, and you incorrectly modify the attributes of Active Directory objects, you can cause serious problems. These problems may require you to reinstall Windows 2003, Exchange 2003 Server, or both. Microsoft cannot guarantee that problems that occur if you incorrectly modify Active Directory object attributes can be solved. Modify these attributes at your own risk.

3. Remove the Exchange attributes from all users who had their mailboxes on the Exchange Virtual Server using Exchange Tasks Wizard in Active Directory Users and Computers. The Remove Exchange Attributes option is available in Exchange Tasks Wizard when you click Advanced Features on the View menu in Active Directory Users and Computers.

4. Install another server that has the same name as the deleted Exchange Virtual Server into the domain. Be sure to specify the same Administrative Group name during the setup, and make sure to set up the server in the same Routing Group that the server used to be in.

5. Upgrade the new server to the same service pack level as the original clustered server.

6. Create storage groups and database names on the new server that have the same names and configuration as were on the deleted Exchange Virtual Server.

7. Restore the Exchange databases from backup, and then reconnect the restored mailboxes to the appropriate user accounts.

For more information about restoring Exchange 2003 databases, see Chapter 23, "Restoring Exchange Server 2003."

Best Practices

If you are planning to increase fault tolerance and availability for servers running Exchange Server 2003, consider using clustering technology according to the role of the servers in your messaging environment. Bridgehead servers and Exchange front-end servers that do not host any user data are clustered using a load-balancing solution, such as Windows Network Load Balancing. On the other hand, you can cluster mailbox servers and public folder servers using the Windows Cluster service.

You can achieve Windows Network Load Balancing through a DNS round-robin configuration, Windows Network Load Balancing, or an alternative hardware or software solution. Use of Windows Network Load Balancing is recommended for load-balancing clusters with less than 32 nodes.

Server clusters based on the Windows Cluster service can be configured using active/passive or active/active configurations. All recommendations for Exchange clustering are for active/passive cluster configurations. Active/active is only supported for two-node clusters. In active/active clustering, you must carefully plan your configuration to allow one node to temporarily own the two Exchange Virtual Servers of this cluster. For example, you should limit the number of mailboxes on each Exchange Virtual Server in an active/active cluster to less than 1900.

When installing a server cluster, remember that all nodes should run the same Windows and Exchange 2003 versions and Service Pack. All nodes of the cluster must belong to the same domain, and all Exchange Virtual Servers of a cluster must belong to the same administrative group and routing group. Do not change the computer name of a cluster node or the network name of an Exchange Virtual Server after configuring resources.

You should also not change the drive letters of the system disks on the nodes. Partition and format all disks on the cluster storage device before adding the first node to your cluster. You must format the disk that will be the quorum resource. All partitions on the cluster storage device must be formatted with NTFS. If the number of drive letters required for Exchange databases and transaction log files exceeds the number of drive letters supported by the operating system, consider using volume mount points or Storage Server Feature Pack.

Only use server cluster hardware that is listed in the Windows Catalog. Configure all nodes identically. Do not mix server applications, or at least keep them on separate nodes. Exchange 2003 is best deployed in server clusters dedicated to running Exchange Server 2003. Do not install Exchange 2003 into the default Cluster Group, however. You should also not delete or rename the default Cluster Group or remove any resources from that resource group. Remember that the Windows Cluster service does not protect your messaging databases. You should perform a complete backup on each node in the cluster.

Chapter 16

Standard Monitoring Tools

About This Chapter

Monitoring Exchange Server 2003 is ideally a proactive process in which the administrator anticipates problems by tracking typical points of failure. When monitoring becomes a matter of responding to critical events or responding when too many users complain, then the administrator is constantly one or more steps behind the latest upcoming problem.

To help you better understand monitoring tools, this chapter first discusses Exchange services and dependencies. Exchange Server 2003 is a complex system that relies on internal components and Windows components to function. To understand what monitoring tools to use to track specific resources or components, you must understand the various services and their dependencies.

Next, this chapter focuses on ways to use Exchange System Manager and IIS Manager to check important components such as queues and database availability, as well as Exchange services. To help automate monitoring processes, this chapter also provides suggestions on how to use Windows Management Instrumentation (WMI) in your organization, and finally, it provides overall best practices in monitoring.

This chapter is an overview of available monitoring tools. It is intended for a small to medium-sized Exchange organization that performs monitoring tasks without using an automated tool such as Microsoft Operations Manager.

Understanding Exchange Service Dependencies

To understand how to monitor an Exchange organization, you must first have a general idea of Exchange architecture. Specifically, you should know about the various services that enable Exchange Server to operate. You should also understand how those services interrelate.

The following is a list of key Exchange services, along with how each service contributes to Exchange functionality, and how each service relates to other services. For an overview of how these services interrelate, see Figure 16-1.

- **IIS Admin**   The IIS Admin service is a core service responsible for managing Internet Information Services (IIS)-related components such as HTTP, Network News Transfer Protocol (NNTP), File Transfer Protocol (FTP), and Simple Mail Transfer Protocol (SMTP). Most of the Exchange components depend on this service to function. For example, the IIS Admin service directly manages the SMTP service. Without SMTP transport, mail messages could not be routed and delivered.

- **System Attendant**   The System Attendant service is a vital part of Exchange. The System Attendant service is responsible for handling communication between Active Directory directory services and Exchange 2003. The System Attendant service includes a DSAccess component. DSAccess is responsible for querying domain controllers and global catalog servers about Exchange-related data, such as configuration and schema information.

  Many services depend on the System Attendant. The Exchange Message Transfer Agent (MTA) and the Microsoft Exchange Information Store service rely on the System Attendant service to start and run.

  Other services also use the System Attendant service. The Remote Procedure Call (RPC) service, the Workstation service, the NT LM Security Support Provider service, and the Event Log service use the System Attendant service to enable Exchange Server to run.

- **Information Store**   The Microsoft Exchange Information Store service manages and maintains Exchange databases. Exchange databases contain mailboxes and public folders. To interface with the databases, the Microsoft Exchange Information Store service uses Extensible Storage Engine (ESE). Internet services and other services depend on the Microsoft Exchange Information Store service. For example, the IMAP4, POP3, and IIS Admin services use the databases. MAPI clients can interface directly with the Exchange store. In turn, the Microsoft Exchange Information Store service requires the System Attendant service, the Web Storage System, and Exchange Installable File System (ExIFS) to be running.

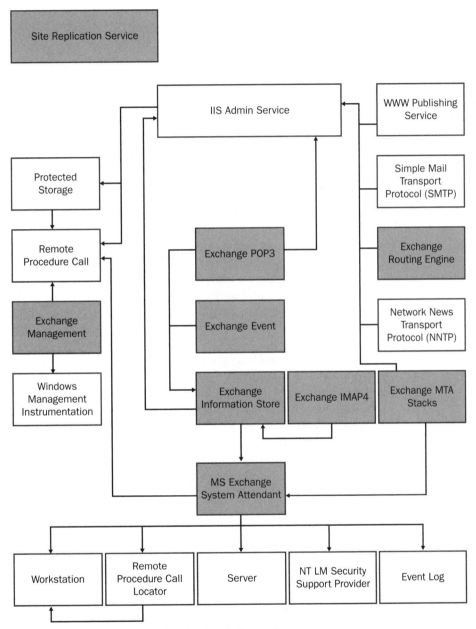

Figure 16-1   Services dependencies for Exchange Server

- **SMTP and MTA**   The transport engine commonly used for Exchange 2000 and later versions is SMTP. SMTP includes a store driver to interface to the Exchange store, a Routing component, a Categorizer to resolve addresses against

Active Directory, and a protocol engine that is used in communicating with other SMTP servers. SMTP depends on a working Exchange environment. The interfaces with the Exchange databases must work, and the IIS components must work for transferring messages. Active Directory and System Attendant must also be functional.

Exchange Message Transfer Agent (MTA) is used primarily in interfacing with systems that do not use SMTP. This includes Exchange 5.5 systems. The MTA service depends on System Attendant and the X.400 service to function.

- **Internet services**   Internet and related services include Outlook Web Access, Outlook Mobile Access, Exchange ActiveSync, NNTP, and so on. These services are integrated with Internet Information Service (IIS) and depend on the IIS Admin service to run.

Monitoring with Exchange System Manager

A helpful resource for both an overview of Exchange health and availability and for daily monitoring is Exchange System Manager. In the Tools folder, and in the Monitoring and Status subfolder, various tools are included. This section discusses how you can use the tools to monitor an Exchange organization.

The monitoring tools available in Exchange System Manager are as follows:

- **Message Tracking Center**   Message Tracking Center is a tool included with Exchange System Manager that tracks the path of a message as it progresses through various queues and servers. You can use Message Tracking Center to check for successful delivery of important messages, diagnose why messages are not being delivered or why messages are stuck in queues, as well as evaluate the general mail flow in an Exchange organization. By specifying criteria such as server, sender or recipient, and date range, you can locate messages and track their flow through Exchange queues.

- **Service and Resource Monitoring**   Exchange System Manager includes a monitoring tool to track services, such as SMTP, and the use of resources, such as a disk or CPU.

- **Link monitoring**   Exchange System Manager includes a tool to monitor link status. Links can be monitored for availability, and an alert can be generated as a notification in case of a down state.

Configuring Monitored Services and Resources

Exchange 2003 includes a method to monitor the condition of server services and resources from a single administrative console within Exchange System Manager. A server or system monitor periodically checks specified services or conditions against a defined threshold value. When the system exceeds the threshold based on that value, the server enters into a warning or critical state. For example, a server monitor might check CPU use. When the CPU use exceeds a defined value of 80 percent for a set amount of time, the system can enter into a warning or critical state and notify the administrator of the problem or launch a process.

The Services snap-in combined with server monitors from within System Manager can help to maintain uptime and server management. If a key service such as System Attendant fails, it can be set to restart under the Recovery tab of the service's Properties window. By default, no action is taken when the system enters a warning or critical state. A notification or script must be configured to run based on created monitors.

A server monitor tracks whether a service is running and then takes action. For example, if you configure a monitor to track the SMTP service and issue a notification when it fails, you will be unaware of the steps leading to the failure. In this case, the monitoring is a notification of actual failure, rather than anticipation and prevention of problems or growing the organization to meet user needs.

Server Monitors

By default, the following services are monitored for each server:

- Microsoft Exchange Information Store
- Microsoft Exchange MTA Stacks
- Microsoft Exchange Routing Engine
- Microsoft Exchange System Attendant
- Simple Mail Transfer Protocol (SMTP)
- World Wide Wed Publishing Service

You can install additional services to monitor, and you can view a list of installed services in the Services tool.

Server monitors are particularly useful for an overview of overall server health. Within a server monitor, the option exists to change the state of a server when a service is not running. For example, the services listed above are all critical to Exchange. Exchange Server cannot run without all of them operating. Therefore, when any or all of the services do not run, the default state is Critical. The other available state is Warning. For other services that may indicate a problem, or for non-critical service stops, the Warning state may be appropriate. These two states help to provide a status on the server and enable an administrator to respond accordingly. A Critical state might warrant immediate attention, for example. Similarly, a Warning state might need to be resolved, but not with the greatest urgency.

Resource Monitors

Resource monitors complement service monitors by providing a more in-depth status of the Exchange organization. Figure 16-2 shows the available resources to monitor. They are as follows:

- **Available virtual memory**   The available virtual memory threshold is a percentage threshold of the virtual memory available to Exchange. You can set both Critical or Warning thresholds. When virtual memory use exceeds a defined threshold, the state changes. You can set the period of time in which virtual memory use exceeds a threshold before the state changes.

- **CPU utilization**   The CPU utilization resource tracks CPU use. You can choose the duration of time before a state is changed and the threshold levels for both critical and warning levels.

- **Free disk space**   In the free disk space resource, you can choose the drive to monitor, as well as the megabytes (MB) free for the Critical state and the Warning state.

- **SMTP queue growth**   When messages travel through the transport system, they reside in queues. Continuous queue growth indicates that messages are not routed properly and are not being delivered. In the SMTP queue growth resource, you can specify the period of time during which a queue may grow. You can specify thresholds for both warning and critical levels.

- **Windows 2000 services**   In addition to adding Windows Server 2003 services to server monitors, you can add Windows 2000 services as a monitored resource.

- **X.400 queue growth**   X.400 queue growth monitoring is similar to SMTP growth monitoring. When an X.400 queue grows for a period of time and does not decrease in size, this might indicate that messages are not being delivered. You can set the thresholds for critical states and warning states according to the use of the Exchange resources in your organization.

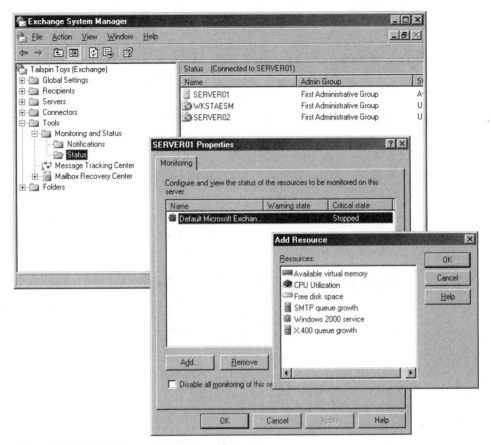

Figure 16-2   Available resources to monitor

Link Monitors

Link monitors are configured through notifications, as explained in the following section. Link monitors are important because links enable message flow and transport. Suppose you have a legacy X.400 messaging system with a connector that was created to enable the MTA to forward and receive e-mail messages. If that connector fails, executing a script or sending an e-mail notification can help to notify you of a problem.

Notification options for link monitoring include the following connectors available to monitor:

- **All connectors**   This option monitors every connector link on the network and issues a notification when any link is down.

- **Any connector in the routing group**   This option limits the connections monitored by restricting them to only the connectors in the local routing group.

- **Custom list of connectors**   You can also create a customized list of connectors to monitor.

Using Notifications

Exchange System Manager includes a tool to help alert you when a resource, link, or server enters into a Critical or Warning state, and to provide some automation in responses. A notification uses defined conditions and executes a script or sends an e-mail message when those defined conditions are met.

A monitoring scenario using notifications requires completion of the following steps:

1. On a server, define resources and services to monitor, as well as the corresponding Warning and Critical states when a service is down, or when a threshold is breached.

2. In the Notifications folder under Monitoring and Status in Exchange System Manager, create a new notification. Figure 16-3 shows notification options and the configuration interface for creating an e-mail notification.

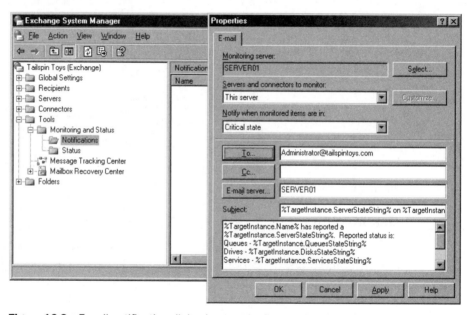

Figure 16-3   E-mail notification dialog box

Notifications can be used to monitor various objects. In the list of options for a notification, you can choose to monitor the following:

- This server
- All servers
- All servers in the routing group to which the chosen server belongs
- All connectors

- Any connector in the routing group to which the server belongs

- A custom list of servers in the Exchange organization

- A custom list of connectors in the Exchange organization

When configuring e-mail notifications, and when monitoring servers in a routing group, it is important to consider how the e-mail message will be delivered. For example, suppose a server is monitored and System Attendant and SMTP services stop. If the server is specified as the mail relay server for notification delivery, then the message will not be delivered. If you use notifications, plan to use an external server for notification. If a server monitors itself and encounters a problem, notification can fail. You should avoid relying only on e-mail notifications to discover problems in a messaging system, because if e-mail routing and transport is not available, then an administrator will not be notified.

Limitations of State Information and System Monitoring

Exchange System Manager monitoring tools provide essential capability to examine a service or resource to determine if it is running as expected. However, Exchange System Manager is not an all-encompassing tool to monitor Exchange servers.

Suppose a problem occurs and e-mail messages are not being delivered. To check the problem with Exchange System Manager, you click on the server or servers impacted, check for services that have stopped, check for other Critical or Warning states, and attempt to determine the cause of the problem. In this case, you might also need to use Windows logs, such as the application log, to try and determine the cause of the error.

When Exchange System Manager refreshes data, especially for service availability and link-state information, this might require some time to update in an organization with many Exchange servers and domain controllers. So the problem might not be visible in Exchange System Manager for many minutes before you realize that you must take action.

To monitor complex environments, or for a more comprehensive monitoring solution, use Exchange Management Pack with Microsoft Operations Manager.

More Info   For more information about Exchange Management Pack, see Chapter 17, "Exchange Server 2003 Management Pack."

Monitoring with Internet Information Services Manager

As shown in Figure 16-1, many Exchange services, including critical services such as SMTP and System Attendant, interface with the IIS Admin service. Complementary services, such as Outlook Web Access, Outlook Mobile Access, and Exchange Active-Sync, rely on Internet Information Services (IIS) to function. You can use Internet Information Services (IIS) Manager to monitor IIS-related services. Additionally, Exchange System Manger complements IIS Manager by providing a means to configure settings, including logging.

Monitoring IIS-Related Services

Depending on your Exchange configuration, you need to run different IIS-related services, such as Outlook Mobile Access, POP3, and IMAP4. For example, Outlook Web Access might be used to access mailboxes through a front-end server. IMAP4 might be enabled as a protocol for mail retrieval. These services must run on the server if Exchange is using them. These services and their related virtual servers also have specific logs.

By default, Exchange installs an HTTP virtual server, named Exchange Virtual Server, the settings of which can be adjusted in Internet Information Services Manager.

You can enable logging for individual Web and File Transfer Protocol (FTP) sites. After you enable logging for a Web or FTP site, all traffic to the site (including virtual directories) is written to the corresponding file for each site. You can also enable logging for specific virtual directories. To enable logging, the user must be a member of the Administrators group on the local computer.

To enable logging on a Web or FTP site:

1. In IIS Manager, expand the local computer, expand the Web or FTP Sites directory, right-click the Web or FTP site for which you want to enable logging, and then click Properties.

2. On the Web Site or FTP Site tab, click the Enable logging check box.

3. In the Active log format list box, click a format. By default, the format is W3C Extended Log File Format.

Note   If you select Open Database Connectivity (ODBC) logging, click Properties and type the ODBC Data Source Name (DSN) and the name of the table within the database into the text boxes. If a user name and password are required to access the database, type the necessary credentials, and click OK.

4. Click Apply, and then click OK.

To enable logging for a specific virtual directory on a site:

1. In IIS Manager, expand the local computer, expand the Web Sites directory, right-click the virtual directory, and click Properties.

2. On the Virtual Directory or Directory tab, select the Log visits check box if it is not selected. By default, the check box is selected.

3. Click Apply, and then click OK.

As shown in Figure 16-4, you can use IIS Manager to configure not only HTTP-related settings, but also Outlook Mobile Access and Exchange ActiveSync logging.

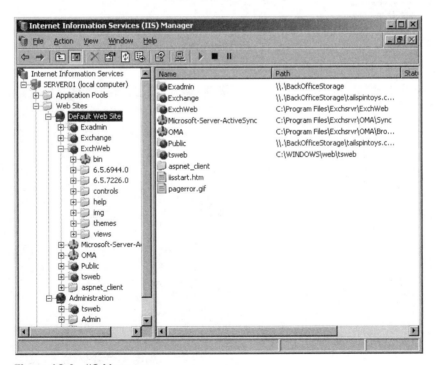

Figure 16-4   IIS Manager

Along with IIS Manager, Exchange System Manager provides an additional interface for configuring logging for virtual servers. Logs can have one of six log formats, as follows:

■ **W3C Extended log file format**   Text-based, customizable format for a single site. This is the default format.

■ **National Center for Supercomputing Applications (NCSA) Common log file format**   Text-based, fixed format for a single site.

■ **IIS log file format**   Text-based, fixed format for a single site.

■ **ODBC logging**   Fixed format for a single site. Data is recorded in an ODBC-compliant database.

■ **Centralized binary logging**   Binary-based, unformatted data that is not customizable. Data is recorded from multiple websites and sent to a single log file. To interpret the data, you need a special parser.

■ **HTTP.sys error logging**   Fixed format for HTTP.sys-generated errors.

Logging for SMTP virtual servers is configured in Exchange System Manager, as shown in Figure 16-5.

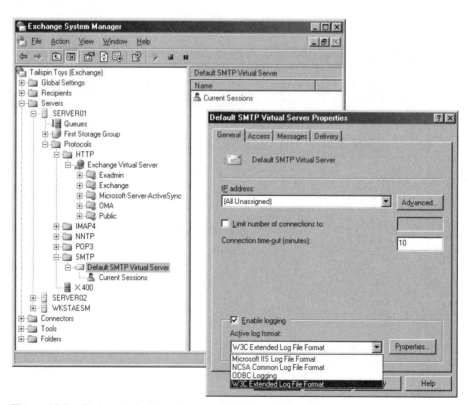

Figure 16-5   Exchange System Manager SMTP logging options

Analyzing Server Logs

After enabling logging, you should institute a system for archiving logs and for analyzing them. You can do this systematically with software or manually. Analyzing IIS logs is an important part of monitoring Exchange.

When you review logs, check for the following:

- Security errors and failures

- SSL-related logs, especially ones that signify SSL failure or misconfiguration

- HTTP failures

- General warnings and errors

You can use logs in combination with other tools to understand problems. For example, suppose you know from a notification that between 1:00 P.M. and 1:17 P.M., mail was not routed to recipients. Checking the SMTP log for this time frame might help to diagnose the problem. For statistics and general analysis, log analyzers are an efficient method of analyzing logs.

Monitoring with Windows Tools

Exchange Server 2003 uses the underlying Windows operating system and hardware to function. Windows Server 2003 comes with a set of tools that can be used for monitoring an Exchange organization, as well as for diagnosing and solving problems.

Windows tools that you can use include the following:

- **Network Monitor**   Network monitor is a tool to monitor traffic on your network. It can monitor packets across defined ports.

- **System Monitor**   The System Monitor tool includes graphs and counters that track performance data for services and components.

- **Event Viewer**   Events written by services are written to Windows logs, such as the application log and the security log. Event Viewer enables you to view these logs.

- **Windows Management Instrumentation (WMI)**   WMI is a flexible management technology that can be used to query components of a computer and obtain system information.

Using Network Monitor

Network monitor is a helpful tool in verifying server connectivity at a low level. To check connectivity between servers, or to check for a particular set of transmitted data on a specified port, you can use Network Monitor. Network Monitor is a network diagnostic tool that monitors local area networks and provides a graphical display of network statistics. Network administrators can use these statistics to perform routine trouble-shooting tasks, such as locating a server that is down, or that is receiving a disproportionate number of work requests.

Using System Monitor

When you monitor Exchange-related services, you should take note not only of the individual services such as ExchangeSA, but also of Exchange components such as queues, which might interface with multiple services. Monitoring the components of System Attendant exclusively to watch for incoming mail queues, or monitoring only the Exchange store without also monitoring disk usage is not as effective as full systems monitoring.

It is important to track the following:

■ Within performance objects related to the Information Store service:

   ■ **Send and receive queue sizes**   The send queue size shows the outbound message queue. If this value grows, this might indicate problems in SMTP transport or routing. Similarly, the receive queue size shows the incoming message queue. If it is too high compared to a normal baseline, this might indicate a transport problem.

   ■ **Messages sent and received per minute**   The rate at which messages are sent, both inbound and outbound, indicates server load. If the number of outbound messages increases rapidly, this might indicate a replicating worm problem. These counters can be used in combination with the message queue sizes. If messages are sent and received to their respective queues, and if the queues grow, then messages are not delivered.

■ Within performance objects related to SMTP transport:

   ■ **Retries**   When an outgoing or incoming message cannot be delivered, the transport mechanism waits for a period of time and then attempts to deliver it again. Monitoring the average retries in comparison with the total messages provides an idea of overall transport health. If there is an excess of messages that are not delivered immediately, a component might be malfunctioning.

   ■ **Queues**   By tracking the queues in Exchange, you can detect problems that lead to performance issues. For example, tracking the Categorizer queue length with the Categorizer Queue Length counter shows messages before they are sent to the local queue for inbound delivery or the queue is marked for resolution through the routing engine. When this number is too high, it might indicate a problem with the overall transport, or with the connections between queues and their mechanisms.

- Within the underlying Network, Disk, Processor, and Memory-related performance objects:

    - **Disk free space and queues**   Necessary disk space varies from server to server within the organization. To help track the available disk space on each computer, you can track usage over time. If disk space use increases significantly within a short period of time, this might signal the need for increased disk space or for the imposition of limits.

    - **Memory and processor**   Exchange heavily uses the paging file. You can monitor the percentage used. If this value increases steadily to use more than 75 percent of the file, or if the typical usage is heavy, you can increase the size of the paging file. Within the processor performance object, you can select the instances of IIS, System Attendant, Exchange store, and Active Directory-related processes.

Alerts in System Monitors

System Monitor includes an interface to set up logs and alerts. You can create a polling interval for a counter and review performance over a period of time with a performance log. You can also create alerts to track performance with counters and send an alert when a specified value threshold is reached.

The notification options in a System Monitor alert are as follows:

- The alert logs an entry in the Event Log.

- A message is sent to a specified administrator.

- A performance data log starts.

- The alert runs an executable or script, with optional command line arguments.

Using Event Viewer

Event Viewer displays detailed information about system events. This information includes the event type, the date and time that the event occurred, the source of the event, the category for the event, the Event ID, the user who was logged on when the event occurred, and the computer on which the event occurred.

Diagnostics Logging Configuration

To determine the amount of information written to the Event Log, set the Logging Level for individual categories on the Diagnostics Logging tab, which you can find in the properties of server objects in Exchange System Manager.

The following logging levels are available for monitoring and troubleshooting:

- **None**   This option disables all logging with the exception of error messages.

- **Minimum**   This option provides simple and crucial information about service operations. This is suitable for most basic monitoring, because it shows warnings and critical errors.

- **Medium**   The medium option includes informational messages, warning messages, and error messages.

- **Maximum**   The maximum option will result in the logging of all information related to the service. It should be used with caution, because it will populate the log with many entries. For example, an e-mail message sent with all services set to Maximum generates over 700 entries. Logs such as the event log have a maximum size. If the logs are filled, added events can overwrite existing information or not be written at all, depending on the configuration.

Using Windows Management Instrumentation (WMI)

Windows Management Instrumentation (WMI) is a framework created to produce a way to monitor an entire enterprise with industry standards. WMI can be used to monitor both hardware and software components as objects. For example, you can use WMI in monitoring the CPU. WMI can be used to monitor the physical state of a CPU, such as the temperature, through existing sensors on the motherboard, or the CPU utilization by a specific service, process, or entire operating system. WMI can also be used to alter system states or provide responses. For example, a script can check for running services, provide alerts when a service stops, and execute diagnostics routines. Through WMI, you can monitor local computers and remote computers in the organization using specific credentials.

A large enhancement made in Exchange Server 2003 is the addition of more WMI classes. These classes can be used to manage and monitor queues, public folders, server and link states, and other components. WMI classes and their capabilities are as follows:

- **ExchangeClusterResource Class**   The *ExchangeClusterResource* WMI class has properties that return information about a Microsoft Exchange cluster resource.

- **ExchangeConnectorState Class**   The *ExchangeConnectorState* WMI class has properties that return information about a Microsoft Exchange connector.

- **ExchangeLink Class**   The *ExchangeLink* WMI class has properties that return information about message-handling links between mail servers. A link can contain zero or more *ExchangeQueue* objects, depending on the current message traffic along the link. In Exchange System Manager, these links are named queues.

- **ExchangeQueue Class**   The *ExchangeQueue* WMI class has properties that return information about the dynamic queues created to transfer individual messages between mail servers. An *ExchangeQueue* is part of an *ExchangeLink*. *ExchangeQueue* objects are not the same as the queues listed in the Exchange System Manager.

- **ExchangeServerState Class**   The *ExchangeServerState* WMI class has properties that return information about the computer running Microsoft Exchange 2000 Server.

- **Exchange_DSAccessDC Class**   The properties of the *Exchange_DSAccessDC* class provide information about Microsoft Active Directory domain controllers that are accessible to the Exchange 2000 Server DSAccess service.

- **Exchange_MessageTrackingEntry Class**   Instances of the *Exchange_MessageTrackingEntry* class provide information about events that have occurred to the message during the time it was under the control of the computer running Microsoft Exchange 2000 Server.

- **Exchange_Mailbox Class**   The *Exchange_Mailbox* WMI class has properties that return information about Microsoft Exchange mailboxes.

- **Exchange_Logon Class**   Instances of *Exchange_Logon* represent the users who are currently logged on to Microsoft Exchange.

- **Exchange_Link Class**   The *Exchange_Link* WMI class has properties that return information about message-handling links between mail servers. A link can contain zero or more *Exchange_Queue* objects, depending on the current message traffic along the link. In the Microsoft Exchange System Manager, these links are named queues.

- **Exchange_FolderTree Class**   Instances of the *Exchange_FolderTree* WMI class provide information about public and private folder trees on Microsoft Exchange servers.

- **Exchange_PublicFolder Class**   The *Exchange_PublicFolder* WMI class provides properties and methods for working with Microsoft Exchange public folders.

- **Exchange_Queue Class**   The *Exchange_Queue* WMI class provides properties and methods for working with Microsoft Exchange queues.

- **Exchange_QueueCacheReloadEvent Class**   Instances of the *Exchange_QueueCacheReloadEvent* class provide information about when the queue's cache was reloaded.

- **Exchange_QueuedMessage Class**   The *Exchange_QueuedMessage* WMI class is the base class for the *Exchange_QueuedX400Message* and *Exchange_QueuedSMTPMessage* classes. The *Exchange_QueuedMessage* class provides information about messages that reside in Microsoft Exchange queues.

- **Exchange_QueuedSMTPMessage Class**   The *Exchange_QueuedSMTPMessage* class provides methods for working with Microsoft Exchange messages currently in an SMTP queue.

- **Exchange_QueuedX400Message Class**   The *Exchange_QueuedX400Message* class provides methods for working with Microsoft Exchange messages currently in an X400 queue.

- **Exchange_QueueSMTPVirtualServer Class**   The *Exchange_QueueSMTPVirtualServer* class returns properties for SMTP queue virtual servers. This class provides two methods in addition to the properties it inherits from the *Exchange_QueueVirtualServer* class.

- **Exchange_QueueVirtualServer Class**   The *Exchange_QueueVirtualServer* class is the base class for the *Exchange_QueueSMTPVirtualServer* and *Exchange_QueueX400VirtualServer* classes.

- **Exchange_QueueX400VirtualServer Class**   The *Exchange_QueueX400VirtualServer* class returns properties for X400 queue virtual servers. This class inherits all its properties from the *Exchange_QueueVirtualServer* class.

- **Exchange_ScheduleInterval Class**   The *Exchange_ScheduleInterval* WMI class provides information about the start and stop time of the public folder replication schedule. Instances of the *Exchange_ScheduleInterval* class are returned as members of an array from the *ReplicationSchedule* Property.

- **Exchange_Server Class**   Instances of the *Exchange_Server* WMI class provide properties and methods for working with Exchange servers.

- **Exchange_SMTPLink Class**   The *Exchange_SMTPLink* class provides methods for controlling an Microsoft Exchange Link. The *Exchange_SMTPLink* class inherits all the properties of the *Exchange_Link* class.

- **Exchange_SMTPQueue Class**   The *Exchange_SMTPQueue* class returns properties for SMTP queues. This class inherits all of its properties from the *Exchange_Queue* class.

- **Exchange_X400Link Class**   The *Exchange_X400Link* class provides methods for controlling a Microsoft Exchange Link. The *Exchange_SMTPLink* class inherits all the properties of the *Exchange_Link* class.

- **Exchange_X400Queue Class**   The *Exchange_X400Queue* class returns properties for X400 queues. This class inherits all of its properties from the *Exchange_Queue* class.

> **Note**   For a definition of WMI providers and resources, especially those specific to Exchange Server 2003, see *http://msdn.microsoft.com/library/ en-us/e2k3/e2k3/_e2k3_WMIIntro.asp.*

The WMI classes in the preceding list are Exchange-specific to help obtain Exchange performance and state data. You can use VBScript or other languages compatible with WMI to create custom indicators. For example, a typically used performance object for System Monitor is MSExchangeIS. Within MSExchangeIS, a particular counter measures how many people are accessing the Exchange store at a particular time.

With VBScript, use the method *GetObject* and assign it to a variable using the *Set* command (set objWMI = GetObject("winmgmts:\root\cimv2")). Then, you can call the counters for the object and write the outcome to a file. The complete script is as follows:

```
'===============================================================
' Name:      Show connected users
' Purpose:   Shows connected users from the MSExchangeIS object
'            in System Monitor.
' Input:     MSExchangeIS object and items in object
' Output:    Writes object items and values into text file (results.txt).
'===============================================================

On Error Resume Next
strComputer = "."
Set objWMIService = GetObject("winmgmts:\\" & strComputer & "\root\cimv2")
Set colItems = objWMIService.ExecQuery("Select * from" _
        & " Win32_PerfRawData_MSExchangeIS_MSExchangeIS")
Set fwrite = CreateObject("Scripting.FileSystemObject")
Set  wr = fwrite.CreateTextFile("results.txt", True)

For Each objItem in colItems
    wr.writeline( "ActiveAnonymousUserCount: " _
                  & objItem.ActiveAnonymousUserCount)
    wr.writeline( "ActiveConnectionCount: " & objItem.ActiveConnectionCount)
    wr.writeline( "ActiveUserCount: " & objItem.ActiveUserCount)
    wr.writeline( "AnonymousUserCount: " & objItem.AnonymousUserCount)
    wr.writeline( "AppointmentInstanceCreationRate: " _
                  & objItem.AppointmentInstanceCreationRate)
    wr.writeline( "AppointmentInstanceDeletionRate: " _
                  & objItem.AppointmentInstanceDeletionRate)
    wr.writeline( "AppointmentInstancesCreated: " _
                  & objItem.AppointmentInstancesCreated)
    wr.writeline( "AppointmentInstancesDeleted: " _
                  & objItem.AppointmentInstancesDeleted)
    wr.writeline( "Caption: " & objItem.Caption)
    wr.writeline( "ConnectionCount: " & objItem.ConnectionCount)
    wr.writeline( "DatabaseSessionHitRate: " & objItem.DatabaseSessionHitRate)
```

```
wr.writeline( "DatabaseSessionHitRate_Base: " _
                  & objItem.DatabaseSessionHitRate_Base)
wr.writeline( "Description: " & objItem.Description)
wr.writeline( "FBPublishCount: " & objItem.FBPublishCount)
wr.writeline( "FBPublishRate: " & objItem.FBPublishRate)
wr.writeline( "Frequency_Object: " & objItem.Frequency_Object)
wr.writeline( "Frequency_PerfTime: " & objItem.Frequency_PerfTime)
wr.writeline( "Frequency_Sys100NS: " & objItem.Frequency_Sys100NS)
wr.writeline( "MaximumAnonymousUsers: " & objItem.MaximumAnonymousUsers)
wr.writeline( "MaximumConnections: " & objItem.MaximumConnections)
wr.writeline( "MaximumUsers: " & objItem.MaximumUsers)
wr.writeline( "Name: " & objItem.Name)
wr.writeline( "PeakPushNotificationsCacheSize: " _
                  & objItem.PeakPushNotificationsCacheSize)
wr.writeline( "PushNotificationsCacheSize: " _
                  & objItem.PushNotificationsCacheSize)
wr.writeline( "PushNotificationsGeneratedPersec: " _
                  & objItem.PushNotificationsGeneratedPersec)
wr.writeline( "PushNotificationsSkippedPersec: " _
                  & objItem.PushNotificationsSkippedPersec)
wr.writeline( "ReadBytesRPCClientsPersec: " _
                  & objItem.ReadBytesRPCClientsPersec)
wr.writeline( "RecurringAppointmentDeletionRate: " _
                  & objItem.RecurringAppointmentDeletionRate)
wr.writeline( "RecurringAppointmentModificationRate: " _
                  & objItem.RecurringAppointmentModificationRate)
wr.writeline( "RecurringAppointmentsCreated: " _
                  & objItem.RecurringAppointmentsCreated)
wr.writeline( "RecurringAppointmentsDeleted: " _
                  & objItem.RecurringAppointmentsDeleted)
wr.writeline( "RecurringAppointmentsModified: " _
                  & objItem.RecurringAppointmentsModified)
wr.writeline( "RecurringApppointmentCreationRate: " _
                  & objItem.RecurringApppointmentCreationRate)
wr.writeline( "RecurringMasterAppointmentsExpanded: " _
                  & objItem.RecurringMasterAppointmentsExpanded)
wr.writeline( "RecurringMasterExpansionRate: " _
                  & objItem.RecurringMasterExpansionRate)
wr.writeline( "RPCOperationsPersec: " & objItem.RPCOperationsPersec)
wr.writeline( "RPCPacketsPersec: " & objItem.RPCPacketsPersec)
wr.writeline( "RPCRequests: " & objItem.RPCRequests)
wr.writeline( "RPCRequestsPeak: " & objItem.RPCRequestsPeak)
wr.writeline( "SingleAppointmentCreationRate: " _
                  & objItem.SingleAppointmentCreationRate)
wr.writeline( "SingleAppointmentDeletionRate: " _
                  & objItem.SingleAppointmentDeletionRate)
wr.writeline( "SingleAppointmentModificationRate: " _
                  & objItem.SingleAppointmentModificationRate)
wr.writeline( "SingleAppointmentsCreated: " _
                  & objItem.SingleAppointmentsCreated)
wr.writeline( "SingleAppointmentsDeleted: " _
                  & objItem.SingleAppointmentsDeleted)
wr.writeline( "SingleAppointmentsModified: " _
                  & objItem.SingleAppointmentsModified)
wr.writeline( "Timestamp_Object: " & objItem.Timestamp_Object)
```

```
        wr.writeline( "Timestamp_PerfTime: " & objItem.Timestamp_PerfTime)
        wr.writeline( "Timestamp_Sys100NS: " & objItem.Timestamp_Sys100NS)
        wr.writeline( "UserCount: " & objItem.UserCount)
        wr.writeline( "WriteBytesRPCClientsPersec: " _
                    & objItem.WriteBytesRPCClientsPersec)
    wr.Close()
Next
```

As shown in the script, this is a convenient method to check a specific component, in this case, connected users.

You can also use the Exchange-specific classes noted above. For example, you can use a script to display all Exchange queues and their properties:

```
'==============================================================
' Name:       Show all queues
' Purpose:    Iterates through all Exchange queues, lists them,
'             and their properties.
' Input:      strComputer is the computer to access
' Output:     Writes name and properties in a text file (output.txt).
'==============================================================

On Error Resume Next
strComputer = "."

const nSpace = "\root\cimv2\applications\exchange"
const Instance = "ExchangeQueue"

Dim strWinMgmts ' Connection string for WMI
Dim objWMIExchange ' Exchange Namespace WMI object
Dim listQueues ' ExchangeQueue collection
Dim objExchangeQueue ' A single ExchangeQueue WMI object

Set fwrite = CreateObject("Scripting.FileSystemObject")
Set wr = fwrite.CreateTextFile("output.txt", True)

' Create the object string, indicating WMI (winmgmts),
' using the current user credentials (impersonationLevel=impersonate),
' on the computer passed to the function in strComputerName, and using the
' CIM namespace for the ExchangeQueue provider.

strWinMgmts = "winmgmts:{impersonationLevel=impersonate}!//" _
            & strComputer & "/" & nSpace

' Get an object using the string you just created.
Set objWMIExchange = GetObject(strWinMgmts)

' The Resources that currently exist appear as a list of ExchangeQueue
' instances in the Exchange namespace.
Set listQueues = objWMIExchange.InstancesOf(Instance)

' Were any ExchangeQueue Instances returned?

If (listQueues.count > 0) Then
    ' Iterate through the list of ExchangeQueue objects.
    For Each objExchangeQueue In listQueues
```

```
wr.writeline( " LinkName = " & "[" _
             & TypeName(objExchangeQueue.LinkName) & "] " _
             & objExchangeQueue.LinkName)
wr.writeline( " ProtocolName = [" _
             & TypeName(objExchangeQueue.ProtocolName) & "] " _
             & objExchangeQueue.ProtocolName)
wr.writeline( " QueueName = [" & TypeName(objExchangeQueue.QueueName) _
             & "] " & objExchangeQueue.QueueName)
wr.writeline( " VirtualServerName = [" _
             & TypeName(objExchangeQueue.VirtualServerName) & "] " _
             & objExchangeQueue.VirtualServerName)
wr.writeline( " GlobalStop = [" & TypeName(objExchangeQueue.GlobalStop) _
             & "] " & objExchangeQueue.GlobalStop)
wr.writeline( " IncreasingTime = [" _
             & TypeName(objExchangeQueue.IncreasingTime) & "] " _
             & objExchangeQueue.IncreasingTime)
wr.writeline( " NumberOfMessages = [" _
             & TypeName(objExchangeQueue.NumberOfMessages) & "] " _
             & objExchangeQueue.NumberOfMessages)
wr.writeline( " SizeOfQueue = [" _
             & TypeName(objExchangeQueue.SizeOfQueue) & "] " _
             & objExchangeQueue.SizeOfQueue)
wr.writeline( " Version = [" & TypeName(objExchangeQueue.Version) _
             & "] " & objExchangeQueue.Version)
wr.writeline( " VirtualMachine = [" _
             & TypeName(objExchangeQueue.VirtualMachine) & "] " _
             & objExchangeQueue.VirtualMachine)
wr.writeline( " MsgEnumFlagsSupported = [" _
             & TypeName(objExchangeQueue.MsgEnumFlagsSupported) _
             & "] 0x" & Hex(objExchangeQueue.MsgEnumFlagsSupported))
wr.writeline( " (Least Significant Bit)")
wr.writeline( " CanEnumFailed = [" _
             & TypeName(objExchangeQueue.CanEnumFailed) & "] " _
             & objExchangeQueue.CanEnumFailed)
wr.writeline( " CanEnumSender = [" _
             & TypeName(objExchangeQueue.CanEnumSender) & "] " _
             & objExchangeQueue.CanEnumSender)
wr.writeline( " CanEnumRecipient = [" _
             & TypeName(objExchangeQueue.CanEnumRecipient) & "] " _
             & objExchangeQueue.CanEnumRecipient)
wr.writeline( " CanEnumLargerThan = [" _
             & TypeName(objExchangeQueue.CanEnumLargerThan) & "] " _
             & objExchangeQueue.CanEnumLargerThan)
wr.writeline( " CanEnumOlderThan = [" _
             & TypeName(objExchangeQueue.CanEnumOlderThan) & "] " _
             & objExchangeQueue.CanEnumOlderThan)
wr.writeline( " CanEnumFrozen = [" _
             & TypeName(objExchangeQueue.CanEnumFrozen) & "] " _
             & objExchangeQueue.CanEnumFrozen)
wr.writeline( " CanEnumNLargestMessages = [" _
             & TypeName(objExchangeQueue.CanEnumNLargestMessages) _
             & "] " & objExchangeQueue.CanEnumNLargestMessages)
wr.writeline( " CanEnumNOldestMessages = [" _
             & TypeName(objExchangeQueue.CanEnumNOldestMessages) _
             & "] " & objExchangeQueue.CanEnumNOldestMessages)
```

```
        wr.writeline( " CanEnumFirstNMessages = [" _
                    & TypeName(objExchangeQueue.CanEnumFirstNMessages) _
                    & "] " & objExchangeQueue.CanEnumFirstNMessages)
        wr.writeline( " CanEnumAll = [" & TypeName(objExchangeQueue.CanEnumAll) _
                    & "] " & objExchangeQueue.CanEnumAll)
        wr.writeline( " CanEnumInvertSense = [" _
                    & TypeName(objExchangeQueue.CanEnumInvertSense) & "] " _
                    & objExchangeQueue.CanEnumInvertSense)
        wr.writeline( " (Most Significant Bit)")
    Next
Else
    wr.writeline( "No ExchangeQueue instances were returned.")
    wr.Close()
End If
```

Configuring Service Recovery Options in Windows 2003

When a service stops unexpectedly or fails to run, a setting in Windows Server 2003 provides an automatic means to respond to the situation. The settings in the Service Recovery tab include three selections: First Failure, Second Failure, and Subsequent Failure. You can choose the proper response according to the type of service failure.

Four options are available when you configure service recovery:

- **Take No Action**   This is the default option. With this option, the service does not attempt to restart, and no action is taken in the event of failure.

- **Restart the Service**   With this option, the service restarts in the event of failure.

- **Run a Program**   There is an option to run a program or script when a service stops. Use this option to specify the program to run.

- **Restart the Computer**   If this service fails to start, the computer will be restarted. If this option is selected, the Restart Computer Options will no longer be grayed out. Additional parameters will be available, such as configuring the length of time to wait until the computer is restarted, as well as the ability to send a broadcast message to computers on the network before the computer restarts.

Figure 16-6 shows the Recovery tab from the services tool.

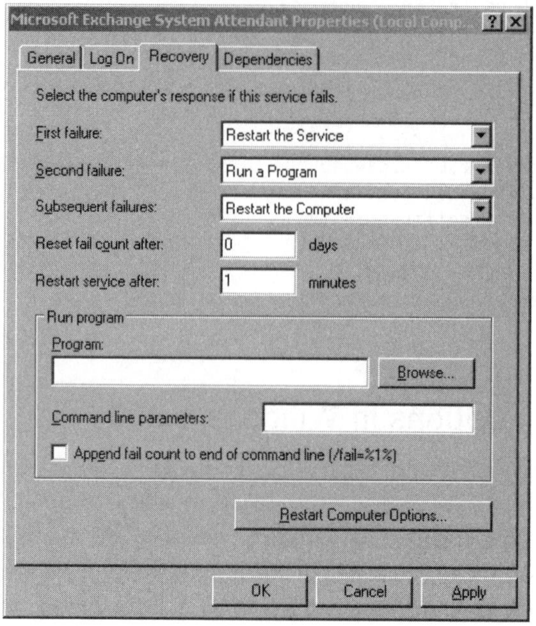

Figure 16-6   Recovery tab

Some services, such as Event Log, Security Accounts Manager, and Net Logon have no recovery options. When they fail, the computer restarts. Other services, such as Windows Time, WMI, and Print Spooler restart automatically for the first and second failures.

When you configure Exchange services in service recovery options, you can use automatic restarting combined with Exchange System Manager notifications to provide a basic level of response to failures, and to receive notifications in the event of failure.

Making a Monitoring Plan

To use the monitoring tools in this chapter, you should formulate a monitoring plan. The plan should include the following:

- **Baseline standards**   To monitor when resources are overloaded, take sample performance and state data for various components. For example, the typical queue length in the organization might be 10. You can monitor performance based on this baseline number. Keep in mind, however, that there might be periods of little use in the organization. If the use varies, you may want to consider having period baseline numbers, some for off-hours typical use, and some for normal use.

- **Service level details** With any monitoring, you should have a goal of server uptime, performance, availability, or some other criteria. Meeting the goal and striving to beat it helps to fine-tune settings for optimal performance. In some cases, there will be public SLAs that you adhere to. Internal targets should reach or exceed these.

- **Data collection specifics** With so many possible tools to use in monitoring the overall organization, as well as specific Exchange components, you should define what tools to use for each monitored component. Additionally, you should consider how to best gather the data, in a centralized, distributed, or hybrid method.

- **Data and report repository plans** After data is collected, it must be stored, and it should be used to generate meaningful reports for trend analysis, capacity planning, and statistics. How often this is done and what is done with the reports depends on the type of data and the organization. For example, a large organization might want general use statistics monthly and server uptime weekly. These might be consolidated as part of a larger, bi-annual review for capacity planning. Consider when to run reporting, because data gathering and consolidation often use up resources, which might result in degraded performance for users.

- **Analysis and capacity planning** With data, reports, and monitored components, evaluating problematic areas, overused resources, and the most frequent sources of failure can help you to proactively use the tools in this chapter and plan for growth.

With an established monitoring plan, detailed and defined tasks, and planning, you can monitor and operate an Exchange organization. With a baseline performance measure, collecting state and performance data, and acting on it, along with planning for the future can help to maintain a healthy system. For another, more automatic solution, you can use Exchange Management Pack with Microsoft Operations Manager (MOM).

More Info For more information about Exchange Management pack, see Chapter 17, "Exchange Server 2003 Management Pack."

Best Practices

Standard monitoring tools are helpful when performing routine Exchange monitoring. They form a solid basis for proactively checking the health of an Exchange organization and correcting problems before the problems result in catastrophic failures.

When using standard monitoring tools, keep the following approaches in mind:

- **Monitor vital Exchange components**   Exchange components rely on each other to run. Moreover, Exchange needs Windows components to function properly. When using standard monitoring tools, keep these interrelationships in mind because problems often involve more than one component.

- **Use Exchange System Manager**   Many common Exchange tasks such as user creation, deletion, message tracking, link state checking, service availability checking, and others can be done with Exchange System Manager. When monitoring an Exchange organization, Exchange System Manager is great preliminary tool to use.

- **Use Windows tools**   In addition to Exchange System Manager, Windows Server includes monitoring tools and logs to help manage your Exchange organization. These are helpful when resolving complex problems or watching for common indicators of errors. For example, using System Monitor to warn of potential queue problems or excessive virtual memory use might prevent problems for occurring.

Chapter 17

Exchange Server 2003 Management Pack

About This Chapter

This chapter discusses the installation and use of Exchange Server 2003 Management Pack for Microsoft Operations Manager 2000 SP1 (MOM 2000 SP1). Specifically, it discusses the following configurations:

- **Centralized** In this configuration, the Exchange organization is contained in a single location, enabling centralized administration.

- **Distributed** The distributed configuration has routing groups and administrative groups in different physical locations.

- **Hybrid** A hybrid configuration includes aspects of both a centralized and a distributed configuration. For example, one resource might be monitored centrally and be located in a specific location, and another resource might be spread across the organization.

In keeping with the practical approach to planning, deploying, administering, and troubleshooting Exchange 2003, this chapter uses test scenarios for each configuration. These scenarios are a guide to better understand the features and technologies of Exchange 2003 Management Pack. You can find worksheets and additional information related to this chapter on the companion CD.

What You Need to Know

To understand this chapter, you should be familiar with Exchange 2003, Windows technologies, and general system administration procedures. In addition, you should have an understanding of Exchange monitoring tools and methods.

> **Note**   For more information on Exchange monitoring tools and methods, see Chapter 16, "Standard Monitoring Tools."

To understand Exchange 2003 Management Pack, you should have at least a working knowledge of Microsoft Operations Manager. Specifically, you should understand Exchange 2003 Management Pack components and how they are integrated with Microsoft Operations Manager. There is a discussion about Exchange Management Pack components later in this chapter.

> **Note**   For more information about Exchange Management Pack and Microsoft Operations Manager, see the Exchange Technical Documentation Library at *http://www.microsoft.com/technet/prodtechnol/exchange/2003/ Library/default.mspx* and the Microsoft Operations Manager product documentation at *http://www.microsoft.com/mom/techinfo/productdoc/ default.mspx.*

Exchange Management Pack Overview

Exchange 2003 Management Pack enables an administrator to simplify and automate monitoring tasks. It is most useful in an environment with multiple servers, domains, and administrators, because it provides a means for tracking and alert of existing and potential problems. Moreover, Exchange Management pack can be deployed in complex topologies to integrate with existing monitoring tools, or as a part of an existing monitoring approach that uses Microsoft Operations Manager.

Exchange 2003 Management Pack is not a standalone application or service that provides a monitoring solution for an Exchange organization. Exchange 2003 Management Pack is an add-in to Microsoft Operations Manager 2000 SP1 (MOM 2000 SP1). Microsoft Operations Manager is the underlying monitoring system that uses Exchange Management Pack to monitor the overall health of servers and their components. To run Exchange Management Pack, you must first install and configure Microsoft Operations Manager.

> **More Info** For more information on Microsoft Operations Manager, see *www.microsoft.com/mom*. For information about installing and configuring Microsoft Operations Manager with Exchange Management Pack, see the installation and configuration sections for each topology in this chapter and worksheets on the companion CD.

Microsoft Operations Manager Components Used by Exchange Management Pack

Because Microsoft Operations Manager is the underlying technology that enables Exchange Management Pack to function, it is important to understand Microsoft Operations Manager components and how Exchange Management Pack uses them. To provide a comprehensive method to monitor an Exchange organization, Exchange Management Pack and MOM 2000 include Rules and Alerts. Rules are a set of specific criteria, such as a percentage of free disk space remaining, or queue size, that are included with Exchange Management Pack. When criteria in the Rules are met, MOM generates an Alert for the administrator according to the severity level of the problem. For alerts that are more critical, a page, or e-mail can be sent the designated administrator. For alerts that are less critical, the notification can be an e-mail to a person or group, a page, or an attempt to resolve the problem by running a script. Rules and Alerts are discussed later in this section.

Although the basic process used by Exchange Management Pack involves checking Rules and generating Alert when Rule conditions and thresholds are met, Exchange Management Pack is integrated with the following Microsoft Operations Manager components:

- **Configuration Group** A configuration group includes the MOM Database, MOM Server, monitored computers, and their associated agents.

- **MOM Server** Also called the data consolidator and agent manager (DCAM), the MOM server is a member server that queries MOM agents and collects data from them.

- **MOM Agents** A MOM Agent is a service that runs on each monitored computer. The agent collects data from components such as System Monitor, logs, WMI, and Event Monitor and transfers the data back to one or more MOM servers.

- **MOM Database** MOM 2000 SP1 requires an operational SQL Server 2000 database. The database can run on the same server as MOM, or on a different server. MOM stores configuration information, event and report data, and Rule data in the SQL database.

Figure 17-1 illustrates MOM 2000 SP1 components.

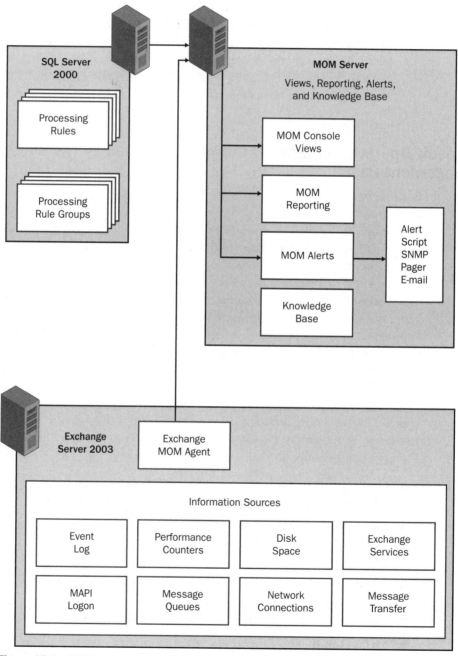

Figure 17-1   MOM and Exchange 2003 Management Pack

Rules

Rules specify how MOM 2000 collects, handles, and responds to information. Rules define the events and threshold conditions for MOM to monitor. When a MOM server receives information from an information source (Windows Management Instrumentation, System Monitor, the event log, and others) that matches a Rule, the responses associated to the Rule are executed. The Exchange 2003 Management Pack includes many predefined Rules, but you can also define your own.

The most common Rule types are:

- **Event Rules**   Event Rules instruct MOM 2000 to generate an alert or run responses when specific events occur. These events can be events that are written to Windows event logs by the Windows components that are being monitored, or they can be events that are generated by MOM. MOM 2000 stores the events and alerts in the MOM database.

- **Timed Event Rules**   Timed Event Rules generate a response or an alert at specified timed intervals. These Rules are used to start monitoring scripts that are included with MOM 2000 for monitoring system components. MOM uses monitoring scripts to generate performance data and also to generate MOM-specific events that are used by other MOM Event Rules.

- **Performance Rules**   Performance Rules collect performance data. You can view this information by using the MOM Monitor snap-in or the MOM Web console. MOM stores performance data in the MOM database.

- **Threshold Rules**   Threshold Rules generate an alert when some measured value, such as CPU usage, exceeds a defined threshold. Threshold Rules can define multiple threshold values, with a separate alert severity level for each of the values.

Alerts

An alert occurs when a MOM agent detects an event or measured value that matches the event or threshold that is defined in a Rule. An alert notifies the administrator about the event that triggered the alert. The alert can trigger the sending of an e-mail message or the running of a script.

Defining Alert Severity Levels

Each Rule in MOM 2000 that generates an alert assigns an alert level that indicates the severity of the event that triggers the alert. You can use the alert severity level to determine the importance of the indicated condition. By default, the more severe alerts are sent to page administrators immediately. Alert severity levels for MOM are described in Table 17-1.

Table 17-1   MOM Alert Severity Levels

Severity level	General description	Paged by default
Service Unavailable	Indicates that a service is no longer running or responding to client requests.	Yes
Security Breach	Indicates that a breach in security is likely to have occurred.	Yes
Critical Error	Indicates errors and events that require immediate attention.	Yes
Error	Indicates an error that requires attention soon.	Yes
Warning	Indicates that an event has occurred that is suspect and is likely to cause an error or critical error soon. Paging is not required, and all related services are currently reachable. But the warning should be investigated and the cause of it determined.	No
Information	Provides information about an expected or required event.	No
Success	Provides notification that a particular operation succeeded.	No

Specific Exchange Management Pack Components

Some Exchange Management Pack components are a part of MOM. Specific Exchange Rules monitor the Exchange organization and the deployed MOM Agents alert to possible downtime. These components were addressed in the preceding section. However, Exchange Management Pack also includes Rule Groups, Reports, and an extensive Knowledge Base to help resolve problems. This section provides an overview on each of these Exchange Management Pack components.

Rule Groups

Exchange 2003 Management Pack includes Rule Groups to organize the Rules as follows:

- **Availability**   The Rules in this Rule Group monitor front-end servers, as well as Exchange services and components, such as MAPI, mailboxes, database availability, and mail flow.

- **Exchange events**   The Rules in this Rule Group check Exchange-related events that are written to the event log in Windows Server 2003 logs and monitor for the following:

  - **Exchange store**   The Exchange store hosts the mailboxes and public folders.

- **System attendant**   The system attendant includes important modules, such as DSAccess, without which the Exchange server system cannot function.

- **Simple Mail Transfer Protocol (SMTP), Message Transfer Agent (MTA), and message routing**   These components are elements of the Exchange 2003 transport engine and must be running on every Exchange 2003 server to guarantee a correctly functioning system.

- **Outlook Web Access, Outlook Mobile Access, and Exchange ActiveSync**   Internet and mobile users can use these components to access mailbox resources through HTTP and HTTP-related protocols.

- **IMAP4 and POP3**   These components are important if Internet users access their mailboxes by using Microsoft Outlook Express or another IMAP4 or POP3 conforming client.

- **DSAccess and Active Directory Connector**   DSAccess manages communication between Exchange 2003 and Active Directory. Active Directory Connector (ADC), on the other hand, is an important tool when integrating an Exchange 5.5 organization with Active Directory.

- **Free/busy information**   Microsoft Outlook users can look up other users' free/busy information to determine availability when scheduling meeting requests. Free/busy information is stored in a hidden system folder on the Exchange server.

- **Health**   Server health includes configuration, security, up-to-date patches and service packs, and operations related to general server functionality. The Rules in this Rule Group monitor server health.

- **Performance Thresholds**   The Performance Thresholds Rule Group uses System Monitor counters mostly to monitor Exchange and server components. For example, disk space usage, mail queue growth, and SMTP performance are monitored. This Rule Group includes thresholds for Rules. An alert is generated when a threshold is reached.

Additionally, Exchange 2003 Management Pack includes Rules to collect data from performance counters and the event log and use it for reports.

Views and Reports

Exchange 2003 Management Pack includes a variety of reports to help you quickly identify Exchange issues. With these reports, you can analyze and graph performance data to understand usage trends, perform accurate load balancing, and manage system capacity.

Exchange reports cover the following:

■ **Exchange 2000 and 2003 Health Monitoring and Operations Reports**
You can use the monitoring and operations reports to analyze database sizes, disk usage, mailboxes, server availability, and the configuration of Exchange servers. For example, you can list database sizes for Exchange servers, where database size (in megabytes) is presented for each server, storage group, and database. The reports in this category are as follows:

   ■ **Exchange Disk Usage**   The Disk Usage report provides data about servers running Exchange based on disk performance counters, presenting daily averages for each counter.

   ■ **Exchange Server Availability**   The report on server availability provides the percentage of server availability for Exchange servers during a specified time period and also lists the reasons for unavailability.

   ■ **Exchange Server Configuration**   The Server Configuration report provides configuration information including computer and operating systems configuration and local disks information.

   ■ **Exchange 2003 Outlook Client Monitoring**   The Exchange 2003 Outlook Client Monitoring report gives you the results of analysis data collected by Exchange 2003 servers monitoring Outlook clients for the end-user's experience in terms of response times and errors.

   ■ **Exchange Mailboxes**   This report shows the distribution of mailboxes across storage groups and databases for Exchange servers.

   ■ **Exchange Database Sizes**   This report shows the total database size on each server, as well as the individual components of the database. For example, if a database contains both a Mailbox store, and a Public Folder store, this report shows the size of each.

■ **Exchange 2000 and 2003 Protocol Usage Reports**   The protocol usage reports obtain data about usage and activity levels for the various mail protocols used by Exchange, such as POP3, IMAP4, and SMTP. You can also obtain usage and activity level reports for Exchange components such as the Information Store, Mailbox Store, Public Folder Store, MTA, and Outlook Web Access. These reports use key performance counters for operations conducted within a specific time period.

■ **Exchange 2000 and 2003 Traffic Analysis Reports**   The traffic analysis reports summarize Exchange mail traffic patterns by message count and size for both Recipient and Sender domains. For example, the Mail Delivered: Top 100 Sender Domains by Message Size report provides a list of the top 100 sender domains sorted by message size during a specific time period, as reported in the Exchange message tracking logs.

- **Exchange Capacity Planning Reports**   By analyzing your daily client logons and messages sent and received, as well as work queues, these capacity planning reports show the Exchange server resource usage and help you plan for current and future capacity needs.

- **Exchange Mailbox and Folder Sizes Reports**   You can use these reports to monitor the size of Exchange mailboxes and folders and to determine your highest growth areas. The reports in this category include top 100 mailboxes by size and message count, and top 100 public folders, by size and message count.

- **Exchange Performance Analysis Reports**   The Queue Sizes report summarizes Exchange performance counters and helps you analyze queue performance.

- **Exchange 5.5 Reports**   In a mixed Exchange organization, you can use Exchange 5.5-specific reports to obtain data about operations that include servers running Exchange Server 5.5, such as reports about average time for mail delivery, as well as pending replication synchronizations and remaining replication updates. There are also several Exchange 5.5 traffic analysis reports available to help analyze SMTP queue length and delivery times to internal mailboxes and external deliveries.

Knowledge Base

The Exchange 2003 Management Pack contains a knowledge base with technical information that can help in troubleshooting. The knowledge base information is available on the Knowledge Base tab when displaying alert details in the MOM console. This information indicates the meaning and importance of the alerts that are generated by a Rule. You can also obtain detailed suggestions about resolutions and links to up-to-date information on the Web. The knowledge base contains predefined information from Microsoft, to which you can add information that is specific to your organization.

Exchange Management Pack in a Centralized Environment

A centralized environment enables Exchange monitoring tasks to be organized into one location, from which an administrator can track both individual servers and the overall organizational health. The single location of a centralized environment contains physical servers, routing groups, and administrative groups. Many small to medium-sized businesses are structured with a central topology. This approach reduces administrative overhead, enables quick on-site troubleshooting, and simplifies monitoring tasks.

An example of a simple, centralized environment is a small office for 100 users located in one building with mailboxes residing on dedicated mail servers. An example of a more complex centralized environment is one in which both remote users, such as sales people, and local users access their mail boxes through Microsoft Outlook Web Access and Microsoft Outlook, respectively. Front-end servers are used for the incoming Outlook Web Access requests, and local users can connect through MAPI.

Monitoring a Centralized Environment

For centralized environments with up to 2000 servers, the single configuration group topology provides a fitting, centralized administrative model. This MOM topology can monitor one or more domains and contains one or more MOM servers. For enterprises monitoring fewer than 50 computers, a single configuration group topology can be used with a single computer that is running all MOM components. For larger organizations, MOM components can be placed on different computers, as shown in Figure 17-2. In the test scenario for the centralized environment, a SQL database is contained on one server. Two MOM servers monitor servers and workstations.

Installation Planning for a Centralized Environment

Before you install Exchange Management Pack or other management packs, MOM, and SQL Server 2000 SP3 or later, and configure Exchange Management Pack to monitor your centralized environment, you must perform an analysis of your current Exchange organization, evaluate the configuration, and decide on a course of action. Planning, dependencies, and considerations are discussed in this section.

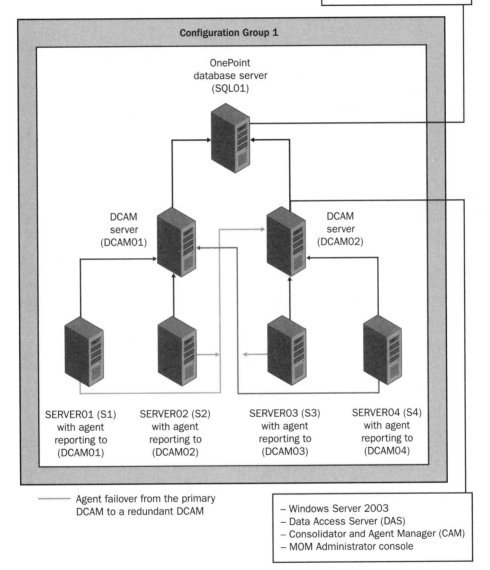

- Windows Server 2003
- SQL Server 2000
- MOM database
- Management Pack Modules

Configuration Group 1

OnePoint
database server
(SQL01)

DCAM
server
(DCAM01)

DCAM
server
(DCAM02)

SERVER01 (S1)
with agent
reporting to
(DCAM01)

SERVER02 (S2)
with agent
reporting to
(DCAM02)

SERVER03 (S3)
with agent
reporting to
(DCAM03)

SERVER04 (S4)
with agent
reporting to
(DCAM04)

Agent failover from the primary
DCAM to a redundant DCAM

- Windows Server 2003
- Data Access Server (DAS)
- Consolidator and Agent Manager (CAM)
- MOM Administrator console

Figure 17-2   MOM single configuration group

Considering Computer Location and Role

You should make a list of existing computers, both servers and workstations, along
with details about their function and role. For ease, it is helpful to represent the com-

puters in a topology diagram. For example, in a test environment, your Exchange organization might consist of one primary domain controller, one secondary domain controller, three Exchange 2003 SP1 servers, and five workstations. You can use this information when deploying Exchange Management Pack by creating planned configuration groups and assigning computers to specific MOM servers. A sample list of computers, their roles, and other information is detailed in Table 17-2.

Table 17-2   Sample Computer Inventory for a Centralized Monitoring Scenario

Name	Domain	IP address	Operating system	Role	Location
SERVERDC01	TAILSPINTOYS.COM	192.168.202.160	Windows Server 2003	Primary domain controller, global catalog server	NOC
SERVERDC02	TAILSPINTOYS.COM	192.168.202.161	Windows Server 2003	Secondary domain controller	NOC
SERVER01	TAILSPINTOYS.COM	192.168.202.112	Windows Server 2003	Exchange mailbox server	NOC
SERVER02	TAILSPINTOYS.COM	192.168.202.113	Windows Server 2003	Exchange front-end server	NOC
SERVER03	TAILSPINTOYS.COM	192.168.202.114	Windows Server 2003	Exchange public folder server	NOC
WKSTA01	TAILSPINTOYS.COM	192.168.202.150	Windows XP SP1	Outlook workstation	Room 202
WKSTA02	TAILSPINTOYS.COM	192.168.202.151	Windows XP SP1	Outlook workstation	Room 203
WKSTA03	TAILSPINTOYS.COM	192.168.202.152	Windows XP SP1	Outlook workstation	Room 204
WKSTA04	TAILSPINTOYS.COM	192.168.202.153	Windows XP SP1	Outlook workstation	Room 100
WKSTA05	TAILSPINTOYS.COM	192.168.202.154	Windows XP SP1	Outlook workstation	Room 101

Computers in an Exchange organization can have many roles, including the following:

- **Active Directory**   There are two main Active Directory roles that an Exchange organization uses:

  - **Domain controller**   Domain controllers help in providing DNS-related services for Exchange. When noting roles, check for primary and secondary domain controllers.

  - **Global catalog servers**   Global catalog servers contain universal group membership information, which is used to grant or deny access to resources.

- **Exchange**   A server running Exchange can also have many roles, such as:

  - Mailbox server

  - Public folder server

  - Free/busy server

  - Offline address list server

  - Front-end server or bridgehead

Considering Hardware, Software, and Bandwidth

To effectively plan for installation of Exchange 2003 Management Pack, you must evaluate existing hardware and software configurations against the requirements for MOM and Exchange Management Pack found on the MOM website, and you must ensure that the MOM components can communicate with each other. Figure 17-1 shows a diagram of the single configuration group topology used in a centralized environment. The MOM servers must communicate with the SQL database running the OnePoint Service and with the agents installed on monitored servers and workstations. It is especially important that you have steady, reliable links between MOM servers and the database server, so that state data is current and so that the administrator is alerted to potential problems and can respond proactively.

> **Note**   To decide on sizing options, you can also use the MOM Performance and Sizing Kit. You can read more about the Performance and Sizing Kit at *http://www.microsoft.com/mom/techinfo/administration/perfsize.asp*.

Dependencies

Each monitored component depends on a working, operational MOM deployment with Exchange 2003 Management Pack installed. Before you can install an agent on a monitored server or workstation, the following prerequisites must be met:

- **SQL server**   The SQL database must be installed and operational. It must interface with MOM and store data such as reports, alerts, configuration data, and so on. You must run Service Pack 3 or later.

- **MOM server**   The MOM server must be installed and configured to import and run Exchange Management Pack.

> **Note**   You can find more deployment instructions, including installation steps for MOM at *http://www.microsoft.com/resources/documentation/ mom/2000sp1/all/deployguide/en-us/default.mspx.*

- **Reporting**   Although reporting is an optional component, if you want to have reporting capabilities, you must install the reporting component during MOM setup. Additionally, you must install reporting prerequisites, such as IIS and Access.

Deploying Exchange Management Pack in a Centralized Environment

After taking an inventory of your existing configuration, you can deploy Exchange Management Pack in your centralized environment. Ensure that all prerequisites are met. For best results, follow the deployments checklists included on the companion CD.

Installing Microsoft Operations Manager

In a single configuration group topology that corresponds to a centralized environment, you must install MOM and related components, as shown in Figure 17-1. One server should run the SQL database, and one or more servers should be MOM servers. This provides redundancy. The test environment is used to demonstrate how to install MOM and prepare it for Exchange Management Pack.

Installing the SQL database

The first step in deploying MOM in preparation for Exchange Management Pack is to install SQL 2000 SP3 on a member server. After you install SQL, run MOM setup, choose the Custom option, and select to install only the database component of the MOM installation. An option available is the database size. Choose a database size that allows for scalability in your environment.

> **More Info**   For a guide to choosing the best size, see the MOM deployment guide, at *http://www.microsoft.com/resources/documentation/mom/2000sp1/all/deployguide/en-us/default.mspx*.

Installing the MOM servers

A primary MOM server, and a backup, failover MOM server are used as the data consolidators and agent managers (DCAMs) in the centralized environment. You should install the primary MOM server first and the secondary server next. The setup program has an option to verify that prerequisites, such as IIS, Access for reporting, SQL, MSDTC log file size, and so on are met. The setup program also provides instructions for how to install and configure the prerequisites.

> **More Info**   You can find more detailed setup instructions on the companion CD.

Upgrading from Exchange 2000 Management Pack

If you have an existing monitoring solution that uses MOM 2000 SP1 with Exchange 2000 Management Pack, you should be aware of several additional steps that you must perform before you install Exchange 2003 Management Pack.

To upgrade from Exchange 2000 Management Pack:

1. Open a Command Prompt window, and locate the command-line ExchangeMP-Config.exe tool.

2. To export a configuration, type **ExchangeMPconfig /s *target-server* /e current-configuration.xml**, where ***target-server*** is the computer from which you want to export the configuration.

3. To import the configuration to the local computer, type **ExchangeMPconfig /i current-configuration.xml**.

> **Note**   To target a specific group, server, or set of servers matched by name, or all servers in the organization, you can use filters in the export step.

Installing the Exchange 2003 Management Pack Report Update

The Exchange Management Pack Report Update tool replaces the Eearept.mdb file that is installed with MOM (Figure 17-3). The update tool contains reports that you can use with Microsoft Office Access. Completing this procedure also updates and adds new SQL Server views and stored procedures in the MOM database.

The update must be installed on:

- The server that contains SQL Server with the Microsoft Operations Manager (OnePoint) database, if it is separate from the Consolidator.

- Each server that contains the Microsoft Operations Manager Consolidator and that has Microsoft Operations Manager Reporting installed.

- Each client computer that has Microsoft Operations Manager Reporting installed.

To install the Exchange 2003 Management Pack Report Update, from the Exchange 2003 Management Pack download, run the Exchange Management Pack Report Update executable to update the reports with the Exchange 2003 versions.

Note   You can download the Exchange 2003 Management Pack from *http:/ /go.microsoft.com/fwlink/?LinkId=25338*. After you install reporting, ensure that you obtain any fixes available to reports, such as the Top CPU Utilization Report, at *http://support.microsoft.com/?linkid=3052&kbid=821014*.

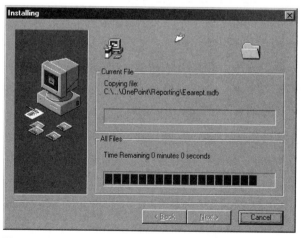

Figure 17-3   Installing screen of the Exchange 2003 Management Pack Report Update

Importing Exchange 2003 Management Pack

To use Exchange 2003 Management Pack, you must first import it into MOM. Exchange Management Pack is not included with MOM. You must download it separately. You can download Exchange Management Pack at *http://go.microsoft.com/ fwlink/?LinkId=25338.*

If you have an existing Exchange 2003 Management Pack with customized settings and configurations, special procedures might apply. For example, if null characters are included in the knowledge base, there are errors during the import process.

> **Note**   For more information about importing an existing Exchange 2003 Management Pack with customized settings, see Microsoft Knowledge Base Article 303841, "Problems Importing MOM Management Packs," at *http://support.microsoft.com/default.aspx?scid=kb;en-us;303841.*

If a Rule has a response with references to more than one script, the import also fails.

> **More Info**   For more information on import failure because a rule has a response with references to more than one script, see Microsoft Knowledge Base Article 305453, "Importing Management Pack Causes MOM to Use All Available Memory and May Produce an Access Violation," at *http://support.microsoft.com/default.aspx?scid=kb;en-us;305453&sd=tech.*

You can import the Exchange 2003 Management Pack from the MOM Administrator Console, as shown in Figure 17-4.

To import the Exchange 2003 Management Pack:

1. Copy Exchange Management Pack.akm from the Exchange 2003 Management Pack download to the Microsoft Operations Manager (MOM) consolidator server.

2. Click Start, point to Programs, point to Microsoft Operations Manager, and then click MOM Administrator Console.

3. In the MOM Administrator Console, go to the Console Root, expand Microsoft Operations Manager, and then click Rules.

4. Right–click Processing Rule Groups, and then select Import Management Pack. The Import Options window opens.

5. Locate the management pack and select Exchange Management Pack.akm.

6. Click Next and then click Finish.

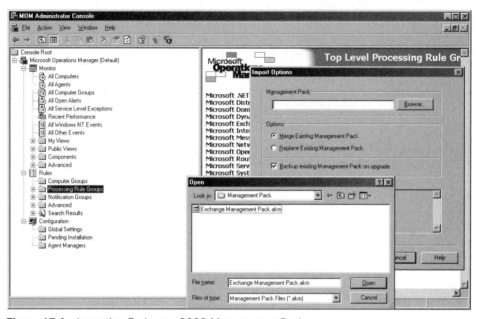

Figure 17-4   Importing Exchange 2003 Management Pack

Installing Configuration Wizard

The Exchange 2003 Management Pack download includes the setup file for Configuration Wizard, ExchangeMPConfig.msi. Use that file to install Configuration Wizard. The computer used for Configuration Wizard installation must have both Exchange System Manager and .NET Framework 1.1 installed.

Installing Exchange Management Pack for a Centralized Environment

The way Exchange Management Pack is deployed in a centralized environment depends on which MOM servers monitor Exchange servers. In the single configuration group scenario shown in Figure 17-1, two MOM servers manage the agents deployed on monitored computers. However, those agents are not automatically deployed. They are deployed after managed computers are added to the MOM server. The MOM servers do not perform software or hardware load balancing. To achieve a desired degree of balancing, you must manually configure which computers will be monitored by which MOM servers. For example, all back-end mailbox servers can be monitored by the first server, and all front-end servers can be monitored by another server. Alternatively, all Exchange-related servers can be monitored by one or more servers, and other components, such as IIS, Active Directory, and SQL can be monitored by another server. Although load balancing is not automatic, MOM does provide failover in case a MOM server fails. Each computer is associated with a primary MOM server. If that server fails, the agent reports to another MOM server in the configuration group, based on the order in which the MOM server was added.

> **Note** Each monitored computer must have only one primary MOM server. No two MOM servers should have Managed Computer Rules for the same computer. A computer that is identified in more than one set of Managed Computer Rules will change its primary MOM server each time there is a managed computer scan.

To ensure that data is collected correctly, you should increase the size of the event logs collected by Windows Server 2003 to at least 20 MB. If logs are full, event logging stops, and MOM does not collect new events. You can also configure the event logs to be overwritten when they become full.

Adding Computers to Monitor to a MOM Server

To add computers to a MOM server, perform the following steps:

1. Define Managed Computer Rules by entering a Rule for each agent, or using wildcards to match a group of computers to monitor.

2. Run an Agent Manager scan on the MOM server to search for computers that match the specified Rules.

3. Check pending installations and accept the desired ones. The computers that match the Rule are listed in the Pending Installation folder under Configuration in the left pane of the MOM Administrator console. To accept agent installation, right-click Pending Installation, and then click Approve All Pending Actions.

4. Process the approved actions by right-clicking Pending Installation and then clicking Process All Approved Actions.

5. Review agent installation to ensure that pending actions have been processed. Additionally, look for error events related to the Agent Manager under Public Views. Additionally, verify that all agents belong to the correct computer groups.

Configuring Exchange Management Pack

Configuration Wizard included with Exchange Management Pack is the primary tool for configuring Exchange Management Pack. However, Exchange Management Pack also includes a command-line tool for expanded functionality. The command-line tool has the capability to import and export configuration files. For example, in a scenario in which you are upgrading from Exchange 2000 Management Pack and want to keep your existing monitoring configuration intact, you must export the existing configuration file using the command-line tool.

Running Configuration Wizard

You must meet the following requirements before running the wizard:

- The user running the tool must have at least Exchange Full Administrator rights for the administrative group or organization that they want to configure, in addition to local administrative rights to each Exchange server, because writing to the registry is required.

- Each server that you want to configure must have Remote Registry Service running.

  The wizard guides you through two options:

- **Default**   This option enables message tracking, service monitoring, mailbox availability, and mail flow options.

- **Custom**   This option enables you to choose which default options to enable or disable.

  Pick the option that is appropriate for what you want to configure. In many cases, the Default option is appropriate.

  On an existing configuration, you must export the existing configuration file and use it as a basis for configuring the new installation. The procedure is the same as that for upgrading from Exchange 2000 Management Pack. For more information, see the section "Upgrading from Exchange 2000 Management Pack" earlier in this chapter.

Configuring for Monitoring Outlook Web Access, Outlook Mobile Access, and Exchange ActiveSync

Additional configuration steps must be performed to enable availability monitoring for Outlook Web Access, Outlook Mobile Access, and Exchange ActiveSync. With the Default option in Configuration Wizard, availability monitoring is automatically enabled. With the Custom option, you can select to enable monitoring of front-end servers. This also enables availability monitoring.

To monitor availability, a synthetic logon process is used, which requires a user account with a mailbox. For the Outlook Web Access logon, Configuration Wizard automatically picks one of the existing back-end test mailboxes created by the configuration wizard that is used by the MAPI logon scripts in Exchange Management Pack. This mailbox name is automatically stored in the HKLM\Software\Exchange MOM\FEMonitoring*front-end servername\BEAccount* registry value on the front-end server.

> **Note**   When configuring a front-end server for availability monitoring, you must select the same Mailbox Access account that is used by the back-end server.

For Outlook Mobile Access and Exchange ActiveSync monitoring, the mailbox of the Mailbox Access account is used for the synthetic logon. Ensure that this mailbox resides on an Exchange 2003 server, because Outlook Mobile Access does not support logging onto an Exchange 2000 mailbox.

Exchange 2003 Management Pack automatically determines the URL used to monitor the front-end services by using a combination of localhost/network card IP and the virtual server and virtual directory information in the Internet Information Services (IIS) metabase. This URL is the local monitoring URL, because the logon request is submitted to the local front-end server, where the logon request is generated.

You also can supply a custom URL to monitor the public URL that is used by your Web and mobile clients. To use a custom URL, you must configure registry entries on each server for which you want the monitoring enabled.

Configure custom URLs as follows:

1. **For Outlook Web Access**   Open Registry Editor and browse to the HKLM\Software\Exchange MOM\FEMonitoring*front-end servername*\ key and create a registry value (type string) named CustomUrls. Enter the custom URL value as a comma-delimited list in this value. For example: ***https:// www.tailspintoys.com/exchange*** or, for multiple URLs, ***https://www.tail- spintoys.com/exchange, https://www.tailspintoys.com/mail***.

> **Note**   Do not append the mailbox name in the URL, for example, *https:// www.tailspintoys.com/exchange/TedBremer*, or the synthetic logon will fail.

2. **For Outlook Mobile Access**   Open Registry Editor and browse to the HKLM\Software\Exchange MOM\FEMonitoring*front-end servername*\ key and create a registry value (type string) named CustomOmaUrls. Enter the custom URL value as a comma-delimited list in this registry value. For example, for a single URL, ***https://www.tailspintoys.com/OMA*** or, for multiple URLs, ***https://www.tailspintoys.com/OMA, https://www.subdomain.tailspin- toys.com/OMA***.

3. **For Exchange ActiveSync**   Open Registry Editor and browse to the HKLM\Software\Exchange MOM\FEMonitoring*front-end servername*\ key

and create a registry value (type string) named CustomEasUrls. Enter the custom URL value in this registry value. For example, ***https://www.tailspintoys.com/ ActiveSync***.

Editing the Configuration File

The configuration for Exchange Management Pack is contained in an XML configuration file. You can edit this file manually to control options, but we recommend that you run Configuration Wizard to have a well-formed, valid XML configuration file. In most cases, the Configuration Wizard creates the configuration file for you. However, if you do not want to use the Configuration Wizard, or if you need to create a configuration file manually, the option exists with the command-line tool.

Table 17-3 includes container options in the configuration file.

Table 17-3   Exchange Management Pack Configuration File Container Objects

Container Object	Description
AdministrativeGroup	This node is a container object for *<Servers>* elements. It also has an *<AdministrativeGroupName>* element. The *AdministrativeGroupName* element contains the name of an administrative group as displayed by Exchange System Manager. There must be exactly one instance of the *AdministrativeGroupName* element and exactly one instance of the Servers element. Parent: *AdministrativeGroups.*
AdministrativeGroups	This node is a container object for the list of administrative groups discriminated in the configuration. It must contain at least one *<AdministrativeGroup>* element. Parent: *Configuration.*
BackEnd	This node is a container object for the configuration options that can be set for a back-end Exchange server: *<ServerName>*, *<MonitorMessageTracking>*, *<ServicesToMonitor>*, *<MailBoxAccessAccount>*, *<MDBAvailabilityMonitoring>*, and *<MailFlowMonitoring>*. The *ServerName* object contains the fully qualified domain name (FQDN) or the NetBIOS name of the server as a string. The *MonitorMessageTracking* object contains a Boolean value that specifies whether Message Tracking is enabled. The other three objects are container objects for other configuration elements. For an input configuration file, each BackEnd node must contain either zero or one instance of each of these objects. The only exception is the ServerName element. Each *BackEnd* instance must contain exactly one instance of the *ServerName* element. For the other elements, not specifying an element means that it will not be configured. An output report must contain exactly one instance of each of these objects. Parent: *Servers*

Table 17-3 Exchange Management Pack Configuration File Container Objects (Continued)

Container Object	Description
Configuration	This is the root node for the XML file. It can contain one child object, the *<AdministrativeGroups>* object, which is a container object for *AdministrativeGroup* configuration information. There must be at least one *AdministrativeGroup* object. There can be more than one *AdministrativeGroup* object. Parent: None
FrontEnd	This node is a container element for configuration information for a front-end Exchange server. It must contain exactly one *<ServerName>* element, which is a string containing the FQDN of the server. It can also contain *<ServicesToMonitor>*, *<FrontEndAvailabilityMonitoring>*, *<MailBoxAccessAccount>*, and *<MonitorMessageTracking>* objects (previously defined). Parent: *Servers*
MailBoxAccessAccount	This node contains the account information for the *MailBoxAccessAccount* for the current server. It contains *<username>* and *<domain>* elements, which are strings and contain the user name and domain name of the Mailbox Access account, respectively. This object is used only in the output configuration report. It is ignored when importing a configuration file, and the user is prompted to enter a user name and password for the Mailbox Access account when running the tool from the command line. Parent: *BackEnd* and *FrontEnd*
MailFlowMonitoring	This node contains four elements: *<ExpectMailFrom>*, *<SendMailToServer>*, *<SendMailToMailbox>* and *<TestMailBox>*. *ExpectMailFrom* and *SendMailToServer* are repeating string elements. They contain the NetBIOS name of the server that they are expecting mail from or that they are supposed to send mail to, respectively. *SendMailToMailbox* is used to specify custom mailboxes (instead of servers) to which the server is supposed to send messages. This element enables customers to use "custom test mailboxes." When using *SendMailToMailbox*, it is mandatory to add *<ServerMailToServer>*Custom*</SendMailToServer>* to the mail flow configuration, otherwise no mail flow message will be sent to the customer mailboxes. There can be multiple instances of all elements. *TestMailBox*, an optional element that can be used to send/receive mail flow messages, should be specified whenever using customer mailboxes to monitor mail flow. Parent: *BackEnd*
MDBAvailabilityMonitoring	This node contains *<MDBToMonitor>* objects. The *MDBToMonitor* object contains the configuration of each MDB. If empty, it means that the configuration will disable MAPI logon availability. Parent: *BackEnd*

Table 17-3   Exchange Management Pack Configuration File Container Objects (Continued)

Container Object	Description
MDBToMonitor	This node contains three elements, *<StorageGroup>*, *<MDB-Name>*, and *<TestMailBox>*, that specify information about an MDB. The first two elements are required and exactly one instance of each element must exist under this node. The *Test-MailBox* element can be present, but it is not required. If it is present, this name is used for the mailbox monitoring account. If not, the default naming scheme is used. Parent: *MDBAvailabilityMonitoring*
Servers	This node is a container object for *<BackEnd>* and *<FrontEnd>* objects. *FrontEnd* and *BackEnd* objects contain the configuration information for front-end or back-end servers, respectively. There can be multiple instances of the *FrontEnd* and the *BackEnd* objects under the server container. No other elements can be in the Servers container object. Parent: *AdministrativeGroup*
ServicesToMonitor	This node contains the services to monitor. It contains the *<ServiceName>* element, which is a string and contains the system name of the service to monitor; for example, SMTPSVC or MSExchangeIS, not Simple Mail Transfer Protocol or Microsoft Exchange Information Store service. This is a repeating element (). Parent: *FrontEnd* or *BackEnd*

Using the Command-Line Interface

The command-line tool is an alternative tool to supplement Configuration Wizard. Using it, you can import a created configuration file into the MOM environment, or export the existing configuration file.

The command-line tool supports both a silent mode, in which you specify all parameters, and an interactive mode, which prompts for input as needed. You can run the command-line tool on any workstation or server, as long as it meets the prerequisites.

ExchangeMPConfig.exe Syntax

You can import and export configurations through the ExchangeMPConfig.exe tool.

To import and apply a configuration, use the following command:

ExchangeMPConfig.exe /i <filename> [/u <domain\username> [/p <password>]]

The required parameters are:

- **/i *filename.xml*** Sets configuration on user's servers based on the information in filename.xml.
  Optional parameters used with **/i** are as follows:

- **/u *username*** The user can use the /u parameter to specify the Mailbox Access account. The user name will be in the DOMAIN\username format. The tool will validate this.

- **/p *password*** The user can use the /p parameter to specify the password for the Mailbox Access account. /u is required.

To export a configuration, use the following command:
ExchangeMPConfig.exe /e *<filename>* [/s *<serverFilter>*] [/a *<adminis-trativeGroupFilter>*]
The required parameters are:

- **/e *filename.xml*** Creates a report named filename.xml that contains the configuration information of the selected servers. If you do not specify a server, information about all servers, even ones that are not monitored, is exported. Filename.xml is the configuration file (configuration.xml) that is used with the /i parameter.
  Optional parameters used with **/e** are as follows:

- **/s *servername*** Specifies the server from which to obtain the configuration file, instead of the default local computer. It can be used in combination with wildcard characters such as * and ?. Check the usage output of the tool for more information.

- **/a *admin group*** Specifies the common name of an administrative group from which to obtain the configuration. If this parameter is set, the tool discovers all Exchange servers in the specified domain, obtains the configuration information from each server, and saves it to the configuration file. It can be used in combination with wildcard characters such as * and ?.

- **/?** Displays the valid command switches for the command and gives a summary of what each does.

Each parameter must be separated by a space from the value associated with the parameter. For example, **/e configuration.xml** is valid, but **/e:configuration.xml**, **/e=configuration.xml**, and **/econfiguration.xml** are not valid.

Table 17-4 lists typical command lines that you can use to run ExchangeMPConfig.exe.

Table 17-4 ExchangeMPConfig.exe Command-line Examples

Command Line	Description
ExchangeMPConfig.exe	This command runs the wizard in GUI mode.
ExchangeMPConfig.exe /i configuration.xml	This command imports the configuration specified in configuration.xml. An error is presented if the local computer does not have the Exchange System Manager tools installed, or the current user does not have permissions to do the required configuration.
	Because no Mailbox Access account is specified on the command line, when the command executes, you are prompted for the Mailbox Access account user name and password only if required by the configuration.
	Note that the password field is not shown. As you type characters in the password, the command prompt pointer remains at the same location. See the runas.exe command included with Windows 2000, or later, for an example.
	Output:
| | ```
C:\> ExchangeMPConfig.exe /i configuration.xml

Mailbox Access Account Username (Domain\account): <name
user entered>
Password:
Configuration Successful.
``` |
| | Output (failure, permissions): |
| | ```
C:\> ExchangeMPConfig.exe /i configuration.xml
Error: You do not have permissions to perform
this operation. Please see
%temp%\ConfigurationLog.log for details.
``` |
| | Output (failure, management tools not installed): |
| | ```
C:\> ExchangeMPConfig.exe /i configuration.xml
Error:  The Exchange System Management tools
are required to run this command. Please
install them and try again. Please see
%temp%\ConfigurationLog.log for details.
``` |
| | Output (failure, other): |
| | ```
C:\> ExchangeMPConfig.exe /i configuration.xml
Error: An error has occurred. Please see
%temp%\ConfigurationLog.log for information.
``` |
| | Output (failure, command line parameters invalid): |
| | ```
C:\> ExchangeMPConfig.exe /iconfiguration.xml
Error:  The command line you specified is
invalid. The invalid parameter was
/iconfiguration.xml. Please correct
the error and try again.
``` |
```

Table 17-4   ExchangeMPConfig.exe Command-line Examples (Continued)

Command Line	Description
ExchangeMPConfig.exe /i configuration.xml /u ExDom\MailAcct	This command functions the same as **ExchangeMPConfig.exe /i configuration.xml**, but because the username is provided, you are not prompted to enter a Mailbox Access account interactively. However, you are still prompted for a Mailbox Access account password only if necessary in the configuration.
	Output:
|  | ```
C:\> ExchangeMPConfig.exe /i configuration.xml
/u ExchDomain\MailAcct
Password:
``` |
ExchangeMPConfig.exe /i configuration.xml /u ExDom\MailAcct /p pass	This command does the same action as the previous command, but the Mailbox Access account password is provided on the command line. The user is not prompted to interactively enter any information when using these parameters.
ExchangeMPConfig.exe /e report.xml	This command generates a configuration file that contains the current configuration information for all Exchange servers. The file format is compliant with the format required for the **/i** parameter.
	Output:
|  | ```
C:\> ExchangeMPConfig.exe /e report.xml
Generating configuration report for the local
system. This operation may take several minutes.
``` |
| | Output (failure, permissions): |
|  | ```
C:\> ExchangeMPConfig.exe /e report.xml
Error: You do not have permissions to perform
this operation. Please see
%temp%\ConfigurationLog.log for details.
``` |
| | Output (failure, monitoring pack not installed): |
|  | ```
C:\> ExchangeMPConfig.exe /e report.xml
Error:  The Exchange Monitoring Pack is not
installed on the local system. Please install
 it and try again. Please see
%temp%\ConfigurationLog.log for details.
``` |
| | Output (failure, other): |
|  | ```
C:\> ExchangeMPConfig.exe /e report.xml
Error: An error has occurred. Please see
%temp%\ConfigurationLog.log for information.
``` |
| | Output (failure, command line parameters invalid): |
|  | ```
C:\> ExchangeMPConfig.exe /econfiguration.xml
Error:  The command line you specified is
invalid. The invalid parameter was
/econfiguration.xml. Please correct the
error and try again.
``` |

Table 17-4   ExchangeMPConfig.exe Command-line Examples (Continued)

Command Line	Description
ExchangeMPConfig.exe /e report.xml /s exch1	This command generates a configuration file. The system is specified with the **/s** parameter and the configuration of that system is retrieved instead of the local system. The listed server name can be the NetBIOS or FQDN name for the Exchange computer.
	In addition to the errors listed in the previous command, the Exchange System Management Tools must be installed on the system where the configuration tool runs. If the tools are not on the local system, you will receive an error. Also, if the specified server cannot be contacted, you will receive an error. Only errors that are different from the above are listed here.
	Output:
| | ```
C:\> ExchangeMPConfig.exe /e report.xml
/s exch1
Generating configuration report for exch1.
This operation may take several minutes.
``` |
| | Output (failure, management tools not installed): |
| | ```
C:\> ExchangeMPConfig.exe /e report.xml
/s exch1
Error:  The Exchange System Management tools
are required to run this command. Please
install them and try again. Please see
%temp%\ConfigurationLog.log for details.
``` |
| | Output (failure, server unreachable): |
| | ```
C:\> ExchangeMPConfig.exe /e report.xml
/s exch1
Error: System exch1 does not exist or cannot
be contacted. Please try again later. Please
see %temp%\ConfigurationLog.log for details.
``` |
```

Table 17-4   ExchangeMPConfig.exe Command-line Examples (Continued)

Command Line	Description
ExchangeMPConfig.exe /e report.xml /a ExAG1	This command works similarly to the previous two commands. It generates a configuration file for the domain specified with the **/a** parameter. All servers running Exchange and the Exchange Management Pack are queried for their current configuration. The administrative group name must be the common name of the administrative group.
	Output:
| | ```
C:\> ExchangeMPConfig.exe /e report.xml
/a ExAG1
Generating configuration report for ExAG1.
This operation may take several minutes.
``` |
| | Output (failure, server unreachable): |
| | ```
C:\> ExchangeMPConfig.exe /e report.xml
/a ExAG1
Error: The Administrative Group ExAG1
cannot be contacted. Please try again later.
Please see %temp%\ConfigurationLog.log
for details.
``` |
| | Output (failure, Exchange 5.5 Admin Group): |
| | ```
C:\> ExchangeMPConfig.exe /e report.xml
/a ExAG1
Error: The Administrative Group ExAG1 is an
administrative group for a version of
exchange not supported by this tool.
This tool only supports Exchange 2000 and
later administrative groups.
``` |
| | Output (failure, other): |
| | ```
C:\> ExchangeMPConfig.exe /e report.xml
/a ExAG1
Error: An error has occurred. Please see
%temp%\ConfigurationLog.log for information.
``` |
| **ExchangeMPConfig.exe /?** | This command displays the usage information for the executable. Usage information is also displayed if the user does not enter valid command line parameters. |

Exchange Management Pack in a Distributed Environment

In a distributed environment, control, administration, and monitoring are not confined to a single location or area. The distributed environment enables routing groups and administrative groups to be monitored from more than one location. For example, an organization might have segregated business units with separate forests, domain trusts, and separate Exchange organizations. In such a scenario, control is not centralized. However, each unit retains control over monitoring and administration. Whenever Exchange messaging systems require separate monitoring and administration, a solution is to use the distributed environment configuration for Exchange Management Pack. With a distributed environment, multiple configuration groups exist for each division within the organization.

Monitoring a Distributed Environment

With multiple configuration groups, many locations can be monitored across one or more domains. MOM includes a multi-homing feature that enables agents to be members of multiple configuration groups. This is similar to a single configuration group in that the agent can report to more than one MOM server. However, in a multiple configuration group scenario, the agent uses multi-homing to report not only to a different MOM server, but also to a MOM server that is a part of another configuration group.

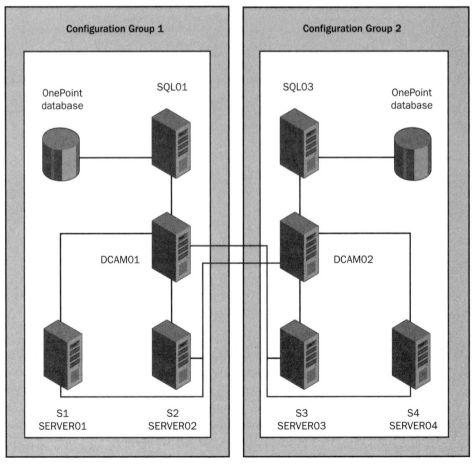

Figure 17-5   MOM multiple configuration groups with multi-homed agents

There are advantages to running a multi-homed agent environment. For example, the agent reports the collected events, alerts, and performance counters to multiple configuration groups in such a way as to have no conflicts between processing of the Rules. Computers with multi-homed agents can belong to a maximum of four configuration groups. Figure 17-5 shows a distributed environment monitoring scenario.

Installation Planning for a Distributed Environment

Installation planning for a distributed environment does not differ greatly from installation planning for a centralized environment. You must, at the very least, consider the following aspects of your existing configuration:

- **Location and role**   You should make a list of each computer in your organization, along with related data, such as the one seen in Table 17-1. List the role, FQDN, IP address, special notes, organizational units, and so on. If possible, create a network diagram of your organization that specifies major servers, groups of workstations and users, and configuration settings. Additionally, you should create a layout of your organization as it relates to Exchange Management Pack and MOM. You can specify which computers will be in specific configuration groups, and which MOM servers will manage the agents on those computers.

- **Bandwidth, hardware, and software requirements**   To have agent multi-homing across multiple configuration groups, the computers in those groups must have constant connectivity to report to MOM servers. The requirements differ according to the size of the organization and amount of monitored services. The computers used to run the SQL servers and MOM servers should follow the general requirements specified earlier regarding both software and hardware.

- **Dependencies**   There are software dependencies involved in installing MOM, such as Access reporting, SQL, IIS, and so on. For a full list, see the "Dependencies" section of the centralized environment installation planning discussion.

Deploying Exchange Management Pack in a Distributed Environment

To deploy Exchange Management Pack in a distributed environment, you must carefully plan and outline how the organization will be structured according to MOM. You must decide how many configuration groups to have, how many MOM servers, how many SQL servers, and which computers will be monitored by which MOM server. Additionally, you must export the existing configuration in an upgrade scenario. For information on how to do this, see the section "Upgrading from Exchange 2000 Management Pack" earlier in this chapter.

Installing Microsoft Operations Manager

After you plan for deployment in the distributed environment, to deploy Exchange Management Pack, follow the steps below. The steps are for one configuration group in a distributed environment. To create additional configuration groups, repeat the following steps.

To deploy a configuration group in a distributed environment:

1. Review the requirements and prerequisites for installation. Install SQL Server 2000 SP3 on a computer. Then, run MOM setup and install the database option. Additionally, install the reporting update on all required computers.

2. Install MOM prerequisites and install one or more MOM servers for the configuration group. Ensure that the Agent Manager has the appropriate security rights to the agent computer.

3. Define the Managed Computer Rules (MCRs) for each MOM server in the properties of the Agent Manager, in the Managed Computer Rules tab. Use the following guidelines when you create Managed Computer Rules:

   - Add computers to the MCRs of only one DCAM within the configuration group. Ensure that MCRs across DCAMs within a configuration group do not overlap. The names must include only English characters.

   - When you enter domain names, use the NetBIOS name, not the Fully Qualified Domain Name (FQDN). NetBIOS names should not exceed 15 characters.

   - When you define Rules for computers that are in workgroups, enter the workgroup name in the Domain field. Computers in workgroups can be added to the MCRs after they have been installed using the manual agent setup.

   - When you enter computer names, you can either enter a specific computer name or enter expressions that match substrings or wildcards. There are many options available for specifying computer names. For more information, search for "Regular Expression" and "Boolean Regular Expression" in MOM Help.

   - If both an Include MCR and an Exclude MCR exist for an agent computer, the Exclude Rule takes priority. Changes to MCRs do not take effect until after the Agent Manager performs a scan.

4. Run a managed computer scan to install agents. Expand Configuration, and then select Agent Managers. Right-click the appropriate Agent Manager and then click Scan Managed Computers Now.

5. Refresh the pending installation list.

6. Review the pending installations by choosing Action on the menu bar and selecting Approve All pending Actions.

7. Process the approved installations.

8. Verify that the agents are installed on the monitored computers and added to the correct computer groups. If the agent computer is not in the expected computer group, you must add it manually.

    To manually add an agent computer to a computer group:

    a. In the left pane, expand Rules, and then click Computer Groups.

    b. Right-click the appropriate computer group, and then select Properties.

    c. In the Computer Rule Properties dialog box, click Included Computers.

    d. Click Add, and then complete the criteria for adding the computer.

    e. Click OK, and then click Apply.

9. Initiate a managed computer scan or wait until the next regularly scheduled scan.

10. After the scan is complete, verify that the agent has been added to the computer group. To do this, locate the agent (in the left pane, expand Monitor, and then click All Agents), right-click the agent computer name, and then click View Computer Groups.

Installing Exchange Management Pack for a Distributed Environment

Installing Exchange Management Pack in a distributed environment requires a similar approach to the installation in a centralized environment. You should consider the following guidelines when installing Exchange 2003 Management Pack in a distributed environment.

- **Import the Management Pack**   To install the Management Pack, you must import the .akm file into MOM. If you are upgrading or have another special scenario, follow the steps to successfully import the management pack.

- **Run Configuration Wizard**   After you download and install Configuration Wizard, run Configuration Wizard and set up the environment for proper Exchange monitoring.

Configuring Exchange Management Pack

After deploying Exchange Management Pack, you can configure it by using Configuration Wizard or the command-line configuration tool.

If you want to monitor front-end servers, Outlook Web Access, Outlook Mobile Access, and Exchange ActiveSync, you must perform additional configuration steps and make changes to the registry. For more information, see the configuration section of the centralized environment scenario.

Exchange Management Pack in a Hybrid Environment

In a hybrid environment, aspects of both the centralized environment and the distributed environment are combined. For example, an Exchange organization might require mailboxes to be separated according to organizational units and divisions, and public folders to be centralized in the company headquarters, because most of the users of public folders are in that location. In this scenario, monitoring and administration of public folders is centralized, while mailbox monitoring and administration is distributed. A hybrid environment enables administrators to share tasks and resources across the entire organization in a specialized way, depending on the needs of groups within the organization.

Monitoring a Hybrid Environment

The hybrid environment does not differ greatly from a centralized environment. It builds upon the centralized idea and allows for flexibility. In the above example of an organization that centralizes public folders and segregates mailboxes, a hierarchy of configuration groups can be used to achieve a monitoring solution with MOM and Exchange Management Pack. A central location can be used to monitor every individual configuration group, as well as public folders. Each configuration group, in turn, monitors Exchange mailboxes. Alerts from each configuration group are forwarded to the central location, producing an overall centralized monitoring with each configuration group having the ability to monitor and control a defined resource.

Figure 17-6 shows a diagram of the multi-tiered configuration group deployment with alert forwarding enabled. This configuration is used for a hybrid environment. Three main components make up the configuration:

- **Master configuration group**   The master configuration group is the group that receives alerts from sub-tier configuration groups. It includes a SQL database and one or more MOM servers to receive data from other configuration groups. A master configuration group can support up to 10 zone configuration groups with up to 120,000 alerts per day forwarded to the master configuration group.

- **Alert forwarding**   Alert forwarding is the process by which data can be sent from a configuration group to a master configuration group. Alert forwarding is used to achieve centralized monitoring by forwarding only alerts and the events that are associated with those alerts. Forwarded alerts keep origin data, for example, data about the originating computer. This separation enables a configuration group to make changes in alert properties without affecting settings in the master configuration group.

- **Sub-tier configuration groups**   Configuration groups that forward alerts to the master configuration group are the last component in the hybrid environment. These configuration groups contain a dedicated SQL database and one or more MOM servers. A maximum of two tiers can be implemented. MOM supports a two-tiered architecture: zone configuration group to master configuration group. Implementing more than two tiers is not supported.

Figure 17-6 illustrates the topology for monitoring a hybrid environment.

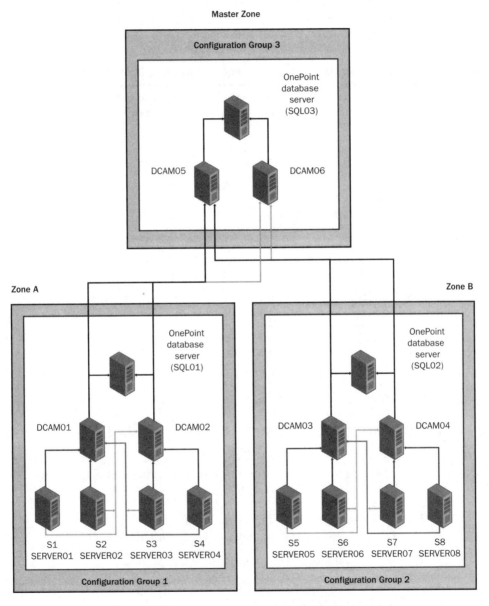

Figure 17-6   Multi-tiered configuration groups with alert forwarding

Installation Planning for a Hybrid Environment

Because of the complexity of a hybrid environment, you must do additional planning before deploying MOM and Exchange Management Pack in the organization. In addition to considering hardware and software requirements, dependencies, bandwidth requirements and potential bottlenecks, you must specify the task of each configuration zone, and what alerts to forward. Configuring alert forwarding is explained later in this chapter.

Table 17-5 shows a sample planning list for deploying a hybrid environment.

Table 17-5   Sample Computer Inventory for a Hybrid Monitoring Scenario

Identifying information	Configuration group	Monitored component	Notes
SERVERDC01	Master	Active Directory	
SERVERSQL01	Master	SQL	
SERVERMOM01	Master	MOM	
SERVERMOM02	Master	MOM	
SERVER01-SERVER09	Master	Exchange	Centralized mailbox servers
WKSTA01-50	Master	Workstations	
SERVERSQL02	Group1	SQL	
SERVERMOM03	Group1	MOM	
SERVERMOM04	Group1	MOM	
SERVER51-SERVER60	Group1	Exchange	Public folder servers
SERVERSQL03	Group2	SQL	
SERVERMOM05	Group2	MOM	
SERVERMOM06	Group2	MOM	
SERVER61-SERVER70	Group2	Exchange	Public folder servers

Deploying Exchange Management Pack in a Hybrid Environment

After you diagram the proposed deployment, consider future and present requirements, and prepare for installation by checking prerequisites, create a checklist to follow when deploying Exchange Management Pack. For example:

1. Verify that the existing Exchange organization functions without problems, such as queue growth, fragmentation, bandwidth and connectivity issues, and so on.

2. Create the master configuration group, including:

    a. Install the SQL server and prerequisites

    b. Install the MOM servers

    c. Install the reporting update

    d. Prepare for Exchange Management Pack deployment

3. Create secondary configuration groups with alert forwarding to the master con-figuration group.

It might seem overly simplistic, but in a large organization that requires cooper-ation between multiple teams and people, ensuring that all team members are work-ing together for a common goal, such as server software updates, is key to a successful deployment.

There are several issues to note when deploying Exchange Management Pack:

■ **Upgrades**   When upgrading from a previous installation of MOM, or from a pre-vious version of Exchange Management Pack, note any custom configurations, Rules, and settings you may need with Exchange 2003 Management Pack. Addi-tionally, you must export the existing configuration, as discussed in the upgrading section of the centralized environment discussion earlier in this chapter.

■ **Additional settings**   At times, you might need to use the command-line tool. For example, when upgrading from Exchange 2000 Management Pack. Also, for front-end servers and for monitoring availability of Outlook Web Access, Outlook Mobile Access, and Exchange ActiveSync, you might need to configure registry settings to function according to your organization.

Installing Microsoft Operations Manager

To import Exchange Management Pack, you must install and configure Microsoft Operations Manager. Follow the procedures for creating a master configuration group and secondary configuration groups when installing MOM.

Installing Exchange Management Pack for a Hybrid Environment

To successfully install Exchange Management Pack, follow the general procedures for installation defined earlier in this chapter. You should do the following:

1. Import the Management Pack into MOM.

2. Install and run Configuration Wizard, or use the command-line tool to configure Exchange Management Pack.

Configuring Exchange Management Pack

Because the hybrid environment uses alert forwarding, you must set up alert forward-ing after installing Exchange Management Pack and running Configuration Wizard.

Both the master configuration group database and the secondary configuration group databases store forwarded alerts. The alerts can be managed individually at the master group level without impacting other configuration groups, or at the configura-tion group level, without impacting the master configuration group. Similarly, responses to alerts are not confined to a single configuration group. Responses specified by a Rule are executed in each configuration group by the MOM server in the group. However, once an alert is forwarded to the master configuration group, a separate response can be executed.

If you have a response for a forwarded alert that you want to run specifically in the master configuration group, you should:

■ Define an alert processing Rule for that alert response in the master configuration group.

■ Specify that the alert response runs on the Consolidator computer.

If you specify that the response is to run on the agent computer, then the response runs on the secondary zone MOM server.

> **Note**   For alerts to be forwarded to the master configuration zone, the Rule that generates the alert must have the same GUID on both the zone configuration group and the master configuration group. A way to ensure that the Rules have the same GUID is to install Management Packs created by Microsoft. However, if custom Rules are created, they must be exported from one configuration group and imported into the master configuration group. If a Rule has no counterpart in the master configuration group, but exists in a zone configuration group, then alert forwarding does not occur. In this case, the zone configuration group continues to use the Rule and generate alerts. The alerts will remain local and will not be forwarded.

When you configure alert forwarding for Exchange, remember that only alerts are forwarded. Event data and performance data are not forwarded to the master configuration group.

Monitoring Important Exchange 2003 Components

Exchange Management Pack includes over 2,000 various Rules to monitor Exchange Server 2003. A benefit of using Exchange Management Pack with MOM is that it can function in various configurations. As shown, Exchange Management Pack functions in a centralized environment, a distributed environment, and a hybrid environment.

The Rules in Exchange Management Pack monitor not only Exchange components, but also components related to Exchange Server. For example, Exchange relies heavily on Active Directory directory services to connect to a mailbox, access address lists, and so on. Exchange relies on DNS for domain resolution and for SMTP routing to function. Active Directory also relies on DNS. Exchange Management Pack accounts for these interdependencies and monitors core Exchange components, as well as Exchange-related components.

Core Exchange components include:

- **System Attendant**   Most of the Exchange services depend on the System Attendant component to function. The System Attendant service is responsible for managing user properties, routing tables, and communication between other Exchange components. For example, the System Attendant service includes a DSAccess component. DSAccess communicates with Active Directory to obtain directory information and store it in cache. The System Attendant also includes a DSProxy component. DSProxy forwards MAPI-based address lookups to a global catalog server. When System Attendant stops, other Exchange services cannot run. It is vital to ensure that System Attendant runs properly, and Exchange Management Pack includes Rules to monitor its functioning.

- **Message Transfer Agent (MTA)**   The MTA includes routing functions for communicating with non-Exchange systems such as Lotus Notes or Novell GroupWise, X.400 messaging systems, and Exchange Server 5.5.

- **SMTP Transport Engine**   The SMTP transport engine is one of the most important components of Exchange Server 2003. The SMTP transport engine processes all incoming and outgoing messages. The engine includes the capability to determine routing, receive mail from MAPI clients for direct access to the Exchange store, and deliver mail to local or remote recipients.

- **Microsoft Exchange Information Store service**   The Microsoft Exchange Information Store service is responsible for maintaining user mailboxes and public folders in databases. It keeps transaction logs, stores data, and manages access to the Exchange databases.

- **Complementary Services**   Exchange includes complementary services for added functionality. For example, services such as POP3 and IMAP4 access, NNTP, Outlook Web Access, Outlook Mobile Access, and Exchange ActiveSync are complementary Exchange services. They can be enabled and disabled according to your organizational needs. Often, the services are disabled by default and configuration is necessary to incorporate them into the environment.

The Rules in Exchange Management Pack are grouped into five main categories. The categories are as follows:

- **Availability Monitoring**   The Rules in this Rule Group monitor for uptime and availability. Core Exchange components, such as System Attendant and Microsoft Exchange Information Store service, are monitored.

- **Exchange Events**   The Rules in this Rule Group search for Exchange-related events written to the Windows event and application logs. When an event occurs, the Rules include responses or generate a warning or alert, notifying of potential system failure.

- **Health Monitoring and Performance Thresholds**   The Rules in this Rule Group primarily monitor queues, available disk space, security, and configuration information.

- **Performance Counter Logging**   The Rules in this Rule Group consist of Performance Rules that check server and Exchange resource use.

- **Report Collection Rules**   The Rules in this Rule Group collect data related to report generation.

Each of these Rule Groups, their features, and included Rules are discussed in the following section.

Monitoring System Availability

Exchange Management Pack includes processing Rule Groups to monitor system availability. These Rules can be enabled and disabled according to your requirements. The Rules monitor the following components:

- **Database Mounted Check**   Events are generated when a database is connected, and when a database is disconnected. An alert is generated by Rules in this Rule Group when a database is disconnected.

- **MAPI Logon Check and Availability Reporting**   A MAPI client, such as Outlook 2003, accesses the databases that store Exchange data. This Rule Group can verify that these operations are successful.

- **Unexpected Service Termination**   When an Exchange service terminates unexpectedly, Exchange logs the event. The Rules in this Rule Group monitor and alert for unexpected service termination.

- **Verify Agent Mailbox Configuration**   The test mailboxes that are used in availability monitoring include Rules to verify that the test mailboxes are correctly installed and configured. The Rules in this Rule Group verify that test mailboxes function properly.

- **Verify Exchange ActiveSync Front-End Availability**   Scripts in this Rule Group perform synthetic Exchange ActiveSync logons and monitor the results to determine the availability of Exchange ActiveSync.

- **Verify Exchange Services**   The Rules in this Rule Group monitor core Exchange services and generate an alert when a service is down or not functioning properly.

- **Verify Mail Flow**   Test messages between sending and receiving servers are sent out periodically through scripts. This is one of the fastest ways to monitor availability. If messages can be sent and delivered, the Exchange servers and their components are functioning.

- **Verify Outlook Mobile Access Front-End Availability**   Scripts in this Rule Group perform synthetic Outlook Mobile Access logons and monitor the results to determine the availability of Outlook Mobile Access.

- **Verify Outlook Web Access Front-End Availability**   Scripts in this Rule Group perform synthetic Outlook Web Access logons and monitor the results to determine the availability of Outlook Web Access.

Database Mounted Check

Two event processing Rules and an alert processing Rule comprise the Database Rule Group. The Rules determine which Exchange databases are not connected. An alert is generated when a database fails to connect or is disconnected. When the severity level is Error or higher, a notification is sent.

MAPI Logon Check and Availability Reporting

MAPI clients, such as Outlook 2003, access the Exchange database directly. The Rules in this Rule Group monitor MAPI availability.

The MAPI Rule Group includes the following Event Rules:

- **Cannot access the Exchange Information Store service**   This Rule generates an alert when the Exchange 2003 - MAPI logon verification script generates the event: Exchange MOM 9982 Problem in accessing Microsoft Exchange Information Store service.

- **The Exchange Information Store service availability cannot be verified**   This Rule checks for the following event: Exchange MOM 9998 Cannot check availability because of WMI, ClusterAutomation, or other unexpected error. An alert is generated when the script that checks for the availability of the server that is running Exchange encounters an unexpected error.

- **MAPI Logon Failure**   This Rule checks for the following event: Exchange MOM 9981 General MAPI logon failure. An alert is generated when the MAPI Logon script that checks for server availability fails a MAPI logon because of problems in accessing Active Directory.

- **Cannot verify Exchange Information Store service availability due to an unexpected error**   This Rule checks for the following event: Exchange MOM 9983 Cannot verify availability of the following test account. An alert is generated when the script that checks for the availability of the server that is running Exchange encounters an unexpected error about the test account.

- **Check mailbox store availability – MAPI logon test**   By default, this Rule runs every five minutes and uses the Exchange 2003 - MAPI logon verification script to check whether the Microsoft Exchange Information Store service is accessible to a client application through a MAPI logon test.

Unexpected Service Termination

Service termination is monitored by Exchange Management Pack. The following Rules are included:

- **Unexpected Exchange-related Service Termination**   These Rules monitor termination of the WWW, IIS, MOM, SMTP, NNTP, and other Exchange services.

- **Unexpected Service Termination**   These Rules monitor server starts, stops, and improper stops.

Verify Agent Mailbox Configuration

The Rules in this Rule Group check whether the test mailbox accounts are correctly configured. The following Event Rules are included:

- **Failure to get MOM test mailbox account information**   The Exchange 2003 - Verify Test Mailboxes script failed in its query of MOM test mailbox accounts.

- **MOM Test account without an Exchange mailbox**   There are some accounts for which the name matches the MOM test mailbox accounts, but these accounts do not have an Exchange mailbox.

- **Exchange Server does not have a MOM test mailbox account**   The test mailbox account is absent.

- **More than one MOM test mailbox account in the same mailbox database (MDB)**   There is more than one MOM test mailbox account for the same mailbox database on this Exchange server. The Exchange Management Pack supports logging on to only one test mailbox per mailbox database.

- **Verify Test Mailboxes**   This Rule is triggered by a timed event. The Rule periodically runs a script that verifies that the test mailboxes are correctly configured.

- **No MOM test mailbox account for some mailbox databases**   The Exchange 2003 - Verify Test Mailboxes script verified that some mailbox databases (MDBs) in this computer do not have a MOM test mailbox account. Without this account, the Exchange Management Pack cannot perform the MAPI logon to check the availability of the specified MDBs. Therefore, it will not be possible to collect data for the MAPI availability reports for any of the specified MDBs.

- **MOM test mailbox account residing on different Exchange server than intended**   The Exchange 2003 - Verify Test Mailboxes script verified that some MOM test mailbox accounts that should be residing on this Exchange server are residing on other servers. When mailboxes reside on an unintended server, it usually indicates an error in creating or moving the account.

Verify Exchange ActiveSync Front-End Availability

Exchange ActiveSync availability is verified by executing synthetic logons to the front-end server housing Exchange ActiveSync. The Rules in this Rule Group include scripts to execute logons, and report successes and failures.

This group includes the following Event Rules:

- **EAS logon failure: Forbidden**   This Rule generates an error when the Mailbox Access account is not enabled for Exchange ActiveSync, or when Exchange ActiveSync is disabled. The alert is generated when the logon scripts cannot log on.

- **Synthetic Exchange ActiveSync logon**   This Rule runs a script every 15 minutes to perform synthetic Exchange ActiveSync logons. The other Rules in this Rule Group rely on the script for event data.

- **Exchange ActiveSync logon failure: Internal Server Error**   This Rule generates an alert when the logon scripts cannot successfully log on because of a server error.

- **Exchange ActiveSync logon failure: Bad Request**   This Rule generates an error when the EAS logon function is not receiving acceptable parameters.

- **Exchange ActiveSync logon failure: General Error**   The Exchange ActiveSync synthetic logon scripts rely on underlying components to function. This script generates an error when a component is unavailable.

- **Exchange ActiveSync logon failure: Server Busy**   This Rule generates an alert when synthetic logon fails because of a busy or overloaded server. This alert is also generated when the Active Directory domain controller cannot return data to the logon scripts because it is overloaded.

Verify Exchange Services

The Verify Exchange Services Rule Group has Rules that use a timed event to periodically determine whether key Exchange services are running. A notification is triggered if the severity level is Error or higher.

There are four views to monitor these results. They are located under Public Views\Exchange 2003\Server Configuration and Security\Script Reporting Events\Service Verification Events:

- **Services not installed**   Lists events where services to be monitored are not installed on the server.

- **Services not running**   Lists events where monitored services are not running.

- **Services registry key is empty**   Lists servers in which the Monitored Services registry key is empty. If no Exchange services are to be monitored on this server, set this registry value to NONE.

- **Unable to read the registry key for services**   Lists servers for the Monitored Services registry key that could not be read, most likely because they are not available.

The Exchange Services Rule Group includes the following Event Rules:

- **Service verification. Check services script**   This Rule is triggered by a timed event that periodically runs the Exchange 2003 - Check service(s) state script to determine whether services specified in a registry key on the Exchange server are running.

- **Service verification. Check Services to monitor registry key**   This Rule runs a script once a day to look for the presence of the Monitored Services entry under HKEY_LOCAL_MACHINE\SOFTWARE\Microsoft\Exchange MOM in the registry.

- **Service verification. Service to be monitored is not installed**   This Rule responds to an event generated by the Service verification - Check Services Script Rule. This Rule periodically runs a script to determine whether a service specified in a registry key on the Exchange server is installed.

- **Exchange-related services not running**   This Rule responds to an event generated by the Service verification - Check Services Script Rule to determine whether a specified service is running.

Verify Mail Flow

Exchange Management Pack uses test accounts to send test e-mail messages between Exchange servers. If you have only one Exchange server, test e-mail messages can be sent from the server to itself. An alert is generated when test messages cannot be delivered or when they time out.

This group includes the following Event Rules:

- **Receive mail flow messages**   This Rule uses the Exchange 2003 – Mail Flow Receiver script and periodically checks mail flow. It generates an alert if message delivery latency exceeds a specified threshold.

- **Mail flow script cannot resolve recipient's address**   This Rule generates an alert if a recipient's address cannot be resolved.

- **An incorrect parameter was sent to the Received Mail script**   This Rule generates an alert when a malformed or unacceptable parameter is passed to the script. The alert contains a description of acceptable values.

- **Mail flow latency exceeded the specified threshold**   This Rule generates an alert when latency threshold is greater than the defined value.

- **General errors in the mail flow scripts**   This Rule generates an alert when a mail flow script stops running.

- **Mail flow message not received** This Rule generates an alert when messages sent by the mail flow verification scripts are not received.

- **Send mail flow messages** This Rule is triggered by a timed event and periodically runs a script that sends a message to one Exchange server to verify that mail is being sent without problems.

- **Clock synchronization problem** This Rule generates an alert when the system clock on the Exchange servers reports negative latency beyond the defined threshold.

Mailbox Access Account

The Mailbox Access account must be able to log on for mail flow to function correctly. Therefore, it has specific rights to enable mail flow scripts to work. An access control entry (ACE) is added and specifies the following rights:

- **ADS_RIGHT_READ_CONTROL** The right to read data from the security descriptor of the object, not including the data in the system access control list (SACL).

- **ADS_RIGHT_DS_READ_PROP** The right to read properties of the object. The ObjectType member of an ACE can contain a GUID that identifies a property set or property. If ObjectType does not contain a GUID, the ACE controls the right to read all the object properties.

- **ADS_RIGHT_DS_LIST_OBJECT** The right to list a particular object. If the user is not granted such a right, and the user does not have ADS_RIGHT_ACTRL_DS_LIST set on the object parent, the object is hidden from the user. This right is ignored if the third character of the dSHeuristics property is '0' or not set.

- **ADS_RIGHT_ACTRL_DS_LIST** The right to list child objects of this object.

> **More Info** For more information about ACE properties, see the Active Directory Service Interfaces (ADSI) enumerations at *http://go.microsoft.com/fwlink/?LinkId=25449*.

This ACE is added directly to the locations listed in Table 17-6.

Table 17-6   Mailbox Access Account ACE Locations

LDAP object	Inherited in the LDAP tree?	ViewStoreStatus
Configuration container	No	No
Exchange organization	No	No
Address lists container	Yes	No
Addressing container	Yes	No
Admin groups container	No	No
Selected admin group container	Yes	Yes
Global settings container	Yes	No
Recipients policies container	Yes	No
System policies container	Yes	No

ViewStoreStatus is a specific Exchange property that enables the account to view database information. The security ID (SID) of the Mailbox Access account is added to the msExchAdmins property so that it appears on Delegation Wizard. The value specified in this property is the pair SID + ",30".

For each test mailbox, the Mailbox Access account has the following rights:

- Delete mailbox storage

- Read permissions

- Full mailbox access

Verify Outlook Mobile Access Front-End Availability

Exchange Management Pack includes Rules to verify Outlook Mobile Access availability. Similar to the Rules in the Exchange ActiveSync group, the Rules in the Outlook Mobile Access group perform synthetic logons to the front-end Exchange server that houses Outlook Mobile Access. An alert is generated when logon is not successful.

This group includes the following Event Rules:

- **Outlook Mobile Access logon failure: ASP.net errors**   An alert is generated when MOM event 22008 occurs. This event signifies that ASP.NET or the Exchange server is configured incorrectly.

- **Outlook Mobile Access logon failure: Outlook Mobile Access configuration errors**   An alert is generated when MOM event 22007 occurs. This event signifies that there is a configuration problem with Outlook Mobile Access and that the IIS metabase might have been corrupted.

- **Outlook Mobile Access logon failure: Mailbox hosted on an Exchange Server version earlier than 2003** An alert is generated when MOM event 22002 occurs. This event signifies that the logon script tried to log on to an Exchange server running a version of Exchange before Exchange 2003.

- **Outlook Mobile Access logon failure: Unable to connect** An alert is generated when MOM event 22001 occurs. This event signifies that a connection cannot be established to the back-end Exchange mailbox.

- **Outlook Mobile Access logon failure: Network problem** An alert is generated when MOM event 22005 occurs. This event signifies that network problems are preventing Outlook Mobile Access operations.

- **Synthetic Outlook Mobile Access logon** This time Event Rule runs every 15 minutes and launches the Exchange 2003 - OMA logon verification script. This script verifies front-end server availability through synthetic Outlook Mobile Access logon.

- **Outlook Mobile Access logon failure: Wireless access is not enabled for the account** An alert is generated when MOM event 22004 occurs. This event signifies that the account is not enabled to use Outlook Mobile Access.

- **General error during synthetic Outlook Mobile Access logon** An alert is generated when MOM events 20907 and 20908 occur. These events signify that the underlying components and services on which the synthetic logon relies are not operational.

- **Outlook Mobile Access logon failure: Unexpected errors** An alert is generated when MOM event 22010 occurs. This event signifies that an unexpected error or exception has occurred when Outlook Mobile Access is processing the logon request.

- **Outlook Mobile Access logon failure: Device type not supported (Web.config file is modified)** An alert is generated when MOM event 22009 occurs. This event signifies that the device is unsupported. A possible cause is that the Web.config file has been modified.

- **Outlook Mobile Access logon failure: Incorrect password or mailbox not created** An alert is generated when MOM event 2003 occurs. This event signifies that the entered password is incorrect, or that the account is not created.

Verify Outlook Web Access Front-End Availability

Outlook Web Access availability is verified through synthetic logons to the front-end Exchange server housing Outlook Web Access. When a login is unsuccessful, a script in the Rules generates an alert.

This group includes the following Event Rules:

- **Outlook Web Access logon failure: Webexception**   Synthetic Outlook Web Access logon attempt failed because of an exception. This Rule generates an alert when a MOM event ID 20003 occurs.

- **Outlook Web Access logon failure: (HTTP error 401) Unauthorized**   This Rule generates an alert when MOM event 20015 occurs. The logon failure is caused by a rejected user name and password combination.

- **General error during synthetic Outlook Web Access logon**   This Rule generates an alert when services or components on which the synthetic logon object relies are not running, are having problems, or refuse connection.

- **Outlook Web Access logon failure: (HTTP error 400) Bad Request**   This Rule generates an alert when MOM event 20014 occurs. The logon failure is caused because the server does not understand the request because of malformed syntax. This is frequently caused by interrupted communications.

- **Outlook Web Access logon failure: (HTTP error 404) Page not found**   This Rule generates an alert when MOM event 20017 occurs. When a connection cannot be established to the Outlook Web Access server, an alert is generated.

- **Outlook Web Access logon failure: Authentication error.**   An alert is generated when a logon attempt fails because of an authentication error. The credentials for Mailbox Access account may be incorrect or changed after initial deployment.

- **Outlook Web Access logon failure: (HTTP error 503) Service Unavailable**   An alert is generated when MOM event 20013 occurs. This event signifies that the server cannot handle the request because of temporary overloading or maintenance of the server.

- **Outlook Web Access logon failure: (HTTP error 407) Proxy Authorization Required**   An alert is generated when MOM event 20018 occurs. This event signifies that a proxy is required. If a proxy server is installed, it might not be relaying connections correctly.

- **Outlook Web Access logon failure: (HTTP error 408) Request Time Out**   When a client request times out waiting for a response, an alert is generated. This Rule generates an alert when MOM event 20019 occurs.

- **Outlook Web Access logon failure: (HTTP error 403) Access forbidden**   An alert is generated when MOM event 20016 occurs. This event signifies that too many users are connected to the server.

- **Outlook Web Access logon failure: General HTTP error**   When the Outlook Web Access server returns an error during a logon try, this Rule uses the related MOM event 20011 to generate an alert.

- **Unexpected error during synthetic Outlook Web Access logon**   When an error occurs during a logon try that is not addressed by a specific error type, MOM event 19999 is written to the log. This Rule generates an alert when the event occurs.

- **Outlook Web Access logon failure: (HTTP error 500) Server returned an unknown error**   An alert is generated when a MOM event 20012 occurs. This event signifies that Outlook Web Access has returned an error, related to either ASP.NET, Kerberos, or to general server malfunction.

- **Synthetic Outlook Web Access logon**   This Rule is a timed event that runs every 15 minutes and uses the Exchange 2003 - Outlook Web Access logon verification script. The script logs on to the front-end Outlook Web Access server and verifies that it is functional.

Monitoring Exchange Events

Exchange service events are logged in the various Windows logs, such as the event logs and the application log. The Exchange Event Monitoring Rule Group checks for various events logged by Exchange-related events. Each service is listed as a separate sub-group.

The following services are monitored:

- **Active Directory Connector (Exchange 2003)**   The Rules in this Rule Group monitor events from the Exchange 2003 Active Directory Connector.

- **DSAccess**   The Rules in this Rule Group monitor events from the Exchange DSAccess service. This service is responsible for the interaction of the servers running with Active Directory.

- **ExCDO**   The Rules in this Rule Group monitor events from the work done on the server running Exchange to support Collaboration Data Objects.

- **Exchange ActiveSync**   The Rules in this Rule Group monitor events from Exchange ActiveSync, which formats and delivers up-to-date notifications to supported mobile devices when new e-mail, calendar, or contact items arrive. When a supported device receives the notification, it will automatically initiate a synchronization session with Exchange to retrieve the new items.

- **Exchange Cluster**   The Rules in this Rule Group monitor events from the Exchange Cluster service.

- **Extensible Storage Engine**   The Rules in this Rule Group monitor events from the Extensible Storage Engine (ESE).

- **Free/Busy Publishing**   The Rules in this Rule Group monitor events related to free/busy publishing.

- **Full Text Indexing**   The Rules in this Rule Group monitor events from the Microsoft Search and MssCi, which Exchange uses for its full-text indexing and querying. When Full Text Indexing is enabled for a given Exchange database, it can perform a search using Advanced Find feature in Outlook.

- **IMAP4**   The Rules in this Rule Group monitor events from the Exchange IMAP4 service.

- **Information Store service**   The Rules in this Rule Group monitor events from the Exchange Information Store service.

- **Message Transfer Agent**   The Rules in this Rule Group monitor events from the Exchange MTA service and other related Exchange components, such as the X.400 gateway.

- **Metabase Update Agent**   The metabase update agent runs under the context of the Exchange System Attendant Service. Its role is to update the IIS metabase configuration so that the SMTP, IMAP4, POP3, Outlook Web Access, and Web services can work properly.

- **MSExchange Address Lists**   The Rules in this Rule Group monitor events from the Exchange Address List service (also known as the Recipient Update Service). Each Exchange mailbox may be referred to by more than one address (these are known as proxy addresses). This service is responsible for stamping the proxy addresses on mail accounts. In most cases, errors occurring in the Address List service are self-correcting. A few errors might require that the Recipient Update Service be updated or rebuilt manually.

- **Outlook Mobile Access**   The Rules in this Rule Group monitor events from Outlook Mobile Access.

- **Outlook Web Access**   This Rule Group contains events that are generated by the World Wide Web Publishing Service (W3SVC), which are relevant for Outlook Web Access deployments. For effective monitoring of Outlook Web Access, administrators should monitor Exchange store alerts (enabled by default), as well as World Wide Web Publishing Service alerts.

- **POP3**   The Rules in this Rule Group monitor events from the Exchange POP3 service.

- **SMTP and Routing**   This Rule Group monitors events from the Internet Information Service (IIS) SMTP service (SMTPSVC). This service is critical to all aspects of Exchange 2003 mail delivery. Included in this Rule Group are transport and routing events written by other Exchange components, such as SMTP connectors.

- **System Attendant**   The Rules in this Rule Group monitor events from the Exchange System Attendant service.

- **Time Service Errors** These Rules provide alerts for events generated by the Windows Time Service (w32time). These errors and warnings must be addressed immediately. Time sync problems can interfere with message tracking and relay and with Kerberos functionality.

Monitoring Health and Performance

The Exchange Management Pack includes Rules to monitor performance indicators such as mail queues, disk use, CPU load, and other thresholds.

The Rules check the following:

- **Free Disk Space Thresholds** Disk space use must be checked to ensure availability and to help plan for upgrades.

- **Mail Queue Thresholds** Thresholds of queue size and latencies included in this Rule Group help provide an alert about potential failures in SMTP transfer.

- **Server Configuration and Security Monitoring** Security and settings can be checked with the Rules in this group.

- **Server Performance Thresholds** Overall server performance dealing with CPU use, latencies, and so on can be checked with Rules in this group.

- **SMTP Remote Queues Thresholds** Outbound queues, growth, and sizes can be checked with this group.

- **Verify Windows Hotfixes** To have uniform application of Windows updates, you can specify them, and have each server checked to verify that they are installed. This can help maintain a consistent and centralized update policy.

Free Disk Space Thresholds

The Rules in this Rule group generate alerts when free space is below the defined threshold. The Check Free Disk Space script classifies each local volume in one of the following categories:

- Exchange 2003 transaction log file volume

- Exchange 2003 SMTP queue directory volume

- Both SMTP queue directories and transaction log file volume

- None of the above categories, and has neither transaction log files nor SMTP queue directories

The script generates warnings and errors based on the threshold breached. For example, if the threshold was breached and a warning was generated, and no action was taken, then the problem is likely to continue. If disk space use grows to a critical point, other thresholds might be breached, in which case more severe alerts are generated.

Each category includes an absolute threshold and a percentage threshold. If you want to customize thresholds, you must determine what the percentage threshold should be, relative to the absolute threshold.

This group includes the following Event Rules:

- **Exchange 2003 Transaction log drive is low on disk space**   An alert is generated when MOM event 9976 occurs. This event signifies that both the percentage and absolute amount of free disk space are below the current warning thresholds for a volume containing Exchange transaction log files.

- **Exchange 2003 Simple Mail Transfer Protocol (SMTP) Queue and Transaction log drive is low on disk space**   An alert is generated when MOM event 9978 occurs. This event signifies that both the percentage and absolute amount of disk free space are below the current warning thresholds for a volume containing both Exchange transaction log files and queues.

- **Exchange 2003 Simple Mail Transfer Protocol (SMTP) Queue drive is low on disk space**   An alert is generated when MOM event 9974 occurs. This event signifies that both the percentage and absolute amount of disk free space are below the current warning thresholds for a volume containing SMTP queues.

- **Exchange 2003 Simple Mail Transfer Protocol (SMTP) Queue drive is very low on disk space**   An alert is generated when MOM event 9973 occurs. This event signifies that both the percentage and absolute amount of disk free space are below the current warning thresholds for a volume containing SMTP queues. This is a more severe alert to notify you when free space is critically below the threshold.

- **Low free disk space**   An alert is generated when MOM event 9972 occurs. This event signifies that both the percentage and absolute amount of disk free space are below the current warning thresholds for a local disk. For Exchange servers, this event refers to volumes other than those containing Exchange transaction log files or Exchange queue files.

- **Exchange 2003 Simple Mail Transfer Protocol (SMTP) Queue and Transaction log drive is very low on disk space**   An alert is generated when MOM event 9977 occurs. This event signifies that both the percentage and absolute amount of disk free space are below the current Critical Error thresholds for a volume containing both Exchange transaction log files and queues. You should resolve this situation immediately, because it is time-consuming to recover from running out of space on the transaction log volume.

- **Check free disk space**   This is the underlying script that checks the percentage of free space of each local disk. By default, it runs every 30 minutes.

- **Very low free disk space** An alert is generated when MOM event 9971 occurs. This event signifies that both the percentage and absolute amount of disk free space are below the current warning thresholds for a local disk. For Exchange servers, this event refers to volumes other than those containing Exchange transaction log files or Exchange queue files.

- **Exchange 2003 Transaction log drive is very low on disk space** An alert is generated when MOM event 9975 occurs. This event signifies that both the percentage and absolute amount of disk free space are below the current warning thresholds for a volume containing Exchange transaction log files.

Mail Queue Thresholds

The two tracked types of queues in this Rule Group are SMTP queues and MTA queues. The Rules in this Rule Group check for the size of the queues to see if messages are processed in a timely manner.

> **Note** If the Exchange organization experiences heavy traffic on a regular basis, the thresholds for the queues might need to be adjusted accordingly.

This group includes the following Performance Processing Rules:

- **Exchange Information Store service Queue of Messages to MTA > 50** This Rule tracks the current number of messages in transit to MSExchangeMTA. It uses the MSExchangeIS Transport Driver performance object.

- **Exchange 2003: SMTP: Local Retry Queue > 50** This Rule tracks the message queue of those messages waiting to be delivered to the database that have previously failed delivery. It tracks the SMTP Server object and its Total Retry Queue Length counter.

- **Exchange 2003: SMTP: Messages Pending Routing > 50** This Rule tracks the number of messages that are categorized but are not routed. It uses the SMTP Server object and its Messages Pending Routing counter.

- **Public Folder Replication: PF Receive Queue consistently > 10 deep** This Rule tracks the Public Folder Replication Receive queue. It uses the MSExchangeIS Public object and the Receive Queue Size counter. Most of the time, this value should be close to zero. When the queue depth is consistently greater than 10, the public folders are not synchronizing with other servers.

- **Mailbox Store: Receive Queue > 25** This Rule tracks the MSExchangeIS Mailbox object and its Receive Queue Size counter. Receive Queue Size is the number of messages in the mailbox store receive queue.

- **Information Store Transport Temp Table Entries > 600**   This Rule tracks the current number of entries in the Microsoft Exchange Information Store service Temp Table that is used by Exchange Transport. It uses the MSExchangeIS Transport Driver object and the TempTable Current counter.

- **MTA Queue Length per Connection > 50**   This Rule uses the MSExchangeMTA Connections object and the Queue Length counter. This counter tracks the outstanding messages queued for transfer to the database and the Pending Reroute queue.

- **Exchange 2003: SMTP: Remote Queue > 500**   This Rule uses the SMTP Server object and the Remote Queue Length counter. It tracks the remote queues, which send messages to other servers. This is a total number for all remote queues.

- **Mailbox Store: Send Queue > 25**   This Rule uses the MSExchangeIS Mailbox object and the Send Queue Size counter. It tracks the number of messages awaiting transfer from the Microsoft Exchange Information Store service to the IIS.

- **Exchange 2003: SMTP: Remote Retry Queue > 500**   This Rule uses the SMTP Server object and Remote Retry Queue Length counter to track the number of messages in the remote queue that cannot be sent to a destination server.

- **Exchange 2003: SMTP: Messages in SMTP Queue Directory > 500**   This Rule tracks the message number of the queue stored on the physical disk. It uses the SMTP NTFS Store Driver object and the Messages In Queue Directory counter.

- **MTA Work Queue > 50**   This Rule tracks the number of messages not yet processed to completion by the MTA. It uses the MSExchangeMTA object and the Work Queue Length counter.

- **Exchange 2003: SMTP: Local Queue > 50**   This Rule uses the SMTP Server object and Local Queue Length counter to track the queue of messages awaiting delivery to the Microsoft Exchange Information Store service.

- **Information Store Queue of Messages from MTA > 25**   This Rule tracks the number of messages in transit from the MTA to the Exchange store. It uses the MSExchangeIS Transport Driver object and the Current Message From MSExchangeMTA counter.

- **Exchange 2003: SMTP: Categorizer Queue > 50**   This Rule tracks the Categorizer queue through the SMTP Server object and Categorizer Queue Length counter. This queue is discussed earlier in the chapter.

Server Configuration and Security

Exchange Management Pack includes Rules to check for and monitor server configuration and security issues. For example, Rules included monitor anonymous SMTP relaying, log file truncation, /3GB switch status, and so on.

This Rule Group includes the following Rules:

- **Verify that the IIS lockdown wizard started** This Rule runs the Microsoft Operations Manager\Rules\Advanced\Scripts\Exchange 2003 - Verify IIS Lockdown script to determine if IIS Lockdown Wizard has been started by verifying registry keys. IIS Lockdown applies only to Windows 2000 servers. On newer servers, the script does not run. The script generates event 8144 when the IIS Lockdown Wizard does not start.

- **SMTP Virtual Server that relays anonymously** A virtual SMTP server can be used to relay anonymously. When you allow anonymous access to your SMTP virtual server and allow all IPs to relay through this virtual server, an alert is generated.

- **Mailboxes homed on a front-end server** When a front-end server contains one or more mailboxes, users cannot access these mailboxes with Outlook Web Access. An alert with event ID 8203 is generated to notify you of the configuration.

- **Verify Message Tracking Log shares are locked down** This Rule runs the Microsoft Operations Manager\Rules\Advanced\Scripts\Exchange 2003 - Verify that Message Tracking Log shares are locked down script, which verifies that the permissions on your message tracking log directories do not contain the Everyone group. This script generates alert 8103 when permissions do contain the Everyone group.

- **URLScan ISAPI filter is disabled** When the URLScan Internet Server Application Programming Interface (ISAPI) filter is not running, an alert is generated, together with event ID 8164. This filter is important only to Windows 2000. It is used to protect Web server security from being compromised by examining HTTP header information and filtering requests based on the URLScan.ini configuration file.

- **Verify that the URLScan ISAPI filter is installed and running** This Rule runs a script to determine if the URLScan ISAPI filter is running.

- **Verify that SMTP Virtual Server cannot anonymously relay (SPAM prevention)** This Rule runs a script that uses Active Directory Service Interface (ADSI) and Collaboration Data Objects (CDO) to determine anonymous relay for each SMTP virtual server. The script generates event 8083 for each virtual server that allows anonymous relay.

- **Check for existence of mailboxes on Front-End Servers** This Rule runs a script to look for mailboxes on front-end servers. Event 8203 is generated for each front-end server that has a mailbox.

- **Verify if SSL should be required** This Rule runs a script to determine when SSL should be required for accessing a resource. If SSL is required and it is not installed, event 9110 is generated.

- **Exchange Transaction Log files are equal to or older than the maximum days allowed** The Microsoft Operations Manager\Rules\Processing Rule Groups\Microsoft Exchange 2003 Server\Server Health Monitoring\Server Configuration Monitoring\ Verify that the Log Files are being truncated by backup (by age modified) script generates an alert when log files are equal to or older than the maximum days configured in the settings.

- **SSL should be required to secure HTTP access to the Exchange server** The Rule generates an alert when there is a server configuration that allows for non-SSL data transmission of sensitive data. Configure Secure Sockets Layer (SSL) for any back-end HTTP virtual server that accepts anonymous and basic authentication and always configure SSL for any front-end server.

- **Message Tracking Logs have 'Everyone' group listed in the ACL permission** To prevent unauthorized users from reading the Message Tracking Log, remove the Everyone group from the access control list (ACL) permission. If this permission is given, an alert is generated.

- **Circular Logging setting is incorrect** For a storage group that must have circular logging enabled, this Rule generates an alert when it is disabled. Similarly, for a storage group that must have circular logging disabled, this Rule generates an alert when it is enabled.

- **Verify that the Log Files are being truncated by backup (by age modified)** The script generates one event per storage group that contains transaction log files greater than or equal to the maximum number of days old allowed. It runs the following script to do this: Microsoft Operations Manager\Rules\Advanced\Scripts\Exchange 2003 - Verify Log Files Are Being Truncated (by age modified) and generates event 8183 when the log files are equal to or greater than two days old, by default.

- **Verify that the SMTP directories are on an NTFS formatted drive** This Rule runs a script to verify that each SMTP directory per SMTP virtual server is on an NTFS file system formatted drive.

- **Verify Circular Logging setting for each Storage Group** The Microsoft Operations Manager\Rules\Advanced\Scripts\Exchange 2003 - Verify Circular Logging settings are correct for each Storage Group script used by this Rule determines whether the circular logging setting is correct for each storage group. The script generates one event per storage group that does not have the circular logging state set correctly.

■ **Value of the HeapDeCommitFreeBlockThreshold registry key is incorrect** On servers with one gigabyte of physical memory, the HKEY_LOCAL_MACHINE\SYSTEM\CurrentControlSet\Control\Session Manager\HeapDecommitFreeBlockThreshold key in the registry should be set to **262144** to help reduce heap fragmentation. This Rule generates an alert when the registry value is different.

■ **Check the value of the HeapDeCommitFreeBlockThreshold registry key** This Rule uses the Microsoft Operations Manager\Rules\Advanced\ Scripts\Exchange 2003 - Check value of HeapDeCommitFreeBlockThreshold registry key script to retrieve the total amount of physical memory on the server and verify that the value for the registry key HKEY_LOCAL_MACHINE\SYS-TEM\CurrentControlSet\Control\Session Manager\HeapDecommitFreeBlock-Threshold is set to **262144** if the computer has equal to or greater than one gigabyte of physical memory.

■ **Verify that Message Tracking is enabled**   This Rule runs a script to determine if Message Tracking is enabled and generates an alert when it is not.

■ **SMTP directories are not on an NTFS formatted drive**   This Rule runs a script to determine if the Queue, Pick Up, and BadMail SMTP directories are not on an NTFS drive.

■ **Message Tracking is not enabled**   You must enable Message Tracking to track undelivered messages and troubleshoot mail flow problems. Event 8043 and an alert are generated when message tracking is disabled.

■ **IIS Lockdown was not found on a server**   On Windows 2000 servers, Exchange runs the IIS Lockdown Wizard. When it is not run, an alert is generated.

Server Performance Thresholds

The Server Performance Thresholds Rules group checks performance counters that can indicate poor performance. These counters include remote procedure call (RPC) requests, disk reads and writes, and CPU use.

The following performance processing Rules are included:

■ **MSExchangeIS:RPC latency > 200 ms**   This Rule checks the latency of RPC requests every minute. If the average latency over five minutes exceeds 200 milliseconds (ms), an alert is generated.

■ **MSExchangeIS: RPC Requests > 25**   This Rule tracks the number of RPC requests serviced by the Microsoft Exchange Information Store service at a particular time. Up to 100 RPC requests can be handled at the same time. However, the value is typically quite low, less than ten, when the server is functioning normally.

- **Disk Write Latencies > 50 ms** When disk write latencies are above 50 milliseconds, an alert is generated.

- **ESE Log Generation Checkpoint Depth > 800** The Microsoft Exchange Information Store service varies startup time based on the log generation checkpoint depth. When this value is above 1000, all databases in the affected storage group are disconnected. When the value increases above the 800 threshold, an alert is generated.

- **Average CPU > 90% for 15 minutes** When the CPU is idle less than ten percent of the time, an alert is generated. Continuous CPU execution of non-idle threads can indicate a hung thread or overall increased server load.

- **Information Store Private Bytes > 1 GB** When a process allocates bytes that cannot be shared, these bytes are named private bytes. When the Microsoft Exchange Information Store service runs at a high stress level for prolonged periods of time, the private bytes can exceed the threshold, which generates an alert.

- **Information Store Virtual Bytes > 2.9 GB** Virtual Bytes is the current size in bytes of the virtual address space the process is using. Use of virtual address space does not necessarily imply corresponding use of either disk or main memory pages. Virtual space is finite, and by using too much, the process can limit its ability to load libraries. When the virtual bytes are greater than the 2.9-gigabyte threshold, an alert is generated.

- **DSAccess:LDAP Search Time > 50 ms avg. over 5 minutes** If the average DSAccess search time is above 50 milliseconds for more than five minutes an alert is generated. This counter measures only the search time for queries over LDAP originating from DSAccess. Long search times for these queries do not necessarily indicate that Active Directory is also experiencing excessive latency. High values for this counter are not necessarily a problem, unless other problems are detected on the server, such as growing SMTP queues.

- **Disk Read Latencies > 50 ms** When disk read latencies are above 50 milliseconds, an alert is generated.

- **Outlook Mobile Access: Last response time> 60 sec** When the Outlook Mobile Access server response time value is greater than 60 seconds, an alert is generated.

SMTP Remote Queues Thresholds

The Rules in this Rule group monitor SMTP queues intended for remote transport. This Rule Group includes the following two Event Rules:

- **Alert for problems in remote Simple Mail Transfer Protocol (SMTP) queues**   When parameters specified in the Verify Remote SMTP Queues Rule are not met, an alert is generated.

- **Verify remote Simple Mail Transfer Protocol (SMTP) queues**   This Rule runs a script every hour to determine remote SMTP queue state. The script generates an event when the specified number in the NumberOfMessages parameter exceeds a certain threshold. By default, the NumberOfMessages value is 200.

Verify Windows Hotfixes

The Rules in the Windows Hotfixes group verify whether all specified Windows hotfixes are installed on servers running Exchange 2003. If a specified hotfix is not installed, an alert is generated.

This Rule Group includes the following Event Rules:

- **Verify required Windows hotfixes**   This Rule runs a script every day to check for hotfixes. You can specify the hotfixes for which the script searched through the HotfixID parameter. The script generates event 9017, listing all required hotfixes that are not installed.

- **The required Windows hotfix is not installed**   When a required hotfix is not installed, this Rule generates an alert.

Performance Counter Logging

This Rule Group contains the rules that log information about the use of the Exchange server and the extent that the server resources are being used. The following child Rule Groups are included:

- Exchange Utilization and Performance
- Server Resource Utilization

Each of the child Rule Groups is discussed next.

Exchange Utilization and Performance Rule Group

The Rules in this Rule Group include performance data about various Exchange components.

The Rules track performance data for the following components:

- **ActiveSync Utilization**   The performance data for ActiveSync use includes I/O requests, notifications sent, notifications received, and number of users.

- **Antivirus**   This Rule Group records the Exchange antivirus utilization by using Exchange performance counters.

- **Client Monitoring**   This Rule Group records performance counters relating to the collection of client performance data by the Exchange server that is sent by Outlook clients newer than Outlook 2002. Data such as RPCs sent and received, number of clients, and latencies is included.

- **DSAccess and Active Directory**   This Rule Group records the utilization of DSAccess to query Active Directory.

- **ESE Database**   Included performance data in this Rule Group are table opens, cache size, and log checkpoint depth.

- **IMAP4 Utilization**   This Rule Group records use of the IMAP4 protocol, such as connections and commands.

- **Mail Queue Logging**   Both MTA and SMTP performance data are included in this Rule Group.

- **Mailbox Store Utilization**   The performance data in this Rule Group tracks mailbox store use. Data, such as local deliveries, messages submitted, client logons, uptime, and recipients is included.

- **Message Transfer Agent Utilization**   This Rule Group records utilization of the message transfer agent (MTA).

- **Outlook Mobile Access Utilization**   This Rule Group records utilization of Outlook Mobile Access.

- **Outlook Web Access Utilization**   This Rule Group records the use of Outlook Web Access.

- **POP3 Utilization**   This Rule Group records utilization of the POP3 protocol

- **Public Folder Store Utilization**   This Rule Group records utilization of Exchange public stores.

- **Remote Procedure Calls**   This Rule Group records data on RPC utilization, such as requests, packets, and packet latency.

- **SMTP Utilization**   This Rule Group records data on SMTP utilization, such as bytes sent, bytes received, messages sent, messages submitted, messages received, and messages delivered.

Server Resource Utilization Rule Group

The Rules in this Rule Group log performance counter information about how the Exchange server is functioning. This data is logged for both the Exchange 2003 views and reports. The following child Rule Groups are included:

- **CPU Usage Logging**   The Rules in this Rule Group log the total CPU usage and the CPU used by several important Exchange-related processes.

- **Disk Capacity Logging**   The Rules in this Rule Group log performance counters that record the available megabytes and percentage of free space for all logical disks.

- **Disk Performance Logging**   The Rules in this Rule Group log the performance counters associated with disk performance: disk read and write rates and latencies and the current disk queue lengths.

- **Memory Usage Logging**   This Rule Group monitors global memory usage and memory usage specific to Exchange.

- **Network Usage Logging**   The Rules in this Rule Group monitor the usage of the network interfaces.

Generating System Reports and Statistics

The Exchange 2003 Management Pack includes several views and reports to help you quickly identify Exchange issues. With these views and reports, you can analyze and graph performance data to understand usage trends, do accurate load balancing, and manage system capacity.

Report Types

Exchange reports cover the following:

- **Exchange 2000 and 2003 Health Monitoring and Operations Reports**
  You can use the monitoring and operations reports to analyze database sizes, disk usage, mailboxes, server availability, and the configuration of Exchange servers. For example, you can list database sizes for Exchange servers, where database size (in megabytes) is presented for each server, storage group, and database. The reports in this category are as follows:

- **Exchange Disk Usage**   This report provides data about servers running Exchange based on disk performance counters, presenting daily averages for each counter.

- **Exchange Server Availability** This report provides the percentage of server availability for Exchange servers during a specified time period and also lists the categories of failure types that could lead to a server being unavailable.

- **Exchange Server Configuration** This report provides configuration information including computer and operating systems configuration and local disk information.

- **Exchange 2003 Outlook Client Monitoring** This report gives you the results of analysis data collected by Exchange 2003 servers monitoring Outlook clients for the end user's experience in terms of response times and errors.

- **Exchange Mailboxes** This report shows the distribution of mailboxes across storage groups and databases for Exchange servers.

- **Exchange Database Sizes** This report shows the total database size on each server, in addition to the individual components of the database. For example, if a database contains both a mailbox store and a public folder store, this report shows the size of each.

> **Note** Exchange Health Monitoring and Operations reports are available only for servers running Exchange 2000 Server and Exchange Server 2003. The other Exchange reports apply to servers running Exchange 5.5 or later.

- **Exchange 2000 and 2003 Protocol Usage Reports** The protocol usage reports obtain data about usage and activity levels for the mail protocols that are used by Exchange, such as POP3, IMAP4, and SMTP. You can also obtain usage and activity level reports for Exchange components, such as Microsoft Exchange Information Store service, mailbox store, public folder store, Exchange MTA, and Outlook Web Access. These reports use key performance counters for operations conducted in a specific time period. The reports include data for Exchange 2000 servers only when the Exchange 2000 Management Pack for Microsoft Operations Manager is installed.

- **Exchange 2000 and 2003 Traffic Analysis Reports** The traffic analysis reports summarize Exchange mail traffic patterns by message count and size for both Recipient and Sender domains. For example, the report Mail Delivered: Top 100 Sender Domains by Message Size provides a list of the top 100 sender domains sorted by message size during a specific time period, as reported in the Exchange message tracking logs. The reports include data for Exchange 2000 servers only when the Exchange 2000 Management Pack for Microsoft Operations Manager is installed.

- **Exchange Capacity Planning Reports** By analyzing your daily client logons and messages sent and received, in addition to work queues, the capacity planning reports show the Exchange server resource usage and help you plan for current and future capacity requirements.

- **Exchange Mailbox and Folder Sizes Reports**   You can use these reports to monitor the size of Exchange mailboxes and folders and to determine your highest growth areas. The reports in this category include top 100 mailboxes by size and message count, and top 100 public folders by size and message count.

- **Exchange Performance Analysis Report**   The Queue Sizes report summarizes Exchange performance counters and helps you to analyze queue performance.

Generating Reports

After you choose a report to generate, you can select options. For example, you can select which servers to include in the report, and the date range.

> **Note**   You must have a printer installed before viewing and generating reports.

A basic report you can use that provides a summary of Exchange availability is the Exchange Availability report. It is part of the Exchange 2000 and 2003 Health Monitoring and Operations Reports group.

To create the report:

1. Select Exchange Server Availability in the Exchange 2000 and 2003 Health Monitoring and Operations Reports group. In the right window pane, there are options to select servers and a time period, as shown in Figure 17-7.

2. Select the desired servers and time periods.

3. Next, you have several output options. You can print the report, save it to HTML, or preview it. A sample Exchange Availability report is shown in Figure 17-8.

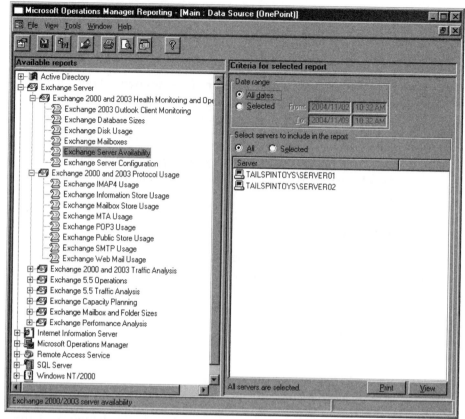

Figure 17-7   Report options

You can archive past reports and generate multiple reports. Archiving reports is useful for monitoring past state and performance data. To save time and generate all reports, and save them to file for later analysis, you can generate multiple reports. To generate multiple reports, from the menu bar, select File, and then select Print or View Multiple Reports.

To archive reports, from the menu bar, select Tools, and then select Archive Previous Reports. With this option, existing reports are archived in the Archive directory in the HTML reports directory categorized by the date of generation.

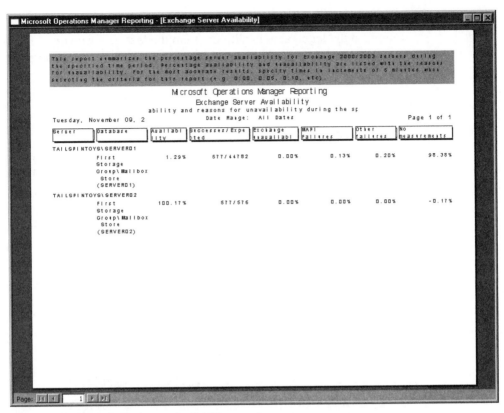

Figure 17-8   Sample Exchange Availability report

Troubleshooting Exchange Management Pack Deployments

When you run Configuration Wizard, you may encounter errors or problems in deployment. This section provides some solutions, best practices, and sources of information for troubleshooting Exchange Management Pack.

Checking the Configuration Log File

When Configuration Wizard runs, it generates a configuration log file at the end. That configuration file includes the settings specific to your organization. You should review the configuration log file to understand potential causes of failure. Configuration Wizard stores the configuration log file in a temporary directory on the hard disk.

To access the ConfigurationLog.xml file, click Start and then click Run. Type %**temp**%**ConfigurationLog.xml** to access the file.

> **Note**   If the logon user is different from the last user who ran Configuration Wizard, the log file will not be found, because the %temp% parameter will point to a different directory.

Checking the Configuration File

In addition to the configuration log file, Configuration Wizard also generates a configuration file used to configure Exchange Management Pack. This includes configuration settings in XML format. This is the file that you can import and export using the command-line configuration tool. You can access the file both through the command-line tool and through Configuration Wizard. Configuration Wizard has an option to save the XML configuration file in the summary page before the configuration is implemented, as shown in Figure 17-9.

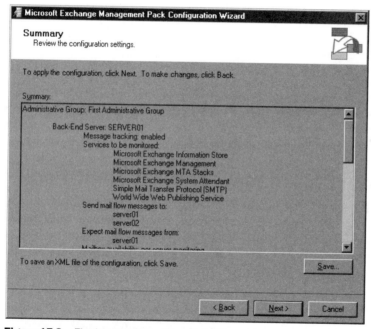

Figure 17-9   Final page of Configuration Wizard

ExMOM 8203 Alert

This alert occurs if you selected a front-end server as the home for the Mailbox Access account mailbox. Front-end servers should not be used to store mailboxes. To fix the problem, move the mailbox to a back-end server or disable one or both of the following Rules:

- Microsoft Exchange Server 2003\Health Monitoring and Performance Thresholds\Server Configuration and Security Monitoring\Check for existence of mailboxes on Front-End Servers

- Microsoft Exchange Server 2003\Health Monitoring and Performance Thresholds\Server Configuration and Security Monitoring\Mailboxes homed in a front-end server

Permission-related Errors When Running the Configuration Tool over the Network

The following error occurs if you attempt to run the configuration tool from a networked mapped drive:

```
Error: Request for the permission of type
System.Security.Permissions.EnvironmentPermission, mscorlib, Version=1.0.5000.0,
Culture=neutral, PublicKeyToken=b77a5c561934e089 failed
```

This error is the result of new security restrictions in the .NET Framework to protect your computer and your network. The Exchange Management Pack Configuration tool must be installed locally to run.

The configuration tool must be installed in a location that belongs to a security policy group with FullTrust permissions. While local drives belong to the "Zone – MyComputer" security policy group, which has FullTrust permissions, network shares and mapped network drives belong to the "Zone – Intranet" security policy group, which has LocalIntranet permissions and might prevent the Configuration Application from executing.

Boolean Data Type Formatting

The configuration file, ConfigurationLog.xml, is in XML format. The entries are case sensitive and accept Boolean values, as defined by W3C. Boolean supports binary-valued logic and can have the following literals: {true, false, 1, 0}.

> **More Info**   For more information about Boolean values, see *http://www.w3.org/TR/2001/REC-xmlschema-2-20010502/#boolean*.

Disabling Mail Flow

Using the wizard, you can disable MAPI logon, message tracking, service monitoring, and mail flow. Disabling mail flow requires extra configuration. To disable mail flow, ensure that the check boxes are not checked in Configuration Wizard during mail flow configuration setup. Configuration Wizard configures mail flow automatically. If you select one server to send to another server, then the wizard configures the second server to wait for messages coming from the first server.

MAPI Logon

When deploying Exchange Management Pack and configuring MAPI logon, ensure that the display name and the alias in Active Directory for the test mailboxes that are used with MAPI logon match exactly. If the display name and alias do not match, then Automatic Name Resolution might not work.

Best Practices

When using Exchange Management Pack with Microsoft Operations Manager, it is important to keep in mind the type of topology that is used in the Exchange organization. Planning, installation, configuration, and use all depend on the way the organization is structured. The centralized, distributed, and hybrid models were discussed in the chapter.

Some best practices for installation and use have already been mentioned in the chapter. For example, before installing Exchange Management Pack, you should evaluate the current monitoring solution, if any, number of servers to monitor, expected database sizes, desired management packs, and so on. In using Exchange Management Pack, configure the Alerts and Rules for your environment. To maximize performance, you can also disable unneeded Rules, set polling intervals for data, create custom Rules for special applications and monitored components, and generate reports to keep track of server and component performance and availability.

Chapter 18

Tuning Exchange Performance

About This Chapter

This chapter provides information about how to tune and improve the performance of Microsoft Exchange Server 2003. Getting your server(s) to operate at peak efficiency is important if you are going to get the most out of Exchange Server 2003. There are a number of new tuning enhancements that you can use, such as link state traffic and virtual address space management.

Storage Configuration for Exchange Server 2003

The following sections provide recommended storage configuration for the various types of Exchange 2003 servers.

SMTP Bridgehead Server

If your Exchange server is a Simple Mail Transfer Protocol (SMTP) bridgehead server, generally the best disk layout is to create one partition that spans multiple disks. Messages arrive on the SMTP interface and are written to the Mailroot directory (which should be on an NTFS file system-formatted system) before being passed through the Advanced Queuing Engine. To get the best performance, span the Mailroot directory over as many disks as possible. A set of disks acting as a single unit is the best way to accomplish this. A set of hardware redundant array of inexpensive disks (RAID) configuration is a good way to go and is largely dictated by the number of disk spindles available, as shown in Table 18-1.

Table 18-1   RAID Recommendations

Number of disks	Recommended hardware RAID level and partitioning
2	RAID1; mirroring; one partition
4 or more	RAID0+1; data striping and mirroring; one partition

Because bridgehead servers primarily pass e-mail messages back and forth between other mail servers, it is important to relocate the SMTP Mailroot directory to the fastest partition.

Note   If your hardware RAID controller has a mirrored, battery-backed, write-back cache, and it allows you to tune the read/write cache ratio, set the ratio to 100 percent write because the server can only acknowledge receipt of a message after it has been written to the disk. Therefore, the faster the server can write to the disk, the more responsive the server is to other computers. Although the message contents must be reread before being relayed to the next computer, the SMTP service has an open file handle to the data, and it can retrieve the contents from the NTFS cache. This doesn't just apply to the SMTP bridgehead servers, but also to any other bridgehead server in your environment.

X.400 Bridgehead Server or Other Connector Server

If your Exchange 2003 server contains many X.400 connectors or if it connects to other messaging systems, such as Lotus cc:Mail, Lotus Notes, Novell GroupWise, or Microsoft Mail, create a separate disk partition for transaction logs, providing you have a sufficient number of spindles. Messages that use these Exchange connectors move data through the Store.exe process and, if the server is under a heavy load, additional performance is gained by splitting the transaction logs from the database. Also. be aware that many connectors use mailboxes to handle their messages, which means that they go through the store to send and receive messages. From an input/ output (I/O) perspective, the I/O requirement of the transaction logs is much less than the databases themselves. Hence, on servers that host connectors, it is reasonable to conclude that the disks on which the databases are installed should be the faster disks. This would be the case on relay and bridgehead servers. Generally, these servers do not host mailboxes for end users. Instead, they host connectors and connect routing groups, which means that you will need faster I/O to move messages through the connectors to their final destinations.

The number of disk spindles available affects your hardware RAID configuration, as shown in Table 18-2.

Table 18-2   RAID Recommendations

Number of disks	Recommended hardware RAID level and partitioning
2 to 4	RAID1; mirroring; two partitions (operating system and pagefile on partition 1 and Exchange on partition 2)
5	RAID5 (drive C) for three disks; binaries and database
	RAID1 (drive D) for two disks; log files
6	RAID5 (drive C) for three disks; binaries and database
	RAID1 (drive D) for two disks; log files
	No RAID (drive E) for one disk; pagefile
N*2	RAID 0+1: Use the number of disks in your strip set and double it for the mirrored disk array.

Although the 6-disk configuration does not use a RAID partition for the pagefile, if high availability of the server is critical, locate the pagefile on a protected partition.

Mailbox and Public Folder Servers

The basic principle when configuring mailbox and public folder servers, is to ensure that your transaction logs are held on a separate spindle to achieve the fastest response time for your users. In addition, this spindle set should be dedicated only to the transaction logs. If you intend to create multiple storage groups on the server, your number one priority, again, is to split the logs onto dedicated spindles. However, to gain any performance, you must have a dedicated spindle set for each storage group's databases as well. Therefore, there are two efforts you can engage in to increase performance. The first is placing your transaction logs on a separate spindle so that control is returned to the user faster. The second is to place your databases for each storage group on a separate spindle so that the overall system performance is improved.

> **Note**   If disk I/O is a primary consideration, then you need to understand that the database activities represent roughly 90 percent of the disk I/O and the transaction log work represents the other 10 percent. That being said, if you need to optimize your Exchange servers for performance and not necessarily for the fastest end-user experience, then your databases should also be quarantined on their own spindle(s). The best case scenario is to have both the databases and the transaction logs quarantined and writing to the fastest disks you can reasonably afford.

You can split the properties database (.edb) files from the streaming database (.stm) files by placing them on separate disks. However, in most cases, you will not need to do this. You will want to do this when you expect to service only Internet Message Access Protocol version 4rev1 (IMAP4) and Post Office Protocol version 3 (POP3) users with large attachments. In this example, the read/write size of the e-mail messages might be larger than the 4 KB that is typically seen with MAPI users on an .edb database. In this case, splitting these files is recommended because you'll be writing larger amounts of information to the .stm file, which should be placed on faster disks than the .edb file.

MAPI and Microsoft Outlook Web Access clients read and write data to and from the .edb file. Technically, these clients communicate to the Store.exe process. Therefore, they have no understanding of .edb files versus .stm files. All other clients use the .stm file. Table 18-3 shows the preferred location that is used by different clients.

Table 18-3   Preferred Client Storage Locations

Client type	Submitting data	Retrieving data
Outlook in MAPI mode	.edb files	.edb files
POP3	.stm files (through SMTP)	.stm files
IMAP4	.stm files (through SMTP)	.stm files
Outlook Web Access	.stm files (but full promotion to .edb files)	.edb files
Installable File System (IFS)	.stm files	.stm files
SMTP	.stm files	Not applicable
SMTP (with MAPI data)	.stm files (but full promotion to .edb files)	Not applicable
Microsoft ActiveX Data Objects (ADO) or OLE DB	.stm files	.stm files
Collaboration Data Objects (CDO) for Exchange 2000	.stm files	.stm files
CDO 1.21	.edb files	.edb files

Note that as disks become larger, it is tempting to purchase fewer, but larger disks to handle user data. Unfortunately, larger disks are often slower. Therefore, you may have sufficient physical disk space, but the performance may not be sufficient for the user load. Ensure that you are purchasing the fastest disks possible for your Exchange deployment and that you have enough of them. In summary, the following are your best guidelines for configuring mailbox servers:

- Create a RAID1 partition for Windows and Exchange binary files.

- Put the pagefile on a separate RAID1 spindle. For mailbox servers, you should never put the pagefile on a non-RAID partition because the loss of the volume causes the server to stop.

- Create one dedicated fault-tolerant partition for each storage group for the transaction logs (for example, RAID1 or RAID0+1). A two-disk RAID1 partition should yield approximately 300 sequential write I/O operations a second. See the Disk I/O Discussion section for additional information.

- Create at least one fault-tolerant partition for your databases. If you have only one array, put all databases on this array. If you have multiple arrays, use one array for each storage group (databases only).

Disk I/O Discussion

How do you know if your drives are healthy? The simplest way to check is to measure how long it takes for a read and write (referred to as the read and write latency) to occur. Take a look at the physical disk\sec per read and sec per write counters for your database drives. The server reports this in seconds, but we generally talk about it in milliseconds (ms). Are the latencies less than 20 ms? If so, this is excellent. If the latencies are larger than 20 ms, it is time to take a look at your disk usage. Do the physical disk\disk transfers/sec counters exceed the maximum throughput of your drives? If you don't know, then you will need to learn how to determine the maximum throughput of your drives.

The best way to determine maximum throughput is to measure it. The Jetstress tool is an excellent way to measure the maximum throughput of your disks. However, to use Jetstress, you have to test your disks in a lab, not in a production environment. So what do you do if you already have a server in production and suspect you have exceeded the maximum throughput? The best thing you can do is make an estimate. Here is a method for doing this:

1. Most disks can do between 130 to 180 I/Os per second.

2. Exchange typically has a Read-to-Write (R:W) ratio of 3:1 or 2:1.

3. It is recommended that you plan to use less than 80 percent disk utilization at peak load.

Now, RAID 0 (striping) has the same cost as no RAID. Reads and writes happen once. RAID 0+1 requires two disk I/Os for every write (the mirrored data is written twice). RAID 5 requires four disk I/Os for every write (two reads, two writes to calculate and write parity). Essentially, this translates into the values as shown in Tables 18-4, 18-5, and 18-6. These are the values you should use when you estimate how much disk throughput is available for users during peak load.

Table 18-4   Estimated Maximum Disk Throughput for No RAID or RAID 0

R:W ratio\disk speed	130 I/Os per second	180 I/Os per second
3:1	104 I/OPS	144 I/OPS
2:1	104 I/OPS	144 I/OPS

Table 18-5   Estimated Maximum Disk Throughput for RAID 0+1 or RAID 10

R:W ratio\disk speed	130 I/Os per second	180 I/Os per second
3:1	83 I/OPS	115 I/OPS
2:1	78 I/OPS	108 I/OPS

Table 18-6   Estimated Maximum Disk Throughput for RAID 5

R:W ratio\disk speed	130 I/Os per second	180 I/Os per second
3:1	59 I/OPS	82 I/OPS
2:1	52 I/OPS	72 I/OPS

The conservative approach will be to assume you can safely get a throughput of 80 I/Os per second for most disks, in a RAID 0+1 configuration. RAID 0+1 is generally recommended for most database drives.

If you have multiple drives (or "spindles") connected in a RAID configuration, multiply the throughput by the number of drives. Thus, ten disks in RAID 0+1 will safely support a load of 800 I/OPS. One customer recently changed disks, going from six small disks to three large disks. After that, users began seeing a lot of Outlook pop-ups while waiting for messages to open or change folders. When the disks were replaced with fewer, larger disks, the three disks were unable to deliver the I/O throughput that six disks were able to deliver. The disks were bottlenecked because I/O latency went up, and so did RPC latency as a consequence. The solution was to put more disks in the RAID configuration. While it might seem perfectly reasonable to move to fewer, larger disks, this example demonstrates how it can get your server into trouble if you reduce the overall I/O of the RAID configuration.

What if your disk's throughput is below the maximum, but the latencies are still high? Then, ensure you are not sharing Storage Area Network drives with another application. When Exchange is competing with another application for I/O, user experience suffers. If you are having a poor latency and think the throughputs are well below the disk maximum throughput, you will have to go back to your disk guru and start troubleshooting. In general, we do not recommend sharing database Storage Area Network spindles with other applications. Never share log drives with any other application because this significantly reduces the throughput as well.

Aligning Exchange I/O Operations with Storage Track Boundaries

Some physical disks maintain 64 sectors per track. When Windows creates a partition, it always does so starting at the sixty-fourth sector, therefore misaligning it with the underlying physical disk. To be certain of disk alignment, use Diskpar.exe, a disk partition tool provided in the Windows 2000 Resource Kit. Diskpar.exe is a command-line utility that can explicitly set the starting offset in the master boot record (MBR). By setting the starting offset, you can track alignment and improve disk performance. Exchange 2003 writes data in multiples of 4 KB I/O operations (4 KB for the databases and up to 32 KB for streaming files). Therefore, make sure that the starting offset is a multiple of 4 KB. Failure to do so may cause a single I/O operation spanning two tracks, causing performance degradation.

Optimizing Memory Usage

This section contains information about monitoring and optimizing memory usage on your servers. Exchange Server 2003 is a resource-hungry platform that will consume large amounts of memory. If the available virtual memory starts to fall too low (below 32 MB), you will begin to see errors recorded in the application log, which is viewable using the Event Viewer tool.

In the application log, an Event ID 9582 warning appears when the largest free block of virtual memory decreases to 32 MB. If the largest block decreases to 16 MB, an Event ID 9582 error appears again. In either case, you are getting close to a server failure and you should restart the Store.exe process at the earliest opportunity. Failure to act on these events can cause sporadic mail delivery and IMAIL conversion failures (Event ID 12800).

In Performance Logs and Alerts, monitor the following counters:

- **VM Largest Block Size counter in the MSExchangeIS object**   A healthy server has more than 200,000,000 bytes (200 MB) as the largest free block. If the value is lower, carefully monitor the server.

- **Pool Pages Bytes in the Memory object**   When the /3GB switch is used in the boot.ini file, memory sizes larger than 200 MB indicate a problem, except when backups are running. During backups, each page in the cache manager is copied into the pool page, which causes an increase in pool page size.

- **Pool Nonpaged Bytes in the Memory object**   When the /3GB switch is used in the boot.ini file, amounts larger than 100 MB indicate a problem.

- **Free System Page Table Entries in the Memory object**   Amounts less than 3000 bytes indicate a problem.

- **Working Set in the Process object**   An upward trend indicates a potential memory leak.

    If a server shows signs of low virtual address space (Event ID 9665), you should adjust the following settings:

    - If the server is running Windows 2000 Advanced Server or Windows Server 2003 and has 1 GB or more of physical memory, set the /3GB switch in the boot.ini file.

    - If the server is running Windows Server 2003 (any edition), configure the /USERVA switch registry key.

    - If the server is running Windows 2000, make sure that Windows 2000 SP3 or later is installed.

    - If the server is running Windows Server 2000 Advanced Server, configure the SystemPages registry key.

    - If the server has 1 GB or more of physical memory, set the HeapDeCommit-FreeBlockThreshold registry parameter.

    - If necessary, tune the store database cache size.

- **Event 9665**   When the Store.exe process starts, Exchange 2003 performs an optimal memory configuration check. If the memory settings are not optimal, you receive an Event 9665 message in the Event Viewer. This message appears in the following instances:

    - The server is running Windows 2000 and the SystemPages value in the registry is set outside the range of 24,000 to 31,000.

    - The server has 1 GB of memory or more and does not have the /3GB switch.

    - The server is running Windows Server 2003, has 1 GB of memory or more and the /3GB switch is set, but the /USERVA setting is not present or is outside the range of 3,030 to 2,970.

    If you see this event, check the SystemPages and HeapDeCommitFree-BlockThreshold settings in the registry, in addition to the /3GB switch and the /USERVA setting in the boot.ini file. SystemPages applies only to Windows 2000. What follows here are the recommendations for these configurations. Many of these configurations include registry value changes.

> **Warning**   Incorrectly editing the registry can cause serious problems that may require you to reinstall your operating system. Problems resulting from editing the registry incorrectly may not be able to be resolved. Before editing the registry, back up any valuable data.

If you want to turn off the memory configuration check, create the registry key shown in Table 18-7.

Table 18-7   Registry Key to Turn Off Memory Configuration Check

Path	HKEY_LOCAL_MACHINE\SYSTEM\CurrentControlSet\ Services\MSExchangeIS\ParametersSystem\
Parameter	Suppress Memory Configuration Notification
Type	REG_DWORD
Setting	1

Note   The memory configuration check does not occur on servers running Microsoft Small Business Server.

- **Setting the /3GB switch in the boot.ini file**   By default, Windows 2000 Advanced Server and Windows Server 2003 allocate 2 GB of virtual address space to user mode processes such as Store.exe. If a server has 1 GB or more of physical memory, set the /3GB switch in the boot.ini file to increase virtual address space.

More Info   For more information about the /3GB switch, see Microsoft Knowledge Base article 328882, "Exchange Memory Use and the 3GB Switch" (http://support.microsoft.com/default.aspx?scid=kb;en-us;328882).

The /3GB switch is designed for Windows 2000 Advanced Server and all editions of Windows Server 2003. Do not set the /3GB switch in Windows 2000 Standard Edition.

- **Configuring /USERVA and SystemPages**   If the server is running Windows 2000, you should set the SystemPages registry key to a value between 24,000 and 31,000. The SystemPages registry key is located in the following path:

    HKEY_LOCAL_MACHINE\SYSTEM\CurrentControlSet\Control\Session   Manager\Memory Management\SystemPages

If the server is running Windows Server 2003, set the SystemPages value to **zero**, and set the /USERVA=3030 parameter in the boot.ini file. These settings let you enter more system page table entries on the server, which is critical for systems that scale-up.

■ **Setting the HeapDeCommitFreeBlockThreshold registry key**   The `Heap-DeCommitFreeBlockThreshold` registry key controls the free space required before the heap manager decommits (or frees up) memory. The default is zero, which means that the heap manager decommits each 4-KB page that becomes available. Over time, virtual address space can become fragmented. On servers that have 1 GB or more of physical memory, you should set the registry key to a higher value to reduce fragmentation. Set the registry key as shown in Table 18-8, and then restart the server.

Table 18-8   HeapDeCommitFreeBlockThreshold Settings

Path	`HKEY_LOCAL_MACHINE\SYSTEM\CurrentControlSet\` `Control\Session Manager`
Parameter	HeapDeCommitFreeBlockThreshold
Type	`REG_DWORD`
Default	Zero
Recommended setting	262144
	This value is the number of blocks in decimal. This value corresponds with a hexadecimal value of 0x00040000.

Exchange Store and Extensible Storage Engine Tuning

Exchange 2003 can handle up to 25 databases per server, 20 for production and five for restore purposes, spread across five storage groups. There are some advantages to filling up a storage group with databases before creating a new storage group. Two advantages of doing this are reduced memory consumption and reduced disk overhead.

However, be aware of some tradeoffs when filling out the storage groups, as follows:

■ You can control logging only at the storage group level.

■ If one database in the group goes offline because of an error, the other databases in that group temporarily go offline and then reconnect (note that this scenario does not apply to out-of-disk-space errors).

■ Only one backup or restore process can occur in a single storage group at any one time.

■ Backing up one database in a storage group stops the online maintenance of all other databases in the storage group.

The most common solution uses a combination of storage groups and databases. For example, a server with two storage groups and three databases in each provides a good balance between performance, resource consumption, and manageability. If this server has sufficient disk spindles, consider using three storage groups with two databases in each. This design provides you with a smaller recovery window if parallel restore of online (streaming) backups is used.

Online Database Maintenance

Each mailbox and public folder store requires periodic online maintenance to be run. By default, each database is set to run online maintenance between the times of 01:00 and 05:00. Online maintenance performs a variety of tasks necessary to keep the store in good health. The tasks performed by the Microsoft Exchange Information Store service include:

1. Purge Indices (public and mailbox stores)

2. Tombstone Maintenance (public and mailbox stores)

3. Dumpster Cleanup (public and mailbox stores)

4. Public Folder Expiry (public stores)

5. Age Folder Tombstone (public stores)

6. Folder Conflict Aging (public stores)

7. Update Server Versions (public stores)

8. Cleanup Secure Folders (public stores)

9. Cleanup Deleted Mailboxes (mailbox stores)

10. Check Messages Table (public and mailbox stores)

If the maintenance window ends before one of the ten tasks above is completed, the last one running is recorded. The last task will be allowed to run until completion, which could exceed the maintenance window. During the next maintenance window, the Microsoft Exchange Information Store service determines the last task in progress and restarts the process, essentially picking up where it left off on the next task.

These operations, performed by online maintenance, have specific performance costs, and you should understand these costs before you implement an online maintenance strategy. One subroutine that is a part of online maintenance is conducting an Active Directory lookup for each user. The more users you have in each database, the more Active Directory searches are made. These searches are used to keep the mailbox store synchronized with any Active Directory changes (specifically looking for deleted mailboxes). The performance cost of this task is negligible on the Exchange server, but it can be significant on Active Directory, depending on the number of users, the number of databases, and the online maintenance times of each database. In a corporate scenario, the online maintenance typically occurs at night, when very few users are logged on and the load on Active Directory servers is very low. The extra domain controller load created by online maintenance should not be a problem in this scenario.

However, in a scenario such as a global deployment where the servers are always available, you may not find that you have Active Directory servers with downtime. In such a scenario, you can stagger the online maintenance schedules to ensure that the domain controllers are not overloaded.

Many of these tasks are disk intensive and only affect the server where the maintenance is being run. During this part of online maintenance, the server may be perceived by users as sluggish if many databases are set to perform online maintenance at the same time. Again, in corporate scenarios, this maintenance would occur at night when the server can easily handle the extra load. In a global data center, it may make sense to stagger the database schedule (in respect to each other on a single server) to spread disk-intensive tasks over a greater period of time.

Online backup requires additional consideration. Backing up an Exchange 2003 database stops the maintenance of any database in that storage group (maintenance restarts if the backup finishes before the maintenance interval has passed). If you have two databases in a single storage group and one is running online maintenance, if a backup is started against either database, the online defragmentation on the database (which is running online maintenance) is stopped. It is critical that the backup time for any database in a storage group not conflict with the maintenance times of any database in the same storage group. If it does, backup stops the online defragmenting part of the online maintenance and the database may never finish defragmenting.

The correct online maintenance strategy can be devised by examining the user profile, such as times of low activity. Note how many users, databases, and servers are in the site and coordinate this information with the online backup strategy.

The defragmentation of the database is performed by the Extensive Storage Engine, not by the Microsoft Exchange Information Store service. The defragmentation begins after at least one of the ten tasks listed above has been completed.

An important note to make about Microsoft Exchange Information Store maintenance and online defragmentation is the large number of changes made to the database. To maintain recoverability of the database, each of the changes made by these tasks is also transacted in the transaction logs. Depending upon the number of changes made in the database during these tasks, a large number of log files can be generated during the maintenance windows.

Backup schedules should also be monitored so they do not overlap with the Exchange Information Store maintenance schedule. Backup will not preempt the ten initial tasks performed by the Microsoft Exchange Information Store service, therefore they will run simultaneously. However, when initiating a backup of a database, the online defragmentation process is suspended until the backup is completed.

Message Promotion on Move Mailbox

Although Internet protocol clients such as IMAP4 and POP3 use the streaming store (.stm file) for reading and writing data, you should understand that the move mailbox function moves data into the .edb file. Therefore, clients who use POP3 and IMAP4 to access their mailboxes may see decreased performance after a mailbox has been moved between databases or servers. When logging on, message size is calculated and a MAPI to MIME conversion occurs in the memory of the server and on the disk of the server. In extreme cases, this can cause very large temporary files to be created on the Exchange 2003 Server.

If you move hundreds or thousands of IMAP4 and/or POP3 mailboxes, you can mitigate potential issues by using the following recommendations. On the destination Exchange server, do both of the following:

1. Make sure the TMP/TEMP environment variables point to a fast RAID0+1 spindle set (up to 12 disks for large mailbox servers). For stand-alone mailbox servers, the system environment TMP/TEMP variables should be adjusted. For clustered servers, the variables should be configured for the service account that the Cluster service is running under.

2. Set the following registry parameters, as shown in Table 18-9 and Table 18-10, to inform the store that it should use approximate instead of exact calculations for message sizes.

Table 18-9   Compatibility Setting (POP3svc)

Location	HKEY_LOCAL_MACHINE\System\CurrentControlSet\ Services\POP3svc\Parameters
Parameter	Compatibility
Type	REG_DWORD
Default setting	Not present
When to change	Change when you want the store to use approximate message size calculations.
	Changing this setting causes some older mail clients (such as Fetchmail) to break. Setting this registry key also breaks RFC-compliance for the POP3 protocol.
Recommended setting	0xfffffffe

Table 18-10   Compatibility Setting (IMAP4svc)

Location	HKEY_LOCAL_MACHINE\System\CurrentControlSet\ Services\IMAP4svc\Parameters
Parameter	Compatibility
Type	REG_DWORD
Default setting	Not present

Table 18-10 Compatibility Setting (IMAP4svc) (Continued)

When to change	Change when you want the store to use approximate message size calculations.
	Changing this setting causes some older mail clients (such as Fetchmail) to break. Setting this registry key also breaks RFC-compliance for the IMAP4 protocol.
Recommended setting	0xfffffffe

After you set these registry parameters, you must restart the Store.exe and Inetinfo processes.

Message Transfer Agent Tuning

Exchange 2003 does not include a Performance Optimization wizard; the majority of Exchange 2003 components are self-tuning. In scenarios in which only Exchange 2003 servers exist in an organization, the message transfer agent (MTA) does almost no processing and, therefore, does not need performance tuning. However, in a mixed environment, the MTA is used for all communications within a site, and possibly between sites, if site connectors using remote procedure calls (RPCs) or X.400 connectors are deployed. The MTA also processes messages coming from or going to other messaging systems, such as Lotus cc:Mail, Lotus Notes, Novell GroupWise, and Microsoft Mail.

In Exchange 2003, the MTA places a much greater load on system resources (CPU, memory, and disk) than in Exchange 5.5, because all messages now go through the Store.exe process. You should consider this increased load when planning the size of your hardware. In a large mixed Exchange 5.5 and Exchange 2000 or Exchange 2003 site, you may want to divide your servers into different routing groups, and dedicate one of the Exchange 2003 servers to handling the Exchange 2000 or Exchange 2003 to Exchange 5.5 MTA communication. The other Exchange 2003 servers in the site can use this dedicated bridgehead server to send messages to the Exchange 5.5 servers, which reduces the MTA processing overhead.

Let's take a look at some of the registry parameters that may require adjustment. Note that increasing the number of threads for a process does not always increase performance; in fact, it may decrease performance. In addition, ensure that you understand the ramifications of lowering or raising one value on the other parts of the Exchange system. For example, consider the relationship between Reliable Transfer Service (RTS) threads and Kernel threads in the MTA. RTS threads are responsible for putting data in the queues; Kernel threads take the data out and move it off the server. If the RTS threads' setting is too high, local queues fill quickly and may prevent the Kernel threads from reading the queue data, causing message transfer to slow.

MSExchangeMTA\Parameters Registry Key Settings

The registry parameters in this section can be found in the following registry key:

`HKEY_LOCAL_MACHINE\System\CurrentControlSet\Services\MSExchangeMTA\Parameters`

The following Table 18-11 through Table 18-18 illustrate, in detail, the parameters that you can set, along with notes and information about those parameters.

Table 18-11   DB Data Buffers Per Object Setting

Parameter	DB data buffers per object
Type	REG_DWORD
Explanation	This value is the number of database server buffers that are configured for each database object. More buffers require more memory, but they make it less likely for a database object to be rolled out to disk because of a lack of buffer space.
Default setting	0x00000003
When to change	Adjust if this MTA communicates with multiple Exchange 5.5 servers either in a site, or between sites. Additionally, you should tune if another messaging connector is homed on this server.
Recommended setting	0x00000006

Table 18-12   Dispatcher Threads Setting

Parameter	Dispatcher threads
Type	REG_DWORD
Explanation	This value is the number of MTA Dispatcher threads, which are responsible for the processing of messages. This is multiplied by three for the three subtypes (Router, Fanout, Result) of Dispatcher thread.
Default setting	0x00000001
When to change	Adjust if this MTA communicates with other Exchange 5.5 servers. Additionally, consider tuning if more than five Exchange 5.5 servers exist in the site, or if groups (that is, distribution lists) are heavily used.
Recommended setting	0x00000003

Table 18-13   10 Kernel Threads Setting

Parameter	Kernel threads
Type	REG_DWORD
Explanation	This value is the number of platform threads that handle the Presentation and Session level of the Open Systems Interconnection (OSI) stack. These threads are at the heart of MTA message processing.
Default setting	0x00000001
When to change	Adjust if this MTA communicates with other Exchange 5.5 servers using RPC over slow or highly latent network connections.
Recommended setting	0x00000003—Standard recommendation.
	0x00000008—If the Exchange 2003 MTA belongs to a site containing more than 15 Exchange 5.5 servers.
	0x0000000C (12)—If the Exchange 2003 MTA belongs to a site containing more than 30 Exchange 5.5 servers.

Table 18-14   Max RPC Calls Outstanding Setting

Parameter	Max RPC Calls Outstanding
Type	REG_DWORD
Explanation	This value is the maximum number of RPC threads. This setting limits the maximum number of RPCs that are guaranteed to be processed at the same time.
Default setting	0x00000032 (50)
When to change	Adjust if you increase the number of Gateway In/Out threads in the Store.exe process, which is recommended in Exchange 5.5 and Exchange 2000 coexistence scenarios.
Recommended setting	0x00000080 (128)

Table 18-15   MDB Users Setting

Parameter	MDB users
Type	REG_DWORD
Explanation	Defines the number of distinguished names to cache from the directory.
Default setting	0x000001F4 (500)
When to change	Adjust when your organization contains more than 1,500 users. Change the value to one-third the size of the global address list (GAL), to a maximum of 5000.
Recommended setting	0x00001388 (5000)

Table 18-16   RTS Threads Setting

Parameter	RTS threads
Type	REG_DWORD
Explanation	RTS threads. This value is the number of platform threads that handle the reliable transfer service element (RTSE) level of the OSI stack.
Default setting	0x00000001
When to change	Adjust if this MTA communicates with multiple Exchange 5.5 servers, either in a site or between sites.
Recommended setting	0x00000003

Table 18-17   TCP/IP Control Blocks Setting

Parameter	TCP/IP control blocks.
Type	REG_DWORD
Explanation	This value is the maximum number of concurrent RFC 1006 (TCP/IP) connections that are supported. This setting controls the number of buffers available for X.400 connections.
Default setting	0x00000014 (20)
When to change	Adjust if hosting more than one X.400 connector on the server.
Recommended setting	Ten control blocks for each hosted X.400 connector, plus one control block for incoming connections.

Table 18-18   Transfer Threads Setting

Parameter	Transfer threads
Type	REG_DWORD
Explanation	This value is the number of MTA Transfer threads. It is multiplied by two for the two subtypes (Transfer In, Transfer Out) of the Transfer thread.
Default setting	0x00000001
When to change	Adjust if this MTA communicates with multiple Exchange 5.5 servers, either in a site or between sites.
Recommended setting	0x00000003

You must restart the MTA before registry adjustments take effect.

> **Note**   After you upgrade your last Exchange 5.5 server, restore the original registry parameters for the MTA. Using the MTA tunings described in Table 18-11 through Table 18-18 in a native mode Exchange organization decreases the performance of your Exchange installation.

MSExchangeIS Registry Key Settings

When messages are received in the MTA from an Exchange 5.5 server or a previous gateway, they are handed off to the Store.exe process, and then they go to the advanced queuing engine. In environments in which many messages reach the MTA at the same time, it is a good idea to increase the number of processing threads between the Store.exe process and MTA. You can monitor the MTA to Store.exe process queue build-ups using either System Monitor or Exchange System Manager.

The registry parameters in this section can be found in the following key:

```
HKEY_LOCAL_MACHINE\System\CurrentControlSet\Services\MSEx-
changeIS\server_name\Private-database_guid
```

The following Table 18-19 and Table 18-20 illustrate, in detail, the parameters that you can set, along with notes and information about those parameters.

Table 18-19   Gateway In Threads Setting

Parameter	Gateway In Threads
Type	REG_DWORD
Explanation	Defines the number of threads available for retrieving messages from the MTA process in the Store.exe process.
Default setting	Not present, but defaults to 0x00000001.
When to change	Adjust if this MTA communicates with multiple Exchange 5.5 servers or other messaging connectors.
Recommended setting	0x00000003
Note	Each thread consumes about 1 MB of virtual memory. Additionally, the actual number of threads created is this value multiplied by the number of databases. This may be an issue on servers with many private databases. For example, if you have ten private databases, and you increase this parameter and the following parameter from 1 to 3 (a total increase of four threads), you actually create 4 x 10 = 40 threads, which together consume 40 MB of virtual memory.

Table 18-20 Gateway Out Threads Setting

Parameter	Gateway Out Threads.
Type	REG_DWORD
Explanation	Defines the number of threads available for sending messages from the Exchange Information Store to the MTA process.
Default setting	Not present, but defaults to 0x00000001.
When to change	Adjust if this MTA communicates with multiple Exchange 5.5 servers or other messaging connectors.
Recommended setting	0x00000003

You should add these parameters to all private databases configured on the server. After you make this change, you must increase the Max RPC Calls Outstanding registry parameter for the MTA process.

Routing Tuning

This section contains information about message routing on your servers. Tuning message routing can significantly increase the speed at which e-mail messages are passed between servers and, subsequently, between users.

Suppressing Link-State Changes

Exchange 2003 includes functionality to automatically detect changes in the state of a link and then flood the other servers in the organization with the updated link state information. Hence, other servers can be told to use an alternative route instead of the lowest-cost primary route. Link state information is broken down into major and minor changes. A major change occurs when the administrator changes the routing topology, such as the addition of a new connector or a cost change. Minor updates occur when the system automatically detects the failure or restoration of a link.

This feature works well in small- to medium-sized organizations. However, in large multi-site environments, mass network fluctuation can cause link update floods for the minor version. To be truly effective, link state data must be broadcast to all the servers in the organization. Additionally, when state changes, the whole link state table is rebroadcast, which can cause significant data to be transmitted over the network. In these scenarios, it may be useful to suppress minor link state changes. To disable minor link state changes, implement the registry parameter shown in Table 18-21.

Table 18-21 SuppressStateChanges Setting

Location	HKEY_LOCAL_MACHINE\System\CurrentControlSet\ Services\RESvc\Parameters
Parameter	SuppressStateChanges

Table 18-21   **SuppressStateChanges Setting (Continued)**

Type	REG_DWORD
Default setting	Not present, but defaults to 0x00000000.
When to change	Change to 0x00000001 to disable broadcast of minor link state changes.

In hub-and-spoke environments in which there is no alternative path between the spoke bridgehead and the hub, Exchange 2003 servers automatically suppress link state changes for that connector. In this scenario, you do not have to enforce the registry parameter described in Table 18-21.

Glitch Retry

If Exchange 2003 tries to route a message to a heavily loaded external SMTP system, such as a virus wall, it can receive a Server Busy error. In these situations, the Exchange transport goes into a state known as "glitch retry." In this state, Exchange 2003 waits 60 seconds before attempting to resend the message, and it repeats this process three times before resorting to other actions. If external SMTP servers are consistently busy, reduce the glitch retry wait time to prevent mass message queuing. Table 18-22 shows the registry parameter that controls this time.

Table 18-22   **GlitchRetrySeconds Setting**

Location	HKEY_LOCAL_MACHINE\System\CurrentControlSet\ Services\SMTPSvc\Queuing
Parameter	GlitchRetrySeconds
Type	REG_DWORD
Default setting	Not present, but defaults to 0x0000003C (60).

Creating Routing Groups

After you create a routing group in Exchange System Manager, information about that group, contained servers, and any connectors associated with the group is broadcast through link state updates to all the other Exchange 2000 and Exchange 2003 servers in the organization. If the routing group is removed, the object becomes orphaned in the link state table; however, the data continues to be broadcast as part of the link state. Removing the group does not cause routing problems, but the link state table will be larger than it should be. The only way to permanently remove all orphaned routing groups from the link state table is to shut down the Exchange 2000 and Exchange 2003 servers in the organization at the same time. Therefore, you should keep the creation and deletion of routing groups in a production Exchange environment to a minimum.

SMTP Transport Tuning

This section contains information about transport tuning on your servers.

Mailroot Directory Location

In Exchange 2003, when messages arrive through SMTP, the data is written to a disk in the form of an NTFS file system file (specifically, an .eml file). By default, these files are written to a directory (<*drive*>:\Program Files\Exchsrvr\Mailroot) on the same disk partition where the Exchange 2003 binary files are installed.

In some scenarios, such as configuring a bridgehead or relay server, relocating the SMTP Mailroot directory to a faster disk partition may improve performance.

In Exchange 2003, you can use Exchange System Manager to move the Mailroot directory. To move the Mailroot directory, use the Messages tab in the SMTP Virtual Server Properties dialog box.

SMTP MaxMessageObjects

The MaxMessageObjects setting correlates to the number of messages that can be queued up at a particular time by SMTP. Each mail message resident in the SMTP queue uses at least 4 KB of memory; therefore, you can experience low memory with a very large queue. Lowering this setting reduces the maximum number of messages that can reside in the queue, thereby decreasing the maximum memory footprint for SMTP. After this limit is reached, each SMTP connection made to the server returns with an out-of-memory error. For example, if this value is reduced to 10,000, SMTP refuses inbound mail after the queue reaches 10,000 messages. Table 18-23 discusses these settings.

Table 18-23 MaxMessageObjects Setting

Location	`HKEY_LOCAL_MACHINE\Software\Microsoft\Exchange\Mailmsg`
Parameter	MaxMessageObjects
Type	`REG_DWORD`
Default setting	Not present, but defaults to 0x000186a0 (100000).
When to change	Adjust if the Exchange 2003 server is running out of memory because the number of incoming messages is too great for the server to process.

Active Directory Connector Tuning

The Active Directory Connector (ADC) requires almost no tuning during typical operation. There are two scenarios in which you might want to consider manually tuning the ADC process: during sleep time and block searching.

Sleep Time

After the ADC has fully replicated Exchange and Active Directory data, it performs replication on the changes made to those directories. In most circumstances, those changes are small. During a connection agreement's activation time, the ADC is permitted to work continuously for five minutes. After that, the ADC sleeps for five minutes to allow other applications, such as replication processing time on domain controller or global catalog servers, to run. However, if a connection agreement is running for the first time or if many changes are made to one of the directories, you may want to permit the ADC to perform the replication without sleeping (and therefore speed up the replication cycle). You can configure the maximum time that the ADC is permitted to work without sleeping and the maximum time the ADC should sleep. Table 18-24 and Table 18-25 discuss these settings.

> **Note**   These changes affect all the connection agreements running on the ADC server, and they may adversely affect other Active Directory applications.

Table 18-24   Max Continuous Sync (Secs) Setting

Location	HKEY_LOCAL_MACHINE\System\CurrentControlSet\Services\MSADC\Parameters
Parameter	Max Continuous Sync (secs)
Type	REG_DWORD
Default setting	Not present, but defaults to 0x0000012c (300).
When to change	Adjust if you want the ADC to continue processing even after replicating solidly for five minutes.
Recommended setting	Set to no more than 20 minutes (1,200 seconds). Setting this value too high can have an adverse effect on Active Directory and other applications.

Table 18-25   Sync Sleep Delay (Secs) Setting

Location	HKEY_LOCAL_MACHINE\System\CurrentControlSet\Services\MSADC\Parameters
Parameter	Sync Sleep Delay (secs)
Type	REG_DWORD
Default setting	Not present, but defaults to 0x0000012c (300).
When to change	Adjust if you want to change the default sleep time of the ADC.

Table 18-25   Sync Sleep Delay (Secs) Setting (Continued)

Recommended setting	Set to a minimum of one minute (60 seconds). Whenever possible, leave this setting at the default. Be careful when raising this value. For example, if you set it to 3,600 seconds (one hour) and set the connection agreement replication schedule for individual 15-minute segments, the ADC may never replicate. It is recommended that you only change the sleep delay when setting the replication schedule to **Always**.

Block Searching

By default, the ADC requests changes from Exchange and Active Directory in blocks of 10,000. If more than 10,000 objects are to be replicated, the ADC requests the first 10,000 entries, processes them, and then prompts you for the next 10,000. If the ADC communicates with directory servers over an error-prone network, it may be useful to reduce the block size. If the ADC receives a partial block caused by a connection failure, the complete block must be replicated again. Reducing the block size reduces the number of repeat replications caused by connection failures. Table 18-26 discusses the Export Block Size Setting parameters.

Table 18-26   Export Block Size Setting

Location	`HKEY_LOCAL_MACHINE\System\CurrentControlSet\` `Services\MSADC\Parameters`
Parameter	Export Block Size
Type	`REG_DWORD`
Default setting	Not present, but defaults to 0x00002710 (10000).
When to change	Adjust if you want the ADC to commit before 10,000 new or changed objects have been received. You would generally lower this value in difficult WAN situations.
Recommended setting	Set as appropriate. If you set the value too low (never go below 100), you receive poor performance from the ADC.

Active Directory Integration Tuning

This section contains information about tuning Active Directory components to optimize Exchange 2003.

Dedicated Active Directory Servers for Exchange

If you have a high concentration of Exchange 2003 servers, you must dedicate a set of global catalog servers for Exchange. Create a dedicated Active Directory site that contains both the Exchange 2003 servers and any dedicated global catalog servers. This results in several positive effects:

- Traffic from systems other than Exchange 2003 is distributed to other Active Directory servers in the organization.

- Performance analysis and management of Active Directory is easier.

- The Exchange administrator has better control over the Active Directory servers that are dedicated for Exchange.

Set PDC Avoidance

Applications other than Exchange can make heavy use of the primary domain controller (PDC) emulator computer. If Exchange 2003 also tries to use the PDC emulator computer for its requests, the performance of the PDC emulator and Exchange can decrease. By default, DSAccess picks up the PDC emulator computer for request, together with other servers in the local Active Directory site. However, you can edit the registry to change this behavior. Table 18-27 shows the registry parameter to set.

Table 18-27 MinUserDc Setting

Location	`HKEY_LOCAL_MACHINE\System\CurrentControlSet\` `Services\MSExchangeDSAccess\Profiles\Default`
Parameter	MinUserDc
Type	`REG_DWORD`
Default setting	Not present, but defaults to 0xffffffff (-1).
When to change	Set this value if the PDC emulator is located in the same Active Directory site as your Exchange 2003 servers. The value that you set relates to the minimum number of domain controllers that must be detected in the same site and same domain before the PDC emulator is excluded from the server list. For example, if you set this value to **3**, DSAccess does not use the PDC for LDAP requests if it detects three or more domain controllers in the Active Directory site. If fewer than three domain controllers are detected, Exchange continues to use the PDC. To force PDC avoidance in all scenarios, set this registry value to **1**.

Use of the /3GB Switch on Active Directory Servers

The Active Directory process uses the Extensible Storage Engine (ESE) for its database. By default, the ESE cache size is 512 MB. However, if you use Windows 2000 Advanced Server or Windows Server 2003 (any edition) for your global catalog servers, and you have more than 2 GB of physical RAM installed, you should set the /3GB switch in the boot.ini file of these servers. This action automatically increases the ESE cache to 1024 MB. In most circumstances, having a larger cache reduces the number of disk reads by 20 to 40 percent and dramatically reduces LDAP response times.

Using Exchange 2003 on Active Directory Servers

For the best scalability and administrative flexibility, Exchange 2003 should be installed on a Windows member server instead of a domain controller or global catalog server. The latter scenario is supported, but you should be aware of the consequences.

Threads in the Lsass.exe (Active Directory) process run at a higher priority than Exchange threads. An increase in the Lsass.exe process can adversely affect Exchange processing time.

If the Exchange server also acts as a domain controller, the server spends resources on other non-Exchange requests, such as user authentication and directory lookups for other applications. This additional activity affects performance on the Exchange 2003 server.

Although DSAccess detects all domain controllers and global catalog servers in the local Active Directory site, it does not use them. All directory requests are sent to the local directory service. Load balancing and failover do not occur in this scenario.

To manage Exchange 2003 services, the administrator must be defined as a local administrator. If Exchange 2003 is running on a domain controller, the Exchange administrator must belong to the Administrators group in the domain. Membership implicitly gives the Exchange administrator additional access to other computers in the domain.

Important   Administrators who have logon access to domain controllers must be trusted in the Active Directory forest because it is possible for these users to elevate their permissions in Active Directory. Administrators who can only log on to member servers cannot elevate their permissions in Active Directory.

Tuning DSAccess on Mailbox Servers

By default, DSAccess caches objects. The cache is broken into two sections: one section for user objects (that is, domain naming context), and the other section for configuration data, such as store and routing objects. User objects are cached for five minutes, and configuration data is cached for 15 minutes. By default, the configuration data cache in Exchange 2003 is 5 MB and the user object is 140 MB.

In very large topologies containing a hundred or more administrative or routing groups, increased performance can be achieved by manually tuning the DSAccess cache sections. Table 18-28 shows the registry parameter to set.

Table 18-28 MaxMemoryConfig Setting

Location	HKEY_LOCAL_MACHINE\System\CurrentControlSet\Services\MSExchangeDSAccess\Instance0
Parameter	MaxMemoryConfig
Type	REG_DWORD
Default setting	Not present, but defaults to 0x00001400 (5 MB).
When to change	Adjust when there are more than 100 administrative or routing groups in the organization.
Recommended setting	0x0000028f5 (approximately 10 MB).

Tuning DSAccess on Branch Office Servers

If you run Exchange 2003 in a large branch office environment, some manual performance adjustments may be necessary to get the best efficiency.

- You must always have LAN-speed access to a global catalog server.

- If there are hundreds of routing groups in the organization, you may notice a mass spike of activity on the local global catalog every 15 minutes. This spike occurs because DSAccess rereads the routing group configuration. In severe cases, the local global catalog may become consumed with this activity. To minimize the burden, you can index the Routing Group Back-Link property (msExchRoutingGroupMembersBL). Use Active Directory Schema Manager to enable the Index This Attribute In Active Directory option for this property.

Increasing the Maximum Active LDAP Queries

If there are many Exchange 2003 servers in a Windows Active Directory site, a very large LDAP load can be put on the Active Directory servers. By default, an Active Directory server is configured to support a maximum of 20 active LDAP queries. If this limit is reached, Active Directory returns the LDAP_ADMIN_LIMIT_EXCEEDED error and stops processing any more LDAP queries. A setting of 20 is generally sufficient for most Active Directory servers, but it is necessary to increase this value when you are running Exchange 2003 on eight-processor servers, or if the LDAP_ADMIN_LIMIT_EXCEEDED error message is logged.

The maximum LDAP queries can be configured through the *MaxActiveQueries* attribute. This setting can be adjusted using the Ntdsutil.exe tool. Increasing this setting uses more memory in the Lsass.exe process on the Active Directory server. Therefore, do not increase this value any higher than is necessary.

To change the MaxActiveQueries setting using NTDSUTIL:

1. Click Start, and then click Run.

2. Type **NTDSUTIL**, and then click OK.

3. Type **LDAP POLICIES**.

4. Type **CONNECTIONS**.

5. Type **CONNECT TO SERVER** *domain_controllor_or_global_catalog_name.*

6. Type **Q**.

7. Type **SHOW VALUES**.

8. Type **SET MAXACTIVEQUERIES TO 40**.

9. Type **COMMIT CHANGES**.

10. Type **SHOW VALUES**.

11. Verify that the new setting is shown.

12. Type **Q**.

13. Type **Q**.

> **Note**   This setting replicates to all Active Directory servers in the forest.
> You do not have to restart the domain controller or global catalog servers
> for this change to take effect.

Disabling Unused Services

For additional performance and security, you may decide to disable certain services from running. For example, although Exchange 2003 requires the Network News Transfer Protocol (NNTP) stack to be installed before Exchange 2003 is installed, if you have no requirements for NNTP access, you can shut down and disable this service after Exchange 2003 is installed. The same is true for POP3 and IMAP4 services.

Do not disable services that Exchange 2003 requires for normal operation. For example, the MTA service is required for internal operations even when working in a native mode Exchange organization. Therefore, you should never disable the MTA or stop it for any long period of time.

Performance Tuning Tools

This section describes the tools that can help you verify the performance of your Microsoft Exchange Server 2003 environment. Some of these tools are installed with Microsoft Windows 2000 Server or Windows Server 2003, and some with Exchange. Table 18-29 outlines these tools and their use.

> **Warning**   Some tools can cause serious, sometimes irreversible, problems if they are used incorrectly. Before you use tools in your production environment, always familiarize yourself with them on test servers first. Be sure to read the documentation associated with any tool and become familiar with the risks involved.

Table 18-29   Exchange Performance Tools

Tool name	Description
Exchange Stress and Performance (ESP)	Use to test stress and performance.
	This tool simulates large numbers of client sessions by concurrently accessing one or more protocol servers.
Jetstress	Use to test the performance and stability of the disk subsystem.
Load Simulator (LoadSim)	Use as a benchmarking tool to test the response of servers to mail loads.
Network Monitor	Use to diagnose issues with server connectivity.
System Monitor (also known as Performance Monitor)	Use for establishing a baseline of performance and for troubleshooting performance issues.

LoadSim and ESP are helpful when you test systems to ensure the health of the systems before going into production. You can use the other tools to help diagnose bottlenecks in production servers.

Exchange Server Stress and Performance 2003

You can use Exchange Server Stress and Performance (ESP) 2003 to simulate arbitrary several client sessions that are concurrently accessing one or more Exchange 2003 servers.

ESP provides modules that simulate client sessions over the following Internet protocols and APIs:

- WebDAV (for Microsoft Office Outlook Web Access)

- Internet Message Access Protocol version 4rev1 (IMAP4)

- Lightweight Directory Access Protocol (LDAP)

- OLE DB

- Network News Transfer Protocol (NNTP)

- Post Office Protocol version 3 (POP3)

- Simple Mail Transfer Protocol (SMTP)

- Exchange ActiveSync

- Outlook Mobile Access

ESP is similar to LoadSim; however, use ESP when you are validating deployments that use mobility features and Internet protocols that LoadSim does not cover.

For more information about ESP, see the documentation that comes with the tool.

Jetstress

Jetstress helps administrators verify the performance and stability of the disk subsystem prior to putting their Exchange server into production.

Jetstress helps verify disk performance by simulating Exchange disk I/O load. Jetstress simulates the Exchange database and log file loads produced by a specific number of users. You use System Monitor, Event Viewer, and Exchange Server Database Utilities together with Jetstress to verify that your disk subsystem meets or exceeds the performance criteria you establish.

With Jetstress, you can perform two types of tests:

1. The Jetstress Disk Performance Test runs for two hours. You can verify the performance and sizing of your storage solution.

2. The Jetstress Disk Subsystem Stress Test runs for 24 hours. You can test your server load using a much larger load over a more significant amount of time.

Note   Running both tests is the best way to verify the integrity performance of your disk subsystem.

After a successful completion of the Jetstress Disk Performance Test and Jetstress Disk Subsystem Stress Test in a nonproduction environment, you are ready for the next step in your Exchange 2003 deployment process. By running the tests, you help ensure that your Exchange 2003 disk subsystem is adequately sized (in terms of performance criteria that you establish) for the user count and user profiles you have established.

For more information about Jetstress, see the documentation that comes with the tool.

Load Simulator 2003

Load Simulator 2003 (LoadSim) simulates the performance load of MAPI clients. Load-Sim helps you determine if each of your servers can handle the load that you intend for it to carry. Another use for LoadSim is to help you validate your deployment plan.

However, LoadSim does not account for all of the factors involved in sizing servers. LoadSim does not simulate the following factors that can affect your server capacity planning:

- Incoming unsolicited commercial e-mail (also known as spam) from the Internet

- Incoming SMTP mail flow from the Internet or other sites within your organization

- Use of non-MAPI protocols for account access, such as POP3 and IMAP4

- Use of mobile devices

- Public folder usage

In addition, LoadSim does not give a complete picture with regard to user experience, and its results should not be interpreted in that aspect.

Best Practices

In this chapter, we have discussed some of the tuning configurations that you can apply to your Exchange deployment so your deployment will run better, faster, and more efficiently. While detailed, this chapter has presented most of the information you will need to support your deployment, regardless of your organization's size.

Best practices would include placing your databases on separate spindles for faster I/O performance, placing your transaction logs for each storage group on a separate spindle for faster end-user response times and tweaking the registry settings in Exchange to maximize performance of your Exchange servers to your unique environment.

Part IV

Troubleshooting Exchange Server 2003

Exchange Server 2003 Troubleshooting Basics

About This Chapter

This chapter discusses general procedures for diagnosing Microsoft Exchange Server 2003 problems, and it explains how to use Microsoft troubleshooting and debugging tools to gather information about the health and configuration of a server running Microsoft Exchange Server 2003. Gathering detailed diagnostics information can be helpful in any troubleshooting event, but especially when you are contacting Microsoft Product Support Services. This chapter also explains how to configure Dr. Watson to send most detailed diagnostics information automatically to Microsoft in the event that Exchange Server crashes.

This chapter assumes that you are familiar with Microsoft Windows server technology, the concepts of Active Directory directory service, and Exchange Server 2003.

More Info   For more information about troubleshooting Windows Server 2003, see Windows Server 2003 Technology Centers at *http://www.microsoft.com/windowsserver2003/technologies*. For information about how to troubleshoot specific Active Directory and Exchange 2003 issues, such as directory access problems or problems related to the Exchange store, see subsequent chapters in this Resource Kit, specifically Chapters 20 through 23. See also the technical article "Troubleshooting Exchange Server 2003 Performance" at *http://www.microsoft.com/technet/prodtechnol/exchange/2003/library/e2k3perf.mspx*.

What You Need to Know

Troubleshooting Exchange 2003 is often difficult because Exchange 2003 is a complex messaging system that depends on other equally complex systems, such as Transmission Control Protocol/Internet Protocol (TCP/IP), DNS, and Active Directory. Replication latencies further contribute to the complexity, because configuration changes might not take effect immediately. If you apply a series of configuration changes overanxiously and without proper analysis of the current system state, you might end up aggravating a problem instead of fixing it. It is important to troubleshoot Exchange 2003 issues in a coordinated way using tried and proven procedures and to document changes that you make during the troubleshooting process.

On the Resource Kit CD   To troubleshoot Exchange 2003 issues in a coordinated way, use the flowcharts that you can find in the \Companion Material\Chapter 19\flowcharts folder on the companion CD.

Unless you are dealing with a mission-critical issue, such as total unavailability of messaging services, we recommend that you adopt the following methodical approach, shown in Figure 19-1, when you troubleshoot Exchange 2003 issues. Mission-critical issues you might want to put on a fast lane, but it is nevertheless a good idea to approach all issues in a coordinated way regardless of their urgency. The following is a tried and proven general troubleshooting approach:

1. **Identify and analyze the issue**   This usually requires checking the affected Exchange server, its components, and installed software. Depending on the nature of the problem, you might also have to check domain controllers, DNS zone information, the configuration of network equipment, and messaging cli-

ents. Event logs, protocol logs, network traces, and dump files can provide valuable information when analyzing an issue.

2. **Understand the components involved**   Before you can troubleshoot an issue, you must understand exactly what is happening. This requires that you study the architecture of the components involved, the dependencies of these components, and their interaction. Subsequent chapters provide detailed information about the architecture of Exchange 2003 components.

> **More Info**   For more information, see the Exchange online book *Exchange Server 2003 Technical Reference Guide* (*http://www.microsoft.com/downloads/details.aspx?FamilyID=3768246d-c9ed-45d8-bece-a666143cba4e&DisplayLang=en*).

3. **Locate the issue**   Knowing the architecture and dependencies of the components involved enables you to determine probable causes of an issue. You can then try to replicate the problem. This is a crucial part of the troubleshooting process. If you can replicate a problem, you can locate the actual issue by altering the configuration and verifying the corresponding system behavior. Change only one setting or configuration at a time so that you can keep track of the behavior before and after the change. Allow for directory replication to propagate the changes throughout the forest and carefully document all changes that you make. After you determine the cause of the problem, check the configuration to find out why the affected component is experiencing a problem.

> **Note**   We recommend that you carefully document all major system changes, including those applied during normal operation. This documentation can provide valuable clues about the likely source of a problem. For example, if message transfer to the Internet is interrupted, and your system documentation indicates that firewalls were recently reconfigured, you might want to look at the configuration of your Internet access point first.

4. **Solve the issue**   Devise a solution to prevent the problem from happening again. Do not apply your solution until you have carefully tested it for side effects in a test lab. For example, service packs contain many solutions for known issues, but you should not apply a service pack without first testing it on a reference system. However, urgent matters might require you to keep testing at a minimum.

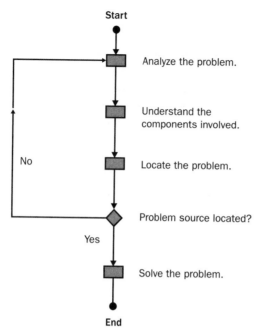

Figure 19-1   Recommended troubleshooting approach

Locating and analyzing a problem are key activities in every troubleshooting incident. Once the trouble spot is located, it is typically straightforward to apply a solution, such as a fix to a known problem or adjusting the system configuration. To locate the source of a problem, however, you must check available system logs and use troubleshooting tools to gather further information. You might also have to run tests to rule out specific components.

If you are dealing with a complex problem, you can get additional information and assistance from the following sources:

- **Microsoft Knowledge Base**   Search or browse through the Knowledge Base at *http://support.microsoft.com/search/?adv=1* to find information about the various Exchange Server 2003 components. Many Knowledge Base articles provide straightforward answers to frequently asked questions or discuss known issues. Some articles clarify which components and configurations are supported by Microsoft, and others explain how to use troubleshooting tools. You can search the Knowledge Base using keywords, header text, or full text.

  The following is a short sample list of troubleshooting articles in the Microsoft Knowledge Base related to unexpected Exchange 2003 behavior:

  - Article 835575, "The System Attendant quits unexpectedly in Exchange Server 2003" (*http://support.microsoft.com/?kbid=835575*)

- Article 835962, "The MTA quits unexpectedly while processing a long address that contains embedded DDA values in Exchange Server 2003" (*http://support.microsoft.com/?kbid=835962*)

- Article 836027, "The Exchange Server 2003 Information Store service does not start, and event IDs 1180 and 5000 are logged" (*http://support.microsoft.com/?kbid=836027*)

- Article 824319 "IIS stops unexpectedly when you use the POP3 RETR command on a server that is running Exchange 2000 Server" (*http://support.microsoft.com/?kbid=824319*)

- **Microsoft TechNet**   TechNet is a central information and community resource designed for IT professionals. The TechNet program includes technical briefings, special offers, the TechNet website, and an electronic newsletter, in addition to a CD subscription. TechNet offers information about Microsoft strategies and industry trends, provides "how-to" information and bug fixes for known problems, and serves as a forum for sharing information, ideas, and opinions with other Exchange specialists. The Microsoft Knowledge Base is a TechNet resource, for example. To subscribe to TechNet, see "TechNet Subscriptions" (*http://www.microsoft.com/technet/abouttn/subscriptions/default.mspx*).

- **Exchange-specific websites and newsgroups**   You can visit numerous websites and newsgroups to obtain information about Exchange Server 2003. For the latest versions of Exchange online books and articles, visit *http://go.microsoft.com/fwlink/?LinkId=21277*. It is also worth visiting the Microsoft Technical Communities website at *http://www.microsoft.com/communities/default.mspx*. For a list of Microsoft newsgroups about Exchange 2003, visit *http://www.microsoft.com/technet/community/newsgroups/server/exchange.mspx*.

- **Microsoft Product Support Services**   If you cannot solve a problem without direct assistance from a support specialist, contact Microsoft Product Support Services online or by phone. For information about Product Support Services, including how to contact them, go to *http://support.microsoft.com*.

General Troubleshooting Tools

You can use the following standard tools to troubleshoot Exchange 2003 issues. Some of these tools are grouped together in the Performance tool that is available in the Administrative Tools program group; others are included in Exchange System Manager; again others might require a fully deployed network management and monitoring system, such as Microsoft Exchange Management Pack for Microsoft Operations Manager. Which tools you use to troubleshoot a system and in which order you use them depends on the problem that you are troubleshooting.

■ **Event Viewer** Many of the internal Exchange 2003 components record events in the Event Log. An event is any occurrence in the system or in a program that might require administrator attention. Event logs can help you identify and diagnose the source of current system problems or help you predict potential issues. Table 19-1 lists various Event Viewer logs that you might find on your Exchange 2003 servers. The standard logs, Application, System, and Security exist in all computer configurations. Others, such as the Directory Service log, are available only in specific configurations, such as on domain controllers.

Table 19-1 Important Windows 2003 Event Viewer logs

Event log	Description
Application log	The Application log contains events that are logged by Exchange 2003 and other applications. Most Exchange 2003 events are logged in the Application log.
System log	The system log contains events that are logged by Microsoft Windows system components. For example, the failure of a driver or other system component to load during startup is recorded in the System log.
Security log	The Security log can record security events, such as valid and invalid logon attempts, as well as events related to resource use, such as creating, opening, or deleting files. An administrator can specify what events are recorded in the Security log. For example, if you enable logon auditing, attempts to log on to the system are recorded in the security log.
Directory Service log	On domain controllers, the Directory Service log contains events from the Active Directory directory service, such as reported connection problems between a server and the global catalog.
File Replication Service log	On domain controllers, the File Replication Service log contains events logged by the Windows File Replication service. For example, file replication failures between domain controllers are recorded in the file replication service log.
DNS log	On Windows DNS servers, the DNS log contains events logged by the DNS Server service. For example, the server might receive invalid DNS update messages from a network client, in which case, the DNS Server service will log a DNS_EVENT_BAD_UPDATE_PACKET warning.

Many system components and programs write events into the application event log. If you are only interested in a specific component, you can filter the events by selecting Filter from the View menu in Event Viewer. Under Event source, you can select the information source that you are interested in. The names of most Exchange 2003 event sources start with MSExchange. For example, the Exchange message transfer agent (MTA) is named MSExchangeMTA, and the event source for the internal transport engine of Exchange 2003 is MSExchangeTransport.

> **Note**   If you want to increase the amount of information that an Exchange component writes to the event log, start Exchange System Manager and display the properties of the server in which you are interested. Click the Diagnostics Logging tab and then select the component of interest from the Services list. Next, select all or individual categories for this component from the Categories list. Then, under Logging Level, determine the amount of information that is written to the event log: None, Minimum, Medium, and Maximum. Keep in mind, however, that increasing the diagnostics logging can quickly fill the event log with irrelevant information, thus generally decreasing the usefulness of the application event log. You should increase the diagnostics logging level only when troubleshooting a server issue. Do not forget to increase the maximum log size for the application event log and activate the option to overwrite events as needed. Perhaps even more importantly, do not forget to reset the diagnostics logging level when you are finished troubleshooting.

- **System Monitor**   System Monitor is part of the Performance tool that is included in the Administrative Tools program group. Among other things, you can use System Monitor to monitor the behavior of Exchange servers in real time. You can determine the number of messages in inbound and outbound message queues, for example, and other information, such as the total number of users currently accessing a mailbox store. It is a good idea to check system health using System Monitor, because performance bottlenecks are often the sources of other problems. Keep in mind, however, that System Monitor does not capture data in a performance log or trace file. To create a performance log, use the Performance Logs and Alerts tool explained below.

  To add performance counters to System Monitor, start the Performance tool and then, in the toolbar, click the Add button indicated by a plus sign (+). Table 19-2 lists important Exchange 2003 performance objects that you can select from the Performance object drop-down list in the Add Counters dialog box. If you select an Exchange 2003 component, you can then find appropriate performance counters under Select counters from list. For example, the Simple Mail Transfer Protocol (SMTP) service (Performance object: SMTP Server) provides counters such as Message Received Total and Message Delivered Total that indicate how many inbound messages have been received and how many messages have been delivered to local mailboxes.

Table 19-2 Important Exchange 2003 Performance Objects

Resource	Performance object
Address lists	MSExchangeAL
Directory Service Access caches	MSExchangeDSAccess Caches
Directory Service Access global counters	MSExchangeDSAccess Global Counters
Directory Service Access processes	MSExchangeDSAccess Processes
Epoxy queues and activity	Epoxy
Mailbox store	MSExchangeIS Mailbox
Public folder store	MSExchangeIS Public
Exchange store	MSExchangeIS
Connector for Lotus Notes	MSExchangeNMC
Message Transfer Agent	MSExchangeMTA
Message Transfer Agent connections	MSExchangeMTA Connections
Connector for Novell GroupWise	MSExchangeGWC
Simple Mail Transfer Protocol	SMTP Server
Exchange routing engine	SMTP Routing

More Info In addition to Exchange 2003-specific performance objects, you should also check performance counters of system objects, such as Memory, Disk, Processor, Process, and Threads. For more information about useful performance objects and troubleshooting performance issues, see the paper *Troubleshooting Exchange Server 2003 Performance* (*http://www.microsoft.com/technet/prodtechnol/exchange/2003/library/e2k3perf.mspx*).

- **Performance Logs and Alerts** This tool is also included in the Performance tool. You can use Performance Logs and Alerts to collect data automatically from local or remote computers. Performance Logs and Alerts is similar to System Monitor in that you can select performance objects, performance counters, and object instances, as well as set sampling intervals for monitoring. You can use this tool to create reports that document system behavior over a specified period of time. These reports can be viewed in the Performance tool, or the data can be exported to a spreadsheet or database for analysis.

> **Tip**   It is a good idea to set up a baseline when the server is running within normal parameters. Comparing the values between the baseline and later reports, you can quickly identify performance issues.

- **Exchange System Manager**   Use the Exchange System Manager Microsoft Management Console (MMC) snap-in to check the state of your servers and the state of Exchange store databases, virtual servers for Internet protocols, and messaging connectors. For example, you can use the Monitoring and Status tool in the Tools container in Exchange System Manager to determine which connectors and bridgehead servers are available and which are not. Select the Status container under Monitoring and Status to display this information. In addition, you can use the Notifications container to configure e-mail or script notifications to alert you automatically when a critical system state is detected.

   You can also use the Queues container object under a server object in Exchange System Manager to list all queues and all messages within those queues that are currently awaiting message transfer on the server. You can freeze a particular message or all messages, which prevents them from being transferred through a connector until you unfreeze the messages. Freezing all messages in a message queue can be useful, for example, if you know that the destination of the message queue is temporarily unavailable, to avoid unnecessary connection attempts and possibly message rerouting. You can also delete a message from a message queue (with or without sending a non-delivery report back to the originator), which might be necessary if a corrupted message is blocking other messages. For more information, see Microsoft Knowledge Base Article 823489, "How to Use Queue Viewer to Troubleshoot Mail Flow Issues," (*http://support.microsoft.com/default.aspx?scid=kb;en-us;823489*).

   Exchange 2003 supports two types of message queues:

   - **System queues**   There are three providers for system queues: SMTP (for the SMTP transport engine), X.400 (for the Exchange message transfer agent (MTA), and MAPI (Connector for Lotus Notes, Connector for Novell GroupWise, and other Exchange Development Kit (EDK)-based connectors).

   - **Link queues**   The SMTP transport engine creates link queues when there are multiple messages bound for the same destination. These queues are listed in the Queues container only when they have messages waiting to be routed. The name of the queue matches the remote delivery destination.

Another important Exchange System Manager component for trouble-shooting is the Message Tracking Center, which you can use to track messages across an Exchange organization. You can track all kinds of messages, including system messages and regular e-mail messages that are going to or coming from a non-Exchange messaging system. For example, public folder replication messages that Exchange stores exchange with each other to synchronize public folder instances on separate servers are system messages. You can use Message Tracking Center to locate messages that have failed to arrive in your users' mailboxes, such as messages that are stuck in a connector's message queue.

Note   Message tracking is not enabled by default. To enabled it, display the properties of the server in Exchange System Manager, and then on the General tab, click the Enable Message Tracking check box. You can also jointly enable message tracking for multiple servers in a server policy. Keep in mind, however, that Message Tracking Center is unable to track messages within a non-Exchange messaging system. Message tracking ends (or begins, in the case of inbound messages) at the messaging connector that connects your Exchange organization to another messaging system.

- **Exchange Management Pack for Microsoft Operations Manager**   Keeping track of issues that involve many servers across an organization can be difficult when you are using standard tools. If you are responsible for a complex organization with multiple Exchange servers, you might want to implement a centralized tool, such as Microsoft Operations Manager (MOM) with the Exchange 2003 Management Pack, for monitoring and alerting, reporting, and trend analysis. The Exchange 2003 Management Pack provides preconfigured scripts, rules, and reports specific to Exchange with which you can monitor an entire Exchange organization or specific servers. The Exchange Management Pack also includes an extensive set of Knowledge Base articles to provide you with background information and troubleshooting information.

  With Exchange Management Pack for Microsoft Operations Manager, you can:

  - Check the system status of multiple Exchange servers from a single console

  - Create sophisticated rules to respond to system events

  - Generate custom reports

  - Handle operational tasks and obtain background information for trouble-shooting

> **More Info**   For more information about the Exchange Management Pack, see Chapter 17, "Exchange Server 2003 Management Pack."

- **Microsoft Exchange Server Best Practices Analyzer Tool (ExBPA)** ExBPA is a tool that you can use to determine if the configuration of an Exchange organization is set according to Microsoft best practices. This can help to proactively identify and resolve configuration problems. You can install ExBPA on a computer that is running Microsoft .NET Framework 1.1. With the proper network access, the tool can examine all your Active Directory directory service and Exchange servers, but you can also specify a specific server, or a reduced set of servers. The ExBPA tool and documentation are available at *http://www.microsoft.com/exchange/downloads/2003/ExBPA/default.asp*.

- **Network Monitor**   Network Monitor is a useful tool for detecting and troubleshooting problems that can occur during communication over the computer network. You can identify problems related to message transfer over a messaging connector or client-to-server connection, find a computer that makes a disproportionate number of protocol requests, and identify unauthorized users on your network. For example, if you are experiencing problems transferring messages over an X.400 connector, tracing the communication between the X.400 systems using Network Monitor can reveal protocol details that would not otherwise be visible.

  Network Monitor is a component of Microsoft Systems Management Server (SMS), but a version with fewer features also ships with the Windows Server 2003 family of operating systems. The operating system version of Network Monitor can capture frames that are sent to or from the computer on which Network Monitor is installed. If you want to capture frames that are sent to or from a remote computer, you must use the Network Monitor component that ships with SMS.

  With Network Monitor, you can:

  - Identify network traffic patterns and network problems

  - Capture frames (also called data packets) directly from the network

  - Display, filter, save, and print the captured frames

  For more information about Network Monitor, see the following Microsoft Knowledge Base articles:

  - 294818, "Frequently Asked Questions About Network Monitor" (*http://go.microsoft.com/fwlink/?linkid=3052&kbid=294818*)

- 148942, "How to Capture Network Traffic with Network Monitor" (*http://go.microsoft.com/fwlink/?linkid=3052&kbid=148942*)

- 168862, "How to Install ISO and TP4 Parser for Network Monitor" (*http://go.microsoft.com/fwlink/?linkid=3052&kbid=168862*)

- **Exchange 2003 Deployment Tools**   Exchange 2003 Deployment Tools is a collection of tools and wizards that you can use to perform integrity checks, and to identify various pre-setup conditions, post-setup conditions, and error conditions. Exchange 2003 Deployment Tools are included in the \Support\Exdeploy folder on the Exchange Server 2003 product CD. You can also download the latest version at *http://www.microsoft.com/downloads/details.aspx?FamilyId=271E51FD-FE7D-42AD-B621-45F974ED34C0&displaylang=en.*

  Two important troubleshooting tools included in Exchange 2003 Deployment Tools are Network Connectivity Tester (Netdiag.exe) and Domain Controller Diagnostic Tool (DCDiag.exe). These are command-line diagnostic tools that help you isolate networking, name resolution, and connectivity problems and analyze the state of domain controllers in a forest or enterprise. These tools perform a series of tests to determine the state of network services, DNS, WINS, and domain controllers and report any problems to assist in troubleshooting. Netdiag and DCDiag are covered in more detail later in this chapter.

- **Exchange 2003 Support Tools**   The Web release tools for Exchange 2003, which you can download at *http://www.microsoft.com/exchange/downloads/2003.asp*, include the following troubleshooting tools:

  - **DNS Resolver Tool**   Simulates the internal code path of the SMTP service and prints diagnostic messages that indicate how DNS name resolution is proceeding.

  - **Error Code Lookup Tool**   Enables you to determine error values from decimal and hexadecimal error codes in the Windows operating systems.

  - **Exchange Domain Rename Fixup Tool**   Enables you to fix attributes after you rename a Windows 2003 domain that contains Exchange 2003 servers.

  - **Exchange Server Stress and Performance 2003 Tool**   Enables you to stress test Exchange 2003 by simulating a large number of Internet client sessions.

  - **Information Store Viewer Tool**   Enables you to work with the low-level contents (raw data) of Exchange store databases using the MAPI interface.

  - **Jetstress Tool**   Enables you to verify the performance and stability of the disk subsystem by simulating Exchange disk input/output (I/O) load.

- **Load Simulator 2003**   Enables you to simulate workload on an Exchange 2003 server caused by MAPI clients.

- **MTA Check Tool**   Enables you to analyze and correct problems in the Exchange MTA.

- **Up-to-Date Notifications Troubleshooting Tool**   Enables you to troubleshoot up-to-date notifications issues that users might be experiencing with wireless devices.

- **WinRoute Tool**   Enables you to analyze the link state routing information that is known to the routing group master.

- **Common TCP/IP and Windows Support Tools**   Windows operating systems support many TCP/IP diagnostic tools that you can use to troubleshoot network issues. These tools are either installed by default or are included in the Windows Support Tools, available in the \Support folder on the Windows 2003 product CD. The following are the most important diagnostic and troubleshooting tools:

  - **Test TCP (TTCP) Tool**   You can use this tool to measure TCP and UDP performance. The TTCP tool is located in the \Valueadd\Msft\Net\Tools folder on the Windows Server 2003 CD.

  - **Address Resolution Protocol (ARP) Tool**   You can use the ARP tool to view and manage the ARP cache on the network interfaces of the local computer.

  - **IP Configuration (IPConfig) Tool**   You can use the IPConfig tool to display current TCP/IP network configuration values, update or release Dynamic Host Configuration Protocol (DHCP) allocated leases, and display, register, or flush DNS names.

  - **NetBIOS over TCP/IP Statistics (NBTStat) Tool**   You can use the NBTStat tool to check the state of current NetBIOS over TCP/IP (NBT) connections, view and update the NetBIOS name cache, and determine the names registered with Windows Internet Name Service (WINS).

  - **Network Statistics (Netstat) Tool**   You can use the Netstat tool to display statistics for current TCP/IP connections.

  - **Name Server Lookup (NSLookup) Tool**   You can use the NSLookup tool to check records, domain host aliases, domain host services, and operating system information by querying DNS servers.

  - **Packet InterNet Groper (PING) Tool**   You can use the PING tool to send Internet Control Message Protocol (ICMP) Echo messages to an IP address on the network to verify IP connectivity.

- **Route Tool**   You can use the Route tool to display the IP routing table and add, edit, or delete IPv4 routes.

- **Trace Route (Tracert) Tool**   You can use the Tracert tool to trace a path to a destination on a TCP/IP network.

- **Network Connectivity Tester (NetDiag) Tool**   As mentioned earlier, you can use NetDiag to test general network connectivity.

- **Domain Controller Diagnostics (DCDiag) Tool**   As mentioned earlier, you can use DCDiag to test network connectivity to Active Directory and DNS name resolution.

Verifying Network Connectivity

Broken network cables; faulty network adapters; incorrect switch, router, or firewall settings; and unavailable name resolution services are examples of issues that can cause Exchange communication to fail. Some networking issues, such as broken network cables, are relatively straightforward to troubleshoot because the problem is persistent. Other issues have sporadic symptoms that do not clearly point to the source of the problem. For example, a faulty network adapter might loose data packets during peak hours but might work properly when data traffic is at moderate levels. To locate the issue, you might have to trace network communication over a lengthy period of time using Network Monitor.

Verifying Connectivity Using Standard TCP/IP Tools

If you suspect that network connectivity issues are causing problems in your Exchange 2003 organization, you should first verify that other computers in the same and other network segments can communicate with the target computer. This is quickly accomplished using standard TCP/IP tools, such as PING and Tracert. For example, if client A cannot communicate with a mailbox server, is client B able to communicate? If other computers can communicate with the target computer, the problem is most likely an issue on that one computer. On the other hand, if no computer can communicate with the target computer, the problem might be related to the target computer itself or to a network device in between.

When troubleshooting TCP/IP connectivity on a client computer or Exchange server, follow these steps:

1. **Check that TCP/IP is installed correctly on the computer.**   You should ping the IP loopback address on the local computer using the following command line: ping 127.0.0.1. The TCP/IP stack should respond immediately. If the command fails, check the application and system event log and look for problems reported by the TCP/IP service. If the command succeeds, ping the IP addresses of your computer's local interface(s). Successful responses indicate that the IP layer on the computer is most likely initialized correctly.

2. **Check that the computer can reach the default gateway.** Next, you should ping the IP address of your default gateway. If this command fails, you should verify the configuration of your TCP/IP stack using the following command line: ipconfig /all. For example, an incorrect subnet mask can cause problems. If you notice incorrect TCP/IP configuration settings, verify the local TCP/IP configuration and the configuration of your Dynamic Host Configuration Protocol (DHCP) servers. Successful responses indicate that your computer is able to communicate with the default gateway at the IP layer, which is a prerequisite for communication with computers in other subnets that are reached through the default gateway.

Note The default gateway must be located on the same TCP/IP subnet as any of the installed network interface(s) on the system. This is determined by comparing the net ID portion of the default gateway (by computing a bitwise AND operation between the subnet mask and the default gateway) and the net ID(s) of any of the installed interfaces. For example, a system with a single network card configured with an IP address of 192.168.202.120 and a subnet mask of 255.255.255.0 would require that the default gateway be of the form 192.168.202.xxx because the net ID portion of the IP interface is 192.168.202.

3. **Check that the computer can reach computers in other network segments.** Next, you should ping the IP address of a computer in another IP subnet. If the command fails, use the Trace Route tool (Tracert <IP address>) to examine the path to the target computer and to locate the point at which the command fails. You should then investigate why the data packets are not routed further. For example, an IP router with an incorrect routing table might route datagrams to the wrong subnet.

Note PING and Trace Route rely on the Internet Control Message Protocol (ICMP), which is often blocked by firewalls. An unsuccessful ping or Tracert does not necessarily mean that IP communication does not work. However, a successful ping or Tracert implies that you can reach the target computer at the IP layer.

4. **Check that the computer can reach the target computer's IP address.**   Next, ping the IP address of the target computer you want to reach. If the command fails, use Tracert to see where and why the datagrams are dropped. Keep in mind that the ICMP protocol may be blocked. If ICMP is blocked, use the Telnet tool to connect to an available TCP port on the server. For example, the SMTP service of an Exchange 2003 server typically listens on the well-known port 25, so you should be able to establish a connection to this port using the following command: telnet <IP address of Exchange server> 25.You can also use Network Monitor on both ends of the network connection to verify that data packets reach their destination.

5. **Check that name resolution works.**   Next, ping the fully qualified host name of the target computer, such as ping SERVER01.tailspintoys.com. You should also ping the NetBIOS name, such as ping SERVER01. The PING tool will accomplish two steps:

   a. Resolve the host or NetBIOS name into an IP address.

   b. Ping the specified host using the IP address obtained.

> **Note**   If you ping a host, the Ping tool will report the host name and IP address to you, such as `Pinging server01.tailspintoys.com [192.168.202.121] with 32 bytes of data`. If a fully qualified host name is returned, then the name was resolved through Domain Name System (DNS). If Ping returns a NetBIOS name instead, such as `Pinging server01 [192.168.202.121] with 32 bytes of data`, then the name was resolved through Windows Internet Naming Service (WINS) or broadcasts.

3. **Check that communication at the application layer works.**   Next, you should attempt to connect to the target computer using an application layer protocol. For example, if the target computer is an Exchange 2003 server, you can use Hypertext Transfer Protocol (HTTP) to establish a connection. Start Internet Explorer and then, in the Address textbox, type the following URL: http://<server name>/Exchange, such as http://SERVER01/Exchange. You can also use Telnet to connect to known TCP ports, such as TCP port 25 to communicate with the SMTP service running on the Exchange server. If communication at the application layer fails although you are able to ping the server name, check that no firewall is blocking the communication and that the application service is started and configured properly on the target computer. For example, if you stop the SMTP service on an Exchange 2003 server, you will not be able to connect that server's TCP port 25.

At this point, you already verified that the target IP address is available at the IP layer. However, an incorrect host record in DNS or WINS might cause name resolution to return an incorrect IP address to the Ping tool. When pinging a host, it is therefore a good idea to double-check the IP address information that Ping returns. If you notice that TCP/IP resolves the host or NetBIOS name into a wrong IP address, verify the configuration of your name resolution services. For example, you can use the NSLookup tool to query DNS for IP address information registered in host (A) and other resource records (RR). You should also check the local computer's HOSTS and LMHOSTS files that you can find in the \Windows\System32\Drivers\Etc folder. Ensure that these files do not contain any invalid entries.

Verifying Connectivity Using Netstat

You can also use the Netstat tool to analyze TCP/IP statistics. For example, the netstat -a command shows the status of all TCP and UDP ports on the local system. Healthy status is usually indicated by 0 bytes in the send and receive queues. If data is blocked in either queue, or if the state is irregular, there is likely a problem with the TCP/IP connection. If not, you are probably experiencing network or application delay.

Verifying Connectivity Using NetDiag

If you have installed Windows 2003 Support Tools on your computer, you can also run NetDiag to perform a series of checks, such as IP configuration tests, NetBT name tests, domain membership tests, and more. For a listing of all available tests and command-line options, open a command prompt and type NetDiag /?. For further information, see also Microsoft Knowledge Base Article 321708 "HOW TO: Use the Network Diagnostics Tool (Netdiag.exe) in Windows 2000" (*http://support.microsoft.com/default.aspx?scid=kb;en-us;321708*).

The following listing is an example of a NetDiag log file showing details regarding network communication on an Exchange 2003 server. As highlighted in the listing, there is a problem with the WINS configuration in the network. To run NetDiag, ensure that you are logged on to the server as a member of the local Administrators group.

```
    Computer Name: SERVER01
    DNS Host Name: server01.tailspintoys.com
    System info : Windows 2000 Server (Build 3790)
    Processor : x86 Family 15 Model 2 Stepping 8, GenuineIntel
    List of installed hotfixes :
        Q147222
Netcard queries test . . . . . . . : Passed
Per interface results:
    Adapter : Local Area Connection
        Netcard queries test . . . : Passed

        Host Name. . . . . . . . . : server01
        IP Address . . . . . . . . : 192.168.202.121
```

```
                  Subnet Mask. . . . . . . . : 255.255.255.0
                  Default Gateway. . . . . . : 192.168.202.1
                  Primary WINS Server. . . . : 192.168.202.121
                  Dns Servers. . . . . . . . : 192.168.202.121

                  AutoConfiguration results. . . . . . : Passed
                  Default gateway test . . . : Passed
                  NetBT name test. . . . . . : Passed
                  [WARNING] At least one of the <00> 'WorkStation Service',
                        <03> 'Messenger Service', <20> 'WINS' names is missing.
                        No remote names have been found.

                  WINS service test. . . . . : Failed
                        The test failed.  We were unable to query the WINS servers.
Global results:
Domain membership test . . . . . . : Passed
NetBT transports test. . . . . . . : Passed
      List of NetBt transports currently configured:
            NetBT_Tcpip_{DFD4C3B5-127F-490D-A2E9-EAB7167698E0}
      1 NetBt transport currently configured.
Autonet address test . . . . . . . : Passed
IP loopback ping test. . . . . . . : Passed
Default gateway test . . . . . . . : Passed
NetBT name test. . . . . . . . . . : Passed
      [WARNING] You don't have a single interface with the
            <00> 'WorkStation Service', <03> 'Messenger Service',
            <20> 'WINS' names defined.
Winsock test . . . . . . . . . . . : Passed
DNS test . . . . . . . . . . . . . : Passed
      PASS - All the DNS entries for DC are registered on
            DNS server '192.168.202.121'.
Redir and Browser test . . . . . . : Passed
      List of NetBt transports currently bound to the Redir
            NetBT_Tcpip_{DFD4C3B5-127F-490D-A2E9-EAB7167698E0}
      The redir is bound to 1 NetBt transport.
      List of NetBt transports currently bound to the browser
            NetBT_Tcpip_{DFD4C3B5-127F-490D-A2E9-EAB7167698E0}
      The browser is bound to 1 NetBt transport.
DC discovery test. . . . . . . . . : Passed
DC list test . . . . . . . . . . . : Passed
Trust relationship test. . . . . . : Skipped
Kerberos test. . . . . . . . . . . : Passed
LDAP test. . . . . . . . . . . . . : Passed
Bindings test. . . . . . . . . . . : Passed
WAN configuration test . . . . . . : Skipped
      No active remote access connections.
Modem diagnostics test . . . . . . : Passed
IP Security test . . . . . . . . . : Skipped
      Note: run "netsh ipsec dynamic show /?" for more detailed information
```

> **Note**   You can run Netdiag with /fix switch to correct issues with DNS and domain controllers automatically, provided you allow dynamic DNS updates. For more information, see Knowledge Base Article 219289, "Description of the Netdiag /fix Switch" (*http://support.microsoft.com/default.aspx?scid=kb;en-us;Q219289*).

Verifying Connectivity Using Network Monitor

If services on an Exchange server appear to be configured correctly, and you are still experiencing problems with application layer protocols; for example, if Outlook is unable to communicate through remote procedure calls (RPCs), you might have to use Network Monitor to capture and analyze network traffic in more detail. It is useful to run Network Monitor at the same time on both ends of the network connection. After you filter the traces on the addresses of the two systems, you can compare the traces to see if data packets have been dropped on their way across the computer network. In such a case, you might want to check all intermediate cabling, hubs, switches, and routers for hardware or configuration errors. It is also a good idea to take a reference trace on a properly functioning system and then compare that reference trace to the trace in question. This comparison can help to isolate a problem quickly.

Gathering Server Information

After you verify that a problem is not specific to a single client computer and that the computer network and network services operate reliably, it is possible to conclude that a problem might be related to the Exchange server itself. Malfunctioning hardware and operating system components, such as device drivers, can cause performance and stability problems on an Exchange server.

> **On the Resource Kit CD**   Unavailable Active Directory domain controllers and global catalog servers can also cause Exchange services to fail, as demonstrated in the document Shutting down the one and only GC in a test environment.doc, which you can find in the \Companion Material\Chapter 02 folder on the companion CD.

Obtaining Diagnostics Information

The first task in troubleshooting is to get an overview of the situation. You must understand exactly how the problem manifests itself and what is causing the problem so that you can be confident that you are not troubleshooting the wrong issue. Accordingly, you should start troubleshooting Exchange server problems with an analysis of the server's system and application event logs, because these logs contain valuable information about the current system behavior.

By default, the services of Exchange Server 2003, such as Microsoft Exchange System Attendant and Microsoft Exchange Information Store, log error events and critical messages to the application event log, but you can also increase the logging level to obtain more information. You can increase the diagnostics logging level by using Exchange System Manager, as mentioned earlier in this chapter. Remember, however, that setting logging levels for the Exchange 2003 services and their internal components too high can quickly fill the event log with irrelevant information. Do not forget to reset the logging level on all categories to None when you are done troubleshooting Exchange 2003.

Exchange System Manager enables you to specify logging levels None through Maximum, which is sufficient for most troubleshooting situations. However, when troubleshooting a particularly complex Exchange problem, you might want to log even more information in the application event log by enabling trace logging. Trace level logging is not exposed in Exchange System Manager. You can only set it using Registry Editor. Keep in mind, however, that trace level logging degrades server performance measurably. You should use trace level logging under the guidance of Microsoft Product Support Services when troubleshooting complex Exchange Server 2003 issues.

Warning   Using Registry Editor incorrectly can cause serious problems that may require you to reinstall your operating system. Microsoft cannot guarantee that problems resulting from the incorrect use of Registry Editor can be solved. Use Registry Editor at your own risk.

To set the diagnostics logging level for Exchange services to trace level, use the following steps:

1. Start Registry Editor and open the Diagnostics registry key of the desired Exchange service in the Windows services database that is available at `HKEY_LOCAL_MACHINE\SYSTEM\CurrentControlSet\Services`. For example, the registry key of the System Attendant is: `HKEY_LOCAL_MACHINE\SYSTEM\CurrentControlSet\Services\MSExchangeSA`.

2. Double-click each entry for the individual diagnostics categories and set the values to **0x7**. For example, you can set the value of the 13 OAL Generator category for the MSExchangeSA service to **0x7** to obtain most detailed information about the generation of offline address books.

3. Restart the Exchange services. Services typically do not have to be restarted for configuration changes to take effect. However, when you edit settings of active Exchange 2003 services in the registry manually, you might have to perform this step because Registry Editor (unlike Exchange System Manager) is not a service control program. In other words, Registry Editor does not inform Service Control Manager (SCM) that the configuration of a service has changed, and so SCM does not instruct the affected service to re-read its configuration settings.

To cope with the amount of information written to the application event log, you can filter for events of interest according to event sources and categories. In Event Viewer, select the Application log, click View, and then click Filter. Under Event source, you can select desired source, such as MSExchangeSA. To display all events of the selected event source, ensure that Category is set to All. Event logs can be viewed locally or remotely, and they can be saved to *.EVT files.

Using Microsoft Product Support Reporting Tools

If you contact Microsoft Product Support Services in a troubleshooting incident, you might need to send your event logs plus additional system, diagnostic, and configuration information to Microsoft, so that the support specialist assigned to your case can locate possible causes of the problem. You can use Microsoft Product Support Reporting Tools (MPS_REPORTS) to gather the required information. You can download the MPS_REPORTS tools at *http://www.microsoft.com/downloads/details.aspx?FamilyId=CEBF3C7C-7CA5-408F-88B7-F9C79B7306C0&displaylang=en#filelist*.

> **Note**   MPS_REPORTS does not change registry settings and does not change the configuration of the operating system.

MPS_REPORTS is a compressed software package that comes in the following editions (a .txt readme file accompanies each edition):

■ **MPSRPT_Alliance.exe**   A general, all-purpose edition of MPS_REPORTS that you can use to capture a broad range of configuration information.

■ **MPSRPT_Cluster.exe**   A cluster edition of MPS_REPORTS that you can use to capture information that is relevant to Windows Cluster Service issues.

- **MPSRPT_Dirsvc.exe**   An edition of MPS_REPORTS that you can use to capture information that is relevant to Directory Services issues.

- **MPSRPT_Exchange.exe**   An edition of MPS_REPORTS that you can use to capture information that is relevant to Exchange 2003 issues.

- **MPSRPT_MDAC.exe**   An edition of MPS_REPORTS that you can use to capture information that is relevant to Microsoft Data Access Components (MDAC) issues.

- **MPSRPT_Network.exe**   An edition of MPS_REPORTS that you can use to capture information that is relevant to networking issues.

- **MPSRPT_Setupperf.exe**   An edition of MPS_REPORTS that you can use to capture information that is relevant to setup and performance issues.

- **MPSRPT_SUS.exe**   An edition that you can use to capture information that is relevant to Software Update Services (SUS) issues.

- **MPSRPT_SQL.exe**   An edition that you can use to capture information that is relevant to SQL Server.

For Exchange 2003 troubleshooting, use the Exchange edition of MPS_REPORTS. After downloading this tool, you can run MPSRPT_Exchange.exe directly on the Exchange server. MPSRPT_Exchange.exe is self-installing and will install itself every time you run the tool, overwriting any previous installation, before running MPSRPT.cmd automatically to gather the reports. You can also install the tool without creating any reports if you start MPSRPT_Exchange.exe with the /Q option. By default, the tool installs itself in %SystemRoot%\MPSReports\Exchange. To gather the reports without installing MPSRPT_Exchange.exe again, you can run the MPSRPT.cmd batch file directly from the \Bin folder.

Lite Mode and Full Mode

MPSRPT_Exchange.exe has two reporting modes: Lite Mode and Full Mode. By default, MPSRPT_Exchange.exe runs in Lite Mode, capturing event logs in both native and CSV format, system startup and crash recovery data (including Boot.ini, Autoexec.nt, and Config.nt, as well as the registry settings that control application and system crash handling), clustering information (if the server is part of a server or Network Load Balancing cluster), system service configuration and trace settings, information about hotfix install history, system diagnostics, network configuration and current state information, inventory of the currently running processes and device drivers on the system, information about installed software, and information about the installation and configuration of Exchange Server.

Full Mode, which is started by using the /F option, creates all of the reports in Lite Mode and adds an inventory of all application files and more system files that are not collected in Lite Mode. Full Mode can take an extended period of time to gather information. You should only run MPSRPT_Exchange.exe in Full Mode when directed by a Microsoft Support Professional. You can find more information about MPSRPT_Exchange.exe in the readme files in the %SystemRoot%\MPSReports\Exchange\Doc folder.

On the Resource Kit CD For step-by-step instructions about how to run MPSRPT_Exchange.exe, see the document named To gather Exchange diagnostics information using MPS_PREPORTS.doc, which you can find in the \Companion Material\Chapter 19 folder on the companion CD.

MPS_REPORTS Dump Files

To run MPSRPT_Exchange.exe, ensure that you are logged on to the server as a member of the local Administrators group. It takes about five to 15 minutes to create the reports. Up to a maximum of approximately 200 megabytes (MB) of hard disk space is required for the reports, depending on the size of the event log files. For your convenience, MPSRPT_Exchange.exe places all generated reports into a .cab file that you can then send to the support specialist who is handling your support incident. Each time you run MPSRPT_Exchange.exe, the tool overwrites any existing report files and creates a new .cab file. If you need to look at an older report, you can extract it from the old .cab file. You can find the .cab files in the %SystemRoot%\MPSReports\Exchange\Cab folder. Windows Explorer can read .cab files directly.

Table 19-3 lists the reports generated by MPSRPT_Exchange.exe in Lite Mode. Most of these reports are plain text files that you can view in Notepad.

Table 19-3 MPSRPT Generated Reports

File Name	Comments
ExchDump_*<date>_<time>*.HTM	Contains current state information of your Exchange organization in Hypertext Markup Language (HTML) format. This file contains information obtained from Active Directory, the metabase, the Windows registry, and the local security database. The Exchange dump file also contains a remote procedure call (RPC) endpoint map.
	Among other things, the Exchange dump contains:
	■ Configuration information for every server (including child objects) and administrative group object in the organization.
	■ Information specific to Active Directory Connector connection agreements.
	■ Information specific to Exchange SMTP. Also includes Recipient Policy and Routing Group information.
	■ Information specific to public folder hierarchies.
	■ Information specific to Recipient Policies.
	■ Information specific to Recipient Update Service and address list configuration.
	■ Information specific to Routing Groups, such as connectors installed and their configuration.
	■ Information specific to the Exchange HTTP components including OWA, IM, OMA, Active Synch and RPC/HTTP.
	■ Information specific to the Internet Information Services (IIS) Web service, access control reports for all valid paths, and user rights information.
	Note that MPSRPT_Exchange.exe uses the ExchDump tool to generate this file. You can also use the ExchDump tool manually, which can be useful if you want to dump configuration about a particular component that you are interested in. For information about how to use the Exch-Dump tool, see Microsoft Knowledge Base Article 839116, "Overview of the ExchDump tool for Exchange 2000 Server and for Exchange Server 2003" (*http://support.microsoft.com/default.aspx?scid=kb;EN-US;839116*).
ExchDump_*<date>_<time>*.XML	Contains the Exchange dump in XML format.
ExchInfo.xsl	A file in Extensible Stylesheet Language (XSL) format that is used in conjunction with <server name>_Exch_Info.xml to render Exchange 2003 configuration information in a Web page.

Table 19-3 MPSRPT Generated Reports (Continued)

File Name	Comments
NetDiag.log	Contains information about the configuration of TCP/IP and the availability of important network services.
<server name>_.NETFramework.CSV	Contains information about Microsoft .NET modules installed on the server in comma separated format.
*<server name>*_.NETFramework.TXT	Contains information about Microsoft .NET modules installed on the server in plain text format.
*<server name>*_Active Directory Connector Setup.log	Contains details about the installation of Active Directory Connector on the local computer (if applicable).
*<server name>*_Application.evt	Contains a dump of the events in the current application even log. You can use Event Viewer to open this file.
*<server name>*_BOOT_INI.TXT	A copy of the current boot.ini file.
*<server name>*_CLUSTER-FILES.CSV	Contains information about the files of the Windows Cluster service installed on the local computer in comma-separated format.
<server name>_CLUSTER-FILES.TXT	Contains information about the files of the Windows Cluster service installed on the local computer in plain text format.
*<server name>*_CLUSTERINFO.TXT	Contains information about the current configuration and state of the local Windows Cluster service.
*<server name>*_CONFIG_AUTO.txt	A copy of the config.nt file of the local computer.
*<server name>*_dcdiag.TXT	Contains domain controller diagnostics information.
*<server name>*_Directory_Service.evt	Contains a dump of the events in the current directory service event log. This log only exists only on domain controllers. You can use Event Viewer to open this file.
*<server name>*_DNS_Server.evt	Contains a dump of the events in the current DNS server event log. This log only exists only on DNS servers. You can use Event Viewer to open this file.
*<server name>*_DRIVERS.CSV	Contains information about the device drivers installed on the local computer in comma-separated format.
*<server name>*_DRIVERS.TXT	Contains information about the device drivers installed on the local computer in plain text format.
*<server name>*_Event-Application.CSV	Contains a dump of the events in the current application event log in comma-separated format.
*<server name>*_EventDirectory Service.CSV	Contains a dump of the events in the current directory service event log in comma-separated format.
*<server name>*_EventDNS Server.CSV	Contains a dump of the events in the current DNS server event log in comma-separated format.

Table 19-3 MPSRPT Generated Reports (Continued)

File Name	Comments
*<server name>*_EventFile Replication Service.CSV	Contains a dump of the events in the current file replication service event log in comma-separated format.
*<server name>*_EventSystem.CSV	Contains a dump of the events in the current system event log in comma-separated format.
*<server name>*_Exchange Server Setup Progress.log	Contains details about the installation of Exchange Server 2003 on the local computer.
*<server name>*_EXCH_ADC.CSV	Contains information about the files and configuration of Active Directory Connector on the local computer in comma-separated format.
*<server name>*_EXCH_ADC.TXT	Contains information about the files of Active Directory Connector on the local computer in plain text format.
*<server name>*_EXCH_ADCREG.TXT	Contains a dump of the registry keys for Active Directory Connector in plain text format.
*<server name>*_EXCH_DIR.CSV	Contains a listing of the files and directories that belong to Exchange 2003 on the local computer in comma-separated format.
*<server name>*_EXCH_DIR.TXT	Contains a listing of the files and directories that belong to Exchange 2003 on the local computer in plain text format.
*<server name>*_EXCH_dsaccess.TXT	Contains information about the domain controllers and LDAP port numbers that the DSAccess component of the Microsoft Exchange System Attendant service is using to communicate with Active Directory.
*<server name>*_EXCH_IMF.TXT	Contains information about Exchange Intelligent Message Filter (IMF), if applicable.
*<server name>*_Exch_Info.xml	Contains general configuration information about the local Exchange 2003 server. You can view this information directly in Internet Explorer. ExchInfo.xsl is used automatically to transform the XML data into a Web page.
*<server name>*_EXCH_NLtest.TXT	Contains information about the success or failure of NetLogon service tests.
*<server name>*_EXCH_REG.TXT	A dump of important Exchange 2003 registry keys.
*<server name>*_EXCH_smtpreg.TXT	Contains a dump of the IIS metabase settings that apply to the SMTP service.
*<server name>*_EXCH_Trace.TXT	Contains RegTrace configuration information. Regtrace is a debugging tool that a troubleshooter can use to capture activities in the Exchange 2003 transport subsystem.
*<server name>*_EXCH_web.config	Contains configuration information about Outlook Mobile Access.

Table 19-3 MPSRPT Generated Reports (Continued)

File Name	Comments
*<server name>*_File_Replication_Service.evt	Contains a dump of the events in the current file replication service event log. This log exists only on domain controllers. You can use Event Viewer to open this file.
*<server name>*_HOTFIX.TXT	Contains a list of hotfixes installed on the local computer.
*<server name>*_IISREG.TXT	Contains a dump of registry keys that apply to Internet Information Services (IIS).
*<server name>*_IPSEC.TXT	Contains information about the IPSec configuration and policies that apply to the local computer.
*<server name>*_metabase.xml	A copy of the current IIS 6.0 metabase.
*<server name>*_MISC.txt	A dump of miscellaneous configuration information, such as environment variables, server name, and network shares.
*<server name>*_MSINFO32.NFO	Complete system configuration in Microsoft System Information format. Start the System Information tool (msinfo32.exe) and then open this file to view the contents.
*<server name>*_netdiag.TXT	Contains detailed diagnostics information about network interface configuration and network communication.
*<server name>*_NETINFO.txt	Contains detailed diagnostics information about the configuration of the TCP/IP protocol stack and related communication protocols.
*<server name>*_PROCESS.CSV	Contains information about the processes and modules currently active on the local computer in comma-separated format.
*<server name>*_PROCESS.TXT	Contains information about the processes and modules currently active on the local computer in plain text format.
*<server name>*_PROGRESS.TXT	Contains detailed information about the actions performed by MPSRPT_Exchange.exe. If you analyze this file, you can see which other tools MPSRPT_Exchange.exe starts to gather the configuration information.
*<server name>*_PSTAT.TXT	Contains system information about the processes currently running on the local computer.
*<server name>*_RECOVERY.TXT	Contains registry settings that apply to Dr. Watson and Session Manager.
*<server name>*_setupact.log	A copy of the setupact.log file that is located in the \Windows directory. The setupact.log file contains information about the actions performed by the Windows Setup program.

Table 19-3   MPSRPT Generated Reports (Continued)

File Name	Comments
*<server name>*_setupapi.log	A copy of the setupapi.log file that is located in the \Windows directory. The setupapi.log file contains information about device and driver installations, service pack installations, and hotfix installations.
*<server name>*_setuperr.log	A copy of the setuperr.log file that is located in the \Windows directory. The setuperr.log file contains information about errors that might have occurred during the installation of the operating system.
*<server name>*_SYSINFO.TXT	Contains general information about the local computer and the operating system.
*<server name>*_System.evt	Contains a dump of the events in the current system event log. You can use Event Viewer to open this file.
*<server name>*_SYSTEM32.CSV	Contains information about important system files in the \Windows\System32 directory in comma-separated format.
*<server name>*_SYSTEM32.TXT	Contains information about important system files in the \Windows\System32 directory in plain text format.
*<server name>*_TRACING.TXT	Contains a dump of registry keys that apply to the Windows security subsystem.
*<server name>*_WLBS.TXT	Contains configuration information about Windows Network Load Balancing, if installed on the local computer.
*<server name>*_WMI_Cons.log	A copy of the Cons.log file that is located in the \Windows\System32\Wbem\Logs directory. The Cons.log file contains trace information about WMI consumers.
*<server name>*_WMI_Frame-Work.log	A copy of the FrameWork.log file that is located in the \Windows\System32\Wbem\Logs directory. The FrameWork.log file contains trace information and error messages for the WMI provider framework and the Win32 Provider.
*<server name>*_WMI_mof-comp.log	A copy of the Mofcomp.log file that is located in the \Windows\System32\Wbem\Logs directory. The Mofcomp.log file contains compilation details from the Managed Object Format (MOF) compiler.
*<server name>*_WMI_setup.log	A copy of the Setup.log file that is located in the \Windows\System32\Wbem\Logs directory. The Setup.log file contains information about the activities performed to add the WMI classes to the WMI repository.
*<server name>*_WMI_wbemess.log	A copy of the Wbemess.log file that is located in the \Windows\System32\Wbem\Logs directory. The Wbemess.log file contains all warning and error messages related to the WMI event subsystem.

Table 19-3 MPSRPT Generated Reports (Continued)

File Name	Comments
*<server name>*_WMI_wbem-prox.log	A copy of the Wbemprox.log file that is located in the \Windows\System32\Wbem\Logs directory. The Wbemprox.log file contains trace information for the WMI proxy server.
*<server name>*_WMI_wmiadap.log	A copy of the WMI_wmiadap.log file that is located in the \Windows\System32\Wbem\Logs directory. The WMI_wmiadap.log file contains error messages related to the WMI AutoDiscoveryAutoPurge (ADAP) process.
*<server name>*_WMI_wmiprov.log	A copy of the WMI_ wmiprov.log file that is located in the \Windows\System32\Wbem\Logs directory. The WMI_wmiprov.log file contains management data and events from WMI-enabled Windows Driver Model (WDM) drivers.

Generating Debugging Information

Even most detailed event log and configuration information might not reveal the source of a problem if you are dealing with an Exchange service that stops responding (hangs) or quits unexpectedly (crashes). For example, the Microsoft Exchange Information Store service might crash due to a system conflict with an unreliable component installed on the server, such as an untested virus scanner. In this situation, Microsoft Product Support Services might have to analyze memory dumps and text files that contain debugging information.

To generate debugging information, you should download Debugging Tools for Windows available at *http://www.microsoft.com/whdc/ddk/debugging/default.mspx*. Debugging Tools for Windows includes debuggers, such as Microsoft Console Debugger (CDB), and other tools, such as a very useful Microsoft Visual Basic script called Autodump Plus (ADPlus.vbs). ADPlus.vbs automates the CDB debugger to produce memory dumps and log files with debug output from user-mode processes or services, such as the Microsoft Exchange System Attendant service or the Microsoft Exchange Information Store service. All Exchange Server 2003 services run as user-mode processes. The only Exchange 2003 component that runs in kernel mode is the Exchange Installable File System (ExIFS) driver.

You can use ADPlus.vbs to provide Microsoft Product Support Services with debugging information if you are experiencing the following problems:

- Exchange services stop responding

- Exchange services consume 100 percent of CPU resources

- Exchange services shut down unexpectedly

> **On the Resource Kit CD**   For an example of how to use the ADPlus.vbs script to generate debugging information, see the document To generate Exchange debugging information using ADPlus.doc, which you can find in the \Companion Material\Chapter 19 folder on the companion CD.

ADPlus Modes of Operation

ADPlus.vbs has two modes of operation: Hang Mode and Crash Mode. Hang mode is used to troubleshoot Exchange services or other processes, such as Internet Information Services (IIS), that stop responding or that consume 100 percent of CPU resources for sustained periods of time or indefinitely. Crash Mode, on the other hand, is used to troubleshoot services or other processes that shut down unexpectedly. It is important to note, however, that you cannot use ADPlus.vbs to troubleshoot an Exchange service that quits unexpectedly during startup. The service must at least start successfully so that you can attach the debugger. If you must troubleshoot a service that terminates unexpectedly upon startup, you must use the Windows CDB debugger directly.

> **Caution**   Do not run Windows debugging tools on a production server unless instructed by a product support specialist. If you want to familiarize yourself with ADPlus.vbs, install and run the debugging tools on a test server.

Generating Memory Dumps in Hang Mode

You can run ADPlus.vbs in hang mode at any time to produce the memory dump of a running process. To generate a memory dump for a hanging Exchange service, however, you must wait until the service stops responding before running ADPlus.vbs. You can then run ADPlus by opening the command prompt, switching to the folder where the debuggers are installed (such as C:\Program Files\Debugging Tools for Windows), and then typing **adplus.vbs** and pressing Enter. If you are running ADPlus.vbs for the first time, a Register Cscript.exe as default script interpreter? dialog box will appear. Click Yes. We recommend that you change the default script interpreter from WScript.exe to CScript.exe. In the Windows Script Host dialog box informing you that the default script interpreter was changed successfully, click OK. A second command prompt will open that lists ADPlus.vbs command line options and usage information.

To run ADPlus.vbs in Hang Mode, you must specify at a minimum two command-line options: one that specifies the mode of operation, and one that specifies a target process to operate against. For example, to produce a memory dump of IIS and all its related services, including the Web service, SMTP service, IMAP4 service, and POP3 service, type **adplus.vbs -hang -iis** and press Enter. Each time you run ADPlus.vbs, the script places memory dumps and debug files in a new, uniquely named folder on the local hard disk. A Windows Script Host dialog box is displayed to inform you of the actual location, but you can also use the **-o** command-line option to specify a name for the debug output folder and files.

To run ADPlus.vbs in hang mode against an Exchange-specific service, you can use the **-pn** or **-p** command-line option to specify the service to which you want to attach. You can use the **-pn** option to specify the process you are interested in by name, such as Store.exe for the Microsoft Exchange Information Store service. Do not forget to specify the file name extension. Using the -p option, you can specify the process by process ID (PID). You can use Task Manager to determine the PID of the hanging process when adding the PID column to the Processes tab (View menu, Select Columns). For example, in Figure 19-2, Store.exe has a PID of 1864, and to create a dump of that process, you can use the command line **adplus.vbs -hang -p 1864**. For more information about the ADPlus.vbs command-line options, type **adplus.vbs -?** and press Enter.

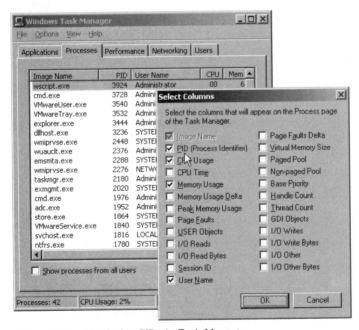

Figure 19-2   Displaying PIDs in Task Manager

When ADPlus.vbs is dumping memory for an Exchange 2003 service, it does so asynchronously to provide an effective snapshot of the entire process, including all threads and loaded libraries at the time ADPlus was run. It is also important to remember that the Exchange service might make remote procedure calls (RPCs) to other processes. It is important to capture all of the processes at the same time to reflect the actual state of Exchange 2003.

Generating Memory Dumps in Crash Mode

ADPlus.vbs works differently in Crash Mode, because the script cannot dump the virtual memory of a process that is not running any longer. If you are troubleshooting an Exchange service that often quits unexpectedly, you must start ADPlus.vbs before the actual crash occurs. You can use the **-notify** command-line option to have ADPlus.vbs send a notification to you or a computer when the crash occurs. Ensure that the Windows Messenger service is started on that computer.

You can activate Crash Mode when you start ADPlus.vbs with the **-crash** command-line option instead of **-hang**. Using the **-pn** or **-p** command-line option, you can specify the Exchange service or other process that you want to monitor. You can additionally specify **the –nodumponfirst** switch that instructs ADPlus.vbs not to create a memory dump when a process experiences a first-chance exception. A first-chance exception can in most cases be handled in the code itself while second-chance exceptions cause the actual process to crash, because there is no code handling the exception. If you do not exclude first-chance exceptions, ADPlus.vbs will most likely create multiple dump files, because first-chance exceptions can occur occasionally during normal operation. Dumping the memory on every first-chance exception will greatly increase hard disk activity (to save those dumps) and these dumps might not be relevant to the component crash.

When ADPlus monitors an Exchange service in crash mode and a fatal error occurs and the service crashes, ADPlus tracks important information about the crash to the event log and performs a memory dump. On the other hand, if no crash occurs, you can press CTRL+C to break into the debugger and detach the debugger from the monitored service. However, you must also restart the monitored Exchange service, because the monitored service is stopped when you detach the debugger.

When a fatal error occurs in a monitored service, ADPlus.vbs performs the following actions:

1.   Pauses the monitored service.

2.   Logs the date and time that the fatal error occurred.

3.   Logs the thread ID and the call stack for the thread that raised the fatal error.

4.   Produces a full memory dump of the monitored service or process.

5.   Exits the CDB debugger and stops the monitored service.

Note If you are running ADPlus in crash mode from the local console, you must remain logged on to the console for the duration of the debug session. When you log out, debugging is cancelled and the monitored service is stopped. To avoid this issue, lock the current session (by pressing CTRL+ALT+DEL, and then click Lock Computer) instead of logging out. Alternatively, you can also run ADPlus.vbs non-interactively from a remote command shell that does not require an interactive logon. You can use the Remote.exe tool included in Debugging Tools for Windows to start a remote command shell through the following command (where remote_server is the name of the server that is running the remote command shell): **remote.exe /c remote_server remoteshell**.

Installing Symbol Files

If you run ADPlus.vbs without further preparation, the script displays a Windows Script Host dialog box informing you that the Windows symbol files are not installed. Symbol files hold the names of global and local variables, as well as function names and other data, such as source-code line numbers, that make it easier to analyze debugging information. Symbol files are created when compiling source code into executables and DLLs, but the symbols are actually not required to run the binaries. The purpose of symbols is to make the debugging process user-friendly. Keeping the symbols separate from executables and DLLs results in smaller and faster binaries.

The Windows Script Host dialog box instructs you to install the symbol files for Windows Server and Exchange Server 2003 so that ADPlus.vbs can resolve function names in the stack trace information of each thread in the processes being debugged. However, you do not need to install symbols if you are planning to send the dump files to Microsoft Product Support Services. Support specialists can take a dump and link it to internal symbol servers in order to see all information. Installing the symbol files is useful if you want to check the crash dump in a debugger yourself, and to avoid the ADPlus.vbs warning that the symbols are missing.

To enable full-featured debugging, you must install the proper symbols for the code that you want to debug, and load these symbols into the debugger. If your server is connected to the Internet, you can also use Microsoft's public symbol store. For more information about how to use this store, see *http://go.microsoft.com/fwlink/?linkid=17363&clcid=0x409*.

If you do not want to use the public symbol store, follow these steps to install the symbol files for Windows 2003:

1. Make sure you have at least one Gigabyte (GB) of available hard disk space to accommodate the symbol package and required temporary files.

2. Go to the Windows Symbols website at *http://www.microsoft.com/whdc/dev-tools/debugging/symbolpkg.mspx#Windows%20symbol%20packages* and download the appropriate symbol package according to your Windows and Service Pack version. Most likely you should download the symbols for the retail version.

3. Double-click the downloaded file, such as Windows2003.x86.fre.rtm.symbols.exe, and then in the License dialog box, read the licensing agreement, and if you agree, click Yes to continue.

4. In the Microsoft Windows Symbols dialog box, verify that C:\Windows\Symbols is specified as the Symbol install directory, and then click OK.

5. In the Microsoft Windows Symbols dialog box informing you that the installation is complete, click OK.

6. Click Start, right-click My Computer, and then click Properties.

7. Click the Advanced tab, and then click Environment Variables.

8. Under System Variables, click New. Create an **_NT_SYMBOL_PATH** environment variable, and then set it to **C:\WINNT\Symbols**.

9. Click OK repeatedly to close all dialog boxes.

To install the symbol files for Exchange 2003, follow these steps:

1. From the Exchange 2003 or Exchange 2003 Service Pack 1 product CD, start the Setup program that you can find in the \Support\Symbols\i386 folder.

2. The Setup program installs the symbol files without further input. You do not need to restart Exchange Server 2003.

3. The Setup program completes automatically. To verify that the symbol files are installed, open the C:\WINDOWS\Symbols\exe folder and check that you can find Exchange-specific .pdb files, such as Store.pdb, which is the symbol file for the Store.exe file of the Exchange Information Store service. In Windows 2003, all symbol files have a .pdb file name extension.

Note   The symbol files that you install must match the software versions of Windows and Exchange Server on the target computer. If you plan to perform user-mode debugging on the server running Exchange Server 2003, then install the symbol files that match the version of Windows running on that system.

Automatic Error Reporting in Exchange Server 2003

Having installed symbol files for Exchange 2003, you can also configure Dr. Watson to generate a symbol table. Error reporting based on Dr. Watson allows you to report fatal software errors to Microsoft. Microsoft collects the error reports, and then uses the information to improve product functionality. By default, when fatal errors occur in Exchange System Manager or an Exchange 2003 service, a notification message is displayed when you log on to the computer to inform you that unexpected events have occurred and to provide you with an option to send an error report to Microsoft. If you do not want to view the standard error reporting dialog box, you can configure Exchange to automatically send service-related error reports to Microsoft.

On the Resource Kit CD   For detailed step-by-step instructions about how to enable automatic service-related error reporting, see the To enable automatic service-related error reporting in Exchange 2003.doc document, which you can find in the \Companion Material\Chapter 19 folder on the companion CD.

Note   Exchange 2003 sends error reports to Microsoft over a secure HTTPS connection. The report, known as a minidump, usually consists of a 10 to 50 kilobyte (KB) compressed file.

By default, Dr. Watson only creates a mini crash dump. To generate a full dump instead, plus a symbol table, start drwtsn32.exe from a command prompt or the Run dialog box, and then click Full under Crash Dump Type and select the Dump Symbol Table check box. Leave all other check boxes selected and click OK. You can also adjust the default Log File Path and Crash Dump path for Dr. Watson files. The default is C:\Documents and Settings\<user account>\Local Settings\Application Data\Microsoft\Dr Watson, but it is a good idea to place this folder on a disk drive other than the system drive. For more information about how to configure Dr. Watson, see the technical article Using Dr. Watson (*http://go.microsoft.com/fwlink/ ?LinkId=15183*).

Best Practices

It is important to troubleshoot Exchange 2003 issues in a coordinated way using tried and proven procedures. You should identify, analyze, and locate the issue before applying configuration changes. Applying configuration changes to a product system without coordination and testing is seldom a good strategy. It is good practice to apply a solution to a problem only after successful testing in a test lab.

Analyzing and locating a problem typically requires checking diagnostics information in event and system logs. Many of the internal Exchange 2003 components record events in the Event Log. Others write system information into protocol logs on the file system (such as IIS services). In a troubleshooting situation, it is useful to increase the diagnostics logging level for the internal components of affected Exchange services. Do not forget to set the diagnostics logging level back to None when you have gathered the required information. To obtain most detailed system information, you can also create system reports using MPS_REPORTS, and you can prepare memory dumps and stack traces using Debugging Tools for Windows. If you are dealing with a complex problem, it is a good idea to contact Microsoft Product Support Services for assistance.

The dump files that you can create using MPS_REPORTS and debugging tools contain an overwhelming amount of details, which makes it difficult to analyze the information. You can address this issue by setting up a baseline dump when the server is running within normal parameters. You can then analyze a problematic dump by comparing it to the baseline dump. Tools, such as Windiff.exe, can be helpful in finding differences between the dump files quickly. The Windiff tool is included in the Windows Platform Software Development Kit (SDK). You can download Windiff at *http://msdn.microsoft.com/library/default.asp?url=/library/en-us/tools/tools/windiff.asp*.

Chapter 20

Troubleshooting Active Directory Communication

About This Chapter

This chapter explains how Microsoft Exchange Server 2003 communicates with Microsoft Active Directory directory service. It will look at the components of Active Directory that impact an Exchange 2003 organization and the tools that an administrator can use to analyze Active Directory and the communication between Exchange and Active Directory to ensure everything is functioning properly.

What You Need to Know

It is assumed that you are familiar with Microsoft Windows server technology, Active Directory directory service, and managing directory information in an Exchange 2003 organization. To familiarize yourself with Windows Server 2003 or Active Directory, see Windows Server 2003 Technology Centers at *http://www.microsoft.com/ windowsserver2003/technologies*. For more information about managing Exchange Server 2003 directory information, see Chapter 9, "Managing Directory Information."

Exchange Server relies heavily on Active Directory directory service and Domain Name System (DNS). For this reason, you must ensure that domain controllers, global catalog servers, and DNS servers in your organization are functioning properly. Similar to the way directory replication errors created problems and inconsistencies in Exchange Server 5.5, problems with Active Directory replication will cause problems with Exchange 2003 configuration information and address lists. Active Directory replication must be functioning properly to ensure that Exchange can communicate and access current information from Active Directory.

Understanding Active Directory Server Roles and Active Directory Replication

Because Exchange uses Active Directory to store Exchange data such as recipient objects, configuration data, schema attributes, and the global address list (GAL), it is important to understand the relationship between Active Directory server roles and Active Directory replication to understand how they impact the Exchange organization.

The Active Directory database is logically separated into directory partitions (or naming contexts), a schema partition, a configuration partition, domain partitions, and application partitions. Each partition is a unit of replication, and each partition has its own replication topology. Replication is performed between directory partition replicas. All domain controllers in the same forest have at least two directory partitions in common: the schema and configuration partitions. In addition, all domain controllers in the same domain share a common domain partition.

Active Directory Server Roles

Several supporting services, such as DNS services, domain controller services, and global catalog services, are critical for the proper functioning of your Exchange organization.

- There must also be enough DNS servers on the network to provide good performance for name resolution.

- There must be enough domain controllers and global catalog servers on the network to provide good performance for authentication and directory lookups.

DNS Servers

DNS services are critical to the operations of your Exchange organization. Windows Server 2003 Active Directory directory service uses DNS as its domain controller location mechanism. When operations, such as authentication, updating, or searching, are performed, Windows Server 2003 computers use DNS to locate Active Directory domain controllers and these domain controllers use DNS to locate each other. For example, when a network user with an Active Directory user account logs in to an Active Directory domain, the user's computer uses DNS to locate a domain controller for the Active Directory domain to which the user wants to log in.

Exchange servers and Exchange clients use DNS for name resolution when locating Exchange servers and global catalog servers. Exchange servers use DNS for routing messages and message delivery. Use of the DNS dynamic update functionality in Windows Server 2003 can reduce administration of DNS zones and ensure that Exchange servers and Exchange clients can find the Exchange servers and global catalog servers in your environment. DNS dynamic updates allow DNS client computers to register and dynamically update their resource records with a DNS server whenever changes occur. Servers running Exchange can dynamically register Host (A) records with DNS. Host records map the DNS domain name of the server to its IP address.

For your Exchange servers to receive Internet mail, a Mail Exchanger (MX) resource record must exist in DNS. MX records can exist on internal DNS servers if you manage your own DNS, or on DNS servers managed by your Internet service provider (ISP). MX records are DNS records that tell other computers the IP address and name of the server in your Exchange organization that receives Internet mail. The MX record must point to the A record associated with the IP address of the Exchange SMTP virtual server that receives Internet mail for your organization. If you are supporting multiple e-mail domains, an MX record must exist for each of those domains for DNS to accept mail for the domain. MX records for your Exchange servers do not register dynamically with DNS.

More Info   For more information about deploying Windows Server 2003 DNS, see the book *Deploying Network Services* in the Microsoft Windows Server 2003 Deployment Kit (*http://www.microsoft.com/resources/documentation/WindowsServ/2003/all/deployguide/en-us/Default.asp*).

Table 20-1 shows the DNS records that are required for proper Active Directory functionality.

Table 20-1   Required DNS Records

Mnemonic	Type	DNS record	Requirements
pdc	SRV	_ldap._tcp.pdc._msdcs.*<DnsDomainName>*	One per domain
gc	SRV	_ldap._tcp.gc._msdcs.*<DnsForestName>*	At least one per forest
gcIPaddress	A	_gc._msdcs.*<DnsForestName>*	At least one per forest
dsaCNAME	CNAME	*<DsaGuide>*._msdcs.*<DnsForestName>*	One per domain controller

Table 20-1   Required DNS Records (Continued)

Mnemonic	Type	DNS record	Requirements
kdc	SRV	_kerberos._tcp.dc._msdcs.*<DnsDomain-Name>*	At least one per domain
dc	SRV	_ldap._tcp.dc._msdcs.*<DnsDomainName>*	At least one per domain
	A	*<DomainControllerFQDN>*	One per domain controller (Domain controllers that have multiple IP addresses can have more than one A resource record.)

> **More Info**   Some Exchange functionality is still dependent on network basic input/output system (NetBIOS) name resolution. These functions include the Exchange Server 2003 Setup program and Exchange Mailbox Merge Wizard (ExMerge). For additional information about requirements for NetBIOS name resolution in an Exchange 2003 organization, view the Microsoft Knowledge Base article 837391, "Exchange Server 2003 and Exchange 2000 Server Require NetBIOS Name Resolution for Full Functionality" (*http://support.microsoft.com/default.aspx?scid=kb;en-us;837391*).

Domain Controllers

Domain controllers contain a copy of the schema and configuration partitions for the Active Directory forest and domain partition for its own domain.

- **Schema partition**   Only one schema partition exists per forest. The schema partition is stored on all domain controllers in a forest. The schema partition contains definitions of all objects and attributes that you can create in the directory, and the rules for creating and manipulating them. Schema information is replicated to all domain controllers in the forest.

  When you create the Exchange organization by running Exchange Setup with the /ForestPrep option, the schema partition is updated with Exchange specific objects and attributes.

- **Configuration partition**   There is only one configuration partition per forest. The configuration partition is stored on all domain controllers in a forest. The configuration partition contains information about the forest-wide Active Directory structure, including what domains and sites exist, which domain controllers exist in each forest, and which services are available. Configuration information is replicated to all domain controllers in a forest.

Exchange stores the majority of its information in the configuration partition, including the topology, connectors, protocols, and service settings for the Exchange organization. Because Active Directory replicates the configuration partition between all domains in the forest, the configuration of the Exchange organization is also replicated throughout the forest.

- **Domain partition**   Domain partitions are stored on each domain controller in a given domain. A domain partition contains information about all domain-specific objects that were created in that domain, including recipient objects, such as users, contacts, and groups. The domain partition is replicated to all domain controllers of that domain but not beyond that domain.

- **Application partition**   Application partitions store information about applications in Active Directory. For example, if you use a DNS that is integrated with Active Directory, you have two application partitions for DNS zones: ForestDN-SZones, which is part of a forest and contains forest zone data, and DomainDN-SZones, which is unique for each domain and contains domain DNS zones. You can designate which domain controllers in a forest host specific application partitions.

All of the Exchange servers in the organization must be able to connect to a domain controller in order to access configuration information. Exchange can use up to 10 domain controllers to perform Active Directory lookups for objects in the local domain. These domain controllers are primarily used to update objects in the local domain or read non-configuration data that is not replicated to global catalog servers.

Configuration Domain Controller

The configuration domain controller is the single domain controller chosen by the Directory Service Access (DSAccess) process (which runs under the control of the System Attendant service) during startup to read and write configuration data. DSAccess uses only a single domain controller for all configuration context requests to reduce issues of replication latency, and to avoid partial directory additions or modifications being made to different domain controllers. Exchange uses the configuration domain controller to read and write all configuration data.

Global Catalog Servers

A global catalog is a Windows Server domain controller that stores two forest-wide partitions—the schema and configuration partitions—plus a complete read/write copy of the domain partition from its own domain and a partial replica of all other domain partitions in the forest. These partial replicas contain a read-only subset of the information in each domain partition.

By default, the partial set of attributes stored in the global catalog includes those attributes most frequently used in search operations, because one of the primary functions of the global catalog is to support clients querying Active Directory.

Exchange uses the services of the global catalog for many purposes, such as message routing and address book lookups. Exchange can use as many as 10 global catalog servers that perform forest-wide queries. All user data is looked up on the global catalog servers.

■ To send and receive e-mail in an Exchange organization, both the e-mail client and the Exchange server must be able to connect to Active Directory global catalog servers.

■ To resolve e-mail addresses for messages sent to recipients in the Exchange organization, the Exchange server must be able to locate the recipient object in the global catalog.

■ To open the GAL, the e-mail client must be able to connect to a global catalog server, either directly or by means of DSProxy. For more information about DSProxy, see the section "Examining DSProxy" later in this chapter.

■ To determine universal group membership, a global catalog server must be available.

Operations Masters

Active Directory defines five operations master roles: the schema master, domain naming master, primary domain controller (PDC) emulator, relative identifier (RID) master, and the infrastructure master. Each role is performed by a domain controller. Each forest can have only one schema master and domain naming master. For the other roles, there is one per domain.

You must carefully monitor the performance of the various operations masters for your Active Directory forest and for each domain. Although these operations masters are not single points of immediate failure, access to services will be affected if these services remain unavailable for an extended period of time, such as permanently shutting down a server holding an operations master role. If you need to shut down a server holding an operations masters role but plan on bringing that server back online again, the role can be transferred to another domain controller. If a server fails and will not be brought back online, you can seize the operations master role. For more information about transferring and seizing operations master roles, see the section "Transferring and Seizing of Operations Master Roles" later in this chapter. Table 20-2 lists each of the operations master roles and the impact if that role is unavailable.

Table 20-2   Operations Master Roles and Availability Impact

Role	Function	Availability impact
Schema master	Contains the master list of object classes and attributes that are used to create all Active Directory objects. The schema master controls all originating updates to the schema and replicates updates to the Active Directory schema to all domain controllers in the forest by using standard replication of the schema partition.	You cannot modify the schema or install applications that modify the schema.
Domain naming master	Controls the addition or removal of domains in the forest. The domain naming master prevents multiple domains with the same domain name from joining the forest.	You cannot add or remove domains from the forest.
PDC emulator	Acts as a Microsoft Windows NT PDC to support any backup domain controllers (BDCs) in a mixed-mode domain.	You cannot change passwords on client computers that do not have the Active Directory client software installed. No replication occurs to Windows NT 4.0 backup domain controllers.
RID master	Allocates blocks of RIDs to each domain controller in the domain. New security principals (user, group, or computer objects) created in a domain are assigned a unique security identifier (SID). This SID consists of a domain SID, which is the same for each security principal that is created in that domain, and a RID, which is unique for each security principal in the domain.	Eventually, domain controllers cannot create new directory objects because each of their RID pools is depleted.
Infrastructure master	Updates object references in its domain that point to objects in another domain. It is responsible for updating group memberships.	Delays displaying updated group membership lists in the user interface when you move users from one group to another.

Active Directory Replication

Replication is the process of updating information in Active Directory from one domain controller to other domain controllers on a network. Whenever an administrator or user performs an action that initiates an update to Active Directory, a domain controller is chosen to perform the update. Active Directory uses a multimaster replication model. *Multimaster* means there are multiple domain controllers, also called masters, that have the authority to modify or control the same information. The replication process synchronizes the movement of updated information between domain controllers. Replication ensures that the same Active Directory information is available to all domain controllers, client computers and servers across the network.

Active Directory must determine which domain controllers replicate data with other domain controllers. Replication occurs between two domain controllers at a time, these domain controllers are known as *replication partners*. Over time, replication synchronizes information in Active Directory for an entire forest of domain controllers. The *replication topology* defines the route by which replication data travels throughout a network. To create a replication topology, Active Directory uses the Knowledge Consistency Checker (KCC) to establish a replication path between domain controllers. The KCC is a built-in process that runs on each domain controller and generates the replication topology for all directory partitions that are contained on that domain controller.

Because all domain controllers within a forest share schema and configuration partitions, Active Directory replicates schema and configuration partitions to all domain controllers. Domain controllers replicate the domain partition with all other domain controllers in the same domain. In addition, domain controllers that host an application partition replicate the application partition.

To optimize replication traffic, a domain controller may have several replication partners for different partitions. Active Directory replicates updates to the directory across domain controllers that contain the updated partition in the forest.

Because Exchange uses domain controllers and global catalog servers to read information stored in Active Directory, replication failure can cause Exchange to access information that is not up-to-date. For example, let's say that you have two domains, DomainA and DomainB. DomainA has two domain controllers, DC-1A and DC-2A that are replication partners, and DomainB has two domain controllers, DC-1B and DC-2B that are replication partners. Replication between DomainA and DomainB occurs between DC-2A and DC-2B.

- You create a mailbox-enabled user on DC-1A. If replication of the user object fails within DomainA, any server reading the domain naming context would not have current knowledge of that user.

- You modify the schema using a domain controller in DomainA. If replication within DomainA was functioning but replication between DomainA and DomainB was not, any server reading the schema naming context from a domain controller in DomainB would have outdated information.

Similarly, if replication of the configuration partition prevented Exchange servers in different domains from knowing of a change in the Exchange configuration, such as adding a connector, Exchange message routing could be impacted.

Active Directory Server Roles and Active Directory Replication Troubleshooting

There are a variety of tools that will allow you to troubleshoot Active Directory. You identify problems in Active Directory using Windows Server tools, Windows Support tools and other tools that you can download. You can identify which servers perform which roles in your Active Directory forest and change the server performing those roles if required. The following section looks at some of the common tools for troubleshooting Active Directory server roles and replication issues. You can find more information about Active Directory by visiting the Windows Server 2003 Technology Centers at *http://www.microsoft.com/windowsserver2003/technologies*.

Tools for Troubleshooting Active Directory

Table 20-3 provides a quick overview of tools you can use to troubleshoot Active Directory and a brief description of their use. Additional information about using some of the tools for troubleshooting follows.

Table 20-3   Tools for Troubleshooting Active Directory

Tool	Description
Event Viewer (eventvwr.msc)	Used to view logged events, such as errors and warnings.
Performance Monitor (perfmon.msc)	Used for establishing a baseline of performance and for troubleshooting performance issues.
LDP (ldp.exe)	Used to perform Lightweight Directory Access Protocol (LDAP) searches against Active Directory. Useful when you want to see what attributes are set to on specific Active Directory object.
	Available on the Windows Server 2003 CD in *<drive>*:\support\tools.
Active Directory Service Interfaces (ADSI) Editor (ADSIEdit.msc)	Used to view and edit attribute values of objects in the configuration, schema, or domain naming context of Active Directory.
	Available on the Windows Server 2003 CD in *<drive>*:\support\tools.
DsAcls (Dsacls.exe)	Used to display and change permissions (access control entries) in the access control list (ACL) of objects in Active Directory. Useful when troubleshooting permissions issues.
	Available on the Windows Server 2003 CD in *<drive>*:\support\tools.
Ping (Ping.exe)	Used to verify configurations and determine whether a specific IP address is accessible.
Network Monitor (netmon.exe)	Used to diagnose issues with server connectivity.

Table 20-3 Tools for Troubleshooting Active Directory (Continued)

Tool	Description
DNS Resolver (Dnsdiag.exe)	Used to troubleshoot Domain Name System (DNS) issues.
	Available at *http://go.microsoft.com/fwlink/?LinkId=25097*.
NSLookup (Nslookup.exe)	Used for testing and troubleshooting DNS servers. Checks records, domain host aliases, domain host services, and operating system information by querying DNS servers.
Active Directory Sites and Services (dssite.msc)	Used to administer the replication of Active Directory data.
Domain Controller Diagnostic Tool (Dcdiag.exe)	Used to analyze the state of domain controllers in a forest or enterprise and report any problems to assist in troubleshooting.
	Available on the Windows Server 2003 CD in *<drive>*:\support\tools.
Network Connectivity Tester (Netdiag.exe)	Used to isolate networking and connectivity problems by performing a series of tests to determine the state of your network client.
	Available on the Windows Server 2003 CD in *<drive>*:\support\tools.
Active Directory Replication Monitor (Replmon.exe)	Used to view the low-level status of Active Directory replication, force synchronization between domain controllers, view the topology in a graphical format, and monitor the status and performance of domain controller replication.
	Available on the Windows Server 2003 CD in *<drive>*:\support\tools.
Replication Diagnostics Tool (Repadmin.exe)	Used to diagnose replication problems between Windows domains, view the replication topology, manually create the replication topology, force replication events between domain controllers, view both the replication metadata and up-to-date vectors, and for monitoring the relative health of an Active Directory forest.
	Available on the Windows Server 2003 CD in *<drive>*:\support\tools.
NTDSUtil (Ntdsutil.exe)	Used to perform database maintenance of Active Directory, manage and control operations master roles, remove metadata left behind by domain controllers that were removed from the network without being properly uninstalled, and create application directory partitions.

Troubleshooting Active Directory Using Event Viewer

You can use the Event View to monitor Active Directory events on domain controllers and global catalog servers. Active Directory events are recorded in the Directory Service event log. By default, Active Directory services record only critical events in the Directory Service event log. You should monitor these events on a regular basis. You should also monitor the DNS Server event log. DNS Server event log contains events logged by the DNS service on computers running Windows configured as a DNS server.

If you are experiencing problems, you can increase the level of logging recorded by Active Directory to allow more verbose logging by modifying the Diagnostics key for NTDS service using the Registry Editor (regedit.exe). Table 20-4 shows the registry key and range of values that can be configured for Active Directory logging.

> **Note** Increasing logging levels should be done to troubleshoot problems. Once the problem has been diagnosed and resolved, logging levels should be return to their original state to avoid event logs from filling up.

Table 20-4 Active Directory Logging

Registry parameter	Description
Path	HKEY_LOCAL_MACHINE\SYSTEM\CurrentControlSet\Services\NTDS\Diagnostics
Parameter	Multiple parameters available, see Figure 20-1
Type	REG_DWORD
Default	0
Value	0 through 5
	0 records on errors and critical information in event log
	5 is verbose logging, all events recorded in event log

For example, if you are troubleshooting Active Directory replication, consider increasing the diagnostic logging level on the Knowledge Consistency Checker, Name Resolution, and Replication Events parameters. The NTDS diagnostics key is pictured in Figure 20-1.

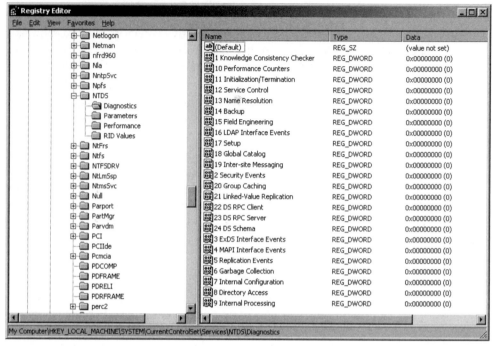

Figure 20-1   NTDS Diagnostics key

You can use the Events and Errors Message Center (*http://www.microsoft.com/technet/support/default.mspx*) to find an explanation, recommended actions, and links to related support material, such as Microsoft Knowledge Base articles, by entering the message source (such as Active Directory) and Event ID for a specific error or event message that you find in the event logs.

Troubleshooting Active Directory Replication Failures

You may encounter replication problems in Active Directory. Although you can resolve most common problems by using Active Directory Sites and Services, advanced utilities and command-line tools exist to analyze replication problems. Some common symptoms of replication failures include new user accounts not being recognized and deleted objects still appearing in Active Directory. Both are indications that directory information is outdated and that a failure in Active Directory replication has occurred.

To monitor, diagnose, and resolve replication problems, you can use the Replmon.exe, Repadmin.exe and Dcdiag.exe tools. The tools are available in the Windows Server 2003 Support Tools, which are included on the Windows Server 2003 CD-ROM.

> **More Info**   For additional information about troubleshooting Active Direc-
> tory, see the whitepaper "Active Directory Operations Guide" (*http://
> www.microsoft.com/windows2000/techinfo/administration/activedirectory/
> adops.asp*).

Refreshing the Replication Topology Using Active Directory Sites and Services

To refresh replication topology, first determine whether you want to refresh the replication topology between sites or the replication topology within a site.

- To regenerate it between sites, run the KCC on the domain controller that holds
  the intersite topology generator role.

- To regenerate it within a site, run the KCC on any domain controller that is not
  the intersite topology generator.

**To determine the domain controller that holds the role of the intersite
topology generator in the site, perform the following steps:**

1. In Active Directory Sites And Services, expand Sites, and then select the site.

2. In the details pane, right-click NTDS Site Settings, and then click Properties.
    The site and server that holds the intersite topology generator role appears
    on the properties page under Inter-Site Topology Generator.

To force the KCC to run, perform the following steps:

1. In Active Directory Sites And Services, in the console tree, expand Sites, expand
    the site that contains the server on which you want to run the KCC, expand Serv-
    ers, and then select the server object for the domain controller that you want to
    run the KCC on.

2. In the details pane, right-click NTDS Settings, click All Tasks, and then click
    Check Replication Topology.

    You use the Active Directory Sites and Services to force replication over a con-
nection. You may be required to force replication if the event log displays replication
inconsistencies or if you receive a message on the domain controller console alerting
you to replication problems.

To force replication over a connection, perform the following steps:

1. In Active Directory Sites And Services, expand the domain controller for the site
    that contains the connection that you use to replicate directory information.

2. In the console tree, click NTDS Settings.

3. In the details pane, right-click the connection that you use to replicate directory information, and then click Replicate Now.

Troubleshooting Replication Problems Using Replication Monitor

Replication Monitor graphically displays the replication topology of connections between servers on the same site. You can view low-level status and performance of replication between domain controllers. You can use Replication Monitor to:

- Display replication information both directly and transitively.

- Display each Update Sequence Number (USN) value, the number of and reason for failed replication attempts, and the flags that are used for direct replication partners. If the failure meets or exceeds an administrator-defined value, Replication Monitor can write to an event log, and then send e-mail notification.

- Poll the server at an administrator-defined interval to obtain current statistics and replication state, and to save a log file's history.

- Show which objects have not yet been replicated from a particular computer.

- Synchronize Active Directory partitions between two domain controllers.

- Trigger the KCC to recalculate the replication topology.

You can run Replication Monitor on any domain controller, member server, or stand-alone computer that runs Windows Server 2003. Figure 20-2 shows an example of monitoring the replication topology using Replication Monitor.

To configure Replication Monitor, perform the following steps:

1. To open Active Directory Replication Monitor, click Start, click Run, type **replmon**, and then click OK.

2. On the View menu, click Options.

3. On the Active Directory Replication Monitor Options page, on the Status Logging tab, click Display Changed Attributes When Replication Occurs, and then click OK.

4. In the console pane, right-click Monitored Servers, and then click Add Monitored Server.

5. In the Add Server To Monitor dialog box, click Add The Server Explicitly By Name, and then click Next.

6. In the Enter The Name Of The Server To Monitor Explicitly box, type the server name, and then click Finish.

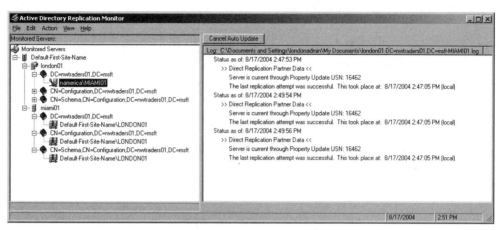

Figure 20-2   Monitoring replication topology using Replication Monitor

Troubleshooting Replication Problems Using Repadmin

You use the Repadmin.exe tool to view the replication topology from the perspective of each domain controller. You can also use Repadmin.exe to manually create the replication topology, force replication events between domain controllers, and view the replication metadata, which is information about the data, and up-to-date state of vectors.

To run the **repadmin** command, you use the following syntax at the command prompt:

repadmin *command arguments* [/u:[*domain*]*user* /pw:[*password* | *]]

To display the replication partners of the domain controller named domaincontroller1, use the syntax:

repadmin /showreps domaincontroller1.contoso.msft

Table 20-5 shows the error messages generated by this command and the root cause for the error.

Table 20-5   Repadmin /Showreps Error Messages

Repadmin error	Root cause
No inbound neighbors.	If no items appear in the "Inbound Neighbors" section of the output generated by the repadmin /showreps command, the domain controller was not able to establish replication links with another domain controller.
Access is denied.	A replication link exists between two domain controllers, but replication cannot be properly performed.

Table 20-5 Repadmin /Showreps Error Messages (Continued)

Repadmin error	Root cause
Last attempt at *<date - time>* failed with the "Target account name is incorrect."	This problem can be related to connectivity, DNS, or authentication issues.
	If it is a DNS error, the local domain controller could not resolve the GUID–based DNS name of its replication partner.
No more end point.	This can be caused because no more end-points are available to establish the TCP session with the replication partner. This error can also result when the replication partner can be contacted, but its remote procedure call (RPC) interface is not registered. This usually indicates that the domain controller's DNS name is registered but with the wrong IP address.
LDAP Error 49.	The domain controller computer account might not be synchronized with the Key Distribution Center (KDC).
Cannot open LDAP connection to local host.	The administration tool could not contact Active Directory.
AD replication has been preempted.	An inbound replication in progress was interrupted by a higher priority replication request, such as a request generated manually by using the repadmin /sync command.
Replication posted, waiting.	The domain controller posted a replication request and is waiting for an answer. Replication is in progress from this source.
Last attempt @never was successful.	The KCC successfully created the replication link between the local domain controller and its replication partner, but because of the schedule or possible bridgehead overload, replication has not occurred.
	A large backlog of inbound replication must be performed on this domain controller.

The Active Directory replication uses USNs maintained by each Active Directory domain controller to track updates to any attribute or property on an Active Directory object. When an object is changed, the USN is advanced and stored with the updated property and with a property that is specific to the domain controller. Each Active Directory-based server also maintains a table of USNs received from replication partners. The highest USN received from each partner is stored in this table.

To display the highest USN on the domain controller named domaincontroller2, use the syntax:

repadmin /showvector dc=contoso,dc=msft domaincontroller2.contoso.msft

To display the connection objects for the domain controller named domaincontroller1, use the syntax:

repadmin /showconn domaincontroller1.microsoft.com

To determine if a change to the user account larryi has replicated to the domain controller named domaincontroller2, use the syntax:

repadmin /showmeta "cn=larryli,ou=designteam,ou=development, dc=namerica,dc=contoso,dc=msft" domaincontroller2.contoso.msft

By running the **repadmin /showmeta** command against each domain controller, you can determine whether all domain controllers have the same replicated values. If a specific domain controller does not have the same value, and the change was made some time ago, you can begin investigating why the computer has not yet received the change.

Troubleshooting Domain Controllers with Dcdiag Tool

You use the Dcdiag.exe tool to analyze the state of a domain controller and report any problems. The Dcdiag.exe tool performs a series of tests to verify different aspects of the system. These tests include connectivity, replication, topology integrity, and inter-site health.

To run the **dcdiag** command, you use the following syntax at the command prompt:

dcdiag *command arguments* [/v /f:*LogFile* /ferr:*ErrLog*]

Table 20-6 describes the common switches you can use with the dcdiag command.

Table 20-6   Dcdiag Switches

Switch	Description
/v	Verbose mode will provide more information in an easier-to-read format that can help you troubleshoot a problem. The /v switch will also provide information about the Flexible Single Master Operation (FSMO) roles.
/f:*LogFile*	Redirects output to a specified log file.
/ferr:*ErrLog*	Redirects fatal error output to a separate log file.
/?	The help switch will provide more information about the other options that are available for the dcdiag command.

Transferring and Seizing of Operations Master Roles

You place operations master roles in a forest when you implement the forest and domain structure. You should transfer an operations master role only when you make a major change to the domain infrastructure. Such changes include decommissioning a domain controller that holds a role and adding a new domain controller that is better suited to hold a specific role.

Transferring Operations Master Roles

Transferring an operations master role means moving it from one functioning domain controller to another. To transfer roles, both domain controllers must be up and running and connected to the network.

To transfer the operations master role for the RID master, PDC emulator, or infrastructure master, perform the following steps:

1. Open Active Directory Users And Computers.

2. In the console tree, right-click Active Directory Users And Computers, and then click Connect To Domain Controller.

3. In the Or Select An Available Domain Controller list section, click the domain controller that will become the new operations master, and then click OK.

4. In the console tree, right-click the domain that contains the server that will become the new operations master, and then click Operations Masters.

5. On the Infrastructure, PDC, or RID tab, click Change, and then click Yes.

To transfer the domain naming master role to another domain controller, perform the following steps:

1. Open Active Directory Domains And Trusts.

2. In the console tree, right-click Active Directory Domains And Trusts, and then click Connect To Domain Controller.

3. In the Or Select An Available Domain Controller list section, click the domain controller that will become the new domain naming master, and then click OK.

4. In the console tree, right-click Active Directory Domains And Trusts, and then click Operations Master.

5. When the name of the domain controller that you selected in step 3 appears, click Change, and then click Yes.

To transfer the schema operations master role, perform the following steps:

1. Open Active Directory Schema.

2. In the console tree, right-click Active Directory Schema, and then click Change Domain Controller.

3. Click Specify Name, type the name of the domain controller that you want to transfer the schema master role to, and then click OK.

4. In the console tree, right-click Active Directory Schema, and then click Operations Master.

5. When the name of the domain controller that you typed in step 3 appears, click Change, and then click Yes.

Seizing Operations Master Roles

Seizing an operations master role means forcing an operations master role on another domain controller, which cannot contact the failed domain controller when you seize the role. You should perform a role seizure only if the original operations master role owner will not be brought back into the environment.

To seize an operations master role for the PDC emulator or infrastructure master, perform the following steps:

1. Open Active Directory Users And Computers.

2. In the console tree, right-click the domain for which you want to seize an operations master role, and then click Operations Masters.

    It may take several seconds for the data to appear because Active Directory Users and Computers is waiting for a response from the current holder of the operations master role.

3. In the Operations Master dialog box, on the Infrastructure, PDC, or RID tab, click Change.

4. In the Active Directory dialog box, click Yes.

5. When an Active Directory dialog box appears, indicating that this computer is a nonreplication partner, click Yes.

6. When an Active Directory dialog box appears, indicating a transfer is not possible, click Yes.

7. In the Active Directory dialog box, click OK, and then click Close.

To use the ntdsutil command to seize an operations master role, perform the following steps:

1. In the Run box, type **cmd**, and then click OK.

2. At the command prompt, type **ntdsutil**, and then press Enter.

3. At the ntdsutil prompt, type **roles**, and then press Enter.

4. At the fsmo maintenance prompt, type **connections**, and then press Enter.

5. At the server connections prompt, type **connect to server** followed by the fully qualified domain name (FQDN) of the domain controller that will be the new role holder, and then press Enter.

6. Type **quit**, and then press Enter.

7. At the fsmo maintenance prompt, type one of the following commands to seize the appropriate operations master, press Enter, type **quit**, and then press Enter.

   - Seize RID master

   - Seize PDC

   - Seize infrastructure master

   - Seize domain naming master

   - Seize schema master

8. At the ntdsutil prompt, type **quit**, and then press Enter.

Understanding the in Exchange 2003 Directory Access Architecture

Because of the tight integration with Active Directory, Exchange 2003 requires that core components of Exchange access directory information in Active Directory. Exchange must also manage recipient data for its e-mail clients, such as Microsoft Office Outlook. DSAccess controls how most components in Exchange interact with Active Directory. The Recipient Update Service (RUS) manages recipient data. For more information about managing Exchange Server 2003 directory information, see Chapter 9, "Managing Directory Information."

The key to optimal Active Directory access is a well-designed DNS and the identification of which domain controllers and global catalog servers are available at the lowest network cost. DSAccess is the component used to discover the Active Directory topology that will be used by other components.

Examining the DSAccess Component

DSAccess is an internal process in Exchange 2003 that is used for accessing and for storing directory information. DSAccess is the centralized mechanism that determines the Active Directory topology, opens the appropriate LDAP connections, and works around server failures by performing the following functions:

- Retrieves information from and writes information to Active Directory, such as configuration data and recipient data.

- Uses cache to provide better performance when querying Active Directory. DSAccess caches configuration and recipient data locally so that this information is available for subsequent queries from other Exchange servers. Caching information locally also reduces the network traffic that is caused by additional queries to Active Directory.

- Constructs a list of available domain controllers and global catalog servers that other Exchange components can query. For example:

  - The message transfer agent (MTA) routes LDAP queries through the DSAccess layer to Active Directory.

  - The store process uses DSAccess to obtain configuration information from Active Directory to connect to databases.

  - The transport process uses DSAccess to obtain information about the connector arrangement to route messages.

Table 20-7 shows the components in Exchange that are dependent on DSAccess to access Active Directory.

Table 20-7 Exchange Components Dependent on DSAccess

Component	Function	Dependency on DSAccess
Exchange Information Store	Maintains the messaging databases that contain all server-based mailboxes and public folders.	User and configuration lookups.
SMTP Categorizer (SMTP CAT)	Communicates with Active Directory to resolve recipient information and determine message restrictions during message transfer.	List of global catalog servers in the topology.
Exchange Routing Engine (RESVC)	Communicates link state information between servers running Exchange 2000 Server and Exchange Server 2003 in the local routing group.	User and configuration lookups.
Message transfer agent (MTA)	Routes messages through X.400 and gateway connectors to non-Exchange messaging systems.	User and configuration lookups.
Directory Service Proxy (DSProxy)	Proxies Active Directory requests for older MAPI clients.	List of global catalog servers in the topology.
Inetinfo	Runs the main IIS process and hosts most of the protocol engines of IIS 6.0.	Message routing.
WebDAV	Provides a Web interface to the Microsoft Exchange Information Store service.	User and configuration lookups.
Exchange Metabase Update (DS2MB)	Replicates settings from Active Directory to the IIS metabase.	Directory changes tracked by update sequence number (USN).

> **Note**   During Exchange Setup components of Internet Information Services (IIS) are enhanced. Even though inetinfo.exe is not part of Exchange, you must consider it when you consider DSAccess dependencies. This is because Exchange relies on the Windows Simple Mail Transfer Protocol (SMTP) service, which is a component of IIS that runs as part of the Inetinfo.exe process, to route all messages.

Constructing a Directory Access Topology

One of the functions of DSAccess is constructing a list of available domain controllers and global catalog servers. By default, each Exchange server uses DSAccess to automatically detect the appropriate domain controllers and global catalog. The setting that controls this default behavior is the Automatically Discover Servers check box near the bottom of the Directory Access tab in the server's Properties dialog box (Figure 20-3).

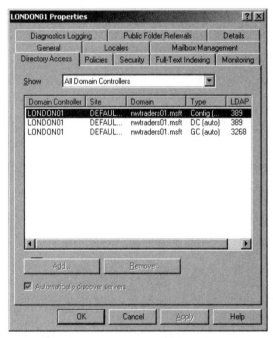

Figure 20-3   Directory Access tab

To discover these servers, DSAccess locates domain controllers and global catalog servers that run Windows Server 2003, or Microsoft Windows 2000 Server Service Pack 3 (SP3) or higher. DSAccess then tests these servers and chooses suitable servers for Exchange services to use to perform Active Directory queries. The default configuration enables DSAccess components to automatically discover the following servers in an Exchange organization:

- A configuration domain controller used to read and write information in the configuration naming partition in Active Directory.

- Up to 10 working domain controllers to perform Active Directory lookups for objects in the local domain.

- Up to 10 working global catalog servers to perform forest-wide queries of user data.

DSAccess is designed to be fault tolerant of failures in the network and Active Directory. If a domain controller or global catalog server fails, all of the Exchange services that used the failed domain controller or global catalog to perform Active Directory queries will fail over to another server and continue to run. The exception to this is when Exchange is installed on a domain controller. DSAccess will no longer failover if Active Directory services are busy or not responding.

Manually Constructing a Directory Access Topology

There are times, such as when troubleshooting problems, that you may want to override the automatic discovery of servers. You can create a manual topology for DSAcess by clearing the Automatically Discover Servers check box.

When you manually create a topology for DSAccess, you no longer have the advantages of automatic failover and load balancing that you have when DSAccess automatically discovers the topology. If a server that you set manually becomes unavailable, the list does not update and Exchange still tries to use the unavailable server, thereby causing Exchange to fail.

> **Note** Because manually constructed topologies do not update automatically, it is strongly recommended that you use the Automatically Discover Servers setting.

To manually create a topology for DSAccess, you must select a server type (from the Show pull down list) to be able to clear the Automatically Discover Servers check box. Once you have cleared the Automatically Discover Servers check box, you can add or remove servers from the topology. To configure the Directory Access tab, perform the following tasks:

1. On the Directory Access tab in the server's Properties dialog box, in the Show list, select the type of servers that you want to view.

   2. Clear the Automatically Discover Servers check box.

      This clears the current list of servers.

   3. Click Add to add servers to or click Remove to remove servers from the topology.

Statically Configuring DSAccess Parameters

DSAccess can be statically configured to channel queries to a specified set of domain controller or global catalog servers using the registry. One possible scenario would be to ensure that front-end servers in a perimeter network can communicate with Active Directory servers. If your firewall supports IP filtering, you may want to configure DSAccess to use specific domain controllers and global catalog servers, and then use IP filtering to ensure that the front-end servers connect to only those domain controllers and global catalog servers.

   DSAccess can be statically configured to tune DSAccess cache to achieve better performance.

Configuring Static Domain Controller and Global Catalog Servers

Upon initialization, DSAccess first reads the registry to determine if any domain controllers or global catalogs have been statically configured. If so, then automatic detection is not performed. Conversely, if no static configurations are made to the registry, DSAccess automatically detects the domain controller or global catalog servers in the topology.

> **Caution**   You should use extreme caution when statically configuring DSAccess. Similar in behavior to other Exchange Server services, DSAccess does not check the validity of the domain controller or global catalog servers that are specified in the registry and does not recognize misspellings or other mistakes made when modifying the registry.

When DSAccess has been statically configured, DSAccess will never fall back and use any other domain controller or global catalog that might otherwise be automatically detected. As a result, if all the statically configured domain controllers or global catalogs are down, then no DSAccess operations will succeed. The following rules apply to DSAccess:

   ■ If global catalogs are statically configured but no domain controllers are specified in the registry, any available domain controller will be automatically detected and used.

- If domain controllers are statically configured but no global catalogs are specified in the registry, any available global catalogs will be automatically detected and used.

- If the configuration domain controller is not statically configured, the configuration domain controller will be taken from the list of available domain controllers (whether this list is found automatically or statically configured).

The domain controllers and global catalogs used for user data are profile-dependent. For this reason, the location in the registry for these settings is specified under the `Profiles\Default` subkey. Because only a single domain controller is used to query the configuration naming partition, configuration domain controller settings are shared among all profiles. For this reason, the registry settings for the configuration domain controller are specified under the `\Instance0` subkey.

Registry settings pertain to a single Exchange Server computer. Any configurations made to the registry must be made to all Exchange Server computers in the topology.

The following registry keys are required to statically configure domain controllers for use by DSAccess:

Registry parameter	Description
Path	`HKEY_LOCAL_MACHINE\System\CurrentControlSet\Services\MSEx-changeDSAccess\Profiles\Default\UserDC1` (`UserDC2`, and so on)
Parameter	`IsGC`
Type	`REG_DWORD`
Value	`0x0`
Parameter	`HostName`
Type	`REG_SZ`
Value	*DC_DomainName.CompanyName.com*
Parameter	`PortNumber`
Type	`REG_DWORD`
Value	`0x185` by default or `0x27C` for SSL (LDAP port number)

The following registry keys are required to statically configure global catalog servers for use by DSAccess:

Registry parameter	Description
Path	HKEY_LOCAL_MACHINE\System\CurrentControlSet\Services\MSExchangeDSAccess\Profiles\Default\UserDC1 (UserDC2, and so on)
Type	REG_DWORD
Value	0x1
Parameter	HostName
Type	REG_SZ
Value	*GC_DomainName.CompanyName.com*
Parameter	PortNumber
Type	REG_DWORD
Value	0xCC4 by default or 0xCC5 for SSL (LDAP port number)

The following registry key is required to statically configure the configuration domain controller used by DSAccess. As mentioned before, the configuration domain controller is shared among all profiles. For this reason, the registry settings for the configuration domain controller are specified under the \Instance0 subkey as shown in the following example:

Registry parameter	Description
Path	HKEY_LOCAL_MACHINE\System\CurrentControlSet\Services\MSExchangeDSAccess\Instance0
Parameter	ConfigDCHostName
Type	REG_SZ
Value	*configDC_DomainName.CompanyName.com*
Parameter	ConfigDCPortNumber
Type	REG_DWORD
Value	0x185 by default or 0x27C for SSL (LDAP port number)

Tuning DSAccess Cache Tuning

Part of the DSAccess API is the directory cache. The cache is broken into two sections: one section for user objects (that is, domain naming context), and the other section for configuration data, such as store and routing objects. The cache is enabled by default and memory is dedicated to the cache when you start Exchange.

All Exchange system queries made through DSAccess are cached for five minutes for user objects, and 15 minutes for configuration data in Exchange 2003. By caching Active Directory queries, Exchange improves responsiveness and decreases the load on the domain controllers. By default, the cache pool is 5 MB for the configuration data cache and 140 MB for cached user objects.

In very large topologies containing more than 100 administrative or routing groups, increased performance can be achieved by manually tuning the DSAccess cache sections. You may also need to change how information is cached when you are troubleshooting DSAccess.

The following registry key is required to manually change the settings for DSAccess cache:

Registry parameter	Description
Path	HKEY_LOCAL_MACHINE\System\CurrentControlSet\Services\MSEx-changeDSAccess
Parameter	CachingEnabled
Type	REG_DWORD
Value	0x1 to enable caching for DSAccess
	0x2 to disable caching for DSAccess

The following registry key is required to manually configure DSAccess cache memory:

Registry parameter	Description
Path	HKEY_LOCAL_MACHINE\System\CurrentControlSet\Services\MSEx-changeDSAccess\Instance0
Parameter	MaxMemoryConfig
Type	REG_DWORD
Value	0x00001400 (5 MB is the default)
	0x0000028f5 (approximately10 MB recommended)

The following registry key is required to manually configure how long DSAccess will cache objects:

Registry parameter	Description
Path	HKEY_LOCAL_MACHINE\System\CurrentControlSet\Services\MSEx-changeDSAccess\Instance0
Parameter	CacheTTL
Type	REG_DWORD
Value	0x600 (600 seconds is the default)

The following registry key is required to manually configure how many entries DSAccess will cache:

Registry parameter	Description
Path	`HKEY_LOCAL_MACHINE\System\CurrentControlSet\Services\MSEx-changeDSAccess\Instance0`
Parameter	`MaxEntries`
Type	`REG_DWORD`
Value	`0x0` (allows an unlimited number by default value)

Examining DSProxy

DSProxy is the Exchange component that provides an address book service to Outlook clients. DSProxy has two functions:

- To emulate a MAPI address book service, and proxy requests to an Active Directory server.

- To provide a referral mechanism so that Outlook clients can directly contact Active Directory servers.

Although its name implies that it provides proxy services only, DSProxy provides both proxy and referral services. MAPI clients running Outlook 2000 Service Release 1 (SR-1) and earlier use the proxy functionality. These earlier clients were designed with the assumption that each Exchange server contains a directory service. This is no longer true in Exchange 2000 and 2003. Therefore, DSProxy emulates a directory service so that these earlier clients can continue to function. In actuality, however, the Exchange server forwards the requests to Active Directory.

Later versions of Outlook, such as Outlook 2000 (SR-2 and later), Outlook 2002, and Outlook 2003, are designed with the assumption that Exchange does not have its own directory service. The very first time one of these later clients contacts the Exchange server, DSProxy refers the client to a global catalog server. The client stores this reference in its registry, and then communicates directly with that global catalog server for all subsequent directory service requests.

DSProxy obtains its list of working global catalog servers from DSAccess, but it does not route its queries through DSAccess. This is because DSProxy uses the Name Service Provider Interface (NSPI) to submit MAPI address book lookups. NSPI is the API used for address book lookups by MAPI clients such as Outlook. DSAccess handles only LDAP queries.

NSPI was introduced with the Exchange 4.0 directory service and was also used in Exchange 5.0 and 5.5. Although Exchange 2003 does not include its own directory service, the DSProxy process emulates NSPI and forwards requests to Active Directory servers. DSProxy does not convert NSPI requests into LDAP or any other protocol; it works by simply forwarding the NSPI request that it receives from the client. Therefore, global catalog servers also natively support NSPI. Domain controllers do not support NSPI because they contain directory information for only the local domain and not the entire directory.

Manually Controlling RFR and NSPI Proxy Servers

After DSAccess builds the list of working global catalog servers, DSAccess forwards the list to DSProxy. In turn, DSProxy removes global catalog servers that are in non-local domains. DSProxy dynamically adds and removes servers as required. The resulting server list that DSProxy uses consists of up to 10 global catalog servers from the same Active Directory site and domain as the Exchange server.

If you want DSAccess to perform automatic topology detection, but you want to control the NSPI Proxy and RFR interface services, you can implement registry parameters.

In some scenarios, you may want to force all Outlook clients, regardless of version, to use NSPI Proxy. You may need to do this if a firewall exists between your user and the Exchange server. Instead of allowing the Exchange server to send a referral to the client and opening a new server/port through the firewall, you can force the client to use the NSPI Proxy service on the Exchange server by setting the following registry key:

Registry parameter	Description
Path	HKEY_LOCAL_MACHINE\System\CurrentControlSet\Services\MSExchangeSA\Parameters
Parameter	No RFR Service
Type	REG_DWORD
Value	0x00000001

To specify the server that should be used for MAPI client proxy service, set the following registry key:

Registry parameter	Description
Path	HKEY_LOCAL_MACHINE\System\CurrentControlSet\Services\MSExchangeSA\Parameters
Parameter	NSPI Target Server
Type	REG SZ or REG MULTI SZ
Value	*<FQDN of the server>*

If you want to specify the server that should be used for MAPI client referral service, set the following registry key:

Registry parameter	Description
Path	`HKEY_LOCAL_MACHINE\System\CurrentControlSet\Services\MSExchangeSA\Parameters`
Parameter	`RFR Target Server`
Type	`REG SZ or REG MULTI SZ`
Value	*<FQDN of the server>*

Recipient Update Service

Exchange uses the Recipient Update Service primarily to generate and update default and customized address lists, and to process changes made to recipient policies. This service ensures the following:

- When new recipient policies or address lists are created, their content is applied to the appropriate recipients in the organization.

- Existing policies are applied to new recipients that are created after the policy or address list has already been established. This keeps recipient information current with minimal administrative overhead.

> **More Info**   For more information about address lists and recipient policies in Exchange Server 2003, see Chapter 9, "Managing Directory Information."

Tasks Performed by the Recipient Update Service

The following tasks are performed by the Recipient Update Service:

- Sets the proxyAddresses attribute for users based on recipient policies. It may not set it if the proxyAddresses attribute is manually added.

- Sets the showInAddressBook attribute based on the address lists present. This attribute defines which objects appear on which address list. It is also needed to resolve names in Outlook or other MAPI clients.

- Sets the homeMDB, homeMTA, and msExchHomeServerName attributes if at least one is already present. It does not change any attribute if it already exists.

- Sets the msExchMailboxGuid attribute if it is not present.

- Sets the legacyExchangeDN attribute if it is not present.

- Sets the displayName attribute if it is not present.

- For groups that have the hideDLMembership attribute equal to TRUE, it adds some non-canonical access control entries (ACEs) into the ACL of that group, to prevent people from seeing the membership of that group.

- Sets the ACL on the "cn=Microsoft Exchange System Objects,DC=*domain*, DC=com" container to reflect administrative rights that are assigned by the Exchange Administration Delegation Wizard.

- Populates the members of the Exchange Enterprise Servers group on each domain of the forest.

Managing the Recipient Update Service

You must have at least one Recipient Update Service for each domain in your organization, and it must be run from an Exchange 2003 (or Exchange 2000) server. For domains without an Exchange server, the Recipient Update Service must be run from an Exchange server outside the domain. If you do not have a Recipient Update Service for a domain, you cannot create recipients in that domain.

In the case where there are multiple domain controllers for a domain, you can set up more than one Recipient Update Service, but each Recipient Update Service must read from and write to a unique domain controller.

Understanding Network Latency and the Recipient Update Service

Network latency can have an impact on the Recipient Update Service. Network latency can cause a newly created mailbox to be unavailable when an administrator looks at the user's properties in Active Directory Users and Computers, or when a user tries to log on to the mailbox for the first time and cannot resolve the mailbox name. Network latency can cause the GAL not to display a newly created recipient.

To help mitigate these problems where you have high network latency in a domain, set up the Recipient Update Service at the local Windows sites. For example, if you have one domain with two Windows sites, Miami and London, a mailbox that is created by the administrator in London may experience a delay before it is processed by the Recipient Update Service in Miami. To reduce the delay, you should configure the Recipient Update Service to use the local domain controller in London.

Remember, the information that is used by the Recipient Update Service is only as current as the domain controller that is accessed by the Recipient Update Service. Active Directory replication failures, such as a failure that prevents changes in a recipient object from being replicated between global catalog servers, can cause Exchange to access information that is not up-to-date. You can use Active Directory Sites and Services to update information between domain controllers in different sites.

Forcing the Recipient Update Service

The Recipient Update Service runs on a regular basis according to the Update interval configured on the properties of the Recipient Update Service object. If you need to force the Recipient Update Service to run, you can select an Update or Rebuild operation from the context menu on the Recipient Update Service object.

Updating Recipient Information

You can perform an Update operation from the Recipient Update Service *(ActiveDirectoryDomainName)* if you need the Recipient Update Service to update newly added recipients in that domain. You can perform a Rebuild operation if you want the Recipient Update Service to evaluate all recipient objects in that domain.

Updating Configuration Information

You can perform an Update or Rebuild operation from the Recipient Update Service *(Enterprise Configuration)* if you need the Recipient Update Service to update the e-mail addresses of the objects that are in the configuration partition of Active Directory, such as the Exchange Information Store object, the MTA object, and the System Attendant object. Troubleshooting the Directory Access Architecture in Exchange 2003.

A variety of tools can be used to troubleshoot directory access problems. Windows Server tools, Exchange System Manager, and Windows Support tools can all be used to help identify the source of problems in directory access. You must also remember that directory access problems can arise from Active Directory replication problems.

Tools for Troubleshooting Exchange

Table 20-8 provides a quick overview of tools that you can use to troubleshoot directory access and a brief description of their use. Additional information about using some of the tools for troubleshooting follows. Information about other useful tools including LDP, Active Directory Sites and Services, and Ping are included in the previous section, "Troubleshooting Active Directory Server Roles and Active Directory Replication."

Table 20-8   Tools for Troubleshooting Directory Access

Tool	Description
Event Viewer (eventvwr.msc)	Used to view logged events, such as errors and warnings.
Exchange System Manager (exchange system manager.msc)	Used to provide a graphical view of an Exchange organization where you can perform many administrative tasks.
Performance Monitor (perfmon.msc)	Used for establishing a baseline of performance and for troubleshooting performance issues.

Table 20-8   Tools for Troubleshooting Directory Access (Continued)

Tool	Description
DNS Manager (dnsmgmt.msc)	Used to administer DNS.
NSLookup (Nslookup.exe)	Used for testing and troubleshooting DNS servers. Checks records, domain host aliases, domain host services, and operating system information by querying DNS servers.
Domain Controller Diagnostic Tool (Dcdiag.exe)	Used to analyze the state of domain controllers in a forest or enterprise and report any problems to assist in troubleshooting. Available on the Windows Server 2003 CD in *<drive>*:\support\tools.
Network Connectivity Tester (Netdiag.exe)	Used to isolate networking and connectivity problems by performing a series of tests to determine the state of your network client. Available on the Windows Server 2003 CD in *<drive>*:\support\tools.

Troubleshooting Directory Access Using Event Viewer

To begin troubleshooting, analyze any errors that appear in the event logs on the Exchange server. You should look at the System event log for general service problems, and at the Application event log for Exchange-specific errors. If you are experiencing problems, you can increase the level of logging to allow more verbose logging by modifying the Diagnostics Logging tab (Figure 20-4) on the properties of the server object. You should also monitor the DNS Server event log on computers running Windows configured as a DNS server for events logged by the DNS service.

Configuring Diagnostics Logging on a Server

Diagnostics logging levels determine which additional Exchange events are written to the Application event log in Event Viewer. You can use diagnostics logging to record significant events that are related to authentication, connections, and user actions.

You configure diagnostics logging separately for each service on each server. MSExchangeDSAccess, MSExchangeAL and MSExchangeSA can help you troubleshoot issues related to directory access. Depending on the level of logging you configure, the service will write a different amount of information to the Application event log. The default level for all services on Exchange servers is None. Table 20-9 shows the categories of errors that can be logged for directory access related services and Table 20-10 shows the diagnostic logging levels available.

Table 20-9   Diagnostics Logging Services

Service	Description
MSExchangeAL	Helps diagnose address list problems. Logs events for LDAP Operations, Service Control, Attribute Mapping, Account Management, and Address List Synchronization categories.
MSExchangeDSAccess	Helps diagnose directory access and topology-related problems, such as Event 2080. Logs events for the following categories: General, Cache, Topology, Config, and LDAP categories.
MSExchangeSA	Helps diagnose the Microsoft Exchange System Attendant, which handles many core Exchange tasks, such as mailbox management, e-mail proxy generation, offline address list generation, and monitoring. Helps diagnose topology-related problems. Logs events for Clean Mailbox, NSPI Proxy, RFR Interface, OAL Generator, Proxy Generation, and RPC Calls categories.

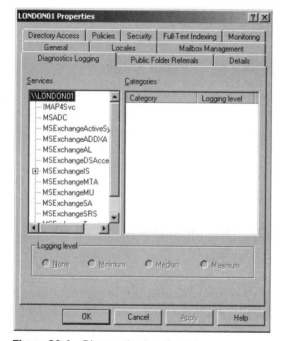

Figure 20-4   Diagnostics Logging tab

When Exchange generates an event less than or equal to the logging level, the event is logged. Events range from significant events (such as application failures) to moderately important events (such as the receipt of messages across a gateway) to events that are relevant only to debugging. Typically, you log only critical events. However, when problems occur, diagnostics logging helps you to change the logging levels to capture more events in greater detail.

Table 20-10 Diagnostics Logging Levels

Logging levels	Description
None	Only critical events, error events, and events with a logging level of zero are logged.
Minimum	Events with a logging level of 1 or lower are logged.
Medium	Events with a logging level of 3 or lower are logged.
Maximum	Events with a logging level of 5 or lower are logged.

To configure diagnostics logging:

1. In Exchange System Manager, navigate to the server.

2. Right-click the server, and then click Properties.

3. On the Diagnostics Logging tab, select an Exchange 2003 service on which you want to set category logging levels.

4. Under Category, select the categories and logging levels that you want to configure.

Using Event Viewer to Monitor DSAccess

You can diagnose most directory related problems by selecting MSExchangeDSAccess on the Diagnostics Logging tab. By setting the Logging Level to Minimum or higher, additional information will be written to the event log.

One event that is often reported that is useful in diagnosing directory related problems is Event 2080. Event 2080 reports certain characteristics of your Active Directory servers, including the roles a server is capable of fulfilling, whether the server is reachable, and so forth. The following is an example of Event 2080. Table 20-11 describes how server characteristics are represented in the event text.

```
Event Type: Information
Event Source: MSExchangeDSAccess
Event Category: Topology
Event ID: 2080
Computer: MyMachine
Description:
Process MAD.EXE (PID=1304). DSAccess has discovered the following servers with the
following characteristics:
(Server name | Roles | Reachability | Synchronized | GC capable | PDC | SACL right |
Critical Data | Netlogon)
In-site:
EXGGHH01.ParentDomain.extest.microsoft.com CDG 7 7 1 1 1 1 7
Out-of-site:
```

Table 20-11   Server Characteristics Reported in Event 2080

Characteristic	Description
Server name	Shows the actual Active Directory server name.
Roles	Shows whether or not the particular server can be used as a configuration domain controller (C), a domain controller (D), or a global catalog server (G). An abbreviation means the server can be used, and a hyphen (-) means the server cannot be used.
Reachability	Shows whether the server is reachable through a TCP/IP connection. These are bit flags, where 0x1 means the server is reachable as a global catalog server (port 3268), 0x2 as a domain controller (port 389), 0x4 as a configuration domain controller (port 389). In the previous example, "7" means that the server is reachable as all three types (0x1 | 0x2 | 0x4 = 0x7).
Synchronized	Shows whether the "isSynchronized" flag set on the rootDSE of the server is TRUE. These values are the same bit flags used in Reachability.
GC capable	Boolean. Specifies whether the server is a global catalog server. 1 indicates it is a global catalog.
PDC	Boolean. Specifies whether the server is a primary domain controller for its domain. 1 indicates it is a PDC.
SACL right	Boolean. Specifies whether DSAccess has the necessary permissions to read the Security Access Control List (SACL) (part of the nTSecurityDescriptor) for the configuration naming context.
Critical Data	Boolean. States whether DSAccess found this Exchange server in the Exchange configuration container.
NetLogon	Shows whether the server is running the NetLogon service. This check requires the use of RPC, and this call may fail for reasons other than a server that is down. For example, firewalls may block this call. So, if there is a 7 in the ninth column, it means that the Net Logon service check was successful for each role (domain controller, configuration domain controller, and global catalog).

Using Event Viewer to Monitor DSProxy

To monitor DSProxy activity, in System Manager, set the NSPI Proxy diagnostics logging level to Maximum on the MSExchangeSA service. A logging level of Maximum is recommended for NSPI Proxy because lower logging levels do not provide much information. Unlike other Exchange components, a setting of Maximum for NSPI Proxy will not overwhelm the event logs with information.

After you set the logging level to Maximum, restart System Attendant. For information about the errors that are generated by the DSProxy service in the event logs, see the whitepaper, "Understanding and Troubleshooting Directory Access" (*http:// www.microsoft.com/downloads/details.aspx?FamilyID=c976433f-f979-4745-b7a6- 9d8446ef6409&displaylang=en*).

Troubleshooting Directory Access Using Performance Monitor

There are different types of behaviors associated with an overloaded Exchange server as compared to an overloaded domain controller. Remember that without Active Directory, Exchange Server 2003 will not run properly and messaging clients such as Outlook 2003 will not be able to perform simple tasks, such as resolving e-mail addresses. DSAccess performance counters will help you troubleshoot whether DSAccess is performing as expected, and warn you about processing delays and latencies that require your attention.

For information about troubleshooting Active Directory server roles, see the book *Troubleshooting Exchange Server 2003 Performance* (*http:// www.microsoft.com/technet/prodtechnol/exchange/2003/library/e2k3perf.mspx*).

Troubleshooting Name Resolution

The majority of Exchange directory access problems are caused by name resolution problems. Therefore, DNS is the first component you should verify. Symptoms of DNS trouble include failures in starting Exchange services and setup failure.

To verify that DNS is configured properly:

1. View the IP address entered into the DNS field on the TCP/IP stack of the Exchange server by typing **ipconfig /all** at the command prompt.
   Verify that the address is correct.

2. Ping the IP address of the DNS server to see if it responds.

3. In the console of the DNS server, verify that the server's IP address is correct.

4. Open the DNS Manager snap-in to verify that the Host record of the Exchange server exists.

5. Verify that the _msdcs, _sites, _tcp, and _udp keys exist in the DNS database. If they do not exist, verify that the DNS IP address has been correctly entered on the TCP/IP stack of the DNS server.

6. View Event Viewer event logs and DNS Server event logs and analyze any errors that appear.

   To use NSLookup to query for a service record:

```
C:\>nslookup
>set type=srv
>_ldap._tcp.domainname.com
```

Note   E-mail clients also experience problems if name resolution is not functioning correctly. The e-mail client must be able to resolve the name of the Exchange server before it can open the mailbox. Microsoft Windows 2000 Professional and later clients rely on DNS to resolve the host name of the Exchange server. Earlier clients rely on WINS to resolve the NetBIOS name of the Exchange server.

More Info   For additional information about troubleshooting e-mail clients not being able to resolve the name of the Exchange server, view the Microsoft Knowledge Base article 297801, "Troubleshooting Check Name Errors" (*http://support.microsoft.com/?id=297801*).

Troubleshooting Recipient Update Service

If the e-mail addresses configured by recipient policies are not being applied to recipients, use the following troubleshooting options:

- **Force an immediate update**   You can force the Recipient Update Service to run immediately by right-clicking the Recipient Update Service object and clicking Update Now.

- **Check for Exchange server and Active Directory server availability**   The Recipient Update Service object is configured with a domain controller and an Exchange server. The Recipient Update Service must be able to connect to both servers in order to run. If one of the servers is not available, you need to manually reconfigure the Recipient Update Service to use a different server.

- **Confirm that the System Attendant service is running**   The Recipient Update Service runs within the System Attendant service, so the System Attendant must be running.

- **Enable Diagnostics Logging on the Exchange server that manages the Recipient Update Service for the MSExchangeSA Proxy Generation category**   After logging is enabled, force the Recipient Update Service to run, and then check the application log for details about what is occurring when the Recipient Update Service attempts to run.

Troubleshooting the Network Infrastructure using Dcdiag and Netdiag

You use the Dcdiag.exe tool to analyze the state of a domain controller and report any problems. Dcdiag will perform the following:

- Verify that the domain can support Active Directory.

- Determine if it is possible to create an Active Directory forest.

- Determine if it is possible to add another domain controller to an existing domain.

- Determine if a Windows 2000, Windows 2003, or Microsoft Windows XP computer can be added to the domain.

- Test replication between domain controllers.

- Report down servers.

- Test that all domain controllers are advertising their presence to other domain controllers.

See "Troubleshooting Domain Controllers with Dcdiag Tool" for information on using the dcdiag command line switches.

You can use netdiag to test network connectivity by testing the following items:

- Network adapter interface information, including the:
  - Host name
  - IP address
  - Subnet mask
  - Default gateway
  - DNS server
  - WINS server
- Domain membership
- Loopback ping test
- Default gateway ping test
- NetBIOS name check
- Winsock test
- DNS test
- Domain controller discovery test
- Trust relationship test
- LDAP test
- Internet Protocol Security (IPSec) test

To run the netdiag command, use the following syntax at the command prompt:
netdiag *command arguments* [/v /f:*LogFile* /ferr:*ErrLog*]

Table 20-12 describes the common switches that you can use with the netdiag command.

Table 20-12   Netdiag Switches

Switch	Description
/v	The tests performed by Netdiag will alert you to many possible problems. You can expand on the result messages by using the /v switch to turn on verbose mode.
/f	The tests performed by Netdiag can result in a large amount of output. It may be necessary to send the resulting information to others to review. Using the /l switch will capture the information to a log file in the same directory as the Netdiag.exe file.
/?	The help switch will provide more information about the other options that are available for Netdiag.

Best Practices

- Exchange relies on a healthy Active Directory directory service.

  - Ensure that the appropriate numbers of directory service servers are deployed and located appropriately to support your Exchange organization.

  - Ensure that directory service servers are functioning correctly.

  - Ensure that Active Directory replication is functioning correctly.

- Exchange relies on DNS to function properly. Ensure that DNS is configured and name resolution is functioning properly.

- Both Active Directory components and services and Exchange components can create problems for Active Directory access. When troubleshooting, be sure to evaluate both areas for possible causes of directory access problems.

Chapter 21

Disaster Recovery Planning for Exchange 2003

About This Chapter

This chapter discusses how to develop a disaster recovery plan for Microsoft Exchange Server 2003. Previous chapters in this Resource Kit have considered various technologies, components, and design issues related to Exchange 2003. This chapter discusses the steps for developing a plan for your company that allows your Exchange organization to be returned to a running state in a minimum amount of time, if a failure or disaster occurs. It discusses how to design your Exchange organization with failures and disasters in mind, the data that you must protect to ensure that Exchange can be recovered, different types of backup strategies, and the tools that an administrator needs to address any recovery issues that might arise.

Chapter 22, "Implementing a Backup Solution," and Chapter 23, "Restoring Exchange Server 2003," discuss the practical tasks of implementing the plan if an actual failure or disaster occurs.

This chapter assumes that you are familiar with Microsoft Windows server technology and Active Directory directory service. To familiarize yourself with Windows

Server 2003 or Active Directory, see Windows Server 2003 Technology Centers at *http://www.microsoft.com/windowsserver2003/technologies.*

Introduction to Disaster Recovery Planning

For most companies, e-mail is no longer a causal business application offered to company employees. E-mail has become critical to day-to-day operations. It is used to communicate with employees, customers, and business partners. Because so many business functions today depend on e-mail availability 24 hours a day, seven days a week, e-mail servers such as Exchange are crucial to business success.

When you plan a disaster recovery strategy, you must consider all possible disasters, both natural and human-caused. You must identify the components and services that can fail and the requirements to restore those components and services, through replacement, replication, or backups.

Although there is no way to prevent failures and disasters, proper planning can minimize the impact of such occurrences on your Exchange organization and users. The goal of a good disaster recovery plan is to identify what is possible, prepare for everything that is plausible, and then document and test the tasks required to return critical business services to a functioning state in the least amount of time.

For more information about planning for disasters and performing backup and restores in an Exchange 2003 environment, see the book "Exchange Server 2003 Disaster Recovery Operations Guide" (*http://go.microsoft.com/fwlink/ ?LinkId=30250*).

Preparing for Disaster Recovery

Disaster recovery planning is a complex process that depends on many factors. Much of how you plan for failures and disasters depends on how critical your company considers e-mail. Other factors that affect your disaster planning are how Exchange is deployed, the hardware and software that support fault tolerance, backups and restores, and budgeting constraints. If possible, disaster planning should start during the design phase of Exchange deployment. This ensures that your design decisions match organizational goals for disaster recovery.

Performing a Business Impact Analysis

A business impact analysis is the initial step that you take when you create a disaster recovery plan. You must identify the risks that can affect your Exchange organization. Risks are problems waiting to happen, the possibility of suffering loss. Risks can be the result of threats, vulnerabilities, or poor design. Threats are events that could disrupt a system component or resource. Examples of threats are natural disasters, such as a wildfire, flood, or earthquake; physical infrastructure disasters, such as broken pipes and fire; and human-caused disasters, such as sabotage and mistakes. Vulnerability is the susceptibility that a system component or resource has to the threat. For example, the closer a building is to an earthquake fault, the more vulnerable it is to an earthquake. The business impact from these disruptions can be a loss of revenue, a loss of customers, a damaged reputation, or disgruntled employees.

Once you know what risks can impact your Exchange organization, you must analyze the impact of those risks, determine what action to take to mitigate those risks, and then gather the processes and tools needed to reduce the potential impact to your Exchange environment in case of a failure or disaster.

Identifying Risks

When you identify risks, you must first consider all the services and components that are required to keep your Exchange environment functioning. This enables you to fully understand the impact that the loss of a service might have on the ability of your company to conduct business. Next, ask yourself what types of failures or disasters would require that you repair or restore these services or components. By identifying risks to your Exchange environment, you can build recovery options into your disaster recovery plan.

In an Exchange environment, possible areas of risk include:

- Loss of information, for example:
    - A single message, mailbox, or public folder
    - A single database (mailbox or public folder)
    - A storage group
    - The Exchange server configuration information stored in Active Directory
    - Loss of the entire server
    - Loss of an entire data center

- Loss of a Microsoft Windows service, for example:
    - Domain Name System (DNS)
    - Internet Information Services (IIS)
    - Domain controller and global catalog services
    - Certificate services

- Loss of supporting hardware services, for example:
    - Network infrastructure components
    - Cluster components

- Loss of service due to inadequate or improper configuration, resulting in:
    - A performance problem

- A security breach
- A denial of service
- A virus outbreak

Analyzing Risks

Risk analysis is the conversion of risk data into risk decision-making information. Risk analysis considers each risk that you have identified, ranks the probability that the disruption will occur, and determines the impact to your business if the disruption occurs. Business impact can be measured in financial terms or with a subjective measurement scale, as long as all risks use the same unit of measurement. This process allows you to prioritize different types of risks when you develop your disaster recovery plan.

Table 21-1 shows an example of risk analysis for some of the risks identified earlier in this chapter using a subjective measurement scale.

Table 21-1   Example of Risk Analysis

Identified Risk	Probability of Occurrence	Business Impact
Single message loss	High	Low
Storage group loss	Low	High

Based on the risk analysis, it is more important to ensure that disaster recovery planning covers the loss of a storage group than the loss of a single message, because although it is less likely to occur, loss of a storage group has a higher impact on your business.

Mitigating Risks

Guidelines for mitigating risks are largely based on the cost to implement a solution versus the loss of business. For example, can your company afford to purchase a standby server that will be used only during a disaster or for spare parts, or is the impact of the temporary loss of the Exchange server not significant enough to warrant the implementation of a standby server? You also need to determine the minimum acceptable levels of customer service and the amount of time that it will take to reach those levels in the event of a failure or disaster.

As with the other elements of business impact analysis, the risk mitigation process begins at the design phase of your deployment of Exchange. Running the Microsoft Active Directory directory service and deploying the hardware solutions and server configurations required for Active Directory have an impact on your ability to recover from disaster. For example, you can mitigate the risk of various types of hardware failure by deploying Windows server clustering and using redundant storage components and network components when you initially deploy your Exchange servers. You can also mitigate the risk of domain controller failure by implementing multiple domain controllers to provide fault tolerance for Active Directory.

More Info For more information about risk management, see Microsoft Solutions Framework at *http://go.microsoft.com/fwlink/?LinkId=5929*.

Evaluating Service Level Agreements

Part of planning your disaster recovery strategy is evaluating service level agreements (SLAs). SLAs are agreements between a service provider and a customer that specifies the services, such as e-mail, that the provider will furnish and defines the customer's expectations for the availability and performance of those services. Availability is often expressed as the percentage of time that a service is available. For example, 99.9 percent availability means that a service is unavailable for 8.75 hours per year. SLAs can be established between a company and outside contractors or hardware and software vendors. SLAs can also be established internally between an IT department and its customers, which are usually business units and end users.

You should evaluate SLAs based on your business impact analysis to ensure that they are not costing your company too much money and effort based on the value to your business. There is a difference between determining what services SLAs should measure and determining the right values to include in the SLAs for maintaining those services. For example, your company has offices worldwide. You originally established an SLA that guaranteed that all messages must be delivered end-to-end throughout the system within five minutes, regardless of the recipient of the message. Once a month, your corporate office sends a message to all users in the global address list (GAL). While the majority of the messages reach their destination within the time frame defined in the SLA, a single office receives the message outside the time frame. This deviation might be viewed as a system failure as defined by your existing SLA. By reviewing the SLA against the business impact analysis, you might find that spending time, effort, and money trying to meet the SLA for that one message arriving at that one office does not focus the efforts of your IT staff effectively. Modifying the SLA to allow for that deviation in message delivery time might be more cost effective and at the same time not have a significant impact on your business. Whereas spending that same time, effort, and money to meet another SLA that ensures that mailbox content is highly available might have a much higher return for your business.

If you are creating a disaster recovery plan for your Exchange organization during the design phase, you can determine the Exchange 2003 deployment and server configurations that are best suited to meet your SLAs.

SLAs typically define the following areas:

- **Allowed downtime**   The maximum allowable downtime that is acceptable for your organization based on your organization's definition of Exchange service availability.

- **Allowed recovery time**   The maximum time allowed for each type of disaster recovery operation. For example, the approximate amount of time required to recover a mailbox, a single database, or an entire server running Exchange 2003.

- **Data loss tolerance**   The tolerance your organization has for either the temporary or permanent loss of Exchange data. For example, your organization might be able to tolerate the temporary loss of mailbox data, such as a single e-mail message, for a period of 24 hours, but might not tolerate the temporary loss of an Exchange database or storage group for more than four hours, because loss of a database or storage group has a much greater business impact than loss of a single e-mail message.

Your Exchange design will have a direct impact on your ability to meet your SLAs. For example, designing your Exchange storage group and database configurations to include large information stores can significantly impact the amount of time required to restore a database to a server. Features in Exchange 2003 and Windows Server 2003 might enable you to challenge the limits that were previously imposed by your SLAs. Examples of such features include the Volume Shadow Copy Service and the Exchange recovery storage group features that reduce the time required to restore Exchange databases.

More Info   The Volume Shadow Copy Service feature in Windows Server 2003 can be used to greatly reduce the time that it takes to back up and restore Exchange 2003. Volume Shadow Copy Service works with backup applications and with disk array hardware and software from third-party vendors to provide a shadow copy-based backup infrastructure. Additional information on using the Volume Shadow Copy Service is covered later in this chapter in the section "Determining a Backup Strategy."

More Info   The Recovery Storage Group feature in Exchange 2003 enables you to mount a second copy of an Exchange mailbox database on the same server as the original database, or on any other Exchange server in the same Exchange administrative group. This capability enables you to recover data from an older backup copy of the database without disturbing user access to current data. The recovery storage group can also be useful in various disaster recovery scenarios, such as the Messaging Dial Tone scenario, in which you provide users with a blank database during disaster recovery, allowing them to send and receive messages, and then use the recovery storage group to restore the user's previous data as it becomes available. For more information about Recovery Storage Groups, see the book "Using Exchange Server 2003 Recovery Storage Groups" (*http://go.microsoft.com/fwlink/?LinkId=23233*).

Table 21-2 lists some of the categories and specific elements of your SLAs that you might want to review as part of planning for disaster recovery.

Table 21-2   SLA Categories and Elements

Categories	Elements
Hours of Operation	Hours that the messaging service is available to users
	Hours reserved for planned downtime (maintenance)
	Amount of advance notice for network changes or other changes that might affect users
Service Availability	Percentage of time that Exchange services are running
	Percentage of time that mailbox stores are mounted
	Percentage of time that domain controller services are running
Disaster Recovery	Amount of time allowed for recovery of each failure type, such as individual database failure, mailbox server failure, or domain controller failure
	Amount of time allowed to provide a backup mail system so users can send and receive e-mail messages without accessing historical data (called Messaging Dial Tone)
	Amount of time allowed to recover data to the point of failure

More Info   For information about the different ways to define Exchange service availability, see the book "Exchange Server 2003 High Availability Guide" (*http://go.microsoft.com/fwlink/?LinkId=30251*).

Identifying Exchange-Related Data

It is important to identify all of your company's critical data and to establish procedures for backing up and restoring that data in the event of a disaster. Critical data includes the contents of the mailboxes and public folders on your servers and the configuration data that is needed to operate servers running Exchange. The data that is backed up on each server depends on the components that are installed on that server. For example, if the Exchange server is a front-end server, there is no mailbox data to back up on that server. In addition, the data that you decide to back up as part of your disaster recovery strategy determines the recovery processes that you can perform.

The following are some examples of the types of data for which you should have back up procedures defined in your disaster recovery plan:

- Microsoft Windows Server 2003 operating system, which includes:

    - The system partition (the disk volume that contains the hardware-specific files that are needed to start Windows, for example, Ntldr, Boot.ini, and Ntdetect.com)

    - The boot partition (the disk volume that contains the Windows operating system files—by default located in the WINDOWS folder—and its support files—by default in the WINDOWS\System32 folder)

- Windows system state data, which includes:

    - The Windows Server 2003 registry

    - Windows Server 2003 boot files

    - Windows Server 2003 protected operating system files

    - The Windows Server 2003 IIS metabase (includes information that affects Exchange 2003, such as protocol settings for Post Office Protocol version 3 (POP3), Internet Message Access Protocol version 4 (IMAP4), Network News Transfer Protocol (NNTP), or HTTP; virtual directories for mailbox, public folder, and instant messaging access; and HTTP security settings)

    - COM+ Class registration database

    - Certificate Services database (if the server is a certificate server)

    - Active Directory directory service (if the server is a domain controller)

    - The SYSVOL directory (if the server is a domain controller)

    - Domain Name Service (DNS) zone information (if the server is running DNS)

    - Cluster service resource registry checkpoints and the quorum disk resource data (if the server is running the Microsoft Cluster Server Cluster service)

- Exchange 2003 databases and log files

- Exchange 2003 message tracking logs

- Exchange 2003 full-text indexing files

- Site Replication Service (SRS) databases. SRS works in conjunction with Active Directory Connector (ADC) to provide replication services from Active Directory to the Exchange 5.x Directory Service.

- Exchange 2003 connector-specific data. Connector-specific configuration data is stored in the registry of the computer where the connector (such as Microsoft Exchange Connector for Novell GroupWise or Microsoft Exchange Connector for Lotus Notes) is installed, as well as in Active Directory. Depending on your backup strategy, there might be additional files that must be backed up and restored manually.

- Packaged application software, such as Windows Server operating system software or Exchange Server 2003 software, along with any service packs or software updates

- Supporting software, such as third-party backup applications, or system management software

- User application software, such as Active Server Pages (ASP) applications, mailbox agents, and workflow software

- Management scripts

Evaluating Your Exchange Design

How you design your Exchange organization affects your ability to recover from a failure or disaster within the definitions of your SLAs.

Ideally, you should consider disaster recovery planning at the same time as you plan your Exchange 2003 deployment. The deployment choices you make directly affect your Exchange 2003 backup and restore options and can reduce the impact of failures and disasters, in some cases minimizing downtime.

Evaluating Server Design

You should design your Exchange servers with fault tolerance in mind. You should review your server design to reduce or eliminate the impact that a single failure can have on your Exchange 2003 organization. For example, you can implement fault tolerance by using redundant server components, storage subsystem components, and network components. In addition, you can implement fault tolerance at the server level by implementing Windows server clustering on your back-end Exchange servers and by installing multiple domain controllers at each site.

- **Server partitioning**   Store your Windows operating system files, Exchange application files, Exchange database files, and transaction log files on separate disks to optimize recovery, improve fault tolerance, and improve performance.

  - By locating your Exchange application files and Windows Server 2003 files on their own disks, you can improve fault tolerance by eliminating a single point of failure. For example, if the disk on which Exchange 2003 is installed fails, Windows Server 2003 continues to function.

  - By locating your Exchange transaction log files and database files on separate disks, you can minimize the impact of a failure and minimize data loss. For example, if you keep your Exchange databases and transaction log files on separate physical hard disks, and the disk containing your databases fails, you can recover to the point of failure by restoring your databases from your last backup and replaying any transaction logs generated since the last backup into the restored databases.

  - By locating your Exchange transaction log files and database files on separate disks, you can improve performance as a result of separating the sequential write only file I/O of the transaction log files from the random read/write file I/O of database files.

> **Tip**   Simple Mail Transfer Protocol (SMTP) queues can be stored on the same drives as the Exchange database files. In some scenarios, such as configuring a bridgehead or relay server, storing the SMTP queues to a separate drive may improve performance.

  Ensure that disks used for Exchange data are dedicated to Exchange and are not being shared with other applications. This is especially necessary in Storage Area Network (SAN) configurations, where the SAN is typically part of the overall network of computing resources for an enterprise and is more likely to be used by other applications. When the SAN is shared by one or more applications, it is important to carefully plan partitioning of the SAN to ensure that disks used by Exchange are in fact dedicated to Exchange data.

- **Data storage**   Implement redundant array of independent disks (RAID) solutions on your disks to match the type of data on each disk. For example, implement storage solutions for your database files (.edb and .stm files) and transaction logs files that ensure reliability, such as RAID-1 (mirrored disk array) or RAID-0+1 (in which data is mirrored and then striped).

Note   We recommend using the best performing storage array possible. In most cases, this is RAID-0+1 but other RAID variations, such as RAID-5, might make sense provided that you understand and plan for their performance impact. It is critical that you test your storage solution before deploying it in a production environment. Use utilities such as Load Simulator 2003 (loadsim.exe) and JetStress (jetstress.exe) to simulate database read/write access before deploying any storage solution, paying special attention that disk latency is under 20 milliseconds (ms) average. For more information and to download these tools, see the Downloads for Exchange Server 2003 website (*http://go.microsoft.com/fwlink/ ?LinkId=25097*).

- **Hard disk space**   Ensure that you provide enough disk space to ensure recoverability and the ability to perform preventative maintenance on the Exchange databases.

  - Ensure that you have adequate hard disk capacity on your Exchange servers to restore both the database and the log files. Depending on how many log files are generated during a week, you could have a backup that is too large to restore to its original location. For example, a server generating 2,000 log files in a week amounts to 10 gigabytes (GB) of log file space, in addition to the space required for the database files.

  - Ensure that you provide enough disk space to perform database maintenance. Database repairs and offline defragmentation of the database files require free disk space. If you use Exchange Server Database Utilities (Eseutil.exe) to repair an Exchange database, you must have sufficient free disk space for Eseutil to run, approximately 20 percent of the size of the database that you are repairing on the same drive as the database. If you are using Eseutil to defragment the database file, you must have 110 percent of the size of the database. Although you can redirect the temp files to another drive, this will dramatically increase the time it takes to repair your database.

Evaluating Storage Design

You should design your Exchange server storage to meet your backup and restore requirements. Review the following areas of your Exchange server design when planning for disaster recovery:

- **Storage group configuration**   Plan your storage group and store configurations to maximize recoverability. Your disaster recovery strategy has an important role in determining how many storage groups and stores your storage solution should support. For example, if you are using Exchange Server 2003 Enterprise Edition, you can use multiple mailbox stores to increase reliability and recoverability by spreading mailboxes across multiple mailbox stores so that the loss of a single store impacts only a subset of users rather than the entire organization. To further isolate users from store failures, locate individual mailbox stores on separate physical disks. In addition, reducing the number of mailboxes per store reduces the time required to recover a damaged store from a backup.

> **Tip**   If you are using Exchange Server 2003 Enterprise Edition, we recommend that you populate each server with the maximum of four storage groups with five stores per storage group (20 stores total) as soon as possible to maximize recoverability.

- **Mailbox server storage sizing**   Plan the size of your Exchange stores to ensure recoverability. Exchange 2003 Enterprise Edition has virtually no set limit on the size of an individual store (up to 16 terabytes), which makes it difficult to calculate the maximum outage times relative to your backup hardware.

    Set size limits for your mailbox stores (and public folder stores) and enforce those size limits so you can estimate the amount of time required to restore a mailbox store and ensure that recovery can occur within the constraints of your SLAs. Setting mailbox size limits for your users can also facilitate reducing the size of mailbox stores. Mailbox size limits can be configured on individual user mailboxes by using Active Directory Users and Computers, or on mailbox stores (either configuring individually or through store policies) by using Exchange System Manager.

Evaluating Your Backup and Restore Infrastructure

You must evaluate how Exchange fits into your backup and restore infrastructure. You must also evaluate whether your backup and restore infrastructure enables you to perform a restore within the amount of time allowed by your messaging SLAs. This includes evaluating whether your backup software limits your ability to provide the adequate recovery of your Exchange servers, or whether utilizing other technologies, such as the Volume Shadow Copy Service will enable you to better meet your SLAs. If your current backup and restore infrastructure does not support Exchange, you must develop an infrastructure that will.

> **Note** Additional information on using the Volume Shadow Copy Service is covered later in this chapter in the section "Determining a Backup Strategy."

Evaluating Backup Software

Each vendor of backup software offers a different mix of features, device support, and cost. As a best practice, you will need to select the technology that best meets your unique requirements. When evaluating your choice of backup software, verify that your backup software:

- Supports the Exchange 2003 online backup API or utilizes the Volume Shadow Copy Service Exchange writer to enable you to successfully perform online backups of Exchange stores without interrupting service to your users.

- Provides support for the backup and restore topology. This may include performing a backup to disk, using a tape drive located on the local server or on a remote server, using a tape library, or using a SAN-based backup solution based on the performance requirements defined in your SLAs.

> **More Info** For detailed information about the advantages and disadvantages of implementing different backup and restore topologies, see the chapter "Backup and Recovery Services" in the Service Blueprints section of the Reference Blueprints topic of the Windows Server System Reference Architecture (*http://www.microsoft.com/technet/itsolutions/techguide/wssra/raguide/default.mspx*).

- Provides good media management if you are backing up to tape. Your software should provide a means of automatically identifying the tapes to make it easier for you to identify and archive large quantities of tapes. This is especially true if you are using a complex tape rotation scheme that requires a large number of tapes.

- Provides the most complete disaster recovery features, such as allowing for a complete server recovery through a disaster recovery disk.

Evaluating Backup Hardware

In addition to evaluating the backup software that you will use for Exchange, you must also evaluate the hardware technology that will support your disaster recovery plan. This includes selecting the type of device and associated tape media supported by the device. The tape media determines the amount of data that can be retained on a single tape. For example, Digital Linear Tape (DLT) format tape drives can transfer data to tape media at 6 to 10 megabytes per second (MB/sec) and typically store 60 GB of data (150 GB compressed), whereas Linear Tape-Open (LTO) tape drives can transfer data to tape media at 20 to 40 MB/sec and typically store 100 GB of data (200 GB compressed).

The device you choose must also fit your infrastructure. For example, you might want to attach a local tape device to the Exchange servers and back them up locally. Alternatively, you might want to implement a centralized backup system that automatically backs up multiple servers (often across a dedicated backup-only LAN or directly from a SAN) to a farm of dedicated backup servers and multiple tape devices.

There are multiple backup technologies available, and what is considered state of the art is rapidly evolving. It is a good idea to educate yourself about the alternatives and features offered by several vendors before choosing a solution.

Evaluating Administrative Requirements

The disaster recovery strategy you choose will have a significant impact on the administrative resources required to perform backup and recovery tasks. When developing your disaster recovery plan, you must evaluate staffing, your administrative model, and any permissions that might be required to recover from a failure or disaster.

Staffing

Evaluate the demand that frequent backups will have on the number of messaging administrators or other staff that are performing backup and restore tasks, and ensure that they are not over extended. Ensure that your staff is fully trained on implementing the disaster recovery plan and that staff practices implementing the plan periodically so that if a failure or disaster occurs, they can implement the plan rapidly, without delays.

Administrative Model

Servers running Exchange 2003 use Active Directory to replicate Exchange object properties and configuration information throughout an entire Active Directory forest. Servers running Exchange 2003 continually communicate with Active Directory domain controllers to access information in Active Directory.

As part of your Exchange 2003 disaster recovery planning, you should familiarize yourself with the dependencies that Exchange 2003 has on Active Directory. All Exchange 2003 directory information (including configuration information for mailboxes, servers, and sites within the Exchange 2003 organization) is stored within Active Directory. Items such as distribution lists and access permissions for users and groups are also stored within Active Directory.

Because of the dependencies of Exchange on Active Directory:

- Exchange administrators must work closely with Windows administrators to ensure that fault-tolerance measures (such as multiple domain controllers) are considered before Active Directory is deployed.

- Exchange administrators who are responsible for disaster recovery must have permissions in Active Directory to read, create, modify, and delete Exchange entries (Table 21-3 and Table 21-4).

- Exchange administrators must consider the impact of different recovery scenarios on Active Directory. Many recovery scenarios, such as single item or single mailbox restores, can utilize the recovery storage group in Exchange 2003 and the production Active Directory forest. But other scenarios, such as recovering mailboxes that were deleted or purged from the system, recovering public folder data, or testing backup and restore procedures in a non-production environment, must use a separate Active Directory forest that hosts a copy of the Exchange organization. A separate Active Directory forest enables administrators to recover a damaged mailbox or public folder from a recovery server that is not a part of the production Exchange organization, or to perform test restores without impacting production servers or the production forest.

More Info For more information about using recovery storage groups, see the book "Using Exchange Server 2003 Recovery Storage Groups" (*http://go.microsoft.com/fwlink/?LinkId=23233*).

- Exchange administrators should work with Active Directory administrators to ensure that any changes to the Exchange organization, such as adding a server or moving users, result in the creation of a new backup of Active Directory to preserve those changes.

Permission Requirements

When developing your disaster recovery plan, ensure that you evaluate the permissions and rights required to perform backup and restore tasks.

Table 21-3 summarizes the permissions required to perform disaster recovery tasks. Table 21-4 summarizes the backup privileges that are extended to members of built-in groups.

Table 21-3   Disaster Recovery Permissions

Task	Minimum permissions
Exchange backups	Domain backup operator
Exchange restore operations	Full Exchange administrator
Windows backups	Local backup operator
Windows restore operations	Local administrator rights

Table 21-4   Accounts and Their Backup Privileges

Account is a member of	Backup privileges
Local Administrators group	Can back up most files and folders on the computer where your account is a member of the local Administrators group.
	If you are a local administrator on an Exchange member server, you cannot back up Exchange database files unless you are also a member of the Backup Operators or Domain Admins groups.
Domain Admins group	Can back up all files and folders on all computers in the domain.
Local Backup Operators group	Can back up all files and folders on the computer where your account is a member of the local Backup Operators group.
Domain Backup Operators group	Can back up all files and folders on all computers in the domain.
Any other domain or local group	Can back up all files and folders that your account owns.
	Can back up files or folders for which your account has Read, Read and Execute, Modify, or Full Control permissions.

Evaluating Monitoring and Maintenance Procedures

Proactive monitoring and maintenance procedures help to prevent or minimize the impact of disasters such as hardware failures. For example, Extensible Storage Engine (ESE) errors being logged in the event logs can indicate a defective hard disk or indicate that a hard disk is about to fail. Review daily, weekly, and monthly procedures to ensure that procedures for monitoring and maintaining the health of your Exchange organization are included, such as:

- Procedure for applying service packs, hotfixes, and firmware updates
- Procedure for monitoring Event Logs

- Procedures for using tools such as Performance Monitor, and programs such as Microsoft Operations Manager (MOM) to generate alerts when components are near or at capacity, or when critical events occur

- Procedure for maintaining server and changing management logs that track changes to servers that might be important when troubleshooting, for example, previous failures, use of non-standard hardware, or the application of QFEs or hot fixes

- Procedure for monitoring daily backups, including procedures for verifying that backups completed successfully

- Procedures for periodically testing restores of backups

> **More Info**   For more information on performing maintenance and monitoring procedures, see Chapter 8, "Operating an Exchange Server 2003 Organization," Chapter 16, "Standard Monitoring Tools," and Chapter 17, "Exchange Server 2003 Management Pack."

Determining a Backup Strategy

Once you have identified the types of loss that can occur and the types of data that you must back up, your next step in developing a disaster recovery plan is to determine a backup strategy that supports your organizational needs and meets your SLAs.

You can use Windows 2003 Backup to implement different backup strategies, or you can use a third-party backup tool that supports the Exchange 2003 online backup API. The Exchange 2003 online backup API automatically identifies and gathers the Exchange 2003 database and transaction log file data required for successful restoration. Every page of the Exchange database is checked for corruption as it is being streamed to the backup media to ensure that you are not backing up a corrupt database. An online backup of Exchange 2003 databases occurs without interrupting service to users. Database backups occur while users are connected to and modifying the databases. Transaction logs generated during the backup are stored with the backup and are used to reconstruct all changes. The backup can be performed to tape or to disk, or a combination in which the data is backed up to disk then streamed to tape.

In addition, you can perform SAN-based snapshot backups that take snapshots of the Exchange databases (also referred to as shadow copies or clones) either while your Exchange databases are online (referred to as a hot-split snapshot) or offline (referred to simply as a snapshot). With the required hardware and software, you can create SAN-based snapshot backups of your Exchange 2003 databases in much less time than it takes to create the same backup set using traditional Exchange backup API backup processes.

SAN-based snapshot backups fall into two general categories: backups that use Volume Shadow Copy Service and backups that do not use Volume Shadow Copy Service.

- **SAN-Based Snapshot Backups Using Volume Shadow Copy Service** This method uses the Volume Shadow Copy Service to coordinate backup requests from a Volume Shadow Copy-compliant backup application with Exchange 2003. Volume Shadow Copy is a framework (included with Microsoft Windows Server 2003) that provides for individual applications to prepare their data to be captured by a point-in-time copy. Exchange 2003 includes a Volume Shadow Copy Service provider that works with the Exchange store and flushes pending transactions from the logs before the point-in-time copy is made. This guarantees a consistent, clean copy of the Exchange databases and log files. Volume Shadow Copy requires Windows Server 2003, Exchange 2003 server, and a Volume Shadow Copy-compatible backup tool. For SAN-based backups, Volume Shadow Copy can be integrated with Volume Shadow Copy-aware transport providers to enable vendor-neutral copy-and-move functionality.

More Info   For detailed information about the Windows Server 2003 Volume Shadow Copy Service, see the technical article "Storage Management Using Windows Server 2003 and Windows Storage Server 2003 Virtual Disk Service and Volume Shadow Copy Service" (*http://go.microsoft.com/ fwlink/?LinkId=26119*). For more information about using Volume Shadow Copy Service with Exchange 2003, see Microsoft Knowledge Base article 822896, "Exchange Server 2003 Data Back Up and Volume Shadow Copy Services" (*http://go.microsoft.com/fwlink/?linkid=3052&kbid=822896*).

- **SAN-Based Snapshot Backups That Do Not Use Volume Shadow Copy Service** This method uses proprietary, vendor-specific solutions to capture point-in-time copies of the Exchange data store and then transports the data elsewhere on the SAN for processing. These solutions can offer performance similar to SAN-based snapshot backups that use Volume Shadow Copy Service.

More Info   For information about backing up Exchange 2003 data by using snapshot backups that do not use Volume Shadow Copy Service, see Microsoft Knowledge Base article 311898, "XADM: Hot Split Snapshot Backups of Exchange" (*http://go.microsoft.com/fwlink/ ?linkid=3052&kbid=311898*).

Note If you implement a SAN-based snapshot solution for Exchange 2003, the vendor of the backup application is your primary support provider for backup and recovery issues, and your storage array vendor is your primary support for storage array issues. For information about specific third-party vendors that provide SAN-based snapshot solutions, see the Exchange Server Partners website (*http://go.microsoft.com/fwlink/?LinkId=30008*).

Understanding Exchange Database Backup Types

The backup types that you can choose from when using a backup application that supports the Exchange backup API include: normal (also referred to as a full backup), copy, differential, incremental, and daily. Table 21-5 describes each of the available types of backups as they apply to Exchange.

Note The backup types listed in the table are the options provided by Windows 2003 Backup (ntbackup.exe). Other backup applications might not provide for all of these backup types, or might use their own terms when describing the type of backup and any requirements. It is important to find out in advance of purchasing backup software or implementing a backup solution exactly what backup types are supported for Exchange.

Table 21-5   Description of Database Backup Types

Backup type	Description
Normal backup	A Normal (or full) backup archives every selected database and all necessary log files. Log files older than the checkpoint and that are no longer required by any database in the storage group are candidates for deletion after the backup completes.
	Advantages:
	Simplest online backup method. Daily Normal backups prevent log files from monopolizing hard disk space.
Copy backup	A Copy backup is the same as a Normal backup, except that transaction log files are not deleted.
	Advantage:
	Enables you to save a copy of your Exchange databases at a specific point in time.

Table 21-5   Description of Database Backup Types (Continued)

Backup type	Description
Differential backup	A Differential backup archives only the transaction log files that are stored on disk. The transaction logs are not deleted. You cannot perform a Differential backup when circular logging is enabled. Advantage: Restoring data from a Differential backup requires only the most recent Normal and Differential backups sets.
Incremental backup	An Incremental backup archives only the transaction log files which have been created since the last Normal or Incremental backup. Log files that were backed up are deleted after the backup completes. You cannot perform an Incremental backup when circular logging is enabled. To restore data from an Incremental backup, you must have the most recent Normal backup and each subsequent Incremental backup set available. Advantage: Incremental backups require the least amount of time to perform, because they back up only new log files that were created since the last backup.
Daily backup	In Exchange 2003, a Daily backup performs the same functions as a Copy backup.

Select a Backup Strategy

Determining the appropriate backup strategy requires evaluating the length of time the backup will take, the number of backup sets required to perform a restore, and the amount of time allowed to complete the restore. The time allowed to complete the restore includes both the time required to transfer database files and log files from the backup media to the server, and the time required to replay any transaction logs generated since the last backup into the restored database. Table 21-6 compares different backup strategies. Use the table to determine the appropriate backup strategy for your company.

Table 21-6   Comparing Backup Strategies

Backup strategy	Time to perform backup	Number of sets required for restore	Time to perform recovery
Copy Daily	Same as a Normal Daily	One backup set	Fastest recovery, but recovers only to last backup, not to point of failure.

Table 21-6   Comparing Backup Strategies (Continued)

Backup strategy	Time to perform backup	Number of sets required for restore	Time to perform recovery
Normal Daily	Longest amount of time to perform backup	One backup set	Second fastest recovery, but unlike Copy, recovers to point of failure by replaying the log files still on disk since last backup.
Normal Weekly plus Daily Incremental	Least amount of time	One Normal weekly backup set plus each daily Incremental backup set	Longest recovery, because each Incremental set must be recovered, then rolled into the database.
Normal Weekly plus Daily Differential	Progressively longer to complete	One Normal weekly backup set plus latest daily Differential set	Second longest recovery, because only one Differential set must be recovered, then rolled into the database.

Selecting a Tape Rotation Strategy

Although it is not an Exchange-specific matter, if you use tapes in your backup solution, how those tapes are reused during your backup cycle is an important consideration. By rotating tapes, you ensure that adequate data versions are always available on tape and that tapes are protected from excessive wear and damage, so that if a failure or disaster occurs, you can restore your Exchange servers.

> **Note**   A common mistake that administrators make is not retiring tapes after a certain number of uses. Tape manufactures provide information on the useful life of their tape media, and it is important to follow their recommendations and remove old tapes and discard them when necessary.

Tape rotation strategies differ according to the number of tapes required and the amount of time the media is kept before it is rotated back into the schedule. They also differ according to how media is taken out of the rotation and archived. Two common tape rotation schemes are Grandfather-Father-Son (GFS) and Tower of Hanoi.

Grandfather-Father-Son

GFS requires 20 tapes (assuming a five-day backup schedule). The tapes are used and labeled as follows:

- Four tapes (Sons) are used to perform incremental or differential backups and are labeled for the day of the week each tape is used; for example, Mon, Tues, Wed, and Thurs. Each tape is reused each week on the day matching its label. These tapes are typically stored on site.

- Four tapes (Fathers) are used to perform Normal (full) backups weekly, on the day that a "Son" media is not used, and are labeled Week 1, Week 2, Week 3, and Week 4. This media is reused monthly. These tapes can be stored on site or off site.

- 12 tapes (Grandfathers) are used to perform Normal backups on the last business day of each month and are labeled with the month and year, for example Month 1/2004, Month 2/2004, etc. The monthly tapes can be archived for permanent storage or recycled on a quarterly or yearly basis depending on your company's requirements. They are stored off site.

Note If a backup exceeds the capacity of a single tape, create a tape set and label it accordingly.

Table 21-7 shows an example of a two-month rotation period using GFS where the first month ends on a Wednesday, and the second month ends on a Friday.

Table 21-7   Grandfather-Father-Son Tape Rotation

Monday	Tuesday	Wednesday	Thursday	Friday
				Week 1
Mon	Tues	Wed	Thurs	Week 2
Mon	Tues	Wed	Thurs	Week 3
Mon	Tues	Wed	Thurs	Week 4
Mon	Tues	Month 1/2004	Thurs	Week 1
Mon	Tues	Wed	Thurs	Week 2
Mon	Tues	Wed	Thurs	Week 3
Mon	Tues	Wed	Thurs	Week 4
Mon	Tues	Wed	Thurs	Month 2/2004

Tower of Hanoi

Tower of Hanoi is a more complex scheme. You perform a Normal backup on five tape sets labeled A, B, C, D, and E.

Tape set A is used every other backup session. For example, if you perform Normal daily backups, start on day one with A and reuse tape set A every other day. The next tape set, B, starts on the first non-A backup day and repeats every fourth backup session. Tape set C starts on the first non-A or non-B backup day and repeats every eighth session. Tape set D starts on the first non-A, non-B, or non-C backup day and repeats every sixteenth session. Tape set E alternates with tape set D and is stored off site.

Table 21-8 shows an example of a month of backups using the Tower of Hanoi tape rotation scheme.

Table 21-8   Tower of Hanoi Tape Rotation

Monday	Tuesday	Wednesday	Thursday	Friday
Tape A	Tape B	Tape A	Tape C	Tape A
Tape B	Tape A	Tape D	Tape A	Tape B
Tape A	Tape C	Tape A	Tape B	Tape A
Tape E	Tape A	Tape B	Tape A	Tape C
Tape A	Tape B	Tape A		

Comparing Tape Rotation Strategies

Table 21-9 compares the advantages and disadvantages of the two common tape rotation schemes.

Table 21-9   Comparing Tape Rotation Strategies

Rotation Scheme	Advantages	Disadvantages
Grandfather-Father-Son	Provides the most secure data protection Allows for weekly offsite archival of tapes Implements monthly archival of tapes Supported by most backup software	Requires more tapes (20 minimum)
Tower of Hanoi	Allows for easy system restores (uses Normal daily backups) Uses fewer tapes than GFS (five minimum)	Difficult rotation strategy that is not as straight-forward to implement unless your backup software supports it (too complex to manually track tape rotation) Long backup times (uses Normal daily backups)

Archiving Backup Media

Tapes are typically removed from the tape rotation and archived monthly, quarterly, or yearly. Depending on the industry that your company is in, you might be required to maintain long-term data archives of e-mail communications to fulfill financial or legal requirements. For any archive or long-term archive strategy, it is important to create a duplicate data set on separate media and store it in a separate physical or geographic location. By having a duplicate set of media, you reduce the risk of vulnerability due to mishandling, natural disaster, inappropriate environmental conditions, or misplacement of your archive data.

Verifying and Validating Database Backups

The time and effort it takes to perform backup operations are only worthwhile if they enable you to successfully recover from a failure. Part of your disaster recovery plan should include verifying and validating database backups to ensure not only that the backup is being completed without error, but also that the correct data is being backed up and that there are no failures in the media that would prevent the data from being restored. You should take the following measures to verify and validate database backups:

- Review the backup log to verify that the backup was successful. For example, if you are using Windows Backup, immediately after each backup is complete, check the backup log created by Backup for errors.

- Review the Application event log in Event Viewer to verify the backup was successful. For example, review the application event log for events generated by "NTBackup" or "ESE." NTBackup event ID 8000 and 8001 indicate the start and end of the backup process, ESE event ID 213 indicates that the backup procedure has successfully completed, whereas NTBackup event ID 8017 indicates a backup failure, as does ESE events 203, 214 and 226.

> **More Info**   For additional information to assist you in troubleshooting events found in the event log, see the Events and Errors Message Center page on the Microsoft TechNet website (*http://www.microsoft.com/technet/ support/eventserrors.mspx*).

- Verify data by restoring the backed up data from your backup media to a test server, a lab forest, or by using the recovery storage group on a production server (if you are verifying a mailbox store backup). Once the data has been restored, ensure that the data can be accessed properly. Restoring data allows you to verify the integrity of your system and identify potential problems before you lose data to a real disaster.

> **Note**   It is not necessary or feasible to perform daily test restore operations for all of the databases on each of your servers. Instead, consider rotating through backups made on various servers so that all of your backups are tested regularly.

Building a Disaster Recovery Toolkit

The time spent searching for parts, utilities and information during a failure or disaster, such as a server outage, can cost your company valuable time and expense. By assembling in advance the components you need to respond quickly when a failure or disaster occurs, you ensure the resolution in the least amount of time possible.

Keeping Spare Hardware Available

To help minimize downtime costs, keep replacement hardware immediately available that duplicates the hardware resources in your server environment. For example, a company might spend a lot of time and resources troubleshooting the cause of a network issue, only to learn that the issue could have been resolved much faster if there had been spare network adapters nearby.

Types of replacement hardware that you should keep available include:

- Alternate or standby servers
- Network adapters
- Video card
- Hard disks
- Hard disk controllers
- Power supplies
- Memory
- Network components such as routers and cables

Having a Crash Cart Available

A crash cart is an assembly of items that enable you to debug a server or service that has failed and that cannot be recovered by rebooting. A crash cart consists of the following items:

- An additional computer (such as a laptop).

- A null modem cable to connect the additional computer to your server.

- Debug symbol files for both the operating system and the application to be debugged.

> **Note**   Whether or not you perform debugging on your own, having a crash cart assembled in advance will facilitate using resources such as Microsoft Product Support Services to troubleshoot any issues you might have.
>
> To download debugging tools for Windows, see the Microsoft Debugging Tools on the Microsoft Windows Driver Development Kit Web page at *http://www.microsoft.com/ddk/debugging/*.

Keeping Software and Documentation Available

Items that you should attach to all servers or keep readily available on a network share to facilitate recovery are:

- Windows installation software and service packs

- Exchange installation software and service packs

- Other software for the server including:

  - Software and firmware updates for your vendor's hardware

  - Antivirus software

  - Backup software

  - Other third-party software

- Documentation on your server that includes:

  - Software version information for Windows, including any service packs and hotfixes

  - Software version information for Exchange, including any service packs and hotfixes

  - Backup schedule details (for example, Normal backups are performed on Fridays with Incremental backups performed Saturday through Thursday)

- RAID array configuration details
- Application and system log archives
- Disaster recovery procedures
- Emergency telephone numbers for:
    - Members of your IT department
    - Microsoft Product Support Services and your technical account manager, if you have one
    - Antivirus support
    - Hardware vendor support
- Relevant Microsoft Knowledge Base articles and white papers, including:
    - Knowledge Base articles that document changes that you made to your server
    - Knowledge Base articles to help you recover your server
    - Disaster recovery white papers

Note It is important to keep your disaster recovery tool kit up-to-date. The utilities and documentation in your toolkit should be maintained and updated on a regular basis.

Best Practices

To reduce downtime resulting from a failure or disaster, apply the following best practices when developing your disaster recovery plan for Exchange 2003:

- Fully document your backup and restore strategy.
- Provide exact step-by-step procedures that your staff will implement in the event of each type of failure or disaster that may occur.
- Ensure that administrators, operators, and support staff within your Exchange 2003 organization have access to various training opportunities and technical reference materials regarding disaster recovery issues.
- Perform occasional disaster recovery simulations in separate, non-production domains. These simulations will familiarize administrators, operators, and support staff with recovery procedures and indicate any deficiencies in your backup and restore strategies.

- Update your disaster recovery plan based on your experiences of performing recovery simulations.

- Review technical articles, such as the Technical Case Study, "Messaging Backup and Restore at Microsoft" (*http://www.microsoft.com/exchange/evaluation/casestudies/casestudy.asp?CaseStudyID=14112*) to understand how other companies have implemented disaster recovery solutions.

- Visit the Disaster Recovery for Exchange 2003 website (*http://www.microsoft.com/ exchange/techinfo/administration/2003/DisasterRecovery.asp*) to find resources to help you prepare for, prevent, and recover from failures and disasters in an Exchange organization.

- Keep abreast of changes in technologies to understand how those changes impact availability and recovery in your Exchange environment. Hardware and software based technologies are constantly improving to provide high levels of availability, and faster, more reliable recovery methods.

Chapter 22

Implementing a Backup Solution

About This Chapter

This chapter explains the processes involved in backing up Exchange Server and the Windows operating system data. Further topics include running Exchange Server 2003 on a Windows Server 2003 platform, and using Windows Backup (NTBackup.exe) to perform the backups.

Backing up Exchange data on a regular basis is an essential part of general Exchange administration. The reason for data backup is to enable you to restore the data at a later date, either in the event of data loss or corruption, or for test purposes. Backing up Exchange and Windows is a relatively simple task, but the backup regime is determined by factors such as backup hardware, backup window durations, and restore constraints. Service-level agreements play a major part in determining backup regimes, and if, for example, your service-level agreement for Exchange specifies that Exchange services must not be down for more than two hours during a disaster, the backup regime must be designed and performed with this goal in mind.

What You Need to Know

Backing up data is possibly the most critical operation within an enterprise, but also the operation with the least quantifiable benefit to the company. Data backup is a kind of insurance policy, and involves various components: hardware, software, and an appropriate backup regime. The latter is probably the most important aspect of all, and is the one with which this chapter is concerned.

Backup is a means to an end, and the end is to restore the data that has been copied to the external media. Backup operations are driven and guided by the possible disaster recovery scenarios. Data must be restored and normal company operations resumed. E-mail and collaboration systems are now some of the most critical systems in the enterprise, so ensuring that data cannot only be recovered, but recovered speedily and reliably, is the prime goal of the backup regime.

In order to start defining a backup regime for Exchange, you must understand the underlying systems and technologies behind Exchange. The Windows services on which it relies, such as Internet Information Services, Simple Mail Transport Protocol, the Domain Name System and others, must be considered. Indeed, Exchange disaster recovery planning must take into account that of the Windows systems and Active Directory domain in order to have proper meaning.

Understanding the Exchange system is also important. Being aware of the interaction between databases and log files helps an administrator understand the likely impact of a certain kind of disaster, and what initial action should be taken, as well as the rest of the recovery processes. Exchange Server 2003 Enterprise Edition enables the creation of multiple databases in multiple storage groups. This enables administrators to create more resilient Exchange servers with different databases and log files on separate hard disk arrays. Understanding what tasks must be undertaken, and the recovery techniques that can be used when a database or log file set is lost or corrupted, is critical to the expedient recovery of data, and therefore to the backup regime that is established.

Information on the design of Exchange Server and its dependencies can be found in Chapter 2, "Exchange Server 2003 Design Basics." Chapter 21, "Disaster Recovery Planning for Exchange 2003," lays out frameworks for disaster recovery planning and backup types and schedules.

Defining the Backup Data

Exchange Server backup operations include many components over and above Exchange data itself. Active Directory databases, which store much of the Exchange configuration settings and objects, must be backed up. Local server configuration repositories, such as the registry and Internet Information Services (IIS) metabase, provide information about Exchange components, such as Internet protocols; and Exchange databases and log files comprise the user data, such as messages and attachments.

The IIS metabase is a data storage location that holds and manages configuration information for IIS and related applications.

Backing up Exchange databases and components with a view to the successful restoration of the data requires an involved set of procedures and a thorough understanding of the way the Exchange transactional database system works. Carefully consider what components need to be backed up in order to restore an entire Exchange server or organization, and also which components would facilitate restoring certain components, such as individual databases. In the event of a disaster, configuration data, such as IIS and Simple Mail Transfer Protocol (SMTP) connector settings, can be recreated manually, but the store databases and log files must be restored from backup and are therefore the priority for any backup regime. Other backup procedures and servers must also be taken into account when considering the backup of Active Directory, an essential service for Exchange but not one that is necessarily installed on the same server.

Note Installing Exchange Server 2003 on a domain controller is a supported configuration but one that is not normally recommended because of the extra processing load and security concerns. Slightly increased complication in the restore procedures is another reason why Exchange running on domain controllers is not a preferred configuration.

Windows Components

When discussing Exchange Server backup, you must include Windows in the process because the Windows backup set is an essential piece of the puzzle. Exchange Server stores its configuration data in many places including the registry, IIS metabase and Active Directory, and these repositories must all be included to produce a full Exchange backup set. Details of the configuration repositories Exchange uses and general Exchange design is covered in Chapter 2, "Exchange Server 2003 Design Basics."

- **The registry** The Windows Registry is used by Exchange to store settings, such as diagnostic logging levels, setup configuration information, and graphical user interface (GUI) settings, such as the ShowSecurityPage, which specifies that the Security tab be shown on the Properties page of Exchange configuration objects. The registry files are located in the Systemroot\System32\config folder.

> **Note**   A copy of the registry is copied to the Systemroot\Repair folder. This can be used to restore registry data using the Windows Server 2003 Recovery Console.

- **The IIS metabase**   The metabase configuration file stores the configuration data for IIS, on which the Exchange server relies. Exchange-related settings that have to do with SMTP virtual servers, HTTP configuration for Outlook Web Access, and for System Manager access and other settings, are stored in Active Directory and copied to the metabase by the Metabase Update Service, a process of the System Attendant. The metabase is a necessary part of the underlying Windows operating system, however, and must be present for IIS (and therefore Exchange) to function. On Windows Server 2003 servers the metabase is stored in an XML file named Metabase.xml and a corresponding metabase schema file, MBSchema.xml, which defines the available attributes for objects described in the metabase. On Windows 2000 Server servers the metabase is stored in binary format in a Metabase.bin file. The metabase files reside in System-root\System32\inetsrv in Windows 2003 and Windows 2000.

- **Active Directory**   The Active Directory is the key repository of configuration for Exchange Server. The backing up of Active Directory is covered in more detail later in this chapter, under "Domain Controllers and Exchange Server 2003."

The System State

The System State refers to a collection of system components of the Windows operating system. The components that make up the System State of a particular server depend on the services the server is running, and they may include the following:

- **Windows Registry**   The registry contains configuration information about the computer and installed operating system, including user profile data, installed software, hardware configuration, and communication ports used. The registry holds configuration information for the Exchange server as detailed above.

- **Boot files**   The boot files required to boot the operating system are ntldr, ntde-tect.com, and bootsect.dat.

- **COM+ class registration database**   This is configuration data relating to COM applications installed on the computer.

- **System files**   System files are required to start, run, and configure Windows. These consist mainly of essential files in the Systemroot folder, and the boot files detailed above.

- **IIS metabase**   The metabase is a plaintext XML file (in Windows 2000 it is a binary file) consisting of the configuration data for IIS. As explained in Chapter 2, IIS is an essential Windows component for Exchange Server 2003.

- **Active Directory directory services**   If the server is a domain controller, the System State backup includes the local copy of Active Directory, which holds information about every object in the Windows domain.

- **SYSVOL directory**   If the server is a domain controller, the SYSVOL folder, which contains copies of the domain's replicated public files, will be backed up as part of the System State. SYSVOL information includes the NETLOGON share for earlier clients, system policies, and group policy settings, including logon scripts.

- **Cluster service information**   If the server is part of a cluster, the System State backup includes the cluster quorum resource.

- **Certificate Services**   If Certificate Services are installed on the server, the System State backup will include the Certificate Services database.

> **Note**   The System State contains the configuration repositories required for a full Exchange Server restore. However, due to dependencies between the components the System State is regarded as a single quantum, which means that only the entire System State can be backed up or restored. To enable the restoration of individual components, these components must be backed up separately. For example, the IIS metabase can be backed up and restored on its own. IIS metabase backup is covered later in this chapter.

The System State data is only one part of a full Windows server backup. Operating system files must also be backed up in order to create a full backup set.

To see exactly what is backed up as part of the System State of your server you can restore it to a different location on the server or on another computer. To do this, use NTBackup and, in the Advanced properties of the restore operation, select Alternate Location. This will restore most of the files involved in the System State backup to the folder you specify, keeping its folder structure in the meantime. If you specify Single Folder in the Advanced settings, all of the files will be restored to the same single folder.

> **Note**   Some components of the System State will not be restored because they cannot be restored to an alternate location. These are the Active Directory files, Certificate Services database, and the COM+class registration database.

Exchange Databases

The data you must back up on an Exchange server depends on the components installed on the server. Mailbox and public folder servers have private and public store databases at the very least. Special functions, such as the Site Replication Service, full-text indexing, and connectors, all have their own data repositories that must be backed up.

The core databases consist of the Exchange database (EDB) and Streaming database (STM) files, along with their dependent transaction log files. The checkpoint file, which keeps track of log files that have been applied to the databases, also forms a part of the core database backup.

Stores and Storage Groups

Exchange mailbox and public folder stores are grouped together in storage groups. An Exchange server can have up to four storage groups, each containing a maximum of five stores.

Each storage group corresponds to an instance of the Extensible Storage Engine (ESE), each of which maintains a single set of log files and one checkpoint file. Figure 22-1 shows the architecture of a single storage group.

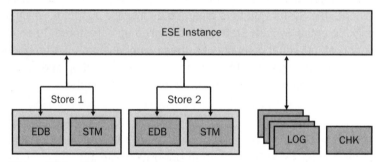

Figure 22-1   Storage group architecture

The core Exchange Server 2003 databases are those that belong to the Information Store service and contain the working data for Exchange, the mailboxes and public folders. The default mailbox store database files are named PRIV1.EDB and PRIV1.STM and the default private store files are PUB1.EDB and PUB1.STM, although different file names can be specified that are more appropriate to the server or the function of the databases. The default locations for these files are c:\program files\exchsrvr\mdbdata, although online backups are independent of file location.

Transaction Logs

During operation, Exchange Server stores database transactions in memory and in transaction log files. As discussed in Chapter 10, this helps to improve the performance of Exchange because it commits the transactions to the databases at a time when the server is not busy, when the Information Store service is stopped, or during an online streaming backup.

The other advantage of transaction logs is the added resilience it gives the database system, which is achieved when the log files and database files are stored on separate disk arrays. Transaction logs hold all of the transactions since the last full or incremental backup, so if the disk with the database files on it breaks, you can restore Exchange up to the point of failure by restoring the last database backup and replaying the transaction logs back into the database. If the disk with the transaction log files fails, however, simply shutting down the Information Store may retain all of the data because the uncommitted transactions are stored in memory and written to the database on shutdown. Restoring the database will leave Exchange with data only up to the point of the backup. Repairing the existing database, however, may result in almost current data, although it may incur some loss of messages through the use of the ESEUtil tool. ESEUtil.exe is a command line maintenance tool for performing offline operations on database files.

Circular Logging

Exchange keeps a record of every database transaction in a set of log files in order that the database information may be restored to its exact state before the disaster. These logs are deleted after a full or incremental backup is performed. When circular logging is on, Exchange writes transaction logs as usual; however, after the checkpoint has been advanced, the inactive portion of the transaction log is discarded and overwritten. This does not mean that Exchange will have only a single transaction log when circular logging is enabled. Large messages and high-volume conditions can cause additional log files to be created. If the total number of unprocessed transactions exceeds 5 MB and more continue to build up, another log file is created to hold these transactions. If the high-volume conditions continue, the log files continue to increase in number until the transactions can be processed completely and reused. After the transaction, processing catches up and the checkpoint is advanced past the transactions in these log files. The log files become inactive and are not removed until a full backup is performed.

While circular logging reduces the amount of disk space required for Exchange, the way the transactions are committed dictates that the databases can be restored only to the point of the last backup. It also limits the backup types to Full and Copy; incremental and differential backups are both concerned only with backing up log files.

Circular logging is disabled by default and is not recommended except on servers that do not contain critical data, such as Network News Transport Protocol (NNTP) servers and bridgehead servers.

Checkpoint Files

During database operation the checkpoint file keeps track of which logs within a storage group have been committed to the databases. The checkpoint file aids in recovery by telling ESE engine what transactions have already been committed, allowing for faster recovery. However, the checkpoint file is not required for transaction log replay; it only saves the ESE from starting with the lowest log and checking every transaction to determine if it has been committed to the database set. The checkpoint file is not backed up by an online Exchange backup, it is backed up only by Volume Shadow Copy service-based backups and offline backups.

Optional Databases and Components

The databases and transaction log files are the most important data to back up. However, depending on the Exchange configuration, there are other components that need to be or should be backed up as part of the standard backup procedures. Some of these components are important, such as cluster quorum logs, and some components are a matter of the needs of the organization and what fits in with your service-level agreements. Certain log files, like message tracking logs for instance, are not critical to the operation of Exchange, but the data they hold may be useful enough to make a part of the backup.

The optional databases and components to back up with Exchange include:

- **Full-text index** Full-text indexes are configured on the public folder store or mailbox store level and contain indexes of words within e-mail messages and attachments for faster searching from client applications, such as Microsoft Office Outlook. The loss of these index files is not critical because they simply represent data that is available in the Information Store databases. However, depending on the size of the index, it may be prudent to back up the files so that in a restore scenario the server will not need to regenerate the index files.

  The files that comprise the full-text index are the catalogs, property store, property store logs, temporary files, and gather logs. The default location of the full text index files is \Program Files\Exchsrvr\ExchangeServer_<*ServerName*>\Projects, where <*ServerName*> is the name of the Exchange server.

- **Message tracking logs** When message tracking is enabled, the message tracking logs keep track of all inter- and intra-server e-mail messages. The logs are shared between servers by a folder share on each server, enabling the tracking of messages from source to destination within an Exchange organization. The message tracking logs are not required for Exchange operation but may be required for compliance with any regional legal regulations.

  The default location for the message tracking logs is the c:\Program Files\Exchsrvr\<*ServerName*>.log folder.

■ **Site Replication Service (SRS)**   SRS is an Exchange Server 2003 directory service that acts like an Exchange 5.5 directory in order to replicate directory data with Exchange 5.5 servers. SRS is present only in organizations with coexistence with Exchange 5.5 servers.

The default location for the SRS is the c:\Program Files\Exchsrvr\Srsdata folder.

SRS is an important component of a mixed Exchange environment, and although it can be recreated with the use of a second Exchange 2003 server, it should be an integral part of the backup procedure. Depending on the service-level agreements set for Exchange services, it is favorable to avoid having to recreate the SRS database as part of a recovery process. Instructions on how to recreate the SRS database can be found in Knowledge Base article 822453, "How to Rebuild a Site Replication Service in Exchange 2003 When You Do Not Have a Backup of the SRS Database" (*http://go.microsoft.com/fwlink/?LinkId= 3052&kbid=822453*).

■ **Exchange cluster data**   Backing up a clustered Exchange server is similar to backing up a stand-alone server except a cluster backup must include the quorum file that holds the cluster configuration data and the Exchange database and log files on the shared disk resource. On a cluster that uses the Majority Node Set, the quorum data is stored on each node rather than the shared disk. The cluster data is backed up as a part of the System State backup on a Windows Server 2003 server. For more information on backing up and restoring Windows Server 2003 clusters, see "Backing up and restoring server clusters" (*http:// www.microsoft.com/resources/documentation/WindowsServ/2003/standard/ proddocs/en-us/Default.asp?url=/resources/documentation/WindowsServ/ 2003/standard/proddocs/en-us/sag_mscsusing_9.asp*).

Volume Shadow Copy Service

The Volume Shadow Copy service framework is a component of Windows Server 2003 and Windows XP that enables the creation of high-fidelity point-in-time images by backup applications. By using these images, or shadow copies of data volumes, the data can be backed up with little effect on the performance of the production server.

Volume images have been available in third-party storage systems for some time, but Volume Shadow Copy service provides a standardized framework for the creation, transport, and restoration of shadow copies within the operating system. Volume Shadow Copy service is a component of the Virtual Disk Service which is designed to bring together storage services uniformly, so different third-party devices can be managed through Windows Server 2003 Disk Management. The Virtual Disk Service is discussed in the next section.

The Volume Shadow Copy service framework provides two methods of creating shadow copies: a complete copy using the clone method, or a differential copy using the copy-on-write method. Each method creates a logical copy of the data at a point in time. The clone method duplicates the whole volume, whereas the copy-on-write method duplicates only the modified data and relies on the original data to construct the logical copy.

- **Clone (split mirror/full copy)**   A clone is a complete copy (or "plex") of the original volume. This method uses hardware or software mirroring and synchronizes the data between each volume until the point at which the shadow copy is made. At this point, the copy becomes read-only and constitutes the full point-in-time copy of the original volume. The data on the copy can then be used for backup, transport to another server, or other procedures. Figure 22-2 illustrates a split-mirror shadow-copy creation process.

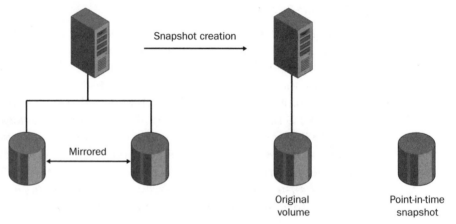

Figure 22-2   Creation of a split-mirror shadow-copy volume

- **Copy-on-write (differential copy)**   A differential copy stores not the whole data but only the changes made to the original data volume. When a change is made to a data block on the original volume, the block to be modified is copied into a differences area (or "diff area"), thus preserving a copy of the data before it was overwritten. At a given time in the future the original volume can be reconstructed by combining the data on the original volume with the diff area to create a logical representation of the volume at that point in the past. Figure 22-3 illustrates the copy-on-write shadow copy creation process.

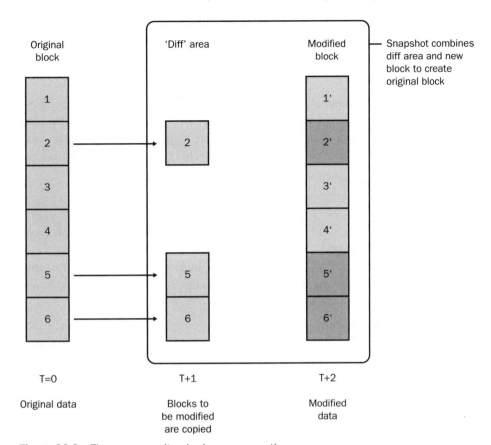

Figure 22-3   The copy-on-write shadow-copy creation process

The Volume Shadow Copy service provided with Windows Server 2003 uses the copy-on-write method to implement Shadow Copies for Shared Folders. Exchange database backups, on the other hand, are typically implemented as clones because the number of pages being changed during normal use would mean that perhaps all of the blocks that make up the database file will have been changed since backup.

Both methods can be implemented in hardware or software but only hardware-based shadow copies are transportable. Transportable shadow copies can be copied to other servers or systems for data mining, backup, or testing purposes and can be implemented by means of masking and unmasking logical disk units. For more information about Windows Server 2003 Volume Shadow Copy service, see the document "How Volume Shadow Copy Service Works," on the Technet website (*http://www.microsoft.com/resources/documentation/WindowsServ/2003/all/techref/en-us/Default.asp?url=/resources/documentation/WindowsServ/2003/all/techref/en-us/W2K3TR_vss_how.asp*).

In order for a backup or restore operation to use Volume Shadow Copy service successfully, the backup software, the application, and the backup device must be programmed to work with it.

Volume Shadow Copy service components fall into the following categories:

■ **Requestor**   A requestor is implemented within the backup software and initiates the creation and deletion of the shadow copy. The requestor informs the Volume Shadow Copy service that it requires a shadow copy and that the Volume Shadow Copy service should coordinate its creation.

■ **Writer**   A writer is a component of an application that takes part in the shadow copy process and whose data is included in the shadow copy. The writer prepares the application data for the shadow copy process and then freezes the application; Exchange Server 2003 includes a Volume Shadow Copy service writer, and in this case the writer purges the current log file to disk and temporarily halts write operations to the Exchange databases before freezing the application. The writer understands the application that is being backed up and how to prepare the application for the backup process.

■ **Provider**   A provider is the component that performs the shadow copy process. When the Volume Shadow Copy service informs the provider that the volume is ready to be backed up, the provider performs the creation of the shadow copy.

The modular structure of the Volume Shadow Copy service framework allows hardware and software manufacturers to produce their own requestors, writers, and providers, and provides additional functionality for their own products through a standard interface. The structure of the Volume Shadow Copy service framework is represented in Figure 22-4. The different Volume Shadow Copy service components may be distributed across servers in this illustration.

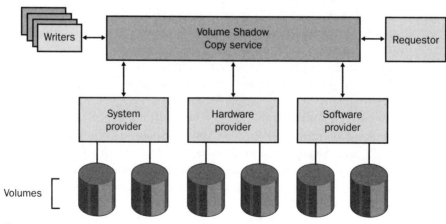

Figure 22-4   The Volume Shadow Copy service framework

NTBackup is a Volume Shadow Copy service requestor that is capable of taking shadow copy backups of volumes. It is a non-component requestor, however, which means that while it prepares the system, including the writer applications, for shadow copy backup, it discards the metadata information provided by the writers and leaves the file selection up to the user or backup application. The Volume Shadow Copy service writer that is a part of Exchange is not supported by NTBackup; only streaming Exchange backups can be performed using NTBackup. Windows also includes a number of Volume Shadow Copy service writers; for example, writers for MSDE, IIS metabase, Event Log, and for domain controllers, an NTDS writer. The software Volume Shadow Copy service provider that comes as part of Windows Server 2003 is named the "Microsoft Software Shadow Copy Provider 1.0" or "Volsnap" and supports only the differential copy method for making shadow copies.

> **Note**   You can list the providers and writers present on a Windows Server 2003 server by using the server tool VSSAdmin.exe. Running the command **vssadmin list writers** from the command line outputs data similar to that below.

```
vssadmin 1.1 - Volume Shadow Copy Service administrative command-line tool
(C) Copyright 2001 Microsoft Corp.

Writer name: 'System Writer'
   Writer Id: {e8132975-6f93-4464-a53e-1050253ae220}
   Writer Instance Id: {d2083dbf-da0d-407b-90b3-0bf535cdac1b}
   State: [1] Stable
   Last error: No error

Writer name: 'FRS Writer'
   Writer Id: {d76f5a28-3092-4589-ba48-2958fb88ce29}
   Writer Instance Id: {025f7540-9807-4753-966d-064079b73d99}
   State: [1] Stable
   Last error: No error

Writer name: 'NTDS'
   Writer Id: {b2014c9e-8711-4c5c-a5a9-3cf384484757}
   Writer Instance Id: {6f02b3f2-604e-4b1f-9909-dc72b0ab0e7a}
   State: [1] Stable
   Last error: No error

Writer name: 'Microsoft Exchange Writer'
   Writer Id: {76fe1ac4-15f7-4bcd-987e-8e1acb462fb7}
   Writer Instance Id: {78eb5ecf-793a-43c2-b3b4-52fc278924b8}
   State: [1] Stable
   Last error: No error

Writer name: 'IIS Metabase Writer'
   Writer Id: {59b1f0cf-90ef-465f-9609-6ca8b2938366}
```

```
    Writer Instance Id: {9e1334df-b6ff-4f47-bfcc-af89ef9a71e4}
    State: [1] Stable
    Last error: No error

Writer name: 'Registry Writer'
    Writer Id: {afbab4a2-367d-4d15-a586-71dbb18f8485}
    Writer Instance Id: {83ec619b-83a3-4757-852e-8e8bb02bb8b2}
    State: [1] Stable
    Last error: No error
```

The Backup Process

When a backup program initiates the creation of a volume shadow copy, it first queries the Volume Shadow Copy service for a list of writers present on the server before informing them that it intends to take a shadow copy backup. The writers then provide relevant metadata to the requestor defining the capabilities of the writer and the requested action for the shadow copy. The metadata provided by the Exchange Server 2003 writer is covered in the next section.

The Volume Shadow Copy service requestor then tells the writers to prepare for shadow copy creation in whatever way is appropriate for that specific writer. For a file system writer this may mean that it should stop all writes to the file system, or perhaps store writes in memory or in a separate disk location. A database writer, such as Exchange, may stop all transactions and stabilize the database by committing all open transactions to the database prior to the backup. This process is initiated by a "freeze" command given by the requestor.

When the writers have prepared their data for shadow copy creation, the provider then makes the shadow copy of the volume. This process takes a matter of seconds, after which a "thaw" command is sent to the writers and the applications resume normal operation.

The Virtual Disk Service

The Virtual Disk Service (VDS) provides a single Windows interface that supports volume management for multi-vendor storage devices. Although the Virtual Disk Service integrates and provides volume information through the Disk Management MMC snap-in, much of its functionality is provided through two command-line utilities, Diskpart and Diskraid.

Diskpart is used to control, extend, and delete partitions on basic and dynamic disks, and Diskraid, one of the Windows Server 2003 Resource Kit tools, is used to configure hardware redundant array of independent disks (RAID) subsystems, creating deleting, extending, and masking/unmasking logical units on a Storage Area Network. In order to manage the underlying storage hardware with these tools, a Volume Shadow Copy service provider must be present for the hardware.

VDS and Shadow Copy Management

In contrast to the copy-on-write method of shadow copy creation used by the Windows Server 2003 provider, hardware providers are able to use the split-mirror or clone method of shadow copy creation. These methods create a separate physical copy of the data on the volume, usually on another logical unit (LUN) on the same Storage Area Network.

Although the Volume Shadow Copy service framework is often used to create shadow copies for local backup of high-fidelity images onto tape media, environments with Storage Area Network–based storage arrays can take advantage of the hardware-based split-mirror technique in order to manage shadow copies for transport to another server for backup, data mining, or for testing purposes. Using volume virtualization on a Storage Area Network system, shadow copies can be transported virtually between servers by simply masking and unmasking the LUNs.

After a clone shadow copy is created, at the moment the clone is split from the original volume it is marked as read-only and no longer touched. The Diskraid command can then be used to mask off the LUN with the clone copy from the original server and unmask it to another server. This process is referred to as "virtual transport" because it takes advantage of the ability of Storage Area Networks to move entire volumes between servers without physically moving any data.

Backing Up Windows

In order to produce a useful backup procedure for Exchange Server 2003 it is essential that the host operating system, Windows 2000 Server or Windows Server 2003, is included in the disaster recovery plan. As discussed in previous chapters, the dependencies of Exchange are such that certain components of Windows, for example Active Directory, IIS metabase, registry, and other operating system components, must be present for Exchange to operate. Components may be restored from backup or reconfigured manually. It is important to be aware of the operating system dependencies for Exchange and the various types of backup that can be used to successfully back up these required components as part of an Exchange disaster recovery plan.

There are two main methods of backing up a Windows server, an image backup or a component backup. A component backup is the backup of the files on the hard disk, such as the operating system files and program files. An image backup is a brick-level backup, performed at the disk level, of the hard disk or volume itself that can be used for quick restore operations.

Image Backup

Image backups refer to the sector-level backing up of an entire hard disk or volume on a server. An image backup includes information about volume partitions, file tables, and the Master Boot Record, as well as the files on the disk.

Image backups are used primarily to provide quick restore in the case of disaster situations because they make it possible to boot the server from a floppy disk or the backup drive itself and replay the backup onto a new hard disk directly. It is not necessary to install Windows beforehand, only to provide a low-level formatted hard disk for the restore. This is the advantage of an image backup over a file or component backup.

Hard disk or volume images have a number of caveats in their preparation and implementation, namely:

- **Special care must be taken when restoring a server from an image file** If implemented incorrectly the restored server may cause conflicts with configuration data in Active Directory or even with a present server of the same name (if the old server has not been removed).

- **Images must be up-to-date** Restoring older images may cause problems and require the server to be removed and added again to the domain or the secure channels to be reset.

- **Server downtime** Creating an image of a server necessarily means downtime for the server being imaged

Image backups can be created using specific hardware or software products. Imaging software can create an image of an operating system in order that it can be restored directly from the storage medium by booting from a floppy disk. Some backup hardware manufacturers provide tape drives with the ability to create an image of a server hard disk by pressing a single button on the device. In the event of the server requiring a rebuild, the server can be booted from the tape device and the image restored directly.

Automated System Recovery

Windows backup provides a process called Automated System Recovery (ASR), which creates a copy backup of an entire Windows server system partition. An ASR backup is used to restore a system quickly in the event of a major system failure. ASR is a kind of hybrid image backup because it produces a backup of the system drive and a helper floppy disk, but rather than enabling restore of the system by streaming a brick-level backup directly from tape it requires the automated installation of Windows from the Windows Server 2003 CD. The recovery of a server using ASR is covered in Chapter 23, "Restoring Exchange Server 2003."

ASR backup sets are for rebuilding a server when all other recovery methods have been exhausted. Examples of other recovery methods are Last Known Good Configuration, Safe Mode, and the Recovery Console.

An ASR backup consists of a tape backup of the system partition and a floppy-based configuration disk, the ASR diskette. The system backup part of ASR creates the following three backup sets on the tape drive:

- **The system partition**   This is a Volume Shadow Copy service-based copy backup of the system volume, usually the C: drive.

- **The System State**   This consists of Windows boot files, COM+class registration database, and the system registry, IIS metabase, cluster registry, and so forth.

- **ASR state information files**   Asr.sif and Asrpnp.sif are files that are copied to the ASR diskette and contain information about hardware devices and configuration.

The ASR diskette consists of three important files:

- **Asr.sif**   Contains information about the server's storage devices, partitions, volumes and removable media.

- **Asrpnp.sif**   Contains information about Plug and Play devices present on the server.

- **Setup.log**   Contains a list of all System State and critical files backed up by the ASR process but plays no part in an ASR restore.

Figure 22-5 shows the backup sets that are part of the ASR backup.

ASR backups can be performed using the Automated System Recovery Wizard within Windows Backup. This wizard guides you through creating a system settings floppy disk and other media that contain the backup of the local system partition.

ASR backups should be performed regularly, especially when configuration changes are made to the server, such as installing software or making changes to System State components.

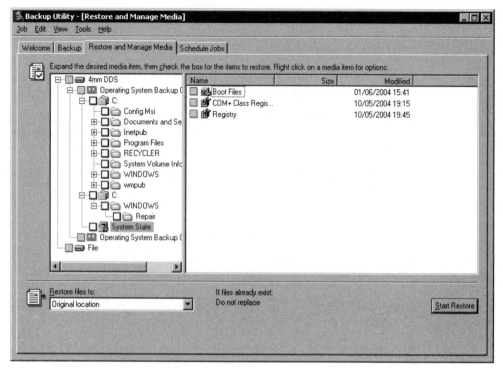

Figure 22-5   The contents of an ASR backup set

Component Backup

Component or file-based backups are used for backing up file servers in order that important files can be restored from tape when the file is corrupted or lost. Component backups are also used for backing up operating system files and configuration in order that the Windows installation can be restored to its previous state from a new Windows installation.

Using simple backup applications such as NTBackup for Windows 2003 you can back up individual files and components within Windows, for example the system files, System State, and executable files installed by applications, in order to restore these components back onto a fresh installation of the operating system. Usually, this type of backup procedure is used for backing up individual files as part of a structured backup procedure, but it can also be used to back up the entire system for disaster situations where the server must be rebuilt.

As part of the backup strategy chosen for the organization, the component backup can be used to back up data files, Exchange databases, and system information, such as the System State, which includes the components discussed earlier in this chapter. For more information about backup strategies and tape rotations, see Chapter 21, "Disaster Recovery Planning for Exchange Server 2003."

Windows Server 2003 backup actually uses image technology in the form of the Volume Shadow Copy Service to perform a shadow copy file backup of the system. Volume Shadow Copy service uses a low-level method of backup creation but also maintains file-level data so individual files can be restored from the image. Volume Shadow Copy service shadow copies are point-in-time copies that ensure that the data being backed up is consistent. For more information about Volume Shadow Copy service backups, see the document "How Volume Shadow Copy Service Works," on the Microsoft TechNet website (*http://www.microsoft.com/resources/documentation/WindowsServ/2003/all/techref/en-us/Default.asp?url=/resources/documentation/WindowsServ/2003/all/techref/en-us/W2K3TR_vss_how.asp*).

If you are using NTBackup to create Volume Shadow Copy service-based backups you should install the post-RTM fix for Windows Server 2003 Backup detailed in Knowledge Base article 833167 (*http://support.microsoft.com/default.aspx?scid=kb;en-us;833167*).

Creating a Windows Backup Set

The Windows Backup utility (NTBackup.exe) provides the ability to create a component-based backup of the operating system and an ASR backup set for disaster recovery purposes.

When NTBackup is run for the first time it starts in wizard mode. When you choose the backup option, wizard mode gives you the choice of backing up the entire server or a subset of the data on the server, as shown in Figure 22-6. If the option All Information On This Computer is chosen, it automatically runs the Automated System Recovery Wizard and creates a tape backup and floppy set, as described above. Choosing Let Me Choose What To Back Up brings you into Backup Or Restore Wizard where you can manually select the components to back up.

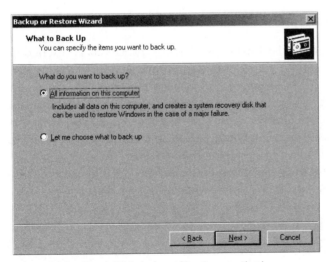

Figure 22-6 The initial choice of backup method

By running the Backup utility and following the Automated System Recovery Wizard, a full ASR backup is created, as described in the previous section. It is important to keep the ASR tape and floppy disk in a safe location in case of a server disaster.

On the Resource Kit CD   The document Performing an ASR backup.doc in the \Companion Material\Chapter 22 folder on the companion CD contains step-by-step instructions to create an ASR backup of a stand-alone server onto direct-attached storage.

Tip   If the ASR diskette is lost or destroyed, it can be recreated by copying the Asr.sif and Asrpnp.sif files from the backup tape to a blank floppy disk. The Setup.log file plays no part in the ASR restore procedure and is not necessary.

The component, or file-based Windows backup is also performed by using the Windows Backup utility. By using the Backup Wizard you can choose to back up everything on the computer (which backs up all files on all local volumes), selected files, or only the System State data. When performing regular backups of a server as part of your backup regime chosen in Chapter 21 you should choose the Backup-selected files, drives, or network data option in order to specify which files and folders to back up.

Backing up Exchange

When defining your standard Exchange backup processes and schedule, consideration must be given to the many different backup methods available. Depending on what the backup is to be used for and also on the overall backup strategy, some backup methods have advantages over others. Exchange 2003 introduces support for backup techniques, which can not only increase the speed and efficiency of backup and restore processes, but also enable the swift transportation of backups for other purposes, such as testing and separate-server backup. These new methods also assist in offloading some of the processing required in producing backups in order that the Exchange server can concentrate more of its resources on serving Outlook and other clients.

This section discusses the various types of backup open to administrators in order to best protect your Exchange environment from minor problems as well as major disasters.

The following are standard backup options available to administrators and backup operators:

- **Streaming backups**   Exchange Server includes a streaming API, into which backup programs can interface in order to create backups of the Exchange databases while the Exchange services are running and servicing clients. This is the most popular type of backup for regular operation because it requires no downtime, and degradation of normal service can be negligible if implemented properly.

- **Offline backups**   This backup method requires that the Information Store service is stopped for the duration of the backup, causing downtime for users and applications that access the Exchange databases. While the Information Store is stopped, the backup is created using a simple file backup process.

- **Shadow copy backups**   Using the new Volume Shadow Copy service framework described earlier in the chapter, backup applications can take advantage of the built in Exchange writer, which enables a shadow copy backup of the Exchange databases while keeping services online.

Streaming or Legacy Backups

Messaging services, particularly e-mail, have become extremely important in modern business. Many environments must keep services running 24 hours a day, seven days a week, with minimal allowance for server downtime. Backup operations must be able to run while servers are online and people are using Exchange.

The streaming API included with Exchange 2003 enables programs to back up the Information Store databases through a steady stream of data from the online database. This method ensures that a consistent backup of the store data can be made without interrupting normal processes. In order to do this, the backup application must be programmed to understand the specific streaming API that Exchange provides.

Normal Backups

A normal, or full-backup job backs up all of the selected information, databases and logs, purging the backed-up log files from the server. Normal backups should be run to ensure that a full backup of the database exists in case of disaster, all transactions are committed to the database, and the transaction logs are purged from the disk. Depending on the amount of data to be backed up, the speed of the backup devices and other factors, normal backups should be performed on a daily basis whenever possible. Because they back up all of the data, normal backups can consume a considerable amount of storage space.

The steps that a normal or full backup process goes through are as follows:

1. The backup application agent communicates with the Information Store service and initiates a backup process.

2. The transfer of the database to backup media starts while transactions are still being written to the transaction log files.

3. As each page in the database is read, its validity is verified against the page's checksum before transferring to backup medium.

4. After the databases have been transferred to backup, the current transaction log is closed and a new log file started, regardless of whether the current log file is full. Log files cannot be copied to tape while they are open, so this enables the backing up of the log file and ensures that the transactions applicable to the database being backed up are also copied to the tape.

5. The closed log files are backed up to tape and the committed log files on disk are truncated.

> **Note**   If all databases in the storage group are backed up, only the log files from the checkpoint log to the highest numbered (closed) log will be backed up to tape. Exchange will copy to backup media all of the log files required to bring the backed up databases back to the present state.

6. The Previous Full Backup section of the header of each backed up database is updated to reflect the time of the backup and the log files required.

7. The backup finishes and the archive bit is cleared.

During a normal backup operation the transaction log files are truncated, or flushed from the disk. This involves the deletion of the logs that have been committed to the databases and backed up to disk. The checkpoint file keeps track of which logs have been committed, while each database's header keeps a note of when it was last backed up and which logs were required. However, under the following circumstances not all of the backed up logs will be truncated:

- **Not all databases within the storage group are selected for backup**   If only some of the databases are backed up, Exchange truncates the logs only to the time of the oldest database backup. So, if one database has not been backed up for a month, that month's worth of logs files will not be truncated. If one of the databases is never backed up, the log files will never be truncated.

- **A database in the same storage group is dismounted**   If one of the databases in the storage group to be backed up is dismounted, Exchange cannot read its header and therefore does not know which log files are required to restore it fully. No log files will be truncated during the backup operation in this case because no calculation can be made as to which ones to keep.

Copy Backups

Copy backups are similar to normal backups because they back up the entire databases and log files onto the backup media. The only difference is that they do not flush any log files or update the Previous Full Backup section of the database header, and they also do not clear the archive attribute of the database files. A copy backup is essentially a ghost backup, and it leaves no trace of it having happened.

Copy backups are specified by selecting the copy backup type under the Advanced Backup Options page, as shown in Figure 22-7.

Copy backups are used primarily for testing purposes, such as performing mock disaster recovery operations.

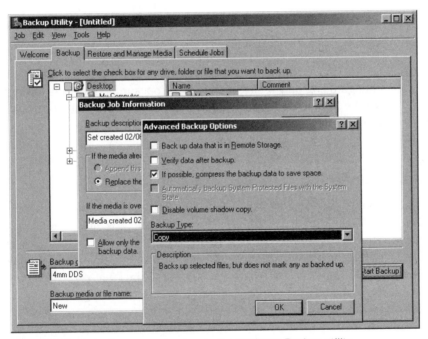

Figure 22-7 Selecting a copy backup in the Windows Backup utility

Differential Backups

Differential backups back up only the log files since the last full backup was made. It uses the archive attribute to determine which log files to back up but does not reset the attribute when it is finished. The point of differential backups is to be able to completely restore the Exchange databases up to the last minute with only the last full backup and the latest differential backup. Making differential backups in between full backups means that restore operations take longer because two backup sets must be restored, but the backups themselves are smaller and quicker because they don't involve backing up the databases.

Since a differential backup does not delete any log files, the size of the backups gets increasingly larger until the next full backup, which then flushes the logs.

The steps that a differential backup process goes through are as follows:

1. The backup application agent communicates with the Information Store service and initiates a backup process.

2. While new transactions are still accepted and processed by the Information Store, the checkpoint file is frozen until the backup is finished.

3. The current log file (E*xx*.log) is closed and a new one started, regardless of how full the log file is.

4. All of the numbered log files, including the one just closed, are copied to tape.

5. The backup finishes.

Note Because the point of a differential backup is to be able to restore Exchange using only a single differential backup plus the last full backup, all of the logs since the last full backup must be present. For this reason, differential backups do not flush the log files.

Incremental Backups

Incremental backups are similar to differential backups in that they copy only the log files to the backup medium. Where incremental backups differ from differential backups is in the deletion of the backed up log files.

Because the log files are deleted each time an incremental backup completes, a complete restore of the Exchange databases requires that each incremental backup taken since the last full backup is restored in order to bring Exchange to the state it was in prior to the disaster.

Note As with a normal backup, which log files are deleted depends on which databases within the storage group are being incrementally backed up and the state of the other databases within the storage group. The group dependency on the same set of transaction logs means that all of the log files up to the checkpoint may not be flushed.

When an incremental or differential backup is performed, it may fail after two seconds and give an error such as the following in the backup log file:

```
Error: LDNEX02\Microsoft Information Store\First Storage Group is not
a valid drive, or you do not have access.
```

The reason for this may be that a full, or normal backup has not been previously performed on the databases. To verify this, check the Database tab on the properties of the individual stores, as shown in Figure 22-8. Perform a full backup on the storage group before attempting a differential or incremental backup.

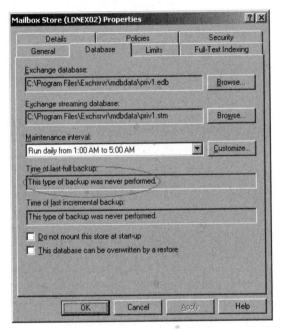

Figure 22-8   Checking the last backup of a mail store

Log File Deletion

It is crucial for the Exchange administrator to verify that the Exchange backups are running and completing properly and also that all of the databases are being backed up. During backup operations, some conditions can cause the checkpoint file to become locked (for example, if the backup application hangs), which can result in a build-up of uncommitted transaction logs on the server. If the server crashes, it may take a number of hours to replay these logs. Also, the Exchange store will automatically be dismounted if the checkpoint file falls more than 1,000 logs behind.

When a data store is dismounted, Exchange cannot determine the state of the database and consequently does not flush any log files. This potentially causes a build up of transaction logs on the server. If a database needs to be in a dismounted state for a prolonged period it may be worth placing it in its own storage group.

Another issue that can occur if log files are not truncated is that you can exhaust the number of available log files. The ESE engine only supports a maximum of 1,048,560 log files per instance. When this occurs, the databases within the storage group will dismount and the following events will be logged in the server's application log:

```
Event Type: Error
Event Source: MSExchangeIS Mailbox
Event Category: Logons
Event ID: 1022
Description: Logon Failure on database <Path_of_Database>. Error: -519

Event Type: Error
Event Source: MSExchangeIS
Event Category: General
Event ID: 9518
Description: Error 0xfffffddc starting Storage Group <Path_of_Storage_Group>
            on the Microsoft Exchange Information Store.
Storage Group - Initialization of Jet failed.
```

Before this limit is reached the following event will be logged to give you advance warning:

```
Event Type:Warning
Event Source:ESE
Event Category:Logging/Recovery
Event ID:514
```

Note   Information Store (2748) <Storage Group Name>: Log sequence numbers for this instance have almost been completely consumed. To begin renumbering from generation 1, the instance must be shut down cleanly, and all log files must be deleted. Backups will be invalidated.

More Info   For more information about this issue and steps you must take to remount your databases, please see Knowledge Base article 830408, "A storage group has shut down and will not remount on Exchange 2000 or on Exchange Server 2003" at *http://support.microsoft.com/?id=830408*.

Offline Backups

An offline backup consists of a copy of the files that make up the Exchange Server databases. To take an offline backup the database must be dismounted and therefore is inaccessible to users. An offline backup is equivalent to a copy backup in that it performs a full backup without purging any log files with the exception that user down-time is involved.

The advantage of the offline backup is it can include all the Exchange configuration data, such as connector information, as well as the databases.

Offline backups require the database to be dismounted and inaccessible to users for the duration of the backup. Also, because the transaction logs are not purged, they build up on the hard disk until a full online backup is taken.

To perform an offline backup of an Exchange storage group, dismount the databases and copy the MDB and STM files from the MDBDATA folder containing the databases. The offline backup can be made using a backup application such as NTBackup or by simply copying the files in Windows Explorer. When the databases are dismounted, the log files are committed to the databases so it is not necessary to back up the log files as well unless they may be used to replay into a previous database backup.

Volume Shadow Copy Service and Shadow Copy Backups

Exchange Server 2003 with Service Pack 1 (SP1) supports full, incremental, differential, and copy backups using the Volume Shadow Copy service. With Volume Shadow Copy service the storage group is the only selectable component for backup; single databases are not selectable. This is because during a normal or incremental backup the logs, which are particular to a storage group, are truncated. However, if one or more databases in a storage group are dismounted, the logs will not be truncated in case those databases become corrupt.

NTBackup in Windows 2003 can act as a Volume Shadow Copy service requestor when it starts a backup operation; this is in fact the default behavior for NTBackup, but it can be deselected in the backup program. However, NTBackup supports only a subset of the possible features of the Volume Shadow Copy service framework. While Volume Shadow Copy service provides the possibility for either split-mirror or copy-on-write shadow copies, the NTBackup requestor uses only the copy-on-write method. Also, as discussed earlier in this chapter, NTBackup is a non-component requestor, which means it discards the metadata provided by the writer applications and leaves the file/component selection up to the user.

If you use Volume Shadow Copy service when backing up Exchange using NTBackup, create separate backup sets for the Exchange data and the System State. When you attempt to back up both within the same procedure, the backup fails and the following is written in the backup log:

```
The 'Microsoft Information Store' returned 'Backup is already active.'
from a call to 'HrESEBackupSetup()' additional data '-'The 'Microsoft
Information Store' returned 'Functions called in an invalid sequence.'
from a call to 'HrESEBackupClose()' additional data '-' The operation
was ended.
```

The reason for this is that NTBackup uses legacy APIs to back up the Exchange data, but because the Volume Shadow Copy service framework has been invoked these APIs think a Volume Shadow Copy service backup is being taken and therefore fails. A post-RTM fix is available that avoids this behavior by disabling the Exchange writer when NTBackup is launched.

The overall Volume Shadow Copy service backup process is shown in Figure 22-9.

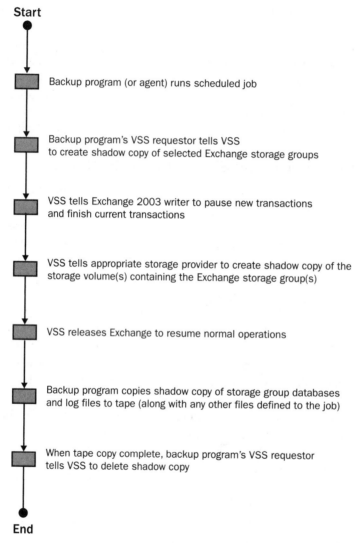

Start

Backup program (or agent) runs scheduled job

Backup program's VSS requestor tells VSS to create shadow copy of selected Exchange storage groups

VSS tells Exchange 2003 writer to pause new transactions and finish current transactions

VSS tells appropriate storage provider to create shadow copy of the storage volume(s) containing the Exchange storage group(s)

VSS releases Exchange to resume normal operations

Backup program copies shadow copy of storage group databases and log files to tape (along with any other files defined to the job)

When tape copy complete, backup program's VSS requestor tells VSS to delete shadow copy

End

Figure 22-9   The Volume Shadow Copy service backup process

Using third-party backup applications, shadow copy backups can be taken of the file system and Exchange databases, depending on the specifications of the requestor application. With a hardware requestor that supports Volume Shadow Copy service, a split-copy shadow copy can be created on a Storage Area Network that creates a copy of the Exchange databases and splits the LUN off for transporting to another system for testing or direct to tape. The masking and unmasking of these shadow copy LUNs on a Storage Area Network speeds up backup and recovery of data by virtually transporting shadow copies of data volumes between servers on the same Storage Area Network.

To create such shadow copies, refer to the documentation with your Storage Area Network hardware or backup software.

Future Exchange 2003-aware volume shadow copy service requestors from storage vendors will be able to create shadow copies periodically during the day, leaving them on disk in case of the need for quick restore. This process is similar to Shadow Copy for Shared Folders which takes shadow copies of user file volumes periodically to enable single file restores when required.

Backing Up the SRS Database

The Site Replication Service (MSExchangeSRS) database is present only in organizations that contain Exchange 5.5 servers. By default, the server that is running the SRS is the first Exchange 2000 or Exchange 2003 server installed into an Exchange 5.5 site although more SRS instances can be installed manually onto other Exchange 2000 or Exchange 2003 servers.

To find out which server is running the SRS, open the Exchange System Manager and look in Tools\Site Replication Services. As in Figure 22-10, the SRS instances are named "Microsoft Exchange Site Replication Service (*computername*)."

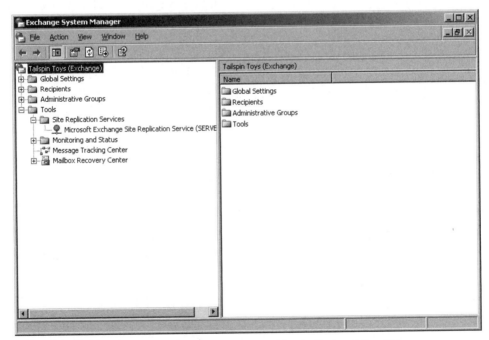

Figure 22-10 Site Replication Service instance entries in System Manager

The SRS database appears beside the Information Store data as a component in NTBackup under *<servername>*\Site Replication Service. To perform an online back up the database select the SRS Storage icon.

Alternately, the SRS database components can be backed up using a file-based backup, but the MSExchangeSRS service must be stopped beforehand as with an offline Exchange database backup.

Backing Up Exchange 2003 Clusters

Exchange 2003 supports 2-node active/active clusters and active/passive clusters of up to 8 nodes on Windows Server 2003, Enterprise Edition and Windows Server 2003 Datacenter Edition. Each node in a cluster can be based on different hardware as long as each component is in the Windows Hardware Compatibility List. Network cards, however, should be identical on each node, in hardware, software, and settings. Clustered Exchange servers have shared storage areas that hold the active data, such as the Exchange databases and log files, so that nodes can fail over and relinquish control of this data to another node. For more information about Windows clusters, see the Windows Server 2003 Clustering Services Technology Center (*http://www.microsoft.com/windowsserver2003/technologies/clustering/default.mspx*).

Clusters differ fundamentally from stand-alone servers in that their services are controlled centrally via the cluster service, and access to the cluster is through a separate, virtual IP address/name which is transparent to clients. One or more Exchange virtual servers exist in the cluster, and each node can also house more than one Exchange virtual server in active/active cluster scenarios.

Backup operations with Exchange cluster servers differs little from those of a stand-alone server because the backup of most of the cluster-specific components is transparent to the administrator. The main differences in a cluster are the shared storage system and cluster quorum, which is stored on the shared storage in a standard cluster or on each node in the case of a majority node-set clusters.

To successfully back up an Exchange cluster, you should create a full computer backup set for each node as well as Exchange database backups for each virtual server in the cluster. Other dynamic data, such as message tracking logs and connector data, should be backed up as normal according to your selected backup regime.

Backing Up the Quorum Data

The quorum data consists of the files on the shared quorum disk and the cluster registry, which resides in the %systemroot%\Cluster\CLUSDB folder on each node. The quorum disk is a separate shared disk that holds the quorum log file that records changes to the quorum database to share with all nodes.

The quorum resources are essential for restoring a cluster, and both the shared disk and the local registry file must be backed up from the node that owns the quorum disk resource.

A System State backup on the node that currently owns the quorum disk includes the quorum log and the local registry components of the cluster data. If you perform a Windows backup set, full-computer backup set, or ASR backup set on this node, the quorum resources will be included. No extra backup operation is required.

Backing Up the Shared Disk Resource

The shared disk resources on an Exchange cluster are the disks that hold the data that must be accessed by any node in the cluster. The Exchange 2003 databases and log files must reside on the shared disks so that they can be accessed by another node in the event of failover.

Backing up the databases and log files on the shared disks uses the same method as on a stand-alone server. Selecting the components to be backed up under the Information Store option in NTBackup will back up those databases and log files accordingly, regardless of the location of those files. Because the Exchange backup works through the Exchange APIs, the backup is run using the System Attendant and Information Store services on each virtual server. Remember, that because of this it is not necessary to make sure you are backing up Exchange from the node that has control of the shared resource. The backup is done through the virtual server rather than physical nodes.

Creating one backup set for the system and boot partitions and the System State data, and another for the Exchange data files, gives you the most flexibility when it comes to restoring nodes and shared data.

Backing Up Certificate Services

Exchange Server 2003 uses a public key-based security infrastructure to encrypt and sign e-mail messages. This framework can be provided by Windows Server 2003 servers running Certificate Services, called certification authority (CA) servers.

Certificate Services can be backed up as part of the System State backup of a CA server backup, or by using the Certification Authority Backup Wizard that is available in the CA MMS snap-in.

When using NTBackup to back up a CA, the IIS metabase is also backed up and restored with the System State. The IIS metabase is used by Certificate Services to display its Web pages for CA management. The manual CA backup process is shown in Figure 22-11.

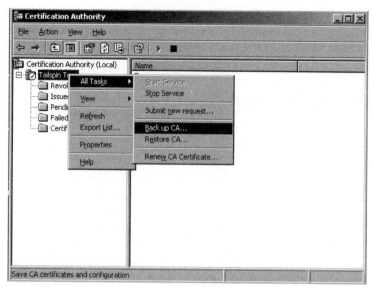

Figure 22-11   Manually backing up a certification authority

When using the backup function of the CA MMC snap-in, make sure the IIS metabase is backed up as well so that it can be restored with the certificate services. The metabase is not a requirement for certificate services, however, and IIS can be reconfigured to support the CA Web pages.

> **Note**   If certificate services are lost and no backup is available, some data in the Exchange server may become inaccessible.

> **More Info**   For more information on backing up a CA, see "Backing up and restoring a certification authority" in the Windows Server 2003 online help (*http://go.microsoft.com/fwlink/?LinkID=25762*).

Backing Up Mail Connector Information

Exchange servers that have connectors to other mail systems, such as Lotus Notes and Novell GroupWise, store connector information in the registry and in Active Directory.

Backing up the System State on the Exchange server that houses the connector and a copy of Active Directory will enable a restore of most of this configuration information when running Exchange Server setup in disaster recovery mode, but each type of connector also requires certain information within the ExchSrvr\Conndata folder to be backed up manually. Such data includes import and export files, configuration files, and correlation tables for foreign systems.

Apart from the connector information stored in the local registry and in Active Directory, the following should be included in the backup:

- **Connector for Lotus Notes**   The Connector for Lotus Notes stores mapping rules and synchronization data in the dxamex and dxanotes subfolders of the Conndata folder. These folders should be backed up along with the Notes client installed on the connector server.

- **Connector for Novell GroupWise**   The Connector for GroupWise stores mapping rules and synchronization data in the dxagwise subfolder, and message data in the \Gwrouter folder and its subfolders. Back these folders up directly using a standard backup job.

These folders should be backed up as part of your regular Windows backup set. If Exchange is installed on the system partition, it will also be included in ASR sets.

Backing Up other Dynamic Data

Other data you may wish to back up includes:

- **Message tracking logs**   To back up the message tracking logs, include the folder Exchsrvr\<*servername*>.log\ in the file-based backup.

- **Full text indexes**   To back up full-text indexes on your Exchange server, perform a file-based backup of the Exchsrvr\ExchangeServer_<*servername*>\Projects\ folder. This folder contains the full-text indexes for all the stores on which indexing is enabled.

Data to Exclude from File-Based Backups of an Exchange Server

Because an online Exchange database backup uses specific Exchange APIs, the process can clash with standard file-based backups in Windows backup. The APIs feed the data from the databases to the backup applications through the Information Store service, in contrast to a file-based backup of the actual database files on the file system. In fact, attempting to back up certain components related to the databases using a non-Exchange-aware backup utility can cause corruption in the databases and cause the backup to fail.

There are therefore a number of components that a backup of an Exchange server should not include:

- **Database and log files**   The databases and some log files are in use during an online Exchange backup and cannot be backed up by simple file-based utilities. Using open-file backup utilities can cause database corruption. The database and log files are backed up by the Exchange backup APIs when using an Exchange-aware backup utility such as NTBackup. When performing a file-based backup, exclude the MDBDATA folders on all volumes, as shown in Figure 22-12.

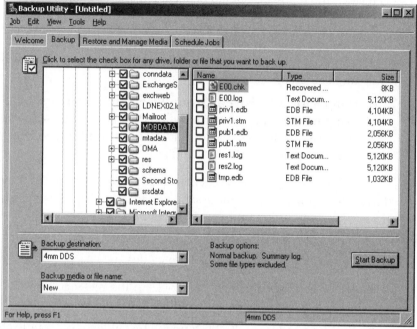

Figure 22-12 Exclude the MDBDATA folders from a backup

- **Installable file system (IFS) drive** Although not present by default in Exchange 2003, the IFS drive can be created to give applications direct file system access to public and private folders. Backing up this drive can cause corruption of the databases and because it is simply a representation of the databases themselves, the IFS drive is backed up through the Exchange APIs.

- **Shared disk resources on cluster servers** Typically, a cluster shared disk resource holding Exchange databases and logs and cluster quorum should not be backed up directly. The databases are backed up using the Exchange APIs and the quorum resource is backed up by the System State option in the backup program.

Automating Backups

When the backup regime for the Exchange servers has been decided, in order to save administrative time and effort these backup jobs can be scheduled using NTBackup and most other backup applications. While saving administrative effort, backup schedules must be carefully organized in order to avoid problems in the event of requiring a restore, such as retrieving tapes and verifying that the tapes hold the correct backup sets.

Once the regime is decided and organized, the process for which is covered in Chapter 21, "Disaster Recovery Planning for Exchange 2003," NTBackup can be used to implement the backup schedule on each server.

> **Tip**   When scheduling Exchange Server backups it is important to set the schedule so that it does not coincide with the daily online maintenance routines run on the databases. These routines are run by the Information Store and the database engine (ESE) and consist of ten discrete tasks, one of which is online defragmentation. If a backup starts on any database in a storage group while online defragmentation is running, defragmentation will be suspended until the backup completes. If online defragmentation is not allowed to finish on each database at least once a week, you will come across problems, such as performance issues, due to the fragmented database and the inability to complete maintenance without defragmenting the databases offline. You should also monitor the Application Event Log to make sure online defragmentation completes every few days at least.

Before scheduling a backup the Task Scheduler service must be running on the server. To make sure this is running, use the Services snap-in to check the status of the service and to change its Startup Type to **Automatic**.

NTBackup can be run and scheduled from the command line or from the GUI. Although the GUI offers ease of use, command line utilities often provide more comprehensive options.

GUI Interface

The Windows Backup application (NTBackup.exe) provides a convenient scheduler as part of the front end. Schedules can be set through the Backup Wizard or by using the manual backup process on the Backup tab.

The backup scheduler can be accessed via the GUI by using the Backup Wizard or the Advanced Mode, both of which go through nearly the same steps. When using Advanced Mode you create a backup job as if it were a one-off, then set a schedule on the Advanced tab toward the end of the process.

> **On the Resource Kit CD**   The document Scheduling an Exchange Backup Using the GUI in the \Companion Material\Chapter 22 folder on the companion CD goes through the steps of creating the scheduled backup.

NTBackup uses the Task Scheduler service to run the backup jobs so that the schedule will not be lost when NTBackup is closed. As can be seen from Figure 22-13, the resulting scheduled backup job is a command line script incorporated into the Task Scheduler.

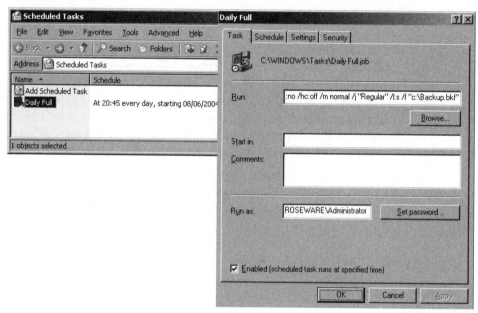

Figure 22-13   A scheduled backup task configured from the GUI

Command Line Interface

As demonstrated above, any backup job can be expressed in terms of a command line script. The command line options allow NTBackup to be easily utilized by other applications or incorporated into scripts. Using the command line options it is possible to configure complex backup jobs and schedule them using the Windows "at" command, which is the command line hook into the Task Scheduler. Figure 22-14 shows a simple scheduled task added from the command line and automatically incorporated into the Windows-based Task Scheduler. The same happens to backup jobs entered from the command line.

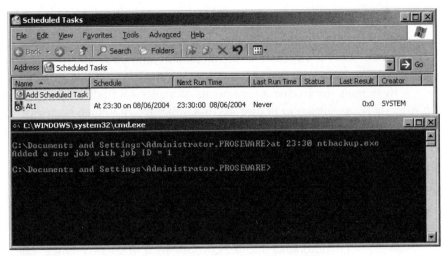

Figure 22-14   Adding scheduled tasks from the command line

When backing up Exchange Server, the command line option has a distinct disadvantage in that there is only a simple switch, /IS *"servername,"* which can be used to back up the entire information store on the server. This switch does not work against Exchange 2003, however, and is there only for use against Exchange 5.5 servers along with the /DS switch that backs up the directory service.

In order to define an Exchange 2003 storage group or store for backup, it is necessary to revert to the GUI version of backup to create a backup selection file (.bks) that defines the selections to back up. To do this you must go through the Backup Wizard and select the components required for backup. Depending on the method used, NTBackup will ask for a folder in which to save the selection file or simply save it in c:\Documents and Settings\<*username*>\Local Settings\Application Data\Microsoft\Windows NT\NTBackup\data along with the backup log files. This file contains a plain text selection that can be modified in Notepad or another text editor. An example of a backup selection file for an Exchange storage group is shown in Figure 22-15. It is advisable, however, to use NTBackup to create and modify these files, and then refer to them in the command-line-based backup job.

Figure 22-15   An example of a backup selection file

Backup Schedule

In order to avoid performance problems due to regular online database maintenance during the night, the backup and maintenance routines should be scheduled so as not to run at the same time.

By default, the Exchange online maintenance routines run between 12 A.M. and 5 A.M. daily, as shown in Figure 22-16. Online maintenance performs some consistency checking of the databases and removes any tombstoned data, such as deleted messages and mailboxes.

Because the online maintenance deletes data and defragments the databases, it is a good idea to run the backup after maintenance has finished if possible. In order to find out how long the maintenance takes, and therefore when to schedule the backup, set the maintenance schedule as long as possible and check the Application Event Log for Event ID 1221 for each store. This information will give you the amount of time the full maintenance requires, from which the maintenance schedule and the backup schedule can be set.

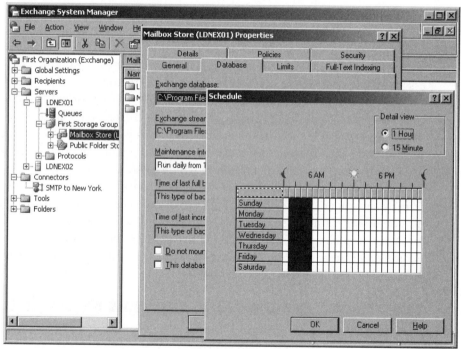

Figure 22-16   The default online database maintenance schedule

Domain Controllers and Exchange 2003

No Exchange Server backup is complete without its directory service, Active Directory. Active Directory must be backed up from a domain controller as part of its System State backup, and is likely to be a separate operation from the backup of Exchange itself.

When Exchange Server is running on a member server it will query a domain controller for data it needs, such as mailbox, user, and public folder configuration. In some situations an Exchange server is also a domain controller, but in most cases the two responsibilities are separated between servers for performance reasons.

A System State backup of a server that is a domain controller will include the Active Directory databases. These databases use the same transactional database technology as Exchange and use database files, transaction logs, reserve transaction logs, and a checkpoint file. For this reason it is not possible to back it up using a file-based backup, and attempting to do so may cause damage to the directory.

The files that make up Active Directory reside in the Systemroot\Ntds folder and are the following:

- **Ntds.dit**   The Active Directory database file
- **Edb.chk**   The database checkpoint file
- **Edb*.log**   The transaction log files, each 10 MB in size
- **Res1.log and Res2.log**   The reserve transaction log files

There are advantages and disadvantages to running Exchange on a domain controller. On the one hand, directory access is faster because lookups do not need to go across the network. On the other hand, the server must perform directory lookups for other machines as well as run Exchange services. Also, Exchange Server normally can fall over its directory requests to another domain controller in case the one it normally queries is not functioning. If the directory service on the Exchange server itself ceases to function, it does not try to query other domain controllers.

> **More Info**   For more information on the impact of Exchange running on domain controllers, see the "Exchange Server 2003 Performance and Scalability Guide" at *http://www.microsoft.com/technet/prodtechnol/exchange/2003/library/perfscalguide.mspx*.

When backing up Active Directory, back up the entire server, including the boot and system partitions. The Automated System Restore backup detailed earlier in this chapter will back up all of the components required for a full restore.

Recommendations for backing up a domain controller:

- **Maintain regular backups of at least one domain controller in each domain**   Active Directory uses circular logging (which cannot be changed) so any restore of the database will restore data only up to the time of the backup. Backups of Active Directory should also be taken whenever significant changes are made to Exchange configuration, for example creating new storage groups, mailboxes, or connectors.

- **Ensure Active Directory backups are within their tombstone lifetime**   Active Directory backups have a time limit on when they can be restored (by default it is 60 days in Windows Server 2003 and 180 days in Windows Server 2003 SP1). See Microsoft Knowledge Base article 216993, "Backup of the Active Directory has 60-Day Useful Life." Windows will refuse to restore an Active Directory backup that is older than the set tombstone lifetime.

In the vast majority of cases, the Active Directory data can be retrieved from a replication partner in the same domain because all Active Directory data is replicated between domain controllers. Backups are useful for when authoritative restores are required, however.

> **More Info**   For more information about backing up domain controllers see the article "Active Directory Disaster Recovery" (*http://go.microsoft.com/fwlink/?LinkID=6270*).

Verifying Database Backups

When backing up Exchange servers it is critical that the backup sets are consistent so that they can be used to restore the data back to the point of the backup. If the data from the Exchange databases is copied onto a tape drive or other backup device without any integrity checks, the data in the backup set may not resemble the data being backed up. This could happen because of a hardware or software fault, or sometimes tapes are not swapped according to the backup regime and backups overwrite other backups.

A number of methods can be used to verify that the data is copied correctly and that a restore procedure using the backup set can work in case of a disaster. Cyclic redundancy checks on the data-copied, verification processes in software and hardware, and test restore procedures can be used to help verify that backups work properly.

- **Verifying the streaming data**   Exchange Server verifies the data prior to backup by reading the checksum at the beginning of each page.

During an Exchange backup using the APIs, the underlying JET engine performs verification on the current database as it is being copied to the backup medium. This helps to prevent bad data being backed up, but it does not verify that the data has been properly transferred to the backup device. This functionality is usually provided in the backup software itself. When JET encounters a problem with the data it is backing up, it is reported only in the Event Log and possibly the backup application log. For this reason, every time a backup is completed, the Event Log and backup logs should be checked either manually or programmatically.

Note A Volume Shadow Copy service backup does not perform the same verification process. Because Volume Shadow Copy service takes a shadow copy at the volume level it uses Exchange APIs within the writer and not the Exchange streaming APIs and merely takes an exact copy of the database on the disk. This process relies on the writer to make sure transactions are not being committed during backup to avoid discrepancies in the backed up data.

■ **Verifying static data backups** Data backed up using the standard file backup process can be verified in a similar way through the backup application. If you specify that the data be verified during backup, the data written to backup media is checked against the data on the disk by means of a cyclic redundancy check. This verification should not be employed when backing up Exchange databases using the streaming APIs, however, because the databases and therefore the CRC values are constantly being modified.

■ **Verifying other data** The best way to verify that a backup operation is successful is to restore the backup onto a separate server. Recreating the domain environment, including restoring Active Directory, and restoring the backed up Exchange data verifies that the backup has worked and also that the restore procedures work.

Performing a full restore of backed up data is the best way of verifying that the backup and the restore processes function properly. This should be executed on a regular basis to ensure that:

■ The operations staff has an understanding of the procedures.

■ The procedures as defined work.

■ The backup processes function as desired.

Best Practices

Backups of critical data are important because they enable you to recover from a disaster situation where loss of data occurs. However, the type of backups and when to back up data is also important. Backup regimes are put in place with the sole view of being able to implement effective restore procedures, and the type of backups that have been taken have a direct bearing on the duration and complexity of the restore.

With the type of backup there are usually trade-offs between storage capacity and restore complexity, and also between backup speed and restore speed. Some companies may choose to minimize their restore complexity and duration by implementing full backups every day. This minimizes the amount of time to restore the data as well as the number of tapes used. However, it also uses up a lot of backup storage space and maximizes the backup duration, which can have a performance effect on the server and also cause problems with daily database maintenance processes.

Whenever a configuration change is made to an Exchange server, for example if connectors are added or removed or registry data modified, particularly if the database locations or mailboxes have moved, it is important to perform a full backup of the system.

Another occasion where a full backup is essential is when the physical topology of the database changes; for example, after an offline defragmentation or repair. When this happens, the database signature changes but the log file signatures do not. Databases only accept data replay from log files with the same signature, so if a database is restored from before the database's signature change it will accept the log files only up to the point of the signature change. Likewise, a later database will not accept log files from before the log change, although this is less likely to be an issue.

Chapter 23

Restoring Exchange Server 2003

About This Chapter

This chapter explains how to recover from failures in an Exchange environment. It covers what you need to know from the rebuilding of individual servers and cluster nodes to the restoration and recovery of Exchange database data and individual configuration components.

An in-depth understanding of Exchange is important when you are restoring a part of the organizational data or configuration. Particularly important is an understanding of the way that databases and log files relate to each other. This chapter assists you in understanding these relationships within the restore and recovery procedures, and also within the directory

The scope of this chapter covers Exchange Server 2003 running in a Windows Server 2003 environment, using the backup tool in Windows Server 2003 (NTBackup.exe) to restore Windows and Exchange data. Some of the methods explained in this chapter might not be applicable to Exchange Server 2003 running on a Windows 2000 Server platform.

What You Need to Know

When a disaster occurs that requires the restoration of an Exchange server or Exchange data such as databases and transaction logs, the procedures used for the restore can depend highly upon prior analysis of the problem that occurred and its surrounding circumstances. After identifying the Exchange components that are no longer functional or present, you can decide the best method by which to restore the environment to its previous, fully functioning state.

Problems such as lost databases resulting from faulty hardware can lead to a situation in which the actual server is still present, as is its configuration data, both on the Exchange server and in Active Directory. In this case, the administrator must restore the databases and perhaps the log files from backup and ensure that the databases mount and that any log replay happens satisfactorily.

Corruption of the Exchange server itself, either loss of configuration data or loss of the entire server necessitates a reinstall of Exchange Server 2003 on the original or additional hardware. This might be an install using the /DisasterRecovery switch in the case of recovering the same server or perhaps a clean install on a different server with a different server name.

This chapter requires understanding of Exchange Server 2003's relationship with Active Directory and other components, such as Internet Information Services (IIS) and the Windows Registry. Knowledge of the database technology is very important when attempting to restore databases to a point in time, and this is covered in Chapter 10, "Configuring Exchange Store Resources."

When deciding on a restore strategy, you must take into account the overall strategy for backup and restore, including:

- **Restoring Windows Server 2003**   Does the server operating system need to be reinstalled on the original server or on separate hardware? In the case of a non-functioning system the server operating system must be reinstalled either on a separate server or on the repaired server.

- **Restoring Exchange Server 2003**   Does the disaster necessitate the reinstall or fresh install of Exchange Server 2003? In scenarios in which local configuration data was lost or corrupted, you must reinstall Exchange over the top to restore default values.

- **Restoring databases**   Has loss of data occurred? The first step might be to restore data from a backup source, including, perhaps, incremental or differential backups from a number of backup events. Data recovery must also be performed in this case.

One of the most important aspects of an Exchange recovery is the user element. If users are to be inconvenienced for a significant amount of time, it is vital to keep them informed of what is going on in order to prevent unrest and possibly also unnecessary load on the Exchange servers while you are performing the recovery. Sometimes users might be required to help in the recovery, for example by changing their Microsoft Office Outlook settings themselves during a recovery procedure in order to take the burden off the administrators.

Restore and Recovery

The terms "restore" and "recovery" are terms that are frequently used interchangeably in the general context of Exchange Server, for example, when speaking of recovering and restoring servers. However, when used in the context of Exchange databases, the terms have distinct meanings.

- **Restore**   Refers to the process of retrieving data from a backup source such as a tape library or file-based backup.

- **Recovery**   Refers to processes used to reconstitute the databases by using the transactions from the transaction logs. Recovery is also known as log file replay.

Recovery Considerations

A successful Exchange recovery operation is dependent on a number of things. Exchange itself depends on the network infrastructure being in place before it will run: Windows Server 2003 and Active Directory must be properly configured so that Exchange can store and access vital configuration data. Additional Windows components, such as the Simple Mail Transfer Protocol (SMTP) and Network News Transfer Protocol (NNTP) services, must be installed and working properly. A solid understanding of Windows Server restore procedures, and more importantly when to perform each recovery method on Windows, is vital to the success of an Exchange restore.

Service level agreements and downtime are important factors to consider when you decide on a recovery procedure. When calculating the time required to perform a restore operation, you must calculate the amount of time required to restore the data from tape (databases and log files) and also the time the Microsoft Exchange Information Store service requires to replay all necessary logs back into the databases. Sometimes a straight recovery of databases takes more time than is acceptable, and a messaging dial tone method, though a longer process, is a better method, because it brings basic services back very quickly.

The messaging dial tone recovery method is one where a new empty database provides immediate service to users, and is covered in detail later in this chapter.

> **Note**   Determining reasonable timescales and processes for recovery is covered in Chapter 21, "Disaster Recovery Planning for Exchange Server 2003."

Proper and efficient communication with the users is essential in the event of a disaster. Users should be kept informed at all times at least of projected recovery completion and restoration of services and perhaps also of the progress of the disaster recovery effort. Messages can be sent to domain machines using the **net send** command (Figure 23-1). This is a simple one-way communication that can be used to inform users of events. Alternatively, instant messaging technology, such as Microsoft Live Communications Server, can be used to convey information to users during such a time (Figure 23-2), and can initiate two-way conversations.

> **Note**   The Messenger service must be enabled for this to work. However, this service might be disabled for security reasons.

Figure 23-1   Sending a message to all users on the network

Figure 23-2   A Messenger popup box on the user's desktop

You should consider these points when formulating your disaster recovery plan, as detailed in Chapter 21, "Disaster Recovery Planning for Exchange 2003," and you can refer to them when performing recovery operations.

Restoring a Windows Server

When problems arise with the Windows operating system on which Exchange is installed, there are a number of techniques that you can use to resolve problems, such as the Chkdsk tool, Last Known Good Configuration, and the Windows Recovery Console. These techniques are covered in the Windows Server 2003 Deployment Kit, found at *http://www.microsoft.com/windowsserver2003/techinfo/reskit/deploy-kit.mspx*, and you should attempt them before restoring the operating system and system backups.

However, sometimes it is necessary to reinstall the operating system on an Exchange server, particularly after hardware failure, such as when the hard disk holds the system partition. If the server is a domain controller, and especially if it is the only domain controller, the restoration process is complicated by the requirement to restore the Active Directory database in addition to the System State and critical operating system files. This scenario is covered later in this chapter.

There are two methods of restoring a Windows Server 2003 server using NTBackup: using Automated System Recovery (ASR) restore and restoring a Windows backup set.

Note   The ASR restore method is available only when running Windows Server 2003.

Restoring Windows Using Automated System Recovery (ASR)

Windows Server 2003 provides a mechanism for automated backup and restore of a Windows server, including the system files and the system state data. Similar to backing up and restoring a full Windows backup set, the Automated System Recovery (ASR) feature automates and speeds up the process of full server restore.

When you restore a full Windows backup set to a new server, you must first of all create a new, full installation of Windows and then restore the Windows backup set and any further backup sets manually using the backup program. Although certain steps can be automated, this is quite a labor-intensive and lengthy process that requires multiple server reboots.

Restoring a server using ASR is for the most part an automated process. You boot the server from the Windows Server 2003 CD and press F2 to select ASR Restore. Insert the ASR Diskette and ensure that the backup device is attached and the relevant tape inserted. The ASR process automatically performs the steps necessary to restore the server completely (Figure 23-3).

```
Windows Server 2003, Enterprise Edition Setup

To restore the configuration of your system, Setup must delete
and recreate all the partitions on the disks listed below.

CAUTION:  All data present on these disks will be lost.

Do you want to continue recreating the partitions?

    •  To continue, press C.  Partitions on all the disks listed
       below will be deleted.

    •  To quit Setup, press F3.  No changes will be made to any
       of the disks on the system.

 ┌─────────────────────────────────────────────────────────────┐
 │4095 MB Disk 0 at Id 0 on bus 0 on symmpi [MBR]                │
 │                                                               │
 │                                                               │
 │                                                               │
 │                                                               │
 │                                                               │
 └─────────────────────────────────────────────────────────────┘

 C=Continue Setup   F3=Quit
```

Figure 23-3   The start of the Automated System Recovery Restore process

On the Resource Kit CD   The ASR Recovery process is detailed step-by-step in the document Performing an ASR Restore, which you can find in the Worksheets\Chapter 23 folder on the companion CD.

An ASR restore requires the ASR backup on tape and the ASR Diskette. The ASR diskette contains two essential files: asr.sif, which contains information about hard disk partitions, removable media, and the recovery media; and asrpnp.sif, which contains information about system devices.

Recreating the ASR Diskette

To recreate the ASR diskette, you must copy the two files, asr.sif and asrpnp.sif, to a blank floppy disk. These files are also contained in the recovery media.

To copy the files from the recovery tape, insert the tape and start NTBackup. It might be necessary to explicitly allow NTBackup to use the tape and then to catalog the tape contents before use.

Restore the asr.sif and asrpnp.sif files from the %windir%\repair folder and copy them onto the floppy disk. You can now use this floppy disk to start the ASR restore process.

Restoring a Windows Backup Set

Using a Windows 2003 backup set, you can restore the files and settings of the server to a new Windows installation. A full Windows backup set consists of the following components:

- **System state**   This typically consists of the boot files, system files, registry, and other essential components. The system state backup is detailed in Chapter 22, "Implementing a Backup Solution."

- **Boot partition**   This is the disk partition from which the computer starts. This partition contains the boot files, such as Ntldr and Boot.ini.

- **System partition**   This is the disk partition on which Windows is installed. It is often the same as the boot partition.

The system state restore restores the name of the server and its system ID, which corresponds to the server's ID in Active Directory. It also restores the registry and IIS metabase settings required by Exchange.

The following procedures outline the steps required to restore a Windows backup set:

1. Reinstall the operating system. The version of Windows should be the same as that of the failed installation, as should the service pack level and the hotfixes installed. The same system drive and directories should be specified. During the component part of Windows setup, you must specify the exact same components as the previous installation; otherwise, you might encounter problems with configuration information restored in the next step. (For example, if IIS is not included in the reinstall but the IIS configuration is restored with the System State, Exchange will not run until IIS is installed and the System State is restored again. For this reason, some restore procedures require a high level of documentation of the existing configuration.)

> **Note**   It is not necessary to specify the same server name when reinstalling the operating system if you are restoring the System State, because this procedure renames the server and makes it a part of the domain.

2. Log on to the server as the administrator. You can now restore the Windows backup set, including the system partition and state, by cataloging the tape or other backup media and restoring to the new Windows installation. Best results are obtained when forcing the backup software (such as NTBackup) to always overwrite files during the restore even if they already exist. Because you are restoring a "seasoned" version of Windows over the top of a fresh version of

Windows, this prevents file mismatches such a incorrect .dlls that would not be resolved if you didn't overwrite files that already exist. Not choosing to force file overwrites at the worst could cause your new installation to be unbootable after the restore, or more likely you will simply be plagued by numerous errors in Windows and in your applications which typically are extremely difficult to pinpoint and resolve. Forcing all files to overwrite in the restore brings the new installation as close as possible back to the original server at the time it was backed up. When this restore is complete you will have to reboot the server again (if you don't then you didn't restore the system state data).

3. If your Windows backup contains Exchange data you should be aware of it as it can impact your recovery if not managed properly. This could either be:

   ■ Exchange application files (in your Exchange installation folder), which you only want to put back if you are intending to restore Exchange by restoring it's application files directly from your backup – as opposed to restoring Exchange files via setup using the /disasterrecovery switch. If you intend to put the Exchange files back by running Exchange setup, it's best to start with a clean installation folder. So in that scenario, you would uncheck the Exchange folder when restoring your Windows backup.

   ■ Exchange Database related files, which might exist on one of the partitions in your Windows backup. This would be files like the .edb and .stm database files, transaction logs, or checkpoint files. First of all, if you are backing those up as part of your Windows or ASR backup, you are needlessly adding large amounts of data to your backup. Unless you are purposefully backing up these database files while those Exchange databases are offline, you are creating a partial backup of the databases files that is not fit for restore. As mentioned in Chapter 21 there is a separate online backup methodology for most Exchange aware backup applications that uses our APIs to backup live databases, instead of backing up their related files directly. If you were to restore a file level backup of those files when restoring your Windows or ASR backup, and then restore again a backup that used the Exchange APIs, you can get mismatched and broken log series, mismatched checkpoint files or other problematic issues that arise from both backups being taken at different times, and the fact that the file level backup doesn't get everything needed like a backup using the Exchange APIs would.

4. When the server reboots after the restore, Windows will typically inform you that one or more services failed to start. This happens because the references to Exchange services in the registry that was restored point to files that are no longer there. This is resolved by reinstalling Exchange server as detailed later in this chapter.

Note   If your backup media comprises an offline server backup (typical with disk imaging solutions that back up all volumes at the sector level), the Exchange binary executables, databases, and all other files will be included in the restore, and you do not need to reinstall Exchange. This is an easier way of restoring Exchange settings and data, but you must keep the offline backups up to date and create them every time Exchange is updated with a service pack or hot fix. The inconvenience of taking offline backups of Exchange makes this an unattractive prospect to perform regularly. However, it is more commonly used to quickly restore to a starting point, as disk imaging restores are typically very speedy and can be put back much faster than installing a clean build of Windows and then restoring a file backup on top.

Depending on whether your Windows backup set includes both the Exchange binary files and offline copies of the database files, the Exchange services might start, but the databases might not mount. The flexibility of choosing what to include of a server's Exchange data in your Windows backup also comes with a corresponding cost in needing to understand how that impacts your backup, restore and recovery options and the procedures you will still need to follow after the operating system backup has been restored during a full server recovery. As part of a Windows file-based backup, the databases will not be backed up, and so you must restore these from an Exchange backup before mounting the databases. If the Exchange binaries are not part of the Windows backup, the Exchange services will not start, and you should reinstall Exchange 2003 using the /DisasterRecovery switch covered later in this chapter.

After restoring the server, it is a good idea to review the event log and test settings and connectivity to other servers before going further. Use the Netdiag and DCDiag tools with the /fix switch to fix any minor networking issues, and troubleshoot further through the event log if necessary. This will help eliminate communication problems with Active Directory and minimize any problems when restoring Exchange server databases and bringing them online.

Repairing Exchange 2003

Sometimes problems arise within an Exchange 2003 server or cluster node that do not require a reinstall of the operating system or a restore of the databases from backup. Typically, such problems arise from missing files or Exchange registry settings.

On many occasions, it might be sufficient to reinstall Exchange 2003 over the top of the existing installation.

Reinstalling Exchange 2003 over a Damaged Installation

Reinstalling Exchange 2003, plus any service packs and hotfixes, can solve problems that arise from file version mismatches, missing files, and missing or corrupt registry entries. Exchange 2003 setup restores the default registry entries for the services and other aspects of Exchange, as well as replacing binary files.

On the Resource Kit CD   For detailed instructions about how to reinstall Exchange 2003 over a damaged installation, see the document Reinstalling Exchange 2003 over a Damaged Installation, which you can find in Worksheets\Chapter 23 on the companion CD.

Note   When reinstalling Exchange 2003 the Exchange services are stopped, and the server will be inaccessible to users until the reinstall is complete.

Reinstalling Exchange 2003 Using the /DisasterRecovery Switch

When Exchange 2003 is installed on a server for the first time, a number of file copies and configuration changes take place to properly register it in the local machine and Active Directory. The binary files are copied to the exchsrvr\bin folder, DLLs registered in the registry, the IIS metabase, and so forth. In addition to the local changes and registrations, the configuration information for the server is added to the configuration naming context of Active Directory.

When an Exchange server no longer functions as a result of hardware failure or the effects of a virus, for instance, and must be rebuilt, the /DisasterRecovery switch can be used to install Exchange 2003 on the replacement server without making any changes to the configuration in Active Directory. This process requires that the Exchange configuration of the server still be present in Active Directory.

The DisasterRecovery switch accomplishes the following:

- Installs the Exchange 2003 binaries
- Restores the default Exchange registry settings for the server
- Re-registers required DLLs and other components

The DisasterRecovery switch does NOT:

- Register the server in Active Directory
- Mount the databases when the Exchange services start after setup completes

Before using the DisasterRecovery switch, you must adhere to some prerequisites:

- The operating system must be the same edition, version, and patch level as on the failed server. It must also be installed on the same volume and path.

- The server hardware should ideally be largely identical, because the system state refers to drivers on the old system. This might not be a problem, however, because the plug-and-play system will recognize the new hardware and install drivers accordingly. The server might require a second reboot after the restoration of the system state in this case.

- Active Directory configuration information for the server must be intact, or the new Exchange installation will not be registered in Active Directory. If this information is not intact, you must use the standard setup procedure to install a new server.

To prepare the recovery server for a /DisasterRecovery reinstall of Exchange you may first need to install the same version of Windows (in the case of a no-boot situation or recovering an Exchange server onto different hardware) and/or restore the Windows backup set off the original server you are rebuilding. If the original Exchange installation is on the system volume, and you restore the server by using an ASR set, the re-installation of Exchange should not be required.

On the Resource Kit CD   You can find a walkthrough of the procedure to restore an Exchange server by using the DisasterRecovery switch in the Companion Material\Chapter 23 folder on the companion CD.

Note   When recovering an Exchange server by using the /DisasterRecovery switch, always install any service packs by using the same switch. This prevents the databases from being mounted when the services start, which can cause problems with the recovery effort.

Restoring Exchange 2003 Information

When the Exchange databases are restored from an online backup, the backup application uses the APIs provided by Exchange 2003 to communicate with the ESE engine through the System Attendant (SA) service to restore the databases and associated transaction log files. By using an offline backup of the Exchange databases, it is possible to avoid the need for using the Exchange APIs or an Exchange-aware backup application. Using NTBackup, it is possible to restore whole storage groups or individual private or public stores, and many backup applications enable you to back up and restore individual mailboxes, as well, often referred to as brick level backups of Exchange by third-party backup applications.

This section covers the restoration of Exchange databases using a number of methods, each of which is particularly useful in certain scenarios. The scenarios covered are:

- Restoring from streaming database backups

- Restoring an offline database backup

- Restoring a Site Replication Service (SRS) database

- Restoring connector-specific data

- Restoring Exchange clusters

- Troubleshooting a failed or incomplete restore

- Using the Recovery Storage Group

- Performing a Messaging Dial Tone Database restore

- Restoring deleted mailboxes

- Restoring Deleted Items

- Restoring public folder data

- Restoring from shadow copy backups

- Restoring to a different server

Restoring Exchange Databases

If a database on your Exchange server becomes unusable, and you have a backup of the database, the first step is to restore the database from your backup set. If the existing database is present but corrupt, and no backup of the databases exists, you can attempt a repair of the data from the existing database by using ESEutil.exe and ISInteg.exe.

ESEutil and ISInteg are command line tools for repairing and recovering database information in situations where corruption and/or loss of data occurs. ISInteg can be used to fix errors within the database structure such as the logical links between database tables. ESEutil is used to modify and fix the physical structure of the database by comparing computed checksum values against those stored in page headers. This process involves checking and fixing the individual tables themselves. Special care should be taken when using these tools as some of their processes, particularly with ESEutil, can result in data loss.

During a restore operation, the backup application talks to the Exchange services through the Exchange backup APIs to coordinate the retrieval of data from the backup media to the server. In addition to the database files, any associated transaction log files are also restored from the backup, and additional log files from incremental or differential backups might be required to be restored on top of any full backups.

The restore operation copies the database files into their original location on the disk, overwriting the existing .edb and .stm files if they are present. Then the log files are copied to a temporary location, specified by the person performing the restore, and replayed back into the database at the end of the restore procedure. A Restore.env file is also copied into the temporary folder, which stores information about the log files, such as the storage group they belong to, the database paths, and the range of log files restored. This file is used specifically for the replaying of the log files to the database, which can be done automatically by the backup program at the end of the restore, or manually, either if the Last Restore Set check box is not checked, or if you need to manually copy log files into the temporary folder for replaying back to the databases.

To restore Exchange data by using NTBackup, first dismount the database(s) you are restoring, leaving the Microsoft Exchange Information Store service running. Select the backup device and set from which you are restoring the databases, either from a file or from removable media, such as a tape device. From the backup set, you must select which components you are restoring (Figure 23-4). After selecting Start Restore, you must specify a temporary location for the log files and Restore.env file on the local drive. If there are no incremental or differential backups to restore, select the Last Restore Set check box.

Note If you are restoring multiple databases from the same storage group concurrently, without performing log replay after each restore, ensure that you specify a different temporary location for each storage group, otherwise you might find that the Restore.env file and perhaps some log files will be overwritten and the restore will fail. This is not a problem when restoring databases from multiple storage groups concurrently however, as a separate subfolder is created for each storage group within the temporary location.

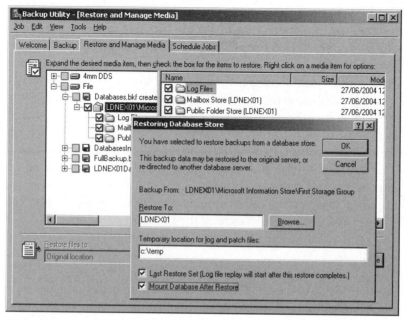

Figure 23-4 Select the Exchange components to be restored during the full restore

The database files are restored to their original location specified in the store properties, and any log files are copied to the temporary folder. If you selected the Last Restore Set check box, a hard recovery process is started by a separate instance of Extensible Storage Engine (ESE) to replay the log files into the recovered database. If you selected the Mount Database After Restore option during restore, the databases will be remounted when the log replay process is completed.

Incorporating Incremental and Differential Backups

If incremental or differential backups of the databases' transaction logs are to be included in the restore, these require separate restore processes for each set. During the restore, you must specify the same temporary log file location as you do for the full backup set restore, so that at the end of the process the entire set of log files are in the same location for hard recovery.

During the log file replay process, the Restore.env file is updated to reflect the new set of log files to be replayed into the databases.

Note It is essential that you restore all incremental or differential backups immediately after restoring the databases and prior to mounting the databases. It is not possible to restore log files after you have mounted the restored databases.

When you restore the final set of log files to the server, select the Last Restore Set check box, so that hard recovery is performed automatically. When the restore is completed and hard recovery has finished, check that the temporary folder that you specified is empty and also check the event log for any errors. An informational event is also created there for each storage group involved in the restore process when hard recovery both begins and ends for a particular storage group, but usually it's much easier to just check the temp directory files to see when files are deleted. If the sub-folder for a storage group in the temporary folder you specify during the restore is not empty, hard recovery has not yet completed for that storage group.

Performing a Manual Hard Recovery

Before hard recovery occurs, the database is in a dirty shutdown state, because it is not synchronized with its log files. If you forget to select the Last Restore Set check box in NTBackup, or if you are copying log files from another location, such as a different hard drive or remote media, you must perform a manual hard recovery before the database will mount.

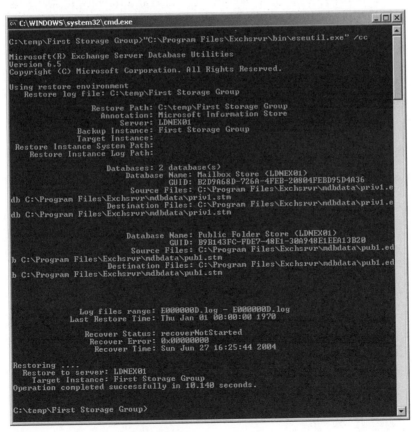

Figure 23-5   A successful hard recovery

To run the hard recovery, use the ESEutil.exe command line tool with the /cc switch. Open a command prompt, and navigate to the temporary location of the Restore.env file and run ESEutil.exe /cc (by default, this is in the c:\Program Files\Exchsrvr\bin folder). Figure 23-5 shows an example output from the hard recovery process.

If you run the ESEUtil command from a different folder, you must also specify the location of the Restore.env file. For example:

C:\Program Files\Exchsrvr\bin\eseutil.exe /cc "C:\temp\First Storage Group"

When hard recovery is complete, you can mount the databases within the storage group.

Restoring an Offline Database Backup

Offline Exchange database backups are copies of the actual database files. To restore an offline backup, you must dismount the store and copy the files into the appropriate location. Unlike an online restore, an offline database backup requires that you determine the folder location in which the database and log files reside. This information should be documented in advance, but if it is not then it can be found in the properties of the store object in Exchange System Manager, or by using ADSIEdit and other Active Directory tools. The location of the database files is important, particularly if you want to restore log data after the restore. In some scenarios it is not desired to restore the log files as well. One example of this is when you are restoring a public folder database up to a certain point in the past and allowing backfill to restore the rest of the data through replication.

> **Note** When performing an online database restore, it is good practice to make an offline (file-based copy) backup of the databases beforehand, in case the restore procedure fails. You can try to repair the old databases if those on the backup media are corrupted or otherwise irretrievable. Ensure that the database is consistent before taking an offline backup or the restore procedure might fail.

You can perform a point-in-time restore or a roll-forward restore. A point-in-time restore involves restoring only the databases, whereas a roll-forward restore replays log files into the restored databases.

Point-in-Time Restore

When restoring an offline backup, you must dismount the databases involved, then copy/move the offline backup to the correct location on the hard drive. Mounting the store will then make the databases accessible to users.

In order to successfully restore and mount an Exchange database, the display names of the storage group and database must be the same as the original, as must that of the administrative group. If the offline restore is onto a different server, storage group, or logical store, or if the Active Directory object was previously deleted, the database will not mount. You must specify that the database can be overwritten by a restore by selecting the This database can be overwritten by a restore check box in the database properties in Exchange System Manager. This allows the system to automatically synchronize the information store with the directory, as the ISINTEG –patch command does with Exchange Server 5.5.

> **Note** The This Database Can Be Overwritten By A Restore check box is not required for all restore operations, only when the GUID of the store object in Active Directory is different from that of the database being restored. This is typically the case in alternate server and when using a Recovery Storage Group, but the check box is not required when restoring a database directly to its original location.

When the database is mounted, it is not possible to replay any log files back to the database.

Roll-Forward Restore

Note the location of the database files on the hard disk. The location of the restored database files is important, particularly if you want to replay log files, as is usually the case particularly in the case of mailbox database restore. Log files store in their header the path to the databases they relate to. Databases do not hold such information, so the location of the log files is unimportant; a fact illustrated by the temporary log file location created during an online database restore.

Before restoring the offline backup, dismount all of the databases in the storage group. It is good practice to save a copy of any database files that you are replacing in case you need to extract data from them later.

Copy the offline database backup into the correct folder and the log files to a temporary location. Before proceeding, check the consistency of each database in the store, and check that the database pairs are matched. In addition, you must identify the low and high anchor logs, which are the first and last logs required to recover all the data. To do this, run the **ESEutil /mh <database name>** command against each database file (Figure 23-6). Ensure the database is in clean shutdown mode by looking for "State: Clean Shutdown," and note the database number under "Last Consistent."

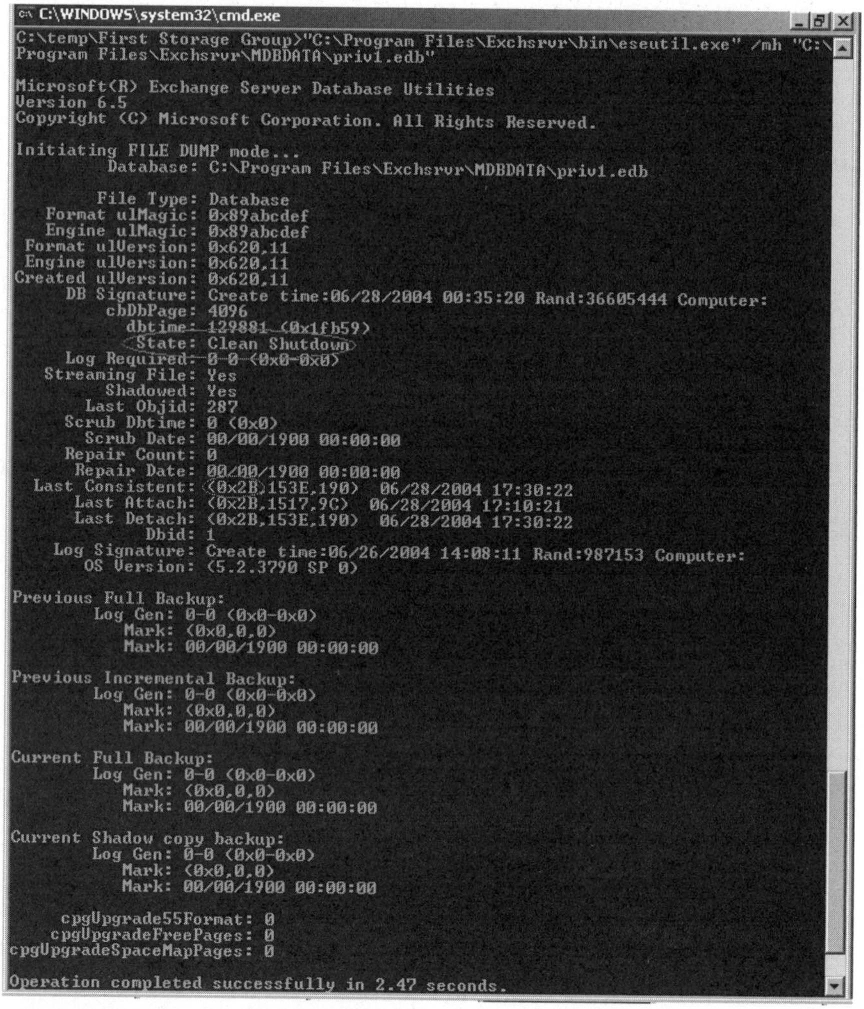

```
C:\WINDOWS\system32\cmd.exe
C:\temp\First Storage Group>"C:\Program Files\Exchsrvr\bin\eseutil.exe" /mh "C:\
Program Files\Exchsrvr\MDBDATA\priv1.edb"

Microsoft(R) Exchange Server Database Utilities
Version 6.5
Copyright (C) Microsoft Corporation. All Rights Reserved.

Initiating FILE DUMP mode...
         Database: C:\Program Files\Exchsrvr\MDBDATA\priv1.edb

        File Type: Database
     Format ulMagic: 0x89abcdef
     Engine ulMagic: 0x89abcdef
   Format ulVersion: 0x620,11
   Engine ulVersion: 0x620,11
  Created ulVersion: 0x620,11
       DB Signature: Create time:06/28/2004 00:35:20 Rand:36605444 Computer:
           cbDbPage: 4096
             dbtime: 129881 (0x1fb59)
              State: Clean Shutdown
       Log Required: 0-0 (0x0-0x0)
     Streaming File: Yes
           Shadowed: Yes
         Last Objid: 287
       Scrub Dbtime: 0 (0x0)
         Scrub Date: 00/00/1900 00:00:00
       Repair Count: 0
        Repair Date: 00/00/1900 00:00:00
    Last Consistent: (0x2B,153E,190)  06/28/2004 17:30:22
        Last Attach: (0x2B,1517,9C)  06/28/2004 17:10:21
        Last Detach: (0x2B,153E,190)  06/28/2004 17:30:22
               Dbid: 1
      Log Signature: Create time:06/26/2004 14:08:11 Rand:987153 Computer:
         OS Version: (5.2.3790 SP 0)

Previous Full Backup:
        Log Gen: 0-0 (0x0-0x0)
           Mark: (0x0,0,0)
           Mark: 00/00/1900 00:00:00

Previous Incremental Backup:
        Log Gen: 0-0 (0x0-0x0)
           Mark: (0x0,0,0)
           Mark: 00/00/1900 00:00:00

Current Full Backup:
        Log Gen: 0-0 (0x0-0x0)
           Mark: (0x0,0,0)
           Mark: 00/00/1900 00:00:00

Current Shadow copy backup:
        Log Gen: 0-0 (0x0-0x0)
           Mark: (0x0,0,0)
           Mark: 00/00/1900 00:00:00

     cpgUpgrade55Format: 0
    cpgUpgradeFreePages: 0
cpgUpgradeSpaceMapPages: 0

Operation completed successfully in 2.47 seconds.
```

Figure 23-6 The output from an ESEUTIL /mh command

From all of the databases present, note the Last Consistent log file; the low anchor is the lowest number log of all, and the high anchor the highest. In Figure 23-6, the log file referred to is E000002B.log. The low anchor is the first log file that will be replayed to the databases. Without the low anchor, none of the subsequent logs can be replayed into the database.

> **Note**   If you do not have the low anchor log file, it might be possible to replay the logs that you do have into those databases with a higher "Last Consistent" log than the lowest log file present. Otherwise, you can delete the log files that are present and mount the consistent databases. By doing this, you lose any chance of replaying the log files.

Next, ensure that the signatures of each database and the low anchor log are the same by executing the following commands:

Eseutil /mh *<database name>* | **find /i "log signature"**

Eseutil /ml *<low anchor log>* | **find /i "signature"**

If the log file has multiple signatures, the first one is the database's own signature. The rest are of databases that were running when the log file was created.

Figure 23-7   Output showing the log file signatures

Next, copy the log files, ensuring that the log files are present in unbroken sequence from the low anchor log to the highest number log file, into the current transaction log file location. It is necessary to verify that the log files all have the matching signatures, are all in unbroken sequence, and that they are not damaged. To do this, run **eseutil /ml E0n**. The n is a number that corresponds to its particular storage group. An example output from this command is shown in Figure 23-8.

```
C:\WINDOWS\system32\cmd.exe                                          _□×

C:\Program Files\Exchsrvr\bin>eseutil.exe /ml "C:\Program Files\Exchsrvr\MDBDATA
\logs\E00

Microsoft(R) Exchange Server Database Utilities
Version 6.5
Copyright (C) Microsoft Corporation. All Rights Reserved.

Initiating FILE DUMP mode...

Verifying log files...
      Base name: E00

      Log file: C:\Program Files\Exchsrvr\MDBDATA\logs\E0000029.log - OK
      Log file: C:\Program Files\Exchsrvr\MDBDATA\logs\E000002A.log - OK
      Log file: C:\Program Files\Exchsrvr\MDBDATA\logs\E000002B.log - OK
      Log file: C:\Program Files\Exchsrvr\MDBDATA\logs\E000002C.log - OK
      Log file: C:\Program Files\Exchsrvr\MDBDATA\logs\E000002D.log - OK
      Log file: C:\Program Files\Exchsrvr\MDBDATA\logs\E00.log - OK

No damaged log files were found.

Operation completed successfully in 2.31 seconds.

C:\Program Files\Exchsrvr\bin>
```

Figure 23-8   Verifying the log files before replay

Any log files that do not share the signature must be removed from the folder. The E0n.chk file should also be deleted. This file determines the log at which to start log replay, and might try to start with a log file later than the low anchor, and thus fail. In the absence of the checkpoint file, Exchange will start log replay at the lowest available log file, which is the low anchor.

The databases can now be mounted, and log file replay will be attempted automatically.

> **Note**   If the checkpoint file is not deleted or removed, log replay will be attempted from the log file referenced in this file. Because the checkpoint is likely to reference a more recent log file than the low anchor, log file replay will fail. In this case, you must start again with the entire restore. Dismounting the database and deleting the checkpoint file does not work, because the database header was updated during the mount process.

Restoring an SRS Database

The Site Replication Service (SRS) database, a copy of the connected Exchange 5.5 directory, is an ESE-based database like the other Exchange databases and should be backed up and restored in a similar way. The Windows backup program, NTBackup, presents the SRS as an Exchange component beside the Microsoft Exchange Information Store service components.

> **Note**   Although the presence of an Exchange 5.5 server in the environment provides a method to restore the SRS in the absence of a backup, this procedure to recreate the SRS is much more complex and time-consuming than restoring the SRS directly back to the Exchange 2003 server. To recreate an SRS in an Exchange 5.5/2003 mixed environment, follow the instructions in the Knowledge Base article Q282061 "How to Rebuild a Site Replication Service Without a Backup" (*http://support.microsoft.com/ default.aspx?kbid=282061*).

To restore the SRS database from backup, select the SRS database to be restored. Restarting the SRS service then completes the recovery. Ensure that the SRS service (MSExchangeSRS) is set to start automatically and that the logon credentials are correct.

If a backup of SRS does not exist or cannot be restored, create a new instance of the SRS on another server in the site, and then delete the original SRS instance. A separate server is required, because Exchange does not allow you to delete the only SRS in a mixed site, and it is not possible to have two instances of SRS on the same server.

Restoring Connector-specific Data

All messaging connectors that come with Exchange store their data in the local registry, Active Directory, or both. The only Exchange connectors that also store data on the file system are Connector for Lotus Notes and Connector for GroupWise. These connectors store their mapping rules and synchronization data in subfolders of the Exchsrvr\Conndata folder, and these folders can be backed up as part of a Windows backup set.

In order to restore the information for these connectors, you must ensure that the configuration data was restored to the local registry and to Active Directory, if necessary. Restoring the files in the Conndata subfolders by using NTBackup restores the connectors to their previous configuration.

For more information on backing up and restoring Exchange connectors, see the Knowledge base article "How to Back Up and Restore Connectors on Exchange 2000" (*http://support.microsoft.com/default.aspx?scid=kb;en-us;328835*).

Restoring Exchange Clusters

Server clustering is a technique for providing failover of services when a disaster occurs. When a single node fails, the services on that node are transferred to another node, which then carries on the duties of that server, providing service to users. Unrecoverable nodes can then be repaired or replaced and later reconnected to the cluster.

This section describes the steps necessary for repairing or replacing a single failed node in a cluster and for recovering from the loss of a shared disk resource.

Depending on the type of cluster recovery, the following information can be useful:

- NetBIOS (network basic input/output system) names of each node

- Network names of each Exchange Virtual Server (EVS)

- Names of cluster groups

- Names of cluster resources

- Names of virtual server storage groups

- Names of virtual server Exchange stores

- IP addresses of virtual servers

It is not essential to detail this information beforehand, unless you are expecting in a particular recovery scenario to be rebuilding the cluster from scratch. It is good practice however, to document such information in case the entire cluster data is destroyed. In the vast majority of recovery scenarios the cluster configuration data can be restored if you have a Windows backup of at least a single node in the cluster and other Exchange Virtual Server configuration data is preserved in Active Directory.

Recovering a Single Cluster Node

If a cluster node fails irretrievably and must be rebuilt before rejoining the cluster, you must reinstall Windows Server and Exchange Server on the node. No Exchange data needs to be restored as it is still available and hopefully running on another node. Similarly, no Exchange configuration needs to be done on the newly built node as the configuration data is within the cluster quorum itself.

To rebuild a cluster node running Exchange Server 2003:

1. Reinstall Windows Server 2003.

2. Configure the cluster service to join the cluster.

3. Install Exchange Server 2003.

The new node will automatically pick up the Exchange cluster resources and will provide Exchange services when the virtual server fails over to that node. You should always test failover when adding a new node to a cluster.

Note Rebuilding a failed cluster node does not require restoring data from backup as the databases and other shared data are present on the shared disks. The rebuilding process involves installing only the binaries and computer settings. The DisasterRecovery switch is not used (and indeed does not work on a cluster) as the settings in Active Directory that the switch reads are particular to the Exchange Virtual Server on the cluster, not the node.

Recovering a Shared Disk Resource

Microsoft recommends using fault tolerant disk arrays (for example RAID1 or RAID5) to reduce the risk of loss of shared storage disks. On occasion however, it might be necessary to manually recover data from a shared disk if the disk or array becomes unusable. The recovery process for a shared disk is slightly different depending on whether the disk stores Exchange data, such as databases and log files, or quorum data, although the process of bringing a replacement disk resource online is the same.

When a disk becomes unusable, the cluster disk resource fails, and with it, the Exchange virtual server or quorum that resides on it fails. The main steps required are replacing the disk and restoring the data onto the new disk. A Physical Disk cluster resource uses the disk signature to identify the physical disk it represents, and when a disk is reformatted with a low-level format or is replaced, the disk signature is different, and the disk resource cannot be brought online.

The ClusterRecovery tool contained in the Windows Server 2003 Resource Kit Tools, which can be downloaded from *http://www.microsoft.com/downloads/ details.aspx?familyid=9d467a69-57ff-4ae7-96ee-b18c4790cffd&displaylang=en*, enables you to replace a failed disk resource with a new disk directly and to transfer the configuration of the old disk, such as failover policies, chkdsk attributes, and timeouts.

Replacing a Lost Storage Disk

When one of the shared disks containing data is lost, insert a new disk and assign it a drive letter in Windows that is different from the original disk. You can then use the ClusterRecovery tool to replace the cluster resource pointing to the failed disk with a new resource for the replacement disk.

Because ClusterRecovery replaces the disk resource, the disk signature is no longer an issue, but it also transfers the resource settings as outlined above.

On the Resource Kit CD   Replacing a failed disk is covered in detail in the worksheet Replacing a failed storage disk.doc that you can find in Companion Material\Chapter 23 on the companion CD.

The general steps are as follows:

1. Replace the disk in the shared storage and start up one of the nodes. Assign a new drive letter to the disk and format it.

2. Start the cluster service on one node and create a physical disk resource for the new disk. The name does not matter, because the ClusterRecovery tool will modify the name.

3. Open ClusterRecovery and select Replace a Physical Disk Resource. Select the old failed resource and the new resource, so that the tool transfers the configuration settings from one to the other.

4. With the new resource still online, change the drive letter mapping to the original drive letter.

5. Restart the cluster service on all nodes.

The lost disk is now successfully replaced, and the next step is to restore the data to the new disk. Log on to the node that is the owner of the shared disk and follow the standard procedures for restoring Exchange data.

Replacing a Lost Quorum Disk

The quorum disk is the shared disk that holds the quorum resource, the resource with the configuration data for the entire cluster. If the quorum resource is lost, the cluster service does not start and the cluster fails.

Depending on the nature of the disaster, the quorum disk may need to be replaced or the quorum restored from backup in order to have the cluster run properly again.

For detailed information on replacing quorum disks and restoring quorum resources, see "Backing up and Restoring Server Clusters" at *http:// www.microsoft.com/resources/documentation/WindowsServ/2003/standard/prod- docs/en-us/Default.asp?url=/resources/documentation/WindowsServ/2003/stan- dard/proddocs/en-us/sag_mscsusing_9.asp.*

Repairing Exchange 2003 Databases after a Failed Restore

On the occasion where database corruption has occurred, despite testing of the backup and restore procedures and of the integrity of the backups, you may encounter a situation where the database backup is not able to be restored to an Exchange server. In this case it is sometimes preferable to repair the existing database rather than restore from an older backup. The best course of action when tackling database corruption is as follows:

- **Try to fix any logical database issues**   Run a few passes on the database with the ISInteg tool. This tool is designed to restore any missing logical links and pointers within the databases and should be run as long as it has an effect on the database.

- **Move mailboxes onto another server in the same organization**   You can isolate problem mailboxes by temporarily moving mailboxes onto another server. The mailbox move process validates the data and allows you to specify how many corrupt items to move.

- **Fix physical database corruption**   In the case of mailboxes that are not moved due to high levels of corruption, data might be retrievable by using ESEUtil on the database.

Using the Recovery Storage Group

It is possible to restore mailbox data directly on a production Exchange 2003 server by using the Recovery Storage Group (RSG). The RSG is a special storage group that allows you to mount a mailbox store on a server for data recovery purposes. Exchange separates the RSG logically from the other storage groups, so the recovered mailbox store is not accessible to Exchange clients, nor can mail be delivered to it, but it is accessed through ExMerge or the Recover Mailbox Data function in order to recover data from the store.

The Recovery Storage Group can be used to recover mailbox stores from the same administrative group as the recovery server, and the database must be from an Exchange 2000 Service Pack 3 server or later. Prior to recovering the database, it must be added to the RSG from a list of mailbox stores within the administrative group.

Recovery Storage Group Scenarios

The recovery storage group was created to aid administrators in the recovery of mailbox data in certain circumstances, notably when the configuration information is still intact in Active Directory. The RSG is useful in the following scenarios:

- **Recovering mistakenly deleted items**   If a user accidentally deletes important data the RSG can be used to quickly restore it without requiring a separate recovery server if it has not been retained via your item retention policies in

Exchange (which is the easiest way to recover accidentally deleted items, as it can be done through the Outlook client).

■ **Merging data from one database into another**   In a disaster recovery scenario such as the Messaging Dial Tone recovery method covered later in this chapter, the mailbox content of the dialtone and restored databases can be merged from one into the other.

■ **Recovering a database onto a separate server**   If performance would be impacted too badly to recover to the original server, the mailbox store can be recovered to a separate server. In cases where you then need to copy the recovered databases back to the original server, you must prepare for the length of time needed to copy it over given the bandwidth utilized, if that's the LAN this could be quite slow. Ideally you would want to simply be able to re-path to the restored database after it has been recovered, or move the database from one logical volume to another so you don't have to copy the entire database files. These techniques are much easier in a SAN storage environment.

Limitations of the Recovery Storage Group

The recovery storage group is useful for restoring mailbox items or for merging databases, but there are a number of limitations to the use of the RSG:

■ Only one RSG is possible per server, so if multiple restore operations need to be carried out you must configure more than one server for recovery. You must be careful not to cause an overlap with the databases being recovered as this will cause confusion for ExMerge and the Recover Mailbox Data wizard. These tools are covered later in this section.

■ Multiple databases can be added to the RSG, but only if they are all from the same original storage group. If you want to restore databases from another storage group you must use an additional RSG on a separate server.

■ The original database must be from an Exchange server version running between Exchange 2000 Service Pack 3 and the version of Exchange running on the recovery server itself.

■ Databases can be restored only onto a server in the same administrative group as the original server.

■ Public folder stores cannot be recovered using the RSG.

■ Shadow copies made using VSS cannot natively in Exchange be restored to an RSG, although third-party VSS solutions may be able to find ways to work around this

■ The original database object must be present in Active Directory and must be in the same storage group as when the backup was taken. If the database object in

Active Directory has been deleted, for example, if the mailboxes have all since been moved to another server or database, the restore will not work.

> **Note**   When recovering a database to an RSG, the database is upgraded to the version of the recovery server. If the database is to be copied directly back to the original server, you must first upgrade the original server to the same version and service pack level as the server running the RSG.

The Recovery Storage Group is not appropriate for the following scenarios:

- **Recovering public folder data**   The Recovery Storage Group works only with mailbox stores.

- **Restoring data from multiple storage groups**   Multiple databases from the same storage group can be added to the Recovery Storage Group during the same operation, but recovery operations using databases from different storage groups require either multiple separate operations or multiple recovery Exchange servers.

- **The Exchange configuration data in Active Directory has changed since the backup**   The Recovery Storage Group relies on the configuration information in Active Directory when restoring and transferring data. If this is not available or has changed significantly, the process will fail.

Recovering Data with the Recovery Storage Group

To perform a recovery of mailbox data using an RSG, you must first create the RSG and specify a mailbox store to recover. The RSG is created in the same way as a normal storage group by right-clicking the server object, and selecting New and Recovery Storage Group. After specifying the paths to the transaction logs and system path location, the RSG is created and is as yet empty. After creating the RSG, it is necessary to add to it the databases that you want to recover. Those databases are created by default in the same location as specified for the transaction log files unless otherwise specified.

If the database is being restored onto a different server from the original, the name of the RSG must be the same as the original storage group. If there is already a storage group of that name on the recovery server, a different name is required. At this point, RSG and database objects are created in Active Directory, but there are no database or log files yet present in the RSG file location. Leave the new store in its unmounted state until the database has been restored into the RSG.

Restoring a database into the RSG is a very similar process to restoring a database into a production storage group. In fact, the Recovery Storage Group becomes the default location for online restores, even if you elect to restore the database to its original location. When a database is added to the RSG, the This database can be overwritten by a restore check box is already enabled. The process, which is performed through the Exchange backup API, is orchestrated as usual by the System Attendant and the Microsoft Exchange Information Store service, so the backup application is unaware that it is copying the data to a different storage group.

> **Note**   As with a standard restore, remember to check the Last Restore Set check box to enable log file replay when the restore is complete. If this is not done, you must perform a hard recovery on the database with the ESEUtil.exe /cc command before the database will start. If you are restoring additional log files manually, you will have to run hard recovery manually.

With the database restored into the RSG, the data in the recovered mailboxes can be merged by using Exchange System Manager into the original mailboxes on the production server. The Recover Mailbox Data function of the Recovery Storage Group can copy or merge data from the recovered mailboxes and in some circumstances can be used as a convenient alternative to ExMerge. If you choose to copy the data, the entire contents of the mailbox, including the folder tree, is copied into a new folder created in the target mailbox, which is named according to the time it was recovered (for example, Recovered Data 6/12/2004 18:05 PM). If the data is merged, the data is copied into its original location in the mailbox.

Restoring Mailbox Data to a Different Database

When restoring mailbox data, it is not possible to select the destination mailbox store. This means that if the mailbox has been moved to another database since the relevant backup was made, the Recover Mailbox Data process will fail and produce a report similar to that in Figure 23-9.

This happens because the database in the RSG is linked to the original database through the msExchOrigMDB attribute in Active Directory. The msExchOrigMDB attribute of the recovery database contains the data from the distinguishedName attribute of the original server so that recovery operations target the correct mailbox store.

```
RecoverMailboxDataFailedBecauseMailboxMoved.txt - Notepad                        [_][□][X]
File  Edit  Format  View  Help
<?xml version="1.0" encoding="unicode" ?>
<taskwizardRun taskName="Recover Mailbox Data" dcName="NYDC01" buildNumber="7226"
 runningAs="Administrator@PROSEWARE.COM">
  <timespan startTime="2004-06-23 23:32:20.393" milliseconds="1672" />
  <recoverMailbox>
    <destination>
      <database>/dc=com/dc=proseware/cn=Configuration/cn=Services/cn=Microsoft
        Exchange/cn=First Organization/cn=Administrative Groups/cn=First Administrative
        Group/cn=Servers/cn=NYEX01/cn=InformationStore/cn=First Storage Group/cn=Mailbox
        Store (NYEX01)
      </database>
    </destination>
  </recoverMailbox>
  <taskSummary errorCount="1" completedCount="0" warningCount="0" errorCode="0x00000000" />
  <items>
    <item adsPath="fergus" class="user">
      <progress code="0" milliseconds="1672">Connecting to source server.</progress>
      <summary isWarning="false" errorCode="0xc1050000">The attempt to log on to the
        Microsoft Exchange Server computer has failed. The MAPI provider failed. Microsoft
        Exchange Server Information Store ID no: 8004011d-0512-00000000</summary>
    </item>
  </items>
</taskwizardRun>
```

Figure 23-9 The Recover Mailbox Data process fails when the mailbox is no longer present

There are two methods for overcoming this by using the Recover Mailbox Data function:

- Move the mailbox back to the original database.

- Change the msExchOrigMDB attribute of the recovery database.

The msExchOrigMDB attribute can be changed using ADSIEdit.msc from the Windows Server 2003 Support Tools. Replace the data in the msExchOrigMDB attribute of the recovery database with the data from the distinguishedName attribute of the database that holds the moved mailbox. Now the Recover Mailbox Data process will complete successfully.

> **Note** If the mailbox was moved to a storage group in a different administrative group, the Recover Mailbox Data process will not work. You must move the mailbox back to its original location or to another mailbox store in the same administrative group as the recovery server.

As an alternative to the Recover Mailbox Data tool, you can use the Mailbox Merge program (ExMerge.exe). This can be used against the recovery database to extract data and import it into a mailbox in one of the production databases. ExMerge can be configured to filter out certain data, such as by date, folder and message subject, and will copy Inbox rules and permissions as well. In a disaster recovery scenario it may be useful to filter out folders such as Sent Items and Deleted Items in order to speed up the process, returning to migrate these folders at a later time.

The Mailbox Merge program should be used instead of Recover Mailbox Data when:

- A subset of the mailbox data is to be restored. ExMerge can filter data by the following criteria:

    - Folder

    - Date: delivery time or last modification time

    - Message subject

- Inbox rules, personal forms, or custom views must be restored.

- You want to recover items from the Dumpster. The Dumpster contains items that have been deleted but have not yet been purged from the system. Deleted items are able to be retrieved from the Dumpster as long as they are younger than the Deleted Items Retention Period.

More Info   For more information about extracting and importing mailbox data using ExMerge, see the document Extracting and importing data with the Mailbox Merge tool, which you can find in the Companion Material\Chapter 23 folder on the companion CD.

For more detail on Recovery Storage Groups, see the whitepaper "Using Exchange Server 2003 Recovery Storage Groups."

Performing a Messaging Dial Tone Database Restore

Restoring database backups from tape onto an Exchange server can take a long time, especially with databases of several gigabytes. The entire restore process for a multi-gigabyte database, including log file restore and replay, might take a number of hours, which is unacceptable in the framework of many companies' service level agreements. The messaging dial tone database restore enables you to resume e-mail service to users while the data restore operation is going on. Service is restored almost immediately by creating a blank mailbox database to temporarily replace the original.

A similar process of high speed recovery with delayed restore was available even before Exchange 2003, but two additional features of Exchange 2003 make it a much more manageable and attractive prospect:

- The Recovery Storage Group

- Outlook 2003 Exchange Recovery Mode

The Recovery Storage Group enables you to perform the restore on the production server, which eliminates the need to recover data on a dedicated server and copy the data over to the production server, which can take a long time.

Outlook 2003 Exchange Recovery Mode enables access to the offline folder store (.ost file) or the Exchange mailbox and enables Outlook to revert back to the previous .ost file when the recovery is finished, rather than having to recreate the .ost file.

These features are covered in the following sections.

When to Use Messaging Dial Tone Recovery

Messaging dial tone database restores apply to the restoration of mailbox databases when a full restore is required; for example, if the hard disk hosting the private data store becomes inoperable. Usually the recovery process is to replace the hard disk and restore the database from backup tape directly onto that disk. This can be a lengthy procedure, which is why this fast recovery method has an advantage.

The Messaging Dial Tone Procedure

The process for the messaging dial tone procedure is as follows:

1. **Create the dial tone database**   If the old database files are present, move them to a separate location (keep them, in case they are needed for repair) and mount the mailbox store. The Microsoft Exchange Information Store service automatically creates a blank database in its place. When users attempt to access their mailbox, the server creates one in place of the lost mailbox and the user is faced with an empty, for the moment, set of folders (Figure 23-10). Also, as with newly created mailboxes, if a message is sent to one of these users, the mailbox appears in the System Manager. The new mailbox retains the same unique ID (msExchMailboxGUID) as previously, which it obtains from the user object. This is important for the transfer of data by using ExMerge after the database restore. Users are able to send and receive messages normally, albeit without their historical data and other settings such as forms, Inbox rules, and views. These are restored later with the data.

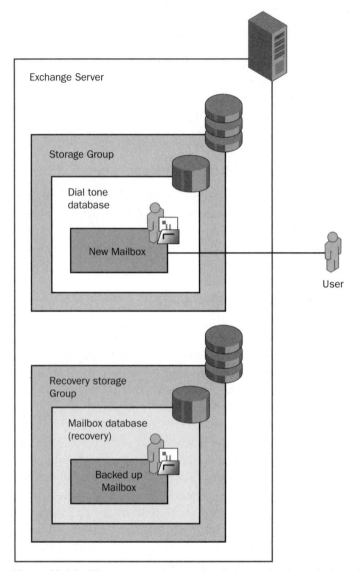

Figure 23-10 The user attaches to the dial-tone database in the original storage group

2. **Create a Recovery Storage Group for the restore of the mailbox database from backup** The RSG should be on the same server as the production mailbox store and, if possible, the database location should be the same logical volume as the dial tone database. Moving databases between locations on the same volume is significantly faster than moving them between volumes.

3. **Restore the database(s) to the Recovery Storage Group** Using the method outlined earlier, restore the mailbox database to the recovery storage group from backup. It is possible to restore multiple databases from the same original storage group at the same time. When the restore process is complete, dismount the database and ensure that it is consistent by using eseutil.exe /mh <database name>.edb and look for the line "State: Clean Shutdown." When restoring additional databases to the recovery storage group, you should remove log files beforehand to avoid any conflicts.

Note As with any database restore, if the log files are available, they should also be restored. Log files cannot be restored into the database after it has been mounted or moved to a normal storage group.

At this point, the users are working with the dial tone database as normal, and the original database is in the Recovery Storage Group (Figure 23-11). The data in the original database in the recovery storage group could now be transferred to the new database by using ExMerge. However, because the data in the original database is greater than that in the dial tone database, it is often preferable to move the data the other way. To do this, you must first swap the databases around.

Note Using ExMerge to extract an import Exchange data leads to the loss of single instance storage within the database. This means that multiple copies of the same messages and attachments may be created and consequently the size of the database file may increase significantly. This is particularly true of environments where users work with large or many attachments.

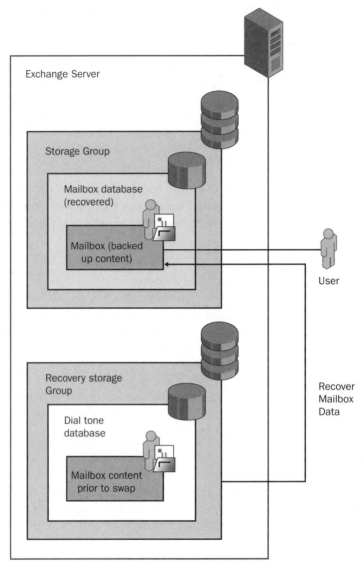

Figure 23-11   The users now access the old data while their mailboxes are populated with messages from the temporary mailbox store

There are a number of advantages to using this method as opposed to moving data to the new database:

a. The data to be transferred from the dial tone database is normally a lot less than if the data is transferred the other way.

b. ExMerge transfers lose single instance storage in the destination database, expanding the size of the database. Less data transferred makes better use of the database volume.

  c. This method ends up with the original database in the original information store, and with it is included other data, such as folder rules, forms, and views.

4. **Swap the databases** The aim of this step is to restore the restored database back into the original storage group and place the dial tone database into the recovery storage group. This can be performed in two ways:

5. **Physically move the databases** If the recovery storage group databases are on the same storage volume as those of the original database, you can swap the locations of the databases by using file copy operations in Windows Explorer. Because the names of the database files might be different in the original store and the recovery storage group stores, you might have to change the references in Exchange System Manager accordingly.

6. **Change the database paths on each store** This method is preferred only if the dial tone and original databases are on different volumes, because it does not require any moving of databases on the file system. To do this, you dismount each database and swap the references to the databases. However, Exchange does not permit you to change the target database to one that already exists, so it is necessary to temporarily move each set of databases to another folder, change the targets to databases that are not present, and then move the databases back to the target location.

On the Resource Kit CD This process is detailed exactly in the worksheet Performing a Dial Tone Database Restore, which you can find in the Worksheets\Chapter 23 folder on the companion CD.

After the databases have been swapped and mounted, the mailboxes in the original database may appear to be disconnected and will not show up in ExMerge. Rather than reconnecting each mailbox, you can simply run the Cleanup Agent from System Administrator, and the mailboxes will be reconnected.

Tip By default, the database file name of the first mailbox store is "priv1.edb and priv1.stm, whereas the database in the recovery storage group is named after the store (for example "Mailbox Store (NYEX01).edb"). It is important to either rename the database files or to set the correct file name when changing the reference in each mailbox store.

1. Move or copy data from the dial tone into the original database

2. With the original database in place and users accessing their old data, the data from the beginning of the restore procedure must be merged into the original mailboxes. To do this you can use the Recover Mailbox Data wizard, select multiple mailboxes concurrently, and merge or copy the data back into users' production mailboxes.

Outlook 2003 Exchange Recovery Mode

During the time that the dial tone database is being used, Outlook 2003 users who are working in Cached Exchange Mode see the dialog box shown in Figure 23-12 when they log on, giving them the choice of connecting to the database or the offline store.

Figure 23-12 Choose whether to connect to the database or the offline store

If users choose to connect to the Exchange server, they can send and receive e-mail using their dial tone mailbox, but the data in the offline file (.ost) is inaccessible. If users choose Work Offline, they can access the offline mailbox but they cannot send or receive e-mail.

During the period when the dial tone database is in operation, users will be prompted each time they open Outlook, so that the online dial tone mailbox and the local offline store are both accessible during this time. With previous versions of Outlook, they do not receive this message, but if they choose to work online, the previous offline (.ost) file could become permanently inaccessible in dial-tone scenarios. This is why the behavior was changed in Outlook 2003 to allow switching between the two until the original database is restored, or swapped.

The reason for this behavior is the encryption key utilized by Outlook for its offline file, which keeps the offline data secure. This key is associated with a GUID stored in the user's mailbox on their Exchange server. When the user connects to the new mailbox, the GUID no longer matches and in order to prevent your local offline data from synchronizing up to a mailbox that was never associated with the offline cache's .ost file, Outlook prevents you from accessing both at the same time. When the dial tone database is replaced with the original database the user will need to use the dialog to reconnect to the online mailbox a final time and Outlook will recognize the original GUID has been restored. Subsequent connections will then no longer invoke the recovery mode choice and the user's online mailbox and offline cache should function together normally again.

Note As long as the dial tone database remains as the production database, users who are using Exchange Cached Mode will always receive the dialog box above, because the encryption key on the .ost file does not match their mailbox in the database. Several things you can do in Outlook (such as trying to force replication when in offline mode) may trigger it into abandoning the .ost along with all its offline data, and the user will receive a pop up warning dialog if they are attempting an operation which will force the exit of this recovery mode in this fashion. If they choose to continue anyway they will lose access to their .ost and return to online mode only. A wise option is to use the Export option on the File menu in Outlook to backup your offline .ost data to a portable .pst file before exiting recovery mode this way, since there is no going back once you OK the warning message. Creating a new user profile in Outlook is another method for breaking out of the recovery mode, which allows you to setup a new online connection with it's own caching (using a new .ost) while still preserving the old profile so that the .ost file could still be accessed from there

Restoring Deleted Mailboxes

When a user's mailbox is deleted through either Exchange System Manager or Active Directory Users and Computers, the system marks the mailbox for deletion in Active Directory and disconnects it from the user object to which it was attached. The default behavior of Exchange 2003 for deleted mailboxes is to retain them for a period before actually deleting them. The default period is 30 days, but this can be changed by using an Exchange system policy or on the properties of the Mailbox Store object directly.

When a mailbox is deleted, the Exchange attributes of the user object are removed, and the mailbox is orphaned. The mailbox exists in the mailbox store, but it is not connected to any user object in Active Directory, and so it is inaccessible using mail clients.

The process of reconnecting and restoring deleted mailboxes depends on the state of the mailbox and other factors. Standard methods of recovering mailboxes are as follows:

- **Reconnect mailboxes individually** Deleted mailboxes that have not reached the retention period, and therefore have not been purged from the system, can be reconnected on an individual basis.

- **Mailbox Recovery Center** The Mailbox Recovery Center enables you to reconnect multiple deleted mailboxes from more than one mailbox store in the organization.

- **Restore using the Recovery Storage Group**   Mailboxes that have been deleted and purged from the system can be restored using the Recovery Storage Group.

- **Restore brick-level backups**   If your backup jobs include a brick-level, or individual mailbox backup, you can restore the mailbox directly from tape.

Reconnecting Mailboxes with the Cleanup Agent

Individual mailboxes can be quickly reconnected to their user object if the user, or another appropriate user, exists in Active Directory. Running the Cleanup Agent in System Manager prompts the system to review the mailboxes that are marked for deletion and those that should be purged, and it marks those that are deleted but still retained with a red cross on the mailbox item. Often, you must run the Cleanup Agent before the deleted mailboxes show up as deleted in System Manager.

This mailbox cleanup process is also performed by online maintenance which runs every night.

When you want to reconnect a deleted mailbox to a user in Active Directory, browse to the mailbox object in Exchange System Manager, right-click it and select Reconnect. This process reinstates the Exchange attributes to that user object and re-establishes the association between the user and the mailbox.

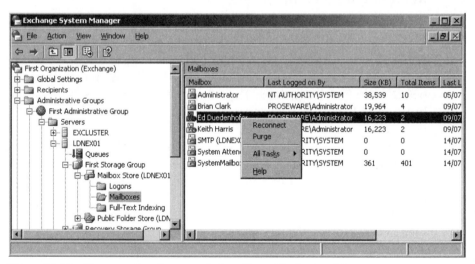

Figure 23-13   Reconnecting disconnected mailboxes in System Manager

> **Note**   When reconnecting a mailbox, you are given a choice of user to which to connect the mailbox. The mailbox can be connected to any user object that is not already mail-enabled or mailbox-enabled. This makes it easy to reassign mailboxes from one user to another simply by deleting and reconnecting them.

After reconnecting the mailbox to an Active Directory user, the mailbox can be accessed as usual with Outlook or another mail client.

Reconnecting Mailboxes with the Mailbox Recovery Center

The Exchange 2003 Mailbox Recovery Center is a tool that enables administrators to reconnect mailboxes in much the same way as the Reconnect command within a mailbox store object. The Mailbox Recovery Center provides the same functionality as the separate command-line only tool called the Mailbox Reconnect Tool (MBConnect.exe) which was included on the Exchange 2000 CD-ROM, and is a comprehensive set of tools for reconnecting multiple mailboxes and re-establishing user object information to bring mailboxes into a usable state. Multiple operations can be performed concurrently from the Mailbox Recovery Center.

The Mailbox Recovery Center gives a consolidated view of the disconnected mailboxes across a number of mailbox stores. Mailbox stores can be added and removed within the Mailbox Recovery Center, and by refreshing the view, disconnected mailboxes appear and disappear accordingly. In addition to the name of the mailbox, the standard view also shows the associated user name, its mailbox store name, and the mailbox directory name. The Full Mailbox Directory Name signifies the original user of the mailbox when it was first created, because it includes the user logon name in the path.

Connecting an orphaned mailbox to a user account is a multi-stage process that involves the following stages:

- **Adding mailbox stores**   You must first add to the Mailbox Recovery Center one or more mailbox stores that contain disconnected mailboxes. The list of mailboxes includes a consolidated view from all of the mailbox stores.

- **Finding a match for each mailbox**   Prior to connecting a mailbox, you must first match it with a user account. The Mailbox Matching Wizard helps perform this task.

- **Resolving conflicts and specifying associated user**   If multiple users or no users are found to which to reconnect, this tool assists in mapping the mailbox to a single user account.

■ **Reconnecting the mailbox**   The Mailbox Reconnect Wizard connects the mailbox to the specified user. This process actually modifies the msExchMailboxGUID of the user object to match the mailbox.

> **Note**   The mailbox GUID is an attribute of the mailbox specified at the mailbox's creation. This value does not change, but the msExchMailboxGUID value of the user object changes according to the mailbox to which it is connected. The msExchMailboxGUID value can be found by using ADSIEdit.msc, or a similar tool, as in Figure 23-14.

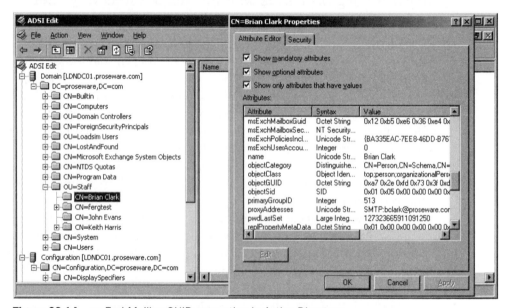

Figure 23-14   msExchMailboxGUID properties in Active Directory

Finding a Match

When reconnecting mailboxes by using the Mailbox Recovery Center, the first operation that you must perform is to find a matching user object for the mailbox. The operation can be performed on multiple mailboxes and automatically finds the user object that best matches the mailbox. The summary page at the end of the operation details the matches found, and the Mailbox Recovery Center view is updated to show the matched user objects.

The following are the outcomes of this operation:

■ **If a direct match is found**   It associates the mailbox with, but does not connect it to, the user it finds.

- **If you must connect the mailbox to another user**   If the user specified is not the desire user, you can right-click the mailbox and choose to Resolve Conflicts. This allows you to specify another user object.

- **If multiple possible users are found**   The Exchange Mailbox Matching Wizard notifies you that multiple possible matches exist. You then use the Conflict Resolution Wizard to provide the list of possible matches from which you can choose the correct user.

> **Note**   The list of possible matches comprises the mailbox's original user and the last user to which the mailbox was connected.

- **If no possible user is found**   You can use the Conflict Resolution Wizard to choose a user object to which to connect the mailbox.

- **If the user object was deleted**   It is possible to recreate the user object by retrieving user settings from the mailbox itself.

Figure 23-15 shows the Mailbox Recovery Center containing orphaned mailboxes. Two of the mailboxes have the same mailbox name, because they were both associated to the same user at a different time.

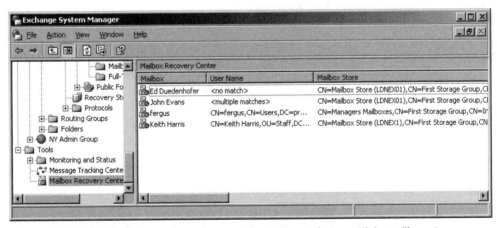

Figure 23-15   The Mailbox Recovery Center with mailboxes from multiple mailbox stores

Resolving Conflicts

When the Mailbox Matching Wizard does not find an appropriate user, or finds more than one appropriate user, you can use the Conflict Resolution Wizard to specify which user to associate with. Using this wizard, you can associate the mailbox with a user object and actually connect the mailbox at a later stage.

The Conflict Resolution Wizard gives you a list of the possible user objects that the Mailbox Matching Wizard found to associate with, from which you can choose a user. If no appropriate user was found, you can browse Active Directory to choose one.

After the Conflict Resolution Wizard finishes, the mailbox has an associated user to which it can connect. In the case of Figure 23-16, Brian Clark has been chosen to connect to John Evans's mailbox, as he would do if taking over John's job.

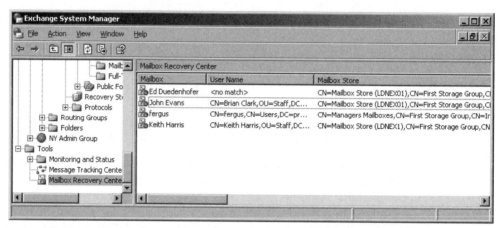

Figure 23-16   Mailboxes have been associated with users ready for reconnection

Reconnecting the Mailbox

As with most operations in the Mailbox Recovery Center, connecting the mailboxes to the user objects can be done on multiple user accounts concurrently. The Mailbox Reconnect Wizard uses the mapping created in the previous stages to change the msExchMailboxGUID attribute of the associated user and thus reconnect the mailbox (Figure 23-17).

The attributes that establish the association between a user account and the physical mailbox are discussed later in this chapter.

> **Note**   If the msExchMailboxGUID attribute of a user object is changed to match the GUID of another mailbox, the user is connected to that mailbox. The msExchMailboxGUID attribute is the only thing that needs to be changed to associate a user object with a mailbox.

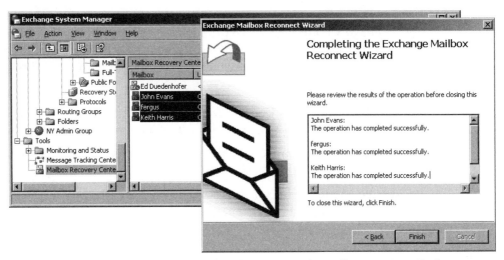

Figure 23-17   The Mailbox Reconnect Wizard reconnects the mailboxes automatically

Exporting User Object Definitions from the Mailbox

Unlike Exchange 2003, Active Directory does not feature any kind of item retention. It does handle deleted items in the same way, but does not feature a built-in method of retrieving items that are marked for deletion. However, if the user object to which the mailbox belongs has already been deleted, the Mailbox Recovery Center provides the ability to recreate the user from the attributes stamped on the mailbox itself.

> **Note**   To retrieve deleted items in Active Directory you must perform an authoritative restore of the Active Directory database.

An Exchange mailbox retains certain information about the original owner, such as the displayName and the UserAccountControl attributes. UserAccountControl is a multi-value attribute that stores the values on the Account Properties tab of a user object in Active Directory Users and Computers.

> **More Info**   For more information about this attribute, see Microsoft Knowledge Base article Q305144, How to Use the UserAccountControl flags to Manipulate User Account Properties (*http://support.microsoft.com/ default.aspx?scid=kb;en-us;Q305144*).

The Exchange Mailbox Export Wizard exports the user objects below to a Lightweight Directory Format (LDF) file that can be imported directly into Active Directory using the LDIFDE.exe or CSVDE.exe command line tools for manipulating Active Directory and other Lightweight Directory Access Protocol (LDAP)-based directories.

- **userAccountControl**   This holds a number of properties, such as whether the account is disabled, trusted for delegation, and many other properties.

- **msExchUserAccountControl**   This attribute is set to "0" to signify that the account is mailbox-enabled.

- **displayName**   This contains the display name of the object as it appears in the Global Address List and other address lists.

- **objectClass**   The type of Active Directory object to create. In this case it is a user.

- **sAMAccountName**   This is the logon name used to support clients and servers with previous versions of Windows. It is one of the standard names used to log on to Windows.

Using the command **LDIFDE –I –f <filename>** you can import the LDF file into Active Directory to create the users and then attach the mailboxes to those new users.

More Info   By default Active Directory does not allow blank passwords for user objects, so in a default environment this command will fail with the error shown in Figure 23-18. You must set policy compliant passwords using LDIFDE. For more information about setting passwords using LDIFDE, see Microsoft Knowledge Base article263991, How to Set a User's Password with Ldifde (*http://support.microsoft.com/default.aspx?scid=kb;en-us;263991*).

```
C:\WINDOWS\system32\cmd.exe

C:\Documents and Settings\Administrator.PROSEWARE>ldifde -i -f c:\ed.ldf
Connecting to "LDNDC01.proseware.com"
Logging in as current user using SSPI
Importing directory from file "c:\ed.ldf"
Loading entries.
Add error on line 1: Unwilling To Perform
The server side error is "Unable to update the password. The value provided for
the new password does not meet the length, complexity, or history requirement of
 the domain."
0 entries modified successfully.
An error has occurred in the program
No log files were written.  In order to generate a log file, please
specify the log file path via the -j option.

C:\Documents and Settings\Administrator.PROSEWARE>_
```

Figure 23-18   The import process fails if blank passwords are not allowed in Active Directory

When the user objects have been recreated in Active Directory, go back to the Mailbox Recovery Center and start the Mailbox Matching Wizard again. The wizard will find the new user objects and assign them. You then use the Reconnect command to connect the mailboxes again.

The user objects, mail-disabled when they were first created using LDIFDE, automatically become mailbox-enabled by the Mailbox Reconnect Wizard, which changes attributes on each user object to point to the mailboxes.

Restoring Mailboxes Using the Recovery Storage Group

After the mailbox retention period expires on a deleted mailbox (by default 30 days), the mailbox is physically purged from the database and is no longer available for reconnection. In this case, to retrieve the mailbox data you must restore the mailbox from your backup media. The Recovery Storage Group can be used to restore the mailbox database directly onto the original server, or another Exchange server in the same administrative group.

When a mailbox user needs to retrieve deleted and purged data from a backup of their mailbox, the Recovery Storage Group can be used to restore the backup of the database and the data transferred from the backup to the original mailbox using ExMerge or the Recover Mailbox Data wizard. However, if the original mailbox has been moved or deleted, it is not possible to retrieve the data from the mailbox in the RSG. If you use ExMerge to retrieve mailboxes from the recovered database, you receive an error, which is written to the ExMerge.log (Figure 23-19).

ExMerge cannot connect to the original mailbox because it needs to match the mailbox GUID of the mailbox in the Recovery Storage Group to its original mailbox, and also to the msExchMailboxGUID attribute of the user object. If the mailbox is disconnected then no user object has this attribute. If the mailbox has been purged there is no mailbox GUID corresponding to that in the recovered database.

To restore the data from the database backup, you can either restore the backup to a separate server and reconnect the mailboxes to user objects for extraction, or restore to the Recovery Storage Group then move the database files into a newly created storage group. To use this method, you must have spare capacity in your Exchange server for a single mail store or database. If you can use a separate storage group, this is preferable, as it limits the chance of error.

Figure 23-19   Errors in the ExMerge log suggest the mailboxes cannot be connected to

To restore a mailbox in this way:

1. Create a Recovery Storage group and add the relevant mailbox store to it.

2. Restore the database to the RSG and mount and dismount the store.

3. Create a new normal storage group and a mailbox store within it. Do not mount the mailbox store.

4. Using Windows Explorer, move the database files from the Recovery Storage group folder to the location of the files for the new storage group. Ensure that the names of the database files referenced in the properties of the mailbox store match the names of the files moved into the folder.

5. Check the This database can be overwritten by a restore check box and mount the store.

In Figure 23-20, the database backup was restored to the Recovery Storage Group and transferred to the "New Mailbox Store," where it was mounted and Brian Clark's mailbox reconnected.

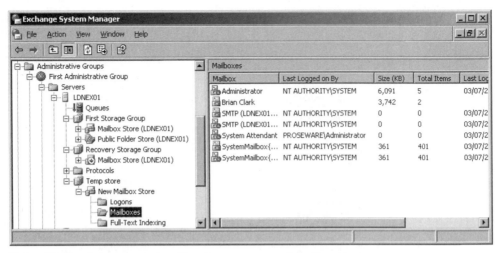

Figure 23-20   A reconnected mailbox from a recovered mailbox store

You now have the restored database running in a production storage group, from which you can reconnect the restored mailboxes to any user object and extract the required data using Outlook or another mail client.

Restoring Deleted Items

To help avoid the necessity of manually restoring deleted items from backup, you should set appropriate values for the deleted item and mailbox retention for mailbox and public folder stores (Figure 23-21). Deleted item retention is covered in Chapter 21, "Disaster Recovery Planning for Exchange 2003."

There is no built-in method of restoring individual items from an Exchange Server 2003 server. With a third-party backup solution, it might be possible to restore deleted items and folders directly; otherwise, you must follow the same process as for restoring deleted mailboxes or public folders. In the case of mailbox data, you must restore the database according to the recovery methods detailed earlier in this chapter and extract the data by using ExMerge or the Recover Mailbox Data wizard. To restore public folder data, you must also use a database restore procedure, as detailed in the next section, Restoring Public Folder Data, and the items must be extracted using a mail client such as Outlook.

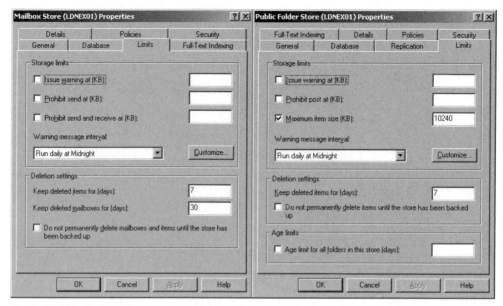

Figure 23-21   Deleted item and mailbox retention settings

Restoring Public Folder Data

Public folders differ fundamentally from mailboxes in that they can be replicated between folder stores on different servers. In a disaster recovery scenario, this replication can act as a natural data recovery mechanism when creating the new replacement Exchange server.

You can restore public folders manually by restoring the public database from backup or, depending on the public folder replication settings, by recreating an empty public store on the recovered server and allowing normal replication to take place.

Recovering Public Folders by Replication

If the public folder data that has been lost due to a disaster on an Exchange server is replicated elsewhere, it is possible to replicate this data back to the recovered server with no extra administrative effort. Simply by recreating the public folder databases on the recovery server, the data replication will take place and repopulate the new database with public folder data from the other servers. This is termed "backfill."

Note Changes made to the local, lost database that were not replicated to other servers will obviously not be restorable using this method. It is a matter of judgment, based on the replication schedule and other circumstances, whether to use this method or to restore the database from backup media and allow hard recovery to replay transactions into the public folder database to bring it up to the point of the disaster.

Whether this method can be used or not depends on the recovery method. In order for the replication to start from where it left off before the database loss, the Active Directory configuration for the lost database must be still present. If it is, the new database on the recovered server will take part in the public folder replication automatically. If it does not, you can simply add the store into the replication list of the relevant public folders.

Recovering Public Folders Using a Restore

If you need to physically restore the public folder database from backup in order to retrieve the data, there are two ways of achieving this: restore to the same public folder store or restore to a separate server.

In some scenarios it is necessary to restore the public folder store from a backup. This requires a database restore either directly over the public database on the production server or via a recovery server as with an Exchange 2000 Server restore. If the server to be restored is the only one with a copy of the lost folders, a restore is the required solution.

A direct restore may be preferred, or necessary, where:

- Public folders are not replicated fully or at all.
- Significant changes have been made to public data since the last backup was not replicated to other Exchange servers.

Note In order to bring the public folders to the state they were in at the moment of the disaster, the log files for the storage group on which the public store resides must be intact. If they are not available, you will only be able to restore to the point of the last backup.

Restoring public folders is not as convenient as mailbox restoration, which can use the Recovery Storage Group. The RSG does not handle public folder stores, so the restoration methods for public folders are the same as those for Exchange 2000.

If you need to restore the whole public folder database, for example, if the database disk is faulty, you can restore the public folder store directly onto the same server from the backup tape. This process should not be used if you need to restore only individual items or folders.

If you wish to retrieve individual folders or items from a public folder backup, restore the databases either to another server in the same administrative group or to a recovery server. Restoration of databases to a separate server are covered in the section "Restoring to a Different Server" later in this chapter.

Shadow Copy Restore

Windows Server 2003 supports restore techniques using the Volume Shadow Copy Service and facilitates the cooperation of third-party snapshot technology and applications such as Exchange to work together in backing up and restoring the application's data. Using snapshot technology restores can be performed much more quickly than with the Exchange streaming APIs, and therefore allows servers to support larger Exchange databases while staying within the restraints of the service level agreement.

Storage Area Network (SAN)-based shadow copy technology can be used to create and manage shadow copies of volumes for testing and recovery purposes. Using the hardware infrastructure of a SAN means this can be done extremely quickly and with very little overhead on the Windows server.

More Info   For more information about the Volume Shadow Copy Service on Windows Server 2003, see Technical Overview of Windows Server 2003 Storage Management (*http://www.microsoft.com/windowsserver2003/techinfo/overview/storage.mspx*) and the Volume Shadow Copy Service Technical Reference (*http://www.microsoft.com/resources/documentation/WindowsServ/2003/all/techref/en-us/Default.asp?url=/resources/documentation/windowsServ/2003/all/techref/en-us/W2K3TR_vss_intro.asp*).

Restoring to a Different Server

Some situations lend themselves to restoring lost Exchange data to a separate server; for example, situations in which an Exchange server is destroyed and the mailbox and public folder data must be back online in as little time as possible, or when hardware limitations require that a separate restore environment is necessary.

In previous versions of Exchange, some database restore operations require a recovery server in a separate logical environment from the production organization. Exchange 2003 also enables restores of mailbox and public folder databases onto other servers in the same environment. Each operation has its uses, and this section covers both of these operations.

Restoring data to a different server in the same forest is useful when you want to retrieve certain items from a public folder store, or if you are limited in your use of the Recovery Storage Group on the production server.

Some circumstances require the use of a separate server in a separate forest environment, for example when a restore operation on a production server would have a serious effect on performance.

Restoring to a Different Server in the Same Forest

In the event of a complete server failure, Exchange mailbox databases can be restored directly onto another server in the same administrative group so that users can quickly gain access to their data while the original server is being rebuilt.

To restore a database to a different server, the storage group and store names must be identical. If the default storage group name, First Storage Group, is being used on both the original and the recovery server, you can optionally rename this storage group on the recovery server and recreate a First Storage Group group for the restored stores. This can help avoid potential log file conflicts and generally separate the recovery procedures from the production environment.

In addition to the same storage group and logical database names, the new server must be of the same Exchange version and service pack.

The restore function of NTBackup enables you to restore databases to different servers (Figure 23-22). By default, the Restore To: field will contain the name of the original server from which the backup came.

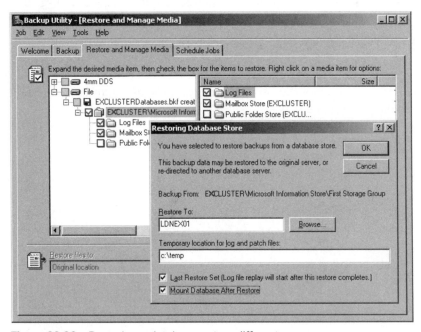

Figure 23-22 Restoring a database onto a different server

Reconnecting Mailboxes Manually

In a disaster recovery scenario, when you have restored the databases from the failed Exchange server onto another production server, because the server on which the mailboxes reside has changed, there is a mismatch between the user objects that own the mailboxes and the mailboxes themselves. User objects remain mailbox-enabled and point towards a mailbox on the old server.

The specific user attributes that determine the mailbox properties are the following:

- **msExchMailboxGUID**   This attribute reflects the Globally Unique ID of the mailbox to which it is associated (the Mailbox GUID). This value singularly links a mailbox to an Active Directory user object.

- **msExchHomeServerName**   This contains the complete distinguished name of the server on which the mailbox resides.

- **homeMDB**   This attribute contains the complete distinguished name of the mailbox server for the mailbox.

- **homeMTA**   This contains the complete distinguished name of the Message Transfer Agent (MTA) of that server.

> **Note**   By changing these attributes alone you can change the target mailbox for a user in the Exchange organization. To change the target to another mailbox on the same server, only the msExchMailboxGUID must be changed.

The attributes of the user objects can be viewed and modified directly using ADSIEdit (Figure 23-23).

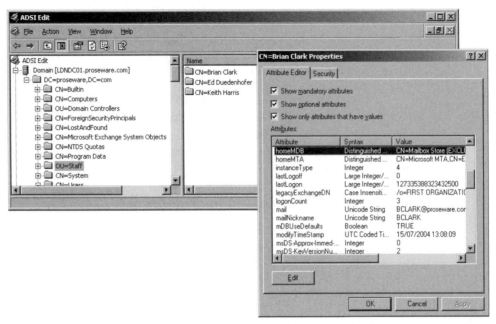

Figure 23-23   Viewing the Active Directory attributes of mailbox-enabled users

To redirect the user objects that point to the failed server over to the recovery server, the System Manager-based method is to reconnect the mailboxes directly within the Mailbox Recovery Center, as detailed earlier in this chapter. To do this, follow these steps:

1. Delete the users' mailboxes.

2. You must first remove the Exchange attributes of the users by deleting their mailboxes. This process does not actually delete the mailboxes, it merely disconnects the users from the mailboxes by removing their related attributes.

> **Caution**   Do not recreate mailboxes for these users. Recreating mailboxes in Active Directory Users and Computers will create a new mailbox for each user with a new GUID and will result in duplicate mailboxes. The mailbox creation process does not check to see if there is an existing mailbox that should be assigned to the user.

3. Add the recovered mailbox store to the Mailbox Recovery Center.

4. This process will parse the recovered mailbox store and show all of the mailboxes that are now in a disconnected state. These will correspond to the users whose attributes have been deleted.

5. Reconnect the Mailboxes

6. Follow the procedures detailed in the previous section, "Reconnecting Mailboxes with the Mailbox Recovery Center." This process will re-establish the four attributes above in each user object and link the mailbox to the user.

The process of reconnecting the mailboxes is easily completed. However, establishing the list of users who must be re-homed and deleting the Exchange attributes from these users is not easy. The user objects might be distributed within Active Directory Users and Computers, and the manual process of manipulating each user object can be difficult.

Reconnecting Mailboxes Programmatically

An alternative method of achieving this is to reconnect the mailboxes programmatically. You can find all the users with mailboxes on a certain server quickly using a script, by parsing the msExchHomeServerName attribute. The script can then modify the other relevant values, homeMDB and homeMTA.

On the Resource Kit CD   The script that performs this operation is named FixHomeServer.wsf, and you can find it in the Companion Material\Scripts folder on the companion CD.

In conjunction with the ListMailboxStores script from Chapter 4, "Upgrading to Exchange Server 2003," which lists the distinguished names of the mailbox stores on an Exchange 2003 server, this script can modify the appropriate attributes of the users whose mailboxes have moved.

The parameters required for this script are:

- **Source server**   This is the server that previously stored the users' mailboxes. The user attributes still point to this server prior to running the script.

- **Target mailbox store**   The mailbox store where the mailboxes now reside. The user attributes will be changed to point towards this store.

- **Enable write mode**   By default, the script will list only mailboxes that will be affected. To enable the changes you must use the –W parameter.

The script is run under the command line script (Figure 23-24) and, by default, outputs simple information about the users affected. In order to display more information about the process, use the verbose mode or log events to the system event log.

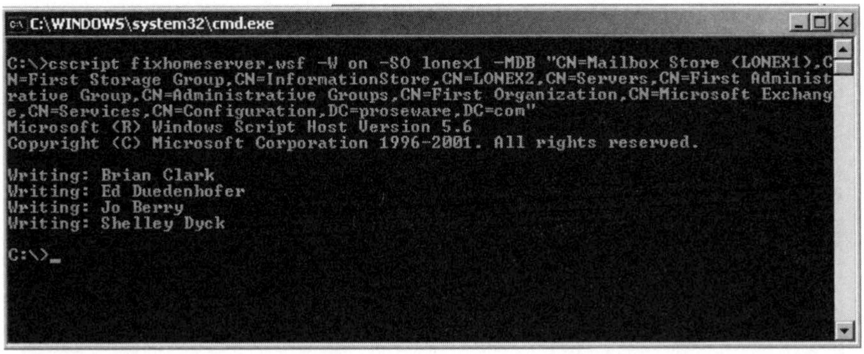

```
C:\WINDOWS\system32\cmd.exe                                           _□×

C:\>cscript fixhomeserver.wsf -W on -SO lonex1 -MDB "CN=Mailbox Store (LONEX1),C
N=First Storage Group,CN=InformationStore,CN=LONEX2,CN=Servers,CN=First Administ
rative Group,CN=Administrative Groups,CN=First Organization,CN=Microsoft Exchang
e,CN=Services,CN=Configuration,DC=proseware,DC=com"
Microsoft (R) Windows Script Host Version 5.6
Copyright (C) Microsoft Corporation 1996-2001. All rights reserved.

Writing: Brian Clark
Writing: Ed Duedenhofer
Writing: Jo Berry
Writing: Shelley Dyck

C:\>_
```

Figure 23-24   Using the FixHomeServer.wsf script to redirect users to the new Exchange server

When the script is run successfully, the users will be able to log on to their mailboxes as before. Outlook 2003 must still be redirected if Exchange is not running on the old server. This can be achieved either manually by changing Outlook profile settings through the Mail settings in Control Panel, or automatically by distributing an Outlook Profile (PRF) file via Group Policy or Systems Management Server, so that each user's profile is updated when they log on or when they open the PRF file. An example of an Outlook PRF file is shown below.

Note   Each of the scripts comes with an instruction document of the same name which contains the required and possible switches for use with the scripts.

Double-clicking a PRF file automatically starts Outlook and imports the settings in the file, so users will be able to start working against the new Exchange server immediately.

Figure 23-25   Changing the Exchange server name in an Outlook profile using a PRF file

Restoring to a Different Server in a Separate Forest

Under certain circumstances, it is not possible to use the Recovery Storage Group or to utilize additional storage groups to assist in data recovery. When you must restore public folder items, or if there are server performance issues with restoring onto the production server, you should use a separate server to perform the restore and recovery.

In a different server recovery scenario, the data is recovered to a separate server and extracted by using a mail client such as Outlook or ExMerge. The extracted data can then be moved onto the production server and imported.

Because of dependencies between the databases and Active Directory, there are a number of prerequisites for the recovery server:

■ Exchange Server must be of the same or higher version and service pack level.

■ The storage group to host the recovered database must have the same display name as the original.

■ The Exchange organization name must match that of the original organization.

- The administrative group name must match that of the original server.

- The storage group and logical database names on the recovery server must match those on the original server.

The databases should be restored directly into the storage group, rather than restoring them via the recovery storage group.

If you need to reconnect multiple mailboxes, you can use the Mailbox Recovery Center, which is introduced earlier in this chapter.

In order to retrieve public folder items, if you have restored both the mailbox and public folder stores, you must connect only one mailbox and log on using this account to access and extract the public folder data to a .pst file.

The white paper "Mailbox Recovery for Microsoft Exchange 2000 Server" describes the processes and requirements for recovering mailboxes to a separate recovery server in greater detail and can be found at *http://support.microsoft.com/ default.aspx?scid=kb;en-us;326278*. The procedures for using an offline recovery server are the same as for Exchange Server 2003.

The legacyExchangeDN Value

When a database is created in Exchange, the legacyDN value is stamped on it, and this value does not change. The legacyExchangeDN attribute is used for backward compatibility with the Exchange 5.5 database but is still required on certain Exchange objects in Exchange 2003.

To restore a database onto another server, the organization name, administrative group name and legacyExchangeDN of the administrative group must all match those of the original server. It is possible to change the organization and administrative group names using Active Directory Sites and Services, but the legacyExchangeDN attribute of these objects and a number of objects below them must also be changed to match those of the original server.

To change the organization and administrative group names, use the Active Directory Sites and Services tool. To show the Exchange services, you must select Show Services Node from the View menu. From here you can manually rename administrative groups and organizations.

> **Note**   In a mixed mode organization it is not possible to change the names of the organization or administrative groups. This is because of potential conflicts in a mixed Exchange 2003/Exchange 5.5 organization. If your organization is in mixed mode, it may be possible to convert it to native mode if there are no Exchange servers earlier than Exchange 2000, or use ADSIEdit or the Legacydn.exe tool which ignore this restriction.

The LegacyDN.exe tool, downloadable from the Microsoft website, can be used to change the attributes required. LegacyDN changes the organization and administrative group names, as well as the legacyExchangeDN attributes of the relevant Exchange objects within the administrative group. For information about how to use LegacyDN.exe, read the instruction document that is part of the tool download.

Best Practices

Restoring and recovering Exchange can be a complex and time consuming task, and a stressful one when the company loses money due to Exchange downtime. Reviewing the different recovery methods in advance of a disaster, and producing a walk-through document in case of disaster, is a must for speedy and efficient recovery. Given a document to walk through, an administrator can make an informed decision as to how to proceed, can provide a reasonable estimate as to the possible outage duration, and more importantly is less likely to make mistakes.

Restoration procedures should not only be well documented, they should also be practiced using a test environment. This helps to train the administrators in restore procedures and also crucially provides inherent testing of the backups.

When restoring an Exchange database it is important to retain a copy of the present databases in a safe location. You can do this by simply moving or copying the database files to another folder or server. In the event that the restore operation does not work, for example, if the backup is corrupt and there are no suitable backup tapes available, the last resort of the administrator is to perform disaster recovery operations on a corrupt database by using the ESEUtil and ISInteg tools. This is a last resort operation, because data loss is likely to occur when using these tools.

The option of reinstalling Exchange from the CD can be used when there are corrupt or missing binary files in the installation, or a mismatch in file versions. The /disasterrecovery switch performs the same operation, because it installs the Exchange binaries and sets local settings such as the registry and IIS metabase, but does not create a new instance of the server in Active Directory. The /disasterrecovery switch is used when rebuilding a failed Exchange server when installing Exchange for the first time on the new installation (where the /reinstall switch is not available).

The new Recovery Storage Group feature is very useful for recovering items and mailboxes in disaster and non-disaster situations while maintaining normal operations on the same server. The dial tone recovery scenario is useful for providing users the ability to send and receive mail in a short amount of time while gradually replaying the old data back into their mailboxes. When swapping over the dial tone and recovered databases, you must pay special attention to the location of the final databases and when you are renaming the databases within the mailbox store object. You cannot change the database file name and location to a database that already exists, so database files might need to be moved to temporary locations while swapping the databases.

The key to a successful and speedy Exchange recovery is to keep it as simple as possible and to automate as many tasks as possible. An administrator should have the information in front of him to allow him to choose the method that has a high possibility of working successfully rather than the method that is quickest or most complex. There are a number of tools and scripts available, within the resource kit and by direct download from the Microsoft website, which can ease recovery operations. In particular, the Mailbox Merge Wizard (ExMerge), the LegacyDN and MtaCheck tools, available from the Exchange website are essential tools for certain recovery operations. Other tasks can be automated by writing scripts; for example, to automatically swap the dial tone and original databases when performing a dial tone database recovery, or to make an offline copy of the database files before restoring on top of them.

Using documented solutions based on particular scenarios, twinned with the correct tools and scripts at hand, an administrator has more chance of recovering essential data with the minimum loss of Exchange downtime and company revenue.

Index

Authors

Kay Unkroth

Kay Unkroth has specialized in Microsoft messaging technologies for more than 12 years. He started his career as a Microsoft support specialist in Central Europe before he founded his own consulting company in 1996. Kay supports Exchange Server administrators in companies of all sizes around the globe through training, consulting, and authoring.

Elizabeth Molony

Elizabeth Molony has been supporting computer technologies for large and small companies for more than 16 years. In 1996, she turned her focus to providing consulting services to companies implementing Microsoft Exchange Server. She has also been working with Microsoft Learning, applying the real-world experience gained from installing, migrating, and supporting Exchange Server to the development of courseware and workshops.

Pav Cherny

Pav Cherny is an author and technology consultant focused on administration, operations, and systems monitoring. Since 1998, he has helped mid-sized and enterprise companies optimize IT environments and implement Microsoft technologies. Pav co-owns Iyou LLC, a solutions company that provides documentation for a variety of industries.

Brian Reid

Brian Reid is a messaging and security specialist with over 10 years' experience with Microsoft technologies. Based in the United Kingdom, Brian is a director of C7 Solutions Ltd., a Microsoft consulting and training company serving clients worldwide, including Microsoft's support and consulting groups, for whom he provides in-depth training on Microsoft Exchange Server and ISA Server. Brian has also written numerous training manuals and books.

Fergus Strachan

Fergus Strachan, MCSE, Managing Director of Corporate OnSite, Ltd. in London, operates a Microsoft Certified Partner company that specializes in infrastructure design and implementation. He has been designing, implementing, and troubleshooting Windows Server- and Exchange Server-based environments for organizations such as banks and government for more than six years.

Bill English

Bill English, MCSE, MCSA, MVP, is an author and educator specializing in collaborative technologies. He is the principal author of *Microsoft SharePoint Products and Technologies Resource Kit* (Microsoft Press), and coauthor of five books on Exchange Server, including *Microsoft Exchange Server 2003 Administrator's Companion* (Microsoft Press). As co-owner of Mindsharp, he conducts private corporate training events for companies of all sizes.